# COGNITIVE
# PSYCHOLOGY

# Key Readings in Cognition

The aim of this series is to make available to senior undergraduate and graduate students key articles in each area of cognition in an attractive, user-friendly format. Many professors want to encourage their students to engage directly with research in their fields, yet this can often be daunting for students coming to detailed study of a topic for the first time. Moreover, declining library budgets mean that articles are not always readily available, and course packs can be expensive and time-consuming to produce. **Key Readings in Cognition** aims to address this need by providing comprehensive volumes, each one of which will be edited by a senior and active researcher in the field. Articles will be carefully chosen to illustrate the way the field has developed historically, as well as current issues and research directions. Each volume will have a similar structure to include:

- an overview chapter, as well as an introduction to sections and articles
- questions for class discussion
- annotated bibliographies
- full author and subject indexes

**Published titles:**

Visual Perception                  *Edited by Steven Yantis*
Cognitive Psychology               *Edited by David A. Balota and Elizabeth J. Marsh*

**Titles in preparation:**

Human Memory                       *Edited by Henry L. Roediger III, Kathleen McDermott, and*
                                   *Elizabeth J. Marsh*
Cognitive Neuroscience             *Edited by Marie Banich*
Applied Cognition                  *Edited by David G. Payne and Douglas Herrmann*

# COGNITIVE PSYCHOLOGY
## Key Readings

Edited by

## David A. Balota
*Washington University in St. Louis*

and

## Elizabeth J. Marsh
*Duke University*

**Psychology Press**
New York and Hove

Published in 2004 by
Psychology Press
270 Madison Avenue
New York, NY 10016
www.psypress.com

Published in Great Britain by
Psychology Press
27 Church Road
Hove, East Sussex
BN3 2FA
www.psypress.co.uk

Psychology Press is an imprint of the Taylor & Francis Group.
Printed in the United States of America on acid-free paper.

10 9 8 7 6 5 4 3 2 1

Library of Congress Cataloging-in-Publication Data

  Cognitive psychology : key readings / edited by David A. Balota and Elizabeth J. Marsh
     p. cm. — (Key readings in cognition)
  Includes bibliographical references and index.
   ISBN 1-84169-064-3 (hbk) — ISBN 1-84169-065-1 (pbk.)
   1. Cognitive psychology.  I. Balota, D. A.  II. Marsh, Elizabeth J.  III. Series.
  BF201.C642 2003
  153—dc21

                                                  2003009115

# Contents

# About the Editors

**David A. Balota** is a cognitive psychologist working in the areas of psycholinguistics and age-related changes in attention and memory. His work has consistently been funded by NIH, NSF, or both. In addition to being on numerous editorial boards, he has been associate editor at the *Journal of Memory and Language* and is currently editor for the *Psychonomic Bulletin and Review.* He has been president of Division 3, Experimental Psychology, chair of the governing board of the Psychonomic Society, and is a fellow of the American Psychological Association, the American Psychological Society, and the American Association for the Advancement of Science.

**Elizabeth J. Marsh** received her PhD in cognitive psychology from Stanford University in 1999. She completed an NIMH-funded postdoctoral research fellowship at Washington University before moving to her present faculty position at Duke University. Her research is focused on human memory, especially autobiographical memories, the acquistion and source of general world knowledge, and memory illusions.

# Acknowledgments

The editors and publishers are grateful to the following for permission to reproduce the articles in this book:

**Reading 1:** D. Marr, *Vision.* Chapter 1: The Philosophy and the Approach (pp. 8–38). San Francisco: W.H. Freeman and Co., 1982. Reprinted with permission.

**Reading 2:** S. Sternberg, Memory-Scanning: Mental Processes Revealed by Reaction-Time Experiments. *American Scientist, 57,* 421–457. Copyright © 1969. Reprinted with permission.

**Reading 3:** J. L. McClelland, D. E. Rumelhart, and G. E. Hinton, *The Appeal of Parallel Distributed Processing.* Chapter 1: Parallel Distributed Processing: Explorations in the Microstructure of Cognition. Cambridge: MIT Press, 1986. Reprinted with permission.

**Reading 4:** C. Sacchett and G. W. Humphreys, Calling a Squirrel a Squirrel but a Canoe a Wigwam: A Category-Specific Deficit for Artefactual Objects and Body Parts. *Cognitive Neuropsychology, 9,* 73–86. Copyright © 1992, by Lawrence Erlbaum Associates. Reprinted with permission.

**Reading 5:** S. E. Petersen, P. T. Fox, M. I. Posner, M. A. Mintun, and M. E. Raichle, Positron Emission Tomographic Studies of the Cortical Anatomy of Single-Word Processing. Reprinted by permission from *Nature, 331,* 585–589. Copyright © 1988, Macmillan Publishers Ltd.

**Reading 6:** U. Neisser, *Pattern Recognition.* Chapter 3: Cognitive Psychology (pp. 46–85). Upper Saddle River, NJ: Prentice Hall, 1967. Reprinted with permission.

**Reading 7:** P. D. Eimas and J. D. Corbit, Selective Adaptation of Linguistic Feature Detectors. *Cognitive Psychology, 4,* 99–109. Copyright © 1973, Elsevier Science (USA). Reproduced with permission from the publisher.

**Reading 8:** D. J. Simons and D. T. Levin, Failure to Detect Changes to People during a Real-World Interaction. *Psychonomic Bulletin & Review, 5,* 644–649. Copyright © 1998, Psychonomic Society, Inc. Reprinted with permission.

**Reading 9:** F. Tong, K. Nakayama, J. T. Vaughan, and N. Kanwisher, Binocular Rivalry and Visual Awareness in Human Extrastriate Cortex. *Neuron, 21,* 753–759. Copyright © 1998. Reprinted by permission of the publisher.

**Reading 10:** E. C. Cherry, Some Experiments on the Recognition of Speech, with One and with Two Ears. *Journal of the Acoustical Society of America, 25,* 975–979. Copyright © 1953, by the American Institute of Physics. Reprinted with permission.

**Reading 11:** J. R. Stroop, Studies of Interference in Serial Verbal Reactions. *Journal of Experimental Psychology, 18,* 643–663. Copyright © 1935. Public domain.

**Reading 12:** M. I. Posner and C. R. R. Snyder, Attention and Cognitive Control. In R. L. Solso (Ed.), *Information Processing and Cognition: The Loyola Symposium* (pp. 55–85). Hillsdale, NJ: Lawrence Erlbaum Associates, 1975. Reprinted by permission of the publisher.

**Reading 13:** S. P. Tipper, Selection for Action: The Role of Inhibitory Mechanisms. *Current Directions in Psychological Science, 1,* 105–109. Copyright © 1992, by Blackwell Publishers. Reprinted with permission.

**Reading 14:** S. M. Kosslyn, T. M. Ball, and B. J. Reiser, Visual Images Preserve Metric Spatial Information: Evidence from Studies of Image Scanning. *Journal of Experimental Psychology: Human Perception & Performance, 4,* 47–60. Copyright © 1978, by the American Psychological Association. Reprinted with permission.

**Reading 15:** R. N. Shepard and J. Metzler, Mental Rotation of Three-Dimensional Objects. *Science, 171,* 701–703. Copyright © 1971, by the American Association for the Advancement of Science. Reprinted with permission.

**Reading 16:** R. A. Finke, S. Pinker, and M. J. Farah, Reinterpreting Visual Patterns in Mental Imagery. *Cognitive Science, 13,* 51–78. Copyright © 1989, by the Cognitive Science Society. Reprinted with permission.

**Reading 17:** M. J. Farah, The Neural Basis of Mental Imagery. Reprinted from *Trends in Neuroscience, 12,* 395–399. Copyright © 1989, with permission from Elsevier Science.

**Reading 18:** F. I. M. Craik and E. Tulving, Depth of Processing and the Retention of Words in Episodic Memory. *Journal of Experimental Psychology: General, 104,* 268–294. Copyright © 1975, by Blackwell Publishers. Reprinted/adapted with permission.

**Reading 19:** E. F. Loftus, D. G. Miller, and H. J. Burns, Semantic Integration of Verbal Information into a Visual Memory. *Journal of Experimental Psychology: Human Learning & Memory, 4,* 19–31. Copyright © 1978, by the American Psychological Association. Reprinted with permission.

**Reading 20:** L. J. Jacoby, V. Woloshyn, and C. Kelley, Becoming Famous without Being Recognized: Unconscious Influences of Memory Produced by Dividing Attention. *Journal of Experimental Psychology: General, 118,* 115–125. Copyright © 1989, by the American Psychological Association. Reprinted with permission.

**Reading 21:** H. L. Roediger III and K. B. McDermott, Creating False Memories: Remembering Words Not Presented in Lists. *Journal of Experimental Psychology: Learning, Memory & Cognition, 21,* 803–814. Copyright © 1995, by the American Psychological Association. Reprinted with permission.

**Reading 22:** A. Baddeley, Working Memory. Reprinted from *Science, 255,* 556–559. Copyright © 1992, American Association for the Advancement of Science. Reprinted with permission.

**Reading 23:** E. Tulving, How Many Memory Systems Are There? *American Psychologist, 40,* 385–398. Copyright © 1985, by the American Psychological Association. Reprinted with permission.

**Reading 24:** D. Bruce, A. Dolan, and K. Phillips-Grant, On the Transition from Childhood Amnesia to the Recall of Personal Memories. *Psychological Science, 11,* 360–364. Copyright © 2000, by Blackwell Publishers. Reprinted with permission.

**Reading 25:** A. M. Collins and M. R. Quillian, Retrieval Time from Semantic Memory. *Journal of Verbal Learning and Verbal Behavior, 8,* 240–247. Copyright © 1969, Elsevier Science (USA), reproduced with permission from the publisher.

**Reading 26:** D. Balota and R. F. Lorch, Jr., Depth of Automatic Spreading Activation: Mediated Priming Effects in Pronunciation but Not in Lexical Decision. *Journal of Experimental Psychology: Learning, Memory & Cognition, 12,* 336–345. Copyright © 1986, by the American Psychological Association. Reprinted with permission.

**Reading 27:** R. Brown and D. McNeill, The "Tip of the Tongue" Phenomenon. *Journal of Verbal Learning and Verbal Behavior, 5,* 325–337. Copyright © 1966, Elsevier Science (USA), reproduced with permission from the publisher.

**Reading 28:** J. D. Bransford and M. K. Johnson, Contextual Prerequisites for Understanding: Some Investigations of Comprehension and Recall. *Journal of Verbal Learning and Verbal Behavior, 11,* 717–726. Copyright © 1972, Elsevier Science (USA), reproduced with permission from the publisher.

**Reading 29:** E. Rosch, C. B. Mervis, W. D. Gray, D. M. Johnson, and P. Boyes-Braem, Basic Objects in Natural Categories. *Cognitive Psychology, 8,* 382–440. Copyright © 1976, Elsevier Science (USA), reproduced/adapted with permission from the publisher.

**Reading 30:** M. I. Posner and S. W. Keele, On the Genesis of Abstract Ideas. *Journal of Experimental Psychology, 77,* 353–363. Copyright © 1968, by the American Psychological Association. Reprinted with permission.

**Reading 31:** D. L. Medin, Concepts and Conceptual Structure. *American Psychologist, 44,* 1469–1481. Copyright © 1989, by the American Psychological Association. Reprinted with permission.

**Reading 32:** V. Fromkin, S. Krashen, S. Curtiss, D. Rigler, and M. Rigler, The Development of Language in Genie: A Case of Language Acquisition beyond the "Critical Period." *Brain and Language, 1,* 81–107. Copyright © 1974, Elsevier Science (USA), reproduced with permission from the publisher.

**Reading 33:** J. Berko, The Child's Learning of English Morphology. *Word, 14,* 150–177. Public domain.

**Reading 34:** J. R. Saffran, R. N. Aslin, and E. L. Newport, Statistical Learning by Eight-Month-Old Infants. *Science, 274,* 1926–1928. Copyright © 1996, American Association for the Advancement of Science. Reprinted with permission.

**Reading 35:** G. F. Marcus, S. Vijayan, S. Bandi Rao, and P. M. Vishton, Rule Learning by Seven-Month-Old Infants. *Science, 283,* 77–80. Copyright © 1999, American Association for the Advancement of Science. Reprinted with permission.

**Reading 36:** V. A. Fromkin, The Non-Anomalous Nature of Anomalous Utterances. *Language, 47,* 27–52. Copyright © 1971, by the Linguistic Society of America. Reprinted with permission.

**Reading 37:** D. A. Swinney, Lexical Access during Sentence Comprehension: (Re)Consideration of Some Context Effects. *Journal of Verbal Learning and Verbal Behavior, 18,* 645–659. Copyright © 1979, Elsevier Science (USA), reproduced with permission from the publisher.

**Reading 38:** N. Geschwind, Language and the Brain. *Scientific American, 226,* 76–83. Copyright © 1972, by Scientific American, Inc. Reprinted with permission.

**Reading 39:** D. A. Robertson, M. A. Gernsbacher, S. J. Guidotti, R. R. W. Robertson, W. Irwin, B. J. Mock, and M. E. Campan, Functional Neuroanatomy of the Cognitive Process of Mapping during Discourse Comprehension. *Psychological Science, 11,* 255–260. Copyright © 2000, by Blackwell Publishers. Reprinted with permission.

**Reading 40:** A. Tversky and D. Kahneman, The Framing of Decisions and the Psychology of Choice. *Science, 211,* 453–458. Copyright © 1981, American Association for the Advancement of Science. Reprinted with permission.

**Reading 41:** A. Tversky and D. Kahneman, Judgment under Uncertainty: Heuristics and Biases. *Science, 185,* 1124–1131. Copyright © 1974, American Association for the Advancement of Science. Reprinted with permission.

**Reading 42:** A. Tversky and T. Gilovich, The Cold Facts about the "Hot Hand" in Basketball. *Chance: New Directions for Statistics and Computing, 2,* 16–21. Copyright © 1989, by Springer-Verlag, Inc. Reprinted with permission.

**Reading 43:** M. L. Gick and K. J. Holyoak, Schema Induction and Analogical Transfer. *Cognitive Psychology, 15,* 1–38. Copyright © 1983, Elsevier Science (USA), reproduced with permission from the publisher.

**Reading 44:** M. K. Kaiser, J. Jonides, and J. Alexander, Intuitive Reasoning about Abstract and Familiar Physics Problems. *Memory and Cognition, 14,* 308–312. Copyright © 1986, by Psychonomic Society, Inc. Reprinted with permission.

**Reading 45:** K. A. Ericsson and N. Charness, Expert Performance: Its Structure and Acquisition. *American Psychologist, 49,* 725–747. Copyright © 1994, by the American Psychological Association. Reprinted with permission.

**Appendix:** From *Research Methods in Psychology* (with InfoTrac), 6th Edition, by D. G. Elmes, B. H. Kantowitz, and H. L. Roediger III. Copyright © 1999. Reprinted with permission of Wadsworth, a division of Thomson Learning. Fax 800-730-2215.

# Cognitive Psychology:
# An Overview

David A. Balota and Elizabeth J. Marsh

The word *cognitive* comes from the Latin word *cognare,* meaning "to know." Hence, cognitive psychology is the study of the behavior of knowing or thought. Although experimental psychologists have studied related issues for well over a century, this area gained considerable impetus during the late '50s and early '60s. During that time, psychologists (along with linguists, computer scientists, and neuroscientists) began to provide empirical evidence and theoretical models to support distinctions among qualitatively different mental operations. For example, in the domain of memory, support shifted from a unitary memory system to the belief that not all memories are the same; that is, short-term memories seem to be qualitatively distinct from long-term memories.

In order to carve out a niche for this burgeoning area of research, Neisser (1967) defined cognitive psychology as the study of all processes by which "a sensory input is transformed, reduced, elaborated, stored, recovered, and used." One might argue that such a definition is too inclusive, as it includes all processes from the input of a stimulus to a subject's response. In fact, the cognitive perspective is a broad one that has extended into historically distinct areas of experimental psychology; for example, there are now thriving fields such as social cognition, cognitive development, and cognitive neuroscience. Moreover, because there is no clear specification that cognition need only involve humans, there is a field of experimental psychology referred to as animal cognition. But surely, once one takes this step, one might question the utility of the label, if indeed *all* experimental psychologists are at some level cognitive psychologists. Instead of specifying the processes that cognitive psychologists are interested in, one might specify the (a) major content areas, (b) modes of study, and (c) theoretical issues.

## Content Areas

Cognitive psychologists are interested in the processes by which patterns and objects are recognized, attended, remembered, imagined, and linguistically elaborated. These basic processes also feed into higher-order decision making and complex problem-solving behavior. Although each of these areas involves a rich and unique set of experimental findings and theoretical developments, the last three decades of research have also indicated that there is considerable overlap across content areas. For example, in developing models

1

of memory, cognitive psychologists must also be sensitive to developments in the area of attention, and vice versa.

For this book, we have chosen readings from each of the major content areas. These readings were selected on the basis of multiple constraints, such as capturing distinct perspectives on a topic, readability for a person with relatively little background in the field, and historical influence. Probably the most disheartening aspect of working on this project has been the loss of other classic papers due to simple space limitations. Hence, this book does not pretend to report *the* set of classic papers, but only a subset of classic papers. We have also peppered these readings with some recent papers that capture important developments within a given domain. However, before the reader jumps into the readings, it is important to be acquainted with some necessary background information. The primary goal of the present chapter is to provide the reader with some appreciation for the methodological tools available to cognitive psychologists, as well as some theoretical and historical context.

## Methods in Cognitive Psychology

Mental processes are by definition internal events—how then, do cognitive psychologists study these hypothesized processes?

Early research relied heavily on introspection, on experimenters' observations of their own thought processes (e.g., Titchener, 1898; Wundt, 1874). Although this approach is intuitively appealing, it quickly fell out of favor due to such problems as inadvertent experimenter bias and the inaccessibility of hypothesized unconscious processes. Ultimately, introspection fell prey to the problem reflected in the following awkward but compelling question "How can one think about thinking without the thinking influencing the thinking that one is thinking about?" Although introspection is no longer the primary method, cognitive psychologists do remain interested in people's subjective experience. For example, subjects may report on how vividly they experience an image or remember an event or how confident they are in a problem's solution.

Although variations on naturalistic observation are used less frequently than in other areas of psychology, cognitive psychologists do sometimes use them to study mental processes. For example, one approach to studying expertise involves the collection of "talk-aloud" protocols, in which subjects verbally describe their thought processes as they solve a problem. Another variation involves diary studies, in which subjects keep daily records of such naturally occurring cognitive processes as intrusive memories or possibly what was occurring when they experienced a troubling tip-of-the-tongue event.

Overwhelmingly, however, cognitive psychologists rely most heavily on the experimental method, in which independent variables are manipulated and dependent variables are measured. The experimental method is favored because it is the only way to establish cause-and-effect relationships. In order to evaluate the results from such experiments, cognitive researchers most often use inferential statistics (e.g., analyses of variance) to estimate the likelihood of a particular pattern of results occurring solely due to chance. If it is highly unlikely (typically less than 5% of the time) that a particular pattern of results has occurred if only chance were operating, then the researcher rejects the conclusion that the results were due only to chance (i.e., the null hypothesis). The researcher instead concludes that the results were due to the influence of the independent variable(s) (i.e., the alternative hypothesis).

The experimental methods that cognitive psychologists use depend in large part upon the area of study. Thus, we will provide an overview of the methods used in a number of distinct areas, including perception, memory, attention, and language processing, along with some discussion of methods that cut across these areas.

## Perceptual Methods

During the initial stage of stimulus processing, an individual encodes/perceives the stimulus. Encoding is the process of translating the sensory energy of a stimulus into a meaningful pattern (see papers in the "Pattern Recognition" section). However, before a stimulus can be encoded, a minimum or threshold amount of sensory energy is required to detect that stimulus. In psychophysics, the *Method of Limits* and the *Method of Constant Stimuli* have been used to determine sensory thresholds. The Method of Limits converges on sensory thresholds by using sub- and supra-threshold intensities of stimuli. From these anchor points, the intensity of a stimulus is gradually increased or decreased until it is at its sensory threshold and is just detectable by the participant. In contrast, the Method of Constant Stimuli converges on a sensory threshold by using a series of trials in which participants decide whether a stimulus was presented or not, and the experimenter varies the intensity of the stimulus. At the Sensory Threshold, participants are at chance at discriminating between the presence and the absence of a stimulus.

Although sensory threshold procedures have been important, these methods fail to recognize the role of nonsensory factors in stimulus processing. Thus, *signal detection theory* was developed to take into account an individual's biases in responding to a given signal in a particular context (Green & Swets, 1966). Figures 1 and 2 display the way signal detection theory can provide insights into the locus of an effect. The basic notion is that target stimuli produce some signal that is always embedded in a background of noise (see Figure 1). As

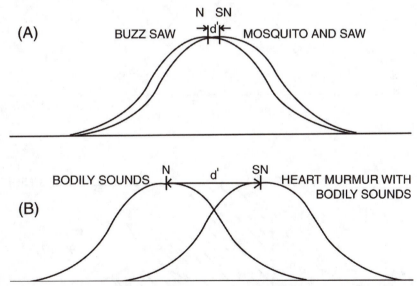

**FIGURE 1** ■ Noise (N) and signal plus noise (SN) distributions with varying amounts of overlap. Figure 1a depicts two virtually overlapping distributions. The sound of a mosquito is very hard to detect, given the background noise of a buzz saw. Figure 1b depicts moderate overlap, such as when a physician listens for a heart murmur in a background of other bodily sounds. The parameter d-prime (d') reflects the distance in standard deviation units between the means of the two distributions. From Lachman, Lachman, and Butterfield (1979), reprinted with permission of Lawrence Erlbaum Associates.

shown, the overlap in the distributions can vary dramatically, and the difference between a noise and a signal plus noise distribution is reflected by a parameter called d prime (d'). Performance in a given task does not only reflect the overlap in the distributions. Also important is the criterion, referred to as Beta, that the participant places to determine when to respond, "Yes, the queried dimension is present." Often, subjects set Beta at a location that maximizes the correct hit rate and minimizes the false alarm rate (see Figure 2a). However, the payoffs for hits (correctly responding "yes" when the stimulus is presented) and correct rejections (correctly responding "absent" when the stimulus is not presented) modulate the likelihood of an individual reporting that a stimulus is present or absent. For example, consider a sonar operator in a submarine listening to signals that could be interpreted as either an enemy ship or background noise. Because it is very important to detect a signal in this situation, the sonar operator may be biased to say "yes," another ship is present, even when the stimulus intensity is very low and could just be background noise. As shown in Figure 2b, this bias will not only lead to a high hit probability, but it will also lead to a high false-alarm probability (i.e., incorrectly reporting that a ship is there when there is only noise). Signal detection theory allows researchers to tease apart the sensitivity that the participant has in discriminating between signal and signal plus noise distributions (reflected by changes in d prime) and any bias that the individual may bring into the decision-making situation (reflected by changes in Beta).

Signal detection theory has been used to illustrate the independent roles of signal strength and response bias not only in perceptual experiments but also in other domains, such as

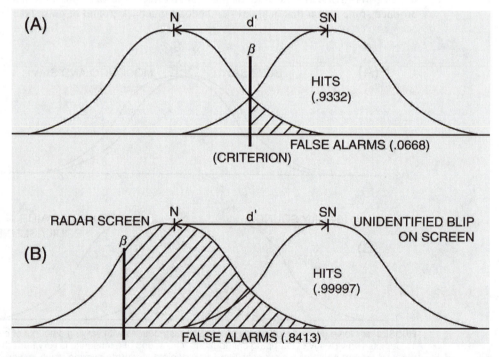

**FIGURE 2** ■ The influence of the placement of the decision criterion (Beta) on hits and false alarm rates. Figure 2a depicts a decision criterion placed to maximize hits and minimize false alarms. Figure 2b depicts a situation where one is very biased to make a hit independent of the accompanying change in false alarms. From Lachman, Lachman, and Butterfield (1979), reprinted with permission of Lawrence Erlbaum Associates.

attention, memory, and decision making. Consistent with the distinction between sensitivity and bias, different variables affect d prime and Beta. Variables such as subject motivation and the proportion of signal trials influence the placement of the decision criterion (Beta) but not the distance between the signal plus noise and noise distributions on the sensory energy scale (d prime). On the other hand, variables such as stimulus intensity influence the distance between the signal plus noise and noise distributions (d prime) but not the placement of the decision criterion (Beta).

## Memory Methods

Ebbinghaus' (1885–1913) classic studies of human memory remain important as one of the first studies to use experimental methods to investigate distinct aspects of memory. One of the methods was the *savings-in-learning* technique, in which he studied and restudied lists of nonsense syllables (e.g., *PUV*) to a criterion of perfect recitation. Memory was defined as the reduction in the number of trials necessary to relearn a list to criterion, relative to the number of trials necessary to first learn a list. Since the work of Ebbinghaus, there has been considerable development in the methods used to study memory.

Researchers often attempt to distinguish between three different aspects of memory: encoding (the initial storage of information), retention (the delay between storage and the use of information), and retrieval (the access of the earlier stored information). For example, one way of investigating encoding processes is to manipulate the participants' expectancies for a memory task (see Craik & Tulving, 1975, paper). During intentional study, participants are explicitly told to study for a later memory test. In contrast, during incidental study, participants are *not* told to study for a memory test. Rather, they are given a secondary task that engages a particular type of processing (e.g., rating the pleasantness of a word versus simply counting its letters). Hyde and Jenkins (1969) found that both the intentionality of learning and the type of encoding influenced later memory performance.

Studies of the retention of information most often involve varying the delay between study and test; of interest are the influences of the passage of time on memory performance. However, researchers soon realized that it is not simply the passage of time that matters but also what occurs during the passage of time (Waugh & Norman, 1965). In order to address this, researchers developed retroactive interference paradigms, in which they manipulate the similarity of post-event information to the original to-be-remembered events. Results from such studies clearly indicate that interference is a powerful modulator of memory performance (see Anderson & Neely, 1996, for a review). The classic paper by Loftus, Miller, and Burns (1978) is an example of interference in an applied setting—namely, eyewitness testimony.

There are two general classes of methods used to tap into memory retrieval processes. On an *explicit memory test,* the participants are presented with a list of materials during an encoding stage, and at some later point in time they are given a test in which they are asked to directly retrieve the earlier presented material. There are three common measures of explicit memory: recall, recognition, and cued recall. During a recall test (akin to a classroom essay test), participants attempt to remember earlier presented material either in the order that it was presented (serial recall) or in any order (free recall). Of interest is how much subjects recall, as well as any intrusions of non-presented items. Researchers often compare the order of information during recall to the initial order of presentation (serial recall functions); order-of-recall data are also informative as to the organizational strategies that individuals invoke during retrieval (measures of subjective organization and clustering). In order to investigate more complex materials such as stories and discourse processing, researchers sometimes measure the propositional structure of the recalled information. The notion is that in order to comprehend a story, individuals rely on a network of interconnected propositions (see Bransford & Johnson, 1972, reading). A proposition is a flexible representation of a sentence that contains a predicate (e.g., an adjective or a verb) and an argument (e.g., a noun or a pronoun). By looking at the recall of the propositions, one can provide insights into the representation that the individuals may have gleaned from a story (Kintsch & van Dijk, 1978).

Of course, there may be memories available that the individual may not be able to produce in a free recall test. Thus, researchers sometimes employ a cued recall test, which is quite similar to free recall, with the exception that the participant is provided with a retrieval cue at the time of recall. In a recognition task, participants are given the earlier presented information and are asked to discriminate this information from new information. The two most common types of recognition tests are the forced choice recognition test and the free choice or yes/no recognition test. On a forced choice recognition test (akin to a classroom multiple choice test), a participant chooses which of two or more items is old. On a yes/no recognition test (akin to a classroom true/false test), a participant indicates whether each item in a large set of items is old or new.

A second general class of memory tests has some similarity to Ebbinghaus' original savings method. These are called *implicit memory tests*. The distinguishing aspect of implicit tests is that participants are not asked to directly recollect an earlier episode. Rather, participants are asked to engage in a task where performance often benefits from earlier exposure to the stimulus items. For example, participants could be presented with a list of words (e.g., elephant, library, assassin) to name aloud during encoding, and then later they would be presented with a list of word fragments (e.g., _le_ _a_ t) or word stems (e.g., ele _ _ _ _ _) to complete. Some of these fragments or stems might reflect earlier presented items, whereas others may reflect new items. In this way, one can measure the benefit (also called priming) of previous exposure to the items compared to novel items. Interestingly, amnesics are often unimpaired in implicit memory tests, yet show considerable impairment in explicit memory tests (see papers by Jacoby, Woloshyn, & Kelly, 1989; and by Tulving, 1985, for further discussion of these dissociations).

## Chronometric Methods

In addition to relying on experiments to discriminate among classes of mental operations, cognitive psychologists have also attempted to provide information regarding the speed of mental operations. Interestingly, this work began well over a century ago with the work of Donders (1868–1969). In an attempt to isolate the speed of mental processes, Donders developed a set of response time tasks that appeared to differ only in a simple component of processing. For example, Task A might have required Process 1 (stimulus encoding), whereas Task B might have required both Process 1 (stimulus encoding) and Process 2 (binary decision). According to Donder's *subtractive method,* cognitive operations can be added and removed without influencing other cognitive operations. This has been referred to as the assumption of pure insertion and deletion. In the previous example, the duration of the binary decision process could have been estimated by subtracting the reaction time in Task A from the reaction time in Task B.

In Sternberg's (1969) classic paper, he points out that the pure insertion assumptions of subtractive factors have some inherent difficulties. For example, the speed of a given process might change when coupled with other processes. Therefore, one cannot provide a pure estimate of the speed of a given process. As an alternative, Sternberg introduced *additive factors logic.* According to additive factors logic, if a task contains distinct processes, there should be variables that selectively influence the speed of each process. Thus, if two variables influence different processes, their effects should be statistically additive. However, if two variables influence the same process, their effects should statistically interact, that is, the effect of one independent variable is dependent upon the level of another independent variable. In this way, additive factor methods allow one to use studies of response latency to provide information regarding the sequence of stages and the manner in which such processes are influenced by independent variables.

Unfortunately, even additive factors logic has some difficulties. Specifically, additive factors logic works if one assumes a discrete serial stage model of information processing, in which the output of a processing stage is not passed on to the next stage until the current stage is complete. However, there is a second class of models that assumes that the output of a given stage can begin to influence the next stage of processing before processing is complete. These are called cascade models; they are so named to capture the notion that the flow of mental processes (like a stream over multiple stones) can occur simultaneously across multiple stages. McClelland (1979) has shown that if one assumes a cascade model, then one cannot use additive factors logic to unequivocally determine the locus of the effects of independent variables.

One cannot consider reaction time measures without considering accuracy because there is an inherent tradeoff between speed and accuracy. Specifically, behaviors typically are less accurate when completed too quickly (e.g., consider the danger associated with driving too fast or the errors associated with solving a set of arithmetic problems under time demands). Most chronometric researchers attempt to ensure that accuracy is quite high, most often above 90% correct, thereby minimizing the concern about accuracy. However, as shown in Figure 3, Pachella (1974) has developed an idealized speed-accuracy tradeoff function that provides estimates of changes in speed across conditions and how such changes might relate to changes in accuracy. Of course, this will depend on the emphasis on speed

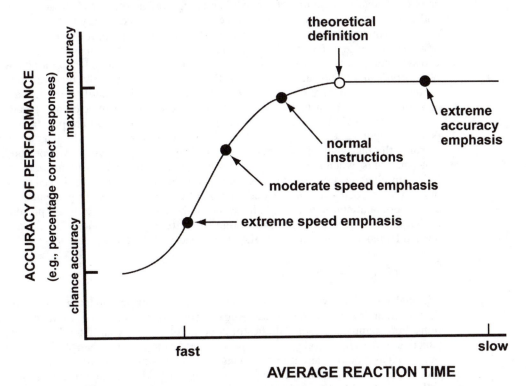

**FIGURE 3** ■ Idealized speed-accuracy operating characteristic, from Pachella (1974), and reprinted with permission of Lawrence Erlbaum Associates.

or accuracy within the experimental setting. The importance of Pachella's conceptualization is that at some locations of the speed-accuracy tradeoff curve, very small changes in accuracy can lead to large changes in response latency and at other locations on this curve, large changes in accuracy can lead to small changes in response latency. More recently, researchers have capitalized on the relation between speed and accuracy to empirically obtain estimates of speed-accuracy functions across different conditions. In these deadline experiments, participants are given a probe that signals the participant to terminate processing at a given point in time. By varying the delay of the deadline, one can track changes in the speed-accuracy function across conditions and thereby determine if an effect of a variable is in encoding or retrieval of information, or both (see Meyer, Osman, Irwin, & Yantis, 1988, for a review).

It is important to note that although the temporal dynamics of virtually all cognitive processes can (and probably should) be measured, attention and language processing are the areas that have relied most heavily on chronometric methods. For example, in the area of word recognition, researchers have used the lexical decision task (participants make word/nonword judgments) and speeded naming performance (speed taken to begin the overt pronunciation of a word) to develop models of word recognition (see Balota & Lorch, 1986, and Swinney, 1979, papers). These studies have looked at stimulus variables such as its syntactic class (e.g., DOG vs. RUN), whether it is more abstract or concrete (e.g., FAITH vs. TRUCK), and the frequency with which a word appears in the English language (e.g., ORB vs. DOG). In addition, eye-tracking methods have been developed that allow one to measure how long the reader looks at a particular word (e.g., fixation and gaze measures) while engaged in more natural reading. Interestingly, in contrast to our intuition, our eyes do not smoothly move across a line of text while reading. Rather, our eyes land at a given location and stay there for about a quarter of a second and then make a very fast movement (called a saccade) that takes only 20 milliseconds (1 millisecond equals 1/1000th of a second) to a new location of text. Eye-tracking data have yielded important insights into the semantic and syntactic processes that modulate the speed of recognizing and integrating a word with other words in the surrounding text (see Rayner & Pollatsek, 1989, for a review).

Researchers in the area of attention have also relied quite heavily on speeded tasks. For example, two common techniques in attention research are interference paradigms and cueing paradigms. In interference paradigms, at least two stimuli are presented that compete for output. An excellent example of this is the *Stroop task,* in which a person is asked to name the ink color of a printed word (see Stroop, 1935, paper). Under conditions of conflict, that is, when the word *green* is printed in red ink, there is a considerable increase in response latency compared to nonconflict conditions (e.g., the word *deep* printed in red ink). In the second class of speeded attention tasks, individuals are presented with visual cues to orient attention to specific locations in the visual field. A target is presented either at that location or at a different location. The difference in response latency to cued and uncued targets is used to measure the effectiveness of the attentional cue.

## Cross-Population Studies

Although cognitive psychologists rely most heavily on college students as their target sample, there is an increasing interest in studying cognitive operations across quite distinct populations. For example, there are studies of cognition from early childhood (see Berko, 1958, paper) to older adulthood that attempt to trace developmental changes in specific operations such as memory, attention, and language processing. In addition, there are studies of special populations that may have a breakdown in a particular cognitive operation. Specifically, there has been considerable work attempting to understand the attentional breakdowns that occur in schizophrenia (Cohen & Serban-Schreiber, 1992) and the memory breakdowns that occur in Alzheimer's disease (Balota & Faust, 2002). Also of interest is the other end of the spectrum, namely, cognition at its best. The point is to understand how the cognitive processes of experts differ from novices in domain-specific ways. For example, categorization researchers have studied expert bird-watchers, decision researchers have studied economists, and attention researchers have studied x-ray technicians and bingo players. Thus, researchers have begun to explore distinct populations (both the skilled and the less skilled) to provide further leverage in isolating cognitive activity.

## Case Studies

After a trauma to the brain, there are sometimes breakdowns in apparently isolated components of cognitive performance (see Farah, 1989; Fromkin et al., 1974; and Sacchett & Humphreys, 1992, papers). Thus, studying these individuals and their deficits may provide insights into the cognitive architecture. For example, there is the classic case of HM, an individual whose medial temporal lobes were removed in an attempt to relieve epilepsy. HM produced severe memory deficits on explicit tests, although his performance on implicit memory tests was relatively intact. This is an example of a *dissociation,* the impairment of one ability but not another. A dissociation suggests that the two processes rely on different brain areas (i.e., that implicit and explicit memory rely on different brain areas).

Of particular interest are *double dissociations,* the finding of both patterns of impairment and sparing. For example, two very different patterns of language impairment have been observed following damage to two different brain areas (see Geschwind, 1972, paper). Broca's aphasics (who have damage to posterior left frontal areas) have relatively spared comprehension processes but difficulty producing fluent speech. In contrast, Wernicke aphasics (who have damage to left temporal areas near where they meet occipital and parietal areas) have impaired comprehension processes but relatively fluent speech production. Double dissociations provide stronger evidence for the two processes being linked to two distinct brain areas; a single dissociation may occur when a process normally conducted by the damaged brain area is rerouted to a different pathway or compensated for via an atypical strategy.

## Measures of Brain Activity

With the increasing technical sophistication of the neurosciences, there has recently been an influx of studies that measure the brain correlates of mental activity (Posner & Raichle, 1994). Although other methods are available, we will review only the three most common here. The first is the *evoked potential* method. In this method, the researcher measures the electrical activity of systems of neurons (i.e., brain waves) as the individual is engaged in some cognitive task. This procedure has excellent temporal resolution but is less specific as to the brain locus of the activity.

An approach that has much better spatial resolution is *Positron Emission Tomography* (PET). In this approach, displayed in Figure 4, the individual receives an injection of a radioactive isotope, which emits signals that are measured by a scanner (see Petersen, Fox, Posner, Mintun, & Raichle, 1988, paper). The notion is that there will be increased blood flow (which carries the isotope) to the most active areas of the brain. In this way, as shown in Figure 5 (see color insert following page 176), one can actually look at the activation in a given slice of the brain as the participant is engaged in a given task. Typically, these scans involve about a minute of some form of cognitive processing (e.g., reading visually presented words). As shown in Figure 6 (see color insert), researchers often subtract out the pattern of blood flow in a different task that primarily differs on the targeted operation (e.g., looking at a fixation cross). Given the window of time necessary for such scans (on

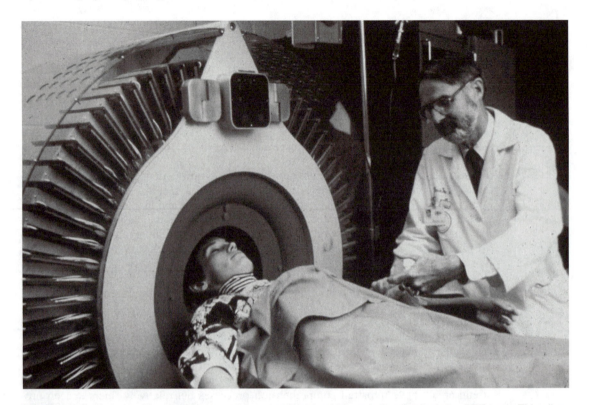

**FIGURE 4** ■ An example of a participant receiving a radioactive isotope before beginning a PET scan. This allows researchers to measure blood flow in targeted areas of the brain while the subject is engaged in a cognitive task, such as word reading.

the order of a minute), the PET approach has some temporal limitations in measuring cognitive operations that last on the order of milliseconds.

A second more recent approach is *functional Magnetic Resonance Imaging* (fMRI). This procedure is less invasive because it does not involve a radioactive injection. A similar "subtraction" logic is used as in the PET scans; researchers compare the correlates of brain activity during two different cognitive processes. However, methodological advances in this area suggest that one can look at a more fine-grained temporal resolution in fMRI, at least compared to PET techniques. Ultimately, the wedding of evoked potential and fMRI signals may provide the necessary temporal and spatial resolution of the neural signals that underlie cognitive processes (see Robertson, Gernsbacher, Guidotti, Robertson, Irwin, Mock, & Campan, 2000; Tong, Nakayama, Vaughan, & Kanwisher, 1998, papers).

## Computational Modeling

Most models of cognition, although grounded in the experimental method, are metaphorical and noncomputational in nature. For example, information-processing models that propose separate short-term and long-term memory stores do so in a descriptive sense. However, there is also an important method in cognitive psychology that uses computationally explicit models (see Marr's 1982 paper). One example of this approach is connectionist/ neural network modeling, in which relatively simple processing units are often layered in a highly interconnected network (see the McClelland, Rumelhart, & Hinton, 1986, paper). Activation patterns across the simple processing units are computationally tracked across time to make specific predictions regarding the effects of stimulus and task manipulations. Computational models are used in a number of ways to better understand the cognitive architecture. First, these models force researchers to be very explicit regarding the underlying assumptions of metaphorical models. Second, these models often can be used to help explain differences across conditions. Specifically, if a manipulation has a given effect in the data, then one may be able to trace that effect in the architecture within the model and pinpoint what part of the model is implicated. Third, these models can provide important insights into different ways of viewing a given set of data. For example, as noted earlier, McClelland (1979) demonstrated that cascadic models could handle data that were initially viewed as supportive of serial stage models.

## Theories in Cognitive Psychology

The primary goal of cognitive psychology is to use the scientific method to understand mental activity. Because mental activity is not directly observable, cognitive science is heavily theory laden. Theories attempt to provide an explanation of the results from a large number of studies and make predictions that can be directly tested in future studies. A good theory should reduce complex behavior to a limited set of principles that explain why some phenomena occur in some circumstances but not in others. However, there are some general limitations to theories that are noteworthy. For example, because most cognitive theory is based on observable independent and dependent variables, theories are less informative regarding the structures and processes hypothesized to intervene between the manipulations and behavior. In fact, Anderson (1976) has argued that behavioral data may not allow one to distinguish between theories that assume very different representations and processes. Theories must then be guided by other criteria such as parsimony, effectiveness, generality, and accuracy. For example, a good theory should be parsimonious, that is, provide an account of a set of data with relatively few assumptions.

Given the difficulty in cognitive theory development, how does one build confidence in a theory? *Converging operations* have been used extensively by cognitive scientists to discriminate among alternative theoretical accounts of particular patterns of data (Garner, Hake, & Eriksen, 1956). Converging operations reflect the use of two or more experimental operations that eliminate an alternative theoretical account of a set of data. If Theory A is consistently supported after being pitted against reasonable competing theoretical accounts of a set of data, then there is increased confidence in Theory A.

In order for the reader to gain some appreciation for cognitive theories, a brief overview of some of the major theoretical issues is presented. Obviously, it would be impossible to cover the richness of theory development in such a limited space. Thus, we have chosen to cover theoretical issues that have stirred controversy in the field. As one will see, these issues consistently arise in the classic papers that were chosen for this volume.

### Bottom-Up versus Interactive Models of Pattern Recognition

Models of perception attempt to explain, in large part, how patterns are recognized. Our intuitions might suggest the following "bottom-up" stream of events: patterns in the environment activate sensory receptive systems (e.g., ears and eyes), and these systems provide signals that are transformed into higher-level representations that provide information regarding the identity of a stimulus pattern. For example, as described in Neisser's paper, the Pandemonium model of letter recognition (Selfridge & Neisser, 1960) is one of the first examples of a bottom-up feature detection model. Stimuli first activate a set of feature detectors (e.g., vertical lines, horizontal lines, oblique patterns, diagonals), and these feature detectors are combined to activate relevant letters (e.g., the letter E would be activated by the presence of three horizontal lines and one vertical line). Ultimately, the most activated letter is selected as the target to report. Interestingly, not long after Selfridge's theoretical model was introduced, results from electrophysiological studies provided some converging evidence for feature-like detectors in nonhuman species (e.g., Hubel & Wiesel, 1962).

Although evidence for feature detectors exists, and the bottom-up approach is intuitively appealing, there is also support for an alternative perspective, called the interactive model, which assumes that pattern recognition is not simply controlled by the stimulus but is aided by pre-existing memory representations. For example, one of the findings in support of an interactive position is the word superiority effect. This is the finding that letters embedded within words are better perceived than letters embedded in nonwords or presented in isolation. The resulting theoretical conundrum is this: How can the word representation influence the letters that make up the word, as the letters must have been already identified in route to recognizing the word? These findings led McClelland (1979) to propose that higher-order mental representations influence recognition via a processing cascade. Specifically, early in perception, before letter recognition has occurred, letter units begin receiving activation, and partial activation is transferred to higher-order representations (e.g., words). These higher-order representations then transmit partial activation back down to the relevant letter representations, actually helping to constrain the perception of those letters.

The interactive perspective with both bottom-up and top-down processes has been very influential because it suggests that the stimulus is not the only source of information. Rather, over time the perceiver adds information to the stimulus information and hence actively constructs the perceptual experience. It is precisely this type of "added" information that provides a way of understanding perceptual illusions and potentially memories of events that never occurred. Our perceptions and memories involve an elaborate interaction between the external stimulus and pre-existing knowledge.

One of the major theoretical debates that has arisen in this area is the extent to which there are interactions among distinct systems within the processing system (see papers by Reicher, 1969; Simons & Levin, 1998; Tong et al., 1998). According to the modular approach (e.g., Fodor, 1983), there are modular (self-contained) systems that only provide feed-forward information from lower-level systems to higher-level systems. On the other hand, some theorists believe in almost complete interactivity across systems. For example, consider the processes by which the meanings of ambiguous words are resolved in sentence contexts. The modular approach suggests that when processing an ambiguous word (e.g., the word *organ* can refer to a musical instrument or a bodily organ), a prior sentence context such as "The musician played both the piano and the organ" does not influence which meaning becomes initially activated (i.e., both the musical instrument meaning and the body meaning of *organ* would become initially activated). The classic paper by Swinney (1979) supports this view. In contrast, the interactive approach suggests that prior sentence context should control which meaning becomes initially activated (i.e., only the contextually relevant meaning becomes activated). Although the original research in this area strongly supported the modular approach, more recent work has indicated that a strong sentence context can influence the initial interpretation of ambiguous linguistic structures (see Gorfein, 2001, for recent discussion of these issues).

## Attentional Selection: "Early or Late"

One of the most difficult issues that cognitive scientists have had to grapple with is how to empirically address and theoretically model human attention. For example, how do people at a crowded party ignore distracting information and focus on (i.e., attend to) one conversation? As in pattern recognition, we all have intuitions regarding attention, but how does one develop a theory of attention based on experimental studies? Researchers have used metaphors such as attentional filters, switches, reservoirs of capacity, spotlights, executive processors, and many more. Although attention research ultimately touches on all areas of cognitive psychology, most researchers work on specific aspects of attention, such as the locus of attentional selection, its relationship to consciousness, and aspects of attentional control and automaticity.

Much of the early theoretical debate focused on the extent to which unattended stimuli are processed. "Early selection" models postulated that selection occurs at a relatively early level in the system, before meaning has been extracted. Support for this notion was initially provided by studies using the dichotic listening task. In the classic paper by Cherry (1953), listeners were given a very demanding primary task to one ear (verbally repeating the information presented over headphones, i.e., shadowing), while information was simultaneously presented to the other ear. The results suggested that participants did not notice much information presented to the unattended ear; for example, they did not even notice a switch to a different language. However, researchers soon realized that attentional selection was not an all-or-none phenomenon. For example, if the unattended channel contains a highly relevant stimulus (e.g., your name), then this information is likely to be recalled (Moray, 1959). Returning to the crowded party example presented earlier, one would be able to tune out most of the other conversations at the party, but if one hears something that is highly relevant to oneself (e.g., one's own name), then it is likely that one would attend to this information. The topic of attentional selection has invoked rather widespread interest not only in studies of healthy young adults but also in the neuropsychological literature. In some patient populations (such as people with attention deficit disorders or schizophrenia), there may be a breakdown in the amount of information getting into the system (i.e., a breakdown in the attentional selection system), thereby overloading any limited capacity aspect of the processing system.

A related issue is the control of attention (see the Posner & Snyder paper). Again, our intuition would suggest that we have control over what we attend. However, researchers have become interested in situations where effects of variables are outside of the individual's attentional control. If we return to the Stroop (1935) paper, described earlier, participants were slower to name the color of a word printed in an incongruent color (e.g., the word *red* printed in blue) than to name the color of a neutral word such as *run*. Some researchers have argued that this interference occurs because words invoke a qualitatively distinct type of processing, referred to as automatic processing. The idea is that words automatically activate their meaning (outside of attentional control), and this automatic processing produces conflict when the color and the word information are inconsistent. Automatic processes are well practiced and under consistent stimulus to response mappings. In the prior example, the word *blue* is read easily due to practice, its meaning is highly processed, and the symbol maps to a consistent meaning. Because these processes have in some sense been wired into the system, they are relatively outside the scope of attentional control. Researchers have addressed theoretically interesting questions regarding development of automaticity such as its time course, the role of conscious control, the influence of practice, and even the neurophysiological substrates. Thus, the distinction between automatic and attentional control processes has been a central theme in current theory development.

## Separate versus Unitary Memory Systems

Our intuition suggests that there are several different memory systems. For example, rehearsing a telephone number until it is dialed seems to be quite distinct from recalling what one had for breakfast, which also seems quite distinct from providing the definition of the low-frequency word *orb* from memory. Indeed, there is a rich history of memory research supporting distinct types of memory systems, such as short-term, long- term, implicit, explicit, and so on. Are these types of memory reflective of distinct memory systems, or are they best understood in terms of a single system that utilizes different processes?

The debate over memory types has had a long tradition in cognitive psychology. For example, Atkinson and Shiffrin (1968) introduced an information-processing model consisting of sensory, short-term, and long-term memory stores (see Waugh & Norman, 1965). This distinction was based in part on apparent qualitative differences between short-term and long-term memories; short-term memories appeared to be coded phonetically, whereas long-term memories were more semantic. However, shortly thereafter, Craik and Lockhart (1972) advanced a unitary view of memory referred to as "levels of processing." The idea was that the level at which information is initially processed determines how well it will be encoded in memory. Memory for information processed at a "shallow" level (e.g., visual features) differs from memory processed at a "deep" (e.g., meaning) level (see the paper by Craik & Tulving, 1975). Thus, the distinction between short- and long-term memories could also be viewed as a distinction between different types of encoding processes.

As noted earlier, distinctions also have been made between explicit (directly recollecting an earlier experience) and implicit memory systems (the benefit from an earlier exposure to a stimulus on an indirect measure). For example, encoding manipulations that lead to a particular result on explicit measures (e.g., recall of a list of words) can produce opposite effects on implicit measures (e.g., perceptual identification of a visually degraded word) (e.g., Jacoby, 1983). The levels-of-processing effect described earlier occurs on explicit but not implicit tests. These dissociations would appear to support distinct memory systems. However, this evidence was challenged by Roediger, Weldon, and Challis (1989), who argued that many of the dissociations that appear in the literature could also be accommodated within the transfer-appropriate-processing (TAP) framework. This approach emphasizes the match between encoding operations and retrieval operations. Roediger et al. noted that studies of implicit memory often emphasized data-driven processes, whereas studies of explicit memory often emphasized conceptually driven processes. They also argued that if dissociations were the criterion for separate systems, we would need many more than just two or three distinct systems.

Finally, even the dissociation between abstract category information and individual episodic experiences has been challenged. That is, do people store representations of each and every episode they encounter, or do they store some sort of general representation that captures only the gist of the individuals' experiences? Posner and Keele (1968), among others, have argued for a distinct representation for prototypes/categories (e.g., DOG) that represent the common attributes of members within a category (e.g., COLLIE, POODLE, BEAGLE). More recent work by Hintzman (1986) and Barsalou (1991) has suggested that this may be an unnecessary distinction. Rather, a model assuming only one type of instance-based memory system can accommodate the evidence supporting qualitatively distinct representations for instances and prototypes (see the paper by Medin, 1989). These theorists argue that the "apparent" distinction between category and instances falls quite naturally from correlations among the features across members within a category. That is, collies, poodles, and beagles all have four legs, bark, have fur, are good pets, and so on. It is the similarity across these features that produce the DOG category.

Although there is still theoretical debate regarding distinct memory systems versus distinct processing engaged by different tasks, it is important to note that there is an accumulation of evidence for some memory system distinctions. For example, as described earlier, results indicate that amnesics perform poorly on explicit memory tasks, whereas their performance on implicit tasks is often normal. Thus, the lesion produced in these individuals would appear to be primarily affecting one system, while leaving the other system intact (Squire, 1987). Moreover, evidence from brain-imaging studies also is beginning to provide evidence for distinct memory systems (Nyberg, Cabeza, & Tulving, 1996). Thus, although it is clearly the case that *some* memory system dissociations are more apparent than real, it is also the case that some system dissociations are in fact real (see the paper by Tulving, 1985).

## Analog versus Propositional Representations of Mental Images

Humans have little difficulty imagining stimuli that are typically perceived via the senses. For example, we have little difficulty imagining a shiny red apple or a yellow school bus. The theoretical issue concerns the form of the representation underlying an image. For example, do mental images demand a qualitatively different form of representation than the representation that we use to process language?

One popular notion of imagery posits that the mental code retains the spatial and sensory properties of the external stimuli we perceive. This would be an *analog* representation. For example, an analog representation of the neighborhood in which we live would preserve the relative distances between houses and their sizes. Accordingly, the time it takes to mentally scan between two objects in a mental image should reflect their relative distance to each other. Many experiments have demonstrated this to be the case (see the Kosslyn, Ball, & Reiser, 1978, paper). The alternative view of imagery posits that mental images are represented as abstract propositions. According to this account, mental images and language rely on the same primitive code, and the brain uses this single form to process all types of information (i.e., "the language of thought," Fodor, 1975). The generation of images occurs after this primitive code is accessed.

The results from recent studies of the neuropsychological underpinnings of mental imagery have informed the debate on analog versus prepositional representations. For example, Kosslyn, Thompson, Kim, and Alpert (1995) used brain imaging to demonstrate that visual images activate areas of the brain dedicated to visual processing. More critically, for both perception and imagery, activations within neural systems were correlated with the size of the stimuli. Thus, there appears to be a link between the neural systems that underlie imagery and actual visual perception. This assertion is further supported by studies of individuals with brain lesions. Researchers have noted dissociations between different aspects of visual imagery, such as the spatial versus the visual nature of the image (e.g., Farah, Hammond, Levine, & Calvanio, 1988). Thus, it is clear that important constraints have been placed on theories of visual imagery by both behavioral and neuropsychological evidence (see papers by Farah, 1989; Kosslyn, Ball & Reiser, 1978; Shepard & Metzler, 1971).

## Connectionist versus Symbolic Representations

One issue that has recently received a considerable amount of attention is the level of description needed for models of higher-level cognition such as language processing and problem solving. For example, how might one build a theory of orthography, phonology, or syntax within a language? One might assume a set of rules, based on linguistic theory, that specifies how the constituents can be combined within a language. For example, a rule might specify that the vowel that precedes the letter *e* at the end of a word, as in *gave*, should be elongated. Such "rules" provide a descriptive account of many phenomena in language processing. Unfortunately, as in most rules, there are many exceptions. For example, according to the previous rule, the word *have* should be pronounced such that it rhymes with *save*. Thus, linguistic models are often forced to provide a separate processing route for such exceptions.

Within the past decade, there has been an increased appreciation for an alternative way of modeling aspects of human cognition, that is, connectionist modeling (see the paper by Rumelhart & McClelland, 1986). Connectionist models typically assume a relatively simple set of processing units that are in distinct layers, with all the processing units within a layer connected to all the processing units in adjacent layers. These models do not assume any rules and are mathematically specified. "Knowledge" of a domain is contained in the values of weighted connections linking units. The connection weights are either built into the models or are adjusted according to a gradual learning algorithm. In the second case, activation patterns are updated based on the frequency of exposure to a given stimulus and the deviation of the correct response to the current output. Interestingly, the general principles of connectionist modeling have been used to account for many aspects of cognitive processes (i.e., pattern recognition, speech production, category learning).

There has clearly been some tension between symbolic rule-based theories and connectionist theories (e.g., Fodor & Pylyshyn, 1988). One might argue that the symbolic models reflect the first wave of cognitive theorizing. These models are often metaphorical in nature, that is, performance can be modeled by a specific set of stages and a specific set of rules at each stage. These models remain central in current theories of human cognition. On the other hand, connectionist models have a level of computational specificity that is quite appealing. Moreover, there is at least some sense of neural plausibility within such connectionist models (i.e., the simple processing units have some surface level resemblance to neurons, whereas rules are difficult to envisage within a neural network). Ultimately, the adequacy of such models may lie in their ability to provide new insights into understanding data. Because both types of models have advantages, it is likely that both will continue to be central to theoretical accounts of human cognition (Spieler & Balota, 1997). The papers by Marcus, Vijayan, Rao, and Vishton (1999) and Saffran, Aslin, and Newport (1996) are excellent recent examples of this theoretical debate in the area of language acquisition by 7- and 8-month-old infants.

## About This Volume

This introductory chapter briefly reviewed the major topics, methods, and theoretical controversies of cognitive psychology.[1] The fundamental theoretical issues will be more fully explored in the classic papers selected for this volume. The papers will expose the readers to some of the specific approaches researchers have developed to gain leverage on these central questions. It is hoped that the combination of this introductory chapter, the introductory sections at the beginning of each of the chapters to follow, and the classic papers will afford the reader some appreciation for the remarkable insights cognitive psychologists have provided into the scientific study of mental processes.

The book includes 11 chapters, in addition to this general introductory chapter. Each of the remaining chapters begins with an introduction to the topic that places the selected papers in their relevant theoretical and historical context. There are three to seven papers in each chapter; some of these have been edited to ease the reader's job. None of these edits, however, dilute the overall main point of the articles. At the close of each chapter, the reader will find a list of suggested readings (each with an explanation for why it might be of interest) and a series of discussion questions. Due to space constraints, we were unable to include all of the papers we wished to include, and thus we encourage the interested reader to take advantage of the many reference sections in this book!

Choosing the papers was an incredibly tough task. We wanted historical papers (true classics), but we also wanted to expose the reader to recent advances. We wanted a mix of empirical, review, and theoretical papers. We wanted to sample from the many methods of cognitive psychology, including case studies, observation, behavioral experiments, connectionist models, and neuroimaging studies. We also wanted to choose papers friendly to undergraduates and beginning graduate students. Even with all these constraints, there are simply too many good papers for us to include them all here. In the end, though, we feel that we have an important set of papers. On average, the papers in this volume have been cited 665 times, and the median number of citations is 417! This is particularly impressive if the reader remembers that many scientific papers are never cited even once, and each section includes one or two recent papers that were not afforded time for citations to accumulate.

We have one last piece of advice for the reader. The reader may be tempted to treat each paper as an independent entity, but, of course, one of the goals of this volume is to stimulate an integrative approach. With the aid of the introductions, the reader should be able to link each paper to larger themes and problems in cognitive psychology. In addition, some of the discussion questions cut across chapters (as do many of the problems in our field!). Any chapter may be read in isolation, but the best experience would be to read the chapters in the order in which they appear.

Many colleagues provided invaluable advice about this volume. In the early stages, Kristi Multhaup made numerous useful suggestions. Sheila Black, Nelson Cowan, Dale Dagenbach, Janet Duchek, Richard Ferraro, Alice Healy, Mark McDaniel, Tram Neill, David Payne, Henry L. Roediger III, Greg Simpson, and Jeffrey Zacks reviewed an early version of the paper list and provided much useful feedback. A number of persistent research assistants helped with technical details, including Shana Blumenthal, Elana Graber, Jeff Templeton, and Daniella Van Hooren. We are grateful for all the assistance we have received with this project.

## NOTE

[1] Portions of this chapter were based in part on papers by Balota and Cortese (2000) and Balota and Watson (2000).

## REFERENCES

Anderson, J. R. (1976). Arguments concerning representations for mental imagery. *Psychological Review, 85,* 249–277.

Anderson, M. C., & Neely, J. H. (1996). Interference and inhibition in memory retrieval. In E. L. Bjork & R. A. Bjork (Eds.), *Memory.* New York: Academic Press.

Atkinson, R. C., & Shiffrin, R. M. (1968). Human memory: A proposed system and its control processes. In W. K. Spence & J. T. Spence (Eds.), *The psychology of learning and motivation: Advances in research and theory* (Vol. 2, pp. 89–195). San Diego, CA: Academic Press.

Balota, D. A., & Cortese, M. J. (2000). Theories in cognitive psychology, in A. Kazdin (Ed.), *Encyclopedia of Psychology* (Volume 2, pp. 153–158). Oxford University Press.

Balota, D. A., & Faust, M. E. (2002). Attention in Alzheimers disease. In F. Boller & S. Cappa (Eds.), *Handbook of Neuropsychology,* 2nd ed. (Vol. 6, pp. 51–80). New York: Elsevier Science.

Balota, D. A., & Lorch, R. F. (1986). Depth of automatic spreading activation: Mediated priming effects in pronunciation but not in lexical decision. *Journal of Experimental Psychology: Learning, Memory and Cognition, 12,* 336–345.

Balota, D. A., & Watson, J. W. (2000). Methods in cognitive psychology, in A. Kazdin (Ed.), *Encyclopedia of Psychology* (Volume 2, pp. 158–162). Oxford University Press.

Barsolou, L. W. (1991). Deriving categories to achieve goals. In G. H. Bower (Ed.), *The psychology of learning and motivation* (Vol. 27, pp. 1–64). San Diego, CA: Academic Press.

Berko, J. (1958). The child's learning of English morphology. *Word, 14,* 150–177.

Bransford, J. D., & Johnson, M. K. (1972). Contextual prerequisites for understanding: Some investigations of comprehension and recall. *Journal of Verbal Learning and Verbal Behavior, 11,* 717–726.

Cherry, E. C. (1953). Some experiments on the recognition of speech, with one and two ears. *Journal of the Acoustical Society of America, 25,* 975–979.

Cohen, J. D., & Servan-Schreiber, D. (1992). Context, cortex, and dopamine: A connectionist approach to behavior and biology in schizophrenia. *Psychological Review, 99,* 45–77.

Craik, F. I. M., & Lockhart, R. S. (1972). Levels of processing: A framework for memory research. *Journal of Verbal Learning and Verbal Behavior, 11,* 671–684.

Craik, F. I. M., & Tulving, E. (1975). Depth of processing and the retention of words in episodic memory. *Journal of Experimental Psychology: General, 104,* 268–294.

Donders, F. C. (1969). On the speed of mental processes. Translated by W. G. Koster, in G. Koster (Ed.), *Attention and performance* (Vol. 2). Amsterdam: North Holland Press. (Original work published in 1868.)

Ebbinghaus, H. (1913). *Memory: A contribution to experimental psychology.* New York: Columbia University Press. (Original work published in 1885.)

Farah, M. J. (1989). The neural basis of mental imagery. *Trends in Neruoscience, 12,* 395–399.

Farah, M. J., Hammond, K. M., Levine, D. N., & Calvanio, R. (1988). Visual and spatial mental imagery: Dissociable systems of representation. *Cognitive Psychology, 20,* 439–462.

Fodor, J. A. (1975). *The language of thought.* New York: Crowell.

Fodor, J. A. (1983). *Modularity of mind.* Cambridge, MA: MIT Press.

Fodor, J. A., & Pylyshyn, Z. W. (1988). Connectionism and cognitive architecture: A critical analysis. *Cognition, 28,* 3–71.

Fromkin, V., Krashen, S., Curtiss, S., Rigler, D., & Rigler, M. (1974). The development of language in Genie: A case of language acquisition beyond the "critical period." *Brain and Language, 1,* 81–107.

Garner, W. R., Hake, H. W., & Eriksen, C. W. (1956). Operationism and the concept of perception. *Psychological Review, 63,* 149–159.

Geschwind, N. (1972). Language and brain. *Scientific American, 226*(4), 76–83.

Gorfein, D. S. (2001). *On the consequences of meaning selection: Perspectives on resolving lexical ambiguity.* Washington, DC: American Psychological Association.

Green, D. M., & Swets, J. A. (1966). *Signal detection theory and psychophysics.* New York: Wiley.

Hintzman, D. L. (1986). "Schema abstraction" in a multiple-trace memory model. *Psychological Review, 93,* 411–427.

Hubel, D. H., & Wiesel, T. N. (1962). Receptive fields, binocular interaction, and functional architecture in the cat's visual cortex. *Journal of Physiology, 160,* 106–154.

Hyde, T. S., & Jenkins, J. J. (1969). Differential effects of incidental tasks on the organization of recall of a list of highly associated words. *Journal of Experimental Psychology, 82,* 472–481.

Jacoby, L. L. (1983). Remembering the data: Analyzing interactive processes in reading. *Journal of Verbal Learning and Verbal Behavior, 22,* 485-508.

Jacoby, L. L., Woloshyn, V., & Kelley, C. (1989). Becoming famous without being recognized: Unconscious influences of memory produced by dividing attention. *Journal of Experimental Psychology: General, 118,* 115–125.

Kintsch, W., & van Dijk, T. A. (1978). Toward a model of text comprehension and production. *Psychological Review, 85,* 363–394.

Kosslyn, S. M., Ball, T. M., & Reiser, B. J. (1978). Visual images preserve metric spatial information: Evidence from studies of image scanning. *Journal of Experimental Psychology: Human Perception & Performance, 4,* 47–60.

Kosslyn, S. M., Thompson, W. L., Kim, I. J., & Alpert, N. M. (1995). Topographical representations of mental images in primary visual cortex. *Nature, 378,* 496–498.

Lachman, R., Lachman, J. L., & Butterfield, E. C. (1979). *Cognitive psychology and information processing: An introduction.* Hillsdale, NJ: Erlbaum.

Loftus, E. F., Miller, D. G., & Burns, H. J. (1978). Semantic integration of verbal information into a visual memory. *Journal of Experimental Psychology: Human Learning & Memory, 4,* 19–31.

Marcus, G. F., Vijayan, S., Rao, S. B., & Vishton, P. M. (1999). Rule learning by seven-month-old infants. *Science, 283,* 77–80.

Marr, D. (1982). *Vision: A computational investigation into the human representation and processing of visual information,* chapter 1. San Francisco, CA: Freeman.

McClelland, J. L. (1979). On the time relations of mental processes: An examination of systems of processes in cascade. *Psychological Review, 86,* 287–330.

McClelland, J. L., Rumelhart, D. E., & Hinton, G. E. (1986). The appeal of parallel distributed processing. In D. E. Rumelhart, J. L. McClelland, & the PDP Research Group (Eds.), *Parallel distributed processing: Explorations in the microstructure of cognition: Volume 1: Foundations* (pp. 1–44). Cambridge, MA: Harvard University Press.

Medin, D. L. (1989). Concepts and conceptual structure. *American Psychologist, 44,* 1469–1481.

Meyer, D. E., Osman, A. M., Irwin, D. E., & Yantis, S. (1988). Modern mental chronometry. Special Issue: Event related potential investigations of cognition. *Biological Psychology, 26,* 3–67.

Moray, N. (1959). Attention in dichotic listening: Affective cues and the influence of instructions. *Quarterly Journal of Experimental Psychology, 11,* 56–60.

Neisser, U. (1967). *Cognitive Psychology* (chap. 3, pp. 46–85).

Nyberg, L., Cabeza, R., & Tulving, E. (1996). PET studies of encoding and retrieval: The HERA model. *Psychonomic Bulletin & Review, 3,* 135–148.

Pachella, R. G. (1974). The interpretation of reaction time in information-processing research. In B. H. Kantowitz (Ed.), *Human Information Processing—Tutorials in performance and cognition.* Hillsdale, NJ: Erlbaum.

Petersen, S. E., Fox, P. T., Posner, M. I., Mintun, M., & Raichle, M. E. (1988). Positron emission tomography studies of the cortical anatomy of single word processing. *Nature, 331,* 585–589.

Posner, M. I., & Keele, S. W. (1968). On the genesis of abstract ideas. *Journal of Experimental Psychology, 77,* 353–363.

Posner, M. I., & Raichle, M. E. (1994). *Images of mind.* New York: Scientific American Library.

Posner, M. I., & Snyder, C. R. R. (1975). Attention and cognitive control. In R. L. Solso (Ed.), *Information processing and cognition: The Loyola Symposium* (pp. 55–85). Hillsdale, NJ: Erlbaum.

Rayner, K., & Pollatsek, A. (1989). *The psychology of reading.* Upper Saddle River, NJ: Prentice-Hall.

Reicher, G. M. (1969). Perceptual recognition as a function of meaningfulness of stimulus material. *Journal of Experimental Psychology, 81,* 275–280.

Robertson, D. A., Gernsbacher, M. A., Guidotti, S. J., Robertson, R. R. W., Irwin, W., Mock, B. J., & Campan, M. E. (2000). Functional neuroanatomy of the cognitive process of mapping during discourse comprehension. *Psychological Science, 11,* 255–260.

Roediger, H. L., Weldon, M. S., & Challis, B. H. (1989). Explaining dissociations between implicit and explicit measures of retention: A processing account. In H. L. Roediger & F. I. M. Craik (Eds.), *Varieties of memory and consciousness* (pp. 3–41). Hillsdale, NJ: Erlbaum.

Rumelhart, D. E., McClelland, J. L., & the PDP Research Group (1986). *Parallel distributed processing: Explorations in the microstructure of cognition: Vol. 1. Foundations.* Cambridge, MA: MIT Press.

Sacchett, C., & Humphreys, G. W. (1992). Calling a squirrel a squirrel but a canoe a wigwam: A category-specific deficit for artefactual objects and body parts. *Cognitive Neuropsychology, 9,* 73–86.

Saffran, J. R., Aslin, R. N., & Newport, E. L. (1996). Statistical learning by 8-month-old infants. *Science, 274,* 1926–1928.

Selfridge, O. G., & Neisser U. (1960). Pattern recognition by machine. *Scientific American, 203,* 60–68.

Shepard, R. N., & Metzler, J. (1971). Mental rotation of three-dimensional objects. *Science, 171,* 701–703.

Simons, D. J., & Levin, D.T. (1998). Failure to detect changes to people during a real-world interaction. *Psychonomic Bulletin & Review, 5,* 644–649.

Spieler, D. H., & Balota, D. A. (1997). Bringing computational models of word naming down to the item level. *Psychological Science, 8,* 411–416.

Squire, L. R. (1987). *Memory and brain.* New York: Oxford University Press.

Sternberg, S. (1969). The discovery of processing stages: Extensions of Donders' method. In W. G. Koster (Ed.), *Attention and performance* (Vol. 2). Amsterdam: North Holland Press.

Stroop, J. R. (1935). Studies of interference in serial verbal reactions. *Journal of Experimental Psychology, 18,* 643–661.

Swinney, D. A. (1979). Lexical access during sentence comprehension: (Re)consideration of some context effects. *Journal of Verbal Learning and Verbal Behavior, 18,* 645–659.

Titchener, E. B. (1898). *A primer of psychology.* New York: Macmillan.

Tong, F., Nakayama, K., Vaughan, J. T., & Kanwisher, N. (1998). Binocular rivalry and visual awareness in human extrastriate cortex. *Neuron, 21,* 753–759.

Tulving, E. (1985). How many memory systems are there? *American Psychologist, 40,* 385–398.

Waugh, N. C., & Norman, D. A. (1965). Primary memory. *Psychological Review, 72,* 89–104.

Wundt, W. (1874). *Principles of physiological psychology.* Leipzig: Englemann.

PART I

# Methods of Cognitive Psychology

# Introduction to Part I:
# Methods of Cognitive Psychology

Consider yourself in the situation of trying to figure out how humans think. How would you approach this topic? The first natural response is to use introspective methods, that is, to think about your own internal processes and possibly write them down and attempt to analyze what they mean. However, you must be cautious because it is possible, and actually likely, that most mental processes are simply not available to such introspective techniques. And how does one think about thinking without the current thinking influencing the thinking that one is interested in? Of course, when confronted with such daunting problems, you might simply punt and start worrying about more tractable issues.

In this chapter, we have included classic papers involving creative and highly influential methods to analyze human cognition. We begin with the paper by the late David Marr, as it provides a framework for reading all the papers in this section (and this book). The paper is aptly entitled "The Philosophy and the Approach." Marr provides insightful analysis of what cognitive scientists should be looking for in a theory of cognition. Marr's framework resulted in part from his experience as a researcher of visual perception. As he describes in the original work on visual perception, there was considerable excitement for single cell recording studies (in the '50s and '60s). These studies indicated that there are specific cells dedicated to analyzing certain types of visual information, such as vertical lines, horizontal lines, intersections, directional movement, and so on. And so, the search began for higher-level cells, such as the Grandmother cell (a neuron that would fire specifically in response to seeing one's Grandmother). But, as Marr points out, even if such a cell were found, what would this tell you? At some level, such neurons (or, more likely, constellation of neurons) must exist, but documenting existence doesn't tell you why the system is wired in this manner or how such neural firing at the single cell level maps onto one's perception of one's Grandmother.

Finding specific visual cells is important but insufficient as a description of how vision works. That is, a complete understanding of vision requires more than a description of the physical hardware. A full theory, Marr argued, involves three distinct levels of analysis. First, it is critical to understand the goal of the computation and why it is important for the organism. Second, you must understand the input and output representations, and how input is translated to the output. Third, one must consider the actual physical implementation, that is, these mental events must be implemented in the human brain. Finding a vertical line detector satisfies the third level of analysis (physical implementation) but does not tell you much about the first or second levels. Marr's classic paper forcefully points out why all three levels of analysis are important, as well as the limitations of each. Marr's arguments hold for all areas of cognition, not just visual perception. When reading the papers in this section, you should keep Marr's framework in mind. The remaining papers represent four different important methodologies: measurement of reaction time, (Sternberg, 1969), computational modeling (McClelland et al., 1986), the case study approach

(Sacchett & Humphreys, 1992), and neuroimaging (Petersen et al., 1988).

Traditionally, cognitive psychologists have used behavioral methods to explore cognition and have not focused on the underlying neural mechanisms (Level 3). To show the power of purely behavioral methods, we have included the classic Sternberg (1969) paper on mental chronometry. It may be surprising to you that response latencies (reaction times) in a simple behavioral task could yield so much insight into cognition. This method assumes that mental operations are performed in real time. Sternberg analyzes a remarkably simple task in which individuals memorize a short string of stimuli (typically, digits) and then decide whether a probe digit is or is not in the stimulus list. The independent variables were whether or not the probe was in the list, and the size of the set held in memory. At first glance, one might question how much leverage on mental operations one can obtain from such a simple task. The critical results were that reaction time was affected by set size, but this set size effect was not modulated by whether or not the probe was in the studied set. As such, Sternberg concluded that subjects serially and exhaustively searched the set for the probe. Sternberg's elegant analysis shows (a) one can use this task to distinguish among a set of very different and plausible models, (b) humans apparently perform this task in a counterintuitive manner, and (c) how such a counterintuitive model might ultimately have considerable functional utility if one assumes a very fast mental scanning operation.

Behavioral methods dominate cognitive psychology; there are many clever methods in addition to mental chronometry (see Meyer, Osman, Irwin, & Yantis, 1988). However, the remaining three papers in this chapter represent alternatives to the behavioral approach. We did this for two reasons. First, you will be exposed to many other classic behavioral approaches in the remaining chapters in this book. Second, we wished for you to see the full range of tools available to the cognitive psychologist, as the behavioral approach alone does not allow analysis at all of Marr's three levels.

The McClelland, Rumelhart, and Hinton (1986) paper provides an introduction to parallel distributed processing (PDP). This is a computational approach for understanding human cognition. It assumes a large number of simple processing units that are highly interconnected, via facilitatory and inhibitory connections. The weights, or strengths, of these connections change and gradually approach the desired outcome as a function of simple learning feedback algorithms. The elegance and power of this approach have been highly influential in the development of models of cognition; modeling forces researchers to be explicit about both representation and processes in their descriptions of performance in a given task. It is noteworthy that the PDP approach would be at Marr's second level of analysis. In their original work, McCelland et al. were quite explicit in pointing out that the apparent similarity between simple processing units and neurons is not critical to their analysis. However, this approach has since been extended to Marr's Level 3 of analysis (physical implementation); there is now considerable work under the general extension called neural net modeling.

In PDP models, there is no one location that provides all the information about a given person or thing, but, rather, features are distributed across many different processing units (see the McClelland et al. example of Sharks and Jets). How are these different features themselves represented and organized? The paper by Sacchett and Humphreys (1992) is informative here. They report a case study of an individual who has no problems with natural objects, but who appears to have a specific deficit in representing artificial objects. As exemplified in the title of the paper, the patient was fine at calling a squirrel a squirrel (a natural object), but when confronted with a canoe (an artificial object), he would call it a wigwam. This is an intriguing observation, as it suggests that a specific brain lesion can disrupt one type of information, artificial things, while leaving other types of information relatively intact. Moreover, as Sacchett and Humphreys noted, there is also evidence in the literature that one can find the opposite pattern in individuals, that is, a loss of natural objects but intact performance on artificial objects (see Warrington & Shallice, 1984). The literature offers two explanations for these results. One position is that the brain has separate systems for natural versus artificial objects, and that such a distinction would be evolutionarily adaptive (e.g., Caramazza & Shelton, 1998). On the other hand, the brain may have separate systems for visual features (which tend to characterize natural objects) versus functional ones (which tend to characterize artificial objects) (e.g., Warrington & McCarthy, 1983; Warrington & Shallice, 1984). Regardless of which feature you believe is the critical one (category membership versus modality), the Sacchett and Humphreys paper is an excellent example of a focused analysis of a single individual. This paper demonstrates that subtle aspects of cognition can be disrupted, while leaving other aspects intact. Neuropsychological case studies have been central to many developments in cognitive psychology, especially in the areas of language and memory processes.

The notion of localized neural activity that is dedicated to accomplishing specific cognitive processes took a significant leap forward with the development of neuroimaging techniques. Clearly, the paper by Petersen, Fox, Posner, Mintun, and Raichle (1988) was the seminal paper in this area. They used positron emission tomography (PET) to study the processing of single words. In PET, a radioactive isotope is intravenously injected in an individual who is about to engage in a cognitive task. As the blood flows to the brain, detector systems localize the radioactive isotope in a specific area of the brain. The argument is that increased blood flow in a given area reflects more cognitive activity in that area. For example, Petersen et al. used a subtraction technique to measure the different areas engaged in passively viewing words, actively reading words, or generating verbs to nouns. They argued that one could subtract the areas activated in the brain during one task (e.g., passively viewing) from the areas

engaged in the next more complex task (e.g., reading aloud) to localize the targeted mental activity (e.g., phonological articulatory operations). The amazing finding in this study is that there were remarkably distinct areas engaged in each of these three component mental operations. At a gross level, passive viewing of words primarily activated areas in the back of the brain, actively reading aloud activated areas in the middle portion of the brain, and generating verbs activated areas more in the front of the brain. There have been many developments in neuroimaging techniques since the original Petersen et al. paper, including more noninvasive methods such as functional magnetic resonance imaging, and procedures that allow the implementation of more standard cognitive psychology paradigms. Clearly, this technique provides an additional important constraint on developing adequate models of cognition.

It is interesting to reflect on the vastly different methods that are being used to tackle human cognition. We have mentioned single cell recording, single case studies, connectionist modeling, neuroimaging, and behavioral analysis. As Marr pointed out, each of these approaches will provide information at a distinct level of our understanding, and it is only through the combination of these methods that ultimately we will converge on the appropriate understanding of human cognition.

## REFERENCES

Caramazza, A., & Shelton, J. R. (1998). Domain specific knowledge systems in the brain: The animate-inanimate distinction. *Journal of Cognitive Neuroscience, 10*, 1–34.

Marr, D. (1982). The philosophy and the appoach. In *Vision: A computational investigation into the human representation and processing of visual information* (chap. 1). San Francisco, CA: Freeman.

McClelland, J. L., Rumelhart, D. E., & Hinton, G. E. (1986). The appeal of parallel distributed processing. In D. E. Rumelhart, J. L. McClelland, & the PDP Research Group (Eds) *Parallel distributed processing: Explorations in the microstructure of cognition: Volume 1: Foundations* (pp. 1–44). Cambridge, MA: Harvard University Press.

Meyer, D. E., Osman, A. M., Irwin, D. E., & Yantis, S. (1988). Modern mental chronometry. *Biological Psychology, 26*, 3–67.

Petersen, S. E., Fox, P. T., Posner, M. I., Mintun, M., & Raichle, M. E. (1988). Positron emission tomographic studies of the cortical anatomy of single word processing. *Nature, 331*, 585–589.

Sacchett, C., & Humphreys, G. W. (1992). Calling a squirrel a squirrel but a canoe a wigwam: A category-specific deficit for artefactual objects and body parts. *Cognitive Neuropsychology, 9,* 73–86.

Sternberg, S. (1969). Memory scanning: Mental processes revealed by reaction time experiments. *American Scientist, 57*, 421–457.

Warrington, E. K., & McCarthy, R. A. (1983). Category-specific access dyspasia. *Brain, 106,* 859–878.

Warrington, E. K., & Shallice, T. (1984). Category-specific semantic impairment. *Brain, 107,* 829–853.

# The Philosophy and the Approach

D. Marr • Massachusetts Institute of Technology

## Background

The problems of visual perception have attracted the curiosity of scientists for many centuries. Important early contributions were made by Newton (1704), who laid the foundations for modern work on color vision, and Helmholtz (1910), whose treatise on psychological optics generates interest even today. Early this century, Wertheimer (1912, 1923) noticed the apparent motion not of individual dots but of wholes, or "fields," in images presented sequentially as in a movie. In much the same way we perceive the migration across the sky of a flock of geese: the flock somehow constitutes a single entity, and is not seen as individual birds. This observation started the Gestalt school of psychology, which was concerned with describing the qualities of wholes by using terms like *solidarity* and *distinctness*, and trying to formulate the "laws" that governed the creation of these wholes. The attempt failed for various reasons, and the Gestalt school dissolved into the fog of subjectivism. With the death of the school, many of its early and genuine insights were unfortunately lost to the mainstream of experimental psychology.

Since then, students of the psychology of perception have made no serious attempts at an overall understanding of what perception is, concentrating instead on the analysis of properties and performance. The trichromatism of color vision was firmly established (see Brindley, 1970), and the preoccupation with motion continued, with the most interesting developments perhaps being the experiments of Miles (1931) and of Wallach and O'Connell (1953), which established that under suitable conditions an unfamiliar three-dimensional shape can be correctly perceived from only its changing monocular projection.[1]

The development of the digital electronic computer made possible a similar discovery for binocular vision. In 1960 Bela Julesz devised computer-generated random-dot stereograms, which are image pairs constructed of dot patterns that appear random when viewed monocularly but fuse when viewed one through each eye to give a percept of shapes and surfaces with a clear three-dimensional structure. An example is shown in Figure 1.1. Here the image for the left eye is a matrix of black and white squares generated at random by a computer program. The image for the right eye is made by copying the left image, shifting a square-shaped region at its center slightly to the left, and then providing a new random pattern to fill the gap that the shift creates. If each of the eyes sees only one matrix, as if the matrices were both in the same physical place, the result is the sensation of a square floating in space. Plainly, such percepts are caused solely by the stereo disparity between matching elements in the images presented to each eye; from such experiments, we know that the analysis of stereoscopic information, like the analysis of motion, can proceed independently in the absence of other information. Such findings are of critical importance because they help us to subdivide our study of perception

**FIGURE 1.1** ■ A random-dot stereogram used extensively by Bela Julesz. The left and right images are identical, except for a central square region that is displaced slightly in one image. When fused binocularly, the images yield the impression of the central square floating in front of the background. (Bela Julesz, 1971, p. 21, fig. 2.4–1)

into more specialized parts which can be treated separately. I shall refer to these as independent modules of perception.

The most recent contribution of psychophysics has been of a different kind but of equal importance. It arose from a combination of adaptation and threshold detection studies and originated from the demonstration by Campbell and Robson (1968) of the existence of independent, spatial-frequency-tuned channels—that is, channels sensitive to intensity variations in the image occurring at a particular scale or spatial interval—in the early stages of our perceptual apparatus. This paper led to an explosion of articles on various aspects of these channels, which culminated 10 years later with quite satisfactory quantitative accounts of the characteristics of the first stages of visual perception (Wilson and Bergen, 1979). I shall discuss this in detail later on.

Recently, a rather different approach has attracted considerable attention. In 1971, Roger N. Shepard and Jacqueline Metzler made line drawings of simple objects that differed from one another either by a three-dimensional rotation or by a rotation plus a reflection (see Figure 1.2). They asked how long it took to decide whether two depicted objects differed by a rotation and a reflection or merely a rotation. They found that the time taken depended on the three-dimensional angle of rotation necessary to bring the two objects into corre-

spondence. Indeed, the time varied linearly with this angle. One is led thereby to the notion that a mental rotation of sorts is actually being performed—that a mental description of the first shape in a pair is being adjusted incrementally in orientation until it matches the second, such adjustment requiring greater time when greater angles are involved.

The significance of this approach lies not so much in its results, whose interpretation is controversial, as in the type of questions it raised. For until then, the notion of a representation was not one that visual psychologists took seriously. This type of experiment meant that the notion had to be considered. Although the early thoughts of visual psychologists were naive compared with those of the computer vision community, which had had to face the problem of representation from the beginning, it was not long before the thinking of psychologists became more sophisticated (see Shepard, 1979).

But what of explanation? For a long time, the best hope seemed to lie along another line of investigation, that of electrophysiology. The development of amplifiers allowed Adrian (1928) and his colleagues to record the minute voltage changes that accompanied the transmission of nerve signals. Their investigations showed that the character of the sensation so produced depended on which fiber carried the message, not how the

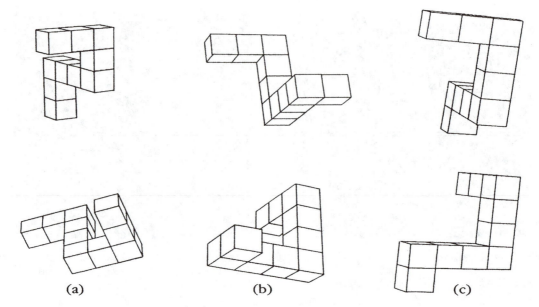

(a)                              (b)                              (c)

**FIGURE 1.2** ■ Some drawings similar to those used in Shepard and Metzler's experiments on mental rotation. The ones Shown in (a) are identical, as a clockwise turning of this page by 80° will readily prove. Those in (b) are also identical, and again the relative angle between the two is 80°. Here, however, a rotation in depth will make the first coincide with the second. Finally, those in (c) are not at all identical, for no rotation will bring them into congruence. The time taken to decide whether a pair is the same was found to vary linearly with the angle through which one figure must be rotated to be brought into correspondence with the other. This suggested to the investigators that a stepwise mental rotation was in fact being performed by the subjects of their experiments.

fiber was stimulated—as one might have expected from anatomical studies. This led to the view that the peripheral nerve fibers could be thought of as a simple mapping supplying the sensorium with a copy of the physical events at the body surface (Adrian, 1947). The rest of the explanation, it was thought, could safely be left to the psychologists.

The next development was the technical improvement in amplification that made possible the recording of single neurons (Granit and Svaetichin, 1939; Hartline, 1938; Galambos and Davis, 1943). This led to the notion of a cell's "receptive field" (Hartline, 1940) and to the Harvard School's famous series of studies of the behavior of neurons at successively deeper levels of the visual pathway (Kuffler, 1953; Hubel and Wiesel, 1962, 1968). But perhaps the most exciting development was the new view that questions of psychological interest could be illuminated and perhaps even explained by neurophysiological experiments. The dearest early example of this was Barlow's (1953) study of ganglion cells in the frog retina, and I cannot put it better than he did:

If one explores the responsiveness of single ganglion cells in the frog's retina using handheld targets, one finds that one particular type of ganglion cell is most effectively driven by something like a black disc subtending a degree or so moved rapidly to and fro within the unit's receptive field. This causes a vigorous discharge which can be maintained without much decrement as long as the movement is continued. Now, if the stimulus which is optimal for this class of cells is presented to intact frogs, the behavioural response is often dramatic; they turn towards the target and make repeated feeding responses consisting of a jump and snap. The selectivity of the retinal neurons and the frog's reaction when they are selectively stimulated, suggest that they are "bug detectors" (Barlow, 1953) performing a primitive but vitally important form of recognition.

The result makes one suddenly realize that a large part of the sensory machinery involved in a frog's feeding responses may actually reside in the retina rather than in mysterious "centres" that would be too difficult to understand by physiological methods. The essential lock-like property resides in each member of a whole class of neurons and allows the cell to discharge only to the appropriate key pattern of sensory stimulation. Lettvin et al. (1959) suggested that there were five different classes of cell in the frog, and Barlow, Hill and Levick (1964) found an even larger number of categories in the rabbit. [Barlow et al.] called these key patterns "trigger features" and Maturana et al. (1960) emphasized another important aspect of the behaviour of these ganglion cells; a cell continues to respond to the same trigger feature in spite of changes in light intensity over many decades. The properties of the retina are such that a ganglion cell can, figuratively speaking, reach out and determine that something specific is happening in front of the eye. Light is the agent by which it does this, but it is the detailed pattern of the light that carries the information, and the overall level of illumination prevailing at the time is almost totally disregarded. (p. 373)

Barlow (1972) then goes on to summarize these findings in the following way:

The cumulative effect of all the changes I have tried to outline above has been to make us realise that each *single neuron can perform a much more complex and subtle task than had previously been thought* (emphasis added). Neurons do not loosely and unreliably remap the luminous intensities of the visual image onto our sensorium, but instead they detect pattern elements, discriminate the depth of objects, ignore irrelevant causes of variation and are arranged in an intriguing hierarchy. Furthermore, there is evidence that they give prominence to what is informationally important, can respond with great reliability, and can have their pattern selectivity permanently modified by early visual experience. This amounts to a revolution in our outlook. It is now quite inappropriate to regard unit activity as a noisy indication of more basic and reliable processes involved in mental operations: instead, we must regard single neurons as the prime movers of these mechanisms. Thinking is brought about by neurons and we should not use phrases like "unit activity reflects, reveals, or monitors thought processes," because the activities of neurons, quite simply, are thought processes.

This revolution stemmed from physiological work and makes us realize that the activity of each single neuron may play a significant role in perception. (p. 380)

This aspect of his thinking led Barlow to formulate the first and most important of his five dogmas: "A description of that activity of a single nerve cell which is transmitted to and influences other nerve cells and of a nerve cell's response to such influences from other cells, is a complete enough description for functional understanding of the nervous system. There is nothing else "looking at" or controlling this activity, which must therefore provide a basis for understanding how the brain controls behaviour" (Barlow, 1972, p. 380).

I shall return later on to more carefully examine the validity of this point of view, but for now let us just enjoy it. The vigor and excitement of these ideas need no emphasis. At the time the eventual success of a reductionist approach seemed likely. Hubel and Wiesel's (1962, 1968) pioneering studies had shown the way; single-unit studies on stereopsis (Barlow, Blakemore, and Pettigrew, 1967) and on color (DeValois, Abramov, and Mead, 1967; Gouras, 1968) seemed to confirm the close links between perception and single-cell recordings, and the intriguing results of Gross, Rocha-Miranda, and Bender (1972), who found "hand-detectors" in the inferotemporal cortex, seemed to show that the application of the reductionist approach would not be limited just to the early parts of the visual pathway.

It was, of course, recognized that physiologists had been lucky: If one probes around in a conventional electronic computer and records the behavior of single elements within it, one is unlikely to be able to discern what a given element is doing. But the brain, thanks to Barlow's first dogma, seemed to be built along more accommodating lines—people *were* able to determine the functions of single elements of the brain. There seemed no reason why the reductionist approach could not be taken all the way.

I was myself fully caught up in this excitement. Truth, I also believed, was basically neural, and the central aim of all research was a thorough functional analysis of the structure of the central nervous system. My enthusiasm found expression in a theory of the cerebellar cortex (Marr, 1969). According to this theory, the simple and regular cortical structure is interpreted as a simple but powerful memorizing device for learning motor skills; because of a simple combinatorial trick, each of the 15 million Purkinje cells in the cerebellum is capable of learning over 200 different patterns and discriminating them from unlearned patterns. Evidence is gradually accumulating that the cerebellum is involved in learning motor skills (Ito, 1978), so that something like this theory may in fact be correct.

The way seemed clear. On the one hand, we had

new experimental techniques of proven power, and on the other, the beginnings of a theoretical approach that could back them up with a fine analysis of cortical structure. Psychophysics could tell us what needed explaining, and the recent advances in anatomy—the Fink-Heimer technique from Nauta's laboratory and the recent successful deployment by Szentagothai and others of the electron microscope—could provide the necessary information about the structure of the cerebral cortex.

But somewhere underneath, something was going wrong. The initial discoveries of the 1950s and 1960s were not being followed by equally dramatic discoveries in the 1970s. No neurophysiologists had recorded new and clear high-level correlates of perception. The leaders of the 1960s had turned away from what they had been doing—Hubel and Wiesel concentrated on anatomy, Barlow turned to psychophysics, and the mainstream of neurophysiology concentrated on development and plasticity (the concept that neural connections are not fixed) or on a more thorough analysis of the cells that had already been discovered (for example, Bishop, Coombs, and Henry, 1971; Schiller, Finlay, and Volman, 1976a, 1976b), or on cells in species like the owl (for example, Pettigrew and Konishi, 1976). None of the new studies succeeded in elucidating the *function* of the visual cortex.

It is difficult to say precisely why this happened, because the reasoning was never made explicit and was probably largely unconscious. However, various factors are identifiable. In my own case, the cerebellar study had two effects. On the one hand, it suggested that one could eventually hope to understand cortical structure in functional terms, and this was exciting. But at the same time the study has disappointed me, because even if the theory was correct, it did not much enlighten one about the motor system—it did not, for example, tell one how to go about programming a mechanical arm. It suggested that if one wishes to program a mechanical arm so that it operates in a versatile way, then at some point a very large and rather simple type of memory will prove indispensable. But it did not say why, nor what that memory should contain.

The discoveries of the visual neurophysiologists left one in a similar situation. Suppose, for example, that one actually found the apocryphal grandmother cell.[2] Would that really tell us anything much at all? It would tell us that it existed—

Gross's hand-detectors tell us almost that—but not why or even how such a thing may be constructed from the outputs of previously discovered cells. Do the single-unit recordings—the simple and complex cells—tell us much about how to detect edges or why one would want to, except in a rather general way through arguments based on economy and redundancy? If we really knew the answers, for example, we should be able to program them on a computer. But finding a hand-detector certainly did not allow us to program one.

As one reflected on these sorts of issues in the early 1970s, it gradually became clear that something important was missing that was not present in either of the disciplines of neurophysiology or psychophysics. The key observation is that neurophysiology and psychophysics have as their business to *describe* the behavior of cells or of subjects but not to *explain* such behavior. What are the visual areas of the cerebral cortex actually doing? What are the problems in doing it that need explaining, and at what level of description should such explanations be sought?

The best way of finding out the difficulties of doing something is to try to do it, so at this point I moved to the Artificial Intelligence Laboratory at MIT, where Marvin Minsky had collected a group of people and a powerful computer for the express purpose of addressing these questions.

The first great revelation was that the problems are difficult. Of course, these days this fact is a commonplace. But in the 1960s almost no one realized that machine vision was difficult. The field had to go through the same experience as the machine translation field did in its fiascoes of the 1950s before it was at last realized that here were some problems that had to be taken seriously. The reason for this misperception is that we humans are ourselves so good at vision. The notion of a feature detector was well established by Barlow and by Hubel and Wiesel, and the idea that extracting edges and lines from images might be at all difficult simply did not occur to those who had not tried to do it. It turned out to be an elusive problem: Edges that are of critical importance from a three-dimensional point of view often cannot be found at all by looking at the intensity changes in an image. Any kind of textured image gives a multitude of noisy edge segments; variations in reflectance and illumination cause no end of trouble; and even if an edge has a clear existence at one point, it is as likely as not to fade out quite soon, appearing only in patches along its length in the image. The common and almost despairing feeling of the early investigators like B. K. P. Horn and T. O. Binford was that practically anything could happen in an image and furthermore that practically everything did.

Three types of approach were taken to try to come to grips with these phenomena. The first was unashamedly empirical, associated most with Azriel Rosenfeld. His style was to take some new trick for edge detection, texture discrimination, or something similar, run it on images, and observe the result. Although several interesting ideas emerged in this way, including the simultaneous use of operators[3] of different sizes as an approach to increasing sensitivity and reducing noise (Rosenfeld and Thurston, 1971), these studies were not as useful as they could have been because they were never accompanied by any serious assessment of how well the different algorithms performed. Few attempts were made to compare the merits of different operators (although Fram and Deutsch, 1975, did try), and an approach like trying to prove mathematically which operator was optimal was not even attempted. Indeed, it could not be, because no one had yet formulated precisely what these operators should be trying to do. Nevertheless, considerable ingenuity was shown. The most clever was probably Hueckel's (1973) operator, which solved in an ingenious way the problem of finding the edge orientation that best fit a given intensity change in a small neighborhood of an image.

The second approach was to try for depth of analysis by restricting the scope to a world of single, illuminated, matte white toy blocks set against a black background. The blocks could occur in any shapes provided only that all faces were planar and all edges were straight. This restriction allowed more specialized techniques to be used, but it still did not make the problem easy. The Binford–Horn line finder (Horn, 1973) was used to find edges, and both it and its sequel (described in Shirai, 1973) made use of the special circumstances of the environment, such as the fact that all edges there were straight.

These techniques did work reasonably well, however, and they allowed a preliminary analysis of later problems to emerge—roughly, what does one do once a complete line drawing has been extracted from a scene? Studies of this had begun sometime before with Roberts (1965) and Guzman

(1968), and they culminated in the works of Waltz (1975) and Mackworth (1973), which essentially solved the interpretation problem for line drawings derived from images of prismatic solids. Waltz's work had a particularly dramatic impact, because it was the first to show explicitly that an exhaustive analysis of all possible local physical arrangements of surfaces, edges, and shadows could lead to an effective and efficient algorithm for interpreting an actual image. Figure 1.3 and its legend convey the main ideas behind Waltz's theory.

The hope that lay behind this work was, of course, that once the toy world of white blocks had been understood, the solutions found there could be generalized, providing the basis for attacking the more complex problems posed by a richer visual environment. Unfortunately, this turned out not to be so. For the roots of the approach that was eventually successful, we have to look at the third kind of development that was taking place then.

Two pieces of work were important here. Neither is probably of very great significance to human perception for what it actually accomplished—in the end, it is likely that neither will particularly reflect human visual processes—but they are both of importance because of the way in which they were formulated. The first was Land and McCann's (1971) work on the retinex theory of color vision, as developed by them and subsequently by Horn (1974). The starting point is the traditional one of regarding color as a perceptual approximation to reflectance. This allows the formulation of a clear computational question, namely, How can the effects of reflectance changes be separated from the vagaries of the prevailing illumination? Land and McCann suggested using the fact that changes in illumination are usually gradual, whereas changes in reflectance of a surface or of an object boundary are often quite sharp. Hence by filtering out slow changes, those changes due to the reflectance alone could be isolated. Horn devised a clever parallel algorithm for this, and I suggested how it might be implemented by neurons in the retina (Marr, 1974a).

I do not now believe that this is at all a correct analysis of color vision or of the retina, but it showed the possible style of a correct analysis. Gone are the ad hoc programs of computer vision; gone is the restriction to a special visual miniworld; gone is any explanation in terms of

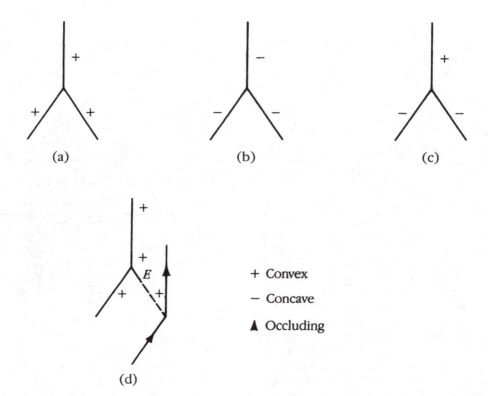

+ Convex

− Concave

▲ Occluding

**FIGURE 1.3** ■ Some configurations of edges are physically realizable, and some are not. The trihedral junctions of three convex edges (a) or of three concave edges (b) are realizable, whereas the configuration (c) is impossible. Waltz catalogued all the possible junctions, including shadow edges, for up to four coincident edges. He then found that by using this catalog to implement consistency relations [requiring, for example, that an edge be of the same type all along its length like edge *E* in (d)], the solution to the labeling of a line drawing that included shadows was often uniquely determined.

neurons—except as a way of implementing a method. And present is a clear understanding of what is to be computed, how it is to be done, the physical assumptions on which the method is based, and some kind of analysis of algorithms that are capable of carrying it out.

The other piece of work was Horn's (1975) analysis of shape from shading, which was the first in what was to become a distinguished series of articles on the formation of images. By carefully analyzing the way in which the illumination, surface geometry, surface reflectance, and viewpoint conspired to create the measured intensity values in an image, Horn formulated a differential equation that related the image intensity values to the surface geometry. If the surface reflectance and illumination are known, one can solve for the surface geometry (see also Horn, 1977). Thus from shading one can derive shape.

The message was plain. There must exist an additional level of understanding at which the character of the information-processing tasks carried out during perception are analyzed and understood in a way that is independent of the particular mechanisms and structures that implement them in our heads. This was what was missing—the analysis of the problem as an information-processing task. Such analysis does not usurp an understanding at the other levels—of neurons or of computer programs—but it is a necessary complement to them, since without it there can be no real understanding of the function of all those neurons.

This realization was arrived at independently and formulated together by Tomaso Poggio in Tübingen and myself (Marr and Poggio, 1977; Marr, 1977b). It was not even quite new—Leon D. Harmon was saying something similar at about the same time, and others had paid lip service to a similar distinction. But the important point is that if the notion of different types of understanding is taken very seriously, it allows the study of the information-processing basis of perception to be made rigorous. It becomes possible, by separating explanations into different levels, to make explicit statements about what is being computed and why and to construct theories stating that what is being computed is optimal in some sense or is guaranteed to function correctly. The ad hoc element is removed, and heuristic computer programs are replaced by solid foundations on which a real subject can be built. This realization—the formulation of what was missing, together with a clear idea of how to supply it—formed the basic foundation for a new integrated approach, which it is the purpose of this book to describe.

## Understanding Complex Information-Processing Systems

Almost never can a complex system of any kind be understood as a simple extrapolation from the properties of its elementary components. Consider, for example, some gas in a bottle. A description of thermodynamic effects—temperature, pressure, density, and the relationships among these factors—is not formulated by using a large set of equations, one for each of the particles involved. Such effects are described at their own level, that of an enormous collection of particles; the effort is to show that in principle the microscopic and macroscopic descriptions are consistent with one another. If one hopes to achieve a full understanding of a system as complicated as a nervous system, a developing embryo, a set of metabolic pathways, a bottle of gas, or even a large computer program, then one must be prepared to contemplate different kinds of explanation at different levels of description that are linked, at least in principle, into a cohesive whole, even if linking the levels in complete detail is impractical. For the specific case of a system that solves an information-processing problem, there are in addition the twin strands of process and representation, and both these ideas need some discussion.

### Representation and Description

A *representation* is a formal system for making explicit certain entities or types of information, together with a specification of how the system does this. And I shall call the result of using a representation to describe a given entity a *description* of the entity in that representation (Marr and Nishihara, 1978).

For example, the Arabic, Roman, and binary numeral systems are all formal systems for representing numbers. The Arabic representation consists of a string of symbols drawn from the set (0, 1, 2, 3, 4, 5, 6, 7, 8, 9), and the rule for constructing the description of a particular integer $n$ is that one decomposes $n$ into a sum of multiples of powers of 10 and unites these multiples into a string with the largest powers on the left and the smallest on the right. Thus, thirty-seven equals $3 \times 10^1 + 7 \times 10^0$, which becomes 37, the Arabic numeral system's description of the number. What this description makes explicit is the number's decomposition into powers of 10. The binary numeral system's description of the number thirty-seven is 100101, and this description makes explicit the number's decomposition into powers of 2. In the Roman numeral system, thirty-seven is represented as XXXVII.

This definition of a representation is quite general. For example, a representation for shape would be a formal scheme for describing some aspects of shape, together with rules that specify how the scheme is applied to any particular shape. A musical score provides a way of representing a symphony; the alphabet allows the construction of a written representation of words; and so forth. The phrase "formal scheme" is critical to the definition, but the reader should not be frightened by it. The reason is simply that we are dealing with information-processing machines, and the way such machines work is by using symbols to stand for things—to represent things, in our terminology. To say that something is a formal scheme means only that it is a set of symbols with rules for putting them together—no more and no less.

A representation, therefore, is not a foreign idea at all—we all use representations all the time. However, the notion that one can capture some aspect of reality by making a description of it using a symbol and that to do so can be useful seems to me a fascinating and powerful idea. But even the simple examples we have discussed introduce some rather general and important issues that arise whenever one chooses to use one particular representation. For example, if one chooses the Arabic numeral representation, it is easy to discover whether a number is a power of 10 but difficult to discover whether it is a power of 2. If one chooses the binary representation, the situation is reversed. Thus, there is a trade-off; any particular representation makes certain information explicit at the expense of information that is pushed into the background and may be quite hard to recover.

This issue is important, because how information is represented can greatly affect how easy it is to do different things with it. This is evident even from our numbers example: It is easy to add, to subtract, and even to multiply if the Arabic or binary representations are used, but it is not at all easy to do these things—especially multiplication—with Roman numerals. This is a key reason why the Roman culture failed to develop mathematics in the way the earlier Arabic cultures had.

An analogous problem faces computer engineers today. Electronic technology is much more suited to a binary number system than to the conventional base 10 system, yet humans supply their data and require the results in base 10. The design decision facing the engineer, therefore, is, Should one pay the cost of conversion into base 2, carry out the arithmetic in a binary representation, and then convert back into decimal numbers on output; or should one sacrifice efficiency of circuitry to carry out operations directly in a decimal representation? On the whole, business computers and pocket calculators take the second approach, and general purpose computers take the first. But even though one is not restricted to using just one representation system for a given type of information, the choice of which to use is important and cannot be taken lightly. It determines what information is made explicit and hence what is pushed further into the background, and it has a far-reaching effect on the ease and difficulty with which operations may subsequently be carried out on that information.

## Process

The term *process* is very broad. For example, addition is a process, and so is taking a Fourier transform. But so is making a cup of tea, or going shopping. For the purposes of this book, I want to restrict our attention to the meanings associated with machines that are carrying out information-processing tasks. So let us examine in depth the notions behind one simple such device, a cash register at the checkout counter of a supermarket.

There are several levels at which one needs to understand such a device, and it is perhaps most useful to think in terms of three of them. The most abstract is the level of *what* the device does and *why*. What it does is arithmetic, so our first task is to master the theory of addition. Addition is a mapping, usually denoted by +, from pairs of numbers into single numbers; for example, + maps the pair (3, 4) to 7, and I shall write this in the form $(3 + 4) \rightarrow 7$. Addition has a number of abstract properties, however. It is commutative: both $(3 + 4)$ and $(4 + 3)$ are equal to 7; and associative: the sum of $3 + (4 + 5)$ is the same as the sum of $(3 + 4) + 5$. Then there is the unique distinguished element, zero, the adding of which has no effect: $(4 + 0) \rightarrow 4$. Also, for every number there is a unique "inverse," written $(-4)$ in the case of 4, which when added to the number gives zero: $[4 + (-4)] \rightarrow 0$.

Notice that these properties are part of the fundamental *theory* of addition. They are true no matter how the numbers are written—whether in binary, Arabic, or Roman representation—and no matter how the addition is executed. Thus part of this first level is something that might be characterized as *what* is being computed.

The other half of this level of explanation has to do with the question of *why* the cash register performs addition and not, for instance, multiplication when combining the prices of the purchased items to arrive at a final bill. The reason is that the rules we intuitively feel to be appropriate for combining the individual prices in fact define the mathematical operation of addition. These can be formulated as *constraints* in the following way:

1. If you buy nothing, it should cost you nothing; and buying nothing and something should cost the same as buying just the something. (The rules for zero.)
2. The order in which goods are presented to the cashier should not affect the total. (Commutativity.)
3. Arranging the goods into two piles and paying for each pile separately should not affect the total amount you pay. (Associativity; the basic operation for combining prices.)
4. If you buy an item and then return it for a refund, your total expenditure should be zero. (Inverses.)

It is a mathematical theorem that these conditions define the operation of addition, which is therefore the appropriate computation to use.

This whole argument is what I call the *computational theory* of the cash register. Its important features are (1) that it contains separate arguments about what is completed and why and (2) that the resulting operation is defined uniquely by the constraints it has to satisfy. In the theory of visual processes, the underlying task is to reliably derive properties of the world from images of it; the business of isolating constraints that are both powerful enough to allow a process to be defined and generally true of the world is a central theme of our inquiry.

In order that a process shall actually run, however, one has to realize it in some way and therefore choose a representation for the entities that the process manipulates. The second level of the analysis of a process, therefore, involves choosing two things: (1) a *representation* for the input and for the output of the process and (2) an *algorithm* by which the transformation may actually be accomplished. For addition, of course, the input and output representations can both be the same, because they both consist of numbers. However this is not true in general. In the case of a Fourier transform, for example, the input representation may be the time domain, and the output, the frequency domain. If the first of our levels specifies what and why, this second level specifies *how*. For addition, we might choose Arabic numerals for the representations, and for the algorithm we could follow the usual rules about adding the least significant digits first and "carrying" if the sum exceeds 9. Cash registers, whether mechanical or electronic, usually use this type of representation and algorithm.

There are three important points here. First, there is usually a wide choice of representation. Second, the choice of algorithm often depends rather critically on the particular representation that is employed. And third, even for a given fixed representation, there are often several possible algorithms for carrying out the same process. Which one is chosen will usually depend on any particularly desirable or undesirable characteristics that the algorithms may have; for example, one algorithm may be much more efficient than another, or another may be slightly less efficient but more robust (that is, less sensitive to slight inaccuracies in the data on which it must run). Or again, one algorithm may be parallel, and another, serial. The choice, then, may depend on the type of hardware or machinery in which the algorithm is to be embodied physically.

This brings us to the third level, that of the device in which the process is to be realized physically. The important point here is that, once again, the same algorithm may be implemented in quite different technologies. The child who methodically adds two numbers from right to left, carrying a digit when necessary, may be using the same algorithm that is implemented by the wires and transistors of the cash register in the neighborhood supermarket, but the physical realization of the algorithm is quite different in these two cases. Another example: Many people have written computer programs to play tic-tac-toe, and there is a more or less standard algorithm that cannot lose. This algorithm has in fact been implemented by W. D. Hillis and B. Silverman in a quite different technology, in a computer made out of Tinkertoys, a children's wooden building set. The whole monstrously ungainly engine, which actually works, currently resides in a museum at the University of Missouri in St. Louis.

Some styles of algorithm will suit some physical substrates better than others. For example, in conventional digital computers, the number of connections is comparable to the number of gates, while in a brain, the number of connections is much larger ($\times 10^4$) than the number of nerve cells. The underlying reason is that wires are rather cheap in biological architecture, because they can grow individually and in three dimensions. In conventional technology, wire laying is more or less restricted to two dimensions, which quite severely restricts the scope for using parallel techniques and algorithms; the same operations are often better carried out serially.

## The Three Levels

We can summarize our discussion in something like the manner shown in Figure 1.4, which illustrates the different levels at which an information-processing device must be understood before one can be said to have understood it completely. At one extreme, the top level, is the abstract computational theory of the device, in which the performance of the device is characterized as a mapping from one kind of information to another, the abstract properties of this mapping are defined precisely, and its appropriateness and adequacy for the task at hand are demonstrated. In the center is

| Computational Theory | Representation and Algorithm | Hardware Implementation |
|---|---|---|
| What is the goal of the computation, why is it appropriate, and what is the logic of the strategy by which it can be carried out? | How can this computational theory be implemented? In particular, what is the representation for the input and output, and what is the algorithm for the transformation? | How can the representation and algorithm be realized physically? |

**FIGURE 1.4** ■ The three levels at which any machine carrying out an information-processing task must be understood.

the choice of representation for the input and output and the algorithm to be used to transform one into the other. And at the other extreme are the details of how the algorithm and representation are realized physically—the detailed computer architecture, so to speak. These three levels are coupled, but only loosely. The choice of an algorithm is influenced for example, by what it has to do and by the hardware in which it must run. But there is a wide choice available at each level, and the explication of each level involves issues that are rather independent of the other two.

Each of the three levels of description will have its place in the eventual understanding of perceptual information processing, and of course they are logically and causally related. But an important point to note is that since the three levels are only rather loosely related, some phenomena may be explained at only one or two of them. This means, for example, that a correct explanation of some psychophysical observation must be formulated at the appropriate level. In attempts to relate psychophysical problems to physiology, too often there is confusion about the level at which problems should be addressed. For instance, some are related mainly to the physical mechanisms of vision—such as afterimages (for example, the one you see after staring at a light bulb) or such as the fact that any color can be matched by a suitable mixture of the three primaries (a consequence principally of the fact that we humans have three types of cones). On the other hand, the ambiguity of the Necker cube (Figure 1.5) seems to demand a different kind of explanation. To be sure, part of the explanation of its perceptual reversal must have to do with a bistable neural network (that is, one with two distinct stable states) somewhere inside the brain, but few would feel satisfied by an ac-

count that failed to mention the existence of two different but perfectly plausible three-dimensional interpretations of this two-dimensional image.

For some phenomena, the type of explanation required is fairly obvious. Neuroanatomy, for example, is clearly tied principally to the third level, the physical realization of the computation. The same holds for synaptic mechanisms, action potentials, inhibitory interactions, and so forth. Neurophysiology, too, is related mostly to this level, but it can also help us to understand the type of representations being used, particularly if one accepts something along the lines of Barlow's views that I quoted earlier. But one has to exercise extreme caution in making inferences from neurophysiological findings about the algorithms and representations being used, particularly until one has a clear idea about what information needs to be represented and what processes need to be implemented.

Psychophysics, on the other hand, is related more directly to the level of algorithm and representation. Different algorithms tend to fail in radically different ways as they are pushed to the limits of their performance or are deprived of critical information. As we shall see, primarily psychophysical evidence proved to Poggio and myself that our first stereo-matching algorithm (Marr and Poggio, 1976) was not the one that is used by the brain, and the best evidence that our second algorithm (Marr and Poggio, 1979) is roughly the one that is used also comes from psychophysics. Of course, the underlying computational theory remained the same in both cases; only the algorithms were different.

Psychophysics can also help to determine the nature of a representation. The work of Roger Shepard (1975), Eleanor Rosch (1978), or Eliza-

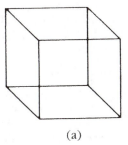
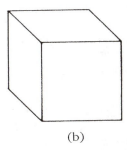
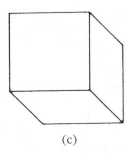

(a)    (b)    (c)

**FIGURE 1.5** ■ The so-called Necker illusion, named after L. A. Necker, the Swiss naturalist who developed it in 1832. The essence of the matter is that the two-dimensional representation (a) has collapsed the depth out of a cube and that a certain aspect of human vision is to recover this missing third dimension. The depth of the cube can indeed be perceived, but two interpretations are possible, (b) and (c). A person's perception characteristically flips from one to the other.

beth Warrington (1975) provides some interesting hints in this direction. More specifically, Stevens (1979) argued from psychophysical experiments that surface orientation is represented by the coordinates of slant and tilt, rather than (for example) the more traditional $(p, q)$ of gradient space. He also deduced from the uniformity of the size of errors made by subjects judging surface orientation over a wide range of orientations that the representational quantities used for slant and tilt are pure angles and not, for example, their cosines, sines, or tangents.

More generally, if the idea that different phenomena need to be explained at different levels is kept clearly in mind, it often helps in the assessment of the validity of the different kinds of objections that are raised from time to time. For example, one favorite is that the brain is quite different from a computer because one is parallel and the other serial. The answer to this, of course, is that the distinction between serial and parallel is a distinction at the level of algorithm; it is not fundamental at all—anything programmed in parallel can be rewritten serially (though not necessarily vice versa). The distinction, therefore, provides no grounds for arguing that the brain operates so differently from a computer that a computer could not be programmed to perform the same tasks.

## Importance of Computational Theory

Although algorithms and mechanisms are empirically more accessible, it is the top level, the level of computational theory, which is critically important from an information-processing point of view. The reason for this is that the nature of the computations that underlie perception depends more upon the computational problems that have to be solved than upon the particular hardware in which their solutions are implemented. To phrase the matter another way, an algorithm is likely to be understood more readily by understanding the nature of the problem being solved than by examining the mechanism (and the hardware) in which it is embodied.

In a similar vein, trying to understand perception by studying only neurons is like trying to understand bird flight by studying only feathers: It just cannot be done. In order to understand bird flight, we have to understand aerodynamics; only then do the structure of feathers and the different shapes of birds' wings make sense. More to the point, as we shall see, we cannot understand why retinal ganglion cells and lateral geniculate neurons have the receptive fields they do just by studying their anatomy and physiology. We can understand how these cells and neurons behave as they do by studying their wiring and interactions, but in order to understand *why* the receptive fields are as they are—why they are circularly symmetrical and why their excitatory and inhibitory regions have characteristic shapes and distributions—we have to know a little of the theory of differential operators, band-pass channels, and the mathematics of the uncertainty principle.

Perhaps it is not surprising that the very specialized empirical disciplines of the neurosciences failed to appreciate fully the absence of computational theory; but it is surprising that this level of approach did not play a more forceful role in the early development of artificial intelligence. For far too long, a heuristic program for carrying out some task was held to be a theory of that task, and the distinction between what a program did and how it did it was not taken seriously. As a result, (1) a style of explanation evolved that invoked the use of special mechanisms to solve particular problems, (2) particular data structures, such as the lists of attribute value pairs called property lists in the LISP programing language, were held to amount to theories of the representation of knowledge, and (3) there was frequently no way to determine whether a program would deal with a particular case other than by running the program.

Failure to recognize this theoretical distinction between *what* and *how* also greatly hampered communication between the fields of artificial intelligence and linguistics. Chomsky's (1965) theory of transformational grammar is a true computational theory in the sense defined earlier. It is concerned solely with specifying what the syntactic decomposition of an English sentence should be, and not at all with how that decomposition should be achieved. Chomsky himself was very clear about this—it is roughly his distinction between competence and performance, though his idea of performance did include other factors, like stopping in midutterance—but the fact that his theory was defined by transformations, which look like computations, seems to have confused many people. Winograd (1972), for example, felt able to criticize Chomsky's theory on the grounds that it cannot be inverted and so cannot be made to run on a computer; I had heard reflections of the same argument made by Chomsky's colleagues in linguistics as they turned their attention to how grammatical structure might actually be computed from a real English sentence.

The explanation is simply that finding algorithms by which Chomsky's theory may be implemented is a completely different endeavor from formulating the theory itself. In our terms, it is a study at a different level, and both tasks have to be done. This point was appreciated by Marcus (1980), who was concerned precisely with how Chomsky's theory can be realized and with the kinds of constraints on the power of the human grammatical processor that might give rise to the structural constraints in syntax that Chomsky found. It even appears that the emerging "trace" theory of grammar (Chomsky and Lasnik, 1977) may provide a way of synthesizing the two approaches—showing that, for example, some of the rather ad hoc restrictions that form part of the com-

putational theory may be consequences of weaknesses in the computational power that is available for implementing syntactical decoding.

## The Approach of J. J. Gibson

In perception, perhaps the nearest anyone came to the level of computational theory was Gibson (1966). However, although some aspects of his thinking were on the right lines, he did not understand properly what information processing was, which led him to seriously underestimate the complexity of the information-processing problems involved in vision and the consequent subtlety that is necessary in approaching them.

Gibson's important contribution was to take the debate away from the philosophical considerations of sense-data and the affective qualities of sensation and to note instead that the important thing about the senses is that they are channels for perception of the real world outside or, in the case of vision, of the visible surfaces. He therefore asked the critically important question, How does one obtain constant perceptions in everyday life on the basis of continually changing sensations? This is exactly the right question, showing that Gibson correctly regarded the problem of perception as that of recovering from sensory information "valid" properties of the external world. His problem was that he had a much oversimplified view of how this should be done. His approach led him to consider higher-order variables—stimulus energy, ratios, proportions, and so on—as "invariants" of the movement of an observer and of changes in stimulation intensity.

"These invariants," he wrote, "correspond to permanent properties of the environment. They constitute, therefore, information about the permanent environment." This led him to a view in which the function of the brain was to "detect invariants" despite changes in "sensations" of light, pressure, or loudness of sound. Thus, he says that the "function of the brain, when looped with its perceptual organs, is not to decode signals, nor to interpret messages, nor to accept images, nor to *organize* the sensory input or to *process* the data, in modern terminology. It is to seek and extract information about the environment from the flowing array of ambient energy" and he thought of the nervous system as in some way "resonating" to these invariants. He then embarked on a broad study of animals in their environments, looking for invariants to which they might resonate. This was the basic idea behind the notion of ecological optics (Gibson, 1966, 1979).

Although one can criticize certain shortcomings in the quality of Gibson's analysis, its major and, in my view fatal shortcoming lies at a deeper level and results from a failure to realize two things. First, the detection of physical invariants, like image surfaces, is exactly and precisely an information-processing problem, in modern terminology. And second, he vastly underrated the sheer difficulty of such detection. In discussing the recovery of three-dimensional information from the movement of an observer, he says that "in motion, perspective information alone can be used" (Gibson, 1966, p. 202). And perhaps the key to Gibson is the following:

> The detection of non-change when an object moves in the world is not as difficult as it might appear. It is only made to seem difficult when we assume that the perception of constant dimensions of the object must depend on the correcting of sensations of inconstant form and size. The information for the constant dimension of an object is normally carried by invariant relations in an optic array. Rigidity is *specified*. (Emphasis added.)

Yes, to be sure, but *how*? Detecting physical invariants is just as difficult as Gibson feared, but nevertheless we can do it. And the only way to understand how is to treat it as an information-processing problem.

The underlying point is that visual information processing is actually very complicated, and Gibson was not the only thinker who was misled by the apparent simplicity of the act of seeing. The whole tradition of philosophical inquiry into the nature of perception seems not to have taken seriously enough the complexity of the information processing involved. For example, Austin's (1962) *Sense and Sensibilia* entertainingly demolishes the argument, apparently favored by earlier philosophers, that since we are sometimes deluded by illusions (for example, a straight stick appears bent if it is partly submerged in water), we see sense-data rather than material things. The answer is simply that usually our perceptual processing does run correctly (it delivers a true description of what is there), but although evolution has seen to it that our processing allows for many changes (like inconstant illumination), the perturbation due to the refraction of light by water is not one of them. And incidentally, although the example of the bent

stick has been discussed since Aristotle, I have seen no philosophical inquiry into the nature of the perceptions of, for instance, a heron, which is a bird that feeds by pecking up fish first seen from above the water surface. For such birds the visual correction might be present.

Anyway, my main point here is another one. Austin (1962) spends much time on the idea that perception tells one about real properties of the external world, and one thing he considers is "real shape" (p. 66), a notion which had cropped up earlier in his discussion of a coin that "looked elliptical" from some points of view. Even so,

> it had a real shape which remained unchanged. But coins in fact are rather special cases. For one thing their outlines are well defined and very highly stable, and for another they have a known and a nameable shape. But there are plenty of things of which this is not true. What is the real shape of a cloud? . . . or of a cat? Does its real shape change whenever it moves? If not, in what posture *is* its real shape on display? Furthermore, is its real shape such as to be fairly smooth outlines, or must it be finely enough serrated to take account of each hair? *It is pretty obvious that there is no answer to these questions—no rules according to which, no procedure by which, answers are to be determined.* (Emphasis added.) (p. 67)

But there *are* answers to these questions. There are ways of describing the shape of a cat to an arbitrary level of precision, and there are rules and procedures for arriving at such descriptions. That is exactly what vision is about, and precisely what makes it complicated.

## A Representational Framework for Vision

Vision is a process that produces from images of the external world a description that is useful to the viewer and not cluttered with irrelevant information (Marr, 1976; Marr and Nishihara, 1978). We have already seen that a process may be thought of as a mapping from one representation to another, and in the case of human vision, the initial representation is in no doubt—it consists of arrays of image intensity values as detected by the photoreceptors in the retina.

It is quite proper to think of an image as a representation; the items that are made explicit are the image intensity values at each point in the array, which we can conveniently denote by $I(x,y)$

at coordinate $(x,y)$. In order to simplify our discussion, we shall negect for the moment the fact that there are several different types of receptor, and imagine instead that there is just one, so that the image is black-and-white. Each value of $I(x,y)$ thus specifies a particular level of gray; we shall refer to each detector as a picture element or *pixel* and to the whole array $I$ as an image.

But what of the output of the process of vision? We have already agreed that it must consist of a useful description of the world, but that requirement is rather nebulous. Can we not do better? Well, it is perfectly true that, unlike the input, the result of vision is much harder to discern, let alone specify precisely, and an important aspect of this new approach is that it makes quite concrete proposals about what that end is. But before we begin that discussion, let us step back a little and spend a little time formulating the more general issues that are raised by these questions.

## The Purpose of Vision

The usefulness of a representation depends upon how well suited it is to the purpose for which it is used. A pigeon uses vision to help it navigate, fly, and seek out food. Many types of jumping spider use vision to tell the difference between a potential meal and a potential mate. One type, for example, has a curious retina formed of two diagonal strips arranged in a V. If it detects a red V on the back of an object lying in front of it, the spider has found a mate. Otherwise, maybe a meal. The frog, as we have seen, detects bugs with its retina; and the rabbit retina is full of special gadgets, including what is apparently a hawk detector, since it responds well to the pattern made by a preying hawk hovering overhead. Human vision, on the other hand, seems to be very much more general, although it clearly contains a variety of special-purpose mechanisms that can, for example, direct the eye toward an unexpected movement in the visual field or cause one to blink or otherwise avoid something that approaches one's head too quickly.

Vision, in short, is used in such a bewildering variety of ways that the visual systems of different animals must differ significantly from one another. Can the type of formulation that I have been advocating, in terms of representations and processes, possibly prove adequate for them all? I think so. The general point here is that because vision is used by different animals for such a wide variety of purposes, it is inconceivable that all seeing animals use the same representations; each can confidently be expected to use one or more representations that are nicely tailored to the owner's purposes.

As an example, let us consider briefly a primitive but highly efficient visual system that has the added virtue of being well understood. Werner Reichardt's group in Tübingen has spent the last 14 years patiently unraveling the visual flight-control system of the housefly, and in a famous collaboration, Reichardt and Tomaso Poggio have gone far toward solving the problem (Reichardt and Poggio, 1976, 1979; Poggio and Reichardt, 1976). Roughly speaking, the fly's visual apparatus controls its flight through a collection of about five independent, rigidly inflexible, very fast responding systems (the time from visual stimulus to change of torque is only 21 ms). For example, one of these systems is the landing system; if the visual field "explodes" fast enough (because a surface looms nearby), the fly automatically "lands" toward its center. If this center is above the fly, the fly automatically inverts to land upside down. When the feet touch, power to the wings is cut off. Conversely, to take off, the fly jumps; when the feet no longer touch the ground, power is restored to the wings, and the insect flies again.

In-flight control is achieved by independent systems controlling the fly's vertical velocity (through control of the lift generated by the wings) and horizontal direction (determined by the torque produced by the asymmetry of the horizontal thrust from the left and right wings). The visual input to the horizontal control system, for example, is completely described by the two terms

$$r(\psi)\dot{\psi} + D(\psi)$$

where $r$ and $D$ have the form illustrated in Figure 1.6. This input describes how the fly tracks an object that is present at angle $\psi$ in the visual field and has angular velocity $\dot{\psi}$. This system is triggered to track objects of a certain angular dimension in the visual field, and the motor strategy is such that if the visible object was another fly a few inches away, then it would be intercepted successfully. If the target was an elephant 100 yd away, interception would fail because the fly's built-in parameters are for another fly nearby, not an elephant far away.

Thus, fly vision delivers a representation in

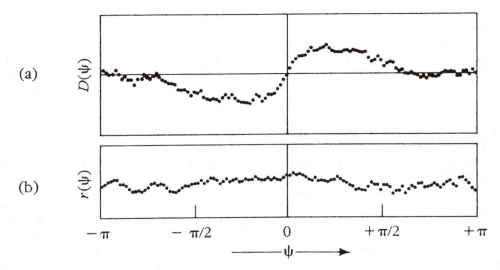

**FIGURE 1.6** ■ The horizontal component of the visual input $R$ to the fly's flight system is described by the formula $R = D(\psi) - r(\psi)\dot{\psi}$, where $\psi$ is the direction of the stimulus and $\dot{\psi}$ is its angular velocity in the fly's visual field. $D(\psi)$ is an odd function, as shown in (a), which has the effect of keeping the target centered in the fly's visual field; $r(\psi)$ is essentially constant as shown in (b).

which at least these three things are specified: (1) whether the visual field is looming sufficiently fast that the fly should contemplate landing; (2) whether there is a small patch—it could be a black speck or, it turns out, a textured figure in front of a textured ground—having some kind of motion relative to its background; and if there is such a patch, (3) $\psi$ and $\dot{\psi}$ for this patch are delivered to the motor system. And that is probably about 60% of fly vision. In particular, it is extremely unlikely that the fly has any explicit representation of the visual world around him—no true conception of a surface, for example, but just a few triggers and some specifically fly-centered parameters like $\psi$ and $\dot{\psi}$.

It is clear that human vision is much more complex than this, although it may well incorporate subsystems not unlike the fly's to help with specific and rather low-level tasks like the control of pursuit eye movements. Nevertheless, as Poggio and Reichardt have shown, even these simple systems can be understood in the same sort of way, as information-processing tasks. And one of the fascinating aspects of their work is how they have managed not only to formulate the differential equations that accurately describe the visual control system of the fly but also to express these equations, using the Volterra series expansion, in a way that gives direct information about the minimum possible complexity of connections of the underlying neuronal networks.

## Advanced Vision

Visual systems like the fly's serve adequately and with speed and precision the needs of their owners, but they are not very complicated; very little objective information about the world is obtained. The information is all very much subjective—the angular size of the stimulus as the fly sees it rather than the objective size of the object out there, the angle that the object has in the fly's visual field rather than its position relative to the fly or to some external reference, and the object's angular velocity, again in the fly's visual field, rather than any assessment of its true velocity relative to the fly or to some stationary reference point.

One reason for this simplicity must be that these facts provide the fly with sufficient information for it to survive. Of course, the information is not optimal and from time to time the fly will fritter away its energy chasing a falling leaf a medium distance away or an elephant a long way away as a direct consequence of the inadequacies of its perceptual system. But this apparently does not matter very much—the fly has sufficient excess energy for it to be able to absorb these extra costs. Another reason is certainly that translating these rather subjective measurements into more objective qualities involves much more computation. How, then, should one think about more advanced visual systems—human vision, for example. What are the issues? What kind of information is vision really delivering, and what are the representational issues involved?

My approach to these problems was very much influenced by the fascinating accounts of clinical neurology, such as Critchley (1953) and Warrington and Taylor (1973). Particularly important was a lecture that Elizabeth Warrington gave at MIT in October 1973, in which she described the capacities and limitations of patients who had suffered left or right parietal lesions. For me, the most important thing that she did was to draw a distinction between the two classes of patient (see Warrington and Taylor, 1978). For those with lesions on the right side, recognition of a common object was possible *provided* that the patient's view of it was in some sense straightforward. She used the words *conventional* and *unconventional*—a water pail or a clarinet seen from the side gave "conventional" views but seen end-on gave "unconventional" views. If these patients recognized the object at all, they knew its name and its semantics—that is, its use and purpose, how big it was, how much it weighed, what it was made of, and so forth. If their view was unconventional—a pail seen from above, for example—not only would the patients fail to recognize it, but they would vehemently deny that it *could* be a view of a pail. Patients with left parietal lesions behaved completely differently. Often these patients had no language, so they were unable to name the viewed object or state its purpose and semantics. But they could convey that they correctly perceived its geometry—that is, its shape—even from the unconventional view.

Warrington's talk suggested two things. First, the representation of the shape of an object is stored in a different place and is therefore a quite different kind of thing from the representation of its use and purpose. And second, vision alone can deliver an internal description of the shape of a viewed object, even when the object was not recognized in the conventional sense of understanding its use and purpose.

This was an important moment for me for two reasons. The general trend in the computer vision community was to believe that recognition was so difficult that it required every possible kind of information. The results of this point of view duly appeared a few years later in programs like Freuder's (1974) and Tenenbaum and Barrow's (1976). In the latter program, knowledge about offices—for example, that desks have telephones on them and that telephones are black—was used to help "segment" out a black blob halfway up an image and "recognize" it as a telephone. Freuder's program used a similar approach to "segment" and "recognize" a hammer in a scene. Clearly, we do use such knowledge in real life; I once saw a brown blob quivering amongst the lettuce in my garden and correctly identified it as a rabbit, even though the visual information alone was inadequate. And yet here was this young woman calmly telling us not only that her patients could convey to her that they had grasped the shapes of things that she had shown them, even though they could not name the objects or say how they were used, but also that they could happily continue to do so even if she made the task extremely difficult visually by showing them peculiar views or by illuminating the objects in peculiar ways. It seemed clear that the intuitions of the computer vision people were completely wrong and that even in difficult circumstances shapes could be determined by vision alone.

The second important thing, I thought, was that Elizabeth Warrington had put her finger on what was somehow the quintessential fact of human vision—that it tells about shape and space and spatial arrangement. Here lay a way to formulate its purpose—building a description of the shapes and positions of things from images. Of course, that is by no means all that vision can do; it also tells about the illumination and about the reflectances of the surfaces that make the shapes—their brightnesses and colors and visual textures—and about their motion. But these things seemed secondary; they could be hung off a theory in which the main job of vision was to derive a representation of shape.

## To the Desirable via the Possible

Finally, one has to come to terms with cold reality. Desirable as it may be to have vision deliver a completely invariant shape description from an image (whatever that may mean in detail), it is almost certainly impossible in only one step. We can only do what is possible and proceed from there toward what is desirable. Thus we arrived at the idea of a sequence of representations, starting with descriptions that could be obtained straight from an image but that are carefully designed to facilitate the subsequent recovery of gradually more objective, physical properties about an object's shape. The main stepping stone toward this goal is describing the geometry of the visible surfaces, since the information encoded in images, for example by stereopsis, shading, texture, contours, or visual motion, is due to a shape's local surface properties. The objective of many early visual computations is to extract this information.

However, this description of the visible surfaces turns out to be unsuitable for recognition tasks. There are several reasons why, perhaps the most prominent being that like all early visual processes, it depends critically on the vantage point. The final step therefore consists of transforming the viewer-centered surface description into a representation of the third-dimensional shape and spatial arrangement of an object that does not depend upon the direction from which the object is being viewed. This final description is object centered rather than viewer centered.

The overall framework described here therefore divides the derivation of shape information from images into three representational stages: (Table 1.1): (1) the representation of properties of the two-dimensional image, such as intensity changes and local two-dimensional geometry; (2) the representation of properties of the visible surfaces in a viewer-centered coordinate system, such as surface orientation, distance from the viewer, and discontinuities in these quantities; surface reflectance; and some coarse description of the prevailing illumination; and (3) an object-centered representation of the three-dimensional structure and of the organization of the viewed shape, together with some description of its surface properties.

This framework is summarized in Table 1.1.

**TABLE 1.1. Representational Framework for Deriving Shape Information from Images**

| Name | Purpose | Primitives |
|---|---|---|
| Image(s) | Represents intensity | Intensity value at each point in the image |
| Primal sketch | Makes explicit important information about the two-dimensional image, primarily the intensity changes there and their geometrical distribution and organization | Zero-crossings<br>Blobs<br>Terminations and discontinuities<br>Edge segments<br>Virtual lines<br>Groups<br>Curvilinear organization<br>Boundaries |
| 2½-D sketch | Makes explicit the orientation and rough depth of the visible surfaces and contours of discontinuities in these quantities in a viewer-centered coordinate frame | Local surface orientation (the "needles" primitives)<br>Distance from viewer<br>Discontinuities in depth<br>Discontinuities in surface orientation |
| 3-D model representation | Describes shapes and their spatial organization in an object-centered coordinate frame, using a modular hierarchical representation that includes volumetric primitives (i.e., primitives that represent the volume of space that a shape occupies) as well as surface primitives | 3-D models arranged hierarchically, each one based on a spatial configuration of a few sticks or axes, to which volumetric or surface shape primitives are attached |

## NOTES

[1] The two dimensional image seen by a single eye.

[2] A cell that fires only when one's grandmother comes into view.

[3] *Operator* refers to a local calculation to be applied at each location in the image, making use of the intensity there and in the immediate vicinity.

## REFERENCES

Adrian, E. D. (1928). *The Basis of Sensation*. London: Christophers. (Reprint ed. New York: Hafner, 1964).

Adrian, E. D. (1947). *The Physical Background of Perception*. Oxford: Clarendon.

Austin, J. L. (1962). *Sense and Sensibilia*. Oxford: Clarendon.

Barlow, H. B. (1953). Summation and inhibition in the frog's retina. *J. Physiol. (Lond)* 119, 69–88.

Barlow, H. B. (1972). Single units and sensation: a neuron doctrine for perceptual psychology? *Perception 1*, 371–394.

Barlow, H. B., Blakemore, C., & Pettigrew, J. D. (1967). The neural mechanism of binocular depth discrimination. *J. Physiol. (Lond) 133*, 327–342.

Barlow, H. B., Hill, R. M., & Levick, W. R. (1964). Retinal ganglion cells responding selectively to direction and speed of image motion in the rabbit. *J. Physiol. (Lond.) 173*, 377–407.

Bishop, P. O., Coombs, J. S., & Henry, G. H. (1971). Responses to visual contours: Spatio-temporal aspects of excitation in the receptive fields of simple striate neurons. *J. Physiol. (Lond.) 219*, 625–657.

Brindley, G. S. (1970). *Physiology of the Retina and Visual Pathway*. Physiological Society Monograph no. 6. London: Edwin Arnold.

Campbell, F. W. C., & Robson, J. (1968). Application of Fourier analysis to the visibility of gratings. *J. Physiol. (Lond.) 197*, 551–566.

Chomsky, N. (1965). *Aspects of the Theory of Syntax*. Cambridge, MA: MIT Press.

Chomsky, N., & Lasnik, H. (1977). Filters and control. *Linguistic Inquiry 8*, 425–504.

DeValois, R. L., Abramov, I., & Mead, W. R. (1967). Single cell analysis of wavelength discrimination at the lateral geniculate nucleus in the macaque. *J. Neurophysiol. 30*, 415–433.

Fram, J. R., & Deutsch, E. S. (1975). On the quantitative evaluation of edge detection schemes and their comparison with human performance. *IEEE Trans. Comput. C–24*, 616–628.

Freuder, E. C. (1974). A computer vision system for visual recognition using active knowledge. MIT A.I. Lab Tech. Rep. 345.

Galambos, R., & Davis, H. (1943). The response of single auditory-nerve fibres to acoustic stimulation. *J. Neurophysiol. 7*, 287–303.

Gibson, J. J. (1966). *The Senses Considered as Perceptual Systems*. Boston: Houghton Mifflin.

Gibson, J. J. (1979). *The Ecological Approach to Visual Perception*. Boston: Houghton Mifflin.

Gouras, P. (1968). Identification of cone mechanisms in monkey ganglion cells. *J. Physiol. (Lond) 199*, 533–547.

Granit, R., & Svaetichin, G. (1939). Principles and technique of the electrophysiological analysis of colour reception with the aid of microelectrodes. *Upsala Lakraef Fath. 65*, 161–177.

Gross, C. G., Rocha-Miranda, C. E., & Bender, D. B. (1972). Visual properties of neurons in inferotemporal cortex of the macaque. *J. Neurophysiol. 35*, 96–111.

Guzman, A. (1968). Decomposition of a visual scene into three-dimensional bodies. In *AFIPS Conf. Proc. 33*, 291–304. Washington, DC: Thompson.

Hartline, H. K. (1938). The response of single optic nerve fibres of the vertebrate eye to illumination of the retina. *Am. J. Physiol. 121*, 400–415.

Hartline, H. K. (1940). The receptive fields of optic nerve fibers. *Am. J. Physiol. 130*, 690–699.

Helmholtz, H. L. F. von. (1910). *Treatise on Physiological Optics*. Translated by J. P. Southall, 1925. New York: Dover.

Horn, B. K. P. (1973). The Binford-Horn LINEFINDER. MIT A.I. Lab. Memo 285.

Horn, B. K. P. (1974). Determining lightness from an image. *Computer Graphics and Image Processing 3*, 277–299.

Horn, B. K. P. (1975). Obtaining shape from shading information. In *The Psychology of Computer Vision*, P. H. Winston, Ed., 115–155. New York: McGraw-Hill.

Horn, B. K. P. (1977). Understanding image intensities. *Artificial Intelligence 8*, 201–231.

Hubel, D. H., & Wiesel, T. N. (1962). Receptive fields, binocular interaction and functional architecture in the cat's visual cortex. *J. Physiol. (Lond.) 166*, 106–154.

Hubel, D. H., & Wiesel, T. N. (1968). Receptive fields and functional architecture of monkey striate cortex. *J. Physiol. (Lond.) 195*, 215–243.

Hueckel, M. H. (1973). An operator which recognizes edges and lines. *J. Assoc. Comput. Mach. 20*, 634–647.

Ito, M. (1978). Recent advances in cerebellar physiology and pathology. In *Advances in Neurology*, R. A. P. Kark, R. N. Rosenberg, and L. J. Shut, Eds., 59–84. New York: Raven Press.

Kuffler, S. W. (1953). Discharge patterns and functional organization of mammalian retina. *J. Neurophysiol. 16*, 37–68.

Land, E. H., & McCann, J. J. (1971). Lightness and retinex theory. *J. Opt Sec. Am. 61*, 1–11.

Lettvin, J. Y., Maturana, R. R., McCulloch, W. S., & Pitts, W. H. (1959). What the frog's eye tells the frog's brain. *Proc. Inst. Rad. Eng. 47*, 1940–1951.

Mackworth, A. K. (1973). Interpreting pictures of polyhedral scenes. *Art. Intel. 4*, 121–137.

Marcus, M. P. (1980). *A Theory of Syntactic Recognition for Natural Language*. Cambridge, MA: MIT Press.

Marr, D. (1969). A theory of cerebellar cortex. *J. Physiol. (Lond.) 202*, 437–470.

Marr, D. (1974a). The computation of lightness by the primate retina. *Vision Res. 14*, 1377–1388.

Marr, D. (1974b). A note on the computation of binocular disparity in a symbolic, low-level visual processor. MIT A.I. Lab. Memo 327.

Marr, D. (1976). Early processing of visual information. *Phil. Trans R. Soc. Lond. B 275*, 483–524.

Marr, D. (1977a). Analysis of occluding contour. *Proc. R. Soc. Lond. B 197*, 441–475.

Marr, D. (1977b). Artificial intelligence—a personal view. *Artificial Intelligence 9*, 37–48.

Marr, D., & Nishihara. H. K. (1978). Representation and recognition of the spatial organization of three-dimensional shapes. *Proc. R. Soc. Lond. B 200*, 269–294.

Marr, D., & Poggio, T. (1976). Cooperative computation of stereo disparity. *Science 194*, 283–287.

Marr, D., & Poggio, T. (1977). From understanding computation to understanding neural circuitry. *Neurosciences Res. Prog. Bull. 15*, 470–488.

Marr, D., & Poggio, T. (1979). A computational theory of human stereo vision. *Proc. R. Soc. Lond. B 204*, 301–328.

Maturana, H. R., Lettvin, J. Y., McCulloch, W. S., & Pitts, W. H. (1960). Anatomy and physiology of vision in the frog (*Rana Pipiens*). *J. Gen. Physiol. 43* (suppl. no. 2, Mechanisms of Vision), 129–171.

Miles, W. R. (1931). Movement in interpretations of the silhouette of a revolving fan. *Am. J. Psychol. 43*, 392–404.

Newton, I. (1704). *Optics*. London.

Pettigrew, J. D., & Konishi, M. (1976). Neurons selective for orientation and binocular disparity in the visual wulst of the barn owl (*Tyto alba*). *Science 193*, 675–678.

Poggio, T., & Reichardt, W. (1976). Visual control of orientation behavior in the fly. Part II. Toward the underlying neural interactions. *Quart. Rev. Biophys. 9*, 377–438.

Reichardt, W., & Poggio, T. (1976). Visual control of orientation behavior in the fly. Part I. A quantitative analysis, *Quart. Rev. Biophys. 3*, 311–375.

Reichardt, W., & Poggio, T. (1979). Visual control of flight in flies. In *Recent Theoretical Developments in Neurobiology*, W. E. Reichardt, V. B. Mountcastle, and T. Poggio, Eds.

Roberts, L. G. (1965). Machine perception of three-dimensional solids. In *Optical and electro optical infomation processing*, J. T. Tippett et at., Eds., 159–197. Cambridge, MA: MIT Press.

Rosch, E. (1978). Principles of categorization. In *Cognition and categorization*, E. Rosch and B. Lloyd, Eds., 27–48. Hillsdale, NJ: Erlbaum.

Rosenfeld, A., & Thurston, M. (1971). Edge and curve detection for visual scene analysis. *IEEE Trans. Comput. C-20*, 562–569.

Schiller, P. H., Finlay, B. L., & Volman, S. F. (1976b). Quantitative studies of single-cell properties in monkey striate cortex. II. Orientation specificity and ocular dominance. *J. Neurophysiol. 39*, 1320–1333.

Shepard, R. N. (1975). Form, formation and transformation of internal representations. In *Information Processing and Cognition: The Loyola Symposium*, R. Solso, Ed., 87–122. Hillsdale, NJ: Erlbaum.

Shepard, R. N., & Metzler, J. (1971). Mental rotation of three-dimensional objects. *Science, 171,* 701–703.

Shirai, Y. (1973). A context-sensitive line finder for recognition of polyhedra. *Artificial Intelligence 4*, 95–120.

Stevens, K. A. (1979). Surface perception from local analysis of texture and contour. Ph.D. dissertation, MIT. (Available as The information content of texture gradients. *Biol. Cybernetics 42* (1981), 95–105; also, The visual interpretation of surface contours. *Artificial Intelligence 17* (1981), 47–74.)

Tenenbaum, J. M., & Barrow, H. G. (1976). Experiments in interpretation-guided segmentation. Stanford Research Institute Tech. Note 123.

Wallach, H., & O'Connell, D. N. (1953). The kinetic depth effect. *J. Exp. Psychol. 45*, 205–217.

Waltz, D. (1975). Understanding line drawings of scenes with shadows. In *The Psychology of Computer Vision*, P. H. Winston, Ed., pp. 19–91. New York: McGraw-Hill.

Warrington, E. K. (1975). The selective impairment of semantic memory. *Quart. J. Exp. Psychol. 27*, 635–657.

Warrington, E. K., & Taylor, A. M. (1973). The contribution of the right parietal lobe to object recognition. *Cortex 3*, 152–164.

Warrington, E. K., & Taylor, A. M. (1978). Two categorical stages of object recognition. *Perception 7*, 695–705.

Wertheimer, M. (1912). Experimentelle Studien uber das Sehen von Bewegung. Zeitschrift f. Psychol. 61, 161–265.

Wilson, H. R., & Bergen, J. R. (1979). A four mechanism model for spatial vision. *Vision Res. 19*, 19–32.

Winograd, T. (1972). *Understanding Natural Language*. New York: Academic Press.

# Memory-Scanning: Mental Processes Revealed by Reaction-Time Experiments[1]

Saul Sternberg

**O**ne of the oldest ideas in experimental psychology is that the time between stimulus and response is occupied by a train of processes or *stages*—some being mental operations—which are so arranged that one process does not begin until the preceding one has ended. This *stage theory* implies that the reaction-time (RT) is a *sum*, composed of the durations of the stages in the series, and suggests that if one could determine the component times that add together to make up the RT, one might then be able to answer interesting questions about mental operations to which they correspond. The study of RT should therefore prove helpful to an understanding of the structure of mental activity.

The use of results from RT experiments to study stages of information processing began about a century ago with a paper, "On the Speed of Mental Processes," by F. C. Donders (1868). It was in this paper that Donders introduced the *subtraction method*—a method for analyzing the RT into its components and thereby studying the corresponding stages of processing.

## 1. Decomposing RT by the Subtraction Method

To use the subtraction method one constructs two different tasks in which RT can be measured, where the second task is thought to require all the mental operations of the first, plus an additional inserted operation. The difference between mean RTs in the two tasks is interpreted as an estimate of the duration of the inserted stage, as shown in Figure 2.1. This interpretation depends on the validity of both the stage theory and an *assumption of pure insertion* which states that changing from Task 1 to Task 2 merely inserts a new processing stage without altering the others.

For example, Wundt (1880, pp. 247–260) developed an application in which RTs were measured when a subject had to respond after he had identified a stimulus, and also when he had to respond after merely detecting its presence. The difference was used as an estimate of the identification time. In this instance the stages shown in Figure 2.1 might be (*a*) stimulus detection, (*b*) stimulus identification, and (*c*) response organization. In an earlier application, Donders (1868) had compared mean RTs in a simple-reaction task (one stimulus and response) and a choice-reaction task (multiple stimuli and responses); he regarded the difference as the duration of the stages of stimulus discrimination and response selection.

This kind of enterprise occupied many psychologists during the last quarter of the nineteenth century. Much of their work was summarized by J. Jastrow (1890) in a popular treatise on *The Time Relations of Mental Phenomena*.

Around the turn of the century the subtraction method became the subject of criticism for two main reasons. First, the differences in mean RT that were observed in some applications varied excessively from subject to subject, and from laboratory to laboratory. In retrospect, this seems to have been caused by the use of tasks and instructions that left the subject's choice of "processing strategy" relatively uncontrolled.[2] Second, introspective reports put into question the assumption of pure insertion, by suggesting that when the task was changed to insert a stage, other stages might also be altered: (For example, it was felt that changes in stimulus-processing requirements might also alter a response-organization stage.) If so, the difference between RTs could not be identified as the duration of the inserted stage. Because of these difficulties, Külpe, among others, urged caution in the interpretation of results from the subtraction method (1895, Secs. 69, 70). But it appears that no tests other than introspection were proposed for distinguishing valid from invalid applications of the method.

A stronger stand was taken in later secondary sources. For example, in a section on the "discarding of the subtraction method" in his *Experimental Psychology* (1938, p. 309), R. S. Woodworth queried "[Since] we cannot break up the reaction into successive acts and obtain the time of each act, of what use is the reaction-time?" And, more recently, D. M. Johnson said in his *Psychology of Thought and Judgment* (1955, p. 5), "The reaction-time experiment suggests a method for the analysis of mental processes which turned out to be unworkable."

Nevertheless, the attempt to analyze RT into components goes on, and there has been a substantial revival in the last few years in the use of RT as a tool for the study of mental processes ranging from perceptual coding to mental arithmetic and problem-solving.[3] The work on memory retrieval described here is part of this revival, and is based heavily on Donders' stage theory. Modern styles of experimentation and data analysis lead

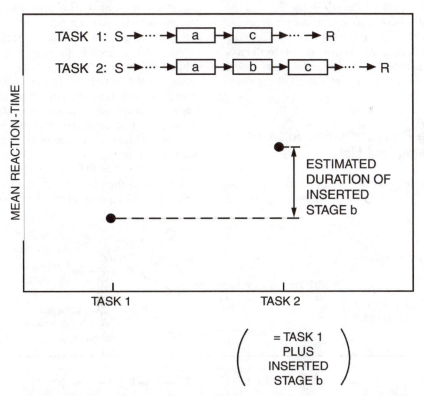

**FIGURE 2.1** ■ Donders' subtraction method. Hypothetical stages between stimulus (S) and response (R) are represented by a, b, and c.

to applications of the stage theory that seem to withstand the early criticisms, and to tests of validity other than introspection.

I shall describe experiments on retrieval from memory that have led to the discovery of some relatively simple search processes. My aim is to convey the general outline rather than the details of this work, so the picture I paint will be somewhat simplified; there will be little discussion of alternative explanations that have been considered and rejected. Such discussions can be found in Sternberg (1966, 1967a, b, and 1969).

The purpose of most of these experiments has been to study the ways in which information is retrieved from memory when learning and retention are essentially perfect. The method is to present a list of items for memorization that is short enough to be within the immediate-memory span. The subject is then asked a question about the memorized list; he answers as quickly as he can, and his delay in responding is measured. By examining the pattern of his RTs, while varying such factors as the number of items in the list and the kind of question asked, one can make inferences about the underlying retrieval processes. Since the aim has been to understand error-free performance, conditions and payoffs are arranged so that in most experiments the responses are almost always correct.

## 2. Judging Presence versus Absence in a Memorized List

The flavor of this approach will become clearer as we consider a particular experiment. Figure 2.2

shows the paradigm of an *item-recognition task.* The stimulus ensemble consists of all potential test stimuli. From among these, a set of *s* elements is selected arbitrarily and is defined as the *positive set;* these items are presented as a list for the subject to memorize. The remaining items are called the *negative set.* When a test stimulus is presented, the subject must decide whether it is a member of the positive set. If it is, he makes a *positive response* (e.g., saying "yes" or operating a particular lever). If not, he makes a *negative response.* The measured RT (sometimes referred to as *response latency*) is the time from test-stimulus onset to response.

Within the item-recognition paradigm, different procedures can be used. One of them, shown at the top of Figure 2.3, is the *varied-set procedure.* Here, the subject must memorize a different positive set on each trial. In one experiment (Exp. 1), for example, the stimulus ensemble consisted of the 10 digits. On each trial a new positive set, ranging randomly over trials from 1 to 6 different digits, was presented sequentially at a rate of 1.2 seconds per digit. Two seconds after the last digit in the set was displayed, a warning signal appeared, followed by a visually-presented test digit. The subject pulled one lever, making a positive response, if the test stimulus was contained in the memorized list. He pulled the other lever, making a negative response, if it was not. After responding to the test stimulus the subject recalled the list. This forced him to retain the items in the presented order, and prevented him from working with the negative set rather than the positive. Regardless of the size of the positive set, the two responses were required equally often. As in the other ex-

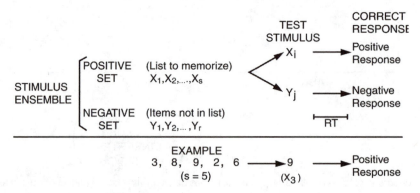

**FIGURE 2.2** ■ Paradigm of item-recognition task (Exps. 1–5).

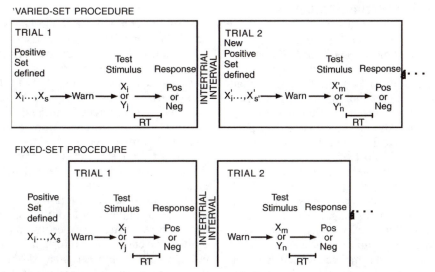

VARIED-SET PROCEDURE

FIXED-SET PROCEDURE

**FIGURE 2.3** ■ Varied-set and fixed-set procedures in item-recognition. A $Y$ represents an item in the negative set. Primes are used in representing trial 2 of the varied-set procedure to show that both the items in the positive set $(X_1, \ldots, X_s)$ and its size ($s$) may change from trial to trial.

periments I shall describe, subjects were relatively unpracticed. The error rate in this kind of experiment can be held to 1 or 2 percent by paying subjects in such a way as to penalize errors heavily while rewarding speed.

Averaged data from eight subjects are shown in Figure 2.4. Mean RT is plotted as a function of the number of symbols in memory—that is, the number of digits in the positive set that the subject committed to memory at the start of the trial.

These data are typical for item-recognition experiments. They show, first, a linear relation between mean RT and the size of the positive set. Second, the latencies of positive and negative responses increase at approximately the same rate. The slope of the line fitted to the means is 38 msec per item in memory; its zero-intercept is about 400 msec. (It happens to be true in these data that latencies of positive and negative responses have approximately the same *values*: the two latency functions have not only the same slope but also the same zero-intercept. This is not a general finding, but results from the particular conditions in this experiment. By varying the relative frequency with which positive and negative responses are required, for example, one can vary the relation between their latencies. But as relative frequency is varied the *slopes* of the two latency functions remain equal and unchanged.) Before considering

the interpretation of these findings, we turn to some general matters regarding search processes.

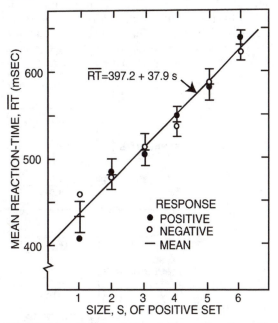

$$\overline{RT} = 397.2 + 37.9\,s$$

RESPONSE
● POSITIVE
○ NEGATIVE
— MEAN

**FIGURE 2.4** ■ Results of Exp. 1: Item-recognition with varied-set procedure. Mean latencies of correct positive and negative responses, and their mean, as functions of size of positive set. Averaged data from eight subjects, with estimates of ±σ about means, and line fitted by least squares to means.

## 3. Two Types of Serial Search

Let *serial search* (or *scanning*) be a process in which each of a set of items is compared one at a time, and no more than once, to a target item. Linear RT-functions, as in Figure 2.4, suggest that subjects in the item-recognition task use a serial search process whose mean duration increases by one unit for each additional comparison. The purpose of the search is to determine whether an agreement (or *match*) exists between the test item and any of the items in the memorized set. Two types of serial search that might serve this purpose need to be considered. In *self-terminating serial search*, the test stimulus is compared successively to one item in memory after another, either until a match occurs (leading to a positive response), or until all comparisons have been completed without a match (leading to a negative response). In *exhaustive serial search*, the test stimulus is compared successively to *all* the memorized items. Only then is a response made—positive if a match has occurred, and negative otherwise. A self-terminating search might require a separate test, after each comparison, to ascertain whether a match had occurred, rather than only one such test after the entire series. On the other hand, an exhaustive search must involve more comparisons, on the average, than a search that terminates when a match occurs.

Suppose that the average time from the beginning of one comparison, to the beginning of the next is the same for each comparison in the series, and is not influenced by the number of comparisons to be made. Then the durations of both kinds of search will increase linearly with the number of memorized items (*list length*). There are, however, important differences. In an exhaustive search the test stimulus is compared to all items in memory before each positive response as well as before a negative response. Hence, the rate at which RT increases with list length—the the slope of the RT-function—is the same for positive and negative responses. In contrast, a self-terminating search stops in the middle of the list, on the average, before positive responses, but continues through the entire list before negatives. The result is that as list length is increased, the latency of positive responses increases at half the rate of the increase for negatives. This difference between the two kinds of search is illustrated on the left side of Figure 2.5.

A second difference between the two types of search, illustrated on the right side of Figure 2.5, is in the serial-position functions for positive responses. In a simple exhaustive search neither the order of search nor the position of the matching item in the list should have any effect on the RT, since all items are compared. A self-terminating

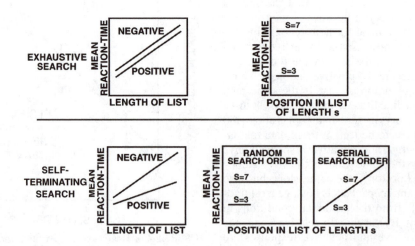

**FIGURE 2.5** ■ Some properties of exhaustive (top) and self-terminating (bottom) serial search. Left: Theoretical RT-functions (mean latencies of positive and negative responses as functions of length of list). Right: Theoretical serial-position functions (mean latency of positive responses as a function of serial position of test item in a list of given length).

search that occurred in a random order, or started at a random point, also would produce flat serial-position curves. But if a self-terminating search started consistently with the first item, and proceeded serially, then the serial-position curves would increase linearly. (If, in addition, list length influenced *only* the search process, then the curves for different list lengths would be superimposed: for example, the time to arrive at the second item in a memorized list would be independent of the length of the list.) Increasing serial-position functions are therefore sufficient (but not necessary) evidence for inferring that a search process is self-terminating.

## 4. High-Speed Exhaustive Scanning

The serial-position curves actually observed in the item-recognition experiment described in Section 2 were relatively flat.[4] Together with this finding, the linearity of the latency functions and the equality of their slopes for positive and negative responses indicate an exhaustive search. The data show also that memory-scanning can proceed at a remarkably high rate. The slope of the mean RT-function, which is an estimate of the time per comparison, was 38 msec, indicating an average scanning rate between 25 and 30 digits per second.

Perhaps because of its high speed, the scanning process seems not to have any obvious correlate in conscious experience. Subjects generally say either that they engage in a self-terminating search, or that they know immediately, with no search at all, whether the test stimulus is contained in the memorized list.

Is high-speed scanning used only when a list has just been memorized and is therefore relatively unfamiliar? The results discussed so far (Figure 2.4) are from the varied-set procedure (Figure 2.3), in which the subject must memorize a new positive set on each trial, and is tested only three seconds after its presentation. How is the retrieval process changed when a person is highly familiar with a particular positive set and has had a great deal of practice retrieving information from it? At the bottom of Figure 2.3 is shown the *fixed-set procedure* in the item-recognition paradigm, in which the same positive set is used for a long series of trials. For example, in one experiment (Exp. 2) subjects had 60 practice trials and 120 test trials

for each positive set. On the average test trial, a subject had been working with the same positive set for ten minutes, rather than three seconds. The sets were sufficiently well learned that subjects could recall them several days later. Sets of one, two, and four digits were used. There were six subjects.

Results are shown in Figure 2.6, and are essentially identical to those from the varied-set procedure. The RT data are linear, the slopes for positive and negative responses are equal, and the average slope is 38 msec per digit. The small difference between the zero-intercepts in the two experiments is not statistically significant. The remarkable similarity of results from the two procedures indicates that the same retrieval process was used for both the unfamiliar and the well-learned lists.

## 5. Active and Inactive Memory

Evidence has accumulated, particularly during the past decade, that there are at least two systems or

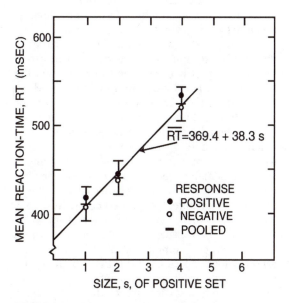

**FIGURE 2.6** ■ Results of Exp. 2: Item-recognition with fixed-set procedure. Mean latencies of correct positive, negative, and pooled responses as functions of size of positive set. Averaged data from six subjects, with estimates of ±σ about pooled means, and line fitted by least squares to those means. For each set size positive responses were required on 27% of the trials.

states of memory for encoded verbal items (e.g., Broadbent, 1958; Waugh & Norman, 1965; Glanzer & Cunitz, 1966; Atkinson & Shiffrin, 1968). The picture that is emerging is roughly as follows: The *long-term store*, or *inactive memory*, is relatively permanent and of large capacity. It receives information from the *short-term store*, a temporary *active memory*[5] of small capacity from which information is rapidly lost unless an active retention process is operating. In the long-term store, the coding of verbal items includes semantic attributes; in the short-term store, however, such items are coded primarily as acoustic or articulatory representations of their spoken names, even when they have been presented visually (see Sperling, 1960; Conrad, 1964; Baddeley, 1966; Wickelgren, 1969). The active process that regenerates the rapidly-decaying traces of a list of items in the short-term store is *rehearsal*, the overtly- or silently-spoken cyclic serial recall of stored items (see Sanders, 1961; Sperling, 1963; Posner & Rossman, 1965; Cohen & Johansson, 1967; Crowder, 1967; Atkinson & Shiffrin, 1968). Rehearsal, which also causes information in the short-term store to be entered in the long-term store, has an approximate maximum rate of from three to seven items per second (Landauer, 1962).

Whereas in the varied-set procedure of Exp. 1 the positive set must have been stored in active memory only, it is reasonable to believe that the set had entered the long-term store in the fixed-set procedure of Exp. 2. However, the similarity of results from the two procedures suggests that the same memory system was being scanned: that is, when information in inactive memory has to be used, it may be entered also in active memory (where it is maintained by rehearsal) and thus becomes more readily available. An experiment that tests this conjecture is described below (Exp. 5).

It appears, then, that the memory of the positive sets in both tasks is maintained by a serial rehearsal process; supporting this notion, subjects reported silent rehearsal of the sets in both experiments. But the estimated rates of high-speed scanning and the fastest silent speech differ by a factor of at least four. Rehearsal is far too slow to be identical to the scanning process. Instead, it should be thought of as a separate process whose only function in these tasks is to maintain the memory that is to be scanned.[6]

## 6. Encoding of the Test Stimulus

In the scanning process inferred from these experiments, some internal representation of the test stimulus is compared to internal representations of the items in the positive set. What is the *nature* of the representations that can be compared at such high speed? Another way to phrase the question is to ask how much processing of the test stimulus occurs before it is compared to the memorized items.

Various considerations lead one to expect a good deal of preprocessing. For example, the idea that items held in active memory are retained as acoustic or articulatory representations of their spoken names introduces the possibility that the test stimulus is processed to the point of naming, and that the name of the test stimulus is compared to the names of the items in the positive set. But two points should be kept in mind regarding this possibility. First, it would require that stored names could be scanned much faster than they could be covertly articulated, since the scanning rate is about four times as fast as people can say names of digits to themselves. Second, unlike other forms of preprocessing, such as image-sharpening or feature-extraction, preprocessing a character to the point of identification or naming would itself require the retrieval of information from memory—that information which relates the character to its name.

In one experiment bearing on this question (Exp. 3), I degraded the test stimulus by superimposing a pattern that had been adjusted to increase the RT without substantially altering the error rate. I then examined the effect of stimulus quality on the function that relates mean RT and the size of the positive set. It is shown below that this effect would depend on the nature of the internal representation of the test-stimulus.

Figure 2.7 shows idealized data from a scanning experiment. The zero-intercept corresponds to the total duration of all processes that occur just once, regardless of the size of the positive set—such as the encoding of the test stimulus to form its representation, and the organization and execution of the motor response. The slope, on the other hand, measures the duration of processes that occur once for each member of the positive set—the comparison operation, and the time to switch from

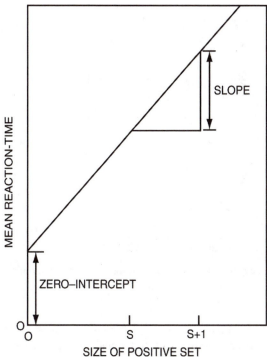

FIGURE 2.7 ■ Idealization of mean RT-function from an item-recognition task.

one item to the next.[7] Figure 2.8 shows a flow diagram of some hypothetical stages between test stimulus and response. The height of a box represents the mean duration of that stage. An effect of stimulus degradation on the *stimulus-encoding stage*, which generates the stimulus representation, would increase the zero-intercept of the RT-function. An effect on the *serial-comparison stage* would increase the slope, since a time increment would be added for each item compared.

Consider two extreme possibilities: First, suppose that the encoding stage did nothing other than transmit an unprocessed image, or direct copy, of the test stimulus. Then degradation could influence only the comparison operation, which occurs once for each member of the positive set; only the slope of the RT-function would change, as in Panel A of Figure 2.9. At the other extreme, suppose that the representation produced by the encoding stage was the *name* of the test stimulus. The input to the serial-comparison stage would be the same, whether or not the test stimulus had been degraded by a superimposed visual pattern; hence degradation could not influence this stage. (For the serial-comparison stage to be influenced by visual degradation, its input would have to be visual, in the sense

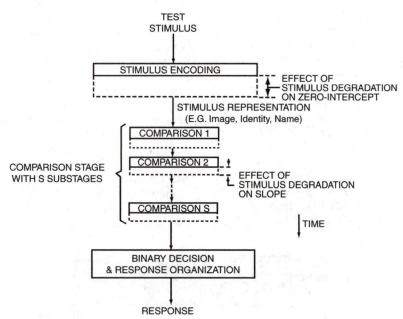

FIGURE 2.8 ■ Some hypothetical stages and substages in item-recognition, and two possible effects of test-stimulus quality on stage and substage durations. Height of box represents mean duration of that stage or substage.

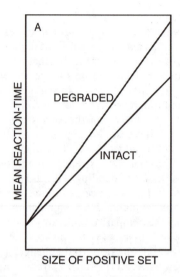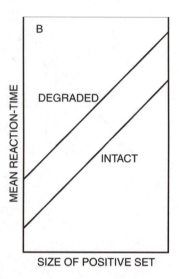

FIGURE 2.9 ■ Two possibilities for the effect of test-stimulus quality on the RT-function. A: Quality influences comparison stage only. B: Quality influences encoding stage only.

of embodying details of the physical stimulus pattern that are not present in the mere name of the stimulus.) Only the encoding stage, then, could be influenced by degradation; and since encoding takes place just once, only the zero-intercept of the RT-function would change, as in Panel B of Figure 2.9. (The absence of a change in slope, however, does not necessarily imply a nonvisual stimulus-representation; the representation could be visual, but highly processed.)

In Exp. 3 each of twelve subjects had positive sets of one, two, and four digits, with test stimuli *intact* in some blocks of trials, and in others *degraded* by a superimposed checkerboard pattern. Intact and degraded numerals are shown in Figure 2.10.

The fixed-set procedure was used. Results for the two sessions are shown separately in Figure 2.11. Consider first the data from the second session, on the right-hand side of the figure. Latencies

of positive and negative responses have been averaged together. The functions for degraded and intact stimuli are almost parallel, but there is a large effect on the zero-intercept, closely approximating the pattern shown in Panel B of Figure 2.9. This indicates that degradation had a large influence on the stimulus-encoding stage, and that the representation generated was sufficiently processed that the serial-comparison stage could proceed as rapidly with degraded as with intact stimuli. The stimulus representation was either nonvisual or, if visual, sufficiently refined in the second session to eliminate any effect of degradation.

The data from this session are an instance of the *additivity* of two effects on RT. There is no interaction between the effect of set size and the effect of stimulus quality; instead, the effect of each of these factors on mean RT is independent of the level of the other. Such additivity supports the theory of a sequence of stages, one stage influ-

FIGURE 2.10 ■ Photographs of intact and degraded numerals used in Exp. 3. Numerals were about 0.6 in. high and were viewed from a distance of about 29 in. Degraded numerals were somewhat more discriminable than they appear in the black-and-white photograph, possibly because of a slight color difference between numerals and checkerboard.

enced by stimulus quality and the other by set size (see Section 7).

Now let us consider the data from the first session, shown on the left hand side of Figure 2.11. Here, where subjects have not yet had much practice with the superimposed checkerboard, there is a 20% increase in the slope of the RT-function, as well as an increase in its zero-intercept. This pattern agrees with neither of the pure cases of Figure 2.9. Stimulus quality apparently *can* influence the duration of comparison operations; hence, the output of the encoding stage must be sensitive to degradation. Findings from the two sessions imply, then, that although the stimulus representation is highly processed; it embodies physical attributes of the test stimulus, rather than being a name or identity. That is, the test-stimulus representation is visual. The memory representations of the positive set that are used in the serial-comparison stage must therefore also be visual, to make comparison, possible. Hence, although items in the posi-

tive set appear to be represented as covertly-spoken names in the course of their rehearsal, this is not the only form in which they are available.

What changed between the first and second sessions so as to virtually eliminate the influence of stimulus quality on the slope of the RT-function? Since the scanning rate with intact stimuli and the effect of degradation on the zero-intercept are approximately the same in the two sessions, it seems unlikely that the type of representation changed. For the present, my interpretation is that the encoding stage became more efficient at removing the effects of the fixed degrading pattern.

Additional support for the idea that the memory representations scanned in the item-recognition task have sensory characteristics, rather than being completely abstracted from the physical stimuli, comes from two other studies. In the first, Chase and Calfee (1969) created four different conditions in the varied-set procedure by representing both the positive set and the test stimulus either visually

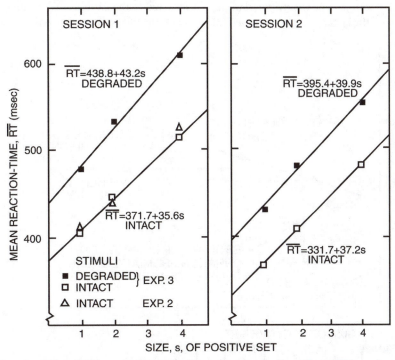

**FIGURE 2.11 ■** Results of Exp. 3: Effect of stimulus quality on item-recognition. Mean RT, based on pooled data from positive and negative responses, as a function of size of positive set for intact and degraded test stimuli. Left-hand and right-hand panels show data from Sessions 1 and 2, respectively. Averaged data from 12 subjects, with lines fitted by least squares. In all conditions positive responses were required on 27% of the trials. Triangles show results from Exp. 2 (Figure 2.6), which was similar.

or aurally. When the set and test item were presented in different modalities, the slope of the RT-function increased by about 30%, indicating a slower scanning rate. If abstract representations were being compared in the same-modality conditions, then the change to different-modality conditions should have altered only the zero-intercept, as in Figure 2.9B. In the second study, Posner, et al. (1969) concluded that when a single letter is presented *aurally* for memorization, the decision whether a *visual* test-letter is the "same" is facilitated by the internal generation of a visual representation of the memorized letter, which obviates the need to identify the test letter. Still further evidence will be discussed below (Exp. 4).

## 7. A Test of the Stage Theory

The work described above is grounded on Donders' stage theory. That is, as in his subtraction method, the effects on mean RT of changes in experimental conditions (factors) have been attributed to the selective effects of these factors on hypothetical

processing stages between stimulus and response. How can we ensure that such inferences are not open to the classical criticism of the subtraction method, that even if information processing *is* organized in functionally different stages, factor effects may not be selective? One answer, of course, is that the test of a method's applicability is whether it produces results that fit together and make sense. But there are two other arguments as well.

The first stems from replacement of the assumption of pure insertion by a weaker and more plausible *assumption of selective influence*. Instead of requiring that a change in the task insert or delete an entire processing stage without altering others, the weaker assumption requires only that it influence the *duration* of some stage without altering others. One example is illustrated in Figure 2.12. To estimate the comparison time by the subtraction method, one would have studied Task 2, in which the positive set has one member, and compared it to a Task 1. Task 1 would have been constructed to measure the zero-intercept directly, by deleting the entire comparison stage. But I sus-

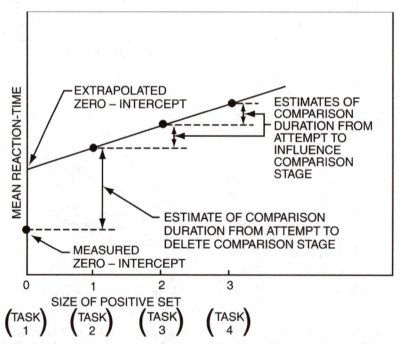

FIGURE 2.12 ■ Example of error from hypothetical attempt to estimate comparison time by deleting the comparison stage altogether, as in the subtraction method, and to use a measured zero intercept. Attempt fails because *deletion* of comparison stage changes the demands placed on other stages, whereas *variation* of the number of comparisons, $s$, ($s \geq 1$) does not.

pect that there *is* no appropriate Task 1, in which deletion of all comparisons would leave the other stages of processing invariant. In this instance, then, the assumption of pure insertion is probably invalid. This is why the important RT-differences in the experiments described above were those between Tasks 2 and 3, 3 and 4, and so on, whose interpretation required only that the comparison stage be selectively *influenced* by set size. Similarly, in studying the pre-processing of the stimulus, instead of entirely eliminating the need to discriminate the stimulus (in an effort to *delete* the hypothetical encoding stage) I examined the effects of making its discrimination more or less difficult, thereby varying the amount of work the stage had to accomplish. Of course, one result of using a factor that influences but does not insert a stage is that we have no estimate of the stage's total duration. But that seems to be of less interest than whether there is such a stage, what influences it, what it accomplishes, and what its relation is to other stages.[8]

In a given experimental situation, the validity of even the weaker assumption of selective influence must be checked, however. We can distinguish those situations where one of the assumptions—influence or insertion—holds, by testing the additivity of the effects of two or more factors on mean RT (Sternberg, 1969). It is this test that provides the second and most telling way of dealing with the classical criticism. Consider a pair of hypothetical stages and a pair of experimental factors, with each factor inserting or selectively influencing one of the stages. Because stage durations are additive (by definition), the changes in mean RT produced by such factors should be independent and additive. That is, the effect of one factor will be the same at all levels of the other,

when the response is measured on a scale of time or its (arithmetic) mean.[9]

In experiments with the fixed-set procedure I have examined four factors, which are listed above the broken line in Figure 2.13. The additivity of five of the six possible factor pairs has been tested and confirmed (1&2, after a session of practice, 1&3, 2&3, 2&4, and 3&4). These instances of additivity support the assumption that the factors selectively influence different stages of processing and, *a fortiori*, confirm the existence of such stages. Another instance of additivity, and the one on which inferences about the structure of the comparison stage strongly depend, is represented by the linearity of the effect of set size: the effect of adding an item to the positive set is independent of the number of items already in the set. Together with other considerations (discussed in Sternberg, 1969) these findings lead to the analysis into processing stages and substages shown below the broken line in Figure 2.13.[10]

## 8. Generality of High-Speed Scanning

Let us turn now to more substantive matters, and consider the generality of the high-speed exhaustive scanning process. Binary classification of digits into sets that are small, randomly-assembled, and relatively unfamiliar is hardly a typical example of memory retrieval. But it is useful to pin down one process fairly well, and explore techniques that reveal it in a relatively pure form, in order to use it as a baseline for the study of other mechanisms.[11]

For one example of a possible alternative to serial search, consider the case where the items in a memorized set share a physical feature whose

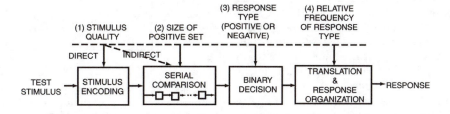

**FIGURE 2.13** ■ Four processing stages in item-recognition. Above the broken line are shown the four factors examined. Below the line is shown the decomposition of RT inferred from additive relations between factor pairs 1&2, 1&3, 2&3, 2&4, and 3&4, the linear effect of factor 2, and other considerations. (The indirect effect of factor 1 on the comparison stage, and the resulting interaction of factors 1&2, is seen in unpracticed subjects only.)

presence distinguishes them from the rest of the stimulus ensemble. Here one might expect subjects to test the stimulus for the presence of the feature rather than compare it to the items in the set one by one. Surprisingly, using letters with a diagonal line-segment as the distinguishing feature, Yonas (1969) showed that subjects start by scanning the set; only after considerable practice do they use the feature test, thereby eliminating the effect of the number of letters in the set.

Another possible alternative to serial search is an "associative" process. Consider the case in which positive items are distinguished by membership in a well-learned category. (For example, the positive set might contain digits only, and the negative set, letters.) To each member of a category is associatively linked its category label, and the binary choice depends on which label is elicited by the test stimulus. The speed of such a process might be independent of the sizes of positive and negative sets (although it might depend on various attributes of the categories that contained them, including *their* sizes; see Landauer & Freedman, 1968). On the other hand, the high speed of scanning might make it more efficient than an associative process, when one of the sets is small. In short, there may be alternative mechanisms for the same task, and which one is used may depend, in part, on which one is more efficient. If this is the case it is a great advantage to understand at least one of the alternatives in some detail.

## 9. Retrieval of Nonsymbolic versus Symbolic Information

Other questions about the generality of the scanning process are raised by its high speed, which precludes its being identified with the subvocalization of numeral names, and also by the influence of stimulus-quality on the scanning rate in Exp. 3 (section 6), which indicates that the stimulus representation is not the name or identity of the numeral. The fact that numerals are patterns with extremely well-learned names may therefore be irrelevant to the scanning process. Of course, numerals have other special properties: they are highly familiar, they are symbols, they represent numerical quantities, and people are practiced at manipulating the numbers they represent. A. M. Treisman and I recently tested the importance of

these properties for memory retrieval, using two different ensembles, one of nonsense forms, and the other of photographs of faces (Exp. 4). To our subjects, both ensembles were unfamiliar, nonsymbolic, unordered, and without well-learned names. We used the fixed-set procedure with sets of size 1 to 4, but found it necessary to display the positive set before each trial in order to help the subjects, who were inexperienced, to maintain it in active memory.

RT data, shown in Figure 2.14, are qualitatively the same as those for digit sets. They show linearity, suggesting a serial process, and equality of slopes for positive and negative responses, indicating exhaustiveness of search. The main difference is in the scanning rate, which seems to depend to some extent on the nature of the stimuli. Even for faces, however, the estimated rate is high—about 18 faces per second. These findings indicate that

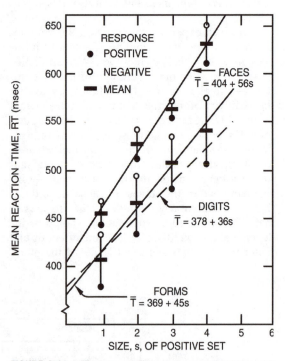

**FIGURE 2.14** ■ Results of Exp. 4: Item-recognition with nonsense forms and photographs of faces. Mean latencies of correct positive and negative responses, and their mean, as a function of size of positive set for the two stimulus ensembles. Averaged data from eight subjects for each ensemble, with lines fitted by least squares to means. Broken line was fitted to data from a similar experiment with an ensemble of numerals.

high-speed exhaustive scanning does not depend on the special properties of numerals mentioned above. They also add further support to the conclusion that the test-stimulus representation in the case of numerals is not the name of the numeral, but is some sort of visual representation.

## 10. Retrieval from Inactive versus Active Memory

A further question about the generality of the high-speed scanning process is raised by the conjecture (section 5) that it occurs only when information is being held in active memory. The similarity of results from the varied-set and fixed-set procedures led to the idea that even when a list is contained in long-term memory, it is transferred into active memory and maintained there by rehearsal in order to be used in the item-recognition task. If that is so, one would expect some change in the process if one prevented the relevant list from being rehearsed (for example, by occupying the active memory with other material). This kind of procedure moves us closer to studying the differences between retrieval from the short-term (active) and long-term (inactive) stores, and thereby understanding the latter by using the former as a baseline.

The procedure in a small preliminary experiment (Exp. 5) is shown in Figure 2.15. At the start of a series of trials the subject memorized a list of 1, 3, or 5 digits, which defined the positive set for the entire series. On each trial a new list of seven letters was presented sequentially, at a rate of two letters per second. A short time after the last letter, there was a brief warning signal, and then one of two things could happen. On a random third of

the trials the subject saw a recall signal, and attempted to recall the seven letters. These trials were used in order to encourage the subject to attend to the letters and retain them in memory until the test event. (Observing and retaining the list of letters was intended to occupy his active memory on all trials and prevent him from rehearsing the positive set.) On the remaining trials the subject saw a test digit. He was required to make a positive or negative response, based on the previously memorized digit set, as quickly as possible consistent with accuracy. This is a difficult task, and required a session of practice for smooth performance. In the series of control trials, which alternated with series of experimental trials, no lists of letters were presented.

Data averaged over the four subjects in this preliminary experiment are shown in Figure 2.16. The lower set of points represents performance in the control condition, which was similar in procedure to Exp. 2. Mainly because of one exceptional subject, the fitted line is somewhat steeper than usual, with a slope of 57 msec per digit. Otherwise the data are typical. In the experimental condition the fitted line is about twice as steep as in the control condition, with a slope of 105 msec per digit. Again, the latencies of positive and negative responses grow at equal rates as set size is increased. The zero-intercepts in the experimental and control conditions differ also, by over 100 msec.

Evidently, the retrieval process is radically altered, with the effective scanning rate halved, when the information to be retrieved is not being rehearsed and is therefore not in active memory. Current notions about the functions of rehearsal include maintenance of short-term memory, and transfer of information into long-term memory (section 5). The results of Exp. 5 suggest a third

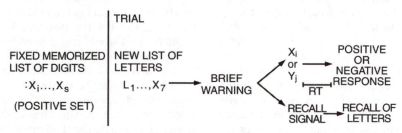

**FIGURE 2.15** ■ Paradigm of Exp. 5: Item-recognition from active and inactive memory. Only the inactive-memory condition is shown. In the active-memory condition, also involving a fixed-set procedure (Figure 2.3), no letters were presented.

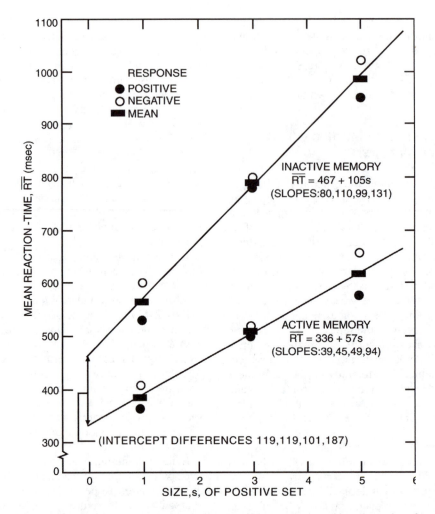

**FIGURE 2.16** ■ Results of Exp. 5: Item-recognition from active and inactive memory. Mean latencies of correct positive and negative responses, and their mean, as functions of size of positive set, in conditions of active and inactive memory. Averaged data from four subjects, with lines fitted by least squares to means. Intercept differences and slopes for the four subjects are listed, the order of subjects being the same in each list.

role—that of making information already stored in long-term memory more rapidly accessible.

At this point there is little basis for selecting among potential explanations for the data from the experimental condition, but experiments are under way that may help to do so. The explanation that I favor, shown in Figure 2.17, is the one that makes plausible two striking aspects of the data: despite the large effect of condition, the linearity of the RT-function and the equality of slopes for positive and negative responses are both preserved. The first two boxes in the figure represent hypo-

thetical stages that might be present in the experimental condition but not in the control. One might be searching for the positive set in inactive memory. This would take a fixed time, regardless of the size of the positive set, and could account for the increase in the zero-intercept. The second added stage might be the serial transfer of each item in the positive set into active memory, with a fixed average time per item transferred, estimated from the data to be about 50 msec. Since all items would be transferred, whether the required response was positive or negative, the slopes of the

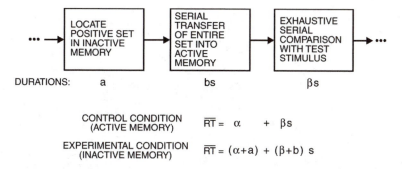

| LOCATE POSITIVE SET IN INACTIVE MEMORY | SERIAL TRANSFER OF ENTIRE SET INTO ACTIVE MEMORY | EXHAUSTIVE SERIAL COMPARISON WITH TEST STIMULUS |

DURATIONS:          a                    bs                    βs

CONTROL CONDITION
(ACTIVE MEMORY)          $\overline{RT} = \alpha + \beta s$

EXPERIMENTAL CONDITION
(INACTIVE MEMORY)          $\overline{RT} = (\alpha + a) + (\beta + b)\ s$

**FIGURE 2.17** ■ One explanation of results of Exp. 5. Left and middle boxes represent hypothetical stages that might be inserted in the inactive-memory condition. Also shown are hypothesized durations of these two stages and the comparison stage, and resulting theoretical RT-functions in which $\alpha$ represents the zero-intercept of the RT-function in the active-memory condition.

functions for both responses would be increased by the same amount. The high-speed scanning stage, which we already know to be exhaustive, would follow. The two added stages are plausible and would account for the important features of the data. But this explanation—particularly the concept of "transferring a set of items into active memory"— needs to be made more precise and then tested.

## 11. An Explanation of Exhaustiveness

As mentioned in section 3, an exhaustive search must involve more comparisons, on the average, than a search that terminates when a match occurs. The exhaustiveness of the high-speed scanning process therefore appears inefficient, and hence implausible. Why continue the comparison process beyond the point at which a match occurs? Figure 2.18 illustrates a system in which an exhaustive search could be more efficient than a self-terminating one for performance in an item-recognition task. A representation of the test stimulus is placed in a comparator. When the scanner is being operated by the "central processor" or "homunculus," H, it delivers memory representations of the items in the list, one after another, to the comparator. If and when a match occurs a signal is delivered to the match register. The important feature of the system is that the homunculus can *either* operate the scanner *or* examine the register. It cannot engage in both of these functions at once, and switching between them takes time.

In this kind of system, if the switching time is long relative to the scanning rate, and if the list is sufficiently short, then an exhaustive search (in which the match register must be examined only once) is more efficient than a self-terminating one (where the register would have to be examined after each comparison). The surprisingly high speed of the scanning process may therefore be made possible by its exhaustiveness. But such a system might have at least one important limitation. After the search was completed, there might be no information available (without further reference to the memory of the list) as to the location in the list of the item that produced the match. The limitation would create no difficulty if the response required of the subject depended only on the presence or absence of an item in the list and not on its location, as in the item-recognition task. But the possibility that high-speed scanning does not yield location information does suggest an experiment to test this theory of exhaustiveness. Suppose we require a subject to give a response that *does* depend on where in the list a matching item is located. Then after each comparison, with information still available as to the location of the item just compared to the test stimulus (e.g., preserved by the position of the scanner in Figure 2.18), it would have to be determined whether this item produced a match (by the homunculus switching from scanner to register). Scanning should then be slower than when only presence or absence has to be judged; it should also be self-terminating, since further comparisons after a match had been detected would be superfluous. Such a process will be called *scanning to locate*.

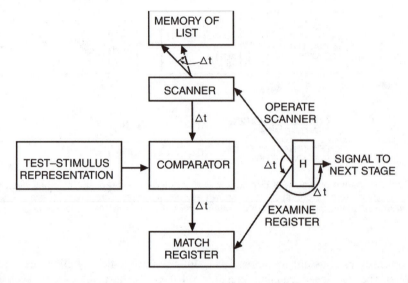

**FIGURE 2.18** ■ A system in which exhaustive scanning could be more efficient than self-terminating scanning. Some loci of possible time delays are represented by $\Delta t$s.

## 12. Retrieval of Contextual Information by Scanning to Locate

In Figure 2.19 is shown the paradigm of a *context-recall task*, one of the experiments devised to test these ideas (Exp. 6). On each trial the subject memorized a new random list of from three to seven different digits, presented visually one after another. The length of the list was varied at random from trial to trial. After a delay and a warning signal, a test item was presented, randomly selected from among all the digits in the list except the last. The test item, then, was always present in the list. The correct response was the spoken name of the item that followed the test item in the memorized list. The idea was that in order to make this response—that is, to recall an item defined by its contextual relation to the test item— the location of the test item in the list might first have to be determined. As in the other experiments described, subjects were encouraged to respond as rapidly as possible, while attempting to maintain a low error rate.

Two aspects of the data are of particular interest: the relation between mean RT and list length; and the relation, for a list of given length, between RT and the serial position of the test item in the list.

Data averaged over six subjects are shown in Figure 2.20. Consider first Panel A. The bars show the percentage of wrong responses, which rises to 25% for lists of length 7. This is much higher than one would like, given an interest in error-free performance. The effect of list-length on mean RT is roughly linear, suggesting a scanning process. (Even closer approximations to linearity have been found in other similar experiments.) With a slope of 124 msec per item, the fitted line is much steeper than the corresponding RT-function in the item-recognition task.

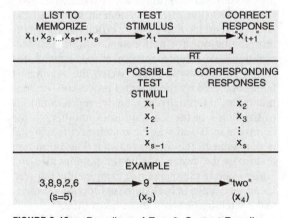

**FIGURE 2.19** ■ Paradigm of Exp. 6: Context-Recall.

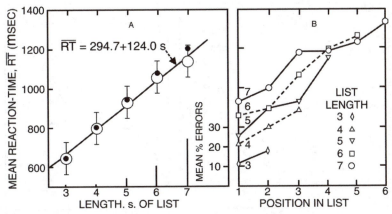

**FIGURE 2.20** ■ Results of Exp. 6: Context-recall. Averaged data from six subjects. A: Effect of list length on percent errors (bars), on mean latency of correct responses (open circles) with estimates of ±σ and line fitted by least squares, and on mean RT of all responses (filled circles). B: Relation between mean RT of correct responses and serial position of the test item in lists of five lengths.

To interpret the slope, we have first to establish if the process is self-terminating, as expected. Evidence on this point is provided by the average serial-position functions shown in Panel B. For each list length, mean RT is plotted as a function of the serial position of the test item in the memorized list. These functions are all increasing, suggesting a self-terminating process that tends to start at the beginning of the list and proceed in serial order.

Now we can interpret the slope of the function in Panel A, if we assume that list length influences only the scanning stage. (Evidence supporting this assumption of selective influence is presented below.) Since an average of about half the items in a list have to be scanned before a match occurs, the slope represents half of the time per item, and implies a scanning rate of about 250 msec per item, or four items per second, in scanning to locate an item in a memorized list. Scanning to locate is therefore about seven times as slow as the high-speed scanning process used to determine the presence of an item in a list. The slowness of the search, and the fact it is self-terminating, lend support to the explanation (section 11) of the exhaustiveness of the high-speed process. Scanning to locate seems to be fundamentally different from scanning for presence.[12]

As mentioned earlier (section 3), if a self-terminating process started consistently at the beginning of a list and proceeded serially, the serial-

position functions would be steep and superimposed, whereas if it started at a random point they would be flat and separated. The functions shown in Panel B lie between these extremes. This is partly because they represent averages of data from several subjects. Data from two subjects in Exp. 6 who represent almost pure cases are shown in Figure 2.21. The estimated scanning rates for these two subjects are almost the same, but their starting strategies appear to be radically different. Subject 1 seems to have started at a random point. This could occur if the presentation of the test item interrupted an ongoing cyclic rehearsal process, and scanning then began at the serial position where rehearsal happened to have stopped. Subject 4, on the other hand, has the superimposed functions that would arise if he had started scanning consistently at the beginning of the list, perhaps by terminating his rehearsal before the test-stimulus appeared. Data from other subjects range between these extremes, presumably because of mixed starting strategies.

One explanation of these results is the following: In order to recall a contextual item, the subject must first determine the test item's location in the memorized list. This is achieved by a slow, self-terminating process of scanning to locate, in which the items in memory are compared successively to the test item until a match occurs. Each nonmatching item that participates contributes to the RT a component time that depends neither on

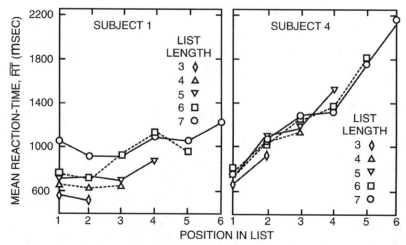

**FIGURE 2.21** ■ Individual data from Exp. 6: Context-recall. Contrasting sets of serial-position functions in lists of five lengths, one set relatively flat and separated, the other steep and, in general, superimposed.

list length nor on the item's position in the list. This component time is occupied by switching to the item, comparing it to the test stimulus, and determining that they have not matched. In the present context-recall task, the occurrence of a match is followed by a shift (e.g., a movement of the scanner in Figure 2.18) from the item that matches the test item to the adjacent response item. For superimposed serial-position functions (as in Figure 2.21) to be possible, we must assume that the duration of the shift operation (as well as other stages, such as stimulus-encoding and response-organization) is independent of the length of the list. Given this assumption, the slope of the RT-function is determined solely by the scanning rate.

The process of scanning to locate is a still more dramatic instance of having to hunt for information even when it is contained in a list that is being rehearsed. In some important sense one does not know what is in one's active memory, other than the single item to which attention is currently directed.[13]

## 13. Independence of Learning and Retrieval from Active Memory

One problem with Exp. 6 is the high error rate, and its marked increase with list length (Figure 2.20A). This makes the RT data somewhat suspect and violates the aim of studying error-free

processes. Moreover, it raises the possibility that the level of learning of the list, which is clearly lower for longer lists, might be contributing to the increase of RT with list length. (For example, suppose that a list embodies a chain of associations and that the recall of a contextual item involves the performance of one of the associations. If the associations in a longer list are weaker, then at least one of the sources of the effect of list length on RT might be an increased associative latency.) In an experiment (Exp. 7) devised to look into these matters, the list was presented once, twice, or three times, as shown in Figure 2.22, to vary how well it was learned. In the one-presentation condition, at the bottom of the figure, the list was presented, and there followed a test stimulus and response, just as in Exp. 6. Again, the list changed from trial to trial, and contained from 3 to 7 digits. In the two-presentation condition, each trial included an additional presentation of its list and an attempt to recall it. In the three-presentation condition there was still another presentation and recall of the list.

Results from six subjects are shown in Figure 2.23. At the bottom, the percent of errors in naming the succeeding digit is shown as a function of list length, for each condition. Added presentations reduced the error rate by a factor of three. At the top of the figure, mean RT is shown as a function of list length, for each of the three conditions. Despite the change in level of learning indicated by the error data, the pattern of RTs shows

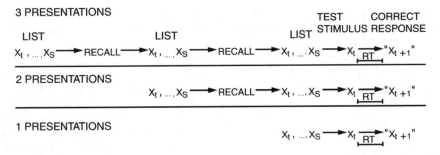

**FIGURE 2.22** ■ Conditions in Exp. 7: Effect of learning on context-recall.

no systematic change with number of presentations.

This invariance indicates that differences in level of learning that are associated with list length do not contribute to the influence of list length on mean RT; and further, that within the limits of the experiment, the rate of scanning to locate is independent of how well a list has been learned.[14] The invariance with level of learning, which is similar to that of the high-speed scanning process over fixed-set and varied-set procedures, is consistent with the interpretation of the context-recall data

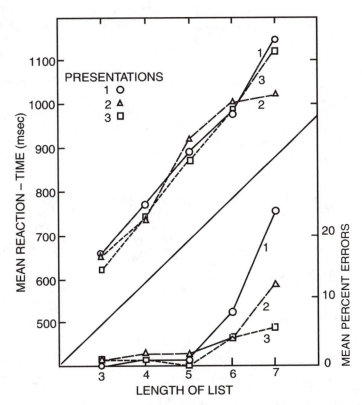

**FIGURE 2.23** ■ Results of Exp. 7: Effect of learning on context-recall. Averaged data from six subjects for one, two, and three presentations of the list. Bottom: mean percent errors in naming contextual item. Top: mean latency of correct responses.

presented in section 11, and adds to the evidence that factors well known to influence learning may have no effect on active-memory functioning. Finally, given the invariance of the retrieval process, the strong influence of number of presentations on error rate suggests that the errors result primarily from faults in learning and retention, rather than in retrieval.

## 14. Recall versus Recognition of Contextual Information

In explaining the difference between findings from the item-recognition and context-recall tasks (Exps. 1–5 *versus* Exps. 6–7) I have emphasized that in one case the response depends merely on presence of an item in the list, and in the other case on its exact location. For an explanation in these terms to be valid, however, certain other differences between the tasks must be shown to be unimportant: one task involves recall, and the other recognition; one requires that for production of the response a memory representation be converted into a particular form—its name—and the other does not; and whereas the number of response alternatives in one task grows with list length, the other always requires a binary choice.

The last experiment to be described (Exp. 8) was designed to evaluate the importance of these factors and to examine further the generality of the process of scanning to locate. A recognition

procedure was used to study the retrieval of contextual information; the resulting *context-recognition task* is shown in Figure 2.24. On each trial the subject attempted to memorize a list of from 3 to 6 different digits, presented visually, one after another. To increase accuracy, the list was actually presented twice, with a recall attempt after the first presentation. The test stimulus was a pair of simultaneously presented digits that had appeared successively somewhere in the list. The subject's task was to decide whether the left-to-right order of the pair was the same as its temporal order in the list, or reversed. He made his response by pulling one of two levers (as in Exps. 1–5).

This experiment seemed to be somewhat risky, since there appeared to be a variety of strategies open to the subject. One possibility was that before its order could be tested, the pair might have to be located in the list by means of a scanning process. This process would be revealed by the relation between RT and the length of the list. Suppose that the test pair is located in the list by scanning for the location of one of its members, according to the self-terminating process described in Section 11. One would then expect that in the context-recognition task mean RT for both same-order and reversed-order responses would increase linearly with list length, and at equal rates, and that the rate of increase would be the same as in the context-recall task.

The same six subjects who performed the context-recall task of Exp. 7 also served (in a balanced

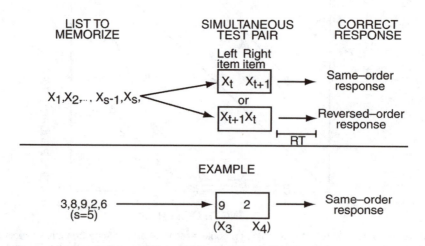

**FIGURE 2.24** ■ Paradigm of Exp. 8: Context-recognition.

order) in the recognition task. RT-functions for both responses (Figure 2.25) are linear, supporting the notion that in this task, also, performance involves a scanning process. For both responses the slope of the fitted line is 114 msec per item.[15] The equality of slopes is consistent with the idea that both responses depend on first locating one of the members of the pair in the list. That this is accomplished by means of a self-terminating process is suggested by the serial-position data: for all subjects, and for both responses, mean RT increased with the serial position of the pair in the list. Averaged serial-position data are shown in Figure 2.26.

RT-functions from the context-recognition and context-recall tasks (Exps. 7 and 8) are compared in Figure 2.27. The fitted lines are parallel, supporting the idea that the same search process (scanning to locate) underlies performance in both tasks. Also shown, for reference, is the RT-function from the item-recognition task of Exp. 1.

These parallel lines provide another striking instance of additive effects on mean RT. Here the additive factors are task (context-recognition *versus* recall) and list length; the absence of interaction indicates that these factors influence processing stages selectively, and helps to justify our interpretations of the data. Apparently, the change

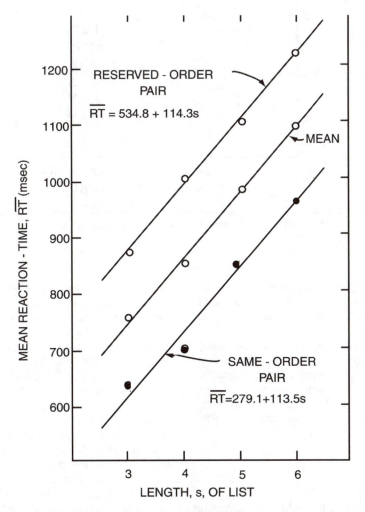

**FIGURE 2.25** ■ Results of Exp. 8: Context-recognition. Averaged data from six subjects. Mean latencies of correct same-order and reversed-order responses, and their mean, with lines fitted by least squares.

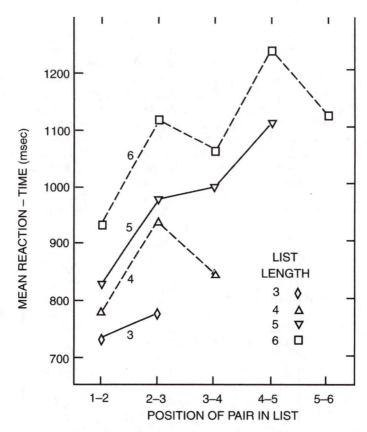

**FIGURE 2.26** ■ Further results of Exp. 8: Context-recognition. Relation between mean RT of correct responses and serial position of the test pair in lists of four lengths. Data were averaged over six subjects and over same-order and reversed-order responses.

from recall to recognition does not influence the scanning stage, and, as assumed in section 12, changes in list length do not influence perceptual and response stages.

One final substantive point about these results concerns their implications for the recognition-recall distinction. It is tempting to think that recognition involves less search, in some sense, than recall. These data reveal at least one search process that is as evident in a recognition task (Exp. 8) as in a recall task (Exp. 7).

## Summary

I have reviewed informally eight experiments on the retrieval of information from human memory, whose interpretation depended on inferences from the structure of RT data to the organization of mental processes. The experiments have led to the discovery of two kinds of memory search that people use in the retrieval of information from short memorized lists. One is a high-speed exhaustive scanning process, used to determine the *presence* of an item in the list; the other is a slow self-terminating scanning process used to determine the *location* of an item in the list. Among other substantive implications of the experiments are: (1) Apparently one *must* scan a list serially to retrieve information from it, even when it is contained in active memory. There is no evidence in any of these data that one can "think about" more than one thing at a time, and thereby simultaneously compare a set of memorized items to a

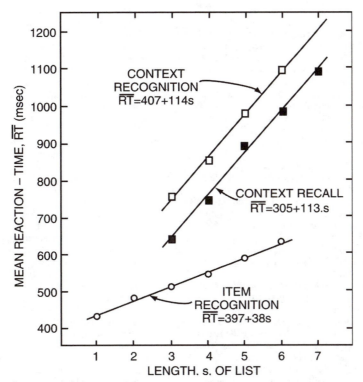

**FIGURE 2.27** ■ Comparison of results from context-recognition, context-recall, and item-recognition tasks. Top: Mean RTs from Exp. 8 (Figure 2.24), averaged over same-order and reversed-order responses. Middle: Mean RTs averaged over the three conditions in the context-recall task of Exp. 7 (Figure 2.22), which used the same subjects as Exp. 8. Bottom: Mean RTs from Exp. 1 (Figure 2.4).

test item. (2) On the other hand, even a well-learned list can be made more readily available by being maintained in active memory. (3) Despite the possibility that retention may depend on a rehearsal process involving covert speech, visual rather than auditory memory-representations are used for comparison to representations of visual stimuli. (4) The same search process can be involved in both recall and recognition tasks.

Many of the inferences from the data were based on a proposal first made by Donders (1868) that the time between stimulus and response be regarded as the sum of the durations of a series of processing stages. Donders' *subtraction method* depends on this *stage theory,* together with an *assumption of pure insertion,* which states that a change in the subject's task can cause the insertion of an additional processing stage without altering the other stages. It was the questioning of

this assumption, and the absence of any objective tests of its validity, that led to the decline of the subtraction method in the late nineteenth century.

The present paper advocates retaining the idea of stages of processing. But it shows how the insertion assumption can sometimes be replaced by a weaker *assumption of selective influence,* and how the validity of either assumption for a given experiment can be tested by determining whether the effects of experimental factors on RT are additive. The main ideas are: (1) if separate stages between stimulus and response have been correctly identified, then for each of these stages it may be easier to find a factor that *influences* it without altering other stages than to find one that *inserts* it without altering other stages; and (2) these factors would then have additive effects on mean RT. The discovery of several sets of such additive factors was critical in the interpretation of the experiments described.

## NOTES

1. Most of the research reported in this paper was supported by Bell Telephone Laboratories and conducted in its Behavioral and Statistical Research Center at Murray Hill, N.J. The work reported as Exp. 4 was done in collaboration with A. M. Treisman of the University of Oxford. I am grateful to C. S. Harris, T. K. Landauer, H. Rouanet, and R. Teghtsoonian for helpful criticisms of the manuscript, and to L. D. Harmon for discussion leading to Exp. 5. R. E. Main assisted with Exps. 4 and 5, B. Barkow with Exps. 7 and 8, and B. A. Nasto with Exps. 4, 5, 7, and 8.

2. For example, Cattell (1886, p. 377) reported that "I have not been able myself to get results by [Wundt's] method. I apparently either distinguished the impression and made the motion simultaneously, or if I tried to avoid this by waiting until I had formed a distinct impression before I began to make the motion, I added to the simple reaction not only a perception, but a volition."

3. See, e.g., Egeth, 1966; Hochberg, 1968; Nickerson, 1967; Posner & Mitchell, 1967; Restle & Davis, 1962; Smith, 1967; Suppes & Groen, 1966.

4. Several investigators have, however, reported marked recency effects in item-recognition tasks: RTs were shorter for test stimuli later in the list (Corballis, 1967; Morin, DeRosa, & Stultz, 1967; Morin, DeRosa, & Ulm, 1967). Without embellishment a theory of exhaustive scanning cannot, of course, handle such findings. The salient procedural characteristics of experiments that produce such recency effects seem to be a fast rate of list presentation and a short interval (less than 1 sec) between the last item in the list and the test item. Findings of Posner et al. (1969), indicate that in this range the time interval between successive stimuli may critically influence the nature and duration of comparison operations.

5. An alternative term is "working memory," used by Newell & Simon, 1963, to refer to the arithmetic unit of a general-purpose computer. See also "Active verbal memory," Ch. 9 in Neisser, 1967, and "Operational memory," section 4 in Posner, 1967.

6. It is sometimes thought that the six or seven objects in the "span of apprehension" are immediately and simultaneously available, being contained in the "psychological present." And the information in active memory has occasionally been identified with this momentary capacity of consciousness (e.g., Miller, 1962, pp. 47–49; Waugh & Norman, 1965). The finding that one must scan one's active memory to ascertain its contents, rather than having immediate access to them, reveals a possible flaw in this argument.

7. This analysis assumes that the mean durations of comparisons leading to matches and to mismatches are equal. Without this assumption all the statements here (and elsewhere in the paper) are correct, except that the slope of the RT-function measures the mean duration of only those comparisons that lead to mismatches, together with the time to switch from one comparison to the next. Any difference between durations of the two kinds of comparison would contribute to a difference between zero intercepts of the latency functions for positive and negative responses.

8. This alternative was preferred by Cattell, 1886, who argued (p. 378) "I do not think it is possible to add a perception to the reaction without also adding a will-act. We can however change the nature of the perception without altering the will-time, and thus investigate with considerable thoroughness the length of the perception time." But he suggested no way to test these assertions.

9. Discussions of various other aspects and modern versions of the subtraction method, including considerations of validity, may be found in Hohle, 1967; McGill & Gibbon, 1965; McMahon, 1963; Smith, 1968; Sternberg, 1964; Sternberg, 1969; and Taylor, 1966.

10. The linear interaction between stimulus quality and set size in Session 1 is attributed to an "indirect" influence of stimulus quality on the duration of the second stage, by way of its effect on the output of the first stage (see section 6, and Sternberg, 1967b). Thus one may sometimes infer a separate stage even when its output is not invariant with respect to a factor that influences its duration, and when as a consequence there is a failure of additivity. In this instance the inference is justified by the form of the interaction (a *linear* increase in the effect of degradation with set size), and the structure of the comparison stage (inferred to be a series of substages).

11. The function of such an experimental baseline is similar to the use of well-understood mathematical models as theoretical baselines (Sternberg, 1963, section 6.6) in which it is the discrepancies between data and model that are of interest.

12. Alternative explanations of the dissimilarity of the two kinds of scanning are possible, of course. One interesting alternative (which existing data cannot reject) is that memory representations that can carry order information are different from those that need only carry item information, and that the observed differences in retrieval result from the fact that different kinds of memory representations are being scanned. However, for this alternative explanation to apply to Exp. 1 (in which subjects had to recognize an item and then recall the entire list in order), it must be possible for both kinds of memory representation to be maintained simultaneously.

13. One traditional view is that the structure of a memorized list is a chain of overlapping associated pairs of items: the subject's task in a context-recall experiment is thought of as the performance of one of the associations in the chain, and the RT measure as an index of associative strength. At the least, this view must be modified to recognize the existence of a search for the representation of the test item in the list. This search is an instance of the obligatory process (usually ignored by association theorists) that locates and activates the memory trace of a stimulus before an associative response to that stimulus can be performed (Rock, 1962). Furthermore, in this experiment, not only does the locating process produce the dominant effect, but also there appears to be *no* influence of associative strength (section 13). One might therefore question whether the traditional view is at all appropriate, at least for lists contained in active memory. It has been challenged from other directions also in recent years (e.g., Slamecka, 1967).

14. If a list could only be either perfectly learned or not learned at all, this conclusion would not be justified, since

restricting the latencies analyzed to those of correct responses would entail the selection of lists that had been learned to the same degree (perfectly) in the three conditions. This objection does not apply here, mainly because correct responses in conjunction with *partially*-learned lists were frequent.

15. Although equal in slope, the RT-functions for the two kinds of response differ by about 250 msec in intercept. The several ways in which one might account for this difference are not discussed in this paper.

# REFERENCES

Atkinson, R. C. & Shiffrin, R. M. Human memory: A proposed system and its control processes. In K. W. Spence and J. T. Spence (Eds.), *The psychology of learning and motivation: Advances in research and theory*. Vol. 2. New York: Academic Press, 1968. Pp. 89–195.

Baddeley, A. D. The influence of acoustic and semantic similarity on long-term memory for word sequences. *Quart. J. Exp. Psychol.*, 1966, *18*, 302–309.

Broadbent, D. E. *Perception and communication*. London: Pergamon Press, 1958.

Cattell, J. McK. The perception time. *Mind*, 1886, *11*, 377–392. Reprinted in *James McKeen Cattell, Man of science*. Lancaster, Pa.: The Science Press, 1947. Pp. 64–79.

Chase, W. G. & Calfee, R. C. Modality and similarity effects in short-term recognition memory. *J. Exp. Psychol.*, 1969, *81*, 510–514.

Cohen, R. L. & Johansson, B. S. Some relevant factors in the transfer of material from short-term to long-term memory. *Quart. J. Exp. Psychol.*, 1967, *19*, 300–308.

Conrad, R. Acoustic confusions in immediate memory. *Brit. J. Psychol.*, 1964, *55*, 75–84.

Corballis, M. C. Serial order in recognition and recall. *J. Exp. Psychol.*, 1967, *74*, 99–105.

Crowder, R. G. Short-term memory for words with a perceptual-motor inter-polated activity. *J. Verb. Learn. Verb. Behav.*, 1967, *6*, 753–761.

Donders, F. C. Over de snelheid van psychische processen. Onderzoekingen gedaan in het Physiologisch Laboratorium der Utrechtsche Hoogeschool, 1868–1869, Tweede reeks, II, 92–120. Transl. by W. G. Koster in W. G. Koster (Ed.), *Attention and performance II. Acta Psychol.*, 1969, *30*, 412–431.

Egeth, H. E. Parallel versus serial processes in multidimensional stimulus discrimination. *Percept. & Psychophys.*, 1966, *1*, 245–252.

Glanzer, M. & Cunitz, A. R. Two storage mechanisms in free recall. *J. Verb. Learn. Verb. Behav.*, 1966, *5*, 351–360.

Hochberg, J. In the mind's eye. In R. N. Haber (Ed.), *Contemporary theory and research in visual perception*. New York: Holt, Rinehart & Winston, 1968. Pp. 309–331.

Hohle, R. H. Component process latencies in reaction times of children and adults. In L. P. Lipsett and C. C. Spiker (Eds.), *Advances in child development and behavior*. Vol. 3. New York: Academic Press, 1967. Pp. 225–261.

Jastrow, J. *The time-relations of mental phenomena. Fact & theory papers No. VI*. New York: N.D.C. Hodges, 1890.

Johnson, D. M. *The psychology of thought and judgment*. New York: Harper, 1955.

Kulpe, O. *Outlines of psychology*. New York: MacMillan, 1895.

Landauer, T. K. Rate of implicit speech. *Percept. Mol. Skills*, 1962, *15*, 646.

Landauer, T. K. & Freedman, J. L. Information retrieval from long-term memory: category size and recognition time. *J. Verb. Learn. Verb. Behav.*, 1968, *7*, 291–295.

McGill, W. J. & Gibbon, J. The general gamma distribution and reaction times. *J. Math. Psychol.*, 1965, *2*, 1–18.

McMahon, L. E. Grammatical analysis as part of understanding a sentence. Unpublished doctoral dissertation, Harvard University, 1963.

Miller, G. A. *Psychology, the science of mental life*. New York: Harper & Row, 1962.

Morin, R. E., DeRosa, D. V., & Stultz, V. Recognition memory and reaction time. In A. F. Sanders (Ed.), *Attention and performance. Acla Psychol.*, 1967, *27*, 298–305.

Morin, R. E., DeRosa, D. V., & Ulm, R. Short-term recognition memory for spatially isolated items. *Psychon. Sci.*, 1967, *9*, 617–618.

Neisser, U. *Cognitive psychology*. New York: Appleton-Century-Crofts, 1967.

Newell, A. & Simon, H. A. Computers in psychology. In R. D. Luce, R. R. Bush, and E. Galanter (Eds.), *Handbook of mathematical psychology*. Vol. 1. New York: Wiley, 1963. Pp. 361–428.

Nickerson, R. S. Categorization time with categories defined by disjunctions and conjunctions of stimulus attributes. *J. Exp. Psychol.*, 1967, *73*, 211–219.

Posner, M. I. Short-term memory systems in human information processing. In A. F. Sanders (Ed.), *Attention and performance. Acta Psychol.*, 1967, *27*, 267–284.

Posner, M. I., Boies, S. J., Eichelman, W. H., & Taylor, R. L. Retention of visual and name codes of single letters. *J.Exp. Psychol. Monogr.*, 1969, *79*, No. 1, Part, 2, 1–16.

Posner, M. I. & Mitchell, R. F. Chronometric analysis of classification. *Psychol. Rev.*, 1967, *74*, 392–409.

Posner, M. I. & Rossman, E. Effect of size and location of informational transforms upon short-term retention. *J. Exp. Psychol.*, 1965, *70*, 496–505.

Restle, F. & Davis, J. H. Success and speed of problem solving by individuals and groups. *Psychol. Rev.*, 1962, *69*, 520–536.

Rock, I. A neglected aspect of the problem of recall: The Höffding function. In J. M. Scher (Ed.), *Theories of the mind*. New York: Free Press, 1962. Pp. 645–659.

Sanders, A. F. Rehearsal and recall in immediate memory. *Ergonomics*, 1961, *4*, 25–34.

Slamecka, N. J. Serial learning and order information. *J. Exp. Psychol.*, 1967, *74*, 62–66.

Smith, E. E. Effects of familiarity on stimulus recognition and categorization. *J. Exp. Psychol.*, 1967, *74*, 324–332.

Smith, E. E. Choice reaction time: an analysis of the major theoretical positions. *Psychol. Bull.*, 1968, *69*, 77–110.

Sperling, G. The information available in brief visual presentations. *Psychol. Monogr.*, 1960, *75* (11, Whole No. 498).

Sperling, G. A model for visual memory tasks. *Hum. Factors*, 1963, *5*, 19–31.

Sternberg, S. Stochastic learning theory. In R. D. Luce, R. R. Bush, and E. Galanter (Eds.), *Handbook of mathematical psychology*. Vol. 2. New York: Wiley, 1963. Pp. 1–120.

Sternberg, S. Estimating the distribution of additive reaction-time components. Paper presented at the meeting of the Psychometric Society, Niagara Falls, Ont., October 1964.

Sternberg, S. High-speed scanning in human memory. *Science*, 1966, *153*, 652–654.

Sternberg, S. Retrieval of contextual information from memory. *Psychon. Sci.*, 1967, *8*, 55–6. (a)

Sternberg, S. Two operations in character-recognition: Some evidence from reaction-time measurements. *Percept. & Psychophys.*, 1967, *2*, 45–53. (b)

Sternberg, S. The discovery of processing stages: Extensions of Donders' method. In W. G. Koster (Ed.), *Attention and performance II. Acta Psychol.*, 1969, *30*, 276–315.

Suppes, P. & Groen; G. Some counting models for first-grade performance data on simple addition facts. Technical Report 90, Institute for Mathematical Studies in the Social Sciences, Stanford University, 1966.

Taylor, D. H. Latency components in two-choice responding. *J. Exp. Psychol.*, 1966, *72*, 481–488.

Waugh, N. C. & Norman, D. A. Primary memory. *Psychol. Rev.*, 1965, *72*, 89–104.

Wickelgren, W. A. Auditory or articulatory coding in verbal short-term memory. *Psychol. Rev.*, 1969, *76*, 232–235.

Woodworth, R. S. *Experimental psychology*. New York: Holt, 1938.

Wundt, W. *Grundzüge der physiologischen Psychologie*, Vol. II, 2nd ed. Leipzig: Engelmann, 1880.

Yonas, A. The acquisition of information-processing strategies in a time-dependent task. Unpublished doctoral dissertation, Cornell University, 1969.

# The Appeal of Parallel Distributed Processing

J. L. McClelland, D. E. Rumelhart, and G. E. Hinton

What makes people smarter than machines? They certainly are not quicker or more precise. Yet people are far better at perceiving objects in natural scenes and noting their relations, at understanding language and retrieving contextually appropriate information from memory, at making plans and carrying out contextually appropriate actions, and at a wide range of other natural cognitive tasks. People are also far better at learning to do these things more accurately and fluently through processing experience.

What is the basis for these differences? One answer, perhaps the classic one we might expect from artificial intelligence, is "software." If we only had the right computer program, the argument goes, we might be able to capture the fluidity and adaptability of human information processing.

Certainly this answer is partially correct. There have been great breakthroughs in our understanding of cognition as a result of the development of expressive high-level computer languages and powerful algorithms. No doubt there will be more such breakthroughs in the future. However, we do not think that software is the whole story.

In our view, people are smarter than today's computers because the brain employs a basic computational architecture that is more suited to deal with a central aspect of the natural information processing tasks that people are so good at. In this chapter, we will show through examples that these tasks generally require the simultaneous consideration of many pieces of information or constraints. Each constraint may be imperfectly specified and ambiguous, yet each can play a potentially decisive role in determining the outcome of processing. After examining these points, we will introduce a computational framework for modeling cognitive processes that seems well suited to exploiting these constraints and that seems closer than other frameworks to the style of computation as it might be done by the brain. We will review several early examples of models developed in this framework, and we will show that the mechanisms these models employ can give rise to powerful emergent properties that begin to suggest attractive alternatives to traditional accounts of various aspects of cognition. We will also show that models of this class provide a basis for understanding how learning can occur spontaneously, as a by-product of processing activity.

## Multiple Simultaneous Constraints

### REACHING AND GRASPING

Hundreds of times each day we reach for things. We nearly never think about these acts of reaching. And yet, each time, a large number of different considerations appear to jointly determine exactly how we will reach for the object. The position of the object, our posture at the time, what else we may also be holding, the size, shape, and anticipated weight of the object, any obstacles that may be in the way—all of these factors jointly determine the exact method we will use for reaching and grasping.

Consider the situation shown in Figure 3.1. Figure 3.1A shows Jay McClelland's hand, in typing position at his terminal. Figure 3.1B indicates the position his hand assumed in reaching for a small knob on the desk beside the terminal. We will let him describe what happened in the first person:

On the desk next to my terminal are several objects—a chipped coffee mug, the end of a com-

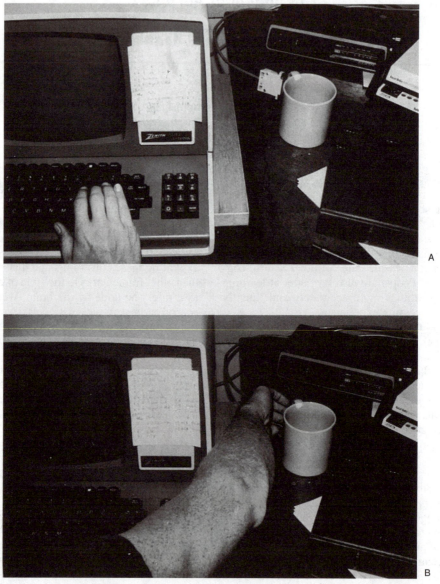

A

B

**FIGURE 3.1** ■ A: An everyday situation in which it is necessary to take into account a large number of constraints to grasp a desired object. In this case the target object is the small knob to the left of the cup. B: The posture the arm arrives at in meeting these constraints.

puter cable, a knob from a clock radio. I decide to pick the knob up. At first I hesitate, because it doesn't seem possible. Then I just reach for it, and find myself grasping the knob in what would normally be considered a very awkward position—but it solves all of the constraints. I'm not sure what all the details of the movement were, so I let myself try it a few times more. I observe that my right hand is carried up off the keyboard, bent at the elbow, until my forearm is at about a 30° angle to the desk top and parallel to the side of the terminal. The palm is facing downward through most of this. Then, my arm extends and lowers down more or less parallel to the edge of the desk and parallel to the side of the terminal and, as it drops, it turns about 90° so that the palm is facing the cup and the thumb and index finger are below. The turning motion occurs just in time, as my hand drops, to avoid hitting the coffee cup. My index finger and thumb close in on the knob and grasp it, with my hand completely upside down.

Though the details of what happened here might be quibbled with, the broad outlines are apparent. The shape of the knob and its position on the table; the starting position of the hand on the keyboard; the positions of the terminal, the cup, and the knob; and the constraints imposed by the structure of the arm and the musculature used to control it—all these things conspired to lead to a solution which exactly suits the problem. If any of these constraints had not been included, the movement would have failed. The hand would have hit the cup or the terminal—or it would have missed the knob.

## THE MUTUAL INFLUENCE OF SYNTAX AND SEMANTICS

Multiple constraints operate just as strongly in language processing as they do in reaching and grasping. Rumelhart (1977) has documented many of these multiple constraints. Rather than catalog them here, we will use a few examples from language to illustrate the fact that the constraints tend to be reciprocal: The example shows that they do not run only from syntax to semantics—they also run the other way.

It is clear, of course, that syntax constrains the assignment of meaning. Without the syntactic rules of English to guide us, we cannot correctly understand who has done what to whom in the following sentence:

The boy the man chased kissed the girl.

But consider these examples (Rumelhart, 1977; Schank, 1973):

I saw the grand canyon flying to New York.
I saw the sheep grazing in the field.

Our knowledge of syntactic rules alone does not tell us what grammatical role is played by the prepositional phrases in these two cases. In the first, "flying to New York" is taken as describing the context in which the speaker saw the Grand Canyon—while he was flying to New York. In the second, "grazing in the field" could syntactically describe an analogous situation, in which the speaker is grazing in the field, but this possibility does not typically become available on first reading. Instead we assign "grazing in the field" as a modifier of the sheep (roughly, "who were grazing in the field"). The syntactic structure of each of these sentences, then, is determined in part by the semantic relations that the constituents of the sentence might plausibly bear to one another. Thus, the influences appear to run both ways, from the syntax to the semantics and from the semantics to the syntax.

In these examples, we see how syntactic considerations influence semantic ones and how semantic ones influence syntactic ones. We cannot say that one kind of constraint is primary.

Mutual constraints operate, not only between syntactic and semantic processing, but also within each of these domains as well. Here we consider an example from syntactic processing, namely, the assignment of words to syntactic categories. Consider the sentences:

I like the joke.
I like the drive.
I like to joke.
I like to drive.

In this case it looks as though the words *the* and *to* serve to determine whether the following word will be read as a noun or a verb. This, of course, is a very strong constraint in English and can serve to force a verb interpretation of a word that is not ordinarily used this way:

I like to mud.

On the other hand, if the information specifying whether the function word preceding the final word is *to* or *the* is ambiguous, then the typical reading of the word that follows it will determine which way the function word is heard. This was shown in an experiment by Isenberg, Walker, Ryder, and Schweikert (1980). They presented sounds half-way between *to* (actually /t^/) and *the* (actually /d^/) and found that words like *joke*, which we tend to think of first as nouns, made subjects hear the marginal stimuli as *the*, while words like *drive*, which we tend to think of first as verbs, made subjects hear the marginal stimuli as *to*. Generally, then, it would appear that each word can help constrain the syntactic role, and even the identity, of every other word.

### SIMULTANEOUS MUTUAL CONSTRAINTS IN WORD RECOGNITION

Just as the syntactic role of one word can influence the role assigned to another in analyzing sentences, so the identity of one letter can influence the identity assigned to another in reading. A famous example of this, from Selfridge, is shown in Figure 3.2. Along with this is a second example in which none of the letters, considered separately, can be identified unambiguously, but in which the possibilities that the visual information leaves open for each so constrain the possible identities of the others that we are capable of identifying all of them.

At first glance, the situation here must seem paradoxical: The identity of each letter is constrained by the identities of each of the others. But since in general we cannot know the identities of any of the letters until we have established the identities of the others, how can we get the process started?

The resolution of the paradox, of course, is simple. One of the different possible letters in each position fits together with the others. It appears then that our perceptual system is capable of exploring all these possibilities without committing itself to one until all of the constraints are taken into account.

### UNDERSTANDING THROUGH THE INTERPLAY OF MULTIPLE SOURCES OF KNOWLEDGE

It is clear that we know a good deal about a large number of different standard situations. Several

**FIGURE 3.2** ■ Some ambiguous displays. The first one is from Selfridge, 1955. The second line shows that three ambiguous characters can each constrain the identity of the others. The third, fourth, and fifth lines show that these characters are indeed ambiguous in that they assume other identities in other contexts. (The ink-blot technique of making letters ambiguous is due to Lindsay and Norman, 1972.)

theorists have suggested that we store this knowledge in terms of structures called variously: *scripts* (Schank, 1976), *frames* (Minsky, 1975), or *schemata* (Norman & Bobrow, 1976; Rumelhart, 1975). Such knowledge structures are assumed to be the basis of comprehension. A great deal of progress has been made within the context of this view.

However, it is important to bear in mind that most everyday situations cannot be rigidly assigned to just a single script. They generally involve an interplay between a number of different sources of information. Consider, for example, a child's birthday party at a restaurant. We know things about birthday parties, and we know things about restaurants, but we would not want to assume that we have explicit knowledge (at least, not in advance of our first restaurant birthday party) about the conjunction of the two. Yet we can imagine what such a party might be like. The fact that the party was being held in a restaurant would modify certain aspects of our expectations for birthday parties (we would not expect a game of Pin-the-Tail-on-the-Donkey, for example), while the fact that the event was a birthday party would inform our expectations for what would be ordered and who would pay the bill.

Representations like scripts, frames, and schemata are useful structures for encoding knowledge, although we believe they only approximate the underlying structure of knowledge representation that emerges from the class of models we consider. Our main point here is that any theory that tries to account for human knowledge using script-like knowledge structures will have to allow them to interact with each other to capture the generative capacity of human understanding in novel situations. Achieving such interactions has been one of the greatest difficulties associated with implementing models that really think generatively using script- or frame-like representations.

## Parallel Distributed Processing

In the examples we have considered, a number of different pieces of information must be kept in mind at once. Each plays a part, constraining others and being constrained by them. What kinds of mechanisms seem well suited to these task demands? Intuitively, these tasks seem to require mechanisms in which each aspect of the information in the situation can act on other aspects, simultaneously influencing other aspects and being influenced by them. To articulate these intuitions, we and others have turned to a class of models we call *Parallel Distributed Processing* (PDP) models. These models assume that information processing takes place through the interactions of a large number of simple processing elements called units, each sending excitatory and inhibitory signals to other units. In some cases, the units stand for possible hypotheses about such things as the letters in a particular display or the syntactic roles of the words in a particular sentence. In these cases, the activations stand roughly for the strengths associated with the different possible hypotheses, and

the interconnections among the units stand for the constraints the system knows to exist between the hypotheses. In other cases, the units stand for possible goals and actions, such as the goal of typing a particular letter, or the action of moving the left index finger, and the connections relate goals to subgoals, subgoals to actions, and actions to muscle movements. In still other cases, units stand not for particular hypotheses or goals, but for aspects of these things. Thus a hypothesis about the identity of a word, for example, is itself distributed in the activations of a large number of units.

## PDP Models: Cognitive Science or Neuroscience?

One reason for the appeal of PDP models is their obvious "physiological" flavor: They seem so much more closely tied to the physiology of the brain than are other kinds of information-processing models. The brain consists of a large number of highly interconnected elements (Figure 3.3) which apparently send very simple excitatory and inhibitory messages to each other and update their excitations on the basis of these simple messages. The properties of the units in many of the PDP models we will be exploring were inspired by basic properties of the neural hardware.

Though the appeal of PDP models is definitely enhanced by their physiological plausibility and neural inspiration, these are not the primary bases for their appeal to us. We are, after all, cognitive scientists, and PDP models appeal to us for psychological and computational reasons. They hold out the hope of offering computationally sufficient and psychologically accurate mechanistic accounts of the phenomena of human cognition which have eluded successful explication in conventional computational formalisms; and they have radically altered the way we think about the time-course of processing, the nature of representation, and the mechanisms of learning.

### The Microstructure of Cognition

The process of human cognition, examined on a time scale of seconds and minutes, has a distinctly sequential character to it. Ideas come, seem promising, and then are rejected; leads in the solution to a problem are taken up, then abandoned and replaced with new ideas. Though the process may

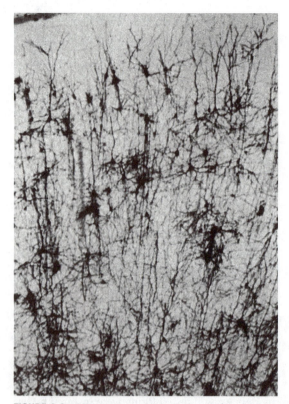

**FIGURE 3.3** ■ The arborizations of about 1 percent of the neurons near a vertical slice through the cerebral cortex. The full height of the figure corresponds to the thickness of the cortex, which is in this instance about 2 mm. (From *Mechanics of the Mind*, p. 84, by C. Blakemore, 1977, Cambridge, England: Cambridge University Press. Copyright 1977 by Cambridge University Press. Reprinted by permission.)

not be discrete, it has a decidedly sequential character, with transitions from state-to-state occurring, say, two or three times a second. Clearly, any useful description of the overall organization of this sequential flow of thought will necessarily describe a sequence of states.

But what is the internal structure of each of the states in the sequence, and how do they come about? Serious attempts to model even the simplest macrosteps of cognition—say, recognition of single words—require vast numbers of microsteps if they are implemented sequentially. As Feldman and Ballard (1982) have pointed out, the biological hardware is just too sluggish for sequential models of the microstructure to provide a plausible account, at least of the microstructure of *human* thought. And the time limitation only gets worse, not better, when sequential mechanisms try to take large numbers of constraints into account. Each additional constraint requires more time in a sequential machine, and, if the constraints are imprecise, the constraints can lead to a computational explosion. Yet people get faster, not slower, when they are able to exploit additional constraints.

Parallel distributed processing models offer alternatives to serial models of the microstructure of cognition. They do not deny that there is a macrostructure, just as the study of subatomic particles does not deny the existence of interactions between atoms. What PDP models do is describe the internal structure of the larger units, just as subatomic physics describes the internal structure of the atoms that form the constituents of larger units of chemical structure.

We shall show that the analysis of the microstructure of cognition has important implications for most of the central issues in cognitive science. In general, from the PDP point of view, the objects referred to in macrostructural models of cognitive processing are seen as approximate descriptions of emergent properties of the microstructure. Sometimes these approximate descriptions may be sufficiently accurate to capture a process or mechanism well enough; but many times, we will argue, they fail to provide sufficiently elegant or tractable accounts that capture the very flexibility and open-endedness of cognition that their inventors had originally intended to capture. We hope that our analysis of PDP models will show how an examination of the microstructure of cognition can lead us closer to an adequate description of the real extent of human processing and learning capacities.

The development of PDP models is still in its infancy. Thus far the models which have been proposed capture simplified versions of the kinds of phenomena we have been describing rather than the full elaboration that these phenomena display in real settings. But we think there have been enough steps forward in recent years to warrant a concerted effort at describing where the approach has gotten and where it is going now, and to point out some directions for the future.

## Examples of PDP Models

In what follows, we review a number of recent applications of PDP models to problems in motor control, perception, memory, and language. In many cases, as we shall see, parallel distributed processing mechanisms are used to provide natural accounts of the exploitation of multiple, simultaneous, and often mutual constraints. We will also see that these same mechanisms exhibit emergent properties which lead to novel interpretations of phenomena which have traditionally been interpreted in other ways.

## Motor Control

Having started with an example of how multiple constraints appear to operate in motor programming, it seems appropriate to mention two models in this domain. These models have not developed far enough to capture the full details of obstacle avoidance and multiple constraints on reaching and grasping, but there have been applications to two problems with some of these characteristics.

### FINGER MOVEMENTS IN SKILLED TYPING

One might imagine, at first glance, that typists carry out keystrokes successively, first programming one stroke and then, when it is completed, programming the next. However, this is not the case. For skilled typists, the fingers are continually anticipating upcoming keystrokes. Consider the word *vacuum*. In this word, the *v*, *a*, and *c* are all typed with the left hand, leaving the right hand nothing to do until it is time to type the first *u*. However, a high speed film of a good typist shows that the right hand moves up to anticipate the typing of the *u*, even as the left hand is just beginning to type the *v*. By the time the *c* is typed the right index finger is in position over the *u* and ready to strike it.

When two successive key strokes are to be typed with the fingers of the same hand, concurrent preparation to type both can result in similar or conflicting instructions to the fingers and/or the hand. Consider, in this light, the difference between the sequence *ev* and the sequence *er*. The first sequence requires the typist to move up from home row to type the *e* and to move down from the home row to type the *v*, while in the second sequence, both the *e* and the *r* are above the home row.

The hands take very different positions in these two cases. In the first case, the hand as a whole stays fairly stationary over the home row. The middle finger moves up to type the *e*, and the index finger moves down to type the *v*. In the second case, the hand as a whole moves up, bringing the middle finger over the *e* and the index finger over the *r*. Thus, we can see that several letters can simultaneously influence the positioning of the fingers and the hands.

From the point of view of optimizing the efficiency of the typing motion, these different patterns seem very sensible. In the first case, the hand as a whole is maintained in a good compromise position to allow the typist to strike both letters reasonably efficiently by extending the fingers up or down. In the second case, the need to extend the fingers is reduced by moving the whole hand up, putting it in a near-optimal position to strike either key.

Rumelhart and Norman (1982) have simulated these effects using PDP mechanisms. Figure 3.4 illustrates aspects of the model as they are illustrated in typing the word *very*. In brief, Rumelhart and Norman assumed that the decision to type a word caused activation of a unit for that word. That unit, in turn, activated units corresponding to each of the letters in the word. The unit for the first letter to be typed was made to inhibit the units for the second and following letters, the unit for the second to inhibit the third and following letters, and so on. As a result of the interplay of activation and inhibition among these units, the unit for the first letter was at first the most strongly active, and the units for the other letters were partially activated.

Each letter unit exerts influences on the hand and finger involved in typing the letter. The *v* unit, for example, tends to cause the index finger to move down and to cause the whole hand to move down with it. The *e* unit, on the other hand, tends to cause the middle finger on the left hand to move up and to cause the whole hand to move up also. The *r* unit also causes the left index finger to move up and the left hand to move up with it.

The extent of the influences of each letter on the hand and finger it directs depends on the extent of the activation of the letter. Therefore, at first, in typing the word *very*, the *v* exerts the greatest control. Because the *e* and *r* are simultaneously pulling the hand up, though, the *v* is typed primarily by moving the index finger, and there is little movement on the whole hand.

Once a finger is within a certain striking distance

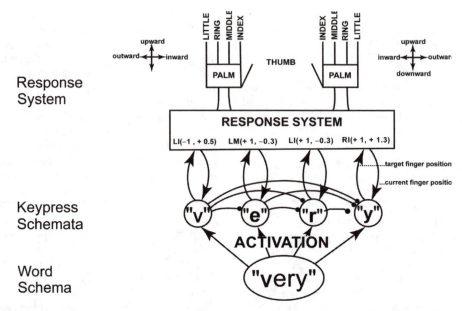

**FIGURE 3.4 ■** The interaction of activations in typing the word *very*. The *very* unit is activated from outside the model. It in turn activates the units for each of the component letters. Each letter unit specifies the target finger positions, specified in a keyboard coordinate system. L and R stand for the left and right hands, and I and M for the index and middle fingers. The letter units receive information about the current finger position from the response system. Each letter unit inhibits the activation of all letter units that follow it in the word: inhibitory connections are indicated by the lines with solid dots at their terminations. (From "Simulating a Skilled Typist: A Study of Skilled Motor Performance" by D. E. Rumelhart and D. A. Norman, 1982, *Cognitive Science, 6*, p. 12. Copyright 1982 by Ablex Publishing. Reprinted by permission.)

of the key to be typed, the actual pressing movement is triggered, and the keypress occurs. The keypress itself causes a strong inhibitory signal to be sent to the unit for the letter just typed, thereby removing this unit from the picture and allowing the unit for the next letter in the word to become the most strongly activated.

This mechanism provides a simple way for all of the letters to jointly determine the successive configurations the hand will enter into in the process of typing a word. This model has shown considerable success predicting the time between successive keystrokes as a function of the different keys involved. Given a little noise in the activation process, it can also account for some of the different kinds of errors that have been observed in transcription typing.

The typing model represents an illustration of the fact that serial behavior—a succession of key strokes—is not necessarily the result of an inherently serial processing mechanism. In this model, the sequential structure of typing emerges from the interaction of the excitatory and inhibitory influences among the processing units.

## REACHING FOR AN OBJECT WITHOUT FALLING OVER

Similar mechanisms can be used to model the process of reaching for an object without losing one's balance while standing, as Hinton (1984) has shown. He considered a simple version of this task using a two-dimensional "person" with a foot, a lower leg, an upper leg, a trunk, an upper arm, and a lower arm. Each of these limbs is joined to the next at a joint which has a single degree of rotational freedom. The task posed to this person is to reach a target placed somewhere in front of it, without taking any steps and without falling down. This is a simplified version of the situation in which a real person has to reach out in front for an object placed somewhere in the plane that vertically bisects the body. The task is not as simple as it looks, since if we just swing an arm out in front of ourselves, it may shift our center of gravity so far forward that we will lose our balance. The problem, then, is to find a set of joint angles that simultaneously solves the two constraints on the task. First, the tip of the forearm must touch the object. Second, to keep from falling down, the person must keep its center of gravity over the foot.

To do this, Hinton assigned a single processor to each joint. On each computational cycle, each processor received information about how far the tip of the hand was from the target and where the center of gravity was with respect to the foot. Using these two pieces of information, each joint adjusted its angle so as to approach the goals of maintaining balance and bringing the tip closer to the target. After a number of iterations, the stick-person settled on postures that satisfied the goal of reaching the target and the goal of maintaining the center of gravity over the "feet."

Though the simulation was able to perform the task, eventually satisfying both goals at once, it had a number of inadequacies stemming from the fact that each joint processor attempted to achieve a solution in ignorance of what the other joints were attempting to do. This problem was overcome by using additional processors responsible for setting combinations of joint angles. Thus, a processor for flexion and extension of the leg would adjust the knee, hip, and ankle joints synergistically, while a processor for flexion and extension of the arm would adjust the shoulder and elbow together.

With the addition of processors of this form, the number of iterations required to reach a solution was greatly reduced, and the form of the approach to the solution looked very natural. The sequence of configurations attained in one processing run is shown in Figure 3.5.

Explicit attempts to program a robot to cope with the problem of maintaining balance as it reaches for a desired target have revealed the difficulty of deriving explicitly the right combinations of actions for each possible starting state and goal state. This simple model illustrates that we may be wrong to seek such an explicit solution. We see here that a solution to the problem can emerge from the action of a number of simple processors each attempting to honor the constraints independently.

## Perception

### STEREOSCOPIC VISION

One early model using parallel distributed processing was the model of stereoscopic depth perception proposed by Marr and Poggio (1976). Their theory proposed to explain the perception of depth in random-dot stereograms (Figure 3.6) in terms of a simple distributed processing mechanism.

Random-dot stereograms present interesting challenges to mechanisms of depth perception. A stereogram consists of two random-dot patterns. In a simple stereogram such as the one shown here,

**FIGURE 3.5** ■ A sequence of configurations assumed by the stick "person" performing the reaching task described in the text, from Hinton (1984). The small circle represents the center of gravity of the whole stick-figure, and the cross represents the goal to be reached. The configuration is shown on every second iteration.

**FIGURE 3.6** ■ Random-dot stereograms. The two patterns are identical except that the pattern of dots in the central region of the left pattern are shifted over with respect to those in the right. When viewed stereoscopically such that the left pattern projects to the left eye and the right pattern to the right eye, the shifted area appears to hover above the page. Some readers may be able to achieve this by converging to a distant point (e.g., a far wall) and then interposing the figure into the line of sight. (From *Vision*, p. 9, by D. Marr, 1982, San Francisco: Freeman. Copyright 1982 by W. H. Freeman & Co. Reprinted by permission.)

one pattern is an exact copy of the other except that the pattern of dots in a region of one of the patterns is shifted horizontally with respect to the rest of the pattern. Each of the two patterns—corresponding to two retinal images—consists entirely of a pattern of random dots, so there is no information in either of the two views considered alone that can indicate the presence of different surfaces, let alone depth relations among those surfaces. Yet, when one of these dot patterns is projected to the left eye and the other to the right eye, an observer sees each region as a surface, with the shifted region hovering in front of or behind the other, depending on the direction of the shift.

What kind of a mechanism might we propose to account for these facts? Marr and Poggio (1976) began by explicitly representing the two views in two arrays, as human observers might in two different retinal images. They noted that corresponding black dots at different perceived distances from the observer will be offset from each other by different amounts in the two views. The job of the model is to determine which points correspond. This task is, of course, made difficult by the fact that there will be a very large number of spurious correspondences of individual dots. The goal of the mechanism, then, is to find those correspondences that represent real correspondences in depth and suppress those that represent spurious correspondences.

To carry out this task, Marr and Poggio assigned a processing unit to each possible conjunction of a point in one image and a point in the other. Since the eyes are offset horizontally, the possible conjunctions occur at various offsets or disparities along the horizontal dimension. Thus, for each point in one eye, there was a set of processing units with one unit assigned to the conjunction of that point and the point at each horizontal offset from it in the other eye.

Each processing unit received activation whenever both of the points the unit stood for contained dots. So far, then, units for both real and spurious correspondences would be equally activated. To allow the mechanism to find the right correspondences, they pointed out two general principles about the visual world: (a) Each point in each view generally corresponds to one and only one point in the other view, and (b) neighboring points in space tend to be at nearly the same depth and therefore at about the same disparity in the two images. While there are discontinuities at the edges of things, over most of a two-dimensional view of the world there will be continuity. These principles are called the *uniqueness* and *continuity* constraints, respectively.

Marr and Poggio incorporated these principles into the interconnections between the processing units. The uniqueness constraint was captured by inhibitory connections among the units that stand for alternative correspondences of the same dot. The continuity principle was captured by excitatory connections among the units that stand for similar offsets of adjacent dots.

These additional connections allow the Marr and Poggio model to "solve" stereograms like the one shown in the figure. At first, when a pair of patterns is presented, the units for all possible correspondences of a dot in one eye with a dot in the other will be equally excited. However, the excitatory connections cause the units for the correct conjunctions to receive more excitation than units for spurious conjunctions, and the inhibitory connections allow the units for the correct conjunctions to turn off the units for the spurious connections. Thus, the model tends to settle down into a stable state in which only the correct correspondence of each dot remains active.

There are a number of reasons why Marr and Poggio (1979) modified this model (see Marr, 1982, for a discussion), but the basic mechanisms of mutual excitation between units that are mutually consistent and mutual inhibition between units that are mutually incompatible provide a natural mechanism for settling on the right conjunctions of points and rejecting spurious ones. The model also illustrates how general principles or rules, such as the uniqueness and continuity principles may be embodied in the connections between processing units, and how behavior in accordance with these principles can emerge from the interactions determined by the pattern of these interconnections.

## PERCEPTUAL COMPLETION OF FAMILIAR PATTERNS

Perception, of course, is influenced by familiarity. It is a well-known fact that we often misperceive unfamiliar objects as more familiar ones and that we can get by with less time or with lower-quality information in perceiving familiar items than we need for perceiving unfamiliar items. Not only does familiarity help us determine what the higher-level structures are when the lower-level information is ambiguous; it also allows us to fill in missing lower-level information within familiar higher-order patterns. The well-known *phonemic restoration effect* is a case in point. In this phenomenon, perceivers hear sounds that have been cut out of words as if they had actually been present. For example, Warren (1970) presented *legi#lature* to subjects, with a click in the location marked by the #. Not only did subjects correctly identify the word legislature; they also heard the missing /s/ just as though it had been presented. They had great difficulty localizing the click, which they tended to hear as a disembodied sound. Similar phenomena have been observed in visual perception of words since the work of Pillsbury (1897).

Two of us have proposed a model describing the role of familiarity in perception based on excitatory and inhibitory interactions among units standing for various hypotheses about the input at different levels of abstraction (McClelland & Rumelhart, 1981; Rumelhart & McClelland, 1982). The model has been applied in detail to the role of familiarity in the perception of letters in visually presented words, and has proved to provide a very close account of the results of a large number of experiments.

The model assumes that there are units that act as detectors for the visual features which distinguish letters, with one set of units assigned to detect the features in each of the different letter-positions in the word. For four-letter words, then, there are four such sets of detectors. There are also four sets of detectors for the letters themselves and a set of detectors for the words.

In the model, each unit has an activation value, corresponding roughly to the strength of the hypothesis that what that unit stands for is present in the perceptual input. The model honors the following important relations which hold between these "hypotheses" or activations: First, to the extent that two hypotheses are mutually consistent, they should support each other. Thus, units that are mutually consistent, in the way that the letter *T* in the first position is consistent with the word *TAKE*, tend to excite each other. Second, to the extent that two hypotheses are mutually inconsistent, they should weaken each other. Actually, we can distinguish two kinds of inconsistency: The first kind might be called between-level inconsistency. For example, the hypothesis that a word begins with a *T* is inconsistent with the hypothesis that the word is *MOVE*. The second might be called mutual exclusion. For example, the hypothesis that a word begins with *T* excludes the hypothesis that it begins with *R* since a word can only begin with one letter. Both kinds of inconsistencies operate in the word perception model to reduce the activations of units. Thus, the letter units in each position compete with all other letter units in the same position, and the word units compete with each other. This type of inhibitory interaction is often called *competitive inhibition*. In addition, there are inhibitory interactions between incompatible units on different levels. This type of inhibitory interaction is simply called *between-level inhibition*.

The set of excitatory and inhibitory interactions between units can be diagrammed by drawing excitatory and inhibitory links between them. The whole picture is too complex to draw, so we illustrate only with a fragment: Some of the interactions between some of the units in this model are illustrated in Figure 3.7.

Let us consider what happens in a system like this when a familiar stimulus is presented under degraded conditions. For example, consider the display shown in Figure 3.8. This display consists of the letters w, o, and r, completely visible, and enough of a fourth letter to rule out all letters other than r and k. Before onset of the display, the activations of the units are set at or below 0. When the display is presented, detectors for the features present in each position become active (i.e., their activations grow above 0). At this point, they begin to excite and inhibit the corresponding detectors for letters. In the first three positions, w, o, and r are unambiguously activated, so we will focus our attention on the fourth position where r and k are both equally consistent with the active features. Here, the activations of the detectors for r and k start out growing together, as the feature detectors below them become activated. As these detectors become active, they and the active letter detectors for w, o, and r in the other positions start to activate detectors for words which have these

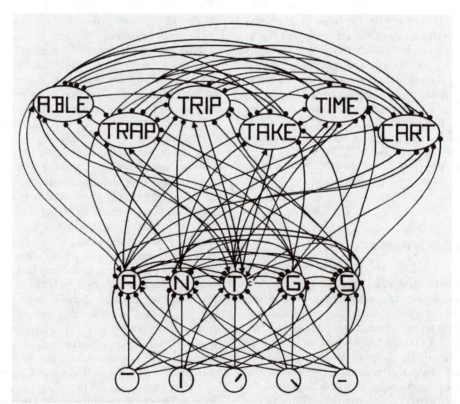

**FIGURE 3.7** ■ The unit for the letter *T* in the first position of a four-letter array and some of its neighbors. Note that the feature and letter units stand only for the first position; in a complete picture of the units needed from processing four-letter displays, there would be four full sets of feature detectors and four full sets of letter detectors. (From "An Interactive Activation Model of Context Effects in Letter Perception: Part 1. An Account of Basic Findings" by J. L. McClelland and D. E. Rumelhart, 1981, *Psychological Review, 88*, p. 380. Copyright 1981 by the American Psychological Association. Reprinted by permission.)

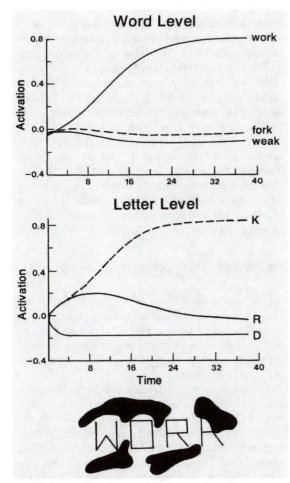

**FIGURE 3.8.** A possible display which might be presented to the interactive activation model of word recognition, and the resulting activations of selected letter and word units. The letter units are for the letters indicated in the fourth position of a four-letter display.

letters in them and to inhibit detectors for words which do not have these letters. A number of words are partially consistent with the active letters, and receive some net excitation from the letter level, but only the word WORK matches one of the active letters in all four positions. As a result, WORK becomes more active than any other word and inhibits the other words, thereby successfully dominating the pattern of activation among the word units. As it grows in strength, it sends feedback to the letter level, reinforcing the activations of the W, O, R, and K in the corresponding positions. In the fourth position, this feedback gives K the upper

hand over R, and eventually the stronger activation of the K detector allows it to dominate the pattern of activation, suppressing the R detector completely.

This example illustrates how PDP models can allow knowledge about what letters go together to form words to work together with natural constraints on the task (i.e., that there should only be one letter in one place at one time), to produce perceptual completion in a simple and direct way.

## COMPLETION OF NOVEL PATTERNS

However, the perceptual intelligence of human perceivers far exceeds the ability to recognize familiar patterns and fill in missing portions. We also show facilitation in the perception of letters in unfamiliar letter strings which are word-like but not themselves actually familiar.

One way of accounting for such performances is to imagine that the perceiver possesses, in addition to detectors for familiar words, sets of detectors for regular subword units such as familiar letter clusters, or that they use abstract rules, specifying which classes of letters can go with which others in different contexts. It turns out, however, that the model we have already described needs no such additional structure to produce perceptual facilitation for word-like letter strings; to this extent it acts as if it "knows" the orthographic structure of English. We illustrate this feature of the model with the example shown in Figure 3.9, where the nonword YEAD is shown in degraded form so that the second letter is incompletely visible. Given the information about this letter, considered alone, either E or F would be possible in the second position. Yet our model will tend to complete this letter as an E.

The reason for this behavior is that, when YEAD is shown, a number of words are partially activated. There is no word consistent with Y, E or F, A, and D, but there are words which match YEA_ (YEAR, for example) and others which match _EAD (BEAD, DEAD, HEAD, and READ, for example). These and other near misses are partially activated as a result of the pattern of activation at the letter level. While they compete with each other, none of these words gets strongly enough activated to completely suppress all the others. Instead, these units act as a group to reinforce particularly the letters E and A. There are no close partial matches which include

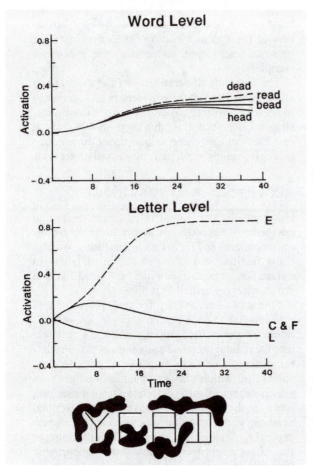

## Word Level

## Letter Level

**FIGURE 3.9** ■ An example of a nonword display that might be presented to the interactive activation model of word recognition and the response of selected units at the letter and word levels. The letter units illustrated are detectors for letters in the second input position.

the letter *F* in the second position, so this letter receives no feedback support. As a result, *E* comes to dominate, and eventually suppress, the *F* in the second position.

The fact that the word perception model exhibits perceptual facilitation to pronounceable nonwords as well as words illustrates once again how behavior in accordance with general principles or rules can emerge from the interactions of simple processing elements. Of course, the behavior of the word perception model does not implement exactly any of the systems of orthographic rules that have been proposed by linguists (Chomsky & Halle, 1968; Venesky, 1970) or psychologists

(Spoehr & Smith, 1975). In this regard, it only approximates such rule-based descriptions of perceptual processing. However, rule systems such as Chomsky and Halle's or Venesky's appear to be only approximately honored in human performance as well (Smith & Baker, 1976). Indeed, some of the discrepancies between human performance data and rule systems occur in exactly the ways that we would predict from the word perception model (Rumelhart & McClelland, 1982). This illustrates the possibility that PDP models may provide more accurate accounts of the details of human performance than models based on a set of rules representing human competence—at least in some domains.

## Retrieving Information from Memory

### CONTENT ADDRESSABILITY

One very prominent feature of human memory is that it is content addressable. It seems fairly clear that we can access information in memory based on nearly any attribute of the representation we are trying to retrieve.

Of course, some cues are much better than others. An attribute which is shared by a very large number of things we know about is not a very effective retrieval cue, since it does not accurately pick out a particular memory representation. But, several such cues, in conjunction, can do the job. Thus, if we ask a friend who goes out with several women, "Who was that woman I saw you with?", he may not know which one we mean—but if we specify something else about her—say the color of her hair, what she was wearing (in so far as he remembers this at all), where we saw him with her—he will likely be able to hit upon the right one.

It is, of course, possible to implement some kind of content addressability of memory on a standard computer in a variety of different ways. One way is to search sequentially, examining each memory in the system to find the memory or the set of memories which has the particular content specified in the cue. An alternative, somewhat more efficient, scheme involves some form of indexing—keeping a list, for every content a memory might have, of which memories have that content.

Such an indexing scheme can be made to work with error-free probes, but it will break down if there is an error in the specification of the retrieval cue. There are possible ways of recovering from such errors, but they lead to the kind of combinatorial explosions which plague this kind of computer implementation.

But suppose that we imagine that each memory is represented by a unit which has mutually excitatory interactions with units standing for each of its properties. Then, whenever any property of the memory became active, the memory would tend to be activated, and whenever the memory was activated, all of its contents would tend to become activated. Such a scheme would automatically produce content addressability for us. Though it would not be immune to errors, it would not be devastated by an error in the probe if the remaining properties specified the correct memory.

As described thus far, whenever a property that is a part of a number of different memories is activated, it will tend to activate all of the memories it is in. To keep these other activities from swamping the "correct" memory unit, we simply need to add initial inhibitory connections among the memory units. An additional desirable feature would be mutually inhibitory interactions among mutually incompatible property units. For example, a person cannot both be single and married at the same time, so the units for different marital states would be mutually inhibitory.

McClelland (1981) developed a simulation model that illustrates how a system with these properties would act as a content addressable memory. The model is obviously oversimplified, but it illustrates many of the characteristics of the more complex models that will be considered in later chapters.

Consider the information represented in Figure 3.10, which lists a number of people we might meet if we went to live in an unsavory neighborhood, and some of their hypothetical characteristics. A subset of the units needed to represent this information is shown in Figure 3.11. In this network, there is an "instance unit" for each of the characters described in Figure 3.10, and that unit is linked by mutually excitatory connections to all of the units for the fellow's properties. Note that we have included property units for the names of the characters, as well as units for their other properties.

Now, suppose we wish to retrieve the properties of a particular individual, say Lance. And suppose that we know Lance's name. Then we can

The Jets and The Sharks

| Name | Gang | Age | Edu | Mar | Occupation |
|---|---|---|---|---|---|
| Art | Jets | 40's | J.H. | Sing. | Pusher |
| Al | Jets | 30's | J.H. | Mar. | Burglar |
| Sam | Jets | 20's | COL. | Sing. | Bookie |
| Clyde | Jets | 40's | J.H. | Sing. | Bookie |
| Mike | Jets | 30's | J.H. | Sing. | Bookie |
| Jim | Jets | 20's | J.H. | Div. | Burglar |
| Greg | Jets | 20's | H.S. | Mar. | Pusher |
| John | Jets | 20's | J.H. | Mar. | Burglar |
| Doug | Jets | 30's | H.S. | Sing. | Bookie |
| Lance | Jets | 20's | J.H. | Mar. | Burglar |
| George | Jets | 20's | J.H. | Div. | Burglar |
| Pete | Jets | 20's | H.S. | Sing. | Bookie |
| Fred | Jets | 20's | H.S. | Sing. | Pusher |
| Gene | Jets | 20's | COL. | Sing. | Pusher |
| Ralph | Jets | 30's | J.H. | Sing. | Pusher |
| Phil | Sharks | 30's | COL. | Mar. | Pusher |
| Ike | Sharks | 30's | J.H. | Sing. | Bookie |
| Nick | Sharks | 30's | H.S. | Sing. | Pusher |
| Don | Sharks | 30's | COL. | Mar. | Burglar |
| Ned | Sharks | 30's | COL. | Mar. | Bookie |
| Karl | Sharks | 40's | H.S. | Mar. | Bookie |
| Ken | Sharks | 20's | H.S. | Sing. | Burglar |
| Earl | Sharks | 40's | H.S. | Mar. | Burglar |
| Rick | Sharks | 30's | H.S. | Div. | Burglar |
| Ol | Sharks | 30's | COL. | Mar. | Pusher |
| Neal | Sharks | 30's | H.S. | Sing. | Bookie |
| Dave | Sharks | 30's | H.S. | Div. | Pusher |

**FIGURE 3.10** ■ Characteristics of a number of individuals belonging to two gangs, the Jets and the Sharks. (From "Retrieving General and Specific Knowledge from Stored Knowledge of Specifics" by J. L. McClelland, 1981, *Proceedings of the Third Annual Conference of the Cognitive Science Society*, Berkeley, CA. Copyright 1981 by J. L. McClelland. Reprinted by permission.)

probe the network by activating Lance's name unit, and we can see what pattern of activation arises as a result. Assuming that we know of no one else named Lance, we can expect the Lance name unit to be hooked up only to the instance unit for Lance. This will in turn activate the property units for Lance, thereby creating the pattern of activation corresponding to Lance. In effect, we have retrieved a representation of Lance. More will happen than just what we have described so far, but for the moment let us stop here.

Of course, sometimes we may wish to retrieve a name, given other information. In this case, we might start with some of Lance's properties, effectively asking the system, say "Who do you know who is a Shark and in his 20s?" by activating

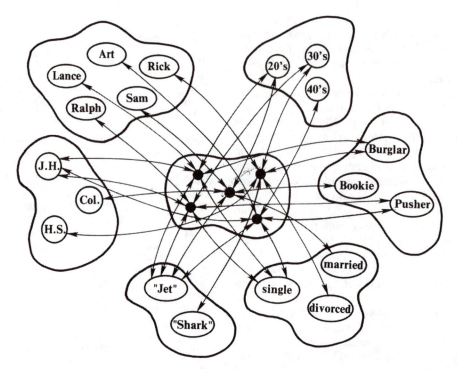

**FIGURE 3.11** ■ Some of the units and interconnections needed to represent the individuals shown in Figure 3.10. The units connected with double-headed arrows are mutually excitatory. All the units within the same cloud are mutually inhibitory. (From "Retrieving General and Specific Knowledge from Stored Knowledge of Specifics" by J. L. McClelland, 1981, *Proceedings of the Third Annual Conference of the Cognitive Science Society*, Berkeley, CA. Copyright 1981 by J. L. McClelland. Reprinted by permission.)

the Shark and 20s units. In this case it turns out that there is a single individual, Ken, who fits the description. So, when we activate these two properties, we will activate the instance unit for Ken, and this in turn will activate his name unit and fill in his other properties as well.

### GRACEFUL DEGRADATION

A few of the desirable properties of this kind of model are visible from considering what happens as we vary the set of features we use to probe the memory in an attempt to retrieve a particular individual's name. Any set of features which is sufficient to uniquely characterize a particular item will activate the instance node for that item more strongly than any other instance node. A probe which contains misleading features will most strongly activate the node that it matches best. This will clearly be a poorer cue than one which contains no misleading information—but it will still

be sufficient to activate the "right answer" more strongly than any other, as long as the introduction of misleading information does not make the probe closer to some other item. In general, though the degree of activation of a particular instance node and of the corresponding name nodes varies in this model as a function of the exact content of the probe, errors in the probe will not be fatal unless they make the probe point to the wrong memory. This kind of model's handling of incomplete or partial probes also requires no special error-recovery scheme to work—it is a natural byproduct of the nature of the retrieval mechanism that it is capable of graceful degradation.

These aspects of the behavior of the Jets and Sharks model deserve more detailed consideration than the present space allows. One reason we do not go into them is that we view this model as a stepping stone in the development of other models, such as the models using more distributed representations, that occur in other parts of this book.

We do, however, have more to say about this simple model, for like some of the other models we have already examined, this model exhibits some useful properties which emerge from the interactions of the processing units.

## DEFAULT ASSIGNMENT

It probably will have occurred to the reader that in many of the situations we have been examining, there will be other activations occurring which may influence the pattern of activation which is retrieved. So, in the case where we retrieved the properties of Lance, those properties, once they become active, can begin to activate the units for other individuals with those same properties. The memory unit for Lance will be in competition with these units and will tend to keep their activation down, but to the extent that they do become active, they will tend to activate their own properties and therefore fill them in. In this way, the model can fill in properties of individuals based on what it knows about other, similar instances.

To illustrate how this might work we have simulated the case in which we do not know that Lance is a Burglar as opposed to a Bookie or a Pusher. It turns out that there are a group of individuals in the set who are very similar to Lance in many respects. When Lance's properties become activated, these other units become partially activated, and they start activating their properties. Since they all share the same "occupation," they work together to fill in that property for Lance. Of course, there is no reason why this should necessarily be the right answer, but generally speaking, the more similar two things are in respects that we know about, the more likely they are to be similar in respects that we do not, and the model implements this heuristic.

## SPONTANEOUS GENERALIZATION

The model we have been describing has another valuable property as well—it tends to retrieve what is common to those memories which match a retrieval cue which is too general to capture any one memory. Thus, for example, we could probe the system by activating the unit corresponding to membership in the Jets. This unit will partially activate all the instances of the Jets, thereby causing each to send activations to its properties. In

this way the model can retrieve the typical values that the members of the Jets have on each dimension—even though there is no one Jet that has these typical values. In the example, 9 of 15 Jets are single, 9 of 15 are in their 20s, and 9 of 15 have only a Junior High School education; when we probe by activating the Jet unit, all three of these properties dominate. The Jets are evenly divided between the three occupations, so each of these units becomes partially activated. Each has a different name, so that each name unit is very weakly activated, nearly canceling each other out.

In the example just given of spontaneous generalization, it would not be unreasonable to suppose that someone might have explicitly stored a generalization about the members of a gang. The account just given would be an alternative to "explicit storage" of the generalization. It has two advantages, though, over such an account. First, it does not require any special generalization formation mechanism. Second, it can provide us with generalizations on unanticipated lines, on demand. Thus, if we want to know, for example, what people in their 20s with a junior high school education are like, we can probe the model by activating these two units. Since all such people are Jets and Burglars, these two units are strongly activated by the model in this case; two of them are divorced and two are married, so both of these units are partially activated.[1]

The sort of model we are considering, then, is considerably more than a content addressable memory. In addition, it performs default assignment, and it can spontaneously retrieve a general concept of the individuals that match any specifiable probe. These properties must be explicitly implemented as complicated computational extensions of other models of knowledge retrieval, but in PDP models they are natural by-products of the retrieval process itself.

# Representation and Learning in PDP Models

In the Jets and Sharks model, we can speak of the model's *active representation* at a particular time, and associate this with the pattern of activation over the units in the system. We can also ask: What is the stored knowledge that gives rise to that pattern of activation? In considering this question, we see immediately an important difference between PDP models and other models of cognitive processes. In most models, knowledge is stored as a static copy of a pattern. Retrieval amounts to finding the pattern in long-term memory and copying it into a buffer or working memory. There is no real difference between the stored representation in long-term memory and the active representation in working memory. In PDP models, though, this is not the case. In these models, the patterns themselves are not stored. Rather, what is stored is the *connection strengths* between units that allow these patterns to be re-created. In the Jets and Sharks model, there is an instance unit assigned to each individual, but that unit does not contain a copy of the representation of that individual. Instead, it is simply the case that the connections between it and the other units in the system are such that activation of the unit will cause the pattern for the individual to be reinstated on the property units.

This difference between PDP models and conventional models has enormous implications, both for processing and for learning. We have already seen some of the implications for processing. The representation of the knowledge is set up in such a way that the knowledge necessarily influences the course of processing. Using knowledge in processing is no longer a matter of finding the relevant information in memory and bringing it to bear; it is part and parcel of the processing itself.

For learning, the implications are equally profound. For if the knowledge is the strength of the connections, learning must be a matter of finding the right connection strengths so that the right patterns of activation will be produced under the right circumstances. This is an extremely important property of this class of models, for it opens up the possibility that an information processing mechanism could learn, as a result of tuning its connections, to capture the interdependencies between activations that it is exposed to in the course of processing.

In recent years, there has been quite a lot of interest in learning in cognitive science. Computational approaches to learning fall predominantly into what might be called the "explicit rule formulation" tradition, as represented by the work of Winston (1975), the suggestions of Chomsky, and the ACT* model of J. R. Anderson (1983). All of this work shares the assumption that the goal of learning is to formulate explicit rules (propositions,

productions, etc.) which capture powerful generalizations in a succinct way. Fairly powerful mechanisms, usually with considerable innate knowledge about a domain, and/or some starting set of primitive propositional representations, then formulate hypothetical general rules, e.g., by comparing particular cases and formulating explicit generalizations.

The approach that we take in developing PDP models is completely different. First, we do not assume that the goal of learning is the formulation of explicit rules. Rather, we assume it is the acquisition of connection strengths which allow a network of simple units to act *as though* it knew the rules. Second, we do not attribute powerful computational capabilities to the learning mechanism. Rather, we assume very simple connection strength modulation mechanisms which adjust the strength of connections between units based on information locally available at the connection.

These issues will be addressed at length in later sections of this book. For now, our purpose is to give a simple, illustrative example of the connection strength modulation process, and how it can produce networks which exhibit some interesting behavior.

## LOCAL VERSUS DISTRIBUTED REPRESENTATION

Before we turn to an explicit consideration of this issue, we raise a basic question about representation. Once we have achieved the insight that the knowledge is stored in the strengths of the interconnections between units, a question arises. Is there any reason to assign one unit to each pattern that we wish to learn? Another possibility—one that we explore extensively in this book—is the possibility that the knowledge about any individual pattern is not stored in the connections of a special unit reserved for that pattern, but is distributed over the connections among a large number of processing units. On this view, the Jets and Sharks model represents a special case in which separate units are reserved for each instance.

Models in which connection information is explicitly thought of as distributed have been proposed by a number of investigators. The units in these collections may themselves correspond to conceptual primitives, or they may have no particular meaning as individuals. In either case, the focus shifts to patterns of activation over these units and to mechanisms whose explicit purpose is to learn the right connection strengths to allow the right patterns of activation to become activated under the right circumstances.

In the rest of this section, we will give a simple example of a PDP model in which the knowledge is distributed. We will first explain how the model would work, given pre-existing connections, and we will then describe how it could come to acquire the right connection strengths through a very simple learning mechanism. A number of models which have taken this distributed approach have been discussed in this book's predecessor, Hinton and J. A. Anderson's (1981) *Parallel Models of Associative Memory*. We will consider a simple version of a common type of distributed model, a *pattern associator*.

Pattern associators are models in which a pattern of activation over one set of units can cause a pattern of activation over another set of units without any intervening units to stand for either pattern as a whole. Pattern associators would, for example, be capable of associating a pattern of

activation on one set of units corresponding to the appearance of an object with a pattern on another set corresponding to the aroma of the object, so that, when an object is presented visually, causing its visual pattern to become active, the model produces the pattern corresponding to its aroma.

## HOW A PATTERN ASSOCIATOR WORKS

For purposes of illustration, we present a very simple pattern associator in Figure 3.12. In this model, there are four units in each of two pools. The first pool, the A units, will be the pool in which patterns corresponding to the sight of various objects might be represented. The second pool, the B units, will be the pool in which the pattern corresponding to the aroma will be represented. We can pretend that alternative patterns of activation on the A units are produced upon viewing a rose or a grilled steak, and alternative patterns on the B units are produced upon sniffing the same objects. Figure 3.13 shows two pairs of patterns, as well as sets of interconnections necessary to allow the A member of each pair to reproduce the B member.

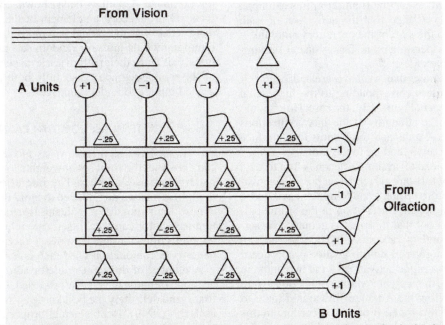

**FIGURE 3.12** ■ A simple pattern associator. The example assumes that patterns of activation in the A units can be produced by the visual system and patterns in the B units can be produced by the olfactory system. The synaptic connections allow the outputs of the A units to influence the activations of the B units. The synaptic weights linking the A units to the B units were selected so as to allow the pattern of activation shown on the A units to reproduce the pattern of activation shown on the B units without the need for any olfactory input.

|  | +1 | −1 | −1 | +1 |  |
|---|---|---|---|---|---|
|  | −.25 | +.25 | +.25 | −.25 | −1 |
|  | −.25 | +.25 | +.25 | −.25 | −1 |
|  | +.25 | −.25 | −.25 | +.25 | +1 |
|  | +.25 | −.25 | −.25 | +.25 | +1 |

|  | −1 | +1 | −1 | +1 |  |
|---|---|---|---|---|---|
|  | +.25 | −.25 | +.25 | −.25 | −1 |
|  | −.25 | +.25 | −.25 | +.25 | +1 |
|  | −.25 | +.25 | −.25 | +.25 | +1 |
|  | +.25 | −.25 | +.25 | −.25 | −1 |

FIGURE 3.13 ■ Two simple associators represented as matrices. The weights in the first two matrices allow the A pattern shown above the matrix to produce the B pattern shown to the right of it. Note that the weights in the first matrix are the same as those shown in the diagram in Figure 3.12.

The details of the behavior of the individual units vary among different versions of pattern associators. For present purposes, we'll assume that the units can take on positive or negative activation values, with 0 representing a kind of neutral intermediate value. The strengths of the interconnections between the units can be positive or negative real numbers.

The effect of an A unit on a B unit is determined by multiplying the activation of the A unit times the strength of its synaptic connection with the B unit. For example, if the connection from a particular A unit to a particular B unit has a positive sign, when the A unit is excited (activation greater than 0), it will excite the B unit. For this example, we'll simply assume that the activation of each unit is set to the sum of the excitatory and inhibitory effects operating on it. This is one of the simplest possible cases.

Suppose, now, that we have created on the A units the pattern corresponding to the first visual pattern shown in Figure 3.13, the rose. How should we arrange the strengths of the interconnections between the A units and the B units to reproduce the pattern corresponding to the aroma of a rose? We simply need to arrange for each A unit to tend to excite each B unit which has a positive activation in the aroma pattern and to inhibit each B unit which has a negative activation in the aroma pattern. It turns out that this goal is achieved by setting the strength of the connection between a given A unit and a given B unit to a value proportional to the product of the activation of the two units. In Figure 3.12, the weights on the connections were chosen to allow the A pattern illustrated there to produce the illustrated B pattern according to this principle. The actual strengths of the connections were set to ±.25, rather than ±1, so that the A pattern will produce the right magnitude, as well as the right sign, for the activations of the units in

the B pattern. The same connections are reproduced in matrix form in Figure 3.13A.

Pattern associators like the one in Figure 3.12 have a number of nice properties. One is that they do not require a perfect copy of the input to produce the correct output, though its strength will be weaker in this case. For example, suppose that the associator shown in Figure 3.12 were presented with an A pattern of (1, −1, 0, 1). This is the A pattern shown in the figure, with the activation of one of its elements set to 0. The B pattern produced in response will have the activations of all of the B units in the right direction; however, they will be somewhat weaker than they would be, had the complete A pattern been shown. Similar effects are produced if an element of the pattern is distorted—or if the model is damaged, either by removing whole units, or random sets of connections, etc. Thus, their pattern retrieval performance of the model degrades gracefully both under degraded input and under damage.

## HOW A PATTERN ASSOCIATOR LEARNS

So far, we have seen how we as model builders can construct the right set of weights to allow one pattern to cause another. The interesting thing, though, is that we do not need to build these interconnection strengths in by hand. Instead, the pattern associator can teach itself the right set of interconnections through experience processing the patterns in conjunction with each other.

A number of different rules for adjusting connection strengths have been proposed. One of the first—and definitely the best known—is due to D. O. Hebb (1949). Hebb's actual proposal was not sufficiently quantitative to build into an explicit model. However, a number of different variants can trace their ancestry back to Hebb. Perhaps the simplest version is:

When unit A and unit B are simultaneously excited, increase the strength of the connection between them.

A natural extension of this rule to cover the positive and negative activation values allowed in our example is:

Adjust the strength of the connection between units A and B in proportion to the product of their simultaneous activation.

In this formulation, if the product is positive, the change makes the connection more excitatory, and if the product is negative, the change makes the connection more inhibitory. For simplicity of reference, we will call this the *Hebb rule*, although it is not exactly Hebb's original formulation.

With this simple learning rule, we could train a "blank copy" of the pattern associator shown in Figure 3.12 to produce the B pattern for rose when the A pattern is shown, simply by presenting the A and B patterns together and modulating the connection strengths according to the Hebb rule. The size of the change made on every trial would, of course, be a parameter. We generally assume that the changes made on each instance are rather small, and that connection strengths build up gradually. The values shown in Figure 3.13A, then, would be acquired as a result of a number of experiences with the A and B pattern pair.

It is very important to note that the information needed to use the Hebb rule to determine the value each connection should have is *locally available* at the connection. All a given connection needs to consider is the activation of the units on both sides of it. Thus, it would be possible to actually implement such a connection modulation scheme locally, in each connection, without requiring any programmer to reach into each connection and set it to just the right value.

It turns out that the Hebb rule as stated here has some serious limitations, and, to our knowledge, no theorists continue to use it in this simple form. More sophisticated connection modulation schemes have been proposed by other workers; most important among these are the delta rule, the competitive learning rule, and the rules for learning in stochastic parallel models. All of these learning rules have the property that they adjust the strengths of connections between units on the basis of information that can be assumed to be lo-

cally available to the unit. Learning, then, in all of these cases, amounts to a very simple process that can be implemented locally at each connection without the need for any overall supervision. Thus, models which incorporate these learning rules train themselves to have the right interconnections in the course of processing the members of an ensemble of patterns.

## LEARNING MULTIPLE PATTERNS IN THE SAME SET OF INTERCONNECTIONS

Up to now, we have considered how we might teach our pattern associator to associate the visual pattern for one object with a pattern for the aroma of the same object. Obviously, different patterns of interconnections between the A and B units are appropriate for causing the visual pattern for a different object to give rise to the pattern for its aroma. The same principles apply, however, and if we presented our pattern associator with the A and B patterns for steak, it would learn the right set of interconnections for that case instead (these are shown in Figure 3.13B). In fact, it turns out that we can actually teach the same pattern associator a number of different associations. The matrix representing the set of interconnections that would be learned if we taught the same pattern associator both the rose association and the steak association is shown in Figure 3.14. The reader can verify this by adding the two matrices for the individual patterns together. The reader can also verify that this set of connections will allow the rose A pattern to produce the rose B pattern, and the steak A pattern to produce the steak B pattern: when either input pattern is presented, the correct corresponding output is produced.

The examples used here have the property that the two different visual patterns are completely uncorrelated with each other. This being the case, the rose pattern produces no effect when the interconnections for the steak have been established, and the steak pattern produces no effect when the interconnections for the rose association are in effect. For this reason, it is possible to add together the pattern of interconnections for the rose association and the pattern for the steak association, and still be able to associate the sight of the steak with the smell of a steak and the sight of a rose with the smell of a rose. The two sets of interconnections do not interact at all.

$$
\begin{bmatrix} - & + & + & - \\ - & + & + & - \\ + & - & - & + \\ + & - & - & + \end{bmatrix}
+
\begin{bmatrix} + & - & + & - \\ - & + & - & + \\ - & + & - & + \\ + & - & + & - \end{bmatrix}
=
\begin{bmatrix} & ++ & -- & - \\ -- & ++ & & \\ & -- & ++ & \\ ++ & -- & & - \end{bmatrix}
$$

FIGURE 3.14 ■ The weights in the third matrix allow either A pattern shown in Figure 3.13 to recreate the corresponding B pattern. Each weight in this case is equal to the sum of the weight for the A pattern and the weight for the B pattern, as illustrated.

One of the limitations of the Hebbian learning rule is that it can learn the connection strengths appropriate to an entire ensemble of patterns only when all the patterns are completely uncorrelated. This restriction does not, however, apply to pattern associators which use more sophisticated learning schemes.

### ATTRACTIVE PROPERTIES OF PATTERN ASSOCIATOR MODELS

Pattern associator models have the property that uncorrelated patterns do not interact with each other, but more similar ones do. Thus, to the extent that a new pattern of activation on the A units is similar to one of the old ones, it will tend to have similar effects. Furthermore, if we assume that learning the interconnections occurs in small increments, similar patterns will essentially reinforce the strengths of the links they share in common with other patterns. Thus, if we present the same pair of patterns over and over, but each time we add a little random noise to each element of each member of the pair, the system will automatically learn to associate the central tendency of the two patterns and will learn to ignore the noise. What will be stored will be an average of the similar patterns with the slight variations removed. On the other hand, when we present the system with completely uncorrelated patterns, they will not interact with each other in this way. Thus, the same pool of units can extract the central tendency of each of a number of pairs of unrelated patterns.

### EXTRACTING THE STRUCTURE OF AN ENSEMBLE OF PATTERNS

The fact that similar patterns tend to produce similar effects allows distributed models to exhibit a kind of spontaneous generalization, extending behavior appropriate for one pattern to other similar patterns. This property is shared by other PDP models, such as the word perception model and the Jets and Sharks model described above; the main difference here is in the existence of simple, local, learning mechanisms that can allow the acquisition of the connection strengths needed to produce these generalizations through experience with members of the ensemble of patterns. Distributed models have another interesting property as well: If there are regularities in the correspondences between pairs of patterns, the model will naturally extract these regularities. This property allows distributed models to acquire patterns of interconnections that lead them to behave in ways we ordinarily take as evidence for the use of linguistic rules.

Here, we describe the model very briefly. The model is a mechanism that learns how to construct the past tenses of words from their root forms through repeated presentations of examples of root forms paired with the corresponding past-tense form. The model consists of two pools of units. In one pool, patterns of activation representing the phonological structure of the root form of the verb can be represented, and, in the other, patterns representing the phonological structure of the past tense can be represented. The goal of the model is simply to learn the right connection strengths between the root units and the past-tense units, so that whenever the root form of a verb is presented, the model will construct the corresponding past-tense form. The model is trained by presenting the root form of the verb as a pattern of activation over the root units, and then using a simple, local, learning rule to adjust the connection strengths so that this root form will tend to produce the correct pattern of activation over the past-tense units. The model is tested by simply presenting the root form as a pattern of activation over the root units and examining the pattern of activation produced over the past-tense units.

The model is trained initially with a small number of verbs children learn early in the acquisition process. At this point in learning, it can only produce appropriate outputs for inputs that it has explicitly been shown. But as it learns more and more verbs, it exhibits two interesting behaviors. First, it produces the standard *ed* past tense when tested with pseudo-verbs or verbs it has never seen. Second, it "overregularizes" the past tense of irregular words it previously completed correctly. Often, the model will blend the irregular past tense of the word with the regular *ed* ending, and produce errors like CAMED as the past of COME. These phenomena mirror those observed in the early phases of acquisition of control over past tenses in young children.

The generativity of the child's responses—the creation of regular past tenses of new verbs and the overregularization of the irregular verbs—has been taken as strong evidence that the child has induced the rule which states that the regular correspondence for the past tense in English is to add a final *ed* (Berko, 1958). On the evidence of its performance, then, the model can be said to have acquired the rule. However, no special rule-induction mechanism is used, and no special language-acquisition device is required. The model learns to behave in accordance with the rule, not by explicitly noting that most words take *ed* in the past tense in English and storing this rule away explicitly, but simply by building up a set of connections in a pattern associator through a long series of simple learning experiences. The same mechanisms of parallel distributed processing and connection modification which are used in a number of domains serve, in this case, to produce implicit knowledge tantamount to a linguistic rule. The model also provides a fairly detailed account of a number of the specific aspects of the error patterns children make in learning the rule. In this sense, it provides a richer and more detailed description of the acquisition process than any that falls out naturally from the assumption that the child is building up a repertoire of explicit but inaccessible rules.

There is a lot more to be said about distributed models of learning, about their strengths and their weaknesses, than we have space for in this preliminary consideration. For now we hope mainly to have suggested that they provide dramatically different accounts of learning and acquisition than are offered by traditional models of these processes. We saw in earlier sections of this chapter that performance in accordance with rules can emerge from the interactions of simple, interconnected units. Now we can see how the aquisition of performance that conforms to linguistic rules can emerge from a simple, local, connection strength modulation process.

We have seen what the properties of PDP models are in informal terms, and we have seen how these properties operate to make the models do many of the kinds of things that they do. The business of the next chapter is to lay out these properties more formally, and to introduce some formal tools for their description and analysis. Before we turn to this, however, we wish to describe some of the major sources of inspiration for the PDP approach.

## Origins of Parallel Distributed Processing

The ideas behind the PDP approach have a history that stretches back indefinitely. In this section, we mention briefly some of the people who have thought in these terms, particularly those whose work has had an impact on our own thinking. This section should not been seen as an authoritative review of the history, but only as a description of our own sources of inspiration.

Some of the earliest roots of the PDP approach can be found in the work of the unique neurologists Jackson (1869/1958) and Luria (1966). Jackson was a forceful and persuasive critic of the simplistic localizationist doctrines of late nineteenth century neurology, and he argued convincingly for distributed, multilevel conceptions of processing systems. Luria, the Russian psychologist and neurologist, put forward the notion of the *dynamic functional system*. On this view, every behavioral or cognitive process resulted from the coordination of a large number of different components, each roughly localized in different regions of the brain, but all working together in dynamic interaction. Neither Hughlings-Jackson nor Luria is noted for the clarity of his views, but we have seen in their ideas a rough characterization of the kind of parallel distributed processing system we envision.

Two other contributors to the deep background of PDP were Hebb (1949) and Lashley (1950). We already have noted Hebb's contribution of the Hebb rule of synaptic modification; he also introduced the concept of cell assemblies—a concrete example of a limited form of distributed processing—and discussed the idea of reverberation of activation within neural networks. Hebb's ideas were cast more in the form of speculations about neural functioning than in the form of concrete processing models, but his thinking captures some of the flavor of parallel distributed processing mechanisms. Lashley's contribution was to insist upon the idea of distributed representation. Lashley may have been too radical and too vague, and his doctrine of equipotentiality of broad regions of cortex clearly overstated the case. Yet many of his insights into the difficulties of storing the "engram" locally in the brain are telling, and he seemed to capture quite precisely the essence of distributed representation in insisting that "there are no special cells reserved for special memories" (Lashley, 1950, p. 500).

In the 1950s, there were two major figures whose ideas have contributed to the development of our approach. One was Rosenblatt (1959, 1962) and the other was Selfridge (1955). In his *Principles of Neurodynamics* (1962), Rosenblatt articulated clearly the promise of a neurally inspired approach to computation, and he developed the *perceptron convergence procedure*, an important advance over the Hebb rule for changing synaptic connections. Rosenblatt's work was very controversial at the time, and the specific models he proposed were not up to all the hopes he had for them. But his vision of the human information processing system as a dynamic, interactive, self-organizing system lies at the core of the PDP approach. Selfridge's contribution was his insistence on the importance of interactive processing, and the development of *Pandemonium*, an explicitly computational example of a dynamic, interactive mechanism applied to computational problems in perception.

In the late 60s and early 70s, serial processing and the von Neumann computer dominated both psychology and artificial intelligence, but there were a number of researchers who proposed neural mechanisms which capture much of the flavor of PDP models. Among these figures, the most influential in our work have been J. A. Anderson, Grossberg, and Longuet-Higgins. Grossberg's mathematical analysis of the properties of neural networks led him to many insights we have only come to appreciate through extensive experience with computer simulation, and he deserves credit for seeing the relevance of neurally inspired mechanisms in many areas of perception and memory well before the field was ready for these kinds of ideas (Grossberg, 1978). Grossberg (1976) was also one of the first to analyze some of the properties of the competitive learning mechanism. Anderson's work differs from Grossberg's in insisting upon distributed representation, and in showing the relevance of neurally inspired models for theories of concept learning (Anderson, 1973, 1977); the work on distributed memory and amnesia owes a great deal to Anderson's inspiration. Anderson's work also played a crucial role in the formulation of the *cascade* model (McClelland, 1979), a step away from serial processing down the road to PDP. Longuet-Higgins and his group at Edinburgh were also pursuing distributed memory models during the same period, and David Willshaw, a member of the Edinburgh group, provided some very elegant mathematical analyses of the properties of various distributed representation schemes (Willshaw, 1981). His insights provide one of the sources of the idea of coarse coding. Many of the contributions of Anderson, Willshaw, and others distributed modelers may be found in Hinton and Anderson (1981). Others who have made important contributions to learning in PDP models include Amari (1977a), Bienenstock, Cooper, and Munro (1982), Fukushima (1975), Kohonen (1977, 1984), and von der Malsburg (1973).

Toward the middle of the 1970s, the idea of parallel processing began to have something of a renaissance in computational circles. We have already mentioned the Marr and Poggio (1976) model of stereoscopic depth perception. Another model from this period, the HEARSAY model of speech understanding, played a prominent role in the development of our thinking. Unfortunately, HEARSAY's computational architecture was too demanding for the available computational resources, and so the model was not a computational success. But its basically parallel, interactive character inspired the interactive model of reading

(Rumelhart, 1977), and the interactive activation model of word recognition (McClelland & Rumelhart, 1981; Rumelhart & McClelland, 1982).

The ideas represented in the interactive activation model had other precursors as well. Morton's *logogen* model (Morton, 1969) was one of the first models to capture concretely the principle of interaction of different sources of information, and Marslen-Wilson (e.g., Marslen-Wilson & Welsh, 1978) provided important empirical demonstrations of interaction between different levels of language processing. Levin's (1976) *Proteus* model demonstrated the virtues of activation-competition mechanisms, and Glushko (1979) helped us see how conspiracies of partial activations could account for certain aspects of apparently rule-guided behavior.

Our work also owes a great deal to a number of colleagues who have been working on related ideas in recent years. Many of these colleagues appear as authors or coauthors of chapters in this book. But there are others as well. Several of these people have been very influential in the development of the ideas in this book. Feldman and Ballard (1982) laid out many of the computational principles of the PDP approach (under the name of *connectionism*), and stressed the biological implausibility of most of the prevailing computational models in artificial intelligence. Hofstadter (1979, 1985) deserves credit for stressing the existence of a subcognitive—what we call microstructural—level, and pointing out how important it can be to delve into the microstructure to gain insight. A sand dune, he has said, is not a grain of sand. Others

have contributed crucial technical insights. Sutton and Barto (1981) provided an insightful analysis of the connection modification scheme we call the *delta rule* and illustrated the power of the rule to account for some of the subtler properties of classical conditioning. And Hopfield's (1982) contribution of the idea that network models can be seen as seeking minima in energy landscapes played a prominent role in the development of the Boltzmann machine, and in the crystallization of the ideas on harmony theory and schemata.

The power of parallel distributed processing is becoming more and more apparent, and many others have recently joined in the exploration of the capabilities of these mechanisms. We hope this chapter represents the nature of the enterprise we are all involved in, and that it does justice to the potential of the PDP approach.

## ACKNOWLEDGMENTS

This research was supported by Contract N00014–79–C–0323, NR 667–437 with the Personnel and Training Research Programs of the Office of Naval Research, by grants from the System Development Foundation, and by a NIMH Career Development Award (MH00385) to the first author.

## NOTE

1. In this and all other cases, there is a tendency for the pattern of activation to be influenced by partially activated, near neighbors, which do not quite match the probe. Thus, in this case, there is a Jet Al, who is a Married Burglar. The unit for Al gets slightly activated, giving Married a slight edge over Divorced in the simulation.

# Calling a Squirrel a Squirrel but a Canoe a Wigwam: A Category-Specific Deficit for Artefactual Objects and Body Parts

Carol Sacchett • Queen Mary's Hospital, Sidcup, Kent, U.K.

Glyn W. Humphreys • University of Birmingham, Edgbaston, Birmingham, U.K.

A single-case study is reported of a patient, CW, with a category-specific deficit for naming artefactual objects and body parts along with good naming of natural objects. Tests using matching rather than naming techniques further suggested that CW had some difficulty in distinguishing between close semantic co-ordinates of artefactual objects. The case provides a double dissociation relative to patients with selective problems in identifying natural objects. Possible reasons for CW's category-specific impairment are discussed.

## Introduction

Category-specific deficits in the visual identification and naming of objects have recently aroused considerable interest (e.g., Humphreys & Riddoch, 1987; McCarthy & Warrington, 1988; Marshall, 1985). For the most part, patients have been documented with problems in the visual identification of objects from natural biological categories (e.g., animals, birds, insects, fruits, and vegetables), whilst having relatively preserved identification of artefactual objects (e.g., clothing, furniture, tools, vehicles). The factors underlying such category-specific deficits, however, remain unclear. For instance, many patients who have difficulty identifying natural objects remain able to identify body parts (e.g., Riddoch & Humphreys, 1987a), suggesting that membership of a biological category is not the critical factor. Nor is it that

natural objects suffer simply because their base-level representations (Rosch et al., 1976) are at the category level (e.g., as with the category "birds") whilst base-level representations of artefacts correspond to nameable items (e.g., chair, car, coat), since this last point also holds for many of the natural categories that can be most impaired (e.g., animals, fruits, and vegetables). Due to the difficulty of specifying the critical factor(s), category-specific problems with natural objects could plausibly reflect deficit(s) at various stages in the object-naming process. For instance, they may be due to patients having problems making fine visual-perceptual distinctions between classes of visually similar objects (e.g., Riddoch & Humphreys, 1987b), to them having impaired stored knowledge (specifying known structural or known semantic properties of objects; e.g., Sartori & Job, 1988; Silveri & Gainotti, 1988; Warrington

& Shallice, 1984), or to problems transmitting information from structural to semantic knowledge systems (Riddoch & Humphreys, 1987a). Hart, Berndt, and Caramazza (1985) further suggested that category-specific problems with natural objects could arise at the name retrieval stage. Their patient, MD, showed intact knowledge of fruits and vegetables when given their names, but selectively poor naming of objects from these categories. However, MD was also somewhat impaired at categorising objects as either fruits or vegetables, suggesting that the problem was not confined to naming.

Category-specific problems in recognising artefactual objects have been noted more infrequently (e.g., Neilsen, 1946), and only assessed quantitatively in two cases (Warrington & McCarthy, 1983; 1987). In both the relevant cases, the patients studied were global aphasics with marked problems in naming *any* objects. Testing was therefore based on picture-word matching techniques. Warrington and McCarthy (1983) reported that their patient was poor at pointing to one of a set of five artefactual objects but relatively good at the same task performed with a set of natural objects with matched name-frequencies. Warrington and McCarthy (1987) reported that their patient was particularly impaired at picture-word matching with small manipulable objects. These two last cases are important in that they suggest that category-specific problems cannot only reflect within-category visual similarity, since categories of natural objects tend to have higher levels of perceptual overlap between their exemplars than do categories of artefactual objects (e.g., see Humphreys, Riddoch, & Quin-lan, 1988). Category-specific deficits for artefactual objects should not occur if within-category visual similarity were the *sole* determining factor. For instance, in at least some cases, problems may reflect impaired knowledge representations, which are to some extent specialised for different types of object.

The present paper reports the case of a patient with a category-specific problem in identifying artefactual objects and body parts visually, who manifests a relatively *preserved* ability to name natural objects. The case provides additional support for the distinction between the recognition and naming procedures developed for natural and artefactual objects. In the General Discussion we consider some of the factors that could give rise to the observed patterns of deficit.

## Case History

CW (born 1949), a right-handed bank employee, was admitted to hospital on April 12, 1988 with a dense right hemiplegia and right facial weakness. He was unable to speak or to respond to questions or commands. A C.T. scan performed one day post-onset revealed a large left fronto-parietal infarct with some midline shift. At two months post-onset, when this study was performed, CW had a right homonymous hemianopia, non-fluent speech production, and some function in the right lower limb.

Formal assessment commenced at five weeks post onset.

### Preliminary Assessments

CW was fairly good at reasoning with visual material, scoring normally on the Ravens Coloured Progressive Matrices (33/36). Auditory comprehension was examined using the Test for Reception of Grammar (T.R.O.G.; Bishop; 1983). CW made no errors with single words or simple sentences (SV, SVO), but made errors on reversible and on embedded sentences. Thus CW's auditory comprehension was moderately impaired, with there being particular difficulties with more complex syntactic constructions.

CW's spontaneous speech was typically high in content but lacking in fluency. It consisted of a number of content words separated by pauses, with a paucity of grammatical structure and function words. Examples of spontaneous speech in conversation and picture description are given in Table 4.1. CW's reading aloud was characterised by visual errors, primarily affecting the word ending. He read aloud 26/39 regular and 24/39 irregular words from the Coltheart, Besner, Jonasson, and Davelaar (1979) lists. There was no evidence of reading being based on sub-word segments.

### Experimental Investigations

The primary experimental investigations concerned CW's problems in naming common objects.

**TABLE 4.1. Examples of CW's Spontaneous Speech in Conversation and in Picture Description (the Cookie Theft Picture)**

*Conversation*

(Context: discussion about CW's progress)
"speech . . . 6 months . . . hundred percent . . . question?"
(Context: discussion about CW's employment)
"bank . . . Japanese . . . sales . . . two hundred million pounds . . . consortium . . ."

*Picture Description*

"cookie jar (reads) . . . cookie . . . chair . . . or stool . . . boy and a girl . . . 'Ssh!' . . . fall over . . . dishes and eh . . . wash up . . . the woman wash . . ."

---

This was first assessed using the Boston Naming Test (Kaplan, Goodglass, Weintraub, & Segal, 1983), which was also used to evaluate item consistency.

## Experiment 1: The Boston Naming Test and Performance Consistency

CW was given the Boston Naming Test on two occasions (May, 24, 1988 and November 29, 1988). Each item was presented in isolation on a card and CW was given unlimited time to respond.

On Test 1 he spontaneously named only 17% of the pictures (10/60). The vast majority of errors occurred because CW was unable to make a response (37/60 trials). He made 7 errors that could broadly be classed as semantic, but rejected 5 of these as incorrect (e.g., PELICAN → "duck or drake . . . but similar;" CANOE → "wigwam . . . no no!"). There were 6 unrelated errors that were all immediately rejected (e.g., OCTOPUS → "windmill . . . no!"). Following a failure to name an object correctly, CW was given a cue consisting of the first phoneme in the object's name. He then named a further 35 items, including 4 of the objects for which semantic errors first occurred and 4 of those for which unrelated responses had previously occurred. Of the 15 items CW failed to name even after being phonemically cued, there were 10 instances of no response and 5 instances where a phonemic cue resulted in an incorrect but semantically related name (e.g., SEAHORSE → "sealion"; HARP → "harmonica"). On the no-response items CW was unable to provide any information that might indicate tacit knowledge of the phonological form of the target (e.g. length, syllable structure, phonological approximation). The name frequencies of the items he named cor-

rectly without cueing were reliably higher than those of items he was unable to name ($F[1,58] = 7.61$, $P < 0.01$; median name frequency for correctly named and unnamed items = 11 and 1 occurrence per million, using the Kuçera & Francis, 1967, word frequency count).

On Test 2 he named 33/60 items correctly. There were semantic errors on 19/27 error trials, no response on 7 trials, and 1 possible derivational error (HANGER → hanging). Of the 19 semantic errors, CW accepted 6 as correct. Phonemic cueing facilitated name retrieval on a further 13 items. The effect of name frequency was not significant ($F[1,58] = 1.58$, $P > 0.05$; median name frequency for correctly named items was 2 per million, whereas it was 1 per million for the items not named).

The items in the Boston Naming Test are not matched across different categories. However, a breakdown of CW's performance on artefacts and natural objects revealed that, although there was little difference on Test 1 (when performance was poor overall), the naming of natural objects was rather better than that of artefacts on Test 2 (Test 1, 2/14 versus 8/46 on natural objects and artefacts respectively; Test 2, 11/14 versus 22/46).

## Consistency

The 10 items that CW named correctly on the first administration of the test were also named correctly on the second administration. CW failed to name 27 items on both occasions, and there was a set of 23 items that were named on the second but not on the first test. It is clear that CW performed better on the second administration of the test, consistent with there being some degree of spontaneous recovery. Along with this recovery, CW tended on the second test to make relatively more semantic than "no-response" errors when he failed to name objects correctly. This suggests that, over time, CW was able to achieve a closer semantic specification for objects, changing his responses from failures to produce any name to producing the names of close semantic co-ordinates. Name frequency affected his performance on Test 1 but not Test 2. In addition there was some degree of item-specific consistency, in the sense that items correctly named on Test 1 were always named correctly on Test 2.

## Experiment 2: Pyramids and Palm Trees

Given CW's poor naming performance, it is important to assess his ability to recognise pictures and to retrieve full semantic information. As a first test of visual access to semantic information, CW was given the pyramids and palm trees test (see Howard & Orchard-Lisle, 1984). The test consists of 52 picture triads, preceded by one example. The subject is required to match a target picture against 1 of 2 test pictures, using associations drawn from real-world knowledge. For example, the subject must choose between a picture of a palm tree and that of a deciduous tree to match against a picture of a pyramid.

CW scored 46/52. This score is less than that achieved by Howard and Orchard-Lisle's control subjects, who made 3 errors or less. There is thus some suggestion of a semantic deficit, though it is by no means marked. All errors involved artefact targets.

## Experiment 3: Picture-Word Matching 1

To investigate CW's visual access to semantic information further, a picture-word matching task was undertaken, using semantic and unrelated distractors.

CW was presented with 32 line drawings of common objects on 3 occasions. On each occasion the examiner (CS) spoke a name that was either the correct target name, the name of a semantic co-ordinate, or an unrelated name. CW was instructed to respond "yes" or "no" according to whether the name corresponded to the picture presented.

In previous studies, anomic patients have been differentiated according to their performance on picture-word matching tests such as that described here. For instance, Howard and Orchard-Lisle (1984) reported a patient (JCU) who accepted the name of a close semantic co-ordinate on 50% of occasions. It was proposed that her picture-naming impairment reflected an imprecise semantic specification for target objects. In contrast, Kay and Ellis (1987) reported a patient (EST) who rejected all semantic distractors, despite having a profound naming impairment. It was proposed that EST's naming impairment arose after correct semantic processing of pictures.

CW accepted the correct name on 28/32 occasions (rejecting it on 4 presentations). He rejected unrelated names on all occasions (32/32), but the names of semantic co-ordinates on only 28/32 presentations. The targets could also be divided on the basis of whether they were natural objects or artefacts. CW both accepted the correct name and rejected the semantic co-ordinate distractor for 10/11 natural objects; in contrast, he did this only for 14/21 artefacts.

As in Experiment 2 (pyramids and palm trees), there is some suggestion of a problem in accessing semantic knowledge about objects from vision, since CW correctly rejects some correct object names and incorrectly accepts the names of some semantic co-ordinates. The problem in accessing semantic knowledge also appears to be worse for artefacts than for natural objects. The category-specificity of the problem was investigated in more detail in Experiment 4.

## Experiment 4: Picture-Word Matching 2 (Effects of Category)

A second picture-word matching test required CW to select one word from a choice of four to match against a line drawing from the Snodgrass and Vanderwart (1980) set. In this test items were drawn from natural and artefactual object classes. The words were presented in the written and auditory modalities simultaneously to ensure that CW identified the words correctly and could maintain them whilst making the judgement.

There were 80 trials, 35 with targets drawn from categories of natural objects (birds, insects, domestic animals, wild animals, vegetables, and fruit), 35 with targets from categories of arte-factual objects (furniture, tools, clothing, musical instruments, transport, and kitchen utensils), and 10 target body parts. On 16/80 trials the distractor words referred to unrelated items (7 "animate" trials, 7 "inanimate" trials, 2 "body part" trials); on the remaining 64 trials the distractor words referred to semantic co-ordinates of the target (e.g., FOX: fox, deer, squirrel, rabbit; SAW: saw, hammer, screwdriver, chisel). No attempt was made to control the visual similarity between targets and the items invoked by distractor names, though it should be noted that visually, similarity will tend to be highest within categories of natural objects (see Humphreys et al., 1988).

CW made no errors on trials where distractor names referred to unrelated items (16/16), and no errors on natural object targets with semantic co-ordinate distractors (28/28). He made 7/28 errors on trials with artefactual targets and 1/8 error with a body-part target when the distractors referred to semantic co-ordinates. When there were semantic co-ordinate distractors, performance was better with natural object targets than with artefactual targets (Fisher exact probability, $P = 0.005$).

These data support those obtained in Experiment 3 and suggest that, although CW is relatively unimpaired at deriving semantic information for natural objects, he has difficulties with artefactual objects. More informally, it was also noted that CW performed considerably more slowly on trials with artefactual relative to natural objects. On 10 occasions, he requested that the item be put to one side and returned to later. In contrast, his responses to natural objects were immediate and no repeats were requested.

## Experiment 5: Naming Natural and Artefactual Objects

In Experiment 5 we returned to access CW's naming ability, but this time contrasting his naming of frequency-matched artefacts, body parts, and natural objects. We also compared his naming ability with his ability to make picture-word matching decisions between semantic co-ordinates (from Experiment 4).

Two sets of 20 line drawings were selected from Snodgrass and Vanderwart's (1980) set. One set contained natural objects selected from the categories of birds, insects, wild animals, and domestic animals. The second set contained artefactual objects selected from the categories clothing, tools,

kitchen utensils, musical instruments, and transport, along with 2 body parts (see Appendix for the full set). Using the measures provided by Snodgrass and Vanderwart, the items were matched on name agreement, image agreement, and name frequency (F[1,38] = 3.44 and 2.30, and F < 1.0 respectively; all $P > 0.05$). The natural objects were less familiar and more complex than the artefacts and body parts (F[1,38] = 24.48 and 13.29 respectively, $P < 0.01$). Also, the names for the natural objects tended to be shorter than those for the artefacts and body parts (e.g., 19/20 of the natural objects had names of either 1 or 2 syllables, compared with 16/20 of the artefacts and body parts). The pictures were presented in random order and CW was simply asked to name each one in turn.

CW spontaneously named 19/20 of the natural objects, making 1 super-ordinate error (ANT → "insect"), which he then self-corrected. He named only 7/20 of the artefacts and body parts correctly, and made 2 semantic/visual errors (SPOON → "fork"; FLUTE → "recorder"). His naming of natural objects was significantly better than his naming of artefacts and body parts ($\chi^2 = 15.82$, $P < 0.005$. The advantage for natural objects over artefactual objects and body parts was not due to the effects of the number of syllables in the names; CW named 5/12 1-syllable artefacts and body parts, relative to 8/8 2- and 3-syllable natural objects.

Of the artefacts and body parts used in this naming test, 14 had also served as targets in Experiment 4 (picture-word matching separated for object category). CW made correct picture-word matches to 13 of these items, of which he was only able to name 5 correctly.

We note here that the advantage for natural objects over artefacts and body parts occurred even though the artefacts and body parts were rated as more familiar and less visually complex.

## General Discussion

CW presents with a category-specific deficit in identifying common artefacts and body parts. In contrast to this, his ability to recognise visually and name natural objects such as animals, birds, insects, fruits, and vegetables, is relatively good. He made few errors in picture-word matching with the latter objects, even when distractors were close semantic co-ordinates (Experiments 2, 3, and 4), and he showed good naming performance (Test 2, Experiment 1; Experiment 5). With artefactual objects and body parts, CW made errors in picture-word matching with semantic distractors, and showed impaired naming. His naming performance was, if anything, rather worse than his ability to select between semantic distractors, since he was poor at naming items on which he succeeded in the matching task.

CW's case supports those of the patients described by Warrington and McCarthy (1983; 1987), as well as going beyond them in showing that impaired identification of artefacts can co-exist with relatively intact naming of natural objects. A patient with a similar problem in naming artefacts, along with relatively preserved naming of animals, has recently been reported by Hillis and Caramazza (1990). Their patient was additionally impaired with fruits and vegetables. CW showed no sign of this. For instance, on the picture-word matching test with semantically related distractors (Experiment 4), CW made no errors on the eight fruits and vegetables used.

From the data we were able to collect with CW, we can propose that the most likely locus of his problem is in accessing semantic information for artefacts and body parts from vision. We conclude this because there was a mild impairment in the pyramid and palm trees test (Experiment 2), and in picture-word matching with semantic distractors (Experiments 3 and 4). Also, although CW's matching performance was better than his naming of the same items (Experiments 4 and 6), it should be acknowledged that picture-word matching is a highly constrained task in which correct selections may take place even when considerable uncertainty still exists (e.g., see Rapp & Caramazza, 1989). In less constrained tasks, such as picture naming, inability to achieve the correct semantic specification for an item could produce an apparently more serious deficit in name retrieval. That is, the apparently better performance on matching than naming is quite consistent with there being a single deficit, in retrieving appropriate semantic descriptors for particular object classes.

In view of this argument for the existence of a semantic deficit, three other findings are of note:

1. CW made semantic errors, which increased proportionately as his naming improved (Experiment 1).

2. His naming was greatly facilitated by phonemic cueing (Experiment 1).
3. There was item-consistency in his naming performance (e.g., all items named correctly on Test 1 in Experiment 1 were named correctly on Test 2).

Of these findings, the semantic errors in naming are most obviously consistent with CW having a semantic impairment. Indeed, the proportional increase in semantic errors over time would also fit with a gradual resolution in the semantic deficit. Initially, CW may have been unable to access any semantic information about particular objects, so that either an unrelated name or no name at all was produced. As the condition resolved, so CW gained access to approximate semantic information, producing relatively more semantic errors. In addition to this, CW incorrectly accepted some semantic errors as correct, something he never did when he made unrelated naming errors (Experiment 1). This again suggests a distinction between the two error types, with CW being more conscious of being incorrect when no rather than when partial semantic information is retrieved.

Also consistent with there being a semantic impairment is the item-consistency manifested in his naming performance. Such item-consistency may not be expected if there were solely a name-retrieval problem (Shallice, 1988).

Perhaps less obviously consistent with the semantic-deficit argument is the finding of a facilitatory effect of phonemic cueing (Experiment 1). Such a facilitatory effect might be thought to occur because the cue mitigates a specific problem in retrieving output phonology. However, if object naming involves a set of cascading processes, in which partial information can be passed between different representations (cf. Ellis, 1985; Humpreys et al., 1988), phonemic cues may help resolve semantic uncertainty by feeding back to facilitate selection amongst a set of semantic candidates (see Ellis, 1985). Cascade mechanisms can also be used to understand the differential effects of name frequency on CW's picture naming on the first and second test sessions in Experiment 1. On Test 1, naming was poor overall and there was an effect of name frequency; on Test 2 naming improved, more semantic errors were made, but there was no effect of name frequency. In Test 1 we assume that, for many items, little semantic information was retrieved. Under this circumstance, items with high name frequencies may sometimes be named if, for these items, minimal semantic information is required for name retrieval. In Test 2 we presume that partial semantic information can be retrieved for most items. In this circumstance, the main constraint may be differentiating between candidate semantic representations rather than accessing semantic information at all. The names of several semantic candidates may then be activated, and the effects of name frequency consequently lessened (see Humphreys et al., 1988, for a similar argument concerning reduced name frequency effects on picture naming for items that activate many semantic candidates during name retrieval).

## Category-Specificity in Visual Object Identification

The category-specificity of CW's impairment supports the argument that our internal representations of the world are to some extent organised along categorical lines. There are good reasons why this should be so. For instance:

1. Associations within and across modalities differ for different object categories (e.g., many artefacts are associated with fine hand manipulations and actions, as are body parts; other natural objects may be more closely associated with sounds, tastes, or type of motion; cf. Allport, 1985; Warrington & McCarthy, 1987; Warrington & Shallice, 1984).
2. The object classes differ in terms of the kinds of information that may be used to select the appropriate object name (e.g., differences in function are important for distinguishing many artefacts and possibly also body parts, whereas differences in precise perceptual characteristics such as facial configuration, colour, and texture are important for distinguishing many other natural objects; see Warrington & Shallice, 1984).
3. Many artefacts contain the same local parts and are distinguished by the local spatial relations between the parts (see Biederman, 1987); many natural objects have the same parts in the same special relations, so that some other form of visual coding—such as the relative scaling of the parts—may be more important.

Category-specific problems in identifying inanimate objects could then arise because:

1. Specific associations are impaired (e.g., with fine hand manipulations, or contrastingly with sound or taste).
2. Stored information concerned with perceptual or with functional distinctions between objects is impaired (e.g., Warrington & McCarthy, 1987).
3. The visual processing routines most crucial for particular object classes are impaired (e.g., routines concerned either with coding the local spatial relations between object parts, or with coding the relative scaling of the parts).

These arguments, for the involvement of different processes in the identification of particular classes of object, are given further weight by emerging evidence for category-specific effects in normal object recognition. Price and Humphreys (1989) showed evidence for different types of perceptual association. They found that surface details (both colour and brightness gradients) influence the identification of natural objects more than that of artefacts. They argued that such effects occur because surface detail facilitates the differentiation between natural objects with similar perceptual structures. Loss of the association between stored knowledge of the perceptual structures of objects and their surfaces may thus be expected to disrupt the identification of natural objects in particular.

Evidence for different visual recognition routines comes from Dickerson and Humphreys (Note 1). They found that the effects of rotation in the plane are greater on natural objects than on artefacts. The relatively small effects of rotation on artefacts may occur because they are identified on the basis of local relations between their parts, which are little changed under within-plane rotations. In contrast, the identification of many natural objects depends on the relative scaling of their parts, a process involving coding the parts with respect to some overall reference frame (cf. Marr & Nishihara, 1978). Coding relative to a perceptual reference frame may be disrupted by within-plane rotation, since the standard frame may be the gravitational vertical. Hence the identification of natural objects suffers under within-plane rotation.

In general, we should look to convergent evidence from normal and from neuropsychological studies in order to understand better the procedures mediating the identification of different types of objects. In CW's case, we can tentatively suggest that there is a problem in retrieving semantic (associative or functional) knowledge about particular object classes. For instance, a failure to retrieve functional knowledge about the uses of different objects might particularly impair the identification of artefacts. In other patients, a failure or a spared ability to retrieve certain kinds of knowledge may render other categories relatively impaired or preserved (e.g. Hillis & Caramazza, 1990, suggest that their patient may have a preserved ability to retrieve information about the characteristic motion of objects, leading to spared naming of animals but not fruits and vegetables). Future work needs to be sensitive to the various different factors that underlie category-specific problems in object identification, and we should not expect the same kind of problem to underlie all cases.

## REFERENCES

Allport, D. A. (1985). Distributed memory, modular subsystems, and dysphasia. In S. Newman & R. Epstein (Eds.), *Current perspectives in dysphasia*. Edinburgh: Churchill Livingstone.

Biederman, I. (1987). Recognition by components: A theory of human image understanding. *Psychological Review, 94*, 115–145.

Bishop, D. (1983). *The Test for the Reception of Grammar*. Manchester: University of Manchester Press.

Coltheart, M., Besner, D., Jonasson, J., & Davelaar, E. (1979). Phonological encoding and deep dyslexia. *Quarterly Journal of Experimental Psychology, 31*, 489–507.

Ellis, A. W. (1985). The production of spoken words: A cognitive neuropsychological perspective. In A.W. Ellis (Ed.), *Progress in the psychology of language. Vol. 2*. London: Erlbaum.

Hart, J., Berndt, R. S., & Caramazza, A. (1985). Category-specific naming deficit following cerebral infarction. *Nature, 316*, 439–440.

Hillis, A. E., & Caramazza, A. (1990). *Category-specific naming and comprehension impairment: A double dissociation*. Report of the Cognitive Neuropsychology Laboratory. Baltimore: The Johns Hopkins University.

Howard, D., & Orchard-Lisle, V. (1984). On the origin of semantic errors in naming: Evidence from the case of a global aphasic. *Cognitive Neuropsychology, 1*, 163–190.

Humphreys, G. W., & Riddoch, M. J. (1987). On telling your fruits from your vegetables: A consideration of category-specific deficits after brain damage. *Trends in Neuroscience, 10*, 145–148.

Humphreys, G. W., Riddoch, M. J., & Quinlan, P. T. (1988). Cascade processes in picture identification. *Cognitive Neuropsychology, 5*, 67–103.

Kaplan, E., Goodglass, H., Weintraub, S., & Segal, H. (1983). *Boston Naming Test*: Philadelphia: Lea & Febinger.

Kay, J., & Ellis, A. W. (1987). A cognitive neuropsychological case study of anomia: Implications for psychological models of word retrieval. *Brain, 110*, 1–17.

Kuçera, H., & Francis, W. (1967). *Computational analysis of present-day American English*. Providence, RI: Brown University Press.

McCarthy, R. A., & Warrington, E. K. (1988). Evidence for modality-specific meaning systems in the brain. *Nature, 334*, 428–430.

Marr, D., & Nishihara, H. K. (1978). Representation and recognition of the spatial organisation of three-dimensional shapes. *Proceedings of the Royal Society of London, B200*, 269–294.

Marshall, J. C. (1988). A fruit by any other name. *Nature, 316*, 388.

Neilsen, J. M. (1946). *Agnosia, apraxia, aphasia: Their value in cerebral localisation*. New York: Hoeber.

Price, C. J., & Humphreys, G. W. (1989). The effects of surface detail on object categorisation and naming. *Quarterly Journal of Experimental Psychology, 41A*, 797–828.

Rapp, B., & Caramazza, A. (1989). General to specific access to word meaning: A claim re-examined. *Cognitive Neuropsychology, 6*, 251–272.

Riddoch, M. J., & Humphreys, G. W. (1987b). A case of integrative visual agnosia. *Brain, 110*, 1431–1462.

Riddoch, M. J., & Humphreys, G. W. (1987a). Visual object processing in optic aphasia: A case of semantic access agnosia. *Cognitive Neuropsychology, 4*, 131–185.

Rosch, E., Mervis, C. B., Gray, W.D., Johnson, D. M., & Boyes-Braem, P. (1976). Basic objects in natural categories. *Cognitive Psychology, 8*, 382–439.

Sartori, G., & Job, R. (1988). The oyster with four legs: A neuropsychological study on the interaction between vision and semantic information. *Cognitive Neuropsychology, 5*, 105–132.

Shallice, T. (1988). *From neuropsychology to mental structure*. Cambridge: Cambridge University Press.

Silveri, M. C., & Gainotti, G. (1988). Interaction between vision and language in category-specific semantic impairment. *Cognitive Neuropsychology, 5*, 677–709.

Snodgrass, J. G., & Vanderwart, M. (1980). A standardised set of 260 pictures: Norms for name agreement, image agreement, familiarity, and visual complexity. *Journal of Experimental Psychology: Human Learning and Memory, 6*, 174–215.

Warrington, E. K., & McCarthy, R. A. (1983). Category-specific access dysphasia. *Brain, 106*, 859–878.

Warrington, E. K., & McCarthy, R. A. (1987). Categories of knowledge: Further fractionation and an attempted integration. *Brain, 100*, 1273–1296.

Warrington, E. K., & Shallice, T. (1984). Category-specific semantic impairment. *Brain, 107*, 829–853.

## REFERENCE NOTE

1. Dickerson, J. & Humphreys, G. W. *Effects of Rotation on the Identification of Different Classes of Object*. Cognitive Science Research Report, University of Birmingham. This work was supported by a grant from the Medical Research Council of Great Britain to the second author.

*Note:* The scores in the appendix overleaf are taken from Snodgrass and Vanderwart (1980). *Name* refers to the percentage of subjects in Snodgrass and Vanderwart's study who gave the same name to each picture. It is a measure of name agreement. *Image* is a rating measure of how closely the picture agrees with subjects' images of the object (1 = low agreement, 5 = high agreement). *Familiarity* and *Complexity* are rating measures of, respectively, how familiar and how complex an object is (1 = unfamiliar or not complex, 5 = very familiar and very complex). *K&F* refers to the frequency of the name of the object, taken from Kucera and Francis's (1967) word count. *Corr.* refers to whether CW named the item correctly or not (1 = correct, 0 = error, 0/1 = self corrected).

## Appendix

| | Name | Image | Familiarity | Complexity | K&F | Corr. |
|---|---|---|---|---|---|---|
| *Natural Objects* | | | | | | |
| chicken | 67 | 3.62 | 2.42 | 3.48 | 37 | 1 |
| duck | 95 | 3.85 | 2.75 | 3.32 | 9 | 1 |
| owl | 100 | 4.10 | 2.22 | 4.22 | 2 | 1 |
| ant | 81 | 2.92 | 2.62 | 3.92 | 6 | 0/1 |
| bee | 60 | 2.78 | 2.68 | 4.75 | 11 | 1 |
| butterfly | 100 | 3.92 | 2.92 | 4.25 | 2 | 1 |
| deer | 76 | 3.72 | 2.22 | 3.55 | 13 | 1 |
| fox | 74 | 3.49 | 1.95 | 4.02 | 13 | 1 |
| mouse | 79 | 4.22 | 2.45 | 3.28 | 10 | 1 |
| rabbit | 100 | 4.20 | 2.95 | 3.28 | 11 | 1 |
| squirrel | 93 | 4.42 | 3.82 | 3.75 | 1 | 1 |
| bear | 88 | 3.62 | 1.98 | 3.68 | 57 | 1 |
| camel | 95 | 3.92 | 2.08 | 3.75 | 1 | 1 |
| lion | 93 | 3.88 | 2.00 | 4.30 | 17 | 1 |
| tiger | 93 | 3.82 | 2.10 | 4.62 | 7 | 1 |
| zebra | 98 | 4.05 | 1.60 | 4.55 | 1 | 1 |
| cow | 93 | 3.92 | 2.42 | 3.85 | 19 | 1 |
| donkey | 86 | 3.48 | 1.88 | 3.35 | 1 | 1 |
| horse | 100 | 4.20 | 3.55 | 3.82 | 117 | 1 |
| sheep | 67 | 3.00 | 1.85 | 3.80 | 23 | 1 |
| **Mean** | 86.9 | 3.76 | 2.42 | 3.88 | 18.4 | |
| *Artefacts and Body Parts* | | | | | | |
| hat | 98 | 3.65 | 3.18 | 2.35 | 56 | 0 |
| glove | 98 | 3.65 | 3.38 | 3.02 | 9 | 0 |
| shoe | 95 | 3.02 | 4.62 | 3.38 | 14 | 1 |
| sock | 100 | 3.72 | 4.52 | 1.62 | 4 | 0 |
| tie | 69 | 4.05 | 3.80 | 2.90 | 23 | 0 |
| axe | 90 | 4.50 | 2.28 | 2.48 | 12 | 0 |
| hammer | 100 | 4.10 | 3.48 | 2.60 | 9 | 0 |
| nail | 98 | 4.73 | 3.28 | 1.80 | 6 | 1 |
| pliers | 88 | 4.22 | 3.38 | 2.20 | 1 | 1 |
| fork | 100 | 4.15 | 4.78 | 2.62 | 14 | 1 |
| scissors | 98 | 4.40 | 3.98 | 2.15 | 1 | 1 |
| spoon | 98 | 4.10 | 4.50 | 2.02 | 6 | 1 |
| accordion | 88 | 3.40 | 2.15 | 4.68 | 1 | 0 |
| flute | 88 | 3.41 | 2.45 | 4.15 | 1 | 1 |
| guitar | 98 | 4.20 | 3.58 | 4.00 | 19 | 0 |
| piano | 81 | 4.02 | 3.42 | 4.58 | 38 | 0 |
| violin | 86 | 4.18 | 2.68 | 4.10 | 11 | 0 |
| helicopter | 95 | 3.42 | 2.55 | 3.80 | 1 | 0 |
| ear | 95 | 4.26 | 4.50 | 2.68 | 29 | 0 |
| eye | 98 | 4.15 | 4.88 | 3.48 | 122 | 0 |
| **Mean** | 93.5 | 3.97 | 3.57 | 3.03 | 18.9 | |

# Positron Emission Tomographic Studies of the Cortical Anatomy of Single-Word Processing

Steven E. Petersen, Peter T. Fox, Michael I. Posner, Mark A. Mintum, and Marcus E. Raichle
• Washington University School of Medicine, St. Louis, Missouri

The use of positron emission tomography to measure regional changes in average blood flow during processing of individual auditory and visual words provides support for multiple, parallel routes between localized sensory-specific, phonological, articulatory and semantic-coding areas.

Language is an essential characteristic of the human species, and has been studied by disciplines ranging from philosophy to neurology. Because language is so complex, cognitive and neurological studies often focus on processing of individual words (lexical items). Cognitive models for lexical processing consider words perceived visually and auditorily to involve separate modality-specific codes, with access in parallel to shared output (articulatory) and meaning (semantic) codes.[1-6] In contrast, the model most widely accepted in the clinical neurological literature argues for serial processing, with an early recoding of visual input into an auditory-based code which is used in turn for semantic and articulatory access.[7,8]

We have used recent advances in the precision of positron emission tomography (PET) for measuring activity-related changes in regional cerebral blood flow to identify brain regions active during three levels of single-word processing. Our results indicate localization of different codes in widely separated areas of the cerebral cortex. The results favour the idea of separate brain areas involved in separate visual and auditory coding of words, each with independent access to supramodal articulatory and semantic systems. These findings fit well with the parallel models, but argue against the obligatory visual-to-auditory recoding and serial nature of the clinical neurological models.

## Methods

Brain blood flow was measured in 17 (11 female, 6 male) right-handed normal volunteers using a bolus intravenous injection of O-labeled water[15] (half-life, 123 s) and a 40-s data acquisition.[9,10] A series of 6–10 blood flow scans were obtained in each subject (10 m interscan interval). Within this series, conditions were designed as a hierarchy of paired comparisons to allow subtractive (task minus control) data analysis (see below).

Stimuli were presented throughout data acquisition. All stimuli were frequent English nouns presented at a rate of one per second. Visually presented words appeared on a colour monitor suspended 300 mm from the subject. Auditory words were presented through hearing-aid type speakers fitted within the ears and driven by a digital tape recorder.

Four behavioural conditions formed a three-level subtractive hierarchy (Table 5.1). Each task state was intended to add a small number of operations to those of its subordinate (control) state.[11] In the first-level comparison, the presentation of single words without a lexical task was compared to visual fixation without word presentation. Note that no motor output or volitional lexical processing was required in this task; rather, simple sensory input and involuntary word-form processing were targeted by this subtraction (sensory task). In the second-level comparison, speaking each presented word was compared with word presentation without speech. Areas involved in output coding and motor control were targeted by this comparison. In the third-level comparison, saying a use for each presented word (for example, if 'cake' was presented, to say 'eat') was compared with speaking presented words. This comparison targeted areas involved in the task of semantic processing (verb-noun association), as distinct from speech, sensory input, and involuntary word-form processing (association task).

Images were analysed by paired (intrasubject) subtraction. Task-state minus control-state subtractions created images of the regional blood flow changes associated with the operations of each cognitive level. Intersubject averaging was used to increase the signal-to-noise ratio of these subtracted images.[12] Averaging required anatomical standardization of all images; this was based on a previously described stereotactic method of anatomical localization for PET images.[13,14]

Statistical significance was determined by distribution analysis of the entire population (both positive and negative) of independent regional changes within each averaged subtracted image. The location and magnitude of these changes were determined using a centre-of-mass computer search algorithm.[15] Each change distribution contained both noise and task-induced responses. During averaging, task-induced responses gained in magnitude relative to image noise, becoming 'outliers' in the distribution.[12] Significant responses, then, were defined using tests for outlier detection.[16] Statistical analysis was two-tiered: first, omnibus testing (gamma-2 statistic) determined whether an image (a distribution) contained any significant responses (any outliers); then, post-hoc analysis by Z-score ascribed significance levels to each response within the population. All distributions reported had a gamma-2 significance level of $P < 0.05$. All cortical responses with a Z-score over 2.17. ($P < 0.03$) are reported.

## Lexical Processing Regions

Regions of activation are enumerated in Tables 5.2–5.4, and the cortical sites of activation are summarized in Figure 5.1. The most striking aspect of Figure 5.1 is that there are relatively few areas of activation added by each task and that these areas are clustered in a few critical parts of the cortex.

Modality-specific primary and non-primary sensory regions were activated by passive auditory or visual presentation of words (Table 5.2, Figure 5.2a and b, see color insert following page 176). No regions were activated for both auditory

**TABLE 5.1. Paradigm Design**

| Subtraction | Control State | Stimulated State | Task |
|---|---|---|---|
| Sensory task | Fixation point only | Passive words | Passive sensory processing Modality-specific word code |
| Output task | Passive words | Repeat words | Articulatory code Motor programming Motor output |
| Association task | Repeat words | Generate uses | Semantic association Selection for action |

The rationale of the three levels stepwise paradigm design is shown. At the second and third level, the control state is the stimulated state from the previous level. Some hypothesized cognitive operations are represented in the third column.

**TABLE 5.2 Sensory Tasks**

| Region | Coordinates (mm) | | | Magnitude |
|--------|---|---|---|-----------|
| | Z | X | Y | |
| Visual | | | | |
| 1. Striate cortex (L) | 10 | 6 | −72 | 2.28† |
| 2. Striate cortex (R) | 10 | −12 | −72 | 2.66† |
| 3. Extrastriate cortex (L) | 2 | 24 | −58 | 3.82‡ |
| 4. Extrastriate cortex (R) | 6 | −26 | −66 | 2.95‡ |
| 5. Inferior lateral occipital cortex (R) | −4 | −34 | −46 | 3.38‡ |
| Auditory | | | | |
| 6. Posterior superior temporal cortex (L) | 14 | 46 | −10 | 2.46† |
| 7. Temporal cortex (R) | 12 | −42 | −16 | 2.76‡ |
| 8. Anterior superior temporal cortex (L) | −2 | 42 | 10 | 3.02‡ |
| 9. Temporoparietal cortex (L) | 14 | 54 | −30 | 2.88‡ |
| 10. Lateral temporal cortex (R) | .8 | −62 | −12 | 3.30‡ |
| 11. Inferior anterior cingulate cortex (L) | 18 | 12 | 44 | 2.34† |

Subtraction conditions: Passive words—Fixation point. For Tables 5.2–5.4, the following conventions are used: the region is given a mnemonic anatomical name associated with the coordinates. The coordinates and magnitudes of response are determined using a three-dimensional search algorithm on the averaged subtraction image. The coordinates are in mm from a 0, 0, 0 point that is at the level of a line drawn between the anterior and posterior commissures ($z = 0$), at the midline of the brain ($x = 0$), and located antero-posteriorly halfway between the commissures ($y = 0$). The magnitudes are the change in blood flow in ml/(100 g × min), and the statistical significance of the points is assessed with a two-stage testing procedure. The distribution of the magnitudes of local blood-flow change is tested for outliers using an omnibus gamma-2 test. For all averaged images presented here, there are statistically significant outliers. The foci with the largest magnitude of blood-flow change are then given a z-score with respect to the population of all local changes within an image. All foci of change with a P-value <0.03 are reported in the tables. † $P < 0.03$, ‡ $P < 0.01$.

In general, the passive presentation subtractions identify modality-specific foci of activation, whereas the higher level subtractions activate similar regions across modalities.

and visual presentation. The areas identified appear to support two different computational levels in each modality, one of passive sensory processing and a second level of modality-specific word-form processing.

For the visual modality, the main cortical activations are in the striate cortex and in a small set of prestriate areas reaching as far anterior as the temporal-occipital boundary. The primary striate responses were similar to those produced by other

**TABLE 5.3. Output Tasks**

| Region | Coordinates (mm) | | | Magnitude |
|--------|---|---|---|-----------|
| | Z | X | Y | |
| Visual | | | | |
| 12. Mouth region, rolandic cortex (L) | 40 | 46 | 0 | 4.34‡ |
| 13. Rolandic cortex (R) | 32 | −52 | 6 | 3.46‡ |
| 14. Buried sylvian cortex (L) | 14 | 31 | 6 | 3.04† |
| 15. Lateral sylvian cortex (R) | 8 | −63 | −4 | 2.96† |
| 16. Premotor cortex (L) | 18 | 48 | 14 | 2.98† |
| 17. Supplementary motor area (SMA) | 50 | −2 | 10 | 3.36† |
| Auditory | | | | |
| 18. Mouth region, rolandic cortex (L) | 42 | 46 | −2 | 3.64‡ |
| 19. Rolandic cortex (R) | 40 | −56 | 2 | 3.78‡ |
| 20. Buried sylvian cortex (L) | 14 | 34 | 10 | 3.17† |
| 21. Lateral sylvian cortex (R) | 12 | −62 | −7 | 3.22‡ |
| 22. Premotor cortex (L) | 26 | 52 | 2 | 3.06† |
| 23. SMA | 52 | 2 | 14 | 2.80† |

Subtraction conditions: Repeat words—Passive visual words. See Table 5.2 legend for details of conventions used.

**TABLE 5.4. Association Tasks**

| Region | Coordinates (mm) | | | Magnitude |
|---|---|---|---|---|
| | Z | X | Y | |
| Visual | | | | |
| 24. Dorsolateral prefrontal cortex (L) | 20 | 44 | 36 | 2.98‡ |
| 25. Lateral prefrontal cortex (L) | 8 | 38 | 36 | 2.96‡ |
| 26. Inferior prefrontal cortex (L) | −6 | −28 | 50 | 2.26† |
| 27. Anterior cingulate | 38 | −6 | 24 | 3.12‡ |
| 28. Inferior anterior cingulate | 28 | −2 | 34 | 2.76‡ |
| Auditory | | | | |
| 29. Inferior prefrontal cortex (L) | −6 | 33 | 43 | 3.10‡ |
| 30. Anterior cingulate | 38 | 7 | 28 | 3.28‡ |
| 31. Inferior anterior cingulate | 28 | 11 | 31 | 3.04‡ |

Subtraction conditions: Generate words—Repeat visual words. See Table 5.2 legend for details of conventions used.

types of visual stimuli.[17,18] However, the regions of extrastriate occipital cortex in Table 5.2 have so far been activated only by the presentation of visual words. These regions may represent a network which codes for visual word form. Lesions near these regions sometimes cause pure alexia, that is, the inability to read words without other language deficits.[19,20] According to some cognitive models,[1,3,21] a visual word form would be generated by a cooperative computational network including feature, letter, and word levels. The multiple areas activated could represent the different levels of such a network.

For auditory processing, areas of activity were found bilaterally in primary auditory cortex, and left-lateralized in temporoparietal cortex, anterior superior temporal cortex, and inferior anterior cingulate cortex. The temporoparietal and anterior superior temporal regions have not been activated by presentation of non-word auditory stimuli.[22–24] The temporoparietal region is near the angular and supramarginal gyri, areas that have been associated in lesion studies with the phonological deficits,[25,26] and is a good candidate for a phonological coding region.

Areas related to motor output and articulatory coding are activated when words are repeated aloud (Table 5.3). In general, similar regions were activated for visual and auditory presentation. The activated regions included primary sensorimotor mouth cortex at a location corresponding to previous descriptions of sensorimotor topography.[27] Also activated were a set of premotor structures including a midline structure (supplementary motor area, SMA) and a set of activations around the sylvian fissure. The left sylvian regions are near Broca's area, a region often viewed as specifically serving language output.[7,8] But sylvian activation was also found in the right hemisphere, and this bilateral sylvian activation was also found when subjects were instructed to simply move their mouths and tongues, arguing against specialization of this region for speech output. Small lesions confined to classically defined Broca's area most frequently cause stuttering and oral apraxia rather than full-blown Broca's aphasia,[28] adding further support to the view that these regions are related to general motor, rather than language-specific output programming.

The association tasks activated two areas of cerebral cortex for both auditory and visual presentation. A left inferior frontal area was identified that almost certainly participates in processing for semantic association. The second area, anterior cingulate gyrus, appears to be part of an anterior attentional system engaged in selection for action. This localization of function was suggested by the performance of a converging experiment in which subjects monitored lists of words for members of a semantic category (such as monitoring for dangerous animals). In the semantic monitoring condition, left-frontal activation was strong and was unaffected by the number of targets in the list, supporting a semantic-processing function. Anterior-cingulate activation, however, was much stronger for lists containing many targets than for those with few, suggesting activation only when target selection was frequent. Similarly, rapid uncued movements and imagined movements activated anterior cingulate,[29] whereas monitoring very low-

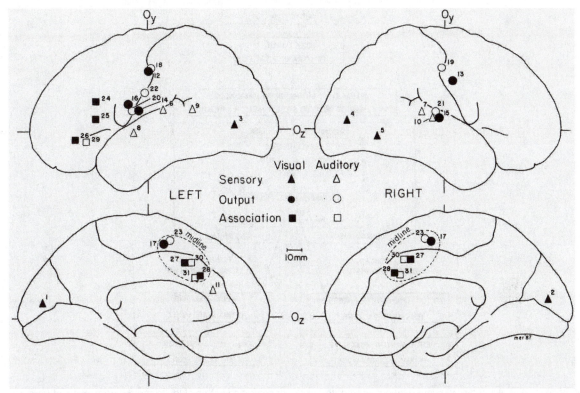

**FIGURE 5.1** ■ Schematic lateral (upper) and medial (lower) surface views of the left and right hemispheres with superimposed cortical activation foci. $O_y$ and $O_x$ are 0 reference planes. Each numbered symbol represents a cortical focus of activation, the number referring to Focus number in Tables 5.2–5.4. The key to the activation conditions is in the figure. Notice that for passive subtractions, there is no overlap between visual (filled triangle) and auditory (open triangle) sensory tasks. There is considerable overlap, however, between presentation modality for the association and output foci.

frequency non-linguistic visual stimuli (J. V. Pardo, P.T.F., M.E.R., unpublished observations) activated neither cingulate nor left-frontal cortex. In accord with these observations, lesions of the anterior cingulate reduced the frequency of movements and speech (akinetic mutism),[30–32] whereas left-frontal lesions produced deficits in word-fluency tests,[33] and in semantic-priming tasks.[34,35]

## Lexical Processing Models

What type of model do these results support? A serial single-route model has been widely accepted in clinical neurology.[7,8] In the serial model, access to semantics is by a phonological code, and access to output is by semantics. Thus, a visual word must be phonologically recoded (said to occur in the angular gyrus) and must establish semantic associations. (Wernicke's area in the posterior temporal lobe) before output coding. Our results are more consistent with multiple-route models in concept,[1–6,36–38] and are also quite inconsistent with the serial neurological model in detail.

First, there is no activation in any of our visual tasks near Wernicke's area or the angular gyrus in posterior temporal cortex. Visual information from occipital cortex appears to have access to output coding without undergoing phonological recoding in posterior temporal cortex. Second, tasks calling for semantic processing of single words activate frontal, rather than posterior, temporal regions. Third, sensory-specific information appears to have independent access to semantic codes and output codes; simple repetition (output tasks) of a presented word failed to activate the left-frontal semantic area (association tasks). A framework consistent with these results is presented in Figure 5.3.

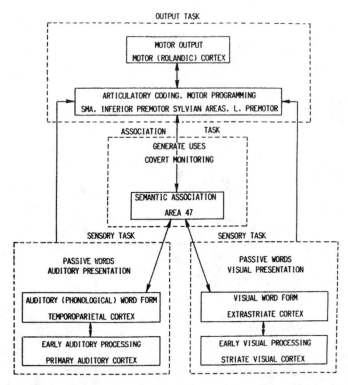

**FIGURE 5.3** ■ A general network relating some of the areas of activation in this study to the different levels of lexical processing. There are many alternative networks consistent with the conditions under which the areas are activated, but this arrangement represents a simple design consistent with our results, and some convergent experiments from other types of studies. The dashed boxes outline the different subtractions. The solid boxes outline possible levels of coding and associated anatomical areas of activation.

The combination of cognitive and neurobiological approaches, of which this study is an example, has given us information about the functional anatomy of perception, attention, motor control, and language. As these endeavours proceed, solutions to the problem of mind-brain interaction that have intrigued us for so long should be illuminated.

## ACKNOWLEDGMENT

This work was supported in part by the Office of Naval Research the National Institute of Health, and by the McDonnell Center for Higher Brain Function and the MacArthur Foundation.

## NOTES

1. LaBerge, D. & Samuels, J. *Cognitive Psychol. 6*, 293–323 (1974).
2. Rumelhart, D. E. & McClelland, J. L. *Psychol. Rev. 89*, 60–94 (1982).
3. Rumelhart, D. E. & McClelland, J. L. *Parallel Distributed Processing* Vols 1 and 2 (MIT, Cambridge, 1986).
4. Carr, T. H. & Pollatsek, A. *Reading Research* Vol. 5, 1–82 (Academic, New York, 1985).
5. Posner, M. I. in *Chronometric Explorations of Mind* (Posner, M. I. & Marin, O. S. M.). (Erlbaum, Englewood Height, NJ, 1978).
6. Coltheart, M. *Attention and Performance XI* (Erlbaum, Hilldale, NJ, 1985).
7. Geschwind, N. *Brain 88*, 237–294, 585–644 (1965).
8. Geschwind, N. *Scient. Am. 241*, 158–168 (1979).
9. Herscovitch, P., Markham, J., & Raichle, M. E. *J. Nucl. Med. 24*, 782–789 (1983).
10. Raichle, M. E., Martin, W. R. W., Herscovitch, P., Mintun, M. A., & Markham, J. *J. Nucl. Med. 24*, 790–798 (1983).
11. Sternberg, S. *Acta Psychol. 30*, 276–315 (1969).
12. Fox, P. T., Mintun, M. A., & Raichle, M. E. *J. Cerebral Blood Flow Metab.* (in the press).
13. Fox, P. T., Perimutter, J. S., & Raichle, M. E. *J. Comp. Assist. Tomogr. 9*, 141–153 (1985).
14. Tailarach, J. et al. *Atlas d'Anatomie Stereotaxique due Telencephale* (Masson, Cie., Park, 1967).
15. Mintun, M. A., Fox, P. T., & Raichle, M. E. *Soc. Neurosci. Abstr. 13*, 850 (1987).

16. Snedecor, G. W. & Corcoran, W. G. *Statistical Methods* (Iowa University Press, Iowa City, 1980).
17. Fox, P. T. et al. *Nature 323,* 806–809 (1986).
18. Fox, P. T., Miezin, F. M., Allman, J. M., Van Essen, D. C., & Raichle, M. E. *J. Neurosci. 7,* 913–922 (1987).
19. Damasio, A. R. & Damasio, H. *Neurology 33,* 1573–1583 (1983).
20. Henderson, V. W. *Brain Lang. 29,* 119–133 (1986).
21. McClelland, J. L. & Rumelhart, D. E. *Psychol. Rev. 88,* 375–407 (1981).
22. Lauter, J., Herscovitch, P., Formby, C., & Raichle, M. E. *Hearing Res. 20,* 199–205 (1985).
23. Mazziota, J. C., Phelps, M. E., Carson, R. E., & Kuhl, D. E. *Neurology 32,* 921–937 (1982).
24. Roland, P., Larson, B., Lassen, N. A., & Skinhoj, E. *J. Neurophysiol. 43,* 118–136 (1980).
25. Roeltgen, D. P., Sevush, S., & Heilman, K. M. *Neurology 33,* 755–765 (1983).
26. Shallice, T. *Brain 104,* 413–429 (1981).
27. Fox, P. T. & Raichle, M. E. *Proc. natn. Acad. Sci. U.S.A. 83,* 1140–1144 (1986).
28. Möhr, J. P. et al. *Neurology 28,* 311–324 (1978).
29. Fox, P. T., Pardo, J. V., Petersen, S. E., & Raichle, M. E. *Soc. Neurosci. Abstr. 13,* 1433 (1987).
30. Masdau, J. C., Schoene, W. C., & Fuhkenstein, H. *Neurology 28,* 1220–1223 (1978).
31. Barris, R. W. & Schuman, H. R. *Neurology 3,* 44–52 (1953).
32. Nielsen, J. M. & Jacobs, L. L. *Bull. L.A. Neurol Soc. 16,* 231–234 (1951).
33. Benton, A. L. *Neuropscychologia 6,* 53–60 (1968).
34. Milberg, W. & Blumstein, S. E. *Brain Lang. 14,* 371–385 (1981).
35. Milberg, W., Blumstein, S. E., & Dworetzky, B. *Brain Lang. 31,* 138–150 (1987).
36. Humphreys, G. W. & Evett, E. J. *Behav. Brain Sci. 8,* 689–740 (1985).
37. Shallice, T., McLeod, P., & Lewis, K. *Q. J. Exp. Psychol. 37A,* 507–532 (1985).
38. Coltheart, M., Davelaar, E., Jonasson, J., & Besner, D. in *Attention and Performance VI* (ed. Dornic, S.) (Academic, New York, 1977).

PART I

# Methods of Cognitive Psychology

## Discussion Questions

1. As Marr points out, there are a number of levels of analysis in understanding human cognition. One might argue that the major breakthroughs will come through studies that have a physiological basis, such as imaging or lesion studies. Discuss the relative importance of each of Marr's levels. For cognitive science, is there more constraint placed on the influence of an independent variable when an area of the brain is activated, as measured through imaging techniques versus an effect on response latency?

2. The results from Sternberg's memory scanning study appear quite counterintuitive. Describe why these results are counterintuitive, and why would humans evolve such a fast scanning operation?

3. Why is it important to develop computational models of cognition? What evidence is there that such models provide new insights into how humans actually perform a task? Is it reasonable to computationally model all aspects of human cognition?

4. What are some possible concerns about results from lesion studies? What, if anything, is wrong with the following statement: Dave has a lesion in the anterior portion of the left temporal lobe and has a particular difficulty in accessing meanings of words. Hence, this is where the processing of meaning of words takes place.

5. As you read the subsequent content sections, be on the alert in identifying which content area of study in cognitive psychology is most ripe for the convergence of each of the methods used in this section.

## Suggested Readings

L. R. Buckner and S. E. Peterson (1998, Neuroimaging, in W. Bechtel & G. Graham [Eds.], *A Companion to Cognitive Science*, pages 413–424, Blackwell Publishers Ltd., Oxford, U.K.) review some of the logic and methods used in neuroimaging and also provide some intriguing examples of how one can draw inferences about underlying cognitive processes from such studies.

F. F. Donders's classic paper (1968, Over de snelheid van psychische processen. Onderzoekingen gedaan in het Psychologisch Laboratorium der Utrechtsche Hoogeschool. *Tweede Reeks, 2,* 92–120. Translated by W. G. Koster, for *Attention and Performance*, Volume 2, which was published in *Acta Psychologia, 30,* 412–430) has been reprinted; it details how one can use chronometric methods to isolate speed of mental processes.

K. A. Ericsson (1998, Protocal analysis. In W. Bechtel & G. Graham (Eds.), A *Companion to Cognitive Science*, pages 425–432, Blackwell Publishers Ltd., Oxford, U.K.) provides a very interesting discussion of the utility of protocol analysis that shows the power of introspective verbal reports on elucidating cognitive processes.

M. J. Farah and J. L. McClelland (1991, A computational model of semantic memory impairment: Modality specificity and emergent category specificity, *Journal of Experimental Psychology: General, 120*, pages 339–357) discuss how a computational model of category-specific deficits can arise from breakdowns in the analysis of perceptual characteristics of items within categories.

C. D. Frith (1998, Deficits and pathologies. In W. Bechtel & G. Graham (Eds.), A *Companion to Cognitive Science*, pages 380–390, Blackwell Publishers Ltd., Oxford, U.K.) provides a short overview of individuals with neuropathological breakdowns and how the distinct behavioral patterns of these individuals can provide constraints for theories of normal cognitive functioning.

R. S. Lockhart (2000, Methods of memory research. In E. Tulving and F. I. M. Craik [Eds.], *The Oxford Handbook of Memory*, pages 45–57, Oxford University Press) provides a nice introductory review to the methods used in memory research.

D. E. Meyer, A. M. Osman, D. E. Irwin, and S. Yantis (1988, Modern mental chronometry. *Biological Psychology, 26*, 3–67) provide a remarkable review of the methods cognitive psychologists have developed to use response latency to measure cognitive operations.

D. E. Rumelhart, J. L. McClelland, and the PDP Research Group (1986, *Parallel Distributed Processing: Explorations in the Microstructure of Cognition, Volume 1: Foundations*, MIT Press, Cambridge, MA) provides, historically the first full treatment of the details and utility of parallel distributed processing systems as applied to a number of distinct domains.

R. Sun (1998, Artificial intelligence. In W. Bechtel & G. Graham (Eds.), *A Companion to Cognitive Science*, pages 341–351, Blackwell Publishers Ltd., Oxford, U.K.) provides a short and useful introduction to the methods that researchers use in the area of artificial intelligence.

PART II

# Pattern Recognition

# Introduction to Part II: Pattern Recognition

Recognizing sensory input as a chair, face, or an auditory word would at first glance appear to be one of the simplest of cognitive operations. We are able to accomplish pattern recognition quite effortlessly and in most cases are highly accurate. Because of the apparent simplicity of such an operation, one might assume that the scientific study of pattern recognition must be well worked out. Clearly, pattern recognition processes would seem to pale in comparison to the complexity of higher-level human cognition such as problem solving, language comprehension, and decision making. Somewhat surprisingly, one finds that even simple pattern recognition is a very difficult and interesting topic to scientifically study. Fortunately, researchers soon began to develop the tools to chip away at understanding the processes involved in pattern recognition.

Ulric Neisser's (1967) chapter on pattern recognition truly energized the field in identifying the problems that one must address in an adequate model of pattern recognition. For example, a major problem is simply the variability in the patterns that our senses receive and yet the constancy in the pattern recognition system. Consider, for example, looking at a chair as one is walking around a room. Even minor movement of the body, the head, or the eyes provides a change in the sensory input. Clearly, simple models that have only stored patterns that serve as matches for the stimulus-driven information (template models) have some problems in accommodating the amazing fluency of our pattern recognition systems.

There would seem to be an endless number of such templates. But what is the alternative to such models? Here, Neisser provides converging evidence for the utility of features in recognizing patterns. These are primitive building blocks for patterns, such as diagonal lines, intersections, oblique patterns, and so on, and are combined en route to recognizing a more complex pattern such as a letter.

Neisser's overview of Selfridge's Pandemonium model of letter recognition provided a critical analysis of the principles involved in cognitive modeling. Here, one can see that there are distinct levels in the model, that is, features, letters, decision systems. In addition, there are both serial stages from the features to the decision components and also parallel components, reflecting the fact that multiple detectors at the feature and letter level are simultaneously receiving input and changing their current state of energy. These principles are widely used in cognitive psychology and are still the basic building blocks in many models. Ultimately, Neisser argues that simple sensory-driven models, bottom-up models, are inadequate to explain the data in pattern recognition, and notes the importance of top-down memory-based influences. If we return to our chair example, one of the reasons the pattern is so easily recognized is that chairs are likely to be perceived in a given context, thereby driving up their activation, via top-down influences. Again, the notion of both stimulus-driven and memory-driven combinations of energy are central to many cognitive models of pattern recognition.

Equally important to his theoretical analysis was Neisser's integration of the tools that researchers could use to provide empirical constraints on the potential models of pattern recognition. He reviews the influential work of developmental psychologists (e.g., Gibson, 1965), important studies in the emerging field of mental chronometry (measuring the speed of mental operations), and intriguing work in animal learning. Moreover, he provides an excellent integration of the single-cell recording literature that provides some metrics of what neurons are doing when a stimulus is presented to a visual field, which ultimately led to the Nobel Prize-winning work by Hubel and Wiesel (1962). Given the theoretical and empirical thrust of Neisser's chapter on pattern recognition, it is not surprising that it is still an excellent read for an introduction to principles that are central to current views.

At the same time that there were breakthroughs in visual pattern recognition, there was an equally rich literature developing in the area of speech recognition. It turns out that human speech pattern recognition appears to be even more difficult to account for than pattern recognition in the visual domain. Consider the amazing ability that people have in quickly adjusting to the different auditory input across speakers, speakers with food in their mouth, speakers who are whispering, and so on. Each of these produces dramatic changes in the physical characteristics of the acoustic input, and yet we somehow effortlessly recognize and comprehend speech. Moreover, in speech, there are no breaks between words that indicate when one word is ending and the next begins, even though people believe there are short silent pauses.

Interestingly, just as visual features were needed to account for visual pattern recognition, researchers in speech recognition recognized the need for a type of primitive feature in speech perception, known as a phonetic feature. For example, the beginning sounds of the stimuli *ba* and *pa* are produced by bringing the lips together and abruptly releasing air; hence these are called bilabial stops. *Da* and *ta* are produced at a different point, by bringing the end of the tongue up to the alveolar ridge at the top of the mouth; hence they are called alveolar stops. Interestingly, although produced at a different location in the mouth, *ba* and *pa* have some similarity and *da* and *ta* have some similarity. Specifically, both *ba* and *da* are voiced sounds and *pa* and *ta* are voiceless sounds. Voicing refers to the synchronicity of the release of air and the vibrations of the vocal cords. For voiced sounds the release of the air occurs simultaneously with the vocal cord vibrations, whereas for voiceless sounds there is a tiny delay between the two events.

The Eimas and Corbit (1973) paper provides an excellent overview of the notion of phonetic feature detectors and also discusses the underlying mechanism. In particular, the authors show how one can use a type of habituation paradigm to provide evidence for the existence of phonological detectors. (Neisser also discusses the utility of using the fatiguing paradigm in the visual domain in his chapter.) In particular, because neural systems will fatigue through repeated stimulation, Eimas and Corbit were interested in whether they could fatigue a featural detector such as voicing. So, they repeatedly exposed subjects to a particular phonetic

segment and found that the underlying phonetic feature was fatigued as reflected in a change in the subject's discrimination threshold. This paper provides an overview of some of the basic speech perception principles, along with fine-tuned experimental work that distinguishes alternative theoretical perspectives. The area of speech perception has afforded considerable insights into the problems of developing a model of this amazing capacity available to humans. It is still the case that modern-day computer-assisted speech-recognition systems are not in the same league as the power of the human speech-recognition system.

We close this section on pattern recognition with two relatively short, and recent, papers that are quite clever in taking novel approaches to this topic. Simons and Levin (1998) ask a question concerning how much information is actually processed during normal visual perception and how deeply that information is processed. Our intuitions suggest that we perceive a very rich visual world at any given point in time. However, Simons and Levin demonstrate that subjects actually have much less information than our intuitions would suggest. For example, participants could not recognize the face of an individual who asked them for directions to a building on campus, even though the request occurred a few seconds earlier. The processes investigated in the Simons and Levin study are very similar to the processes that allow film editors to get away with mistakes such as scenes where people switch positions, they have different clothing, or even new objects mysteriously appear or disappear across scenes. The phenomenological experience of richly processing visual information appears at least in part to be a constructive aspect of visual perception.

The Tong et al. paper also deals with intriguing aspects of the phenomenological experience of pattern recognition, that is, binocular rivalry. A basic problem for the visual system is to somehow coordinate the perception of a single world even though it is being perceived by two eyes separated in space. Typically, this process works quite well, producing a stable world. In binocular rivalry experiments by Tong et al., one stimulus (a face) was presented to one eye and a second stimulus (a house) was simultaneously presented to the other eye. In such situations, people perceive either a house or a face at a given point in time and these percepts switch back and forth across time, even though the external stimulus is identical. Tong et al. were interested in the nature of the brain activity during the two phenomenological experiences. Is it comparable to a situation where two stimuli are presented successively across time to the two eyes? In order to address this issue, they used functional magnetic resonance imaging to provide an estimate of the brain activity in targeted areas that were already known to be critical for face and house processing. The results indicated that the neural activity in the targeted areas during binocular rivalry experiments were the same areas that were activated when one or the other stimulus was presented alone. The Tong et al. paper is an excellent example of the use of modern brain-imaging techniques to better understand the nature of phenomenological experience in visual perception and reflects a growing reliance on this type of tool to provide constraints in understanding human cognition.

## REFERENCES

Eimas, P. D., & Corbit, J. (1973). Selective adaptation of linguistic feature detectors. *Cognitive Psychology, 4,* 99–109.

Gibson, E. J. (1965). Learning to read. *Science, 148,* 1066–1072.

Hubel, D. H., & Wiesel, T. N. (1962). Receptive fields, binocular interaction and functional architecture in the cat's visual cortex. *Journal of Physiology, 160,* 106–154.

Neisser, U. (1967). *Cognitive Psychology* (chap. 3, pp. 46–85). Englewood Cliffs, NJ: Prentice-Hall.

Simons, D. J., & Levin, D. T. (1998). Failure to detect changes to people during a real-world interaction. *Psychonomic Bulletin & Review, 5,* 644–649.

Tong, F., Nakayama, K., Vaughan, J. T., & Kanwisher, N. (1998). Binocular rivalry and visual awareness in human extrastriate cortex. *Neuron, 21,* 753–759.

# Pattern Recognition

Ulric Neisser

The problem of pattern recognition, or stimulus equivalence, is ubiquitous in psychology. This reading considers the solutions that have been proposed from the time of Gestalt psychology to the present, including recent techniques developed for computer programs. The two main theoretical approaches are "template-matching," in which each new input is compared with a standard, and "feature-analysis," in which the presence of particular parts or particular properties is decisive. The various theories are examined in the light of relevant observations, including recognition tests with displaced, rotated, or ill-defined figures; studies of decision time and visual search; stopped-image experiments, single-cell physiological recording; and certain developmental studies of visual discrimination. It is concluded that recognition is mediated, in part, by a hierarchy of "feature analyzers."

By some process that operates on iconically-stored information, the subject "reads out" a letter—he recodes a visual pattern into an essentially auditory one. What can we say about this process? How does the subject know an *A* when he sees one?

The obvious answer, that he knows because it looks like an *A*, is not very helpful and may even be wrong. One could argue with equal force that it looks like an *A* only because he knows what it is. Neither statement exhausts the issue, because not all *A*s look alike. There are capital *A*s and small *A*s and elite *A*s and pica *A*s and script *A*s and block

*A*s; large *A*s and small *A*s; slanted *A*s and straight *A*s. There are configurations, like the one in Figure 6.1, which look like an *A* in certain contexts and like an *H* in others. Finally, there are hand-printed and handwritten *A*s, whose variety is truly astonishing. A few genuine hand-printed specimens are shown enlarged in Figure 6.2. They are all recognizable; no subject misidentified any of them in an actual experiment (see Neisser & Weene, 1960, where the method of collecting such specimens is described). Nevertheless, they are quite diverse. If all of these are *A*s "because they look alike," we must consider what process creates

**FIGURE 6.1** ■ The effect of context on letter-recognition (after Selfridge, 1955).

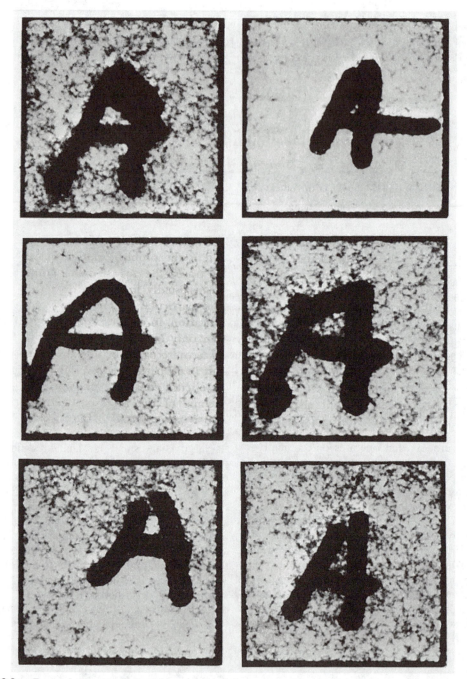

**FIGURE 6.2** ■ Recognizable specimens of hand-printed *A*s.

their similarity. And if they look alike only because they are classified as *A*s, we must consider what mechanism might do the classifying.

This problem has many names. In the language of behaviorism, it is a matter of stimulus generalization or of stimulus equivalence. In the terminology of Gestalt psychology, it is the problem of contact between perceptual process and memory trace: the so-called "Höffding step." Among philosophers, the question is usually formulated in terms of "universals" and of "abstraction from particulars." For Bruner and his associates, it is the problem of categorization. In computer technology, it is called "character recognition" when only letters and numbers are to be identified, or more generally "pattern recognition." It does not arise only in tachistoscopic perception but in all perception, and not only with *A*s but with all sets of stimuli that elicit a consistent response.

The present chapter surveys some of the available data on human pattern recognition, in an effort to relate them to the theories that have been proposed. The first section below considers the nature of the problem, rather briefly. Then, two further sections deal with some of the empirical observations that are too frequently ignored in current speculation. After a brief theoretical excursion to consider the simplest possible models, those involving "template-matching," empirical findings appear again in a section on decision-time and search experiments. After the reader has been introduced to some widely used ideas by way of a model of visual search, the main theoretical review deals with Hebb's "part" theory and the "feature" theories of Bruner, Selfridge, and Sutherland. Since even these approaches leave many problems unsolved, the next chapter will take up some further notions, especially focal attention and figural synthesis.

## The Nature of the Problem

The problem of pattern recognition has been formulated here in connection with tachistoscopic experiments, but it must be dealt with in general terms. Whenever a stimulus evokes a single response consistently, we can say that it is being "recognized." The problem for theory is to describe the processes of recognition. It is a difficult problem because many different stimuli may be equiva-

lent in producing the same reaction. Following Bruner, Goodnow, and Austin (1956), I will treat the consistent response as a category and use "categorization" as a synonym for "pattern recognition."

This does not mean that either of these words is a synonym for "perception." Bruner's claim that "all perception is necessarily the end-product of a categorization process" (1957b, p. 124) must be rejected. Many cognitive processes, such as iconic storage itself, do not involve categorizing to any serious extent. Of course, the nervous system has only a finite capacity to discriminate, so very similar inputs must often give rise to the same iconic pattern. In a sense, one might say that these are "categorized together." This use of the term makes it uninteresting, however, since even a photographic plate is categorial in the same way. There is little value in speaking of "pattern recognition" or "categories" unless genuinely diverse inputs lead to a single output. A stage of cognition which preserves the shape, size, position, and other formal characteristics of the stimulus should be called "literal," or perhaps "analog," but not "categorial." The transient icon is probably "analog" in this sense, and some of the more permanent forms of visual memory may also be.

It is true that categorization is involved whenever a subject *names* what he sees. But not all responding is naming, and Bruner's claim that "neither language, nor the tuning that one could give an organism to direct any other form of overt response, could provide an account (of perceptual experience) save in generic or categorial terms" (1957b, p. 125) should not go unquestioned. Visual tracking, drawing, and beating a rhythm are examples of overt responses that may sometimes be analog instead of categorial. This is not a mere matter of definition. The act of drawing often *is* categorial, reflecting only stereotypes and expectations instead of the real form of the stimulus. Yet it hardly follows that all drawing is of this sort, or that the interplay between categorial and literal processes cannot be studied. Even where tachistoscopic recognition of letters is concerned, some reservations are appropriate. The task obviously does demand rapid categorization: the subject must assign one of 26 names to each figure before the icon has faded. Nevertheless, we should bear in mind that this may not be typical of all, or even most, cognitive activity. Not all situations demand classification so explicitly as does a choice among 26 well-defined alternatives; not all classification, even when it occurs, is made under time pressure.

Within the letter-recognition situation, the main theoretical problem is that of "stimulus equivalence." How does it happen that so many different visual configurations are all called "A"? If this were not the case, theorizing would be relatively simple. Even then, however—even if every *A* were an exact foveal replica of a centrally stored prototype—we would still find that one critical step demanded a theoretical explanation. A new *A* presented to the eye would still be only a peripheral event; recognition requires that it make contact with appropriate centrally stored information.

It was this step which the Gestalt psychologists called the "Höffding function" (Köhler, 1940; Rock, 1962), after the nineteenth-century Danish psychologist who saw it as a necessary refinement of simple association theory (Höffding, 1891). To say that the sight of bread gives rise to the idea of butter "by virtue of previous association," as was (and is) so commonly assumed, is to miss a crucial step. The present sight of bread, as a stimulus or a perceptual process, is not generally associated with butter; only stored memories of bread are associated in this way. Hence we must assume that the present event is somehow identified as bread first, i.e., that it makes contact with "memory traces" of earlier experiences with bread. Only then can the preexisting association be used. Association cannot be effective without prior pattern recognition.

According to the Gestalt psychologists, a very simple mechanism would suffice for the Höffding step if only all glimpses of bread (or all *A*s) were alike, even to their position on the retina. In that case the "memory trace" or central representation could be an exact copy of the perceptual event that had occurred previously. It would be "aroused" or "contacted" by overlap; perhaps all of its neurons would be simultaneously fired by their mates in the perceptual system. Such an arrangement is depicted in Figure 6.3a.

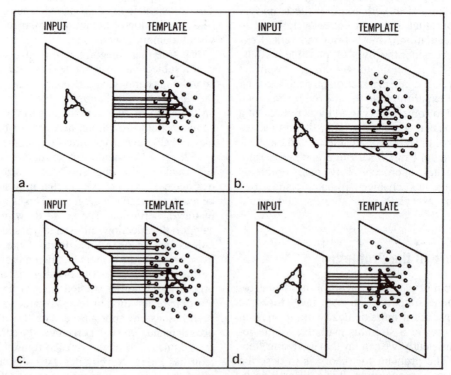

**FIGURE 6.3** ■ Problems of template-matching. Figure 6.3a shows an input which matches the template; 6.3b, a mismatch due to change of position; 6.3c, a change of size; 6.3d, change of orientation.

This solution (which the Gestalt psychologists rejected in its simple form) is one example of an approach to pattern recognition in terms of "prototypes," or "canonical forms," that is most often called *template-matching* (Selfridge & Neisser, 1960; Uhr, 1963; Gibson, 1963). A new figure is identified by noting its coincidence, or congruence, with a basic model. Template-matching is not uncommon in daily life. To determine if a particular fingerprint was made by one of his suspects, a detective may superimpose it, successively, on the prerecorded prints of each one until he obtains a match. Even then, the new print and the standard will probably not be quite identical: the sample will be smudged or distorted or partially incomplete. Nevertheless, the detective will be satisfied as long as the match is reasonably good, and better than any other. In a sense, he computes a correlation coefficient between the two patterns and asks if it is near 1.00.

Höffding observed that simple template-matching has some obvious inadequacies as a theory of pattern recognition. Ordinary experience suggests that we can recognize a form even in a new retinal position (Figure 6.3b) and despite size changes (Figure 6.3c) or rotations (Figure 6.3d), although any of these operations must destroy the congruence necessary for recognition. Thus one must choose between elaborating the template model considerably and abandoning it altogether. As Hebb has pointed out, "it is hard to reconcile an unlocalized afferent process with a structural (and hence localized) mnemonic trace" (1949, p. 15).

Unlike the Gestalt psychologists, who never gave up the notion of templates altogether, Hebb himself chose the second alternative. To him, and no doubt to most of those concerned with the problem today, it seems likely that patterns are identified in terms of their "attributes." These attributes may just be the lines and angles which make up the figure—this is Hebb's interpretation—or they may be more complex. In the "feature" theories of Selfridge (1959) and Sutherland (1959), figures are identified in terms of attributes like "concavity" and "horizontality," which are characteristics of the whole rather than simple parts. Such theories have many advantages over those based on templates, but they too will need considerable elaboration before they explain the observed facts.

## Empirical Observations: Displacement and Rotation

There is little doubt that familiar patterns are recognized no matter where they happen to fall on the retina of the eye. This creates a problem for any template theory: how is the right prototype to be found? To be sure, we might assume that any familiar form must *already* have fallen on every conceivable position of an adult's retina, leaving so many templates behind that contact with one becomes inevitable. Whatever the plausibility of this approach may be, it will hardly work if the pattern to be recognized is unique. But are unfamiliar patterns indeed recognizable in new positions? If a new form is exposed in one retinal locus, will it subsequently appear familiar, and be properly named, if it is presented to another?

In general, the answer is "yes." Köhler (1940) cites an experiment by Becher which demonstrates this point; Wallach and Austin (1954) mention four others which went unpublished because the experimenters had been trying to prove the contrary. Undiscouraged, Wallach and Austin carried out an experiment of their own, trying to find at least some small effect of retinal position on recognition. Their critical stimulus was Figure 6.4, which tends to be seen as a "dog" when presented horizontally and as a "chef" when presented vertically. Given at 45°, it becomes an ambiguous figure. In general, a subject who has seen a "biased"—i.e., unambiguous—version of such a figure tends afterwards to see the ambiguous one with the same bias. Wallach and Austin tried to use this "aftereffect" as a sensitive index of pattern recognition. How will the ambiguous pattern be seen if both unambiguous versions have already been presented to the subject, each at a different retinal position? Will it be "controlled" by the previous exposure which happened to share the same retinal locus? They

**FIGURE 6.4** ■ Ambiguous figure used by Wallach and Austin (1954) and Rock (1956).

found this to be the case and concluded that "traces" are somehow "localized" in the nervous system.

Although this result does seem to show some effect of input position, it should not be given too much weight. There are many reasons why a test stimulus might have been more readily interpreted in terms of the pattern that had appeared on the same side of the visual field than of the contralateral one. They share the same relations with the visually given framework, and may even share specific feelings of eyestrain. If such explanations seem *ad hoc*, we must remember that the persistence of recognition despite changes in the locus of the input is a far-ranging and biologically useful principle, which we should not abandon lightly. Its wide generality can be illustrated by a familiar psychological demonstration. Take off your shirt and ask someone to trace a letter of the alphabet on your back with his finger. You will have little difficulty in identifying the letter he marks out, although it is quite unlikely that such a pattern ever appeared on your back before! This indifference to locus, and even to modality, is a remarkable phenomenon. In many ways, it seems closely akin to the transferability of motor skills. Having learned to make letters with a pencil in your hand, you can also make them, perhaps a little awkwardly, with one held in your teeth or your toes or even the crook of your elbow. We will consider whether these motor equivalences may have the same basis as the perceptual ones.

While the process of pattern recognition may indeed be indifferent to the *locus* of the input, its *orientation* seems to be more critical. Everyday experience testifies to the perceptual changes which can be produced by rotation. Turn a square by 45° and you get a diamond instead; rotate a page of this book by 90° and you will find it difficult to read. The phenomenal effects of visual rotations have often been discussed (e.g., Arnheim, 1954, pp. 65–70). However, there was little serious experimentation in this area before the intricate series of studies by Rock (1956, also Rock & Heimer, 1957). Using the "chef-dog" figure (Figure 6.4) in the manner of Wallach and Austin, he found that rotation of the retinal image does not prevent recognition of relatively simple figures. They can be easily identified despite any change of orientation. However, the results suggest that this is only true as long as the subject knows which

side of the figure is supposed to be "the top." Phenomenal orientation is all-important. An ambiguous figure tilted at 45° is *not* identified in terms of a previously exposed upright version *unless* the subject knows (through instructions) or perceives (with the aid of a tilted framework) that such a rotation has occurred. On the other hand, recognition encounters no difficulty if the head, and thus the retina, is itself turned 90°. This is apparently because the subject, aware of his own head movement, still knows which part of the stimulus pattern is really "up." Interestingly enough, a concurrent rotation of the stimulus, which together with the head movement actually leaves retinal orientation unchanged, *does* impair recognition—again, unless the subject knows about it.

In short, while it is true that patterns can be recognized despite rotation, this accomplishment depends on a rather complex mechanism. The perceiver must isolate from the figure, or construct within the figure, a directed axis of orientation which defines some part as the top and another as the bottom. Only then is he able to identify it as pertaining to an earlier pattern which was also specifically oriented. Without this intervening stage of processing, recognition may not occur. These findings deserve careful consideration by pattern-recognition theorists, especially those who have been tempted by simple accounts based on peripheral neurology.

Rock's principle of phenomenal orientation holds only for what he called "simple" figures; it breaks down for reading, and for the identification of partial and ill-defined patterns. In the Höffding tradition, Rock and Heimer regard this as proof that "traces preserve their original orientation" after all (1957, p. 510). To me, it seems more likely that these tasks are affected because they involve eye movements. To read a page turned by 90°, the eyes would have to move up-and-down rather than left-to-right—not an easy change to make in such an overlearned motor skill. This explanation makes it easy to understand why a rotation of 180° (turning the page upside down) is less troublesome than one of 90°. The residual difficulty at 180° may appear because the necessary saccadic movements are then in the opposite direction.

Kolers, Eden, and Boyer (1964) have studied the effect of various rotations and transformations on reading speed. Rotation of the whole line or

a. Each letter is inverted with left-right order unchanged.

b. Here the whole line has been turned through 180 degrees.

c. detrevni ton era yeht tub tfel ot thgir morf nur srettel ehT

**FIGURE 6.5** ■ Transformations of text like those used by Kolers, Eden, and Boyer (1964). Figure 6.5a shows inversion of individual letters; 6.5b the inversion of the line as a whole; 6.5c, a left-right reversal.

page through 180° (Figure 6.5b) is surprisingly easy to cope with. Kolers has pointed out that the Greeks once used a style of writing called *Boustrephedon* in which every other line was rotated in this way! Other transformations, such as arraying the letters from right-to-left (Figure 6.5c) or inverting each one individually (Figure 6.5a), produce much greater difficulties. On first consideration, these results seem paradoxical. Figure 6.5b involves *both* inversion (from top-to-bottom) *and* reversion (from left-to-right), yet it is easier than the lines which contain only a "single" transformation! However, such a finding makes perfect sense from Rock's viewpoint. Figure 6.5b is the only transform in which all the letters have the same relationship to each other, and to a phenomenally given "top" of the line, as in normal text. This relationship, and not retinal orientation itself, is what distinguishes 6 from 9 or u from n. When it is disrupted, reading becomes much more difficult.

However, it would be misleading to break off the discussion at this point. Other observations with rotated figures seem to carry a different implication or at least confuse matters considerably. For the most part, these are observations on children. It has been remarked (for example, by Arnheim, 1954) that preschoolers often look at pictures without bothering to turn them right-side-up, and draw letters in reversed or inverted form. This suggests that their perceptual processes are relatively more "indifferent to orientation" than those of adults. Yet it would certainly be hard to believe that the complex reorienting mechanisms used by Rock's subjects would be still more effective in children! Moreover, Ghent and her collaborators (Ghent, 1960; Ghent & Bernstein, 1961) have shown clearly that children are *not* good at identifying rotated figures. Even though this book is not primarily concerned with developmental

psychology, a short digression to deal with these apparent paradoxes cannot be avoided.

The important distinction to be made here is between active compensation for rotation, which Rock demonstrated in adults, and the simple failure to distinguish between two orientations of a figure. Both can lead to the same overt result. After all, many properties of figures remain invariant no matter how they have been turned. A rotated A still has a sharp point, a rotated P still has a closed loop, a Y still has a central acute angle, a C remains rounded. If recognition is based on the presence of critical features such as these, rather than on templates, it can also display "indifference to rotation." A subject who identified all rounded letters as Cs would recognize a C in any orientation whatever, though of course he could not distinguish it from an O. If such simple and "orientation-proof" features are particularly important for pattern recognition in children, a number of superficially conflicting observations can be understood.

One paradigmatic experiment in this area is that of Gibson, Gibson, Pick, and Osser (1962). The children in their study were given a standard form like those at the left of Figure 6.6 and were to pick out any other forms that were "exactly like" it from a row that included at least one standard as well as the numerous transformations shown in the figure. The focus of Gibson et al.'s interest was on errors of commission: What kinds of incorrect stimuli would the children select? It turned out that some transforms, like the "perspective" shifts in columns 10 and 11 of Figure 6.6, were erroneously chosen by many children of all ages. Others, like the breaks and closures illustrated in columns 12 and 13, were rarely mistaken for the standards by any subject. However, the rotations (in columns 5–9) showed a clear developmental trend. Preschool children found them difficult to

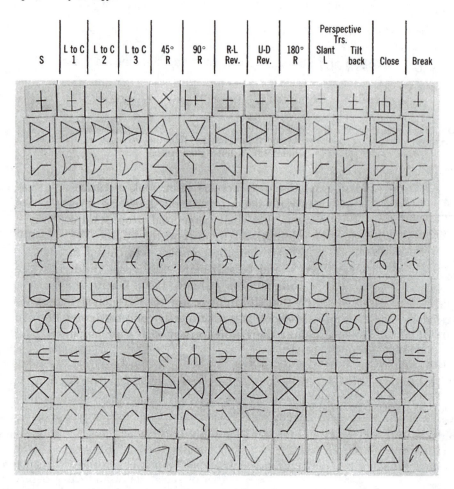

**FIGURE 6.6** ■ Stimuli used by Gibson, Gibson, Pick, and Osser (1962).

distinguish from the standards, while older children had much less trouble.

This result fits well with the general observations about preschool indifference to rotation and makes it clear that a confusion, a lack of discrimination, is involved. We need only suppose that the younger children are liable to notice just those features and properties that fail to distinguish between a pattern and some rotational transform of it. Even when these children make a correct match, they do so on the basis of simpler processes than an adult would use.

On such an interpretation, Ghent's findings are no longer paradoxical. She briefly displayed a single figure, having warned the children that it might be upside down in some cases. Afterward,

they were asked to pick it out of an array of figures that were all right-side-up. With both meaningful (Ghent, 1960) and meaningless (Ghent & Bernstein, 1961) stimuli, the children made more errors when the first figure was inverted than when its orientation matched that of the subsequent display. And, especially, in the first study, younger children made more errors than their older schoolmates. We may assume that here too, perception was fragmentary, and that the partial cues obtained in the brief exposure often led the children astray. The "bottom" of a rotated figure may have looked like the bottom of some other figure in the set of alternatives, for example. Adults in such an experiment might have noticed more during the brief flash, might have reconstructed the figure as a whole, and might have "rotated it mentally" before comparing it with the standard, as they did in Rock's experiment. Such complex processing was apparently beyond the capacity of most of the children. In this situation, then, fragmentary perception often prevented the children from matching a stimulus to its rotated twin correctly; in the experiment of Gibson et al., fragmentary perception led to frequent confusions between them.

In a tachistoscopic study with adults, Mandes and Ghent (1963) showed that single figures are harder to recognize if the critical feature is at the bottom or at the right than if it is near the top or left. Their subjects did not know what orientation any particular figure would have. This finding is reminiscent of Bryden's (1960) work. He showed that the left end of a string of figures is better reported than the right. Bryden went further, however, and showed that his tendency can be reversed if the subjects are told to scan from right-to-left. Mandes and Ghent might have made the same finding if they had used similar instructions. Such results, like those of Rock and Heimer (1957), show again that what matters for adults is how the subject "takes" the figure. Only where eye movements are involved, or at least highly overlearned scanning directions (Bryden's subjects could not reverse their letter scanning), are adults unable to compensate for rotations that they know about.

So much for displacement and rotation; what about size? It would seem to be just as important a variable as orientation, but there are very few relevant experiments. Ordinary experience does suggest that retinal size, at least, is of little importance for recognition. Hebb (1949, p. 91) assumes that this is true, buttressing his argument with animal experiments. Unquestionably, a person who stood 3 feet away when he was introduced to you will be recognizable in a fresh glance when he is across the room, his retinal image much diminished. But in such a situation there are many other cues, and you would probably "recognize" him even with his back turned. A study of this problem with the reversible-figure method of Rock (1956) and Wallach and Austin (1954) would be extremely useful. My hunch is that the results would bear out the principles established by Rock and Heimer (1957) for orientation. If the subject *knows* that a present figure has been somehow enlarged with respect to a past one, recognition should be easy; without this knowledge it may not occur.

What is the relation of all this to the familiar constancies of shape and size? The letters on this page keep their phenomenal shapes even when you tilt the book backward and skew the retinal image; they stay the same apparent size despite great changes in the retinal projection when the book is moved back and forth. Is this because they have already been recognized? Although we cannot go into the intricacies of perceptual constancy here, it is clear that the best answer is "no." Even unfamiliar objects would keep their shapes and sizes through such transformations. Instead, it seems that the constancies operate *before* recognition, to make recognition possible. This is not an invariable principle, however: there have been occasional demonstrations that size or shape judgments are affected by an identification already made.

## Empirical Observations: Ill-Defined Categories and Expectancies

In theoretical accounts of pattern recognition, easily specified transformations like displacement and rotation have played the most prominent part. Any such transform leads to what may be called a "well-defined category." The analogy here is to Minsky's definition of a "well-defined problem" as one which provides "some systematic way to decide when a proposed solution is acceptable" (1961, p. 9). By this definition, the group of all patterns produced by rotating a given figure through any number of degrees is a well-defined category: there are fixed criteria for deciding whether any new figure belongs to it. But, just as many interesting problems turn out to be "ill-defined" (see Reitman, 1964, 1965, for discussion of this point), so also do most categories lack clear-cut boundaries and formulations. The As in Figure 6.2 are unmistakable, but none of them is a simple transformation of any other, or of a standard. A little reflection shows that an *A* is actually a difficult thing to define.

Ill-defined categories are the rule, not the exception, in daily life. The visual distinctions between dogs and cats, or between beauty and ugliness, are ill-defined, just like the conceptual differences between creative science and hack work, or health and neurosis. So are the EEG patterns which indicate a particular stage of sleep, the X-ray shadows which suggest a tumor, the style of painting which identifies a Picasso, or the features which continue to characterize the face of a friend through the years.

In all such cases, there are two possibilities. The simple alternative is that an apparently "ill-defined" category is actually definable by some feature of the situation that has escaped the investigator's attention. The much-publicized work of the ethologists (e.g., Tinbergen, 1951) has shown that this is often true in animals. The situation which elicits fighting in the stickleback fish is no vaguely defined "hostile act," but a red spot of a certain kind. Similar discoveries are sometimes made about human perception, as when Hess (1965) recently discovered that the attractiveness of a face depends in part on whether its pupils are dilated.

However, much as these simple solutions might appeal to the cognitive theorist, it is clear that they will not work for many important categories. Attempts at mechanical pattern recognition have made this obvious. There is real need for a mechanical or computable way to distinguish among EEG patterns, for example, and a great deal of sophisticated effort has been expended to develop systems with this capacity, but no satisfactory ones have been built. Their failure is eloquent testimony that the criteria involved are anything but simple. Much effort has also gone into the recognition of handwritten or hand-printed letters. Some of these programs have achieved considerable success, but only with the aid of considerable complexity. The mechanisms by which they succeed will be discussed later. The point to be noted here is that genuinely ill-defined categories do exist and are regularly used by people in their daily activities. Any serious account of human pattern recognition will have to deal with them.

Assignment to a category is not always the endpoint of a cognitive process; it can be the beginning. Theories of pattern recognition do not only have to explain what mechanisms might lead to identification, but also how prior identification might affect these mechanisms. The stimulus which is identified as "13" when the subject is expecting numbers becomes "B" when he expects letters (Bruner & Minturn, 1955); the pattern which is readily described as an "S" on one occasion may be called a "5" or a "snake" or even a "meaningless blur" on others, or go unnoticed altogether. These are the familiar effects of "set" or "expectancy." Some "set" effects were ascribed to prior-

ity of encoding, following the argument of Harris and Haber (1963). The same factor may be at work more generally. In terms of a template theory, one might suppose that the subject who expects numbers tries out "13" before he gets around to "B" and becomes somehow committed to it. The same principle could be used in an attribute model: The subject may look for different features when he is set for numbers than when he expects letters.

Nevertheless, it seems wise to stress the relationship between sets and ill-defined categories here. We have seen how many forms the letter *A* can take; does a subject who expects "a letter" have all of them in readiness, along with every version of *B, C, D, . . . Z?* Evidently, what he has in readiness is an ill-defined category. The same conclusion follows from an experiment by Leeper (1935), who asked subjects to identify figures such as those of Figure 6.7. He found that verbal cues like "It is a musical instrument" were powerful aids to pattern recognition. Note that the figure at the lower right, which remains difficult even with this hint, becomes easy to organize if you are specifically told that it represents a violin. Yet "violin" itself is an ill-defined category, so far as its visual properties are concerned: What exactly do violins look like?

A more recent experiment by Bugelski and Alampay (1961) shows how such effects can be induced even without explicit verbal instructions. After showing several pictures of animals, they presented subjects with the ambiguous "rat-man" for identification (Figure 6.8). Most saw it as a rat, while subjects without special pretraining generally see the man instead. It is evident that the experimental group had formed a "set" for animals, ill-defined though such a category may be.

Categorial sets do not always succeed in affecting visual organization. When he used a more complex figure that could be given two alternative interpretations, both relatively compelling, Leeper (1935) found verbal cues to be ineffective, while another procedure—the use of appropriately similar *visual* presentations—had a marked effect. This represents not merely a "set" but a species of visual memory. It is evident that we do not fully understand the powers and limitations of perceptual sets. It is equally evident that any theory of pattern recognition must reckon with them, and especially with their ill-defined characteristics.

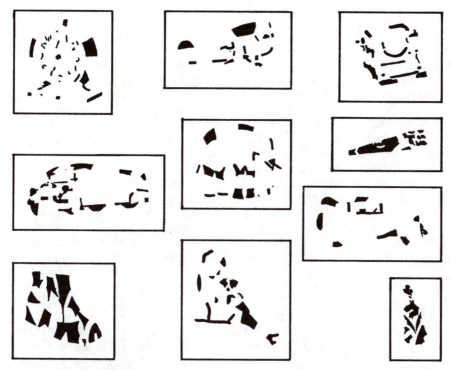

**FIGURE 6.7** ■ Figures used by Leeper (1935).

## Theories of Pattern Recognition: Template-Matching

In the face of all these data, is a template theory possible? How could an input which was displaced, enlarged, or rotated find its template? How could a single template correlate well with every member of an ill-defined category?

The Gestalt psychologists had a simple answer to all these apparently difficult questions: "similarity." The present *A*, however it may be shaped and wherever it may be located, is similar to past *A*s; the present perceived loaf of bread is similar to previously perceived loaves, and thus to their "traces." Somehow the two similar mental or neural processes make contact, and we read "A" or go on to think of butter. Unfortunately, this answer offers little comfort to the theorist. Without some definition or criterion of similarity, no empirical prediction is possible; we are left to guess whether any particular stimulus will be recognized or not. Without any explicit model or mechanism, the notion of "similarity" is only a restatement of the observed

fact that some inputs are recognized while others are not. Yet psychologists have rarely suggested any supplementary mechanisms in connection

**FIGURE 6.8** ■ Rat-man figure used by Bugelski and Alampay (1961).

with a template theory. Lashley's (1942) theory of "interference patterns," vague as it is, was perhaps the only serious attempt of this sort.

Far more specific solutions to Höffding's problem have been offered, however, in the attempt to program computers so they might recognize alphabetic characters or other patterns. Although many programmers have turned away from template-matching altogether, as we shall see, others have made it workable for a limited range of patterns. This is usually done by inserting a level of analysis *between* the input and the template. In this procedure, called "preprocessing," certain operations are routinely applied to the input at an early level. In general, preprocessing operations are of two kinds. One, only slightly interesting for our purposes, produces more accurate matches sim-

ply by "cleaning up" the input. This is almost essential for artificial systems, because they usually start with photographs or printed material which contains numerous small imperfections. A handprinted A, converted to a crude mosaic for input to a computer, will generally include many isolated dots and blanks which are of no significance (Figure 6.9a). Indeed, even machine-printed material is surprisingly liable to such flaws. A simple cleanup program which fills small holes (Figure 6.9b) and eliminates isolated points (Figure 6.9c) can simplify the task of identification considerably. These are extremely *local* processes, and the transformations they produce are quite independent of the gross form or actual identity of the letter. Local processes which are functionally similar to these certainly operate in human vision to over-

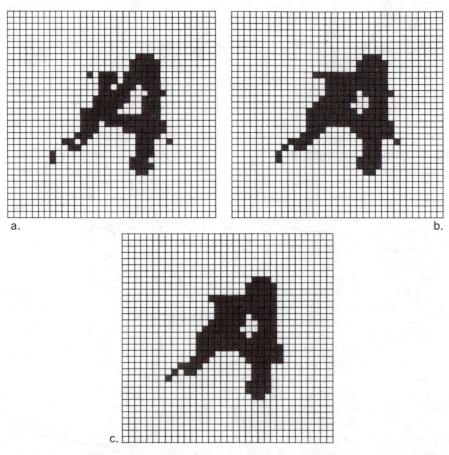

FIGURE 6.9 ■ Local preprocessing of a hand-printed *A* by a computer, after Selfridge and Neisser (1960). In Figure 6.9a, all grid squares touched by the lines are filled in; in Figure 6.9b, "outliers" are eliminated; in 6.9c, "holes" are filled.

come the disturbances created by nystagmus, scattered light, intraocular irregularities, and so on.

Local preprocessing is, perhaps, of minor theoretical interest. But, in computers, a more powerful possibility is available: The input figure can be *normalized*. Regardless of where it first appears, it can be effectively moved so that its center (defined in some geometrical sense) coincides with the center of the input area. It can then be symmetrically expanded or contracted until its height and width reach some standard value, and rotated until its longest axis reaches a fixed orientation. If the actual identifying processes operate only on this normalized "image," they will be indifferent to changes in the position, size, and orientation of the original input. There are many preprocessing schemes which will accomplish this. The model put forward by Pitts and McCulloch (1947, recently reviewed by Arbib, 1964), was perhaps the first to be suggested, and is often cited in this context. They proposed a specific—and rather complex—transformation which would give the same output for every member of certain well-defined categories. Today their procedure seems particularly vulnerable to the criticisms which follow.

The hypothesis that an additional level of processing intervenes between the input and the template is not entirely farfetched. Something very like "normalization" occurs when we move our eyes to fixate an object of interest, manipulate the retinal size of letters by holding a book at a preferred distance, or turn a picture right-side-up to look at it. Viewed as a theory of pattern recognition in man, normalization implies that there are internal information processes which play the same role as these external adjustments. Certainly, the general observation that recognition *is* indifferent to position, and perhaps to size, lends some support to this theory, though we shall see that other interpretations are available. More specific support comes from the studies with rotated figures, which showed that an adult subject is able to "take" a figure as having its "top" turned toward the bottom of the page. That is, he seems to rotate it subjectively, to normalize it, before he tries to identify it.

Although normalization and template-matching together can account for many aspects of human pattern recognition, they can hardly be the whole story. We have seen that in children, at least, there is another basis for stimulus equivalence. An even more convincing argument stems from the existence of ill-defined categories, for which no single template could be adequate. The *A*s in Figure 6.2 illustrate this point. Every one was actually identified as an *A* by all the subjects of our letter-recognition experiment (Neisser & Weene, 1960), without any use of context. Yet some of them are rather like *R*s, and others like *H*s or *4*s, if only their quantitative overlap with hypothetical templates is considered.

A final argument against a template theory is the frequent observation that small details can have a great influence on the category to which a pattern is assigned. The difference between a *Q* and an *O* is minute compared with the shape differences between *O*s, but it is decisive. The curvature of a small line segment can alter the expression of a cartoon face completely. The theoretical significance of this observation is not that the category is ill-defined (though it may be, in the case of facial expressions) but that such a critical feature would be quite insignificant in an overall comparison between a specimen *Q* and a template. It is evident, then, that figures are not always categorized on the basis of their overall, global properties.

Before turning to the attribute theories which these observations suggest, one more aspect of template-matching must be considered. The process of identification is not quite complete even after an input, from a well-defined category, has been normalized. There still remains the task of determining *which* template overlaps or correlates with the new pattern most strongly. The matching process must be carried out with each of the relevant alternatives, or at least with many of them. Here there are two theoretical alternatives which have given rise to a good deal of discussion: are the necessary comparisons conducted one at a time or all at once?

The successive alternative is sometimes designated by the misleading term "scanning" (e.g., Wiener, 1948). The intended analogy is with genuinely spatial searches, as when the sky is scanned with a radar beam in search of aircraft. But the search for a fitting template is not carried out through a real space, unless, as seems unlikely, the several templates are neatly laid out in different parts of the brain. Used in this way, the metaphor leads to confusion between a possibly sequential consideration of alternatives, on the one hand, and several genuinely spatial scans on the other.

One kind of real "scanning" occurs when we examine a scene, or a list, by moving our eyes across it. In fact, a successive "scanning" readout can occur even without eye movements. These genuine progressions through different spatial positions must be clearly distinguished from the sequential conduct of a series of different *operations*, like a number of template comparisons. (To add to the confusion, some authors have proposed a kind of "scan" as a solution to one aspect of Höffding's problem: the input which occurs at a new retinal [and cortical] *position* may be somehow swept across the visual cortex until it finds a match at the old locus. I find it hard to take this notion seriously, though others do. It is logically equivalent to normalization for position only.)

A sequential search through alternative templates is not the only way to locate a match. We may also imagine that all of them are examined simultaneously, "in parallel." Such systems are not difficult to visualize. An array of tuning forks operates as a parallel recognition system for frequency, for example. If a fork of unknown pitch is struck near such an array, it is "compared with" the whole array at once and "arouses" only the fork which has a similar resonant frequency. (The Gestalt psychologists had a system of this sort in mind when they spoke of contact "by similarity" between perceptual process and trace.) Given the resources of electronic or neural circuitry, highly complex parallel systems can be constructed. The curiously shaped magnetic numerals which appear on many bank checks are "read" by a computer with 14 parallel recognition circuits, one for each character of the American Bankers Association "alphabet." The machine is so constructed that all circuits examine a representation of the input letter simultaneously, and the circuits are matched to the shapes of the letters so that not more than one of them is ever tempted to respond (Evey, 1959).

The distinction between sequential and parallel processing, which has arisen here in the context of template-matching, is just as relevant if recognition is based on properties or features. In such models, we can also ask whether the critical operations are carried out one at a time or all at once. Before elaborating on the theoretical consequences of these two alternatives, we must look at some observations on the temporal characteristics of human performance. Since extra cognitive operations must take more time in sequential systems,

but not necessarily in parallel ones, such data are very relevant.

## Empirical Observations: Decision-Time and Visual Search

In a disjunctive reaction experiment, the subject must make one of $n$ different responses, depending on which of $n$ stimuli has appeared. Such reaction times can be used to study the speed of categorization. On the sequential theory, one would expect longer decision times with more alternatives; this is indeed the classical result, usually attributed to Merkel. Hick reopened the question in 1952 with an experiment in which the dependence of reaction time on $n$ took a particularly neat form. Every time he doubled the number of alternatives, the reaction time was increased by a fixed amount. This meant that the time was a linear function of the logarithm of $n$; i.e., of the amount of "stimulus information." This was precisely what might be expected from some sequential feature-testing models; ideally, doubling the number of alternatives would mean that one more binary feature was needed to distinguish them. For a template theory, Hick's results were less comforting. If each of $n$ templates were successively correlated with an input, the total time might be expected to grow linearly with $n$, not with log $n$.

Very much more linear functions do actually appear in a slightly different kind of experiment which, following Sternberg (1967), may be called "character-classification." Here the subject has only two responses, which we may call "yes" and "no" even if they are actually switch-closures. Sternberg (1963, 1966) used the digits from *0* through *9* as stimuli, assigning one, two, or four of them to the "yes" category and the remainder to "no." The average decision time increased by about 35 to 40 msecs. for every additional digit assigned to the smaller ("yes") set. He concluded that there is "an internal serial-comparison process whose average rate is between 25 and 30 symbols per second" (1966, p. 652).

The sequential-testing model also provides a good fit to the data of other experimenters, including Nickerson and Feehrer (1964), Shepherd (1964), Kaplan and Carvellas (1965), and Kaplan, Carvellas, and Metlay (1966). Kaplan and his collaborators do not measure classification-time directly. Instead, they estimate it from search rates, following a suggestion I had made earlier (Neisser, 1963b). If a subject successively examines the items on a list, looking for a particular target, his search rate can easily be converted into a measure of the average time spent with any single item. On a template model, this is the time needed to compare the item with a template of the target. If there are several targets, any of which can terminate the search, the subject must make several template comparisons for every item he examines. If he makes the comparisons sequentially, one after the other, the time-per-item must depend on the number of potential targets. The search procedure corresponds rather closely to Sternberg's character-classification experiments, despite superficial differences between the two paradigms. The termination of a search with "I've found it!" (or some key-pressing equivalent) is like a "yes" response, and the act of continuing the search corresponds to "no."

Kaplan's group has used several different variants of the search technique and found evidence for sequential processing in all of them. In the first experiment of Kaplan, Carvellas, and Metlay (1966), the subject glanced at a small group of letters which were the targets for a given trial, and then looked through a line of 10 letters in an effort to find them all. Search time was recorded by eye-movement photography. In a second experiment described in the same paper, subjects had to search for and cancel certain letters in a block of newspaper copy; their search rate (between cancellations) was measured by hand-movement photography. A third method was used by Kaplan and Carvellas (1965). They asked subjects to scan an array flashed on a screen, in search of any member of a predefined set of letters. In this study the search rate was not measured directly; it was inferred, as in my own experiments, from the variation of total time with the position of the target in the display. (The method is illustrated with some of my own data in Figure 6.10. A straight line has been fitted to the observed search times by the method of least squares; its slope shows how much additional time is needed for each additional item examined.) Each of the Kaplan experiments found that time-per-item increased linearly with the number of different targets for which the subject was searching.

Results like these seem to give strong support to a sequential theory. However, another set of findings makes quite a different impression. Some of this work has been reviewed by Leonard (1961); more recent references are cited by Morin, Konick, Troxell, and McPherson (1965). In essence, it

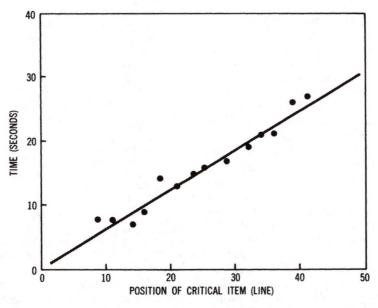

FIGURE 6.10 ■ A line fitted to a set of observed search times. Its slope estimates the scanning rate (Neisser, 1964a).

appears that Merkel's principle simply fails to apply when letters, numbers, or words are the stimuli, and their names are the responses. The time needed to respond then does *not* depend on how many numerals are used in the experiment, nor on the range of vocabulary from which a word is chosen (Pierce & Karlin, 1957). The number of alternatives is also unimportant if the stimuli and responses are highly "compatible," as when Leonard (1959) required his subjects to press down with the finger that had just been stimulated. Even with other material, the number of alternative possible stimuli may cease to affect reaction time after a great many trials (Mowbray & Rhoades, 1959). However, not all familiar or well-practiced materials display this freedom from Merkel's principle. Morin et al. (1965) showed that the time needed to name colors, symbols, animals, and the faces of friends *does* grow with the number of alternatives; only for letters did they find no increase. There is evidently something special about the patterns used in reading, and about overlearned responses. We will consider later what it might be.

One might be tempted to account for these findings with a modified template theory, perhaps by assuming that naive subjects examine templates sequentially while practiced ones can do it in parallel. However, I do not believe that even this view is tenable. Instead, some form of feature or attribute theory seems to be necessary in cases where the number of alternatives does not matter. To clarify this point, I must briefly discuss some experiments carried out by my associates and myself at Brandeis University (Neisser, 1963b; Neisser, Novick, & Lazar, 1963; Neisser & Lazar, 1964; Neisser & Beller, 1965; Neisser & Stoper, 1965). Our experimental materials were 50-line lists, like the one in Figure 6.11a. Each contained a single "target letter" at an unpredictable position. As soon as the list appeared, the subject began scanning down from the top, looking for the target (*K* in Figure 6.11a). When he found it, he turned a switch which stopped a clock, and the total search time was recorded. From a dozen such times, the scanning time-per-item can be reconstructed by the method discussed earlier and illustrated in Figure 6.10. With practice in simple scans of this sort, subjects readily reach speeds of ten lines per second or more. The final speed depends, among other things, on the difficulty of the discrimination required. It takes much longer to find the *Z* in Figure 6.12b than in Figure 6.12a.

| a. | b. |
|---|---|
| EHYP | ZVMLBQ |
| SWIQ | HSQJMF |
| UFCJ | ZTJVQR |
| WBYH | RDQTFM |
| OGTX | TQVRSX |
| GWVX | MSVRQX |
| TWLN | ZHQBTL |
| XJBU | ZJTQXL |
| UDXI | LHQVXM |
| HSFP | FVQHMS |
| XSCQ | MTSDQL |
| SDJU | TZDFQB |
| PODC | QLHBMZ |
| ZVBP | QMXBJD |
| PEVZ | RVZHSQ |
| SLRA | STFMQZ |
| JCEN | RVXSQM |
| ZLRD | MQBJFT |
| XBOD | MVZXLQ |
| PHMU | RTBXQH |
| ZHFK | BLQSZX |
| PNJW | QSVFDJ |
| CQXT | FLDVZT |
| GHNR | BQHMDX |
| IXYD | BMFDQH |
| QSVB | QHLJZT |
| GUCH | TQSHRL |
| OWBN | BMQHZJ |
| BVQN | RTBJZQ |
| FOAS | FQDLXH |
| ITZN | XJHSVQ |
| VYLD | MZRJDQ |
| LRYZ | XVQRMB |
| IJXE | QMXLSD |
| RBOE | DSZHQR |
| DVUS | FJQSMV |
| BIAJ | RSBMDQ |
| ESGF | LBMQFX |
| QGZI | FDMVQJ |
| ZWNE | HQZTXB |
| QBVC | VBQSRF |
| VARP | QHSVDZ |
| LRPA | HVQBFL |
| SGHL | HSRQZV |
| MVRJ | DQVXFB |
| GADB | RXJQSM |
| PCME | MQZFVD |
| ZODW | ZJLRTQ |
| HDBR | SHMVTQ |
| BVDZ | QXFBRJ |

**FIGURE 6.11** ■ Lists for visual searching (Neisser, 1964a). In Figure 6.11a, the target is *K*; in 6.11b, the target is a line that does not contain the letter *Q*.

A template theory would suggest that the subject compares each letter on the list with a template of the target and stops only if it fits. This seems extremely unlikely. Subjects insist that they

| a. | b. |
|---|---|
| ODUGQR | IVMXEW |
| QCDUGO | EWVMIX |
| CQOGRD | EXWMVI |
| QUGCDR | IXEMWV |
| URDGQO | VXWEMI |
| GRUQDO | MXVEWI |
| DUZGRO | XVWMEI |
| UCGROD | MWXVIE |
| DQRCGU | VIMEXW |
| QDOCGU | EXVWIM |
| CGUROQ | VWMIEX |
| OCDURQ | VMWIEX |
| UOCGQD | XVWMEI |
| RGQCOU | WXVEMI |
| GRUDQO | XMEWIV |
| GODUCQ | MXIVEW |
| QCURDO | VEWMIX |
| DUCOQG | EMVXWI |
| CGRDQU | IVWMEX |
| UDRCOQ | IEVMWX |
| GQCORU | WVZMXE |
| GOQUCD | XEMIWV |
| GDQUOC | WXIMEV |
| URDCGO | EMWIVX |
| GODRQC | IVEMXW |

FIGURE 6.12 ■ Lists for visual searching (Neisser, 1964a). The target is *Z* in both lists.

do not "see" individual letters at all, that everything is a blur from which the target "stands out." The times involved suggest that practiced subjects take in several lines at a glance. Indeed, tasks which require line-by-line examination (e.g., "which line of Fig. 6.11b does not contain a *Q*?") produce much slower search rates. Nor do search times increase linearly with the width of the column, as a letter-template view might suggest. (They do increase slightly, however, for reasons which we are still exploring.)

One of our most interesting findings was that multiple searches take no longer than simple ones, provided that the subjects are sufficiently practiced. It is possible to look for "*Z* or *K*" as rapidly as for one of these targets alone. In fact, a subject can look for any of 10 targets just as rapidly as for a single one (Neisser, Novick, & Lazar, 1963). This finding is theoretically important, since it seems to rule out sequential comparison as the mechanism involved. However, 10 targets is not a remarkable number in terms of human cognitive capacity. The experienced readers in a "newsclip" agency

are a case in point. Such a reader can search through the daily paper at over 1,000 words a minute, looking for any reference to the agency's clients, of whom there are usually hundreds. The feasibility of multiple searches in such a practical context suggests that our own results are not due to artifacts or to demand characteristics.

## Theories of Pattern Recognition: A Simple Feature-Analyzing Model

The general tenor of these results suggested an interpretation in terms of parallel processing and separate features, based on the more general "Pandemonium" model proposed by Selfridge (1959). A brief account of this interpretation may be helpful, even though I now believe that it should be substantially modified. Such an account will at least show an attribute model in explicit form and prepare the reader for the more general theories which follow.

The fundamental assumption was that the cognitive system used in searching is hierarchically organized. At its first level are "analyzers" which test the input for the presence of various specific features. The details of these features are not known: they might be parts of letters, certain kinds of gaps between them, even global properties like roundness, angularity, or the occurrence of parallel lines. There must be very many such analyzers, all operating simultaneously on every relevant portion of the input. Behind them, the model postulated a level of "letter-analyzers." These are not at all like templates; they do not resemble the input patterns. Instead, each one responds to a particular weighted, probabilistic combination of tests at the earlier level. No single attribute is uniquely necessary to arouse the Z-analyzer, for example; various combinations can do so. Moreover, in tasks where isolated letters are to be identified (e.g., tachistoscopic recognition), a given set of features will generally arouse more than one letter-analyzer. Identification then depends on which is most strongly aroused. Dominant activity by a single one was thought of as the equivalent of "seeing" the letter, and thus as the prerequisite for an identifying response.

In the search situation, letter-analyzers other than those for the target can be effectively "turned off," while all the feature-analyzers continue to test the input. This means that activity is confined to the feature level until the target actually appears. As a result, the irrelevant letters themselves are not seen. Practice is effective because it brings different and faster first-level analyzers into play. In many cases, these are sensitive to features that characterize whole blocks of letters, rather than to properties of letters individually. In more difficult discriminations, no really fast analyzers ever suffice, and so practice does not have much effect on the search rate.

When the subject is asked to look for any of several targets, in a multiple search task, more first-level operations are needed than before. Again, however, no letter-analyzers become active until a target has been found. Because the operations at the feature level are in parallel, the extra ones do not increase the search time. The subject should not be thought of as waiting until all the feature-analyzers have finished with a given stimulus-item or group, before proceeding to the next one. Instead, he settles on a fixed scan rate, one that allows most of the necessary feature-processing to occur on most glances. Occasionally, some of it remains unfinished; this is one source of the frequent errors of omission in these experiments.

The principle of "parallel processing," which distinguished this model from certain other theories of pattern recognition, actually appeared in it in two distinguishably different forms. First, the feature-analyzers of the model were thought to be *spatially parallel*; the same operations can be carried out simultaneously all over the effective portion of the retina. A Z anywhere in the field immediately arouses the analyzers for acute angles, parallels, etc., and thus eventually activates the Z-analyzer. It is this postulate which no longer seems plausible to me. In addition, the feature-analyzers are *operationally parallel*. That is, they work independently of one another; the test for acute angles is in no way contingent on any other test outcome. Indeed, in the model the analyzers were supposed to operate *simultaneously,* as well as independently, and it is this simultaneity which appears in the experiments with multiple targets. Nevertheless, an operationally parallel system could be "simulated" even on a computer that carries out only one operation at a time. Its defining property is not simultaneity, but the fact that no analyzer depends on the course or the outcome of processing by the others.

These two concepts of parallel processing can be further clarified by considering their opposites, which may be called *serial* and *sequential* processing, respectively. A spatially serial activity is one which analyzes only a part of the input field at any given moment. The reading of letters from a tachistoscopic display is a good example of serial processing. On the other hand, the term *sequential* refers to the manner in which a process is organized; it is appropriate when the analysis consists of successive, interrelated steps. A model involving feature-analyzers is sequential if the output of earlier analyzers determines which ones are to be applied later.

Any particular scheme for sequential analysis can be specified in terms of the familiar type of diagram called a "decision tree" because it has so many alternative "branches." For an example of such a tree, it will be helpful to consider Feigenbaum's (1963) EPAM program, the "Elementary Perceiver and Memorizer" (see also Feigenbaum & Simon, 1962, 1963). EPAM actually develops its decision tree—which Feigenbaum calls a "discrimination net"—as a result of encounters with stimuli. A very simple and partially developed EPAM tree is illustrated in Figure 6.13.

Given a nonsense syllable, this tree would apply two tests, and thereby identify it as one of four possible alternatives. Tests *2a* and *2b* are never *both* applied, whatever the input may be; instead the outcome of test *1* assigns the input to one "branch" or the other, and the second test is contingent on the branch chosen. This system is extremely efficient, since it reduces the number of necessary tests to a minimum. On the other hand, it is quite vulnerable to error, since even a single misstep will put the program irrevocably on the wrong branch. By contrast, a single malfunctioning test will generally have little effect in an operationally parallel program.

This use of EPAM as an illustrative example is very far from doing it justice. Two of its other accomplishments should not go unmentioned. First, if EPAM misclassifies a syllable—as must happen when no test in the system happens to distinguish it from another syllable already incorporated—a new test will be invented, and new branches grown accordingly. For example, the tree in Figure 6.13 would sort *DEF* to the same terminal as *DAX*, but if it found that they differed in some respect—perhaps in whether or not the *last* letter

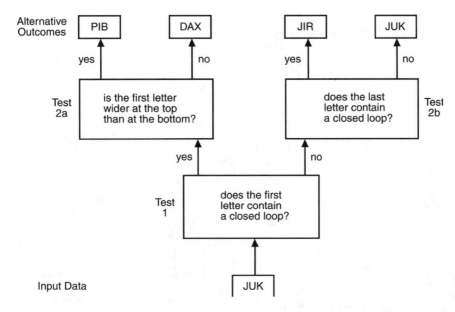

FIGURE 6.13 ■ A decision tree which might have been developed by Feigenbaum's (1963) EPAM program.

was wider at the top than the bottom—a test based on this difference would replace the present DAX terminal and lead to two distinct branches. Second, "response" syllables can be associated with terminals, so that the presentation of a "stimulus" produces a particular "response," which may itself reenter the decision tree. In this way EPAM can gradually learn serial lists of syllables. A more elaborate version, called EPAM-III (Simon & Feigenbaum, 1964), is also able to learn paired associates. Many of the ordinary phenomena of rote learning, including the effects of serial position, intraserial similarity, familiarization, and the like, appear in EPAM to a degree which matches human performance quantitatively as well as qualitatively. For present purposes, EPAM is only of interest as a model of pattern recognition, where its relentlessly sequential approach does not seem quite appropriate.

The data on searching for more than one target are perhaps the strongest reason for supposing that visual cognition is operationally parallel, at least at some levels. Additional targets must require additional analyzers, and in a sequential model this would mean a longer series of tests. However, there are other reasons for rejecting the sequential model as well. Perception generally does seem to have the redundancy, wastefulness, and freedom from

gross misrepresentation that characterize a parallel process. This point has been noted by Brunswik (1956, pp. 91–92), and by others also. Moreover, one might expect a parallel process to resist introspection, since so much unrelated activity is going on simultaneously. The early stages of perception do have precisely this quality. So do some kinds of thinking, as we shall see later on.

## Theories of Pattern Recognition: Features and Parts

We must turn now from this particular model of the way letters are identified to more general conceptions of pattern recognition, especially those based on some kind of feature analysis. It is appropriate to begin with the work of Oliver Selfridge, on which the visual search model was based. Selfridge (1955, 1956) was one of the first workers in the computer field to recognize the complexity of the problem. My Figure 6.1 for example, is taken from his discussion of context effects, in a paper (1955) which introduced the notions of preprocessing and feature extraction as well. In 1959, he proposed a more systematic model for pattern recognition, called "Pandemonium," which is represented in Figure 6.14. In a

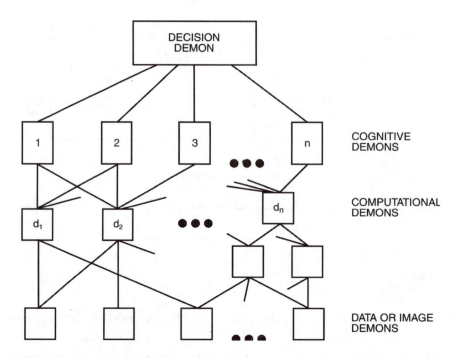

- **FIGURE 6.14** ■ Parallel processing in Selfridge's (1959) "Pandemonium" program.

Pandemonium, each possible pattern (perhaps each letter of the alphabet) is represented by a demon (the "cognitive demons," in the upper row of Figure 6.14). Being egotistic, such a demon incessantly looks for evidence (suitable results offered by inferior "computational demons") that he is being depicted in the "image," or input. To the extent that he finds such evidence, he shouts loudly, and the loudest shout in his Pandemonium is taken by the "decision demon" as identifying the stimulus. The computational demons perform operations of varying complexity on the input, all simultaneously. They are the feature-analyzers of the search model, while the cognitive demons correspond to the letter-analyzers.

Such a theory is far removed from template-matching, and also from sequential testing, as a comparison among Figures 6.3, 6.13, and 6.14 will illustrate. In principle, a Pandemonium can recognize *any* pattern, as long as some weighted combination of the features being tested serves to distinguish category-members from nonmembers. The features to be analyzed (by the computational demons) may be of any desired sort. Whole-qualities ("Does it have a closed perimeter?" "Is it con-

cave downward?") are as eligible as partial ones ("Does it have a little *Q*-defining stroke at the bottom?"). Moreover, a Pandemonium can easily improve its performance through learning. It need only be told, trial by trial, whether its identification of the preceding pattern was correct, so it can increase or decrease certain "weights" associated with the cognitive demon that was selected. (These weights govern the cognitive demon's dependence on the particular computational demons which shouted on the trial in question.) Because of its ability for self-improvement, a Pandemonium can deal with truly "ill-defined" patterns. The programmer or designer need not have *a priori* definitions of the categories which it is to recognize. Even a "set" for an ill-defined category is conceivable, based on a temporary increase in the weights given to certain features. It is also worth noting that a Pandemonium with a large and redundant array of computational demons is not very sensitive to malfunction or error. If one demon fails to shout, the others may well be loud enough without him.

The Pandemonium conception has been applied to several real problems in automatic pattern recognition, including the translation of hand-sent

Morse code and the identification of hand-printed letters (see Selfridge & Neisser, 1960, for a summary of this work). In the case of hand-printed letters (Doyle, 1960), a system with about 30 rather complex feature-analyzers was simulated on a general-purpose computer. In operation, it was first presented with several hundred letters as examples from which to "learn." During this phase, each input was accompanied by its correct identification. In the test phase, unfamiliar letters—all drawn from the same pool as those in Figure 6.2—were presented and identified with close to 90 percent accuracy.

Other theorists have also preferred features to templates. N. S. Sutherland (1957, 1959), started from the discriminative capacities of animals rather than from the design of automata, arrived at a theory very similar to Selfridge's, and has continued to develop it (1963a, 1963b). The term "analyzer" was introduced by him. He argued that, if an animal can discriminate between two stimuli, it must possess some mechanism which reacts differentially to the two; discrimination learning consists of attaching suitable responses to the outputs of the right analyzers. The experimenter can infer a good deal about the analyzers by noting (a) what patterns can and cannot be discriminated by the animal, and (b) what new patterns can elicit the same response in a transfer test.

Sutherland's original work was done with octopuses (Sutherland, 1957). These animals easily discriminate between vertical strokes and horizontal ones, but apparently cannot distinguish a line sloping 45° to the right from one which slopes 45° to the left. This led Sutherland to assume that they possess analyzers for verticality (specifically, for the ratio of maximum vertical extent to square root of area) and horizontality, but not for other inclinations. The theory was subsequently elaborated to deal with differences in discriminative capacity between octopuses and rats, and to include other hypothetical analyzers as well.

Bruner, too, has emphasized that pattern recognition depends on the identification of specific features or *attributes* of the stimulus. "That thing is round and nubbly in texture and orange in color and of such-and-such size—therefore an orange" (1957b, p. 124). Less interested in specific mechanisms than Selfridge or Sutherland, he has devoted more attention to other aspects of the pattern-recognition process. These include the various effects of set and expectancy on recognition, and the processes which serve to verify tentative identifications by "match-mismatch signals" or "confirmation checks."

All of these theories share a willingness to postulate rather complex processes at the level of feature-analysis. Selfridge's computational demons extract properties like "concave downward." Sutherland assumes the existence of analyzers for "horizontality." Bruner speaks of such attributes as "round" or "nubbly in texture." How does the organism come to have such useful and highly specific systems? Bruner is not specific on this point, but Sutherland (1959) argues explicitly that they must be innate. For Selfridge, too, they are effectively "inborn" and unmodifiable. A Pandemonium can modify the weights assigned to various feature-tests, but it cannot construct any new ones. Those originally provided by the programmer must suffice.

Many psychologists find it unlikely that the organism could start out with such highly differentiated and well-adapted structures. They would prefer to think that the feature-analyzers themselves are developed by experience. One such alternative has been explored by Uhr (1963; see also Uhr, Vossler, & Uleman, 1962) in a computer program. His program incorporates a level of feature-analyzers, whose combined outputs lead to recognition just as in a Pandemonium. But Uhr's feature-analyzers are simply $5 \times 5$ matrices of black and white (much smaller than the figures being categorized). They can contain *any* arbitrary local pattern, and function like templates for the portion of the input they happen to cover. At the start, the operating set of analyzers is chosen at random from among the $(2)^{25}$ possible matrices of this sort, but it is subject to change as the result of experience. Old "features" (i.e., specific matrices) are discarded if they do not contribute to correct recognition, and new ones are then tried. He has achieved considerable success with this program, not only in recognizing letters but with other ill-defined patterns as well.

Uhr's program, while it is more susceptible to modification by experience than the other theories we have considered, still has a good deal of initial structure. Some theorists, however, have assumed that the organism starts out with very little structure and must acquire virtually *everything* from experience. Ideally, one might think of the newborn nervous system as only a randomly connected network of neurons, which develops complexity gradually through commerce with the environment. This assumption leads to what are called "neural net" theories. If such a network could actually develop the functional equivalent of analyzers within a plausible number of trials—which is doubted by Minsky and Selfridge (1961)—the analyzers to appear first might be relatively simple and local. The attributes they could detect might well be elementary *parts* of figures, rather than wholistic features like roundness. Such, at least, was the argument made by Hebb (1949) in his influential book, which is still the most thoughtful and wide-ranging discussion of visual cognition that we have.

Hebb's account of pattern recognition in the mature individual resembles the other feature-oriented theories in many respects. The first level of processing is assumed to consist of "cell-assemblies" which act much like feature-analyzers or demons. However, the only features extracted at this level are lines, angles, and contours. In effect, this model (like Uhr's) is a cross between a feature and a template theory: the "features" are really simple templates for parts. To solve Höffding's problem—that response does not seem to depend on retinal locus—Hebb uses spatially parallel processing. The cell-assemblies, or part-templates, are reduplicated all over the input region, and corresponding ones are connected together. In this way, a line of a particular orientation (say) excites what is effectively the same assembly wherever it happens to appear. The cell-assemblies themselves are supposedly combined by selective experience into what Hebb calls "phase sequences," whose role is similar to that of cognitive demons.

Hebb's reason for restricting himself to parts, instead of the more general class of features later envisaged by other theorists, is his fundamental assumption that the entire system develops from an undifferentiated neural net on the basis of experience. However, we may well ask whether cell-assemblies would actually be formed, and maintain their integrity, under the conditions he describes. This question has been frequently raised, and modifications of the theory have been suggested to make the cell-assembly a more plausible product of visual experience (e.g., Milner, 1957). Other neural net theories, like Rosenblatt's (1958) "Perceptron," have been challenged on similar

grounds: could such a net ever learn any nontrivial categorization? Minsky thinks not (1961; also Minsky & Selfridge, 1961), and indeed the achievements of the "Perceptron" have not substantiated the early claims of its proponents. There is no doubt that any attempt to develop a powerful cognitive system out of randomness, whether as psychologically sophisticated as Hebb's or as naive as Rosenblatt's, faces grave difficulties. (Further discussion of the "Perceptron" may be found in the review of pattern recognition by Uhr, 1963 and in Arbib, 1964.)

Problems of perceptual development are, strictly speaking, outside the scope of this book. However, we cannot ignore another difficulty faced by such theories. Even if part-templates do exist, it is hard to see how they could account for pattern recognition in adults. One obvious source of difficulty is the identification of ill-defined patterns. The *A*s of Figure 6.2 do seem to have properties in common, but congruent angles and lines are hardly the whole story. Moreover, there seems to be a complex, nonlocal, and innate feature-analyzer at the very heart of Hebb's theory, in the form of what he calls "primitive unity" (1949, p. 19). Even persons opening their eyes for the first time, after a cataract operation, see visual objects as separate and individual wholes. As far as Hebb is concerned, this elementary figure-ground segregation is simply a fact outside his explanatory system. To me, it indicates the presence of at least some feature-analyzers that do not look at parts, but at properties of whole figures. If analyzers of this sort are present from the beginning, why not assign them some serious role in later pattern recognition? We will see that this means at least a partial retreat from the notion of parallel processing, and we will examine the arguments for making such a retreat. First, however, an empirical detour is necessary. A review of pattern recognition would hardly be complete without consideration of some recent experiments that bear specifically on the differences among parts, features, and templates.

## Empirical Observations: Features and Parts

One important line of research in recent years has been the study of perceptual fragmentation. Under certain stimulus conditions, perceived figures break into segments, some or all of which may disappear. The effect can be observed in a particularly striking way with the optical technique known as the "stopped image" (Pritchard, Heron, & Hebb, 1960; Pritchard, 1961). In this procedure, eye movements are compensated for and cannot produce any shift of the optical image on the retina; that is, they do not change the proximal stimulus. Perceived figures soon disappear in whole or in part when this is done, presumably because of "fatigue" at the retina or elsewhere in the visual system. Similar effects occur even with ordinary ocular fixation on figures which are faint or defocused (McKinney, 1963, 1966).

The disappearance of parts in these experiments is not haphazard. Lines come and go as wholes, for example, so that triangles generally lose one side at a time, while the letter *T* loses either its entire upright or its entire crosspiece. Parallel lines tend to appear and disappear together, even at considerable separations. Curvilinear figures often undergo simplification and gap-completion. Whenever possible, the fragmentation tends to produce meaningful patterns rather than nonsensical ones. Figure 6.15 illustrates this phenomenon. A monogram breaks into recognizable letters more often than into unnamable fragments; a word characteristically loses exactly those letters which will leave another definable word behind; the eye in a profile disappears and reappears as a unit. As Hebb points out in his stimulating review (1963), the occurrence of fragmentation tends to support the notion that there are functional subsystems in perception, even if the nature of the fragments is not always what would have been predicted from his theory. Certainly, it gives little comfort to a template hypothesis.

A particularly interesting result is that of McKinney (1966). He used the figures illustrated in Figure 6.16 as fragmentation targets. One group of subjects was shown the patterns labeled *1, 2, 3, 4, 5,* and *6,* with the indication that each was a letter. Another group was given patterns *7, 2, 8, 4, 9,* and *6.* They were *not* told to expect letters, and thought of all the patterns as meaningless. In the upshot, patterns *2, 4,* and *6* (shown to both groups) underwent far less fragmentation for subjects who saw them as letters than for those who took them to be meaningless designs! McKinney interprets his data in terms of the verbal labels ("L," "T," and "V") used by the first group of subjects, and thus as resulting from "neural firing in the language centre" (1966, p. 241). However, another possible interpretation should not be overlooked.

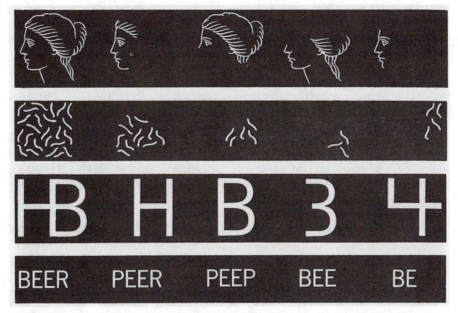

**FIGURE 6.15** ■ Perceptual fragmentation in "stopped images." The figures at the left are stimulus patterns; the others are typical products of fragmentation (from Pritchard, 1961).

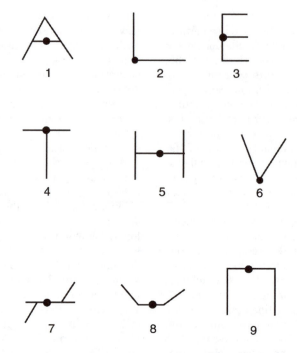

**FIGURE 6.16** ■ Patterns used in McKinney's (1966) study of fragmentation.

We have already referred to Orne's (1959, 1962a) observation that every experiment has "demand characteristics"—that all subjects try to figure out what is expected of them, and most subjects try to behave accordingly. Sometimes it is difficult to make sense of an experiment, and under those conditions subtle cues from the experimenter's behavior may be particularly important. In other instances, demand characteristics may arise simply from the nature of the task. This is a very real possibility in fragmentation studies. A subject who is shown letters under conditions where they soon become indistinct and asked to "report if any portion of the letter seems to break up and disappear" may interpret his task as one of holding it together as long as possible. On the other hand, a subject shown meaningless patterns may interpret similar instructions in the opposite way to see if he can break them up.

It should be carefully noted that the demand-characteristic interpretation does not suggest that the subject is deceiving the experimenter, or reporting phenomena which he has not actually seen. Common experience shows that the effect of in-

tention on the perception of ambiguous figures is very great. Merely by "trying," we can affect the way Figures 6.4, 6.8, or 6.18 appear to us. It seems more than likely that a similar kind of "trying" could affect the appearance of the stimuli in a fragmentation experiment.

A second kind of data relevant to these issues comes from microelectrode studies of neural functioning. Strictly speaking, neuroanatomy and physiology are outside the limits of this book, but an exception is justified in the case of work so widely cited by pattern-recognition theorists. The major contributions in this field are by Lettvin, Maturana, McCulloch, and Pitts (1959), and by Hubel and Wiesel (1959, 1962; also Hubel, 1963).

Lettvin and his collaborators were able to record the activities of single fibers in the optic nerves of unanesthetized frogs, while presenting various visual stimuli. These fibers are not direct extensions of the first layer of receptors; they come from the intermediate ganglion cells of the eye. Hence, if any feature-analyzers occur early in the frog's visual system, Lettvin et al. expected to record their *out*put in the optic nerve. They had come to suspect the existence of such analyzers from Selfridge's arguments about pattern recognition and hoped to demonstrate their physiological reality. In this, they were astonishingly successful.

Each fiber in the frog's optic nerve seems to have its own "receptive field"—a useful physiological term due to Hartline, which denotes the region of retina where stimulation can produce some activity in the fiber. The frog's fibers turn out to be quite selective in the *kind* of stimulation which must appear in their receptive fields to produce a response. One type of fiber, termed a "net convexity detector" (or, less formally, as a "bug perceiver") responds if a small dark object enters the receptive field or moves about in it, and continues to respond if the object becomes stationary in the field. Such fibers do not respond to large moving edges, nor to changes in the overall illumination. Other fiber types found included "sustained contrast detectors," "moving edge detectors," and "net dimming detectors." All of them have rather obvious significance in the life of the frog, as he catches flies, escapes from the looming shadows of predators, and the like. The results seem to show clearly that complex *features* of the input, not simply its parts, are abstracted very early in the visual system. (For a more detailed introduction to this work, see Arbib, 1964.)

Hubel and Wiesel used a similar method, but their experimental animal was the cat, and their most interesting recordings were from cells in the visual cortex rather than those in the optic nerve. They found cells that were much concerned with the *orientation* of stimuli on the retina. Many of these had what Hubel and Wiesel called "simple fields." These fields were divided into excitatory and inhibitory areas in such a way that a particularly oriented edge, at just the right position, gave a much stronger response than any other stimulus. In other "complex" fields, the exact position of the edge seemed irrelevant as long as it was somewhere in a relatively large area, but its orientation remained critical. Hubel and Wiesel surmised that these latter cells could be fired by any of a cluster of the former, more specific ones. As in the case of Lettvin et al.'s fiber types, these elements were all reduplicated throughout the input area; that is, they were spatially parallel. Unlike the optic-nerve fibers of the frog, however, related cells in the cat's cortex were generally close to one another.

These data pose particular problems for neural net theories, at both of the levels discussed earlier. The notion that "cell-assemblies" are developed by experience alone becomes especially suspect. Experience is not likely to modify the retina of the frog, nor to produce neat anatomical arrangements in the feline cerebrum. Moreover, the Lettvin et al. data also pose a challenge of the second kind. Even at early levels of the visual system, there seem to be analyzers for complex attributes of the input, not just for parts. While this finding is compatible with a model like that of Selfridge (1959), it cannot easily be reconciled with Hebb's views.

The observations of Hubel and Wiesel are not as troublesome in this respect. They suggest an analysis in terms of oriented line-segments, which could fit a part-template interpretation of pattern recognition if one is willing to assume that the templates are innately given. Such an interpretation has been particularly attractive to Sutherland, whose "analyzers" for horizontality and verticality were very much like oriented and generalized line-segments to start with. In recent papers (1963a, 1963b) he has explicitly incorporated the Hubel-Wiesel discoveries into his theorizing. On the assumption that the octopus has more cells sensitive to horizontal orientation than to vertical, and more of either than of the obliquely-oriented kind, Sutherland has been able to explain a wide range of results.

It seems clear that this theoretical approach is a fruitful one. Parallel analyzers for specifically oriented line-segments may well be a part of man's visual equipment, as they are of the cat's. Nevertheless, we must face the fact that most of the data about human pattern recognition cannot be accounted for by analyzers of this sort. They hardly even explain our ability to recognize rotated figures under the right circumstances, as discussed above, let alone our recognition of ill-defined figures. Other arguments against taking such mechanisms as the cornerstones of theory have been presented by Gyr, Brown, Willey, and Zivian (1966).

A third set of experiments that deserve mention here are certain studies of pattern recognition in young children, carried out by Eleanor Gibson and her associates at Cornell University (see Gibson, 1965, for a general review). Their study of rotational and perspective transformations (Gibson, Gibson, Pick, & Osser, 1962) has already been mentioned. Using the same techniques, Pick (1965) has attempted a very direct test of the

| Features | A | B | C | E | K | L | N | U | X | Z |
|---|---|---|---|---|---|---|---|---|---|---|
| **Straight segment** | | | | | | | | | | |
| Horizontal | + | | | + | + | | | | | + |
| Vertical | | + | | + | + | + | + | | | |
| Oblique / | + | | | + | | | | | + | + |
| Oblique \ | + | | | + | | | + | | + | |
| **Curve** | | | | | | | | | | |
| Closed | | + | | | | | | | | |
| Open vertically | | | | | | | | + | | |
| Open horizontally | | | + | | | | | | | |
| Intersection | + | + | | + | + | | | | + | |
| **Redundancy** | | | | | | | | | | |
| Cyclic change | | + | | + | | | | | | |
| Symmetry | + | + | + | + | + | | | + | + | |
| **Discontinuity** | | | | | | | | | | |
| Vertical | + | | | + | | | | | + | |
| Horizontal | | | | | + | + | + | | | + |

FIGURE 6.17 ■ One possible set of distinctive features for letters (from Gibson, 1965). Each letter is characterized by those features marked "+" in its column.

template theory (she prefers the term "prototype"), as opposed to feature-analysis. She first taught 60 kindergarten children to distinguish each of three standard shapes (like those in Figure 6.6) from several of its transforms. The "confusion items" presented to each child all involved the *same* three transforms of every standard. For a particular child, these might include changing one line to a curve, rotating by 45°, and right-left reversal. When the child could successfully distinguish each standard from all of the corresponding confusion items, he was transferred to a new task. One group now had to distinguish the *same standards* from new confusion items, involving novel transformations; this should have been easy if templates of the standards had been developed during training. A second group of subjects was transferred to new standards, but the new confusion items were generated by applying the *same transforms;* this should have been easy if analyzers for the relevant dimensions had been developed during training. In fact, it was this second group which transferred more readily, thereby supporting the analyzer rather than the template theory. Even the template group, however, outperformed a third set of subjects who received *both* new standards and new templates.

The Gibson group assumes that letters are rec-

ognized by a feature-analytic process, very like Selfridge's Pandemonium. Pick's data support this view, although her stimuli were not actual letters but only letter-like forms. In addition, Gibson, Osser, Schiff, and Smith (1963), strongly influenced by the Jakobson-Halle notion of "distinctive features" in spoken language, made an explicit attempt to discover the critical features by which letters are identified. They began with several alternative sets of features based chiefly on speculation; one such set appears in Figure 6.17. (Notice that some are rather global, like the "cyclic change" which is characteristic of *B* and *E*.) If this set were the correct one, one might expect to find more visual confusions between letters that differ by only a few features, like *B* and *E*, than between letters different in many, like *B* and *C*. To some extent, this expectation was confirmed in empirical results obtained from four-year-old children in a matching task. However, the findings were not clear-cut.

All of these data tend to support the view that pattern recognition involves some kind of hierarchy of feature-analyzers. Nevertheless, there is reason to doubt that any theory which involves only parallel processing, whether of features or parts, can be adequate.

# Selective Adaptation of Linguistic Feature Detectors[1]

Peter D. Eimas[2] and John D. Corbit • Brown University

Using a selective adaptation procedure, evidence was obtained for the existence of linguistic feature detectors, analogous to visual feature detectors. These detectors are each sensitive to a restricted range of voice onset times, the physical continuum underlying the perceived phonetic distinctions between voiced and voiceless stop consonants. The sensitivity of a particular detector can be reduced selectively by repetitive presentation of its adequate stimulus. This results in a shift in the locus of the phonetic boundary separating the voiced and voiceless stops.

Converging evidence from electrophysiological studies of single neurons in animals (e.g., Lettvin et al., 1959; Hubel & Wiesel, 1962) and from psychophysical studies of human perception (Blackmore & Campbell, 1969; Blackmore & Sutton, 1969) indicates that there are detector mechanisms in the brain that are uniquely sensitive to particular and relatively restricted patterns of stimulation. In this study of speech perception, we attempted to demonstrate the existence of feature detectors for linguistic information by use of a selective adaptation procedure. The acoustic dimension that was investigated was voice onset time (VOT), variations in which are sufficient for the perceived distinctions between the voiced and voiceless stop consonants of English in initial position[3] (Lisker & Abramson, 1970).

Voice onset time is defined as the time between the release burst and laryngeal pulsing (Lisker & Abramson, 1964). Very short lags in the onset of voicing are perceived in English as voiced stops, [b, d, g], whereas relatively long lags in the onset of voicing are perceived in English as voiceless stops, [p, t, k]. It is possible to produce synthetic speech with variations in VOT. Figure 7.1 shows two spectrograms of synthetic speech which illustrate two values along the VOT continuum. The sound pattern shown in the upper spectrogram has a short (10 msec) lag in VOT and is perceived in its acoustic form as a voiced stop, in this instance as [b] plus the vowel [a]. The lower spectrogram depicts a sound with a longer (100 msec) lag in voicing, which is perceived as a voiceless stop, [p] in this case, plus the vowel [a].

The perception of series of synthetic speech varying continuously in VOT alone has been found to be very nearly categorical for English listeners (Abramson & Lisker, 1970; Wolf, 1972). That is, for these series of stimuli the percept exists only in one of two stages: the voiced or voiceless stop.

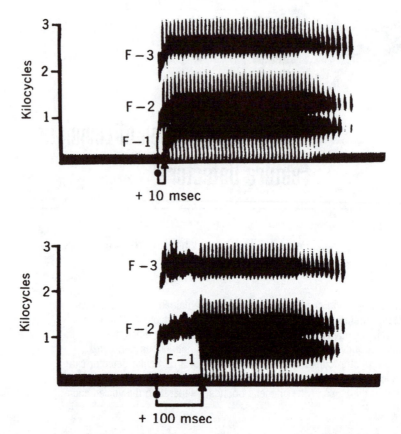

**FIGURE 7.1** ■ Spectrograms of synthetic speech showing two values of voice onset time: a slight voicing lag represented by [ba] in the upper figure and a long voicing lag in the lower figure, represented by [pa]. The symbols F-1, F-2, and F-3 represent the first three formants, that is, the relatively intense bands of energy in the speech signal. (Courtesy of L. Lisker & A. S. Abramson.)

As a consequence, listeners are able to assign stimuli to phonetic categories with great consistency. Moreover, their ability to detect differences between stimuli is limited by their ability to assign differential labels to the stimuli. The latter is evidenced by marked peaks in the discriminability functions at the region of the phonetic boundary; that is, the discrimination of a given difference in VOT is considerably better when two stimuli lie in different phonetic categories than when the two stimuli are from the same phonetic category.

Of particular interest is the fact that the categorical nature of the perception of the VOT continuum appears to be universal. That is, it is characteristic not only of adult speakers of English but also of adult speakers of other languages, e.g., Thai, and

more importantly it is present in preverbal human infants as young as 1 month of age (Eimas et al., 1971). The apparent universality of this phenomenon suggests that it is a manifestation of the basic structure of the human brain.

Another line of evidence consistent with this idea comes from the cross-language research of Lisker and Abramson (1964). They found that the manner in which speakers of 11 diverse languages divided the VOT continuum was notably consistent. The phonetic tokens produced by these speakers, although not the same for all languages, nevertheless tended to fall at three modal values of VOT. Two of these values are used for the English voiced and voiceless stops. English does not use the third distinction, long voicing lead, found in Thai, for example.[4] It would seem reasonable that this uniformity in producing voicing distinctions is matched by specialized perceptual structures. These structures might well take the form of detectors that are differentially tuned to the acoustic consequences of the modes of production (see Lieberman, 1970, for an extended discussion of the relation between the processes of speech production and speech perception).

# Experiment 1

Our experimental plan to obtain evidence for these linguistic feature detectors was based on a selective adaptation procedure. We reasoned that if there are linguistic feature detectors mediating the perception of the voiced and voiceless stops, then repeated presentation of the feature (i.e., appropriate VOT value) to which a given detector is sensitive should fatigue the detector and reduce its sensitivity. As a consequence, the manner in which stimuli are assigned to phonetic categories would be altered, especially for those stimuli near the phonetic boundary where both detectors may be somewhat sensitive to the same VOT values. In order to test this idea, we first obtained identification functions for two series of stop consonants, the bilabial stops [b, p] and the apical stops [d, t], when listeners were in the normal unadapted state. Next, identification functions were obtained for the same series of stimuli after adaptation by repeated presentations of good exemplars of both modes of voicing.

## Method

### STIMULI

The stimuli were two series of 14 synthetic speech stimuli prepared by means of a computer-controlled parallel resonance synthesizer by Lisker and Abramson (1970). For greater detail concerning the construction of synthetic speech by a computer-controlled synthesizer the reader is referred to Mattingly (1968). To produce variations in VOT in the context of the English stop consonants, the onset of the first formant relative to the onset of the second and third formants is varied and the second and third formants are excited by a noise source rather than a periodic source when the first formant is absent (see Figure 7.1 for two examples

of VOT). In the [b, p] series the VOT values ranged from –10 msec (short voicing lead) to +60 msec (relatively long voicing lag) in 5-msec steps except for the final two stimuli which were separated by 10 msec. The [d, t] series had VOT values ranging from 0 msec (voicing and first formant onset coincident with the onset of the second and third formants) to +80 msec. The difference between stimuli was 5 msec except for the final four stimuli in which the difference was 10 msec. The acoustic differences between the two series were in the starting frequency and direction of the second- and third-formant transitions, these differences being sufficient cues for the perceived phonetic differences, that is, for the perceived differences between [b] and [d] and between [p] and [t] (Liberman et al., 1967).

### PROCEDURE

To obtain the initial identification functions when the listeners were in an unadapted state, the 14 stimuli from each series were presented binaurally by means of a tape recorder at a comfortable listening level. For both series, which were presented separately, the order of presentation was randomized, and 50 identification responses were obtained for each stimulus. The interval between stimuli was always 3 sec. Next, identification functions were obtained after selective adaptation. For example, if the detector assumed to underlie perception of the voiced stops were to be adapted, listeners were exposed to repetitive presentations of a [b] with a VOT value of –10 msec or to a [d] with a VOT value of 0 msec for 2 min at the beginning of each session, and then for 1 min before each stimulus was to be identified. When adapting the detector for the voiceless stops, either a [p] with a VOT value of +60 msec or a [t] with a VOT value of +80 msec was repeatedly presented before each identification response. There were eight adaptation conditions in all: each of the two series was identified after adaptation with [b], [d], [p], and [t]. In any single adaptation session, listeners heard 2 min (150 presentations) of the adapting sound pattern, with each presentation being 500 msec in duration and separated by 300 msec of silence. Next 70 adaptation trials were administered in which each individual adaptation trial consisted of 1 min of the adapting stimulus (75 presentations), followed by 500 msec of silence and then a single stimulus to be identified. Five seconds elapsed before the next trial occurred, and short breaks were given every 14 trials. For any session, the adapting stimulus and series to be identified were randomly determined as was the order in which the individual stimuli were presented for identification. There was a total of 16 adaptation sessions, with at least 24 hr between sessions, yielding 10 identification responses to each stimulus of both series under each of the four adaptation conditions.

### SUBJECTS

The subjects were two undergraduate students and one graduate student at Brown University who were paid for their participation. Two of the subjects had previous experience in listening to synthetic speech.

## Results and Discussion

In Figure 7.2, the identification functions for a single subject are shown. In each instance, adaptation caused a notable shift in the phonetic boundary and moreover, the direction of the shifts in the locus of the phonetic boundary was uniformly consistent; the boundary moved closer to the adapting stimulus indicating a greater number of identification responses representing the unadapted mode of voicing had occurred. After adaptation with a voiced stop, the listener gave more identifi-

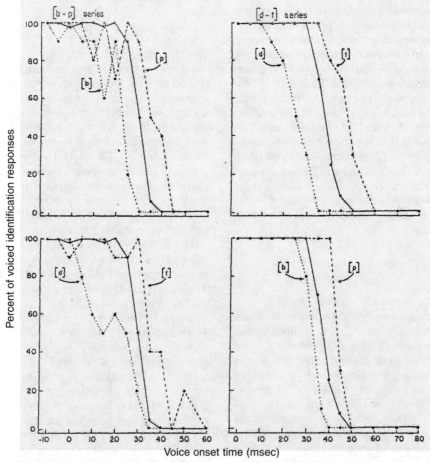

**FIGURE 7.2** ■ Percentages of voiced identification responses ([b or d]) obtained with and without adaptation for a single subject. The functions for the [b, p] series are on the left and those for the [d, t] series are on the right. The solid lines indicate the unadapted identification functions and the dotted and dashed lines, the identification functions after adaptation. The phonetic symbols indicate the adapting stimulus.

cation responses belonging to the voiceless category, especially when attempting to identify stimuli near the original phonetic boundary. Conversely, after adaptation with a voiceless stop, a greater number of identification responses belonged to the voiced category. Again the effect was most pronounced for stimuli near the phonetic boundary.

Of particular interest was the finding that the shifts in the locus of the phonetic boundary occurred when the adapting stimulus and identification stimuli were from different series. For example, adaptation with a bilabial stop produced an approximately equivalent effect on the identification of both bilabial and apical stops. These cross-series effects rule out explanations based on adaptation of the sound pattern as a phonetic unit. If this were the case, it is difficult to understand, for example, how alterations in the system underlying perception of [b] would likewise affect perception of the apical stops. In addition, given the acoustic differences between the two series with respect to the second- and third-formant transitions, and the cross-series adaptation effects, it is unlikely that what was, in fact, selectively adapted were detectors for simple acoustic information. Rather the evidence indicates that detectors for those complex aspects of the sound pattern that both series had in common, namely, voice onset time, were selectively adapted.

The identification functions for the remaining two subjects were very similar to those shown in Figure 7.2. In all, there were 24 instances of attempted adaptation, eight adapting conditions for each of three subjects. In each instance there was a shift in the phonetic boundary, and furthermore

the direction of the shift was always toward the voicing distinction that had been adapted, i.e., more identification responses belonged to the unadapted mode of voicing. The individual data are shown in Table 7.1. The mean shift in the locus of the phonetic boundary was 8.0 msec. It should be noted that the effects of adaptation were not symmetrical: the mean shift was 6.1 msec after adaptation with voiced stops and 10.0 msec after adaptation with voiceless stops. In addition for all listeners the mean magnitude of the boundary shift was only slightly (less than 2 msec) contingent upon the adapting stimulus and the identification series belonging to the same class of stop consonants (i.e., bilabial or apical).

Although we have not systematically investigated the time-course of recovery from adaptation, some preliminary investigations indicated that recovery is no more than 50% complete at the end of 90 sec and that complete recovery will require 30 min or more.

## Experiment 2

Given the categorical nature of the perception of the stop consonants as most markedly evidenced by a peak in the discriminability function of adjacent stimuli at the region of the phonetic boundary, we reasoned that the peak would shift after selective adaptation of one of the voicing detectors. That is, inasmuch as the ability to discriminate these stimuli has been found to be closely related to the ability to apply differential phonetic labels, then any shift in the locus of the phonetic boundary should be paralleled by a corresponding shift in

**TABLE 7.1. Shift in the Locus of the Phonetic Boundary in Milliseconds of VOT for the Identification Experiment**

| Identification Series | Subjects | Adapting Stimulus | | | |
|---|---|---|---|---|---|
| | | [b] | [p] | [d] | [t] |
| [b, p] | 1 (29.0)[a] | +6.3 | −13.8 | +.5 | −15.0 |
| | 2 (28.8) | +7.5 | −6.8 | +2.8 | −16.3 |
| | 3 (30.0) | +7.5 | −7.5 | +10.0 | −7.5 |
| | X̄ (29.3) | +7.1 | −9.4 | +4.4 | −12.9 |
| [d, t] | 1 (42.5) | +3.8 | −8.0 | +3.5 | −10.0 |
| | 2 (37.5) | +5.3 | −4.8 | +8.0 | −14.5 |
| | 3 (37.5) | +5.5 | −6.0 | +12.0 | −10.0 |
| | X̄ (39.2) | +4.9 | −6.3 | +7.8 | −11.5 |

[a] The number in parentheses shows the locus of the unadapted phonetic boundary.

the peak of the discriminability functions. To verify this we obtained discriminability functions for the [b, p] series before and after adaptation with the voiceless stop [p].

## Method

### STIMULI

The stimuli to be discriminated were 11 synthetic speech patterns taken from the [b, p] series of Experiment 1. The VOT values ranged from 0 to +50 msec in 5-msec steps. The adapting stimulus had a VOT value of +60 msec and was perceived uniformly as [p] plus the vowel [a].

### PROCEDURE

The psychophysical method of ABX was used to measure discriminability. For any set of three stimuli, the first stimulus A differed from the second stimulus B, and the third stimulus X was identical to the first stimulus or to the second stimulus. The listeners' task was to indicate whether the third stimulus was the same as the first or the second stimulus. Sets of stimuli to be discriminated were arranged by pairing each stimulus with the stimulus two steps (10 msec) removed. That is, the discriminability of VOT values 0 and +10, +5, and +15, and so forth was measured. There are 9 such pairs in all and 4 permutations for each pair (ABA, ABB, BAB, and BAA) for a total 36 possible triads.

To obtain the discriminability function without adaptation the 36 triads were presented to the listeners in random order. The stimuli within each triad were separated by 1.5 sec and each triad was separated by 5 sec. A total of 24 measures were obtained for each stimulus pair.

The procedure used to obtain the discriminablity function when the listeners were adapted was the same as that used during the identification study, except that in place of a single stimulus to be identified a randomly selected ABX triad was presented for discrimination. Twenty-four measures were obtained from each listener for each pair of stimuli.

### SUBJECTS

Two of the subjects had served as listeners in the first experiment and together with the third sub-

ject had had extensive experience in listening to synthetic speech.

## Results

Figure 7.3 depicts the mean discriminability function for the three subjects. We have used an average function in this instance since the individual functions were more variable than were the individual identification functions. This variability was most likely a function of the greater difficulty of the discrimination task. However, the effects evident in the group function also appear in each of the individual functions. Exposure to the voiceless stop [p] radically altered the discrimination function. There was a shift in the peak of the discrimination function that corresponded to the shift in the locus of the phonetic boundary, demonstrating in a novel manner that discrimination of the stop consonants is closely related to the ability to

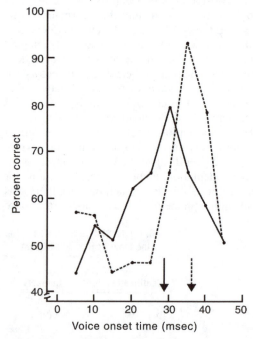

**FIGURE 7.3** ■ The group discriminability function. The points are plotted midway between the two values of voice onset time being discriminated. The dashed line represents the discriminability function after adaptation with [p]. The arrows indicate the locus of the phonetic boundaries found from identification functions with (dashed arrow) and without (solid arrow) adaptation with [p].

differentially identify the stimuli. The magnitude of the shift was 5 msec for two listeners and 10 msec for the third listener. The discriminability function clearly shows that after adaptation, when the likelihood is increased that the stimuli being discriminated belong to the same phonetic class, discriminability is at or very near chance. Conversely, for those stimuli which after adaptation have a greater probability of being assigned to different phonetic categories, there is a marked increase in the level of discrimination.

## General Discussion

The fact that repeated presentation of a member of one of the voicing categories dramatically reduces the sensitivity of the system to members of that category may be explained by assuming two linguistic feature detectors, each of which is tuned to a restricted range of VOT values and mediates the perception of one of the two voicing distinctions found in the stop consonants.

To explain how these detectors might operate to produce the identification and discrimination functions that are obtained with and without experimentally induced adaptation, the following assumptions are needed: (a) There exist detectors that are differentially sensitive to a range of VOT values with greatest sensitivity (as might be measured, in principle, by the output signal of the detector) occurring at the modal production value for a particular voicing distinction (Lisker & Abramson, 1964). (b) Some VOT values excite both detectors, but, all other things being equal, only the output signal with the greater strength reaches higher centers of processing and integration. (c) The phonetic boundary will lie at the VOT value that excites both detectors equally, all other factors being equal. (d) After adaptation, the sensitivity of a detector is lessened; that is, the output signal is weakened or decreased. Furthermore, for purposes of simplicity, the signal strength is assumed to decrease equally for the entire range of VOT values to which the detector is sensitive. From this it follows that selective adaptation shifts the phonetic boundary by shifting the point of equilibrium along the VOT continuum. If we further assume (e) that no distinction is made by higher-order processing elements between two output signals from the same detector, that is, no distinction

is made when the same detector is excited by two different values of VOT, then the peaked discriminability functions are readily accounted for.

The existence of linguistic feature detectors for the voicing distinctions among the stop consonants has a number of important implications. First, it provides a mechanism whereby infants can perceive the VOT continuum in a nearly categorical manner. Second, it adds credence to theoretical descriptions of the basic sound units of language based on distinctive features (Halle, 1962; Jakobson, Fant, & Halle, 1963). And finally it provides an example of a complex analysis of linguistic information in a manner at least analogus to that previously demonstrated in the visual system.

### NOTES

1. We thank Dr. F. S. Cooper for generously making available the facilities at the Haskins Laboratories and Drs. R. M. Church, D. J. Getty, and A. M. Liberman for their critical comments. We also thank Mrs. Catherine G. Wolf for her assistance in conducting these experiments. Supported by PHS Grants HD 05331 and MH 16608.
2. Department of Psychology, Brown University, Providence, Rhode Island 02912.
3. It should be noted that the cues underlying the voicing distinctions discussed in the present paper apply to sound segments in absolute initial position. Although, as Lisker and Abramson (1964) noted, voice onset time does effectively separate stop categories in sentences, there is some effect of embedding the various stops in continuous speech. As a consequence we have limited our research to voicing distinctions in initial positions, where voice onset time is relatively insensitive to contextual effects (Lisker & Abramson, 1967).
4. Inasmuch as this distinction, long voicing lead, does not exist in English and in fact may not be detectable by adult English speakers, we have restricted our research to the two voicing distinctions found in English.

### REFERENCES

Abramson, A. S. & Lisker, L. Discriminability along the voicing continuum: cross-language tests. In *Proceedings of the Sixth International Congress of Phonetic Sciences, Prague, 1967*. Prague: Academia, 1970, 569–573.

Blakemore, C. & Campbell, F. W. On the existence of neurons in the human visual system selectively sensitive to the orientation and size of retinal images. *Journal of Physiology*, 1969, *203,* 237–260.

Blakemore, C. & Sutton, P. Size adaptation: A new aftereffect. *Science*, 1969, *166,* 245–257.

Eimas, P. D., Siqueland, E. R., Jusczyk, P., & Vigorito, J. Speech perception in infants. *Science*, 1971, *171,* 303–306.

Halle, M. Phonology in generative grammar. *Word*, 1962, *18,* 54–72.

Hubel, D. H. & Wiesel, T. N. Receptive fields, binocular interaction and functional architecture in the cat's visual cortex. *Journal of Physiology*, 1962, *160,* 106–154.

Jakobson, R., Fant, C. G. M., & Halle, M. *Preliminaries to Speech Analysis.* Cambridge, Massachusetts: M. I. T. Press, 1963.

Lettvin, J. Y., Maturana, H. R., McCulloch, W. S., & Pitts, W. H. What the frog's eye tells the frog's brain. *Proceedings of the Institute of Radio Engineers*, New York *47,* 1959, 1940–1951.

Liberman, A. M., Cooper, F. S., Shankweiler, D. P., & Studdert-Kennedy, M. Perception of the speech code. *Psychological Review*, 1967, *74,* 431–461.

Lieberman, P. Towards a unified phonetic theory. *Linguistic Inquiry*, 1970, *1,* 307–322.

Lisker, L. & Abramson, A. S. A cross-language study of voicing in initial stops: acoustical measurements. *Word*, 1964, *20,* 384–422.

Lisker, L. & Abramson, A. S. Some effects of context on voice onset time in English stops. *Language and Speech*, 1967, *10,* 1–28.

Lisker, L. & Abramson, A. S. The voicing dimension: some experiments in comparative phonetics. In *Proceedings of the Sixth International Congress of Phonetic Sciences, Prague, 1967*. Prague: Academia, 1970, 563–567.

Mattingly, I. G. Synthesis by rule of General American English. Supplement to *Status Report on Speech Perception*, April 1968. New Haven: Haskins. Laboratories.

Wolf, C. G. The perception of step consonants by children. Unpublished Masters Thesis, Brown University, 1972.

# Failure to Detect Changes to People during a Real-World Interaction

Daniel J. Simons • Harvard University
Daniel T. Levin • Kent State University

Recent research on change detection has documented surprising failures to detect visual changes occurring between views of a scene, suggesting the possibility that visual representations contain few details. Although these studies convincingly demonstrate change blindness for objects in still images and motion pictures, they may not adequately assess the capacity to represent objects in the real world. Here we examine and reject the possibility that change blindness in previous studies resulted from passive viewing of 2-D displays. In one experiment, an experimenter initiated a conversation with a pedestrian, and during the interaction, he was surreptitiously replaced by a different experimenter. Only half of the pedestrians detected the change. Furthermore, successful detection depended on social group membership; pedestrians from the same social group as the experimenters detected the change but those from a different social group did not. A second experiment further examined the importance of this effect of social group. Provided that the meaning of the scene is unchanged, changes to attended objects can escape detection even when they occur during a natural, real-world interaction. The discussion provides a set of guidelines and suggestions for future research on change blindness.

**D**espite our impression that we retain the visual details of our surroundings from one view to the next, we are surprisingly unable to detect changes to such details. Recently, experiments from a number of laboratories have shown that people fail to detect substantial changes to photographs of objects and real-world scenes when the ability to detect retinal differences is eliminated (Blackmore, Brelstaff, Nelson, & Troscianko, 1995; Grimes, 1996; Henderson, 1997; McConkie & Currie, 1996; O'Regan, Deubel, Clark, & Rensink, 1997; Pashler, 1988; Phillips, 1974; Rensink, O'Regan, & Clark, 1997; Simons, 1996; for a review see Simons & Levin, 1997). That is, when retinally localizable information signaling a change is masked by an eye movement or a flashed blank screen, observers have difficulty detecting changes to the visual details of a scene. These findings of "change blindness" suggest that observers lack a precise visual representation of their world from one view to the next. Although we have known for some time that memory for scenes is often distorted, sometimes quite sparse, subject to suggestions, and influenced by expectations and goals (Bartlett, 1932/1977; Brewer & Treyens, 1981; Loftus, 1979; Nickerson & Adams, 1979), studies of change blindness suggest that such details may not be retained even from one instant to the next, a claim that is consistent with earlier studies of the integration of information from successive fixations (Bridgeman & Mayer, 1983; Dennett, 1991; Hochberg, 1986; Irwin, 1991; McConkie & Currie, 1996; Pashler, 1988; Rayner & Pollatsek, 1992).

Given the richness of our visual world, it is perhaps unsurprising that we cannot represent all the visual details of every object and instead must focus on a few important objects. Recent models of attention have argued that observers can fully represent the details of only a few centrally attended objects in a scene. For example, models based on object files (e.g., Treisman, 1993) suggest that we can simultaneously represent several distinct objects in our environment, updating our representations for changes in their properties and features. Such models suggest the possibility that representations of centrally attended objects are relatively detailed even if those for peripheral objects are not.

A recent series of studies directly examined the role of attention in the detection of changes to natural images (Rensink et al., 1997). In their "flicker paradigm," an original version and a modified version of an image were presented in rapid alternation (240 msec each), with a blank screen (80-msec duration) interposed between them, producing a flickering appearance. On each trial, subjects were asked to identify the changing part of the image as soon as they saw it. Consistent with earlier studies of integration across views (for a review, see Irwin, 1991), observers rarely noticed changes during the first cycle of alternation and often required many cycles to detect the change. The change detection process requires observers to shift their attention among the objects in the scene, actively searching for a change. As predicted by models of object files, changes to objects that independent raters consider to be the center of interest of a scene are detected in significantly fewer alternations than changes to peripheral objects. That is, changes to the details of attended objects are detected more readily.

Clearly, focused attention to an object is helpful and possibly necessary for change detection, as evidenced by such "center of interest" effects

(O'Regan, Rensink, & Clark, 1996; Rensink et al., 1997; Tarr & Aginsky, 1996, July) and by findings of more successful change detection when explicit cues specify the location or the type of change (Aginsky, Tarr, & Rensink, 1997). However, attention may not be sufficient for change detection. In fact, observers often fail to detect changes even when attention is focused directly on the changing object (Levin & Simons, 1997; O'Regan et al., 1997; Simons, 1996). In a recent series of studies, we used motion pictures to directly examine the ability to detect changes to attended objects (Levin & Simons, 1997). These brief motion pictures depicted a simple action performed by a "single" actor. During the film, the actor was replaced by a different person. For example, in one film an actor walked through an empty classroom and began to sit in a chair. The camera then changed, or "cut," to a closer view and a different actor completed the action. Even though the actors were easily discriminable and were the focus of attention, only 33% of the 40 participants reported noticing the change from one actor to another (Levin & Simons, 1997).

Although the motion picture experiments demonstrate that attention alone is not sufficient for a complete representation of the visual details of an object, they do not fully assess our ability to represent objects in the real world. Motion picture perception is similar in many ways to perception in the real world, but motion pictures are still a subset of a complete visual experience (Arnheim, 1933/1966). Most importantly, they are viewed passively and may not completely engage the processes necessary for a complete representation of attended objects. Furthermore, cuts from one view to another in motion pictures may artificially hamper our ability to detect changes. Although cuts are similar in some ways to eye movements, they also instantaneously change the simulated observation point. This artificial jump in viewing position may somehow disrupt the ability to detect changes even if it has little effect on our understanding of a scene. Similar objections might be raised about most studies documenting change blindness (for a discussion, see Simons & Levin, 1997). In all previous studies of change blindness, exposure to scenes has been mediated via photographs, computer displays, or television monitors. Perhaps people can more fully represent the details of a scene when they are direct participants, interacting with the objects in the real world.

Here we assess this possibility by taking the study of change blindness into the real world. Rather than changing the sole actor in a video, we changed the subjects' conversation partner during a typical daily interaction.

## Experiment 1

In Experiment 1, we created a situation that allowed us to surreptitiously substitute one individual for another in the middle of a natural, real-world interaction. The situation we chose was asking directions of a pedestrian on a college campus.[1] We temporarily interrupted this interaction by carrying a door between the experimenter and the pedestrian. While the experimenter was occluded by the door, another experimenter took his place and continued the interaction after the door had passed. If change-detection failures are based on the passive nature of mediated stimuli, these substitutions should be clearly detectable.

## Method

### SUBJECTS

A total of 15 pedestrians were approached on the campus of Cornell University. They ranged in approximate age from 20 to 65. Only pedestrians walking alone or together with one other person (two cases) were approached.

### PROCEDURE

An experimenter carrying a campus map asked unsuspecting pedestrians for directions to a nearby building (see Figure 8.1a). Pedestrians had a clear view of the experimenter starting from a distance of approximately 20 m as they walked down a sidewalk. After the experimenter and pedestrian had been talking for 10–15 sec, two other experimenters carrying a door rudely passed between them. As the door passed, the first experimenter grabbed the back of the door, and the experimenter who had been carrying that part of the door stayed behind and continued to ask for directions (Figure

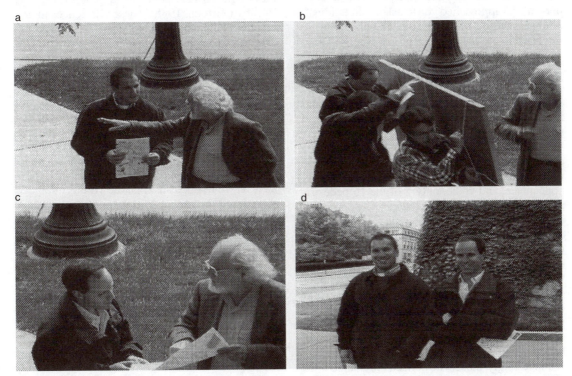

**FIGURE 8.1** ■ Frames from a video of a subject from Experiment 1. Frames a–c show the sequence of the switch. Frame d shows the two experimenters side by side.

8.1c). The first experimenter kept his map during the interruption, and the second experimenter produced an identical copy of the map after the door passed. The door blocked the pedestrian's view for approximately 1 sec (Figure 8.1b). From the subject's perspective, the door briefly occluded his/her conversation partner, and when it was gone, a different person was revealed. As the door passed, subjects typically made eye contact with the second experimenter before continuing to give directions.[2] The entire interaction took 2–5 min. The two experimenters wore different clothing and differed in height by approximately 5 cm (Figure 8.1d). Their voices were also clearly distinguishable.

After a pedestrian finished giving directions, the experimenter told him/her, "We're doing a study as part of the psychology department [experimenter points to the psychology building next door] of the sorts of things people pay attention to in the real world. Did you notice anything unusual at all when that door passed by a minute ago?" Responses were noted by the experimenter, and if subjects failed to report the change, they were directly asked, "Did you notice that I'm not the same person who approached you to ask for directions?" After answering this question, all subjects were informed about the purpose of the experiment.

## Results and Discussion

If change blindness results from the passive nature of mediated stimuli, then these real-world substitutions should be detected. When asked if they had noticed anything unusual, most pedestrians reported that the people carrying the door were rude. Yet, despite clear differences in clothing, appearance, and voice, only 7 of the 15 pedestrians reported noticing the change of experimenters. Those who did not notice the change continued the conversation as if nothing had happened (in fact, some pedestrians who did notice the change also continued the conversation!). Pedestrians who did not notice the change were quite surprised to learn that the person standing in front of them was different from the one who initiated the conversation. One pedestrian who reported noticing nothing unusual nonetheless claimed to have noticed the change when asked directly.

Interestingly, those who noticed the change were all students of roughly the same age as the experimenters (approximately 20–30 years old). Those who failed to detect the change were slightly older than the experimenters (approximately 35–65 years old). One possible explanation for this difference is that younger pedestrians were more likely to expend effort encoding those features that would differentiate the experimenters because the experimenters were roughly of their own generation. In contrast, older pedestrians would likely encode the experimenters without focusing on features that could differentiate the two of them, instead viewing them as members of a social group other than their own. This hypothesis draws on findings from social psychology that members of one's own social group ("in-group") are treated differently from members of social groups distinctly apart from one's own ("out-group"). Upon encountering a member of an in-group, people tend to focus attention on individuating features and to pay little attention to the person's social-group membership. In contrast, for members of out-groups, people direct more attention to attributes associated with the out-group as a whole and generally do not focus on features that distinguish one individual from others in the group (see, e.g., Rothbart & John, 1985). These differences in processing of members of in-groups and out-groups extend to many aspects of cognition. For example, people are likely to assume that members of out-groups are collectively less variable on a variety of traits and variables (Judd & Park, 1988; Linville, Fischer, & Salovey, 1989). This tendency to code group-specifying information for members of out-groups can even determine what represents a visual feature for a particular category (Levin, 1996).

Applying these differences in the coding of in-groups and out-groups to the findings of Experiment 1, we hypothesize that the younger subjects considered themselves members of the same social group as the experimenters and older subjects considered the experimenters to be members of an out-group. To test this hypothesis, we changed the appearance of the experimenters so that they could be classified as members of an out-group by the younger subjects.

## Experiment 2

To examine the role of social group membership in the detection of changes, a second experiment was conducted using the same procedure as the

**FIGURE** 8.2 ■ The experimenters dressed as construction workers for Experiment 2.

first, but with one critical change: The same two experimenters dressed as construction workers (see Figure 8.2). The experimenters again wore different clothing: One wore a construction hat with writing on the front, a large tool belt, and a light blue shirt, and the other wore a newer hat without writing, no tool belt, and a black shirt. The experiment was conducted in the same location as Experiment 1, which happened to be approximately 50 m from a construction site. As in Experiment 1, an experimenter approached a pedestrian to ask for directions to a building on campus. During the conversation, the experimenters were switched. Unlike in the first experiment, all 12 pedestrians who participated in Experiment 2 were from the younger age group (Cornell graduate or undergraduate students), the group that had always detected the change in Experiment 1. The questions asked of the subjects were identical to those of Experiment 1 except that subjects were informed immediately after providing directions that the experimenters were not actually construction workers but were doing a study as part of the psychology department.

## Results and Discussion

In contrast to the younger pedestrians in Experiment 1, all of whom noticed the change, only 4 of the 12 pedestrians in Experiment 2 reported noticing the switch when asked if they had seen anything unusual. Five subjects failed to report the change and were surprised to learn of the switch. An additional 3 subjects reported noticing nothing unusual but then claimed to have noticed the switch of experimenters. Unlike pedestrians who clearly noticed the change, these 3 pedestrians could not accurately describe any of the differences between the experimenters, suggesting that the demands of the task led them to report noticing the change even though they probably had not. Thus, subjects from the same age group that had successfully detected the change in Experiment 1 detected it only 33% of the time in Experiment 2.

When the experimenters appeared to be members of an out-group, thereby decreasing the likelihood that students would code individuating features, the ability to detect a change to the centrally attended object in a scene was dramatically reduced. One subject who failed to detect the change essentially stated our predicted hypothesis: She said that she had just seen a construction worker and had not coded the properties of the individual. That is, she quickly categorized the experimenter as a construction worker and did not retain those features that would allow individuation. Even though the experimenter was the center of attention, she did not code the visual details and compare them across views. Instead, she formed a representation of the category, trading the visual details of the scene for a more abstract understanding of its gist or meaning.

## General Discussion

These simple experiments build on classic findings of failures of eye-witness identification (e.g., Loftus, 1979) and distortions in memory (Bartlett, 1932/1977) as well as recent demonstrations of change blindness for objects (Pashler, 1988; Phillips, 1974; Simons, 1996), photographs (Aginsky et al., 1997; Grimes, 1996; O'Regan et al., 1996; Rensink et al., 1997), and motion pictures (Levin & Simons, 1997; Simons, 1996; Simons & Levin, 1997). Yet, unlike earlier demonstrations, this experiment shows that people may not notice changes to the central object in a scene even when the change is almost instantaneous and happens in the middle of an ongoing, natural event. Attention alone does not suffice for change detection, even in the real world. Instead, successful change detection probably requires effortful encoding of precisely those features or properties that will distinguish the original from the changed object.

One potential objection to our results derives from the pragmatics of the interaction. Specifically, subjects may have detected the change but the social demands of the situation precluded them from reporting it. This possibility is substantially diminished by the subjects in each experiment who reported noticing nothing unusual but then reported noticing the switch. Although these subjects probably did not notice the change, the social demands of the situation encouraged them to report having noticed the switch when asked directly. Thus, the demands of the situation seem biased to increase reports of the switch rather than to decrease them.

Another possible objection is that the task of giving directions distracted subjects from focusing their attention on the experimenters. That is, subjects were focused on the map rather than their conversational partner. Anecdotally at least, subjects appeared focused on the interaction and the conversation, often making eye contact with the experimenters, hearing their voices, and taking turns in a conversation. Although we believe the results are not specific to this situation, ongoing

experiments using a different type of interaction are directly examining the possible distraction caused by the map and possible disruptions to the representation of the first experimenter caused by the unusual nature of the interruption.

A more fundamental question involves assessing the similarity of the experimenters. Clearly, no one would be surprised if pedestrians failed to notice a substitution of identically dressed identical twins. The inability to notice small changes is unsurprising because such changes naturally occur between views. For example, people rarely notice variation in the position and orientation of moveable objects such as body parts (Levin & Simons, 1997). If we constantly noticed such changes, they would likely detract from our ability to focus on other, more important aspects of our visual world. Change detection as a method relies on the tendency of our visual system to assume an unchanging world. The fact that we do not expect one person to be replaced by another during an interaction may contribute to our inability to detect such changes. A critical question for future research is why some changes are more likely to be detected than others. Clearly we would be quite surprised if subjects missed a switch between enormously different people (e.g., a switch from a 4 ft 9 in. female of one race to a 6 ft 5 in. male of another). The change in this case would alter not only the visual details of the person, but also their category membership. If, as suggested by other recent findings of change blindness, we retain only abstracted information and not visual details from one view to the next, changes to category membership may well be detectable. Abstraction of category information is clearly central to coding other people (e.g., the effects of in-group and out-group discussed earlier) and may underlie the representation of other objects across views as well.

What, then, separates inconsequential changes to details from changes that are worth noting? Although there is no easy answer to this question, we would like to propose several guidelines or heuristics for identifying consequential changes for future studies of change blindness. These guidelines, used individually or together, can help constrain the generation of significant changes to scenes.

First, significant changes to a scene should be easily verbalizable, and often verbalized (see

Simons, 1996). Changes that are easily verbalized likely cross a category boundary, making them more likely to be detected. The best example of this principle is the change in the color of the experimenter's shirt in Experiment 2. Both shirt colors (blue and black) have basic color names.

Second, the original and changed objects should be easily discriminable in simultaneous viewing. Everyone is familiar with the comics page game of finding differences between two extremely similar images. In such cases, the change is camouflaged, making it difficult to detect even when both the original and changed version are present. In our experiment, as in most studies of change blindness (see Simons & Levin, 1997), changes generally meet this criterion (e.g., the difference in shirt colors is plainly visible in Figure 8.2).

Third, changes should affect the immediate functional needs of the perceiver. For example, changes to the spatial configuration of objects or their parts can be significant, even if they are not easy to verbalize. Spatial layout information is crucial to navigation and other immediate needs of the organism. For our experiments, variation in the configuration of facial features is precisely the information used in identifying other people; hence the person change should be readily detectable.

Fourth, naive subjects should predict successful change detection. If change blindness is counterintuitive, we can be certain that the change is not trivial. For our experiments, individuals unfamiliar with our research consistently predicted that the change of experimenters would be plainly detectable. To examine this possibility for our experiments, we informally polled a class of 50 introductory psychology students by reading them the following description of our event: "You are walking on the Cornell campus and a man with a puzzled look asks you to help him find Olin library. You stop and give him directions. While you are giving directions, two people carrying a door rudely walk between you and the lost pedestrian. After the door has passed, the person you were giving directions to is now a different person wearing different clothes." By a show of hands, they claimed without exception that they would detect the change.

By applying these four heuristics, researchers can be fairly certain that a change is detectable and that change blindness would be an important finding. In our experiments, the change from one experimenter to another met all of these criteria. Yet, a substantial number of pedestrians failed to detect the switch. Taken together, these experiments show that even substantial changes to the objects with which we are directly interacting will often go unnoticed. Our visual system does not automatically compare the features of a visual scene from one instant to the next in order to form a continuous representation; we do not form a detailed visual representation of our world. Instead, our abstract expectations about a situation allow us to focus on a small subset of the available information that we can use to check for consistency from one instant to the next.

## ACKNOWLEDGMENT

The authors contributed equally to this report, and authorship order was determined arbitrarily. Thanks to Leon Rozenblit, Carter Smith, Julia Noland, and Joy Beck for helping to carry out the experiments and to Linda Hermer for reading an earlier draft of the manuscript. D.J.S. was supported by NSF and Jacob K. Javits fellowships, and parts of this research appeared in his doctoral thesis. Correspondence should be addressed to D. J. Simons, Department of Psychology, Harvard University, 820 William James Hall, 33 Kirkland St., Cambridge, MA 02138 (e-mail: dsimons@wjh.harvard.edu) or D. T. Levin, Department of Psychology, Kent State University, P.O. Box 5190, Kent, OH 44242–0001 (e-mail: dlevin@kent.edu).

## NOTES

1. The idea for this experimental situation came from a comedy television show that used a similar event. Thanks to Ron Rensink for bringing it to our attention.
2. Although some subjects made more eye contact than others, the vantage point of our hidden camera precluded a precise analysis of the effect of eye contact on detection of the change; the initial eye contact between the second experimenter and the pedestrian was masked by the door. In all cases, subjects made extensive eye contact after completing their directions, and most pedestrians did make eye contact immediately before and after the arrival of the door, suggesting that eye contact does not guarantee successful detection of the change.

## REFERENCES

Aginsky, V., Tarr, M. J., & Rensink, R. A. (1997). The stability of color, location, and object presence in mental representations of natural scenes. *Investigative Ophthalmology & Visual Science, 38,* S1009.

Arnheim, R. (1966). *Film as art.* Berkeley: University of California Press. (Original work published 1933.)

Bartlett, F. C. (1977). *Remembering: A study in experimental and social psychology.* Cambridge: Cambridge University Press. (Original work published 1932.)

Blackmore, S. J., Brelstaff, G., Nelson, K., & Troscianko, T. (1995). Is the richness of our visual world an illusion? Transsaccadic memory for complex scenes. *Perception, 24,* 1075–1081.

Brewer, W. F., & Treyens, J. C. (1981). Role of schemata in memory for places. *Cognitive Psychology, 13,* 207–230.

Bridgeman, B., & Mayer, M. (1983). Failure to integrate visual information from successive fixations. *Bulletin of the Psychonomic Society, 21,* 285–286.

Dennett, D. C. (1991). *Consciousness explained.* Boston: Little, Brown.

Grimes, J. (1996). On the failure to detect changes in scenes across saccades. In K. Akins (Ed.), *Perception: Vol. 2. Vancouver studies in cognitive science* (pp. 89–110). New York: Oxford University Press.

Henderson, J. M. (1997). Transsaccadic memory and integration during real-world object perception. *Psychological Science, 8,* 51–55.

Hochberg, J. (1986). Representation of motion and space in video and cinematic displays. In K. R. Boff, L. Kaufman, & J. P. Thomas (Eds.), *Handbook of perception and human performance: Vol. 1. Sensory processes and perception* (pp. 22.21–22.64). New York: Wiley.

Irwin, D. E. (1991). Information integration across saccadic eye movements. *Cognitive Psychology, 23,* 420–456.

Judd, C. M., & Park, B. (1988). Out-group homogeneity: Judgments of variability at the individual and group levels. *Journal of Personality & Social Psychology, 54,* 778–788.

Levin, D. T. (1996). Classifying faces by race: The structure of face categories. *Journal of Experimental Psychology: Learning, Memory, & Cognition, 22,* 1364–1382.

Levin, D. T., & Simons, D. J. (1997). Failure to detect changes to attended objects in motion pictures. *Psychonomic Bulletin & Review, 4,* 501–506.

Linville, P. W., Fischer, G. W., & Salovey, P. (1989). Perceived distributions of the characteristics of in-group and out-group members: Empirical evidence and a computer simulation. *Journal of Personality & Social Psychology, 57,* 165–188.

Loftus, E. F. (1979). *Eyewitness testimony.* Cambridge, MA: Harvard University Press.

McConkie, G. W., & Currie, C. B. (1996). Visual stability across saccades while viewing complex pictures. *Journal of Experimental Psychology: Human Perception & Performance, 22,* 563–581.

Nickerson, R. S., & Adams, M. J. (1979). Long-term memory for a common object. *Cognitive Psychology, 11,* 287–307.

O'Regan, J. K., Deubel, H., Clark, J. J., & Rensink, R. A. (1997). Picture changes during blinks: Not seeing where you look and seeing where you don't look. *Investigative Ophthalmology & Visual Science, 38,* S707.

O'Regan, J. K., Rensink, R. A., & Clark, J. J. (1996). "Mud splashes" render picture changes invisible. *Investigative Ophthalmology & Visual Science, 37,* S213.

Pashler, H. (1988). Familiarity and visual change detection. *Perception & Psychophysics, 44,* 369–378.

Phillips, W. A. (1974). On the distinction between sensory storage and short-term visual memory. *Perception & Psychophysics, 16,* 283–290.

Rayner, K., & Pollatsek, A. (1992). Eye movements and scene perception. *Canadian Journal of Psychology, 46,* 342–376.

Rensink, R. A., O'Regan, J. K., & Clark, J. J. (1997). To see or not to see: The need for attention to perceive changes in scenes. *Psychological Science, 8,* 368–373.

Rothbart, M., & John, O. P. (1985). Social categorization and behavioral episodes: A cognitive analysis of the effects of intergroup contact. *Journal of Social Issues, 41,* 81–104.

Simons, D. J. (1996). In sight, out of mind: When object representations fail. *Psychological Science, 7,* 301–305.

Simons, D. J., & Levin, D. T. (1997). Change blindness. *Trends in Cognitive Sciences, 1,* 261–267.

Tarr, M. J., & Aginsky, V. (1996, July). *From objects to scenes: Speculations on similarities and differences.* Paper presented at the Scene Recognition Workshop, Max-Planck-Institut für Biologische Kybernetik, Tübingen.

Treisman, A. (1993). The perception of features and objects. In A. Baddeley & L. Weiskrantz (Eds.), *Attention: Selection, awareness, and control: A tribute to Donald Broadbent* (pp. 5–35). Oxford: Oxford University Press, Clarendon Press.

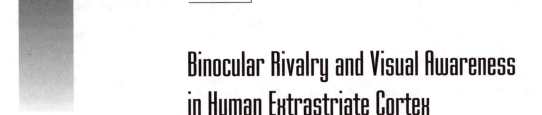

# Binocular Rivalry and Visual Awareness in Human Extrastriate Cortex

Frank Tong • Harvard University

Ken Nakayama • Harvard University

J. Thomas Vaughan • Massachusetts General Hospital

Nancy Kanwisher • Massachusetts General Hospital and

Massachusetts Institute of Technology

## Summary

We used functional magnetic resonance imaging (fMRI) to monitor stimulus-selective responses of the human fusiform face area (FFA) and parahippocampal place area (PPA) during binocular rivalry in which a face and a house stimulus were presented to different eyes. Though retinal stimulation remained constant, subjects perceived changes from house to face that were accompanied by increasing FFA and decreasing PPA activity; perceived changes from face to house led to the opposite pattern of responses. These responses during rivalry were equal in magnitude to those evoked by nonrivalrous stimulus alternation, suggesting that activity in the FFA and PPA reflects the perceived rather than the retinal stimulus, and that neural competition during binocular rivalry has been resolved by these stages of visual processing.

## Introduction

Binocular vision normally leads to a single stable interpretation of the visual world. But when discrepant monocular images are presented to the two eyes, they rival for perceptual dominance such that only one monocular image is perceived at a time while the other is suppressed from awareness (e.g., Levelt, 1965). This phenomenon of binocular rivalry was originally thought to reflect competition between the inputs from each eye, either in the lateral geniculate nucleus or primary visual cortex (V1) (e.g., Blake, 1989). However, single unit recordings in alert monkeys have revealed that only a small percentage of neurons in V1/V2 (9%), V4 (18%), and MT (12%) show increased activity when their preferred stimulus is perceived during rivalry, and that some neurons in V4 (9%) and MT (11%) actually fire more when their preferred stimulus is phenomenally suppressed (Logothetis and Schall, 1989; Leopold and Logothetis, 1996).

These single unit studies suggest that competitive interactions in binocular rivalry are not restricted to monocular neurons in V1 (see also Sengpiel and Blakemore, 1994) but continue to occur at much higher levels of the visual pathway, such as V4 and MT, well after inputs from the two eyes have converged in V1. However, these studies do not reveal if or when this competition is resolved, such that neural activity no longer reflects the presence of the suppressed stimulus and solely reflects the perceived stimulus. Although most neurons (84%) in the inferotemporal cortex of monkeys show significant changes in neural activity corresponding to perceived changes in a rivalrous stimulus, these neural changes are only about half the magnitude of those evoked by nonrivalrous stimulus changes (Sheinberg and Logothetis, 1997). If binocular rivalry were fully resolved, one would expect to find equivalent neural modulations for perceived changes during rivalry and actual stimulus changes.

The present study used functional magnetic resonance imaging (fMRI) to investigate whether activity in human extrastriate cortex is correlated to visual awareness during binocular rivalry, and, more specifically, whether activity changes during rivalry might be comparable to those found during nonrivalrous stimulus alternation. If equivalent responses were found in a specific neural region, this would indicate that binocular rivalry is resolved by this stage of the visual pathway. Such brain regions would not only provide a neural basis for phenomenal dominance and suppression during rivalry, but might also provide insights regarding visual awareness under general conditions of perceptual ambiguity (Crick, 1996; Leopold and Logothetis, 1996).

We capitalized on the stimulus-selective response properties of two high-level visual areas: the human fusiform face area (FFA), which responds selectively to faces as compared to a variety of nonface stimuli (Kanwisher et al., 1997; McCarthy et al., 1997; Tong et al., submitted), and the parahippocampal place area (PPA), which responds strongly to houses and places but not to faces (Epstein and Kanwisher, 1998). The differential response properties of these two regions allowed us to measure changes in fMRI signals during rivalry and nonrivalry alternations.

Three types of fMRI scans were performed: localizer, rivalry, and nonrivalry scans. On localizer scans, alternating sequences of nonrivalrous faces and houses were binocularly presented in order to functionally localize each subject's FFA and PPA. The FFA was defined as the region in the mid-fusiform gyrus that responded significantly more to faces than houses, and the PPA was defined as the region in the parahippocampal gyrus that responded significantly more to houses than faces. These two areas served as the regions of interest for subsequent rivalry and nonrivalry scans.

On rivalry scans, a face image was presented to one eye and a house image was presented to the other eye while subjects maintained fixation (see Figure 9.1a in color insert following page 176).

Subjects used a button box to report when their dominant percept switched to that of a face or house. On subsequent nonrivalry scans, the stimulus alternated between nonrivalrous monocular presentations of either face or house alone using the identical temporal sequences reported during previous rivalry scans in the same subject (see Figure 9.1b in color insert). Subjects maintained fixation and reported when the stimulus switched to a face or house. For rivalry and nonrivalry scans, fMRI activity in the predefined FFA and PPA was monitored every second and later analyzed in an event-related fashion time-locked to the subject's report of a change in percept.

## Results

### Localizer Scans

The FFA and PPA regions of interest were successfully localized in all subjects. The anatomical locus and extent of these regions were highly consistent with those described in previous studies (Kanwisher et al., 1997; McCarthy et al., 1997; Epstein and Kanwisher, 1998). The size of the FFA ranged from 4 to 8 voxels across the three subjects with unilateral FFA regions and comprised a total of 22 voxels in a subject with a bilateral FFA (median FFA size across subjects = 6.5 voxels; voxel size = $3.25 \times 3.25 \times 7$ mm). The PPA appeared bilaterally in all subjects and ranged in size from 25 to 49 voxels (median size = 36.5 voxels).

Figure 9.2a (see color insert) shows the localized FFA and PPA of one subject in two adjacent near-axial slices. Whereas the FFA is lateralized to the right fusiform gyrus in this subject, the PPA occurs bilaterally in parahippocampal cortex. Figure 9.2b (see color insert) shows the time course of MR signal for the FFA and PPA during localizer scans, averaged across all four subjects. During each of the 16 s stimulus periods, the FFA responded vigorously to sequentially presented faces but only weakly to houses, whereas the PPA responded strongly to houses and weakly to faces.

### Rivalry Scans

All subjects reported strong perceptual alternations between a face-dominant and a house-dominant percept while they maintained fixation on the

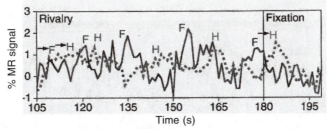

**FIGURE 9.3** ■ Example of Raw Data from Rivalry Scan
Raw MR time course (expressed in percent signal change relative to fixation baseline) showing FFA (solid line) and PPA (dotted line) activity from part of a rivalry scan. While the subject (S1) viewed a rivalrous face/house stimulus or static fixation point. All reported switches to a face percept (F) or house percept (H) have been shifted forward by 4 s (as illustrated by arrows) to compensate for the lag in the hemodynamic fMRI response. (This time shift was not applied to any other analysis or figure.)

rivalrous face/house stimulus. The mean duration of these face percepts and house percepts were of comparable length for each subject but varied in length between subjects (ranging from 2.5 to 5.5 s). The perceptual durations of each subject were distributed according to a gamma-shaped function, as typically found in binocular rivalry studies (e.g., Levelt, 1965).

Figure 9.3 shows the raw fMRI activity and reported perceptual switches of one subject during a portion of a rivalry scan. (Note that for this figure alone, perceptual responses have been shifted forward by 4 s to compensate for the lag in the hemodynamic fMRI response). Even in the raw MR time course, a correspondence between FFA activity, PPA activity, and perceptual awareness could be seen (cf. Brown and Norcia, 1997). FFA activity was generally greater during face than house percepts, whereas PPA activity was greater during house than face percepts.

Average fMRI time course functions for each subject were constructed by separately averaging FFA and PPA signal intensities over all occurrences of a perceptual switch in a given direction (i.e., house to face versus face to house) time-locked to each reported switch. Figure 9.4a shows the average time course of subject S1. Changes from a house percept to a face percept were accompanied by a sharp rise in FFA activity and a sharp fall in PPA activity (left panel), whereas changes from face to house led to the opposite pattern of activity (right panel). These fMRI responses corresponded to the direction of the perceptual switch and thus the content of visual awareness.

Figure 9.5 reveals that all four subjects showed the same qualitative pattern of fMRI responses during rivalry. Switches to the *preferred* percept

of a given region (e.g., house to face switches for the FFA) always led to significant increases in fMRI activity within the specified time window of –2 to +4 s (Figure 9.5a; 8/8 cases), whereas switches to a *nonpreferred* percept led to significant decreases in activity (Figure 9.5c; 7/8 cases). These fMRI responses were closely linked to the time of the reported perceptual switch in all subjects. For all reliable fMRI changes during rivalry, the initial peak or trough always occurred within a narrow time window of –2 to 0 s. These initial extrema significantly preceded the subject's own behavioral response (mean = –0.9 s; t[14] = 4.5; p < 0.001) and appeared to reflect the time of the perceptual switch itself. Final extrema in fMRI activity occurred 1 to 4 s after the subject's response, with durations ranging from 2 to 6 s from the initial to the final peak or trough.

The duration and magnitude of fMRI responses corresponded to the duration of the subject's reported percept. This is illustrated in Figure 9.6, which shows that for subject S2 during switches from face to house, increases in the perceived duration of house led to larger and longer responses from the PPA (rising activity, left panel) and FFA (falling activity, right panel). Enough observations of varying percept durations were collected to reveal this increase in fMRI response magnitude and duration as a function of percept duration in three out of four subjects.

The above results indicate that FFA and PPA activity is tightly linked to visual awareness during rivalry, reflecting both the content and duration of each percept. The observed changes in fMRI activity as a function of percept duration further indicate that our measure of fMRI signals is sufficiently sensitive to detect rather small

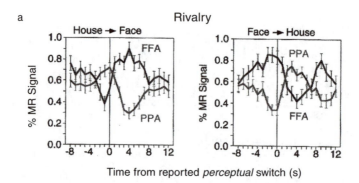

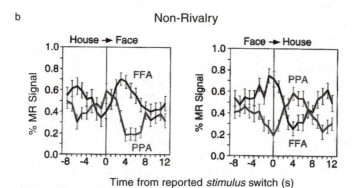

**FIGURE 9.4** ■ Rivalry versus Nonrivalry Data for Subject S1
Average FFA and PPA activity during reported house-to-face switches (left) or face-to-house switches (right) for rivalry (a) and nonrivalry (b) scans for one subject (S1). Vertical line indicates the time of the subject's response (averaged to the nearest second). Vertical bars represent ±1 SEM.

differences in fMRI responses and unlikely to be limited by response saturation. These points will be relevant when we next compare the magnitude of fMRI responses found during rivalry versus nonrivalry.

## Rivalry Versus Nonrivalry Scans

In order to determine the extent to which FFA and PPA activity reflected the perceived as opposed to the retinal stimulus, fMRI signal changes during rivalry were compared with nonrivalrous changes in the retinal stimulus itself. Figure 9.4b shows the average fMRI time course during reported nonrivalrous stimulus switches for subject S1. Inspection of the rivalry and nonrivalry figures (Figures 9.4a and 9.4b) reveals a striking resemblance, not only in the qualitative pattern of FFA and PPA responses but also in the amplitude of these activity changes. This similarity can be seen for all sub-

jects in Figure 9.5 by comparing individual fMRI responses for rivalry (columns a and c) and nonrivalry (columns b and d).

In order to quantify the effects of rivalry versus nonrivalry across subjects, the sign-preserving amplitude of each fMRI response (i.e., final minus initial peak or trough value) was measured for each condition, subject, switch type, and region of interest, as shown in Figure 9.5. The resulting scatterplot in Figure 9.7 reveals a remarkable correspondence in the fMRI responses found across subjects during rivalry (ordinate) versus nonrivalry (abscissa). All points cluster tightly around the line of identical amplitudes of MR responses for rivalry and nonrivalry. A line of best fit accounted for 94% of the variance ($R^2$), and yielded a slope of 0.91 and an intercept of 0.05, which did not significantly differ from a theoretical slope of 1 or intercept of 0. These results indicate that FFA and PPA responses during perceived changes in an

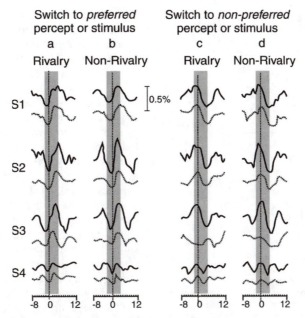

**FIGURE 9.5** ■ Rivalry versus Nonrivalry Data for All Subjects
FFA (solid) and PPA (dotted) time courses for switches to a preferred or nonpreferred percept (rivalry) or stimulus (nonrivalry) for all four subjects. Error bars representing ± 1 SEM indicate when activity reached a maximum or minimum within the specified time window of –2 to +4 s (gray region). Scale depicts 0.5% MR signal change. Switches to a preferred percept (a) or stimulus (b) led to significant increases in activity in 16 of 16 cases (t > 3.3; p < 0.05 Bonferroni corrected). Nonpreferred switches (c and d) led to significant decreases in activity in 14 of 16 cases (S3 showed nonsignificant PPA changes for both rivalry and nonrivalry).

ambiguous rivalrous stimulus are of equal magnitude to those evoked by unambiguous changes in the stimulus itself. This strongly suggests that competitive neural interactions underlying binocular rivalry have been resolved by the time visual information reaches the FFA or PPA.

Overall, the timing of fMRI responses for rivalry and nonrivalry were quite similar (see Figure 9.5). The initial extrema for all reliable fMRI responses during nonrivalry always occurred within a narrow window of –1 to +1 s (relative to the reported switch) as compared to –2 to 0 s for

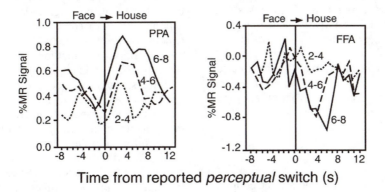

Time from reported *perceptual* switch (s)

**FIGURE 9.6** ■ Effect of Percept Duration
Average PPA (right) and FFA (left) activity for perceived face-to-house switches during rivalry for one subject (S2). Data are plotted as a function of the duration of the house percept: dotted lines, 2–4 s; dashed lines, 4–6 s; solid lines, 6–8 s.

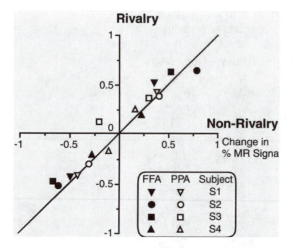

**FIGURE 9.7** ■ fMRI Response Amplitudes for Rivalry versus Nonrivalry. Scatterplot comparing the amplitude of fMRI responses during rivalry (ordinate) and nonrivalry (abscissa) for each region, switch type, and subject (obtained from data shown in Figure 9.5). Positive points in the top right quadrant reflect increases in fMRI activity during switches to a preferred percept or stimulus; negative points in the bottom left quadrant reflect decreases in activity during nonpreferred switches. Note that all points cluster tightly around the line of identical amplitudes of fMRI responses for rivalry and nonrivalry.

rivalry. The somewhat earlier fMRI response for rivalry than nonrivalry (−0.9 s versus −0.1 s, respectively; $t[14] = 4.6$; $p < 0.001$) likely reflects the fact that subjects required more time to determine when a perceptual switch during rivalry had occurred, as well as the fact that a brief face/house blend was sometimes perceived during these switches. Final extrema for fMRI responses were generally comparable for rivalry and nonrivalry (mean = 2.9 s, range = +1 to +4 s for rivalry; mean = 3.3 s, range = +2 to +4 s for nonrivalry; $t[14] = 1.58$; ns), whereas the duration of fMRI responses, estimated by the time difference between the final and initial extrema, were somewhat longer for rivalry than nonrivalry (3.9 s versus 3.4 s, respectively; $t(14) = 2.17$; $p < 0.05$).

## Discussion

The present study demonstrates a tight coupling between human visual awareness and neural activity in two extrastriate areas. When subjects viewed a rivalrous face/house stimulus, they re-

ported spontaneous alternations every few seconds between a face percept and a house percept, consistent with previous binocular rivalry studies (e.g., Levelt, 1965; Blake, 1989). Even though the retinal stimulation remained constant, perceptual alternations during rivalry were accompanied by time-locked fMRI responses in the FFA and PPA that were correlated with the content of visual awareness. Perceived switches from house to face led to sharp increases in FFA activity and decreases in PPA activity; perceived switches from face to house led to the opposite pattern of fMRI responses. Similar fMRI responses occurred when subjects viewed actual alternations between a nonrivalrous face stimulus and house stimulus using the same temporal sequence reported by the subject on previous rivalry scans. Indeed, fMRI responses accompanying phenomenal changes during rivalry were identical in magnitude to those evoked by changes in the stimulus itself.

Our results provide an upper bound for the stage of processing at which binocular rivalry is resolved. Single unit studies of alert monkeys have revealed that only a small percentage of neurons in V1/V2, V4, and MT show increased activity when their preferred stimulus is perceived during rivalry and that some neurons in V4 and MT actually show activity changes corresponding to the suppressed stimulus (Logothetis and Schall, 1989; Leopold and Logothetis, 1996). This suggests that rivalrous information from the two eyes may not be resolved into a single dominant percept by these stages of the visual pathway. Although most neurons in inferotemporal cortex follow the perceived stimulus during rivalry, these neural changes are only about half the magnitude of those observed during nonrivalrous stimulus alternation (Sheinberg and Logothetis, 1997). In contrast, our results demonstrate that in the FFA and PPA, neural responses to a change in perceptual awareness with the stimulus held constant are as large as responses to a change in the stimulus itself. This suggests that competitive neural interactions underlying binocular rivalry are resolved by the time visual information reaches the FFA and PPA.

These findings provide an important contribution to our understanding of the neural basis of binocular rivalry. A number of previous studies have used EEG (e.g., Lansing, 1964; Cobb et al., 1967; Brown and Norcia, 1997) or MEG (Tononi et al., 1998) to demonstrate correlations between neural activity and human visual awareness during rivalry. However, these techniques provide rather coarse information about the cortical locus of awareness-related responses. A recent fMRI study of binocular rivalry used a design similar to ours to ask the orthogonal question of which brain regions are active during reported perceptual alternations (independent of the direction of the switch) compared to intervals in which no alternation occurred (Lumer et al., 1998). They found that parietal and frontal regions were more strongly activated by reported perceptual switches during rivalry than by reported stimulus switches during nonrivalry. They also briefly mention some evidence of fusiform activity correlated with the content of perception. Our study goes beyond these earlier reports to provide specific data regarding the cortical locus of competitive interactions in binocular rivalry and the role of the FFA and PPA in visual awareness.

The identity in neural response for perceived changes during rivalry and actual stimulus changes during nonrivalry suggests that activity in the FFA and PPA reflects the perceived rather than the retinal stimulus. Consistent with this conclusion, recent studies have shown that FFA responses are strongly modulated by voluntary selective attention when the stimulus is held constant (Wojciulik et al., 1998) and that the FFA and PPA are respectively activated during mental imagery of faces or places, even when no visual stimulus is present at all (O'Craven and Kanwisher, submitted). In the present study, we found that these areas also respond during spontaneous reversals of perception during rivalry, demonstrating that awareness-related changes in these regions can occur without effortful voluntary acts of selective attention or mental imagery. These findings support the notion that multiple extrastriate regions such as the FFA and PPA participate in our awareness of specific attributes of the visual world.

## Experimental Procedures

### SUBJECTS

Four experienced observers, ages 20–39, served as subjects. Subjects were right-handed healthy adults with normal or corrected-to-normal visual acuity and normal stereo-depth perception. All subjects reported vigorous binocular rivalry (i.e.,

frequent periods of exclusive phenomenal dominance) in a prior psychophysical testing session.

### MRI ACQUISITION

Scanning was done on a 3T GE scanner at the MGH-NMR Center (Charlestown, MA), using a quadrature bilateral surface coil which provided a high signal-to-noise ratio in posterior brain regions. High resolution anatomical and functional images were collected using six or seven slices, oriented either parallel or perpendicular to the subject's brain stem and centered over the occipito-temporal junction to encompass the FFA and PPA. Standard fMRI procedures were used (gradient echo, EPI acquisition, TE = 30 ms, flip angle = 90°, TR = 2 s for localizer scans; faster TR of 1 s for better temporal resolution on rivalry and nonrivalry scans). A bite bar minimized head motion.

### LOCALIZER SCANS

Each subject's FFA and PPA were functionally localized based on two or three localizer scans (Figure 9.1), using previously described methods (Kanwisher et al., 1997). The FFA included all contiguous voxels in the mid-fusiform gyrus, which responded significantly more to faces than houses, whereas the PPA included all voxels in parahippocampal gyrus, which responded significantly more to houses than faces, using a minimum significance threshold of $p < 10^{-6}$ for each. Only after the precise regions of interest were established based on the independent localizer data did we proceed with subsequent rivalry and nonrivalry analyses.

### RIVALRY AND NONRIVALRY SCANS

The rivalrous stimulus consisted of a superimposed face and house separately defined by red and green luminance variations (Figure 9.1a). When seen through a red filter over one eye and a green filter over the other, only the face was visible through one eye and only the house through the other eye (filters transmitted <4% of the unmatched versus matched luminance color). The nonrivalrous face and nonrivalrous house were defined by either red or green luminance variations alone (Figure 9.1b), which led to alternating monocular presentation through the filters. Both the color assignment (green face and red house or vice versa) and the placement of the filters (green left and red right or vice versa) were counterbalanced across the four subjects. The face/house stimulus subtended 5°–8° of visual angle. Centered within the stimulus was a dark circular fixation point which could be seen through both eyes.

Each subject received five or six rivalry scans and an equal number of nonrivalry scans. For rivalry scans, the rivalrous face/house stimulus was continuously presented for two 75 s periods interleaved within three 15 s fixation periods during which a central fixation point was presented on a yellow square (5°–8° in width). Subjects maintained fixation and reported when their dominant percept changed to that of a "face," "house," or "blend" by pressing one of three keys on a button box. Subjects were instructed to report face/house blends if they persisted over time and not to report blends that were briefly perceived during switches. Nonrivalry scans were identical to rivalry scans with the exception that the stimulus alternated between monocular presentations of either face or house alone using the identical temporal sequence reported on a previous rivalry scan in the same subject. When a blend was reported during rivalry (which happened infrequently), a face/house blend was presented for the corresponding nonrivalry stimulus period.

Activity in the FFA and PPA was analyzed relative to the time of each reported switch. A "face" response was coded as a valid house-to-face switch if it was immediately preceded by "house" or if an intervening "blend" response occurred <2 s prior to the "face" response. A house-to-face switch further required that the report of "face" last a minimum of 2 s before the next response. This was done because a brief face percept or face stimulus followed by "house" typically yielded a small and unreliable MR signal change that was soon followed by the opposite fMRI response (corresponding to house). By contrast, longer durations led to longer, larger, and more reliable responses (see Figure 9.6). The same method was used to code whether a "house" response was a valid face-to-house switch.

Percent MR signal change was calculated using each subject's average signal intensity during fixation epochs (shifted by 5 s to approximate the expected hemodynamic lag) as a baseline. This time shift was only used to calculate baseline fMRI activity and was not applied to any other analysis.

FFA and PPA activity data were sorted (to the nearest second) relative to the time of each reported switch to generate an average time course plot (see Figure 9.4). The average time course plot of each subject comprised an average of 40–121 observations. The amplitude of fMRI change during reported switches for each subject, viewing condition, switch type, and region of interest was measured within the restricted time window of –2 to +4 s as shown in Figure 9.5. This method provided the simplest and most direct measure of fMRI response magnitudes, requiring minimal *a priori* assumptions regarding the precise shape or temporal lag of the hemodynamic response. To test the statistical significance of these fMRI activity changes, peak and trough fMRI values were compared using a conservative Bonferroni corrected test ($t > 3.3$; $p < 0.05$) to account for the number of implicit comparisons within the restricted time window of –2 to +4s.

## ACKNOWLEDGMENTS

We would like to thank members of the MGH-NMR Center for technical assistance and Patrick Cavanagh, Janine Mendola, Bruce Rosen, John Rubin, Adriane Seiffert, Paul Downing, and Zoe Kourtzi for comments on this manuscript. This study was supported by an NSERC postgraduate scholarship to F. T.; grants from NIMH, the Human Frontiers Science Program, and the Dana Foundation to N. K.; and an AFOSR grant to K. N.

## REFERENCES

Blake, R. (1989). A neural theory of binocular rivalry. *Psychol. Rev. 96*, 145–167.

Brown, R. J., and Norcia, A. M. (1997). A method for investigating binocular rivalry in real-time with the steady-state VEP. *Vision Res. 37*, 2401–2408.

Cobb, W. A., Morton, H. B., and Ettlinger, G. (1967). Cerebral potentials evoked by pattern reversal and their suppression in visual rivalry. *Nature 216*, 1123–1125.

Crick, F. (1996). Visual perception: rivalry and consciousness. *Nature 379*, 485–486.

Epstein, R., and Kanwisher, N. (1998). A cortical representation of the local visual environment. *Nature 392*, 598–601.

Kanwisher, N., McDermott, J., and Chun, M. M. (1997). The fusiform face area: a module in human extrastriate cortex specialized for face perception. *J. Neurosci. 17*, 4302–4311.

Lansing, R. W. (1964). Electroencephalographic correlates of binocular rivalry in man. *Science 146*, 1325–1327.

Leopold, D. A., and Logothetis, N. K. (1996). Activity changes in early visual cortex reflect monkeys' percepts during binocular rivalry. *Nature 379*, 549–553.

Levelt, W. J. M. (1965). On Binocular Rivalry (Assen, the Netherlands: Royal VanGorcum).

Logothetis, N. K., and Schall, J. D. (1989). Neural correlates of subjective visual perception. *Science 245*, 761–763.

Lumer, E. D., Friston, K. J., and Rees, G. (1998). Neural correlates of perceptual rivalry in the human brain. *Science 280*, 1930–1934.

McCarthy, J. C., Puce, A., Gore, J. C., and Allison, T. (1997). Face-specific processing in the human fusiform gyrus. *J. Cogn. Neurosci. 9*, 604–609.

Sengpiel, F., and Blakemore, C. (1994). Interocular control of neuronal responsiveness in cat visual cortex. *Nature 368*, 847–850.

Sheinberg, D. L., and Logothetis, N. K. (1997). The role of temporal cortical areas in perceptual organization. *Proc. Natl. Acad. Sci. USA 94*, 3408–3413.

Tononi, G., Srinivasan, R., Russell, D. P., and Edelman, G. M. (1998). Investigating neural correlates of conscious perception by frequency-tagged neuromagnetic responses. *Proc. Natl. Acad. Sci. USA 95*, 3198–3203.

Wojciulik, E., Kanwisher, N., and Driver, J. (1998). Modulation of activity in the fusiform face area by covert attention: an fMRI study. *J. Neurophysiol. 79*, 1574–1578.

PART II

# Pattern Recognition

## Discussion Questions

1. Neisser reviews considerable evidence showing that context influences pattern recognition. Review the details of one of the examples, and provide a description of how context might aid in pattern recognition. Do you think that context actually produces an influence on more perceptual components of pattern recognition or more the conscious guessing aspects of pattern recognition? Review relevant evidence.
2. In speech perception, there are a limited set of phonetic features that are combined to produce phonological segments. This appears to be a common aspect of all languages. However, humans have considerably more flexibility in producing and perceiving sounds. Why would languages evolve with this constraint?
3. There is clear evidence for a limited set of features that are the building blocks in both the visual and the auditory processing of language. Review the evidence for such features and discuss why you think models built on simple features may or may not be complete.
4. Given that our eyes receive input from different spatial locations, why don't we perceive two different perspectives of the world? What insights does the Tong et al. study provide on this aspect of pattern recognition?
5. One might argue that the Simons and Levine study is a classic example of a top-down influence on perception. Describe the additional constraints that humans might use to process visual information in seemingly simple situations. What are the limitations of the Simons and Levine study?

## Suggested Readings

I. Biederman and E. E. Cooper (1991, Priming contour-deleted images: Evidence for intermediate representations in visual object recognition. *Cognitive Psychology, 23,* 393–419) develop an important theory of pattern recognition in which patterns are broken down into larger organized groups of features (called geons) that are used en route to pattern recognition. This paper provides some interesting support for this theoretical framework.

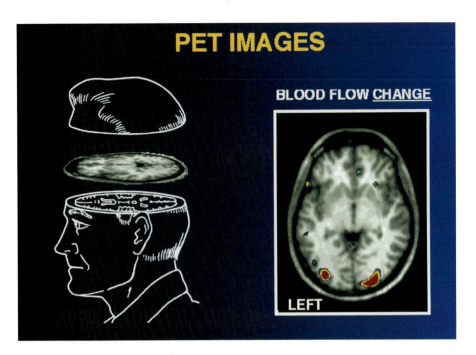

**FIGURE 5** ■ In PET, blood flow change is measured in a slice of the human brain.

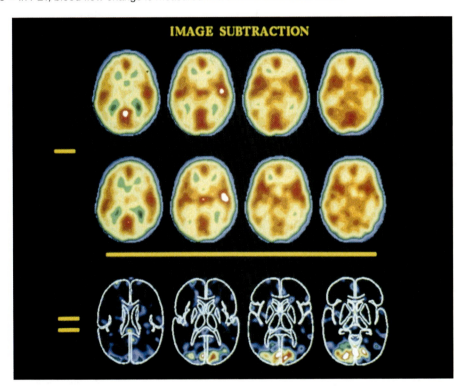

**FIGURE 6** ■ Three sets of PET images for a set of slices of brain activity. The top panel reflects the activation pattern for a word reading scan; the second panel reflects the activation pattern for a fixation scan. The third row reflects the subtraction of the second row from the first row; this isolates patterns of brain activation specific to word reading. As shown, it is difficult to decipher particular areas that are differentially activated in the two scans in the top two rows. But the subtraction method allows one to make this discrimination; in this case, it isolates the occipital areas (back of the brain) as more engaged in reading words than simply fixating.

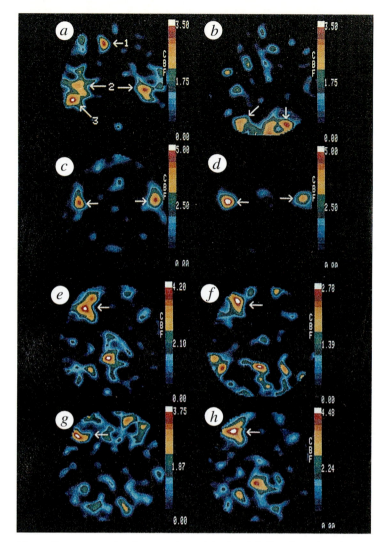

**FIGURE 5.2** ■ *a* and *b*, auditory versus visual comparison. A horizontal slice through averaged subtraction image represents blood flow change when blood flow during fixation is subtracted from blood flow present during presentation of word stimuli at 1 Hz (sensory task). Slice in *a* and *b* is taken 1.6 cm above AC–PC line. Foci of activity present at this level include temporoparietal cortex, bilateral superior posterior temporal cortex, inferior anterior cingulate for auditory presentation, and some occipital cortical activation for visual presentation. Note the non-overlapping distributions of activity for visual and auditory presentation in *a* and *b* during passive presentation. *c* and *d*, auditory versus visual comparison. A horizontal slice through an averaged subtraction image representing blood flow change when blood flow during passive presentation of words is subtracted from blood flow during vocal repetition of presented words (output task). Slice is taken 4.0 cm above AC–PC line. The foci present for both auditory and visual presentation are located on rolandic cortex, just anterior and superior to regions activated by somatosensory stimulation of the lips and probably represent the mouth representation of primary motor cortex. *e* and *f*, auditory versus visual comparison. A horizontal slice through an averaged subtraction image representing blood flow change when blood flow during repetition of presented words is subtracted from blood flow during vocalization of an appropriate use for the presented word (such as presentation of 'cake' . . . output might be 'eat') (cognitive subtraction). Slice is taken 0.8 cm below AC–PC line. Foci for both presentation modalities occur in inferior anterior frontal cortex, probably area 47 of Brodmann. Those areas of activation are strongly left-lateralized. *g* and *h*, comparison of activation in two semantic tasks. The slice on the right (*h*) is from the same condition as *e*; *g*, the blood flow change when the blood flow during passive presentation of words at 2.5 Hz is subtracted from blood flow during a condition where the subject is asked to monitor this string of words for members of a specific semantic category. In the semantic monitoring task, there is no motor output during the scan. Subjects are asked after the scan for a gross estimate of the percentage of target words. The similar foci of activation in these two different semantic tasks implicate this region in semantic processing. Slice is taken 0.6 cm below AC–PC line.

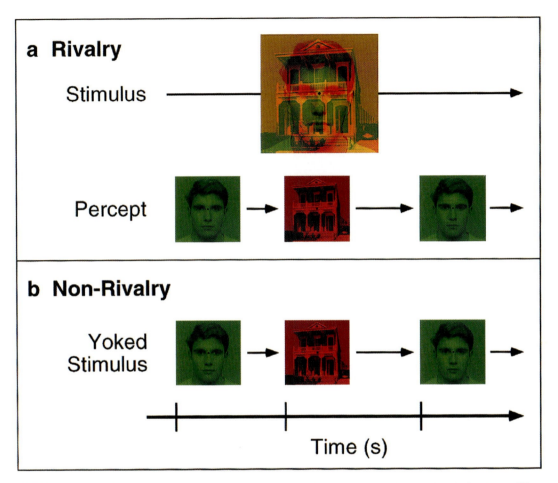

**FIGURE 9.1** ■ Experimental Design and Stimuli. (a) Ambiguous face/house stimulus used in rivalry scans. When viewed through red and green filter glasses, only the face could be seen through one eye and only the house through the other eye. This led to vigorous binocular rivalry as indicated by reported alternations between a face percept and house percept (typically every few seconds). (b) A timeline illustrating how nonrivalry scans presented nonrivalrous monocular images of either face or house alone using the same temporal sequence derived from the perceptual report of a previous rivalry scan.

**a**

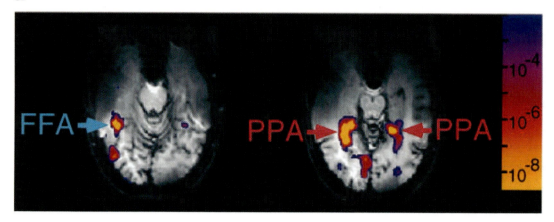

**b**

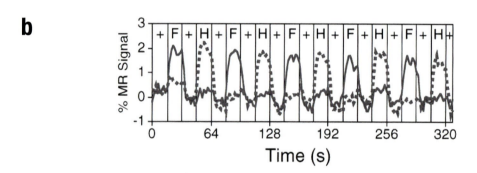

FIGURE 9.2 ■ Localizer Data: FFA and PPA (a) Two adjacent near-axial slices showing the localized FFA and PPA of one subject (S1). The FFA was localized as the region in the fusiform gyrus that responded more to faces than to houses. The PPA was localized as the region in the parahippocampal gyrus that responded more to houses than to faces. (These images follow radiological convention with the left hemisphere shown on the right and vice versa.) (b) MR time course on localizer scans showing FFA (solid line) and PPA (dotted line) activity (expressed in percent signal change relative to fixation baseline) averaged across all four subjects. Subjects viewed sequentially presented faces (F), houses (H), or a static fixation point (+).

P. K. Kuhl, K. A. Williams, F. Lacerda, K. N. Sevens, and B. Lindblom (1992, Linguistic experience alters phonetic perception in infants by 6 months of age. *Science, 225,* 606–608) conducted this important cross-linguistic study that tracks the formation of phonetic categories as a function of early experience and uncovers some language-specific influences on the nature of these early phonetic spaces.

G. R. Loftus, A. P. Shimamura, and C. A. Johnson (1985, How much is an icon worth? *Journal of Experimental Psychology: Human Perception and Performance, 11,* 1–13) describe a series of experiments that detail the utility of a brief visual sensory store, referred to as iconic memory in pattern recognition.

M. McCloskey (1991, Networks and theories: The place of connectionism in cognitive science. *Psychological Science, 2,* 287–295) discusses the utility of connectionist models in developing cognitive models and identifies some potential pitfalls of this approach.

K. Rayner and A. Pollatsek (1989, *The Psychology of Reading.* Englewood Cliffs, NJ: Prentice Hall) review the literature on reading, from basic aspects of perception to higher-level comprehension and syntactic analyses. This book provides an excellent integration of basic psycholinguistic theory and the rigors of experimental psychology.

G. M. Reicher (1969, Perceptual recognition as a function of meaningfulness of stimulus material. *Journal of Experimental Psychology, 81,* 275–280) presents an important study on the word superiority effect, in which people excel at recognizing the letters embedded in a word better than the letters embedded in a nonword. The importance of this finding is that the author has eliminated a series of accounts that are simply due to guessing, thereby suggesting that the results reflect a truly top-down influence on perception.

M. S. Seidenberg and J. L. McClelland (1989, A distributed developmental model of word recognition and naming. *Psychological Review, 96,* 523–568) review the rich literature on word recognition and develop a connectionist model of speeded word naming and lexical decision performance. The model handles a considerable amount of the data without the spelling to sound rules or lexical representations necessary in most available models. For an important alternative account, see M. Coltheart, B. Curtis, P. Atkins, and M. Haller (1993, Models of reading aloud: Dual-route and parallel-distributed-processing approaches. *Psychological Review, 100,* 589–608).

R. M. Warren and R. P. Warren (1970, Auditory illusions and confusions. *Scientific American, 223,* 30–36) review the evidence of a top-down influence on speech perception. In some sense, this is an auditory analogue to the Reicher (1969) study mentioned previously but suggests that such top-down influences may be even more pervasive in speech perception in which people actually hear phonetic segments, based on surrounding contextual information.

PART III

# Attention

# Introduction to Part III: Attention

One might argue that the topic of attention is one of the most contentious and at the same time most important areas in the evolution of cognitive psychology. The controversial nature of attention research stems from the homunculus problem; that is, the question of what is doing the attending. In addition, controversy invariably arises when a problem is relevant to issues of conscious and unconscious processing. The importance of attention springs from its centrality to virtually all topics studied in cognitive psychology, from simple pattern recognition to higher-order decision making. Indeed, the influence of attentional research has extended into many domains of behavioral science including social and clinical psychology.

We begin with Cherry's paper on attentional selection in listening. At the onset, it is noteworthy that Cherry had a primary appointment in a department of electronics and had an engineering orientation. As Cherry notes, the attentional issue (although he carefully avoids the term *attention*) addressed in his studies might be best reflected in a natural listening situation at a cocktail party. Here there may be multiple speakers at a given time, along with a background of other sources of auditory information and conversations. Cherry addressed how humans select a single message to attend to and the extent to which unattended information also receives some processing. In his first series of studies, he explored the types of information that humans use to pull out a single connected message from multiple simultaneous messages (the statistical filtering problem). From an engineering perspective, this turns out to be a rather difficult problem because the acoustic properties of the signal are not sufficient by themselves to isolate one speech stream. People, however, easily can do this. They apparently use higher-order linguistic structures about the message content to keep the attentional system on a single speaker. The second set of studies addressed what people pick up from the unattended ear. This is akin to how much information from background speakers one can pick up when one is attending to a specific speaker. Cherry's results suggest that individuals are remarkably poor at processing unattended information (even the language of the message), and could never report any of the words presented to the unattended channel. Critically, this result supported the notion that the meaning of unattended information does not get into the processing system, and was thus viewed as support for an early selection model of attention (see Broadbent, 1958). Cherry's work helped establish an experimental paradigm to study processing unattended signals, and nicely documented the difficulties encountered by an engineering framework in accommodating the power of the human attentional system. Cherry's paper is relatively conversational in tone, which prompted a recent replication by Wood and Cowen (1995) in a more controlled setting.

Although the work by Cherry and others originally supported an early selection view of attention, later work suggests that in some cases meaning is sometimes processed in the unattended channel. One such study was by Moray (1959). Consistent with the early selection model and Cherry's original work, Moray found that subjects did not remember a word from the unattended channel even if it had been repeated 40 times. However, if the person's own name was presented to the unattended channel, the subject often did report hearing his or her own name. Returning to the cocktail party phenomenon, apparently one doesn't pick up much from non-attended conversations, unless one's own name occurs and redirects attention. This suggests either that meaning does get into the system even from unattended channels (as suggested by the late selection model, Deutsch & Deutsch, 1963; Norman, 1968) or that unattended information is attenuated, but not completely eliminated (as suggested by the early selection, filter attenuation model by Treisman, 1960). Clearly, Cherry's surprising findings of little processing of unattended information motivated much work on the locus of attentional selection.

In the early shadowing experiments, the subject controlled which ear to direct attention to. However, in some situations, it appears that one cannot totally control where attention is directed. The extent to which humans can exert control over what is or is not attended was explored in Stroop's (1935) classic paper, based on his doctoral dissertation. This remains one of the most highly cited papers in psychology, and the Stroop effect still is the topic of considerable study. As in many cases, the beauty of Stroop's work is in its elegant simplicity. The stimuli were color words (e.g., BLUE) that were printed in various ink colors. Subjects were simply asked to read aloud the words (Experiment 1) or name the ink colors (Experiment 2). In Experiment 1, reading words was relatively unaffected by inconsistent ink color (e.g., say BLUE when the word BLUE was printed in RED ink). However, in Experiment 2, a conflict between the word and ink color (e.g., say RED when the word BLUE was printed in RED) considerably slowed ink-naming performance. This basic pattern is called the Stroop effect. It is driven in part by the automaticity of reading; that is, reading is such a well-practiced process that it is hard not to attend to the words when naming ink colors. Stroop addressed many issues that are still of interest today, such as the influence of practice on the Stroop effect. Stroop even investigated sex differences.

The Stroop effect is still a major workhorse in studies of attention. For example, it takes attentional control to reduce interference from the inconsistent words when naming ink colors. Accordingly, individuals with deficits in attentional control (those with dementia of the Alzheimer's type or schizophrenia) show exaggerated Stroop effects (Cohen & Servan-Schreiber, 1992; Spieler, Balota & Faust, 1996). These individuals have increased difficulty suppressing irrelevant information (in the case of ink color naming, the words). This simple effect has also been central to developing computational models of attention (e.g., Cohen, Dunbar, & McClelland, 1990). Moreover, some researchers have suggested that an increased Stroop interference effect reflects breakdowns in specific brain systems, especially anterior aspects of the frontal lobes. For the interested reader, McLeod (1991)

provides an excellent review of the work on the Stroop effect.

The classic paper by Posner and Snyder provides an important follow-up to the Stroop paper. Posner and Snyder were interested in a distinction between automatic processes (which we have little or no control over) and attentional processes (which we clearly control). The Stroop effect has been considered an excellent example of the contribution of the two systems in which one has to exert conscious control (naming the ink color) over the more automatically activated pathway (reading the word). Even for highly practiced subjects, one cannot totally eliminate the competition from the word reading dimension, as in Stroop's original studies. The beauty of the Posner and Snyder chapter is the development of operational distinctions between automatic and attentional mechanisms. For example, they suggested that automatic processes are relatively fast acting and independent of conscious control. On the other hand, attentional mechanisms are relatively slow to engage and under conscious control. Posner and Snyder presented some intriguing studies about how automatic and attentional mechanisms may be extended even into the realm of emotional experience. This distinction between automatic and intentional (attentional, controlled) processes is fundamental to many domains in psychology. For example, the classic papers by Jacoby in the memory section also hinge upon the distinction between automatic and controlled processes. Moreover, recent work on the topic of racial prejudice suggests that fast-acting automatic prejudice may eventually be suppressed across time by a slower, more controlled mechanism (for an example, see Payne, 2001).

We end this section of readings with a short paper by Tipper. The interesting question addressed by Tipper is what happens to the non-selected information during a selection task. Is this non-selected information actually inhibited (pushed below some baseline level of activation) or is this information simply ignored (not processed)? Tipper reviews several intriguing paradigms that suggest that non-selected representations are actually suppressed below baseline levels of activation. For example, in one study, individuals were asked to name the red object in a display with both a red object and a green distracter object. Was the green distracter object simply ignored or did the act of selecting the red object lead to the suppression of the green object? The intriguing result, called negative priming, is that subjects were relatively slow to name the green object, suggesting that the non-selected green object was truly inhibited during the initial selection event. Interestingly, as Tipper points out, there is some evidence of decreased negative priming in individuals with Alzheimer's disease or schizophrenia. This finding of a deficit in attentional mechanisms converges nicely with the results on Stroop noted previously. Although much

research has focused on this topic, we should also note that there is still some controversy regarding the mechanism underlying negative priming experiments (see Neill, Valdes & Terry, 1994, for a discussion). There is little doubt, however, that the work by Tipper and others helped focus researchers on the critical distinction between interference and inhibition in attentional selection.

In closing, it is important to remember that these papers afford only a glimpse of the exciting early work on attention. For example, Treisman provides a comprehensive framework for understanding how attention is used to combine features in recognizing patterns (e.g., Treisman, 1996). Logan (1990) has provided an important alternative to the concept of automaticity. Farah (1990) and Ramachandran and Blakeslee (1998) have provided rich descriptions of attentional breakdowns in distinct types of neuropsychological cases. Luck (1999), among others, is actively exploring different types of imaging techniques to better understand aspects of attentional selection. Ultimately, the work in attention will have ramifications for all areas of cognition and will provide insights into central issues concerning consciousness and the ever-present homunculus problem.

## REFERENCES

Broadbent, D. E. (1958). *Perception and communication.* London: Pergamon.

Cherry, E. C. (1953). Some experiments on the recognition of speech, with one and two ears. *Journal of the Acoustical Society of America, 25,* 975–979.

Cohen, J. D., Dunbar, K., & McClelland, J. L. (1990). On the control of automatic processes: A parallel distributed processing account of the Stroop effect. *Psychological Review, 97,* 332–361.

Cohen, J. D., & Servan-Schreiber, D. (1992). Context, cortex, and dopamine: A connectionist approach to behavior and biology in schizophrenia. *Psychological Review, 99,* 45–77.

Deutsch, J. A., & Deutsch, D. (1963). Attention: Some theoretical considerations. *Psychological Review, 70,* 80–90.

Farah, M. J. (1990). *Visual agnosia: Disorders of object recognition and what they tell us about normal vision.* Cambridge, MA: MIT Press.

Logan, G. D. (1990). Repetition priming and automaticity: Common underlying mechanisms? *Cognitive Psychology, 22,* 1–35.

Luck, S. J. (1999). Direct and indirect integration of event-related potentials, functional magnetic resonance images, and single-unit recordings. *Human Brain Mapping, 8,* 15–120.

McLeod, C. M. (1991). Half a century of research on the Stroop effect: An integrative review. *Psychological Bulletin, 109,* 163–203.

Moray, N. (1959). Attention in dichotic listing: Affective cues and the influence of instructions. *Quarterly Journal of Experimental Psychology, 11,* 56–60.

Neill, W. T., Valdes, L. A., & Terry, K. M. (1995). Selective attention and the inhibitory control of cognition. In F. N. Dempster & C. J. Brainerd (Eds.), *Interference and inhibition in cognition* (pp. 207–255). San Diego, CA: Academic Press.

Norman, D. A. (1968). Toward a theory of memory and attention. *Psychological Review, 75,* 522–536.

Payne, B. K. (2001). Prejudice and perception: The role of automatic and controlled processes in misperceiving a weapon. *Journal of Personality and Social Psychology, 81,* 181–192.

Posner, M. I., & Snyder, C. R. R. (1975). Attention and cognitive control. In R. L. Solso (Ed.), *Information processing and cognition: The Loyola Symposium* (pp. 55–85). Hillsdale, NJ: Erlbaum.

Ramachandran, V. S., & Blakeslee, S. (1998). *Phantoms in the Brain.* New York: William Morrow.

Spieler, D. H., Balota, D. A., & Faust, M. E. (1996). Stroop performance in healthy younger and older adults and in individuals with dementia of the Alzheimer's type. *Journal of Experimental Psychology: Human Perception and Performance, 22,* 461–479.

Stroop, J. R. (1935). Studies of interference in serial verbal reactions. *Journal of Experimental Psychology, 18,* 643–661.

Tipper, S. P. (1992). Selection for action: The role of inhibitory mechanisms. *Current Directions in Psychological Science, 1,* 105–109.

Treisman, A. M. (1960). Contextual cues in selective listening. *Quarterly Journal of Experimental Psychology, 12,* 242–248.

Treisman, A. (1996). The binding problem. *Current Opinion in Neurobiology, 6,* 171–178.

Wood, N. L., & Cowan, N. (1995). The cocktail party phenomenon revisited: Attention and memory in the classic selective listening procedure of Cherry (1953). *Journal of Experimental Psychology: General, 124,* 243–262.

# Some Experiments on the Recognition of Speech, with One and with Two Ears*

E. Colin Cherry • Imperial College, University of London, England, and Research Laboratory of Electronics, Massachusetts Institute of Technology, Cambridge, Massachusetts

This paper describes a number of objective experiments on recognition, concerning particularly the relation between the messages received by the two ears. Rather than use steady tones or clicks (frequency or time-point signals) continuous speech is used, and the results interpreted in the main statistically.

Two types of test are reported: (a) the behavior of a listener when presented with two speech signals simultaneously (statistical filtering problem) and (b) behavior when different speech signals are presented to his two ears.

## 1. Introduction

The experiments described herein are intended as a small contribution to the solution of the general problem of the recognition of speech. They are designed to be essentially objective and behavioristic; that is, the "subject" under test (the listener) is regarded as a transducer whose responses are observed when various stimuli are applied, whereas his subjective impressions are taken to be of minor importance.

A great deal of work has been done relating to aural discrimination, mostly using two kinds of stimulus: (a) pure tones, which may be regarded as separable in frequency; and (b) acoustic "clicks," or impulses, considered as separable in time.[1] It is suggested that a third kind of discrimination is possible and amenable to experimental treatment, namely statistical separation. Speech signals form stimuli in this class, and we appear to possess powers of such discrimination. For example, we decide that a person is speaking English and not, say, French; again we can listen to one speaker when another is speaking simultaneously. These are acts of recognition and discrimination.

The tests to be described are in two groups. In the first, two different spoken messages are presented to the subject simultaneously, using both ears. In the second, one spoken message is fed to his right ear and a different message to his left ear. The results, the subject's spoken reconstructions, are markedly different in the two cases; so also are the significances of these results. Before examining such possible significance, it will be better to describe some of the experiments.

* This work, supported in part by the Signal Corps, the Air Materiel Command, and the U.S. Office of Naval Research, was carried out by the author at M.I.T. while there as a Visiting Professor under a Fulbright grant, and is presented with the kind permission of Professor J. B. Wiesner.

## 2. The Separation of Two Simultaneously Spoken Messages

The first set of experiments relates to this general problem of speech recognition: how do we recognize what one person is saying when others are speaking at the same time (the "cocktail party problem")? On what logical basis could one design a machine ("filter") for carrying out such an operation? A few of the factors which give mental facility might be the following:

a. The voices come from different directions.
b. Lip-reading, gestures, and the like.
c. Different speaking voices, mean pitches, mean speeds, male and female, and so forth.
d. Accents differing.
e. Transition-probabilities (subject matter, voice dynamics, syntax . . . ).

All of these factors, except the last (e), may, however, be eliminated by the device of recording two messages on the same magnetic-tape, spoken by the same speaker. The result is a babel, but nevertheless the messages may be separated.

The logical principles involved in the recognition of speech seem to require that the brain have a vast "store" of probabilities, or at least of probability-rankings. Such a store enables prediction to be made, noise or disturbances to be combated, and maximum-likelihood estimates to be made. Shannon[2] has already reported that prediction is readily possible in the case of printed language, and has described experiments in which a subject is required to guess the successive letters or words of a hidden written message; our present experiments are somewhat analogous, but are carried out with speech, at normal rates of speaking.

Those holding the strict behaviorist view may rightly object that it is inadmissable to speak of "storage of probability-rankings in the brain," because these are not directly observable; the only probabilities which can be discussed are those of the subject's responses. Acknowledging this, we may turn the problem around from one of psychology to one of engineering and ask: On what logical principles could one design a machine whose reaction, in response to speech stimuli, would be analogous to that of a human being? How could it separate one of two simultaneous spoken messages? The tests described here merely purport to show that we ourselves have such power, with the suggestion that we can assess probability-rankings of words, phonemic sounds, syntactical endings, and other factors of speech.

In the first experiment the subject is presented with the two mixed speeches recorded on tape and is asked to repeat one of them word by word or phrase by phrase. He may play the tape as many times as he wishes and in any way. His task is merely to separate one of the messages. He repeats the various identified portions verbally, but is not allowed to write them down.

The following is one example of two messages, showing his reconstructions; the subject matters are markedly distinct in this case.

MESSAGE 1(A) "It may mean that ~~our~~ religious convictions, legal systems and politics have been so successful in accomplishing their ~~ends~~ AIMS during the past 2,000 years, that there has been no need to change our outlooks about them. Or it may mean that the outlook has not changed for other reasons. I ~~will leave~~ BELIEVE IN the first hypothesis ~~is~~ AND IN those who are willing to defend it, and choose the second. As the reader may have guessed, I am interested in learning how obsolete structure of languages preserves obsolete metaphysics."

MESSAGE 1(B) "This very brief discussion will serve to give a slight indication of the really complex nature of the causes and uses of birds' colors, and may serve to suggest a few of the many possibilities that may underlie them. There is a very great opportunity here for close and careful observation of the habits of birds in a free state, with a view to shedding light on these problems. But the observer, in interpreting what he sees, must ever be on his guard lest he lose sight of alternative explanation."

The phrases recognized have been underlined and error indicated by the sub-scripts. No transpositions of phrases between the messages occurred in this example; in other examples extremely few transpositions arose, but where they did they could be highly probable from the text. The next example illustrates this point (indicated by asterisks).

MESSAGE 2(A) "He came ~~out~~ of nowhere special: <sub>FROM</sub> a cabin like any other out West. ~~His folks*~~ were <sub>HE SPOKE TO</sub> nobody special; pleasant, hardworking people like many others. Abe was a smart boy but not too smart He could do a good day's work on the farm, though he'd just as soon stand around and talk. ~~He told funny*~~ stories: he was strong and <sub>PROFESSIONAL TRAINING</sub> kind. He'd never try to hurt you, or cheat you, or fool you. Young Abe worked at odd jobs and read ~~law~~ books at night. Eventually he found his way <sub>WAR</sub> into local politics. And it was ~~then that people listening*~~ <sub>LEADING POSITION IN</sub> <sub>THE WORLD</sub> to his speeches, began to ~~know~~ there was <sub>NOTICE</sub> something special about Abe Lincoln. Abe talked about running <sub>THE</sub> country as though it were something ~~you~~ could do. It was just a matter of people <sub>HE</sub> getting along. He had nothing against anybody, rich or poor, who ~~went~~ his own way and let the other <sub>GO</sub> fellow go his. No matter how mixed up things got, Abe made you feel that the answer was somewhere ~~among~~ those old rules that everybody knows: no <sub>AMONGST</sub> hurting, no cheating, no fooling."

Notice here the recognition in phrases, the highly likely errors and transpositions, and the consistency of any initial grammatical mistake. Similar factors were observed in all the samples taken.

At the subjective level the subject reported very great difficulty in accomplishing his task. He would shut his eyes to assist concentration. Some phrases were repeatedly played over by him, perhaps 10 to 20 times, but his guess was right in the end. In no cases were any long phrases (more than 2 or 3 words) identified wrongly.

MESSAGE 2(B) "In attaining its ~~present*~~ position, the <sub>SPECIAL</sub> Institution has constantly kept before it three objectives—the education of men, the advancement of knowledge and service to ~~industry*~~ and the na- <sub>OTHERS</sub> tion. It aims to give its students such a combination of humanistic, scientific and professional training as will fit them to take leading positions in <sub>THE</sub> world in which science, engineering and architecture are of basic importance. This training ~~is especially~~ planned to prepare students, accord- <sub>HAS BEEN</sub> ing to their desires and aptitudes, to become practicing engineers or architects, investigators, business executives ~~or~~ teachers. The useful <sub>AND</sub> knowledge and mental discipline gained in this training are, however, so broad and fundamental as to constitute an excellent general preparation ~~for other careers~~* Realizing that the institu- <sub>PEOPLE GETTING ALONG</sub> tion ~~trains~~ for life and for ~~citizenship~~ as <sub>TRAINING</sub> <sub>ASSOCIATIONSHIP (?)</sub> well as for a career, its staff seeks to cultivate in each student a strong character, high ideals, and a sense of social responsibility, as well as a keen intellect."

In a variation of the experiment the subject was given a pencil and paper, and permitted to write down the words and phrases as he identified them. Subjectively speaking, his task then became "very much easier." Times were shortened. It appears that the long-term storage provided assists prediction.

Numerous tests have been made, using pairs of messages of varying similarity. Some test samples consisted of adjacent paragraphs out of the same book. The results were consistently similar; the messages were almost entirely separated.

However, it was considered possible to construct

messages which could not be separated with such a low frequency of errors. Such a test is described in the next section.

## 3. Inseparable Spoken Messages, Use of Cliches or "Highly Probable Phrases"

As a final test in this series, using the same speaker recorded as speaking two different messages simultaneously, a pair of messages was composed which could not be separated by the listening subject. The messages were composed by selecting, from reported speeches in a newspaper, 150 clichés and stringing them together with simple conjunctions, pronouns, etc., as continuous speeches. For example, a few of the clichés were:

1. I am happy to be here today,
2. The man in the street,
3. Stop beating about the bush,
4. We are on the brink of ruin,

and the like. The corresponding sample of one speech was as follows:

> "I am happy to be here today to talk to the man in the street. Gentlemen, the time has come to stop beating about the bush—we are on the brink of ruin, and the welfare of the workers and of the great majority of the people is imperiled," and so forth.

It is remarkably easy to write such passages by the page.† Now a cliché is, almost by definition, a highly probable chain of words, and on the other hand the transition probability of one cliché following another specific one is far lower. The subject, as he listened to the mixed speeches in an endeavor to separate one of them was observed to read out complete clichés at a time; it appeared that recognition of one or two words would ensure his predicting a whole cliché. But he picked them out in roughly equal numbers from both speeches; in such artificially constructed cases, message separation appeared impossible. The speeches were of course read with normal continuity, and with natural articulatory and emotional properties, during their recording.

It is suggested that techniques such as those described in the preceding sections may be extended so that they will shed light on the relative importance of the different types of transition probabilities in recognition. For instance, speeches of correct "syntactical structure" but with no meaning and using few dictionary words may readily be constructed. (Lewis Carroll's "Jabber-Wocky" is such an instance; similarly, "meaningful" speeches with almost zero (or at least unfamiliar) syntactical or inflexional structure [Pidgin English].) Again, continuous speaking of dictionary words, which are relatively disconnected, into "meaningless phrases" is possible; the word-transition probabilities may be assessed *a priori*, with the assistance of suitable probability tables. Further experiments are proceeding.

## 4. Unmixed Speeches; One in the Left Ear and One in the Right

The objective, and subjective, results of a second series of tests were completely different. In these tests one continuous spoken message was fed into a headphone on the subject's left ear and a different message applied to the right ear. The messages were recorded, using the same speaker.[1]

The subject experiences no difficulty in listening to either speech at will and "rejecting" the unwanted one. Note that aural directivity does not arise here; the earphones are fixed to the head in the normal way. To use a loose expression, the "processes of recognition may apparently be switched to either ear at will." This result has surprised a number of listeners; although of course it is well known to anyone who has made hearing tests. It may be noteworthy that when one tries to follow the conversation of a speaker in a crowded noisy room, the instinctive action is to turn one ear toward him, although this may increase the difference between the "messages" reaching the two ears.

The subject is instructed to repeat one of the messages concurrently while he is listening[3] and to make no errors. Surprising as it may seem this proves easy; his words are slightly delayed behind those on the record to which he is listening. One marked characteristic of his speaking voice is its monotony. Very little emotional content or

---

† Comment upon this fact has appeared in the *New Yorker* under the name of Mr. Arbuthnot.

stressing of the words occurs at all. Subjectively, the subject is unaware of this fact. Also he may have very little idea of what the message that he has repeated is all about, especially if the subject matter is difficult. But he has recognized every word, as his repeating proves.

But the point of real interest is that if the subject is subsequently asked to repeat anything of what he heard in his other (rejected-message) ear, he can say little about it at all, except possibly that sounds were occurring.

Experiments were made in an attempt to find out just what attributes, if any, of the "rejected" message are recognized.

## 5. Language of "Rejected" Ear Unrecognized

In a further set of tests the two messages, one for the right ear and one for the left, started in English. After the subject was comfortably repeating his right-ear message, the left-ear message was changed to German, spoken by an Englishman. The subject subsequently reported, when asked to state the language of the "rejected" left-ear message, that he "did not know at all, but assumed it was English." The test was repeated with different, unprepared listeners; the results were similar. It is considered unfair to try this particular test more than once with the same listener.

It was considered that a further series of tests might well indicate the level of recognition which is attained in the "rejected" ear, raising the questions, Is the listener aware even that it is human speech? male or female? and the like.

## 6. What Factors of the "Rejected" Message Are Recognized?

In this series of tests the listening subjects were presented at their right-hand ears with spoken passages from newspapers, chosen carefully to avoid proper names or difficult words, and again instructed to repeat these passages concurrently without omission or error. Into their left ears were fed signals of different kinds, for different tests, but each of which started and ended with a short passage of normal English speech in order to avoid any troubles that might be involved in the listener's "getting going" on the test. The center, major, por-

tions of these rejected left-ear signals thus reached the listener while he was steadily repeating his right-ear message.

Again no one listening subject was used for more than one test; none of them was primed as to the results to be expected. The center, major, portions of the left-ear signals for the series of tests were, respectively:

a. Normal male spoken English—as for earlier tests.
b. Female spoken English—high-pitched voice.
c. Reversed male speech (i.e., same spectrum but no words or semantic content).
d. A steady 400-cps oscillator.

After any one of these tests, the subject was asked the following questions:

1. Did the left-ear signal consist of human speech or not?
2. If yes is given in answer to (1), can you say what it was about, or even quote any words?
3. Was it a male or female speaker?
4. What language was it in?

The responses varied only slightly. In no case in which normal human speech was used did the listening subjects fail to identify it as speech; in every such instance they were unable to identify any word or phrase heard in the rejected ear and, furthermore, unable to make definite identification of the language as being English. On the other hand the change of voice—male to female—was nearly always identified, while the 400-cps pure tone was always observed. The reversed speech was identified as having "something queer about it" by a few listeners, but was thought to be normal speech by others.

The broad conclusions are that the "rejected" signal has certain statistical properties recognized, but that detailed aspects, such as the language, individual words, or semantic content are unnoticed.

## 7. Similar Messages in the Two Ears, but with Time Delay between Them

Subjectively speaking, the effect of listening normally, with both ears, to a single message is a very different sensation from that of listening with one ear to one of two different messages as in the earlier tests. This raises the question of how we correlate the signals reaching our two ears so that we are able to decide to listen either to both at the same time (when identical or "correlated") or only to one, rejecting the other.

This question suggested the following experiment. Suppose we apply identical messages to the two ears of a listening subject, but with a very long delay between them. What will be the effect if this delay is steadily reduced, as the message proceeds, until eventually the two ears are stimulated simultaneously and identically?

Preliminary experiments suggest that the basis of correlation (using the word in the popular, not the mathematical, sense) of the messages reaching the two ears depends upon the magnitude of the delay between the ears. When this is very short, of the order of milliseconds, there will exist a considerable connection between the actual sounds, or their spectra; but with longer delays, of the order of seconds, the relation is more a semantic one, or one of word and phrase identification.

The following experiment was carried out with a number of subjects. A long passage of speech was recorded on magnetic tape and subsequently run through two reproducing machines in cascade, with a length of tape between them. The subject, who was unprimed as to the nature and purpose of the experiment, was instructed in exactly the same way as in the earlier experiments; namely, he was asked to repeat the message reaching his right ear, without omission or error. As he was doing this the two machines were slowly pushed together, reducing the delay between the ears. At some stage the subject would exclaim: "My other ear is getting the same thing" or some equivalent remark. Some of them said nothing until asked afterwards and then stated the word or words first recognized as being the same. Nearly all subjects reported that they had recognized words or phrases, at some stage, in the rejected ear message as being the same as those in the accepted ear message.

The surprising thing here is that such words were recognized at all, because in earlier tests, using different texts for the two ears, not a single word of the rejected ear was identified. The delay at which recognition first occurred in the present tests varied considerably between the different listeners acting as subjects but mostly lay between 6

sec and 2 sec.

Experiments of a similar nature, but using very short delays of the orders of milliseconds or tens of milliseconds, are not reported here in connection with the present study. They are of interest mainly for the subjective effects produced.

## 8. The Switching of One Message Periodically between the Two Ears

This experiment was suggested by the results of earlier ones described in Sections 4, 5, and 6. When listening to and repeating concurrently a message received in one ear while a different message is being presented to the other ear, it is found that a very short time interval is required to transfer the attention from the one ear to the other. Thus it was thought that, if a single message was switched between the ears at approximately the time period of this reaction time (not under the control of the listening-speaking subject), his recognition facility might be completely confounded and he would be unable to repeat the words.

A long sample of English speech was recorded on tape and subsequently applied to the right or left headphone of the subject, alternately, by an automatic switch which could be thrown (a) randomly and (b) periodically, at any required rate. When the switching speed was very slow (say a 1-sec period) the subject repeated 100 percent correctly; when very fast (say 1/20–1/50 sec period) most subjects repeated the majority of the words, though they varied in their ability considerably, reporting that they listened as though to both ears simultaneously. The point that matters is that an optimum period of switching could be found at which the fraction of words repeated by the subjects was a minimum. The flatness of this minimum varied between the subjects; the approximate average value of the minimum switching rate was $1/6$–$1/7$ sec, for a complete cycle of switching.

Somewhat surprisingly, little difference in the results was found between the uses of random and periodic switching; so the former was abandoned. The variations between the subjects in their abilities, the flatness of the minima, and other factors tended to make such experiments rather inconclusive. Instead, therefore, a method of switching was sought which could virtually stop any subject repeating any of the words. It was found that if, while the reversing switch was in operation, a very short gap of silence was introduced, the effect upon the subject's responses was most marked. The switching cycle was thus: right ear/silence/left ear/silence—periodically, at about 6 to 7 cps. The silence interval needed to be no greater than 10 msec.

A comparison measurement was made with each subject. Firstly, the ear-phone signals were not reversed, though the silence gap was introduced, the subjects thus listened to both ears, with the periodic (<10 msec) interval as interruption. Word scores were 95 to 100 percent correct. Then the reversal of the earphones was introduced; the word scores fell to less than 20 percent correct.

It may be considered that these results might be accounted for by the inherent noise introduced by the switching interruption of the speech; there are several factors which assist in denying this.

a. The noise is at an extremely low level when the switching rate is as slow as 6 to 7 per sec.
b. A subject might get a high score with a silence gap of <1 msec but this would inevitably fall if the gap was opened. The noise is substantially unchanged.
c. Miller and Licklider's results of experiments[4] carried out with periodically interrupted speech

(both ears simultaneously) show that a 6-cps interruption of 50 percent of the time, that is, square-wave modulation of the speech, gave a word-articulation score as high as 75 percent; the noise introduced presumably being much the same as in our present experiment. The test material was somewhat different in their case, being individual monosyllabic words, not connected speech.

## ACKNOWLEDGMENTS

Acknowledgment of the very great assistance offered by many patient subjects is gratefully made. The author wishes also to thank Professor J. B. Wiesner, Massachusetts Institute of Technology, and Professor Willis Jackson, Imperial College, London, for their assistance in affording the necessary facilities.

## NOTES

1. M. R. Rosenzweig, *Am. J. Physiol. 167* (No. 1) (October, 1951).
2. C. E. Shannon, *Bell System Tech. J. XXX*(50) (1951).
3. D. E. Broadbent, *J. Exptl. Psychol. 43* (April, 1952).
4. G. A. Miller and J. C. R. Licklider, *J. Acoust. Soc. Am. 22*(167) (1950).

READING 11

# Studies of Interference in Serial Verbal Reactions

J. Ridley Stroop • George Peabody College

## Introduction

Interference or inhibition (the terms seem to have been used almost indiscriminately) has been given a large place in experimental literature. The investigation was begun by the physiologists prior to 1890 (Bowditch and Warren, J. W., 1890) and has been continued to the present, principally by psychologists (Lester, 1932). Of the numerous studies that have been published during this period only a limited number of the most relevant reports demand our attention here.

Münsterberg (1892) studied the inhibiting effects of changes in common daily habits such as opening the door of his room, dipping his pen in ink, and taking his watch out of his pocket. He concluded that a given association can function automatically even though some effect of a previous contrary association remains.

Müller and Schumann (1894) discovered that more time was necessary to relearn a series of nonsense syllables if the stimulus syllables had been associated with other syllables in the meantime. From their results they deduced the law of associative inhibition which is quoted by Kline (1921, p. 270) as follows: "If $a$ is already connected with $b$, then it is difficult to connect it with $k$, $b$ gets in the way." Nonsense syllables were also used by Shepard and Fogelsonger (1913) in a series of experiments in association and inhibition. Only three subjects were used in any experiment

and the changes introduced to produce the inhibition were so great in many cases as to present novel situations. This latter fact was shown by the introspections. The results showed an increase in time for the response which corresponded roughly to the increase in the complexity of the situation. The only conclusion was stated thus: "We have found then that in acquiring associations there is involved an inhibitory process which is not a mere result of divided paths but has some deeper basis yet unknown" (p. 311).

Kline (1921) used "meaningful" material (states and capitals, counties and county seats, and books and authors) in a study of interference effects of associations. He found that if the first associative bond had a recall power of 10 percent or less, it facilitated the second association; if it had a recall power of 15 percent to 40 percent, the inhibitory power was small; if it had a recall power of 45 percent to 70 percent, the inhibiting strength approached a maximum; if the recall power was 70 percent to 100 percent, the inhibition was of medium strength and in some cases might disappear or even facilitate the learning of a new association.

In card sorting, Bergström (1893 and 1894), Brown (1914), Bair (1902), and Culler (1912) found that changing the arrangement of compartments into which cards were being sorted produced interference effects. Bergström (1894, p. 441) concluded that "the interference effect of an association

193

194 ■ Cognitive Psychology

bears a constant relation to the practice effect, and is, in fact, equivalent to it." Both Bair and Culler found that the interference of the opposing habits disappeared if the habits were practiced alternately.

Culler (1912), in the paper already referred to, reported two other experiments. In one experiment the subjects associated each of a series of numbers with striking a particular key on the typewriter with a particular finger; then the keys were changed so that four of the numbers had to be written with fingers other than those formerly used to write them. In the other experiment the subjects were trained to react with the right hand to "red" and with the left hand to "blue." Then the stimuli were interchanged. In the former experiment an interference was found which decreased rapidly with practice. In the latter experiment the interference was overbalanced by the practice effect.

Hunter and Yarbrough (1917), Pearce (1917), and Hunter (1922) in three closely related studies of habit interference in the white rat in a T-shaped discrimination box found that a previous habit interfered with the formation of an "opposite" habit.

Several studies have been published which were not primarily studies of interference, but which employed materials that were similar in nature to those employed in this research, and which are concerned with why it takes more time to name colors than to read color names. Several of these studies have been reviewed recently by Telford (1930) and by Ligon (1932). Only the vital point of these studies will be mentioned here.

The difference in time for naming colors and reading color names has been variously explained. Cattell (1886) and Lund (1972) have attributed the difference to "practice." Woodworth and Wells (1911, p. 52) have suggested that, "The real mechanism here may very well be the mutual interference of the five names, all of which, from immediately preceding use, are 'on the tip of the tongue,' all are equally ready and likely to get in one another's way." Brown (1915, p. 51) concluded "that the difference in speed between color naming and word reading does not depend upon practice" but that (p. 34) "the association process in naming simple objects like colors is radically different from the association process in reading printed words."

Garrett and Lemmon (1924, p. 438) have accounted for their findings in these words, "Hence

it seems reasonable to say that interferences which arise in naming colors are due not so much to an equal readiness of the color names as to an equal readiness of the color recognitive processes. Another factor present in interference is very probably the present strength of the associations between colors and their names, already determined by past use." Peterson (1918 and 1925) has attributed the difference to the fact that, "One particular response habit has become associated with each word while in the case of colors themselves a variety of response tendencies have developed." (1925, p. 281.) As pointed out by Telford (1930), the results published by Peterson (1925, p. 281) and also those published by Lund (1927, p. 425) confirm Peterson's interpretation.

Ligon (1932) has published results of a "genetic study" of naming colors and reading color names in which he used 638 subjects from school grades 1 to 9 inclusive. In the light of his results he found all former explanations untenable (He included no examination of or reference to Peterson's data and interpretation.) and proceeded to set up a new hypothesis based upon a three factor theory, a common factor which he never definitely describes and special factors of word reading and color naming. He points out that the common factor is learned but the special factors are organic. He promises further evidence from studies now in progress.

The present problem grew out of experimental work in color naming and word reading conducted in Jesup Psychological Laboratory at George Peabody College for Teachers. The time for reading names of colors had been compared with the time for naming colors themselves. This suggested a comparison of the interfering effect of color stimuli upon reading names of colors (the two types of stimuli being presented simultaneously) with the interfering effect of word stimuli upon naming colors themselves. In other words, if the word "red" is printed in blue ink how will the interference of the ink-color "blue" upon reading the printed word "red" compare with the interference of the printed word "red" upon calling the name of the ink-color "blue"? The increase in time for reacting to words caused by the presence of conflicting color stimuli is taken as the measure of the interference of color stimuli upon reading words. The increase in the time for reacting to colors caused by the presence of conflicting word stimuli is taken as the measure of the interference of word stimuli upon naming colors. A second problem grew out of the results of the first. The problem was, What effect would practice in reacting to the color stimuli in the presence of conflicting word stimuli have upon the reaction times in the two situations described in the first problem?

## Experimental

The materials employed in these experiments are quite different from any that have been used to study interference.[1] In former studies the subjects were given practice in responding to a set of stimuli until associative bonds were formed between the stimuli and the desired responses, then a change was made in the experimental 'set up' which demanded a different set of responses to the same set of stimuli. In the present study pairs of conflicting stimuli, both being inherent aspects of the same symbols, are presented simultaneously (a name of one color printed in the ink of another color—a word stimulus and a color stimulus). These stimuli are varied in such a manner as to maintain the potency of their interference effect. Detailed descriptions of the materials used in each of the three experiments are included in the reports of the respective experiments.

### Experiment I: The Effect of Interfering Color Stimuli upon Reading Names of Colors Serially

#### MATERIALS

When this experiment was contemplated, the first task was to arrange suitable tests. The colors used on the Woodworth-Wells colorsheet were considered but two changes were deemed advisable. As the word test to be used in comparison with the color test was to be printed in black it seemed well to substitute another color for black as an interfering stimulus. Also, because of the difficulty of printing words in yellow that would approximate the stimulus intensity of the other colors used, yellow was discarded. After consulting with Dr. Peterson, black and yellow were replaced by brown and purple. Hence, the colors used were red, blue, green, brown, and purple. The colors were arranged so as to avoid any regularity of occurrence and so that each color would appear twice in each column

and in each row, and that no color would immediately succeed itself in either column or row. The words were also arranged so that the name of each color would appear twice in each line. No word was printed in the color it named but an equal number of times in each of the other four colors; i.e., the word "red" was printed in blue, green, brown, and purple inks; the word "blue" was printed in red, green, brown, and purple inks; etc. No word immediately succeeded itself in either column or row. The test was printed from fourteen-point Franklin lowercase type. The word arrangement was duplicated in black print from same type. Each test was also printed in the reverse order which provided a second form. The tests will be known as "Reading color names where the color of the print and the word are different" (RCNd),[2] and "Reading color names printed in black" (RCNb).

#### SUBJECTS AND PROCEDURE

Seventy college undergraduates (14 males and 56 females) were used as subjects. Every subject read two whole sheets (the two forms) of each test at one sitting. One half of the subjects of each sex, selected at random, read the tests in the order RCNb (Form 1), RCNd (Form 2), RCNd (Form 1) and RCNb (Form 2), while the other half reversed the order thus equating for practice and fatigue on each test and form. All subjects were seated so as to have good daylight illumination from the left side only. All subjects were in the experimental room a few minutes before beginning work to allow the eyes to adjust to light conditions. The subjects were volunteers and apparently the motivation was good.

A ten-word sample was read before the first reading of each test. The instructions were to read as quickly as possible and to leave no errors uncorrected. When an error was left the subject's attention was called to that fact as soon as the sheet was finished. On the signal "Ready! Go!" the sheet which the subject held face down was turned by the subject and read aloud. The words were followed on another sheet (in black print) by the experimenter and the time was taken with a stop watch to a fifth of a second. Contrary to instructions 14 subjects left a total of 24 errors uncorrected on the RCNd test, 4 was the maximum for any subject, and 4 other subjects left 1 error each on the RCNb test. As each subject made 200 reactions on each test this small number of errors was considered negligible. The work was done under good daylight illumination.

## RESULTS

Table 11.1 gives the means ($m$), standard deviations ($\sigma$), differences ($D$), probable error of the difference ($PE_d$), and the reliability of the difference ($D/PE_d$) for the whole group and for each sex.

Observation of the bottom line of the table shows that it took an average of 2.3 seconds longer to read 100 color names printed in colors different from that named by the word than to read the same names printed in black. This difference is not reliable which is in agreement with Peterson's prediction made when the test was first proposed. The means for the sex groups show no particular difference. An examination of the means and standard deviations for the two tests shows that the interference factor caused a slight increase in the variability for the whole group and for the female group, but a slight decrease for the male group.

Table 11.2 presents the same data arranged on the basis of college classification. Only college years one and two contain a sufficient number of cases for comparative purposes. They show no differences that approach reliability.

## Experiment 2: The Effect of Interfering Word Stimuli upon Naming Colors Serially

### MATERIALS

For this experiment the colors of the words in the *RCNd* test, described in Experiment 1, were printed in the same order but in the form of solid squares (■) from 24-point type instead of words. This sort of problem will be referred to as the "Naming color test" *(NC)*. The *RCNd* test was employed also but in a very different manner from that in Experi-

ment 1. In this experiment the colors of the print of the series of names were to be called in succession ignoring the colors named by the words; e.g., where the word "red" was printed in blue it was to be called "blue," where it was printed in green it was to be called "green," where the word "brown" was printed in red it was to be called "red," etc. Thus color of the print was to be the controlling stimulus and not the name of the color spelled by the word. This is to be known as the "Naming color of word test where the color of the print and the word are different" *(NCWd)*. (See Appendix *B*.)

### SUBJECTS AND PROCEDURE

One hundred students (88 college undergraduates, 29 males and 59 females, and 12 graduate students, all females) served as subjects. Every subject read two whole sheets (the two forms) of each test at one sitting. Half of the subjects read in the order *NC, NCWd, NCWd, NC*, and the other half in the order *NCWd, NC, NC, NCWd*, thus equating for practice and fatigue on the two sets. All subjects were seated (in their individual tests) near the window so as to have good daylight illumination from the left side. Every subject seemed to make a real effort.

A ten-word sample of each test was read before reading the test the first time. The instructions were to name the colors as they appeared in regular reading line as quickly as possible and to correct all errors. The methods of starting, checking errors, and timing were the same as those used in Experiment 1. The errors were recorded and for each error not corrected, twice the average time per word for the reading of the sheet on which the error was made was added to the time taken by the stop watch. This plan of correction was arbitrary but seemed to be justified by the situation. There were two kinds of failures to be accounted for: first, the failure to see the error: and second, the failure to correct it. Each phase of the situation gave the sub-

**TABLE 11.1.** The Mean Time in Seconds for Reading One Hundred Names of Colors Printed in Colors Different from That Named by the Word and for One Hundred Names of Colors Printed in Black

| Sex | No. Ss. | RCNd | $\sigma$ | RCNb | $\sigma$ | D | $PE_d$ | $D/PE_d$ |
|---|---|---|---|---|---|---|---|---|
| Male | 14 | 43.20 | 4.98 | 40.81 | 4.97 | 2.41 | 1.27 | 1.89 |
| Female | 56 | 43.32 | 6.42 | 41.04 | 4.78 | 2.28 | .72 | 3.16 |
| Male and Female | 70 | 43.30 | 6.15 | 41.00 | 4.84 | 2.30 | .63 | 3.64 |

**TABLE 11.2. Showing Data of Table 12.1 Arranged on the Basis of College Classification**

| College Year | No. Ss. | RCNd | σ | RCNb | σ | D | D/PE$_d$ |
|---|---|---|---|---|---|---|---|
| 1st | 35 | 43.9 | 6.31 | 41.7 | 5.58 | 2.2 | .38 |
| 2d | 20 | 44.9 | 6.74 | 41.8 | 4.32 | 3.1 | .57 |
| 3d | 8 | 39.8 | 4.62 | 39.2 | 3.73 | .6 | .16 |
| 4th | 7 | 40.8 | 3.60 | 39.2 | 2.93 | 1.6 | .51 |

ject a time advantage which deserved taking note of. Since no accurate objective measure was obtainable and the number of errors was small the arbitrary plan was adopted. Fifty-nine percent of the group left an average of 2.6 errors uncorrected on the NCWd test (200 reactions) and 32 percent of the group left an average of 1.2 errors uncorrected on the NC test (200 reactions). The correction changed the mean on the NCWd test from 108.7 to 110.3 and the mean of the NC test from 63.0 to 63.3.

## RESULTS

The means of the times for the NC and NCWd tests for the whole group and for each sex are presented in Table 11.3 along with the difference, the probable error of the difference, the reliability of the difference, and the difference divided by the mean time for the naming color test.

The comparison of the results for the whole group on the NC and NCWd test given in the bottom line of the table indicates the strength of the interference of the habit of calling words upon the activity of naming colors. The mean time for 100 responses is increased from 63.3 seconds to 110.3 seconds or an increase of 74 percent. (The medians on the two tests are 61.9 and 110.4 seconds respectively.) The standard deviation is increased in approximately the same ratio from 10.8 to 18.8. The coefficient of variability remains the same to the third decimal place ($\sigma/m = .171$). The difference between means may be better evaluated when ex-

pressed in terms of the variability of the group. The difference of 47 seconds is 2.5 standard deviation units in terms of the NCWd test or 4.35 standard deviation units on the NC test. The former shows that 99 percent of the group on the NCWd test was above the mean on the NC test (took more time); and the latter shows that the group as scored on the NC test was well below the mean on the NCWd test. These results are shown graphically in Figure 11.1 where histograms and normal curves (obtained by the Gaussian formula) of the two sets of data are superimposed. The small area in which the curves overlap and the 74 percent increase in the mean time for naming colors caused by the presence of word stimuli show the marked interference effect of the habitual response of calling words.

The means for the sex groups on the NCWd test show a difference of 3.6 seconds which is only 1.16 times its probable error; but the means on the NC test have a difference of 8.2 seconds which is 5.17 times its probable error. This reliable sex-difference favoring the females in naming colors agrees with the findings of Woodworth-Wells (1911), Brown (1915), Ligon (1932), etc.

The same data are arranged according to college classification in Table 11.4. There is some indication of improvement of the speed factor for both tests as the college rank improves. The relative difference between the two tests, however, remains generally the same except for fluctuations which are probably due to the variation in the number of cases.

**TABLE 11.3. The Mean Time for Naming One Hundred Colors Presented in Squares and in the Print of Words Which Name Other Colors**

| Sex | No. Ss. | NCWd | σ | NC | σ | D/NC | D | PE$_d$ | D/PE$_d$ |
|---|---|---|---|---|---|---|---|---|---|
| Male | 29 | 111.1 | 21.6 | 69.2 | 10.8 | .61 | 42.9 | 3.00 | 13.83 |
| Female | 71 | 107.5 | 17.3 | 61.0 | 10.5 | .76 | 46.5 | 1.62 | 28.81 |
| Male and Female | 100 | 110.3 | 18.8 | 63.3 | 10.8 | .74 | 47.0 | 1.50 | 31.38 |

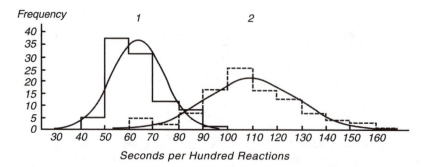

FIGURE 11.1 ■ Showing the effect of interference on naming colors. (No interference [1]; interference [2].)

## Experiment 3: The Effects of Practice upon Interference

### MATERIALS

The tests used were the same in character as those described in Experiments 1 and 2 (*RCNb*, *RCNd*, *NC*, and *NCWd*) with some revision. The *NC* test was printed in swastikas (卐) instead of squares (■). Such a modification allowed white to appear in the figure with the color, as is the case when the color is presented in the printed word. This change also made it possible to print the *NC* test in shades which more nearly match those in the *NCWd* test. The order of colors was determined under one restriction other than those given in section 2. Each line contained one color whose two appearances were separated by only one other color. This was done to equate, as much as possible, the difficulty of the different lines of the test so that any section of five lines would approximate the difficulty of any other section of five lines. Two forms of the tests were printed; in one the order was the inverse of that in the other.

### SUBJECTS AND PROCEDURE

Thirty-two undergraduates in the University of Arizona (17 males and 15 females), who offered their services, were the subjects. At each day's sitting 4 half-sheets of the same test were read, and the average time (after correction was made for errors according to the plan outlined in Experiment 2) was recorded as the day's score. Only a few errors were left uncorrected. The largest correction made on the practice test changed the mean from 49.3 to 49.6. The plan of experimentation was as follows:

| Day | 1 | 2 | 3 | 4 | 5 | 6 | 7 |
|-----|------|------|----|------|------|------|------|
| Test | RCNb | RCNd | NC | NCWd | NCWd | NCWd | NCWd |

| Day | 8 | 9 | 10 | 11 | 12 | 13 | 14 |
|-----|------|------|------|------|----|------|------|
| Test | NCWd | NCWd | NCWd | NCWd | NC | RCNd | RCNd |

On the 1st day the *RCNb* test was used to acquaint the subjects with the experimental procedure and improve the reliability of the 2d day's test. The *RCNd* test was given the 2d day and the 13th day to obtain a measure of the interference developed by practice on the *NC* and *NCWd* tests. The *RCNd* test was given the 14th day to get a measure of the effect of a day's practice upon the newly developed interference. The *NC* test was given the 3d and 12th days, just before and just after the real practice series, so that actual change in interference on the *NCWd* test might be known. The test schedule was followed in regular daily order with

TABLE 11.4. **Showing the Data of Table III Arranged on the Basis of College Classification**

| Class | No. Ss. | *NCWd* | σ | *NC* | σ | *D* | *D/NC* | *D/PE*$_d$ |
|-------|---------|--------|------|------|------|------|--------|-----------|
| 1st yr | 17 | 116.5 | 24.9 | 70.9 | 15.9 | 45.6 | .64 | 22.7 |
| 2d yr | 37 | 114.4 | 18.0 | 66.1 | 10.6 | 48.3 | .73 | 32.6 |
| 3d yr | 12 | 106.1 | 14.0 | 62.8 | 7.0 | 43.3 | .69 | 41.2 |
| 4th yr | 22 | 96.6 | 16.8 | 57.8 | 8.9 | 38.8 | .67 | 30.3 |
| Graduates | 12 | 111.2 | 19.4 | 59.9 | 11.5 | 51.3 | .86 | 37.6 |

two exceptions. There were two days between test days 3 and 4, and also two between test days 8 and 9, in which no work was done. These irregularities were occasioned by weekends. Each subject was assigned a regular time of day for his work throughout the experiment. All but two subjects followed the schedule with very little irregularity. These two were finally dropped from the group and their data rejected.

All of the tests were given individually by the author. The subject was seated near a window so as to have good daylight illumination from the left side. There was no other source of light. Every subject was in the experimental room a few minutes before beginning work to allow his eyes to adapt to the light conditions. To aid eye-adaptation and also to check for clearness of vision each subject read several lines in a current magazine. Every subject was given Dr. Ishihara's test for color vision. One subject was found to have some trouble with red-green color vision; and her results were discarded though they differed from others of her sex only in the number of errors made and corrected.

RESULTS

The general results for the whole series of tests are shown in Table 11.5, which presents the means, standard deviations, and coefficients of variability for the whole group and for each sex separately, together with a measure of sex differences in terms of the probable error of the difference. Table 11.6,

**TABLE 11.5.** Showing the Effects of Practice on the NCWd Test upon Itself, upon the NC Test, and upon the RCNd Test in Terms of Mean Scores, Standard Deviations ($\sigma$), and Coefficients of Variability (s/m) for Thirty-two College Students

| Sex | No. Ss. | Initial Tests | | | | | | Days of Practice on the NCWd Test | | | | | | | |
|---|---|---|---|---|---|---|---|---|---|---|---|---|---|---|---|
| | | RCNb | $\sigma$ | RCNd | $\sigma$ | NC | $\sigma$ | 1 | $\sigma$ | 2 | $\sigma$ | 3 | $\sigma$ | 4 | $\sigma$ |
| Male | 17 | 19.8 | 1.8 | 19.6 | 2.5 | 30.6 | 3.6 | 51.2 | 8.5 | 41.6 | 7.8 | 38.2 | 7.6 | 37.3 | 8.0 |
| Female | 15 | 18.3 | 2.9 | 19.1 | 3.4 | 26.5 | 2.8 | 47.8 | 4.2 | 39.1 | 4.4 | 35.8 | 3.4 | 33.7 | 3.7 |
| M & F | 32 | 19.1 | 2.6 | 19.4 | 3.0 | 28.7 | 3.5 | 49.6 | 7.1 | 40.5 | 6.4 | 37.1 | 6.1 | 35.7 | 6.5 |

| | Sex Differences | | | | | | | | | | | | | | |
|---|---|---|---|---|---|---|---|---|---|---|---|---|---|---|---|
| M & F | 1.5 | | .5 | | 4.1 | | 3.4 | | 2.5 | | 2.4 | | 3.6 | | |
| $PE_d$ | .49 | | .70 | | .76 | | 1.55 | | 1.47 | | 1.36 | | 1.45 | | |
| $D/PE_d$ | 3.06 | | .71 | | 5.39 | | 2.19 | | 1.70 | | 1.76 | | 2.48 | | |

| Sex | Coefficients of Variability | | | | | | | | | | | | | | |
|---|---|---|---|---|---|---|---|---|---|---|---|---|---|---|---|
| Male | .09 ± 0.11 | | .13 ± .015 | | .12 ± .014 | | .17 ± .020 | | .19 ± .022 | | .20 ± .024 | | .22 ± .026 | | |
| Female | .16 ± .024 | | .18 ± .028 | | .11 ± .016 | | .09 ± .013 | | .11 ± .017 | | .09 ± .014 | | .11 ± .017 | | |
| M & F | .14 ± .012 | | .15 ± .013 | | .12 ± .010 | | .14 ± .012 | | .16 ± .014 | | .17 ± .014 | | .18 ± .016 | | |

| Sex | No. Ss. | Days of Practice on the NCWd Test | | | | | | | | Final Tests | | | | | |
|---|---|---|---|---|---|---|---|---|---|---|---|---|---|---|---|
| | | 5 | $\sigma$ | 6 | $\sigma$ | 7 | $\sigma$ | 8 | $\sigma$ | NC | $\sigma$ | RCNd | $\sigma$ | RCNd | $\sigma$ |
| Male | 17 | 36.3 | 7.4 | 33.9 | 7.3 | 33.5 | 6.7 | 33.4 | 7.1 | 25.9 | 4.2 | 37.3 | 13.7 | 22.2 | 4.8 |
| Female | 15 | 32.8 | 4.3 | 32.3 | 4.0 | 31.6 | 3.3 | 31.5 | 3.3 | 23.6 | 1.9 | 32.0 | 6.2 | 21.8 | 6.1 |
| M & F | 32 | 34.9 | 6.2 | 33.2 | 5.4 | 32.6 | 5.5 | 32.8 | 6.1 | 24.7 | 3.2 | 34.8 | 11.7 | 22.0 | 5.5 |

| | Sex Differences | | | | | | | | | | | | | | |
|---|---|---|---|---|---|---|---|---|---|---|---|---|---|---|---|
| M & F | 3.5 | | 1.6 | | 1.9 | | 1.9 | | 2.3 | | 5.3 | | .4 | | |
| $PE_d$ | 1.41 | | 1.34 | | 1.23 | | 1.30 | | .77 | | 2.56 | | 1.31 | | |
| $D/PE_d$ | 2.48 | | 1.19 | | 1.54 | | 1.46 | | 2.99 | | 2.07 | | .31 | | |

| Sex | Coefficients of Variability | | | | | | | | | | | | | | |
|---|---|---|---|---|---|---|---|---|---|---|---|---|---|---|---|
| Male | .20 ± .024 | | .22 ± .026 | | .20 ± .024 | | .21 ± .025 | | .16 ± .019 | | .37 ± .048 | | .22 ± .026 | | |
| Female | .13 ± .020 | | .12 ± .019 | | .10 ± .016 | | .11 ± .016 | | .08 ± .012 | | .19 ± .030 | | .28 ± .045 | | |
| M & F | .18 ± 0.16 | | .16 ± .014 | | .17 ± .015 | | .19 ± .015 | | .13 ± .011 | | .34 ± .031 | | .25 ± .022 | | |

The score is the average time for four trials of 50 reactions each.

**TABLE 11.6. A Summary of the Means in Table V, Showing the Effect of Practice in the NCWd Test upon the NCWd, the NC, and the RCNd Tests**

| Test | NCWd | | | NC | | | RCNd | | |
|---|---|---|---|---|---|---|---|---|---|
| Sex | M | F | M & F | M | F | M & F | M | F | M & F |
| Initial Score | 51.2 | 47.8 | 49.6 | 30.6 | 26.5 | 28.7 | 19.6 | 19.1 | 19.4 |
| Final Score | 33.4 | 31.5 | 32.8 | 25.9 | 23.6 | 24.7 | 37.3 | 32.0 | 34.8 |
| Gain | 17.8 | 16.3 | 16.8 | 4.7 | 2.9 | 4.0 | −17.7 | −12.9 | −15.4 |
| Percent Gain | 34.8 | 34.1 | 33.9 | 15.4 | 10.9 | 13.9 | −90.3 | −67.5 | −79.3 |

Minus sign shows loss.

which is derived from Table 11.5 summarizes the practice effects upon the respective tests. The graphical representation of the results in the practice series gives the learning curve presented in Figure 11.2.

## The Effect of Practice on the *NCWd* Test upon Itself

The data to be considered here are those given in the section of Table 11.5 under the caption "Days of Practice on the *NCWd* Test." They are also presented in summary in the left section of Table 11.6 and graphically in Figure 11.2. From all three presentations it is evident that the time score is low-

ered considerably by practice. Reference to Table 11.6 shows a gain of 16.8 seconds or 33.9 percent of the mean of the 1st day's practice. The practice curve is found to resemble very much the 'typical' learning curve when constructed on time units. The coefficient of variability is increased from .14 ± .012 to .19 ± .015. This difference divided by its probable error gives 2.60 which indicates that it is not reliable. The probability of a real increase in variability, however, is 24 to 1. Hence, practice on the *NCWd* test serves to increase individual differences.

An examination of the data of the sex groups reveals a difference in speed on the *NCWd* test which favors the females. This is to be expected

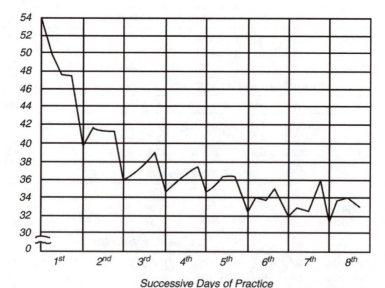

Seconds
per Fifty Reactions

**FIGURE 11.2** ■ Mean scores for the group in each of the four half-sheets of the *NCWd* test, which constituted the daily practice.

as there is a difference in favor of females in naming colors. Though the difference is not reliable in any one case it exists throughout the practice series; indicating that the relative improvement is approximately the same for the two groups. This latter fact is also shown by the ratio of the difference between the halves of practice series to the first half. It is .185 for the males and .180 for the females.

## The Effect of Practice on the NCWd Test upon the NC Test

The middle section of Table 11.6 shows a gain on the *NC* test of 4.0 seconds or 13.9 percent of the initial score. This is only 23.7 percent of the gain on the *NCWd* test which means that less than one fourth of the total gain on the *NCWd* test is due to increase in speed in naming colors. The improvement is greater for the males, which is accounted for by the fact that there is more difference between naming colors and reading names of colors for the males than for the females.

## The Effects in the *RCNd* Test of Practice on the *NCWd* and *NC* Tests

The right section of Table 11.6 shows that the practice on the *NCWd* and *NC* tests resulted in heavy loss in speed on the *RCNd*. A comparison of the right and left sections of the table shows that the loss on the *RCNd* test, when measured in absolute units, is practically equal to the gain on the *NCWd* test; when measured in relative units it is much greater. It is interesting to find that in 10 short practice periods the relative values of opposing stimuli can be modified so greatly. There is little relation, however, between the gain in one case and the loss in the other. The correlation between gain and loss in absolute units is .262 ± .11, while the correlation between percent of gain and percent of loss is .016 ± .17, or zero. This is what one might expect.

From a consideration of the results of the two applications of the *RCNd* test given in the final tests of Table 11.5 it is evident that the newly developed interference disappears very rapidly with practice. From one day to the next the mean decreases from 34.8 to 22.0 seconds. This indicates that renewing the effectiveness of old associations which are being opposed by newly formed ones is easier than strengthening new associations in opposition to old, well-established ones.

The variability of the group is increased by the increase in interference due to practice on the *NCWd* test. The coefficient of variability increases from .15 ± .013 to .34 ± .031, the difference divided by its probable error being 5.65. This is not surprising as the degree of the interference varies widely for different subjects. Its degree is determined by the learning on the practice series which is shown by the individual results to vary considerably. One day's practice on the *RCNd* test reduced the variability from .34 ± .031 to .25 ± .022. The decrease in variability is 2.3 times its probable error.

The data from this experiment present interesting findings on the effect of practice upon individual differences. The results which have already been discussed separately are presented for comparison in Table 11.7.

These results show that practice increases individual differences where a stimulus to which the subjects have an habitual reaction pattern is interfering with reactions to a stimulus for which the subjects do not have an habitual reaction pattern (the word stimulus interfering with naming colors, *NCWd* test); but decreases individual differences where a stimulus to which the subjects do not have an habitual reaction pattern is interfering with reactions to a stimulus for which the subjects have an habitual reaction pattern (the color stimulus

**TABLE 11.7. The Effects of Practice on the NCWd Test and the RCNd Test upon the Coefficient of Variability for the Group**

| Test | No. Ss. | Coefficients of Variability | | D | $PE_d$ | $D/PE_d$ |
| | | Initial | Final | | | |
|---|---|---|---|---|---|---|
| *NCW* | 32 | .14 | .19 | .05 | .034 | 2.60 |
| *RCNd* | 32 | .34 | .25 | .09 | .037 | 2.33 |

interfering with reading words—*RCNd* test). There are two other variables involved, however: initial variability and length of practice. Thus in the *NCWd* test the initial variability was less, the difficulty greater, and the practice greater than in the *RCNd* test. These findings lend some support to Peterson's hypothesis, "Subjects of normal heterogeneity would become more alike with practice on the simpler processes or activities, but more different on the more complex activities" (Peterson and Barlow, 1928, p. 228).

A sex difference in naming colors has been found by all who have studied color naming and has been generally attributed to the greater facility of women in verbal reactions than of men. There is some indication in our data that this sex difference may be due to the difference in the accustomed reaction of the two sexes to colors as stimuli. In other words responding to a color stimulus by naming the color may be more common with females than with males. This difference is probably built up through education. Education in color is much more intense for girls than for boys as observing, naming, and discussing colors relative to dress is much more common among girls than among boys. The practice in naming colors in the *NCWd* test decreased the difference between the sex groups on the *NC* test from a difference 5.38 times its probable error to a difference 2.99 times its probable error. This decrease in the difference due to practice favors the view that the difference has been acquired and is therefore a product of training.

# Summary

1. Interference in serial verbal reactions has been studied by means of newly devised experimental materials. The source of the interference is in the materials themselves. The words red, blue, green, brown, and purple are used on the test sheet. No word is printed in the color it names but an equal number of times in each of the other four colors; i.e., the word "red" is printed in blue, green, brown, and purple inks; the word "blue" is printed in red, green, brown, and purple inks; etc. Thus each word presents the name of one color printed in ink of another color. Hence, a word stimulus and a color stimulus both are presented simultaneously. The words of the test are duplicated in black print and the colors of the test are duplicated in squares or swastikas. The difference in the time for reading the words printed in colors and the same words printed in black is the measure of the interference of color stimuli upon reading words. The difference in the time for naming the colors in which the words are printed and the same colors printed in squares (or swastikas) is the measure of the interference of conflicting word stimuli upon naming colors.

2. The interference of conflicting color stimuli upon the time for reading 100 words (each word naming a color unlike the ink-color of its print) caused an increase of only 2.3 seconds or 5.6 percent over the normal time for reading the same words printed in black. This increase is not reliable. But the interference of conflicting word stimuli upon the time for naming 100 colors (each color being the print of a word which names another color) caused an increase of 47.0 seconds or 74.3 percent of the normal time for naming colors printed in squares.

These tests provide a unique basis (the interference value) for comparing the effectiveness of the two types of associations. Since the presence of the color stimuli caused no reliable increase over the normal time for reading words ($D/PE_d = 3.64$) and the presence of word stimuli caused a considerable increase over the normal time for naming colors (4.35 standard deviation units) the associations that have been formed between the word stimuli and the reading response are evidently more effective than those that have been formed between the color stimuli and the naming response. Since these associations are products of training, and since the difference in their strength corresponds roughly to the difference in training in reading words and naming colors, it seems reasonable to conclude that the difference in speed in reading names of colors and in naming colors may be satisfactorily accounted for by the difference in training in the two activities. The word stimulus has been associated with the specific response "to read," while the color stimulus has been associated with various responses: "to admire," "to name," "to reach for," "to avoid," etc.

3. As a test of the permanency of the interference of conflicting word stimuli to naming colors eight days practice (200 reactions per day) were

given in naming the colors of the print of words (each word naming a color unlike the inkcolor of its print). The effects of this practice were as follows: (1) It decreased the interference of conflicting word stimuli to naming colors but did not eliminate it. (2) It produced a practice curve comparable to that obtained in many other learning experiments. (3) It increased the variability of the group. (4) It shortened the reaction time to colors presented in color squares. (5) It increased the interference of conflicting color stimuli upon reading words.

4. Practice was found either to increase or to decrease the variability of the group depending upon the nature of the material used.

5. Some indication was found that the sex difference in naming colors is due to the difference in the training of the two sexes.

## NOTES

The writer wishes to acknowledge the kind assistance received in the preparation of this thesis. He is indebted to Dr. Joseph Peterson for encouragement, helpful suggestions, and criticism of the manuscript; to Major H. W. Fenker, a graduate student in psychology, for helpful suggestions relative to preparation of the manuscript; to Drs. J. Peterson, S. C. Garrison, M. R. Schneck, J. E. Caster, O. A. Simley, W. F. Smith, and to Miss M. Nichol for aid in securing subjects; to some 300 college students who served as subjects; and to William Fitzgerald of The Peabody Press for substantial assistance in the printing of the test materials.

1. Descoeudres (1914) and also Goodenough and Brian (1929) presented color and form simultaneously in studying their relative values as stimuli.
2. In Appendix A will be found a key to all symbols and abbreviations used in this paper.

## REFERENCES

Bair, J. H., The practice curve: A study of the formation of habits. *Psychol. Rev. Monog. Suppl.*, 1902 (No. 19), 1–70.

Bergström, J. A., Experiments upon physiological memory. *Amer. J. Psychol.*, 1893, *5*, 356–359.

Bergström, J. A., The relation of the interference of the practice effect of an association. *Amer. J. Psychol.*, 1894, *6*, 433–442.

Bowditch, H. P. and Warren, J. W., The knee-jerk and its physiological modifications. *J. Physiology*, 1890, *11*, 25–46.

Brown, Warner, Practice in associating color names with colors. *Psychol. Rev.*, 1915, *22*, 45–55.

Brown, Warner, Habit interference in card sorting. *Univ. of Calif. Studies in Psychol.*, 1914, V, i, No. 4.

Cattell, J. McK., The time it takes to see and name objects. *Mind*, 1886, *11*, 63–65.

Culler, A. J., Interference and adaptability. *Arch. of Psychol.*, 1912, *3* (No. 24), 1–80.

Descoeudres, A., Couleur, forme, ou nombre. *Arch. de Psychol.*, 1914, *14*, 305–341.

Garrett, H. E. and Lemmon, V. W., An analysis of several well-known tests. *J. Appld. Psychol.*, 1924, *8*, 424–438.

Goodenough, F. L. and Brian, C. R., Certain factors underlying the acquisition of motor skill by pre-school children. *J. Exper. Psychol.*, 1929, *12*, 127–155.

Hunter, W. S. and Yarbrough, J. U., The interference of auditory habits in the white rat. *J. Animal Behav.*, 1917, *7*, 49–65.

Hunter, W. S., Habit interference in the white rat and in the human subject. *J. Comp. Physiol.*, 1922, *2*, 29–59.

Kline, L. W., An experimental study of associative inhibition. *J. Exper. Psychol.*, 1921, *4*, 270–299.

Lester, O. P., Mental set in relation to retroactive inhibition. *J. Exper. Psychol.*, 1932, *15*, 681–699.

Ligon, E. M. A., Genetic study of color naming and word reading. *Amer. J. Psychol.*, 1932, *44*, 103–121.

Lund, F. H., The role of practice in speed of association. *J. Exper. Psychol.*, 1927, *10*, 424–433.

Müller, G. E. and Schumann, F., Experimentelle Beiträge zu Unter-suchung des Gedächtnisses. *Zsch. f. Psychol.*, 1894, *6*, 81–190.

Münsterberg, Hugo, Gedächtnisstudien. *Beiträge zur Experimentellen Psychologie*, 1892, *4*, 70.

Pearce, Bennie D., A note on the interference of visual habits in the white rat. *J. Animal Behav.*, 1917, *7*, 169–177.

Peterson, J. and Barlow, M. C., *The Effects of Practice on Individual Differences*. The 27th Year Book of Nat. Soc. Study of Educ., Part II, 1928, 211–230.

Peterson, J., Lanier, L. H., and Walker, H. M., Comparisons of white and negro children. *J. Comp. Psychol.*, 1925, *5*, 271–283.

Peterson, J. and David, Q. J., *The Psychology of Handling Men in the Army*. Minneapolis, Minn. Perine Book Co., 1918, pp. 146.

Shepard, J. F. and Fogelsonger, H. M., Association and inhibition. *Psychol. Rev*, 1913, *20*, 291–311.

Telford, C. W., Differences in responses to colors and their names. *J. Genet. Psychol.*, 1930, *37*, 151–159.

Woodworth, R. S. and Wells, F. L., Association tests. *Psychol. Rev. Monog. Suppl.*, 1911, *13* (No. 57), pp. 85.

## Appendix A

### A Key to Symbols and Abbreviations

*NC*    Naming Colors.
*NCWd*  Naming the Colors of the Print of Word Where the Color of the Print and the Word are Different.
*RCNb*  Reading Color Names Printed in Black Ink.
*RCNd*  Reading Color Names Where the Color of the Print and the Word are Different.
*D*    Difference.
$D/PE_d$  Difference divided by the probable error of the difference.
*M & F*  Males and Females.
$PE_d$  Probable error of the difference.
$\sigma$    Sigma or standard deviation.
$\sigma/m$   Standard deviation divided by the mean.

# Attention and Cognitive Control[1]

Michael I. Posner and Charles R. R. Snyder
• University of Oregon

## Introduction

To what extent are our conscious intentions and strategies in control of the way information is processed in our minds? This seems to be a question of importance to us both as psychologists and as human beings. Yet as Shallice (1972) has pointed out, most theorists in psychology have avoided consideration of the relationship between conscious and unconscious mental events. While psychological writers rarely deal with this distinction directly, the reader of psychological publications can hardly avoid it. On the one hand, the pages of journals are full of studies in which the "strategies" or "optional processes" of the subject are used to explain the results obtained; on the other hand, we are told that human memory is an associational machine that operates entirely without control of the subjects' strategies (Anderson & Bower, 1973). Both of these views need to be accommodated. Even the most cognitive of theorists recognizes that people are not always able to adapt their thought processes to the strategies required by the task, and Anderson and Bower (1973) explicitly recognize that their strategy-free memory system must be coupled to other strategy-dependent systems.

In this paper we review studies designed to provide some experimental analysis of how conscious strategies interact with automatic activation processes to determine performance.

As a first step toward an understanding of conscious control of cognition, we examine in detail the characteristics of purely "automatic" processes. We are all introspectively familiar with thoughts, ideas, or feelings that seem to intrude upon us rather than occur as a result of our intentions to produce them. We propose three operational indicants of whether a process is "automatic," as we will use the term: The process occurs without intention, without giving rise to any conscious awareness, and without producing interference with other ongoing mental activity. Even with these stringent requirements it is possible to show that many complex but habitual mental processes can operate automatically and thus, in principle, be strategy independent.

Many theorists have proposed a fixed processing stage at which limited-capacity attentional effects are to be found. Sometimes the stage is early in processing and sometimes late, but the idea is that some types of operations are not capacity limited while others are. Our view is different; we see a specific mechanism of limited capacity. This mechanism can be committed flexibly to different stages, depending upon many factors. Thus, it is necessary for us to develop operational methods for distinguishing whether a given process is being performed in an "automatic" or "conscious" mode.

Many cognitive tasks may be viewed as combining automatic activation and conscious strategies. By reviewing a number of experimental results we try to see how well our distinction aids in furthering the investigation and understanding of these tasks. In particular, we try to illustrate how a number of disparate paradigms demonstrate similar principles.

Perhaps the problems of cognitive control have been discussed in an effort to understand the nature of emotion. Signals with emotional significance seem more intrusive than other signals. Some have used this to argue that emotions have a special status in memory and thereby serve to guide our conscious cognitions. We introduce some experiments aimed at understanding the way emotional information is activated in the memory system and how that activation affects our conscious cognitions.

## Automatic Pathway Activation

### Intention

#### STROOP EFFECT

There is excellent evidence that subjects cannot choose to avoid processing aspects of an input item that they desire to ignore. The Stroop effect is based upon this difficulty (Dyer, 1973). When given the task of naming the ink color of the words in Figure 12.1, one intends to avoid reading the words, but it is not possible to do so completely.

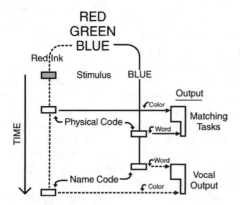

**FIGURE 12.1** ■ A schematic explanation of the Stroop effect. Two internal look-up processes produce representations of the ink color name (dashed line) and the word name (solid line) respectively. If the task is one of physical matching, ink colors arrive at output first and interfere with word matching. If the task is one of naming, words arrive at output first and interfere with ink colors. These interference effects result from the time course of the look-up process.

There is now a great deal of evidence that supports the kind of explanation for this effect which is outlined in Figure 12.1 (Dyer, 1973; Hintzman, Carre, Eskridge, Owens, Shaff, & Sparks, 1972; Keele, 1973; Morton & Chambers, 1973; Murray, Mastronadi, & Duncan, 1972). First, the usual Stroop effect arises because of competition between vocal responses to the printed word and the ink color. Keele (1973) demonstrated the importance of output interference by showing that noncolor words, which produce a small interference over a nonword control with a vocal output, produce no such interference when a key press output is used. Second, the direction of interference depends upon the time relations involved. Words are read faster than colors can be named; thus, a colornaming response receives stronger interference from the word than the reverse. Colors can be matched physically faster than can words, so that a matching response results in greater interference from colors on words than the reverse (Murray et al., 1972). Third, words often facilitate the vocal output to colors with which they share a common name (Hintzman et al., 1972).

These three results suggest that color naming and reading go on in parallel and without interference until close to the output. If they result in lookup of the same name, the overall reaction time is speeded; if they produce different names and a vocal output is required, the word tends to compete with the color name and reaction time is increased. One puzzle that remains is this: Why does a vocal response to color names interfere so much more than words that are not color names? After all, both have well-learned names stored in the memory system. The answer lies in the close semantic associations existing between color names and in the fact that prior activation of an item affects the time for look-up of its name, a phenomenon to which we now turn.

#### MEMORY ACTIVATION

One can use the Stroop effect to investigate the automatic activation pattern of a word in the memory system (Warren, 1972, 1974). Warren presented an auditory item or items, followed after a brief interval by a single visual word printed in colored ink. The only task set for the subject was to name the color of ink as quickly as possible. Warren's results showed clearly that the time

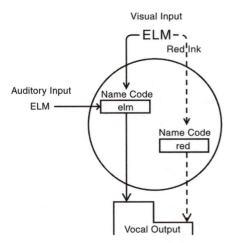

Visual Input

ELM

Red Ink

Auditory Input

ELM

Name Code

elm

Name Code

red

Vocal Output

**FIGURE 12.2** ■ Amount of interference (milliseconds) with color naming as a function of associative strength: condition: high forward, 95; medium forward, 50; low forward, 20; high backward, 0. An auditory word activates its name code. When the following visual word shares the same pathway it will arrive at output first and produce greater interference with color naming. The lower panel shows supportive data for this theory from Warren (1974).

for naming the ink color increased with the associative strength between the auditory word and the visual word. As shown in Figure 12.2, only associative strength in the forward direction is important; there is no effect of backward associative strength from the visual word to the prior auditory word.

The Warren effect can be explained by a logic quite similar to the one shown in Figure 12.1. An auditory word activates a pathway in the nervous system which consists of its auditory representation, its name, and a motor program for its production. When the visual word shares some of the same pathway (e.g., name and motor program) its processing rate is increased. Thus, the word name is delivered more quickly and/or more strongly to the output mechanisms, and thus produces more interference with saying the ink color name. There is no incentive in the task for the subject to activate items related to the auditory word. They are not asked to form associations nor need they be required to recall the auditory items to show the effect. Even when, as sometimes happens, subjects become aware that they are having difficulty in processing related items, they do not seem to be able to shut off the activation process.

The Warren results show why interference in the Stroop effect is greatest for color names, intermediate for associated words, and least for unrelated words. This is due to a general tendency of a word to activate related items. This effect occurs without any apparent intention by the subject. The effect of automatic activation on reaction time drops sharply with delay (Warren, 1972), but the well-known tendency for related words to be reported as "old" on recognition memory tests (Underwood, 1965) suggests that at least on some occasions the effects remain present for a considerable time.

## Awareness

### STROOP STUDIES

Recently, Conrad (1974) showed that the subject may be quite unaware of the activation pattern created by input words. She presented to her subjects sentences that ended with an ambiguous word (e.g., pot). The word was either disambiguated by context or not. Following the oral presentation of the sentence, she showed her subjects a single visual word in colored ink. The subjects' task was to name the color of the ink. In agreement with the Warren effect, she showed that the time to name the color of ink was longer when the word was related to the sentence. This was true both for the ambiguous word itself and for words related to either one of the word's meanings. The size of the interference effect was approximately equal whether the sentence had been disambiguated by context or not. These results are illustrated in Figure 12.3. Since the sentences disambiguated by context are consciously perceived in only one way, the finding that both meanings of the ambiguous word are activated is evidence that the activation pattern is not dependent on the subject's conscious percept.

The results of the Conrad experiment seem to us to be striking support for the kind of automatic activation of lexical memory proposed by Anderson and Bower (1973). They postulate that individual items of a proposition look-up related facts in parallel. Context has its effect as the activation patterns of the different lexical items are combined. The importance of context and the fact that we are rarely aware of ambiguity suggest that the equality of activation found by Conrad will change rapidly as one meaning or another comes to dominate.

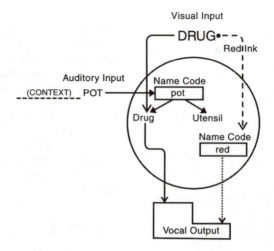

**Amount of Interference (msec) with Color Naming as a Function of Context**

| Context | Word Itself | Appropriate Category | Inappropriate Category |
|---|---|---|---|
| Ambiguous | 73 | 77 | 77 |
| Unambiguous | 58 | 61 | 50 |

**FIGURE 12.3** ■ (Top) The ambiguous word "pot" activates its lexical pathway irrespective of its linguistic context. A following visual word related to either pathway produces greater interference with color naming than a neutral word. Lower panel shows supportive data from Conrad (1974).

Her findings show that it is possible to develop psychological experiments that reveal memory processes relatively free of context and strategy effects.

### DICHOTIC LISTENING

The Stroop demonstrations all involve the automatic activation of a word meaning when subjects are attending to the channel on which it arrives. One might well argue that form and color are integral dimensions (Garner & Felfoldy, 1970), and thus the inability of the subject to ignore the word while attending to color is a very special phenomenon. Suppose instead that the subject attends to another set of items entirely. Will automatic activation still occur?

Much evidence on this comes from studies of dichotic listening. For example, Lewis (1970) has shown that when subjects are shadowing items to one ear, an item occurring on the unattended channel which has the same semantic meaning as an attended item will slow his rate of shadowing.

Mackay (1973) and Lackner and Garrett (1973) have shown that an unattended lexical item may serve to disambiguate the meaning of an attended sentence. In these experiments there is a semantic relationship between the attended and unattended items; thus, the effect could depend upon having an already activated locus in memory related to the unattended item.

Recent work (Corteen & Wood, 1972; von Wright, Anderson, & Stenman, 1975) has eliminated this problem. They first condition subjects to produce a galvanic skin response (GSR) to particular words. They then show that the GSR occurs when these words are presented on an unattended channel during dichotic listening. In the von Wright data, the size of the GSR to semantic associates of the conditioned stimulus was as large when they occurred on the unattended channel as on the attended channel. These results could only occur if semantic classification of the unattended word had taken place. Thus, the dichotic listening studies suggest that very complicated processing, including even stereotyped responses such as the

GSR, occur when the subject's attention is focused elsewhere.

In these studies the subjects have relatively little incentive to shift attention to the nonshadowed ear. Attempts to test awareness of unattended information have involved assessing breakdowns in shadowing, obtaining reports of unusual or obscene items, and measuring recognition memory for unattended items. Overall, it seems fair to conclude that a large amount of automatic processing still occurs when the subject's attention is focused on different items.

## Parallel Processing

The Stroop method of studying automatic activation requires subjects to attend to a particular position in space, although to the ink color rather than to the word. The dichotic method has subjects attending to a particular modality, though not the channel within that modality to which the unattended item is presented. Is there evidence that unattended items activate semantically related information even when they occur to an unattended modality? The results of several experiments (Greenwald, 1970a, b; Lewis, 1970) indicate that subjects are not successful in filtering out information occurring on a modality that they are instructed to ignore when it has a close semantic relationship to the attended information. Thus, it appears that the intention to ignore a modality will not prevent it from affecting attended processing.

Recent studies have provided another technique for examining the buildup of information on an unattended modality. We know from many reaction time studies that subjects are slow to respond to information occurring on a channel that is not the expected one. This might suggest that the buildup of information about the unexpected stimulus is being delayed because the subject is actively attending elsewhere. A more careful analysis raises doubts about this view, however. Consider the results of the following experiment (Posner & Summers, unpublished). In this experiment, subjects are required to classify a single item as to whether or not it is an animal name. On half the trials the stimulus is an animal name, while on the other half it is not. In pure blocks the stimulus is always auditory or always visual, while in mixed blocks it may be either. In addition, sometimes the subject has a warning signal in advance of the stimulus, and at other times he has no warning signal.

When the word is visually presented to the subject, his reaction time is generally fast, provided that he either (1) has a warning signal, or (2) knows the channel of entry. But if neither of these are obtained, his reaction time is quite long (see Figure 12.4). One might imagine that the subject has his eyes closed or defocussed. However, one feature of the data argues against this interpretation. Although the reaction times under these low attention conditions are long, the accuracy is high. It is as though the buildup of information goes on regardless of whether the subject is attending or not. If he is not attending, the response time is slow, but accurate. We think this is because the quality of information builds up at the same rate with or without attention.

Suppose instead of merely making the subject uncertain about the modality on which the information will arrive, his attention is carefully

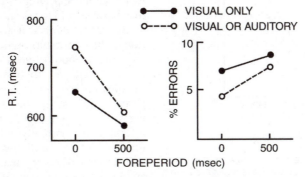

**FIGURE 12.4** ■ Reaction time (left) and errors (right) in classifying a visual word as an animal name as a function of amount of warning (foreperiod) and whether or not the words are all visual or mixed visual and auditory. (After unpublished experiments by Posner and Summers.)

directed to the wrong modality. LaBerge (1973) reported such a study. The task involved a classification response on the auditory modality (1000- versus 990-Hz tone) or on the visual modality (yellow versus orange light). In pure blocks the subject knew the modality that would be used. In mixed blocks he received the expected modality on .85 of the trials and the signal on the unexpected modality on .15 of the trials. A 1000-Hz tone or an orange light was used as a cue stimulus to rivet the subject's attention on the expected modality prior to the signal stimulus. The results for reaction time show that the method was extremely successful (see Figure 12.5). In the pure blocks and when the expected modality was presented in the mixed blocks, the subjects were fast and reaction times were nearly equal. This shows that subjects were attending to the expected modality. When a stimulus on the unexpected modality occurred, subjects were very slow but showed the most accuracy. In this experiment, which requires fine discriminations, error rates are always high, but they are lowest in just those conditions where the subject's attention is directed to the wrong channel of entry.

One explanation of these cross modality results is that information from the unattended channel is building up in the normal way even though the subject is not attending to it. When he switches attention he is able to execute a response that is more accurate because the information quality is

higher. Other interpretations are possible. Since the input remains present until the subject responds, he may take more samples once he has shifted attention. There are studies in the literature where errors occur *more* frequently to unexpected items than to expected ones. Indeed, the increase in accuracy so prominent in Figure 12.5 is not found in another condition of the same study in which subjects are involved in a detection rather than a discrimination task. In studies where errors increase when an unexpected event occurs, there are usually many rapid false responses which are made as though an anticipation of the expected event.

Clearly the cross modality data by themselves are not totally convincing. However, coupled with the results of the Stroop and the dichotic listening studies, there begins to build a picture of stimulus information automatically activating those internal representations that have been habitually associated with it. Note that this view, which is similar to those presented by LaBerge (1975) and Keele (1973), has the nice feature of making the automaticity of a perceptual pathway closely related to the degree of learning or experience that the subject has had to particular associations. This is the same position that has long been used in the area of motor skills (Fitts & Posner, 1967).

## A View of Conscious Attention

Many psychologists have identified conscious attention with the limited-capacity processing system discussed by Broadbent (1958, 1971). The idea of the unity of conscious experience compared to the diversity of input stimulation makes such an identification appealing, and we also have followed that basic idea. However, the processing system as Broadbent defined it also had a definite location in the information-processing sequence. Specifically, it stood between stimulation and access to the associative structure of long-term memory. This feature has proven unacceptable because experiments of the type outlined earlier in this reading made it clear that access to long-term memory information is virtually unlimited. This led to efforts to identify the limited-capacity mechanism with other particular mental operations, for example, the view (Keele, 1973) that memory lookup was not limited but that response execution was. These efforts are not entirely successful. Some

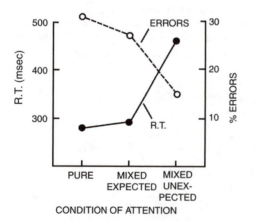

FIGURE 12.5 ■ Reaction time (left ordinate) and errors (right ordinate) as a function of whether signals are all in one modality (pure) or whether they are mixed and subjects are induced to focus on one modality (expected). (After LaBerge, 1973.)

habitual outputs, such as are involved in the GSR (Corteen & Wood, 1972) or eye movements, may occur without involvement of the limited-capacity system, whereas memory look-up with weak retrieval cues may involve a great deal of conscious capacity.

## Limited-Capacity Mechanism

Instead we identify conscious processing with a brain mechanism of limited capacity which may be directed toward different types of activity. For example, it may be directed toward a particular structure in the memory system, a particular input channel or response. If it should be so directed, it will be less available for processing other items. This lack of availability does not prevent automatic activation of the type we discussed earlier.

### ECONOMY

One major objection to this rather intuitive view of active attention seems to be that it would lack economy. This objection has been raised in response to the idea that emotional words are suppressed from consciousness, but it applies as well to our more general view. In Broadbent's (1973) words,

> It seems to require a biologically unlikely kind of machinery. It seems to mean that the part of the brain which analyzes inputs from the environment, and which is presumably quite complicated, is preceded by another and duplicate part of the brain which carries the same function, deciding what is there in order to reject or accept items for admission to the machinery which decides what is there. (p. 67)

If, however, the conscious mechanism is primarily designed not to decide what is there, but to produce integrated actions to often antagonistic habitual responses, its function is not really duplicative. Moreover, the limited-capacity mechanism may serve an important inhibitory function. By giving priority to a particular pathway, it prevents other pathways from having access to any but their habitual response systems (Shallice, 1972). It does not seem worthwhile to debate the general issue, except to suggest that Broadbent's point need not be fatal to the view that we are putting forward.

### PATHWAY INHIBITION

*Theory.* Another major objection to our view of automatic pathway activation is that it provides for facilitatory but no inhibitory effects within the memory system. This aspect of the theory is very likely in error (Milner, 1957). It is well known that repeated auditory presentation of a word may lead to an alteration of its perceptual quality (Warren, 1970). It is difficult to know the basis of this effect, but it has suggested to some that repetition inhibits input pathways. Eimas and Corbit (1973) have shown that repeated presentation of a phoneme leads to a shift in the phonemic boundary. It is not yet clear that this shift is due to inhibition (fatigue) of the pathway, as they argue. In any case, a successful demonstration of inhibition of a pathway resulting from repeated stimulation would not require great modification of our views, since such inhibition would be pathway specific and differ markedly from the widespread inhibition of all signals resulting from commitment of the central processor.

More serious for our views is the theoretical integration presented by Walley and Weiden (1973). They argue that selective attention results entirely from lateral inhibitory processes in the sensory-memory system. They do not distinguish between automatic pathway effects and effects of conscious attention. Their views are of importance, but it seems to us that they would have great difficulty in handling the abundant evidence for facilitation due to pathway activation and would also have trouble dealing with the kind of interference found by Warren (1972). Warren has shown that reaction time to name the base word of the Stroop following activation by a related item is facilitated, while the time to name the ink color is retarded. This would not lend itself easily to a lateral inhibition account. The cost benefit experimental results outlined below also seem difficult to accommodate to a lateral inhibition view, at least unaided by additional assumptions.

## Cost Benefit Analysis

### THEORY

The views of automatic and conscious processing we have been setting forth lend themselves to a summary statement (see Figure 12.6) that dictates the kind of experimental inquiry we have been

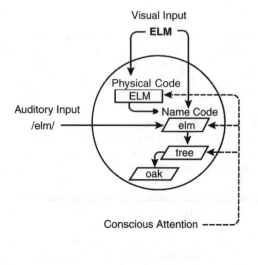

**FIGURE 12.6** ■ A schematic diagram of the role of conscious attention in selecting levels of the automatic activation process upon which to base an output: dashed line, strategic attentional control; solid line, automatic pathway.

following. An input item will automatically activate a specfic pathway in the nervous system. Any item that shares the same pathway will be processed more rapidly and thus be facilitated. This is needed to account for the data obtained by Warren and Conrad. However, as long as the activation pattern is confined to the memory system, there will be no cost or inhibition of the processing of items whose pathways are not activated. This produces a kind of one-way set, in which the nervous system is set to process an item, but is not set against any other item. According to this view, stimulating the memory system in this way produces facilitation but no inhibition.

Once a subject invests his conscious attention in the processing of a stimulus, the benefit obtained from pathway activation is increased, and this benefit is accompanied by a widespread cost or inhibition in the ability of *any* other signals to rise to active attention. This position follows from the limited-capacity nature of the conscious processor. New items still continue to activate input pathways in a purely automatic way, but they are not easily associated to nonhabitual responses. This results in the usual two-sided set familiar in the psychological literature. Subjects do well when the ex-

pected stimulus occurs, but are slow in responding to or miss entirely any unexpected item.

## EXPERIMENTS

In previous papers we have reported in detail the experimental work that has resulted from the cost benefit analysis (Posner & Snyder, 1974). The basic design is to present a single priming item which is either a signal of the same type to which the subject will respond or a neutral warning signal. By manipulating the probabilities that the prime will be a valid cue to the stimulus item, we hoped to vary the degree of active attention that the subject commits to the prime. According to our theoretical view, when the subject commits little processing capacity to the prime, he should benefit from automatic pathway activation but show no cost. When he actively attends to the prime, he should show benefits from both automatic activation and conscious attention, and these should be accompanied by costs on those trials when the prime is not a valid cue to the target.

To calculate benefit we subtracted the reaction times when the prime matched the array from the reaction times obtained following the neutral warning signal. To calculate cost, we subtracted reaction times obtained following the neutral warning signal from those obtained when the prime mismatched the array. The error data were generally high when the reaction times were long.

The most favorable results are those obtained from "yes" reaction times when the array is a pair of letters that must be matched for physical identity and the prime is either of high validity (prime matches array on .8 of the "yes" trials) or of low validity (prime matches array on .2 of the "yes" trials). Figure 12.7 provides a cost benefit analysis obtained from these studies as a function of the time by which the prime led the array.

Two features of these data are of primary interest. When the prime is of low validity (upper panel, Figure 12.7), there is benefit but no cost. When the prime is of high validity, the benefit begins to accrue more rapidly than does the cost. According to our view, benefit should begin to accrue rapidly after the presentation of the prime as the input pathways are activated. It should be closely time-locked to presentation of the prime. Cost is associated with the commitment of the conscious processor to the prime. This should occur more slowly

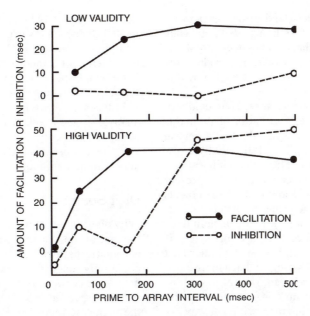

**FIGURE 12.7** ■ Amount of facilitation (benefit) or inhibition (cost) produced by a prime stimulus in relation to a neutral control. The upper panel illustrates a low-validity prime to which subject is not supposed to pay attention; the lower panel illustrates a high-validity prime that is supposed to involve subjects' active attention. (From Posner & Snyder, 1975.)

and depend upon the use the subject intends to make of the prime. The lower panel of Figure 12.7 confirms the striking asymmetry of cost and benefit in the condition where the prime is a valid cue. A comparison of the cost function in the upper and lower panels confirms the degree of flexibility that the experimental situation produces in the amount of cost.

The asymmetry in the time course and flexibility of cost and benefit can be demonstrated in data obtained from other studies (Comstock, 1973; Posner & Boies, 1971; Posner & Klein, 1973). In these studies the attention given to a primary letter-matching task is assessed by the degree of interference (cost) in reaction time to a secondary auditory probe. The facilitation in processing the second letter, produced by varying amounts of prior exposure to the first, increases sharply over the first 150 msec of input and levels out after 300 msec. It is very similar in form to those shown in Figure 12.7 and illustrates close time-locking to the input signal. Cost functions are far more flexible in form. They begin quickly when the subject is given incentive to process the first letter actively. For example, Comstock (1973) turned off the first letter after 15 msec and followed it by a masking

field. The cost function for the auditory probe rose sharply within the first 50 msec after first letter presentation. According to our view the subject must have been timing his attention to coincide closely with the letter onset so that he would not miss it. On the other hand, when the first letter is left in the field for 2 seconds, no cost in processing the probe is found until well after 1 second (Posner & Klein, 1973).

## Strategies

Although these findings provide support for our distinction between pathway activation and conscious attention, other results of our studies (Posner & Snyder, 1975) raise problems for it. A complete account of our data requires a knowledge of the strategy the subject used in this task. This task required subjects to perform a match between the two array items. We found clear evidence that subjects also tend to match the prime item against the array. This strategy serves to improve reaction time and reduce error performance on those occasions when the prime and array match, while hurting performance on those occasions when they do not match. Evidence of this strategy appears in the "no" responses. Subjects tend to be faster in rejecting a pair of letters as being identical when they are given a prime that matches neither of them. However, such strategies would not produce the temporal differences in cost and benefit shown in Figure 12.7

We found a task for which there is no evidence of any automatic pathway facilitation at all. In this task subjects are given either a digit or a neutral warning signal (+) as a prime, followed by a row of letters that might or might not contain a single digit. Their task is to indicate if a digit is present in the array. The results show that when subjects are instructed to use the prime to match deliberately against the array, they show both benefit from a matching prime and cost from a mismatch; if they are not so instructed, they show neither cost nor benefit. These results suggest that a more complete model will include an analysis of how strategies imposed by the task affect the way the attentional mechanism interacts with pathway activation. We turn to this question in the next section.

## Strategies and Conscious Control

Many tasks have been studied in recent years which require subjects to make a rapid response to a simple display. The stimuli are familiar ones that come from a particular location and have well-learned semantic associations. The experimenter provides the subject with a specific task the subject is to accomplish with these stimuli. Although subjects usually can carry out the task assigned, they often have to overcome certain automatic tendencies in order to do so. For example, if the display comes from a certain position (e.g., left of the screen) they find it most natural to respond with the key in the same relative position (e.g., left key) (Simon, 1969). If the word used in the display is an unmarked adjective (e.g., good), they find it easier to respond with a key that is also unmarked (e.g., true) (Seymour, 1973). If they are required to say whether a word is a member of a previously memorized list, they are slow to reject a word that has been used in the experimental situation before, even though they correctly rejected it previously (Atkinson & Joula, 1973). These automatic associations tend to speed certain responses and slow others. The subject often appears to overcome these tendencies with practice, but it is doubtful if he

does so completely in the usual laboratory experiment. Experimenters usually do one of two things with these tendencies: (1) counterbalance and ignore them, or (2) incorporate them into the model but with a status exactly identical to a component the subject can employ or not employ at will.

In this section we try to examine a few tasks in an effort to see if a distinction between automatic activation and conscious strategies can aid in developing a more consistent account of what often appear to be conflicting results.

### Digit Search

Why doesn't the digit search task we discussed at the end of the last section show any evidence of automatic pathway activation? At the time we could only report that this experiment was somehow an exception to our belief that activating a pathway speeded processing of items that shared the pathway. Indeed, we still have no complete explanation, but it seems clear that the strategy of the subject may be rather special in this task. A number of experimental studies are consistent with the view that the human memory system has relatively separate storage areas for letters and digits (Brand, 1971; Jonides & Gleitman, 1972; Posner, 1970; Sanders & Schroots, 1968). There is also some conflicting evidence (Nickerson, 1973), but suppose for the moment that there is a reasonably strong separation between the two types of stimuli in the memory system.

If a subject is asked to determine whether a digit is present in a field of letters, he need simply check to see whether there is activation in that area of memory that represents digits. Notice what happens to this strategy if the subject receives a priming digit. In this case, the priming digit and the digit that is presented in the array will both activate information in the digit area of memory. Thus, the subject will have to make a more careful analysis of the activation in order to determine if the activation pattern is from a priming digit or if it is from one that is in the array. This could very easily slow the subject down, thus counteracting any automatic effect of pathway activation. Experimenters will recognize this hypothesis as entirely *post hoc*, and our data provide no direct confirmation of it.

However, this view provides insight into some interesting discrepancies in the experimental literature. Two studies in which subjects are asked to look for a digit in a field of letters are an experiment by Jonides and Gleitman (1972) and one by Lively and Sanford (1972).

In the Jonides and Gleitman study, when subjects are asked to look for a target item of the opposite class, the array size makes absolutely no difference in the rate of their responses. There is a completely flat function relating the number of items in the array to reaction time. In what appears at first to be a virtually identical condition, Lively and Sanford required subjects to tell whether an array, which consisted of one, two, or four letters, contained a single probe item. On some trials the probe item was a digit; on other trials it was a letter. If one examines those occasions where the probe item was a digit, there is a distinct slope about half that when the probe item is of the same class.

Why the discrepancy between these results? The reason becomes clear when we consider the way in which the subject can use his attentional processes. In the work by Jonides and Gleitman, the subject may ask himself whether there is activation in the area of memory represented by the digits. If there is, he can respond "yes," and if not, "no." In the Lively and Sanford study, activation in the digit, area is sufficient basis for a "no" response, but the subject cannot respond "yes" in the absence of such stimulation. Rather, he must shift his attention to the letter area and ask if there is a match in the letter category. If shifts of attention are relatively slow, it is not a very useful strategy to keep one's attention on the digits. Thus, the slope could result from a combination of different strategies adopted to solve this task.

## Lexical Decisions

A distinction between automatic activation and conscious attention is also useful in understanding the lexical decision task (Rubenstein, Lewis, & Rubenstein, 1971). These experiments have shown that when subjects are asked to judge whether a string of letters is a word, judgments occur more rapidly following a semantically related item than an unrelated item (Schvaneveldt & Meyer, 1973).

Two mechanisms might produce this effect. The first is based on the concept of automatic activation. According to this view, activation of a particular memory location spreads to nearby locations. The increase in activity in these locations makes it easier to access information stored there. The second model assumes a limited-capacity system that can read out of only one memory location at a time. Time is required to shift from one location to another, and the shifting time increases with the distance between locations. Thus, the association effect occurs because shifting to nearby locations is faster than shifting to more distant locations.

To test these two models, Schvaneveldt and Meyer (1973) presented three words in a simultaneous vertical array. The first and third word were associatively related. They examined whether improvement in the processing of the third word was reduced when the middle word was unrelated. The location-shifting model predicts that an intervening item will abolish the advantage of the association between the first and third items, while the automatic activation model does not. Their initial results conform to the automatic activation model. But the materials were presented simultaneously and there was little real control over the order in which the subject examined them.

Subsequently, work by Meyer, Schvaneveldt, and Ruddy (1973) presents evidence somewhat more favorable to the location-shifting view. In this study they found evidence that the advantage of an association between two words is reduced by an unrelated intervening item, particularly when it is a nonword and thus uses a different output, as well as input, pathway.

The evidence used to choose between automatic activation and location shifting is biased. If both are true, as we believe from our results, one will expect to find facilitation when the items are separated by an unrelated item, and the experimenter will conclude that the effects are due only to automatic activation. In order to separate the automatic from the conscious effects, one may examine what happens to a nonword or unrelated word that occurs following a priming word as compared to one following a neutral condition such as a warning signal. If the facilitation of a word by another word is accompanied by an increase in reaction time to unrelated items, one might argue for an attentional explanation. If the benefit for an associated word is not accompanied by a cost to the unrelated word, a more automatic process seems required. We would expect that attentional mechanisms would be especially important when the frequency of related words is high, and automatic activation when the frequency of related words is low.

## Matching Task

A number of years ago one of us reported it was faster to respond "same" to two identical letters than it was when the letters had only their name in common (Posner & Mitchell, 1967). The reason presented for this difference was that with identical letters subjects could respond on the basis of visual information alone and thus emit their response before the letter names were available. In a number of subsequent papers, converging operations were presented that support this position (Posner, 1969, 1973; Posner, Lewis, & Conrad, 1972).

However, an astute reader of this paper will realize that there are now two different explanations for the same phenomenon. One is the levels-of-processing account I have just mentioned. The second is the view that two identical letters will share more of the same pathway than letters that agree only in name. Notice that the first account is a somewhat optional one, since the subject could choose to withhold responding in all cases until he verified the letter name; the second account rests upon an automatic facilitation of the pathway.

The best evidence favoring the second account is an experiment by Eichelman (1970) in which he required subjects to name letters as quickly as possible. Eichelman's subjects, showed an improved reaction time when the letter was repeated on successive trials. This repetition effect was greater for physically identical letters than for those having only their name in common. Eichelman proposed a pathway-activation account of these results. It is also possible to handle these results on the basis of a processing-levels explanation. The idea is that the name of a stimulus presented on a trial is stored along with the visual information. On the next trial the subject first attempts to match the new input to the item presented on the previous trial. If there is a match, he emits the same response without having to identify the new input item. For some time it seemed that this explanation would do. However, subsequently both Warren (1970) and Kirsner (1972)[3] showed that naming was facilitated by presentation of a prior item to which no response was required, and Posner and Boies (1971) reported that physical matches became relatively

faster than mismatches as a function of the time by which the first of two items led the second. These results favored a pathway explanation.

The advantage due to pathway activation in the matching and naming experiments is in the range of 30–50 msec. This is about half the general advantage found for physical matches over name matches.

The advantage of physical matches over name matches may consist of two different components. One involves the specific level of information on which the subject may base his response, and the other refers to the general advantage of an activated pathway. In a naming experiment subjects appear to benefit from automatic activation primarily. In simultaneous matching tasks the level-of-processing component seems to dominate. In successive matching, both factors may be involved.

## Summary

We feel that subjects can program their conscious attention to (1) receive information from a particular input channel or area of memory and (2) perform particular operations upon received information. These programs, which are under the conscious control of the subject, we have been calling *strategies*. Strategies cannot prevent the automatic activation processes discussed earlier. This inability of attention to prevent the build-up of information through automatic activation is in agreement with ideas that have been advocated by Keele (1973), LaBerge (1975), and Shiffrin (1975).

However, strategies do have a profound effect on what subjects perceive consciously, act upon, and report later. To claim that these effects are not perceptual seems to be a rather peculiar use of the term. Evidence shows clearly that subjects may activate memorial pathways even at the level of representation that underlies physical matching (Posner, 1969) and can thus increase the rate at which information enters the conscious processing system. Increases in the rate of information processing of this type improve both speed and accuracy. Shiffrin (1975) has presented evidence that knowledge of the source of input does not improve $d'$ measures. On the other hand, Smith and Blaha (1969) have shown $d'$ changes when subjects know where in the visual field a signal will occur. Our data do not resolve this conflict, but our feeling is that the main importance of a strategy that turns the subject's attention to an input channel or memory pathway is not so much to facilitate the selected item (benefit) as it is to reduce the likelihood of interruption from outside the selected domain (cost).

The act of maintaining concentration on a pathway requires effort. This is additional evidence that it does not turn off the automatic pathway effects of other stimuli. Rather, concentration serves to reduce the probability that these other stimuli will intrude upon the conscious processor. If such intrusion were completely impossible, it would not be necessary to break off this writing so frequently to respond to various real and imagined stimuli. In the study of emotions and attitudes, psychologists have addressed the question of why stimuli outside of consciousness sometimes intrude upon our thought processes. We turn now to examine this issue in the light of the distinctions discussed in this chapter.

## The Place of Value in a Judgment of Fact

Perhaps no place is the distinction between automatic and conscious processes more needed than in the study of the role of emotions, affects, and feelings on perception. The "new look" in perception argued that emotional responses to a word influenced our identification of that word (Erdelyi, 1974). How could identification depend on something (emotional response) that cannot arise unless the word is identified? According to our argument this confuses two senses of identification. One involves the activation of the pathway of interest (i.e., the word name and its habitual associates), and the other involves our conscious awareness of that representation. Studies reviewed earlier in this reading (Corteen & Wood, 1972; von Wright et al., 1975) suggest that the former may occur without the latter ever occurring.

If one makes a distinction between automatic and conscious processes, the problem of the role of emotions in perception may be divided into two parts. First, at what level of processing is emotional information accessed in the memory system? Are the emotional attributes of an item stored as an association to the item name, or are they attributes by which names are organized? This latter view, which has been advocated by Osgood,

Suci, and Tannenbaum (1955) and more recently by Wickens (1972), holds that emotional connotations are primary semantic attributes that may be contacted prior to word identification. Second, how does the emotional response to a word, however produced, affect our awareness of that word?

The second question has been addressed by recent experimental investigations that suggest that the emotional response to a stimulus may serve to change the rehearsal pattern. Erdelyi and Applebaum (1973) show that an emotional symbol (swastika) captures the subject's attention in a way that reduces the information he is able to report from the rest of a complex display. This suggests that emotional stimuli will often demand attention. Broadbent (1973) has shown that emotional words affect the tachistoscopic recognition of words that follow them in a list. He finds that following the presentation of a nasty word, a subject reduces the range of cues he takes in from the next word. He is less likely to report the first and last letter, but more likely to report adjacent ones. This is similar to the effects found with other stressors (Broadbent, 1958, 1971) and may be related to what one finds with a heightened sense of alertness that commits the central processor to an early stage in the buildup of information (Posner, 1974). Broadbent suggests that the effects of an emotional word upon the report of the next word might also intervene between the emotional classification and the awareness of a given word. Of course, the time between classification and conscious awareness is short in tachistoscopic studies and one might expect weak effects, but the principle that emotional words can affect the conscious processor seems to have been established.

These results do not tell us whether emotion is contacted at a relatively early level in the processing of an item, or whether emotion is treated as a higher level semantic dimension. Since the material treated in this paper seems to show that even higher level semantic dimensions may be contacted rapidly and automatically, the fact that emotions affect the direction of our conscious attention does not give them any special status within the memory system.

## Impression Formation

In order to attack this question, we wanted to have a paradigm in which we could vary the strength of the emotional response to an item and see how it affected the factual processing of item information. Many recent investigations of the memorial representation of affect have involved the emotional connotation or evaluation of trait-descriptive adjectives. Asch (1946) investigated the impressions people formed of others, based on a series of adjective traits describing a given person. This has led to a series of experimental investigations (Anderson, 1972) in which people have attempted to form deliberate conscious impressions of others from listening to a set of trait-descriptive adjectives. It is clear from these studies that people can form such impressions. Moreover, Anderson and Hubert (1965) and Anderson and Farkas (1973) have argued that the storage of such information is separate from the specific set of adjectives by which the information is conveyed. They argue that the memory underlying the emotion or evaluation is abstracted from the adjectives and stored separately from the adjectives themselves. The basis for this view is that if asked to recall the adjectives in a given list, the subjects show a relatively strong recency effect, but if asked to rate their overall impression of the person, the primacy effect is stronger.

Our goal was to develop a firmer notion of the memory structures that underlie the emotional classification and to compare them with those that mediate retention of the individual adjectives. In particular we sought to understand the level at which emotional information makes contact with a decision about the presence of a particular trait as a descriptor of a person. The experiments used a memory scanning task developed by Sternberg (1966).

## Retrieval of Item and Value Information

In order to observe the relationship between emotion and item information, we provided subjects with three kinds of sentences. The sentences always consisted of a single proper name followed by one to four adjectives. The adjectives might be all positive in emotional tone, all negative in emotional tone, or a mixture of positive and negative emotional tones. Words were selected from norms provided by Anderson. The sequence of events is illustrated in Figure 12.8. Following the sentences, subjects were given a single probe word. On half the trials, the probe matched one of the words in the sentence, and on half it did not. Subjects were to respond as rapidly as possible to the question of whether the item in the probe matched an item in the sentence.

The basic results of the experiment are quite simple. For "yes" responses reaction times did not differ for positive, negative, or neutral lists. The "no" responses can be broken down into two types, those in which the emotional tone matched the list and those in which it did not. We compared the two types of "no" responses averaged across conditions where the list was positive and where it was negative (see Figure 12.9). This is a particularly sensitive comparison since the probes are the same words in both conditions but follow arrays of differing emotional tone. The results show a small but significantly faster reaction time when the emotional response is opposite to that of the list than when it is identical. This is accompanied by a reduction in error when the emotional response did not match the list. While the difference in reaction times between matching and mismatching "no" responses did not change systematically as a function of size of the list, the error differences changed sharply as a function of size of the list. When the list consisted of four items, there was a much higher probability that the subject would make an error when the emotional response matched the list than when it did not match. What do these results tell us about the relationship of the item information and the emotion?

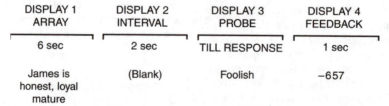

| DISPLAY 1 ARRAY | DISPLAY 2 INTERVAL | DISPLAY 3 PROBE | DISPLAY 4 FEEDBACK |
|---|---|---|---|
| 6 sec | 2 sec | TILL RESPONSE | 1 sec |
| James is honest, loyal mature | (Blank) | Foolish | −657 |

**FIGURE 12.8** ■ Sequence of events in the studies of the role of affect on judgments about the presence of probe adjective.

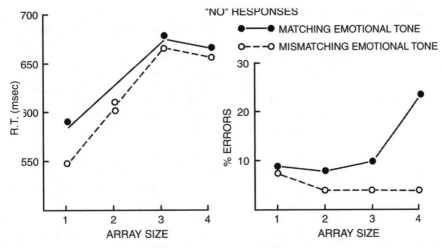

FIGURE 12.9 ■ Reaction time (left) and errors (right) in "no" judgments as a function of array size when the probe word either matches the array items in emotional tone (e.g., both positive) or mismatches them (e.g., array positive and probe negative).

## Models

There are clear effects of the impression on the task. When the emotional tone of the probe does not match that of the list, subjects are facilitated in responding "no."

There are several possible ways this result might occur. Suppose that the emotional information was present relatively more quickly than the factual information. This might be the case if the subject consciously prepared to match on the basis of emotional tone. One would expect subjects to be able to reject the mismatching emotional tone without any required search of the factual information, and this would produce a flat slope relating mismatching "no" responses to array size. However, there is no tendency for the slope to be reduced when the probe emotion mismatches.

Another view supposes that each word consists of an item and an emotional attribute associated with it. Thus, the adjective "loyal" is associated directly with its denotative and connotative meanings. In this view, a probe word may be rejected as matching any array word more quickly if the mismatch involves both item and emotion than if it involves only item information. Lively and Sanford (1972) have adopted exactly this model for their account of what happens when a subject receives a list consisting of digits and gets a probe that is a consonant. Such a model does not fit our data, since

the slope of the "no" reaction time to mismatching emotions is at least as great as for matching emotions.

In their Loyola Symposium paper Atkinson, Herrmann, and Wescourt (1974) suggest that the slope of reaction time versus array size for probes that are outside the category of the list serves as a measure of the degree of semantic analysis required prior to contact with the information representing the category of the probe. They suggest that relatively flat slopes are obtained when the subject has to process little semantic meaning of the probe, and steeper slopes are obtained as the semantic processing required in order to determine the category is increased.

The overall results of the reaction time and error data obtained from our experiment seem most consistent with the following analysis of the relation of emotional information to item information. Suppose there are two independent memory structures. One memory structure consists of the list of trait adjectives that the subject reads in the sentence. The other memory structure consists of an abstracted impression based on an integration of the values presented by the individual adjectives. The time to search the memory structure representing the traits would increase as a function of number of items in the list. On the other hand, the impression would tend to get stronger as we increase the number of items on which it is based;

thus, one might expect a reduction in reaction time. Since judgments based on the emotional classification alone would only be reliable for mismatching "no" responses, one would expect errors to pile up for matching "no" responses when the output of the emotional structure occurred prior to the output of the list array. This could account for the high error rate obtained with four-item arrays.

To test this idea we performed an experiment in which subjects received the same lists as described previously, but were asked to determine if the probe item had the same emotional content as in the previous list. Two types of "yes" responses are possible: first, those to probe items that were on the list, and second, those that were not identical but shared the same emotional tone. The results (see Figure 12.10) support our two-process view of the matching task. The role of the number of items is to increase reaction times for those items that match, but to reduce it for those that mismatch. The two functions come together at about four-item lists.

In brief, what seems to happen is the formation of two memory structures, one consisting of a list of item names, and the other consisting of a generalized emotional response to the items. These separate memory structures appear to be oppositely affected by item length. The data seem most consistent with the view that each memory structure has an output to the binary decision. In cases where

the two decisions agree, there seems to be relatively little effect on overall reaction time or errors. In cases where they disagree, however, there appears to be a lengthening of reaction time as if there were some tendency to make the conflicting response. However, the tendency seems slight unless we let the times for the output get very close together. In that case, there seems to be a very difficult decision to be made and a high probability of error.

These data agree with the view of two separate memory systems laid down by the list items (Anderson & Hubert, 1965). However, they do not agree with the view that emotional information concerning the impression is handled in any different way than other semantic dimensions in the memory system. Rather, it appears that evaluations are handled very much like other semantic dimensions. When a number of items have the same emotional content, information is integrated to produce an overall impression against which to evaluate input.

It would be of interest to examine the extent to which the conscious strategy to extract an evaluation is a necessary condition for obtaining the results we have presented. Currently we know only that subjects need no instruction to be influenced by the evaluative components, but we do not know whether they intend to extract such information either because they realize it is useful in the task or simply find it of interest. Manipulations of the probability that the evaluative information will serve as a valid cue to perform the task correctly might help us to deal with this question.

## Long-Term Memory

In the psychological literature there are a number of studies that compare the retenton of specific item information with the retention of more abstracted information that stands for a set of items. Much of this literature has used dot patterns to serve as the item instances. If subjects are required to classify a set of patterns into a category, they seem to abstract from that category a prototype or central tendency that comes to stand for that category (Posner, 1969; Reed, 1972). We speculated that the abstraction of emotional information and its storage in terms of an impression would be somewhat the same as found in the previous work with patterns. To study this, we set up an

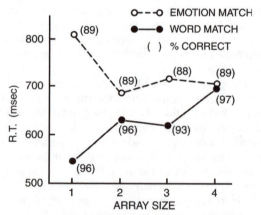

**FIGURE 12.10** ■ Reaction time and percentage correct for "yes" responses when subjects are instructed to match the emotional tone of probe and array deliberately. Word matches are those in which the particular probe adjective was a member of the array; for emotion matches the probe word was not in the array but had the same emotional tone.

experiment in which the subjects had to learn a list of ten adjectives associated with each of six proper names. Two types of test trials were given: list trials and name trials. On list trials, subjects were shown a name and four adjectives selected from those associated with that name, and they were then probed with a trait that was either from that list or not. On name trials, the subject was merely given the name that was being tested, followed after the same retention interval by a single probe adjective. On the name trials we attempted to assess the long-term memory structure that represented the set of items associated with the person's name, while on the list trials we attempted to replicate the results we obtained in the previous experiment.

The results obtained in the previous experiments were replicated on the list trials. Once again, reaction time to "no" responses that mismatched in emotional tone were faster than for "no" responses that matched in tone. On the name trials we found that the reaction time to mismatching "no" responses was 200–400 msec faster than for matching "no" responses or for "yes" responses. The memory system that came to stand for the emotional response was more available to the subject than that which represented the individual items.

Several alternative explanations of this result are possible. It could be that the subject actively attended to the emotional classification of the list, or it could be that the memory system representing the emotion resisted forgetting more than that of the individual item. Further work will be needed to separate these two accounts.

## Summary

Our results, then, taken together with the recent work of Broadbent (1973) and Erdelyi and Applebaum (1973), suggest an overall account of the role of emotion at least when it arises from the evaluative aspect of words. Emotional information is stored as a high level but habitual associate to given words or constellations of words. One would expect that the presentation of an item would automatically activate associated emotional responses. These responses might feed back to affect the conscious mechanism guiding its processing of the various kinds of information associated with the input item. The complexity of

this view fits with the rather diverse results that have been obtained in many experiments involving emotional items. Doubtless, what becomes conscious will be a function not only of the level of emotionality raised by the automatic process, but also by strategies used in different experiments. Thus, the presence of emotional information may lead in some contexts to perceptual vigilance, and, in other cases, to perceptual defense. Investigations of the emotional responses to items would seem to profit from the kind of methodology obtainable with trait-descriptive adjectives where a variety of different individual items may be combined to produce a single emotional trace system. Perhaps the most interesting area for study will be how well emotional material transfers from the situation in which it is learned to other tests.

## Overview

### Summary

This paper discussed the distinction between automatic activation processes which are solely the result of past learning and processes which are under current conscious control. Automatic activation processes are those which may occur without intention, without any conscious awareness and without interference with other mental activity. They are distinguished from operations performed by the conscious processing system since the latter system is of limited capacity and thus its commitment to any operation reduces its availability to perform any other operation. Many current cognitive tasks were analyzed in terms of the interaction of automatic activation processes with strategies determined by task instructions. Concentration on a source of signals serves to reduce interference from outside that source. Outside signals still intrude, particularly when they are classified by the memory system as having emotional significance.

### Prospects

Where are the views outlined in this paper taking us? I am afraid that it is in two directions, which may well turn out to produce a kind of research schizophrenia. The first direction is toward an understanding of the more detailed mechanisms that subserve the functions of pathway activation, levels of processing, and conscious attention (Posner, 1974). This effort leads to the creation of ever simpler tasks, toward a comparison of behavioral data with evoked potential and single-cell studies, and a closer coordination between human and animal studies. The relative stereotypy of "automatic activation" processes gives hope that a mechanistic and analytic approach may work. In contrast, they will not by themselves allow us to say much about how people will actually perform tasks.

The goal of understanding human performance requires an analysis of strategies useful in particular task environments (Newell & Simon, 1972). In part, this involves an effort to understand how strategies modify and build upon "automatic retrieval" processes. Our studies of the effects of emotion on judgment were addressed to that goal. We hope that further efforts along this line will aid us in understanding how much our prior learning biases the way we can think in a particular task environment.

## NOTES

1. This research was supported by the National Science Foundation under Grant GB 40310X. The paper was written while the first author was Visiting Professor of Psychology at Yale University and Haskins Laboratories.
2. Now at Purdue University.
3. Unlike Eichelman, Kirsner found no greater facilitation when the new item was physically identical (visual-visual) over when they shared only the name (auditory-visual). This could have resulted from slower decay of name activation with an auditory prime.

## REFERENCES

Anderson, J. R. & Bower, G. H. *Human Associative Memory*. Washington, D.C.: Winston, 1973.

Anderson, N. H. Information inflation: A Brief Survey. Technical Report No. 24. University of California, San Diego: Center for Human Information Processing, 1972.

Anderson, N. H. & Parkas, A. J. New light on order effects in attitude change. *Journal of Social Psychology*, 1973, **28**, 88–93.

Anderson, N. H. & Hubert, S. Effects of concomitant verbal recall on order effects in personality impression formation. *Journal of Verbal Learning and Verbal Behavior*, 1965, **2**, 531–539.

Asch, S. Forming impressions of personality. *Journal of Abnormal and Social Psychology*, 1946, **41**, 258–290.

Atkinson, R. C., Herrmann, D. J., & Wescourt, K. T. Search processes in recognition memory. In R. L. Solso (Ed.), *Theories in Cognitive Psychology*. Hillsdale, New Jersey: Lawrence Erlbaum Associates, 1974.

Atkinson, R. C. & Joula, J. F. Factors influencing speed and accuracy of word recognition. In S. Kornblum (Ed.), *Attention and Performance IV*. New York: Academic Press, 1973.

Brand, J. Classification without identification in visual search. *Quarterly Journal of Experimental Psychology*, 1971, **23**, 178–186.

Broadbent, D. E. *Perception and Communication*. London: Pergamon, 1958.

Broadbent, D. E. *Decision and Stress*. London and New York: Academic Press, 1971.

Broadbent, D. E. *In Defence of Empirical Psychology*. London: Methuen, 1973.

Comstock, E. M. Processing capacity in a letter-matching task. *Journal of Experimental Psychology*, 1973, **100**, 63–72.

Conrad, C. Context effects in sentence comprehension: A study of the subjective lexicon. *Memory & Cognition*, 1974, **2**, 130–138.

Corteen, R. S. & Wood, B. Autonomic responses to shock associated words in an unattended channel. *Journal of Experimental Psychology*, 1972, **97**, 308–313.

Dyer, F. N. The Stroop phenomenon and its use in the study of perceptual, cognitive and response processes. *Memory & Cognition*, 1973, **1**, 106–120.

Eichelman, W. H. Stimulus and response repetition effects for naming letters. *Perception & Psychophysics*, 1970, **7**, 94–96.

Eimas, P. D. & Corbit, J. D. Selective adaptation of linguistic feature detectors. *Cognitive Psychology*, 1973, **6**, 99–109.

Erdelyi, M. H. A new look at the new look: Perceptual defense and vigilance. *Psychological Review*, 1974, **81**, 1–25.

Erdelyi, M. H., & Applebaum, G. A. Cognitive masking. *Bulletin of the Psychonomics Society*, 1973, **1**, 59–61.

Fitts, P. M. & Posner, M. I. *Human Performance*. Monterey, California: Brooks Cole, 1967.

Garner, W. R. & Felfoldy, G. L. Integrality of stimulus dimensions in various types of information processing. *Cognitive Psychology*, 1970, **1**, 225–241.

Greenwald, A. G. A double stimulation test of ideomotor theory with implications for selective attention. *Journal of Experimental Psychology*, 1970, **84**, 392–398. (a)

Greenwald, A. G. Selective attention as a function of signal rate. *Journal of Experimental Psychology*, 1970, **86**, 48–52. (b)

Hintzman, D. L., Carre, F. A., Eskridge, V. L., Owens, A. M., Shaff, S. S., & Sparks, E. M. "Stroop" effect: Input or output phenomenon. *Journal of Experimental Psychology*, 1972, **95**, 458–459.

Jonides, J. & Gleitman, H. A conceptual category effect in visual search: o as letter or as digit. *Perception & Psychophysics*, 1972, **12**, 457–460.

Keele, S. W. *Attention and Human Performance*. Pacific Palisades, California: Good-year, 1973.

Kirsner, K. Naming latency facilitation: An analysis of the encoding component in reaction time. *Journal of Experimental Psychology*, 1972, **95**, 171–176.

LaBerge, D. H. Identification of two components of the time to switch attention. In S. Kornblum (Ed.), *Attention and Performance IV*. New York: Academic Press, 1973.

LaBerge, D. H. Attention and automatic information processing. In P. M. A. Rabbit (Ed.), *Attention and Performance V*. London: Academic Press, 1975, in press.

Lackner, J. R. & Garrett, M. F. Resolving ambiguity effects of biasing context in the unattended ear. *Cognition*, 1973, **1**, 359–374.

Lewis, J. Semantic processing of unattended messages using dichotic listening. *Journal of Experimental Psychology*, 1970, **85**, 225–228.

Lively, B. L. & Sanford, B. J. The use of category information in a memory search task. *Journal of Experimental Psychology*, 1972, **93**, 379–385.

Mackay, D. G. Aspects of the theory of comprehension, memory and attention. *Quarterly Journal of Experimental Psychology*, 1973, **25**, 22–40.

Meyer, D. E., Schvaneveldt, R. W., & Ruddy, M. G. Activation of lexical memory. Paper presented at the meeting of the Psychonomic Society, St. Louis, Missouri, 1973.

Milner, P. M. The cell assembly: Mark II. *Psychological Review*, 1957, **64**, 242–252.

Morton, J., & Chambers, S. M. Selective attention to words and colors. *Quarterly Journal of Experimental Psychology*, 1973, **25**, 387–397.

Murray, D. J., Mastronadi, J., & Duncan, S. Selective attention to "physical" versus "verbal" aspects of colored words. *Psychonomic Science*, 1972, **26**, 305–307.

Newell, A. & Simon, H. A. *Human Problem Solving*. Englewood Cliffs, New Jersey: Prentice-Hall, 1972.

Nickerson, R. S. Can characters be classified directly as digits versus letters or must they be identified first? *Memory & Cognition*, 1973, **1**, 477–484.

Osgood, C. E., Suci, G. H., & Tannenbaum, P. H. *The Measurement of Meaning*. Urbana, Illinois: The University of Illinois Press, 1955.

Posner, M. I. Abstraction and the process of recognition. In G. Bower (Ed.), *The psychology of Learning and Motivation*. Vol. 3. New York: Academic Press, 1969.

Posner, M. I. On the relationship between letter names and superordinate categories. *Quarterly Journal of Experimental Psychology*, 1970, **22**, 279–287.

Posner, M. I. Coordination of codes. In W. G. Chase (Ed.), *Visual Information Processing*. New York: Academic Press, 1973.

Posner, M. I. Psychobiology of attention. In M. S. Gazzaniga & C. Blakemore (Eds.), *Handbook of Psychobiology*. New York: Academic Press, 1975, in press.

Posner, M. I. & Boies, S. W. Components of attention. *Psychological Review*, 1971, **78**, 391–408.

Posner, M. I. & Klein, R. M. On the functions of consciousness. In S. Kornblum (Ed.), *Attention and Performance IV*. New York: Academic Press, 1973.

Posner, M. I., Lewis, J., & Conrad, C. Component processes in reading: A performance analysis. In J. Kavanaugh & I. Mattingly (Eds.), *Language by Ear and by Eye*. Boston: MIT Press, 1972.

Posner, M. I. & Mitchell, R. F. Chronometric analysis of classification. *Psychological Review*, 1967, **74**, 392–409.

Posner, M. I. & Snyder, C. R. R. Facilitation and inhibition in the processing of signals. In P. M. A. Rabbit (Ed.), *Attention and Performance V*. London: Academic Press, 1975, in press.

Reed, S. K. Pattern recognition and categorization. *Cognitive Psychology*, 1972, **3**, 382–407.

Rubenstein, H., Lewis, S. S., & Rubenstein, M. A. Evidence for phonemic recoding in visual word recognition. *Journal of Verbal Learning and Verbal Behavior*, 1971, **10**, 645–657.

Sanders, G. F. & Schroots, J. J. F. Cognitive categories and memory space II: The effect of temporal versus category recall. *Quarterly Journal of Experimental Psychology*, 1968, **20**, 373–379.

Schvaneveldt, R. & Meyer, D. E. Retrieval and comparison processes in semantic memory. In S. Kornblum (Ed.), *Attention and Performance IV*. New York: Academic Press, 1973.

Seymour, P. H. K. Judgment of verticality and response availability. *Bulletin of the Psychonomic Society*, 1973, **1**, 196–198.

Shallice, T. Dual functions of consciousness. *Psychological Review*, 1972, **79**, 383–393.

Shiffrin, R. M. The locus and role of attention in memory systems. In P. M. A. Rabbitt (Ed.), *Attention and Performance V*. London: Academic Press, 1975, in press.

Simon, J. R. Reaction toward the source of stimulation. *Journal of Experimental Psychology*, 1969, **81**, 174–176.

Smith, S. W. & Blaha, J. Preliminary report summarizing the result of location uncertainty experiments. Institute for Research in Vision, Ohio State University, 1969.

Sternberg, S. High speed scanning in human memory. *Science*, 1966, **153**, 652–654.

Underwood, B. J. False recognition produced by implicit verbal responses. *Journal of Experimental Psychology*, 1965, **70**, 122–129.

von Wright, J. M., Anderson, K., & Stenman, U. Generalization of conditioned GRSs in dichotic listening. In P. M. A. Rabbitt (Ed.), *Attention and Performance V*. London: Academic Press, 1975, in press.

Walley, R. E. & Weiden, T. D. Lateral inhibition and cognitive masking: A neuropsychological theory of attention. *Psychological Review*, 1973, **80**, 284–302.

Warren, R. E. Stimulus encoding in memory. Unpublished doctoral dissertation, University of Oregon, 1970.

Warren, R. E. Stimulus encoding and memory. *Journal of Experimental Psychology*, 1972, **94**, 90–100.

Warren, R. E. Association, directionality and stimulus encoding. *Journal of Experimental Psychology*, 1974, **102**, 151–158.

Wickens, D. D. Characteristics of word encoding. In A. W. Melton & E. Martin (Eds.), *Coding Processes in Human Memory*. Washington, D.C.: Winston, 1972.

READING 13

# Selection for Action:
# The Role of Inhibitory Mechanisms

Steven P. Tipper • McMaster University

The need for selection in action is ubiquitous. Consider a simple example: If you want to pick up a particular glass from a table containing many other glasses, your hand must be *selectively* directed to that glass, the target, and away from the others, the *distractors*. The mechanisms that enable such selection are still under investigation. They have been studied under the heading of attention: The target is viewed as the central focus of awareness and intention. The dominant position has been that selection is primarily based on excitation processes. The analogy typically used is that of a spotlight of attention that is able to move through space. When the spotlight falls on a particular distal stimulus, the neuronal internal representations reflecting the initial perceptual analysis of that stimulus receive further processing. In contrast, according to the general consensus, the internal representations of ignored stimuli, while initially receiving perceptual analysis, then passively decay.[1]

**W**ithout denying the role of excitation processes in attention, it is reasonable to surmise that inhibitory processes acting on the internal representations of to-be-ignored competing stimuli may also play a role. Selection is remarkably efficient; for example, humans can select a visual target object that is superimposed over a distractor when the display is presented for only 0.1 s. Given this efficiency, dual mechanisms acting on both the target and the distractor seem plausible.[2] Indeed, Wundt,[3] the first experimental psychologist, stressed the importance of inhibitory mechanisms acting on the internal representations of distractor stimuli.

## Evidence for Inhibition

To observe whether the internal representations of an ignored distractor stimulus are associated with inhibition, one can use a *priming* procedure based on the following logic: If an ignored stimulus is inhibited during selection of a target, then processing of a subsequent stimulus requiring the inhibited internal representations will be impaired. For example, in one study, subjects viewed a prime display consisting of a red picture superimposed over a green one and were asked to name what the red picture was (see Figure 13.1). The subsequent probe display also consisted of a red picture superimposed over a green picture, and the subject was again asked to give the name of the red picture. In the control condition, neither of the pictures in the prime display was related to the subsequent probe, but in the ignored repetition condition, the distractor in the prime display was the same as the target in the probe display. Results showed longer reaction times (RTs) in the ignored repetition condition. This phenomenon has been termed *negative priming*, in contrast to the usual facilitatory effects produced when subjects attend to a prime.[2,4]

## Object-Centered Inhibition

A central consideration concerns the internal representations that are inhibited. An assumption made by many models of attention is that attentional processes operate on spatial coordinates.[5] In these models, attention is moved between different spatial loci, and mechanisms inhibit or excite a particular spatial location. However, the perceptual system has evolved to extract information concerning *objects* in the environment so that action may be directed to such objects. Hence, it

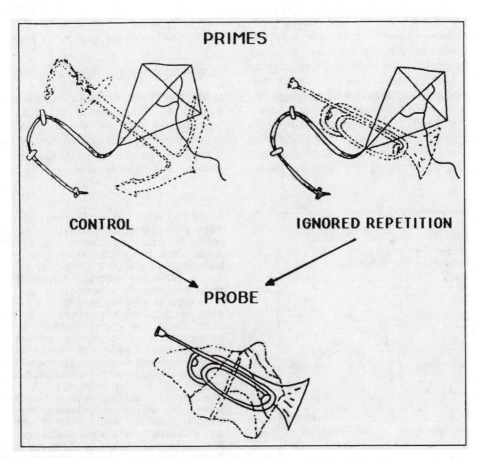

**FIGURE 13.1** ■ Sample displays from a study demonstrating negative priming. Subjects were required to name the red object (solid line) while ignoring a green distractor (broken line). In the control prime display, the target and distractor were unrelated to the subsequent probe, but in the ignored repetition condition, the ignored prime was the same as the subsequent probe target. Negative priming was revealed by longer reaction times to name the probe after presentation of the ignored repetition prime than after the control prime. The probe target was superimposed over a neutral, meaningless distractor.

follows that attentional mechanisms that enable selective action would access object-centered representations, also.

Evidence that the inhibitory mechanisms that enable us to ignore stimuli act on object-centered representations comes from a series of experiments in which subjects reported the spatial locus of a target stimulus with a key-press response while ignoring a distractor. RTs to a target presented in the same location as a previously ignored prime were increased (see Figure 13.2a). However, the inhibition did not transfer between different loci on the computer screen. If, as shown in Figure 13.2b the prime display could appear only in the top four positions, and the subsequent probe stimuli could appear only in the bottom four positions, no negative priming was observed, even though the ignored prime and the subsequent probe had retinal location and motor response in common.[6] This result suggests that neither a specific region on the retina nor a specific motor representation is inhibited. Taken together, these results might appear to indicate that the representation of a particular spatial location is inhibited, as negative priming was observed only when the ignored

prime and subsequent probe were in the same position on the computer screen, as in Figure 13.2a.

However, the results for static stimuli tell only part of the story. When the prime stimuli were perceived to be moving down the screen, disappearing behind occluding surfaces and then reappearing as the probe display (Figure 13.2c), robust negative priming was observed. Although the spatial relations between prime and probe are very similar in Figures 13.2b and 13.2c, negative priming was obtained only with displays of the latter type—with movement. Such data suggest that when an object is perceived to be moving, inhibition moves with the object, as would be predicted by a theory proposing object-centered (as opposed to location-based) mechanisms of attention.[7]

## Goal-Dependent Inhibition

If inhibition acts on object-centered representations, at what stage does it act? From the retinal input through to the response, the object gives rise to successive representations: initially, perceptual representations of its physical attributes, such as its color and location; subsequently, representa-

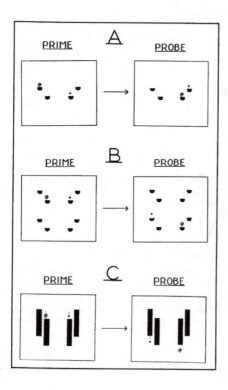

FIGURE 13.2 ■ Sample displays from a study indicating that object-based representations play a role in negative priming. Subjects were required to press one of four keys, spatially compatible with four loci on the screen, to report the position of the target @ while ignoring the distractor +. Then, 350 ms after response to the prime display, probe stimuli were presented, again requiring report of the locus of the target @ with a key press. (a) In one condition, the prime and probe displays appeared in the same place on the screen. In an ignored repetition trial, the ignored prime and subsequent target probe appeared in the same location. Significant negative priming was obtained in this situation relative to a control condition in which there was no spatial overlap between the ignored prime and target probe loci, (b) In another condition, the prime display was presented in four loci near the top of the screen, and the probe stimuli were presented lower on the screen. The subjects moved their eyes to fixate at the center of the appropriate display area before viewing each display. This illustration represents an ignored repetition trial in which the ignored prime appeared in approximately the same retinal coordinates, and was associated with the same key press, as the subsequent target probe. No negative priming was obtained in this situation. (c) If the prime and probe loci were the same as in (b) but specified with continuous columns, and the prime display appeared to move down the screen, disappearing behind the occluding columns, and then reappearing as the probe display, highly consistent negative priming was observed.

tions of its semantic identity (e.g., "dog"); and, finally, representations of the action to be taken. The stage at which inhibition acts varies with the task. When the subject must name the category (e.g., "animal"), the inhibition appears to act at the stage of semantic representations. Driver and I[8] compared the amount of negative priming when a picture of an object was the ignored prime and the word name of that object was the target probe with conditions in which the picture (or the word) was used in both roles. In the first case, only the semantic representation of the two stimuli was the same; in the second, both the perceptual and the semantic representations were the same; but the second case produced no more inhibition (no greater increment in RT) than the first. Furthermore, the inhibition did not act at the stage of the response, because the degree of inhibition was the same whether the first and second response differed (a key press to the prime, followed by naming of the probe) or were the same. Thus, in tasks requiring report of semantic information, inhibition was not associated with perceptual features or specific response properties of the stimulus.

When the task is changed, inhibition may act at a different stage. In the study illustrated in Figure 13.3[9] the subject had to move her hand as fast as possible from a start position to press the button adjacent to a red target light, while ignoring a yellow light at another locus. In this task, inhibition depended on the spatial relation between the hand, the target stimulus, and the distracting stimulus. If the distracting stimulus lay between the hand and the target, it retarded the response, and that location was inhibited (i.e., it was responded to more slowly when it became the location of the target on the next trial). But if the distractor lay beyond the target, it did not interfere with the response and there was little inhibition. Thus, when the hand started at the bottom of the board (Figure 13.3a) and moved to a target at Position 6, a distracting yellow light at Position 2 interfered and was inhibited, but at Position 8, it did not interfere and was not inhibited. When the hand started at the top of the board (Figure 13.3b), the opposite was true: A distractor at Position 8 interfered and was inhibited, but not one at Position 2. In this task, the visual input was held constant by controlling

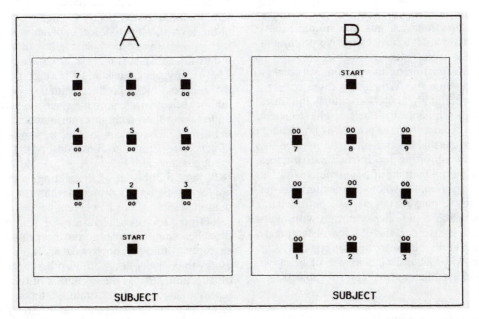

**FIGURE 13.3** ■ Diagram of a stimulus board used to study action-centered mechanisms of attention. The subject had to reach from the starting position to press the button where a red light appeared while ignoring a yellow light. The numbers on this diagram label the positions of the lights, but the numbers were not present on the board during the experiment. The board is not drawn to scale. (a) Setup when the reach moved away from the subject's body. (b) Setup when the reach moved backward, toward the subject's body.

the position in the display that was visually fixated just prior to the appearance of the target and distractor. Therefore, inhibition appeared to be based on the specific actions to be produced, rather than on visual perceptual representations.

Thus, the inhibitory mechanisms of attention are flexible. The behavioral goals of the task, whether semantic identification or manual reaching, determine what representations of a stimulus will be accessed and inhibited by attention. We may speculate that during semantic identification, selective attention inhibits information represented in inferior temporal lobes, whereas during selective reaching toward objects, representations in the parietal-frontal system are manipulated by attention.[10]

## Implications for Clinical Populations

A model proposing inhibition of distracting information as a mechanism of selection makes predictions concerning the nature of the inhibition in different subject populations. It is possible that breakdowns in the ability to inhibit irrelevant information may be an initial stage in general breakdowns in cognitive processes. Clearly, selective information processing is crucial for all higher cognitive functioning. Thus, the simple experiments that are able to reveal negative-priming effects may be useful tests for detecting breakdowns in cognitive functioning in syndromes as diverse as schizophrenia and Alzheimer's disease.

More specifically, those individuals in clinical populations who appear to be less able to attend selectively to stimuli in the presence of distractors (relative to normal control subjects) may be less efficient at inhibiting the intrusive distractors. Research with a number of populations with less efficient selection, for whom distracting information impairs response to targets, has confirmed this prediction. Schizophrenics, children with attentional deficit disorder, the elderly, obsessionals, and young adults who score high on cognitive failures tend to produce less evidence of negative-priming effects than normal control subjects.[11]

## The Need for Further Study

There are a number of reasons why further study of selective inhibition mechanisms will be fruitful. First, the requirement to select one source of information from competing information may be a ubiquitous problem in information processing systems. For example, not only does perceptual input have to be selected to control action, but access to particular memories when many representations may be simultaneously active, and maintaining a particular train of thought when other ideas may be triggered, also requires efficient selection. It may not be unreasonable to assume that the same successful algorithm adopted by evolution to enable goal-directed behavior is employed in different information processing situations. That is, the same inhibitory mechanism may be widespread in brain activity. Thus, computational models that attempt to simulate the remarkable perceptual-motor performance achieved by humans have to consider how selective action, in the service of biological goals, is achieved. Such modelling efforts would formalize the theories and enable more coherent predictions to be made.[12]

Second, if the underlying neurophysiology is investigated, links between the physiological level and formal modeling will provide the converging evidence for a complete account of selective attention. Inhibition is clearly an important concept at the level of physiological explanation. Indeed, the first step toward an understanding of the physiological mechanisms has recently been achieved. That is, my colleagues and I have demonstrated that it is possible to produce animal models of inhibitory selective attention mechanisms. Macaques undertaking the reaching experiments illustrated in Figure 13.3 have demonstrated negative-priming effects very similar to those observed in undergraduate students.[13]

In sum, inhibition of distracting information appears to be an important mechanism of information selection. For a coherent account of such selection processes, a variety of research approaches should converge on the problem. For example, within psychophysical analysis, it is necessary to consider how various other mechanisms of selection, such as the excitation of the internal representations of target stimuli, interact with the inhibition mechanisms discussed here. Furthermore, different levels of analysis are required. Formal computational models are necessary to explicitly identify and test properties of the theory, and neurophysiological studies of selective attention will provide constraints on models arising from psychophysical research.

## ACKNOWLEDGMENTS

The research described here was supported by the National Sciences and Engineering Research Council of Canada.

## NOTES

1. A. H. C. Van dor Heijden, *Short-Term Visual Information Forgetting* (Routledge & Kegan Paul, London, 1981).
2. S. P. Tipper, The negative priming effect: Inhibitory effects of ignored primes. *The Quarterly Journal of Experimental Psychology, 37A*, 571–590 (1985).
3. W. Wundt, *Principles of Physiological Psychology*, 5th ed., E. Titchener, Ed. (MacMillan, New York, 1904) (Original work published 1874).
4. E. C. Dajrymple-Alford and B. Budayr, Examination of some aspects of the Stroop Colour-word test, *Perceptual and Motor Skills, 23*, 1211–1214 (1966); W. J. Neill and R. L. Westberry, Selective attention and the suppression of cognitive noise, *Journal of Experimental Psychology: Learning, Memory, and Cognition, 13*, 327–334 (1987).
5. M. I. Posner, Orienting of attention. *The Quarterly Journal of Experimental Psychology, 32*, 3–25 (1980).
6. See S. P. Tipper, J. C. Brehaut, and J. Driver, Selection of moving and static objects for the control of spatially directed action, *Journal of Experimental Psychology: Human Perception and Performance*, 16, 492–504 (1990).
7. See also N. Kanwlsher and J. Driver, Objects, attributes, and visual attention: Which, what, and where, *Current Directions in Psychological Science, 1*, 26–31 (1992); S. P. Tipper, J. Driver, and B. Weaver, Object-centred inhibition of return of visual attention, *The Quarterly Journal of Experimental Psychology, 43A*, 289–298 (1991).
8. S. P. Tipper and J. Driver, Negative priming between pictures and words: Evidence for semantic analysis of ignored stimuli, *Memory and Cognition, 16*, 64–70 (1988); S. P. Tipper, G. MacQueen, and J. Brehaut, Negative priming between response modalities: Evidence for the central focus of inhibition in selective attention, *Perception and Psychophysics, 43*, 45–52 (1988).
9. S. P. Tipper, C. Lortie, and G. C. Baylis, Selective reaching: Evidence for action-centered attention, *Journal of Experimental Psychology: Human Perception and Performance* (in press).
10. L. G. Ungerleider and M. Mishkin, Two cortical visual systems, in *Analysis of Visual Behavior*, D. J. Ingle, M. A. Goodale, and R. J. W. Mansfield, Eds. (MIT Press, Cambridge, MA, 1982).
11. A. Beech, T. Powell, J. McWilliams, and G. Claridge, Evidence for reduced "cognitive inhibition" in schizophrenia, *British Journal of Clinical Psychology, 28*, 109–116 (1989); L. Hasher, E. R. Stoltzfus, R. T. Zacks, and B. Rympa, Age and inhibition, *Journal of Experimental Psychology: Learning, Memory, and Cognition, 17*, 163–169 (1991); S. P. Tipper, Less attentional selectivity as a result of declining inhibition in older adults, *Bulletin of the Psychonomic Society, 29*, 45–47 (1991).
12. G. Haughton and S. P. Tipper, A model of the dynamics of selective attention, In *Inhibitory Mechanisms of Attention. Memory and Language*. D. Dagenbach and T. Carr, Eds. (Academic Press, Orlando, FL, in press).
13. M. Taffe, B. O. Moore, S. P. Tipper, and G. C. Baylis, Action-based spatial attention in normal and lippocampal lesioned monkeys, *Society for Neuroscience Abstracts, 18*, 479.9 (1991).

## RECOMMENDED READING

W. T. Neill, (1989). Lexical ambiguity and context: An activation-suppression model. In *Resolving Semantic Ambiguity*, D. S. Gorfien, Ed. (Springer-Verlag, New York).

# Attention

## Discussion Questions

1. Cherry was careful to take an engineering perspective to his work and avoid the direct discussion of issues related to attention. Do you think there is something missing in Cherry's explanation? Be specific concerning what aspects of attention might be missing.

2. One of the ways that Posner and Snyder distinguished between automatic and attentional processes is the presence of facilitation and inhibition. In particular, controlled or attentional processes produce both facilitation and inhibition, whereas automatic processes produce only facilitation. However, the Stroop task (a task that some believe reflects automatic processes) produces inhibition in response latencies. How can one explain Stroop performance within the Posner and Snyder framework?

3. The work by Tipper suggests that information that is not attended to is actually suppressed below some baseline. How could one distinguish this perspective from the possibility that the information that is not attended to is simply coded with a "don't attend" tag, and the apparent inhibition is simply a type of interference, instead of a true suppression below baseline?

4. There is some evidence of a breakdown in attentional selection in different populations such as individuals with Schizophrenia and individuals with Dementia of the Alzheimer's Type. How might such breakdowns produce the hallucinations that sometimes occur in schizophrenia and the memory impairments that occur in individuals with Dementia of the Alzheimer's Type?

5. Driving is a task that is highly dependent on attentional operations. Consider the aspects of attention that are involved in driving and how the use of cell phones might be particularly disruptive during driving.

## Suggested Readings

There is a series of monographs entitled *Attention and Performance* that provides excellent overviews of recent developments in Attention.

E. Bisiach and C. Luzzatti (1978, Unilateral neglect of representational space, *Cortex, 14,* 129–133) describe an amazing case of unilateral neglect that extends into the utilization of an image representation of a very well-known place and reverses depending upon perspective taking in the image.

D. E. Broadbent (1958, *Perception and Communication*. London: Pergamon) wrote truly a classic book on attention and was critical in providing a review of experimental approaches to the topic of attention and the critical role it plays in many dimensions of cognition.

M. Corbetta, F. M. Miezin, G. L. Shulman, and Steve Petersen (1993, A PET study of visuospatial attention. *Journal of Neuroscience, 13*, 1202–1226) provide one of the first neuroimaging studies demonstrating the role of the parietal lobe in shifting attention in healthy individuals.

N. Cowan (1993, Activation, attention, and short-term memory, *Memory & Cognition, 21*, 162–167) presents an interesting argument that relates attention to memory processes. In this paper he presents the case that active short-term memory should be conceived as that area of memory that is currently attended. The relation between attention and memory has become critical in recent models.

D. L. LaBerge and S. J. Samuels (1974, Toward a theory of automatic information processing in reading. *Cognitive Psychology, 6*, 293–323) provide a theory of how automaticity develops in reading and how this modulates where attention is directed as reading skill develops.

G. D. Logan (1990, Repetition priming and automaticity: Common underlying mechanisms? *Cognitive Psychology, 22*, 1–35) provides an important alternative model of automaticity that suggests that this can be thought of as a continuum of retrieving individual traces.

S. J. Luck and S. P Vecera (2002, Attention. In H. Pashler [Series Ed.] & S. Yantis [Volume Ed.], *Stevens' Handbook of Experimental Psychology: Vol. 1. Sensation and Perception* [3rd ed., pp. 235–286]. New York: Wiley) provide an excellent review of more recent developments in the area of attention, which also integrates some interesting cognitive neuroscience work.

D. Kahneman (1973, *Attention and Effort*. Englewood Cliffs, NJ: Prentice-Hall) provides an excellent book reviewing basic aspects of attention and develops an alternative to attention selection, emphasizing a capacity view of attention. Performance within this view is dependent upon the attentional demands of a given task, along with the available capacity that an individual has available, among other factors.

V. S. Ramachandran and S. Blakeslee (1998, *Phantoms in the Brain*. New York: William Morrow) present a number of amazing observations concerning specific brain lesions and how they relate to distortions in phenomenological experience.

A. M. Treisman and G. Gelade (1980, A feature-integration theory of attention, *Cognitive Psychology, 12*, 97–136) develop a theory of pattern recognition and visual search that helps solve the binding problem, that is, the direction of attention serves to bind features of a given target together. Also, see A. Treisman (1986, Features and objects in visual processing. *Scientific American, 255,* 114–125) for a very readable discussion of her model and lots of interesting examples of how features are coordinated in visual search tasks.

W. Schneider and R. M. Shiffrin (1977, Controlled and automatic human information processing: I. Detection, search, and attention. *Psychological Review, 84*, 1–66) wrote an excellent paper providing a theory of automaticity and experimental approaches to tease apart automatic and attention-demanding processes.

PART IV

# Imagery

# Introduction to Part IV: Imagery

We can easily imagine "in the mind's eye" people or objects that are not physically present. Such mental imagery is commonplace, involved in many everyday tasks. The hungry person might imagine a slice of freshly baked apple pie. An athlete might visualize her performance prior to competition. You might mentally re-trace your steps as you try to remember where you last saw your (missing) keys.

In the introductory chapter, we described the theoretical debate regarding how these kinds of mental images are represented in the mind. Are mental images supported by the same type of code as other types of information (e.g., words), or is there something different underlying mental images? Pylyshyn (1973) argued that, like language, mental images could be supported by propositions. By a proposition, we simply mean a predicate-argument combination. An argument is an object, and a predicate involves a relationship between arguments. For example, the sentence "The cat is on the windowsill" involves two objects ("cat," "windowsill") and one relation ("on"). How could a simple representation like this yield the vivid images we experience? One possibility is that images are somehow computed from the combination of propositions, and our phenomenal experiences of "mental images" are simply epiphenomenon of underlying rich and detailed propositional representations. Although researchers have agreed this might be possible, many studies (including the Kosslyn paper in this section) have been aimed at showing that the representations formed via imagery are *qualitatively* different and are not affected in the same ways by manipulations that affect propositional representations.

Kosslyn reported several elegant studies demonstrating that mental images have different characteristics than do representations formed without imagery. In one classic study (Kosslyn, 1976), subjects evaluated properties of animals, either with or without imagery instructions. Two types of animal properties were used. One-half were very typical ones (e.g., a cat's paw) that happened to be physically small; the remaining properties were less typical (e.g., a cat's head) but physically larger. In the control group, subjects simply verified whether or not the property characterized the target animal. In the imagery conditions, subjects formed an image of the target animal and indicated when they "saw" the property. As suggested by the semantic memory literature, subjects in the control condition were faster to verify that typical properties were characteristic. More interestingly, the opposite pattern occurred in the imagery conditions; subjects were faster to verify the presence of the physically large but less typical properties. It was as if subjects in the imagery conditions were looking at a real picture and the larger properties of the animals were easier to see.

The classic paper by Kosslyn, Ball, and Reiser (1978) makes a similar point—namely, that mental images retain spatial information. For example, in one study, subjects memorized a map of an imaginary island with seven locations (e.g., hut, tree, pond). Working from a mental image of the island, subjects focused on a target location and then imagined a black dot moving to a second location on the map. They pressed a key upon "arriving" at the target location. The farther apart in physical distance on the map the two island locations, the longer it took subjects to complete the mental scanning task. Interestingly, this relationship was strongly linear, as if participants were visually scanning a real map. The other three experiments in the paper led to similar conclusions. Only when imagery was required did increased distance between objects lead to slower reaction times.

Both the papers described thus far support the idea that images preserve the spatial and size properties of their real-world correspondents. We now turn to two classic papers aimed at under-standing what people can do with their images. The Shepard and Metzler (1971) paper involves the mental rotation of images; the Finke et al. (1989) paper involves the reinterpretation of ambiguous mental images.

Shepard and Metzler (1971) required subjects to make same-different judgments about pairs of three-dimensional objects. In order to make this decision, objects had to be mentally rotated either around the vertical axis or in the picture plane. For "same" pairs, the required rotation was manipu-lated to be between 0 and 180 degrees. Shepard and Metzler's data are beautiful, showing a clear linear relationship between the size of the rotation required and the amount of time needed to make the "same" judgment; this effect occurred for both types of rotations. Again, it is as if the subjects were rotating a real object, instead of an imagined object. All subjects' introspective reports were consistent with the idea that they were actually mentally rotating the objects in order to make their judgments.

Finke, Pinker, and Farah (1989) showed that subjects could combine mental images and place a novel interpretation on them. For example, in one study, subjects were read the instruction "Imagine the letter 'D.' Rotate it 90 degrees to the right. Put the number '4' above it. Now remove the horizontal segment of the '4' to the right of the vertical line." The subject put a verbal label on the constructed image ("sailboat") and also drew it. Given that subjects followed instructions (as verified by their drawing of their image), almost 70% of images were labeled correctly. These data clearly indicate that humans have a very powerful and flexible imagery system.

More recently, researchers have become interested in the neural underpinnings of mental imagery. Of interest is whether mental imagery activates the same neural regions as those normally involved in visual perception. Some of the early research in this area is reviewed in the Farah (1989) paper. Brain imaging studies (e.g., ERP, PET, fMRI) suggest that visual areas such as occipital, temporal, and parietal cortex are involved in mental imagery. For example, in one study, subjects who were told to form images of concrete words (e.g., *apple*) showed more blood flow to occipital areas

than did subjects who only studied the words without imagery instructions (Goldenberg et al., 1987). Similarly, patient data suggest the involvement of visual areas in mental imagery tasks (e.g,. Bisiach & Luzzatti, 1978). People with impaired perception show parallel deficits in mental imagery; for example, a person who has a problem recognizing faces will have a problem imaging faces as well (Shuttleworth, Syring, & Allen, 1982). Together, the results from imaging and patient studies line up nicely with the behavioral studies; across methodologies, the data suggest that representations formed via imagery are qualitatively different from propositional representations.

The neural approach also provides further insights into the behavioral imagery tasks described thus far. For example, tasks involving mental manipulation of co-present stimuli (e.g., the Shepard mental rotation task) appear to be more lateralized to the right hemisphere of the brain. Tasks that require generation of images from memory (e.g., some of the Kosslyn tasks described earlier) may be more lateralized to the left hemisphere. Such differences are interesting as they remind us that "mental imagery" is not a single process but likely involves a number of component processes (cf. Kosslyn, 1987). It's almost as if the brain has evolved an amazing capacity to simulate its underlying processes internally via mental imagery.

## REFERENCES

Bisiach, E., & Luzzatti, C. (1978). Unilateral neglect of representational space. *Cortex, 14,* 129–133.

Farah, M. J. (1989). The neural basis of mental imagery. *Trends in Neruoscience, 12,* 395–399.

Finke, R. A., Pinker, S., & Farah, M. J. (1989). Reinterpreting visual patterns in mental imagery. *Cognitive Science, 13,* 51–78.

Goldenberg, G., Podreka, I., Steiner, M., & Willmes, K. (1987). Patterns of regional cerebral blood flow related to memorizing of high and low imagery words: An emission computer tomography study. *Neuropsychologica, 25,* 473–485.

Kosslyn, S. M. (1976). Can imagery be distinguished from other forms of internal representation? Evidence from studies of information retrieval times. *Memory & Cognition, 4,* 291–297.

Kosslyn, S. M. (1987). Seeing and imagining in the cerebral hemispheres: A computational approach. *Psychological Review, 94,* 148–175.

Kosslyn, S. M., Ball, T. M., & Reiser, B. J. (1978). Visual images preserve metric spatial information: Evidence from studies of image scanning. *Journal of Experimental Psychology: Human Perception & Performance, 4,* 47–60.

Pylyshyn, Z. W. (1973). What the mind's eye tells the mind's brain: A critique of mental imagery. *Psychological Bulletin, 80,* 1–24.

Shepard, R. N., & Metzler, J. (1971). Mental rotation of three-dimensional objects. *Science, 171,* 701–703.

Shuttleworth, E. C., Syring, V., & Allen, N. (1982). Further observations on the nature of prosopagnosia. *Brain & Cognition, 1,* 307–322.

# Visual Images Preserve Metric Spatial Information: Evidence from Studies of Image Scanning

Stephen M. Kosslyn • Harvard University

Thomas M. Ball • Johns Hopkins University

Brian J. Reiser • New York University

Four experiments demonstrated that more time is required to scan further distances across visual images, even when the same amount of material falls between the initial focus point and the target. Not only did times systematically increase with distance but subjectively larger images required more time to scan than did subjectively smaller ones. Finally, when subjects were not asked to base all judgments on examination of their images, the distance between an initial focus point and a target did not affect reaction times.

Introspections about visual imagery very often include references to "scanning" across images. Kosslyn (1973) attempted to demonstrate that scanning of images is a functional cognitive process, and his experiment indicated that more time was required to traverse greater distances across mental images. However, in the course of scanning longer distances,[1] people in Kosslyn's experiment also passed over more parts of the imaged object. For example, in scanning from the motor to the porthole of an imaged speedboat, a person passed over the rear deck and part of the cabin; in scanning from the motor to the more distant anchor, one scanned over all of these parts plus the front deck and bow. Given this confounding, then, we have no way of knowing whether Kosslyn's results were a consequence of people actually scanning over a quasi-pictorial, spatial image. One could argue that the image itself was epiphenom-enal in this situation and that the apparent effects of distance actually were a consequence of how people accessed some sort of underlying list structure. Parts separated by greater distances on the image might simply be separated by more entries in a list of parts of the object.

The notion that scanning corresponds to processing a list structure, and not the spatial "surface" image (see Kosslyn, 1975, 1976; Kosslyn & Pomerantz, 1977), recently seemed to receive support from Lea (1975). In a typical experiment, people evaluated from memory the relative locations of objects in a circular array. Lea asked his subjects to learn the array via imagery. Following this, they were given the name of one object and asked to name the first, second, or $n$th item in a given direction. Lea found that the time to respond depended on the number of intervening items between an initial focus point and the target, but not on the actual distance separating a pair of objects in the array. The interpretation of these results is muddied, however, because Lea never insisted that his subjects base all judgments on actual processing of the image itself. That is, subjects were not told to count the items as they appeared in their image but only to count the appropriate number of steps to the target. It is reasonable to suppose that these people encoded the circular array both as a list and as an image. Given that imagery tends to require more time to use in this sort of task than do nonimaginal representations (Kosslyn, 1976), subjects may have actually arrived at most judgments through processing nonimaginal list structures. If so, then it is not surprising that actual distance separating pairs did not affect retrieval times.

The present experiments, then, test the claim that distance affects time to scan images by removing the confounding between distance and the number of intervening items scanned across. If images really do preserve metric spatial information, and images themselves can in fact be scanned, then actual distance between parts of an imaged object should affect scanning time. If the apparent effects of distance observed by Kosslyn (1973) were in fact due to accessing some sort of ordered list, however, then only ordinal relations between parts—not actual interval distances—should affect the time needed to shift one's attention from one part of an image to another.

## Experiment 1

This experiment is an attempt to distinguish between the effects of scanning different distances and scanning over different numbers of intervening items. The people who participated in the experiment scanned visual images of three letters arrayed on a line, "looking" for a named target. Upon mentally focusing on the target, the subject classified it according to whether it was upper- or lowercase. In scanning to the target letter, one had to traverse one of three distances and pass over zero, one, or two intervening letters; letter arrays were constructed such that each distance appeared equally often with each number of intervening items, allowing us to consider each variable independently of the other.

The present claim is that distance per se affects time to scan an image. However, we also expect

people to take more time in scanning over more items since each item presumably must be "inspected" as it is scanned over, which requires an increment of time. The present claim does not speak to the issue of which factor affects image scanning more—distance or number of intervening items; we are primarily concerned with demonstrating that effects of distance are not simply an artifact of how many things must be scanned over.

## Method

### MATERIALS

We constructed two books of stimuli, each containing 36 arrays of letters. Each array consisted of three letters spaced along a 20.32-cm long line. Each array contained two letters of one case, and one of the other; each case (upper and lower) was represented equally often across arrays. Target letters were placed 5.08, 10.16, and 15.24 cm from the point of focus (one of the two ends of the line), and zero, one, or two other letters intervened between the target and point of focus. Intervening items were spaced at equal intervals between the target and focus point. The arrays were constructed such that each distance occurred equally often with each number of intervening items. Each of these nine conditions was represented by eight arrays, half of which had an uppercase letter as the target and half of which had a lowercase letter as the target. Further, for half of each target type in each condition, the focus point was specified as the left end of the line, and for half it was the right end. We did not use letters whose upper- and lowercases seemed difficult to distinguish (c, k, o, p, s, u, v, w, x, z). The remaining 16 letters of the alphabet were used as targets and distractors. Each of these letters appeared at least once as a target in each case, at each distance, and with each number of intervening items, but not with every possible combination of these variables (this would have required far more trials than we used). The arrays were randomly divided into two sets, which were placed in separate books, and the order of arrays was randomized within each book (with the constraint that no more than three consecutive targets could be of the same case).

We also constructed a tape recording. The tape contained 72 trials of the form "1 . . . cover . . . left . . . A." Each trial was coordinated with an array in the books. The first word named the trial number and was followed 5 sec later by the word *cover* (which was the signal to conceal the array and to construct an image). Two seconds thereafter the word *left* or *right* was heard (indicating point of focus, each word appearing on half of the trials, as noted above). Finally, 3 sec after this, the name of a letter in the corresponding array was heard. Presentation of the letter delivered a pulse to a voice-activated relay that started a reaction time clock (which was stopped by the subject's pressing either of two response buttons). A new number was presented 10 sec after the letter, and the sequence was repeated with a new trial.

## PROCEDURE

Written instructions describing the experimental procedure were given to the subject and then were reviewed orally by the experimenter. It was emphasized that we were interested in studying how people process visual mental images, and therefore we wanted the subject always to use an image in performing this task—even if this did not seem the most efficient strategy. These general instructions preceded every experiment reported in this article. Before we are willing to make inferences about imagery from data, we want to be sure that those data were in fact produced via imagery processing.

The subject was told that he or she would soon see simple arrays of letters. We explained that the task was to study an array and then to shut one's eyes and mentally picture the array as it appeared on the page. We would next ask the subject to focus on one end of the image and then to scan to a given letter in the array. As soon as the target letter was clearly in focus, we wanted the subject to "look" at the letter: If it were uppercase, he or she should push one button; if it were lowercase, the other button should be pushed.

Following this, we explained the meanings of the tape-recorded cues that accompanied the arrays. Upon hearing a number, the subjects were to turn to the next page in the book in front of them, which would have that number at the top (pages were numbered consecutively). They should study this array until hearing the word *cover*, at which point they should cover the array with a small piece of cardboard and mentally image the array. While visualizing the array, they then would hear the word *right* or *left*, directing them to "mentally

stare" at that end of the line. They should continue to focus at that end until hearing the next word, which would be the name of a letter in the array. At this point the subjects were to scan to the named letter and classify it according to its case. Eight practice trials (half upper- and half lowercase, in a random order) preceded the actual test trials. The subjects were questioned during these trials to ensure that they were performing the task as instructed. The subjects were asked to perform the task as quickly as possible while keeping errors to an absolute minimum.

This procedure, then, prevented the subjects from initially encoding an array differently depending on the point of focus or the distance of a target or the number of intervening letters. The order of the two books was counterbalanced over subjects, as was the hand (dominant/nondominant) assigned for indicating each case. Each person was interviewed at the conclusion of the 20-min tape recording and was asked to estimate the percentage of time he or she actually followed instructions while performing the task. Further, we asked each subject to attempt to discern the purposes and motivations of the present experiment.

## SUBJECTS

Twelve Johns Hopkins University students volunteered to participate as subjects to fulfill a course requirement. Although 2 of these people reported noticing distance effects during the course of the experiment, and 2 people reported observing that it was easier when there were no intervening items, no subject reported noticing both effects, and no subject deduced any part of the hypothesis independently of noticing his or her behavior during the task. Data from 1 additional potential subject were discarded because she estimated complying with the imagery instructions only 60% of the time, and data from another potential subject were discarded because his mean reaction times were more than twice the means of all the other subjects. The 12 remaining subjects reported complying with the instructions at least 75% of the time.

## Results

An analysis of variance was performed on the data. Only reaction times from correct responses were

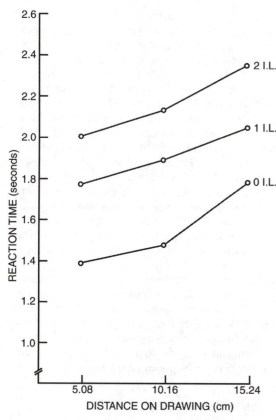

**FIGURE 14.1** ■ The results of Experiment 1: Classification times when subjects scanned different distances over zero, one, or two intervening letters (I.L.).

used, and errors and wild scores were replaced by the mean of the other scores in that condition for that subject. A wild score was defined as one that exceeded twice the mean of the other scores in that cell for that subject; only one score per cell could be so defined, however. Because we wished to generalize over both subjects and items, we used the Quasi $F$ statistic, $F'$ (Clark, 1973).

As expected, scanning times increased as subjects had to scan further distances to reach the target letter, $F'$ (2, 30) = 9.89, $p < .01$. In addition, times also increased when subjects had to scan across more intervening letters before reaching the target, $F'$ (2, 27) = 22.65, $p < .01$. Interestingly, as is evident in Figure 14.1 the effects of distance were the same regardless of how many intervening items were scanned over; there was no interaction between the two variables ($F' < 1$). This lack of interaction also indicates, of course, that the ef-

fects of intervening items were the same for each of the three distances—which is what one would expect if this effect reflects time necessary to "inspect" each of the intervening letters. Finally, there was no difference in time to categorize letters of different case or to scan left versus right, nor were any other effects or interactions significant.

Errors tended to increase with increasing reaction times. For the 5.08-, 10.16-, and 15.24-cm conditions, errors were .7%, 3.1%, and 1.4%, respectively. Although errors for the 10.16-cm distances were relatively high, they were not significantly higher than the errors for the 15.24-cm condition ($p > .1$). For the zero, one, and two intervening item conditions, errors were .7%, 2.1%, and 2.4%, respectively. Thus, it does not appear as if speed-accuracy trade-offs affected the data.

## Discussion

We found that more time is required to scan further distances across an image. In addition, more time also is required when one scans over more items. Our findings argue against the idea that people were not really scanning a spatial image but rather simply processing a serially ordered list of letters. If so, we should only have found an effect of number of intervening items (if scanning the list were self-terminating). There is no reason to expect such a list to have metric distance from each end to be associated with each letter. Furthermore, we found effects of distance even when the target letter was not separated from the focus point by any intervening letters. Finally, we found that it took the same amount of time to scan right to left as it did to scan in the opposite direction. This last result replicates that of Kosslyn (1973) when his subjects were asked to remember and then to scan visual images (left-to-right scanning was easier, however, when subjects encoded and used verbal descriptions of the pictures instead of images). Thus, image scanning would seem to involve processes or mechanisms different from those highly practiced ones used during reading.

Given the existence of two independent effects of distance and number of intervening letters, one might be tempted to ask which factor is the more important. This is a nonsensical question: By increasing the range of distances, we surely could make distance account for the lion's share of the variance in scanning times—and by decreasing the range of distances, we could diminish the importance of this variable. In addition, we could probably manipulate the importance of number of intervening items by making the distractors more or less difficult to discriminate from the targets. Furthermore, the present claim is not that distance is more important than other variables, but only that images do preserve metric distance information—and that such information can be used in real-time processing, affecting the operating characteristics of cognitive processes.

One might argue that the effects of distance on scanning time really reflect nothing more than the enthusiastic cooperation of our subjects, who somehow discerned the purpose of the experiment and manipulated their responses accordingly. Although 2 of our subjects did hypothesize distance effects, they claimed to do so by introspecting upon their performance during the task; no subject confessed to consciously manipulating his or her responses. Nevertheless, we would be more comfortable with a task that was more difficult to second-guess and manipulate.

## Experiment 2

This experiment involves scanning between the 21 possible pairs of seven locations on an imaged map. Each of these distances was different, and the task seemed sufficiently complex to thwart any attempts to produce intentionally a linear relationship between distance and reaction time. Since the critical question is whether images preserve metric information, it is important that scanning times be a function of some known distance—otherwise, variations in scanning time cannot be taken to necessarily reflect amount of distance traversed. Thus, we wished to ensure that subjects scanned only the shortest distance between two points. In order to do so, we altered the instructions slightly and asked these people to imagine a black speck moving along a direct path across the image. After memorizing the map, these subjects imaged it, focused on a location, and then decided whether a given named object was in fact on the map. If so, the subjects were asked to scan to the named object on the image and to push a button when they "arrived" there; if not, they pushed another button. The time necessary to scan between all possible pairs of locations was measured. As before, we

expected times to increase with distance (although not necessarily linearly, as rates may be variable).

## Method

### MATERIALS

A map of a fictional island was constructed containing a hut, tree, rock, well, lake, sand, and grass. Each distance between all 21 pairs was at least .5 cm longer than the next shortest distance. The precise location of each object was indicated by a red dot; these locations are indicated by a small $x$ in Figure 14.2.

A tape recording was constructed containing 84 pairs of words. Each location was named 12 times and then followed 4 sec later by another word; on 6 of these trials, the second word did not name a location on the map. The "false" objects were things that could have been sensibly included on the map (e.g., "bench"). On the other 6 trials, the first word was followed by the name of each of the other locations. Thus, every pair of locations occurred twice, once with each member appearing first. The order of pairs was randomized, with the constraint that the same location could not occur twice within three entries, and no more than

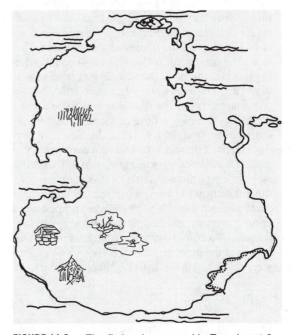

**FIGURE 14.2** ■ The fictional map used in Experiment 2.

4 true or 4 false trials could occur in a row. Presentation of the second word also started a clock. A new trial began 8 sec after the probe word was presented. The test trials were preceded by 8 practice trials naming pairs of cities in the United States for "true" items.

The subjects first were asked to learn the locations of the objects on the map by drawing their relative positions. The subjects began by tracing the locations on a blank sheet placed over the map, marking the locations of the red dots centered on the objects; this procedure allowed them to see the locations themselves in isolation. Next, they studied the map, closed their eyes and imaged it, and then compared their image to the map until they thought their image was accurate.

The map then was removed, and the subjects drew the locations on a blank sheet of paper. Following this, the subjects were allowed to compare their drawings with the original. This procedure was repeated until all points were within .64 cm of the actual location. Between 2 and 5 drawings were required for subjects to reach this criterion.

Next, subjects were told that they would hear the name of an object on the map. They were to picture mentally the entire map and then to focus on the object named. Subjects were told that 5 sec after focusing on the named object, another word would be presented; if this word named an object depicted on the map, the subjects were to scan to it and depress one button when they arrived at the dot centered on it. The scanning was to be accomplished by imaging a little black speck zipping in the shortest straight line from the first object to the second. The speck was to move as quickly as possible, while still remaining visible. If the second word of a pair did not name an object on the map, the subjects were to depress the second button placed before them. The clock was stopped when either button was pushed, and response times were recorded. As before, we interviewed subjects in the course of the practice trials, making sure that they were following the instructions about imagery use.

Eleven new Johns Hopkins University students served as paid volunteers in this experiment. Data from 2 additional people were not analyzed because, when queried afterwards, they reported having followed the imagery instructions less than 75% of the time during the task.

## Results

Only times from correct "true" decisions (where a distance was actually scanned) were analyzed. As before, wild scores were eliminated prior to analysis. A wild score was now defined as one twice the size of the mean of the other score for that distance and the scores for the next shortest and longest distances; only one score in any adjacent row of six could be so eliminated. Data were analyzed in two ways, over subjects and over items. We first analyzed each subject's times for the different distances in an analysis of variance. As expected, times consistently increased with increasing distance, $F(20, 200) = 13.69$, $p < .001$. In addition, we averaged over subjects and calculated the mean reaction time for each pair. The best fitting linear function was calculated for these data by the method of least squares; not only did times increase linearly with increasing distance but the correlation between distance and reaction time was .97. These data are illustrated in Figure 14.3.

Errors occurred on only 1.3% of the trials and were distributed seemingly at random; more errors did not occur for the shorter distances. Finally, subjects drew maps after the experiment. Not surprisingly, the correlation between the drawn and actual distances between all possible pairs of points was quite high, $r = .96$.

## Discussion

Time to scan across visual mental images again increased linearly with the distance to be scanned. This demonstration supports the claim that images are quasi-pictorial entities that can in fact be processed and are not merely epiphenomenal. One of the defining properties of such a representation is that metric distances are embodied in the same way as in a percept of a picture, and the present data suggest that this characteristic is true of visual mental images.

Interestingly, a number of subjects reported that they had to slow down when scanning the shorter distances, because the four objects at the lower left of the map were "cluttered together." The data

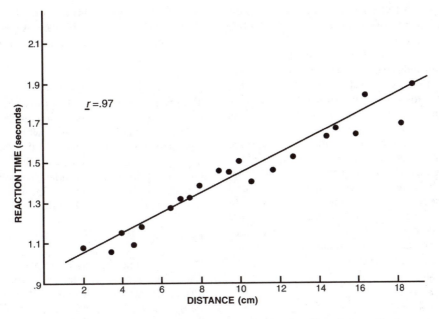

**FIGURE 14.3** ■ The results of Experiment 2: Time to scan between all pairs of locations on the imaged map.

show no sign of this, however, providing further grounds for taking with a grain of salt subjects' interpretations of their introspections. This experiment seems immune to the potential failings of Experiment 1; somewhat surprisingly, no subjects reported suspecting the hypothesis when it was explained to them afterwards.

## Experiment 3

Given the results of the first two experiments, how can we explain Lea's (1975) failure to find increases in reaction times as distances increased? We earlier suggested that this failure was a consequence of his instructions: Subjects were not told to base all judgments on consultation of their images, but only to start off from an imaged location and to "scan" a certain number of objects from there. Although these people initially began with an image, the actual decisions could have been generated via processing of items in a list. If so, only ordinal—and not interval—relations among items (objects in the array, in Lea's case) should affect time to sort through the list. Effects of actual distance ought to occur only when one scans the spatial image itself, which seems to represent interval information about distance. If we find dis-

tance effects even when people do not scan images, we are in trouble: We could not then infer that effects of metric distance implicate scanning of quasi-pictorial images.

A second hypothesis for why Lea failed to obtain effects of distance on time to scan also involves his instructions. Lea did not insist that his subjects always construct the entire array ahead of time; instead, subjects were told simply to image a starting place and then to decide which object was some number of locations away. Perhaps distance only affects time to shift attention between locations in an image when the locations are both "in view" simultaneously. That is, if an entire image is not kept in mind at once, the distance relations between visible and invisible locations may not be represented; these relations could be an "emergent" property of constructing the whole image from its component parts. One might shift to an "invisible" part by generating a sequence of individual images representing intervening locations and not by actually scanning across an image. In this case, interval distance would not be expected to affect time to shift attention between parts.

The following experiment examines the hypotheses described above. In one group, subjects were asked to focus on a given location on an image of the map used in Experiment 2 and then to judge whether a named object was on the map. Unlike the people in Experiment 2, however, these people were not required to consult their images when making their judgments, but simply were asked to reach decisions as quickly as possible. In a second group, subjects also performed the basic task of Experiment 2, but with one major modification. When focusing on the initial location, these people were asked to "zoom in" on it until that object filled their entire image, causing the remainder of the island to "overflow." These people were told, however, that they must "see" an image of the second named object before responding positively (if in fact it was on the map). The two groups, then, were each instructed to perform in a way that Lea's subjects may have acted spontaneously.

## Method

### MATERIALS

The same materials used in Experiment 2 were also used here.

### PROCEDURE

Subjects in both groups learned to draw the map as did subjects in the previous experiment. The procedure differed from that of Experiment 2 only in the following ways:

*1. Rapid Verification Control Group.* These subjects were given instructions like those of Experiment 2, except that no mention was made of scanning the image. After focusing on an initially named object, these people were simply to decide as quickly as possible whether the second object of a pair was in fact on the map. As before, subjects were urged to keep errors to a minimum.

*2. Image Overflow Group.* These subjects were given instructions that differed from those of Experiment 2 in two ways: First, these people were asked to "zoom in" on the initially named object until the rest of the map had "overflowed" (i.e., was no longer visible in) their image. Second, they were instructed to be sure to "see" a second named object of a pair before responding positively. These subjects were not told to scan to the second object if it was on the map but only to be sure to "see" it

prior to responding; no mention was made of a flying black speck or the like. As before, speed with accuracy was stressed in both groups.

### SUBJECTS

Twenty-two new Johns Hopkins University students volunteered as paid subjects in this experiment. Half of these subjects were randomly assigned to one group, half to the other. An additional 3 people were assigned to the Image Overflow Group but were not included, because after the experiment they reported having followed the instructions less than 75% of the time.

## Results

Data were analyzed as in Experiment 2. In the Rapid Verification Group, there were significant differences in time to evaluate different pairs, $F(20, 200) = 2.59$, $p < .01$. As is evident in Figure 14.4 however, times did not increase systematically with distance. In fact, the relationship between distance and verification time was negligible, $r = .09$.

In the Image Overflow Group, in contrast, times did increase systematically with distance. Not only were times to evaluate different pairs significantly different from each other, $F(20, 200) = 4.59$, $p < .01$, but there was a respectable correlation between distance on the map and evaluation time, $r = .89$.

We also performed three additional analyses of variance, one comparing the results from each group with the data obtained in Experiment 2 and one comparing the two groups with each other. Not surprisingly, there were less effects of distance in data from the Rapid Verification Control Group than in the Image Overflow Group or in Experiment 2 ($p < .01$ for the interaction of distance and instructions in both cases). In addition, subjects in the Rapid Verification Control Group made decisions more quickly than those in either other condition ($p < .01$ for both comparisons). The comparison between the results of the Image Overflow Group and the findings of Experiment 2 produced a somewhat surprising result, or rather, lack thereof: In this case, the effects of distance were identical for both instructions ($F < 1$). Furthermore, there was no significant difference overall in verification times (the mean for Experiment 2 was 1.428 sec versus 1.685 sec for the Image Over-

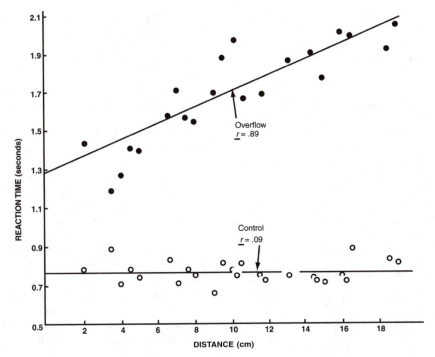

**FIGURE 14.4** ■ The results of Experiment 3: The effects of distance on response times for the Imagery Overflow and the Rapid Verification Control Groups.

flow Group), $F(1, 20) = 1.04$, $p > .1$. If "zooming in" increases the subjective size of an image, it should also increase the "distance" between portions of that image; hence, we would have expected that more time should have been required by subjects in the Image Overflow Group.

The error rate in the Rapid Verification Control Group was 3.3%, whereas there were only 1.4% errors in the Image Overflow Group. As before, errors did not tend to increase with shorter distance for the Image Overflow Group, and seemed randomly distributed for the Rapid Verification Control Group. No subjects deduced the purposes or predictions of this experiment.

## Discussion

When people were not required to base decisions upon consultation of their images, evaluation times did not increase with the distance between a focus point and a probed object that was in fact on the map. This result allows us to argue against a non-imagery interpretation of the scanning results ob-

tained in the preceding experiments: If the effects of distance obtained previously were due to local activation and scanning through an abstract list structure (e.g., perhaps a graph with "dummy nodes" interposed to mark off increasing distance), then we should have found effects of distance here. Distance per se seems to affect response times only when people actually scan their images. Thus, Lea's (1975) results may simply reflect the fact that his subjects were not told to respond only after seeing the probed object in their image. Clearly, before we draw inferences about image processing from some data, we must be certain that such data were produced when people did in fact use their images. The instructions administered in the present experiments and elsewhere (Kosslyn, 1973, 1975, 1976) seem capable of inducing subjects to use imagery, even if other means of performing a task are available.

Lea's results were probably not a consequence of subjects' not having the entire array in their images prior to processing it, as witnessed by the results of the Image Overflow Group. Although these people only had the focus location in their images, times nevertheless increased with distance to a probed object. We were surprised by these results, which were not expected. This finding seems to indicate that one may construct images such that portions are "waiting in the wings," ready to be processed if necessary. Thus, subjects seemed to have scanned to parts that were not visible initially in their images but were available in a non-activated portion of the image.

There is one hitch in the above explanation of the data obtained from the Image Overflow Group: If these people "zoomed in" closer to the imaged map than did those in Experiment 2, the subjective distances between parts should have been greater in the Image Overflow condition. If so, then more time should have been required to scan these enlarged images, which was not the case. One explanation of this disparity rests on a procedural difference between the Image Overflow condition and Experiment 2: Subjects in Experiment 2 were instructed to image a small black speck flying between parts. This task may have required more effort than the simple shift-of-attention instruction used in the present experiment, and thus slowed down scanning. In addition, it is possible that subjects in the two experiments simply scanned at different rates: If people in the Overflow condition scanned relatively quickly, perhaps because distances traversed were on the average relatively large, then we would not necessarily expect any differences in scanning times between the two conditions. The following experiment eliminated the difference in instructions and used a within-subjects design; we hoped that a given person would adopt a constant scanning rate for different materials.

# Experiment 4

In this experiment we investigated whether more time is required to scan across subjectively larger images. We worried that if we used stimuli as complex as those included on the map, people might have to "zoom in" (if the image were small) or "pan back" (if it were large) in order to "see" parts clearly. Kosslyn (1975) demonstrated that parts of subjectively smaller images are more difficult to identify than parts of larger ones, and this, may also be true of parts of "overflowed" images. Not only could difficulty in identifying parts of relatively complex images obfuscate effects of scanning images of different subjective sizes, but people may adjust their scanning rates in accordance with the difficulty in identifying parts. Pilot data lent credence to these fears, encouraging us to use more simple stimuli, where the parts were readily identifiable.

Thus, in this experiment people imaged one of three schematic faces at one of three subjective sizes. The faces had either light or dark eyes, and the eyes were one of three distances from the mouth. These people first focused on the mouth of an imaged face and then shifted their attention to the eyes and decided whether a probe correctly described them. As in Experiment 1, these instructions made no mention of a flying speck or the like. If distances determine scanning times, then subjectively smaller images should be scanned more quickly than larger ones. In addition, the effects of increased distance should become more pronounced with larger images, since when size is multiplied, so are the distances.

## Method

### MATERIALS

Six schematic faces were constructed. The eyes were 7.62, 10.16, or 12.70 cm above the mouth; for each distance, one face was constructed with light eyes and one was constructed with dark eyes. The faces are illustrated in Figure 14.5.

Twelve copies of each face were made and used in nine basic conditions, each of which was represented by eight stimuli. These conditions were defined by three subjective sizes—overflow, full size, and half size—and the three distances. Within a condition, half of the faces had light eyes and half had dark eyes. Further, half of the faces with each eye color were paired with the word *dark* and half with the word *light* on an accompanying tape recording, producing an equal distribution of true and false probes. The faces were then randomized and placed in a booklet, with the constraint that no given distance or size could occur twice within 3 trials.

A tape recording also was made. This tape contained stimuli consisting of three parts: First, the number of the trial was given. Second, 5 sec later the word *cover* was presented, followed 1 sec later

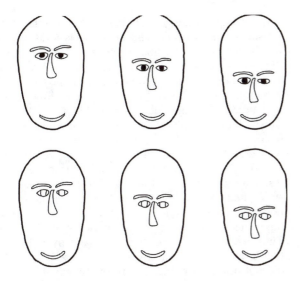

**FIGURE 14.5** ■ The schematic faces used in Experiment 4.

by one of three cues—overflow, full size, or half size. These stimuli indicated the size at which the subject should construct his or her image. Finally, 5 sec later the word *light* or *dark* was presented, which also started a clock. Ten sec after this, a new number was presented and another trial began. For half of the trials in each size condition, the final word described the eyes of the imaged face, and for half it did not. The 72 test trials were preceded by 8 practice trials.

### PROCEDURE

The subjects were told that they were going to see schematic faces one at a time. As soon as a trial number occurred on a tape recording, they should turn to the corresponding page of the book in front of them, exposing a drawing of a face. The subjects were asked to study the drawing well enough to form an accurate visual mental image of it with their eyes closed. After 5 sec, the subjects would hear the word *cover*, at which point they would conceal the face with a small piece of cardboard; shortly thereafter they would hear a size specification, either overflow, full size, or half size. Upon hearing the word *overflow*, the subjects were to image the face so large that only the mouth was visible. Upon hearing *full size*, they were to image it as large as possible while still being able to "see"

all of it at once in their image; as soon as this image was constructed, they were to mentally focus on the mouth and wait there until hearing the next stimulus on the tape. Upon hearing *half size*, they were to image the face at half of the length of the full-size version, again focusing on the mouth. Following this, the subjects were told they would hear either the word *light* or *dark*. At this point, they were to "glance" up at the eyes in their image and see if they were appropriately described. If so, they were to push one button; if not, they were to push the other. Hand of response was counterbalanced over subjects; as before, the clock stopped as soon as either button was pushed, and response times were recorded. Subjects were asked to respond as quickly as possible, but always to base decisions on inspection of the image (as in Experiment 1). During the 8 practice trials preceding the test items (half true, half false, including all three size conditions and all three distances), the subjects were asked repeatedly to describe their mental activity, and any misconceptions about the task were corrected.

### SUBJECTS

Sixteen new Johns Hopkins University students volunteered to participate for pay; data from an additional subject were discarded because this person reported not following the instructions at least 75% of the time.

## Results

Only times from correct decisions were included in an analysis of variance; errors and occasional wild scores (defined as in Experiment 1) were replaced by the mean of the remaining scores in that condition for that subject. As expected, times increased with further separation between the mouth and eyes, $F(2, 30) = 10.81$, $p < .01$. In addition, times increased as subjective size of the image increased, $F(2, 30) = 17.33$, $p < .01$. As is evident in Figure 14.6 increases in distance did have increasingly larger effects as the subjective size increased; the interaction between size and distance was in fact significant, $F(4, 60) = 3.47$, $p < .025$. Examination of Figure 14.6 reveals, however, that the effects of distance were not appreciably different in the full-size and half-size conditions. A marginally significant interaction between type of

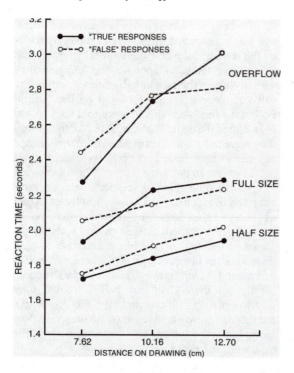

FIGURE 14.6 ■ The results of Experiment 4: The time required to classify eyes located three distances from the mouth of faces imaged at three subjective sizes (overflow, full size, and half size).

response (true or false) and distance, $F(2, 30) = 2.80$, $.05 < p < .10$, led us to consider separately data from true and false responses. As in the main analysis, distance and size both affected decision times for both types of responses ($p < .01$ in all cases in separate analyses of variance of the true and false responses). However, whereas the effects of distance increased with size for true responses, $F(4, 60) = 5.58$, $p < .01$, they did not increase for false responses ($F < 1$). Furthermore, for true responses there was some difference between the effects of distance in the full-size and half-size conditions. We observed that times increased an average of 109 msec for every additional 2.54 cm separating the eyes and mouth on the face in the half-size condition. On this basis, we predicted that time to scan a face twice as long ought to be 2.050, 2.274, and 2.486 sec, respectively, for the three increasing distances. These predictions were clearly off the mark; a chi-square test comparing these expected results with the observed results

was very significant, $\chi^2 = 23.8$, $p < .001$. We then considered the possibility that our subjects adjusted not the length of their images, but the area. If so, then we expected that 1.858, 2.019, and 2.167 sec, respectively, should be required to scan the three distances on a full-sized image; these estimates also failed to fit the data, $\chi^2 = 33.18$, $p < .001$. This failure was much more severe for the middle distance than the ends (the deviation from the expected for the shortest distance was not significant [$p > .2$], whereas the deviation for the longest was barely significant at the .05 level). We then speculated that subjects neither halved the lengths nor halved the areas but reduced size by performing some kind of a compromise between the two. Thus, we simply averaged our estimates from the two procedures and discovered that these means did not deviate significantly from the actual observed mean reaction times, $\chi^2 = 5.06$, $p > .05$; again, the best fit here was with the two extreme distances, $\chi^2 = 1.12$, $p > .5$.

Finally, error rates again tended to be positively correlated with reaction times. For true responses, error rates for the 7.62-, 10.16-, and 12.70-cm stimuli were 6.25%, 4.69%, and 6.25% for the overflow condition; 1.56%, 1.56%, and 4.69% for the full-size condition; and 7.81%, 1.56%, and 3.12% for the half-size condition. For the false responses, error rates for the 7.62-, 10.16-, and 12.70-cm stimuli were 7.81%, 7.81%, and 10.94% for the overflow condition; 3.12%, 7.81%, and 6.25% for the full-size condition; and 4.69%, 3.12%, and 1.56% for the half-size condition. In two cases, the 7.62-cm items incurred more errors than the 12.70-cm ones (true half-size false half size); $t$ tests evaluating these differences were not significant, but the "true" comparison was marginal, $t(15) = 1.86$, $.05 < p < .1$. Thus, the faces incorporating the shortest distance from the mouth to the eyes may have been evaluated faster than they should have been, because of a lowered response criterion. If so, then the slope of the half-size condition (i.e., effects of increased distance on scanning time) may be steeper than is merited by scanning effects per se. In addition, in one case the errors for corresponding distance were greater for the half size than the over flow condition (true, 7.62 cm); this difference was not significant, $t(15) = 1.00$, $p > .1$, belying a speed-accuracy trade-off here. Finally, no subject deduced the purposes or motivation of this experiment.

## Discussion

As expected, people again required more time to scan further distances across their images. This was reflected in three results. First, times increased with further separation between the mouth and eyes of the imaged stimuli; second, more time was generally required to scan across subjectively larger images; and third, there were increasingly large effects of increased distance (on the stimuli) for subjectively large images. This last result was observed only with "true" responses, however. Although there was some difference in slope (i.e., the effects of increases in distance on the face) between the full-size and half-size conditions, these differences were not as large as would be expected if length were varied. This may have been because (a) people sometimes varied the area of their images and sometimes varied the length, or usually used a compromise of the two measures when determining how to scale the images and/or (b) people may have performed some other sort of processing when evaluating short distances on subjectively small images. That is, with the half-size images, the 7.62-cm separation may have seemed so slight that the eyes were visible even as one focused on the mouth. If so, scanning may not have been necessary to evaluate the imaged eyes, and these times thus may have been faster than predicted. This would result in a larger difference between the times necessary to evaluate eyes of faces with short and long distances than we expected—and hence less of a difference in the effects of increased distance in the half- and full-size conditions. The error rates suggested that subjects may in fact have been doing some more rapid, but less cautious, processing for the shortest distance in the half-size condition.

The failure to obtain slope differences for different-sized images on the false trials is not easily explained. There is some evidence, however (see Kosslyn, 1975), that people have more difficulty in using images to arrive at a "false" decision; the present data may simply reflect inconsistent use of imagery on the trials where the probed color was not in fact on the image.

Finally, it is worth noting that the results of this experiment allow us to eliminate one more possible nonimagery interpretation of the scanning effects. That is, one could claim that the closer two objects or parts are, the more likely it is that they will be grouped into the same "chunk" during encoding. Presumably, parts encoded into the same chunk are retrieved in sequence more quickly than parts in different chunks. In this experiment, size of an image was not manipulated until after the drawing was removed, precluding systematic differences in encoding among the three size conditions. Thus, the fact that subjectively larger images generally required more time to scan than did smaller ones seems to run counter to the notion that spatial extent affected scan times only because of a confounding between distance and the probability of being encoded into a single unit.

## General Discussion

The present experiments converge in demonstrating that people can scan the distances embodied in images. More time was required to scan further distances, even when the same number of items fell between the focus and target locations. In addition, subjectively larger images required more time to scan than did subjectively smaller ones. Somewhat surprisingly, we found that the effects of distance persisted even when a person "zoomed in" on one part, such that the remainder of the image seemed to overflow. These results suggest that a part of an image may exist "waiting in the wings," ready to be activated into consciousness if needed. Finally, there were no effects of distance on decision times when people did not actually use their images, even though an image had been generated and focused upon. These results taken together indicate that images are pictorial in at least one respect: Like pictures, images seem to embody information about actual interval spatial extents. The present experiments support the claim that portions of images depict corresponding portions of the represented object(s) and that the spatial relations between portions of the imaged object(s) are preserved by the spatial relations between the corresponding portions of the image. These qualities are apparent in our introspections, and the present experiments suggest that people can operate on the representations we experience as quasi-pictorial mental images.

Given our results, how do we account for Lea's (1975) failure to find systematic effects of distance on evaluation times? First, the results of Experiment 3 suggest that Lea's results may simply reflect his failure to ensure that subjects responded only after "seeing" the target in their image. If left to their own devices in making decisions, subjects would probably find a nonimagery strategy to be faster, and such a nonimagery strategy would not result in distance influencing decision times. Second, Lea's task was so difficult (the mean reaction times reach as high as 8 sec) that effects of distance (which are measured in milliseconds, not seconds) may simply have been drowned out by the nonscanning components of this task. Finally, even if imagery were used, Lea's ordered search task, which involved counting successive items, may have induced subjects to generate a sequence of separate images, each representing an object in the array, rather than to attempt to hold and then scan a complex image (see Kosslyn, 1975, for evidence that more complex images are more difficult to maintain). Weber, Kelley, & Little (1972) report that people can "verbally prompt" sequences of images, and something like this may have occurred in Lea's experiment. If so, then we have no reason to expect distance to affect response times.

In closing, it seems worthwhile to consider briefly two possible conceptualizations of how image scanning might operate. The most obvious notion (two variants of which were suggested by Kosslyn, 1973) is that scanning consists of moving an activated region over a spatial representation, somewhat like moving a spotlight across an unlit billboard. However, the spatial display used in representing images presumably also is used in representing sensory input from the eyes (see Hebb, 1968; Segal & Fusella, 1970) and hence only need represent information from some limited visual arc that corresponds to the scope of the eyes. If so, then one ought to find that one "hits the edge of the billboard" if one scans too far in any given direction. Many people report, however, being able to scan to objects "behind" them in an image and even being able to scan in a seemingly continuous circle across all four walls of an imaged room. There is another way of conceptualizing image scanning that deals with these sorts of observations naturally and easily.

In the Kosslyn & Shwartz (1977) computer simulation of visual mental imagery, it was most elegant to treat scanning as a kind of image transformation, in the same class as mental rotation and size alteration. Here, scanning consists of moving an image across the image display structure, the center of which is posited to be most highly activated (and hence, portions of the image falling under the center are most sharply in focus). In this case, the analogy would be to moving a billboard or sequence of billboards under a fixed spotlight. According to this notion, then, scanning 360° around one in an image would be accomplished by continuously constructing new material at the edge and shifting it across the image display. If nothing else, this approach may have heuristic value by leading us to look for similarities among scanning and other image transformations.

In conclusion, the present results converge in supporting the claim that the experienced quasi-pictorial surface image is functional and is not simply an epiphenomenal concomitant of more abstract "deep" processes. Comprehensive models of memory will probably have to include more than the sort of propositional list structures currently in vogue (e.g., Anderson, 1976, Anderson & Bower, 1973).

## ACKNOWLEDGMENTS

This work was supported by National Institute of Mental Health Grant 1 R03 MH 27012–01 and National Science Foundation Grant BNS 76–16987 awarded to the first author. We thank Phil Greenbarg and Dan Estridge for technical assistance.

## NOTES

1. We will use terms like *distance* and *size* in referring to mental images, even though images themselves—not being objects—do not have such physical dimensions. Nevertheless, we claim that images represent these dimensions in the same way that they are encoded in the representations underlying the experience of seeing during perception. Thus, we experience images as if we were seeing a large or small object, or one at a relatively near or far distance from us. In addition, the apparent distances between parts of an imaged object are experienced in the same way that one would experience apprehending the distances when seeing the parts of the object. We will use the term *quasi-pictorial* in referring to these sorts of pictorial properties of an image, because an image—not being an object—cannot have the physical properties of an actual picture. For convenience, we will refer to an imaged object that is experienced as being some subjective size as if the image were that size, and we will refer to apparent distances on an imaged object as if they were distances on the image itself.

# REFERENCES

Anderson, J. R. *Language, Memory, and Thought*. Hillsdale, N.J.: Erlbaum, 1976.

Anderson, J. R. & Bower, G. H. *Human Associative Memory*. New York: Wiley, 1973.

Clark, H. H. The language-as-fixed-effect fallacy: A critique of language statistics in psychological research. *Journal of Verbal Learning and Verbal Behavior* 1973, *12*, 335–359.

Hebb, D. O. Concerning imagery. *Psychological Review*, 1968, *75*, 466–477.

Kosslyn, S. M. Scanning visual images: Some structural implications. *Perception & Psychophysics*, 1973, *14*, 90–94.

Kosslyn, S. M. Information representation in visual images. *Cognitive Psychology*, 1975, *7*, 341–370.

Kosslyn, S. M. Can imagery be distinguished from other forms of internal representation? Evidence from studies of information retrieval time. *Memory & Cognition*, 1976, *4*, 291–297.

Kosslyn, S. M. & Pomerantz, J. R. Imagery propositions, and the form of interval representations. *Cognitive Psychology*, 1977, *9*, 52–76.

Kosslyn, S. M. & Shwartz, S. P. A simulation of visual imagery. *Cognitive Science*, 1977, *1*, 265–295.

Lea, G. Chronometric analysis of the method of loci. *Journal of Experimental Psychology: Human Perception and Performance*, 1975, *1*, 95–104.

Segal, S. J. & Fusella, V. Influence of imaged pictures and sounds on detection of visual and auditory signals. *Journal of Experimental Psychology*, 1970, *83*, 458–464.

Weber, R. J., Kelley, J., & Little, S. Is visual imagery sequencing under verbal control? *Journal of Experimental Psychology*, 1972, *96*, 354–362.

# Mental Rotation of Three-Dimensional Objects

Roger N. Shepard and Jacqueline Metzler
• Department of Psychology, Stanford University

The time required to recognize that two perspective drawings portray objects of the same three-dimensional shape is found to be (i) a linearly increasing function of the angular difference in the portrayed orientations of the two objects and (ii) no shorter for differences corresponding simply to a rigid rotation of one of the two-dimensional drawings in its own picture plane than for differences corresponding to a rotation of the three-dimensional object in depth.

Human subjects are often able to determine that two two-dimensional pictures portray objects of the same three-dimensional shape even though the objects are depicted in very different orientations. The experiment reported here was designed to measure the time that subjects require to determine such identity of shape as a function of the angular difference in the portrayed orientations of the two three-dimensional objects.

This angular difference was produced either by a rigid rotation of one of two identical pictures in its own picture plane or by a much more complex, nonrigid transformation, of one of the pictures, that corresponds to a (rigid) rotation of the three-dimensional object in depth.

This reaction time is found (i) to increase linearly with the angular difference in portrayed orientation and (ii) to be no longer for a rotation in depth than for a rotation merely in the picture plane. These findings appear to place rather severe constraints on possible explanations of how subjects go about determining identity of shape of

differently oriented objects. They are, however, consistent with an explanation suggested by the subjects themselves. Although introspective reports must be interpreted with caution, all subjects claimed (i) that to make the required comparison they first had to imagine one object as rotated into the same orientation as the other and that they could carry out this "mental rotation" at no greater than a certain limiting rate; and (ii) that, since they perceived the two-dimensional pictures as objects in three-dimensional space, they could imagine the rotation around whichever axis was required with equal ease.

In the experiment, each of eight adult subjects was presented with 1600 pairs of perspective line drawings. For each pair the subject was asked to pull a right-hand lever as soon as he determined that the two drawings portrayed objects that were congruent with respect to three-dimensional shape and to pull a left-hand lever as soon as he determined that the two drawings depicted objects of different three-dimensional shapes. According to

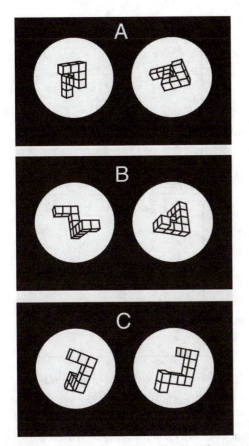

**FIGURE 15.1** ■ Examples of pairs of perspective line drawings presented to the subjects. (A) A "same" pair, which differs by an 80°rotation in the picture plane; (B) a "same" pair, which differs by an 80° rotation in depth; and (C) a "different" pair, which cannot be brought into congruence by *any* rotation.

a random sequence, in half of the pairs (the "same" pairs) the two objects could be rotated into congruence with each other (as in Figure 15.1A and B), and in the other half (the "different" pairs) the two objects differed by a reflection as well as a rotation and could not be rotated into congruence (as in Figure 15.1C).

The choice of objects that were mirror images or "isomers" of each other for the "different" pairs was intended to prevent subjects from discovering some distinctive feature possessed by only one of the two objects and thereby reaching a decision of noncongruence without actually having to carry out any mental rotation. As a further precaution,

the ten different three-dimensional objects depicted in the various perspective drawings were chosen to be relatively unfamiliar and meaningless in overall three-dimensional shape.

Each object consisted of ten solid cubes attached face-to-face to form a rigid armlike structure with exactly three right-angled "elbows" (see Figure 15.1) The set of all ten shapes included two subsets of five: within either subset, no shape could be transformed into itself or any other by any reflection or rotation (short of 360°). However, each shape in either subset was the mirror image of one shape in the other subset, as required for the construction of the "different" pairs.

For each of the ten objects, 18 different perspective projections—corresponding to one complete turn around the vertical axis by 20° steps—were generated by digital computer and associated graphical output ($I$). Seven of the 18 perspective views of each object were then selected so as (i) to avoid any views in which some part of the object was wholly occluded by another part and yet (ii) to permit the construction of two pairs that differed in orientation by each possible angle, in 20° steps, from 0° to 180°. These 70 line drawings were then reproduced by photo-offset process and were attached to cards in pairs for presentation to the subjects.

Half of the "same" pairs (the "depth" pairs) represented two objects that differed by some multiple of a 20° rotation about a vertical axis (Figure 15.1B). For each of these pairs, copies of two appropriately different perspective views were simply attached to the cards in the orientation in which they were originally generated. The other half of the "same" pairs (the "picture-plane". pairs) represented two objects that differed by some multiple of a 20° rotation in the plane of the drawings themselves (Figure 15.1A). For each of these, one of the seven perspective views was selected for each object and two copies of this picture were attached to the card in appropriately different orientations. Altogether, the 1600 pairs presented to each subject included 800 "same" pairs, which consisted of 400 unique pairs (20 "depth" and 20 "picture-plane" pairs at each of the ten angular differences from 0° to 180°), each of which was presented twice. The remaining 800 pairs, randomly intermixed with these, consisted of 400 unique "different" pairs, each of which (again) was presented twice. Each of these "different" pairs corresponded to one "same" pair (of either the "depth" or "picture-plane" variety) in which, however, one of the three-dimensional objects had been reflected about some plane in three-dimensional space. Thus the two objects in each "different" pair differed, in general, by both a reflection and a rotation.

The 1600 pairs were grouped into blocks of not more than 200 and presented over eight to ten 1-hour sessions (depending upon the subject). Also, although it is only of incidental interest here, each such block of presentations was either "pure," in that all pairs involved rotations of the same type ("depth" or "picture-plane"), or "mixed," in that the two types of rotation were randomly intermixed within the same block.

Each trial began with a warning tone, which was followed half a second later by the presentation of a stimulus pair and the simultaneous onset of a timer. The lever-pulling response stopped the timer, recorded the subject's reaction time and terminated the visual display. The line drawings, which averaged between 4 and 5 cm in maximum linear extent, appeared at a viewing distance of about 60 cm. They were positioned, with a center-to-center spacing that subtended a visual angle of 9°, in two circular apertures in a vertical black surface (see Figure 15.1A to C).

The subjects were instructed to respond as quickly as possible while keeping errors to a minimum. On the average only 3.2 percent of the responses were incorrect (ranging from 0.6 to 5.7 percent for individual subjects). The reaction-time data presented below include only the 96.8 percent correct responses. However, the data for the incorrect responses exhibit a similar pattern.

In Figure 15.2 the overall means of the reaction times as a function of angular difference in orientation for all correct (right-hand) responses to "same" pairs are plotted separately for the pairs differing by a rotation in the picture plane (Figure 15.2A) and for the pairs differing by a rotation in depth (Figure 15.2B). In both cases, reaction time is a strikingly linear function of the angular difference between the two three-dimensional objects portrayed. The mean reaction times for individual subjects increased from a value of about 1 second at 0° of rotation for all subjects to values ranging from 4 to 6 seconds at 180° of rotation, depending upon the particular individual. Moreover, despite

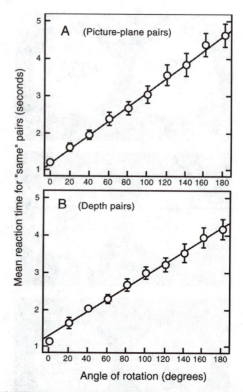

FIGURE 15.2 ■ Mean reaction times to two perspective line drawings portraying objects of the same three-dimensional shape. Times are plotted as a function of angular difference in portrayed orientation: (A) for pairs differing by a rotation in the picture plane only; and (B) for pairs differing by a rotation in depth. (The centers of the circles indicate the means and, when they extend far enough to show outside these circles, the vertical bars around each circle indicate a conservative estimate of the standard error of that mean based on the distribution of the eight component means contributed by the individual subjects.)

such variations in slope, the *linearity* of the function is clearly evident when the data are plotted separately for individual three-dimensional objects or for individual subjects. Polynomial regression lines were computed separately for each subject under each type of rotation. In all 16 cases the functions were found to have a highly significant linear component ($P < .001$) when tested against deviations from linearity. No significant quadratic or higher-order effects were found ($P > .05$, in all cases).

The angle through which different three-dimensional shapes must be rotated to achieve congruence is not, of course, defined. Therefore, a function like those plotted in Figure 15.2 cannot be constructed in any straightforward manner for the "different" pairs. The *overall* mean reaction time for these pairs was found, however, to be 3.8 seconds—nearly a second longer than the corresponding overall means for the "same" pairs. (In the postexperimental interview, the subjects typically reported that they attempted to rotate one end of one object into congruence with the corresponding end of the other object; they discovered that the two objects were *different* when, after this "rotation," the two free ends still remained noncongruent.)

Not only are the two functions shown in Figure 15.3 both linear but they are very similar to each other with respect to intercept and slope. Indeed, for the larger angular differences the reaction times were, if anything, somewhat shorter for rotation in depth than for rotation in the picture plane. However, since this small difference is either absent or reversed in four of the eight subjects, it is of doubtful significance. The determination of identity of shape may therefore be based, in both cases, upon a process of the same general kind. If we can describe this process as some sort of "mental rotation in three-dimensional space," then the slope of the obtained functions indicates that the average rate at which these particular objects can be thus "rotated" is roughly 60° per second.

Of course the plotted reaction times necessarily include any times taken by the subjects to decide how to process the pictures in each presented pair as well as the time taken actually to carry out the process, once it was chosen. However, even for these highly practiced subjects, the reaction times were still linear and were no more than 20 percent lower in the "pure" blocks of presentations (in which the subjects knew both the axis and the direction of the required rotation in advance of each presentation) than in the "mixed" blocks (in which the axis of rotation was unpredictable). Tentatively, this suggests that 80 percent of a typical one of these reaction times may represent some such process as "mental rotation" itself, rather than a preliminary process of preparation or search. Nevertheless, in further research now underway, we are seeking clarification of this point and others.

## REFERENCES AND NOTES

1. Mrs. Jih-Jie Chang of the Bell Telephone Laboratories generated the 180 perspective projections for us by means of the Bell Laboratories' Stromberg-Carlson 4020 microfilm recorder and the computer program for constructing such projections developed there by A. M. Noll. See, for example, A. M. Noll, *Computers Automation* **14**, 20 (1965).
2. We thank Mrs. Chang [see: (*1*)] and we also thank Dr. J. D. Elashoff for her suggestions concerning the statistical analyses. Assistance in the computer graphics was provided by the Bell Telephone Laboratories. Supported by NSF grant GS-2283 to R.N.S.

# Reinterpreting Visual Patterns
# in Mental Imagery

Ronald A. Finke • Texas A&M University
Steven Pinker • Massachusetts Institute of Technology
Martha J. Farah • Carnegie-Mellon University

In a recent paper, Chambers and Reisberg (1985) showed that people cannot reverse classical ambiguous figures in imagery (such as the Necker cube, duck/rabbit, or Schroeder staircase). In three experiments, we refute one kind of explanation for this difficulty: that visual images do not contain information about the geometry of a shape necessary for reinterpreting it or that people cannot apply shape classification procedures to the information in imagery. We show, that given suitable conditions, people can assign novel interpretations to ambiguous images which have been constructed out of parts or mentally transformed. For example, when asked to imagine the letter "D" on its side, affixed to the top of the letter "J", subjects spontaneously report "seeing" an umbrella. We also show that these reinterpretations are not the result of guessing strategies, and that they speak directly to the issue of whether or not mental images of ambiguous figures can be reconstrued. Finally, we show that arguments from the philosophy literature on the relation between images and descriptions are not relevant to the issue of whether images can be reinterpreted, and we suggest possible explanations for why classical ambiguous figures do not spontaneously reverse in imagery.

At least since Berkeley's time, the question of whether mental images can be ambiguous has held a central place in the debate over the nature of imagery. It is easy to see why the two issues are so closely related. The process of perception begins with the geometry of the retinal images, and ends with a description of objects in the world. The controversy over imagery has largely concerned whether images are like early perceptual representations containing information about the geometric properties of visual inputs, or like later cognitive representations containing information about the conceptual categories of interpreted objects (Kosslyn & Pomerantz, 1977; Pylyshyn, 1973). If memory images preserve some of the geometric information in perceptual representations, it should be possible for the imager to recognize the presence of an object category in an image that was not originally assigned when the object was first seen. In the most dramatic case, an imager should be able to observe an ambiguous figure, such as a Necker cube or a duck/rabbit, see it as one object (e.g., a duck), form a visual image of it when it is no longer present, and then be able to see it as the other object (e.g., a rabbit). On the other hand, if memory images are records of the conceptual category or interpretation assigned to the stimulus when it was viewed, and information about its geometric properties is lost or not readily accessible to interpretative processes, then a reassignment of the category of an object should be impossible; the imager should be stuck with whatever interpretation he or she assigned to the stimulus when it was visible.

Several experimental investigations have cast doubt on people's ability to recategorize images of ambiguous figures. An experiment reported by Reed (1974) explored whether subjects could detect "hidden" figures in images of patterns that were composed of combinations of geometric forms. For example, one of the patterns was formed by superimposing two equilateral triangles, one pointing up, and the other pointing down, positioned such that the vertex of one was centered on the base of the other. After a brief retention interval, the subjects were shown a second pattern, and their task was to say whether or not that pattern was a part of the first pattern. Reed found that subjects could easily detect only those parts that would enter into a structural description of the pattern, such as one of the equilateral triangles, but not a part that cuts across the elements of such a description, such as a parallelogram. Reed and Johnson (1975) later found that the parts not fitting into the original composition of a complex pattern could be detected much more easily when subjects could inspect the original patterns at the time of testing, than when they had to rely on a memory image. Because subjects in these experiments could rarely detect the hidden parts in their images, these results suggested that images, unlike visually perceived forms, cannot be reinterpreted or reorganized. Rather, what is detected in an image may depend entirely on how the imagined pattern was initially conceived (see also the relevant work of Hinton, 1979 and Stevens & Coupe, 1978).

These findings conflict with the observations of other imagery theorists who have claimed that the ability to "see" new patterns in an image is one of the prime functions of imagery, for example, in scientific and artistic creativity (Shepard, 1978). More importantly, there are demonstrations that people *can* detect new patterns in transformed images. Pinker and Finke (1980) reported a series of experiments in which subjects were able to "see" shapes that emerged in the projection of a three-dimensional configuration of objects after it was mentally rotated. Shepard and Feng (reported in Shepard & Cooper, 1982) demonstrated that subjects could quickly name the letter resulting from a transformation (rotation, reflection, or some combination of the two) of a starting letter. For example, when given the transformation "rotate 90 degrees" and the starting letter "N," subjects could reconstrue the resulting image as a "Z." In an experiment similar to those of Reed, Slee (1980, Experiment 3) found that subjects were able to judge, with success rates greater than chance, whether various geometric forms were present as embedded figures in patterns they had imagined. In another experiment, Slee demonstrated that subjects could construct a mental image from separately viewed pieces and then detect emergent forms resulting from a reorganization of the imagined pieces according to the Gestalt laws of proximity and common fate. Hollins (1985) had a group of subjects imagine a grid and mentally fill in certain squares specified in terms of their Cartesian coordinates. On different trials, the experimenter dictated patterns of filled-in squares resembling a dog, a pitcher, a wall plug, a car, and a telephone. Subjects were able to say what the resulting image depicted on about half of the trials.

Related indirect evidence comes from experiments on visual synthesis of parts. Palmer (1977) had subjects mentally synthesize patterns by mentally superimposing two visually presented parts consisting of connected line segments. They then had to match the synthesized pattern against visual probes. The task was easiest when the subpatterns corresponded to perceptually "good" geometric figures such as triangles and boxes, as opposed to open or disconnected collections of line segments. However, subjects reported that even when the original subpatterns were not "good," they "looked" for emergent "good" figures in the synthesized whole, with greater or lesser success on different trials. Apparently, at least some subjects were quite successful with this strategy: Their matching times were uniformly fast for shapes synthesized out of good, moderately good, and bad parts. Thompson and Klatzky (1978) obtained this effect more uniformly by having subjects mentally superimpose sets of visually presented angles and lines that together defined unified geometric shapes such as a parallelogram. They found that subjects really did treat the result as an emergent single form: When matching these patterns against probe stimuli, they were no slower when they had synthesized the pattern by superimposing two or three parts than when they had actually seen the pattern in its entirety.

However, a paper has appeared recently whose authors try to make a strong case that the reconstrual of mental images is impossible. Chambers and Reisberg (1985) conducted a set of four experiments aimed at assessing whether people can reinterpret an ambiguous figure stored in a mental image. In their experiments, subjects inspected ambiguous forms, such as the "duck/rabbit" figure commonly used to demonstrate multistability in visual perception (e.g., Attneave, 1971), and were then instructed to form mental images of the forms and to try to see the reversals in their images. Although the subjects were previously trained in detecting such reversals using other types of reversible figures, they never once reported the correct reversal in their imagery. This negative finding persisted even when the subjects were screened for high imagery vividness. In addition, the subjects *were* able to reverse the figures when they later drew the figures from memory and inspected their drawings. Chambers and Reisberg concluded that mental images are therefore not subject to reconstrual, in contrast to visually perceived forms, because images do not contain uninterpreted information; the implication is that images are *nothing but* interpretations or construals. Chambers and Reisberg also offer reasons why the earlier demonstrations of emergent pattern recognition in images should not be considered as bona fide examples of reconstruing an image. They attempt to draw further support for their claims from arguments in the philosophical literature on imagery, which putatively show that images must consist of or at least be accompanied by interpretations, rather than being raw percept-like entities.

The issue of whether images can be reconstrued is of crucial importance to the study of imagery and mental representation. If reconstrual is possible, then images are not *just* conceptual or symbolic representations, but must also contain some of the geometric information available to interpretive processes in perception. In this article we examine the general claim, made most recently by

Chambers and Reisberg, that people cannot reconstrue images, and the explanation for such a deficit that would claim that images lack "uninterpreted" information pertaining to the geometry of an object, or that such information is sealed off from the procedures that derive conceptual interpretations from visual geometric information. We show that, on the contrary, given suitable conditions people can reconstrue, reinterpret, or assign a novel conceptual description to a pattern represented in an image. Furthermore, we argue that (a) there are no sound arguments why such abilities should not be considered as examples of reconstrual; (b) there are alternative explanations of why duck/rabbit figures, Necker cubes, and the like would be difficult to reverse in an image even if people do possess the ability to reconstrue imagined patterns in general; and (c) arguments in the philosophical literature on imagery, such as those cited by Chambers and Reisberg, have no relevance to this strictly empirical question.

To begin with, we report three demonstrations of experiments in which subjects are presented with descriptions of a pattern, and are then asked to report new patterns that are embedded in the described figure, or are asked to identify the name of a new object that the described pattern depicts. These new objects were unlikely to have been predicted from the initial description, since the initial description implied a construal of the pattern very different from the one we expected subjects to be able to make.

Such a demonstration is necessary because the previous literature on seeing emergent patterns in images does not provide evidence on image reconstrual that is sufficiently strong to convince a skeptic. Chambers and Reisberg point out that in most cases of apparent image reconstrual, subjects could have generated images of candidate reconstruals and compared each candidate against the original images, until a match was found. For example, in the Shepard and Feng study, subjects could have imagined each letter of the alphabet to compare it with a rotated "N," stopping when they generated a "Z," and noted its structural identity with the rotated "N." Chambers and Reisberg argue that hypothesizing an interpretation and then verifying it against an image is not the same as spontaneously assigning a novel interpretation to the image based on its inherent geometric properties. Although we will argue later that such a distinction is not a useful one, it would still be useful to show that subjects can report a novel appropriate construal of an imagined pattern in cases where a pattern must first be construed according to one description, and then another construal is detected which has a vanishingly small chance of being hypothesized a priori.

There are other weaknesses in the previous findings of image reconstrual that motivate the present studies as well: First, it is possible that the reconstrual of the imagined stimulus was noticed during the perceptual encoding of the stimulus, and was not actually detected for the first time in the image. Second, the reconstrual rates are so low that one might view the occasional reconstrual of an image as the exception rather than the rule. Accordingly, we will present the results of new studies in which the task is simple enough to elicit high reconstrual rates (if subjects do indeed possess such a capacity), in which the new interpretation of a pattern could not have been the result of some subjects having encoded that interpretation while the stimulus was actually visible, and in which the subjects are not asked to verify *whether* a form is present in an image, but must *discover* *which* form is actually present.

# Experiment 1

In this experiment, we asked subjects to superimpose or juxtapose mental images of familiar patterns, such as alphanumeric characters and simple geometric forms, to see if they could mentally detect any new patterns as a result of their combination. In particular, we were interested to see whether subjects could "reparse" the features in one imagined form when the other was combined with it, enabling them to recognize patterns that were not present in either form separately.

Our task differs from those of Reed (1974) and Slee (1980) in one important respect: Instead of requiring that a single imagined form be reorganized or reconstrued in order to detect certain features, in our task the features to be detected would not be available until two imagined forms were combined in the proper way. For example, subjects would be asked to imagine an upper case "X" superimposed upon an upper case "H," which should result in the depiction of a butterfly, a bowtie, the letter "M," four right triangles, or other

recognizable forms. Thus, subjects would be given the information necessary to create an ambiguous image (e.g., a form that could be construed either as a "superimposed H and X" or as a "butterfly"), and would be tested for their ability to assign an alternative construal to the image and report it.

## Method

### SUBJECTS

Twelve undergraduate students at the State University of New York at Stony Brook served as subjects, in partial fulfillment of a research requirement in an introductory psychology course.

### PROCEDURE

The subjects were tested individually in one-hour sessions. They were told that the experiment would investigate certain characteristics of mental imagery, and that they would be asked to visualize patterns formed out of combinations of familiar symbols or shapes. The experimenter would then ask them to describe any new features or patterns that they could detect while inspecting their mental images. Because the experimenter would be in contact with the subjects throughout the experiment, we were careful to use a naive experimenter in this and all following experiments, as recommended by Intons-Peterson (1983).

The experiment began by showing the subjects two demonstrations of what we wanted them to try to do using their imagery. For example, they were first told that they might be asked to "imagine a square," and were shown a drawing of a black outlined square on a white background, to illustrate exactly how their initial mental image should look. This was followed by the instruction "Now add a diagonal line connecting the upper right-hand corner and the lower left-hand corner," and by the presentation of a second drawing in which the line was added to the square in the described manner. This second drawing depicted how the subject's image should look after the second pattern was added to it. The experimenter then pointed out on this drawing examples of emergent forms that could be detected, such as two right triangles having a common hypotenuse, the letter "Z," and an upside-down "N."

The subjects were told that in the actual imagery

task they were to report as many of these emergent forms as they were able to detect. In every case, they were to line up the described patterns in their images so that end points or edges would always match up. Letters were always to be imagined as capital letters. When reporting the emergent patterns, they were to be as precise as possible about the relative size, orientation or position of the patterns. If they didn't know the name of a particular form or shape, they were to describe it in their own words.

Following the demonstrations, the experimenter instructed the subject to close his or her eyes, and then read descriptions of one of six pairs of experimental patterns, shown in Figure 16.1. These were selected on the basis of two criteria: (a) The individual patterns were all familiar, consisting of letters, numbers, or simple geometric forms,

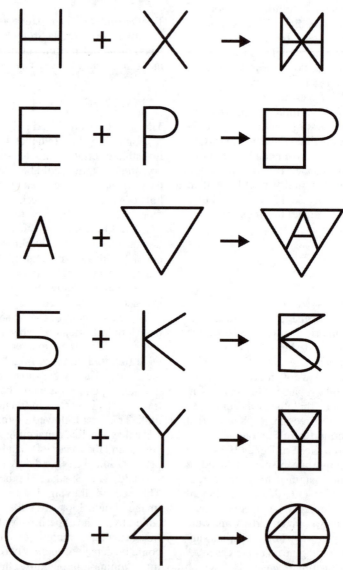

**FIGURE 16.1** ■ In Experiment 1, subjects were instructed to imagine superimposing or juxtaposing the first two patterns in each row. The patterns shown to the right of the arrows are those that would result if the imagined synthesis were performed correctly.

making them easy to imagine, and (b) their super-position yielded a pattern that consisted of or contained novel entities associated with conceptual labels. Some of these entities consisted of simple geometric forms (e.g., "triangle"); others consisted of depictions of objects or figures in some conceptual category (e.g., "butterfly," "the number eight"). The experimenter then instructed the subjects to report any emergent forms that they detected in their images, while always keeping their eyes closed, and then wrote their descriptions down on a response sheet. After the subjects reported that they could not detect any more emergent forms, they were asked to say whether or not they had formed a clear mental image. Following this, they were asked to open their eyes and to draw the final pattern that they had imagined. Then they were asked to inspect their drawing and to report any additional emergent forms that they could now detect but that they hadn't seen in their images. This same procedure was repeated for all six pairs of patterns. The patterns were imagined in random order across the 12 subjects, resulting in a total of 72 imagery reports.

We also asked subjects at the end of the experiment to report whether or not they had any difficulties finding the emergent forms in their images, and if so, to explain what problems they encountered.

## Results and Discussion

In scoring the number of emergent forms reported, we adopted conservative conventions. First, only those forms that would *not* have been present in either of the individually described patterns were counted. For example, in the pair in which the letters "H" and "X" were to be combined in an image (see Figure 15.1), subjects might report detecting the letter "M" and a sideways letter "T," but only the former would be counted as an emergent form. This is because the letter "T" could be detected in the letter "H" alone. In addition, when the same emergent form could appear two or more times in the imagined pattern, reports of that form were counted only once. We also distinguished between geometric and symbolic emergent forms; for example, between reports of detecting "two adjacent squares" and "the number eight." Although we expected that the geometric forms might be easier to detect, reports of symbolic forms might

be better examples of reconstruing images, or assigning them new interpretations. Finally, we did not count reports of isolated features (such as "curved lines" or "brackets"), or reports of forms that could not be verified from the subjects' drawings of what they had imagined.

The results showed that an abundance of emergent forms were detected in the constructed images. Summing across all subjects and stimulus patterns, there were 120 reports of geometric forms and 39 reports of symbolic forms during the imagery task. Of the 12 subjects, all 12 reported at least one novel geometric form, and 9 of the 12 reported at least one novel symbolic form. Of the emergent symbolic forms reported, 29 of the reports were of alphanumeric characters, and 10 were of other types of familiar shapes. Some of the more interesting emergent symbolic forms detected in imagery were a "tilted hourglass" in the "H" and "X" combination, a "5-sided diamond" or "pentagon" in the "A" and "inverted triangle" combination, and a sideways "grain silo" in the "E" and "P" combination. Subjects' drawings revealed that they superimposed the patterns correctly on 68 of the 72 trials, and the subjects reported having formed a clear image 86.1% of the time. The number of different emergent forms based on the images ranged from 8 to 21 across different subjects. The distribution of reports of emergent geometric and symbolic forms for each stimulus pair is presented in Table 16.1.[1]

In sum, we have shown that people are capable of "seeing" shapes in images even when those shapes did not enter into the description or decomposition of the shape initially provided to the subject. We cannot be sure why our findings differ so strongly from those of Reed (1974) and of Reed and Johnsen (1975), who had reported that people are largely unsuccessful at detecting structurally "hidden" forms in imagined patterns. One possibility is that Reed's subjects had to reinterpret, from memory, whole, previously seen patterns that were fairly complex (consisting of 6–16 line segments). Recent experiments by Kosslyn, Reiser, Farah, and Fliegel (1983) have shown that the parts of an image are not generated all at once; instead, it takes a certain amount of time to generate each part. Because the parts begin to fade as soon as they are generated, patterns that cut across several old parts may not be entirely present in an image at a single instant, depending on the total number

TABLE 16.1. Number of Correct Reports of Emergent Patterns in Experiment 1 for Each Pair of Stimulus Patterns

| Stimulus Patterns | Type of Emergent Pattern | | | |
| | Image | | Drawing | |
| | Geometric | Symbolic | Geometric | Symbolic |
| --- | --- | --- | --- | --- |
| "H" + "Y" | 16 | 16 | 2 | 7 |
| "E" + "P" | 12 | 8 | 1 | 1 |
| "A" + Triangle | 22 | 3 | 2 | 6 |
| "5" + "K" | 16 | 4 | 5 | 8 |
| Squares + "Y" | 39 | 4 | 0 | 4 |
| Circle + "4" | 15 | 4 | 1 | 5 |

*Note.* The number of reports are summed over the 12 experimental subjects. The emergent patterns reported in the drawings include only those that were not detected in the subjects' mental images.

of parts that must be generated to create the image. Thus in the Reed studies, the initial parsing of the complex pattern into parts may have obviated opportunities for the subjects to have detected cross-cutting patterns. In the present experiment, the assembled patterns were relatively simple (consisting of 4–8 line segments).

## Experiment 2

The previous demonstrations of emergent recognition might be limited, however, in one respect. Very few of the emergent symbolic forms corresponded to what might be regarded as reconstruals of the entire pattern. By way of contrast, recall that Chambers and Reisberg (1985) found that textbook examples of ambiguous figures, where the whole pattern would have to be reconstrued, and not just some of its parts, could not be perceptually "reversed" in imagery. Their negative findings suggest that people may not be able to change the entire interpretation of an imagined pattern, although they may still be able to detect some emergent features or parts that they did not anticipate. That is, while people might be capable of verifying aspects of the appearance of an object in an image, they do not have the ability to determine what other interpretations the geometric properties of an imagined shape are capable of supporting, because the image itself contains no information that is not part of a conceptual interpretation.

In Experiment 2, we modified our imagery task to see whether subjects could ever recognize that

an entire image corresponded to a familiar form associated with a particular symbol or interpretation that they would not have assigned in advance. We started with a familiar pattern, like a letter or number, and then asked subjects to imagine transforming the pattern until it would correspond to a different pattern which they would be called on to identify.

## Method

### SUBJECTS

The 12 subjects who participated in Experiment 1 also participated in this experiment, again receiving research credit in an introductory psychology course at Stony Brook.

### PROCEDURE

Subjects were told that they would begin each trial by hearing the name of a familiar pattern, whereupon they were to form a mental image of it. The experimenter would then ask them to imagine altering the appearance of the pattern in various ways, and to try to identify the resulting pattern.

As in Experiment 1, two demonstrations were provided to illustrate exactly how the imagery task was to be performed. For example:

Imagine the letter "Q." Put the letter "O" next to it on the left. Remove the diagonal line. Now rotate the figure 90 degrees to the left. The pattern is the number "8." There were six image transformation trials for each subject; these are shown

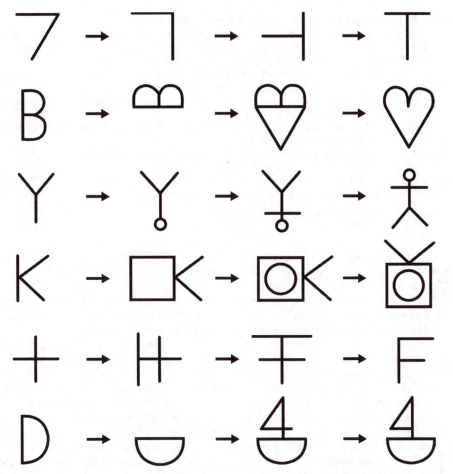

**FIGURE 16.2** ■ In Experiment 2, subjects were instructed to begin by imagining the patterns shown at the left of each row and then to imagine transforming the patterns as the illustration depicts. The final patterns in each sequence are the emergent patterns that subjects were to try to recognize. (Descriptions of these sequences that were read to subjects are provided in Table 16.2.)

in Figure 16.2. Descriptions for these sequences are presented in Table 16.2. At the end of the transformation sequence, the experimenter recorded the subject's identification of the final pattern; the correct identifications were, respectively, the letter "T," a "heart," a "stick figure," a "TV set," the letter "F," and a "sailboat." As in Experiment 1, they performed the imagery task while keeping their eyes closed. They were then asked to report whether or not they had formed a clear mental image of the final pattern. After opening their eyes, they were asked to draw the pattern from memory, and to try to identify it from the drawing if they did not do so during imagery. This procedure was repeated for all trials. The order of transformation sequences was randomized, and at the end of the experiment the subjects were

asked to report any difficulties they might have had transforming their images.

## Results and Discussion

The results are presented in Table 16.3, according to how accurately the imagined transformation was performed, based on the subjects' drawings. A "correct" transformation refers to one that was perfectly correct, a "partial" transformation refers to one that exhibited some minor perturbation or error, but was otherwise accurate, and a "wrong" transformation refers to one that differed substantially from that intended by the description. The identifications were also distinguished according

**TABLE 16.2. Transformation Sequences Read to Subjects in Experiment 2**

"Imagine the number '7'. Make the diagonal line vertical. Move the horizontal line down to the middle of the vertical line. Now rotate the figure 90 degrees to the left." (The letter "T")

"Imagine the letter 'B'. Rotate it 90 degrees to the left. Put a triangle directly below it having the same width and pointing down. Remove the horizontal line." (A heart)

"Imagine the letter 'Y'. Put a small circle at the bottom of it. Add a horizontal line halfway up. Now rotate the figure 180 degrees." (A stick figure)

"Imagine the letter 'K'. Place a square next to it on the left side. Put a circle inside of the square. Now rotate the figure 90 degrees to the left." (A TV set)

"Imagine a 'plus'. Add a vertical line on the left side. Rotate the figure 90 degrees to the right. Now remove all lines to the left of the vertical line." (The letter "F")

"Imagine the letter 'D'. Rotate it 90 degrees to the right. Put the number '4' above it. Now remove the horizontal segment of the '4' to the right of the vertical line." (A sailboat)

*Note.* See Figure 16.2 for illustrations of these sequences.

to whether they were correct as intended (the "correct" identifications), clearly wrong (the "incorrect" identifications), or were different from those intended but were also consistent with the final pattern in the sequence (the "alternative" identifications). The latter consisted of reports, for example, of a "double scoop ice cream cone" instead of the "heart," an "upside-down umbrella" instead of the "sailboat," and a "flower with roots" instead of the "stick figure." We report them separately because, though not scored as "correct," they may still be considered legitimate interpretations of the final pattern.

The intended transformations were correctly performed in 59.7% of the trials. As the data in Table 16.3 indicate, when this was true, subjects correctly identified the emergent symbol 58.1% of the time. Nine out of the 12 subjects made at

least one of these correct identifications. Alternative image identifications were made on 11.6% of these trials. Thus when the images were transformed correctly, an appropriate reconstrual of one sort or another was made 69.7% of the time (and by 10 of the 12 subjects).

Identifications made while inspecting the drawings refer only to those trials on which the pattern was not correctly identified in imagery, but include trials on which an alternative interpretation was given to the imagined pattern. Of the 18 trials on which subjects failed to identify the correct pattern, but had transformed the pattern correctly, correct drawing identifications were made 83.3% of the time. None of the drawing identifications were of the "alternative" variety.

The partial transformations occurred on 20.8% of the trials. Of these, correct image identifications

**TABLE 16.3. Emergent Pattern Identifications According to Accuracy of Mental Transformations in Experiment 2**

| Pattern Identifications | Accuracy of Transformation | | |
|---|---|---|---|
| | Correct | Partial | Wrong |
| | Based on Mental Image | | |
| Correct | 25 | 2 | 0 |
| Alternative | 5 | 5 | 0 |
| Wrong | 13 | 8 | 14 |
| | Based on Drawing | | |
| Correct | 15 | 8 | 0 |
| Alternative | 0 | 0 | 0 |
| Wrong | 3 | 5 | 14 |

*Note.* Responses are summed across the 12 experimental subjects. Identifications of emergent patterns in the drawings were attempted only when the patterns were not correctly identified in the mental images.

were made only 13.3% of the time, whereas alternative identifications were now made 33.3% of the time. The percentage of correct drawing identifications fell to 53.3%. Counting these correct construals made on the basis of partially flawed images brings the number of subjects who made at least one correct reinterpretation up to 11 out of 12.

The wrong transformations were performed on 19.4% of the trials. It is significant that no correct or alternative identifications were given under these conditions, in contrast to the 63.8% of the trials with correct or partial transformations in which subjects reported a correct or alternative interpretation (this difference is significant, $\chi^2(1)$ = 17.38; $p < .01$). This suggests that reports of the target interpretation were contingent on assembling the pattern correctly in the images, and were not the result of anticipations on the basis of the verbal descriptions of the transformations.

The subjects reported having formed clear mental images of the final patterns on 91.7% of the trials. Five of the 12 also reported having had some difficulty mentally rotating the patterns.

Taken together, these results show quite clearly that most subjects, and not necessarily people selected for high spatial or imaginal ability, are capable of understanding a description of a pattern, imagining the pattern according to the description, imagining a specified transformation of the pattern, and then assigning a new interpretation or construal to the entire transformed pattern. We can be confident that this reconstrual was done on the basis of information available in the image, because the construction of the image according to the description had to be performed almost perfectly for the resultant pattern to have been identified correctly. We can thus reject any claim that recognition of emergent patterns in imagery, or reconstrual of an imagined pattern, can never occur.

# Experiment 3

Of course, it is still possible that despite our efforts to disguise what the emergent patterns were going to be, subjects could have been making intelligent guesses about at least some of them, on the basis of knowing what shapes and features were to be combined during the transformation sequence. As a further test of our interpretation of the previous results, we now seek evidence that subjects' ability to reconstrue their images does not depend on their ability to guess, on the basis of information about the features and transformations involved, what the proper reconstruals are likely to be. That is, we seek to ensure that the correct guesses about the identity of the emergent patterns in Experiment 2 could not have been made at some point in the middle of the transformation sequence, using partial information from the first few transformational steps, such as associations to the names of the parts or to the descriptions of the transformation operations, to narrow down the range of possible patterns that could have emerged at the end.

We therefore conducted an experiment similar to Experiment 2, except that now the subjects would be asked to guess what the emergent pattern would be after each step in the transformation sequence. If some emergent patterns are not identified until the final step, we may then rule out, as an alternative explanation, use of a guessing strategy based upon partial information gained after the transformation has begun.

## Method

### SUBJECTS

A new group of 12 subjects participated, drawn from the same pool as in the previous experiments.

### PROCEDURE

The general procedure was similar to that of Experiment 2, with the following exceptions: First, a new set of six transformation sequences were used; these consisted of three steps as opposed to four, and were structured in such a way that the emergent patterns would be hard to identify until the very end of the sequence. Also, none of the emergent patterns corresponded to alphanumeric characters, which further reduced the chance of premature correct guessing. Finally, the subjects were specifically instructed to try to guess what the emergent pattern would be after each step. If they correctly identified the emergent pattern prior to the final step, they were asked to explain how they came up with that answer. If they failed to identify the emergent pattern correctly after the final step, they were asked to try to identify it from their drawings.

The two demonstration sequences depicted a square being transformed into a kite, and a circle being transformed into a railroad crossing sign. The six experimental sequences are illustrated in Figure 16.3, and the corresponding descriptions given to the subjects are presented in Table 16.4.

Each of the sequences began by naming a letter, which could be upper- or lower-case. In the second step of the transformation, there were three possible rotations, or three possible additions. In the final step, there were two possible rotations, three possible additions, or one deletion. As shown in Figure 16.3, the emergent patterns symbolized, in order, a musical note, a yield sign (or wine

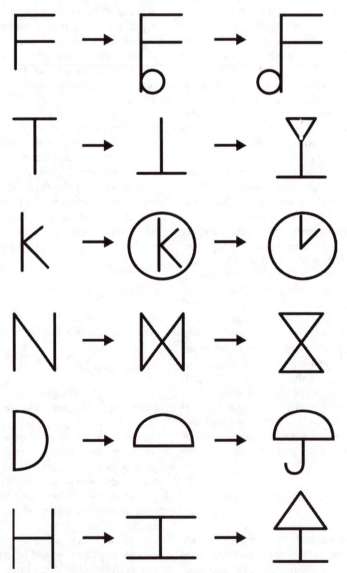

**FIGURE 16.3** ■ In Experiment 3, subjects were instructed to begin by imagining the patterns shown at the left of each row, and then to imagine transforming the patterns as the illustration depicts. In addition, they were asked to try to guess what the emergent patterns (shown at the right) would be at the end of each step in the transformation sequence. (Descriptions of these sequences that were read to subjects are provided in Table 16.4.)

**TABLE 16.4. Transformation Sequences Read to Subjects in Experiment 3**

"Imagine a capital letter 'F'. (Guess #1). Connect a lowercase letter 'b' to the vertical line in the 'F'. (Guess #2). Now flip the loop of the 'b' around so that it's now on the left side of the vertical line." (Final Identification).

"Imagine a capital letter 'T'. (Guess #1). Rotate the figure 180 degrees. (Guess #2). Now add a triangle to the top of the figure, positioned so that its base is at the very top and it appears to be pointing down." (Final Identification).

"Imagine a lowercase letter 'k'. (Guess #1). Surround the letter with a circle. (Guess #2). Now remove the lower half of the letter, below the point where the lines intersect." (Final Identification).

"Imagine a capital letter 'N'. (Guess #1). Connect a diagonal line from the top right corner to the bottom left corner. (Guess #2). Now rotate the figure 90 degrees to the right." (Final Identification).

"Imagine a capital letter 'D'. (Guess #1). Rotate the figure 90 degrees to the left. (Guess #2). Now place a capital letter 'J' at the bottom." (Final Identification).

"Imagine a capital letter 'H'. (Guess #1). Rotate the figure 90 degrees to the right. (Guess #2). Now place a triangle at the top, with its base equal in width to that of the figure." (Final Identification).

*Note.* See Figure 16.3 for illustrations of these sequences.

glass), a clock face, an hourglass (or Roman numeral "10"), an umbrella, and a pine tree.

## Results and Discussion

Unlike Experiment 2, in this study we did not accept any "alternative" identifications, and only the previously designated symbols counted as "correct" identifications. The number of correct identifications for all sequences, conditions, and levels of transformation accuracy are presented together in Table 16.5. Of most immediate interest, the emergent patterns were never identified at the end of the first step of the transformation sequence, and were identified only 4.2% of the time at the end of the second step (each based on 72 observations). In the latter case, the only pattern that was correctly anticipated was the hourglass, which is also the only pattern formed simply by a rotation of the pattern immediately preceding it (see again Figure 16.3). Each of the three subjects who correctly anticipated this pattern reported that he or she had decided to try mentally rotating the second pattern as part of the strategy for guessing. This procedure, therefore, was mostly successful in controlling for the possibility that the emergent patterns might have been identified prior to the final step.

Drawings revealed that the correct transformations were performed on 66.7% of the trials, and of these, the emergent patterns were correctly identified in imagery 47.9% of the time. Eleven of the 12 subjects reported at least one target object. Partial transformations occurred on 19.4% of the tri-

als, and 28.6% of these yielded correct final image identifications. Wrong transformations occurred on the remaining 15.3% of the trials, resulting in only a single correct image identification.

Overall, half of the subjects reported having had at least some difficulty inspecting and transforming their images. However, even when the mental transformation was wrong, or only partially correct, there were reports of emergent patterns that, although technically "incorrect" by our scoring criterion, were nevertheless consistent with the distorted final image. For example, one subject, who failed to rotate mentally the letter "H" before adding a triangle on top of it, reported recognizing a "steeple". Another subject, who imagined the lines in the upper half of the lowercase letter "k" to be equal in length and touching the surrounding circle, reported recognizing "a pie with one piece missing."

## General Discussion

The successful identifications in these experiments show that the kind of object a mental image corresponds to need not be assigned during an act of perception, but can also be discovered in the act of transforming and inspecting an image. If so, images must contain enough information about the geometry of a pattern that its category can be assigned after the image is formed, in much the same way that categorial or symbolic descriptions are assigned to visually perceived patterns. Thus, the

TABLE 16.5. Emergent Pattern Identifications for Each Transformation Sequence in Experiment 3

| Emergent Pattern | Number of Trials | Identification Condition | | | |
|---|---|---|---|---|---|
| | | Guess #1 | Guess #2 | Final Image | Drawing |
| Correct Transformations | | | | | |
| Musical Note | 9 | 0 | 0 | 8 | 1 |
| Yield Sign | 6 | 0 | 0 | 0 | 3 |
| Clock Face | 4 | 0 | 0 | 0 | 4 |
| Hourglass | 10 | 0 | 2 | 2 | 2 |
| Umbrella | 11 | 0 | 0 | 10 | 1 |
| Pine Tree | 8 | 0 | 0 | 1 | 4 |
| Total | 48 | 0 | 2 | 21 | 15 |
| Partial Transformations | | | | | |
| Musical Note | 2 | 0 | 0 | 0 | 0 |
| Yield Sign | 5 | 0 | 0 | 2 | 1 |
| Clock Face | 4 | 0 | 0 | 1 | 1 |
| Hourglass | 1 | 0 | 1 | 0 | 0 |
| Umbrella | 0 | 0 | 0 | 0 | 0 |
| Pine Tree | 2 | 0 | 0 | 0 | 1 |
| Total | 14 | 0 | 1 | 3 | 3 |
| Wrong Transformations | | | | | |
| Musical Note | 1 | 0 | 0 | 0 | 0 |
| Yield Sign | 1 | 0 | 0 | 1 | 0 |
| Clock Face | 4 | 0 | 0 | 0 | 0 |
| Hourglass | 1 | 0 | 0 | 0 | 0 |
| Umbrella | 1 | 0 | 0 | 0 | 0 |
| Pine Tree | 2 | 0 | 0 | 0 | 1 |
| Total | 10 | 0 | 0 | 1 | 1 |

Note. Responses are summed across the 12 experimental subjects. Identifications of emergent patterns in the drawings were attempted only when the patterns were not correctly identified in the mental images.

explanation of Chambers and Reisberg's results cannot be that images are nothing but conceptual interpretations, nor that images lack information about the geometry of a shape that would be necessary for reconstruing it, nor that the information in images is inaccessible to procedures mapping geometric information onto conceptual categories.

Having presented new evidence that reconstruals of images are possible, thus refuting the strong position that images are nothing but interpretations, we turn to Chambers and Reisberg's arguments. In the rest of this paper, we will ask whether our experiments are valid tests of the hypothesis that image reconstrual is impossible, and whether the philosophical arguments cited by Chambers and Reisberg establish that images are not reinterpretable. Finally, we examine why certain kinds of image reconstrual, such as reversals of duck/rabbits and Necker cubes, do not seem to be possible, whereas other kinds, such as those in-

volving a rotated-D + J/umbrella or a rotated-N/Z, are possible.

## Processing Geometric Information in Images versus Assigning a New Interpretation to Images: A Valid Distinction?

There are two reasons why proponents of Chambers and Reisberg's view might not accept subjects' performance in these experiments as legitimate examples of reversing an ambiguous figure in imagery. The first is that in our experiments, unlike those of Chambers and Reisberg, subjects were not given a single figure that could be described in two ways and then asked to discover the second description in imagery. Instead, they were told to construct a figure piece by piece, and only the resulting pattern had a simple description. Thus, one might say, there could be no *re*construal in these experiments, because there was no initial construal that had to be switched away from.

In fact, such an objection does not apply. All of the stimuli used in these experiments had at least two interpretations or construals, for example, "H and X superimposed" versus "butterfly"; "inverted Y with a circle and crossbar attached" versus "stick figure"; "F with a mirror-reversed b attached" versus "musical note"; and so on. Furthermore, in each of these cases the subject started out with only one of these interpretations (since the images were constructed on the basis of those interpretations) and in successful cases "switched to" or "saw" the alternative one. The fact that one of the two interpretations was invariably characterized by a complex articulated description rather than by a single word, unlike the case of a duck/rabbit, is of little theoretical importance. There is no basis for considering the patterns used in this experiment to be any less ambiguous than the duck/rabbit, especially since we can be sure that the complex description had to have been psychologically real or entertained by the subjects in some way in order for them to have created the appropriate image. For that matter, some of the ambiguous figures used by Chambers and Reisberg, such as the Necker cube and Schroeder staircase, also do not have one-word labels attached to each interpretation.

The main value of the traditional reversible figures is that in general, at least one of the interpretations is not perceived immediately (for reasons we will discuss later). Thus, the reversal is surprising to the perceiver (and hence is a provocative demonstration of perceptual ambiguity), and an experimenter can be confident that in an image reconstrual experiment, the subject was not aware of both interpretations when the figure was first perceived. But in our experiments, figures were provided to the subject via verbal descriptions that afforded no opportunity for the subject to detect the second interpretation before the image was completed. Since the patterns were never physically presented to the subjects, there is no need to worry that both construals could have been made during perception. Therefore, the fact that our stimuli do not contain two simply characterized but mutually incompatible descriptions is of no concern. As Chambers and Reisberg point out (p. 319), "the critical test of whether images can be reconstrued hinges on whether subjects can *dis-*

*cover* an unanticipated, uncued shape in an image" [emphasis theirs]. That is precisely what we have demonstrated.

The second possible objection to our results can already be found in their paper when they discuss the earlier demonstrations of the detection of novel patterns in images (e.g., Pinker & Finke, 1980; Reed, 1974; Slee, 1980; and by extension, Shepard and Feng). These demonstrations are all clearly incompatible with the strongest position that one could take on the issue (a position they associate with Fodor, 1981 and Casey, 1976), namely that images are nothing but symbols of a particular thing, so there is no issue of "reading" or "interpreting" an image, because the interpretation must be there at the outset. The reason that even Chambers and Reisberg must distance themselves from this strongest view is that nothing in the *interpretation* of the letter "M" (e.g., that it is the grapheme for the phoneme /m/, the 13th letter of the alphabet, or the first letter in *mother*) allows one to determine that it is also an inverted "W." Similarly, nothing in the interpretation of two adjacent "X"s allows one to determine that a diamond is embedded in it, and nothing in the interpretation of a "J" affixed to a sideways "D" allows one to determine that it depicts an umbrella. Rather, it is the geometry of the pattern that allows these inferences to be made. Since these inferences *can* be made, subjects must have more than the pure symbolic or conceptual residue of these visual patterns available to them.

Chambers and Reisberg deal with this problem by conceding to the imagery system some ability to process geometric information that nonetheless falls short of the ability to construe or reconstrue a pattern. Specifically, they attribute subjects' performance in supposedly reinterpreting images to a two-stage process of replacement or alteration of an initial image, yielding a new distinct image, followed by detection of an isomorphism between the original image and the altered or new one. For example, subjects don't actually see a parallelogram in an image of two adjacent Roman numeral 10's; they start off with an image of a parallelogram, and add or replace parts of it until a form isomorphic to the two juxtaposed Roman numerals results. This "isomorphism," the fact that the two images "have a common form," is detected, and possibly confirmed by exchanging the two distinct images ("parallelogram with segments added" versus "adjacent Roman numeral 10's") and verifying the commonness of form.

There are two reasons why this argument would not work here. First, in experimental paradigms such as ours, in which subjects are not asked to verify the presence of a given pattern but to report *any* pattern that they see, the subject would be required to arrive at an image isomorphic to the target image by a process of trial and error. Regardless of how likely that might have been in earlier studies, it is out of the question in the present demonstrations, where the alternative interpretations of the forms were not supplied to the subjects for verification or even guessed by the subjects before their images were complete. We can safely estimate that there is a near-zero probability that subjects randomly selected a musical note, a TV set, or an umbrella to test for isomorphism with permuted images of F's, K's, circles, and J's in just the cases where we designed the patterns to correspond to these figures.

But even if subjects somehow manage to select the appropriate target figure to juxtapose with the first image, they still have to represent enough information about the geometry of the two images that isomorphic shapes can be recognized as such, and this information has to be fed into a process that can detect isomorphism. Chambers and Reisberg are willing to attribute this ability—detection of "isomorphism" or "common form"—to the imagery system. They also concede that people can detect "unanticipated particulars" in an image; that "one can also be surprised by relations inside an image," such as the size of an image and the color of its background; and that one must "inspect the image to learn how it appears." They refer to an "imagery medium" that allows one to assess the appearance of images, and say that "imagery and perception seem to share a mode of representation, a mode that respects the metric properties of space." Furthermore, images include information about figure and ground, orientation, and depth relations. Chambers and Reisberg are vague as to what exactly they claim the imagery system can do, but it is clear that in these passages they do not deny that it can represent and process some kinds of geometric information concerning the appearance of a figure.

The problem is that one cannot both attribute these properties to the imagery system and also deny that it is possible to construe or reconstrue

an image, that is, to determine what categories of objects the image depicts. That is because representing geometric information about an object, and being able to verify whether particular geometric configurations are present, is in general a sufficient condition for construal to take place. The process of assigning a particular description, interpretation, or construal to an object in perception is nothing but representing the geometric properties of the visual input and determining whether certain relations are satisfied; Marr (1982) even defines the function of the visual system as deriving a description of the world via computations on the geometry of the optical input. For example, construing a pattern of lines as an example of the letter "A" involves determining whether two of the lines form an upward-pointing angle and the third one joins them part way down their lengths. Barring telepathy, what else could construal in perception be? So if the imagery system can represent and submit to analysis the spatial configuration of a pattern, there is nothing to prevent it from assigning an interpretation, including a new interpretation, to that pattern, by applying some of the same processes that are used at some stage of perception. If one can represent in an image the information that a pattern consists of two lines forming an upward-pointing angle, and a third horizontal line joining them midway down their lengths, and can access that information (as Chambers and Reisberg appear willing to concede), there is nothing to prevent one from assigning, as one does in perception, the description "/a/, the first letter in the alphabet" to that pattern, even if such a description was not in mind when the image was first formed. And that is exactly what our subjects did.

In sum, Chambers and Reisberg attempt to remove themselves from this dilemma by drawing a distinction where no distinction can be drawn. If they hold to the extreme view that images are nothing but symbolic descriptions or construals, with geometric information sloughed off or inaccessible, they cannot account for people's ability to detect new pattens in an image or to verify that a part is present in an image. On the other hand, if they allow that images preserve geometric information, and attribute to the imagery system the power to inspect images to learn how they appear, to detect commonality of form between two images, or to note and be surprised by relations inside an image, they cannot maintain that it lacks the abilty to assign a novel interpretation to an image, because assigning an interpretation to a pattern is nothing but the ability to detect relations and properties in the appearance of an object and determining the commonality of form with representations stored in memory.

## What's Wrong with the Philosophical Arguments against the Possibility of Image Reconstrual[2]

Chambers and Reisberg cite arguments from the philosophical literature (e.g., Casey, 1976; Fodor, 1981); that they interpret as saying that (p. 318) "there is no issue of 'reading' or 'interpreting' an image. The image is created as a symbol of some particular thing, and so the interpretation is there at the outset. . . . without a construal process, there is no possibility for reconstrual." We argue that their claim collapses two points, one conceptual and one empirical, and is based on a hidden and dubious premise. The *conceptual* point made by Fodor (which he attributed to Wittgenstein) is that images are only capable of representing by virtue of their being interpreted entities, not because of their being "pictorial" and hence "resembling" external objects. (The problem is that pictures are inherently ambiguous in terms of what they *could* represent: a picture of Richard Nixon could be a representation of Nixon, of a president, of a man, etc.). We have no quarrel with this point. The *hidden premise*, which is what allows Chambers and Reisberg to use this conceptual argument to make claims about the empirical nature of imagery, is that if an entity is *interpreted*, it cannot be *re*interpreted. This leads them to the *empirical* claim that mental images in fact cannot be reinterpreted. Note that without the hidden premise, the conceptual point would not motivate the empirical claim.

The problem with the argument is that there is no basis for the hidden premise that an interpreted entity is in principle incapable of being reinterpreted. Interpreted entities could indeed be reinterpreted, if they had both an uninterpreted aspect or part and an interpreted aspect or part, and if the uninterpreted aspect or part contained enough information that the original interpreted aspect or part could be replaced by a new one. To take a crude example, an image could be an interpreted entity by virtue of its consisting of a picture plus a caption, the caption being the interpretation. If the picture contained the requisite information and was accessible to a suitable process, a new caption could be put in place of the old one. On the other hand, to take an equally crude example, an image could be nothing but a sentence summarizing the interpretation. In that case, the geometric information necessary to replace the sentence with another one consistent with the represented object may be absent, and reinterpretation would be impossible. Both of these examples are consistent with the claim that images represent by virtue of their being interpreted entities. In other words, there may exist two kinds of interpreted entities: those that can be reinterpreted and those that cannot. Whether human visual images are of the first kind or the second kind is strictly an empirical question.[3]

The point can be made without talking about pictures in the head. Consider two machines. Both of them have video cameras aimed at checkerboards. Both register the distribution of light intensities in the projections of the checkerboards by storing them digitally in a "bit map" memory. Both have algorithms that can take as input the information in the bit maps, and use that information to verify whether certain geometric patterns are instantiated by the pattern of checkers in the scene; for example, whether they constitute an example of the letter "X." An assertion to that effect could be stored in memory, and in a sense would serve as an "interpretation" of the checkerboard pattern. When the checkerboard is removed from the camera's view, however, one machine erases its bit map and the other stores it in a file. Later, the machines are called on to determine whether some new object was instantiated in the now-absent checkerboard (i.e., whether it can be given a new interpretation), for example, a tilted "+" (assuming that "+"s are "X"s whose segments meet at right angles). The second machine can retrieve its bit map, allow its geometric property-verification algorithms to process the information in it, determine the answer, and store it as a new interpretation. The first machine is incapable of this. (It would also be unable to detect the "+" if it had recorded the bit map but was incapable of retrieving it and feeding it into the verification algorithm. Note also that for the purposes of this example, the arrangement of checkers and the pattern in question could be anything whatsoever—such as a duck/rabbit.) Clearly, one can ask whether the human capacity for recalling and recognizing visual patterns more closely resembles the capabilities of the first machine or the second machine, and the question of people's ability to reconstrue an image is basically a version of this conceptually straightforward question.

To summarize, the inherent ambiguity of pictures makes them unsuitable to serve by themselves as representations of objects. Therefore images, if they represent, must consist of or contain interpretations. These are conceptual points that we do not argue with. However, images may or may not be the kind of interpreted entity that is susceptible to *re*interpretation. This is an empirical question, and our experiments show that the answer to it is that such reinterpretation is possible.

## Why Don't Classical Ambiguous Figures Reverse in Imagery?

We have tried to show that Chambers and Reisberg do not have a clear interpretation of their findings: The claim that visual images cannot ever be given new construals, because they contain no accessible uninterpreted geometric information, is empirically false, and the middle ground they attempt to occupy, in which images contain accessible geometric information but nonetheless cannot be reinterpreted, is logically inconsistent. However, we do not wish to diminish the value of their empirical demonstrations that classical ambiguous figures cannot be reversed when imagined. Though our experiments show that the strongest negative claims cannot be maintained, Chambers and Reisberg's findings still demand an interpretation. (Furthermore, there are other reasons to suspect that there are limitations on people's power of reconstrual: In experiments on mental superimposition of visual parts such as Palmer (1977) and Thompson and Klatzky (1978), the mentally synthesized emergent shape generally does not attain the same holistic status in perception as when that shape was actually presented to subjects visually.)

One possibility is that there is no principled difference between the classical ambiguous figures and our transformed patterns, and that the empirical differences are due either to confounded factors, such as the complexity of the Necker cube and the Schroeder staircase, or the salience and succinctness of the labels for each interpretation

of the duck/rabbit, giving rise to Stroop-like interference blocking the reinterpretation. However, it is difficult to motivate an account based on such factors, and for what it is worth, most observers note that the process of trying to reverse classical ambiguous figures "feels" different from the processes involved in our demonstrations. Thus, it is possible that the two kinds of reconstrual are different for principled reasons. Here we suggest one possibility.

What is distinctive about classic ambiguous figures? First, it is difficult for perceivers to reverse the figures at will (though they can influence the likelihood of a reversal by shifting attention to one or another part of the figure.) Second, it is not just the interpretation of the entire figure that changes, but the representation of the geometric disposition of each of the features of the figure (which are also ambiguous) that changes as well. For example, in the duck/rabbit figure, the directions of the object's front-back and top-bottom axes with respect to the viewer's axes change in the reversal: The duck is typically pointing up and to the right, whereas the rabbit points down and to the left, and the paired appendages are at the front of the duck pointing in its frontward direction but at the top of the rabbit pointing up and back. In the Necker cube, there is also a reassignment of the objects' axes with respect to the viewer: Some convex edges and vertices become concave and vice versa, and the relative distances of each segment from the viewer change. In the Schroeder staircase, this happens as well, and there is, in addition, a figure-ground reversal and a shift of the boundaries between major parts (see Hoffman & Richards, 1984).

In a naturalistic, visual environment these features can often be assigned by bottom-up analysis alone (using stereopsis, for example), but in line drawings the features are all locally ambiguous, and are thought to be resolved by global constraints on the coherence of the object as a whole. Multiple crude analyses of both parts and wholes are computed simultaneously, and those tentative representations for parts that are consistent with certain tentative representations for the whole mutually reinforce each other to the exclusion of all other analyses in a "cooperative" or "relaxation" process (Attneave, 1971; Feldman & Ballard, 1982; Hinton, 1981). For example, the lowermost horizontal edge of a Necker cube can be represented as convex if and only if the leftmost vertical edge is represented as convex and if and only if the cube is represented as being viewed from above. For ambiguous figures, two global representations are possible, each with a consistent set of representations of the parts. It is assumed that they mutually inhibit each other and thus one global representation dominates, reinforces one set of part representations, and then fatigues, allowing the other global representation to dominate and thus boost the alternative representations for each of its parts. Thus, reversals involve a set of simultaneous mutually consistent changes in the representations of the geometric properties of the parts of the objects relative to the object, and of the object relative to the viewer.

The reconstrued patterns in the present experiments, however, had the assignments of the relative dispositions of their features specified during the verbal descriptions. Thus although our subjects had to reassign the *conceptual* interpretation of each part, they did not have to switch the assignments of *geometric dispositions* of each of the parts by using compatibility relations with each other and with the global object. For example, subjects were told to rotate a "D" counterclockwise and put it on top of a "J"; this specifies the representation of the direction and location of the semicircle in a way that is compatible with the interpretation required by the construal of the object as a depiction of an umbrella. Subjects had to be able to interpret the resulting collection of parts as an exemplar of a different conceptual category, but they did not have to reverse figure and ground, convex and concave, or near and far for each of the features of the pattern.

This difference could be the critical factor distinguishing our results from those of Chambers and Reisberg, for two possible reasons. One is that the global resolution of local geometric ambiguity may require that the whole pattern be active at one time in the visual representation; images, in contrast, consist of dynamically fading and regenerated parts (Kosslyn, 1975; Kosslyn et al., 1983).[4] The other is that the positive feedback loop that resolves local geometric ambiguities may occur at an early stage of visual representation preceding the stage at which memory-generated information can be inserted to create a visual image. Marr (1982), Ullman (1984), Treisman and Gelade (1980), and Pinker (1984), for example, distinguish

between "early" or "low-level" vision, and "late" or "high-level" vision. Low-level vision is assumed to go on automatically and independently of the perceiver's goals or beliefs, to consist of parallel processing across the entire visual field, and to output a representation consisting of the values of a small set of local features for every location in the visual field. "High-level" vision can depend on the goals and knowledge of the perceiver, and it consists of "routines" that apply within an attentional "spotlight" moved sequentially over the visual field in order to detect the presence of feature conjunctions, global and topological properties, and entire objects. Many of the feature representations that reverse in classical ambiguous figures, such as disposition relative to the viewer and the object, convexity versus concavity, figure versus ground, and major part boundaries, are probably computed by early visual processes, which would include the global disambiguation process discussed above. Imagery, on the other hand, does not seem to extend down to these early, automatic visual processes, but interacts with higher level visual routines (see Finke, 1987; Jolicoeur, Ullman, & Mackay, 1986; Pinker, 1984; and Ullman, 1984; for general reviews, and Pinker, 1980, and Pinker & Finke, 1980, for evidence that, specifically, images occur after the stage in which three-dimensional information is assigned). Thus the nonreversibility of classical ambiguous figures in imagery may be due not to images lacking nonconceptual geometric information, which we have shown is false, but to images being unable to affect the low-level process that uses global object consistency to disambiguate the basic geometric properties of local features.

The accounts discussed above are by no means definitive; additional research on these two complex and poorly understood processes (image generation and global disambiguation) and their interaction is needed. However, we hope to have shown not only that images maintain enough geometric information to support conceptual reconstrual, but to have made a more general point as well. One problem with debates over visual imagery is that imagery and perception are treated as monolithic entities, and coarse common sense notions such as "construal" or "interpretation" are applied categorically to them. As we have argued elsewhere (see Farah, 1984; Finke, 1980, 1987; Pinker, 1984), such an approach will inevitably lead to the appearance of paradoxes. This can be avoided if one assumes that imagery, like perception, consists of a set of distinct information processing stages, each dedicated to a different level or type of analysis.

## ACKNOWLEDGMENTS

This research was supported by NIMH Grant 1R01MH3980901 to Ronald A. Finke, by NSF Grant 85–18774 to Steven Pinker, and by ONR Grant N00014–86–K–0094 and NIH Program Project Grant NS–06209–21, and NIH Grant R23–NS–23458–01 to Martha J. Farah.

We thank Ned Block, James Greeno, Stephen Kosslyn, Howard Kurtzman, Steven Palmer, Ross Thompson, and Barbara Tversky for helpful comments and suggestions.

## NOTES

1. Because the alternative predictions of this experiment were that subjects would report either 0 or more than 0 new construals of the imagined patterns, no relevant statistical analyses can be performed on the data (see also Chambers & Reisberg, 1985).
2. We are grateful to Ned Block for his assistance in formulating the arguments in this section.
3. One could state that once an image is reinterpreted (say, once the picture gets a new caption), it becomes a *new* image. That is, our experimental phenomena *must* have consisted of subjects replacing one image with another, because an image with a new interpretation must be a new image; the old one would be gone. But this statement would just be a stipulation of what the word "image" is allowed to mean, and would have no relevance to the scientific issue of the nature of the mechanisms underlying imagery.
4. Chambers and Reisberg consider a simpler version of this possibility, and dismiss it based on the results of Hochberg's (1970) demonstration that subjects can reverse ambiguous figures under anorthoscopic viewing conditions, that is, when they see only a portion of the figure at a time as the figure is moved behind a narrow slit. This finding is cited as evidence that reconstrual can take place when subjects have only piecemeal access to the parts of a figure. However, anorthoscopic perception is achieved only when the figure moves behind a viewing window above a certain critical speed, and is a topic of interest in the psychology of vision precisely because under these conditions subjects do not mentally glue together separately perceived parts, but rather perceive a whole figure via the application of an automatic, low-level perceptual process. This contrasts with what is known about the structure of mental images, which are generated and maintained a part at a time (see Kosslyn, 1980, Chapters 6 and 7).

## REFERENCES

Attneave, F. (1971). Multistability in perception. *Scientific American, 225*, 62–71.

Casey, E. (1976). *Imagining: A phenomenological study.* Bloomington, IN: Indiana University Press.

Chambers, D. & Reisberg, D. (1985). Can mental images be ambiguous? *Journal of Experimental Psychology: Human Perception and Performance, 11*, 317–328.

Farah, M. J. (1984). The neurological basis of mental imagery: A componential analysis. *Cognition, 18*, 245–271.

Feldman, J. A., & Ballard, D. (1982). Connectionist models and their properties. *Cognitive Science, 6*, 205–254.

Finke, R. A. (1980). Levels of equivalence in imagery and perception. *Psychological Review, 87*, 113–132.

Finke, R. A. (1987). Feature interactions in imagery and perception. Manuscript submitted for publication.

Fodor, J. A. (1981). Imagistic representation. In N. Block (Ed.), *Imagery* (pp. 63–86). Cambridge, MA: MIT Press.

Hinton, G. E. (1979). Some demonstrations of the effects of structural descriptions in mental imagery. *Cognitive Science, 3*, 231–250.

Hinton, G. E. (1981). *A parallel computation that assigns canonical object-based frames of reference.* Proceedings of the International Joint Conference on Artificial Intelligence, Vancouver, British Columbia, Canada.

Hochberg, J. (1970). Attention, organization and consciousness. In D. Mostofsky (Ed.), *Attention: Contemporary theory and analysis* (pp. 99–124). New York: Appleton-Century-Crofts.

Hoffman, D. D., & Richards, W. A. (1984). Parts of recognition. *Cognition, 18*, 65–96.

Hollins, M. (1985). Styles of mental imagery in blind adults. *Neuropsychologia, 23*, 561–566.

Intons-Peterson, M. J. (1983). Imagery paradigms: How vulnerable are they to experimenters' expectations? *Journal of Experimental Psychology: Human Perception and Performance, 9*, 394–412.

Jolicoeur, P., Ullman, S., & Mackay, M. (1986). Curve tracing: A possible basic operation in the perception of spatial relations. *Memory & Cognition, 14*, 129–140.

Kosslyn, S. M. (1975). Information representation in visual images. *Cognitive Psychology, 7*, 341–370.

Kosslyn, S. M. (1980). *Image and mind.* Cambridge, MA: Harvard University Press.

Kosslyn, S. M., & Pomerantz, J. R. (1977). Imagery, propositions, and the form of internal representations. *Cognitive Psychology, 9*, 52–76.

Kosslyn, S. M., Reiser, B. J., Farah, M. J., & Fliegel, S. L. (1983). Generating visual images: Units and relations. *Journal of Experimental Psychology: General, 112*, 278–303.

Marr, D. (1982). *Vision.* San Francisco: Freeman.

Palmer, S. E. (1977). Hierarchical structure in perceptual representation. *Cognitive Psychology, 9*, 441–474.

Pinker, S. (1980). Mental imagery and the third dimension. *Journal of Experimental Psychology: General, 109*, 354–371.

Pinker, S. (1984). Visual cognition: An introduction. *Cognition, 18*, 1–63.

Pinker, S., & Finke, R. A. (1980). Emergent two-dimensional patterns in images rotated in depth. *Journal of Experimental Psychology: Human Perception and Performance, 6*, 244–264.

Pylyshyn, Z. W. (1973). What the mind's eye tells the mind's brain: A critique of mental imagery. *Psychological Bulletin, 80*, 1–24.

Reed, S. K. (1974). Structural descriptions and the limitations of visual images. *Memory & Cognition, 2,* 329–336.

Reed, S. K., & Johnson, J. A. (1975). Detection of parts in patterns and images. *Memory & Cognition, 3,* 569–575.

Shepard, R. N. (1978). Externalization of mental images and the act of creation. In B. S. Randhawa & W. E. Coffman (Eds.), *Visual learning, thinking, and communication* (pp. 133–190). New York: Academic.

Shepard, R. N., & Cooper, L.A. (1982). *Mental images and their transformations.* Cambridge, MA: MIT Press.

Slee, J. A. (1980). Individual differences in visual imagery ability and the retrieval of visual appearances. *Journal of Mental Imagery, 4,* 93–113.

Stevens, A., & Coupe, P. (1978). Distortions in judged spatial relations. *Cognitive Psychology, 10,* 422–437.

Thompson, A. L., & Klatzky, R. L. (1978). Studies of visual synthesis: Integration of fragments into forms. *Journal of Experimental Psychology: Human Perception and Performance, 4,* 244–263.

Treisman, A. M., & Gelade, G. (1980). A feature-interaction theory of attention. *Cognition, 12,* 97–136.

Ullman, S. (1984). Visual routines. *Cognition, 18,* 97–159.

# The Neural Basis of Mental Imagery

Martha J. Farah • Carnegie-Mellon University

Visual mental imagery, or 'seeing with the mind's eye', has been the subject of considerable controversy in cognitive science. At issue is whether images are fundamentally different from verbal thoughts, whether they share underlying mechanisms with visual perception, and whether information in images is represented in a spatial (i.e., map-like) format. Research on the neural systems underlying imagery brings a new source of evidence to bear on these cognitive science controversies, as well as on the cerebral localization of imagery processes. Emerging from this work is the view that mental imagery involves the efferent activation of visual areas in prestriate occipital cortex, parietal and temporal cortex, and that these areas represent the same kinds of specialized visual information in imagery as they do in perception. In addition, different components of imagery processing appear to be differentially lateralized, with the generation of mental images from memory depending primarily upon structures in the posterior left hemisphere, and the rotation of mental images depending primarily upon structures in the posterior right hemisphere.

What color are the stars on the American flag? To answer, you probably formed a mental image of the flag, and 'saw' that the stars are white. The question to which this article is addressed is, what neural events underlie this ability to form and use mental images? More specifically, what is the relation between the neural bases of mental imagery and visual perception? Are mental imagery processes lateralized to one hemisphere? And, finally, what are the implications of neuroscientific data for our understanding of mental imagery at the functional, or 'information-processing' level of description used in cognitive science?

## What the Mind's Eye Tells the Brain's Visual Cortex

The subjective similarity of seeing and imagining suggests that common internal representations might underlie these two experiences. In support of this hypothesis, cognitive psychologists such as Finke,[1] Kosslyn,[2] Paivio,[3] and Shepard[4] have used a variety of ingenious experimental paradigms to gather evidence that imagery and perception have similar behavioral consequences, and that imagery and verbal thought have different behavioral consequences. However, for reasons to be discussed in the last section of this reading, not all cognitive psychologists have found these behavioral demonstrations persuasive. It is therefore of interest to turn to neuropsychological and physiological evidence on these issues.

With respect to the relation between imagery and perception, the relevant evidence can be divided into two categories: brain imaging data that implicate activity in cortical visual processing areas during imagery; and studies of brain-damaged patients showing selective deficits in imagery ability that parallel the patients' perceptual deficits. In the first category are electrophysiological and regional blood flow studies of normal subjects during imagery.

One approach has been to record event-related potentials (ERPs) to visual stimuli while subjects hold mental images.[5] If imagery has a systematic effect on the ERP, then there must be some common brain locus at which imagery and perceptual processing interact. More important, if the interaction between imagery and perception is content-specific—for example, if imaging an *H* affects the ERP to visually presented *H*s more than the ERP to visually presented *T*s, and imaging a *T* affects the ERP to *T*s more than the ERP to *H*s—then the interaction must be taking place in neural structures where information about the differences between *H*s and *T*s is preserved, that is, in common neural representations. Imagery was found to have a content-specific effect on the ERP within the first 200 ms of stimulus processing, and this effect was localized at the occipital and posterior temporal recording sites, as shown in Figure 17.1.

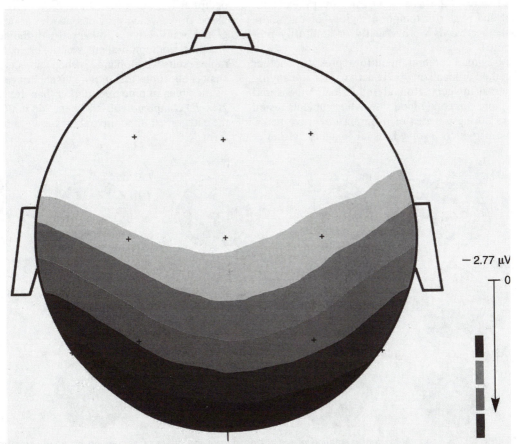

**FIGURE 17.1** ■ Topographic representation of the distribution of the effect of imagery on the visual ERP, obtained by subtracting the ERP to the stimulus when the image and stimulus do not match from the ERP to the stimulus when the image and stimulus match, at 173 ms after stimulus presentation (the latency of the first negative peak of the visual ERP).

Furthermore, the inference that the image-percept interaction was occurring in modality-specific visual cortex is strengthened by the fact that the time course of the effect of imagery on the ERP was the same as that of the first negative peak of the visual ERP waveform, which is believed to originate in extrastriate visual cortex.[6]

The act of generating a mental image from memory also has discernible effects on the ERP.[7] ERPs were recorded to words under two instructional conditions: to encode the word (baseline condition), and to encode the word and form an image of its referent (image condition). The difference between the ERPs to the words in these two conditions should reflect the brain electrical activity synchronized with the generation of mental images. This difference measure, represented in Figure 17.2, was also maximal over the occipital and posterior temporal regions of the scalp, whether words were visually or auditorily presented.

Regional cerebral blood flow provides another method of localizing brain activity accompanying mental imagery. Roland and Friberg[8] measured regional cerebral blood flow while subjects rested and during a series of different cognitive tasks, one of which involved visual imagery: visualiz- ing a walk through one's neighborhood making alternating right and left turns starting at one's front door. This task caused massive blood flow to the posterior regions of the brain, including the occipital, posterior parietal and posterior inferior temporal areas important for higher visual processing. Goldenberg et al.[9] devised a simpler imagery task, along with a control task differing from the imagery task only in the absence of imagery. They gave groups of normal subjects the same auditorily presented lists of concrete words to learn under different instructional conditions: one group was told just to listen to the words and try to remember them; and the other group was told to visualize the referents of the words as a mnemonic strategy. Imagery was associated with more blood flow to the occipital lobes, particularly the left inferior occipital region, and with high co-variation of blood flow (which provides another index of regional brain activity), bilaterally, in the occipital and posterior temporal areas of the brain. Comparable results were obtained when subjects tried to answer questions that require visual imagery (e.g., 'is the green of pine trees darker than the green of grass?') compared with those that do not (e.g., 'is the categorical imperative an ancient grammatical form?').[10]

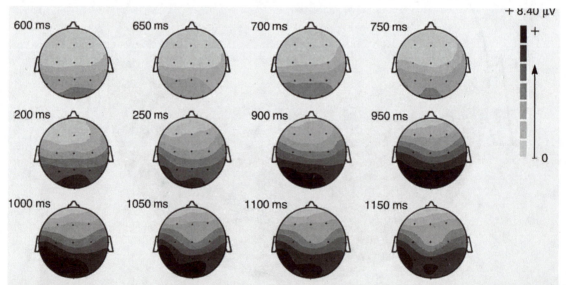

**FIGURE 17.2** ■ Topographic representation of the distribution of the effect of generating an image from memory, obtained by subtracting the ERP to auditorily presented words when subjects passively listen to the words from the ERP to the same stimuli when subjects generate mental images of the words' referents. The effect is shown at 50 ms intervals beginning 600 ms after word onset (upper left diagram) and continuing left to right, and top row to bottom row, through 1150 ms after word onset.

The results of the brain imaging studies implicate occipital, temporal and parietal cortex in mental imagery, the same areas that subserve visual perception. Although it is difficult to distinguish activity in primary visual cortex from that in visual association areas on the basis of these techniques, the ERP results suggest that primary visual cortex is probably not involved: imagery has its earliest effect on the visual ERP at the latency of the first negative component, a component with a presumed extrastriate origin. This is consistent with the results of single-unit recordings in conscious monkeys, showing cognitive effects on neuronal activity in secondary, but not primary, visual cortex.[11]

If mental imagery does consist of endogenously generated activity in cortical visual areas, then patients with damage to those areas should have imagery deficits that parallel their perceptual deficits. Studies of the effects of focal brain damage on imagery are generally consistent with this prediction. For example, color vision may be impaired after brain damage with relative preservation of other visual capacities, and in these cases, the ability to imagine color is often compromised as well.[12] De Renzi and Spinnler[13] investigated various color-related abilities in a large group study of unilaterally brain-damaged patients, and found an association between impairment on color vision tasks, such as the Ishihara test of color blindness, and color imagery tasks, such as verbally reporting the colors of common objects from memory. This is what one would expect to find if the color of mental images were represented in the same neural substrate as the color of visual percepts.

The specializations of the 'two cortical visual systems' for representing visual location and appearance information also appear to apply to mental imagery.[14] A patient with visual disorientation following bilateral posterior parietal lesions could not localize visual stimuli, although he was able to recognize them, and his imagery abilities paralleled his perceptual abilities. He was unable to describe the layout of furniture in his home or the locations of shops in his neighborhood from memory, despite his ability to give accurate and detailed descriptions of the appearances of objects from memory. A patient with visual agnosia following bilateral inferior temporal lesions showed the opposite pattern of perceptual and imagery abilities. He was impaired at recognizing objects, but not localizing them, and he was unable to draw or describe the appearances of objects from memory, despite his ability to give accurate descriptions of the spatial locations of objects and landmarks from memory. In a review of the literature for similar cases, we found that in most published reports of patients with selective 'what' or 'where' deficits in visual perception for whom imagery was tested, parallel imagery impairments were found.

More selective impairments of perceptual functioning within each of the two cortical visual systems also exist, and have correlates in imagery. For example, the neglect syndrome, characterized by a failure to detect visual stimuli in the side of space opposite a parietal lesion, has been shown by Bisiach and his colleagues to manifest itself in imagery. In one study,[15] two right parietal-damaged patients were asked to form an image of the famous Piazza del Duomo in Milan, with which the patients had been familiar before their brain damage. When asked to imagine viewing it from the position marked 'A' in Figure 17.3, and to describe the view, both patients omitted from their descriptions the landmarks that would have fallen on the left side of that scene and named only the landmarks marked 'a' on the map. When the patients were asked to repeat the task from the opposite vantage point, at position 'B', they omitted the landmarks previously included in their descriptions, which now fell on the left of the imagined scene, and named only landmarks marked 'b' on the map.

The functioning of the ventral visual system can also be partially impaired, resulting in recognition deficits for certain classes of stimuli and not others. In these cases, imagery deficits again parallel the perceptual deficits. For example, in further testing of the agnosic patient described earlier, a selective impairment was found for imaging stimuli that could be roughly categorized as 'living things', paralleling his greater recognition impairment for those stimuli.[16] Shuttleworth, Syring and Allen[17] reviewed the literature on cases of prosopagnosia (agnosia for faces) and found that impaired imagery for faces was common. Of their own prosopagnosic patient, they report that she had 'no voluntary visual recall (revisualization) of faces but was able to revisualize more general items such as buildings and places'.

In sum, several lines of evidence converge in implicating cortical visual processing areas in

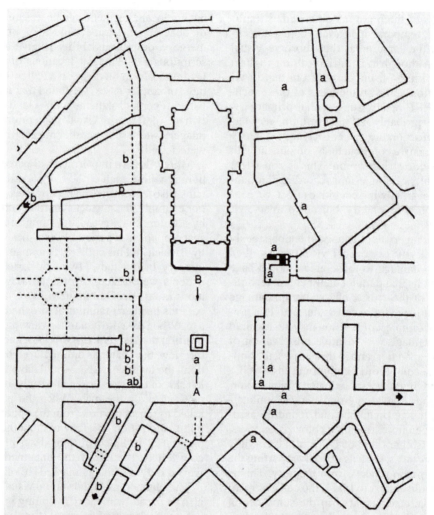

**FIGURE 17.3** ■ Map of the Piazza del Duomo in Milan, showing the two positions 'A' and 'B' from which patients were asked to imagine viewing the Piazza, and the landmarks that they recalled from each imagined position, labeled 'a' and 'b', respectively.

mental imagery. Electrophysiological and regional blood flow measures demonstrate activity in visual areas while normal subjects form mental images. In addition, localized damage to these areas results in selective imagery deficits that parallel the more evident visual perceptual deficits.

## Hemispheric Specialization for Mental Imagery

Many higher perceptual and cognitive functions are carried out more proficiently or even exclu-

sively by one hemisphere, and the question therefore arises whether there is any cerebral asymmetry for mental imagery. Ehrlichmann and Barrett[18] pointed out the existence of a widespread assumption that imagery is a specialized function of the right hemisphere, but found little support for this assumption in their critical review of the literature. Farah[19] suggested that different components of mental imagery ability might have different neuroanatomic loci, and identified a subset of cases of loss of imagery whose profile of abilities and deficits indicated a loss of the image generation process—the ability to form a visual mental image from stored long-term visual memory information. In this subset of cases, the predominant site of damage was the posterior left hemisphere. Subsequent cases have been consistent with this localization (see reference 20) and have suggested a relation between the inability to recognize multiple forms that sometimes follows left posterior brain damage[21] and the inability to generate a normally detailed image from memory, which is believed to require the synthesis of separately stored parts of the image.[2] Language and verbal memory need not be impaired in such cases, despite the laterality of the lesion, indicating that imagery and verbal thought depend upon at least partially distinct neural processes.[1]

The results of research with split-brain patients are also consistent with left hemisphere specialization for generating images. In one experiment, carried out with patient JW,[22] a single hemisphere was presented with an upper case letter and asked to classify the corresponding lower case letter as ascending (e.g., 'f'), descending (e.g., 'g') or neither, a judgement that requires generating a mental image. Only the left hemisphere of this patient could perform the task. In contrast, both hemispheres could correctly classify the lower case letters when viewing them, and both could associate the upper case letters with the corresponding lower case forms in free vision, implicating image generation *per se* as the cause of the right hemisphere's failure in the imagery task. With a different imagery task that did not require visualizing details, judging whether a named animal was larger or smaller than a goat, both of JW's hemispheres performed well, consistent with the idea that the left hemisphere is specialized for synthesizing images that have distinct parts.[23] Two other split-brain patients have been tested on image-generation tasks so far. Like JW, LB showed left hemisphere superiority for the generation of detailed visual images, although his right hemisphere was above chance in at least one image-generation task.[24] Results from patient VP are less clear: she showed initial left hemisphere superiority, but her right hemisphere eventually attained comparable levels of performance.[23] It should be noted that the right hemisphere of this patient is also capable of speech.

Research with normal subjects has also, on the whole, supported the hypothesis of left hemisphere specialization for image generation. For example,

imagery has a larger effect on perception in the right than in the left hemifield,[25, 26] generating images interferes more with right-than with left-hand motor performance,[27,28] and causes greater suppression of EEG a-rhythm over the left than over the right hemisphere.[29] The results of the brain imaging studies with normal subjects mentioned earlier, in which images were formed while brain activity was monitored, are also relevant: all showed left-sided foci of activity.[7–10] Nevertheless, some studies have shown the opposite trend, for greater right than left hemisphere involvement in image-generation tasks[30, 31] and these exceptions may indicate that factors such as practice, individual differences and task requirements modulate the roles of the hemispheres in image generation.[32]

In addition to recalling from memory the appearances of stimuli that are absent, we can also use mental imagery to decide how a stimulus currently in view would look if it were spatially transformed.[33] For example, in deciding whether the pairs of objects depicted in Figure 17.4 are identical or mirror images of one another, you probably mentally rotated them. The process of mental image rotation can be dissociated by brain damage from mental image generation,[34] implying that different neural systems are involved, and the available evidence suggests some degree of right hemisphere superiority for mental rotation. For example, Ratcliff[35] assessed the ability of patients with penetrating head wounds to carry out a mental rotation task, and found that the right posteriorly damaged patients were most impaired at this task. Papanicolaou et al.[36] measured regional cerebral blood flow and evoked potentials to task-irrelevant visual probe flashes while normal subjects performed the mental rotation task shown in Figure 17.4. They found greater blood flow to the right than to the left hemisphere (especially the right parietal region), and greater suppression of probe-evoked potentials over the right than over the left hemisphere, when subjects performed mental rotation than when they passively viewed the same stimuli. Using a lateralized stimulus-presentation technique, Cohen[25] found evidence that normal subjects rotate mental images with their right hemispheres, and Corballis and Sergent[24] used a similar task to document normal mental rotation ability in the right but not the left hemisphere of split-brain patient LB.

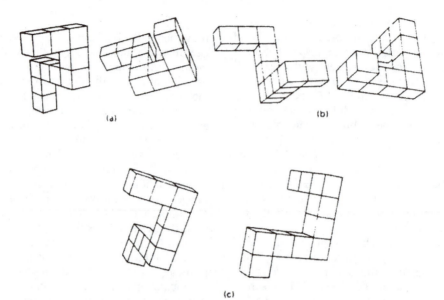

FIGURE 17.4 ■ Are the objects in each of these pairs identical or is one a mirror image of the other? Response time data from normal subjects indicate that most people answer this question by mentally rotating the objects.[33]

## The Functional Architecture of Mental Imagery: Constraints from Neuropsychology

It has proved difficult for cognitive psychologists to gather decisive evidence on certain issues concerning mental imagery. Data that seem to support the visual nature of images, and the map-like or pictorial format of images, can also be explained in terms of non-visual and propositional (i.e., language-like) representations. Anderson[37] has argued that this is an inherent limitation of the kinds of data used by cognitive psychologists. If one can control and measure only the inputs and outputs to a 'black box', then there will always be alternative theories of the internal processing stages that can account for any set of input-output data. For example, the finding that people take longer to 'scan' mentally across subjectively larger mental images appears to support a spatial format for mental images.[2] However, Pylyshyn[38] has suggested that the underlying representations are propositional, and that the scanning times reflect subjects' interpretation of imagery instructions as instructions to *simulate* the scanning of a visual percept.

The neuroscientific data reviewed earlier provide a new source of evidence on these questions.

The dissociability of imagery impairments from impairments in verbal thought suggests that thinking in images is distinct from thinking in language. The existence of common neural substrates for imagery and perception demonstrates rather directly that imagery is a function of the visual system and, insofar as occipital representations are retinotopically mapped, carries the further implication that images also have this format. Finally, in addition to addressing questions about imagery that cognitive scientists have already asked, this new source of data suggests new insights about the functional architecture of mental imagery: the dissociability of imagery impairments after dorsal and ventral damage, for example, implies that the normal visual imagery system includes separate subsystems for representing visual appearance and spatial location information.[39]

### ACKNOWLEDGMENTS

The writing of this article was supported by ONR contract N0014–86–0094, NIH grant NS23458, the Alfred P. Sloan Foundation, and NIH program project grant NS06209 to the Aphasia Research Center of the Boston University School of Medicine. The author thanks Frank Peronnet and his colleagues at INSERM, Unit 280, for their collaboration on the ERP studies, and the anonymous reviewers of this paper for many helpful suggestions.

## SELECTED REFERENCES

1. Finke, R. A. (1980) *Psychol. Rev.* 87, 113–132.
2. Kosslyn, S. M. (1980) *Image and Mind* Harvard University Press.
3. Paivio, A. (1971) *Imagery and Verbal Processes* Holt, Rinehart and Winston.
4. Shepard, R. N. (1978) *Am. Psychol.* 33, 125–137.
5. Farah, M. J., Peronnet, F., Gonon, M. A., and Giard, M. H. (1988) *J. Exp. Psychol. (Gen.)* 117, 248–257.
6. Lesevre, N. and Joseph, J. P. (1980) in *Evoked Potentials* (Barber, C., Ed.), MIT Press.
7. Farah, M. J., Peronnet, F., Welsberg, L., and Monheit, M. A. *J. Cog. Neurosci.* (in press).
8. Roland, P.E. and Friberg, L. (1985) *J. Neurophysiol.* 53, 1219–1243.
9. Goldenberg, G., Podreka, I., Steiner, M., and Willmes, K. (1987) *Neuropsychologia* 25, 473–486.
10. Goldenberg, G., Podreka, I., Steiner, M., Deecke, L., and Willmes, K. (1988) in *Cognitive and Neuropsychological Approaches to Mental Imagery* (Denis, M., Englekamp, J., and Richardson, J. T. E., Eds), pp. 363–373, Martinus Nijhoff.
11. Moran, J. and Desimone, R. (1985) *Science* 229, 782.
12. Beauvois, M. F. and Saillant, B. (1985) *Cog. Neuropsychol.* 2, 1–48.
13. DeRenzi, E. and Spinnler, H. (1967) *Cortex* 3, 194–217.
14. Levine, D. N., Warach, J., and Farah, M. J. (1985) *Neurology* 35, 1010–1018.
15. Bisiach, E. and Luzzatti, C. (1978) *Cortex* 14, 129–133
16. Farah, M. J., Hammond, K. M., Mehta, Z., and Ratciff, G. (1989) *Neuropsychologia* 27, 193–200.
17. Shuttleworth, E. C., Syring, V., and Allen, N. (1982) *Brain Cog.* 1, 302–332.
18. Ehrlichman, H. and Barrett, J. (1983) *Brain Cog.* 2, 39–52.
19. Farah, M. J. (1984) *Cognition* 18, 245–272.
20. Farah, M. J., Levine, D. N., and Calvanio, R. (1988) *Brain Cog.* 8, 147–164.
21. Kinsbourne, M. and Warrington, E. K. (1962) *J. Neurol. Neurosurg. Psychiatry* 25, 339–344.
22. Farah, M. J., Gazzaniga, M. S., Holtzman, J. D., and Kosslyn, S. M. (1985) *Neuropsychologia* 23, 115–118.
23. Kosslyn, S. M., Holtzman, J. D., Farah, M. J., and Gazzaniga, M. S. (1985) *J. Exp. Psychol. (Gen.)* 114, 311–341.
24. Corballis, M. C. and Sergent, J. (1988) *Neuropsychologia* 26, 13–26.
25. Cohen, G. (1975) in *Attention and Performance (Vol. 5)* (Rabbit, P. M. A. and Dornic, S., Eds), pp. 20–32, Academic Press.
26. Farah, M. J. (1986) *Neuropsychologia* 24, 541–551.
27. Lempert, H. (1987) *Neuropsychologia* 25, 835–839.
28. Lempert, H. (1989) *Neuropsychologia* 27, 575–579.
29. Rugg, M. D. and Venables, P. H. (1980) *Neurosci. Lett.* 16, 67–70.
30. Kosslyn, S. M. (1988) *Science* 240, 1621–1626.
31. Sergent, J. (1989) *J. Exp. Psychol. (Hum. Percept. Perform.)* 15, 170–178.
32. Farah, M. J. *J. Exp. Psychol. (Hum. Percept. Perform.)* (in press).
33. Shepard, R. N. and Cooper, L. A. (1982) *Mental Images and Their Transformations* MIT Press.
34. Farah, M. J. and Hammond, K. M. (1988) *Cognition* 29, 29–46.
35. Ratcliff, G. (1979) *Neuropsychologia* 17, 49–54.
36. Papanicolaou, A. C. et al. (1987) *Electroencephalogr. Clin. Neurophysiol.* 66, 515–520.
37. Anderson, J. R. (1978) *Psychol. Rev.* 85, 249–277.
38. Pylyshyn, Z. W. (1981) *Psychol. Rev.* 88, 16–45.
39. Farah, M. J., Hammond, K. L., Levine, D. N., and Calvanio, R. (1988) *Cog. Psychol.* 20, 439–462.

# Imagery

## Discussion Questions

1. Outline the debate surrounding the underlying mental representation of images; that is, do you think the representation is propositional or analog (e.g., retaining the properties of the external stimuli)? Why?
2. Reread the last sentence of the imagery introduction: "It's almost as if the brain has evolved an amazing capacity to simulate its underlying processes internally via mental imagery." Discuss the relationship between imagery and perception, and speculate about why imagery may have evolved.
3. Not all imagery tasks depend upon the same brain regions. Which (if any) of the patients described by Farah would likely have trouble with the Shepard mental rotation task?
4. Using Marr's criteria, do we have a complete theory of mental imagery? That is, can mental imagery be understood at all three levels of Marr's theory? Link the papers in this section to the different levels, as appropriate.
5. One of the problems with studying mental images is to obtain objective measures of performance, rather than subjective reports of image quality. Summarize the methods with which researchers have studied imagery. Can you think of any other methods that do not rely on introspection? Do you think introspection should be used to study imagery?

## Suggested Readings

D. Chambers and D. Reisberg (1985, Can mental images be ambiguous? *Journal of Experimental Psychology: Human Perception & Performance, 11*, 317–328) argue that people cannot re-interpret an ambiguous mental image even though they can easily re-interpret a drawing of that image. After reading the classic paper by Finke, Pinker, and Farah (1989), how do you interpret these data?

S. M. Kossyln (1976, Can imagery be distinguished from other forms of internal representation? Evidence from studies of information retrieval times. *Memory & Cognition, 4*, 291–297) wrote this classic, which we alluded to in our introduction, but space precluded its inclusion in this volume. The interested reader should read the original.

S. M. Kosslyn, N. M. Alpert, W. L. Thompson, V. Maljkovic, S. Weise, C. F. Chabris, S. E. Hamilton, S. L. Rauch, and F. S. Buonanno (1993, Visual mental imagery activates topographically organized visual cortex: PET investigations. *Journal of Cognitive Neuroscience, 5,* 263–287) used positron emission tomography to study whether mental images activate visual areas of the brain.

S. M. Kosslyn, B. J. Reiser, M. J. Farah, and S. L. Fliegel (1983, Generating visual images: Units and relations. *Journal of Experimental Psychology: General, 112,* 278–303) examined the underlying representations of images and how those components are combined to form images.

A. Paivio (1971, *Imagery and Verbal Processes.* New York: Holt, Reinhart, & Winston) is the originator of dual code theory, which posits that there are both verbal and visual codes for information.

Z. W. Pylyshyn (1973, What the mind's eye tells the mind's brain: A critique of mental imagery. *Psychological Bulletin, 80,* 1–24) takes the other side of the debate and argues that propositional representations might underlie mental images.

J. Zacks, B. Rypma, J. D. E. Gabrieli, B. Tversky, and G. H. Glover (1999, Imagined transformations of bodies: An fMRI investigation. *Neuropsychologica, 37,* 1029–1040) used functional magnetic imagining techniques to study the neural underpinnings of taking another person's perspective, a variation on the mental rotation tasks discussed in this chapter.

PART V

# Memory

# Introduction to Part V: Memory

There are several prerequisites for remembering an event. First, the event must have been perceived and encoded; although this may seem obvious, remember from the Simons and Levin (1998) paper that people sometimes fail to encode such major details as the face of a person with whom they were talking! Of course, after initial encoding of the event, the memory must be retained over some period of time (often years). During this time, many other similar events also occur, and these may modify the original encoded event. Finally, memories must be somehow accessed, that is, the memory must be retrieved with a particular (potentially limited) set of retrieval cues. Memory research is often organized around these three stages: encoding, retention/storage, and retrieval. The first three papers in this section have been chosen in part because each investigates a memory process that places primary emphasis on only one of these stages.

We begin with the classic encoding paper by Craik and Tulving (1975). Their experiments support that memories are always being formed as a by-product of attentional and perceptual processes, and the levels of processing (LOP) have considerable consequence for later memory (Craik & Lockhart, 1972). During the orienting phase in these experiments, subjects answered different types of questions for each of a series of words. For example, some subjects decided if BEAGLE was presented in capital letters (structural processing), others whether it rhymed with LEGAL (phonetic processing), and others whether it was an example of an animal (semantic processing). The questions were easy, and subjects had no problem answering them. However, the type of question answered at study determined how well the words were remembered, even if subjects were unaware of the upcoming memory test. Memory was best for items processed semantically, next best after phonetic processing, and worst after structural processing. Across experiments, deeper semantic processing at study yielded better memory. Later research refined this conclusion; it is not necessarily that semantic encoding is best but, rather, memory benefits most from whichever encoding task promotes study of the features (normally semantic) emphasized by the retrieval test (Morris, Bransford, & Franks, 1977).

Even if an event is encoded in a particular way, its memory trace can still be affected by later events. That is, later events can *interfere* with retrieval of the original event. In fact, one could easily argue that interference has dominated much of the work in the area of memory (see Anderson & Neely, 1996, for a review). The classic paper by Loftus, Miller, and Burns (1978) provides an applied example of interference: in eyewitness testimony. The concern is that the eyewitness' testimony may be contaminated by exposure to new information and suggestions after the crime. Loftus and colleagues had subjects watch a slide show of a traffic accident; the critical slide showed a yield sign to half the subjects. Subjects then answered a series of questions, including "Did another car pass the red Datsun while it was stopped at the stop sign?" Of interest was which slide subjects chose in a later two-alternative forced-choice test: the yield sign or the stop sign.

Chance would be 50% correct; subjects who received misinformation scored reliably below chance (41%). Clearly, the misinformation (stop sign) interfered with subjects' ability to remember the original event (yield sign).

There are many different memory tests, and what is remembered is in part dependent upon the type of test that is used at retrieval (e.g., Tulving & Pearlstone, 1966). The Jacoby, Woloshyn, and Kelley (1989) paper provides an important contrast between two classes of tests, namely, between explicit and implicit memory tests. Explicit memory tests require subjects to consciously think back to the study phase. In contrast, implicit tests allow one to infer memory via performance on seemingly "nonmemory" tasks that do not require subjects to consciously retrieve studied items. Consider one of the Jacoby et al. experiments, in which subjects read a list composed entirely of nonfamous names (e.g., Sebastian Weisdorf). Half the subjects studied the names with divided attention; they monitored an audio recording of digits for runs of odd numbers, whereas the remaining subjects allocated full attention to the names. All subjects later judged the fame (an implicit test) of famous names, new nonfamous names, and studied nonfamous names. After the fame judgment task, they received a recognition test (an explicit test) to indicate which names had been studied during the first phase. When subjects had studied the names with full attention, recognition memory was high and subjects did not inflate the fame of the studied nonfamous names. However, when the names had been studied under divided attention, recognition was reduced and the studied nonfamous names were viewed as more famous than new nonfamous names. That is, subjects inflated the fame of the studied nonfamous names; their familiarity due to the study phase (a form of implicit memory) was misinterpreted as fame.

The subjects in the Jacoby et al. paper incorrectly interpreted familiarity (a form of memory) as fame. In many other situations, people make a different mistake: they believe they remember something that did not in fact occur. Memory illusions are informative about how the memory system normally functions, in the same way that visual illusions inform us about the visual system (e.g., Roediger, 1996). A powerful example is the Roediger and McDermott (1995) paper on false memories. This paper is already a classic; seven years after publication, it has already been cited over 300 times. The paradigm is popular for its simplicity and because it yields a much higher rate of false memories than is typical. Subjects simply study lists of related words (e.g., *bed, rest, awake, tired . . .* ) and later are likely to falsely recall and recognize a nonpresented related word (*sleep*). These false memories are held with unusually high confidence and are remarkably immune to warnings (e.g., McDermott & Roediger, 1998). Theories of memory must accommodate not only the findings on veridical memory but also memory illusions such as this one.

The encoding-storage-retrieval conceptualization of memory is a unitary one. That is, frameworks such as LOP do not separate memory into different brain-based systems. Many other approaches to memory involve separation of the concept "memory" into two or more separate entities. One

influential example is Atkinson and Shiffrin's (1971) model of memory, which separated memory into a short-term and a long-term store. As described in the Baddeley (1992) paper, a single short-term store has been replaced by a multicomponent working memory system. Baddeley has argued for modality-specific slave systems that store, rehearse, and manipulate a limited amount of information, whereas a central executive controls the slave systems. More recently, Baddeley has argued for another component to working memory—namely, an episodic buffer (Baddeley & Wilson, 2002).

Like short-term memory, long-term memory has also been subdivided into separate systems. Tulving's classic (1985) paper argues for the separation of at least procedural, semantic, and episodic memories. And many researchers have continued to divide these categories into further types of memory (e.g., see Squire and Zola-Morgan's 1991 subdivision of procedural memory). The Tulving (1985) paper describes criteria for naming a separate memory system such as patient data and neuroimaging data (see the methods papers by Petersen et al., 1988, and Sacchett & Humphreys, 1992, for examples). In addition, behavioral methods can be used to document different subjective experiences associated with the systems, and dissociations between tasks. Returning to the example of implicit versus explicit memory, one can see how such patterns fit the criteria of two different systems. Explicit memory is associated with conscious remembering, whereas implicit memory is not. In the false fame task, explicit memory was affected by divided attention, whereas implicit memory was not. Some researchers believe that patient data is the most powerful evidence supporting multiple systems. For example, consider the classic case of the amnesic HM (e.g., Milner, 1959). He had a severe deficit on explicit tests (such as recalling words from a list) but showed perfectly normal practice effects (a form of implicit memory). Together, these results support separate brain systems for implicit versus explicit memory.

Some researchers have proposed a memory system specific to personal memories (e.g., Conway & Pleydell-Pearce, 2000). The development of this system is proposed to extend into early childhood and, as such, explains the classic problem of childhood amnesia. This refers to the finding that people remember disproportionately few memories from early childhood. In support of this personal memory system, Bruce et al. (2000) provided evidence that people "knew" that personal events had happened in the childhood amnesia period, even though they could not consciously recollect them. This knowing is likely due to exposure to family stories, photographs, logic, and so on. Why can't the subjects consciously remember the events? Numerous explanations have been explored. As noted earlier, one possibility is that a personal memory system is needed, and it has not yet developed during the period of childhood amnesia. A processing explanation is also possible: Memories encoded prior to language acquisition may be encoded in a way that is not consistent with later verbal retrieval cues.

The debate on how to classify memory tasks continues. Critics argue that we should not invoke a separate memory system for each type of memory test. In at least some cases, dissociations can be explained via the different processes emphasized by the tests. However, different processes must be ultimately realized in the human brain. At this point in time, researchers are advocating a more complicated, hybrid approach: the components of processing framework (e.g., Moscovitch, 1994). The basic idea is that each task requires multiple component processes, and any given pair of tasks may overlap in none, some, or all component processes. When two tests are dissociated, they differ in at least one component process—but not necessarily all (Hintzman, 1990). Brain-imaging techniques have the potential of being particularly useful in determining when a collection of component processes constitute a separate system (for a discussion of these issues, see Roediger, Buckner, & McDermott, 1999).

## REFERENCES

Anderson, M. C., & Neely, J. H. (1996). Interference and inhibition in memory retrieval. In E. L. Bjork & R. A. Bjork (Eds.), *Memory*. San Diego: Academic Press.

Atkinson, R. C., & Shiffrin, R. M. (1971). The control of short-term memory. *Scientific American, 225,* 82–90.

Baddeley, A. (1992). Working memory. *Science, 255,* 556–559.

Baddeley, A., & Wilson, B. A. (2002). Prose recall and amnesia: Implications for the structure of working memory. *Neuropsychologica, 40,* 1737–1743.

Bruce, D., Dolan, A., & Phillips-Grant, K. (2000). On the transition from childhood amnesia to the recall of personal memories. *Psychological Science, 11,* 360–364.

Conway, M. A., & Pleydell-Pearce, C. W. (2000). The construction of autobiographical memories in the self-memory system. *Psychological Review, 107,* 261–288.

Craik, F. I. M., & Lockhart, R. S. (1972). Levels of processing: A framework for memory research. *Journal of Verbal Learning & Verbal Behavior, 11,* 671–684.

Craik, F. I. M., & Tulving, E. (1975). Depth of processing and the retention of words in episodic memory. *Journal of Experimental Psychology: General, 104,* 268–294.

Hintzman, D. L. (1990). Human learning and memory: Connections and dissociations. *Annual Review of Psychology, 41,* 109–139.

Loftus, E. F., Miller, D. G., & Burns, H. J. (1978). Semantic integration of verbal information into a visual memory. *Journal of Experimental Psychology: Human Learning & Memory, 4,* 19–31.

Jacoby, L. L., Woloshyn, V., & Kelley, C. (1989). Becoming famous without being recognized: Unconscious influences of memory produced by dividing attention. *Journal of Experimental Psychology: General, 118,* 115–125.

McDermott, K. B., & Roediger, H. L., III (1998). Attempting to avoid illusory memories: Robust false recognition of associates persists under conditions of explicit warnings and immediate testing. *Journal of Memory & Language, 39,* 508–520.

Milner, B. (1959). The memory defect in bilateral hippocampal lesions. *Psychiatric Research Reports, 11.*

Morris, C. D., Bransford, J. D., & Franks, J. J. (1977). Levels of processing versus transfer appropriate processing. *Journal of Verbal Learning & Verbal Behavior, 16,* 519–533.

Moscovitch, M. (1994). Memory and working with memory: Evaluation of a component process model and comparisons with other models. In D. L. Schacter and E. Tulving (Eds.), *Memory systems 1994.* Cambridge, MA: MIT Press.

Petersen, S. E., Fox, P. T., Posner, M. I., Mintun, M., & Raichle, M. E. (1988). Positron emission tomographic studies of the cortical anatomy of single word processing. *Nature, 331,* 585–589.

Roediger, H. L., III (1996). Memory illusions. *Journal of Memory & Language, 35,* 76–100.

Roediger, H. L., III, Buckner, R. L., & McDermott, K. B. (1999). Components of processing. In J. K. Foster and J. Marko (Eds.), *Memory: Systems, process, or function?* (pp. 31–65). Oxford: Oxford University Press.

Roediger, H. L., III, & McDermott, K. B. (1995). Creating false memories: Remembering words not presented in lists. *Journal of Experimental Psychology: Learning, Memory, & Cognition, 21,* 803–814.

Sacchett, C., & Humphreys, G. W. (1992). Calling a squirrel a squirrel but a canoe a wigwam: A category-specific deficit for artefactual objects and body parts. *Cognitive Neuropsychology, 9,* 73–86.

Simons, D. J., & Levin, D. T. (1998). Failure to detect changes to people during a real-world interaction. *Psychonomic Bulletin & Review, 5,* 644–649.

Squire, L. R., & Zola-Morgan, S. (1991). The medial temporal lobe memory system. *Science, 253,* 1380–1386.

Tulving, E. (1985). How many memory systems are there? *American Psychologist, 40,* 385–398.

Tulving, E., & Pearlstone, Z. (1966). Availability versus accessibility of information in memory for words. *Journal of Verbal Learning & Verbal Behavior, 5,* 381–391.

# Depth of Processing and the Retention of Words in Episodic Memory

Fergus I. M. Craik and Endel Tulving

• University of Toronto, Toronto, Ontario, Canada

## Summary

Experiments were designed to explore the levels of processing framework for human memory research proposed by Craik and Lockhart (1972). The basic notions are that the episodic memory trace may be thought of as a rather automatic by-product of operations carried out by the cognitive system and that the durability of the trace is a positive function of "depth" of processing, where depth refers to greater degrees of semantic involvement. Subjects were induced to process words to different depths by answering various questions about the words. For example, shallow encodings were achieved by asking questions about typescript; intermediate levels of encoding were accomplished by asking questions about rhymes; deep levels were induced by asking whether the word would fit into a given category or sentence frame. After the encoding phase was completed, subjects were unexpectedly given a recall or recognition test for the words. In general, deeper encodings took longer to accomplish and were associated with higher levels of performance on the subsequent memory test. Also, questions leading to positive responses were associated with higher retention levels than questions leading to negative responses, at least at deeper levels of encoding.

While information-processing models of human memory have been concerned largely with structural aspects of the system, there is a growing tendency for theorists to focus, rather, on the *processes* involved in learning and remembering. Thus the theorist's task, until recently, has been to provide an adequate description of the characteristics and interrelations of the successive stages through which information flows. An alternative approach is to study more directly those processes involved in remembering—processes such as attention, encoding, rehearsal, and retrieval—and to formulate a description of the memory system in terms of these constituent operations. This alternative viewpoint has been advocated by Cermak (1972), Craik and Lockhart (1972), Hyde and Jenkins (1969, 1973), Kolers (1973a), Neisser (1967), and Paivio (1971), among others, and it represents a sufficiently different set of fundamental assumptions to justify its description as a new paradigm, or at least a miniparadigm, in memory research. How should we conceptualize learning and retrieval operations in these terms? What changes in the system underlie remembering? Is the "memory trace" best regarded as some copy of the item in a memory store (Waugh & Norman, 1965), as a bundle of features (Bower, 1967), as the record resulting from the perceptual and cognitive analyses carried out on the stimulus (Craik & Lockhart,

1972), or do we remember in terms of the encoding operations themselves (Neisser, 1967; Kolers, 1973a)? Although we are still some way from answering these crucial questions satisfactorily, several recent studies have provided important clues.

The incidental learning situation, in which subjects perform different orienting tasks, provides an experimental setting for the study of mental operations and their effects on learning. It has been shown that when subjects perform orienting tasks requiring analysis of the meaning of words in a list, subsequent recall is as extensive and as highly structured as the recall observed under intentional conditions in the absence of any specific orienting task; further research has indicated that a "process" explanation is most compatible with the results (Hyde, 1973; Hyde & Jenkins, 1969, 1973; Walsh & Jenkins, 1973). Schulman (1971) has also shown that a semantic orienting task is followed by higher retention of words than a "structural" task in which the nonsemantic aspects of the words are attended to. Similar findings have been reported for the retention of sentences (Bobrow & Bower, 1969; Rosenberg & Schiller, 1971; Treisman & Tuxworth, 1974) and in memory for faces (Bower & Karlin, 1974). In all these experiments, an orienting task requiring semantic or affective judgments led to better memory performance than tasks involving structural or syntactic judgments. However, the involvement of semantic analyses is not the whole story: Schulman (1974) has shown that congruous queries about words (e.g., "Is a SOPRANO a singer?") yield better memory for the words than incongruous queries (e.g., "Is MUSTARD concave?"). Instruction to form images from the words also leads to excellent retention (e.g., Paivio, 1971; Sheehan, 1971).

The results of these studies have important theoretical implications. First, they demonstrate a continuity between incidental and intentional learning—the operations carried out on the material, not the intention to learn, as such, determine retention. The results thus corroborate Postman's (1964) position on the essential similarity of incidental and intentional learning, although the recent work is more usually described in terms of similar processes rather than similar responses (Hyde & Jenkins, 1973). Second, it seems clear that attention to the word's meaning is a necessary prerequisite of good retention. Third, since retrieval conditions are typically held constant in

the experiments described above, the differences in retention reflect the effects of different encoding operations, although the picture is complicated by the finding that different encoding operations are optimal for different retrieval conditions (e.g., Eagle & Leiter, 1964; Jacoby, 1973). Fourth, large differences in recall under different encoding operations have been observed under conditions where the subjects' task does not entail organization or establishment of interitem associations; thus the results seem to take us beyond associative and organization processes as important determinants of learning and retention. It may be, of course, that the orienting tasks actually do lead to organization as suggested by the results of Hyde and Jenkins (1973). Yet, it now becomes possible to entertain the hypothesis that optimal processing of individual words, qua individual words, is sufficient to support good recall. Finally, the experiments may yield some insights into the nature of learning operations themselves. Classical verbal learning theory has not been much concerned with processes and changes within the system but has concentrated largely on manipulations of the material or the experimental situation and the resulting effects on learning. Thus at the moment, we know a lot about the effects of meaningfulness, word frequency, rate of presentation, various learning instructions, and the like, but rather little about the nature and characteristics of underlying or accompanying mental events. Experimental and theoretical analysis of the effects of various encoding operations holds out the promise that intentional learning can be reduced to, and understood in terms of, some combination of more basic operations.

The experiments reported in the present paper were carried out to gain further insights into the processes involved in good memory performance. The initial experiments were designed to gather evidence for the depth of processing view of memory outlined by Craik and Lockhart (1972). These authors, proposed that the memory trace could usefully be regarded as the by-product of perceptual processing; just as perception may be thought to be composed of a series of analyses, proceeding from early sensory processing to later semantic-associative operations, so the resultant memory trace may be more or less elaborate depending on the number and qualitative nature of the perceptual analyses carried out on the stimulus.

It was further suggested that the durability of the memory trace is a function of depth of processing. That is, stimuli which do not receive full attention, and are analyzed only to a shallow sensory level, give rise to very transient memory traces. On the other hand, stimuli that are attended to, fully analyzed, and enriched by associations or images yield a deeper encoding of the event, and a long-lasting trace.

The Craik and Lockhart formulation provides one possible framework to accommodate the findings from the incidental learning studies cited above. It has the advantage of focusing attention on the processes underlying trace formation and on the importance of encoding operations; also, since memory traces are not seen as residing in one of several stores, the depth of processing approach eliminates the necessity to document the capacity of postulated stores, to define *the* coding characteristic of each store, or to characterize the mechanism by which an item is transferred from one store to another. Despite these advantages, there are several obvious shortcomings of the Craik and Lockhart viewpoint. Does the levels of processing framework say any more than "meaningful events are well remembered?" If not, it is simply a collection of old ideas in a somewhat different setting. Further, the position may actually represent a backward step in the study of human memory since the notions are much vaguer than any of the mathematical models proposed, for example, in Norman's (1970) collection. If we already know that the memory trace can be precisely represented as

$$l = \lambda e^{-\psi n^{1-\gamma}}$$

(Wickelgren, 1973), then such woolly statements as "deeper processing yields a more durable trace" are surely far behind us. Third, and most serious perhaps, the very least the levels position requires is some independent index of depth—there are obvious dangers of circularity present in that any well-remembered event can too easily be labeled *deeply processed*.

Such criticisms can be partially countered. First, cogent arguments can be marshaled (e.g., Broadbent, 1961) for the advantages of working with a rather general theory—provided the theory is still capable of generating predictions which are distinguishable from the predictions of other theo-

ries. From this general and undoubtedly true starting point, the concepts can be refined in the light of experimental results suggested by the theoretical framework. In this sense the levels of processing viewpoint will encourage rather different types of question and may yield new insights. A further point on the issue of general versus specific theories is that while strength theories of memory are commendably specific and sophisticated mathematically, the sophistication may be out of place if the basic premises are of limited generality or even wrong. It is now established, for example, that the trace of an event can be readily retrieved in one environment of retrieval cues, while it is retrieved with difficulty in another (e.g., Tulving & Thomson, 1973); it is hard to reconcile such a finding with the view that the probability of retrieval depends only on some unidimensional strength.

With regard to an independent index of processing depth, Craik and Lockhart (1972) suggested that, when other things are held constant, deeper levels of processing would require longer processing times. Processing time cannot always be taken as an absolute indicator of depth, however, since highly familiar stimuli (e.g., simple phrases or pictures) can be rapidly analyzed to a complex meaningful level. But within one class of materials, or better, with one specific stimulus, deeper processing is assumed to require more time. Thus, in the present studies, the time to make decisions at different levels of analysis was taken as an initial index of processing depth.

The purpose of this article is to describe experiments carried out within the levels of processing framework. The first experiments examined the plausibility of the basic notions and attempted to rule out alternative explanations of the results. Further experiments were carried out in an attempt to achieve a better characterization of depth of processing and how it is that deeper semantic analysis yields superior memory performance. Finally, the implications of the results for an understanding of learning operations are examined, and the adequacy of the depth of processing metaphor questioned.

## Experimental Investigations

Since one basic paradigm is used throughout the series of studies, the method will be described in detail at this point. Variations in the general method will be indicated as each study is described.

## General Method

Typically, subjects were tested individually. They were informed that the experiment concerned perception and speed of reaction. On each trial a different word (usually a common noun) was exposed in a tachistoscope for 200 msec. Before the word was exposed, the subject was asked a question about the word. The purpose of the question was to induce the subject to process the word to one of several levels of analysis, thus the questions were chosen to necessitate processing either to a relatively shallow level (e.g., questions about the word's physical appearance) or to a relatively deep level (e.g., questions about the word's meaning). In some experiments, the subject read the question on a card; in others, the question was read to him. After reading or hearing the question, the subject looked in the tachistoscope with one hand resting on a *yes* response key and the other on a *no* response key. One second after a warning "ready" signal the word appeared and the subject recorded his (or her) decision by pressing the appropriate key (e.g., if the question was "Is the word an animal name?" and the word presented was TIGER, the subject would respond *yes*). After a series of such question and answer trials, the subject was unexpectedly given a retention test for the words. The expectation was that memory performance would vary systematically with the depth of processing.

Three types of question were asked in the initial encoding phase. (a) An analysis of the physical structure of the word was effected by asking about the physical structure of the word (e.g., "Is the word printed in capital letters?"). (b) A phonemic level of analysis was induced by asking about the word's rhyming characteristics (e.g., "Does the word rhyme with TRAIN?"). (c) A semantic analysis was activated by asking either categorical questions (e.g., "Is the word an animal name?") or "sentence" questions (e.g., "Would the word fit the following sentence: 'The girl placed the ____ on the table'?"). Further examples are shown in Table 18.1. At each of the three levels of analysis, half of the questions yielded *yes* responses and half *no* responses.

The general procedure thus consisted of explaining the perceptual-reaction time task to a single subject, giving him a long series of trials in which both the type of question and *yes–no* decisions were randomized, and finally giving him an unexpected retention test. This test was either free recall ("Recall all the words you have seen in the perceptual task, in any order"); cued recall, in which some aspect of each word event was represented as a cue; or recognition, where copies of the original words were represented along with a number of distractors. In the initial encoding phase, response latencies were in fact recorded: A millisecond stop clock was started by the timing mechanism which activated the tachistoscope, and the clock was stopped by the subject's key response. Typically, over a group of subjects, the same pool of words was used, but each word was rotated through the various level and response combinations (CAPITALS?—*yes*: SENTENCE?—no, and so on). The general prediction was that deeper level questions would take longer to answer but would yield a more elaborate memory trace which in turn would support higher recognition and recall performance.

## Experiment 1

### METHOD

In the first experiment, single subjects were given the perceptual-reaction time test; this encoding

**TABLE 18.1. Typical Questions and Responses Used in the Experiments**

| Level of Processing | Question | Answer | |
|---|---|---|---|
| | | Yes | No |
| Structural | Is the word in capital letters? | TABLE | table |
| Phonemic | Does the word rhyme with WEIGHT? | crate | MARKET |
| Category | Is the word a type of fish? | SHARK | heaven |
| Sentence | Would the word fit the sentence: "He met a ____ in the street"? | FRIEND | cloud |

phase was followed by a recognition test. Five types of question were used. First, "Is there a word present?" Second, "Is the word in capital letters?" Third, "Does the word rhyme with _____?" Fourth, "Is the word in the category _____?" Fifth, "Would the word fit in the sentence ____?" When the first type of question was asked ("Is there a word present?"), on half of the trials a word was present and on half of the trials no word was present on the tachistoscope card; thus, the subject could respond *yes* when he detected any wordlike pattern on the card. (This task may be rather different from the others and was not used in further experiments; also, of course, it yields difficulties of analysis since no word is presented on the negative trials, these trials cannot be included in the measurement of retention.)

The stimuli used were common two-syllable nouns of 5, 6, or 7 letters. Forty trials were given; 4 words represented each of the 10 conditions (5 levels × *yes–no*). The same pool of 40 words was used for all 20 subjects, but each word was rotated through the 10 conditions so that, for different subjects, a word was presented as a rhyme-*yes* stimulus, a category-*no* stimulus and so on. This procedure yielded 10 combinations of questions and words; 2 subjects received each combination. On each trial, the question was read to the subject who was already looking in the tachistoscope. After 2 sec, the word was exposed and the subject responded by saying *yes* or *no*—his vocal response activated a voice key which stopped a millisecond timer. The experimenter recorded the response latency, changed the word in the tachistoscope, and read the next question; trials thus occurred approximately every 10 sec.

After a brief rest, the subject was given a sheet with the 40 original words plus 40 similar distractors typed on it. Any one subject had actually only seen 36 words as no word was presented on negative "Word present?" trials. He was asked to check all words he had seen on the tachistoscope. No time limit was imposed for this task. Two different randomizations of the 80 recognition words were typed; one randomization was given to each member of the pair of subjects who received identical study lists. Thus each subject received a unique presentation-recognition combination. The 20 subjects were college students of both sexes paid for their services.

## RESULTS AND DISCUSSION

The results are shown in Table 18.2. The upper portion shows response latencies for the different questions. Only correct answers were included in the analysis. The median latency was calculated for each subject; Table 18.2 shows mean medians. Although the five question levels were selected intuitively, the table shows that in fact response latency rises systematically as the questions necessitated deeper processing. Apart from the sentence level, *yes* and *no* responses took equivalent times. The median latency scores were subjected to an analysis of variance (after log transformation). The analysis showed a significant effect of level, $F(4, 171) = 35.4$, $p < .001$, but no effect of response type (*yes–no*) and no interaction. Thus, intuitively deeper questions—semantic as opposed to structural decisions about the word—required slightly longer processing times (150–200 msec).

Table 18.2 also shows the recognition results. Performance (the hit rate) increased substantially from below 20% recognized for questions concerning structural characteristics, to 96% correct for sentence-*yes* decisions. The other prominent feature of the recognition results is that the *yes* responses to words in the initial perceptual phase were accompanied by higher subsequent recognition than the *no* responses. Further, the superiority of recognition of *yes* words increased with depth (until the trend was apparently halted by a ceiling effect). These observations were confirmed by analysis of variance on recognition proportions (after arc sine transformation). Since the first level (word present?) had only *yes* responses, words from this level were not included in the analysis.

**TABLE 18.2. Initial Decision Latency and Recognition Performance for Words as a Function of Initial Task (Experiment 1)**

| Response Type | Level of Processing | | | | |
|---|---|---|---|---|---|
| | 1 | 2 | 3 | 4 | 5 |
| Response latency (msec) | | | | | |
| Yes | 591 | 614 | 689 | 711 | 746 |
| No | 590 | 625 | 678 | 716 | 832 |
| Proportion recognized | | | | | |
| Yes | .22 | .18 | .78 | .93 | .96 |
| No | | .14 | .36 | .63 | .83 |

Type of question was a significant factor, $F(3, 133)$ = 52.8, $p < .001$, as was response type (yes–no), $F(1, 133) = 40.2$, $p < .001$. The Question × Response Type interaction was also significant, $F(3, 133) = 6.77$, $p < .001$.

The results have thus shown that different encoding questions led to different response latencies; questions about the surface form of the word were answered comparatively rapidly, while more abstract questions about the word's meaning took longer to answer. If processing time is an index of depth, then words presented after a semantic question were indeed processed more deeply. Further, the different encoding questions were associated with marked differences in recognition performance: Semantic questions were followed by higher recognition of the word. In fact, Table 18.2 shows that initial response latency is systematically related to subsequent recognition. Thus, within the limits of the present assumptions, it may be concluded that deeper processing yields superior retention.

It is of course possible to argue that the higher recognition levels are more simply attributable to longer study times. This point will be dealt with later in the paper, but for the present it may be noted that in these terms, 200 msec of extra study time led to a 400% improvement in retention. It seems more reasonable to attribute the enhanced performance to qualitative differences in processing and to conclude that manipulation of levels of processing at the time of input is an extremely powerful determinant of retention of word events. The reason for the superior recognition of *yes* responses is not immediately apparent—it cannot be greater depth of processing in the simple sense, since *yes* and *no* responses took the same time for each encoding question. Further discussion of this point is deferred until more experiments are described.

Experiment 2 is basically a replication of Experiment 1 but with a somewhat tidier design and with more recognition distractors to remove ceiling effects.

## Experiment 2

### METHOD

Only three levels of encoding were used in this study: questions concerning typescript (uppercase or lowercase), rhyme questions, and sentence questions (in which subjects were given a sentence frame with one word missing). During the initial perceptual phase 60 questions were presented: 10 *yes* and 10 *no* questions at each of the three levels. Question type was randomized within the block of 60 trials. The question was presented auditorily to the subject; 2 sec later the word appeared in the tachistoscope for 200 msec. The subject responded as rapidly as possible by pressing one of two response keys. After completing the 60 initial trials, the subject was given a typed list of 180 words comprising the 60 original words plus 120 distractors. He was told to check all words he had seen in the first phase.

All words used were five-letter common concrete nouns. From the pool of 60 words, two question formats were constructed by randomly allocating each word to a question type until all 10 words for each question type were filled. In addition, two orders of question presentation and two random orderings of the 180-word recognition list were used. Three subjects were tested on each of the eight combinations thus generated. The 24 subjects were students of both sexes paid for their services and tested individually.

### RESULTS AND DISCUSSION

The left-hand panel of Figure 18.1 shows that response latency rose systematically for both response types, from case questions to rhyme questions to sentence questions. These data again are interpreted as showing that deeper processing took longer to accomplish. At each level, positive and negative responses took the same time. An analysis of variance on mean medians yielded an effect of question type, $F(2, 46) = 46.5$, $p < .001$, but yielded no effect of response type and no interaction.

Figure 18.1 also shows the recognition results. For *yes* words, performance increased from 15% for case decisions to 81% for sentence decisions— more than a five-fold increase in hit rate for memory performance for the same subjects in the same experiment. Recognition of *no* words also increased, but less sharply from 19% (case) to 49% (sentence). An analysis of variance showed a question type (level of processing) effect, $F(2, 46) = 118$, $p < .001$, a response type (*yes–no*) effect, $F(1, 23) = 47.9$, $p < .001$, and a Question Type × Response Type interaction, $F(2, 46) = 22.5$, $p < .001$.

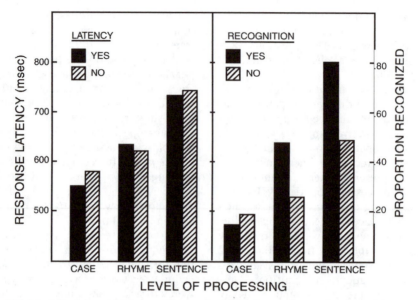

**FIGURE 18.1** ■ Initial decision latency and recognition performance for words as a function of the initial task (Experiment 2).

Experiment 2 thus replicated the results of Experiment 1 and showed clearly (a) Different encoding questions are associated with different response latencies—this finding is interpreted to mean that semantic questions induce a deeper level of analysis of the presented word, (b) positive and negative responses are equally fast, (c) recognition increases to the extent that the encoding question deals with more abstract, semantic features of the word, and (d) words given a positive response are associated with higher recognition performance, but only after rhyme and category questions.

The data from Figure 18.1 are replotted in Figure 18.2, in which recognition performance is shown as a function of initial categorization time. Both *yes* and *no* functions are strikingly linear, with a steeper slope for *yes* responses. This pattern of data suggests that memory performance may simply be a function of processing *time* as such (regardless of "level of analysis"). This suggestion is examined (and rejected) in this article, where we argue that level of analysis, not processing time, is the critical determinant of recognition performance.

Experiments 3 and 4 extended the generality of these findings by showing that the same pattern of results holds in recall and under intentional learning conditions.

## Experiment 3

### METHOD

Three levels of encoding were again included in the study by asking questions about typescript (case), rhyme, and sentences. On each trial the question was read to the subject; after 2 sec the word was exposed for 200 msec on the tachistoscope. The subject responded by pressing the rel-

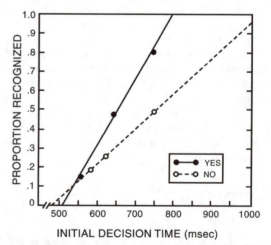

**FIGURE 18.2** ■ Proportion of words recognized as a function of initial decision time (Experiment 2).

evant response key. At the end of the encoding trials, the subject was allowed to rest for 1 min and was then asked to recall as many words as he could. In Experiment 3, this final recall task was unexpected—thus the initial encoding phase may be considered an incidental learning task—while in Experiment 4, subjects were informed at the beginning of the session that they would be required to recall the words.

Pilot studies had shown that the recall level in this situation tends to be low. Thus, to boost recall, and to examine the effects of encoding level on recall more clearly, half of the words in the present study were presented twice. In all, 48 different words were used, but 24 were presented twice, making a total of 72 trials. Of the 24 words presented once only, 4 were presented under each of the six conditions (three types of question × yes–no). Similarly, of the 24 words presented twice, 4 were presented under each of the six conditions. When a word was repeated, it always occurred as the 20th item after its first presentation; that is, the lag between first and second presentations was held constant. On its second appearance, the same *type* of question was asked as on the word's first appearance but, for rhyme and sentence questions, a different *specific* question was asked. Thus, when the word TRAIN fell into the rhyme-*yes* category, the question asked on its first presentation might have been "Does the word rhyme with BRAIN?" while on the second presentation the question might have been "Does the word rhyme with CRANE?" For case questions the same question was asked on the two occurrences since each subject was given the same question throughout the experiment (e.g., "Is the word in lowercase?"). This procedure was adopted as early work had shown that subjects' response latencies were greatly slowed if they had to associate *yes* responses to both uppercase and lowercase words.

A constant pool of 48 words was used for all subjects. The words were common concrete nouns. Five presentation formats were constructed in which the words were randomly allocated to the various encoding conditions. Four subjects were tested on each format: Two made *yes* responses with their right hand on the right response key while two used the left-hand key for *yes* responses. The 20 student subjects were paid for their services. They were told that the experiment concerned perception and reaction time; they were

warned that some words would occur twice, but they were not informed of the final recall test.

## RESULTS AND DISCUSSION

Response latencies are shown in Table 18.3. For each subject and each experimental condition (e.g., case–*yes*) the median response latency was calculated for the eight words presented on their first occurrence (i.e., the four words presented only once, and the first occurrence of the four repeated words). The median latency was also calculated for the four repeated words on their second presentation. Only correct responses were included in the calculation of the medians. Table 18.3 shows the mean medians for the various experimental conditions. There was a systematic increase in response latency from case question to sentence questions. Also, response latencies were more rapid on the word's second presentation—this was especially true for *yes* responses. These observations were confirmed by an analysis of variance. The effect of question type was significant, $F(2, 38) = 14.4$, $p < .01$, but the effect of response type was not ($F < 1.0$). Repeated words were responded to reliably faster, $F(1, 19) = 10.3$, $p < .01$ and the Number of Presentations × Response Type (*yes–no*) interaction was significant, $F(1, 19) = 5.33$, $p < .05$.

Thus, again, deeper level questions took longer to process, but *yes* responses took no longer than

**TABLE 18.3. Response Latencies for Experiments 3 and 4**

| Condition | Case | Rhyme | Sentence |
|---|---|---|---|
| 1st presentation | | | |
| Incidental (Exp. 3) | | | |
| Yes | 689 | 816 | 870 |
| No | 705 | 725 | 872 |
| Intentional (Exp. 4) | | | |
| Yes | 687 | 796 | 897 |
| No | 685 | 768 | 911 |
| 2nd presentation | | | |
| Incidental (Exp. 3) | | | |
| Yes | 616 | 689 | 771 |
| No | 634 | 725 | 856 |
| Intentional (Exp. 4) | | | |
| Yes | 609 | 684 | 793 |
| No | 599 | 716 | 866 |

*Note.* Mean medians of response latencies are presented.

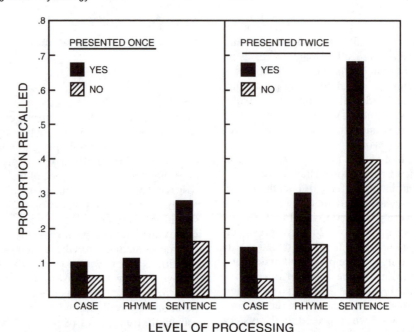

FIGURE 18.3 ■ Proportion of words recalled as a function of the initial task (Experiment 3).

*no* responses. The extra facilitation shown by positive responses on the second presentation may be attributable to the greater predictive value of *yes* questions. For example, the second presentation of a rhyme question may remind the subject of the first presentation and thus facilitate the decision.

Figure 18.3 shows the recall probabilities for words presented once or twice. There is a marked effect of question type (sentence > rhymes > case); retention is again superior for words given an initial *yes* response and recall of twice-presented words is higher than once-presented words. An analysis of variance confirmed these observations. Semantic questions yielded higher recall, $F(2, 38) = 36.9$, $p < .01$; more *yes* responses than *no* responses were recalled, $F(1, 19) = 21.4$, $p < .01$; two presentations increased performance, $F(1, 19) = 33.0$, $p < .01$. In addition, semantically encoded words benefited more from the second presentation, as shown by the significant Question Level × Number of Presentations interaction, $F(2, 38) = 10.8$, $p < .01$.

Experiment 3 thus confirmed that deeper levels of encoding take longer to accomplish and that *yes* and *no* responses take equal encoding times. More important, semantic questions led to higher recall performance and more *yes* response words were recalled than *no* response words. These basic results thus apply as well to recall as they do to recognition. Experiments 1–3 have used an incidental learning paradigm; there are good reasons to believe that the incidental nature of the task is *not* critical for the obtained pattern of results to appear (Hyde & Jenkins, 1973). Nevertheless, it was decided to verify Hyde and Jenkins' conclusion using the present paradigm. Thus, Experiment 4 was a replication of Experiment 3, but with the difference that subjects were informed of the final recall task at the beginning of the session.

## Experiment 4

### METHOD

The material and procedures were identical to those in Experiment 3 except that subjects were informed of the final free recall task. They were told that the memory task was of equal importance to the initial phase and that they should thus attempt to remember all words shown in the tachistoscope. A 10-min period was allowed for recall. The subjects were 20 college students, none of whom had participated in Experiments 1, 2, or 3.

## RESULTS AND DISCUSSION

The response latencies are shown in Table 18.3. These data are very similar to those from Experiment 3, indicating that subjects took no longer to respond under intentional learning instructions. Analysis of variance showed that deeper levels were associated with longer decision latencies, $F(2, 38) = 27.7$, $p < .01$, and that second presentations were responded to faster, $F(1, 19) = 18.9$, $p < .01$. No other effect was statistically reliable.

With regard to the recall results, the analysis of variance yielded significant effects of processing level, $F(2, 38) = 43.4$, $p < .01$, of repetition, $F(1, 19) = 69.7$, $p < .01$, and of response type (*yes–no*), $F(1, 19) = 13.9$, $p < .01$. In addition, the Number of Presentations × Level of Processing interaction, $F(2, 38) = 12.4$, $p < .01$, and the Number of Presentations × Response Type (*yes–no*) interaction, $F(1, 19) = 7.93$, $p < .025$, were statistically reliable. Figure 18.4 shows that these effects were attributable to superior recall of sentence decisions, twice-presented words and *yes* responses. Words associated with semantic questions and with *yes* responses showed the greatest enhancement of recall after a second presentation.

To further explore the effects of intentional versus incidental conditions more comprehensive analyses of variance were carried out, involving the data from both Experiments 3 and 4. For the latency data, there was no significant effect of the intentional-incidental manipulation, nor did the intentional-incidental factor interact with any other factor. Thus, knowledge of the final recall test had no effect on subjects' decision times. In the case of recall scores, intentional instructions yielded superior performance, $F(1, 38) = 11.73$, $p < .01$, and the Intentional-Incidental × Number of Presentations interaction was significant, $F(1, 38) = 5.75$, $p < .05$. This latter effect shows that the superiority of intentional instructions was greater for twice-presented items. No other interaction involving the incidental-intentional factor was significant. It may thus be concluded that the pattern of results obtained in the present experiments does not depend critically on incidental instructions.

The findings that intentional recall was superior to incidental recall, but that decision times did not differ between intentional and incidental conditions, is at first sight contrary to the theoretical notions proposed in the introduction to this article. If recall is a function of depth of processing and

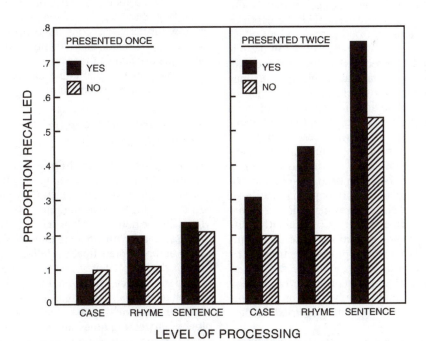

**FIGURE 18.4** ■ Proportion of words recalled as a function of the initial task (Experiment 4).

depth is indexed by decision time, then clearly differences in recall should be associated with differences in initial response latency. However, it is possible that further processing was carried out in the intentional condition, *after* the orienting task question was answered, and was thus not reflected in the decision times.

## Discussion

Experiments 1–4 have provided empirical flesh for the theoretical bones of the argument advanced by Craik, and Lockhart (1972). When semantic (deeper level) questions were asked about a presented word, its subsequent retention was greatly enhanced. This result held for both recognition and recall; it also held for both incidental and intentional learning (Hyde & Jenkins, 1969, 1973; Till & Jenkins, 1973). The reported effects were both robust, and large in magnitude: Sentence–*yes* words showed recognition and recall levels which were superior to case–*no* words by a factor ranging from 2.4 to 13.6. Plainly, the nature of the encoding operation is an important determinant of both incidental and intentional learning and hence of retention.

At the same time, some aspects of the present results are clearly inconsistent with the depth of processing formulation outlined in the introduction. First, words given a *yes* response in the initial task were better recalled and recognized than words given a *no* response, although reaction times to *yes* and *no* responses were identical. Either reaction time is not an adequate index of depth, or depth is not a good predictor of subsequent retention. We will argue the former case. If depth of processing (defined loosely as increasing semantic-associative analysis of the stimulus) is decoupled from processing time, then on the one hand the independent index of depth has been lost, but on the other hand, the results of Experiments 1–4 can be described in terms of qualitative differences in encoding operations rather than simply in terms of increased processing times. The following section describes evidence relevant to the question of whether retention performance is primarily a function of "study time" or the qualitative nature of mental operations carried out during that time.

The results obtained under intentional learning conditions (Experiment 4) are also not well accommodated by the initial depth of processing notions. If the large differences in retention found in Experiments 1–3 are attributable to different depths of processing in the rather literal sense that only structural analyses are activated by the case judgment task, phonemic analyses are activated by rhyme judgments, and semantic analyses activated by category or sentence judgments, then surely under intentional learning conditions the subject would analyse and perceive the name and meaning of the target word with all three types of question. In this case equal retention should ensue (by the Craik and Lockhart formulation), but Experiment 4 showed that large differences in recall were still found.

A more promising notion is that retention differences should be attributed to *degrees of stimulus elaboration* rather than to differences in depth. This revised formulation retains the important point (borne out by Experiments 1–4) that the qualitative nature of encoding operations is critical for the establishment of a durable trace, but gets away from the notions that semantic analyses necessarily always follow structural analyses and that no meaning is involved in shallow processing tasks.

For the moment, the term *depth* is retained to signify greater degrees of semantic involvement. Before further discussions of the theoretical framework are presented, the following section describes attempts to evaluate the relative effects of processing time and the qualitative nature of encoding operations on the retention of words.

## Processing Time versus Encoding Operations

As a first step, the data from Experiment 2 were examined for evidence relating the effects of processing time to subsequent memory performance. At first sight, Experiment 2 provided evidence in line with the notion that longer categorization times are associated with higher retention levels—Figure 18.2 demonstrated linear relationships between initial decision latency and subsequent recognition performance. However, if it is processing time which determines performance, and not the qualitative nature of the task, then *within one task*, longer processing times should be associated with superior memory performance. That is, with the qualitative differences in processing held constant, performance should be determined by the time taken to make the initial decision. On the other hand, if differences in encoding operations are critical for differences in retention, then memory performance should vary between orienting tasks, but within any given task, retention level should not depend on processing time.

This point was explored by analyzing the data from Experiment 2 in terms of fast and slow categorization times. The 10 response latencies for each subject in each condition were divided into the 5 fastest responses and the 5 slowest responses. Next, mean recognition probabilities for the fast and slow subsets of words were calculated across all subjects for each condition. The results of this analysis are shown in Figure 18.5; mean medians for the response latencies in each subset are plotted against recognition probabilities. If processing *time* were crucial, then the words which fell into the slow subset for each task should have been recognized at higher levels than words which elicited fast responses. Figure 18.5 shows that this did not happen. Slow responses were recognized little better than fast responses within each level of analysis. On the other hand, the qualitative nature of the task continued to exert a very large effect on recognition performance, suggesting again that it is the nature of the encoding operations and not processing time which determines memory performance.

For both *yes* and *no* responses, slow case categorization decisions took longer than fast sentence decisions. However, words about which subjects had made sentence decisions showed higher levels of recognition; 73% as opposed to 17% for *yes* responses and 45% as opposed to 17% for *no* responses. No statistical analysis was thought necessary to support the conclusion that task rather than time is the crucial aspect in these experiments.

## ACKNOWLEDGMENT

The research reported in this article was supported by National Research Council of Canada Grants A8261 and A8632 to the first and second authors, respectively. The authors gratefully acknowledge the assistance of Michael Anderson, Ed Darte, Gregory Mazuryk, Marsha Carnat, Marilyn Tiller, and Margaret Barr.

## REFERENCE NOTE

1. Moscovitch, M. & Craik, F. I. M. *Retrieval Cues and Levels of Processing in Recall and Recognition.* Unpublished manuscript, 1975. (Available from Morris Moscovitch, Erindale College, Mississauga, Ontario, Canada).

## REFERENCES

Begg, I. Recall of meaningful phrases. *Journal of Verbal Learning and Verbal Behavior*, 1972, *11*, 431–439.
Bobrow, S. A. & Bower, G. H. Comprehension and recall of sentences. *Journal of Experimental Psychology*, 1969, *80*, 55–61.

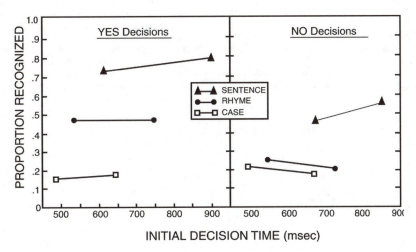

**FIGURE 18.5** ■ Recognition of words as a function of task and initial decision time: Data partitioned into fast and slow decision times (Experiment 2).

Bower, G. H. A multicomponent theory of the memory trace. In K. W. Spence & J. T. Spence (Eds.), *The Psychology of Learning and Motivation* (Vol. 1). New York: Academic Press, 1967.

Bower, G. H. & Karlin, M. B. Depth of processing pictures of faces and recognition memory. *Journal of Experimental Psychology*, 1974, *103*, 751–757.

Broadbent, D. E. *Behaviour*. London: Eyre & Spottiswoode, 1961.

Cermak, L. S. *Human Memory: Research and Theory*. New York: Ronald, 1972.

Craik, F. I. M. & Lockhart, R. S. Levels of processing: A framework for memory research. *Journal of Verbal Learning and Verbal Behavior*, 1972, *11*, 671–684.

Craik, F. I. M. & Watkins, M. J. The role of rehearsal in short-term memory. *Journal of Verbal Learning and Verbal Behavior*, 1973, *12*, 599–607.

Eagle, M. & Leiter, E. Recall and recognition in intentional and incidental learning. *Journal of Experimental Psychology*, 1964, *68*, 58–63.

Horowitz, L. M. & Prytulak, L. S. Redintegrative memory. *Psychological Review*, 1969, *76*, 519–531.

Hyde, T. S. Differential effects of effort and type of orienting task on recall and organization of highly associated words. *Journal of Experimental Psychology*, 1973, *79*, 111–113.

Hyde, T. S. & Jenkins, J. J. Differential effects of incidental tasks on the organization of recall of a list of highly associated words. *Journal of Experimental Psychology*, 1969, *82*, 472–481.

Hyde, T. S. & Jenkins, J. J. Recall for words as a function of semantic, graphic, and syntactic orienting tasks. *Journal of Verbal Learning and Verbal Behavior*, 1973, *12*, 471–480.

Jacoby, L. L. Test appropriate strategies in retention of categorized lists. *Journal of Verbal Learning and Verbal Behavior*, 1973, *12*, 675–682.

Kolers, P. A. Remembering operations. *Memory & Cognition*, 1973, *1*, 347–355. (a)

Kolers, P. A. Some modes of representation. In P. Pliner, L. Krames, & T. Alloway (Eds.), *Communication and Affect: Language and Thought*. New York: Academic Press, 1973. (b)

Kolers, P. A. & Ostry, D. J. Time course of loss of information regarding pattern analyzing operations. *Journal of Verbal Learning and Verbal Behavior*, 1974, *13*, 599–612.

Lockhart, R. S., Craik, F. I. M., & Jacoby, L. L. Depth of processing in, recognition and recall: Some aspects of a general memory system. In J. Brown (Ed.), *Recognition and Recall*. London: Wiley, 1975.

Neisser, U. *Cognitive Psychology*. New York: Appleton-Century-Crofts, 1967.

Norman, D. A. (Ed.). *Models of Human Memory*. New York: Academic Press, 1970.

Paivio, A. *Imagery and Verbal Processes*. New York: Holt, Rinehart & Winston, 1971.

Postman, L. Short-term memory and incidental learning. In A. W. Melton (Ed.), *Categories of Human Learning*. New York: Academic Press, 1964.

Rosenberg, S. & Schiller, W. J. Semantic coding and incidental sentence recall. *Journal of Experimental Psychology*, 1971, *90*, 345–346.

Schulman, A. I. Recognition memory for targets from a scanned word list. *British Journal of Psychology*, 1971, *62*, 335–346.

Schulman, A. I. Memory for words recently classified. *Memory & Cognition*, 1974, *2*, 47–52.

Sheehan, P. W. The role of imagery in incidental learning. *British Journal of Psychology*, 1971, *62*, 235–244.

Sutherland, N. S. Object recognition. In E. C. Carterette & M. P. Friedman (Eds.), *Handbook of Perception* (Vol. 3). New York: Academic Press, 1972.

Till, R. E. & Jenkins, J. J. The effects of cued orienting tasks on the free recall of words. *Journal of Verbal Learning and Verbal Behavior*, 1973, *12*, 489–498.

Treisman, A. & Tuxworth, J. Immediate and delayed recall of sentences after perceptual processing at different levels. *Journal of Verbal Learning and Verbal Behavior*, 1974, *13*, 38–44.

Tulving, E. Episodic and semantic memory. In E. Tulving & W. Donaldson (Eds.), *Organization of Memory*. New York: Academic Press, 1972.

Tulving, E. & Thomson, D. M. Encoding specificity and retrieval processes in episodic memory. *Psychological Review*, 1973, *80*, 352–373.

Tulving, E. & Watkins, M. J. Structure of memory traces. *Psychological Review*, 1975, *82*, 261–275.

Walsh, D. A. & Jenkins, J. J. Effects of orienting tasks on free recall in incidental learning: "Difficulty," "effort," and "process" explanations. *Journal of Verbal Learning and Verbal Behavior*, 1973, *12*, 481–488.

Waugh, N. C. & Norman, D. A. Primary memory. *Psychological Review*, 1965, *72*, 89–104.

Wickelgren, W. A. The long and the short of memory. *Psychological Bulletin*, 1973, *80*, 425–438.

READING 19

# Semantic Integration of Verbal Information into a Visual Memory

Elizabeth F. Loftus • University of Washington
David G. Miller • University of Houston
Helen J. Burns • University of Washington

A total of 1,242 subjects, in five experiments plus a pilot study, saw a series of slides depicting a single auto–pedestrian accident. The purpose of these experiments was to investigate how information supplied after an event influences a witness's memory for that event. Subjects were exposed to either consistent, misleading, or irrelevant information after the accident event. Misleading information produced less accurate responding on both a yes–no and a two-alternative forced-choice recognition test. Further, misleading information had a larger impact if introduced just prior to a final test rather than immediately after the initial event. The effects of misleading information cannot be accounted for by a simple demand-characteristics explanation. Overall, the results suggest that information to which a witness is exposed after an event, whether that information is consistent or misleading, is integrated into the witness's memory of the event.

Almost two centuries ago, Immanuel Kant (1781/ 1887) spoke of the human tendency to merge different experiences to form new concepts and ideas. That tendency has crucial implications for one's ability to report his or her experiences accurately. When one has witnessed an important event, such as a crime or an accident, one is occasionally exposed to subsequent information that can influence the memory of that event. This occurs even when the initial event is largely visual and the additional information is verbal in nature (Loftus, 1975; Pezdek, 1977). For instance, in a previous study, subjects saw films of complex fast-moving events such as automobile accidents or classroom disruptions (Loftus, 1975). Immediately afterward, the subjects were asked a series of questions, some of which were designed to present accurate, consistent information (e.g., suggesting the existence of an object that did exist in the scene), while others presented misleading information (e.g., suggesting the existence of an object that did not exist in the original scene). Thus, a subject might have been asked, "How fast was the car going when it ran the stop sign?" when a stop sign actually did exist (Experiment 1). Or the subject might have been asked, "How fast was the white sports car going when it passed the barn while traveling along the country road?" when no barn existed

(Experiment 3). These subjects were subsequently asked whether they had seen the presupposed objects. It was found that such questions increased the likelihood that subjects would later report having seen these objects. It was argued that the questions were effective because they contained information—sometimes consistent, sometimes misleading—which was integrated into the memorial representation of the event, thereby causing a reconstruction or alteration of the actual information stored in memory.

In these earlier experiments, the original event was presented visually, the subsequent information was introduced verbally via questionnaires, and the final test was also verbal in nature. In the present experiments, a recognition procedure was used; it involved showing a series of slides depicting a complex event and afterward exposing subjects to verbal information about the event. This study phase was followed by a recognition test in which the subjects were presented with target pictures identical to ones seen before and distractor pictures altered in some way. The first reason for this change was that if one subscribes to the view that verbal and visual information are stored separately, one could argue that Loftus's (1975) final test, being verbal in nature, helped subjects access the subsequent verbal information, thereby resulting in an incorrect response.

The second reason for using a recognition test procedure was that if recognition is assumed to be a relatively passive and simple process of matching stimuli to specific locations in a content-addressable storage system, one would expect a representation of the actual (or true) scene to result in a match, whereas an alteration would fail to match. In other words, if the original visual scene is stored

in memory, presenting the subject with the original stimulus might result in a match between the memory representation and the stimulus. If the original scene had been transformed so that an altered version was stored in memory, presenting the subject with the original stimulus would not result in a match between the memorial representation and the stimulus.

These considerations motivated the present series of studies. Before turning to them, we describe a pilot study in some detail, since the materials and procedures were similar to those used in the remaining experiments.

## Pilot Experiment

In a pilot experiment (Loftus, Salzberg, Burns, & Sanders, Note 1), a series of 30 color slides, depicting successive stages in an auto–pedestrian accident, was shown to 129 subjects. The auto was a red Datsun seen traveling along a side street toward an intersection having a stop sign for half of the subjects and a yield sign for the remaining subjects. These two critical slides are shown in Figure 19.1. The remaining slides show the Datsun turning right and knocking down a pedestrian who is crossing at the crosswalk. Immediately after viewing the slides, the subjects answered a series of 20 questions. For half of the subjects, Question 17 was, "Did another car pass the red Datsun while it was stopped at the stop sign?" The remaining subjects were asked the same question with the words "stop sign" replaced by "yield sign." The assignment of subjects to conditions produced a factorial design in which half of the subjects received consistent or correct information, whereas

**FIGURE 19.1** ■ Critical slides used in the acquisition series.

the other half received misleading or incorrect information. All subjects then participated in a 20-min filler activity, which required them to read an unrelated short story and answer some questions about it. Finally, a yes–no recognition test was administered either immediately or 1 week later. The two critical slides (i.e., those containing the stop and yield signs) were randomly placed in the recognition series in different positions for different groups of subjects.

The results indicated that relative to the case in which consistent information is received, misleading information resulted in significantly fewer hits (correct recognitions of the slide actually seen) and slightly more false alarms (false recognitions of the slide not actually seen). With misleading information, the percentage of hits was 71 and the percentage of false alarms was 70, indicating that subjects had zero ability to discriminate the sign they actually saw from the sign they did not see.

Some aspects of the data from this study preclude a clear interpretation of the results and beg for a variation in design. Most of the subjects responded "yes" to the slide shown first in the recognition series, even though the opposite sign had been seen and mentioned in the questionnaire. This indicates that the two critical slides are so similar that subjects failed to make any distinction between them. Perhaps when the second slide appeared, some subjects responded "yes" again, thinking it was the same slide, while others felt obliged to respond "no," having already responded "yes" to the earlier slide. For these reasons, a forced-choice recognition test seemed necessary, since it eliminates the problem of successive recognition tests and forces the subjects to discriminate between the two critical slides.

## Overview of the Experiments

In Experiment 1, subjects were presented with the acquisition series of slides, an intervening questionnaire, and a final forced-choice recognition test. It is shown that misleading information results in substantially less accurate responding than does consistent information. Next, we consider the possibility that subjects are simply agreeing with the information in their questionnaires, fully remembering what they actually saw. Experiment 2 was actually a demonstration designed to show that

the results thus far cannot be explained simply by the demand characteristics of the procedure. In Experiment 3, we asked whether information presented verbally has a different effect depending on whether it is introduced immediately after the initial event (i.e., at the beginning of the retention interval) or just prior to the final test (i.e., at the end of the retention interval). It was found that misleading information has a greater impact when presented just prior to a recognition test rather than just after the initial event. Finally, we addressed the question of whether the verbally presented information actually results in a transformation of an existing representation or whether it is simply a supplementation phenomenon. To answer this issue, one needs to know whether the original sign entered memory in the first place. If not, then the subsequent verbal information may simply introduce a sign where none existed, supplementing the existing memorial representation. If the sign originally did get into memory, the subsequent information has caused either an alteration in the original representation (i.e., one sign replaced the other in memory) or the creation of a new, stronger representation that successfully, competes with the original one, rendering the latter so dramatically suppressed as to be, for all intents and purposes, gone. Experiment 4, in conjunction with Experiment 3, indicates that the traffic sign is encoded by most subjects when they view the series of slides. Experiment 5 demonstrates the generality of the findings with other materials.

## Experiment 1

### Method

Subjects were 195 students from the University of Washington who participated in groups of various sizes. With a few exceptions, the procedure was similar to that used in the pilot experiment. The subjects saw the same series of 30 color slides, seeing each slide for approximately 3 sec. Approximately half of the subjects saw a slide depicting a small red Datsun stopped at a stop sign, whereas the remaining subjects saw the car stopped at a yield sign. Immediately after viewing the acquisition slides, the subjects filled out a questionnaire of 20 questions. For half of the subjects, Question 17 was, "Did another car pass the red Datsun while it was stopped at the stop sign?" For the other half, the same question was asked with the words "stop sign" replaced with "yield sign." Thus, for 95 subjects, the sign mentioned in the question was the sign that had actually been seen; in other words, the question contained consistent information. For the remaining 100 subjects, the question contained misleading information.

After completing the questionnaire, the subjects participated in a 20-min filler activity that required them to read an unrelated short story and answer some questions about it. Finally, a forced-choice recognition test was administered. Using two slide projectors, 15 pairs of slides were presented, each pair of slides being projected for approximately 8 sec. One member of each pair was old and the other was new. For each pair, the subjects were asked to select the slide that they had seen earlier. The critical pair was a slide depicting the red Datsun stopped at a stop sign and a nearly identical slide depicting the Datsun at a yield sign. The slides that the subjects actually saw varied in the left and right positions.

## Results

The percentage of times a subject correctly selected the slide he or she had seen before was 75 and 41, respectively, when the intervening question contained consistent versus misleading information, $Z = 4.72, p < .001$. If 50% correct selection is taken to represent chance guessing behavior, subjects given consistent information performed significantly better than chance, $Z = 5.10, p < .001$, whereas those given misleading information performed significantly worse than chance, $Z = 1.80$, $p < .05$ (one-tailed test).

## Experiment 2

Some time ago, Orne (1962) proposed that certain aspects of any psychological experiment may provide clues, or *demand characteristics*, that permit observant subjects to discern the experimental hypothesis. Obliging subjects may then try to confirm that hypothesis. In the context of the present paradigm, it is possible that some or all of the subjects not only remembered what traffic sign they observed but also remembered what sign was

presupposed on their questionnaire and then "went along" with what they believed to be the experimental hypothesis and chose the sign from their questionnaire. A slightly different version of this position would argue that at the time of the final test, subjects said to themselves, "I think I saw a stop sign, but my questionnaire said 'yield sign,' so I guess it must have been a yield sign." Experiment 2 was designed to investigate this possibility.

## Method

The method was similar to that of Experiment 1 with a few exceptions. Ninety subjects saw the slide series. Half of them saw a stop sign, and half a yield sign. Immediately after slides, the subjects filled out the questionnaire. For 30 subjects, the critical question was, "Did another car pass the red Datsun while it was stopped at the intersection?" In other words, it did not mention a sign. For 30 other subjects, the critical question mentioned a stop sign, and for the remaining 30 it mentioned a yield sign. Thus, for one third of the subjects, the key question contained a true presupposition; for one third, the presupposition was false; and for the remaining one third, the question made no reference to a sign at all. A 20-min filler activity occurred, followed by a forced-choice recognition test.

Finally, the subject was given a "debriefing questionnaire." It stated,

> The study in which you have just been involved was designed to determine the effects of subsequent information on eye-witness testimony. In the beginning, you saw a series of slides which depicted an accident. One of the slides contained either a stop sign or a yield sign. Later you were given a questionnaire. One of the questions on this questionnaire was worded to assume that you had seen either a stop sign or a yield sign or else it contained no information about what kind of sign you saw.
>
> Please indicate which sign you think you saw and what was assumed on your questionnaire.

|                | My Questionnaire |
| I Saw          | Mentioned        |
| A stop sign    | A stop sign      |
| A yield sign   | A yield sign     |
|                | No sign          |

This final debriefing questionnaire permitted a subject to claim, for example, that he or she had seen a stop sign but that the questionnaire had mentioned a yield sign. In other words, it gave the subjects the opportunity to be completely "insightful" about their condition in the experiment.

## Results

Of the 90 subjects who took the forced-choice recognition test, 53 chose the correct sign; 37 chose the incorrect sign. As in the previous experiment, accuracy depended on whether the subject had been given consistent, misleading, or no information on the intervening questionnaire. This relationship can be seen in Table 19.1.

The subjects who chose the correct sign during the forced-choice test were more than three times as likely as incorrect subjects to be completely correct on the debriefing questionnaire. Overall, 43% of the subjects choosing the correct sign accurately responded to the debriefing questionnaire, whereas only 14% of the incorrect subjects were completely accurate, $Z = 2.96$, $p < .01$. Again, whether the subjects responded accurately to the debriefing questionnaire depended on whether they had been given consistent, misleading, or no information on their intervening questionnaires.

Of central concern was the performance of subjects who had been given misleading information and who had subsequently chosen incorrectly on their forced-choice test. For example, they saw a stop sign, read that it was a yield sign, and subsequently chose the yield sign on the forced-choice test. These subjects were the ones who may have been acting the way the experimenter wanted them to act. They may have been deliberately choosing the sign mentioned on their questionnaire although

fully remembering what they saw. Yet, when given the debriefing questionnaire that afforded them the opportunity to say, "I think I saw the stop sign, but my questionnaire said yield," only 12% did so.

## Experiment 3

The issue that motivated Experiment 3 was whether the information introduced subsequent to an event has a different impact when it is introduced immediately after the event than when it is introduced just prior to the final test. To determine this, we varied the time interval between the initial slides and the final forced-choice test. The intervening questionnaire was presented either immediately after the acquisition slides or it was delayed until just prior to the final test.

### Method

Subjects were 648 students from the University of Washington who either participated for course credit or were paid for their participation. They participated in groups of various sizes.

The procedure was nearly identical to that used in Experiments 1 and 2, with the major variations being the retention interval and the time of the intervening questionnaire. Subjects saw each acquisition slide for approximately 3 sec. Half saw the key slide that contained a stop sign, and half saw a yield sign. A questionnaire was administered, followed by a forced-choice recognition test. The forced-choice test occurred after a retention interval of either 20 min, 1 day, 2 days, or 1 week, with 144 subjects tested at each interval. Half of the subjects at each retention interval answered the questionnaire immediately after viewing the

**TABLE 19.1. Data from Experiment 2**

| Information Given | Incorrect Subjects on Forced-Choice Test | | Correct Subjects on Forced-Choice Test | |
|---|---|---|---|---|
| | *n* | % Correct on Debriefing Questionnaire | *n* | % Correct on Debriefing Questionnaire |
| Consistent | 9 | 22 | 21 | 52 |
| Misleading | 17 | 12 | 13 | 31 |
| None | 11 | 9 | 19 | 42 |
| Weighted *M* | | 14 | | 43 |

acquisition slides (immediate questionnaire), and the other half answered it just before the final forced-choice test (delayed questionnaire). In addition, 72 subjects saw the slides, received the questionnaire immediately afterward, and immediately after that were given the forced-choice test. For purposes of analysis, we consider this group to have been tested at a retention interval of zero.[1]

Except at the zero retention interval, all subjects read a short, unrelated "filler" story for 20 min and then answered some questions about it. Subjects who were given the immediate questionnaire completed the filler activity after answering the questionnaire. Subjects who were given the delayed questionnaire completed the filler activity after viewing the acquisition slides.

Question 17 on the questionnaire was the critical question. It mentioned either a stop sign, a yield sign, or no sign at all. Equal numbers of subjects received each version. Thus, one third of the subjects were given consistent information, one third were given misleading information, and one third were given no information at all relevant to a traffic sign.

In the final forced-choice recognition test, sub-jects were asked to choose the slide they had seen before and give a confidence rating from 1 to 3, where 1 indicated the subject was sure of the answer and 3 indicated a guess.

## Results and Discussion

Proportions of correct responses as a function of retention interval are displayed separately for subjects in different conditions in Figure 19.2. The data for subjects tested at a retention interval of zero appear twice in Figure 19.2, once under immediate questionnaire and once under delayed questionnaire, because the questionnaire occurred, by definition, both immediately after the slides and just prior to the final test. In a sense, it was both an immediate and a delayed questionnaire.

Before presenting statistical analyses, we shall point out some major observations. First, for both the immediate and delayed questionnaire, longer retention intervals led to worse performance. Type of information given also had an effect: Relative to a control in which subjects were given no information, consistent information improved their performance and misleading information hindered it.

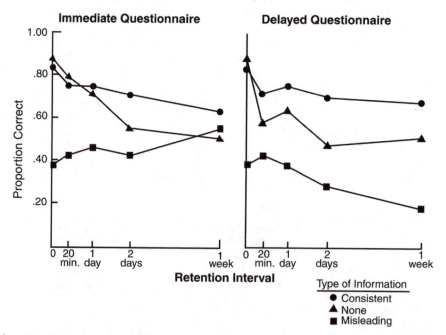

**FIGURE 19.2** ■ Proportion of correct responses as a function of retention interval displayed separately for subjects given an immediate questionnaire and subjects given a delayed questionnaire in Experiment 3. (The curve parameter is type of information the subject received during the retention interval.)

The functions obtained when no relevant information was given show the usual forgetting over time. By 2 days, subjects were performing at chance level. Immediately after viewing the slides, however, there was relatively good memory for them (up to 87% correct).

The first analysis considered only the immediate-questionnaire data. A 5 (retention intervals) × 3 (types of information) analysis of variance of the arc sine transformed proportions was conducted (Mosteller & Tukey, 1949, p. 189). All $F$ tests reported here are with $MS_e = .01$ and $p < .01$, unless otherwise indicated. The analysis showed that longer retention intervals led to less accurate performance, $F(4, \infty) = 5.67$. Further, the type of information to which a subject was exposed affected accuracy, $F(2, \infty) = 50.19$, and there was an interaction between these factors, $F(8, \infty) = 5.19$. A test for monotonic trend for the subjects who were given consistent information yielded a significant trend, $F(1, \infty) = 10.38$. Similarly, the trend was significant for subjects given inconsistent and no information, $F(1, \infty) = 4.43$ and $F(1, \infty) = 43.13$, respectively.

The second analysis considered the data from subjects who received a delayed questionnaire. A 5 × 3 analysis of variance of the arc sine transformed proportions indicated that longer retention intervals led to less accurate performance, $F(4, \infty) = 13.37$. Type of information and the interaction were also significant, $F(2, \infty) = 90.91$, and $F(8, \infty) = 2.98$, respectively. Again, the monotonic trends for each of the three types of information also reached significance: $F(1, \infty) = 5.92$ for subjects given consistent information, 14.05 for inconsistent information, and 35.85 for no information (all $ps < .05$).

## CONSISTENT INFORMATION

Not surprisingly, when a subject is exposed to information that essentially repeats information previously encoded, recognition performance is enhanced. With an immediate questionnaire, the visual and verbal repetitions are massed, whereas with a delayed questionnaire, they are spaced. Whereas in most memory tasks, successive repetitions affect memory less than do repetitions that are spaced apart in time (Hintzman, 1976), this outcome was not obtained in the present experiment. A popular explanation for the spacing ef-

fect is in terms of voluntary attention. The subject chooses to pay less attention to the second occurrence of an item when it closely follows the first occurrence than he does when the interval between the two is longer. In the present case, it appears as if the subject may have paid more attention to the second occurrence when it closely followed the first, resulting in memory enhancement that was able to survive longer retention intervals.

## MISLEADING INFORMATION

When misleading information occurs immediately after an event, it has a different effect than when it is delayed until just prior to the test. The immediate procedure results in a nearly monotonically increasing function, whereas the delayed procedure leads to a monotonically decreasing function. This result makes intuitive sense. When false information is introduced immediately after an event, it has its greatest impact soon. Therefore, when the test was immediate, such subjects performed well below chance. But after an interval of, say, 1 week, both the event and the misleading information apparently had faded such that the subject performed near chance levels. On the other hand, when the misleading information was delayed, it was able to influence the subjects' choice more effectively as the delay increased. Presumably, the weaker the original trace, the easier it is to alter.

To see more clearly the effects of an immediate versus a delayed questionnaire, we excluded the data for subjects tested at a retention interval of zero and collapsed the data over the four remaining retention intervals. The results of these computations are shown in Figure 19.3. The proportion correct is presented as a function of the type of information given, with the immediate versus delayed questionnaire data shown separately. It is again evident that the delayed questionnaire had a larger impact than the immediate one when the subjects were given misleading information: When misleading information was introduced immediately after the incident, 46% of the subjects were correct; however, when it was delayed until just prior to the final test, that percentage dropped to 31.5%, $Z = 2.06$, $p < .05$.

We should mention here that Dooling and Christiaansen (1977) have found a different effect of misleading information. They found that such information had a greater effect on memory

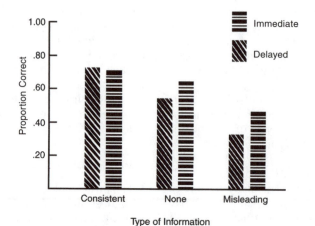

**FIGURE 19.3** ■ Proportion of correct responses for subjects given different types of information in Experiment 3. (Data for subjects given an immediate questionnaire are shown separately from data for those given a delayed questionnaire.)

distortion when it occurred before the retention interval rather than afterward. As these investigators rightfully point out, there are so many differences between their experimental paradigm and ours that it is difficult to essay a resolution of the difference in results. Our subsequent manipulation focuses on one particular detail of the material to be remembered, and a peripheral detail at that. In Dooling and Christiaansen's task, the subsequent information consists of the name of a famous person about whom subjects already have a great deal of knowledge stored in memory. Unfortunately, neither they nor we have been able to come up with an appealing hypothesis for why these paradigmatic differences should lead to different results.

Surprisingly, it appears that even when the questionnaire contained no information relevant to the traffic sign, performance on this key item was somewhat better when subjects were interrogated immediately after the event rather than later. Although this difference failed to reach significance by a Z test involving all four retention intervals, $Z = 1.41$, $.10 < p < .20$, it held up for those retention intervals that, showed some memory performance above chance. For the 20-min and 1-day intervals, the immediate questionnaire had about a 15% advantage over the delayed. Perhaps the early questionnaire permitted the subjects to review the incident in order to answer questions about it, and in the course of this review, some of them refreshed their memory for the traffic sign even though they were not specifically queried on this detail.

## CONFIDENCE RATINGS

Recall that subjects indicated how confident they were in their responses, circling "1" if they felt certain and "3" if they were guessing. The rating "2" was used for intermediate levels of confidence. Figure 19.4 illustrates how these ratings varied as a function of the type of information a subject was exposed to, the timing of that information, and whether the response was correct or incorrect.

A $3 \times 2 \times 2$ unweighted-means analysis of variance (Winer, 1962, p. 241) was performed on all but the zero retention-interval data. This analysis included the 576 subjects who were unambiguously given either an immediate or a delayed questionnaire. The error for all F tests is .493, and $p < .01$ unless otherwise indicated.

Type of information affected confidence, $F(2, 564) = 9.15$, as did whether the subject responded correctly or incorrectly, $F(1, 564) = 23.64$; in other words, subjects were more confident if correct than if incorrect (1.92 vs. 2.18). The main effect of timing (whether the questionnaire was answered immediately or whether it was delayed) was not significant ($F < 1$). The Response Accuracy × Type of Information interaction was marginally significant, $F(2, 564) = 2.71$, $.05 < p < .10$, while the other two-way interactions were not ($Fs < 1$). Finally, the triple interaction reached significance, $F(2, 564) = 5.01$. It is evident from Figure 19.4 that a subject's confidence is boosted by being told anything, whether it is true or not. Further, delaying

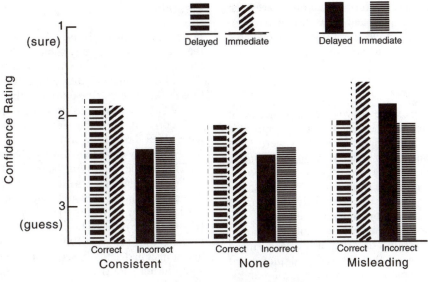

**FIGURE 19.4** ■ Mean confidence ratings as a function of type of information given, immediate versus delayed questionnaire, and correct versus incorrect responses in Experiment 3.

misleading information raises confidence in incorrect responses above the corresponding value associated with correct responses.

To summarize the major results, there appear to be two discernible consequences of exposing a subject to misleading information. First, the likelihood is lowered that a subject will correctly recognize the object previously seen. This is particularly true if the information is introduced just prior to the final test. Second, the misleading information affects a subject's confidence rating. Generally subjects are more confident of their correct responses than their incorrect ones. However, when exposed to delayed misleading information, they are less confident of their correct responses.

## Experiment 4

Loftus (1975) argued that the information contained in a questionnaire influences subsequent choices because that information is integrated into an existing memorial representation and thereby causes an alteration of that representation. This view assumes that when a person sees the initial event, the items of interest are actually encoded at the time of viewing. In the context of the present stimuli, this position would hold that when a person sees a stop sign, for example, the sign gets into memory (i.e., is encoded). If a subsequent questionnaire reports that the sign was a yield sign, that information might, according to this view, enter the memory system and cause an alteration of the original representation. The subject can now be assumed to have a yield sign incorporated into his memorial representation of the event.

A question arises as to whether the stop sign actually got into memory in the first place. If it did not, then the subsequent verbal information may simply be introducing a sign where none existed. In other words, the existing memorial representation of the accident is simply supplemented. On the other hand, if the sign was encoded into memory, then the subsequent information may have caused what is functionally a transformation of the original representation. Thus, it is theoretically important to determine whether subjects attend to and/or encode the sign. A portion of the data from Experiment 3 suggests that people do. Notice in Figure 19.2 that when no information is contained in the questionnaire, subjects show some ability to discriminate the sign they saw from the one they did not, up to and including a retention interval of 1 day. For these subjects, the sign must have been encoded, otherwise performance would have been at chance level. Experiment 4 was designed to provide a further test of whether subjects encoded the sign they saw in the acquisition series.

## Method

Ninety subjects were shown the same series of slides described above, each slide for approximately 3 sec. Following the series, they were given a sheet of paper with a diagram on it similar to that shown in either Figure 19.5a or 19.5b. Forty-five subjects received Diagram 19.5a, and 45 received 19.5b. The instructions were to fill in as many details as could be remembered.

The reason for using two versions of the diagram stems from an observation made during a pilot study. Recall that the slides depict a red Datsun traveling along a side street toward an intersection. From there the car turns right and knocks over a pedestrian in the crosswalk. If the diagram contains no sketch of the car (5a), the subjects tend to concentrate their attention on details at the crosswalk, which is where the accident took place. They may have seen the sign at the corner, but do not draw it, since it does not seem important to the accident. What is needed is a way to focus their attention on the intersection, and the placing of a car near the intersection as in Figure 19.5b appeared to be a way of accomplishing this. The experiment lasted less than 10 min.

## Results

For purposes of analysis, we counted as correct the drawing made by any subject who either drew the sign he had seen or wrote its name. Over all, 45% of the subjects indicated the correct sign. Of those subjects given the outline without a car (Figure 19.5a), 36% correctly drew the stop sign, while 32% correctly drew the yield sign. Of those subjects given the outline with a car (Figure 19.5b), 60% correctly drew the stop sign, while 52% correctly drew the yield sign. An analysis of variance of the arc sine transformed proportions indicated that more subjects depicted a sign when a car was used to direct their attention to the intersection (Figure 19.5b) than when the diagram contained no car (5a), $F(1, \infty) = 19.94$, $MS_e = .01$. Whether the subject had actually seen a stop sign or a yield sign did not significantly affect the likelihood of drawing the correct sign, $F(1, \infty) = 1.51$, $MS_e = .01$, $p < .20$. The interaction also failed to reach significance ($F < 1$). Three of the 50 subjects who saw a yield sign incorrectly drew a stop sign in their diagram; none of the "stop sign" subjects drew a yield sign.

The results indicate that when subjects view the particular series of slides used throughout these experiments, at least half of them (and perhaps more) do encode the correct sign. The data from subjects given Diagram 5b (with a car to focus their attention on the intersection) indicate that over half have encoded the sign to the point of including it in their diagrams. Others may also have encoded it, but this was not revealed by the present procedure.

## Experiment 5

The purpose of Experiment 5 was to demonstrate the generality of our studies beyond the single-stimulus pair used in the previous studies.

## Method

A new series of 20 color slides depicting an autopedestrian accident was shown to 80 subjects. A male pedestrian is seen carrying some items in one hand and munching on an apple held with the other. He leaves a building and strolls toward a parking lot. In the lot, a maroon Triumph backs out of a parking space and hits the pedestrian.

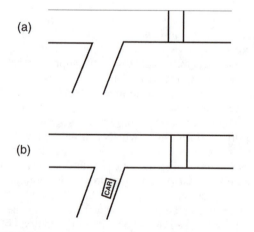

**FIGURE 19.5** ■ Diagrams used in Experiment 4.

Four of the 20 slides were critical. One version of each critical slide contained a particular object (such as a pair of skis leaning against a tree), while the other version contained the identical slide with a changed detail (a shovel leaning against a tree). Each subject saw only one version of the critical slides, and each critical slide was seen equally often across subjects.

Following the slides, which had been seen at a 3-sec rate, subjects completed a 10-min unrelated filler activity. Then they read a three-paragraph description of the slide series supposedly written by another individual who had been given much more time to view the slides. The description contained four critical sentences that either did or did not mention the incorrect critical object. For example, if the subject had seen skis leaning against a tree, his statement might include a sentence that mentioned "the shovel leaning against the tree." The statements were designed so that the mention or nonmention of a critical incorrect detail was counterbalanced over subjects for the four critical items.

After an interval of 10 min, subjects were given a forced-choice recognition test. Using two slide projectors, 10 pairs of slides were presented. The 4 critical pairs were randomly intermixed with the remaining filler pairs. One member of each pair had been seen before, whereas the other had not. The slides that the subject had actually seen varied in the left and right positions.

## Results

The percentage of times a correct selection occurred was 55.3 when the intervening statement contained misleading information and 70.8 when it contained no information. For purposes of analysis, two proportions were calculated for each of the 4 critical slide pairs. One was the proportion of correct selections when misleading information had intervened, and the other, when no information had intervened. A $t$ test for related measures indicated that the mean percentages (given above) were statistically different from each other, $t(3) = 9.34$, $SE_{diff} = 1.66$.

## Discussion

The analysis of Experiment 5 permits us to generalize our findings beyond the single stop-sign-

yield-sign stimulus pair. In the present experiment, subjects who saw a slide containing a particular detail, A, but who were given the information that the slide contained Detail B, were subsequently more likely than control subjects to select on a forced-choice recognition test a slide containing B rather than a slide with A.

Note that even with misleading information, subjects were correct about 55% of the time, a figure that is much higher than the approximately 42% figure obtained with the stop-yield stimuli in Experiment 3 after a comparable retention interval. There is probably good reason for this. Any particular object, such as a shovel, can assume many forms. The particular shovel that any subject imagines while reading the story may not agree with the version shown during the recognition test. A subject can then successfully reject the slide containing the shovel, not because he or she recognizes the other slide (containing the skis) but because of not having seen the particular shovel presented during the recognition test.

With common traffic signs, this would not tend to happen. If a subject imagines a stop sign while answering a question that mentions a stop sign, the imagined sign will certainly match the stop sign that would be presented during the recognition test.

## General Discussion

When a person witnesses an important event, he or she is often exposed to related information some time afterward. The purpose of the present experiments was to investigate how the subsequent information influences memory for the original event.

In the pilot experiment, subjects saw a series of slides depicting an accident, and afterwards they were exposed to a questionnaire that contained either consistent or misleading information about a particular aspect of the accident. The misleading information caused less accurate responding on a subsequent yes–no recognition test. Similarly, in Experiment 1, misleading information resulted in poorer performance on a forced-choice recognition test. For example, in one condition, subjects saw a stop sign but a subsequent question suggested it was actually a yield sign. Some time later they were given a forced-choice test and asked to choose the sign they thought they had seen. Over half of these subjects incorrectly chose the yield sign.

It has been suggested that the reason this happens is that when the misleading information is presented, it is introduced into the memorial representation for the accident and causes an alteration of that representation. Another interpretation is that subjects are simply agreeing with the information contained in their questionnaires, even though they actually remember what they saw. This is a demand-characteristics explanation. Experiment 2 showed that when subjects were told that they might have been exposed to misleading information and were asked to state whether they thought they had, most of them persisted in claiming that they had seen the incorrect item.

A second interpretation of the forced-choice results is that the original sign information may not have been encoded in the first place. If it had not been encoded, then the subsequent question may have introduced a sign where none existed. In other words, the phenomenon may be one of supplementation. On the other hand, if the sign got into the original memory (i.e., was encoded), then the subsequent information caused either an alteration in the original representation or the creation of a new, stronger representation that competed with the original representation. Experiment 4 showed that at least half of the subjects encoded the initial sign to the point where it was included in a drawing they made of the incident.

The paradigm used throughout this research involves two critical time intervals: the time between the initial event and the presentation of subsequent information and the final test for recollection of the event. In Experiment 3, these intervals were examined. Subjects received their final test after a retention interval of 0 min, 20 min, 1 day, 2 days, or 1 week. The subsequent information was introduced either immediately after the initial event or just prior to the final test. The usual retention-interval results were observed: poorer performance after long intervals than after short ones. Of major interest was the finding that misleading information had a larger impact if presented just prior to a recognition test rather than just after the initial event.

We have noted two interpretations for our results, namely that either the subsequent information alters the original memory or both the original and the new information reside in memory, and

the new competes with the old. Unfortunately, this extremely important issue cannot be resolved with the present data. Those who wish to maintain that the new information produces an alteration cannot prove that the earlier information will not one day spontaneously reappear. Those who wish to hold that new and old information both exist in memory will argue that a person who responds on the basis of new information alone does so because the proper retrieval cue or the right technique has not been used. The value of the present data lies in the fact that they clear up a number of alternative explanations for previously published phenomena. Furthermore, they indicate something about the conditions under which new information is more or less likely to affect accuracy.

The present work bears some resemblance to earlier work on the influence of verbal labels on memory for visually presented form stimuli. Much of the earlier work was designed to test the Gestalt hypothesis that progressive memory changes in the direction of a "better" figure occur autonomously. Riley (1962), in an excellent review of that earlier literature, concluded that the hypothesis of autonomous change is probably not testable. Despite this drawback, the work on verbal labels was useful in revealing that reproductions and recognition memory (Carmichael, Hogan, & Walter, 1932; Daniel, 1972) of simple forms were affected by the labels applied to those forms. The present work represents a much needed extension in that it reveals that these effects occur not only with artificial forms but also with highly naturalistic scenes under conditions that have a high degree of ecological validity. Further, the present work convincingly demonstrates both the integration of information from more than one source into memory and the use of that information to reconstruct a "memory" that was never actually experienced.

## ACKNOWLEDGMENT

This research was supported by grants to the first author from the Urban Mass Transportation Administration and from the National Institute of Mental Health. Special thanks are due to R. Abelson, W. Cole, C. MacLeod, G. Loftus, T. Nelson, E. Tulving, and S. Woods for reading and commenting on an earlier draft of this article. R. Shiffrin suggested Experiment 2.

## NOTE

1. A better design would have orthogonally varied the two critical intervals, namely, the interval between the slides and the questionnaire and the interval between the questionnaire and the recognition test. However, such a design would have required nearly three times as many subjects to obtain reasonably stable proportions in each cell, and the authors' colleagues were already becoming distressed at the rapidity with which these experiments were depleting the psychology department's subject pool. We doubt that any conclusions would be changed as a result of the fuller design.

## REFERENCE NOTE

1. Loftus, E. F., Salzberg, P. M., Burns, H. J., & Sanders, R. K. *Destruction of a Visual Memory by Verbal Information*. Paper presented at the annual meeting of the Psychonomic Society, Denver, November 1975.

## REFERENCES

Carmichael, L., Hogan, H. P., & Walter, A. A. An experimental study of the effect of language on the reproduction of visually perceived form. *Journal of Experimental Psychology*, 1932, *15*, 73–86.

Daniel, T. C. Nature of the effect of verbal labels on recognition memory for form. *Journal of Experimental Psychology*, 1972, *96*, 152–157.

Dooling, D. J. & Christiaansen, R. E. Episodic and semantic aspects of memory for prose. *Journal of Experimental Psychology: Human Learning and Memory*, 1977, *3*, 428–436.

Hintzman, D. L. Repetition and memory. In G. H. Bower (Ed.), *The Psychology of Learning and Motivation* (Vol. 10). New York: Academic Press, 1976.

Kant, I. [*Critique of Pure Reason*] (Translated by J. M. D. Meiklejohn). London: George Bell, 1887. (Originally published, 1781.)

Loftus, E. F. Leading questions and the eyewitness report. *Cognitive Psychology*, 1975, *7*, 560–572.

Mosteller, F., & Tukey, J. W. The uses and usefulness of binomial probability paper. *Journal of the American Statistical Association*, 1949, *44*, 174–212.

Orne, M. T. On the social psychology of the psychological experiment: With particular reference to demand characteristics and their implications. *American Psychologist*, 1962, *17*, 776–783.

Pezdek, K. Cross-modality semantic integration of sentence and picture memory. *Journal of Experimental Psychology: Human Learning and Memory*, 1977, *3*, 515–524.

Riley, D. A. Memory for form. In L. Postman (Ed.), *Psychology in the Making*. New York: Knopf, 1962.

Winer, B. J. *Statistical Principles in Experimental Design*. New York: McGraw-Hill, 1962.

# Becoming Famous without Being Recognized: Unconscious Influences of Memory Produced by Dividing Attention

Larry L. Jacoby and Vera Woloshyn • McMaster University
Colleen Kelley • Williams College

The familiarity of names produced by their prior presentation can be misinterpreted as fame. We used this false fame effect to separately study the effects of divided attention on familiarity versus conscious recollection. In a first experiment, famous and nonfamous names were presented to be read under conditions of full versus divided attention. Divided attention greatly reduced later recognition memory performance but had no effect on gains in familiarity as measured by fame judgments. In later experiments, we placed recognition memory and familiarity in opposition by presenting only nonfamous names to be read in the first phase. Recognizing a name as earlier read on the later fame test allowed Ss to be certain that it was nonfamous. Divided attention at study or during the fame test reduced list recognition performance but had no effect on familiarity. We conclude that conscious recollection is an attention-demanding act that is separate from assessing familiarity.

Folk wisdom suggests that we benefit from experience by consciously remembering those experiences and applying the knowledge gained from them to the current situation. In contrast, research shows that many effects of prior experience on later performance can occur independently of the ability to consciously recollect the experience (see Richardson-Klavehn & Bjork, 1988, for a review). In this article, we provide further evidence that the past can be used to influence present performance without the intervention of conscious recollection. We show that divided attention, in comparison with full attention, can radically reduce a person's ability to recognize an item as previously presented while leaving intact the effects of that prior presentation on judgment. Furthermore, this potential for unconscious influence of the past leads to a role for conscious recollection that is directly counter to that advanced by folk wisdom. Rather than being a prerequisite for producing effects of the past, conscious recollection can be a means of escaping misleading effects of the past.

The task that we used required subjects to judge whether a name was famous. In the first phase of each experiment, people read a list of names. Then those old names were mixed with new famous and new nonfamous names in a test of fame judgments. On the basis of earlier research (Jacoby, Kelley, Brown, & Jasechko, 1989; Neely & Payne, 1983), we expected that the familiarity of a name produced by its being read in the first phase would be mistaken for the familiarity that characterizes a famous name; that is, reading either a famous name or a nonfamous name in the first part of the experiment would produce a higher probability of calling the name "famous" on the later test. We expected that divided attention would reduce people's ability to recognize a name as previously read but would have no effect on gains in the familiarity of the name produced by its prior reading.

When one is unable to consciously recollect having read a name, any remaining effect of reading it on its familiarity can be considered an unconscious influence of memory. We have found it useful to think about such effects of the past in terms of Polanyi's (1958) distinction between tool and object (Jacoby & Kelley, 1987). Memory can be used unconsciously as a tool to accomplish a present task, or it can be made the object of reflection for conscious remembering. That framework predicts a difference in focus of attention and processing requirements for conscious recollection, in comparison with unconscious uses of memory. Conscious recollection is seen as involving an act that is separate from the use of memory as a tool to help accomplish some present task.

The notion of conscious recollection as a separate act highlights the possibility that consciousness sometimes serves to oppose unconscious influences of the past that would otherwise prevail. For example, we can use conscious recollection to avoid repeating our stories to the same audience or to avoid unconscious plagiarism. In these cases, recognition in the form of conscious recollection is not a prerequisite for effects of the past, but instead it serves as a means of avoiding undesirable effects of the past. The opposition of conscious and unconscious influences of memory can also be used as a methodological tool to provide a clear separation of the two in performance.

In the second and third experiments, we placed conscious recollection in opposition to effects of reading a name on the judgment of its fame. We arranged the situation so that recognition of a name as previously read allowed subjects to be certain that it was nonfamous. Only nonfamous names were presented in the first phase of the experiment,

and subjects were told that this was the case. Reading a nonfamous name has the unconscious influence of increasing the familiarity of that name and makes it more likely that the name will later mistakenly be called "famous." Conscious recollection of the name as read in the earlier list opposes this unconscious influence and allows one to be certain that the name is nonfamous. Given this arrangement, any increase in the probability of mistakenly calling a nonfamous name "famous" must result from an unconscious influence of the past because conscious recollection of the name as previously read in the list of nonfamous names would dictate an opposite response. Thus placing the two in opposition allows one to separate the effects of conscious recollection from unconscious influences of the past.

There is some evidence that manipulations of attention have a larger effect on conscious recollection than on uses of memory that do not require awareness of the past. When sufficient care is taken to ensure that items are truly unattended, little or no evidence of memory is found on a recognition memory test or a recall test (Fisk & Schneider, 1984; Moray, 1959), which leads to the claim that attention is necessary for memory. However, Eich (1984) found evidence of memory after divided attention by using a test that did not require conscious recollection. Homophones were presented to the unattended channel in a dichotic-listening task, accompanied by a word that biased the homophone to its less common interpretation (e.g., *taxi-fare*). Although divided attention reduced recognition of the homophones to chance, memory for their prior presentation was indirectly revealed by biased spelling of the homophones on a later test. Similarly, Koriat and Feuerstein (1976) showed differential effects of an attention manipulation on conscious recollection, in comparison with memory, as measured by an increased probability of producing earlier presented words on a free-association test. Grand and Segal (1966) used a similar indirect measure of memory and also showed differential effects of a manipulation of attention on that measure, in comparison with recall.

We expected parallels between the effects of divided attention on normal subjects' memory performance and amnesics' performance on memory tasks (e.g., Craik, 1982). Amnesics do show some ability to recognize items, but it appears to be based simply on the familiarity of items, rather than on any ability to consciously recollect a particular prior occurrence. Huppert and Piercy (1978) found that their Korsakoff patients could make recency judgments at an above-chance level, but they tended to judge items presented frequently as having been presented recently and vice versa. In other words, amnesics based both types of judgments on the memory strength or familiarity of the item and so were unable to discriminate between frequency and recency. In contrast, subjects with normal memories could use their recollection of particular occurrences of an item to disentangle the effects of recency and frequency of presentation. Similarly, divided attention at study may prevent later recollection of an event but may not prevent increments in the general familiarity of an item. That familiarity could then be used as a basis for a variety of judgments, such as recency, frequency, or general familiarity of an item.

The goal in our first experiment was to further document that divided attention, in comparison with full attention, during study can produce a large decrement in list-recognition memory performance while having little or no effect on an unconscious use of memory as a tool. Famous names and nonfamous names were presented to be read aloud under conditions of divided or full attention. Gains in familiarity of names were tracked by changes in performance on a later fame-judgment test, and list-recognition memory was assessed with a standard recognition test. We expected a dissociation between gains in familiarity and list-recognition performance, such that previously read names would be judged as famous but not recognized after divided attention. However, familiarity can serve as one basis for calling an item "old" on a test of recognition memory (e.g., Jacoby & Dallas, 1981; Mandler, 1980). Consequently, we did not expect list-recognition performance in the divided-attention condition to be near chance because dividing attention was not expected to disrupt gains in familiarity. Conscious recollection or the retrieval of study context serves as an alternative basis for recognition memory judgments and is the basis for list recognition that we expected to be influenced by the dividing of attention during study.

In later experiments, we placed conscious recollection in opposition to gains in familiarity by presenting only nonfamous names in the first phase of the experiments. We also investigated whether conscious recollection requires an attention-demanding act that is separate from other uses of the past by dividing attention during the fame test (Experiment 3). When attention is divided during study (Experiment 2) or during the test (Experiment 3), old nonfamous names might continue to gain false fame, although subjects are told that all old names are nonfamous. Dividing attention during study or during the test may prevent the processing necessary to consciously recollect a name as previously read while leaving intact the effects of reading a name on its familiarity.

## General Method

Throughout the three experiments, we used one basic paradigm. Variations in the general method are indicated as each experiment is described.

### Subjects

The subjects were volunteers from an introductory psychology course at McMaster University who served in an experiment for course credit. Subjects were randomly assigned to conditions and were tested individually.

### Tasks and Materials

In the first phase of each experiment, names were presented to be read aloud under conditions of either full or divided attention. In the divided-attention condition, subjects read the names while listening to a very long continuous string of numbers with target sequences embedded in the string. Subjects were to search for runs of three odd-numbered digits. Names read in the first phase were mixed with new famous and new nonfamous names for a test of list recognition or fame judgments. For the list-recognition test, subjects judged whether a name had been read in the first phase of the experiment. For the fame-judgment test, subjects judged whether a name was a famous one. List recognition indicated a conscious use of memory. An increase in the probability that a name would be judged famous because of its prior presentation potentially indicated an unconscious use of memory.

The listening task used in the divided-attention conditions was one previously used by Craik

(1982). Forty-three sequences of 3 odd numbers occurred within a list of 224 random numbers. The restrictions that we used to construct the list were that a minimum of 1 and a maximum of 8 numbers must occur between the end of one and the beginning of the next target sequence. Also, not more than 3 even numbers could occur in sequence. The number of target sequences presented was determined by the length of the study list or, in Experiment 3, the length of the test list.

A pool of famous and nonfamous names, including first and last names, was used as materials for the experiments. We attempted to find famous names of the sort that the majority of people could recognize as famous but that were not so famous that most subjects could specify the achievement that led to fame. This criterion for the choice of famous names was meant to make it likely that people would base their judgments of fame on the familiarity of the name rather than on their ability to recall what the named person had done to become famous. Data from other experiments done in our lab were used to select famous names identified as famous by 60%–70% of students from the same undergraduate population as tested here. Nonfamous names were matched with the famous names according to the following characteristics: length of first and last name, sex indicated by the first name, and the nationality of origin of the last name. Examples of nonfamous names are Sebastian Weisdorf, Valerie Marsh, and Adrian Marr. Examples of famous names are Satchel Paige, Minnie Pearl, and Christopher Wren.

The presentation order of names for both study and test lists was random with the restriction that not more than three names of one type (famous vs. nonfamous or old vs. new) could be presented before one name of each of the other types. Two study lists were prepared in such a way that names that were old for the fame judgment test when one study list was used were new when the other study list was used and vice versa. Two random presentation orders of items in each study list were used to produce four combinations of study list and random order. Each combination was used equally often.

## Procedure

Names were presented by means of an Apple computer interfaced with a Zenith monitor. In the first phase of each experiment, the names appeared for 2 s; the initial letter of each first and last name was capitalized. There was a 1-s blank interval after the presentation of each name. For the listening task used in the divided-attention condition, digits were presented in a continuous stream at a 12-s rate per digit. The auditory presentation of digits slightly preceded the visual presentation of names.

Subjects were instructed to read presented names aloud during the first phase of each experiment. Those in a full-attention condition were told that we were interested in their speed and accuracy of pronouncing names and that their pronunciation of names was being recorded. Although a microphone was placed on top of the monitor to make the instructions more credible, neither pronunciations nor latencies were actually recorded. Subjects in a divided-attention condition were told that the task of reading names aloud was meant only to interfere with the more important task of listening for runs of three odd-numbered digits. They were instructed to devote as little attention as possible to their pronunciation of the names and to concentrate on the listening task, pressing a key whenever they heard a target in the listening task. Accuracy of performance on the listening task was recorded.

Before the test of fame judgments, subjects were informed that the famous names were not as extremely famous as Wayne Gretzky or Pierre Trudeau. They were also told that they would not be asked to describe what a named person had done to become famous. These instructions encouraged subjects to use familiarity as a basis for their fame judgments. Subjects made their fame judgments by pressing a key on the right for "famous" and a key on the left for "nonfamous." After their decision, the message "Press center key when ready" appeared on the screen. Pressing the center key resulted in the presentation of another name for a judgment of its fame. This sequence of events was repeated until all of the names in a list had been tested. Each judgment and its latency were recorded by the computer.

For the test of recognition memory, old names and new names were intermixed and printed in columns on a sheet of paper. Subjects were instructed to circle names that they had read in the first phase of the experiment.

## Analyses

Decision-time analyses were for correct judgments only (judgments of famous names as famous and nonfamous names as nonfamous). Times for errors were also examined but are not reported because they were based on fewer observations and were not obtainable for all subjects. An examination of the error times did not reveal any effects that compromise conclusions drawn on the basis of times of correct responses. A log transformation of each subject's decision times was used to lessen the impact of extreme scores on the means. The significance level for all tests was set at $p < .05$.

## Experiment 1

### Method

#### SUBJECTS AND DESIGN

The subjects were 64 students enrolled in an introductory psychology course; 32 subjects were randomly assigned to each of two (full vs. divided) attention conditions. For each subject, the fame-judgment test was followed by the list-recognition memory test. Within subjects, prior presentation of names (old vs. new) was factorially combined with fame of the names (famous vs. nonfamous) for each of the two types of test.

#### MATERIALS AND PROCEDURE

A list of 65 names was presented to be read in the first phase of the experiment. The first 5 names in the list included 3 famous and 2 nonfamous names that served only as fillers (not tested later). The remaining 60 names included 30 famous and 30 nonfamous names. Of those, 20 famous and 20 nonfamous names were mixed with 20 new famous and 20 new nonfamous names for the fame-judgment test. The remaining 10 names of each type were mixed with 10 new famous and 10 new nonfamous names for the recognition memory test.

Before the fame-judgment test, subjects were informed that half of the names that they read in the first phase were famous and half were nonfamous, and so recognition of a name as previously read provided no information about its fame. The procedure used in the fame-judgment test was as described in the General Method section. After the fame-judgment test, subjects were given the list-recognition memory test. Names were presented on a sheet of paper, and subjects were told to circle names that they had read in the first phase of the experiment.

### Results and Discussion

Subjects in the divided-attention condition missed an average of 5.3 of 27 targets in the listening task. The pronunciation of names was generally accurate even when attention was divided. An average of 2.41 of the names presented in the first phase were mispronounced, not pronounced, or stumbled over when attention was divided.

Famous names were more likely to be judged famous (.59) than were nonfamous names (.19), $F(1, 62) = 282$, $MS_e = 0.035$ (see Table 20.1). Names that had been read in the first phase of the experiment were more likely to be judged famous (.46) than were names that were new at the time of test (.32), $F(1, 62) = 159.78$, $MS_e = 0.007$. Although reading a name earlier did produce a bias toward calling the name "famous," the discriminability between famous and nonfamous names was not influenced by previously reading the names; that is, the interaction between prior presentation and the fame of names did not approach significance. An analysis of judgment times showed that old famous names were judged famous more rapidly than were new famous names (1,167 vs. 1,270 ms), $F(1, 62) = 12.75$, $MS_e = 26,921$. There was also a tendency for old nonfamous names to be rejected more slowly than were new nonfamous names (1,456 vs. 1,417 ms), $F(1, 62) = 3.62$, $MS_e = 13,738$, $p < .06$.

Of most importance for our purposes, dividing attention did not affect the gain in familiarity of names produced by their having been read earlier. Neither the main effect of attention condition nor any interaction involving the manipulation of attention approached significance in any of the analyses of fame judgments. This lack of an effect of the manipulation of attention on fame judgments is in marked contrast with the large effect of attention on list recognition memory performance. An analysis of the probabilities of calling a name "old" (see Table 20.1) showed that old names were more likely to be called "old" than were new names and that the effect of prior presentation interacted with the manipulation of attention. The probabil-

**TABLE 20.1. Fame and Recognition Judgments: Experiment 1**

| Condition | New F | New NF | Old F | Old NF |
|---|---|---|---|---|
| Fame | | | | |
|   Full attention | .49 | .13 | .66 | .25 |
|   Divided attention | .53 | .14 | .66 | .25 |
| Recognition | | | | |
|   Full attention | .04 | .05 | .70 | .60 |
|   Divided attention | .13 | .13 | .47 | .39 |

*Note.* F = famous names; NF = nonfamous names. The numbers are the probabilities of responding "famous" for fame judgments and the probabilities of responding "old" for recognition judgments.

ity of a hit was higher and the probability of a false alarm was lower in the full-attention condition (.65 and .04) than in the divided-attention condition (.43 and .13). There were also a significant main effect of fame, $F(1, 62) = 5.75$, $MS_e = 0.021$, and a significant interaction between fame and prior presentation, $F(1, 62) = 11.13$, $MS_e = 0.014$. Old famous names were more likely to be called "old" (.59) than were old nonfamous names (.50), whereas there was no difference in the probabilities of mistakenly calling new famous names (.09) and new nonfamous names (.09) "old." The Attention × Prior Presentation × Fame interaction was not significant ($F < 1$); that is, old famous names did not hold a significantly larger advantage over old nonfamous names in the full-attention condition than in the divided-attention condition.

The data are consistent with the claim that dividing attention reduces list-recognition memory performance, whereas it has no effect on gains in familiarity. The effects of reading a name on a later judgment of its fame largely replicate results reported by Neely and Payne (1983). Those effects remain unchanged when attention is divided while one reads names, even though divided attention, in comparison with full attention, has a large effect on list-recognition performance. This dissociation between effects on familiarity and recognition is similar to dissociations observed in the memory performance of amnesics (e.g., Huppert & Piercy, 1978) and is also similar to differential effects of attention observed by others (Eich, 1984; Koriat & Feuerstein, 1976).

One interpretation of the dissociation between familiarity and item recognition that we observed would be that familiarity relies on the priming of

preexisting units (Morton, 1969), whereas conscious recollection relies on a different mechanism. However, the priming interpretation is implausible, given that the gain in fame due to reading a name was as large for nonfamous names (with no preexisting representation) as for famous names. Elsewhere (Jacoby & Brooks, 1984; Jacoby & Kelley, 1987) we have discussed other reasons for rejecting priming accounts of unconscious influences of memory. Effects on familiarity seem better viewed as resulting from adding new information to memory rather than from priming preexisting knowledge.

## Experiment 2

To preclude the possibility that our measure of familiarity actually reflects some instances of conscious recollection, we placed gains in familiarity and conscious recollection in opposition to one another to further separate the two processes. In our second experiment, all names presented in the first phase were nonfamous; thus conscious recollection of a name as old allowed subjects to be certain that the name was nonfamous. Familiarity without conscious recollection would yield the opposite response, calling a name "famous." Attention was either full or divided during list presentation.

Subjects in the divided-attention condition were not necessarily helpless victims of the false fame effect. If they suspected that their fame judgments were influenced by prior presentation of nonfamous names but realized that their list-recognition memory was poor, they might react by being less willing than subjects in the full-attention condition to call any name "famous." Such a strategy would reduce the probability of judging both old and new names as famous, but it would eliminate confusion between prior presentation and fame only if all the new famous names were more familiar than the old nonfamous names. To assess the possibility of such a change in criterion across attention conditions, we did a signal-detection analysis, using the probability of calling a famous name "famous" as a measure of hits and the probability of calling a new nonfamous name "famous" as a measure of false alarms. If divided attention changes subjects' criterion, we would see a change in the probability of calling both famous and nonfamous names "famous" without a corresponding change in discrimination between the two types of names.

## Method

### SUBJECTS AND DESIGN

The subjects were 40 undergraduates enrolled in an introductory psychology course; 20 subjects were randomly assigned to each of two attention conditions (full vs. divided). Names on the fame-judgment test were famous, nonfamous and earlier read (old nonfamous), or nonfamous and not earlier read (new nonfamous).

### MATERIALS AND PROCEDURE

In the first phase of the experiment, subjects read a list of 40 nonfamous names aloud under conditions of either full or divided attention. The listening task used in the divided-attention condition was the same as in the first experiment except that digits were presented at a 2-s rate. The first 5 and the last 5 names read in the first phase of the experiment were mixed with 10 new nonfamous names and were later presented for a test of recognition memory. The remaining 30 old nonfamous names were mixed with 30 new nonfamous names and 60 new famous names and presented for fame judgments. Multiple formats of the list read in the first phase were constructed in such a way that across formats the names appeared equally often as old nonfamous names or as new nonfamous names in the fame-judgment test. The old nonfamous names used in the recognition memory test remained constant across formats and so were not balanced with those used as new nonfamous names on that test.

After reading names in the first phase of the experiment, subjects were informed that all of the names that they had read were nonfamous ones and that those names would be presented with new famous and new nonfamous names for judgments of fame. The procedure for the fame judgment test was as described in the General Method section. After the fame-judgment test, the test of list recognition was given. Names were presented on a sheet of paper, and subjects were instructed to circle names that they had read in the first phase of the experiment. Because of experimenter error, 20 subjects in each of the attention conditions com-

pleted the test of fame judgments, but only the last 15 subjects tested in each condition were given the test of recognition memory.

## Results and Discussion

An average of 1.5 of 12 targets were missed in the listening task used in the divided-attention condition. Pronunciation of names was not recorded.

We measured the probability of calling a name "famous" (see Table 20.2) for each of the three types of name (famous, old nonfamous, and new nonfamous) and each of the two attention conditions (full and divided). We first compared performances on the famous and the new nonfamous names to test for any differences between the two attention conditions in discriminability or criterion used for fame judgments. That analysis revealed that famous names were more likely to be judged famous than were new nonfamous names, $F(1, 38) = 86.70$, $MS_e = 2.29$. Also, subjects in the divided-attention condition were less willing to judge a name to be famous, regardless of its true status, than were subjects in the full-attention condition, $F(1, 38) = 10.59$, $MS_e = 3.28$. We performed a signal-detection analysis by using fame judgments to obtain estimates of $d'$ (discriminability) and of $\beta$ (criterion for judging a name as famous) for each subject and then entering those estimates into an analysis of variance. That analysis revealed that $d'$ did not differ between the two attention conditions, $F(1, 38) < 1$. However, $\beta$ was higher in the divided-attention condition (2.48) than in the full-attention condition (1.46), $F(1, 38) = 5.12$, $MS_e = 2.037$.

**TABLE 20.2. Fame and Recognition Judgments: Experiment 2**

| Condition | Famous Name: New | Nonfamous Name New | Nonfamous Name Old |
|---|---|---|---|
| Fame | | | |
| Full attention | .62 | .31 | .19 |
| Divided attention | .49 | .17 | .27 |
| Recognition | | | |
| Full attention | — | .00 | .63 |
| Divided attention | — | .11 | .30 |

Note. The numbers are the probabilities of responding "famous" for fame judgments and the probabilities of responding "old" for recognition judgments.

The use of a higher criterion by subjects in the divided-attention condition than in the full-attention condition was probably meant to protect themselves against being misled by familiarity. Unlike subjects in the full-attention condition, subjects in the divided-attention condition could not rely on list recognition to avoid the misleading effects of familiarity. As will be shown, list-recognition performance was very poor in the divided-attention condition. The lack of a difference in $d'$ provides evidence that there was no qualitative difference between the two conditions in the basis used for fame judgments.

Most important were the effects of the attention manipulation on the probabilities of mistakenly judging old and new nonfamous names "famous." An analysis of those data revealed an interaction between attention condition and type of nonfamous name, $F(1, 38) = 22.21, MS_e = 1.00$. As predicted, in the full-attention condition, old nonfamous names were less likely to be judged famous than were new nonfamous names, whereas the opposite was true in the divided-attention condition. An analysis of times for correctly rejecting nonfamous names produced results that were consistent with those from the analysis of probabilities. That analysis revealed a main effect of type of nonfamous name, $F(1, 38) = 5.93, MS_e = 16,989$, and a significant interaction between type of nonfamous name and attention condition, $F(1, 38) = 12.45, MS_e = 16,989$. In the full-attention condition, old nonfamous names were rejected more rapidly than were new nonfamous names (1,256 vs. 1,430 ms), whereas in the divided-attention condition, old nonfamous names required approximately the same amount of time to be rejected as did new nonfamous names (1,203 vs. 1,171 ms). An anlysis of the speed of correctly accepting famous names as being famous failed to reveal a significant difference between the two attention conditions.

According to the recognition memory data (see Table 20.2), divided attention, in comparison with full attention, to the reading of names radically reduced list-recognition performance. The probability of calling a name "old" was higher in the full-attention than in the divided-attention condition, $F(1, 28) = 8.41, MS_e = 0.023$, and higher for names that were old (hits) than those that were new (false alarms), $F(1, 28) = 155.50, MS_e = 0.016$. The interaction between attention condition and

hits versus false alarms was also significant, $F(1, 28) = 42.79, MS_e = 0.016$. The probability of a hit was much higher and the probability of a false alarm was much lower in the full-attention (.63 and .00) than in the divided-attention (.30 and .11) condition.

The results closely conformed to our expectations. The good list recognition of old nonfamous names in the full-attention condition allowed those names to be less likely to be called "famous" and more quickly rejected than were new nonfamous names. In contrast, dividing attention radically reduced list recognition. The failure to recognize old nonfamous names in combination with a gain in their familiarity is revealed by the finding that old nonfamous names were more likely to be called "famous" than were new nonfamous names in the divided-attention condition.

The results of these analyses lead us to conclude that gains in familiarity can be unaccompanied by list recognition. Given that old nonfamous names were more likely to be mistakenly called "famous" than were new nonfamous names, some of the old names must have gained familiarity without being recognized in the divided-attention condition. We also examined the stronger claim that divided attention, in comparison with full attention, while reading names had *no* effect on gains in familiarity. Because any recognized names (either hits or false alarms) would be called "nonfamous," the effects of familiarity gains can occur only for nonrecognized names. We used group data to estimate the probability of calling nonrecognized names "famous" separately for each of the two attention conditions. First, we used the recognition memory data to estimate the number of nonrecognized old and new nonfamous names on the fame test. That involved subtracting the estimated number of recognized names (based on the probability of calling a name "old") from 30 (the number of old and the number of new nonfamous names on the fame judgment test). Then we computed the probability of calling a nonrecognized name "famous" by dividing the number of names called "famous" by our estimated number of nonrecognized names for each combination of conditions (see Table 20.3).

These data are consistent with the claim that the manipulation of attention had no effect on gains in familiarity produced by reading a name. The only effect of attention evident in those data is that

**TABLE 20.3. Probability of Judging a Nonrecognized Name Famous**

| Condition | Famous Name: New | Nonfamous Name | |
|---|---|---|---|
| | | New | Old |
| Full attention | .62 | .31 | .51 |
| Divided attention | .49 | .19 | .39 |

subjects in the divided-attention condition were less willing to call any name "famous" than were subjects in the full-attention condition. This is simply the effect of divided attention on the criterion (discussed earlier) that subjects used for fame judgments. For nonrecognized names, old nonfamous names were more likely to be mistakenly called "famous" than were new nonfamous names, presumably because of the greater familiarity of old nonfamous names. This difference between old and new nonfamous names was identical in the two attention conditions.

To make our comparison of "corrected" fame judgments legitimate, it is not necessary to assume that list-recognition performance provides an accurate estimate of the absolute probability of list recognition when one is making fame judgments. Rather, it is necessary only that any source of error in that estimate not be different for the two attention conditions. The absolute probability of list recognition when one is making fame judgments probably did differ from that on the test of recognition memory. The delay between previously reading a name and the test of recognition memory was longer than that delay for the test of fame judgments. Also, the probability of recognizing an item on a direct test of list recognition is likely to be higher than the probability of using list recognition to monitor performance on a task such as fame judgments (Jacoby, Kelley, Brown, & Jasechko, 1989). However, there is no reason to think that the effects of these factors differed for the two attention conditions.

Subjects in the full-attention condition could use list recognition to avoid being misled by the familiarity of old nonfamous names. Such a use of conscious recollection may be a generally important function. The influence of divided attention on the probability of judging an old nonfamous name as famous is similar to the "sleeper effect" observed in studies of social psychology (e.g.,

Cook, Gruder, Hennigan, & Flay, 1979; Hovland, Lumsdaine, & Sheffield, 1949). In those experiments, a message from a low-reliability source had little impact on attitudes measured immediately after the communication, but it did influence attitudes measured after a delay. Hovland et al. suggested that on the immediate test, the content of the message was discounted because its low-reliability source was readily accessible. However, discounting became less likely after a delay because the source of the message was forgotten. In a manner analogous to the impact of the delay in the sleeper effect, dividing attention while one is reading names made it less likely that conscious recollection of source (list recognition) could be used to reject old nonfamous names and resulted in those names' being more likely than new nonfamous names to be called famous. In other experiments, Jacoby, Kelley, Brown, and Jasechko (1989) showed that lengthening the retention interval between reading a name and its test can produce effects on fame judgments that are similar to those produced by dividing attention.

## Experiment 3

Whereas attention in the first two experiments was divided during study, we investigated the effects of dividing attention during the fame-judgment test in Experiment 3. We predicted that dividing attention during the test would prevent conscious recollection and produce effects that are similar to those produced by the dividing of attention during study. Whereas the dividing of attention during study prevents processing that is important for later conscious recollection, the dividing of attention during the test might limit a person's ability to make use of his or her memory for that processing in an act of recognition. In our example of trying not to repeat oneself, monitoring the past to avoid repetition is an attention-demanding act that might be impossible under conditions of divided attention.

### Method

#### SUBJECTS AND DESIGN

The design was the same as that in Experiment 2, except that the manipulation of attention was during the fame test rather than during the original reading of nonfamous names. Judging fame while doing the listening task was quite difficult, tempting subjects to neglect the listening task. Consequently, performance on the listening task was used as a criterion for using subjects' data in the divided-attention condition. For subjects' data to be included, they could not miss more than 25% of the targets presented in the listening task. This rather stringent criterion ensured that subjects were dividing attention between the two tasks. Eleven subjects were not included in the study for failure to meet the criterion. The remaining subjects were 32 undergraduates enrolled in an introductory psychology course; there were 16 subjects in each of the two attention (full vs. divided) conditions. Names on the fame-judgment test were either famous, nonfamous and earlier read (old nonfamous), or nonfamous and not earlier read (new nonfamous).

## MATERIALS AND PROCEDURE

The materials and procedure were the same as in Experiment 2, except for the change in when the attention manipulation occurred. During the fame-judgment test, subjects in the full-attention condition only made fame judgments, whereas those in the divided-attention condition simultaneously engaged in the task of listening for a series of three odd-numbered digits. Five famous and five nonfamous names were added as fillers to the beginning of the test lists used in Experiment 2. These additional names were presented for fame judgments to subjects in both attention conditions but were added to allow subjects in the divided-attention condition to settle into the listening task before presentation of the main test list. Presentation of names for fame judgments was controlled by the computer. One second after a fame judgment, the next name to be judged was presented. For the listening task, subjects responded verbally, saying "Now" when they detected a target sequence of three odd digits. If during the test phase subjects completed one full cycle through the list of 224 numbers used in the listening task, the list was repeated without interruption. Recognition memory was not tested.

## Results and Discussion

Subjects in the divided-attention condition missed an average of 6.5 of 52 targets in the listening task.

In a first analysis of the probability of calling a name "famous" (see Table 20.4) for each combination of conditions, we compared performance on famous and new nonfamous names to test for differences between the two attention conditions in accuracy of discrimination or in the criterion used for fame judgments. Famous names were more likely to be called "famous" than were new nonfamous names, $F(1, 30) = 163.92$, $MS_e = 0.012$. Although subjects in the full-attention condition were slightly more willing to call a name "famous" than were subjects in the divided-attention condition, neither the main effect of attention condition nor the interaction of attention with fame was significant. A signal-detection analysis indicated no significant effects of attention condition on either the criterion used for judging a name famous or the accuracy of discrimination between famous and new nonfamous names.

Our central interest was in differences between the two attention conditions in performance on new nonfamous and old nonfamous names. An analysis of those probabilities showed that old nonfamous names were more likely to be called "famous" than were new nonfamous names, $F(1, 30) = 6.20$, $MS_e = 0.005$. More important, the interaction between previously reading a name and attention condition was significant, $F(1, 30) = 28.52$, $MS_e = 0.005$. As predicted, old nonfamous names were more likely to be called "famous" than were new nonfamous names in the divided-attention condition, whereas the opposite was true in the full-attention condition. This pattern of results is consistent with the interpretation that subjects in the full-attention condition used list recognition of names as a basis for rejecting old nonfamous names. Subjects whose attention was divided were left without sufficient resources to perform this list-recognition memory check.

Judgment times were consistent with this conclusion. An analysis of times to correctly reject

**TABLE 20.4.** Probability of Judging a Name Famous

| Condition | Famous Name: New | Nonfamous Name New | Old |
|---|---|---|---|
| Full attention | .54 | .18 | .13 |
| Divided attention | .49 | .14 | .28 |

nonfamous names showed a main effect of prior presentation of the name, $F(1, 30) = 11.43$, as well as a significant interaction between prior presentation and attention condition, $F(1, 30) = 4.89$, $MS_e = 31,389$. Old nonfamous names were rejected more rapidly than were new nonfamous names in the full-attention condition (1,278 vs. 1,526 ms), whereas there was no difference in the times to reject old and new nonfamous names in the divided-attention condition (1,534 vs. 1,582 ms). List recognition served as a basis for quickly rejecting old nonfamous names in the full-attention condition but could be used less often in the divided-attention condition. The two conditions did not differ in time taken to correctly call a famous name "famous" ($F < 1$).

We also examined the possibility that divided attention during the test had *no* effect on access to gains in familiarity as measured by fame judgments. Recognition data were not collected in this experiment. However, we used recognition data from Experiment 2 to estimate the probability of calling nonrecognized names famous in the full-attention condition. The use of list-recognition performance from one experiment in order to "correct" fame judgments in another experiment is more conservative than is using data for both types of judgment from the same experiment. To examine any differential effects of attention at test in responding to nonrecognized names, we made the strong assumption that dividing attention completely eliminated list recognition. Under that conservative assumption, it was unnecessary to correct fame judgments for list recognition in the divided-attention condition. According to these computations, the difference between the probabilities of mistakenly responding "famous" to old and new nonrecognized names in the full-attention condition (.35 vs. .18) was approximately the same as that in the divided-attention condition (.28 vs. .14). The small effect of attention condition that remained probably stemmed from the fact that dividing attention does not completely eliminate list recognition. Therefore, some proportion of items in the divided-attention condition were not susceptible to the false fame effect because they were recognized and quickly rejected as nonfamous. Regardless, one can conclude that divided attention, in comparison with full attention, when subjects were making fame judgments radically reduced the use of list recognition to reject

nonfamous names but left in place the effects of prior presentation on the names' familiarity.

The effects of dividing attention while one is making fame judgments were almost identical to those of dividing attention during the initial presentation of nonfamous names. Recognition can suffer equally from a deficit in study or from a deficit in retrieval processing. For both study and retrieval, more demanding cognitive forms of processing that require attentional resources may be necessary for recognition (e.g., Craik, 1982; Jacoby, 1982; Warrington & Weiskrantz, 1982).

The separability of the tool versus object functions of memory is seen when conscious recollection is used to monitor unconscious effects of the past. There may be large individual differences in the extent to which people monitor the past as a source of influence. The effects that we observed in the divided-attention condition may reflect individual differences in such monitoring. It was necessary to reject more than a third of the subjects tested in the divided-attention condition on the grounds of poor performance on the listening task. Subjects who did poorly on the listening task produced a pattern of results similar to that produced by subjects in the full-attention condition. Perhaps subjects who were unable to do the listening task while making fame judgments could not stop monitoring the past. In this regard, one of the authors (Jacoby) found it impossible to perform the listening task while judging fame and claimed to be unable to stop attempting to recognize the names. Those who were able to perform the listening task adequately while making fame judgments claimed that a "laid-back," largely uncritical approach to the fame judgment task was necessary.

## General Discussion

We were successful in making names famous without their being recognized. By doing so, we extended results of earlier experiments (Eich, 1984; Koriat & Feuerstein, 1976) that have shown differential effects of attention on conscious recollection, in comparison with other uses of memory. Dividing attention influenced people's ability to consciously recollect having read a name, as measured by list recognition, but left in place effects of reading a name on its familiarity, as indexed by fame judgments. Familiarity has been proposed as one of two processes in models of retrieval (e.g., Atkinson & Juola, 1974; Glucksberg & McCloskey, 1981; Jacoby & Brooks, 1984; Mandler, 1980). Assessing familiarity is said to often be a rapid process that enables subjects to respond quickly, whereas a second, often slower retrieval process generates further information before specifying a response. The results of our experiments provide strong evidence of the existence of these multiple bases for judgments. The differential effects of dividing attention on fame judgments and on list-recognition memory judgments provide one source of such evidence.

Our strategy of placing conscious recollection in opposition to effects on familiarity provides more conclusive evidence that conscious recollection and assessing familiarity serve as alternative bases for judgments. Effects on familiarity are an unconscious influence of memory in that they do not depend on conscious recollection. We can be certain that this is the case because in our later experiments, conscious recollection would produce a judgment that was opposite to that produced by gains in familiarity. In contrast to the conclusions that can be drawn from our experiments, Gillund and Shiffrin (1984) used different procedures and concluded that they were unable to find any convincing evidence of multiple bases for recognition memory decisions. Our strategy of placing different bases for judgments in opposition allows their clear separation.

## A Processing Account of Unconscious Influences

In other studies of the relation between attention and memory, researchers found that when attention to items was eliminated during study, later recognition performance was near chance (e.g., Fisk & Schneider, 1984). Rather than attempting to fully eliminate attention, we ensured some processing of names in our experiments by requiring subjects to read the names aloud in both divided- and full-attention conditions. Under those circumstances, the pattern of results produced by the dividing of attention during study was similar to that observed for amnesics by Huppert and Piercy (1978). Mandler (1980) interpreted results of this sort as showing that amnesics preserve the ability to assess familiarity without the capability of con-

scious recollection or memory for study context. This deficit has been said to result from amnesics' inability to form a memory representation of study context (e.g., Hirst, 1982). Similarly, divided attention during study can be described as producing a failure to store study context (Craik, 1982). The results of our experiments would then be interpreted as showing that divided attention did not influence memory for content (memory for the names as shown by fame judgments) but did influence memory for context (as shown by list-recognition memory judgments).

However, the conclusion that the dividing of attention prevented subjects from encoding context must be treated with caution. A test of list recognition is a direct test of memory in that people are instructed to base their decisions on their ability to report study context. Performance on indirect memory tests can reveal effects of reinstating context even when context cannot be reported (Kelley, Jacoby, & Hollingshead, in press). When attention was divided during study, context may have been represented in some form that would support performance on an indirect test but not on a direct test of memory. Also, an account in terms of an inability to store context ignores the parallel results produced by the dividing of attention during the test and the dividing of attention during study. We prefer to describe the effects of dividing attention in terms of differences in processing so as to emphasize that parallel and to emphasize other relations among effects on different types of task.

By emphasizing differences in processing, one can reveal relations among tasks that would be ignored if one described effects as produced by a failure to *add* a representation of study context to that of the content of studied material. In this vein, Dywan and Jacoby (1988) showed that people's susceptibility to familiarity errors is correlated with performance on other tasks. Dywan and Jacoby used the fame-judgment task to investigate differences among the aged in their memory performance. As in the later experiments reported here, Dywan and Jacoby placed effects on familiarity in opposition to conscious recollection by presenting only nonfamous names to be read. The difference between the probability of calling an old nonfamous name "famous" and that of calling a new nonfamous name "famous" served as a measure of the likelihood of a familiarity error for each subject and was correlated with the subject's performance on other tasks. Dywan and Jacoby found that subjects who were likely to make a familiarity error were also more likely to make errors when copying a complex figure and were less likely to cluster words by category when recalling a categorized list than were subjects who were unlikely to make a familiarity error. The processing disrupted by divided attention could also be involved in monitoring of the sort necessary to note relations among items in a categorized list and to avoid copying errors. The correlation between familiarity errors and clustering calls into question the claim that memory for context is fully separate from memory for content. Indeed, there are other data to show that memory for temporal relations (an aspect of memory for context) depends on noting relations among items in a list, the same activity required for clustering. Winograd and Soloway (1985) found better recency judgments for related pairs than for unrelated pairs of words. They argued that subjects are reminded of the earlier item when they encounter the second related item and that reminding establishes a relation that supports recency judgments.

Craik (e.g., 1982) used the term *elaboration* to refer to the type of processing that is influenced by the dividing of attention and is important for remembering the context in which an event occurred. We agree with Craik in many ways, but we hesitate to adopt the term *elaboration. Elaboration* usually refers to differences in the processing of meaning, and we do not believe that the effects of dividing attention that we observed were produced by such differences. It is not clear that nonfamous names have any meaning, and in any case, subjects were required only to pronounce the names, a task that does not encourage the processing of meaning. One could consider famous names to be more meaningful to subjects than nonfamous names. If it is the processing of the meaning of individual items that is influenced by the dividing of attention and is responsible for effects on list recognition, one would expect an interaction between manipulations of attention and the meaningfulness of those items. The list of names read in our first experiment did include famous, as well as nonfamous, names. List-recognition performance in that experiment showed a main effect of divided attention and a main effect of famous versus nonfamous names (meaningfulness of names)

but did not reveal a significant interaction between those two factors. In this vein, interactions between manipulations of the processing of meaning and state differences, such as intoxication, that are thought to reflect differences in attention are also often not found (Hartley, Birnbaum, & Parker, 1978). We think the processing influenced by divided attention is better described as reflection (Johnson, 1983) or as treating memory as an object (Jacoby & Kelley, 1987). One possibility is that treating an experience as an object is necessary to define that experience as a separate event and is also necessary for conscious recollection and comparison of that event with other events.

In contrast to our results, divided attention does not always simulate the effects of amnesia. Nissen and Bullemer (1987) found that both normal subjects and amnesics improved with practice on a serial reaction time task that comprised a repeating 10-trial sequence. Unlike the normal subjects, the amnesics were not aware of the repeating sequence. Divided attention during training was meant to produce results for normal subjects that paralleled those of amnesics: learning in the absence of ability to report the repeating sequence. However, divided attention disrupted the learning of normal subjects, as well as their ability to become aware of the repeating patterns. We speculate that the secondary task used by Nissen and Bullemer had its effects on learning by disrupting the continuity of the repeating sequence of trials in the serial reaction time task, thereby producing a change in segmentation. The structure of a task, as well as the ability to verbalize relations, can probably be affected by the dividing of attention. To anticipate the effects of divided attention on memory, it is probably necessary to more fully specify the relation between the secondary task used to divide attention and the requirements of the criterial task (Broadbent, 1989; Neisser, 1980).

## Conscious Recollection as a Separate Act

The rationale underlying our experiments was that conscious recollection often serves to oppose unconscious influences of memory. When unopposed by conscious recollection, reading a name that one is told is nonfamous increases the probability that that name will later be called "famous." Conscious recollection is required to discriminate the familiarity produced by having recently read a name from the familiarity produced by the name's being a famous one. As well as making nonfamous names seem famous, unconscious influences of the past can serve to increase the accuracy of perception (e.g., Jacoby & Dallas, 1981), reduce the subjective loudness of a background noise (Jacoby, Allan, Collins, & Larwill, 1988), and reduce the judged difficulty of anagrams (Jacoby & Kelley, 1987). Jacoby and Kelley (1987) and Jacoby, Kelley, and Dywan (1989) found it useful to think about these unconscious influences of the past versus conscious recollection in terms of Polanyi's (1958) distinction between tool and object. According to the tool/object distinction, familiarity and other unconscious influences of the past stem from the use of memory as a tool to perceive and interpret later events. When used as a tool, memory for a prior event is incorporated into an ongoing activity rather than treated as an object of reflection. Specifying the source of familiarity requires a change in the focus of attention from the task at hand to reflecting on the past; that is, conscious recollection requires an act that is separate from the use of memory as a tool and serves to attribute effects of the past to their source. Even when it is possible to specify the source, people may fail to do so spontaneously.

In this regard, perhaps the most interesting finding from our experiments is that dividing attention during the test produced essentially the same results as did dividing attention while subjects earlier read nonfamous names. Dividing attention at the time of test reduced the likelihood of conscious recollection while leaving in place the effects of earlier reading a name on its familiarity, which made it likely that old nonfamous names would mistakenly be called "famous." This finding is consistent with the claim that conscious recollection is an attention-demanding act that is separate from other uses of memory. Recognition of an item as previously presented is not always automatic or spontaneous even when that item gives rise to a feeling of familiarity.

Questions about automaticity have most often centered on whether the encoding of some type of information is automatic (e.g., Hasher & Zacks, 1979). Treating recollection as a separate act encourages the use of manipulations such as the dividing of attention both at the time of test and during study. In contrast to our results, Baddeley, Lewis, Eldridge, and Thomson (1984) observed very small effects of varying attention at test and concluded that retrieval from memory is largely automatic. A potentially important difference between their experiments and ours is that they instructed their subjects to recall or recognize items. In our experiments, list recognition was not a primary objective for subjects but, rather, served as a means of avoiding being misled by familiarity when judging fame. That is a difference between spontaneous and directed recognition. Perhaps gaining the orientation toward conscious recollection (treating memory as an object), rather than the act of retrieval itself, is what demands attention.

In most investigations of conscious recollection, researchers have relied on directly asking people to report on the past or to recognize an item as previously presented. Those procedures might lead to an overestimate of the probability of "spontaneous" recollection. Fame judgments provided us with a measure of spontaneous recollection. Subjects were not directly asked to consciously recollect names as previously read, but recollection of the source of a name's familiarity would produce a fame judgment that was opposite to that produced by a failure to recollect the source. That arrangement allows one to use effects on fame judgments to infer whether recollection of earlier reading a name was spontaneous—recollected when people were not directly asked to do so. In that light, our results show that spontaneous recollection is less likely when attention is divided at the time of test.

People may neglect to spontaneously recollect even when they have the attentional capacity to do so if directed. Jacoby, Kelley, Brown, and Jasechko (1989) showed that people make errors in fame judgments that could be avoided if they were directly asked to consciously recollect earlier reading a name (make list-recognition judgments), as well as making fame judgments. In other words, errors that reflect a failure to monitor unconscious influences of the past can arise because of people's failure to spontaneously attempt conscious recollection even when they could consciously recollect the relevant experience in response to a direct question. The most common cause of unconscious influences may be a failure to spontaneously note or realize the significance of some earlier event rather than an inability to do so when directly asked (Bowers, 1984). By focusing on the test as the locus for manipulations, we have an opportunity to learn more about the situations that encourage self-monitoring (e.g., Snyder, 1974), as well as about types of monitoring that are important to avoid unconscious influences of the past.

Counter to folk wisdom, conscious recollection can serve as a means of avoiding misleading effects of the past rather than being a prerequisite for effects of the past. Placing conscious recollection in opposition to misleading effects of the past has the advantage of clearly separating conscious from unconscious influences of memory. Our results suggest that the retrieval orientation required for monitoring the past as a potential source of effects on performance is functionally independent from other uses of memory. Dividing attention at test selectively interfered with the use of list recognition to reject old nonfamous names. Manipulations at test provide an additional means of exploring the relation between different functions of memory.

## ACKNOWLEDGMENTS

This research was supported by a grant to Larry L. Jacoby from the Canadian National Science and Engineering Research Council.

We thank Gus Craik, Marcia Johnson, and Ronald Kinchla for their comments on an earlier version of this article. We also thank Ian Begg for his suggestions concerning the analyses of data and Ann Hollingshead for collecting and analyzing the data.

## REFERENCES

Atkinson, R. C., & Juola, J. F. (1974). Search and decision processes in recognition memory. In D. H. Krantz, R. C. Atkinson, R. D. Luce, & P. Suppes (Eds.), *Contemporary developments in mathematical psychology: Vol. 1. Learning, memory and thinking* (pp. 243–293). San Francisco: Freeman.

Baddeley, A., Lewis, V., Eldridge, M., & Thomson, N. (1984). Attention and retrieval from long-term memory. *Journal of Experimental Psychology: General, 113*, 518–540.

Bowers, K. S. (1984). On being unconsciously influenced and informed. In K. S. Bowers & D. Meichenbaum (Eds.), *The unconscious reconsidered* (pp. 227–273). New York: Wiley.

Broadbent, D. E. (1989). Lasting representations and temporary processes. In H. L. Roediger & F. I. M. Craik (Eds.), *Varieties of memory and consciousness: Essays in honor of Endel Tulving.* Hillsdale, NJ: Erlbaum.

Cook, T. D., Gruder, C. L., Hennigan, K. M., & Flay, B. R. (1979). History of the sleeper effect: Some logical pitfalls in accepting the null hypothesis. *Psychological Bulletin, 86*, 662–679.

Craik, F. I. M. (1982). Selective changes in encoding as a func-

tion of reduced processing capacity. In F. Klix, J. Hoffman, & E. van der Meer (Eds.), *Cognitive research in psychology* (pp. 152–161). Berlin: Deutscher Verlag der Wissenschaffen.

Dywan, J., & Jacoby L. L. (1988). *Effects of aging on source monitoring: Differences in susceptibility to false fame.* Manuscript submitted for publication.

Eich, E. (1984). Memory for unattended events: Remembering with and without awareness. *Memory & Cognition, 12*, 105–111.

Fisk, A. D., & Schneider, W. (1984). Memory as a function of attention, level of processing, and automatization. *Journal of Experimental Psychology: Learning, Memory, and Cognition, 10*, 181–197.

Gillund, G., & Shiffrin, R. M. (1984). A retrieval model for both recognition and recall. *Psychological Review, 91*, 1–67.

Glucksberg, S., & McCloskey, M. (1981). Decisions about ignorance: Knowing that you don't know. *Journal of Experimental Psychology: Human Learning and Memory, 7*, 311–325.

Grand, S., & Segal, S. J. (1966). Recovery in the absence of recall: An investigation of color-word interference. *Journal of Experimental Psychology, 72*, 138–144.

Hartley, J. T., Birnbaum, I. M., & Parker, E. S. (1978). Alcohol and storage deficits: Kind of processing? *Journal of Verbal Learning and Verbal Behavior, 5*, 635–647.

Hasher, L., & Zacks, R. T. (1979). Automatic and effortful processes in memory. *Journal of Experimental Psychology: General, 108*, 356–388.

Hirst, W. (1982). The amnesic syndrome: Descriptions and explanations. *Psychological Bulletin, 91*, 435–460.

Hovland, C. I., Lumsdaine, A. A., & Sheffield, F. D. (1949). *Experiments on mass communication.* Princeton, NJ: Princeton University Press.

Huppert, F. A., & Piercy, M. (1978). The role of trace strength in recency and frequency judgments by amnesic and control subjects. *Quarterly Journal of Experimental Psychology, 30*, 346–354.

Jacoby, L. L. (1982). Knowing and remembering: Some parallels in the behavior of Korsakoff patients and normals. In L. S. Cermak (Ed.), *Human memory and amnesia* (pp. 97–122). Hillsdale, NJ: Erlbaum.

Jacoby, L. L., Allan, L. G., Collins, J. C., & Larwill, L. K. (1988). Memory influences subjective experience: Noise judgments. *Journal of Experimental Psychology: Learning, Memory, and Cognition, 14*, 240–247.

Jacoby, L. L., & Brooks, L. R. (1984). Nonanalytic cognition: Memory, perception and concept learning. In G. H. Bower (Ed.), *The psychology of learning and motivation: Advances in research and theory, Vol. 18* (pp. 1–47). New York: Academic Press.

Jacoby, L. L., & Dallas, M. (1981). On the relationship between autobiographical memory and perceptual learning. *Journal of Experimental Psychology: General, 110*, 306–340.

Jacoby, L. L., & Kelley, C. M. (1987). Unconscious influences of memory for a prior event. *Personality and Social Psychology Bulletin, 13*, 314–336.

Jacoby, L. L., Kelley, C. M., Brown, J., & Jasechko, J. (1989). Becoming famous overnight: Limits on the ability to avoid unconscious influences of the past. *Journal of Personality and Social Psychology, 56*, 326–338.

Jacoby, L. L., Kelley, C. M., & Dywan, J. (1989). Memory attributions. In H. L. Roediger & F. I. M. Craik (Eds.), *Varieties of memory and consciousness: Essays in honor of Endel Tulving* (391–422). Hillsdale, NJ: Erlbaum.

Johnson, M. K. (1983). A modular model of memory. In G. H. Bower (Ed.), *The psychology of learning and motivation: Advances in research and theory, Vol. 17* (pp. 81–123). New York: Academic Press.

Kelley, C. M., Jacoby, L. L., & Hollingshead, A. (in press). Direct versus indirect tests of memory for source: Judgments of modality. *Journal of Experimental Psychology: Learning, Memory, and Cognition.*

Koriat, A., & Feuerstein, N. (1976). The recovery of incidentally acquired information. *Acta Psychologica, 40*, 463–474.

Mandler, G. (1980). Recognizing: The judgment of previous occurrence. *Psychological Review, 87*, 252–271.

Moray, N. (1959). Attention in dichotic listening: Affective cues and the influence of instructions. *Quarterly Journal of Experimental Psychology, 11*, 56–60.

Morton, J. (1969). Interaction of information in word recognition. *Psychological Review, 76*, 165–178.

Neely, J. H., & Payne, D. G. (1983). A direct comparison of recognition failure rates for recallable names in episodic and semantic memory tests. *Memory & Cognition, 11*, 161–171.

Neisser, U. (1980). The limits of cognition. In P. Jusczyk & R. Klein (Eds.), *The nature of thought: Essays in honor of D. O. Hebb* (pp. 115–132). Hillsdale, NJ: Erlbaum.

Nissen, M. J., & Bullemer, P. (1987). Attentional requirements of learning: Evidence from performance measures. *Cognitive Psychology, 19*, 1–32.

Polanyi, M. (1958). *Personal knowledge: Towards a post-critical philosophy*. Chicago: University of Chicago Press.

Richardson-Klavehn, A., & Bjork, R. A. (1988). Measures of memory. *Annual Review of Psychology, 39*, 475–543.

Snyder, M. (1974). The self-monitoring of expressive behavior. *Journal of Personality and Social Psychology, 30*, 526–537.

Warrington, E. K., & Weiskrantz, L. (1982). Amnesia: A disconnection syndrome? *Neuropsychologia, 20*, 233–248.

Winograd, E., & Soloway, R. M. (1985). Reminding as a basis for temporal judgments. *Journal of Experimental Psychology: Learning, Memory, and Cognition, 11*, 262–271.

READING 21

# Creating False Memories: Remembering Words Not Presented in Lists

Henry L. Roediger III and Kathleen B. McDermott • Rice University

Two experiments (modeled after J. Deese's 1959 study) revealed remarkable levels of false recall and false recognition in a list learning paradigm. In Experiment 1, subjects studied lists of 12 words (e.g., *bed, rest, awake*); each list was composed of associates of 1 nonpresented word (e.g., *sleep*). On immediate free recall tests, the nonpresented associates were recalled 40% of the time and were later recognized with high confidence. In Experiment 2, a false recall rate of 55% was obtained with an expanded set of lists, and on a later recognition test, subjects produced false alarms to these items at a rate comparable to the hit rate. The act of recall enhanced later remembering of both studied and nonstudied material. The results reveal a powerful illusion of memory: People remember events that never happened.

False memories—either remembering events that never happened, or remembering them quite differently from the way they happened—have recently captured the attention of both psychologists and the public at large. The primary impetus for this recent surge of interest is the increase in the number of cases in which memories of previously unrecognized abuse are reported during the course of therapy. Some researchers have argued that certain therapeutic practices can cause the creation of false memories, and therefore, the apparent "recovery" of memories during the course of therapy may actually represent the creation of memories (Lindsay & Read, 1994; Loftus, 1993). Although the concept of false memories is currently enjoying an increase in publicity, it is not new; psychologists have been studying false memories in several laboratory paradigms for years. Schacter (in press) provides an historical overview of the study of memory distortions.

Bartlett (1932) is usually credited with conducting the first experimental investigation of false memories; he had subjects read an Indian folktale, "The War of the Ghosts," and recall it repeatedly. Although he reported no aggregate data, but only sample protocols, his results seemed to show distortions in subjects' memories over repeated attempts to recall the story. Interestingly, Bartlett's repeated reproduction results never have been successfully replicated by later researchers (see Gauld & Stephenson, 1967; Roediger, Wheeler, & Rajaram, 1993); indeed, Wheeler and Roediger (1992) showed that recall of prose passages (including "The War of the Ghosts") actually improved over repeated tests (with very few errors) if short delays occurred between study and test.[1]

Nonetheless, Bartlett's (1932) contribution was an enduring one because he distinguished between *reproductive* and *reconstructive* memory. Reproductive memory refers to accurate, rote production of material from memory, whereas reconstructive memory emphasizes the active process of filling in missing elements while remembering, with errors frequently occurring. It generally has been assumed that the act of remembering materials rich in meaning (e.g., stories and real-life events) gives rise to reconstructive processes (and therefore errors), whereas the act of remembering more simplified materials (e.g., nonsense syllables, word lists) gives rise to reproductive (and thus accurate) memory. Bartlett (1932) wrote that "I discarded nonsense materials because, among other difficulties, its use almost always weights the evidence in favour of mere rote recapitulation" (p. 204).

The investigators of false memories have generally followed Bartlett's (1932) lead. Most evidence has been collected in paradigms that use sentences (Bransford & Franks, 1971; Brewer, 1977), prose passages (Sulin & Dooling, 1974), slide sequences (Loftus, Miller, & Burns, 1978), or videotapes (Loftus & Palmer, 1974). In all these paradigms, evidence of false memories has been obtained, although the magnitude of the effect depends on the method of testing (McCloskey & Zaragoza, 1985; Payne, Toglia, & Anastasi, 1994). The predominance of materials that tell a story (or can be represented by a script or schema) can probably be attributed to the belief that only such materials will cause false memories to occur.

There is one well-known case of false memories being produced in a list learning paradigm: Underwood (1965) introduced a technique to study false recognition of words in lists. He gave subjects a continuous recognition task in which they decided if each presented word had been given previously in the list. Later words bore various relations to previously studied words. Underwood showed that words associatively related to previously presented words were falsely recognized. Anisfeld and Knapp (1968), among others, replicated the phenomenon. Although there have been a few reports of robust false recognition effects (Hintzman, 1988), in many experiments the false recognition effect was either rather small or did not occur at all. For example, in a study by L. M. Paul (1979), in which synonyms were presented at various lags along with other, unrelated lures, the false recognition effect was only 3% (a 20% false-alarm rate for synonyms and a 17% rate for unrelated lures). Gillund and Shiffrin (1984) failed

to find any false recognition effect for semantically related lures in a similar paradigm. In general, most research on the false recognition effect in list learning does little to discourage the belief that more natural, coherent materials are needed to demonstrate powerful false memory effects. Interestingly, most research revealing false memory effects has used recognition measures; this is true both of the prose memory literature (e.g., Bransford & Franks, 1971; Sulin & Dooling, 1974) and the eyewitness memory paradigm (Loftus et al., 1978; McCloskey & Zaragoza, 1985). Reports of robust levels of false recall are rarer.

We have discovered a potentially important exception to these claims, one that reveals false recall in a standard list learning paradigm. It is represented in an experimental report published by Deese in 1959 that has been largely overlooked for the intervening 36 years, despite the fact that his observations would seem to bear importantly on the study of false memories. Deese's procedure was remarkably straightforward; he tested memory for word lists in a single-trial, free-recall paradigm. Because this paradigm was just gaining favor among experimental psychologists at that time and was the focus of much attention during the 1960s, the neglect of Deese's report is even more surprising. However, since the Social Science Citation Index began publication in 1969, the article has been cited only 14 times, and only once since 1983. Most authors mentioned it only in passing, several authors apparently cited it by mistake, and no one has followed up Deese's interesting observations until now, although Cramer (1965) reported similar observations and did appropriately cite Deese's (1959) article. (While working on this article, we learned that Don Read was conducting similar research, which is described briefly in Lindsay & Read, 1994, p. 291.)[2]

Deese (1959) was interested in predicting the occurrence of extralist intrusions in single-trial free recall. To this end, he developed 36 lists, with 12 words per list. Each list was composed of the 12 primary associates of a critical (nonpresented) word. For example, for the critical word *needle*, the list words were *thread, pin, eye, sewing, sharp, point, pricked, thimble, haystack, pain, hurt,* and *injection.* He found that some of the lists reliably induced subjects to produce the critical nonpresented word as an intrusion on the immediate free recall test. Deese's interest was in determining why some lists gave rise to this effect, whereas others did not. His general conclusion was that the lists for which the associations went in a backward (as well as forward) direction tended to elicit false recall. That is, he measured the average probability with which people produced the critical word from which the list was generated when they were asked to associate to the individual words in the list. For example, subjects were given *sewing, point, thimble*, and so on, and the average probability of producing *needle* as an associate was measured. Deese obtained a correlation of .87 between the probability of an intrusion in recall (from one group of subjects) and the probability of occurrence of the word as an associate to members of the list (from a different group). Our interest in Deese's materials was in using his best lists and developing his paradigm as a way to examine false memory phenomena.

Our first goal was to try to replicate Deese's (1959) finding of reliable, predictable extralist intrusions in a single-trial, free-recall paradigm. We found his result to be surprising in light of the literature showing that subjects are often extremely accurate in recalling lists after a single trial, making few intrusions unless instructed to guess (see Cofer, 1967; Roediger & Payne, 1985). As previously noted, most prior research on false memory phenomena has employed measures of recognition memory or cued recall. Deese's paradigm potentially offers a method to study false recollections in free recall. However, we also extended Deese's paradigm to recognition tests. In Experiment 1, we examined false recall and false recognition of the critical nonpresented words and the confidence with which subjects accepted or rejected the critical nonpresented words as having been in the study lists. In Experiment 2, we tested other lists constructed to produce extralist intrusions in single-trial free recall, to generalize the finding across a wider set of materials. In addition, we examined the extent to which the initial false recall of items led to later false recognition of those same items. Finally, we employed the remember–know procedure developed by Tulving (1985) to examine subjects' phenomenological experience during false recognition of the critical nonpresented items. We describe this procedure more fully below.

## Experiment 1

The purpose of Experiment 1 was to replicate Deese's (1959) observations of false recall by using six lists that produced among the highest levels of erroneous recall in his experiments. Students heard and recalled the lists and then received a recognition test over both studied and nonstudied items, including the critical nonpresented words.

## Method

### SUBJECTS

Subjects were 36 Rice University undergraduates who participated as part of a course project during a regular meeting of the class, Psychology 308, Human Memory.

### MATERIALS

We developed six lists from the materials listed in Deese's (1959) article. With one exception, we chose the six targets that produced the highest intrusion rates in Deese's experiment: *chair, mountain, needle, rough, sleep,* and *sweet*. As in Deese's experiment, for each critical word, we constructed the corresponding list by obtaining the first 12 associates listed in Russell and Jenkins's (1954) word association norms. For example, the list corresponding to *chair* was *table, sit, legs, seat, soft, desk, arm, sofa, wood, cushion, rest*, and *stool*. In a few instances, we replaced 1 of the first 12 associates with a word that seemed, in our judgment, more likely to elicit the critical word. (The lists for Experiment 1 are included in the expanded set of lists for Experiment 2.)

The 42-item recognition test included 12 studied and 30 nonstudied items. There were three types of nonstudied items, or lures: (a) the 6 critical words, from which the lists were generated (e.g., *chair*), (b) 12 words generally unrelated to any items on the six lists, and (c) 12 words weakly related to the lists (2 per list). We drew the weakly related words from Positions 13 and below in the association norms; for example, we chose *couch* and *floor* for the *chair* list. We constructed the test sequence in blocks; there were 7 items per block, and each block corresponded to a studied list (2 studied words, 2 related words, 2 unrelated words, and the critical nonstudied lure). The order of the blocks corresponded to the order in which lists had been studied. Each block of test items always began with a studied word and ended with the critical lure; the other items were arranged haphazardly in between. One of the two studied words that were tested occurred in the first position of the study list (and therefore was the strongest associate to the critical item); the other occurred somewhere in the first 6 positions of the study list.

## PROCEDURE

Subjects were tested in a group during a regular class meeting. They were instructed that they would hear lists of words and that they would be tested immediately after each list by writing the words on successive pages of examination booklets. They were told to write the last few items first (a standard instruction for this task) and then to recall the rest of the words in any order. They were also told to write down all the words they could remember but to be reasonably confident that each word they wrote down did in fact occur in the list (i.e., they were told not to guess). The lists were read aloud by the first author at the approximate rate of 1 word per 1.5 s. Before reading each list, the experimenter said "List 1, List 2," and so on, and he said "recall" at the end of the list. Subjects were given 2.5 min to recall each list.

After the sixth list, there was brief conversation lasting 2–3 min prior to instructions for the recognition test. At this point, subjects were told that they would receive another test in which they would see words on a sheet and that they were to rate each as to their confidence that it had occurred on the list. The 4-point rating scale was 4 for *sure that the item was old* (or studied), 3 for *probably old*, 2 for *probably new*, and 1 for *sure it was new*. Subjects worked through the recognition test at their own pace.

At the end of the experiment, subjects were asked to raise their hands if they had recognized six particular items on the test, and the critical lures were read aloud. Most subjects raised their hands for several items. The experimenter then informed them that none of the words just read had actually been on the list and the subjects were debriefed about the purpose of the experiment, which was a central topic in the course.

## Results

### RECALL

The mean probability of recall of the studied words was .65, and the serial position curve is shown in Figure 21.1. The curve was smoothed by averaging data from three adjacent points for each position because the raw data were noisy with only six lists. For example, data from the third, fourth, and fifth points contributed to the fourth position in the graph. The first and the last positions, however, were based only on the raw data. The serial

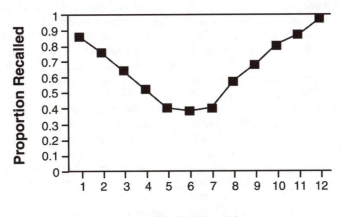

**Serial Position**

**FIGURE 21.1** ■ Probability of correct recall in Experiment 1 as a function of serial position. Probability of recall of the studied words was .65, and probability of recall of the critical nonpresented item was .40.

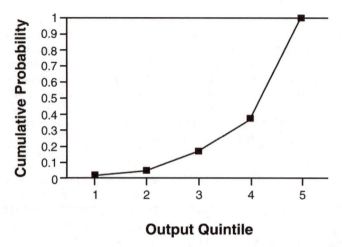

**Output Quintile**

**FIGURE 21.2** ■ Recall of the critical intrusion as a function of output position in recall. Quintiles refer to the first 20% of responses, the second 20%, and so on.

position curve shows marked recency, indicating that subjects followed directions in recalling the last items first. A strong primacy effect is also apparent, probably because the strongest associates to the critical target words occurred early in the list. The critical omitted word was recalled with a probability of .40, or with about the same probability as items that had been presented in the middle of the list (see Figure 21.1). Therefore, items that were not presented were recalled at about the same rate as those that were presented, albeit those in the least favorable serial positions.

The average output position for recall of the critical nonpresented word was 6.9 (out of 8.6 words written down in lists in which there was a critical intrusion). The cumulative production levels of the critical intrusion for those trials on which they occurred is shown in Figure 21.2 across quintiles of subjects' responses. The critical intrusion appeared only 2% of the time in the first fifth of subjects' output but 63% of the time in the last quintile. Thus, on average, subjects recalled the critical nonstudied item in the last fifth of their output, at the 80th percentile of recalled words ($6.9 \div 8.6 \times 100$).

Other intrusions also occurred in recall, albeit at a rather low rate. Subjects intruded the critical lure on 40% of the lists, but any other word in the English language was intruded on only 14% of the lists. Therefore, subjects were not guessing wildly in the experiment; as usual in single-trial free recall, the general intrusion rate was quite low.

Nonetheless, subjects falsely recalled the critical items at a high rate.

RECOGNITION

The recognition test was given following study and recall of all six lists, and thus the results were likely affected by prior recall. (We consider this issue in Experiment 2.) The proportion of responses for each of the four confidence ratings are presented in Table 21.1 for studied (old) items and for the three different types of lures: unrelated words, weakly related words, and the critical words from which the lists were derived. Consider first the proportion of items subjects called old by assigning a rating of 3 (*probably old*) or 4 (*sure old*). The hit rate was 86% and the false-alarm rate for the standard type of unrelated lures was only 2%, so by usual criteria subjects showed high accuracy. The rate of false alarms was higher for the weakly related lures (.21) than for the unrelated lures, $t(35) = 7.40$, $SEM = .026$, $p < .001$. This outcome replicates the standard false-recognition effect first reported by Underwood (1965). The false-recognition rate for weakly related lures was greater than obtained in many prior studies (e.g., L. M. Paul, 1979), and the rate for the critical nonpresented words was dramatically larger than the rate for the weakly related words. As shown in Table 21.1, the false-alarm rate for the critical nonstudied lures (.84) approached the hit rate (.86), $t(35) < 1$, $SEM = .036$, *ns*.

**TABLE 21.1. Recognition Results for Experiment 1: The Proportion of Items Classified as Sure Old (a Rating of 4), Probably Old (3), Probably New (2), or Sure New (1) and the Mean Ratings of Items as a Function of Study Status**

| Study Status | Old | | New | | Mean Rating |
|---|---|---|---|---|---|
| | 4 | 3 | 2 | 1 | |
| Studied | .75 | .11 | .09 | .05 | 3.6 |
| Nonstudied | | | | | |
|     Unrelated lure | .00 | .02 | .18 | .80 | 1.2 |
|     Weakly related lure | .04 | .17 | .35 | .44 | 1.8 |
|     Critical lure | .58 | .26 | .08 | .08 | 3.3 |

Consider next the results based on subjects high-confidence responses (i.e., when they were sure the item had appeared in the study list and rated it a "4"). The proportion of unrelated and weakly related lures falling into this category approached zero. However, subjects were still sure that the critical nonstudied items had been studied over half the time (.58). The hit rate for the studied items remained quite high (.75) and was reliably greater than the false-alarm rate for the critical lures, $t(35)$ = 3.85, $SEM$ = .044, $p < .001$. It is also interesting to look at the rates at which subjects classified items as *sure new*. Unrelated lures were correctly rejected with high confidence 80% of the time. Related lures received this classification only 44% of the time, and critical lures were confidently rejected at an even lower rate, 8%, which is similar to the rate for studied words (5%).

Table 21.1 also presents the mean ratings for the four types of items on the 4-point scale. This measure seems to tell the same story as the other two: The mean rating of the critical lures (3.3) approached that of studied items (3.6); the difference did reach significance, $t(35)$ = 2.52, $SEM$ = .09, $p < .05$. In general, the judgments subjects provided for the critical lures appeared much more similar to those of studied items than to the other types of lures.

## Discussion

The results of Experiment 1 confirmed Deese's (1959) observation of high levels of false recall in a single-trial, free-recall task, albeit with six lists that were among his best. We found that the critical nonpresented items were recalled at about the same level as items actually presented in the middle of the lists. This high rate of false recall was not due to subjects guessing wildly. Other intrusions

occurred at a very low rate. In addition, we extended Deese's results to a recognition test and showed that the critical nonpresented items were called old at almost the same level as studied items (i.e., the false-alarm rate for the critical nonpresented items approximated the hit rate for the studied items). The false-alarm rate for the critical nonpresented items was much higher than for other related words that had not been presented. Finally, more than half the time subjects reported that they were sure that the critical nonstudied item had appeared on the list. Given these results, this paradigm seems a promising method to study false memories. Experiment 2 was designed to further explore these false memories.

## Experiment 2

We had four aims in designing Experiment 2. First, we wanted to replicate and extend the recall and recognition results of Experiment 1 to a wider set of materials. Therefore, we developed twenty-four 15-item lists similar to those used in Experiment 1 and in Deese's (1959) experiment. (We included expanded versions of the six lists used in Experiment 1.) Second, we wanted to examine the effect of recall on the subsequent recognition test. In Experiment 1 we obtained a high level of false recognition for the critical nonpresented words, but the lists had been recalled prior to the recognition test, and in 40% of the cases the critical item had been falsely recalled, too. In Experiment 2, we examined false recognition both for lists that had been previously recalled and for those that had not been recalled. Third, we wanted to determine the false-alarm rates for the critical nonpresented items when the relevant list had not been presented previously (e.g., to determine the false-alarm rate for *chair* when related words had not been presented in the list). Although we considered it remote, the possibility existed that the critical nonpresented items simply elicit a high number of false alarms whether or not the related words had been previously presented.

The fourth reason—and actually the most important one—for conducting the second experiment was to obtain subjects' judgments about their phenomenological experience while recognizing nonpresented items. We applied the procedure developed by Tulving (1985) in which subjects are asked to distinguish between two states of awareness about the past: remembering and knowing. When this procedure is applied in conjunction with a recognition test, subjects are told (a) to judge each item to be old (studied) or new (nonstudied) and (b) to make an additional judgment for each item judged to be old: whether they remember or know that the item occurred in the study list. A *remember* experience is defined as one in which the subject can mentally relive the experience (perhaps by recalling its neighbors, what it made them think of, what they were doing when they heard the word, or physical characteristics associated with its presentation). A *know* judgment is made when subjects are confident that the item occurred on the list but are unable to reexperience (i.e., remember) its occurrence. In short, remember judgments reflect a mental reliving of the experience, whereas know judgments do not. There is now a sizable literature on remember and know judgments (see Gardiner & Java, 1993; Rajaram & Roediger, in press), but we will not review it here except to say that evidence exists that remember–know judgments do not simply reflect two states of confidence (high and low) because variables can affect remember–know and confidence (sure–unsure) judgments differently (e.g., Rajaram, 1993).

Our purpose in using remember–know judgments in Experiment 2 was to see if subjects who falsely recognized the critical nonpresented words would report accompanying remember experiences, showing that they were mentally reexperiencing events that never occurred. In virtually all prior work on false memories, it has been assumed that subjects' incorrect responses indicated false remembering. However, if Tulving's (1985) distinction is accepted, then responding on a memory test should not be equated with remembering. Fur-

ther metamemorial judgments such as those obtained with the remember–know procedure are required to determine if subjects are remembering the events. In fact, in most experiments using the remember–know procedure, false alarms predominantly have been judged as know responses (e.g., Gardiner, 1988; Jones & Roediger, 1995). This outcome would be predicted in our experiment, too, if one attributes false recognition to a high sense of familiarity that arises (perhaps) through spreading activation in an associative network. Therefore, in Experiment 2 we examined subjects' metamemorial judgments with respect to their false memories to see whether they would classify these memories as being remembered or known to have occurred.

In Experiment 2, subjects were presented with 16 lists; after half they received an immediate free recall test, and after the other half they did math problems. After all lists had been presented, subjects received a recognition test containing items from the 16 studied lists and 8 comparable lists that had not been studied. During the recognition test, subjects made old–new judgments, followed by remember–know judgments for items judged to be old.

## Method

### SUBJECTS

Thirty Rice University undergraduates participated in a one hour session as part of a course requirement.

### MATERIALS

We developed 24 lists from Russell and Jenkins's (1954) norms in a manner similar to that used for Experiment 1. For each of 24 target words, 15 associates were selected for the list. These were usually the 15 words appearing first in the norms, but occasionally we substituted other related words when these seemed more appropriate (i.e., more likely to elicit the nonpresented target as an associate). The ordering of words within lists was held constant; the strongest associates generally occurred first. An example of a list for the target word *sleep* is: *bed, rest, awake, tired, dream, wake, night, blanket, doze, slumber, snore, pillow, peace, yawn, drowsy.*

The 24 lists were arbitrarily divided into three sets for counterbalancing purposes. Each set served equally often in the three experimental conditions, as described below. The reported results are based on only 7 of the 8 lists in each set because the critical items in 2 of the lists inadvertently appeared as studied items in other lists; dropping 1 list in each of two sets eliminated this problem and another randomly picked list from the third set was also dropped, so that each scored set was based on 7 lists. With these exceptions, none of the critical items occurred in any of the lists.

## DESIGN

The three conditions were tested in a within-subjects design. Subjects studied 16 lists; 8 lists were followed by an immediate free recall test, and 8 others were not followed by an initial test. The remaining 8 lists were not studied. Items from all 24 lists appeared on the later recognition test. On the recognition test, subjects judged items as old (studied) or new (nonstudied) and, when old, they also judged if they remembered the item from the list or rather knew that it had occurred.

## PROCEDURE

Subjects were told that they would be participating in a memory experiment in which they would hear lists of words presented by means of a tape player. They were told that after each list they would hear a sound (either a tone or a knock, with examples given) that would indicate whether they should recall items from the list or do math problems. For half of the subjects, the tone indicated that they should recall the list, and the knock meant they should perform math problems; for the other half of the subjects, the signals were reversed. They were told to listen carefully to each list and that the signal would occur after the list had been presented; therefore, subjects never knew during list presentation whether the list would be recalled. Words were recorded in a male voice and presented approximately at a 1.5-s rate. Subjects were given 2 min after each list to recall the words or to perform multiplication and division problems. Recall occurred on 4 inch by 11 inch sheets of paper, and subjects turned over each sheet after the recall period, so the recalled items were no longer in view. The first part of the experiment took about 45 min.

The recognition test occurred about 5 min after the test or math period for the 16th list. During this time, subjects were given instructions about making old–new and remember–know judgments. They were told that they would see a long list of words, some of which they had heard during the earlier phase of the experiment. They were to circle either the word *old* or *new* next to each test item to indicate whether the item had been presented by means of the tape player. If an item was judged old, subjects were instructed that they should further distinguish between remembering and knowing by writing an *R* or *K* in the space beside the item. Detailed instructions on the remember–know distinction were given, modeled after those of Rajaram (1993). Essentially, subjects were told that a remember judgment should be made for items for which they had a vivid memory of the actual presentation; know judgments were reserved for items that they were sure had been presented but for which they lacked the feeling of remembering the actual occurrence of the words. They were told that a remember judgment would be made in cases in which they remembered something distinctive in the speaker's voice when he said the word, or perhaps they remembered the item presented before or after it, or what they were thinking when they heard the word. They were always told to make the remember–know judgment about a word with respect to its presentation on the tape recorder, not whether they remembered or knew they had written it down on the free recall test. In addition, they were instructed to make remember–know judgments immediately after judging the item to be old, before they considered the next test item.

The recognition test was composed of 96 items, 48 of which had been studied and 48 of which had not. The 48 studied items were obtained by selecting 3 items from each of the 16 presented lists (always those in Serial Positions 1, 8, and 10). The lures, or nonstudied items, on the recognition test were 24 critical lures from all 24 lists (16 studied, 8 not) and the 24 items from the 8 nonstudied lists (again, from Serial Positions 1, 8, and 10). The 96 items were randomly arranged on the test sheet and beside each item were the words *old* and *new*; if subjects circled old, they made the remember–know judgment by writing *R* or *K* in the space next to the word. All subjects received exactly the same test sheet; counterbalancing of lists was achieved by having lists rotated through the three conditions (study + recall, study + arithmetic, and nonstudied) across subsets of 10 subjects.

After the recognition test, the experimenter asked subjects an open-ended question: whether they "knew what the experiment was about." Most subjects just said something similar to "memory for lists of words," but 1 subject said that she noticed that the lists seemed designed to make her think of a nonpresented word. She was the only subject who had no false recalls of the critical nonpresented words; her results were excluded from those reported below and replaced by the results obtained from a new subject. After the experiment, subjects were debriefed.

## Results

### RECALL

Subjects recalled the critical nonpresented word on 55% of the lists, which is a rate even higher than for the 6 lists used in Experiment 1. The higher rate of false recall in Experiment 2 may have been due to the longer lists, to their slightly different construction, to the fact that 16 lists were presented rather than only 6, or to different signals used to recall the lists. In addition, in Experiment 1 the lists were read aloud by the experimenter, whereas in Experiment 2 they were presented by means of a tape player. Regardless of the reason or reasons for the difference, the false-recall effect was quite

robust and seems even stronger under the conditions of Experiment 2.

The smoothed serial position curve for studied words is shown in Figure 21.3, where marked primacy and recency effects are again seen. As in Experiment 1, subjects recalled the critical nonpresented items at about the rate of studied items presented in the middle of the lists. Subjects recalled items in Positions 4–11 an average of 47% of the time, compared with 55% recall of nonpresented items. Therefore, recall of the critical missing word was actually greater than recall for studied words in the middle of the list; this difference was marginally significant, $t(29) = 1.80$, $SEM = .042$, $p = .08$, two-tailed.

### RECOGNITION

After subjects had heard all 16 lists, they received the recognition test and provided remember–know judgments for items that were called old on the test. We first consider results for studied words and then turn to the data for the critical nonpresented lures.

Table 21.2 presents the recognition results for items studied in the list. (Keep in mind that we tested only three items from each list [i.e., those in Positions 1, 8, and 10].) It is apparent that the hit rate in the study + recall condition (.79) was greater than in the study + arithmetic condition (.65), $t(29) = 5.20$, $SEM = .027$, $p < .001$, indicating

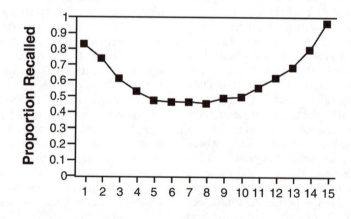

**FIGURE 21.3** ■ Probability of correct recall in Experiment 2 as a function of serial position. Probability of recall of the studied words was .62, and probability of recall of the critical nonpresented item was .55.

**TABLE 21.2. Recognition Results for Studied Items and Critical Lures in Experiment 2**

| Item Type and Condition | Proportion of Old Responses | | |
|---|---|---|---|
| | Overall | R | K |
| Studied | | | |
| Study + recall | .79 | .57 | .22 |
| Study + arithmetic | .65 | .41 | .24 |
| Nonstudied | .11 | .02 | .09 |
| Critical lure | | | |
| Study + recall | .81 | .58 | .23 |
| Study + arithmetic | .72 | .38 | .34 |
| Nonstudied | .16 | .03 | .13 |

*Note.* R = remember judgment; K = know judgment.

that the act of recall enhanced later recognition. Further, the boost in recognition from prior recall was reflected in a greater proportion of remember responses, which differed reliably, $t(29) = 4.87$, $SEM = .033$, $p < .001$. Know responses did not differ between conditions, $t(29) < 1$. The false-alarm rate for items from the nonstudied lists was .11, with most false positives judged as know responses.

Recognition results for the critical nonpresented lures are also shown in Table 21.2. The first striking impression is that the results for false-alarm rates appear practically identical to the results for hit rates. Therefore, to an even greater extent than in Experiment 1, subjects were unable to distinguish items actually presented from the critical lures that were not presented. Table 21.2 also shows that the act of (false) recall in the study + recall condition enhanced later false recognition relative to the study + arithmetic condition, in which the lists were not recalled. In addition, after recalling the lists subjects were much more likely to say that they remembered the items from the list, with remember judgments being made 72% of the time (i.e., .58 ÷ .81 × 100) for words that had never been presented. When the lists were presented but not recalled, the rate of remember judgments dropped to 53%, although this figure is still quite high. Interestingly, the corresponding percentages for items actually studied were about the same: 72% for remember judgments for lists that were recalled and 63% for lists that were not recalled.

One point that vitiates the correspondence between the results for studied and nonstudied items in Table 21.2 is that the false-alarm rates for the

types of items differed when the relevant lists had not been studied. The rate for the regular list words was .11, whereas the rate for the critical lures (when the relevant prior list had not been studied) was .16, $t(29) = 2.27$, $SEM = .022$, $p = .03$, two-tailed. However, the difference was not great, and in both cases false alarms gave rise to more know responses than remember responses.

One further analysis is of interest. In the study + recall condition, we can consider recognition results for items that were produced in the recall phase (whether representing correct responding or false recall) relative to those that were not produced. Although correlational, such results provide an interesting pattern in comparing the effects of prior correct recall to prior false recall on later recognition. Table 21.3 shows the results of this analysis, including the means for studied items and for the critical items. For the studied items, recognition of items that had been correctly recalled was essentially perfect, and most old responses were judged to be remembered. Items not produced on the recall test were recognized half the time, and responses were evenly divided between remember and know judgments. These effects could have been due to the act of recall, to item selection effects, or to some combination. Nonetheless, they provide a useful point of comparison for the more interesting results about the fate of falsely recalled items, as shown in Table 21.3

The recognition results for the falsely recalled critical items closely resemble those for correctly recalled studied items. The probability of recognizing falsely recalled items was quite high (.93),

**TABLE 21.3. Proportion of Items Judged to Be Old on the Recognition Test in the Study + Recall Condition of Experiment 2 as a Function of Whether the Items Were Produced on the Immediate Free Recall Test**

| Condition | Production Rate of Free Recall | Recognition | | |
|---|---|---|---|---|
| | | Overall | R | K |
| Studied | | | | |
| Produced | .62 | .98 | .79 | .19 |
| Not produced | .38 | .50 | .26 | .24 |
| Critical lure | | | | |
| Produced | .55 | .93 | .73 | .20 |
| Not produced | .45 | .65 | .38 | .27 |

*Note.* R = remember judgment; K = know judgment.

and most of these items were judged to be remembered (.73) rather than known (.20). More remarkably, the critical items that were not produced were later (falsely) recognized at a higher rate (.65) than were items actually studied but not produced (.50); this difference was marginally significant, $t(29) = 1.81$, $SEM = .083$, $p = .08$, two-tailed. In addition, these falsely recognized items were judged to be remembered in 58% of the cases (i.e., .38 ÷ .65 × 100), or at about the same rate as for words that were studied but not produced (52%). These analyses reveal again the powerful false memory effects at work in this paradigm, with people falsely remembering the critical nonstudied words at about the same levels (or even greater levels) as presented words.

## General Discussion

The primary results from our experiments can be summarized as follows: First, the paradigm we developed from Deese's (1959) work produced high levels of false recall in single-trial free recall. In Experiment 1, with 12-word lists, subjects recalled the critical nonstudied word after 40% of the lists. In Experiment 2, with 15-word lists, false recall increased, occurring on 55% of the occasions. Second, this paradigm also produced remarkably high levels of false recognition for the critical items; the rate of false recognition actually approached the hit rate. Third, the false recognition responses were frequently made with high confidence (Experiment 1) or were frequently accompanied by remember judgments (Experiment 2). Fourth, the act of recall increased both accurate recognition of studied items and the false recognition of the critical nonstudied items. The highest rates of false recognition and the highest proportion of remember responses to the critical nonstudied items occurred for those items that had been falsely recalled.

We discuss our results (a) in relation to prior work and (b) in terms of theories that might explain the basic effects. We then discuss (c) how the phenomenological experience of remembering events that never happened might occur, and (d) what implications our findings might have for the wider debates on false memories.

## Relation to Prior Work

Prior work by Underwood (1965) has shown false recognition for lures semantically related to studied words, but as we noted in the introduction, these effects were often rather small in magnitude. In our experiments, we found very high levels of false recall and false recognition. Our recognition results are similar to those obtained by investigators in the 1960s and 1970s who used prose materials and found erroneous recognition of related material. For example, Bransford and Franks (1971) presented subjects with sentences that were related and created a coherent scene (e.g., The rock rolled down the mountain and crushed the hut. The hut was tiny.). Later, they confidently recognized sentences that were congruent with the meaning of the complex idea, although the sentences had not actually been presented (e.g., The rock rolled down the mountain and crushed the tiny hut.). Similarly, Posner and Keele (1970) showed subjects dot patterns that were distortions from a prototypic pattern. Later, they recognized the prototype (that had never been presented) at a high rate, and forgetting of the prototype showed less decline over a week than did dot patterns actually presented. Jenkins, Wald, and Pittenger (1986) reported similar observations with pictorial stimuli.

In each of the experiments just described, and in other related experiments (see Alba & Hasher, 1983, for a review), subjects recognized events that never happened if the events fit some general schema derived from the study experiences. A similar interpretation is possible for our results, too, although most researchers have assumed that schema-driven processes occur only in prose materials. Yet the lists for our experiments were generated as associates to a single word and therefore had a coherent form (e.g., words related to sleep or to other similar concepts). The word *sleep*, for example, may never have been presented in the list, but was the "prototype" from which the list was generated, and therefore our lists arguably encouraged schematic processing.

Although our results are similar to those of other research revealing errors in memory, several features distinguish our findings. First, we showed powerful false memory effects in both recall and recognition within the same paradigm. The findings just cited, and others described below, all used recognition paradigms. Although some prior studies have reported false recall (e.g., Brewer, 1977; Hasher & Griffin, 1979; Spiro, 1980), these researchers used prose materials. Second, we showed that subjects actually claimed to remember most of the falsely recognized events as having occurred on the list. The items did not just evoke a feeling of familiarity but were consciously recollected as having occurred. Third, we showed that the effect of prior recall increased both accurate and false memories and that this effect of recall was reflected in remember responses.

## Explanations of False Recall and False Recognition

How might false recall and false recognition arise in our paradigm? Actually, the earliest idea about false recognition—the implicit associative response—still seems workable in helping to understand these phenomena, although today we can elaborate on the idea with new models now available. Underwood (1965) proposed that false recognition responses originated during encoding when subjects, seeing a word such as *hot*, might think of an associate *(cold)*. Later, if *cold* were presented as a lure, they might claim to recognize its occurrence in the list because of the earlier implicit associative response.

Some writers at the time assumed that the associative response had to occur consciously to the subject during study, so it was implicit only in the sense that it was not overtly produced. Another possible interpretation is that the subject never even becomes aware of the associative response during study of the lists, so that its activation may be implicit in this additional sense, too. Activation may spread through an associative network (e.g., Anderson & Bower, 1973; Collins & Loftus, 1975), with false-recognition errors arising through residual activation. That is, it may not be necessary for subjects to consciously think of the associate while studying the list for false recall and false recognition to occur. On the other hand, the predominance of remember responses for the critical lures on the later recognition test may indicate that the critical nonpresented words do occur to subjects during study of the list. That may be why subjects claim to remember them, through a failure of reality monitoring (Johnson & Raye, 1981).

In further support of the idea that associative processes are critically important in producing false recall, Deese (1959) showed that the likelihood of false recall in this paradigm was predicted well by the probability that items presented in the list elicited the critical nonpresented word in free association tests. In other words, the greater the likelihood that list members produced the critical nonpresented target word as an associate, the greater the level of false recall (see also Nelson, Bajo, McEvoy, & Schreiber, 1989). It is worth noting that some of Deese's lists that contained strong forward associations—including the famous "butterfly" list used in later research—did not lead to false recall. The particular characteristics of the lists that lead to false memories await systematic experimental study, but in general Deese reported that the lists that did not lead to false recall contained words that did not produce the critical targets as associates. The butterfly list did not elicit even one false recall in Deese's experiment.

If false recall and false recognition are produced by means of activation of implicit associative responses, then the reason our false-recognition results were more robust than those usually reported may be that we used lists of related words rather than single related words. Underwood (1965) and others had subjects study single words related to later lures on some dimension, and they showed only modest levels of false recognition, or in some cases none at all (Gillund & Shiffrin, 1984). In the present experiments, subjects studied lists of 12–15 items and the false-recognition effect was quite large. Hall and Kozloff (1973), Hintzman (1988), and Shiffrin, Huber, and Marinelli (1995) have shown that false recognition is directly related to the number of related words in a list. For example, Hintzman (1988, Experiment 1) presented from 0 to 5 items from a category in a list and showed that both accurate recognition of studied category members, as well as false recognition of lures from that category, increased as a function of category size. False recognition increased from about 8% when no category members were included in the list to around 35% when five category members occurred in the list. (These percentages were estimated from Hintzman's Figure 11.) Our lists were not categorized, strictly speaking, but the words were generally related. For our 15-item lists in Experiment 2 that did not receive recall tests, false recognition was 72%; the corresponding figure for recalled lists was 81%. It will be interesting to see if longer versions of standard categorized lists will produce false recognition at the same levels as the lists we have used and whether the average probability that items in the list evoke the lure as an associate will predict the level of false recognition. We are now conducting experiments to evaluate these hypotheses.

If the errors in memory occurring on both recall and recognition tests arise from associative processes, then formal models of associative processing might be expected to predict them. At least at a general level, they would seem to do so. For example, the search of associative memory (SAM) model, first proposed by Raaijmakers and Shiffrin (1980) and later extended to recognition by Gillund and Shiffrin (1984), provides for the opportunity of false recognition (and presumably recall) by means of associative processes. Although it was not the main thrust of their paper, Shiffrin et al. (1995) demonstrated that the SAM model did fit their observation of an increased tendency to produce false alarms to category members with increases in the number of category exemplars presented.

Recently, McClelland (in press) has extended the parallel distributed processing (PDP) approach to explaining constructive memory processes and memory distortions. This model assumes that encoding and retrieval occur in a parallel distributed processing system in which there are many simple but massively interconnected processing units. Encoding an event involves the activation of selected units within the system. Retrieval entails patterns of reactivation of the same processing units. However, because activation in the model can arise from many sources, a great difficulty (for the model and for humans) lies in the failure to differentiate between possible sources of prior activation (McClelland, in press). Therefore, because what is encoded and stored is a particular pattern of activity, subjects may not be able to reconstruct the actual event that gave rise to this activity. For example, if presenting the words associated with *sleep* mimics the activity in the system as occurs during actual presentation of the word *sleep*, then the PDP system will be unable to distinguish whether or not the word actually occurred. Consequently, the PDP system would give rise to false memory phenomena, as McClelland (in press) describes.

As the examples above show, associative models can account for false-recall and false-recognition results, although we have not tried fitting specific models to our data. To mention two other models based on different assumptions, Hintzman's (1988) MINERVA 2 model, which assumes independent traces of events, modeled well the effect of increasing category size on the probability of identifying an item from the category as old; this was true both for correct recognition and false recognition. In addition, Reyna and Brainerd (1995) have also applied their fuzzy-trace theory to the problem of false memories.

Although most theorists have assumed that the false memory effects arise during encoding, all remembering is a product of information both from encoding and storage processes (the memory trace) and from information in the retrieval environment (Tulving, 1974). Indeed, false remembering may arise from repeated attempts at retrieval, as shown in Experiment 2 and elsewhere (e.g., Ceci, Huffman, Smith, & Loftus, 1994; Hyman, Husband, & Billings, 1995; Roediger et al., 1993). Retrieval processes may contribute significantly to the false recall and false recognition phenomena we have observed. Subjects usually recalled the critical word toward the end of the set of recalled items, so prior recall may trigger false recall, in part. Also, in the recognition test, presentation of words related to a critical lure often occurred prior to its appearance on the test; therefore, activation from these related words on the test may have enhanced the false recognition effect by priming the lure (Neely, Schmidt, & Roediger, 1983). The illusion of memory produced by this mechanism, if it exists, may be similar to illusions of recognition produced by enhanced perceptual fluency (Whittlesea, 1993; Whittlesea, Jacoby, & Girard, 1990). Indeed, one aspect of our results on which the theories outlined above remain mute is the phenomenological experience of the subjects: They did not just claim that the nonpresented items were familiar; rather, they claimed to remember their occurrence. We turn next to this aspect of the data.

## Phenomenological Experience

In virtually all previous experiments using the remember–know procedure, false alarms have been predominantly labeled as know experiences (e.g.,

Gardiner & Java, 1993; Jones & Roediger, 1995; Rajaram, 1993). The typical assumption is that know responses arise through fluent processing, when information comes to mind easily, but the source of the information is not readily apparent (Rajaram, 1993). In addition, Johnson and Raye (1981) have noted that memories for events that actually occurred typically provide more spatial and temporal details than do memories for events that were only imagined. For these reasons, when we conducted Experiment 2 we expected that the false alarms in our recognition tests would, like other recognition errors, be judged by subjects to be known but not remembered. Yet our results showed that, in our paradigm, this was not so. Subjects frequently reported remembering events that never happened. Clearly, false memories can be the result of conscious recollection and not only of general familiarity.

Furthermore, in our current experiments we found that the act of recall increased both overall recognition and remembering of presented items and of the critical nonpresented items. We assume that generation of an item during a free recall test solidifies the subject's belief that memory for that item is accurate and increases the likelihood of later recognition of the item; why, however, should recall enhance the phenomenological experience of remembering the item's presentation? The enhanced remember responses may be due to subjects' actually remembering the experience of recalling the item, rather than studying it, and confusing the source of their remembrance; similarly, it could be that subjects remember thinking about the item during the study phase and confuse this with having heard it. Each of these mistakes would represent a source monitoring error (Johnson, Hashtroudi, & Lindsay, 1993). Note that our instructions to subjects about their remember–know responses specified that they were to provide remember judgments only when they remembered the item's actual presentation in the list (i.e., not simply when they remembered producing it on the recall test). Nonetheless, despite this instruction, subjects provided more remember responses for items from lists that had been recalled in Experiment 2.

The most promising approach to explaining such false remembering comes from an attributional analysis of memory, as advocated by Jacoby, Kelley, and Dywan (1989). They considered cases in which the aftereffects of past events were misattributed to other sources, but more importantly for present concerns, they considered cases in which subjects falsely attributed current cognitive experience to a concrete past event when that event did not occur. They hypothesized that the ease with which a person is able to bring events to mind increases the probability that the person will attribute the experience to being a memory. They also argued that the greater the vividness and distinctiveness of the generated event, the greater the likelihood of believing that it represents a memory (Johnson & Raye, 1981). Thus, in our paradigm, if subjects fluently generate (in recall) or process (in recognition) the word *sleep* (on the basis of recent activation of the concept) and if this fluency allows them to construct a clear mental image of how the word would have sounded if presented in the speaker's voice, then they would likely claim to remember the word's presentation. The act of recall increases the ease of producing an event and may thereby increase the experience of remembering. Jacoby et al.'s (1989) analysis offers promising leads for further research.

## Implications

The results reported in this article identify a striking memory illusion. Just as perceptual illusions can be compelling even when people are aware of the factors giving rise to the illusion, we suspect that the same is true in our case of remembering events that never happened. Indeed, informal demonstration experiments with groups of sophisticated subjects, such as wily graduate students who knew we were trying to induce false memories, also showed the effect quite strongly.

Bartlett (1932) proposed a distinction between reproductive and reconstructive memory processes. Since then, the common assumption has been that list learning paradigms encourage rote reproduction of material with relatively few errors, whereas paradigms using more coherent (schematic) material (e.g., sentences, paragraphs, stories, or scenes) are necessary to observe constructive processes in memory retrieval. Yet we obtained robust false memory effects with word lists, albeit with ones that contain related words. We conclude that any contrast between reproductive and reconstructive memory is ill-founded; all remembering is constructive in nature. Materials may differ in how readily they lead to error and false memories, but these are differences of a quantitative, not qualitative, nature.

Do our results have any bearing on the current controversies raging over the issue of allegedly false memories induced in therapy? Not directly, of course. However, we do show that the illusion of remembering events that never happened can occur quite readily. Therefore, as others have also pointed out, the fact that people may say they vividly remember details surrounding an event cannot, by itself, be taken as convincing evidence that the event actually occurred (Johnson & Suengas, 1989; Schooler, Gerhard, & Loftus, 1986; Zaragoza & Lane, 1994). Our subjects confidently recalled and recognized words that were not presented and also reported that they remembered the occurrence of these events. A critic might contend that because these experiments occurred in a laboratory setting, using word lists, with college student subjects, they hold questionable relevance to issues surrounding more spectacular occurrences of false memories outside the lab. However, we believe that these are all reasons to be more impressed with the relevance of our results to these issues. After all, we tested people under conditions of intentional learning, with very short retention intervals, in a standard laboratory procedure that usually produces few errors, and we used college students—professional memorizers—as subjects. In short, despite conditions much more conducive to veridical remembering than those that typically exist outside the lab, we found dramatic evidence of false memories. When less of a premium is placed on accurate remembering, and when people know that their accuracy in recollecting cannot be verified, they may even be more easily led to remember events that never happened than they are in the lab.

## ACKNOWLEDGMENTS

This research was supported by Grant F49620–92–J–0437 from the Air Force Office of Scientific Research. We thank Ron Haas and Lubna Manal for aid in conducting this research. Also, we thank Endel Tulving for bringing the Deese (1959) report to our attention. The manuscript benefited from comments by Doug Hintzman, Steve Lindsay, Suparna Rajaram, and Endel Tulving.

## NOTES

1. Bartlett's (1932) results from the serial reproduction paradigm—in which one subject recalls an event, the next subject reads and then recalls the first subject's report, and so on—replicates quite well (e.g., I. H. Paul, 1959). However, the repeated reproduction research, in which a subject is tested repeatedly on the same material, is more germane to the study of false memories in an individual over time. To our knowledge, no one has successfuly replicated Bartlett's observations in this paradigm with instructions that emphasize remembering (see Gauld & Stephenson, 1967).
2. Some people know of Deese's (1959) paper indirectly because Appleby (1986) used it as the basis of a suggested classroom demonstration of déjà vu.

## REFERENCES

Alba, J. W., & Hasher, L. (1983). Is memory schematic? *Psychological Bulletin*, *93*, 203–231.

Anderson, J. R., & Bower, G. H. (1973). *Human associative memory*. Washington, DC: V. H. Winston,

Anisfeld, M., & Knapp, M. (1968). Association, synonymity, and directionality in false recognition. *Journal of Experimental Psychology*, *77*, 171–179.

Appleby, D. (1986). Déja vu in the classroom. *Network*, *4*, 8.

Bartlett, F. C. (1932). *Remembering: A study in experimental and social psychology*. Cambridge, England: Cambridge University Press.

Bransford, J. D., & Franks, J. J. (1971). The abstraction of linguistic ideas. *Cognitive Psychology*, *2*, 331–350.

Brewer, W. F. (1977). Memory for the pragmatic implications of sentences. *Memory & Cognition*, *5*, 673–678.

Ceci, S. J., Huffman, M. L. C., Smith, E., & Loftus, E. F. (1994). Repeatedly thinking about non-events. *Consciousness and Cognition*, *3*, 388–407.

Cofer, C. N. (1967). Does conceptual organization influence the amount retained in free recall? In B. Kleinmuntz (Ed.), *Concepts and the structure of memory* (pp. 181–214). New York: Wiley.

Collins, A. M., & Loftus, E. F. (1975). A spreading-activation theory of semantic processing. *Psychological Review*, *82*, 407–428.

Cramer, P. (1965). Recovery of a discrete memory. *Journal of Personality and Social Psychology*, *1*, 326–332.

Deese, J. (1959). On the prediction of occurrence of particular verbal intrusions in immediate recall. *Journal of Experimental Psychology*, *58*, 17–22.

Gardiner, J. M. (1988). Functional aspects of recollective experience. *Memory & Cognition*, *16*, 309–313.

Gardiner, J. M., & Java, R. I. (1993). Recognizing and remembering. In A. Collins, S. Gathercole, & P. Morris (Eds.), *Theories of memory* (pp. 168–188). Hillsdale, NJ: Erlbaum.

Gauld, A., & Stephenson, G. M. (1967). Some experiments related to Bartlett's theory of remembering. *British Journal of Psychology*, *58*, 39–49.

Gillund, G., & Shiffrin, R. M. (1984). A retrieval model for both recognition and recall. *Psychological Review*, *91*, 1–67.

Hall, J. F., & Kozloff, E. E. (1973). False recognitions of associates of converging versus repeated words. *American Journal of Psychology, 86,* 133–139.

Hasher, L., & Griffin, M. (1979). Reconstructive and reproductive processes in memory. *Journal of Experimental Psychology: Human Learning and Memory, 4,* 318–330.

Hintzman, D. L. (1988). Judgments of frequency and recognition memory in a multiple-trace memory model. *Psychological Review, 95,* 528–551.

Hyman, I. E., Husband, T. H., & Billings, F. J. (1995). False memories of childhood experiences. *Applied Cognitive Psychology, 9,* 181–197.

Jacoby, L. L., Kelley, C. M., & Dywan, J. (1989). Memory attributions. In H. L. Roediger III & F. I. M. Craik (Eds.), *Varieties of memory and consciousness: Essays in honour of Endel Tulving* (pp. 391–422). Hillsdale, NJ: Erlbaum.

Jenkins, J. J., Wald, J., & Pittenger, J. B. (1986). Apprehending pictorial events: An instance of psychological cohesion. In V. McCabe & G. J. Balzano (Eds.), *Event cognition: An ecological perspective* (pp. 117–133). Hillsdale, NJ: Erlbaum.

Johnson, M. K., Hashtroudi, S., & Lindsay, D. S. (1993). Source monitoring. *Psychological Bulletin, 114,* 3–28.

Johnson, M. K., & Raye, C. L. (1981). Reality monitoring. *Psychological Review, 88,* 67–85.

Johnson, M. K., & Suengas, A. G. (1989). Reality monitoring judgments of other people's memories. *Bulletin of the Psychonomic Society, 27,* 107–110.

Jones, T. C., & Roediger, H. L., III. (1995). The experiential basis of serial position effects. *European Journal of Cognitive Psychology, 7,* 65–80.

Lindsay, D. S., & Read, J. D. (1994). Psychotherapy and memories of childhood sexual abuse: A cognitive perspective. *Applied Cognitive Psychology, 8,* 281–338.

Loftus, E. F. (1993). The reality of repressed memories. *American Psychologist, 48,* 518–537.

Loftus, E. F., Miller, D. G., & Burns, H. J. (1978). Semantic integration of verbal information into a visual memory. *Journal of Experimental Psychology: Human Learning and Memory, 4,* 19–31.

Loftus, E. F., & Palmer, J. C. (1974). Reconstruction of automobile destruction: An example of the interaction between language and memory. *Journal of Verbal Learning and Verbal Behavior, 13,* 585–589.

McClelland, J. L. (in press). Constructive memory and memory distortions: A parallel-distributed processing approach. In D. L. Schacter, J. T., Coyle, G. D. Fischbach, M. M. Mesulam, & L. E. Sullivan (Eds.), *Memory distortion.* Cambridge, MA: Harvard University Press.

McCloskey, M., & Zaragoza, M. (1985). Misleading postevent information and memory for events: Arguments and evidence against memory impairment hypotheses. *Journal of Experimental Psychology: General, 114,* 1–16.

Neely, J. H., Schmidt, S. R., & Roediger, H. L., III. (1983). Inhibition from related primes in recognition memory. *Journal of Experimental Psychology: Learning, Memory, and Cognition, 9,* 196–211.

Nelson, D. L., Bajo, M., McEvoy, C. L., & Schreiber, T. A. (1989). Prior knowledge: The effects of natural category size on memory for implicitly encoded concepts. *Journal of Experimental Psychology: Learning, Memory, and Cognition, 15,* 957–967.

Paul, I. H. (1959). Studies in remembering: The reproduction of connected and extended verbal material. *Psychological Issues, 1* (Monograph 2), 1–152.

Paul, L. M. (1979). Two models of recognition memory: A test. *Journal of Experimental Psychology: Human Learning and Memory, 5,* 45–51.

Payne, D. G., Toglia, M. P., & Anastasi, J. S. (1994). Recognition performance level and the magnitude of the misinformation effect in eyewitness memory. *Psychonomic Bulletin & Review, 1,* 376–382.

Posner, M. I., & Keele, S. W. (1970). Retention of abstract ideas. *Journal of Experimental Psychology, 83,* 304–308.

Raaijmakers, J. G. W., & Shiffrin, R. M. (1980). SAM: A theory of probabilistic search of associative memory. In G. H. Bower (Ed.), *The psychology of learning and motivation* (Vol. 14, pp. 207–262). New York: Academic Press.

Rajaram, S. (1993). Remembering and knowing: Two means of access to the personal past. *Memory & Cognition, 21,* 89–102.

Rajaram, S., & Roediger, H. L., III. (in press). Remembering and knowing as states of consciousness during recollection. In J. D. Cohen & J. W. Schooler (Eds.), *Scientific approaches to the question of consciousness.* Hillsdale, NJ: Erlbaum.

Reyna, V. F., & Brainerd, C. J. (1995). Fuzzy-trace theory: An interim synthesis. *Learning and Individual Differences, 7,* 1–75.

Roediger, H. L., III, & Payne, D. G. (1985). Recall criterion does not affect recall level or hypermnesia: A puzzle for generate/recognize theories. *Memory & Cognition, 13,* 1–7.

Roediger, H. L., III, Wheeler, M. A., & Rajaram, S. (1993). Remembering, knowing, and reconstructing the past. In D. L. Medin (Ed.), *The psychology of learning and motivation: Advances in research and theory* (pp. 97–134). San Diego, CA: Academic Press.

Russell, W. A., & Jenkins, J. J. (1954). *The complete Minnesota norms for responses to 100 words from the Kent-Rosanoff Word Association Test.* (Tech. Rep. No. 11, Contract NS ONR 66216, Office of Naval Research). University of Minnesota.

Schacter, D. L. (in press). Memory distortion: History and current status. In D. L. Schacter, J. T. Coyle, G. D. Fischbach, M. M. Mesulam, & L. E. Sullivan (Eds.), *Memory distortion.* Cambridge, MA: Harvard University Press.

Schooler, J. W., Gerhard, D., & Loftus, E. F. (1986). Qualities of the unreal. *Journal of Experimental Psychology: Learning, Memory, and Cognition, 12,* 171–181.

Shiffrin, R. M., Huber, D. E., & Marinelli, K. (1995). Effects of category length and strength on familiarity in recognition. *Journal of Experimental Psychology: Learning, Memory, and Cognition, 21,* 267–287.

Spiro, R. J. (1980). Accommodative reconstruction in prose recall. *Journal of Verbal Learning and Verbal Behavior, 19,* 84–95.

Sulin, R. A., & Dooling, D. J. (1974). Intrusion of a thematic idea in retention of prose. *Journal of Experimental Psychology, 103,* 255–262.

Tulving, E. (1974). Cue-dependent forgetting. *American Scientist, 62,* 74–82.

Tulving, E. (1985). Memory and consciousness. *Canadian Psychologist*, 26, 1–12.

Underwood, B. J. (1965). False recognition produced by implicit verbal responses. *Journal of Experimental Psychology*, 70, 122–129.

Wheeler, M. A., & Roediger, H. L., III. (1992). Disparate effects of repeated testing: Reconciling Ballard's (1913) and Bartlett's (1932) results. *Psychological Science*, 3, 240–245.

Whittlesea, B. W. A. (1993). Illusions of familiarity. *Journal of Experimental Psychology: Learning, Memory, and Cognition*, 19, 1235–1253.

Whittlesea, B. W. A., Jacoby, L. L., & Girard, K. (1990). Illusions of immediate memory: Evidence of an attributional basis for feelings of familiarity and perceptual quality. *Journal of Memory and Language*, 29, 716–732.

Zaragoza, M. S., & Lane, S. M. (1994). Source misattributions and the suggestibility of eyewitness memory. *Journal of Experimental Psychology: Learning, Memory, and Cognition*, 20, 934–945.

# Working Memory

Alan Baddeley

The term working memory refers to a brain system that provides temporary storage and manipulation of the information necessary for such complex cognitive tasks as language comprehension, learning, and reasoning. This definition has evolved from the concept of a unitary short-term memory system. Working memory has been found to require the simultaneous storage and processing of information. It can be divided into the following three subcomponents: (i) the central executive, which is assumed to be an attentional-controlling system, is important in skills such as chess playing and is particularly susceptible to the effects of Alzheimer's disease; and two slave systems, namely (ii) the visuospatial sketch pad, which manipulates visual images and (iii) the phonological loop, which stores and rehearses speech-based information and is necessary for the acquisition of both native and second-language vocabulary.

The question of whether memory should be regarded as a single unitary system or whether it should be fractionated into two or more subsystems formed one of the major controversies within cognitive psychology during the mid-1960s. During that time, evidence began to accumulate in favor of a dichotomy (*1*). Some of the most convincing evidence came from the study of brain-damaged patients; those suffering from the classic amnesic syndrome appeared to have gross disruption of the capacity to form new lasting memories but showed preserved performance on a range of tasks that were assumed to test short-term memory (*2*). Conversely, a second type of patient was identified who appeared to show normal long-term learning but had a short-term memory span limited to one or two items (*3*). It was suggested that such patients had a deficit in short-term storage, in contrast to the long-term storage deficit that occurs in the amnesic syndrome. This finding, together with

considerable evidence from the study of normal subjects, appeared by the late 1960s to argue for a dichotomous view of memory, such as that proposed by Atkinson and Shiffrin (*4*).

By the early 1970s it was becoming clear that the two-component model was running into difficulties. One of its problems was inherent in the neuropsychological evidence that initially appeared to support it so strongly. Atkinson and Shiffrin (*4*) suggested that the short-term store within their model acted as a working memory, being necessary for learning, for the retrieval of old material, and for the performance of many other cognitive tasks. If that were the case, one would expect patients with a grossly defective short-term store to show many other cognitive problems, including impaired long-term learning. In fact, such patients appeared to have a normal long-term learning capacity and surprisingly few cognitive handicaps.

Pursuing this issue was difficult because patients with a pure short-term memory deficit are rare. We therefore attempted to simulate this condition in unimpaired subjects by using a dual-task technique (5). We argued as follows: if the digit-span procedure depends on the short-term store, with the number of digits retained determined by the capacity of the store, then it should be possible to interfere systematically with the operation of the working memory system by requiring the subject to remember digits while performing other cognitive tasks. As the concurrent digit load is increased, the remaining short-term capacity would decrease and the interference would increase, with performance presumably breaking down as the digit load reached the capacity of the system.

Reasoning, comprehension, and learning tasks all showed a similar pattern. As concurrent digit load increased, performance declined, but the degree of disruption fell far short of that predicted. Subjects whose digit memory was at full capacity could reason and learn quite effectively.

These results, together with others, encouraged the abandonment of the idea of a single unitary short-term store that also functions as a working memory. Instead, we proposed the tripartite system shown in Figure 22.1, which comprises an attentional controller and the central executive, supplemented by two subsidiary slave systems. The articulatory or phonological loop was assumed to be responsible for maintaining speech-based information, including digits in the digit span test, whereas the visuospatial sketch pad was assumed to perform a similar function in setting up and manipulating visuospatial imagery.

The concept of working memory has increasingly replaced the older concept of short-term memory (6). Research has subsequently tended to concentrate on one of two complementary but somewhat different approaches. One of these defines working memory as the system that is necessary for the concurrent storage and manipulation of information; tasks are devised that combine processing and storage, and the capacity of such tasks to predict a range of other cognitive skills, such as reading, comprehension, and reasoning, is tested. This psychometric approach, which has flourished most strongly in North America, frequently focuses on the extent to which performance on working memory tasks can predict individual differences in the relevant cognitive skills.

An alternative approach, which has been more favored in Europe, uses both dual-task methodology and the study of neuropsychological cases in an attempt to analyze the structure of the working memory system. Most effort has been devoted to the two slave systems, on the grounds that these offer more tractable problems than the more complex central-executive system.

The two approaches are complementary, and both have strengths and weaknesses; the psychometric correlational approach has the advantage that it can tackle what is probably the most crucial component of the system, the central executive, and can furthermore work directly on problems of practical significance, such as reading comprehension or the reasoning tasks used in tests of intelligence. The weakness of this approach lies in the reliance on complex working memory tasks that have a somewhat arbitrary construction and that do not readily lend themselves to a more detailed analysis of the component processes. The dual-task and neuropsychological approach can be utilized to successfully analyze the constituent processes of the slave systems but has made less headway in teasing apart the complexities of the executive controller.

## Individual Differences in Working Memory

The essence of the psychometric approach is to develop tasks that require the combined storage and manipulation of information and to correlate performance on these tasks with the performance of practically and theoretically important cognitive skills. One influential study in this area was carried out by Daneman and Carpenter (7), who examined the processes involved in reading comprehension. They devised a series of working memory tasks, one of which required subjects to

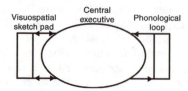

**FIGURE 22.1** ■ A simplified representation of the Baddeley and Hitch working memory model (5).

read aloud or listen to a series of short sentences while retaining the last word from each sentence for subsequent immediate recall. Hence, subjects might read or hear: "The sailor sold the parrot. The vicar opened the book." They should then respond "parrot, book." The test typically starts with two sentences and increases to a point at which subjects are no longer able to recall all the terminal words. This point is designated the subject's working memory span.

Daneman and Carpenter, and others using similar techniques, typically found a correlation coefficient of about 0.5 or 0.6 between working memory span and reading comprehension, as measured by standardized tests (8). The span task does not have to involve language processing because similar correlations are found when simple arithmetic, combined with word recall, is substituted for sentence processing (9).

Subsequent studies have indicated that students with high working memory span were better at coping with "garden path sentences," which contain misleading context, and that they are better at drawing inferences from text, suggesting that they have a better grasp of its meaning (10).

A second area in which the individual differences approach has been applied to the analysis of working memory is concerned with the study of reasoning and concentrates particularly on tasks that have traditionally been used to measure intelligence. One example of this is the working memory analysis by Carpenter, Just, and Shell (11) of performance on the Raven's matrices task, a test in which one sector is missing from a complex pattern and the subject is required to choose which of six possible options offers the best completion. Christal (12) has also shown that working memory tests provide improved prediction of technical learning capacity in U.S. Air Force recruits, when compared with more scholastic measures.

Kyllonen and Christal (13) have carried out a series of studies, each involving several hundred subjects who were required to perform a number of standardized tests of reasoning of the type used to assess intelligence as well as a range of tasks that had been devised to estimate working memory capacity. For each study, their results suggested a very high correlation between working memory capacity and reasoning skill. They concluded, however, that the two concepts, although closely related, were not synonymous; reasoning perfor-

mance was more dependent on previous knowledge than was working memory, which in contrast appeared to be more dependent on sheer speed of processing.

## Components of Working Memory

Although concurrent storage and processing may be one aspect of working memory, it is almost certainly not the only feature; indeed, Baddeley, Barnard, and Schneider and Detweiler (14) all suggest that the coordination of resources is the prime function of working memory, with memory storage being only one of many potential demands that are likely to be made on the system.

One proposed role for the central executive is that of coordinating information from two or more slave systems. This feature of the central executive was used in an attempt to test the proposal that Alzheimer's disease is associated with a particularly marked deficit in central executive functioning (15). Patients with Alzheimer's disease, and both young and elderly normal subjects, were required to perform two tasks concurrently, one visual and one verbal. The difficulty of each task was adjusted so that the Alzheimer patients were making the same proportion of errors as the control subjects, and subjects were then required to perform both tasks at the same time. Normal elderly subjects were no more impaired than young controls by this requirement to coordinate, whereas the Alzheimer patients showed a marked impairment in performance on both the memory and tracking tasks when required to combine them (16). As the disease progressed, performance on the individual tracking and memory span tasks held up very well (Figure 22.2), whereas performance on the combined tasks deteriorated markedly, as would be predicted by the hypothesis of a central executive deficit in Alzheimer's disease (17).

## The Slave Systems of Working Memory

Although an analytic approach to the central executive is beginning to bear fruit, there is no doubt that considerably more progress has been made with the simpler task of understanding the peripheral slave systems of working memory. The dual-task paradigm has been used to demonstrate the

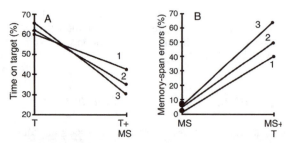

**FIGURE 22.2** ■ Dual-task performance of patients with Alzheimer's disease in a series of three sequential tests (1, 2, and 3) 6 months apart. T, tracking task; MS, memory span task. Normal subjects did not show a difference between single and dual-task conditions. Data from Baddeley et al. (*17*).

separability of the memory systems responsible for learning by means of visuospatial imagery and of learning by rote repetition. Imagery is disrupted by the requirement of performing a visuospatial task, such as tracking a spot of light moving on a screen, by certain types of eye movement, or by the presentation of irrelevant visual material during learning (*18*).

There are separable spatial and visual components, with different tasks differentially recruiting the two. Farah (*19*) distinguishes one imagery component that is principally concerned with the representation of pattern information and that involves the occipital lobes from a second more spatial component that seems to be dependent on parietal lobe functioning. Neuropsychological evidence supports this dichotomy, with some patients having great difficulty in imaging and recalling such visual features as the shape of the ears of a spaniel dog or the color of a pumpkin but having no difficulty in spatial tasks such as describing routes or locating towns on maps; other patients show exactly the reverse pattern of deficits (*20*).

Having found ways of separately disrupting spatial and verbal processing, one can explore the relative contribution of different subsystems to complex tasks. One example of this application concerns the nature of the cognitive processes involved in playing chess. The literature reviewed by Holding [in (*21*)] indicates that both visual and verbal coding have been claimed to be crucial by different studies that principally rely on subjective report. We have sought more objective evidence through a series of experiments that utilize

the secondary-task technique to disrupt either the phonological loop, the sketch pad system, or the central executive. Our first study involved memory for complex chess positions and tested subjects ranging from the modest club player to the international grand master. As expected, expertise correlated highly with memory performance, but all subjects showed the same basic pattern: no disruption from the concurrent verbal task but clear impairment from the tasks occupying the visuospatial sketch pad or the central executive. A second study required subjects to choose the optimum next move from a complex middle-game position and found exactly the same pattern. Disruption of verbal activity had no effect, whereas visuospatial disruption was clear, and this problem-solving task was even more susceptible to central executive disruption than the task in the first study (*22*).

## Analyzing the Phonological Loop

The phonological loop is probably the simplest and most extensively investigated component of working memory. It lies closest to the earlier concept of short-term memory and has been investigated most extensively with the memory-span procedure. It is assumed to comprise two components, a phonological store that can hold acoustic or speech-based information for 1 to 2 seconds, coupled with an articulatory control process, somewhat analogous to inner speech. This system serves two functions; it can maintain material within the phonological store by subvocal repetition, and it can take visually presented material such as words or nameable pictures and register them in the phonological store by subvocalization.

This simple model is able to give a good account of a rich range of laboratory-based findings. These include the following:

1. *The acoustic similarity effect.* This is the observation that the immediate ordered recall of items is poorer when they are similar rather than dissimilar in sound (*23*). Hence, hearing and repeating dissimilar words such as "pit, day, cow, pen, rig," is easier than a phonologically similar sequence such as "man, cap, can, map, mad." This phenomenon is assumed to occur because the basic code involved in the store is phonological; simi-

lar items have fewer distinguishing cues than dissimilar items and are therefore more susceptible to being forgotten. Similarity of meaning does not have this effect, suggesting that this subsystem does not reflect semantic coding.

2. *The irrelevant speech effect.* This refers to a reduction in recall of lists of visually presented items brought about by the presence of irrelevant spoken material (*24*). Once again, the semantic characteristics of the material are not important, with a language that is unfamiliar to the subject being just as disruptive as words in his or her native tongue and nonsense syllables being as disruptive as meaningful words. The effect is not due to simple distraction, because loud bursts of noise have little or no effect (*25*). These results are interpreted under the assumption that disruptive spoken material gains obligatory access to the phonological memory store.

3. *The word-length effect.* This provides evidence on the nature of the subvocal rehearsal process. Memory span for words is inversely related to spoken duration of the words. Subjects can generally remember about as many words as they can say in 2 seconds (*26*). This phenomenon accounts for differences in digit span when subjects are tested in different languages; languages in which digits tend to have long vowel sounds or more than one syllable take longer to rehearse and lead to shorter memory spans (*27*). The model can also explain the marked tendency for digit span in children to increase with age; as children get older, they are able to rehearse faster (*28*).

4. *Articulatory suppression.* It is possible to disrupt the use of subvocal rehearsal by requiring subjects to utter some repeated irrelevant sound, such as the word "the." This process, known as articulatory suppression prevents the subjects from rehearsing the material they are trying to remember and thus removes the effect of word length. Suppression also prevents subjects from registering visually presented material in the phonological store. Recall of such visual material is reduced, and the acoustic similarity effect is abolished (*29*).

The performance of neuropsychological patients with impaired short-term memory can also be explained as a deficit in the phonological store. They typically show no evidence of phonological coding in memory tasks when presentation is visual, no word length effect, and no influence of articu-

latory suppression, suggesting that these patients make little or no use of their defective phonological short-term store (*30*).

## The Function of the Phonological Loop

Patients with a specific phonological loop deficit seem to have remarkably few signs of general cognitive impairment. Although they typically have difficulty in comprehending certain types of complex sentences, interpretation of results in this area remains controversial (*31*). The most commonly held view is that the phonological store serves as a backup system for comprehension of speech under taxing conditions but may be less important with simple, clearly presented material.

In recent years we have been exploring another possible function of this system, namely, its role in long-term phonological learning, such as acquiring the vocabulary of one's native, or even a foreign, language. In one study, we asked a patient with a very specific short-term phonological memory deficit to learn eight items of Russian vocabulary, a language with which the patient was unfamiliar; we compared the results with the patient's capacity to learn to associate arbitrary pairs of words in the patient's native language (*32*). People tend to learn pairs of familiar words in terms of their meaning, and, as expected, the patient's performance on this task was entirely normal. In contrast, the patient failed to learn the Russian words with auditory presentation and was severely impaired relative to control subjects even when presentation was visual. This result suggests that short-term phonological storage is important for new long-term phonological learning. Subsequent studies with normal adults have shown that factors that influence the phonological loop, such as articulatory suppression, word length, and phonological similarity, strongly influence foreign vocabulary acquisition yet show no effect on learning to associate pairs of familiar words (*33*).

Evidence for the importance of the phonological loop in native-language learning comes from a number of sources. Gathercole and Baddeley (*34*) studied a group of children with a specific language disorder and found that their most striking cognitive deficits occurred in a task involving hearing and repeating back unfamiliar nonwords; on this nonword repetition task, 8-year-old children with the language development of 6-year-olds functioned like 4-year-olds. Further investigation suggested that this was due neither to perceptual difficulties nor to difficulties in speech production but probably resided in the operation of the phonological short-term store.

A subsequent study assessed the role of the phonological short-term store in the development of vocabulary across the normal range (*35*). A sample of 118 children was tested after starting school between the ages of 4 and 5 years. Their capacity for nonword repetition was measured, as was their nonverbal intelligence and their vocabulary, which was tested by speaking a series of words to the children and requiring them to point to appropriate pictures. Nonword repetition proved to be highly correlated with vocabulary and to be a powerful predictor of vocabulary 1 year later.

In an experimental simulation of new word learning (*36*), we taught children new names for toy monsters. Two groups were tested that were matched for nonverbal intelligence but that differed in nonword repetition capacity. Those with low capacity showed poor learning, particularly in the case of unfamiliar invented names.

Service (*37*) has studied the acquisition of English as a second language by young Finnish children. Service took a number of measures of cognitive skill before the course began, including measures of nonverbal intelligence and of nonword repetition capacity. Two years later the children's performances on a range of tests of English language were correlated with these earlier measures. Once again, nonword repetition capacity, which is assumed to depend on short-term phonological storage, was clearly the best predictor of subsequent success. Thus, the evidence supports the view that short-term phonological memory is crucial in the acquisition of vocabulary.

## Conclusion

The concept of a working memory system that temporarily stores information as part of the performance of complex cognitive tasks is proving to be productive. Studies that have utilized the individual difference approach have linked working memory to performance on a range of important tasks, including language comprehension and reasoning. The more analytic approach has shown that the concept forms a useful conceptual tool in understanding a range of neuropsychological deficits, which in turn have thrown light on normal cognitive functioning.

Working memory stands at the crossroads between memory, attention, and perception. In the case of the slave systems, the phonological loop, for example, probably represents an evolution of the basic speech perception and production systems to the point at which they can be used for active memory. Any adequate model of the phonological loop is thus likely to overlap substantially with an adequate model of speech perception and speech production. The visuospatial sketch pad is probably intimately related to the processes of visual perception and action. The central executive clearly reflects a system concerned with the attentional control of behavior, with subsequent developments almost certainly depending on parallel developments in the study of attention and of the control of action. If these links can be sustained and developed, the concept of working memory is likely to continue to be a fruitful one.

The author is the director of the Medical Research Council, Applied Psychology Unit, Cambridge CB2 2EF, United Kingdom.

## REFERENCES AND NOTES

1. See A. D. Baddeley [*Human Memory: Theory and Practice* (Allyn and Bacon, Needham Heights, MA, 1990), pp. 39–66] for a review.
2. —— and E. K. Warrington, *J. Verb. Learn. Verb. Behav.* **9**, 176 (1970); B. Milner, in *Amnesia*, C. W. M. Whitty and O. L. Zangwill, Eds. (Butterworths, London, 1966), pp. 109–133.
3. T. Shallice and E. K. Warrington, *Q. J. Exp. Psychol.* 22, 261 (1970); A. Basso, H. Spinnler, G. Vallar, E. Zanobio, *Neuropsychologia 20*, 263 (1982); G. Vallar and T. Shallice, *Neuropsychological Impairments of Short-Term Memory* (Cambridge Univ. Press, Cambridge, 1990).
4. R. C. Arkinson and R. M. Shiffrin, in *The Psychology of Learning and Motivation: Advances in Research and Theory*, K. W. Spence, Ed. (Academic Press, New York, 1968), vol. 2, pp. 89–195.
5. A. D. Baddeley and G. J. Hitch, in *The Psychology of Learning and Motivation*, G. A. Bower, Ed. (Academic Press, New York, 1974), vol. 8, pp. 47–89.
6. R. G. Crowder, *Acta. Psychol. 50*, 291 (1982).
7. M. Daneman and P. A. Carpenter, *J. Verb. Learn. Verb. Behav. 19*, 450 (1980).
8. A. D. Baddeley, R. Logie, I. Nimmo-Smith, N. Brereton, *J. Mem. Lang. 24*, 119 (1985); M. E. J. Masson and G. A. Miller, *J. Educ. Psychol. 75*, 314 (1983).

9. J. V. Oakhill, N. Yuill, A. J. Parkin, *J. Res. Read.* **9**, 80 (1986); M. L. Turner and R. W. Engle, *J. Mem. Lang.* **28**, 127 (1989).

10. M. Daneman and P. A. Carpenter, *J. Exp. Psychol. Learn. Mem. Cogn.* **9**, 561 (1983); J. V. Oakhill, *Br. J. Educ. Psychol.* **54**, 31 (1984).

11. P. A. Carpenter, M. A. Just, P. Shell, *Psychol. Rev.* **97**, 404 (1990).

12. R. E. Christal, *Armstrong Laboratory Human Resources Directorate Technical Report AL-TP-1991-0031* (Brooks Air Force Base, TX, 1991).

13. P. C. Kyllonen and R. E. Christal, *Intelligence 14*, 389 (1990).

14. A. D. Baddeley, *Working Memory* (Oxford Univ. Press, Oxford, 1986); P. Barnard, in *Progress in the Psychology of Language*, A. Ellis, Ed. (Erlbaum, London, 1985), vol. 2, pp. 197–258; W. Schneider and M. Detweiler, in *The Psychology of Learning and Motivation*, G. H. Bower, Ed. (Academic Press, New York, 1987), vol. 21, pp. 54–119.

15. J. T. Becker, in *Alzheimer's Disease: Advances in Basic Research and Therapies*, R. J. Wurtman, S. H. Corkin, J. H. Growdon, Eds. (Center for Brain Sciences and Metabolism Charitable Trust, Cambridge, 1987), pp. 343–348; H. Spinnler, S. Della Sala, R. Bandera, A. D. Baddeley, *Cogn. Neuropsychol. 5*, 193 (1988).

16. A. D. Baddeley, R. Logie, S. Bressi, S. Della Sala, H. Spinnler, *Q. J. Exp. Psychol. 38A*, 603 (1986).

17. A. D. Baddeley, S. Bressi, S. Della Sala, R. Logie, H. Spinnler, *Brain*, in press.

18. L. R. Brooks, *Q. J. Exp. Psychol. 19*, 289 (1967); A. D. Baddeley, S. Grant, E. Wight, N. Thomson, in *Attention and Performance*, P. M. A. Rabbitt and S. Dornic, Eds. (Academic Press, London, 1973), vol. 5, pp. 205–217 {see R. H. Logie and A. D. Baddeley [in *Imagery: Current Developments*, J. Richardson, D. Marks, P. Hampson, Eds. (Routledge and Kegan Paul, London, 1990), pp. 103–128] for a review}; A. D. Baddeley and K. Lieberman, in *Attention and Performance*, R. S. Nickerson, Ed. (Erlbaum, Hillsdale, NJ, 1980), vol. VIII, pp. 521–539.

19. M. J. Farah, *Psychol. Rev. 95*, 307 (1988).

20. ——, K. M. Hammond, D. N. Levine, R. Calvanio, *Cogn. Psychol. 20*, 439 (1988).

21. D. H. Holding, *The Psychology of Chess Skill* (Erlbaum, Hillsdale, NJ, 1985); A. D. Baddeley, in *Attention: Selection Awareness and Control*, A. D. Baddeley and L. Weiskrantz, Eds. (Oxford Univ. Press, Oxford, in press).

22. T. W. Robbins et al., in preparation.

23. R. Conrad, *Br. J. Psychol. 55*, 75 (1964); A. D. Baddeley, *Q. J. Exp. Psychol. 18*, 302 (1966).

24. H. A. Colle and A. Welsh, *J. Verb. Learn. Verb. Behav. 15*, 17 (1976); P. Salamé and A. D. Baddeley, *ibid. 21*, 150 (1982).

25. H. A. Colle, *ibid. 19*, 722 (1980); P. Salamé and A. D. Baddeley, *Ergonomics 30*, 1185 (1987).

26. A. D. Baddeley et al., *J. Verb. Learn. Verb. Behav. 14*, 575 (1975).

27. N. C. Ellis and R. A. Hennelley, *Br. J. Psychol. 71*, 43 (1980); M. Naveh-Benjamin and T. J. Ayres, *Q. J. Exp. Psychol. 38*, 739 (1986).

28. R. Nicolson, in *Intelligence and Learning*, M. P. Friedman, J. P. Das, N. O'Connor, Eds. (Plenum, London, 1981), pp. 179–184; G. J. Hitch and M. S. Halliday, *Philos. Trans. R. Soc. London B 302*, 325 (1983); C. Hulme, N. Thomson, C. Muir, A. Lawrence, *J. Exp. Child Psychol. 38*, 241 (1984).

29. A. D. Baddeley, V. J. Lewis, G. Vallar, *Q. J. Exp. Psychol. 36*, 233 (1984); D. J. Murray, *J. Exp. Psychol. 78*, 679 (1968).

30. G. Vallar and A. D. Baddeley, *J. Verb. Learn. Verb. Behav. 23*, 151 (1984).

31. G. Vallar and T. Shallice, Eds., *Neuropsychological Impairments of Short-Term Memory* (Cambridge Univ. Press, Cambridge, 1990).

32. A. D. Baddeley, C. Papagno, G. Vallar, *J. Mem. Lang. 27*, 586 (1988).

33. C. Papagno, T. Valentine, A. D. Baddeley, *ibid.*, in press; C. Papagno and G. Vallar, *Q. J. Exp. Psychol. 44A*, 47 (1992).

34. S. Gathercole and A. D. Baddeley, *J. Mem. Lang. 29*, 336 (1990).

35. ——, *ibid. 28*, 200 (1989).

36. ——, *Br. J. Psychol. 81*, 439 (1990).

37. E. Service, *University of Helsinki General Psychology Monograph* (Univ. of Helsinki Press, Helsinki, Finland, 1989), no. B9.

38. This article was written while I was visiting the University of Texas at Austin, where I was supported by the Wechsler Chair of Human Performance. I am grateful to S. Della Sala, S. Gathercole, R. Logie, K. Patterson, and H. Spinnler for their contributions to this and related papers.

# How Many Memory Systems Are There?

Endel Tulving • University of Toronto

Memory is made up of a number of interrelated systems, organized structures of operating components consisting of neural substrates and their behavioral and cognitive correlates. A ternary classificatory scheme of memory is proposed in which procedural, semantic, and episodic memory constitute a "monohierarchical" arrangement: Episodic memory is a specialized subsystem of semantic memory, and semantic memory is a specialized subsystem of procedural memory. The three memory systems differ from one another in a number of ways, including the kind of consciousness that characterizes their operations. The ternary scheme overlaps with dichotomies and trichotomies of memory proposed by others. Evidence for multiple systems is derived from many sources. Illustrative data are provided by experiments in which direct priming effects are found to be both functionally and stochastically independent of recognition memory.

**S**olving puzzles in science has much in common with solving puzzles for amusement, but the two differ in important respects. Consider, for instance, the jigsaw puzzle that scientific activity frequently imitates. The everyday version of the puzzle is determinate. It consists of a target picture and jigsaw pieces that, when properly assembled, are guaranteed to match the picture. Scientific puzzles are indeterminate: The number of pieces required to complete a picture is unpredictable; a particular piece may fit many pictures or none; it may fit only one picture, but the picture itself may be unknown; or the hypothetical picture may be imagined, but its component pieces may remain undiscovered.

This article is about a current puzzle in the science of memory. It entails an imaginary picture and a search for pieces that fit it. The picture, or the hypothesis, depicts memory as consisting of a number of systems, each system serving somewhat different purposes and operating according to somewhat different principles. Together they form the marvelous capacity that we call by the single name of *memory*, the capacity that permits organisms to benefit from their past experiences. Such a picture is at variance with conventional wisdom that holds memory to be essentially a single system, the idea that "memory is memory."

The article consists of three main sections. In the first, I present some pretheoretical reasons for hypothesizing the existence of multiple memory systems and briefly discuss the concept of *memory system*. In the second, I describe a ternary classificatory scheme of memory—consisting of procedural, semantic, and episodic memory—and briefly compare this scheme with those proposed by others. In the third, I discuss the nature and logic of evidence for multiple systems and describe some experiments that have yielded data revealing independent effects of one and the same act of learning, effects seemingly at variance with the idea of a single system. I answer the question posed in the title of the article in the short concluding section.

## Pretheoretical Considerations

### Why Multiple Memory Systems?

It is possible to identify several a priori reasons why we should break with long tradition (Tulving, 1984a) and entertain thoughts about multiple memory systems. I mention five here.

The first reason in many ways is perhaps the most compelling: No profound generalizations can be made about memory as a whole, but general statements about particular kinds of memory are perfectly possible. Thus, many questionable claims about memory in the literature, claims that give rise to needless and futile arguments, would become noncontroversial if their domain was restricted to parts of memory.

Second, memory, like everything else in our world, has become what it is through a very long evolutionary process. Such a process seldom forms a continuous smooth line, but is characterized by sudden twists, jumps, shifts, and turns. One might expect, therefore, that the brain structures and mechanisms that (together with their behavioral and mental correlates) go to make up memory will also reflect such evolutionary quirks (Oakley, 1983).

The third reason is suggested by comparisons with other psychological functions. Consider, for instance, the interesting phenomenon of *blindsight:* People with damage to the visual cortex are blind in a part of their visual field in that they do not see objects in that part, yet they can accurately point to and discriminate these objects in a forced-choice situation (e.g., Weiskrantz, 1980; Weiskrantz, Warrington, Sanders, & Marshall, 1974). Such facts imply that different brain mechanisms exist for picking up information about the visual environment. Or consider the massive evidence for the existence of two separate cortical pathways involved in vision, one mediating recognition of objects, the other their location in space (e.g., Mishkin, Ungerleider, & Macko, 1983; Ungerleider & Mishkin, 1982). If "seeing" things—something that phenomenal experience tells us is clearly unitary—is subserved by separable neural-cognitive systems, it is possible that learning and remembering, too, appear to be unitary only because of the absence of contrary evidence.

The fourth general reason derives from what I think is an unassailable assumption that most, if not all, of our currently held ideas and theories about mental processes are wrong and that sooner or later in the future they will be replaced with more adequate concepts, concepts that fit nature better (Tulving, 1979). Our task, therefore, should be to hasten the arrival of such a future. Among other things, we should be willing to contemplate the possibility that the "memory-is-memory" view is wrong and look for a better alternative.

The fifth reason lies in a kind of failure of imagination: It is difficult to think how varieties of learning and memory that appear to be so different on inspection can reflect the workings of one and the same underlying set of structures and processes. It is difficult to imagine, for instance, that perceptual-motor adaptations to distorting lenses and their aftereffects (e.g., Kohler, 1962) are mediated by the same memory system that enables an individual to answer affirmatively when asked whether Abraham Lincoln is dead. It is equally difficult to imagine that the improved ability to make visual acuity judgments, resulting from many sessions of practice without reinforcement or feedback (e.g., Tulving, 1958), has much in common with a person's ability to remember the funeral of a close friend.

If we reflect on the limits of generalizations about memory, think about the twists and turns of evolution, examine possible analogies with other biological and psychological systems, believe that most current ideas we have about the human mind are wrong, and have great difficulty apprehending sameness in different varieties of learning and memory, we might be ready to imagine the possibility that memory consists of a number of interrelated systems. But what exactly do we mean by a *memory system?*

### The Concept of System

We could think of a system simply as a set of correlated processes: Processes within a system are more closely related to one another than they are to processes outside the system. Such an abstract and relatively innocuous definition could be used by those students of memory who, for whatever reasons, are reluctant to consider biology when they think about psychology. It would not distort too many claims I will make about memory systems. However, a more concrete conceptualization—one that refers to the correlation of behavior and thought with brain processes and postulates the verifiable, real existence of memory systems (e.g., Tulving, 1984a)—is preferable because it points to stronger tests of such existence.

Memory systems constitute the major subdivisions of the overall organization of the memory complex. They are organized structures of more elementary operating components. An operating component of a system consists of a neural substrate and its behavioral or cognitive correlates. Some components are shared by all systems, others are shared only by some, and still others are unique to individual systems. Different learning and memory situations involve different concatenations of components from one or more systems. The relatedness of such situations in a natural classification scheme of learning and memory varies directly with the extent to which they entail identical components (Tulving, in press).

Although there is no one-to-one correspondence between tasks and systems (e.g., Kinsbourne, 1976; Tulving, in press), they are nonetheless systematically related: A given memory system makes it possible for organisms to perform memory tasks that entail operating components unique to that system. This means, among other things, that intervention with the operation of a system—even if it occurs through a single component of the system—affects all those learning and memory performances that depend on that system. The widespread but systematic effects of a single toxin or microorganism, for example (Rozin, 1976), reflect the fact that many specific memory performances are subserved by the affected system.

Different systems have emerged at different stages in the evolution of the species, and they emerge at different stages in the development of individual organisms. Thus, they can be ordered from "lower" to "higher" systems (or from less to more advanced), provided that it is clearly understood that such attributions are meaningful only with respect to comparisons between combinations of systems, on the one hand, and individual systems alone, on the other (Schiller, 1952). When a

new memory system with specialized novel capabilities evolves or develops, it enables the organism to increase the number, and the sophistication, of its memory functions. In this sense, the combination of the new system and the older ones is "higher," or more advanced than the older ones alone. As an analogy, we can think of an airplane with an autopilot as a more advanced or higher system than one without it, but we would not think of the autopilot alone as a higher system than the airplane.

## Procedural, Semantic, and Episodic Memories

### A Ternary Classification

Let me now switch gears and discuss a classification scheme according to which memory consists of three major systems. I will refer to them as procedural, semantic, and episodic, primarily for the sake of continuity with previous usage, although these are not necessarily the best terms. The three systems constitute what might be called a *monohierarchical* arrangement (cf. Engelien, 1971). The system at the lowest level of the hierarchy, procedural memory, contains semantic memory as its single specialized subsystem, and semantic memory, in turn, contains episodic memory as its single specialized subsystem. In this scheme, each higher system depends on, and is supported by, the lower system or systems, but it possesses unique capabilities not possessed by the lower systems.

Procedural memory enables organisms to retain learned connections between stimuli and responses, including those involving complex stimulus patterns and response chains, and to respond adaptively to the environment. Semantic memory is characterized by the additional capability of internally representing states of the world that are not perceptually present. It permits the organism to construct mental models of the world (Craik, 1943), models that can be manipulated and operated on covertly, independently of any overt behaviour. Episodic memory affords the additional capability of acquisition and retention of knowledge about personally experienced events and their temporal relations in subjective time and the ability to mentally "travel back" in time.

The monohierarchical relation among the systems means that only procedural memory can operate completely independently of the other systems. This necessarily happens when an organism does not possess either of the two more advanced systems, and it may happen with higher organisms when situations do not call for the use of the other systems. Semantic memory can function independently of episodic memory but not independently of procedural memory. And episodic memory depends on both procedural and semantic memory in its workings, although, as already mentioned, it also possesses its own unique capabilities. The monohierarchical arrangement also implies that certain kinds of double dissociations between learning and memory tasks are precluded (Tulving, in press).

The monohierarchical scheme discussed here represents a revision of the ideas I had expressed about the relations among procedural, semantic, and episodic memory in *Elements of Episodic Memory* (Tulving, 1983). The revised scheme (Tulving, 1984b), anticipated by Lieury (1979), was prompted by the comments of critics such as Kihlstrom (1984), Lachman and Naus (1984), McCauley (1984), Seamon (1984), Tiberghien (1984), and Wolters (1984). It helps to improve the fit between facts and theory, and it does away with some problems of internal consistency of the earlier formulation.

Each system differs in its methods of acquisition, representation, and expression of knowledge. Each also differs in the kind of conscious awareness that characterizes its operations. Let us briefly consider these differences, taking each in turn.

Acquisition in the procedural system requires overt behavioral responding, whereas covert responding—cognitive activity, or "mere observation"—may be sufficient for the other two. We could also say that the characteristic mode of learning is *tuning* in the procedural system, *restructuring* in the semantic system, and *accretion* in the episodic system, along the general lines suggested by Rumelhart and Norman (1978), as long as we keep in mind the implications of the monohierarchical relation among the systems.

The representation of acquired information in the procedural system is prescriptive rather than descriptive: It provides a blueprint for future action without containing information about the past (Dretske, 1982). It may be conceptualized in terms of the "stage-setting" metaphor of Bransford, McCarrell, Franks, and Nitsch (1977), a metaphor akin to Craik's (1983) suggestion that the consequences of learning may take the form of "subtle alterations of the system" (p. 345). It can also be specified in terms of changing probabilities of specific responses to specific stimuli (Mishkin, Malamut, & Bachevalier, 1984). When we are dealing with procedural memory, I agree with Bransford et al. (1977) and with Craik (1983) that it is inappropriate to talk about discrete "memory traces."

Representations in the semantic system, however, are different from those in the procedural system; they describe the world without prescribing any particular action. Representations in both the semantic and episodic systems are isomorphic with the information they represent (Dretske, 1982). Representations in episodic memory additionally carry information about the relations of represented events to the rememberer's personal identity as it exists in subjective time and space (e.g., Claparede, 1911/1951; Tulving, 1983).

Expression of knowledge (Spear, 1984) also differs in the three systems. Only direct expression is possible in procedural memory; overt responding according to a relatively rigid format determined at the time of learning is obligatory (Hirsh, 1974; Mishkin & Petri, 1984). On the other hand, acquired knowledge in both semantic and episodic memory can be expressed flexibly, in different behavioral forms. Such knowledge may manifest itself, under conditions far removed from those of original learning, in behaviors quite dissimilar to the behavior entailed in such learning. Overt behavior corresponding to actualized knowledge is only an optional form of expression. In episodic memory, the typical mode of "expression" of remembering is recollective experience, based on synergistic ecphory. It occurs when the organism is in the "retrieval mode" (Tulving, 1983) or has a particular "attitude" (Bartlett, 1932).

The three memory systems are characterized by different kinds of consciousness (Tulving, 1985). Procedural memory is associated with anoetic (nonknowing) consciousness, semantic memory with noetic (knowing) consciousness, and episodic memory with autonoetic (self-knowing) consciousness. This arrangement is schematically depicted in Figure 23.1.

Anoetic (nonknowing) consciousness represents

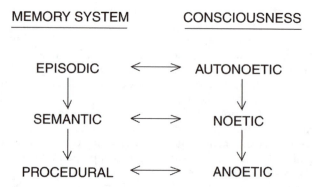

MEMORY SYSTEM          CONSCIOUSNESS

EPISODIC   ⟵⟶   AUTONOETIC

SEMANTIC   ⟵⟶   NOETIC

PROCEDURAL   ⟵⟶   ANOETIC

**FIGURE 23.1** ■ Schematic arrangement of three memory systems and three kinds of consciousness. *Note.* An arrow means "implies."

one of the end points of the continuum: It refers to an organism's capability to sense and to react to external and internal stimulation, including complex stimulus patterns. Plants and very simple animals possess anoetic consciousness as do computers and learning machines that have knowledge and that can improve it (e.g., Hayes-Roth, Klahr, & Mostow, 1980).

Noetic (knowing) consciousness is an aspect of the semantic memory system. It makes possible introspective awareness of the internal and external world. We can say that the object of noetic consciousness is the organism's knowledge of its world. Noetic consciousness is to such knowledge as the knowledge is to the world. Lower animals, very young children, and people suffering from brain damage may lack episodic memory and autonoetic consciousness but may have fully developed noetic consciousness.

Autonoetic (self-knowing) consciousness is a necessary correlate of episodic memory. It allows an individual to become aware of his or her own identity and existence in subjective time that extends from the past through the present to the future. It provides the familiar phenomenal flavor of recollective experience characterized by "pastness" and subjective veridicality. It can be impaired or lost without impairment or loss of other forms of consciousness.

## Other Classificatory Schemes

The ternary classificatory scheme I have described is quite closely related to schemes proposed by other multiple-memory theorists. Although most of these represent various kinds of dichotomies,

some tripartite divisions have also been suggested. Ruggiero and Flagg (1976), for instance, have distinguished among "stimulus-response," "representational," and "organized" memory, and a similar scheme has been adopted by Oakley (1981) who referred to the three varieties as "associative," "representational," and "abstract." The first of these categories is analogous to procedural memory in that it involves the learning and retention of stimulus-response connections and chains; the second is similar to episodic memory in that it represents the capability of forming and storing particular representations of situations and events together with their spatiotemporal context; the third is analogous to semantic memory in that it enables the organism to store context-free facts abstracted from specific instances.

Oakley (1981) has made a systematic attempt to relate the dichotomies suggested by other multiple-system theorists (e.g., Hirsch, 1974; Iversen, 1976; Moore, 1979; O'Keefe & Nadel, 1978; Olton, Becker, & Handelmann, 1979) to his own tripartite scheme. More recent proposals for memory dichotomies include the "knowing how" versus the "knowing that" systems of Cohen and Squire (Cohen, 1984; Cohen & Squire, 1980; Squire & Cohen, 1984), and a similar distinction between the habit system and the "memory" system made by Mishkin and his associates (e.g., Mishkin, Malamut, & Bachevalien 1984; Mishkin & Petri, 1984). The "knowing how" and habit systems are akin to Oakley's associative memory, the "knowing that" and "memory" systems to Oakley's combined representational and organized memory systems.

Some other recent distinctions are more difficult

to compare with either Oakley's (1981) scheme or the ternary scheme discussed in this article. Thus, for instance, Warrington and Weiskrantz's (1982) "semantic" system seems to encompass more than just the associative or the procedural system, and their "cognitive mediational" system transcends the representational or the episodic system. Schacter and Moscovitch's (1984) "early" and "late" systems appear to be analogous to procedural and (undeveloped) semantic systems in the ternary scheme, but this conjecture must await further evaluation.

Some other taxonomic schemes reflect different orientations to the classification problem altogether. Thus, for instance, Pribram's (1984) hierarchical classification of varieties of "cognitive learning" in primates goes considerably beyond simple dichotomies, which he eschewed. In Johnson's (1983) multiple-entry modular memory system the three modules ("subsystems") have no fixed relation to one another but interact variably and continually in different tasks. In her scheme, therefore, no system operates by itself, as the procedural system of the ternary scheme does in some organisms (animals, infants, brain-damaged patients).

On the basis of his review of the literature, Oakley (1981) suggested that the neural substrate of associative memory is subcortical, that representational memory processes depend on both the neocortex and the septo-hippocampal structures, and that abstract memory is subserved by the neocortex. Pribram (1984) also has identified brain structures involved in different kinds of learning. These kinds of suggestions necessarily remain tentative and uncertain, not only because of the paucity of relevant data but also because of the lack of systematic knowledge of functional composition of the kinds of tasks that have been used in lesion and stimulation experiments. Observation that performance on a task is impaired following some treatment, for instance, does not tell us why it is impaired or which of the many functional components of the task has been affected. Especially problematic in this respect are comparisons and assumed parallels between animal and human learning tasks.

Given the diversity of evidence that different theorists have brought to bear upon the enterprise and the different backgrounds from which they come, we should be more pleased with the overall agreement among theorists than concerned about their differences. Some open problems may be worth mentioning, however.

The first concerns the number of major systems. Just about everyone agrees on the reality of a major division between procedural memory (stimulus-response memory, associative memory) on the one hand and the "other kind" on the other. The currently popular open question has to do with what this "other kind" is and whether it is one or two. Many investigators say "one." Different versions corresponding to the "one" position have been promulgated or approvingly mentioned, among others, by Anderson and Ross (1980), Baddeley (1984), Craik (1983, in press), Hintzman (1984), Jacoby (1983a, 1983b), Kihlstrom (1984), Klatzky (1984), Lachman and Naus (1984), McCloskey and Santee (1981), McKoon and Ratcliff (1979), Moscovitch (1982), and Roediger (1984). Some others say "two" (e.g., Herrmann, 1982; Herrmann & Harwood, 1980; Kinsbourne & Wood, 1975, 1982; Oakley, 1981; O'Keefe & Nadel, 1978; Olton, 1984; Ruggiero & Flagg, 1976; Shoben, Wescourt, & Smith, 1978; Warrington, 1981; Wood, Ebert, & Kinsbourne, 1982; Wood, Taylor, Penny, & Stump, 1980). A large majority of the students of learning and memory have yet to join the debate on either side.

A second problem has to do with the identity of the two nonprocedural systems and the nature of the relation between them. It is not immediately clear how we can evaluate suggestions such as those made by Ruggiero and Flagg (1976), as well as Oakley (1981), that representational memory in animals corresponds to episodic memory in humans, or the suggestion of Olton (1984) that animals have episodic memory, too. The ideas make good sense: The ability to register, store, and make use of information concerning past events does characterize episodic memory just as it characterizes abstract memory. On the other hand, it is unclear whether animals possess the capability of recollecting past events as being a "part of" their own past in the same way as people do. There is mounting evidence that brain-damaged patients who have lost their ability to recollect specific episodes and to acquire new ones, and who do not have what I have called autonoetic consciousness, nonetheless can not only use previously learned semantic knowledge (e.g., Cermak & O'Connor, 1983) but can also extract new semantic knowledge from learning episodes (e.g., Glisky, Schacter, & Tulving, 1984; Schacter, Harbluk, & McLachlan, 1984). This fact suggests that animals, too, might be capable of acquiring information about aspects of past events even if they do not possess any system similar to the episodic system in humans. Thus, the distinction between representational and abstract memory in animals (Oakley, 1981) need not quite correspond to the one between episodic and semantic memory in humans. Of course, as long as we think of episodic memory in humans as being merely *analogous* to forms of animal memory, such as Olton's working memory (Olton, 1984, in press), and do not insist on the two being identical, or even homologous, we are probably on firm ground.

A third problem has to do with the order of development of the two nonprocedural systems. I agree with Kinsbourne and Wood (1975), and I think that in both phylogenetic and ontogenetic development, the semantic system precedes the episodic one. Others (e.g., Lachman & Naus, 1984; Seamon, 1984) believe that the order is reversed. The classificatory schemes of Ruggiero and Flagg (1976) and Oakley (1981) imply the developmental priority of representational (analogous to episodic) memory, in agreement with Lachman and Naus and with Seamon. The matter clearly needs attention, thought, and clarification. (See Schacter & Moscovitch, 1984, for a discussion.)

## Nature and Logic of Evidence

### Evidence for Memory Systems

Evidence for classificatory schemes of memory such as those proposed by Ruggiero and Flagg (1976) and Oakley (1981) is derived from experiments in which the effects of brain lesions or brain stimulation (Olton, in press) are observed on the performance of two or more learning or memory tasks. The basic form of findings relevant to making distinctions among memory systems is one in which a particular lesion or a particular type of stimulation affects the performance on one task but not on the other. We can refer to such a finding as demonstrating a functional dissociation of tasks. Many such findings reported in the literature have been reviewed by Hirsh (1974), O'Keefe and Nadel (1978), and by Oakley (1981, 1983).

The ternary classification I have described here is supported by two different sets of evidence. One has to do with the distinction between procedural and propositional memory; such evidence has been reviewed by Baddeley (1984), Moscovitch (1982), and Squire and Cohen (1984), among others. The second type of evidence concerns the episodic/semantic distinction, and its various aspects have been discussed and reviewed by Kinsbourne and Wood (1975, 1982), Parkin (1982), Rozin (1976), Schacter and Tulving (1982), Tulving (1983, 1984b), and Wood, Ebert, and Kinsbourne (1982), among others. I will make no attempt to summarize this evidence here. Instead, I will discuss and analyze a particular kind of experiment, yielding a particular kind of result, that appears as one of the more interesting and promising pieces of the puzzle.

The experiment is one in which people are shown familiar words and are then given two different "memory" tests on the studied, as well as unstudied, words. In one test, recognition memory, they have to remember whether they saw the test word in the study list. Performance on this test can be assumed to depend on, or at least to be greatly facilitated by, the episodic system. In the other, a word fragment completion test, people have to "think of" a word that matches a graphernic fragment. Thus, for instance, if the fragment is o hur, they have to come up with the word *yoghurt;* if the fragment is e d l m, they have to complete it as *pendulum*. Although people can complete a certain percentage of word fragments on the basis of their general knowledge of words, prior presentation of the words in the study list enhances their completion performance.

Inspired by the classic studies of Warrington and Weiskrantz (1970, 1974), we did an experiment in which we compared recognition memory and fragment completion (Tulving, Schacter, & Stark, 1982). Although we found a sizable reduction in recognition over a seven-day interval, we found very little such forgetting in fragment completion. The relevant data are summarized in Figure 23.2. The data mimic other similar patterns of functional dissociation between tasks (for example, see Jacoby & Dallas, 1981; Kihlstrom, 1980; Shoben, Wescourt, & Smith, 1978). But an even more interesting factor yielded by our experiment was that levels of performance on the two tasks of word recognition and fragment completion were not

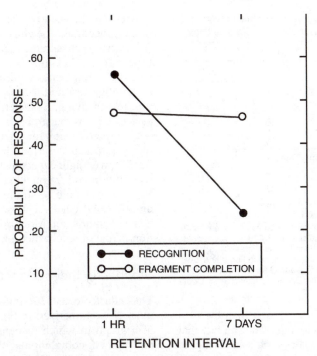

**FIGURE 23.2** ■ Recognition memory and primed fragment completion performance as a function of retention interval. *Note.* Recognition memory = hit rate minus false alarm rate. Data are from "Priming Effects In Word-Fragment Completion Are Independent of Recognition Memory" by E. Tulving, D. L. Schacter, and H. Stark, 1982, *Journal of Experimental Psychology: Human Learning and Memory, 8*, pp. 336–342. Copyright 1982 by the American Psychological Association.

correlated at all. It is this lack of correlation, or stochastic independence, between recognition and fragment completion that greatly encourages thoughts about different memory systems. To place the finding into proper perspective and to appreciate its implications, however, we should first consider a simple, well-known fact about memory.

## Contingency Analyses of Measures of Memory

The well-known fact comes from list-item experiments in which a person studies a list of familiar words and is then given two different tests, a recognition test and a recall test. All such experiments show that recognition is easier than recall. They also show that there is a good positive correlation between recognition and recall when individual items are taken as units of analysis: The probability of recall is greater for items that can be recognized than for those that cannot. (For an interesting exception, see Broadbent & Broadbent, 1975, the discussion by Rabinowitz, Mandler, &

Patterson, 1977, and the rebuttal by Broadbent & Broadbent, 1977.)

Let us look at data from a particular version of this kind of an experiment (Ogilvie, Tulving, Paskowitz, & Jones, 1980). University students studied a list of familiar words, shown one at a time, for three seconds each. They were then given two tests: first a standard yes/no recognition test, and second a cued-recall test with extralist cues, either associatively related to, or rhyming with, target words.

The results of the experiment, for both associative cues and rhyming cues, are summarized in Table 23.1. In both cases, the data are tabulated in a contingency table that represents four possible outcomes: (a) target word both recognized and recalled, (b) target word recognized but not recalled, (c) target word not recognized but recalled, or (d) target word neither recognized nor recalled.

The fact we should note about these two sets of data is the positive correlation, or association, between recall and recognition: The proportion of recalled words that are also recognized (shown at

**TABLE 23.1. Results of the Ogilvie et al. (1980) Experiment: Probability of Recall with Associative and Rhyming Cues**

| Recognition | Recall 1 | Recall 0 | Total |
|---|---|---|---|
| | Associative Cues | | |
| 1 | .47 | .20 | .67 |
| 0 | .05 | .28 | .33 |
| Total | .52 | .48 | |
| | Rhyming Cues | | |
| 1 | .20 | .50 | .70 |
| 0 | .02 | .28 | .30 |
| Total | .22 | .78 | |

*Note.* The conditional probability of recognition given recall, P(Rn | Rc), is .90 for associative cues and .91 for rhyming cues. Data are from the experiment described in "Three-Dimensional Memory Traces: A Model and Its Application to Forgetting" by J. C. Ogilvie, E. Tulving, S. Paskowitz, and G. V. Jones, 1980, *Journal of Verbal Learning and Verbal Behavior, 19*, 405–415. Copyright 1980 by Academic Press, Inc.

the bottom of Table 23.1 is greater than the proportion of all test words recognized. The fact that recognition thus conditionalized on recall is higher than overall recognition means that the two measures, recall and recognition, are positively correlated, or dependent, in this contingency analysis.

Now we are ready to consider what happens when we make what appears to be a minor change in the procedure. The change is that we use word fragments as cues in the recall test. Otherwise the procedure is the same: presentation of familiar words for study, one at a time, followed first by a recognition test and then by a fragment completion test (Tulving, Schacter, & Stark, 1982). Because we know that graphemic word fragments are very effective cues for recall (see, for example, the experiment described by Tulving, 1976, pp. 52–53), we might expect that the relation between recognition and fragment completion in this new experiment would be similar to that between recognition and cued recall, namely one of dependence. But it is not. More often than not, the relation is one of stochastic independence.

## Stochastic Independence

The data from the Tulving et al. (1982) experiment are summarized in Figure 23.3 in the form of a graph in which recognition conditionalized on fragment completion is plotted against overall recognition. Figure 23.3 shows that in four different conditions of the experiment—study list words and recognition test lures tested after one hour and after one week—conditionalized recognition did

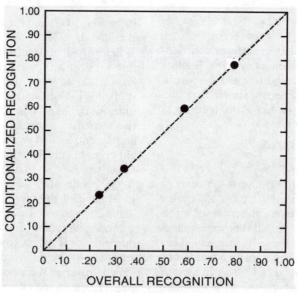

**FIGURE 23.3 ■** Probability of recognition conditionalized on fragment completion as a function of overall recognition hit rate.
*Note.* Data are from "Priming Effects in Word-Fragment Completion Are Independent of Recognition Memory" by E. Tulving, D. L. Schacter, and H. Stark, 1982, *Journal of Experimental Psychology: Human Learning and Memory, 8*, pp. 336–342. Copyright 1982 by the American Psychological Association.

not differ from overall recognition. Such a state of affairs means that recognition and fragment completion in this experiment were completely uncorrelated, or stochastically independent of one another.

This is a remarkable result: A word's appearance in the study list enhances the subject's ability to generate the word to its fragment cue, but such enhancement is identical for the remembered words and for those not remembered. Thus, we have here two manifestations of one and the same single act of learning, one measured by recognition, the other by the enhanced ability to complete fragments, and the two seem to have nothing in common. Note that the positive dependence between recognition and cued recall observed in the Ogilvie et al. (1980) experiment and in many other similar studies (e.g., Rabinowitz et al., 1977) rules out the possibility that the stochastic independence is simply an artifact of the method of successive testing or of the contingency analysis.

The finding of stochastic independence between recognition and fragment completion has been replicated by Light, Singh, and Capps (1984) with both young and older subjects and in our own laboratory with both normal subjects (e.g., Chandler,

1983) and with amnesic patients (Schacter, McLachlan, Moscovitch, & Tulving, 1984). Similar findings of stochastic independence between measures of memory have been reported by Jacoby and Witherspoon (1982) who compared recognition memory with tachistoscopic identification of study list words under conditions where tachistoscopic identification, like fragment completion, shows benefits of earlier exposure in the study list.

Let us consider the experiment done by Chandler (1983). Her design was patterned after that of the Tulving et al. (1982) experiment, but it comprised many more conditions. Subjects studied either short (12 words) or long (48 words) lists and were then tested in two sessions, one immediately after study, the other 24 hours later, under two sets of recall instructions, one emphasizing the correspondence between test fragments and study list words, the other leaving this connection unspecified. The design of Chandler's experiment made it possible to examine the correlation between recognition and recall in 32 separate conditions, 16 entailing words seen on the study list, and the other 16 entailing words not seen in the experiment before the recognition test. Chandler's data are shown in Figure 23.4. The outcome is

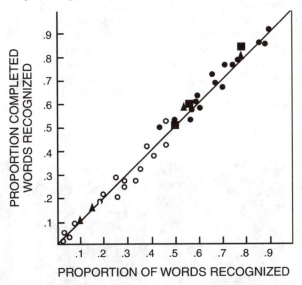

**FIGURE 23.4** ■ Probability of recognition conditionalized on fragment completion, anagram solution, and face identification as a function of overall recognition hit rate.
*Note.* Fragment completion data are shown in circles. Data are from "Does Retrieval Strategy Determine the Relation between Episodic Recognition and Semantic Priming?" by C. Chandler, 1983, unpublished master's thesis, University of Toronto, Toronto, Canada. Used by permission of the author. Anagram solution data are shown in squares and are based on work done by H. Mable in E. Tulving's laboratory, University of Toronto, Toronto, Canada. Face identification data are shown in triangles and are based on work by A. Eillis in E. Tulving's laboratory.

**FIGURE 23.5** ■ Examples of shadow faces used in the Ellis experiments.

uniform: Conditionalized recognition is essentially identical with simple recognition, that is, recognition and fragment completion are stochastically independent.

In other work in our laboratory, we have obtained results showing stochastic independence between recognition and two other tasks that do not require remembering of a particular learning episode but that do reveal the effects of learning of the kind that manifests itself in enhanced fragment completion or tachistoscopic identification, learning that is named *direct priming*, or simply *priming*. One of these is the anagram-solution task. People are given scrambled letters of a word, such as *tinekt* and *hubels*, and they have to rearrange the letters to make a word, such as *kitten* and *bushel*. It is known that anagram solutions show priming effects derived from earlier exposure to the target words (e.g., Dominowski & Ekstrand, 1967; Jablonski & Mueller, 1972).

In one experiment, patterned after Tulving et al. (1982), but using anagram solutions instead of fragment completion, Harriet Mable tested subjects in two test sessions, one on the day of study, the other 24 hours later. Her results, for study-list words and recognition-test lures, and from the same-day test and a test given 24 hours later, are indicated by the four filled triangles in Figure 23.4.

The other task is what we call the shadow face identification task. At the time of the study, subjects are shown shadow faces of the kind depicted in Figure 23.5, and then 24 hours later, they are tested for recognition of these faces and for their ability to "perceive" faces on the basis of fragments of the faces of the kind shown in Figure 23.6. Note that the question put to the subjects here, as in fragment completion and anagram solutions, is not whether they saw the face before, but whether they can "see" the face, to construct it in their own minds, on the basis of fragmentary cues.

**FIGURE 23.6** ■ Fragmented shadow faces corresponding to those shown In Figure 23.5.

The faces, inspired by Mooney (1956), were drawn by Anne Ellis. Ellis also carried out three preliminary experiments with these materials. Results from these three experiments with the face-identification task are indicated by the three filled squares in Figure 23.4.

## Independence Is Not Independence

Stochastic independence between a measure of learning that requires remembering particular episodes (recognition) and measures that do not require it ("primed" fragment completion, tachistoscopic identification, anagram solutions, and identification of faces) seems to represent a reliable phenomenon. What does it mean, and how does it fit into the picture of multiple memory systems?

To answer these questions, it is first necessary to distinguish between *stochastic independence* and what has been called *functional independence*. Stochastic independence is the name given to the relation between two events in which the probability of their joint occurrence is equal to the product of the probabilities of the occurrence of each event alone. It is based on subject items as units of analysis, and its occurrence requires no systematic manipulation of any independent variables. Functional independence, on the other hand, refers to the relation between two dependent variables in a situation in which one variable does and the other one does not vary as a *function* of an independent variable. Functional independence could also be called functional dissociation, or cross-over interaction (see Loftus, 1978).

It is important to realize that there is no necessary logical connection between these two kinds of independence. We could say that "independence is not independence"; it all depends on how relations are specified. It is perfectly possible to find one kind of independence in a particular situation and not the other. Because this simple fact does not seem to be widely known but is important, it may be worth emphasis and a concrete illustration.

Consider an imaginary set of data shown in Table 23.2. Each of three subjects, A, B, and C, is tested for the knowledge of each of three items, 1, 2, and 3, in two tests, X and Y. Each subject either succeeds (receiving a score of 1), or fails (receiving a score of 0), with respect to a given item on a

**TABLE 23.2.  A Set of Imaginary Data from an Experiment in Which Three Subjects Are Tested with Three Items on Each of Two Tests, X and Y**

| Subjects | Items | | | Sum |
|---|---|---|---|---|
| | 1 | 2 | 3 | |
| A | 1, 1 | 1, 1 | 1, 1 | 3, 3 |
| B | 1, 0 | 1, 1 | 0, 1 | 2, 2 |
| C | 1, 0 | 0, 0 | 0, 1 | 1, 1 |
| Sum | 3, 1 | 2, 2 | 1, 3 | |

*Note.* The first entry in each pair is the score on Test X, and the second entry is the score on Test Y.

given test. The data in Table 23.2 can be arranged to show that the two tests, X and Y (or two dependent variables), are (a) perfectly positively correlated, (b) perfectly negatively correlated, and (c) perfectly uncorrelated, all at the same time. Thus, if we take subjects as the units of analysis (for each subject, the data are pooled over all three items), X and Y are perfectly positively correlated ($r = 1.0$), but if we take items as the units (each item is given a score on each test, with the data pooled over all subjects), X and Y are perfectly negatively correlated ($r = -1.0$). The fact that one and the same set of data can show positive and negative correlations simultaneously has been previously pointed out and discussed by Mandler (1959). Here we note the additional point that a given set of data can show *zero* correlation simultaneously with positive and negative correlations between the same dependent variables. Thus, when we rearrange the data in Table 23.2 into a fourfold contingency table, as shown in Table 23.3, it turns out that the two measures, X and Y, are completely independent stochastically.

The independence of functional and stochastic independence has two important implications for the pursuit of our puzzle. One, explanations constructed to account for functional independence may leave stochastic independence unexplained. Two, findings of stochastic independence are much

**TABLE 23.3.  Data from Table 2 Rearranged in the Form of a Contingency Table**

| Test X | Test Y | | Total |
|---|---|---|---|
| | 1 | 0 | |
| 1 | 4 | 2 | 6 |
| 0 | 2 | 1 | 3 |
| Total | 6 | 3 | |

more relevant to the classification problem than findings of functional independence, because they impose tighter constraints on theory.

Functional independence has been demonstrated in many experiments. Much of the evidence in support of multiple memory systems of the kind discussed by Oakley (1981) takes the form of functional dissociations, and so do results that have been used to support the distinction between procedural and propositional memory (e.g., Cohen & Squire, 1980). I used experiments demonstrating functional independence in arguing for the distinction between episodic and semantic memory systems (Tulving, 1983).

Although functional dissociations can be interpreted as supporting ideas concerning multiple memory systems, the evidence they provide is not compelling. It is perfectly possible to interpret data showing functional independence without any need to postulate different systems (Roediger, 1984). For example, one of the more thoroughly investigated functional dissociations—that between recognition and free recall (Anderson & Bower, 1972; Kintsch, 1970; McCormack, 1972; Tulving, 1976)—can be readily interpreted within the generation-recognition model (Watkins & Gardiner, 1979). This model assumes that one of two stages of processing in recall is absent in recognition and that the other stage is common to the retrieval tasks. The discrepant stage is responsible for the functional independence between recognition and recall, whereas the common stage underlies the positive correlation or dependence of the two measures.

Evidence provided by stochastic independence is somewhat more compelling: Stochastic independence cannot be explained by assuming that the two comparison tasks differ in only one or a few operating components (information, stages, processes, mechanisms). As long as there is any overlap in those operating components that are responsible for differences in what is retrieved, some positive dependence between the measures should appear. Perfect stochastic independence implies complete absence of such overlap.

Although more compelling, observations of stochastic independence alone will not settle the question of the reality of memory systems. Much more converging evidence is necessary, and some of it already exists. Thus, we know that priming effects show much slower forgetting than, say, recogni-

tion (e.g., Tulving et al., 1982), that cross-modality transfer is smaller in fragment completion than in recognition (e.g., Ellis & Collins, 1983), that amnesic patients who have great difficulty with recall and recognition show near-normal priming effects (e.g., Graf & Schacter, in press), and that alcoholic intoxication impairs recognition memory but not priming effects in fragment completion (e.g., Parker, Schoenberg, Schwartz, & Tulving, 1983). Additional evidence will most likely be obtained by students of memory working under the banners of neuropsychology, comparative psychology, developmental psychology, cognitive psychology, and other disciplines concerned with plasticity of experience and behavior (Oakley, 1983; Olton, in press; Tulving, in press).

The results I have described here only suggest that the kind of learning reflected in fragment completion and other similar tasks is subserved by a system other than episodic memory. They alone do not tell us what this other system is. We could speculate that fragment completion is basically a procedural memory task, or basically a semantic memory task, but such conclusions are purely conjectural. At the present stage of our knowledge, it is no less plausible to entertain the hypothesis that fragment completion reflects the operation of some other, as yet unknown, memory system, perhaps a precursor to episodic memory. We could refer to this unknown system as the QM system (QM for question mark) and keep our eyes and minds open for evidence for and against its hypothesized existence.

## How Many Systems?

The puzzle of memory systems is not and will not be an easy one to solve. Many difficulties have to be overcome before we can expect more rapid progress. We assume that both memory systems and memory tasks (performances, manifestations, achievements) are composed of, or can be broken down into, more elementary constituents (I have referred to them in this article as operating components), but we do not yet know how to relate one to the other in the world of empirical observations. In the absence of such rules of the game, interpretation of existing evidence from the point of view of multiple memory systems is uncertain and frustrating. The difficulty is compounded by the clever and inventive strategies that learners and rememberers frequently use when confronted with laboratory tasks, strategies that drive wedges between what the experimenter thinks he or she is observing and what the observed organism is in fact doing. A familiar bane of learning and memory researchers is the omnipresent possibility that identical behaviors and responses are produced by different underlying processes and mechanisms. Sometimes crucial theoretical distinctions may depend on fine differences in observed patterns of data, requiring discriminations beyond the resolving power of conventional methodology.

How then, with few facts yet available to guide us and many intractable problems to dampen our enthusiasm, can we expect to answer the question posed in the title of this article? We follow the same procedure that we use when we tackle other puzzles in our science: We exercise our imagination, trying to see beyond the visible horizon, reaching beyond what is given. As long as our imagination is eventually bridled and disciplined by nature's facts, we need not worry about thinking thoughts that transcend our knowledge.

Because I have discussed three systems in this article, in agreement with a number of other friends of multiple learning and memory systems, the answer "three" to our main question would not be entirely amiss at the present time. But if we try to imagine what might lie beyond our currently limited horizon we may decide that a better answer might be "at least three and probably many more."

Whether this or some other answer will prove to come closest to "carving nature at its joints" is something that only the future will show. What matters for the present is that the question is being asked by an increasing number of students of memory. There is no guarantee, of course, that just by asking the question we will get an answer that is acceptable to science. What is absolutely guaranteed, however, is that we will not get the answer unless we pose the question. We cannot solve puzzles that do not exist.

## NOTES

### EDITOR'S NOTE

This article is based on a Distinguished Scientific Contribution Award address presented at the meeting of the American Psychological Association, Toronto, Canada, August 26, 1984.

Award addresses, submitted by award recipients, are pub-lished as received except for minor editorial changes designed to maintain *American Psychologist* format. This reflects a policy of recognizing distinguished award recipients by eliminating the usual editorial review process to provide a forum consistent with that employed in delivering the award address.

### AUTHOR'S NOTE

This work was supported by the Natural Sciences and Engineering Research Council of Canada (Grant No. A8632) and by a Special Research Program Grant from the Connaught Fund, University of Toronto. I would like to thank Fergus Craik and Daniel Schacter for their comments on the article and Janine Law for help with library research and the preparation of the manuscript.

## REFERENCES

Anderson, J. R., & Bower, G. H. (1972). Recognition and retrieval processes in free recall. *Psychological Review, 79,* 97–123.

Anderson, J. R., & Ross, B. H. (1980). Evidence against a semantic-episodic distinction. *Journal of Experimental Psychology: Human Learning and Memory, 6,* 441–465.

Baddeley, A. (1984). Neuropsychological evidence and the semantic/episodic distinction. *Behavioral and Brain Sciences, 7,* 238–239.

Bartlett, F. C. (1932). *Remembering: A study in experimental and social psychology.* Cambridge, MA: University Press.

Bransford, J. D., McCarrell, N. S., Franks, J. J., & Nitsch, K. E. (1977). Toward unexplaining memory. In R. Shaw & J. Bransford (Eds.), *Perceiving, acting and knowing* (pp. 431–466). Hillsdale, NJ: Erlbaum.

Broadbent, D. E., & Broadbent, M. H. (1975). The recognition of words which cannot be recalled. In P. M. A. Rabbitt & S. Dornic (Eds.), *Attention and performance* (Vol. 5, pp. 575–590). New York: Academic Press.

Broadbent, D. E., & Broadbent, M. H. (1977). Effects of recognition on subsequent recall: Comments on "Determinants of recognition and recall: Accessibility and generation" by Rabinowitz, Mandler, and Patterson. *Journal of Experimental Psychology: General, 106,* 330–335.

Cermak, L. S., & O'Connor, M. (1983). The anterograde and retrograde retrieval ability of a patient with amnesia due to encephalitis. *Neuropsychologia, 21,* 213–234.

Chandler, C. (1983). *Does retrieval strategy determine the relation between episodic recognition and semantic priming?* Unpublished master's thesis, University of Toronto, Toronto, Canada.

Claparède, E. (1911). Reconnaissance et moiite. [Recognition and me-ness]. *Archives de Psychologie, 11,* 79–90. (English translation in D. Rapaport [Ed. and Trans.], *Organization and pathology of thought,* 1951, New York: Columbia University Press.)

Cohen, N. J. (1984). Preserved learning capacity in amnesia: Evidence for multiple memory systems. In L. Squire & N. Butters (Eds.), *Neuropsychology of memory* (pp. 83–103). New York: Guilford Press.

Cohen, N. J., & Squire, L. R. (1980). Preserved learning and retention of pattern analyzing skill in amnesia: Dissociation of knowing how and knowing that. *Science*, *210*, 207–209.

Craik, K. (1943). *The nature of explanation*. Cambridge, MA: University Press.

Craik, F. I. M. (1983). On the transfer of information from temporary to permanent memory. *Philosophical Transactions of the Royal Society London*, *B302*, 341–359.

Craik, F. I. M. (in press). Paradigms in human memory research. In L.-G. Nilsson & T. Archer (Eds.), *Perspectives in learning and memory*. Hillsdale, NJ: Erlbaum.

Dominowski, R. L., & Ekstrand, B. R. (1967). Direct and associative priming in anagram solving. *Journal of Experimental Psychology*, *74*, 84–86.

Dretske, F. (1982). The informational character of representations. *Behavioral and Brain Sciences*, *5*, 376–377.

Ellis, A. W., & Collins, A. F. (1983). *Repetition priming of word fragment completion is modality-specific and independent of conscious episodic memory: A replication and extension of Tulving, Schacter, and Stark (1982)*. Unpublished manuscript, University of Lancaster, Lancaster, U.K.

Engelien, G. (1971). *Der Begriff der Klassifikation* [The concept of classification]. Hamburg: Helmut Buske Verlag.

Glisky, E., Schacter, D. L., & Tulving, E. (1984, August). *Vocabulary learning in amnesic patients: Method of vanishing cues*. Paper presented at the meeting of the American Psychological Association, Toronto, Canada.

Graf, P., & Schacter, D. L. (in press). Implicit and explicit memory for new associations in normal and amnesic subjects. *Journal of Experimental Psychology: Learning, Memory and Cognition*.

Hayes-Roth, F., Klahr, P., & Mostow, D. J. (1980, May). *Knowledge acquisition, knowledge programming, and knowledge refinement* (Report No. R–2540-NSF). Santa Monica, CA: Rand Corporation.

Herrmann, D. J. (1982). The semantic-episodic distinction and the history of long-term memory typologies. *Bulletin of the Psychonomic Society*, *20*, 207–210.

Herrmann, D. J., & Harwood, J. R. (1980). More evidence for the existence of separate semantic and episodic stores in long-term memory. *Journal of Experimental Psychology: Human Learning and Memory*, *6*, 467–478.

Hintzman, D. L. (1984). Episodic versus semantic memory: A distinction whose time has come—and gone? *Behavioral and Brain Sciences*, *7*, 240–241.

Hirsh, R. (1974). The hippocampus and contextual retrieval of information from memory: A theory. *Behavioral Biology*, *12*, 421–444.

Iversen, S. D. (1976). Do hippocampal lesions produce amnesia in animals? *International Review of Neurobiology*, *119*, 1–49.

Jablonski, E. M., & Mueller, J. H. (1972). Anagram solution as a function of instructions, priming, and imagery. *Journal of Experimental Psychology*, *94*, 84–89.

Jacoby, L. L. (1983a). Perceptual enhancement: Persistent effects of an experience. *Journal of Experimental Psychology: Learning, Memory, and Cognition*, *9*, 21–38.

Jacoby, L. L. (1983b). Remembering the data: Analyzing interactive processes in reading. *Journal of Experimental Psychology: General*, *22*, 485–508.

Jacoby, L. L., & Dallas, M. (1981). On the relationship between autobiographical memory and perceptual learning. *Journal of Experimental Psychology: General*, *110*, 306–340.

Jacoby, L. L., & Witherspoon, D. (1982). Remembering without awareness. *Canadian Journal of Psychology*, *36*, 300–324.

Johnson, M. K. (1983). A multiple-entry, modular memory system. In G. H. Bower (Ed.), *The psychology of learning and motivation* (Vol. 17, pp. 81–123). New York: Academic Press.

Kihlstrom, J. F. (1980). Posthypnotic amnesia for recently learned material: Interactions with "episodic" and "semantic" memory. *Cognitive Psychology*, *12*, 227–251.

Kihlstrom, J. F. (1984). A fact is a fact is a fact. *Behavioral and Brain Sciences*, *7*, 243–244.

Kinsbourne, M., & Wood, F. (1975). Short-term memory processes and the amnesic syndrome. In D. Deutsch & J. A. Deutsch (Eds.), *Short-term memory* (pp. 258–291). New York: Academic Press.

Kinsbourne, M., & Wood, F. (1975). Short-term memory processes and the amnesic syndrome. In D. Deutsch & J. A. Deutsch (Eds.), *Short-term memory* (pp. 258–291). New York: Academic Press.

Kinsbourne, M., & Wood, F. (1982). In L. S. Cermak (Ed.), *Human memory and amnesia*. Hillsdale, NJ: Erlbaum.

Kintsch, W. (1970). Models for free recall and recognition. In D. A. Norman (Ed.), *Models of human memory* (pp. 333–374). New York: Academic Press.

Klatzky, R. L. (1984). Armchair theorists have more fun. *Behavioral and Brain Sciences*, *7*, 244.

Kohler, I. (1962). Experiments with goggles. *Scientific American*, *206*, 62–72.

Lachman, R., & Naus, M. J. (1984). The episodic/semantic continuum in an evolved machine. *Behavioral and Brain Sciences*, *7*, 244–246.

Lieury, A. (1979). La memoire episodique est-elle emboitee dans la memoire semantique? [Is episodic memory embedded in semantic memory?] *L'Annee Psychologique*, *79*, 123–142.

Light, L. L., Singh, A., & Capps, J. L. (1984). *The dissociation of memory and awareness in young and older adults*. Manuscript submitted for publication.

Loftus, G. R. (1978). On interpretation of interactions. *Memory & Cognition*, *6*, 312–319.

Mandler, G. (1959). Stimulus variables and subject variables: A caution. *Psychological Review*, *66*, 145–149.

McCauley, R. N. (1984). Inference and temporal coding in episodic memory. *Behavioral and Brain Sciences*, *7*, 246–247.

McCloskey, M., & Santee, J. (1981). Are semantic memory and episodic memory distinct systems? *Journal of Experimental Psychology: Human Learning and Memory*, *7*, 66–71.

McCormack, P. D. (1972). Recognition memory: How complex a retrieval system? *Canadian Journal of Psychology*, *26*, 19–41.

McKoon, G., & Ratcliff, R. (1979). Priming in episodic and semantic memory. *Journal of Verbal Learning and Verbal Behavior*, *18*, 463–480.

Mishkin, M., Malamut, B., & Bachevalier, J. (1984). Memories and habits: Two neural systems: In G. Lynch, J. L. McGaugh, & N. M. Weinberger, (Eds.), *The neurobiology of learning and memory* (pp. 65–77). New York: Guilford Press.

Mishkin, M., & Petri, H. L. (1984). Memories and habits: Some implications for the analysis of learning and retention.

In L. Squire & N. Butters (Eds.), *Neuropsychology of memory* (pp. 287–296). New York: Guilford Press.

Mishkin, M., Ungerleider, L. G., & Macko, K. A. (1983). Object vision and spatial vision: Two cortical pathways. *Trends in Neurosciences, 6,* 414–417.

Mooney, C. (1956). Closure with negative after-images under flickering light. *Canadian Journal of Psychology, 10,* 191–199.

Moore, J. W. (1979). Information processing in space-time by the hippocampus. *Physiological Psychology, 7,* 224–232.

Moscovitch, M. (1982). Multiple dissociations of function in amnesia. In L. S. Cermak (Ed.); *Human memory and amnesia* (pp. 337–370). Hillsdale, NJ: Erlbaum.

Oakley, D. A. (1981). Brain mechanisms of mammalian memory. *British Medical Bulletin, 37,* 175–180.

Oakley, D. A. (1983). The varieties of memory: A phylogenetic approach. In A. Mayes (Ed.), *Memory in animals and humans* (pp. 20–82). Wokingham, England: Van Nostrand Reinhold.

Ogilvie, J. C., Tulving, E., Paskowitz, S., & Jones, G. V. (1980). Three-dimensional memory traces: A model and its application to forgetting. *Journal of Verbal Learning and Verbal Behavior, 19,* 405–415.

O'Keefe, J., & Nadel, L. (1978). *The hippocampus as a cognitive map.* Oxford: Clarendon Press.

Olton, D. S. (1984). Comparative analysis of episodic memory. *Behavioral and Brain Sciences, 7,* 250–251.

Olton, D. S. (in press). Learning and memory: Neural and ethological approaches to its classification. In L.-G. Nilsson & T. Archer (Eds.), *Perspectives in learning and memory.* Hillsdale, NJ: Erlbaum.

Olton, D. S., Becker, J. T., & Handelmann, G. E. (1979). Hippocampus, space, and memory. *Behavioral and Brain Sciences, 2,* 313–365.

Parker, E. S., Schoenberg, R., Schwartz, B. L., & Tulving, E. (1983, November). *Memories on the rising and falling blood alcohol curve.* Paper presented at the meeting of the Psychonomic Society, San Diego, CA.

Parkin, A. (1982). Residual learning capability in organic amnesia. *Cortex, 18,* 417–440.

Pribram, K. H. (1984). Brain systems and cognitive learning processes. In H. L. Roitblat, T. G. Bever, & H. S. Terrace (Eds.), *Animal cognition* (pp. 627–656). Hillsdale, NJ: Erlbaum.

Rabinowitz, J. C., Mandler, G., & Patterson, K. E. (1977). Determinants of recognition and recall: Accessibility and generation. *Journal of Experimental Psychology: General, 106,* 302–329.

Roediger, H. L. III (1984). Does current evidence from dissociation experiments favor the episodic/semantic distinction? *Behavioral and Brain Sciences, 7,* 252–254.

Rozin, P. (1976). The psychobiological approach to human memory. In M. R. Rosenzweig & E. L. Bennett (Eds.), *Neural mechanisms of learning and memory* (pp. 3–46). Cambridge, MA: MIT Press.

Ruggiero, F. T., & Flagg, S. F. (1976). Do animals have memory? In D. L. Medin, W. A. Roberts, & R. T. Davis, (Eds.), *Processes of animal memory* (pp. 1–19). Hillsdale, NJ: Erlbaum.

Rumelhart, D. E., & Norman, D. A. (1978). Accretion, tuning, and restructuring: Three modes of learning. In J. W. Cotton & R. Klatzky (Eds.), *Semantic factors in cognition* (pp. 37–53). Hillsdale, NJ: Erlbaum.

Schacter, D. L., Harbluk, J. L., & McLachlan, D. R. (1984). Retrieval without recollection: An experimental analysis of source amnesia. *Journal of Verbal Learning and Verbal Behavior, 23,* 593–611.

Schacter, D. L., McLachlan, D. R., Moscovitch, M. & Tulving, E. (1984, August). *Tracking memory disorders over time.* Paper presented at the meeting of the American Psychological Association, Toronto, Ontario, Canada.

Schacter, D. L., & Moscovitch, M. (1984). Infants, amnesics, and dissociable memory systems. In M. Moscovitch (Ed.), *Infant memory* (pp. 173–216). New York: Plenum.

Schacter, D. L., & Tulving, E. (1982). In R. L. Isaacson & N. E. Spear (Eds.), *Expression of knowledge* (pp. 33–65). New York: Plenum.

Schiller, F. (1952). Consciousness reconsidered. *Archives of Neurology and Psychiatry, 67,* 199–227.

Seamon, J. G. (1984). The ontogeny of episodic and semantic memory. *Behavioral and Brain Sciences, 7,* 254.

Shoben, E. J., Wescourt, K. T., & Smith, E. E. (1978). Sentence verification, sentence recognition, and the semantic-episodic distinction. *Journal of Experimental Psychology: Human Learning and Memory, 4,* 304–317.

Spear, N. E. (1984). Behaviors that indicate memory: Levels of expression. *Canadian Journal of Psychology, 38,* 348–367.

Squire, L. R., & Cohen, N. J. (1984). Human memory and amnesia. In G. Lynch, J. L., McGaugh, & N. M. Weinberger (Eds.), *The neurobiology of learning and memory* (pp. 3–64). New York: Guilford Press.

Tiberghien, G. (1984). Just how does ecphory work? *Behavioral and Brain Sciences, 7,* 255–256.

Tulving, E. (1958). The relation of visual acuity to convergence and accommodation. *Journal of Experimental Psychology, 55,* 530–534.

Tulving, E. (1976). Ecphoric processes in recall and recognition. In J. Brown (Ed.), *Recall and recognition* (pp. 361–371). London, England: Wiley.

Tulving, E. (1979). Memory research: What kind of progress? In L. G. Nilsson (Ed.), *Perspectives on memory research: Essays in honor of Uppsala University's 500th anniversary* (pp. 19–34). Hillsdale, NJ: Erlbaum.

Tulving, E. (1983). *Elements of episodic memory.* New York: Oxford University Press.

Tulving, E. (1984a). Multiple learning and memory systems. In K. M. J. Lagerspetz & P. Niemi (Eds.), *Psychology in the 1990's* (pp. 163–184). North Holland: Elsevier Science Publishers B. V.

Tulving, E. (1984b). Precis of elements of episodic memory. *Behavioral and Brain Sciences, 7,* 223–268.

Tulving, E. (1985). Memory and consciousness. *Canadian Psychology, 26,* 1–12.

Tulving, E. (in press). On the classification problem in learning and memory. In L.-G. Nilsson & T. Archer (Eds.), *Perspectives on learning and memory.* Hillsdale, NJ: Erlbaum, in press.

Tulving, E., Schacter, D. L., & Stark, H. (1982). Priming effects in word-fragment completion are independent of recognition memory. *Journal of Experimental Psychology: Human Learning and Memory, 8,* 336–342.

Ungerleider, L. G., & Mishkin, M. (1982). Two cortical visual systems. In D. J. Ingle, M. A. Goodale, & R. J. W. Mansfield (Eds.), *Analysis of visual behavior* (pp. 549–586). Cambridge, MA: MIT Press.

Warrington, E. K. (1981). Neuropsychological evidence for multiple memory systems. *Acta Neurologica Scandinavica, 64*(Suppl. 89), 13–19.

Warrington, E. K., & Weiskrantz, L. (1970). The amnesia syndrome: Consolidation or retrieval? *Nature, 228,* 628–630.

Warrington, E. K., & Weiskrantz, L. (1974). The effect of prior learning on subsequent retention in amnesic patients. *Neuropsychologia, 12,* 419–428.

Warrington, E. K., & Weiskrantz, L. (1982). Amnesia: A disconnection syndrome? *Neuropsychologia, 20,* 233–248.

Watkins, M. J., & Gardiner, J. (1979). An appreciation of generate-recognize theory of recall. *Journal of Verbal Learning and Verbal Behavior, 18,* 687–704.

Weiskrantz, L. (1980). Varieties of residual experience. *Quarterly Journal of Experimental Psychology, 32,* 365–386.

Weiskrantz, L., Warrington, E. K., Sanders, M. D., & Marshall, J. (1974). Visual capacity in the hemianopic field following a restricted occipital ablation. *Brain, 97,* 709–728.

Wolters, G. (1984). Memory: Two systems or one system with many subsystems? *Behavioral and Brain Sciences, 7,* 256–257.

Wood, F., Ebert, V., & Kinsbourne, M. (1982). The episodic-semantic distinction in memory and amnesia: Clinical and experimental observations. In L. S. Cermak (Ed.), *Human memory and amnesia* (pp. 167–193). Hillsdale, NJ: Erlbaum.

Wood, F., Taylor, B., Penny, R., & Stump, D. (1980). Regional cerebral bloodflow response to recognition memory versus semantic classification tasks. *Brain and Language, 9,* 113–122.

# On the Transition from Childhood Amnesia to the Recall of Personal Memories

Darryl Bruce, Angela Dolan, and Kimberly Phillips-Grant
• Saint Mary's University

When adults are asked to report and date personal memories of their pasts, they show childhood amnesia, that is, diminished recall of experiences over the childhood years. This way of demonstrating the phenomenon was supplemented in the present study with a more direct approach: Participants reported events of early childhood that they knew they had experienced (because of family stories, photographs, etc.) but did not actually remember. The resulting cumulative relative frequency distributions produced by the two methods were substantially different, with the median age of remembered events being 6.07 years and of known events, 3.20 years. We suggest that the mean of these two ages, 4.64 years, gives a good indication of when childhood amnesia is eclipsed by personal memories in adults' recall of their personal pasts.

Childhood amnesia is the impoverished recall by adults of autobiographical memories from early childhood. By autobiographical memory, we mean what Tulving (1972) referred to as *episodic memory*. Brewer (1986) recommended calling it *personal memory* and then later (Brewer, 1996), *recollective memory*. In the present report, we use these three terms interchangeably. Our particular concern was to estimate when the transition from childhood amnesia to the recollection of personal memories occurs. At what age does the hegemony of the former give way to the dominance of the latter? Although it might be thought that the question has long since been answered, consideration of the literature indicates otherwise.

There are two sets of extant data that bear on the problem. One concerns the earliest age at which adults can report personal memories. To determine this, some researchers have requested individuals to describe and date their earliest personal recollections (e.g., Dudycha & Dudycha, 1933; Kihlstrom & Harackiewicz, 1982; Mullen, 1994). Others have asked participants to report a number of experiences that occurred before a specified age (Waldfogel, 1948) or simply from childhood (Crovitz & Quina-Holland, 1976) and then to date when they happened. Yet other studies have probed memories for target events known to have taken place when the participants were of various childhood ages (e.g., Eacott & Crawley, 1998; Usher & Neisser, 1993; Winograd & Killinger, 1983). The results of these investigations indicate that although the time of the earliest personal memories of adults is variable, it tends to be somewhere between 3 and 4 years of age.

In a second set of relevant studies, researchers

have examined recall of personal memories from a range of years. In addition to the research that has focused on the childhood years, there have been a number of significant investigations of the retention of autobiographical memories over the life span (e.g., Crovitz & Schiffman, 1974; Rubin, 1982; Rubin & Schulkind, 1997; Rubin, Wetzler, & Nebes, 1986). Concerning childhood amnesia, it is research by Wetzler and Sweeney (1986) that is perhaps definitive. They documented poorer memory for events over the childhood years as compared with that predicted by an extension of a power function that describes the forgetting of personal memories from age 8 and above, at least for college students. Wetzler and Sweeney concluded that childhood amnesia is an especially useful construct for ages below 5, though judging from findings reported by Winograd and Killinger (1983), the phenomenon may extend up through age 6.

Putting together, then, the central findings from the two kinds of research—the earliest retrievable personal memories of adults are from the 4th year of life and childhood amnesia ranges up to the end of age 6—we may infer that the shift from childhood amnesia to the recollection of personal memories occurs sometime within an interval whose bounds are 3.0 and 7.0 years. But exactly where in that interval is the shift? To answer that question, it may be useful to take a psychophysical perspective and consider the transition from childhood amnesia to the availability of episodic memories as akin to an absolute threshold. In the context of a distribution of childhood memories sampled from a range of childhood years, the threshold may be taken as that age beyond which 50% of the remembered events occurred (see Usher & Neisser, 1993, for similar reasoning). In other words, the median age of such a distribution provides an estimate of when recollective memory begins to outweigh childhood amnesia. For example, the median age of a personal memory calculated from Waldfogel's (1948) data is 6.31 years. The correspondence between a threshold determined in this manner and a threshold obtained in a psychophysical procedure is, of course, not identical. A major difference is that a distribution of childhood personal memories ordinarily consists of data from different subjects. The threshold is thus a between-subjects estimate. In psychophysics, the distribution is based on a single subject,

and the threshold is therefore a within-subject estimate.

Nonetheless, the threshold analogy has an important implication, namely, that the median of a distribution of childhood personal memories is a biased estimate of the transition from childhood amnesia to remembering autobiographical experiences. The bias results from approaching the threshold only from the perspective of personal memories. A more desirable procedure would be to converge on the transition from two directions—first, by determining the median age of a distribution of childhood personal memories and, second, by determining the median age of a distribution of childhood events for which one is amnesic—and then averaging the two estimates. Such a solution is analogous to the method of limits for establishing an absolute threshold. In that method, the threshold is approached from above by diminishing a detectable stimulus to the point where it is no longer detectable (a descending series of stimuli) and from below by increasing a nondetectable stimulus until it is detectable (an ascending series). The estimates are then averaged to give a threshold value absent any directional bias.

The plan for the present study, then, was to produce two distributions of events that individuals experienced at different childhood ages. One was obtained by asking subjects to retrieve personal memories from childhood, that is, to describe events that they remembered happening, and then date them. The other was generated by asking participants to describe childhood events that they knew happened but could not remember, and then date them. The two distributions represent what is in essence the remember-know distinction that has become familiar through the efforts of Gardner (1988), Tulving (1985), and other investigators. To *remember* an event denotes an awareness or consciousness of the event as a part of one's personal past. To *know* an event from one's past means that the knowledge comes from a source other than self-knowing. Hereafter, we frequently refer to these as remember and know memories, respectively. The former constitute personal recollections, and the latter may be said to belong to the phase of childhood amnesia (cf. Perner & Ruffman, 1995). An estimate of the transition from childhood amnesia to the retrievability of childhood episodic memories may be obtained by averaging the median ages of the remember and know distributions.

Implicit in our thinking is that the median age of know memories should be lower than that of remember memories. Research by Hyman, Gilstrap, Decker, and Wilkinson (1998) and Waldfogel (1948) indicates this as a likely outcome. Hyman et al. explicitly requested subjects to provide know memories; Waldfogel simply asked his subjects to designate which of the childhood events they reported were not ones they remembered but had been told about. In both investigations, childhood events known but not remembered were estimated to have occurred at an earlier age on balance than those actually recollected. This finding was not the major focus of the two studies and so was not obtained or described in a manner that permits an answer to the question posed here. Nonetheless, it provides support for anticipating that the distribution of know memories is likely to have a lower median age than that of remember memories.

## Method

Participants described two personal events from the first 8 years of their lives, one that they could recollect and one that they only knew had happened to them. After each report, they estimated how old they were at the time and then judged their confidence in their estimate. Approximately half the subjects described the remember event first and the know event second; the other half performed the tasks in the reverse sequence. Report order was alternated across successive testing sessions. Because subjects were tested individually or in pairs, departures from such alternation occasionally occurred to ensure that the two report orders were used to about the same degree as testing proceeded.

Subjects wrote their information in test booklets. On the first page after the cover sheet (which asked for some biographical information), each participant described an event (either remember or know) from his or her childhood. On the second page, the participant estimated how old he or she was at the time and gave a confidence judgment for this estimate. The third and fourth pages requested, respectively, a description of another childhood event (either know or remember) and

then an age estimate for that event and a confidence judgment. Instructions for completing each page were presented by tape recorder and appeared on the page itself. After listening to each taped segment, subjects summarized in their own words what they were to do. They did not turn any pages of the test booklets until told by the experimenter to do so.

Participants were told that the personal events they reported should be from the first 8 years of their lives. Each experience was to be briefly described (2–4 sentences) and was to be something that could be written in the form "such and such happened to me at such and such a place at such and such a time" (cf. Rubin, 1982). For the remember memory, the instructions requested an event that was

> a personal recollection. In other words, you actually remember the occurrence of the event. It is a personal memory. A personal memory is one in which you are able to become consciously aware again of some aspects of the event, of what happened, or of what you experienced at the time. Perhaps you have an image of the event or you can reexperience one or more specific details about its occurrence.

In the case of a know memory, the participant was instructed to relate an event that

> you know happened, but it is not a personal memory. In other words, you know the event occurred but you cannot consciously recollect any aspect of the event's occurrence, of what happened, or of what you experienced at the time. Instead, your knowledge of the event is based on an external source of information, perhaps your parents and/or other family members, friends, pictures, photo albums, diaries, or family stories.

After completing each report, subjects turned to the next page, which featured a horizontal 8-in. time line. Major ticks appeared at the left end of the line and at 1-in. intervals thereafter. Below the line, the ticks were labeled from "0" to "8." The phrase "Age (in years) at time of event" appeared below the numbers. Minor ticks, which were not labeled, occurred every 0.25 in. (quarter-year intervals). The subjects were instructed to mark a vertical line intersecting the time axis at the age they thought they were when the event just reported had happened. If a line was drawn between two tick marks, the estimate was taken as the lower bound of the interval. Otherwise, a tick mark through which a vertical line passed gave the subject's age directly. Individuals were not told in advance that they would be required to give an age estimate after describing a childhood event, though in reporting the second of their two events, it seems likely that they would have anticipated having to do so. After dating an event, subjects checked one of five statements (from "not at all sure" to "certain") to indicate how confident they were in their estimate.

At the conclusion of testing, the experimenter asked participants for permission to contact their parents or other people who might authenticate the events they had reported and verify how old they were at the time. Letters were sent to the appropriate persons, asking them to verify the event descriptions and to make corrections or additions as necessary. Each recipient was also asked to estimate the age of the participant when each event occurred, using the same time line that subjects had used for that purpose.

A total of 113 introductory psychology students were tested. The data of 18 were rejected for a variety of reasons. The main one was that participants reported repetitive childhood experiences ($n = 12$), thereby rendering dating problematic. It may be noted, too, that we decided in advance that if individuals reported the fact of being born as a know event, we would not include their data. One subject did so and is 1 of the group of 18 who were excluded from the sample. The findings, then, are based on the reports of the remaining 95 subjects—70 females and 25 males. Their ages ranged from 18.3 to 33.5 years, with a median of 20.6 years. Participants received course bonus points for their service.

## Results

### Age Estimates and Confidence Judgments

Judged mean age was significantly younger for know events, 3.35 years ($SD = 1.86$), than for remember events, 5.85 years ($SD = 1.49$), $F(1, 93) = 104.79$, $MSE = 2.86$, $p < .001$. Neither the order in which the two childhood events were reported

nor the interaction of order and type of event had a statistically reliable effect on estimated age, $F(1, 93) < 1$ and $F(1, 93) = 1.63$, $MSE = 2.86$, $p > .05$, respectively. Accordingly, we ignored report order in constructing the distributions of remember and know events, with each distribution representing the data of 95 subjects.

When remember events were reported first and know events second, mean confidence judgments were 4.00 ($SD = 0.94$) for remember events and 3.17 ($SD = 1.18$) for know events (higher numbers indicate greater confidence). When events were reported in the reverse order, the comparable means were 4.00 ($SD = 1.14$) and 3.94 ($SD = 1.05$). Analysis of variance indicated a statistically significant interaction between type of event and order of report, $F(1, 93) = 8.00$, $MSE = 0.87$, $p < .01$. A simple effects analysis confirmed that participants were reliably less confident in their age estimates for know events than for remember events only when the know events were reported second, $F(1, 93) = 18.09$, $MSE = 0.87$, $p < .001$.

### Validity of Event Reports and Age Estimates

Seventy-six subjects permitted us to write individuals—typically their parents—to validate the content of the reported events and the age of the subjects when the events occurred. Fifty-seven replies were received. Of these, 2 indicated that the know events described were repetitive happenings. The data from the corresponding subjects were therefore excluded (these subjects are included in the 12 instances mentioned earlier of subjects whose data were rejected for this reason). The final tally, then, was 55 replies to 74 mailings, a return rate of 74% relative to letters sent out and 58% relative to the total number of subjects who provided usable data.

Of the 55 remember events, parents judged 49 to have happened as described and 2 to have occurred save for minor differences in the details. They had no knowledge of the remaining 4 events. For the 55 know memories, the corresponding frequencies were 45, 9, and 1. In sum, parents largely agreed with the event descriptions their children provided.

Parents' mean estimates of their children's ages at the time of the events were 5.71 years ($SD = 1.76$) for 50 remember events and 3.05 years ($SD$

= 1.86) for 53 know events. (Parents did not give estimates for events they did not know happened, and one parent neglected to date both reported events.) The comparable estimates by participants were 5.55 years ($SD = 1.54$) and 3.26 years ($SD = 1.92$). The differences between the corresponding means for parents and children were not statistically significant, $F(1, 98) < 1$ and $F(1, 104) < 1$, respectively.

Because most of the event descriptions contained an indication of how old subjects were at the time—an age was stated or an otherwise strong cue was provided—it is possible that parents were biased in making their age assessments. However, a comparison of the mean estimates of parents and children for only those remember ($n = 16$) and know ($n = 20$) events whose descriptions contained no information about age also showed that the means of parents and children did not differ significantly, both $Fs < 1$.

## Content of Events

We conducted a content analysis of the events along the lines of that reported by Mullen (1994, Experiment 3). The following descriptive categories were used: topic, location, affect, and people

involved. This analysis uncovered few differences between remember and know events, and those differences found lent credence to the distinction: Thus, in keeping with the estimated later occurrence of remember events compared with know events, a somewhat greater proportion of remember events than know events took place out-of-doors—.44 versus .23—and know events never contained direct descriptions of affect whereas .34 of the remember events did.

## Comparison with Prior Findings

As in Waldfogel's (1948) research, subjects in the present investigation were asked to describe experiences from the first 8 years of their lives. Hence, it is of interest how closely the estimated ages of personal memories in the present study parallel those observed by Waldfogel. His subjects gave an age at the time of each event in whole years (i.e., 4 years old, 5 years old, etc.), and he reported the data in 1-year intervals (i.e., 4–5, 5–6, etc.). For comparison purposes, the current data were categorized in the same way. Figure 24.1 graphs the cumulative relative frequency distribution of personal memories as a function of age for each study. The number of recollective memories

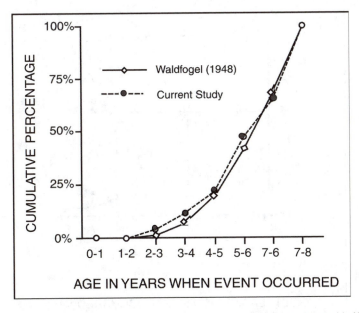

**FIGURE 24.1** ■ Cumulative relative frequency distributions for personal memories reported in Waldfogel (1948) and the current study.

on which the two functions are based differs widely—95 in the present study and 6,487 in Waldfogel's research (to secure so many observations, Waldfogel tested 124 subjects on two separate occasions and obtained slightly more than 52 different remembered events on average from each subject). Nevertheless, it is evident that the functions are remarkably similar.

## Distributions of Remember and Know Memories

Cumulative relative frequency distributions of remember and know memories appear in Figure 24.2. The data are plotted in quarter-year intervals. The distributions are graphed in a manner that illustrates the implication of each. Thus, the percentages of know events are cumulated backward from age 8 to age 0 and illustrate the decline of childhood amnesia with increasing age. The percentages of remember events are cumulated forward from age 0 to age 8 and indicate the increased recallability of childhood experiences as age increases.

The horizontal line in Figure 24.2, drawn from the 50% value on the $y$-axis, intersects each function at what may be considered a threshold. The

perpendicular lines that intersect the $x$-axis show that the thresholds differ markedly for the two functions. The median was 3.20 years for the know distribution and 6.07 years for the remember distribution. The arithmetic average of the two, 4.64 years, may be taken as an estimate of when childhood amnesia begins to be outweighed by the retrievability of personal memories.

## Discussion

The demise of childhood amnesia has always been assessed indirectly; that is, it has been inferred from a gradual increase in the recall of personal memories from childhood beginning about age 2. The current study introduced a more direct approach—asking participants to describe and date childhood events that they could not recollect but knew they had experienced as the result of knowledge from sources other than self-knowing. The procedure appears to be a viable one. Moreover, it indicates that indirect estimates overstate the duration of childhood amnesia. Seen from the perspective of childhood events that are merely known to have happened, childhood amnesia appears to wane earlier than is suggested by functions de-

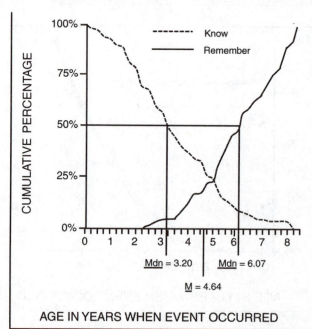

**FIGURE 24.2** ■ Cumulative relative frequency distributions for know and remember events.

scribing the recall of personal memories over the childhood years.

A few caveats may be raised with regard to the present study. One concerns the finding that the median age of know events was lower than that for remember events. It could be argued that this pattern is purely an artifact of which events parents consider noteworthy and hence relate to their children. Perhaps they favor ones that occurred at a very early age in a child's life. Although this is a possibility, an equally plausible assumption, and the one made here, is that childhood events that are noteworthy in the eyes of parents and later shared with children are likely to occur at any age during childhood, but that the events adults subsequently report as known are ones they cannot recollect because of childhood amnesia.

Another reservation may be the analogy we have drawn between the psychophysical method of limits and the current remember-know procedure. We concede that the correspondence is far from complete. We also acknowledge that the analogy may have implications, though none are intended, for how people search autobiographical knowledge for the events of their childhoods. In our judgment, however, such reservations are outranked by the analogy's heuristic usefulness, which is to prompt examination of childhood amnesia from both sides of the fence—from the perspective of know events that are obscured by such amnesia as well as of remember events that are not.

What, now, of 4.64 years as an estimate of the age at which childhood amnesia yields to autobiographical recollections? It is, of course, an average, and there will be variability about that average. For example, it has been found that the age of personal memories remembered from childhood varies as a function of type of event (Usher & Neisser, 1993), age of the subject (Kihlstrom & Harackiewicz, 1982), and birth order, gender, and cultural group of the subject (Mullen, 1994). Moreover, it bears repeating that 4.64 years is an estimate of when autobiographical memories of adults gain ascendancy over childhood amnesia. Such dominance is not given by the age of the earliest recollective memory—typically between 3 and 4 years. The latter is an estimate of the onset of retrievable childhood experiences, and the two ages—transition and onset—are not the same. We note, too, that the data described here do not imply that children can be in a transitional state in which they suffer amnesia for some experiences yet have autobiographical memories for others. The findings do point to such a state of affairs in adult memories, however, a suggestion in keeping with the findings of many other investigations (e.g., Rubin & Schulkind, 1997; Usher & Neisser, 1993).

From a theoretical perspective, the estimated transition age of 4.64 years squares nicely with theories of childhood amnesia that attribute its decline to cognitive developments during the later preschool years. We refer in particular to the development of language, social, and narrative skills (e.g., Fivush & Schwarzmueller, 1998; Nelson, 1993; Pillemer, 1992), of a second memory system responsible for one's personal history (Pillemer & White, 1989), and of encoding that is consistent with adult retrieval schemes (Schachtel, 1947; Winograd & Killinger, 1983). The current findings seem especially compatible with the views of Perner and Ruffman (1995), which take as their point of departure Tulving's (1985) claim that knowledge of having experienced an event is essential for episodic memory. Perner and Ruffman presented evidence indicating that the ability to remember an event as experienced develops between 3 and 6 years of age. The implication is that childhood amnesia lasts up to age 3 and relaxes its hold between ages 3 and 6 as the capacity to encode personal events for the long run develops. The fundamental fact of the present study—the eclipse of know by remember memories around 4.5 years of age—is in accord with this idea. At the same time, the finding seems at odds with the position of Howe and Courage (1997) that "the end of infantile amnesia" (p. 499) occurs late in the 2nd year of life.

## ACKNOWLEDGMENTS

Financial support was provided by the Social Sciences and Humanities Research Council of Canada. We thank Faizal Junus and Veronica Stinson for their assistance with the collection and analysis of the data and Harry Bahrick, John Robinson, Eugene Winograd, and an anonymous reviewer for their helpful comments on an earlier version of the manuscript.

## REFERENCES

Brewer, W. F. (1986). What is autobiographical memory? In D. C. Rubin (Ed.), *Autobiographical memory* (pp. 25–49). Cambridge, England: Cambridge University Press.

Brewer, W. F. (1996). What is recollective memory? In D. C. Rubin (Ed.), *Remembering our past: Studies in autobiographical memory* (pp. 19–66). Cambridge, England: Cambridge University Press.

Crovitz, H. F., & Quina-Holland, K. (1976). Proportion of episodic memories from early childhood by years of age. *Bulletin of the Psychonomic Society, 7*, 61–62.

Crovitz, H. F., & Schiffman, H. (1974). Frequency of episodic memories as a function of their age. *Bulletin of the Psychonomic Society, 4*, 517–518.

Dudycha, G. J., & Dudycha, M. M. (1933). Some factors and characteristics of childhood memories. *Child Development, 4*, 265–278.

Eacott, M. J., & Crawley, R. A. (1998). The offset of childhood amnesia: Memory for events that occurred before age 3. *Journal of Experimental Psychology: General, 127*, 22–33.

Fivush, R., & Schwarzmueller, A. (1998). Children remember childhood: Implications for childhood amnesia. *Applied Cognitive Psychology, 12*, 455–473.

Gardner, J. M. (1988). Functional aspects of recollective experience. *Memory & Cognition, 16*, 309–313.

Howe, M. L., & Courage, M. L. (1997). The emergence and early development of autobiographical memory. *Psychological Review, 104*, 499–523.

Hyman, I. E., Jr., Gilstrap, L. L., Decker, K., & Wilkinson, C. (1998). Manipulating remember and know judgments of autobiographical memories: An investigation of false memory creation. *Applied Cognitive Psychology, 12*, 371–386.

Kihlstrom, J. F., & Harackiewicz, J. M. (1982). The earliest recollection: A new survey. *Journal of Personality, 50*, 134–148.

Mullen, M. K. (1994). Earliest recollections of childhood: A demographic analysis. *Cognition, 52*, 55–79.

Nelson, K. (1993). The psychological and social origins of autobiographical memory. *Psychological Science, 1*, 1–8.

Perner, J., & Ruffman, T. (1995). Episodic memory and autonoetic consciousness: Developmental evidence and a theory of childhood amnesia. *Journal of Experimental Child Psychology, 59*, 516–548.

Pillemer, D. B. (1992). Preschool children's memories of personal circumstances: The fire alarm study. In U. Neisser & E. Winograd (Eds.), *Affect and accuracy in recall: Studies of "flashbulb" memories* (pp. 121–137). Cambridge, England: Cambridge University Press.

Pillemer, D. B., & White, S. H. (1989). Childhood events recalled by children and adults. In H. W. Reese (Ed.), *Advances in child development and behavior: Vol. 21* (pp. 297–340). Orlando, FL: Academic Press.

Rubin, D. C. (1982). On the retention function for autobiographical memory. *Journal of Verbal Learning and Verbal Behavior, 21*, 21–38.

Rubin, D. C., & Schulkind, M. D. (1997). Distribution of important and word-cue autobiographical memories in 20-35-, and 70-year-old adults. *Psychology and Aging, 12*, 524–535.

Rubin, D. C., Wetzler, S. E., & Nebes, R. D. (1986). Autobiographical memory across the life span. In D.C. Rubin (Ed.), *Autobiographical memory* (pp. 202–221). Cambridge, England: Cambridge University Press.

Schachtel, E. G. (1947). On memory and childhood amnesia. *Psychiatry, 10*, 1–26.

Tulving, E. (1972). Episodic and semantic memory. In E. Tulving & W. Donaldson (Eds.), *Organization of memory* (pp. 381–403). New York: Academic Press.

Tulving, E. (1985). Memory and consciousness. *Canadian Psychology, 26*, 1–12.

Usher, J. A., & Neisser, U. (1993). Childhood amnesia and the beginnings of memory for four life events. *Journal of Experimental Psychology: General, 122*, 155–165.

Waldfogel, S. (1948). The frequency and affective character of childhood memories. *Psychological Monographs, 62*(4, Whole No. 291).

Wetzler, S. E., & Sweeney, J. A. (1986). Childhood amnesia: An empirical demonstration. In D. C. Rubin (Ed.), *Autobiographical memory* (pp. 191–201). Cambridge, England: Cambridge University Press.

Winograd, E., & Killinger, W. A., Jr. (1983). Relating age at encoding in early childhood to adult recall: Development of flashbulb memories. *Journal of Experimental Psychology: General, 112*, 413–422.

PART V

# Memory

## Discussion Questions

1. Why is it important to study impairments of memory? In your answer, draw upon both memory errors in normal subjects and deficits in patients.
2. Do you think implicit and explicit memory tests tap different memory systems? Why or why not?
3. Much research on memory is done in the lab using simple materials like words or pictures. Do the papers included here suggest that the results should generalize to more real-world situations? Why or why not? To aid your thinking about generalizations, you might look up the Neisser (1978) and Banaji and Crowder (1989) papers listed in the "Additional Suggested Readings" section.
4. What do you think is the relationship between perceiving (as in the pattern recognition section of this book) and encoding?
5. Roediger (2000) wrote a paper entitled "Why Retrieval Is the Key Process in Understanding Human Memory." From what you've read thus far, why do you think he might have made this assertion? Do you think one of the three memory stages (encoding, storage, retrieval) is key to understanding human memory?

## Suggested Readings

J. R. Anderson and L. J. Schooler (1991, Reflections of the environment in memory. *Psychological Science, 2,* 396–408) argued that the variables that affect memory in the lab (e.g., frequency of study) reflect important environmental variables. For example, topics covered repeatedly in the *New York Times* have a greater probability of being covered again, just as repeatedly studied lab events have a greater probability of later being retrieved.

M. H. Banaji and R. G. Crowder (1989, The bankruptcy of everyday memory. *American Psychologist, 44,* 1185–1193) argued that generalizing memory research to everyday situations may not be necessary and comes at the cost of experimental control.

G. H. Bower (1981, Mood and memory. *American Psychologist, 36,* 129–148) describes how memory is influenced by your mood at study and test. In general, memory is sensitive to a number of contextual factors, such as your physical location and physiological state. That is, memory is best when these factors are the same at test as at study.

M. K. Johnson and C. L. Raye (1981, Reality monitoring. *Psychological Review, 88,* 67–85) describe how people decide whether memories actually happened (as opposed to only being imagined).

E. F. Loftus (1993, The reality of repressed memories. *American Psychologist, 48,* 518–537) describes several alleged cases of recovered memories of sexual abuse and evaluates them from the perspective of a cognitive psychologist.

U. Neisser (1978, Memory: What are the important questions? In M. M. Gruneberg, P. E. Morris, & R. N. Skyes (Eds.), *Practical Aspects of Memory* (pp. 3–24). London: Academic Press) argued for study of more ecologically valid situations and the need to generalize memory research beyond laboratory paradigms.

H. L. Roediger (2000, Why retrieval is the key process to understanding human memory. In E. Tulving (Ed.), *Memory, Consciousness and the Brain: The Tallinn Conference* [pp. 52–75]). Philadelphia: Psychology Press) argued that retrieval is the most important of the three stages of memory processing.

D. C. Rubin (1982, On the retention function for autobiographical memory. *Journal of Verbal Learning and Verbal Behavior, 21,* 21–38) describes remembering across the life span. Contrary to the predictions of laboratory studies of forgetting over time, older adults remember a disproportionate number of personal memories from the time period corresponding to the ages of 20–30.

H. Schmolck, E. A. Buffalo, and L. R. Squire (2000, Memory distortions develop over time: Recollections of the O. J. Simpson trial verdict after 15 and 32 months. *Psychological Science, 11,* 39–45) evaluated the accuracy of people's memory for hearing the news of the O. J. Simpson trial verdict. This paper both reviews older research on so-called flashbulb memories and investigates one variable (the passage of time) that may affect their accuracy.

A. D. Wagner, D. L. Schacter, M. Rotte, W. Koutstaal, A. Maril, A. M. Anders, B. R. Rosen, and R. L. Buckner (1998, Building memories: Remembering and forgetting of verbal experiences as predicted by brain activity. *Science, 281,* 1188–1191) used brain activity during encoding of words to predict later remembering.

# Using and Accessing Pre-Existing Knowledge Structures

# Introduction to Part VI:
# Using and Accessing Pre-Existing
# Knowledge Structures

Humans have an enormous storehouse of knowledge that needs to be quickly and efficiently searched. For example, an adult is likely to have 40,000 to 50,000 distinct words in his or her vocabulary. Much information has been stored about each of these words. For example, stored information about the word *dog* likely includes its relations to many other words (e.g., a dog is a mammal, chases cats, has four legs, is furry, etc.), syntactic class (e.g., the word *dog* is most typically a noun but can take on other forms), and phonological form (e.g., *dog* has one syllable that begins with a voiced plosive). Obviously, simple words are only the tip of the iceberg; much of our knowledge consists of relations among more complex concepts. For example, you likely know that Mark Twain was a great American writer; that he was from Hannibal, Missouri; and that he wrote about such classic characters as Huckleberry Finn and Tom Sawyer.

The papers in this section present experimental approaches for understanding how humans represent and access such vast knowledge bases. The first paper by Collins and Quillian (1969) is an excellent example of the influence of computer modeling in providing testable hypotheses about knowledge representation. In particular, Quillian's dissertation in artificial intelligence suggested that an economical way to store large amounts of information about natural categories (e.g., ANIMALS, FISH, BIRDS . . . ) would be to assume a hierarchical structure, in which features are stored at the highest level that applies to all of its category members. For example, because all animals eat and have skin, these features will be stored at the Animal level, instead of being redundantly associated with each of the animals. The consequence of this type of representation is that in verifying the sentence A CANARY HAS SKIN, one first has to access that a CANARY is a BIRD and then must access the knowledge that BIRDS are ANIMALS to find the relevant feature that ANIMALS HAVE SKIN. Our intuitions might suggest that we store the relevant information directly at the CANARY level. Collins and Quillian report evidence from an ingenious experiment that provides support for the view that humans organize large amounts of information hierarchically, much like the efficient and economical framework that was developed in Quillian's artificial intelligence work. Subjects were slower to verify A CANARY HAS SKIN than A CANARY CAN SING; properties represented at the categorical level (skin) take longer to access than those represented at the concept level (singing). Although it is clear that alternative approaches to knowledge representation may better reflect human knowledge representation (e.g., Smith, Shoben & Rips, 1974), the Collins and Quillian study provided the foundation to empirically addressing and conceptualizing this fundamental issue.

The spreading activation framework of Collins and Loftus (1975) is an alternative way of conceptualizing knowledge representation. Instead of a hierarchical structure, they proposed a network of interconnected nodes representing conceptual information. Retrieval involves activation of a node,

and this activation spreads through the network to other related nodes. This spreading activation mechanism is used in many cognitive models and has face resemblance to neurons sending signals along axons to connected neurons. Motivated by the spreading activation framework, Balota and Lorch (1986) addressed the following simple issue: If activation really spreads automatically within an interconnected network, then one should find evidence of activation beyond directly related concepts. In order to test this, they used a semantic priming paradigm, in which subjects were sequentially presented with two words on a given trial and were simply asked to name aloud the second word. Some words were directly related, such as *tiger-stripes*, but others were indirectly related, such as *lion-stripes*, and some were unrelated such as *chair-stripes*. The results indicated that compared to the unrelated condition, *lion* did in fact facilitate (prime) *stripes*, albeit less so than *tiger*. This was taken as evidence that *lion* activated the concept *tiger*, and then activation spread to the target *stripes*, thereby providing support for the notion of a spread of activation beyond directly connected nodes. Interestingly, McNamara and Altarriba (1988) later found that one could find priming from *mane* to *stripes*, via both *lion* and *tiger*, suggesting that activation can spread across two intervening nodes. If one conservatively estimates that each word is directly connected to 5 other words, then one would have an explosion of 525 activated nodes every time a word is presented.

Of course, if every one of the activated nodes became consciously available, then the explosion of information would overwhelm the processing system. Fortunately, in most, and probably the vast majority of, cases, activated concepts do not become consciously available (see the Posner & Snyder, 1975, reading). Unfortunately, this can also produce a very troubling aspect of cognition. Specifically, there are instances when one attempts to retrieve something, but the activation is not sufficient to push the item over the conscious threshold. This can be a very frustrating and uneasy experience and is exemplified by the tip of the tongue (TOT) phenomenon, which was explored in the classic paper by Brown and McNeill (1966). For example, suppose you were asked to produce a word that fits the following definition: "A navigational instrument used in measuring angular distances, especially the altitude of the sun, moon, and stars at sea." You feel that you know the answer to this definition, but may not be able to retrieve the word. Interestingly, when people are in a TOT state, Brown and McNeill found that they often had partial correct information available, such as the number of syllables, the first letter of the word, and sometimes even the stress pattern. This would appear to be a situation where a representation is activated in memory, but the appropriate form of the word does not have sufficient activation to push the retrieval over threshold. The amazing observation here is that even though subjects cannot retrieve the form of the word, they appear to be sensitive to the activation of "parts" of the knowledge structure, and in fact, the degree of activation later predicts recognition of the correct form. This fractionation between partial activation in memory and the inability to retrieve the referent produces a peculiar and uneasy state of consciousness.

The final paper in this area addresses how pre-existing knowledge structures influence our memory and comprehension of new information. Bransford and Johnson's (1972) subjects studied passages that were meaningful at the sentence level, but for which it was difficult to ascertain the passages' overall messages. Consider the first few sentences from one of their passages: "The procedure is actually quite simple. First, you arrange things into different groups. Of course, one pile may be sufficient, depending on how much there is to do. If you have to go somewhere else due to lack of facilities, that is the next step." Bransford and John found that both memory and comprehension dramatically suffered when the theme was unavailable to the subjects. However, and quite amazingly, in one study, subjects doubled their memory performance when two simple words, *washing clothes*, were provided as a title before the passage was presented. Moreover, Bransford and Johnson found that it was not sufficient to receive the title after the passage was read. In this case, performance was quite comparable to a condition in which subjects never received the title. In order to provide the necessary glue to hold the sentences together, the context needed to be available as the sentences were read. This study is quite important in focusing researchers on the interaction between pre-existing higher-order conceptual information and the information available in individual sentences.

In closing, it is worth noting that there have been a number of advances in current views of knowledge representation and utilization. For example, Kintsch (1994) has developed a more formal model of comprehension performance that nicely specifies the relation between online sentence processing and higher-level knowledge structures. Moreover, recent studies suggest that concepts are represented as sets of distributed features, rather than as unitary elements (e.g., McRae, Sa, & Seidenberg, 1997). Here, one can see a resemblance to notions that are discussed in the classic papers on pattern recognition and in categorization. Finally, with the advent of large electronic databases, there have been recent attempts to define knowledge structures with respect to word co-occurrence. That is, of interest is the extent to which certain words co-occur with other words in these large databases of text (e.g., Landauer, & Dumais, 1997; Lund, Burgess, & Atchley, 1995). Clearly, the manner in which humans represent and access the rich storehouse of knowledge available continues to be a very active area of study.

## REFERENCES

Balota, D. A., & Lorch, R. F. (1986). Depth of automatic spreading activation: Mediated priming effects in pronunciation but not in lexical decision. *Journal of Experimental Psychology: Learning, Memory and Cognition, 12,* 336–345.

Bransford, J. D., & Johnson, M. K. (1972). Contextual prerequisites for understanding: Some investigations of comprehension and recall. *Journal of Verbal Learning and Verbal Behavior, 11,* 717–726.

Brown, R., & McNeill, D. (1966). The "tip-of-the-tongue" phenomenon. *Journal of Verbal Learning and Verbal Behavior, 5,* 325–337.

Collins, A. M., & Loftus, E. F. (1975). A spreading activation theory of semantic processing. *Psychological Review, 82,* 407–428.

Collins, A. M., & Quillian, M. R. (1969). Retrieval time from semantic memory. *Journal of Verbal Learning and Verbal Behavior, 8,* 240–247.

Kintsch, W. (1994). Text comprehension, memory, and learning. *American Psychologist, 49,* 294–303.

Landauer, T. K., & Dumais, S. T. (1997). A solution to Plato's Problem: The latent semantic analysis theory of acquisition, induction, and representation of knowledge. *Psychological Review, 104,* 211–240.

Lund, K., Burgess, C., & Atchley, R. A. (1995). Semantic and associative priming in high-dimensional semantic space. In Cognitive Science Society (Ed.), *Proceedings of the 17th Annual Conference of the Cognitive Science Society* (pp. 660–665). Hillsdale, NJ: Erlbaum.

McRae, K., Sa, V. R. de, & Seidenberg, M. S. (1997) On the nature and scope of featural representations of word meaning. *Journal of Experimental Psychology: General, 126,* 99–130.

McNamara, T. P., & Altarriba, J. (1988). Depth of spreading activation revisted: Semantic mediated priming occurs in lexical decisions. *Journal of Memory and Language, 27,* 545–559.

Posner, M. I., & Snyder, C. R. R. (1975). Attention and cognitive control. In R. L. Solso (Ed.), *Information processing and cognition: The Loyola Symposium* (pp. 55–85). Hillsdale, NJ: Erlbaum.

Smith, E. E., Shoben, E. J., & Rips, L. J. (1974). Structure and process in semantic memory: A featural model for semantic decision. *Psychological Review, 81,* 214–241.

# Retrieval Time from Semantic Memory[1]

Allan M. Collins and M. Ross Quillian

• Bolt Beranek and Newman, Inc., Cambridge, Massachusetts

To ascertain the truth of a sentence such as "A canary can fly," people utilize long-term memory. Consider two possible organizations of this memory. First, people might store with each kind of bird that flies (e.g., canary) the fact that it can fly. Then they could retrieve this fact directly to decide the sentence is true. An alternative organization would be to store only the generalization that *birds* can fly, and to infer that "A canary can fly" from the stored information that a canary is a bird and birds can fly. The latter organization is much more economical in terms of storage space but should require longer retrieval times when such inferences are necessary. The results of a true-false reaction-time task were found to support the latter hypothesis about memory organization.

Quillian (1967, 1969) has proposed a model for storing semantic information in a computer memory. In this model each word has stored with it a configuration of pointers to other words in the memory; this configuration represents the word's meaning. Figure 25.1 illustrates the organization of such a memory structure. If what is stored with canary is "a yellow bird that can sing" then there is a pointer to bird, which is the category name or *superset* of canary, and pointers to two *properties*, that a canary is yellow and that it can sing. Information true of birds in general (such as that they can fly, and that they have wings and feathers) need not be stored with the memory node for each separate kind of bird. Instead, the fact that a canary can fly can be inferred by retrieving that a canary is a bird and that birds can fly. Since an ostrich cannot fly, we assume this information is stored as a property with the node for ostrich, just as is done in a dictionary, to preclude the inference that

an ostrich can fly. By organizing the memory in this way, the amount of space needed for storage is minimized.

If we take this as a model for the structure of human memory, it can lead to testable predictions about retrieving information. Suppose a person has only the information shown in Figure 25.1 stored on each of the nodes. Then to decide "A canary can sing," the person need only start at the node canary and retrieve the properties stored there to find the statement is true. But, to decide that "A canary can fly," the person must move up one level to bird before he can retrieve the property about flying. Therefore, the person should require more *time* to decide that "A canary can fly" than he does to decide that "A canary can sing." Similarly, the person should require still longer to decide that "A canary has skin," since this fact is stored with his node for animal, which is yet another step removed from canary. More directly, sentences

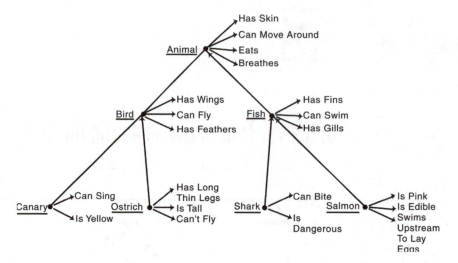

**FIGURE 25.1** ■ Illustration of the hypothetical memory structure for a 3-level hierarchy.

which themselves assert something about a node's supersets, such as "A canary is a bird," or "A canary is an animal," should also require decision times that vary directly with the number of levels separating the memory nodes they talk about.

A number of assumptions about the retrieval process must be made before predictions such as those above can be stated explicitly. First, we need to assume that both retrieving a property from a node and moving up a level in a hierarchy take a person time. Second, we shall assume that the times for these two processes are additive, whenever one step is dependent on completion of another step. This assumption is equivalent to Donders' assumption of additivity (Smith, 1968) for the following two cases: (a) When moving up a level is followed by moving up another level, and (b) when moving up a level is followed by retrieving a property at the higher level. Third, we assume that the time to retrieve a property from a node is independent of the level of the node, although different properties may take different times to retrieve from the same node. It also seems reasonable to assume that searching properties at a node and moving up to the next level occur in a parallel rather than a serial manner, and hence are not additive. However, this assumption is not essential, and our reasons for preferring it are made clear in the Discussion section.

We have labeled sentences that state property relations P sentences, and those that state superset relations S sentences. To these labels numbers are appended. These indicate the number of levels the model predicts it would be necessary to move through to decide the sentence is true. Thus, "A canary can sing" would be a PO sentence, "A canary can fly" would be a P1 sentence, and "A canary has skin" would be a P2 sentence. Similarly, "A canary is a canary" would be an SO sentence, "A canary is a bird" would be an S1 sentence, and "A canary is an animal" would be an S2 sentence.

It follows from the assumptions above that the time differences predicted for PO, P1, and P2 sentences are entirely a result of moving from one level in the hierarchy to the next. Thus, the increase in time from SO to S1 should be the same as from PO to P1 since both increases are a result of moving from level O to level 1. Likewise, the time increase from S1 to S2 should equal the time increase from P1 to P2. In fact, if we assume that the time to move from one level to the next is not dependent on which levels are involved, all the time increases (from PO to P1, P1 to P2, SO to S1, and S1 to S2) should be equal.

Recently, reaction time (RT) has been used as a measure of the time it takes people to retrieve information from memory. By constructing a large number of true sentences of the six types discussed and interspersing these with equal numbers of false sentences, we can measure the reaction time for Ss to decide which sentences are true and which are false. Thus, this method can be used to test the prediction we have derived from the model and our assumptions about the retrieval process.

A caution is in order here: Dictionary definitions are not very orderly and we doubt that human memory, which is far richer, is even as orderly as a dictionary. One difficulty is that hierarchies are not always clearly ordered, as exemplified by dog, mammal, and animal. Subjects tend to categorize a dog as an animal, even though a stricter classification would interpose the category mammal between the two. A second difficulty is that people surely store certain properties at more than one level in the hierarchy. For example, having leaves is a general property of trees, but many people must have information stored about the maple leaf directly with maple, because of the distinctiveness of its leaf. In selecting examples, such hierarchies and instances were avoided. However, there will always be $S$s for whom extensive familiarity will lead to the storing of many more properties (and sometimes supersets) than we have assumed. By averaging over different examples and different subjects, the effect of such individual idiosyncrasies of memory can be minimized.

# Method

Three experiments were run, with eight $S$s used in each experiment. The $S$s were all employees of Bolt Beranek and Newman, Inc. who served voluntarily and had no knowledge of the nature of the experiment. Because of a faulty electrical connection, only three $S$s gave usable data in Expt. 3. The same general method was used for all three experiments, except in the way the false sentences were constructed.

## APPARATUS

The sentences were displayed one at a time on the cathode ray tube (CRT) of a DEC PDP-1 computer.[2] The timing and recording of responses were under program control.[3] Each sentence was centered vertically on one line. The length of line varied from 10 to 34 characters (approximately 4–11° visual angle). The $S$ sat directly in front of the CRT with his two index fingers resting on the two response buttons. These each required a displacement of ¼ in. to trigger a microswitch.

## PROCEDURE

The sentences were grouped in runs of 32 or 48, with a rest period of approximately 1 min between runs. Each sentence appeared on the CRT for 2 sec, and was followed by a blank screen for 2 sec before the next sentence. The $S$ was instructed to press one button if the sentence was generally true, and the other button if it was generally false, and he was told to do so as accurately and as quickly as possible. The $S$ could respond anytime within the 4 sec between sentences, but his response did not alter the timing of the sentences. Each $S$ was given a practice run of 32 sentences similarly constructed.

## SENTENCES

There were two kinds of semantic hierarchies used in constructing sentences for the experiments, 2-level and 3-level. In Figure 25.1, a 2-level hierarchy might include bird, canary, and ostrich and their properties, whereas the whole diagram represents a 3-level hierarchy. A 2-level hierarchy included true PO, P1, SO and S1 sentences; a 3-level hierarchy included true P2 and S2 sentences as well. Examples of sentence sets with 2-level and 3-level hierarchies are given in Table 25.1.[4] As illustrated in Table 25.1, equal numbers of true and false sentences were always present (but in random sequence) in the sentences an $S$ read. Among both true and false sentences, there are the two general kinds: Property relations (P), and superset relations (S).

In Expt 1, each $S$ read 128 two-level sentences followed by 96 three-level sentences. In Expt 2, each $S$ read 128 two-level sentences, but different sentences from those used in Expt 1. In Expt 3, a different group of $S$s read the same 96 three-level sentences used in Expt 1. Each run consisted of sentences from only four subject-matter hierarchies.

To generate the sentences we first picked a hierarchical group with a large set of what we shall call *instances* at the lowest level. For example, baseball, badminton, etc. are instances of the superset game. Different instances were used in each sentence, because repetition of a word is known to have substantial effects in reducing RT (Smith, 1967). In constructing S1 and S2 sentences, the choice of the category name or superset

TABLE 25.1. Illustrative Sets of Stimulus Sentences

| Sentence Type | True Sentences | Sentence Type[a] | False Sentences |
|---|---|---|---|
| **Expt 1, 2-level** | | | |
| PO | Baseball has innings | P | Checkers has pawns |
| P1 | Badminton has rules | P | Ping pong has baskets |
| SO | Chess is chess | S | Hockey is a race |
| S1 | Tennis is a game | S | Football is a lottery |
| **Expt 1, 3-level** | | | |
| PO | An oak has acorns | P | A hemlock has buckeyes |
| P1 | A spruce has branches | P | A poplar has thorns |
| P2 | A birch has seeds | P | A dogwood is lazy |
| SO | A maple is a maple | S | A pine is barley |
| S1 | A cedar is a tree | S | A juniper is grain |
| S2 | An elm is a plant | S | A willow is grass |
| **Expt 2, 2-level** | | | |
| PO | Seven-up is colorless | PO | Coca-cola is blue |
| P1 | Ginger ale is carbonated | P1 | Lemonade is alcoholic |
| SO | Pepsi-cola is Pepsi-cola | SO | Bitter lemon is orangeade |
| S1 | Root beer is a soft drink | S1 | Club soda is wine |

[a] There were no distinctions as to level made for false sentences in Expt 1.

was in most cases obvious, though in a case such as the above 2-level example, sport might have been used as the superset rather than game. To assess how well our choices corresponded with the way most people categorize, two individuals who did not serve in any of the three experiments were asked to generate a category name for each S1 and S2 sentence we used, e.g., "tennis is ____." These two individuals generated the category names we used in about ¾ of their choices, and only in one case, "wine is a drink" instead of "liquid", was their choice clearly not synonymous.

In generating sentences that specified properties, only the verbs "is," "has," and "can" were used, where "is" was always followed by an adjective, "has" by a noun, and "can" by a verb. To produce the PO sentence one of the instances such as baseball was chosen that had a property (in this case innings) which was clearly identifiable with the instance and not the superset. To generate a P1 or P2 sentence, we took a salient property of the superset that could be expressed with the restriction to "is," "has," or "can." In the first example of Table 25.1, rules were felt to be a very salient property of games. Then an instance was chosen, in this case badminton, to which the P1 property seemed not particularly associated. Our assumption was that, if the model is correct, a typical S would decide whether badminton has rules or not

by the path, badminton is a game and games have rules.

In Expt 1, false sentences were divided equally between supersets and properties. No systematic basis was used for constructing false sentences beyond an attempt to produce sentences that were not unreasonable or semantically anomalous, and that were always untrue rather than usually untrue. In Expt 2, additional restrictions were placed on the false sentences. The properties of the false PO sentences were chosen so as to contradict a property of the instance itself. In example 3 of Table 25.1, "Coca-cola is blue" contradicts a property of Coca-cola, that it is brown or caramel-colored. In contrast, the properties of false P1 sentences were chosen so as to contradict a property of the superset. In the same example, alcoholic was chosen, because it is a contradiction of a property of soft drinks in general. The relation of elements in the false SO and S1 sentences can be illustrated by reference to Figure 25.1. The false SO sentences were generated by stating that one instance of a category was equivalent to another, such as "A canary is an ostrich." The false S1 sentence was constructed by choosing a category one level up from the instance, but in a different branch of the structure, such as "A canary is a fish."

The sequence of sentences the S saw was randomly ordered, except for the restriction to four hierarchies in each run. The runs were counter-balanced over *S*s with respect to the different sentence types, and each button was assigned true for half the *S*s, and false for the other half.

## Results and Discussion

In analyzing the data from the three experiments, we have used the mean RT for each *S*'s correct responses only. Error rates were on the average about 8% and tended to increase where RT increased.

### Deciding a Sentence Is True

The data from all three experiments have been averaged in Figure 25.2. To evaluate the differences shown there for true sentences, two separate analyses of variance were performed: one for the 2-level runs and one for the 3-level runs. For the 2-level data the difference between P sentences and S sentences was significant, $F(1, 60) = 19.73$, $p < .01$, the difference between levels was significant $F(1, 60) = 7.74$, $p < .01$, but the interaction

was not quite significant, $F(1, 60) = 2.06$. For the 3-level data, the difference between P and S sentences was significant, $F(1, 60) = 27.02$, $p < .01$, the difference between levels was significant, $F(2, 60) = 5.68$, $p < .01$, and the interaction was not significant, $F < 1$.

Our prediction was that the RT curves for PO, P1, and P2 sentences and for SO, S1, and S2 sentences should be two parallel straight lines. The results are certainly compatible with this prediction, except for the SO point, which is somewhat out of line. It was anticipated that presenting the entire sentence on the CRT at one time would permit the *S*s to answer the SO sentences, e.g., "A maple is a maple," by pattern matching. That they did so was substantiated by spontaneous reports from several *S*s that on the SO sentences they often did not even think what the sentence said. Overall, the underlying model is supported by these data.

It can also be concluded, if one accepts the model and disregards the SO point as distorted by pattern matching, that the time to move from a node to its superset is on the order of 75 msec, this figure being the average RT increase from PO to

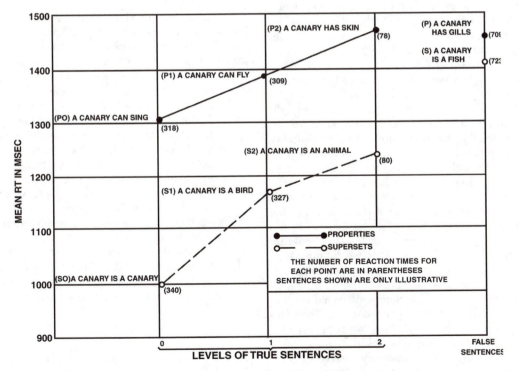

**FIGURE 25.2** ■ Average reaction times for different types of sentences in three experiments.

P1, P1 to P2, and S1 to S2. The differences between S1 and P1 and between S2 and P2, which average to about 225 msec, represent the time it takes to retrieve a property from the node at the level where we assume it is stored.

We have assumed that retrieval of properties at a node and moving up to the superset of the node are parallel processes, but this was not a necessary assumption. In actual fact the computer realization of the model completes the search for properties at a node *before* moving up one level to its superset. If the property search is assumed to be complete before moving up to the next level, then the 75 msec would have to be divided into two processes: (a) the time spent searching for properties, and (b) the time to move up to the superset. If such an assumption is made, then there is no clear prediction as to whether the increases for P sentences should parallel the increases for S sentences. If, given an S-type sentence, the *S* could dispense with process (a) above, then the slope of the curve for S sentences would be less than for P sentences; if he could not, then the prediction of two parallel lines would still hold. However, the fact that the time attributable to retrieving a property from a node is much longer than the time to move from one node to the next suggests that the processing is in fact parallel. It is unlikely that a search of all the properties at a node could be completed before moving up to the next level in less than 75 msec, *if* it takes some 225 msec actually to retrieve a property when it is found at a node. This might be reasonable if most of the 225 msec was spent in verification or some additional process necessary when the search at a node is successful, but attributing most of the 225 msec to such a process involves the unlikely assumption that this process takes much longer for P sentences than for S sentences. If it were the same for both sentence types, then it would not contribute to the difference (the 225 msec) between their RTs.

Since any other systematic differences between sentence types might affect RTs, we did three further checks. We computed the average number of letters for each sentence type and also weighted averages of the word-frequencies based on the Thorndike-Lorge (1944) general count. Then we asked four *S*s to rate how important each property was for the relevant instance or superset, e.g., how important it is for birds that they can fly. In general, we found no effects that could account for

the differences in Figure 25.2 on the basis of sentence lengths, frequency counts, or subject ratings of importance. The only exception to this is that the higher frequency of superset words such as bird and animal in the predicates of S1 and S2 sentences may have lowered the averages for S1 and S2 sentences relative to those for P sentences.

## Deciding a Sentence Is False

There are a number of conceivable strategies or processes by which a person might decide a sentence is false. All of these involve a search of memory; they fall into two classes on the basis of how the search is assumed to terminate.

### THE CONTRADICTION HYPOTHESIS

Under this hypothesis, false responses involve finding a contradiction between information stored in memory and what the statement says. For example, if the sentence is "Coca-cola is blue," the *S* searches memory until he finds a property of Coca-cola (that it is brown or caramel colored) which contradicts the sentence.

The Contradiction Hypothesis was tested by the construction of false sentences for Expt 2. We predicted that the RT increase from PO to P1 found for true sentences might also be found for false sentences. The difference found was in the right direction, but it was negligibly small (7 msec). Similarly, it was thought that if *S*s search for a contradiction, false SO sentences should produce faster times than the false S1 sentences since there is one less link in the path between the two nodes for an SO sentence. (This can be seen by comparing the path in Figure 25.1 between canary and ostrich as in SO sentences to the path between canary and fish as in S1 sentences.) The difference turned out to be in the opposite direction by 59 msec on the average, $t(7) = 2.30$, $p < .1$. If anything, one should conclude from the false SO and S1 sentences in Expt 2 that the closer two nodes are in memory, the longer it takes to decide that they are not related in a stated manner.

### THE UNSUCCESSFUL SEARCH HYPOTHESIS

This is a generalization of what Sternberg (1966) calls the "self-terminating search," one of the two models he considered with regard to his RT studies of short-term memory search. Under this hypothesis an *S* would search for information to decide that a given sentence is true, and, when the search fails, as determined by some criterion, he would respond false. One possible variation, suggested by the longer RTs for false responses, would be that *S*s search memory for a fixed period of time, responding true at any time information is found that confirms the statement is true, and responding false if nothing is found by the end of the time period. Such a hypothesis should lead to smaller standard deviations for false sentences than for true sentences, but the opposite was found for Expt 2, where it could be checked most easily.

## THE SEARCH AND DESTROY HYPOTHESIS

We developed another variation of the Unsuccessful Search Hypothesis after the Contradiction Hypothesis proved unsatisfactory and *S*s had been interrogated as to what they thought they were doing on false sentences. Under this hypothesis we assume the *S* tries to find paths through his memory which connect the subject and predicate of the sentence (e.g., the path "canary → bird → animal → has skin" connects the two parts of "A canary has skin"). Whenever he finds such a path he must check to see if it agrees with what is stated in the sentence. When the *S* has checked to a certain number of levels or "depth" (Quillian, 1967), all connections found having been rejected, the *S* will then respond false. Under this hypothesis, the times for false sentences will be longer, in general, and highly variable depending upon how many connective paths the *S* has to check out before rejecting the statement. For instance, assuming people know Coca-cola comes in green bottles, a statement such as "Coca-cola is blue" would on the average take less time than "Coca-cola is green." This is because the *S* would have to spend time checking whether or not the above path between Coca-cola and green (i.e., that its bottles are green) corresponds to the relation stated in the sentence.

This hypothesis would explain the longer times in Expt 2 for sentences such as "A canary is an ostrich" as compared with "A canary is a fish" in terms of the greater number of connections between canary and ostrich that presumably would have to be checked out. This difference in the number of connections would derive from the greater number of properties that are common to two nodes close together in the network, such as canary and ostrich, than are common to nodes further apart and at different levels, such as canary and fish.

Finding contradictions can be included in this hypothesis, as is illustrated with "Gin is wet." Here the *S* might make a connection between gin and wet through the path "gin is dry and dry is the opposite of wet." Seeing the contradiction, he rejects this as a basis for responding true, but continues to search for an acceptable path. In this example, if he searches deep enough, he will find the path "gin is liquor, and liquor is liquid, and liquid is wet" which is, in fact, what the sentence requires. The point we want to emphasize here is that even though a contradiction can be used to reject a path, it cannot be used to reject the truth of a statement.

There are certainly other possible hypotheses, and it is possible that a combination of this hypothesis with the Contradiction Hypothesis may be necessary to explain false judgments. Needless to say, the process by which a person decides that a statement is false does not seem to be very simple.

# Conclusion

In a computer system designed for the storage of semantic information, it is more economical to store generalized information with superset nodes, rather than with all the individual nodes to which such a generalization might apply. But such a storage system incurs the cost of additional processing time in retrieving information. When the implications of such a model were tested for human *S*s using well-ordered hierarchies that are part of the common culture, there was substantial agreement between the predictions and the data.

There is no clear picture that emerges as to how people decide a statement is false. Our current hypothesis, that people must spend time checking out any interpretations that are possible (see the discussion of the Search and Destroy Hypothesis), should be testable, but even corroborative evidence would not clear up many of the questions about such decisions.

The model also makes predictions for other RT tasks utilizing such hierarchies. For instance, if *S*s are given the task of deciding what common category two instances belong to, then RT should reflect the number of supersets the $S$ must move through to make the decision. (Consider fish and bird, vs. shark and bird, vs. shark and canary; see Figure 25.1). Such RT differences should parallel those in our data. Furthermore, if utilizing a particular path in retrieval increases its accessibility temporarily, then we would expect prior exposure to "A canary is a bird" to have more effect in reducing RT to "A canary can fly" than to "A canary can sing." There are many similar experiments which would serve to pin down more precisely the structure and processing of human semantic memory.

## NOTES

1. This research was supported by the Aerospace Medical Research Laboratories, Aerospace Medical Division, Air Force Systems Command, Wright-Patterson Air Force Base, Ohio, under Contract No. F33615-67-C-1982 with Bolt Beranek and Newman, Inc. and also partly by Advanced Research Projects Agency, monitored by the Air Force Cambridge Research Laboratories, under Contract No. F19628-68-C-0125.

2. Now at the University of Massachusetts, Amherst.
3. The authors thank Ray Nickerson for the use of his program and for his help in modifying it to run on BBN's PDP-1.
4. To obtain the entire set of true sentences for Expt 1 order NAPS Document NAPS-00265 from ASIS National Auxiliary Publications Service, c/o CCM Information Sciences, Inc., 22 West 34th Street, New York, New York 10001; remitting $1.00 for microfiche or $3.00 for photocopies.

## REFERENCES

Quillian, M. R. Word concepts: A theory and simulation of some basic semantic capabilities. *Behavioral Sci.*, 1967, *12,* 410–430.

Quillian, M. R. The Teachable Language Comprehender: A simulation program and theory of language. *Communications Assn. Comp. Mach.*, 1969, (In press).

Smith, E. E. Effects of familiarity on stimulus recognition and categorization. *J. Exp. Psychol.*, 1967, *74,* 324–332.

Smith, E. E. Choice reaction time: An analysis of the major theoretical positions. *Psychol. Bull.*, 1968, *69,* 77–110.

Sternberg, S. High-speed scanning in human memory. *Science*, 1966, *153,* 652–654.

Thorndike, E. L. and Lorge, I. *The Teacher's Word Book of 30,000 Words.* New York: Columbia Univ. Press, 1944.

# Depth of Automatic Spreading Activation: Mediated Priming Effects in Pronunciation but Not in Lexical Decision

David A. Balota • Washington University
Robert F. Lorch, Jr. • University of Kentucky

Lexical decision and pronunciation experiments were conducted to investigate whether activation automatically spreads beyond directly associated concepts within the memory network. Prime-target pairs were constructed such that there was a relation between the prime (e.g., *lion*) and the target (e.g., *stripes*) only through a mediating concept (e.g., *tiger*). The lexical decision results yielded facilitation of directly related priming conditions (e.g., *lion–tiger* and *tiger–stripes*); however, the mediated condition (e.g., *lion–stripes*) did not facilitate performance compared to either a neutral prime or an unrelated prime condition. In contrast, the pronunciation results yielded facilitation of both directly related and mediated priming conditions. The results were viewed as supporting the notion that activation spreads beyond directly related concepts in semantic memory. It is suggested that characteristics of the lexical decision task masked the appearance of a mediated priming effect. Implications of an automatic spread of activation beyond directly related concepts are discussed.

Spreading activation is an important explanatory construct that was developed within network theory as a fundamental memory retrieval mechanism (Anderson & Bower, 1973; Collins & Loftus, 1975; Collins & Quillian, 1969). According to this framework, concepts are represented in memory as nodes and relations are represented as associative pathways between the nodes. When part of the memory network is activated, activation spreads along the associative pathways to related areas in memory. This spread of activation serves to make these related areas of the memory network more available for further cognitive processing.

The concept of spreading activation has been a widely used explanatory construct. Theorists have argued that spreading activation is the underlying search mechanism involved in such tasks as category exemplar production (Loftus, 1973), semantic priming in lexical decisions (Neely, 1977), sentence verification (Loftus, 1973), episodic sentence and word recognition (Anderson, 1983a, 1983b), and perceptual word recognition (McClelland & Rumelhart, 1981). Moreover, spreading activation is now viewed as playing a role in reading comprehension (Foss, 1982; Kieras, 1981; Stanovich & West, 1983) and language processing (Anderson, 1976; McDonald & Hayes-Roth, 1978).

Several important properties of the activation process have been experimentally uncovered. First, the spread of activation is automatic as opposed to being under strategic control (Balota, 1983; Neely, 1977). Second, the amount of activation of a concept node is a function of the "length" of the associative pathway (a reflection of the strength of association) between that node and the source of activation (Lorch, 1982). Third, the amount of activation spreading from a given node along a pathway is a function of the strength of that pathway relative to the sum of the strengths of all paths emanating from that node (Reder & Anderson, 1980). Fourth, because concepts are assumed to be associated within a network of associations, activation may spread not only to directly related concepts but also from those concepts to concepts further in the memory network, that is, multiple steps within the network.

The "multiple-step" assumption of spreading activation theory has been particularly important in accounting for a variety of memory retrieval phenomena. For example, in accounting for category verification response latency, Collins and Quillian (1969) emphasized the number of concept nodes that activation would need to traverse within the memory network. Anderson (1976) has viewed episodic sentence recognition as a parallel spread of activation from terminal concept nodes across intervening concepts until a crucial intersecting concept is sufficiently activated. Within a similar framework, Ratcliff and McKoon (1981) have suggested that differences in asymptotic levels of activation produced by episodic primes are due to the number of intervening concepts between the prime and the target within the memory representation.

Although the multiple-step assumption is widely used, there are both conceptual and empirical reasons to challenge its validity. First, with respect to the conceptual concern, an extensive spread of activation could become unwieldy very quickly. For example, imagine a network in which each node is directly connected to only five other concept nodes. The initial step in the activation process would result in the activation of only five associates. Activation spreading from those associates would activate 25 more nodes, and a third step in the process would result in the activation of an additional 125 nodes! Realizing the potential difficulty with such a mechanism, Anderson (1976, p. 123) postulated a default dampening process where all activated concepts that are not the focus of attention revert back to their resting level of activation after some interval (see Anderson, 1983a, p. 265, for a more recent discussion of this issue).

The second concern with the multiple-step assumption is that, despite its prominence, it has not received any direct empirical support. In order to test multiple-step activation directly, it is necessary to demonstrate that the concepts that are presumably only related via multiple links do not also have a direct association. In fact, it was because of a failure to consider the possibility of direct associations that Collins and Quillian's (1969) initial test of multiple-step activation was not definitive (see Conrad, 1972; Smith, Shoben, & Rips, 1974). The only study that has attempted to eliminate direct associations (de Groot, 1983) appears to indicate that activation only spreads a single step within the memory network (i.e., "one-step" activation). Because of the importance of the de Groot study to spreading activation theory and to the present experiments, we shall describe her major results briefly.

de Groot conducted a series of semantic priming lexical decision experiments to test the depth of spreading activation. She constructed a set of triads in which there was a direct relation between the first and second word (e.g., *bull–cow*) and the second and third word (e.g., *cow–milk*) but no direct relation between the first and third word (*bull–milk*). de Groot argued that if subjects were able to make a lexical decision to *milk* more quickly in the mediated prime condition (*bull–milk*) than in the neutral prime condition (*blank–milk*), then this would suggest that activation had spread across two associative pathways from *bull* to *cow* to *milk*. Hence, this would provide evidence for multiple-step spreading activation. Based on a series of seven lexical decision experiments, de Groot concluded that activation spreads to directly related concepts but does not spread any further within the memory network.

There are several reasons to be reluctant to accept de Groot's conclusion. First, all current theories predict less priming facilitation in a mediated priming condition (*bull–milk*) than in a related priming condition (*cow–milk*). This prediction is based on the assumption that the amount of activation available at a node depends on its distance from the source of activation. Given the relatively small priming effects de Groot reports for directly related concepts (26 ms in Experiment 1); the amount of facilitation expected for the mediated condition would be quite small. Thus, with de Groot's materials, considerable power would be required to detect the small predicted effect in the mediated condition.

The second reason for questioning de Groot's conclusion is that the results of her first four experiments provided some weak support for a multiple-step activation process. Two of the experiments demonstrated reliable facilitation of response latencies in the mediated condition and all four experiments showed a tendency towards facilitation in error rates in the mediated condition. Unfortunately, there were no analyses of error rates reported.

The final point to be made regarding de Groot's results concerns her last three experiments. de Groot hypothesized that the lack of clear mediated priming effects for the initial four experiments may have been due to subjects adopting a strategy that canceled out any small effect of multiple-step activation. Specifically, she suggested that subjects in a lexical decision task conduct a postlexical access search for a relation between the prime and target words because of an implicit assumption that words appear in meaningful context and because the detection of a relation indicates that the target must be a word. If a relation is readily available (i.e., related prime condition), subjects can respond quickly that the target is a word. However, de Groot suggested that if a relation is not easily retrieved, then subjects may lose track and reprocess the material until they either make some sense out of the target in the context or reach a response deadline. If the subjects in de Groot's experiments were unable to find a relation in the mediated condition, such a rechecking strategy may have overridden a multiple-step activation process. The use of a postlexical search strategy would thus explain both the failure to observe facilitation in the mediated condition and the finding of inhibition in the unrelated prime condition.

In an attempt to prevent the postlexical access search, de Groot presented the primes too briefly for subjects to be aware of their identity. The rationale was that the primes would be unavailable for a search for a relation between the prime and target. Although priming facilitation was demonstrated for related priming conditions using this procedure (Experiments 5 and 6), there was no evidence of mediated priming (Experiment 7). However, two observations suggest that this demonstration is not definitive. First, there was again a tendency for a lower error rate in the mediated condition compared to the neutral condition, suggesting there may have been some priming in accuracy for the former condition. Second, de Groot's procedure may not have adequately provided a threshold presentation of the prime items across subjects. In fact, about half of de Groot's subjects reported that they had seen some of the primes. This is noteworthy because Dagenbach and Carr (1985) have provided evidence that related prime conditions can produce either facilitation or inhibition effects depending on the subject's actual threshold. Because thresholds were not individually determined in de Groot's study, facilitation and inhibition effects could have combined across subjects to produce the null effect in the mediated condition of the threshold priming experiment.[1]

Because of the above concerns with de Groot's study and the importance of her results to spreading activation theory, the present series of experiments was conducted to discriminate further between the one-step and multiple-step activation models. The first experiment replicated de Groot's basic design with two major changes. First, we used a different set of mediated items. One concern we had was that some of de Groot's mediated pairs were actually items involving a weak direct relation (e.g., *shepherd–wool*).[2] If so, this would increase the tendency toward mediated priming effects observed in some of de Groot's experiments. Because a test of multiple-step activation rests on the adequacy of the mediated pairs, we have taken a conservative approach and eliminated such items in the present experiments.

Our second change from de Groot's procedure was that we included a between-subjects manipulation of stimulus onset asynchrony (SOA) between the prime and the target. One group of subjects received a 250-ms prime target SOA whereas the second group received a 500-ms SOA. de Groot included only a 240-ms SOA. The 500-ms SOA in the present study was included to test whether one might find evidence of multiple-step activation at a longer SOA. Because activation must traverse an additional link in the mediated conditions, one might need more time for prime processing (Collins & Loftus, 1975; but see Ratcliff & McKoon, 1981).

The observation of interest in Experiment 1 was whether subjects would be faster to recognize a target word *(stripes)* when preceded by an indirectly related word *(lion)* than when preceded by a neutral or unrelated word. Because *lion* and *stripes* appear to be related only by their common associate *tiger*, such an effect would suggest that activation has spread from *lion* to *tiger* to *stripes*.

Finally, control Experiment 1a tested priming effects for the first link in our mediated pairs (i.e., from *lion* to *tiger*). As noted above, it is important to establish strong direct priming across the first links in the triads because the degree of activation of the first link sets a theoretical limit on the observed priming across both links in the triads.

## Lexical Decision Experiments

### Method

#### SUBJECTS

Twenty undergraduate students participated in Experiment 1a and 64 students participated in Experiment 1. Of the 32 subjects in each SOA condition of Experiment 1, 20 subjects were recruited from the University of Kentucky and 12 subjects were recruited from Iowa State University. The assignment of lists and conditions to subjects was completely counterbalanced at both universities. Subjects in the control Experiment 1a were recruited from the University of Kentucky. All subjects participated in the experiments in partial fulfillment of a course requirement.

#### APPARATUS

Stimulus presentation and data collection were controlled by an Apple II plus computer that was interfaced with a Zenith data systems video monitor. The computer included a Thunderclock tim-

ing board that was used for obtaining millisecond reaction times.[3] Subjects made word/nonword responses by pressing either the "1" or "0" key on the Apple keyboard.

#### MATERIALS

The critical stimuli were based on a set of 56-word triads. In each triad, the first and second words *(lion–tiger)* were directly related and the second and third words *(tiger–stripes)* were directly related, but the first and third words *(lion–stripes)* were associated only indirectly by their relations to the second word.

Because of the importance of developing an adequate set of items, the above characterization of the triads was validated in two ways. First, an independent sample of 115 psychology undergraduates produced associates to the mediated prime words (e.g., *lion*). Each student produced eight associates to each of 14 mediated prime words, which were randomly selected from the original set of 56. The assumption underlying this task is that if the mediated target (e.g., *stripes*) does not occur across associates given either within a subject or across subjects, then it is highly unlikely that there is a direct association from the mediated prime to the mediated target. One potential problem with this task is the possibility of subjects chaining associates. That is, a subject may produce *tiger* to *lion* and then produce *stripes* to *tiger*. The instructions given to the subjects emphasized the importance of avoiding such chains and that it was crucial that subjects always produce associates only to the first item.

The results of this production study indicated that out of the original 56 triads in the target set, there were eight cases in which the mediated target was produced to the mediated prime item (e.g., *rain* was produced as an associate to *dry*). In each of the cases in which the mediated target was produced there was some potential that the subject chained their responses, because the mediating word (e.g., *wet*) was produced before the mediated target in every case. Moreover, there were only two cases that produced the mediated target to the mediated prime more than once. However, because of the importance of obtaining a set of items in which there was no direct relation between the mediated prime and target, we adopted a conservative approach and eliminated these eight items from our target pool. Thus, all reported data analyses are based on the remaining 48 items. It is important to note that the mediated targets were never produced for these 48 items despite a total of 12,880 associates produced across our subjects. The Appendix displays the critical 48 triads.

Our second attempt to validate our characterization of the triads involved an independent sample of 149 psychology students. The students were asked to rate the degree of association for word pairs constructed from the triads. Each subject was presented a list of 65 word pairs to rate on a 5-point scale, ranging from *strongest association* (5) to *no association* (1). The 65 word pairs consisted of: 9 practice items; 14 mediated pairs constructed from the first and third words of the same triads (e.g., *lion–stripes*); 14 related first-link pairs constructed from the first two words of the same triads (*lion–tiger*); 14 related second-link pairs constructed from the last two words of the same triads (*tiger–stripes*); and 14 unrelated pairs constructed by randomly pairing the second and third words of different triads (e.g., *fantasy–stripes*). Four different lists of 65 word pairs were constructed such that a given triad was represented once on a list but occurred in each pairing condition across lists.

The results of the rating experiment confirmed our expectations for the 48 critical triads that were selected based on the production study. Both the related first-link pairs and the related second-link pairs were rated as being highly associated ($M = 4.19$, $SD = .35$ for the first-link related pairs; $M = 4.01$, $SD = .43$ for the second-link related pairs). The mediated pairs were rated as considerably lower ($M = 2.05$, $SD = .58$). The unrelated pairs were rated the lowest ($M = 1.41$, $SD = .41$). Although the mediated pairs were rated as somewhat more associated than the unrelated pairs, we attribute this to subjects occasionally finding the mediated association for these items in the untimed rating task. We will later discuss speeded response latency data, which also suggests that there was no direct relation for the mediated pairs.

Although the data for only the 48 triads that did not produce any evidence of a direct relation for the mediated pairs will be reported, all original 56 triads were used to construct four types of prime-target pairs for the lexical decision experiments.[4] The third words in the triads served as the target

words in all priming conditions. The related condition paired the second and third words of the same triads (e.g., *tiger–stripes*). The mediated condition paired the first and third words of the same triads (e.g., *lion–stripes*). The neutral condition used the word *blank* as the prime word (see de Groot, Thomassen, & Hudson, 1982). The unrelated condition paired target words with primes selected from other triads. For a given target, the pool of potential unrelated primes consisted of the related prime words of the other 55 triads and of primes for nonword trials. This meant that there was an 11% probability for a prime to be repeated once for a given subject, so a restriction was placed on the sampling process to prevent a given prime from occurring in the same trial block. The random pairing of prime and target words for the unrelated condition was done independently for each subject.

In addition to the critical word pairs, stimuli were constructed for nonword trials. For each word target, a nonword was generated that matched it in number of letters (the range was three to nine letters). Nonwords were constructed by changing two, three, or four letters in a middle- to high-frequency word. Nonwords were constructed from words that did not serve as stimuli in the experiment. All nonwords were pronounceable. Each nonword was paired with a word prime that did not have any obvious relation to the nonword.

After the stimuli were constructed, they were assigned to four different lists that differed in the assignment of target stimuli to priming conditions. A target word or nonword occurred only once within a given list; each target occurred in each priming condition once across the four lists. Each list consisted of three blocks of word pairs. The initial block of 48 practice items included: 6 neutrally primed nonwords; 18 word-primed nonwords; 6 neutrally primed words; 6 word targets paired with related primes; and 12 word targets paired with unrelated primes. The two test blocks of experimental items each began with 4 buffer items and contained an additional 28 word pairs and 28 nonword pairs. The four priming conditions were equally represented for the word trials in each test block, and there were 21 word-primed nonword trials and 7 neutrally primed nonword trials. The order of presentation of items within each block was randomized independently for each subject. Each subject received only one list.

## PROCEDURE

Subjects were instructed that they would be presented with a pair of stimuli on each of many trials. They were told that the initial stimulus in a pair would be a common English word on 75% of the trials and the word *blank* on the remaining trials. They were instructed that the second stimulus would be either a common English word or a pronounceable nonword. Subjects were told to read the first word to themselves but that their major task was to decide whether the second stimulus was a word or nonword. They were to indicate their decision by pressing the "0" key if the second stimulus was a word or the "1" key if it was not a word. Both speed and accuracy were emphasized in the instructions. The experimenter remained in the lab during the first 10–15 practice trials to insure that the subject fully understood the instructions.

The exact sequence of events on each trial was as follows: (a) a row of three asterisks separated by blank spaces was presented in the center of the screen for 360 ms; (b) a blank screen was presented for 360 ms; (c) a warning tone was presented for 140 ms; (d) a blank screen was presented for 360 ms; (e) the prime word was presented (for 200 ms for the 250 ms SOA condition in Experiment 1 and the control Experiment 1a, and 450 ms for the 500 ms SOA condition for Experiment 1); (f) a dark interval was presented for 50 ms; (g) the target word was presented until the subject pressed either one of two keys to indicate word or nonword; (h) if the subject responded incorrectly, the message "ERROR!!!" was presented until the subject pressed one of the two response keys; (i) a 3-s intertrial interval was included before the next trial.

There were three break periods in the experiments. Subjects received a 20-s break after 24 practice trials and 2-min breaks before each of the test blocks. Subjects participated individually and the experiment was conducted in a small, quiet lab room. Throughout an experimental session, the subject was seated comfortably approximately 50 cm from the video monitor.

## DESIGN

Experiment 1 was a 2 × 4 (SOA × Prime) mixed-factor design with SOA being a between-subjects factor and prime type being a within-subjects factor. Experiment 1a included only the within-subjects factor of prime type (related vs. neutral vs. unrelated).

## Results

In all experiments, an analysis of variance (ANOVA) was initially conducted on the subjects' mean performance per condition to determine if there were any main effects or interactions. Subjects were treated as the only random factor in this analysis. However, because items served in different conditions for different subjects, the error variance due to items was included in the Subject × Condition interactions and therefore the effects should also generalize across items. Planned comparisons were conducted to specify the nature of any significant main effects or interactions. Unless otherwise noted, all tests that are referred to as significant have $p$ values $< .05$.

Each subject's mean response latency was calculated for each of the conditions in both experiments. Response latencies exceeding 1 s were eliminated from all analyses. The mean outlier rate was 2.2% for Experiment 1a and 2.1% for Experiment 1.

Consider the results for Experiment 1a first. There were reliable differences in response times for the three priming conditions, $F(2, 38) = 16.81$, $MS_e = 912$. Paired comparisons indicated that responses in the related condition (mean response latency = 524 ms, error rate = 2.9%) were significantly faster than responses in both the neutral (mean response latency = 576 ms, error rate = .9%) and unrelated conditions (mean response latency = 565 ms, error rate = 3.3%). The 11-ms difference between the neutral and unrelated conditions was not reliable, $t(19) = 1.24$. There were no significant differences in error rates across the prime conditions.

In sum, the 52-ms facilitation effect observed for the related condition demonstrates a strong relation between the first and second words in the stimulus triads. This finding establishes a necessary condition for predicting mediated priming; namely, that there is considerable activation spreading at least to the second word in our triads. We will now consider the results of Experiment 1 to establish whether activation spreads beyond that point.

The results of Experiment 1 are summarized in

**TABLE 26.1. Mean Response Latency and Percent Error Rates as a Function of Prime Condition and Stimulus Onset Asynchrony (SOA) in Experiment 1**

| | Prime Condition | | | | | | | |
|---|---|---|---|---|---|---|---|---|
| | Related | | Mediated | | Neutral | | Unrelated | |
| SOA | Latency | % Error | Latency | % Error | Latency | % Error | Latency | % Error |
| 250 | 519 | 3.2 | 559 | 3.4 | 562 | 6.5 | 564 | 4.9 |
| 500 | 535 | 1.9 | 574 | 5.2 | 565 | 4.0 | 583 | 4.6 |
| M | 527 | 2.6 | 567 | 4.3 | 564 | 5.3 | 574 | 4.8 |

Table 26.1. The results of a 2 × 4 (SOA × Priming Condition) mixed-factor ANOVA yielded a highly significant effect of prime, $F(3, 186) = 22.51$, $MS_e = 1227$; however, neither the effect of SOA nor the interaction between prime and SOA approached significance, both $Fs(1, 62) < 1$. Paired comparisons confirmed the apparent differences among priming conditions: Responses were significantly faster in the related condition than in each of the remaining three conditions; there were no differences among the remaining three conditions.

Using the neutral condition as a baseline for computing priming effects in the related, mediated, and unrelated conditions, it appears in Table 26.1 that facilitation and inhibition effects vary across the SOAs. However, separate contrasts of these changes in facilitation and inhibition effects indicated that none of these contrasts approached significance, all $ts(62) < 1.16$. Finally, it should also be noted that the difference between the unrelated and neutral prime conditions did not reach significance at the 500-ms SOA condition, $t(31) = 1.80$.

A comparable ANOVA on the percent error data yielded a significant main effect of prime condition, $F(3, 168) = 2.76$, $MS_e = .009$; however, again neither the effect of SOA nor the interaction between SOA and prime reached significance, both $Fs < 1.70$. The main effect of prime condition was due to fewer errors in the related condition than in the neutral or unrelated conditions. However, it is noteworthy that separate comparisons at the 250-ms SOA condition indicated that both the mediated and related conditions produced significantly fewer errors than the neutral condition. The unrelated condition did not significantly differ from the remaining prime conditions. Similar comparisons at the 500-ms SOA condition indicated that the related condition produced significantly fewer errors than either the mediated or unrelated conditions.

The results from the lexical decision experiments provide very little evidence of a multiple-step activation process. Large facilitation effects were observed for the directly related priming conditions of both Experiments 1 and 1a, demonstrating single-step activation of the associative pathways connecting the first and second words, and the second and third words in the triads. In fact, the 52-ms facilitation produced in the related condition of control Experiment 1a is considerably larger than the 26-ms effect reported by de Groot (1983). Because this effect size limits the size of the mediated effect, the present experiment should have provided a more sensitive test for mediated priming. However, there was no evidence that response latency was facilitated in the mediated condition. Collapsing across the two SOAs, the mediated condition was actually 3 ms slower than the neutral prime condition. Finally, there was some tendency for lower error rates in the mediated condition than in the neutral condition at the 250-ms SOA (but not the 500-ms SOA), just as de Groot reported. Thus, the overall pattern of data is quite consistent with de Groot's lexical decision results and conclusion that activation only spreads one step within the memory network.

## Pronunciation Experiments

Although the results of the lexical decision experiments clearly support the single-step activation model, the use of the lexical decision task to test the model may limit the generalizability of this conclusion. Because of the importance of the present results to spreading activation theory, it is necessary to provide converging evidence that activation only spreads one step within the memory network.

As was noted in the introduction, de Groot was

concerned that the lexical decision task encourages processing strategies that may override any effects due to activation processes. Consistent with de Groot's concerns, several recent investigations have provided evidence for postaccess processes in the lexical decision task (Balota & Chumbley, 1984; Chumbley & Balota, 1984; Lorch, Balota, & Stamm, in press; Lupker, 1984; Seidenberg, Waters, Sanders, & Langer, 1984; West & Stanovich, 1982). de Groot specifically suggested that subjects may conduct a postaccess check to determine if there is any direct relation between the prime and target. Because such a postaccess checking strategy might obscure multiple-step activation effects, de Groot attempted to prevent this strategy by presenting the prime items at threshold. However, as we noted earlier, the results from her threshold experiments are open to alternative explanations.

An alternative approach to studying lexical access processes is to use a speeded pronunciation task. The advantage of the pronunciation task compared to the lexical decision task is that it does not require the subject to make a binary decision. As a consequence, it should be less likely to promote task-specific strategies that might obscure effects due to automatic lexical access processes. Thus, Experiment 2 replicates the design of Experiment 1 using a pronunciation task. Experiment 2a is a control experiment analogous to Experiment 1a to ensure that pronunciation priming occurs across the first link of the stimulus triads.

## Method

### SUBJECTS

Fifty-six undergraduates participated in Experiment 2. Twenty-eight subjects participated in each SOA condition. Twenty-six subjects participated in the control Experiment 2a. All subjects were recruited from the University of Kentucky and participated as partial fulfillment of a course requirement.

### APPARATUS

The same Apple computer and timing device that was used in the earlier experiments was used in the pronunciation experiments. A Lafayette model 6602A voice key was interfaced with the computer.

Pronunciation latency was measured to the nearest millisecond (see note 3).

### MATERIALS

The word triads employed in the lexical decision experiments were used as the basis for constructing prime-target pairs in the pronunciation experiments. The assignment of triads to priming conditions (related, mediated, neutral, unrelated) was counterbalanced across four lists as described for the lexical decision experiments. The nonword stimuli were excluded to discourage subjects from adopting grapheme to phoneme (lexical bypass) pronunciation strategies. Finally, 16 phonologically irregular buffer items (e.g., *live, pint, save*) were included in order to further discourage such pronunciations. If subjects did use grapheme to phoneme conversion rules as the basis for performing the pronunciation task, then they would be expected to mispronounce the irregular words.

A stimulus list consisted of a block of 32 practice items and two test blocks of 40 items each. Each test block began with four buffer items and included eight phonologically irregular pairs and seven word pairs representing each of the four priming conditions. Again, only the data from the 48 triads that did not produce any mediating associations in the norming study will be reported here. The order of presentation of pairs within blocks was randomized independently for each subject.

### PROCEDURE

Subjects were instructed that they would see a pair of words on each trial in the experiment. They were informed that the first word would usually be a common English word but that it would be the word *blank* on 25% of the trials. Subjects were instructed to read the first word to themselves and to say the second word aloud as quickly as they could without mispronouncing it. The sequence of events on each trial was the same as in the lexical decision experiments, with the following exceptions. First, the subject pronounced the target item instead of pressing a response key. Second, the following message was presented on each trial immediately after a pronunciation was detected: "If you correctly pronounced the word, press the '0' button, otherwise press the '1' button." This procedure was necessary to exclude occasional mispronunciations and extraneous sounds (e.g., a cough) from being counted as correct responses. As in the earlier experiments, pressing one of the two keys initiated a 4-s intertrial interval.

## Results

Consider the results for the control experiment first. The mean outlier rate was 4.1% (again using the 1-s criterion) and subjects indicated an error or premature triggering of the voice key on 1% of the trials. Because there were few errors and we were unable to distinguish inadvertent triggerings of the voice key from actual mispronunciations, our major concern in the present discussion will be response latencies.[5]

The results of the control experiment were that mean response latency was significantly faster in the related condition (525 ms) than in the neutral condition (546 ms) or unrelated condition (550 ms). The difference between the neutral and unrelated conditions was not reliable, $t(25) < 1$. Thus, the results of the control experiment indicated activation of the first link within the triads. We shall next consider the findings of Experiment 2 to determine whether there was any evidence of activation spreading beyond the initial associative link.

The mean outlier rate in Experiment 2 was 1.9% and the error rate was 1.7% (see note 5). The response latency results are shown in Table 26.2. Response latencies varied across priming conditions, $F(3, 162) = 14.80$, $MS_e = 671$. Most important, the mediated condition was faster than the neutral condition, $t(55) = 3.77$. Thus, unlike Experiment 1, Experiment 2 produced a mediated facilitation effect. Finally, the SOA manipulation had no main effect and did not interact with priming condition, both $Fs < 1$.

Because of the importance of providing evidence for mediated priming, pairwise comparisons were conducted to directly compare the means at each of the two SOAs. These comparisons indicated that the mediated condition was significantly faster than the neutral condition at both the 250-ms SOA, $t(27) = 2.01$, $p < .05$ (one tailed), and the 500-ms SOA, $t(27) = 3.18$. Furthermore, the mediated condition was significantly faster than the unrelated condition at both the 250-ms SOA, $t(27) = 2.64$, and again at the 500-ms SOA, $t(27) = 2.19$. In addition to these results, responses were slower in the mediated condition than in the related condition at the 250-ms SOA, $t(27) = 2.65$, but this difference did not reach significance at the 500-ms SOA, $t(27) < 1$. Although the mediated condition was not significantly slower than the related condition at the 500-ms SOA, it is important to note that this was due to a few large reversals in the 500-ms SOA condition. In fact, 21 out of 28 subjects demonstrated faster response latencies in the related condition than in the mediated condition, $p < .05$ by sign test. Finally, the neutral and unrelated conditions did not differ at either SOA, both $ts(27) < 1.17$.

The results of the pronunciation experiment are in sharp contrast to the results of the lexical decision experiment and provide clear evidence for multiple-step spreading activation. Facilitation effects were observed for the mediated pairs at both SOAs, suggesting that activation did spread across the mediating association between the prime and target words of these items.

In order to test whether the apparent differences in the mediated facilitation effects between the lexical decision Experiment 1 and the pronunciation Experiment 2 were significant, an overall 2 × 2 × 2 (Task × SOA × Mediated vs. Neutral) ANOVA was conducted. The results of this analysis yielded a significant interaction between task and prime, $F(1, 116) = 6.70$, $MS_e = 997$. None of the remaining interactions approached significance.

**TABLE 26.2. Mean Pronunciation Latencies as a Function of Prime Condition and Stimulus Onset Asynchrony (SOA) in Experiment 2**

| SOA | Prime Condition | | | |
| | Related | Mediated | Neutral | Unrelated |
| --- | --- | --- | --- | --- |
| 250 | 545 | 558 | 570 | 574 |
| 500 | 553 | 558 | 583 | 576 |
| M | 549 | 558 | 577 | 575 |

## General Discussion

The present results are straightforward. The lexical decision results yielded strong priming effects between the first and second links of each triad but very little evidence of a priming effect in the mediated condition. These results provide a replication of de Groot's (1983) lexical decision experiments. Based on these results, one would suggest that activation spreads only one step within the memory network. Because of recent concerns in the literature that strategic decision processes could possibly obscure the contributions of a multiple step activation process in the lexical decision paradigm, a pronunciation experiment was conducted with the same materials. In contrast to the lexical decision results, the pronunciation results indicated clear mediated priming effects. This was the case even though the pronunciation results yielded smaller priming effects in the related conditions. The results of the pronunciation experiment suggest that activation spreads at least two steps deep in the memory network.

Before considering the implications of these results, it is necessary to address the possibility that the mediated facilitation found in the pronunciation experiment was due to some slight direct relation that may have existed for some percentage of our prime-target pairs. Three findings argue against this possibility. First, there should have been facilitation for mediated items in the lexical decision experiments if some of the prime-target pairs involved direct associations. In the present lexical decision experiments, reliable priming effects were observed for related prime-target pairs but not for mediated prime-target pairs. Second, a very conservative criterion was used for the inclusion of the mediated prime-target pairs in these experiments. None of the targets were produced to the mediated primes in 12,880 responses in the free association task. Third, if the mediated priming effects were due to a few items having weak direct associations, one would expect the mediated pairs that were rated as most strongly associated (see Method section) to be the items responsible for the effect. In order to address this possibility, a median split based on the mean ratings per item was conducted. The mean rating for the lower half of the mediated pairs was 1.45 (very similar to the unrelated condition, mean rating = 1.41), whereas the mean rating for the upper half was 2.64 (still considerably lower than the directly related pairs that had ratings of 4.19 and 4.01). A comparison of the priming effects for the items in the lower half (16-ms facilitation) and upper half (18-ms facilitation) indicated that there was very little relation between the item ratings and the priming effects observed in the pronunciation experiments. Furthermore, the correlation between the ratings of the mediated pairs and the size of

their corresponding facilitation effects (i.e., the difference between the mediated condition and the mean of the neutral and unrelated conditions) did not approach significance, $r = -.017$. Thus, the observed priming effects were not being produced by items that had higher ratings because of some weak direct associations. For the above three reasons, we believe that the facilitation effects observed in the mediated condition of the pronunciation experiments were due to activation spreading across a mediating node between the prime and target nodes.

The remainder of the present discussion will deal with two broad issues: (a) How are the pronunciation and lexical decision results to be reconciled with each other and with the de Groot research? (b) What are the implications of the present research for spreading activation theory?

## Lexical Decision and Pronunciation Tasks

Given the finding that pronunciation was facilitated by the existence of a mediating association between the prime and target, how are we to explain the lack of mediated priming effects in the lexical decision experiments? Following de Groot (1983), we suggest that there are two different influences of a semantic relation in a lexical decision task. The first process reflects spreading activation and influences the speed of lexical access via increased activation of a lexical representation. The second process is a postaccess check for a relation between the prime and target word. Subjects might develop this checking strategy by noticing that: (a) some of the primes and targets are related, and (b) such relations indicate that a "word" response is appropriate. Although the detection of a relation presumably follows lexical access and would therefore seem an inefficient basis for a response, the existence of a prime-target relation is probably very salient information for subjects. Further, it should be emphasized that the lexical decision task is not simply a reflection of lexical access but is a binary choice discrimination task. Thus, subjects can be expected to make their decision based on any information that discriminates word from nonword stimuli (Balota & Chumbley, 1984; Chumbley & Balota, 1984).

Let us consider how the spreading activation and postaccess checking processes operate in the lexical decision task. First, presentation of a non-neutral prime causes an automatic spread of activation to related concept nodes. As a consequence, lexical access is facilitated for both related and mediated target items, although the amount of facilitation is less for mediated items. After lexical access is completed for the target word, the subject then checks to determine whether there is a prime-target association. This postaccess checking process is assumed to be sensitive only to the existence of relatively strong associations (e.g., associations that are activated beyond some criterion). As soon as an association is detected, the subject responds that the target is a word. If no association is detected before a temporal deadline is reached, a decision is made based on any relevant information that has accrued to that point. This was presumably the case for the mediated, unrelated, and neutral conditions where no direct associations were available before the deadline was reached. The major difference between processing in the lexical decision and pronunciation task is that no postaccess check is performed in the pronunciation task. Rather, after lexical access is achieved in the pronunciation task, the subject retrieves the articulatory code for the stimulus and says the word.

Consider how this model of processing in the two tasks accounts for the major results of the current investigation. First, responses were faster in the related condition than in the neutral or unrelated conditions because spreading activation facilitated lexical access in the related conditions of both tasks. Related items in the lexical decision task benefitted additionally from the fact that the postaccess check located a relation before the deadline, whereas responses to targets in all other conditions were delayed until after the deadline was reached. This mechanism explains why facilitation of related items was greater in the lexical decision task (52 ms in Experiment 1a and 37 ms in Experiment 1) than in the pronunciation task (22 ms in Experiment 2a and 28 ms in Experiment 2). Next, mediated targets were responded to faster than neutral or unrelated items in the pronunciation task because spreading activation from the mediated prime facilitated lexical access. Further, the magnitude of the facilitation was less than for related items because the degree of activation of the target would be predicted to be less for mediated than for related targets. Although lexical ac-

cess should also have been facilitated for mediated targets in the lexical decision task, no facilitation was observed. According to the model, this is because subjects failed to detect a relation between the prime and target during the postaccess check and therefore had to delay responding until the deadline on the checking process was reached. Finally, although response latencies did not differ for the mediated and neutral conditions in the lexical decision task, there was some indication that fewer errors occurred in the mediated condition. In all five of de Groot's (1983) experiments (240-ms SOA) and in the 250-ms SOA condition of the present experiment (but not at the 500-ms SOA), accuracy was higher in the mediated condition than in the neutral or unrelated conditions. The model attributes this apparent facilitation effect in the mediated condition to spreading activation from the prime to the target. The resulting higher activation levels of mediated targets relative to neutral or unrelated targets constituted extra evidence that the target was, indeed, a word. Thus, although response latency was not facilitated in the mediated condition of lexical decision because of the deadline mechanism of the postaccess check, accuracy was affected at the shortest SOA.

Although the hypothesis of a postaccess checking strategy unique to the lexical decision task accounts for many of the major findings of the current study, the resulting processing model is quite complex. We have presented some arguments concerning the plausibility of such a processing strategy. In addition, there is independent evidence of its existence. Koriat (1981) has demonstrated that the presence of a backward association from the target word to the prime influences lexical decision performance. This finding suggests that subjects are searching for a prime-target relation after the target is recognized. Seidenberg et al. (1984) replicated Koriat's findings for the lexical decision task and have further demonstrated that the presence of backwards associations does not affect performance in the pronunciation task. These results support the hypothesis of a postaccess checking strategy in the lexical decision but not in the pronunciation task.

We have argued that a critical difference between the lexical decision and pronunciation tasks is that the former task requires a binary choice discrimination, whereas the latter task does not. It might be argued that the critical difference between our use of the two procedures was that the lexical decision task included nonwords, whereas the pronunciation task did not. Although nonwords could have been included in the pronunciation task, we opted to exclude them for three reasons. First, there is some evidence that the inclusion of nonwords does not influence pronunciation performance, at least when sentence contexts are used as primes (West & Stanovich, 1982). Second, we thought that the presence of nonwords might increase the likelihood that subjects would rely on grapheme to phoneme conversion rules as opposed to lexical access routes. If lexical bypass routes were used then this would decrease the sensitivity of the task for detecting a mediated priming effect. Third, it is possible that the inclusion of nonwords in a pronunciation task might encourage subjects to adopt a word/nonword decision strategy before making their pronunciations. Although this possibility would make the pronunciation task more similar to the lexical decision task, it would also encourage the binary decision aspect of the lexical decision task we were attempting to avoid.

There is one final point to note regarding the recent comparisons of lexical decision and pronunciation performance. Past studies have consistently yielded larger effects of experimental manipulations in lexical decision tasks than pronunciation tasks. Compared to pronunciation performance, lexical decision performance has yielded larger effects of word frequency (Balota & Chumbley, 1984), semantic variables such as meaningfulness and category dominance (Chumbley & Balota, 1984), backward priming (Seidenberg et al., 1984), syntactic priming (Seidenberg et al., 1984), list probability manipulations (Neely & Ross, 1985; Seidenberg et al., 1984), and inhibition in sentential contexts (West & Stanovich, 1982). Based on such a pattern, one might argue that the lexical decision task is simply a more sensitive measure of variables that influence lexical access because of potential grapheme to phoneme lexical bypass routes in the pronunciation task (see Coltheart, Davelaar, Jonasson, & Besner, 1977). The present results are the first demonstration of a lexical manipulation that produces a larger effect in the pronunciation task than in the lexical decision task. Thus, the lexical decision task cannot simply be viewed as a more sensitive task; rather, it is a task that involves qualitatively different processes than the pronunciation task.

In sum, we propose that response latencies in lexical decisions were not facilitated by mediated primes because subjects searched for a direct relation between the prime and target and direct relations were not readily available for mediated prime-target pairs. Such postaccess searches occur because of the decision aspects of the lexical decision task. When a task was used that did not involve postaccess search processes (i.e., pronunciation), response latency was facilitated by mediated primes. This result supports the multiple-step activation model.

## Multiple-Step Spreading Activation

Most models of spreading activation assume that activation spreads to directly related concepts and, from those concepts, more deeply into the memory network. This aspect of spreading activation theory has been a crucial component in accounting for a wide variety of cognitive performance. However, the assumption of multiple-step activation has received no direct empirical support until now. The results of the present study and those reported by den Heyer and Briand (in press) using numerical stimuli are the first direct empirical support for the multiple-step activation model.

The assumptions of spreading activation theory are supported not only by the finding of mediated facilitation but also by the finding that the mediated priming effect was smaller than the directly related priming effect (also, see den Heyer & Briand, in press). This result is consistent with two important assumptions of spreading activation theory (Anderson, 1976; Collins & Loftus, 1975). First, mediated priming effects should be smaller than related priming effects because the amount of activation reaching a node in memory is assumed to depend on the "distance" from the source of the activation (Becker, 1980, Experiment 5; de Groot et al., 1982; Lorch, 1982, but see Becker, 1980, Experiments 2 & 4; Neely, 1977). The distance between the prime and target in the mediated condition should have been, on average, twice as long as the distance between the prime and target in the related condition. Second, activation should decrease as it traverses an intermediate concept because the amount of activation emanating from any particular concept is proportional to the strength of all pathways emanating from that concept (Anderson, 1976; Reder & Anderson,

1980). Thus, one should find a reduction as activation traverses the intermediate concept because it travels not only along the associative pathway to the target but also along any other associative pathways emanating from the intermediate concept. Although both factors should reduce the activation reaching the target in the mediated condition, the independent contributions of these factors cannot be discerned from the present results.

The conclusion that activation involves multiple steps raises an important theoretical issue. Specifically, how does the system deal with the potentially enormous amount of information made available by a multiple-step activation process? For example, suppose that multiple-step activation processes occur in language processing. If one considers that an average reading rate is 250 words per minute and that possibly half of the words are content words, then a two-step activation process (with each concept directly connected to five other concepts) would activate as many as 50 concepts during a single second of reading. If the spread of activation is truly automatic, then the activation process itself will incur little cost in resources in the course of making a great deal of potentially relevant information available for further processing. But how does the system then select the most pertinent information from the activated set without incurring heavy costs? One possibility is that only activated intersections receive further processing (Anderson, 1976; Collins & Quillian, 1969). Despite the popularity of this concept, however, there is little direct evidence for a selection process based on intersecting searches. Thus, the present finding of mediated priming effects raises the important issue of how relevant information is selected for further processing from a multitude of activated representations.

Finally, it is of historical importance to note that there has been a long tradition of research and debate concerning mediational effects. In fact, one important issue in verbal learning research was whether one could produce true mediational positive transfer effects in a paired-associate learning situation (see Kjeldergaard, 1968). Concerns regarding direct versus indirect associations producing positive transfer effects were dominant then as they are today. The present research provides continuity with this basic research interest and strongly indicates that there is a measurable impact of indirectly related information.

## ACKNOWLEDGMENT

We thank David Lowe for his technical assistance in conducting this research and Curtis Becker, Annette de Groot, Ken den Heyer, Janet Duchek, James Neely, and Henry L. Roediger III for their helpful comments on an earlier draft of this manuscript.

## NOTES

1. de Groot did find in her masking Experiment 7 that the inhibition for the unrelated condition was eliminated, which is consistent with the notion that subjects were unable to conduct the postaccess search for a relation in this experiment. However, a post hoc partitioning of subjects into those subjects who were above threshold and those who were below threshold indicated that the elimination of the inhibition for the unrelated condition was primarily due to the group of subjects that were above threshold. The suprathreshold group was actually 16 ms faster in the unrelated condition, compared to the neutral baseline, whereas the subthreshold subjects were 9 ms slower in the unrelated condition. Thus, for those subjects who should have been the least likely to conduct the postaccess check, there was still some evidence of inhibition. Finally, because the unrelated primes did not come from the same stimulus set as the related primes, and it is unclear how these items were selected, it is possible that the inhibition effects observed at de Groot's short stimulus onset asynchronies could have been due to characteristics of the prime items.

2. It should be noted that de Groot's stimuli were not presented in English, and therefore one has to be cautious in making any strong statements regarding weak associations in the English translation of her stimuli.

3. Because there were no hardware modifications to synchronize the timer with the location of the signal on the CRT, response latency was not actually measured to the nearest millisecond (see Reed, 1979). Any such error, however, should occur randomly across conditions.

4. The results of the present experiments only include those 48 triads for which there were no mediated targets produced to the mediated primes in the production task. The production task was conducted after the experiments were conducted as an extra source of information about such weak associations. Thus, all list construction included the original 56 items. All major trends in the data were not influenced by this restriction to only 48 items. The counterbalancing of items across lists was not affected by this change.

5. We did conduct analyses on the percentage of trials that subjects pressed the "1" button to discard the previous trial. In the control Experiment 2a the percentages were 0.3% for the related condition, 3.8% for the neutral condition and 0.6% for the unrelated condition. The percentages for Experiment 2 were 0.9% for the related condition, 2.1% for the mediated condition, 2.4% for the neutral condition, and 1.3% for the unrelated condition. Analyses of variance did not yield any significant effects of condition.

# REFERENCES

Anderson, J. R. (1976). *Language, memory and thought.* Hillsdale, NJ: Erlbaum.

Anderson, J. R. (1983a). *The architecture of cognition.* Cambridge, MA: Harvard University Press.

Anderson, J. R. (1983b). A spreading activation theory of memory. *Journal of Verbal Learning and Verbal Behavior, 22,* 261–295.

Anderson, J. R., & Bower, G. H. (1973). *Human associative memory.* Washington, DC: Winston.

Balota, D. A. (1983). Automatic semantic activation and episodic memory encoding. *Journal of Verbal Learning and Verbal Behavior, 22,* 88–104.

Balota, D. A., & Chumbley, J. I. (1984). Are lexical decisions a good measure of lexical access? The role of word frequency in the neglected decision stage. *Journal of Experimental Psychology: Human Perception and Performance, 10,* 340–357.

Becker, C. A. (1980). Semantic context effects in visual word recognition: An analysis of semantic strategies. *Memory & Cognition, 8,* 493–512.

Chumbley, J. I., & Balota, D. A. (1984). A word's meaning affects the decision in lexical decision. *Memory & Cognition, 12,* 590–606.

Collins, A., & Loftus, E. (1975). A spreading activation theory of semantic processing. *Psychological Review, 82,* 407–428.

Collins, A., & Quillian, M. (1969). Retrieval time from semantic memory. *Journal of Verbal Learning and Verbal Behavior, 8,* 240–248.

Coltheart, M., Davelaar, E., Jonasson, J. T., & Besner, D. (1977). Access to the internal lexicon. In S. Dornic (Ed.), *Attention and performance VI* (pp. 535–555). New York: Academic Press.

Conrad, C. (1972). Cognitive economy in semantic memory. *Journal of Experimental Psychology, 92,* 149–154.

Dagenbach, D., & Carr, T. H. (1985). *Now you see it, now you don't: Relations between semantic activation and awareness.* Manuscript submitted for publication.

de Groot, A. M. B. (1983). The range of automatic spreading activation in word priming. *Journal of Verbal Learning and Verbal Behavior, 22,* 417–436.

de Groot, A. M. B., Thomassen, A. J. W. M., & Hudson, P. T. W. (1982). Associative facilitation of word recognition as measured from a neutral prime. *Memory & Cognition, 10,* 358–370.

den Heyer, K., & Briand, K. (in press). Priming single digit numbers: Automatic spreading activation dissipates as a function of distance between prime and target. *American Journal of Psychology.*

Foss, D. J. (1982). A discourse on semantic priming. *Cognitive Psychology, 14,* 590–607.

Kieras, D. (1981). Component processes in the comprehension of simple prose. *Journal of Verbal Learning and Verbal Behavior, 20,* 1–23.

Kjeldergaard, P. M. (1968). Transfer and mediation in verbal learning. In T. R. Dixon & D. L. Horton (Eds.), *Verbal behavior and general behavior theory* (pp. 67–96). Englewood Cliffs, NJ: Prentice-Hall.

Koriat, A. (1981). Semantic facilitation in lexical decisions as a function of prime-target association. *Memory & Cognition, 8,* 587–598.

Loftus, E. F. (1973). Activation of semantic memory. *American Journal of Psychology, 86,* 331–337.

Lorch, R. F. (1982). Priming and search processes in semantic memory: A test of three models of spreading activation. *Journal of Verbal Learning and Verbal Behavior, 21,* 468–492.

Lorch, R. F., Balota, D. A., & Stamm, E. G. (in press). *Locus of inhibition effects in the priming of lexical decisions: Pre- or post-lexical access? Memory & Cognition.*

Lupker, S. J. (1984). Semantic priming without association: A second look. *Journal of Verbal Learning and Verbal Behavior, 23,* 709–733.

McClelland, J. I., & Rumelhart, D. E. (1981). An interactive activation model of context effects in letter perception: Part 1. An account of basic findings. *Psychological Review, 88,* 375–407.

McDonald, D., & Hayes-Roth, F. (1978). Inferential searches of knowledge networks as an approach to extensible language-understanding systems. In D. Waterman & F. Hayes-Roth (Eds.), *Pattern-directed inference systems.* New York: Academic Press.

Neely, J. H. (1977). Semantic priming and retrieval from lexical memory: Roles of inhibitionless spreading activation and limited capacity attention. *Journal of Experimental Psychology: General, 106,* 226–254.

Neely, J. H., & Ross, K. L. (1985, May). *Effects of the probability of related primes on semantic priming and nonword facilitation effects in lexical decision and pronunciation tasks.* Paper presented at the meeting of the Midwestern Psychological Association, Chicago, IL.

Ratcliff, R., & McKoon, G. (1981). Does activation really spread? *Psychological Review, 88,* 454–462.

Reder, L. M., & Anderson, J. R. (1980). A partial resolution of the paradox of interference: The role of integrating knowledge. *Cognitive Psychology, 12,* 447–472.

Reed, A. V. (1979). Microcomputer display timing. Problems and solutions. *Behavior Research Methods and Instrumentation, 11,* 572–576.

Seidenberg, M. S., Waters, G. S., Sanders, M., & Langer, P. (1984). Pre- and postlexical loci of contextual effects on word recognition. *Memory & Cognition, 12,* 315–328.

Smith, E. E., Shoben, E. J., & Rips, L. J. (1974). Structure and process in semantic memory: A feature model for semantic decisions. *Psychological Review, 81,* 214–241.

Stanovich, K. E., & West, R. F. (1983). On priming by a sentence context. *Journal of Experimental Psychology: General, 112,* 1–36.

West, R. F., & Stanovich, K. E. (1982). Source of inhibition in experiments on the effect of sentence context on word recognition. *Journal of Experimental Psychology: Learning, Memory, and Cognition, 8,* 395–399.

# Appendix

## Stimulus Triads

| Mediated | Related | Target | Mediated | Related | Target |
|----------|---------|--------|----------|---------|--------|
| Lion | Tiger | Stripes | Cat | Mouse | Cheese |
| Beach | Sand | Box | Summer | Winter | Snow |
| War | Peace | Quiet | Wedding | Ring | Finger |
| Birthday | Cake | Pie | Tooth | Brush | Hair |
| Deer | Animal | Vegetable | Sport | Baseball | Glove |
| Breeze | Blow | Bubbles | Rough | Smooth | Silk |
| Oyster | Pearl | Necklace | Cry | Baby | Bottle |
| Eyes | Nose | Smell | Bull | Cow | Milk |
| Minute | Hour | Glass | Tree | Maple | Syrup |
| Soap | Water | Drink | Pen | Pencil | Lead |
| Priest | Church | Bell | Beer | Wine | Grape |
| Ceiling | Floor | Carpet | Day | Night | Dark |
| Hand | Foot | Kick | Wrist | Watch | Clock |
| Bat | Ball | Bounce | White | Black | Coal |
| Lemon | Sour | Sweet | Navy | Army | Tank |
| Sky | Blue | Color | Pretty | Ugly | Duckling |
| Hard | Soft | Cotton | Moon | Sun | Hot |
| Tea | Coffee | Bean | Window | Door | Knob |
| Phone | Number | Letter | School | Bus | Stop |
| Nurse | Doctor | Lawyer | Valley | Mountain | Peak |
| Reality | Fantasy | Island | Gas | Oil | Slick |
| Knife | Gun | Trigger | Flower | Rose | Thorn |
| Circle | Square | Dance | Heavy | Light | Feather |
| Fast | Slow | Turtle | Pants | Shirt | Collar |

# The "Tip of the Tongue" Phenomenon

Roger Brown and David McNeill[1] • Harvard University

The "tip of the tongue" (TOT) phenomenon is a state in which one cannot quite recall a familiar word but can recall words of similar form and meaning. Several hundred such states were precipitated by reading to Ss the definitions of English words of low frequency and asking them to try to recall the words. It was demonstrated that while in the TOT state, and before recall occurred, Ss had knowledge of some of the letters in the missing word, the number of syllables in it, and the location of the primary stress. The nearer S was to successful recall the more accurate the information he possessed. The recall of parts of words and attributes of words is termed "generic recall." The interpretation offered for generic recall involves the assumption that users of a language possess the mental equivalent of a dictionary. The features that figure in generic recall may be entered in the dictionary sooner than other features and so, perhaps, are wired into a more elaborate associative network. These more easily retrieved features of low-frequency words may be the features to which we chiefly attend in word-perception. The features favored by attention, especially the beginnings and endings of words, appear to carry more information than the features that are not favored, in particular the middles of words.

**W**illiam James wrote, in 1893:

Suppose we try to recall a forgotten name. The state of our consciousness is peculiar. There is a gap therein; but no mere gap. It is a gap that is intensely active. A sort of wraith of the name is in it, beckoning us in a given direction, making us at moments tingle with the sense of our closeness and then letting us sink back without the longed-for term. If wrong names are proposed to us, this singularly definite gap acts immediately so as to negate them. They do not fit into its mould. And the gap of one word does not feel like the gap of another, all empty of content as both might seem necessarily to be when described as gaps. (p. 251)

The "tip of the tongue" (TOT) state involves a failure to recall a word of which one has knowledge. The evidence of knowledge is either an eventually successful recall or else an act of recognition that occurs, without additional training, when recall has failed. The class of cases defined by the conjunction of knowledge and a failure of recall is a large one. The TOT state, which James described, seems to be a small subclass in which recall is felt to be imminent.

For several months we watched for TOT states in ourselves. Unable to recall the name of the street on which a relative lives, one of us thought of *Congress* and *Corinth* and *Concord* and then looked up the address and learned that it was *Cor-*

*nish*. The words that had come to mind have certain properties in common with the word that had been sought (the "target word"): all four begin with *Co*; all are two-syllable words; all put the primary stress on the first syllable. After this experience we began putting direct questions to ourselves when we fell into the TOT state, questions as to the number of syllables in the target word, its initial letter, etc.

Woodworth (1934), before us, made a record of data for naturally occurring TOT states and Wenzl (1932, 1936) did the same for German words. Their results are similar to those we obtained and consistent with the following preliminary characterization. When complete recall of a word is not presently possible but is felt to be imminent, one can often correctly recall the general type of the word; *generic* recall may succeed when particular recall fails. There seem to be two common varieties of generic recall. (a) Sometimes a part of the target word is recalled, a letter or two, a syllable, or affix. Partial recall is necessarily also *generic* since the class of words defined by the possession of any *part* of the target word will include words other than the target. (b) Sometimes the abstract form of the target is recalled, perhaps the fact that it was a two-syllable sequence with the primary stress on the first syllable. The whole word is represented in *abstract form recall* but not on the letter-by-letter level that constitutes its identity. The recall of an abstract form is also necessarily *generic*, since any such form defines a class of words extending beyond the target.

Wenzl and Woodworth had worked with small collections of data for naturally occurring TOT states. These data were, for the most part, provided by the investigators; were collected in an unsystematic fashion; and were analyzed in an impressionistic non-quantitative way. It seemed to us that such data left the facts of generic recall in doubt. An occasional correspondence between a retrieved word and a target word with respect to number of syllables, stress pattern or initial letter is, after all, to be expected by chance. Several months of "self-observation and asking-our-friends" yielded fewer than a dozen good cases and we realized that an improved method of data collection was essential.

We thought it might pay to "prospect" for TOT states by reading to *S* definitions of uncommon English words and asking him to supply the words. The procedure was given a preliminary test with nine *S*s who were individually interviewed for 2 hrs each.[2] In 57 instances an *S* was, in fact, "seized" by a TOT state. The signs of it were unmistakable; he would appear to be in mild torment, something like the brink of a sneeze, and if he found the word his relief was considerable. While searching for the target *S* told us all the words that came to his mind. He volunteered the information that some of them resembled the target in sound but not in meaning; others he was sure were similar in meaning but not in sound. The *E* intruded on *S*'s agony with two questions: (a) How many syllables has the target word? (b) What is its first letter? Answers to the first question were correct in 47% of all cases and answers to the second question were correct in 51% of the cases. These outcomes encouraged us to believe that generic recall was real and to devise a group procedure that would further speed up the rate of data collection.

## Method

### Subjects

Fifty-six Harvard and Radcliffe undergraduates participated in one of three evening sessions; each session was 2 hrs long. The *S*s were volunteers from a large General Education Course and were paid for their time.

#### WORD LIST

The list consisted of 49 words which, according to the Thorndike-Lorge *Word Book* (1952) occur at least once per four million words but not so often as once per one million words. The level is suggested by these examples: *apsenepotism, cloaca, ambergris,* and *sampan*. We thought the words used were likely to be in the passive or recognition vocabularies of our *S*s but not in their active recall vocabularies. There were 6 words of 1 syllable; 19 of 2 syllables; 20 of 3 syllables; 4 of 4 syllables. For each word we used a definition from *The American College Dictionary* (Barnhart, 1948) edited so as to contain no words that closely resembled the one being defined.

#### RESPONSE SHEET

The response sheet was laid off in vertical columns headed as follows:

*Intended word* (+ *One I was thinking of*).
                    (– Not).
Number of syllables (1–5).
Initial letter.
Words of similar sound. (1. Closest in sound)
                        (2. Middle              )
                        (3. Farthest in Sound)
Words of similar meaning.
Word you had in mind if not intended word.

## Procedure

We instructed Ss to the following effect.

In this experiment we are concerned with that state of mind in which a person is unable to think of a word that he is certain he knows, the state of mind in which a word seems to be on the tip of one's tongue. Our technique for precipitating such states is, in general, to read definitions of uncommon words and ask the subject to recall the word.

1. We will first read the definition of a low-frequency word.
2. If you should happen to know the word at once, or think you do, or, if you should simply not know it, then there is nothing further for you to do at the moment. Just wait.
3. If you are unable to think of the word but feel sure that you know it and that it is on the verge of coming back to you then you are in a TOT state and should begin at once to fill in the columns of the response sheet.
4. After reading each definition we will ask whether anyone is in the TOT state. Anyone who is in that state should raise his hand. The rest of us will then wait until those in the TOT state have written on the answer sheet all the information they are able to provide.
5. When everyone who has been in the TOT state has signaled us to proceed, we will read the target word. At this time, everyone is to write the word in the leftmost column of the response sheet. Those of you who have known the word since first its definition was read are asked not to write it until this point. Those of you who simply did not know the word or who had thought of a different word will write now the word we read. For those of you who have been in the TOT state two eventualities are possible. The word read may strike you as definitely the word you have been seeking. In that case please write '+' after the word, as the instructions at the head of the column direct. The other possibility is that you will not be sure whether the word read is the one you

have been seeking or, indeed, you may be sure that it is not. In this case you are asked to write the sign '–' after the word. Sometimes when the word read out is not the one you have been seeking your actual target may come to mind. In this case, in addition to the minus sign in the leftmost column, please write the actual target word in the rightmost column.
6. Now we come to the column entries themselves. The first two entries, the guess as to the number of syllables and the initial letter, are required. The remaining entries should be filled out if possible. When you are in a TOT state, words that are related to the target word do almost always come to mind. List them as they come, but separate words which you think resemble the target in sound from words which you think resemble the target in meaning.
7. When you have finished all your entries, but before you signal us to read the intended target word, look again at the words you have listed as "Words of similar sound." If possible, rank these, as the instructions at the head of the column direct, in terms of the degree of their seeming resemblance to the target. This must be done without knowledge of what the target actually is.
8. The search procedure of a person in the TOT state will sometimes serve to retrieve the missing word before he has finished filling in the columns and before we read out the word. When this happens please mark the place where it happens with the words "Got it" and *do not provide any more data.*

## Results

### Classes of Data

There were 360 instances, across all words and all Ss, in which a TOT state was signaled. Of this total, 233 were positive TOTs. A positive TOT is one for which the target word is known and, consequently, one for which the data obtained can be scored as accurate or inaccurate. In those cases where the target was not the word intended but some other word which S finally recalled and wrote in the rightmost column his data were checked against that word, his effective target. A negative TOT is one for which the S judged the word read out not to have been his target and, in addition, one in which S proved unable to recall his own functional target.

The data provided by S while he searched for

the target word are of two kinds; explicit guesses as to the number of syllables in the target and the initial letter of the target; words that came to mind while he searched for the target. The words that came to mind were classified by S into 224 words similar in sound to the target (hereafter called "SS" words) and 95 words similar in meaning to the target (hereafter called "SM" words). The S's information about the number of syllables in, and the initial letter of the target may be inferred from correspondences between the target and his SS words as well as directly discovered from his explicit guesses. For his knowledge of the stress pattern of the target and of letters in the target, other than the initial letter, we must rely on the SS words alone since explicit guesses were not required.

To convey a sense of the SS and SM words we offer the following examples. When the target was *sampan* the SS words (not all of them real words) included: *Saipan, Siam, Cheyenne, sarong, sanching,* and *sympoon*. The SM words were: *barge, house-boat,* and *junk*. When the target was *caduceus* the SS words included: *Casadesus, Aeschelus, cephalus,* and *leucosis*. The SM words were: *fasces, Hippocrates, lictor,* and *snake*. The spelling in all cases is S's own.

We will, in this report, use the SM words to provide baseline data against which to evaluate the accuracy of the explicit guesses and of the SS words. The SM words are words produced under the spell of the positive TOT state but judged by S to resemble the target in meaning rather than sound. We are quite sure that the SM words are somewhat more like the target than would be a collection of words produced by Ss with no knowledge of the target. However, the SM words make a better comparative baseline than any other data we collected.

## General Problems of Analysis

The data present problems of analysis that are not common in psychology. To begin with, the words of the list did not reliably precipitate TOT states. Of the original 49 words, all but *zither* succeeded at least once; the range was from one success to nine. The Ss made actual targets of 51 words not on the original list and all but five of these were pursued by one S only. Clearly none of the 100 words came even close to precipitating a TOT state in all 56 Ss. Furthermore, the Ss varied in their

susceptibility to TOT states. There were nine who experienced none at all in a 2-hr period; the largest number experienced in such a period by one S was eight. In out data, then, the entries for one word will not usually involve the same Ss or even the same number of Ss as the entries for another word. The entries for one S need not involve the same words or even the same number of words as the entries for another S. Consequently for the tests we shall want to make there are no significance tests that we can be sure are appropriate.

In statistical theory our problem is called the "fragmentary data problem."[3] The best thing to do with fragmentary data is to report them very fully and analyze them in several different ways. Our detailed knowledge of these data suggests that the problems are not serious for, while there is some variation in the pull of words and the susceptibility of Ss there is not much variation in the quality of the data. The character of the material recalled is much the same from word to word and S to S.

## Number of Syllables

As the main item of evidence that S in a TOT state can recall with significant success the number of syllables in a target word he has not yet found we offer Table 27.1. The entries on the diagonal are instances in which guesses were correct. The order of the means of the explicit guesses is the same as the order of the actual numbers of syllables in the target words. The rank order correlation between the two is 1.0 and such a correlation is significant with a $p < .001$ (one-tailed) even when only five items are correlated. The modes of the guesses correspond exactly with the actual numbers of syllables, for the values one through three; for words of four and five syllables the modes continue to be three.

When all TOTs are combined, the contributions to the total effects of individual Ss and of individual words are unequal. We have made an analysis in which each word counts but once. This was accomplished by calculating the mean of the guesses made by all Ss for whom a particular word precipitated a TOT state and taking that mean as the score for that word. The new means calculated with all words equally weighted were, in order: 1.62; 2.30; 2.80; 3.33; and 3.50. These values are close to those of Table 1 and *rho* with the actual numbers of syllables continues to be 1.0.

**TABLE 27.1. Actual Numbers of Syllables and Guessed Numbers for All TOTs in the Main Experiment**

|  | Guessed Numbers | | | | | No | | |
|  | 1 | 2 | 3 | 4 | 5 | Guess | Mode | Mean |
|---|---|---|---|---|---|---|---|---|
| Actual numbers |  |  |  |  |  |  |  |  |
| 1 | 9 | 7 | 1 | 0 | 0 | 0 | 1 | 1.53 |
| 2 | 2 | 55 | 22 | 2 | 1 | 5 | 2 | 2.33 |
| 3 | 3 | 19 | 61 | 10 | 1 | 5 | 3 | 2.86 |
| 4 | 0 | 2 | 12 | 6 | 2 | 3 | 3 | 3.36 |
| 5 | 0 | 0 | 3 | 0 | 1 | 1 | 3 | 3.50 |

We also made an analysis in which each $S$ counts but once. This was done by calculating the mean of an $S$'s guesses for all words of one syllable, the mean for all words of two syllables, etc. In comparing the means of guesses for words of different length one can only use those $S$s who made at least one guess for each actual length to be compared. In the present data only words of two syllables and three syllables precipitated enough TOTs to yield a substantial number of such matched scores. There were 21 $S$s who made guesses for both two-syllable and three-syllable words. The simplest way to evaluate the significance of the differences in these guesses is with the Sign Test. In only 6 of 21 matched scores was the mean guess for words of two syllables larger than the mean for words of three syllables. The difference is significant with a $p = .039$ (one-tailed). For actual words that were only one syllable apart in length, $S$s were able to make a significant distinction in the correct direction when the words themselves could not be called to mind.

The 224 SS words and the 95 SM words provide supporting evidence. Words of similar sound (SS) had the same number of syllables as the target in 48% of all cases. This value is close to the 57% that were correct for explicit guesses in the main experiment and still closer to the 47% correct already reported for the pretest. The SM words provide a clear contrast; only 20% matched the number of syllables in the target. We conclude that $S$ in a positive TOT state has a significant ability to recall correctly the number of syllables in the word he is trying to retrieve.

In Table 27.1 it can be seen that the modes of guesses exactly correspond with the actual numbers of syllables in target words for the values one through three. For still longer target words (four and five syllables) the means of guesses continue to rise but the modes stay at the value three. Words of more than three syllables are rare in English and the generic entry for such words may be the same as for words of three syllables; something like "three or more" may be used for all long words.

## Initial Letter

Over all positive TOTs, the initial letter of the word $S$ was seeking was correctly guessed 57% of the time. The pretest result was 51% correct. The results from the main experiment were analyzed with each word counting just once by entering a word's score as "correct" whenever the most common guess or the only guess was in fact correct; 62% of words were, by this reckoning, correctly guessed. The SS words had initial letters matching the initial letters of the target words in 49% of all cases. We do not know the chance level of success for this performance but with 26 letters and many words that began with uncommon letters the level must be low. Probably the results for the SM words are better than chance and yet the outcome for these words was only 8% matches.

We did an analysis of the SS and SM words, with each $S$ counting just once. There were 26 $S$s who had at least one such word. For each $S$ we calculated the proportion of SS words matching the target in initial letter and the same proportion for SM words. For 21 $S$s the proportions were not tied and in all but 3 cases the larger value was that of the SS words. The difference is significant by Sign Test with $p = .001$ (one-tailed).

The evidence for significantly accurate generic recall of initial letters is even stronger than for syllables. The absolute levels of success are similar but the chance baseline must be much lower for letters than for syllables because the possibilities are more numerous.

## Syllabic Stress

We did not ask $S$ to guess the stress pattern of the target word but the SS words provide relevant data. The test was limited to the syllabic location of the primary or heaviest stress for which *The American College Dictionary* was our authority. The number of SS words that could be used was limited by three considerations. (a) Words of one syllable had to be excluded because there was no possibility of variation. (b) Stress locations could only be matched if the SS word had the same number of syllables as the target, and so only such matching words could be used. (c) Invented words and foreign words could not be used because they do not appear in the dictionary. Only 49 SS words remained.

As it happened all of the target words involved (whatever their length) placed the primary stress on either the first or the second syllable. It was possible, therefore, to make a 2 × 2 table for the 49 pairs of target and SS words which would reveal the correspondences and noncorrespondences. As can be seen in Table 27.2 the SS words tended to stress the same syllable as the target words. The $C^2$ for this table is 10.96 and that value is significant with $p < .001$. However, the data do not meet the independence requirement, so we cannot be sure that the matching tendency is significant. There were not enough data to permit any other analyses, and so we are left suspecting that $S$ in a TOT state has knowledge of the stress pattern of the target, but we are not sure of it.

## Letters in Various Positions

We did not require explicit guesses for letters in positions other than the first, but the SS words provide relevant data. The test was limited to the following positions: first, second, third, third-last, second-last, and last. A target word must have at least six letters in order to provide data on the six

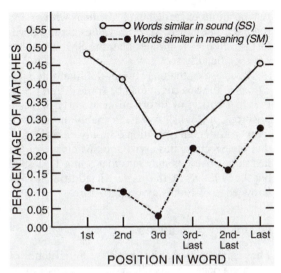

**FIGURE 27.1** ■ Percentages of letter matches between target words and SS words for six serial positions.

positions; it might have any number of letters larger than six and still provide data for the six (relatively defined) positions. Accordingly we included the data for all target words having six or more letters.

Figure 27.1 displays the percentages of letters in each of six positions of SS words which matched the letters in the same positions of the corresponding targets. For comparison purposes these data are also provided for SM words. The SS curve is at all points above the SM curve; the two are closest together at the third-last position. The values for the last three positions of the SS curve quite closely match the values for the first three positions. The values for the last three positions of the SM curve, on the other hand are well above the values for the first three positions. Consequently the *relative* superiority of the SS curve is greater in the first three positions.

The letter-position data were also analyzed in such a way as to count each target word just once, assigning each position in the target a single score representing the proportion of matches across all $S$s for that position in that word. The order of the SS and SM points is preserved in this finer analysis. We did Sign Tests comparing the SS and SM values for each of the six positions. As Figure 27.1 would suggest the SS values for the first three positions all exceeded the SM values with $p$s less than .01 (one-tailed). The SS values for the final

**TABLE 27.2. Syllables Receiving Primary Stress in Target Words and SS Words**

| SS Words | Target Words | |
| --- | --- | --- |
|  | 1st Syllable | 2nd Syllable |
| 1st syllable | 25 | 6 |
| 2nd syllable | 6 | 12 |

two positions exceeded the SM values with $ps$ less than .05 (one-tailed). The SS values for the third-last position were greater than the SM values but not significantly so.

The cause of the upswing in the final three positions of the SM curve may be some difference in the distribution of information in early and late positions of English words. Probably there is less variety in the later positions. In any case the fact that the SS curve lies above the SM curve for the last three positions indicates that $S$ in a TOT state has knowledge of the target in addition to his knowledge of English word structure.

## Chunking of Suffixes

The request to $S$ that he guess the initial letter of the target occasionally elicited a response of more than one letter; e.g., *ex* in the case of *extort* and *con* in the case of *convene*. This result suggested that some letter (or phoneme) sequences are stored as single entries having been "chunked" by long experience. We made only one test for chunking and that involved three-letter suffixes.

It did not often happen that an $S$ produced an SS word that matched the target with respect to all of its three last letters. The question asked of the data was whether such three-letter matches occurred more often when the letters constituted an English suffix than when they did not. In order to determine which of the target words terminated in such a suffix, we entered *The American College Dictionary* with final trigrams. If there was an entry describing a suffix appropriate to the grammatical and semantic properties of the target we considered the trigram to be a suffix. There were 20 words that terminated in a suffix, including *fawning, unctuous*, and *philatelist*.

Of 93 SS words produced in response to a target terminating in a suffix, 30 matched the target in their final three letters. Of 130 SS words supplied in response to a target that did not terminate in a suffix only 5 matched the target in their final three letters. The data were also analyzed in a way that counts each $S$ just once and uses only $Ss$ who produced SS words in response to both kinds of target. A Sign Test was made of the difference between matches of suffixes and matches of endings that were not suffixes; the former were more common with $p = .059$ (one-tailed). A comparable

Sign Test for SM words was very far from significance. We conclude that suffix-chunking probably plays a role in generic recall.

## Proximity to the Target and Quality of Information

There were three varieties of positive TOT states: (1) Cases in which $S$ *recognized* the word read by $E$ as the word he had been seeking; (2) Cases in which $S$ *recalled* the intended word before it was read out; (3) Cases in which $S$ *recalled* the word he had been seeking before $E$ read the intended word and the recalled word was not the same as the word read. Since $S$ in a TOT state of either type 2 or type 3 reached the target before the intended word was read and $S$ in a TOT state of type 1 did not, the TOTs of the second and third types may be considered "nearer" the target than TOTs of the first type. We have no basis for ordering types 2 and 3 relative to one another. We predicted that $Ss$ in the two kinds of TOT state that ended in recall (types 2 and 3) would produce more accurate information about the target than $Ss$ in the TOT state that ended in recognition (type 1).

The prediction was tested on the explicit guesses of initial letters since these were the most complete and sensitive data. There were 138 guesses from $Ss$ in a type 1 state and 58 of these, or 42%, were correct. There were 36 guesses from $Ss$ in a type 2 state and, of these, 20, or 56%, were correct. There were 59 guesses from $Ss$ in a type 3 state and of these 39, or 66%, were correct. We also analyzed the results in such a way as to count each word only once. The percentages correct were: for type 1, 50%; type 2, 62%; type 3, 63%. Finally, we performed an analysis counting each $S$ just once but averaging together type 2 and type 3 results in order to bring a maximum number of $Ss$ into the comparison. The combining action is justified since both type 2 and type 3 were states ending in recall. A Sign Test of the differences showed that guesses were more accurate in the states that ended in recall. than in the states that ended in recognition; one-tailed $p < .01$. Supplementary analyses with SS and SM words confirmed these results. We conclude that when $S$ is nearer his target his generic recall is more accurate than when he is farther from the target.

Special interest attaches to the results from type

2 TOTs. In the method of our experiment there is nothing to guarantee that when *S* said he recognized a word he had really done so. Perhaps when *E* read out a word, *S* could not help thinking that that was the word he had in mind. We ourselves do not believe anything of the sort happened. The single fact that most *S*s claimed fewer than five positive TOTs in a 2-hr period argues against any such effect. Still it is reassuring to have the 36 type 2 cases in which *S* recalled the intended word *before* it was read. The fact that 56% of the guesses of initial letters made in type 2 states were correct is hard-core evidence of generic recall. It may be worth adding that 65% of the guesses of the number of syllables for type 2 cases were correct.

## Judgments of the Proximity of SS Words

The several comparisons we have made of SS and SM words demonstrate that when recall is imminent *S* can distinguish among the words that come to mind those that resemble the target in form from those that do not resemble the target in form. There is a second kind of evidence which shows that *S* can tell when he is getting close (or "warm").

In 15 instances *S*s rated two or more SS words for comparative similarity to the target. Our analysis contrasts those rated "most similar" (1) with those rated next most similar (2). Since there were very few words rated (3) we attempted no analysis of them. Similarity points were given for all the features of a word that have now been demonstrated to play a part in generic recall—with the single exception of stress. Stress had to be disregarded because some of the words were invented and their stress patterns were unknown.

The problem was to compare pairs of SS words, rated 1 and 2, for overall similarity to the target. We determined whether each member matched the target in number of syllables. If one did and the other did not, then a single similarity point was assigned the word that matched. For each word, we counted, beginning with the initial letter the number of consecutive letters in common with the target. The word having the longer sequence that matched the target earned one similarity point. An exactly comparable procedure was followed for sequences starting from the final letter. In sum, each word in a pair could receive from zero to three similarity points.

We made Sign Tests comparing the total scores for words rated most like the target (1) and words rated next most like the target (2). This test was only slightly inappropriate since only two target words occurred twice in the set of 15 and only one *S* repeated in the set. Ten of 12 differences were in the predicted direction and the one-tailed $p = .019$. It is of some interest that similarity points awarded on the basis of letters in the middle of the words did not even go in the right direction. Figure 27.1 has already indicated that they also do not figure in *S*s' judgments of the comparative similarity to the target of pairs of SS words. Our conclusion is that *S* at a given distance from the target can accurately judge which of two words that come to mind is more like the target and that he does so in terms of the features of words that appear in generic recall.

## Conclusions

When complete recall of a word has not occurred but is felt to be imminent there is likely to be accurate generic recall. Generic recall of the *abstract form* variety is evidenced by *S*'s knowledge of the number of syllables in the target and of the location of the primary stress. Generic recall of the *partial* variety is evidenced by *S*'s knowledge of letters in the target word. This knowledge shows a bowed serial-position effect since it is better for the ends of a word than for the middle and somewhat better for beginning positions than for final positions. The accuracy of generic recall is greater when *S* is near the target (complete recall is imminent) than when *S* is far from the target. A person experiencing generic recall is able to judge the relative similarity to the target of words that occur to him and these judgments are based on the features of words that figure in partial and abstract form recall.

## Discussion

The facts of generic recall are relevant to theories of speech perception, reading, the understanding of sentences, and the organization of memory. We have not worked out all the implications. In this section we first attempt a model of the TOT process and then try to account for the existence of generic memory.

## A Model of the Process

Let us suppose (with Katz and Fodor, 1963, and many others) that our long-term memory for words and definitions is organized into the functional equivalent of a dictionary. In real dictionaries, those that are books, entries are ordered alphabetically and bound in place. Such an arrangement is too simple and too inflexible to serve as a model for a mental dictionary. We will suppose that words are entered on keysort cards instead of pages and that the cards are punched for various features of the words entered. With real cards, paper ones, it is possible to retrieve from the total deck any subset punched for a common feature by putting a metal rod through the proper hole. We will suppose that there is in the mind some speedier equivalent of this retrieval technique.

The model will be described in terms of a single example. When the target word was *sextant*, Ss heard the definition: "A navigational instrument used in measuring angular distances, especially the altitude of sun, moon, and stars at sea." This definition precipitated a TOT state in 9 Ss of the total 56. The SM words included: *astrolabe, compass, dividers*, and *protractor*. The SS words included: *secant, sextet*, and *sexton*.

The problem begins with a definition rather than a word and so S must enter his dictionary backwards, or in a way that would be backwards and quite impossible for the dictionary that is a book. It is not impossible with keysort cards, providing we suppose that the cards are punched for some set of semantic features. Perhaps these are the semantic "markers" that Katz and Fodor (1963) postulate in their account of the comprehension of sentences. We will imagine that it is somehow possible to extract from the definition a set of markers and that these are, in the present case: "navigation, instrument, having to do with geometry." Metal rods thrust into the holes for each of these features might fish up such a collection of entries as: *astrolabe, compass, dividers*, and *protractor*. This first retrieval, which is in response to the definition, must be semantically based and it will not, therefore, account for the appearance of such SS words as *sextet* and *sexton*.

There are four major kinds of outcome of the first retrieval and these outcomes correspond with the four main things that happen to Ss in the TOT experiment. We will assume that a definition of each word retrieved is entered on its card and that it is possible to check the input definition against those on the cards. The first possible outcome is that *sextant* is retrieved along with *compass* and *astrolabe* and the others and that the definitions are specific enough so that the one entered for *sextant* registers as matching the input and all the others as not-matching. This is the case of correct recall; S has found a word that matches the definition and it is the intended word. The second possibility is that *sextant* is not among the words retrieved and, in addition, the definitions entered for those retrieved are so imprecise that one of them (the definition for *compass*, for example) registers as matching the input. In this case S thinks he has found the target though he really has not. The third possibility is that *sextant* is not among the words retrieved, but the definitions entered for those retrieved are specific enough so that none of them will register a match with the input. In this case, S does not know the word and realizes the fact. The above three outcomes are the common ones and none of them represents a TOT state.

In the TOT case the first retrieval must include a card with the definition of *sextant* entered on it but with the word itself incompletely entered. The card might, for instance, have the following information about the word: two-syllables, initial s, final t. The entry would be a punchcard equivalent of S_ _T. Perhaps an incomplete entry of this sort is James's "singularly definite gap" and the basis for generic recall.

The S with a correct definition, matching the input, and an incomplete word entry will know that he knows the word, will feel that he almost has it, that it is on the tip of his tongue. If he is asked to guess the number of syllables and the initial letter he should, in the case we have imagined, be able to do so. He should also be able to produce SS words. The features that appear in the incomplete entry (two-syllables, initial s, and final t) can be used as the basis for a second retrieval. The subset of cards defined by the intersection of all three features would include cards for *secant* and *sextet*. If one feature were not used then *sexton* would be added to the set.

Which of the facts about the TOT state can now be accounted for? We know that Ss were able, when they had not recalled a target, to distinguish between words resembling the target in sound (SS words) and words resembling the target in meaning only (SM words). The basis for this distinction in the model would seem to be the distinction between the first and second retrievals. Membership in the first subset retrieved defines SM words and membership in the second subset defines SS words.

We know that when S had produced several SS words but had not recalled the target he could sometimes accurately rank-order the SS words for similarity to the target. The model offers an account of this ranking performance. If the incomplete entry for *sextant* includes three features of the word then SS words having only one or two of these features (e.g., *sexton*) should be judged less similar to the target than SS words having all three of them (e.g., *secant*).

When an SS word has all of the features of the incomplete entry (as do *secant* and *sextet* in our example) what prevents its being mistaken for the target? Why did not the S who produced *sextet* think that the word was "right?" Because of the definitions. The forms meet all the requirements of the incomplete entry but the definitions do not match.

The TOT state often ended in recognition; i.e., S failed to recall the word but when E read out *sextant* S recognized it as the word he had been seeking. The model accounts for this outcome as follows. Suppose that there is only the incomplete entry S_ _T in memory, plus the definition. The E now says (in effect) that there exists a word *sextant* which has the definition in question. The word *sextant* then satisfies all the data points available to S; it has the right number of syllables, the right initial letter, the right final letter, and it is said to have the right definition. The result is recognition.

The proposed account has some testable implications. Suppose that E were to read out, when recall failed, not the correct word *sextant* but an invented word like *sekrant* or *saktint* which satisfies the incomplete entry as well as does *sextant* itself. If S had nothing but the incomplete entry and E's testimony to guide him then he should "recognize" the invented words just as he recognizes *sextant*.

The account we have given does not accord with intuition. Our intuitive notion of recognition is that the features which could not be called were actually in storage but less accessible than the features that were recalled. To stay with our example, intuition suggests that the features of *sextant* that

could not be recalled, the letters between the first and the last, were entered on the card but were less "legible" than the recalled features. We might imagine them printed in small letters and faintly. When, however, the E reads out the word *sextant*, then S can make out the less legible parts of his entry and, since the total entry matches E's word, S recognizes it. This sort of recognition should be "tighter" than the one described previously. *Sekrant* and *saktint* would be rejected.

We did not try the effect of invented words and we do not know how they would have been received but among the outcomes of the actual experiment there is one that strongly favors the faint-entry theory. Subjects in a TOT state, after all, sometimes recalled the target word without any prompting. The incomplete entry theory does not admit of such a possibility. If we suppose that the entry is not S_ _T but something more like S*ex tan*T (with the italicized lower-case letters representing the faint-entry section) we must still explain how it happens that the faintly entered, and at first inaccessible, middle letters are made accessible in the case of recall.

Perhaps it works something like this. The features that are first recalled operate as we have suggested, to retrieve a set of SS words. Whenever an SS word (such as *secant*) includes middle letters that are matched in the faintly entered section of the target then those faintly entered letters become accessible. The match brings out the missing parts the way heat brings out anything written in lemon juice. In other words, when *secant* is retrieved the target entry grows from S*ex tan*T to SE*x t*ANT. The retrieval of *sextet* brings out the remaining letters and S recalls the complete word—*sextant*.

It is now possible to explain the one as yet unexplained outcome of the TOT experiment. Subjects whose state ended in recall had, before they found the target, more correct information about it than did Ss whose state ended in recognition. More correct information means fewer features to be brought out by duplication in SS words and so should mean a greater likelihood that all essential features will be brought out in a short period of time.

All of the above assumes that each word is entered in memory just once, on a single card. There is another possibility. Suppose that there are entries for *sextant* on several different cards. They might all be incomplete, but at different points, or, some might be incomplete and one or more of them complete. The several cards would be punched for different semantic markers and perhaps for different associations so that the entry recovered would vary with the rule of retrieval. With this conception we do not require the notion of faint entry. The difference between features commonly recalled, such as the first and last letters, and features that are recalled with difficulty or perhaps only recognized, can be rendered in another way. The more accessible features are entered on more cards or else the cards on which they appear are punched for more markers; in effect, they are wired into a more extended associative net.

## The Reason for Generic Recall

In adult minds words are stored in both visual and auditory terms and between the two there are complicated rules of translation. Generic recall involves letters (or phonemes), affixes, syllables, and stress location. In this section we will discuss only letters (legible forms) and will attempt to explain a single effect—the serial position effect in the recall of letters. It is not clear how far the explanation can be extended.

In brief overview this is the argument. The design of the English language is such that one word is usually distinguished from all others in a more-than-minimal way, i.e., by more than a single letter in a single position. It is consequently *possible* to recognize words when one has not stored the complete letter sequence. The evidence is that we do not store the complete sequence if we do not have to. We begin by attending chiefly to initial and final letters and storing these. The order of attention and of storage favors the ends of words because the ends carry more information than the middles. An incomplete entry will serve for recognition, but if words are to be produced (or recalled) they must be stored in full. For most words, then, it is eventually necessary to attend to the middle letters. Since end letters have been attended to from the first they should always be more clearly entered or more elaborately connected than middle letters. When recall is required, of words that are not very familiar to S, as it was in our experiment, the end letters should often be accessible when the middle are not.

In building pronounceable sequences the English language, like all other languages, utilizes only a small fraction of its combinatorial possibilities (Hockett, 1958). If a language used all possible sequences of phonemes (or letters) its words could be shorter, but they would be much more vulnerable to misconstruction. A change of any single letter would result in reception of a different word. As matters are actually arranged, most changes result in no word at all; for example: *textant, sixtant, sektant*. Our words are highly redundant and fairly indestructible.

Underwood (1963) has made a distinction for the learning of nonsense syllables between the "nominal" stimulus which is the syllable presented and the "functional" stimulus which is the set of characteristics of the syllable actually used to cue the response. Underwood reviews evidence showing that college students learning paired-associates do not learn any more of a stimulus trigram than they have to. If, for instance, each of a set of stimulus trigrams has a different initial letter, then *S*s are not likely to learn letters other than the first, since they do not need them.

Feigenbaum (1963) has written a computer program (EPAM) which simulates the selective-attention aspect of verbal learning as well as many other aspects. ". . . EPAM has a *noticing order for letters of syllables*, which prescribes at any moment a letter-scanning sequence for the matching process. Because it is observed that subjects generally consider end letters before middle letters, the noticing order is initialized as follows: first letter, third letter, second letter" (p. 304). We believe that the differential recall of letters in various positions, revealed in Figure 27.1 of this paper, is to be explained by the operation in the perception of real words of a rule very much like Feigenbaum's.

Feigenbaum's EPAM is so written as to make it possible for the noticing rule to be changed by experience. If the middle position were consistently the position that differentiated syllables, the computer would learn to look there first. We suggest that the human tendency to look first at the beginning of a word, then at the end and finally the middle has "grown" in response to the distribution of information in words. Miller and Friedman (1957) asked English speakers to guess letters for various open positions in segments of English text that were 5, 7, or 11 characters long. The percentages of correct first guesses show a very clear serial position effect for segments of all three lengths. Success was lowest in the early positions, next lowest in the final positions, and at a maximum in the middle positions. Therefore, information was greatest at the start of a word, next greatest at the end, and least in the middle. Attention needs to be turned where information is, to the parts of the word that cannot be guessed. The Miller and Friedman segments did not necessarily break at word boundaries but their discovery that the middle positions of continuous text are more easily guessed than the ends applies to words.

Is there any evidence that speakers of English do attend first to the ends of English words? There is no evidence that the eye fixations of adult readers consistently favor particular parts of words (Woodworth and Schlosberg, 1954). However, it is not eye fixation that we have in mind. A considerable stretch of text can be taken in from a single fixation point. We are suggesting that there is selection within this stretch, selection accomplished centrally; perhaps by a mechanism like Broadbent's (1958) "biased filter."

Bruner and O'Dowd (1958) studied word perception with tachistoscopic exposures too brief to permit more than one fixation. In each word presented there was a single reversal of two letters and the S knew this. His task was to identify the *actual* English word responding as quickly as possible. When the *actual* word was AVIATION Ss were presented with one of the following: VAIATION, AVITAION, AVIATINO. Identification of the actual word as AVIATION was best when S saw AVITAION, next best when he saw AVIATINO, and most difficult when he saw VAIATION. In general, a reversal of the two initial letters made identification most difficult, reversal of the last two letters made it somewhat less difficult, reversal in the middle made least difficulty. This is what should happen if words are first scanned initially, then finally, then medially. But the scanning cannot be a matter of eye movements; it must be more central.

Selective attention to the ends of words should lead to the entry of these parts into the mental dictionary, in advance of the middle parts. However, we ordinarily need to know more than the ends of words. Underwood has pointed out (1963), in connection with paired-associate learning, that while partial knowledge may be enough for a stimulus syllable which need only be recognized it will not suffice for a response item which must be pro-

duced. The case is similar for natural language. In order to speak one must know all of a word. However, the words of the present study were low-frequency words, words likely to be in the passive or recognition vocabularies of the college-student Ss but not in their active vocabularies; stimulus items, in effect, rather than response items. If knowledge of the parts of new words begins at the ends and moves toward the middle we might expect a word like *numismatics*, which was on our list, to be still registered as NUM_ _ICS. Reduced entries of this sort would in many contexts serve to retrieve the definition.

The argument is reinforced by a well-known effect in spelling. Jensen (1962) has analyzed thousands of spelling errors for words of 7, 9, or 11 letters made by children in the eighth and tenth grades and by junior college freshmen. A striking serial position effect appears in all his sets of data such that errors are most common in the middle of the word, next most common at the end, and least common at the start. These results are as they should be if the order of attention and entry of information is first, last, and then, middle. Jensen's results show us what happens when children are forced to produce words that are still on the recognition level. His results remind us of those bluebooks in which students who are uncertain of the spelling of a word write the first and last letters with great clarity and fill in the middle with indecipherable squiggles. That is what should happen when a word that can be only partially recalled must be produced in its entirety. End letters and a stretch of squiggles may, however, be quite adequate for recognition purposes. In the TOT experiment we have perhaps placed adult Ss in a situation comparable to that created for children by Jensen's spelling tests.

There are two points to clarify and the argument is finished. The Ss in our experiment were college students, and so in order to obtain words on the margin of knowledge we had to use words that are very infrequent in English as a whole. It is not our thought, however, that the TOT phenomenon occurs only with rare words. The absolute location of the margin of word knowledge is a function of S's age and education, and so with other Ss we would expect to obtain TOT states for words more frequent in English. Finally the need to produce (or recall) a word is not the only factor that is likely to encourage registration of its middle letters. The amount of detail needed to specify a word uniquely must increase with the total number of words known, the number from which any one is to be distinguished. Consequently the growth of vocabulary, as well as the need to recall, should have some power to force attention into the middle of a word.

## NOTES

1. Now at the University of Michigan.
2. We wish to thank Mr. Charles Hollen for doing the pretest interviews.
3. We wish to thank Professor Frederick Mosteller for discussing the fragmentary data problem with us.

## REFERENCES

BARNHART, C. L. (Ed.) *The American College Dictionary*. New York: Harper, 1948.

BROADBENT, D. E. *Perception and Communication*. New York: Macmillan, 1958.

BRUNER, J. S. AND O'DOWD, D. A note on the informativeness of words. *Language and Speech*, 1958, *1*, 98–101.

FEIGENBAUM, E. A. The simulation of verbal learning behavior. In E. A. Feigenbaum and J. Feldman (Eds.) *Computers and Thought*. New York: McGraw-Hill, 1963. Pp. 297–309.

HOCKETT, C. F. *A Course in Modern Linguistics*. New York: Macmillan, 1958.

JAMES, W. *The Principles of Psychology*, Vol. I. New York: Holt, 1893.

JENSEN, A. R. Spelling errors and the serial-position effect. *J. Educ. Psychol.*, 1962, *53*, 105–109.

KATZ, J. J. AND FODOR, J. A. The structure of a semantic theory. *Language*, 1963, *39*, 170–210.

MILLER, G. A. AND FRIEDMAN, E. A. The reconstruction of mutilated English texts. *Inform. Control*, 1957, **1**, 38–55.

THORNDIKE, E. L. AND LORGE, I. *The Teacher's Word Book of 30,000 Words*. New York: Columbia *Univer.*, 1952.

UNDERWOOD, B. J. Stimulus selection in verbal learning. In C. N. Cofer and B. S. Musgrave (Eds.) *Verbal Behavior and Learning: Problems and Processes*. New York: McGraw-Hill, 1963. Pp. 33–48.

WENZL, A. Empirische und theoretische Beiträge zur Erinnerungsarbeit bei erschwerter Wortfindung. *Arch. Ges. Psychol.*, 1932, *85*, 181–218.

WENZL, A. Empirische und theoretische Beiträge zur Erinnerungsarbeit bei erschwerter Wortfindung. *Arch. Ges. Psychol.*, 1936, *97*, 294–318.

WOODWORTH, R. S. *Psychology.* (3rd ed.). New York: Holt, 1934.

WOODWORTH, R. S. AND SCHLOSBERG, H. *Experimental Psychology.* (Rev. ed.). New York: Holt, 1954.

READING 28

# Contextual Prerequisites for Understanding: Some Investigations of Comprehension and Recall[1]

John D. Bransford and Marcia K. Johnson
• State University of New York, Stony Brook

The present paper presents a series of studies showing that relevant contextual knowledge is a prerequisite for comprehending prose passages. Four studies are reported, each demonstrating increased comprehension ratings and recall scores when Ss were supplied with appropriate information before they heard test passages. Supplying Ss with the same information subsequent to the passages produced much lower comprehension ratings and recall scores. Various explanations of the results are considered, and the role of topics in activating cognitive contexts is discussed.

The present paper sketches a general approach to some problems of comprehension and memory. Several studies are reported which employ an experimental paradigm that seems particularly adaptable to such problems and that has been useful in developing the point of view proposed here.

Probably the most well-developed approach to comprehension stems from theories based on transformational linguistics (e.g., Chomsky, 1957, 1965, 1968; Postal, 1964). Sentences are assumed to have both superficial and underlying (deep) structures. The surface structure characterizes the phonological shape of the sentence, but the deep structural information is presumed necessary for characterizing sentence meaning (see Katz &

Postal, 1964). According to Katz & Postal (p. 12), the semantically interpreted deep structural relations underlying sentences constitute a full analysis of their cognitive meaning. Comprehension thus involves the recovery and interpretation of the abstract deep structural relations underlying sentences, and sentence memory involves retention of the deep structural but not necessarily the surface structural forms. Many studies have demonstrated the importance of deep structure in sentence perception and memory tasks (e.g., Bever, Lackner, & Kirk, 1969; Blumenthal, 1967, Blumenthal & Boakes, 1967; Perfetti, 1969; Rohrman, 1968; Sachs, 1967; Wanner, 1968).

However, several lines of research support the notion that performance in comprehension and memory tasks has a broader base than simply the semantically interpreted deep structural relations underlying linguistic inputs. Kintsch (1972), for example, has shown that Ss often know more than a sentence specifies directly. The results of experiments by Bransford and Franks (1971), Bransford, Barclay, and Franks (1972) and by Johnson, Bransford, & Solomon (in press) indicate that the information Ss use in a sentence memory task may originate from the integration of information from several related sentences and may include ideas not directly expressed in the acquisition materials.

For example, Johnson, Bransford, and Solomon (in press) presented Ss with short passages like either (a) "The river was narrow. A beaver hit the log that a turtle was sitting beside and the log flipped over from the shock. The turtle was very surprised by the event" or (b) "The river was narrow. A beaver hit the log that a turtle was sitting on and the log flipped over from the shock. The turtle was very surprised by the event." After acquisition, the Ss were read a list of recognition sentences and asked to indicate which sentences they had actually heard during the acquisition task. Those Ss hearing passage (b) were much more likely to think they had heard the novel sentence, "A beaver hit the log and knocked the turtle into the water," than those hearing passage (a). The Ss' understanding of the acquisition sentences apparently involved a realization of the probable consequences of the situations suggested by the input sentences; Ss frequently thought they had heard information which could only have been inferred.

The experiments mentioned above lend considerable support to the idea that Ss do not simply interpret and store the meanings of sentences per se. Rather, Ss create semantic products that are a joint function of input information and prior knowledge. The present paper focuses directly on the role played by prior knowledge in comprehension. Its purpose is to show that not only is prior knowledge reflected in the S's performance in tasks involving the comprehension of linguistic information, but that certain knowledge may be necessary for the meaningful processing of the information in the first place. In the experiments presented below, the availability of prior knowledge is manipulated in order to assess its influence on Ss' ability to comprehend and remember linguistic materials.

# Experiment I

The information presented to the Ss consisted of a passage in which the sentences followed rules of normal English construction and the vocabulary items were used in non-metaphorical ways. The prediction tested was that Ss who received the appropriate prerequisite knowledge would be able to comprehend the passage quite easily, and hence would subsequently be able to recall it relatively well. On the other hand, Ss who did not have access to the appropriate knowledge should find the passage difficult to understand and recall. The prerequisite knowledge was in the form of a picture that provided information about the context underlying the stimulus passage. The passage did not simply describe the contextual picture, but instead described various events that could happen given the context as a conceptual base.

## Method

The experiment consisted of an acquisition phase, followed by two tasks—comprehension rating and recall. There were five independent groups of Ss with 10 Ss per group. In addition to the No Context (1) Ss (who simply heard the passage) and the Context Before Ss (who saw the appropriate context picture before they heard the passage), there were three other groups of Ss. Context After Ss first heard the passage and then saw the appropriate picture. Since it was assumed that contextual information is necessary for the ongoing process of comprehension, the Context After Ss were expected to assign lower comprehension ratings and recall less than the Context Before Ss. Partial Context Ss were shown a picture before the passage was presented. The partial context picture contained all of the objects represented in the appropriate context picture, but the objects were rearranged. It was assumed that the availability of concrete representations of the objects would be equal for the Partial Context and Context Before groups. However, the comprehension and recall performances of the former group were expected to be lower since the relations among the objects in the partial context picture constituted an inappropriate conceptual base for the passage. Finally, No Context (2) Ss heard the passage twice. This group was included to assess the effects of repetitions in the absence of context.

## Materials

The passage was as follows:

> If the balloons popped, the sound wouldn't be able to carry since everything would be too far away from the correct floor. A closed window would also prevent the sound from carrying, since most buildings tend to be well insulated. Since the whole operation depends on a steady flow of electricity, a break in the middle of the wire would also cause problems. Of course, the fellow could shout, but the human voice is not loud enough to carry that far. An additional problem is that a string could break on the instrument. Then there could be no accompaniment to the message. It is clear that the best situation would involve less distance. Then there would be fewer potential problems. With face to face contact, the least number of things could go wrong.

The appropriate- and partial-context pictures are shown in Figures 28.1 and 28.2, respectively.

### PROCEDURE

The Ss assigned to a given condition were tested as a group in a single session. All Ss were told that they were going to hear a tape-recorded passage and were asked to attempt to comprehend and remember it. They were informed that they would later be asked to recall the passage as accurately as they could. The Context Before and Partial Context Ss were given 30 seconds to inspect their respective pictures before the start of the recorded passage. The No Context (2) group heard the same recording twice. After acquisition, there was a 2-minute delay before Ss rated the passage. During this interval, Ss received recall sheets, Context After Ss were allowed 30 seconds to inspect the appropriate picture, and instructions about how to use the comprehension scale were given. A seven-point scale was used, with 1 indicating the passage was very difficult to comprehend, 4 indicating moderate, and 7 indicating very easy. Immediately after the rating task, Ss were asked to recall the passage as accurately as they could and were told that if they could not remember it word for word, they should write down as many ideas as possible. Seven minutes were allowed for recall.

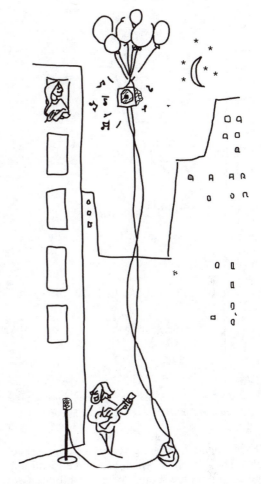

FIGURE 28.1 ■ Appropriate context picture for Experiment I.

### SUBJECTS

The Ss were 50 male and female high school students who volunteered to participate in the experiment.

## Results

We have adopted the following standard procedure for scoring recall protocols of sentence materials or prose passages: Idea units are designated a priori and correspond either to individual sentences, basic semantic propositions, or phrases. Maximum possible scores for the materials used

FIGURE 28.2 ■ Partial context picture for Experiment I.

in Experiments I–IV are given in the appropriate tables. The protocols, which cannot be identified as to condition, are scored independently by two judges against the list of idea units. Paraphrases are allowed. Interjudge reliability for materials such as those used in the present experiments ranges from .91 to .99. Any differences in the assignment of scores to Ss are resolved by a third judge. These adjusted scores are then used in the final analysis of the data.

The mean comprehension rating and the mean number of ideas recalled for each group in Ex-

periment I are given in Table 28.1. For both comprehension and recall scores, Dunnett's test was used to compare the Context Before condition with each of the other four conditions. The comprehension ratings were higher in the Context Before condition than in each of the other four conditions; all values of $d(5, 45) \geq 4.19$, $p < .005$. The Ss in the Context Before condition also recalled a greater number of ideas than Ss in each of the other four conditions; all values of $d(5, 45) \geq 4.12$, $p < .005$. An inspection of the data in Table 28.1 suggests that, relative to the No Context (1) condition, hearing the passage twice, receiving the context after or receiving the partial context before, increased comprehension ratings somewhat. Relative to the No Context (1) condition, these manipulations had little effect on recall scores.

## Discussion

The presentation of the appropriate semantic context had a marked effect on both comprehension ratings and recall. All Ss presumably knew the lexical meanings of the words and were familiar with the sentence structures used in the passage. Comprehension ratings and recall were relatively low, however, when Ss did not receive the appropriate context before they heard the passage.

The large difference in recall between the Context Before and the No Context (1) groups could be due to various factors. For example, knowledge of the appropriate context could simply provide information that allowed Ss to generate (at recall) ideas based on preexperimental experiences, and many of these ideas could have overlapped with those in the passage. If this were an important factor, the Context After Ss should also have been able to augment recall by guessing or generating ideas from the picture. Providing the Ss with the appropriate context after they heard the passage did not, however, produce an increment in recall.

One might also argue that the Context Before

TABLE 28.1. Mean Comprehension Ratings and Mean Number of Ideas Recalled, Experiment I

|  | No Context (1) | No Context (2) | Context After | Partial Context | Context Before | Maximum Score |
|---|---|---|---|---|---|---|
| Comprehension | 2.30 (.30)[a] | 3.60 (.27) | 3.30 (.45) | 3.70 (.56) | 6.10 (.38) | 7 |
| Recall | 3.60 (.64) | 3.80 (.79) | 3.60 (.75) | 4.00 (.60) | 8.00 (.65) | 14 |

[a] Standard error in parentheses.

group benefited from a more available set of retrieval cues (i.e., the elements of the picture—balloons, wire, window, etc.) relative to the No Context group. There are data to suggest that retrieval cues are important for recall and that it is important that these cues be present at input (e.g., Tulving & Osler, 1968). The elements of the picture were available to the Partial Context *S*s before they heard the passage, yet their recall was far below that of the Context Before group. What the partial context picture lacked was the appropriate information about the relations among the concrete elements. Understanding the relations in the appropriate context was a prerequisite for understanding the events suggested by the passage. Although considerable research is needed to assess the relative contributions of comprehension versus retrieval processes to remembering, it seems clear that there is little reason to expect retrieval cues to augment recall for prose appreciably if *S*s have not understood the meaning of a passage. On the other hand, comprehension per se does not necessarily guarantee subsequent recall. Pilot studies using the passage in Experiment I indicate that recall scores for the Context Before *S*s can be increased by supplying them with key words as retrieval cues.

The comparison of the No Context (2) and Context Before groups can be viewed as a transfer of training design, where the No Context (2) group receives Learn A, Learn A, Test A and the Context Before group receives Learn B, Learn A, Test A where Learn B represents time taken to study the prerequisite context. For *S*s in the present experiment, it was more beneficial to transfer from B to A than it was to spend time trying to learn A. Generally, this should be the case if the context in question is truly a prerequisite for comprehension.

The finding that neither Context After, nor Partial Context, nor No Context (2) groups showed augmented recall relative to No Context (1) *S*s was somewhat surprising, although these groups were expected to be clearly inferior to the Context Before group. Eventually, it will be important to characterize those situations under which these types of treatments will benefit the *S*s' performance. For present purposes, however, the major points are the clear advantage of the Context Before group and the resulting picture of the comprehension process that is supported by the general pattern of the results.

In Experiment I, it was very unlikely that the appropriate prerequisite context was (in all its details) part of the preexperimental knowledge of the *S*s. If one generally characterizes comprehension as a process requiring appropriate semantic contexts, then the conditions under which existing structures become activated are extremely important. If a passage does not provide sufficient cues about its appropriate semantic context, the *S* is in a problem-solving situation in which he must find a suitable organization of his store of previous knowledge. Experiments II, III, and IV involve materials for which the appropriate contexts should be part of the preexperimental knowledge of most *S*s. Some *S*s are given a cue (a topic for the passage) that should help activate a suitable context.

It should be noted that the experiments to follow are similar to a set of studies that became available in the literature at the time the present paper was being written: Dooling and Lachman (1971) found that providing the topic of a passage affected subsequent recall. The present studies are included here, however, because (*a*) the passages used are relatively straightforward linguistic descriptions whereas those used by Dooling and Lachman were explicitly metaphorical; and (*b*) the present studies include conditions where *S*s receive knowledge of the topic after hearing the passage in order to determine whether recall increments are simply due to *S*s' abilities to generate probable statements about familiar topics.

## Experiments II, III, and IV

The results of Experiments II, III, and IV will be presented and discussed after the procedures have been described since the three studies were similar in design.

### Method

These experiments were similar to Experiment I in that the acquisition phase, consisting of a single auditory presentation of the materials, was followed by comprehension rating and recall tasks. The rating scale was the same as that used in Experiment I. The conditions in each of the studies were as follows. *Experiment II:* A No Topic group (17 *S*s) heard a passage and received no additional information; a Topic After group (17 *S*s) received the topic of the passage after acquisition and prior to the rating and recall tasks; a Topic Before group (18 Ss) received the topic prior to the presentation of the passage. *Experiment III:* Topic After (10 Ss) and Topic Before (11 Ss) conditions. *Experiment IV:* No Topic (9 Ss), Topic After (11 Ss), and Topic Before (11 Ss) conditions.

### MATERIALS

Materials for Experiments II and III consisted of passages A and B, respectively. Passage B is a slightly longer version of Passage A. Experiments II and III were conducted under different conditions and no comparisons of Ss' performance on Passages A and B were planned or conducted.

## Passage A:

The procedure is actually quite simple. First you arrange things into different groups depending on their makeup. Of course, one pile may be sufficient depending on how much there is to do. If you have to go somewhere else due to lack of facilities that is the next step, otherwise you are pretty well set. It is important not to overdo any particular endeavor. That is, it is better to do too few things at once than too many. In the short run this may not seem important, but complications from doing too many can easily arise. A mistake can be expensive as well. The manipulation of the appropriate mechanisms should be self-explanatory, and we need not dwell on it here. At first the whole procedure will seem complicated. Soon, however, it will become just another facet of life. It is difficult to foresee any end to the necessity for this task in the immediate future, but then one never can tell.

## Passage B:

The procedure is actually quite simple. First you arrange things into different groups. Of course, one pile may be sufficient depending on how much there is to do. If you have to go somewhere else due to lack of facilities that is the next step, otherwise you are pretty well set. It is important not to overdo things. That is, it is better to do too few things at once than too many. In the short run this

may not seem important but complications can easily arise. A mistake can be expensive as well. At first the whole procedure will seem complicated. Soon, however, it will become just another facet of life. It is difficult to foresee any end to the necessity for this task in the immediate future, but then one never can tell. After the procedure is completed one arranges the materials into different groups again. Then they can be put into their appropriate places. Eventually they will be used once more and the whole cycle will then have to be repeated. However, that is part of life.

The materials used in Experiment IV were less like a paragraph than those used in Experiments I–III and the sentences were presented as sentences, rather than in paragraph form. In order of presentation, the sentences were:

> A newspaper is better than a magazine/ A seashore is a better place than the street/ At first it is better to run than to walk/ You may have to try several times/ It takes some skill but it's easy to learn/ Even young children can enjoy it/ Once successful, complications are minimal/ Birds seldom get too close/ Rain, however, soaks in very fast/ Too many people doing the same thing can also cause problems/ One needs lots of room/ If there are no complications, it can be very peaceful/ A rock will serve as an anchor/ If things break loose from it, however, you will not get a second chance/

### EXPERIMENT II PROCEDURE

All Ss were tested simultaneously. Assignment of Ss to conditions was made by randomizing the instruction sheets in blocks of the three experimental treatments and passing the resulting stack of booklets out in normal classroom fashion. The written instructions told the Ss to listen carefully to the passage that E would read to them and that they would later be asked to recall it as accurately as possible. The instruction sheet for the Topic Before Ss included the additional sentence, "The paragraph you will hear will be about washing clothes." Immediately after the passage was read, Ss opened their comprehension rating instructions. For the Context After Ss, these instructions included the sentence, "It may help you to know that the paragraph was about washing clothes." Approximately 2 minutes after the end of acquisition, Ss were reminded to recall as accurately as possible and instructed to write down at least the essential ideas. Five minutes were allowed for recall.

### EXPERIMENT III PROCEDURE

The Ss were tested in groups corresponding to the two conditions. Both groups heard the same tape recording of Passage B. All instructions and the topic (again, "washing clothes") were given verbally by E. Acquisition instructions informed Ss that they would later be asked to recall all the essential ideas of the passage. There was a 1-minute interval between the end of acquisition and the comprehension rating and a 1-minute interval between the rating and recall tasks. Six minutes were allowed for recall.

### EXPERIMENT IV PROCEDURE

All Ss were tested simultaneously with a procedure similar to that used in Experiment II. The topic (which was presented on the acquisition instruction sheet and on the comprehension rating instruction sheet for Topic Before and Topic After groups, respectively) was "making and flying a kite." The sentences were read by E and there was a 2-second interval between the end of one sentence and the beginning of the next. Six minutes were allowed for recall.

### SUBJECTS

In Experiment II the Ss were 52 male and female students enrolled in a course in human learning at the State University of New York, Stony Brook.

The Ss for Experiments III ($N = 21$) and IV ($N = 31$) were male and female high school student volunteers.

## Results

Mean comprehension ratings and mean recall scores for conditions in Experiments II and III are presented in Table 28.2 and those for Experiment IV are presented in Table 28.3.

### EXPERIMENT II

Comprehension ratings were higher in the Topic Before condition than in either the No Topic or the Topic After conditions, Dunnett's test (3, 49) = 4.46 and 4.80, $p < .005$, respectively. Likewise, recall was greater in the Topic Before condition than in the No Topic or Topic After conditions, $d(3, 49) = 3.97$ and $4.20$, $p < .005$, respectively.

### EXPERIMENT III

Both comprehension ratings and recall scores were higher in the Topic Before condition than in the Topic After condition: the $F$s (1, 19) were 12.24 for comprehension and 20.03 for recall, $p < .005$ in both cases.

### EXPERIMENT IV

In the analysis of the comprehension ratings, the Topic Before scores were higher than the No Topic scores, $d(3, 28) = 2.01$, $p < .05$. However, there was no significant difference between ratings of the Topic Before and Topic After Ss, $p < .05$. Recall of the Topic Before Ss was superior to that of both No Topic and of Topic After Ss, $d(3, 28) = 2.49$ and $2.68$, $p < .05$, respectively.

**TABLE 28.2. Mean Comprehension Ratings and Mean Number of Ideas Recalled**

| | Experiment II | | | | Experiment III | | |
|---|---|---|---|---|---|---|---|
| | No Topic | Topic After | Topic Before | Maximum Score | Topic After | Topic Before | Maximum Score |
| Comprehension | 2.29 (.22)[a] | 2.12 (.26) | 4.50 (.49) | 7 | 3.40 (.48) | 5.27 (.27) | 7 |
| Recall | 2.82 (.60) | 2.65 (.53) | 5.83 (.49) | 18 | 3.30 (.66) | 7.00 (.43) | 20 |

[a] Standard error in parentheses.

TABLE 28.3. Mean Comprehension Ratings and Mean Number of Ideas Recalled, Experiment IV

|  | No Topic | Topic After | Topic Before | Maximum Score |
|---|---|---|---|---|
| Comprehension | 2.44 (.47)[a] | 3.82 (.52) | 4.00 (.59) | 7 |
| Recall | 3.22 (.55) | 3.18 (.57) | 5.54 (.76) | 14 |

[a] Standard error in parentheses.

## Discussion

The results of Experiments II, III, and IV indicate that prior knowledge of a situation does not guarantee its usefulness for comprehension. In order for prior knowledge to aid comprehension, it must become an activated semantic context. As in Experiment I, it appears that for maximum benefit the appropriate information must be present during the ongoing process of comprehension. Comprehension and recall scores of the Topic After groups were generally much lower than those of the Topic Before groups. In short, the effect of topic in Experiments II, III, and IV was similar to that of context in Experiment I.

Lachman and his associates (Pompi & Lachman, 1967; Dooling & Lachman, 1971) suggested that knowledge of the topic facilitates retention by functioning as a mnemonic device. In recognition, Ss score higher on theme-related words because they match test words to the theme. In recall, a reconstructive process (with the theme the mediating schema) is emphasized. The present writers view the role of the topic as something more than a schema for generating lexical matches or associations, however. Its critical role appears to be in helping Ss create contexts that can be used to comprehend the passages in the first place. At least in the present experiments, Topic After groups were at a considerable disadvantage relative to Topic Before groups. Most importantly, knowledge of the topic of a passage may be neither necessary nor sufficient for optimal comprehension. Note, for example, that the context supplied in Experiment I did not contain information about the topic of the stimulus passage. The topic would be something like "Possible breakdowns in communication during a serenade." The picture simply supplied information about a basic situation that could have been developed in many different directions. The stimulus passage discussed just one of the many possible sets of events that could have

taken place. The picture greatly improved comprehension and recall scores, despite the fact that Ss in the Context Before group had no more explicit prior information about the topic than Ss in the other groups. Moreover, knowledge of the topic alone is not sufficient for optical comprehension of the passage in Experiment I. Pilot studies indicate that Ss receiving the topic of this passage before hearing it were still clearly inferior to Context Before Ss. The topic "possible breakdowns in communication during a serenade" is not sufficient to suggest the kind of contextual information communicated by the appropriate context picture.

It is interesting that in all the experiments, the absence of an appropriate semantic context seemed to have an effect on memory that is similar to that found when Ss are led to focus on nonsemantic aspects of linguistic inputs. For example, attention to the orthographic properties of sentences or words (rather than attention to their semantic features) causes a considerable decrement in recall (Bobrow & Bower, 1969; Hyde & Jenkins, 1969). In the present experiments all Ss presumably tried to process the information semantically, yet attention to semantic properties alone will not guarantee the availability of an adequate context for comprehension of prose.

Additional evidence that contexts are important for processing incoming information is that many of the Ss in the present experiments who were not provided with the context or topic prior to hearing the passage reported that they actively searched for a situation that the passage might be about; generally they were unable to find one suitable for understanding the entire passage, although they could make parts of it make sense. The extent to which context availability becomes a problem will certainly vary with the circumstances. Many sentences provide cues that allow one to create contextual structures that are sufficient for processing sentences seemingly in isolation. In other cases one will need additional information, such as that built up by perceptual context or previous linguistic context, in order to comprehend.

The notions that certain cognitive structures may be prerequisites for knowledge acquisition, or that such structures may influence perception and recall, have, of course, been discussed by many investigators (e.g., Arnheim, 1971; Ausubel, 1960; Bartlett, 1932; Gombrich, 1961, Piaget, 1950; and Winograd, 1971). Although at present it is not possible to provide a precise statement synthesizing these views and specifying mechanisms and processes operating during the acts of comprehending and remembering, the present results do emphasize the crucial role of semantic contexts. The experimental manipulation of context availability may constitute a useful strategy for investigating the interaction of prior knowledge and present input events.

## NOTE

1. This research was supported in part by a Research Foundation of the State University of New York summer research fellowship to the second author. Senior authorship was decided by tossing a coin. We wish to thank Brian O'Callaghan, guidance counselor, and the students of Ward Melville High School, East Setauket, New York, for their cooperation.

## REFERENCES

Arnheim, R. *Visual Thinking*. Berkeley: University of California Press, 1971.

Ausubel, D. P. *Educational Psychology: A Cognitive View*. New York: Holt, Rinehart and Winston, Inc., 1968.

Bartlett, F. C. *Remembering*. Cambridge: Cambridge University Press, 1932.

Bever, T. G., Lackner, J. R., & Kirk, R. The underlying structures of sentences are the primary units of immediate speech processing. *Perception and Psychophysics*, 1969, *6*, 225–234.

Blumenthal, A. Prompted recall of sentences. *Journal of Verbal Learning and Verbal Behavior*. 1967, *6*, 203–206.

Blumenthal, A. & Boakes, R. Prompted recall of sentences: A further study. *Journal of Verbal Learning and Verbal Behavior*, 1967, *6*, 674–675.

Bobrow, S. A. & Bower, G. H. Comprehension and recall of sentences. *Journal of Experimental Psychology*, 1969, *80*, 455–461.

Bransford, J. D., Barclay, J. R., & Franks, J. J. Sentence memory: A constructive versus interpretive approach. *Cognitive Psychology*, 1972, *3*, 193–209.

Bransford, J. D. & Franks, J. J. The abstraction of linguistic ideas. *Cognitive Psychology*, 1971, *2*, 331–350.

Chomsky, N. *Syntactic Structures*. London: Mouton and Company, 1957.

Chomsky, N. *Aspects of the Theory of Syntax*. Cambridge: M.I.T. Press, 1965.

Chomsky, N. *Language and Mind*. New York: Harcourt, Brace and World, 1968.

Dooling, D. J. & Lachman, R. Effects of comprehension on retention of prose. *Journal of Experimental Psychology*, 1971, *88*, 216–222.

Gombrich, E. H. *Art and Illusion*, New York: Pantheon Books, 1961.

Hyde, T. S. & Jenkins, J. J. Differential effects of incidental tasks on the organization of recall of a list of highly associated words. *Journal of Experimental Psychology*, 1969, *82*, 472–481.

Johnson, M. K., Bransford, J. D., & Solomon, S. Memory for tacit implications of sentences. *Journal of Experimental Psychology*, in press.

Katz, J. J. & Postal, P. M. *An Integrated Theory of Linguistic Descriptions*. Cambridge: M.I.T. Press, 1964.

Kintsch, W. Notes on the structure of semantic memory. In E. Tulving and W. Donaldson (Eds.), *Organization of Memory*. New York: Academic Press, 1972.

Perfetti, C. R. Lexical density and phrase structure depth as variables in sentence retention. *Journal of Verbal Learning and Verbal Behavior*, 1969, *8*, 719–724.

Piaget, J. *The Psychology of Intelligence*. London: Routledge and Kegan Paul, Ltd., 1947.

Pompi, K. F. & Lachman, R. Surrogate processes in the short-term retention of connected discourse. *Journal of Experimental Psychology*, 1967, *75*, 143–150.

Postal, P. M. Underlying and superficial linguistic structure. *Harvard Educational Review*, 1964, *34*, 246–266.

Rohrman, N. L. The role of syntactic structure in the recall of English nominalizations. *Journal of Verbal Learning and Verbal Behavior*, 1968, *7*, 904–912.

Sachs, J. Recognition memory for syntactic and semantic aspects of connected discourse. *Perception and Psychophysics*, 1967, *2*, 437–422.

Tulving, E. & Osler, S. Effectiveness of retrieval cues in memory for words. *Journal of Experimental Psychology*, 1968, *77*, 593–601.

Wanner, H. E. On remembering, forgetting and understanding sentences: a study of the deep structure hypothesis. Unpublished doctoral dissertation. Harvard University, 1968.

Winograd, T. Procedures as a representation for data in a computer program for understanding natural language. Report No. MAC TR-84, Massachusetts Institute of Technology, Project MAC, 1971.

# Using and Accessing Pre-Existing Knowledge Structures

## Discussion Questions

1. Balota and Lorch (1986) suggested that activation spreads across multiple steps within the semantic network. If this is the case, then why aren't we in a constant overload concerning activated representations? Integrate your answer with some of the concepts from the papers on "Attention."
2. There are two classic ways in which meaning is represented. One perspective is that the meaning of a word reflects a prototype of all previous occurrences with that word. Another perspective suggests that meaning reflects lists of features. Describe how the two sets of papers within this section fall within these two camps.
3. The tip of the tongue (TOT) phenomenon reflects a particularly uncomfortable stage wherein one is on the verge of retrieving a word or a name from memory but can't quite output it. Do you believe that TOTs indeed produce such an uncomfortable state, and, if so, why might this be more distressful than other failures of the cognitive system?
4. Bransford and Johnson found that if the title was presented after the passage, there was relatively poor memory for the passage. Why might this be surprising, and why might you predict this pattern?
5. Given that the human knowledge base appears to be constantly expanding as we age, how might one consider implementing such a physical system in a limited system such as the human brain? What are the limits that the physical system places on the knowledge base? Also, what modeling perspective might one take to accommodate this enormous capacity?

## Suggested Readings

J. R. Anderson (1976, *Language, Memory, and Thought*. Hillsdale, NJ: Erlbaum) provides an amazingly comprehensive book that introduces a theory of human cognition, along with empirical tests. The theory involves an associative network model and a long-term memory that encodes propositional knowledge about the world, along with a production system that acts on the prepositional network to perform tasks. This work serves as the foundation of subsequent comprehensive volumes in J. R. Anderson (1983, *The Architecture of Cognition.* Cambridge, MA: Harvard University Press) and in J. R. Anderson (1990, *The Adaptive Character of Thought.* Hillsdale, NJ: Erlbaum)

D. A. Balota (1983, Automatic semantic activation and episodic memory encoding. *Journal of Verbal Learning and Verbal Behavior, 22*, 88–104) shows under some conditions that one can find automatic spreading activation from primes onto targets in lexical decision performance, even though the primes are sufficiently degraded to minimize conscious awareness. The intriguing twist in this study is that the effect has little influence on later interpretation of lexical items.

F. C. Bartlett (1932, *Remembering: A Study in Experimental and Social Psychology.* London: Cambridge University Press) provides a wonderful read on the influence of cultural and expectancy-based influences on both memory and perception.

T. K. Landauer and S. T. Dumais (1997, A solution to Plato's Problem: The latent semantic analysis theory of acquisition, induction, and representation of knowledge. *Psychological Review, 104*, 211–240) and K. Lund, C. Burgess, and R. A. Atchley (1995, Semantic and associative priming in high-dimensional semantic space. In Cognitive Science Society [Ed.], *Proceedings of the 17th Annual Conference of the Cognitive Science Society* [pp. 660–665]. Hillsdale, NJ: Erlbaum.) have taken a very different approach to knowledge representation, which exploits large databases of text to explore how the meanings of words develop and are embedded in networks of other meanings. This is critical work that helps ground semantics based on naturally occurring co-occurrence metrics.

W. Kintsch and T. A. van Dijk (1978, Toward a model of text comprehension and reproduction. *Psychological Review, 85*, 363–394) and W. Kintsch (1988, The use of knowledge in discourse processing: A construction-integration model. *Psychological Review, 95*, 163–182) provide an important model of comprehension performance that incorporates aspects of representation, working memory, and integration processes to provide predictions about memory performance, readability, and online measures of reading. In addition to its impact on basic models of comprehension, this framework has been particularly important in education research.

J. H. Neely (1977, Semantic priming and retrieval from lexical memory: Roles of inhibitionless spreading activation and limited capacity attention. *Journal of Experimental Psychology: General, 106*, 226–254) provides a wonderful study of semantic priming effects and distinguishes between automatic and attentional processes that are based on the Posner and Snyder (1975, see readings on "Attention"). J. H. Neely (1991, Semantic priming effects in visual word recognition: A selective review of current findings and theories, in D. Besner & G. W. Humphreys [Eds.], *Basic Processes in Reading: Visual Word Recognition,* Hillsdale, NJ: Erlbaum) still gives the best review of the semantic priming literature.

R. Ratcliff and G. McKoon (1988, A retrieval theory of priming. *Psychological Review, 95*, 385–408) provide a very different perspective on priming, which emphasizes the prime and target serving as a compound cue for a search of memory. This is an intriguing alternative to the standard models and a nice integration of priming work with standard models of memory retrieval.

R. C. Schank, R. C. and R. P. Abelson (1977, *Scripts, Plans, Goals, and Understanding.* Hillsdale, NJ: Erlbaum) provide a key contribution that specifies the importance of higher-order representations that serve as organizing systems for clusters of knowledge. This is related to the importance of understanding knowledge structures above simple associative networks.

A. Stevens and P. Coupe (1978, Distortions in judged spatial relations. *Cognitive Psychology, 10*, 411–437) present some interesting evidence that spatial knowledge is also organized hierarchically, which places some interesting distortions, in that many people wrongly assume that San Diego is west of Reno; because of the higher-order "state" category, California is viewed as west of Nevada.

PART VII

# Categorization

# Introduction to Part VII: Categorization

By categorization, we mean the grouping of similar concepts. For example, robins, sparrows, and crows can all be categorized as "birds." Categorization is a fundamental aspect of learning and representing knowledge that occurs not only in adults but also in children (e.g., Gelman & Markman, 1986) and animals such as pigeons (e.g., Herrnstein, Loveland, & Cable, 1976).

It is very useful to be able to group together like items into categories. Such grouping allows prediction of item attributes based solely on knowledge of category membership. For example, knowing that a novel object can be classified as a "chair" provides a wealth of information, such as its function, its nonliving status, and information about where one might find it. As such, categories serve the principle of cognitive economy. That is, relying on a category membership is more cognitively efficient than always having to retrieve identifying and other trait information for each and every object encountered. (For an experimental demonstration of cognitive economy, see the classic paper by Collins and Quillian in the "Knowledge" chapter of this book.)

Historically, there have been several different theoretical perspectives on the bases underlying categories. For example, the classical view posits that there are critical and defining features for category membership (e.g., see Bruner, Goodnow, & Austin, 1956). According to this view, the concept of "bird" might be defined by the characteristics of flying, having feathers, singing, and building nests. A new item would only be classified as a category member if it had all of these features. This is in contrast to probabilistic theories, in which category membership is still based upon object attributes, but these features are typical of category membership, rather than required. Typical category members (e.g., robin) have more of the category's properties (e.g., small and flies) than do atypical exemplars (e.g., ostrich) (Rosch & Mervis, 1975). Similarity between category members is then defined by overlap in features.

Rosch et al. (1976) proposed that categories have a hierarchical structure, much as biological taxonomies do. The most general level of the hierarchy is the superordinate level (e.g., furniture), in the middle is the basic level (e.g., chair), and the most specific level is the subordinate (e.g., rocking chair). Rosch et al. argued that the basic level is the most specific level at which members share a number of features. In a series of elegant experiments, they demonstrated the privileged status of the basic level. Items at the basic level overlap in listed attributes and in physical outlines; basic level names are learned first by children and are used naturally by adults to label objects.

Rosch et al. (1976) suggested that basic level items might be simplified even further, resulting in a prototype that captures a category's most typical features. Posner and Keele (1968) experimentally investigated subjects' formation of prototypes. Their experiments began by giving subjects experience with four different categories; subjects learned to classify distortions of a nonpresented prototype (e.g., a random dot pattern). In the second phase, subjects classified studied distortions, novel distortions, and the nonstudied prototype. Subjects made more errors when classifying novel distortions but were just as good at classifying the nonstudied prototype as old items. Posner and Keele interpreted this result as suggesting that information about the gist of the category had in fact been extracted.

The Posner and Keele (1968) paper is a classic, in part because it suggested that complex categorization behavior can be produced from relatively arbitrary patterns. It preceded the debate on whether the prototype is naturally abstracted during the study of exemplars versus later being computed from stored exemplars. More recent research suggests that each individual stimulus is stored, and categorization reflects the convergence of similar traces (e.g., Hintzman, 1986; Nosofsky & Johnasen, 2000).

The probabilistic view takes as its starting point that category members are similar to one another on various dimensions, and that the most typical (or prototypical) category members maximize these dimensions. Rosch argued that the resultant categories parallel the basic structure of the world. This may be the case for biological categories, but we have many nonbiological categories. Medin (1989) points to goal-derived categories, such as "things to take out of the house in case of a fire" (Barsalou, 1985). For these categories, the dimensions on which to maximize similarity cannot follow from the structure of the natural world.

The crucial point made by Medin (1989; Murphy & Medin, 1985) is that similarity is unconstrained. Any two objects can be seen as similar on some dimension. Both televisions and artichokes are objects found on Earth; both meteors and paper clips are nonliving; both chipmunks and lichen are found in forests. In order to assess similarity, a dimension for evaluation (e.g., living versus nonliving) has to be chosen. Medin argued that people have theories to constrain the dimension on which similarity is assessed. Thus, theories such as "things to take out of the house in case of fire" pinpoint the dimension on which to assess the similarity of objects. In this example, the result is similarity ratings based on perceived value, not on structural or perceptual features, as tends to be the case for natural categories.

We close by noting two recent trends in the categorization. First, researchers have begun to bolster their claims about the underlying mental representations of categories via neurological data from patients and neuroimaging studies (see the paper by Sacchett & Humphreys, 1992; see also Ashby & Waldron, 2000; Nosofsky & Zaki, 1998). Second, researchers are also very interested in social categories (Wyer & Srull, 1989), such as how people represent the categories of black versus white people (e.g., Hamilton & Sherman, 1994). Understanding the human tendency to simplify complex sets of information into more simple categories clearly extends beyond describing simple relations between exemplars of natural categories.

## REFERENCES

Ashby, F. G., & Waldron, E. M. (2000). The neuropsychological bases of category learning. *Current Directions in Psychological Science, 9,* 10–14.

Barsalou, L. W. (1985). Ideals, central tendency, and frequency of instantiation as determinants of graded structure in categories. *Journal of Experimental Psychology: Learning, Memory, & Cognition, 11,* 629–654.

Bruner, J. S., Goodnow, J. J., & Austin, G. A. (1956). *A study of thinking.* New York: Wiley.

Gelman, S. A., & Markman, E. M. (1986). Categories and induction in young children. *Cognition, 23,* 183–209.

Hamilton, D. L., & Sherman, J. W. (1994). Stereotypes. In R. S. Wyer, Jr., & T. K. Srull (Eds.), *Handbook of social cognition, Vol. 1: Basic processes* (pp. 1–68). Hillsdale, NJ: Erlbaum.

Herrnstein, R. J., Loveland, D. H., & Cable, C. (1976). Natural concepts in pigeons. *Journal of Experimental Psychology: Animal Behavior Processes, 2,* 285–302.

Hintzman, D.L. (1986). "Schema abstraction" in a multiple-trace memory model. *Psychological Review, 93,* 411–428.

Medin, D. L. (1989). Concepts and conceptual structure. *American Psychologist, 44,* 1469–1481.

Murphy, G. L., & Medin, D. L. (1985). The role of theories in conceptual coherence. *Psychological Review, 92,* 289–316.

Nosofsky, R. M., & Johansen, M. K. (2000). Exemplar-based accounts of "multiple-system" phenomena in perceptual categorization. *Psychonomic Bulletin & Review, 7,* 375–402.

Nosofsky, R. M., & Zaki, S. R. (1998). Dissociations between categorization and recognition in amnesic and normal individuals: An exemplar-based interpretation. *Psychological Science, 9,* 247–255.

Posner, M. I., & Keele, S. W. (1968). On the genesis of abstract ideas. *Journal of Experimental Psychology, 77,* 353–363.

Rosch, E., & Mervis, C. B. (1975). Family resemblances: Studies in the internal structure of categories. *Cognitive Psychology, 7,* 573–605.

Rosch, E., Mervis, C. B., Gray, W. D., Johnson, D. M., & Boyes-Braem, P. (1976). Basic objects in natural categories. *Cognitive Psychology, 8,* 382–440.

Sacchett, C., & Humphreys, G. W. (1992). Calling a squirrel a squirrel but a canoe a wigwam: A category-specific deficit for artefactual objects and body parts. *Cognitive Neuropsychology, 9,* 73–86.

Wyer, R. S., Jr., & Srull, T. K. (1989). Memory and cognition in its social context. Hillsdale, NJ: Erlbaum.

# Basic Objects in Natural Categories

Eleanor Rosch, Carolyn B. Mervis, Wayne D. Gray,
David M. Johnson, and Penny Boyes-Braem

• University of California, Berkeley

Categorizations which humans make of the concrete world are not arbitrary but highly determined. In taxonomies of concrete objects, there is one level of abstraction at which the most basic category cuts are made. Basic categories are those which carry the most information, possess the highest category cue validity, and are, thus, the most differentiated from one another. The four experiments define basic objects by demonstrating that in taxonomies of common concrete nouns in English based on class inclusion, basic objects are the most inclusive categories whose members: (a) possess significant numbers of attributes in common, (b) have motor programs which are similar to one another, (c) have similar shapes, and (d) can be identified from averaged shapes of members of the class.

The world consists of a virtually infinite number of discriminably different stimuli. One of the most basic functions of all organisms is the cutting up of the environment into classifications by which nonidentical stimuli can be treated as equivalent. Yet there has been little explicit attempt to determine the principles by which humans divide up the world in the way that they do. On the contrary, it has been the tendency both in psychology and anthropology to treat that segmentation of the world as originally arbitrary and to focus on such matters as how categories, once given, are learned or the effects of having a label for some segment. A typical statement of such a position is: ". . . the physical and social environment of a young child is perceived as a continuum. It does not contain any intrinsically separate 'things.' The child, in due course, is taught to impose upon this environment a kind of discriminating grid which serves to distinguish the world as being composed of a large number of separate things, each labeled with a name" (Leach, 1964, p. 34). It is the contention of the present paper that such a view would be reasonable only if the world were entirely unstructured; that is, using Garner's (1974) definition of *structure*, if the world formed a set of stimuli in which all possible stimulus attributes occurred with equal probability combined with all other possible attributes.

## Principles of Categorization

The aim of the present research is to show that the world does contain "intrinsically separate things." The world is structured because real-world attributes do not occur independently of each other. Creatures with feathers are more likely also to have wings than creatures with fur, and objects with the visual appearance of chairs are more likely to have functional sit-on-ableness than objects with the appearance of cats. That is, combinations of attributes of real objects do not occur uniformly. Some pairs, triples, or *n*tuples are quite probable, appearing in combination sometimes with one, sometimes another attribute; others are rare; others logically cannot or empirically do not occur.

By *category* we mean a number of objects which are considered equivalent. Categories are generally designated by names, e.g., *dog, animal*. A *taxonomy* is a system by which categories are related to another by means of class inclusion. The greater the inclusiveness of a category within a taxonomy, the higher the level of abstraction. Each category within a taxonomy is entirely included within one other category (unless it is the highest level category) but is not exhaustive of that more inclusive category (see Kay, 1971). Thus, the term *level of abstraction* within a taxonomy refers to a particular level of inclusiveness. A familiar taxonomy is the Linnean system for the classification of animals.

We will argue that categories within taxonomies of concrete objects are structured such that there is generally one level of abstraction at which the most basic category cuts can be made. In general, the basic level of abstraction in a taxonomy is the level at which categories carry the most information, possess the highest cue validity, and are, thus, the most differentiated from one another. The basic level of abstraction can be described both in general terms of cognitive economy and in the specific language of probabilistic cue validity (Brunswik, 1956).

## Cognitive Economy

To categorize a stimulus means to consider it, for purposes of that categorization, not only equivalent to other stimuli in the same category but also different from stimuli not in that category. On the one hand, it would appear to the organism's advantage to have as many properties as possible predictable from knowing any one property (which, for humans, includes the important property of the category name), a principle which would lead to formation of large numbers of categories with the finest possible discriminations between categories. On the other hand, one purpose of categorization is to reduce the infinite differences among stimuli to behaviorally and cognitively usable proportions. It is to the organism's advantage

not to differentiate one stimulus from others when that differentiation is irrelevant for the purposes at hand. The basic level of classification, the primary level at which cuts are made in the environment, appears to result from the combination of these two principles; the basic categorization is the most general and inclusive level at which categories can delineate real-world correlational structures.

## Cue Validity

Cue validity is a probabilistic concept; the validity of a given cue $x$ as a predictor of a given category $y$ (the conditional probability of $y/x$) increases as the frequency with which cue $x$ is associated with category $y$ increases and decreases as the frequency with which cue $x$ is associated with categories other than $y$ increases. [The precise mathematical form used to compute the conditional probability $y/x$ has varied (Beach 1964a, 1964b; Reed, 1972).] The power of cue validity information of the internal structure of categories has been demonstrated for both natural and for controlled artificial categories (Rosch & Mervis, 1975). The cue validity of an entire category may be defined as the summation of the cue validities for that category of each of the attributes of the category. (Note that category cue validity is not a probability: (a) its value may exceed 1, (b) it does not have the same set theoretic properties as a probability.[1]

A category with a high total cue validity is, by definition, more differentiated from other categories than one of lower total cue validity. A working assumption of the present research is that in the real world information-rich bundles of perceptual and functional attributes occur that form natural discontinuities and that basic cuts in categorization are made at these discontinuities. Suppose that basic objects (e.g., *chair, car*) are at the most inclusive level at which there are attributes common to all or most members of the category. Then total cue validities are maximized at that level of abstraction at which basic objects are categorized. That is, categories one level more abstract will be superordinate categories (e.g., *furniture, vehicle*) whose members share only a few attributes among each other. Categories below the basic level will be subordinate categories (e.g., *kitchen chair, sports car*) which are also bundles of predictable attributes and functions, but contain many attributes which overlap with other categories (for example, *kitchen chair* shares most of its attributes with other kinds of chairs).

Superordinate categories have lower total cue validity than do basic level categories because they have fewer common attributes. Subordinate categories have lower total cue validity than do basic because they also share most attributes with contrasting subordinate categories. That basic objects are categories at the level of abstraction which maximizes cue validity is another way of asserting that basic objects are the categories which best mirror the correlational structure of the environment.

This paper reports a series of converging experiments whose purpose was to define further and to provide evidence supporting the concept of basic level objects.

## Converging Operational Definitions of Basic Objects

Basic objects are the most inclusive categories which delineate the correlational structure of the environment. However, real-world correlational structure itself provides a number of aspects which could serve as the point of departure for the present analysis. Four such aspects are explored in our experiments.

### Outline of Experiments 1 through 4

#### EXPERIMENT 1

Some ethnobiologists have asserted a claim somewhat similar to that of the present study—i.e., there is a level of biological classification which corresponds to "natural groupings" of organisms which possess "bundles" of correlated features and which are "obviously" different from other organisms (Berlin, 1972; Bulmer, 1967; Bulmer & Tyler, 1968; Rosaldo, 1972). Berlin (1972) has also argued for an evolutionary theory of plant names. Berlin has identified natural grouping at the level of the genus (oak, maple) and has amassed considerable evidence in support of the claim that the first plant names to evolve in a language refer to this level. For our purposes, the work of ethnobiologists is limited by three factors. First, it

refers only to biological classes; second, the claims for natural groupings are generally supported only by the ethnographer's mention of a few correlated attributes (a tendency being corrected in Berlin's current ethnobotanical studies—see Berlin, Breedlove, & Raven, 1966); and finally, the location of natural groupings at a particular level of abstraction is defined by linguistic—taxonomic, rather than psychological, criteria (see Berlin, Breedlove, & Raven, 1973). The purpose of the first experiment in this paper is to provide a systematic empirical study of the co-occurrence of attributes in the most common taxonomies of man-made and biological objects in our own culture.

#### EXPERIMENT 2

Among the attributes of objects are the ways in which humans habitually use or interact with them. For example, when performing the action of sitting down on a chair, a sequence of body and muscle movements are typically made which are aspects of the functions of chairs. It is not important here to determine whether material attributes or action sequences are more fundamental (although Piaget, 1952, has argued for the ontogenetic significance of sensori-motor schemata in concept development). Our claim is that groups of objects in a given culture require highly similar motor patterns in their use; and these motor patterns serve as common attributes in the construction of categories.

The purpose of Experiment 2 is to develop systematic techniques to operationalize and specify in some detail the actual motor programs which adults employ when using or interacting with common objects. The hypothesis is that when motor programs are measured, basic level objects will be the most inclusive categories at which consistent motor programs are employed for all objects of a class. Categories subordinate to the basic level should be characterized by essentially the same attributes and motor programs as the basic level.

#### EXPERIMENT 3

An aspect of the meaning of a category of objects, inseparable from the attributes and motoric uses of the objects, is the way the objects "look." Appearance is, perhaps, the most difficult of all characteristics of objects to define. Shape is a very general and important aspect of objects. Included within what we call shape are the structural relationships of the parts of an object to each other—for example, the visual representation of the legs, seat, and back of a chair and of the way in which those parts of the chair are placed in relation to one another. Hence, shape is probably a salient visual cue in normal recognition of objects. Pilot studies showed that objects are quite recognizable from only the outline tracing of a two-dimensional projection of their shapes. Indeed, objects were as recognizable from such outlines as from lists of criterial attributes or from full views of parts of the objects.

In order to measure similarity of shape between two objects, we normalized outline drawings of the objects for size and orientation, juxtaposed them, and computed the ratio of overlapped to nonoverlapped area. Experiment 3 examines the hypothesis that with this measure of similarity of shape, the basic level of categorization is the most inclusive level at which the objects of a class begin to look very much alike.

EXPERIMENT 4

If the basic level is the most inclusive level at which shapes of objects of a category are similar, the basic level might also be the most inclusive level at which an average shape of an object can be recognized. Thus, the basic level may be the most inclusive level at which it is possible to form a mental image of some "average" member of the class. This would be the most abstract level at which it is possible to have a relatively concrete image.

# Experiment 1: Attributes

Experiment 1 has three parts. First, the major source of data was obtained by asking subjects to list attributes of object names derived from nine taxonomies. Second, an independent group of subjects judged the truth of the attributes which had been most frequently listed by the first group of subjects. Third, subjects listed attributes of visually present objects as a check on the nature and validity of the attribute lists obtained when object names were used in the first part of the experiment.

## Methods

### Attribute Listing

#### SUBJECTS

Subjects were 200 students in undergraduate psychology courses.

#### STIMULI

The stimuli were 90 object names belonging to three levels of abstraction in nine taxonomies (Table 29.1). These stimuli were chosen systematically according to two principles: One, as the study was an attempt to investigate the categorization of real-world material objects, the stimuli should represent the most common categories of concrete objects in our culture; two, as all of the hypotheses concerned levels of abstraction in classification of objects, specific stimuli had to be those for which relationships of class inclusion, superordination, and subordination both existed as potentials in the English language and were reliably agreed upon by normal speakers of English.

A measure of the most common superordinate categories of concrete objects was obtained in the following manner: The population of categories of concrete nouns in common use in English was determined by the concrete nouns with a word frequency of 10 or greater from the Kučera and Francis (1967) sample of written English. A superordinate category was considered in common use if at least four of its members met this criterion. Categories were eliminated if: (a) all of the items bore a part—whole relationship to the only reasonable superordinate (e.g., parts of the body, parts of buildings), (b) if there was linguistic ambiguity amongst possible superordinates (e.g., *animal* is commonly used as a synonym for *mammal*), and (c) if the superordinate cross-cut a large number of other taxonomic structures (e.g., *food*).

By these criteria, only one biological category, *bird*, could be included in the study. Because biological taxonomies were the only ones in which hypotheses concerning basic objects based on independent linguistic evolutionary data existed, it was necessary to amend the inclusion criteria. A biological category was included if at least one member of the category (or the superordinate noun itself) achieved a Kučera and Francis frequency

**TABLE 29.1. The Nine Taxonomies Used as Stimuli**

| Superordinate | Basic Level | Subordinates | |
|---|---|---|---|
| | | **Nonbiological taxonomies** | |
| Musical instrument | Guitar | Folk guitar | Classical guitar |
| | Piano | Grand piano | Upright piano |
| | Drum | Kettle drum | Base drum |
| Fruit[a] | Apple | Delicious apple | Mackintosh apple |
| | Peach | Freestone peach | Cling peach |
| | Grapes | Concord grapes | Green seedless grapes |
| Tool | Hammer | Ball-peen hammer | Claw hammer |
| | Saw | Hack hand saw | Cross-cutting hand saw |
| | Screwdriver | Phillips screwdriver | Regular screwdriver |
| Clothing | Pants | Levis | Double knit pants |
| | Socks | Knee socks | Ankle socks |
| | Shirt | Dress shirt | Knit shirt |
| Furniture | Table | Kitchen table | Dining room table |
| | Lamp | Floor lamp | Desk lamp |
| | Chair | Kitchen chair | Living room chair |
| Vehicle | Car | Sports car | Four door sedan car |
| | Bus | City bus | Cross country bus |
| | Truck | Pick up truck | Tractor-trailer truck |
| | | **Biological taxonomies** | |
| Tree | Maple | Silver maple | Sugar maple |
| | Birch | River birch | White birch |
| | Oak | White oak | Red oak |
| Fish | Bass | Sea bass | Striped bass |
| | Trout | Rainbow trout | Steelhead trout |
| | Salmon | Blueback salmon | Chinook salmon |
| Bird | Cardinal | Easter cardinal | Grey tailed cardinal |
| | Eagle | Bald eagle | Golden eagle |
| | Sparrow | Song sparrow | Field sparrow |

[a] Fruit is not considered a biological taxonomy by the criteria in Berlin (1972).

of 10 or more. Thirteen superordinate categories met the new criteria: musical instrument, fruit, tool, clothing, furniture, vehicle, vegetable, toy, weapon, bird, tree, fish, and snake.

The second criterion for choosing items was the item's "taxonomic depth" in common English. To test our hypothesis, a class inclusion hierarchy with at least three levels of abstraction is needed: a basic level (such as *hammer*), a superordinate (such as *tool*), and subordinates into which the basic level can be further subdivided (such as *claw hammer* and *ball-peen hammer*). In order to determine taxonomic depth in common English for our potential items, the following procedure was followed: For each of the 13 categories, lists were constructed of the items in that category which appeared 10 or more times in the Battig and Montague (1969) tabulations. (These are tabulations of the frequen-

cies with which instances were produced in response to the category name.) Five judges were given the lists. Judges were asked to give the superordinate (or superordinates if they felt more than one was appropriate) for each item and to list any or all subordinates of the item (i.e., any classifications into which the item could be further subdivided).

The final nine taxonomies used in the experiment each included at least three basic level objects which met the following criteria: (a) All five judges agreed unanimously on listing that superordinate as the single superordinate for the item, and (b) For each basic level object, there were at least two common subordinate items listed by all five judges. In addition, for biological taxonomies, we checked the official taxonomic legitimacy of listed subordinates before including them.

## PROCEDURE

The stimuli were divided into 10 sets of nine items each. Each set consisted of items at only one level of abstraction. Thus, there was one set of superordinate of items, three sets of basic level items, and six sets of subordinate level items. For the basic level items, there was never more than one item per set which belonged to a given superordinate category, and for the subordinate items each set contained only one item from a given basic level (which entailed also from a given superordinate) category.

Subjects were tested in groups, and 20 different subjects received each of the 10 sets. Each item was printed at the top of a page and the nine pages of items in a set assembled in a different randomized order for each subject. Subjects were given 1½ min per item to write down all of the attributes of each object which they could think of. They were asked to avoid simple free associations. (For the complete text of the instructions, see Rosch, Mervis, Gray, Johnson, & Boyes-Braem, Note 1.)

An initial tally was made, and only attributes which were listed by at least six subjects were used as data in the final tabulation.

## Judgments of Attributes

A new group of subjects was asked to judge the truth of the attributes which had been listed by six or more subjects in the free listing experiment; they were not asked to introduce attributes themselves.

### SUBJECTS

Subjects were students in a seminar. Seven completed and returned the judgment forms out of interest in the experiment.

### STIMULI

Separate forms for each of the 27 basic level items were rated by each subject. All of the attributes which had been listed six or more times for a basic level item, its superordinate, or its subordinates in the previous part of the experiment were listed, in random order, down the left side of the page. Across the top of the page were written the superordinate category name, the basic level name, and the two subordinate level names.

## PROCEDURE

Potential subjects were given forms for all 27 basic level items (which were arranged in different random order for each subject) and asked to judge whether each of the attributes listed down the side of the page was true of each category listed across the top. (The text of the instructions is available in Rosch et al., Note 1.) Subjects took the forms home with them; completed forms were collected at the regular seminar meeting the following week.

## Attributes of Physically Present Objects

Both the free listing of attributes and the judgment of attributes in the previous parts of this experiment relied on subjects' retrieval from memory of object characteristics from their names. A further question was whether attribute lists produced by a subject listing the attributes of 20 different visually present objects of a category would correspond with the lists obtained from the previous 20 subjects listing attributes from memory for the object name.

Two paid subjects were employed for the task. Stimulus sets consisted of one basic level item from each of the nine taxonomies: guitar, apple, hammer, pants, chair, car, tree, fish, and bird (the use of the supposed superordinates for the biological taxonomies will be explained in the results section). The subjects' task was to find 20 different examples of each of the items listed above, and (timing themselves with a stopwatch) to list as many attributes of each item as possible in 1½ min. Subjects were told to start with the objects in their own homes when applicable (such as chair and pants) and then to find the other items in the appropriate places: supermarkets, hardware stores, the street, or pictures in books. For fish, one subject visited the Steinhart Aquarium at Golden Gate Park, one rated pictures in the Crescent Book series *Color Treasury of Aquarium Fish* (1972). For birds, both subjects used both *Birds of North America: A Guide to Field Identification* (1966) and *The Golden Book of Bird Stamps* (1966), each picking 20 different pictures from the books using tables of random numbers. Subjects were given essentially the same instructions for listing attributes as the first group of subjects except that they were told not to list functional attributes (which they found themselves simply repeating without further consideration for each instance of the object once they had thought of the attribute).

The protocols for each subject were tallied separately in the same manner as had been the protocols for the 20 subjects listing attributes for each object name in the initial free listing condition.

## Results and Discussion

Table 29.2 shows the number of attributes listed six or more times for each level of abstraction. The left-hand columns show the tallies obtained from the attribute listings in the first part of the experiment. The right-hand columns show the judge-amended tallies; in computing these tallies, an attribute was added or subtracted only when all seven judges agreed that it belonged or did not belong at the appropriate level. Appendix 1 shows examples of the judge-amended attributes: a list of all of the judge-amended attributes for each of the nine taxonomies is available in Rosch et al., Note 1.

The basic hypothesis of the study was that the basic level would be the most inclusive level in a taxonomy at which a cluster of attributes, believed to be common to the class named, would be listed. An initial glance at Table 29.2 shows that the results for the nonbiological and the biological taxonomies are quite different—that is, what we had taken to be the superordinate level for the biological items showed all the signs of being basic level objects at least for our subjects. The first test of

significance was, therefore, a test of whether results for the biological and non-biological categories (e.g., the level at which a marked increase in attributes occurred) differed significantly; such a test was necessary before the substantive hypothesis of the study could be tested. For each category, the proportion of basic level attributes contributed by the increase in attributes between the hypothesized superordinate and the hypothesized basic level was computed. The difference in that proportion between the nonbiological and the biological categories was computed separately for the raw and the judge-amended tallies. Both proved significant: raw tallies, $t(7) = 3.72$, $p < .01$; judge-amended tallies, $t(7) = 4.11$, $p < .01$. This finding supports the idea that for our subjects, the hypothesized superordinate appeared to be the basic level for the biological taxonomies.

Tests of the difference in number of attributes between superordinate and basic level categories were performed for the nonbiological taxonomies to test the hypothesis that basic level items would contain more attributes than superordinate level items. The tests were significant: raw tallies, $t(5) = 4.75$, $p < .01$; judge-amended tallies, $t(5) = 10.07$, $p < .001$. The second prediction from the substantive hypothesis, that the number of attributes added at the subordinate level would be significantly fewer than the number added at the basic level, was also supported for the nonbiological taxonomies: raw tallies, $t(5) = 4.28$, $p < .01$; judge-amended tallies, $t(5) = 6.43$, $p < .001$. (Neither

**TABLE 29.2. Number of Attributes in Common at Each Level of Abstraction**

| | Number of Attributes in Common | | | | | |
| | Raw Tallies | | | Judge-Amended Tallies | | |
| Category | Super-ordinate | Basic Level | Sub-ordinate | Super-ordinate | Basic Level | Sub-ordinate |
|---|---|---|---|---|---|---|
| Nonbiological taxonomies | | | | | | |
| Musical instrument | 1 | 6.0 | 8.5 | 1 | 8.3 | 8.7 |
| Fruit | 7 | 12.3 | 14.7 | 3 | 8.3 | 9.5 |
| Tool | 3 | 8.3 | 9.7 | 3 | 8.7 | 9.2 |
| Clothing | 3 | 10.0 | 12.0 | 2 | 8.3 | 9.7 |
| Furniture | 3 | 9.0 | 10.3 | 0 | 7.0 | 7.8 |
| Vehicle | 4 | 8.7 | 11.2 | 1 | 11.7 | 16.8 |
| Biological taxonomies | | | | | | |
| Tree | 9 | 10.3 | 11.2 | 10 | 11.0 | 11.5 |
| Fish | 6 | 8.7 | 9.3 | 8 | 9.7 | 10.0 |
| Bird | 11 | 14.7 | 15.3 | 14 | 16.0 | 16.5 |

hypothesis could be tested for the biological taxonomies since we had not obtained attribute lists for levels of classification superordinate to the hypothesized superordinates.) Thus, for those categories in which the location of basic level objects is clear, the basic level does appear to be the most inclusive level at which objects have clusters of attributes in common.

In an additional analysis, attributes were coded separately as nouns, adjectives, or functional attributes. The majority (seven out of 10) of the total number of attributes listed for the superordinates of the non-biological taxonomies were functional attributes of a very general nature. The percentage of gain in function, noun, and adjective attributes for basic level over superordinate and for subordinate over basic level was tested for significance by the Sign Test. Both nouns and adjectives increased significantly more than functional attributes between the superordinate and basic level. For the subordinate level, however, those few attributes which were added were almost exclusively adjectives rather than nouns (Sign test, $p < .05$).

The foregoing analysis was based upon attributes elicited by category names. In the last part of the experiment, attributes elicited by objects were compared with those obtained using object names. (Because this part of the experiment was undertaken after the name elicited analyses had been completed, *tree*, *fish*, and *bird* were treated as basic level objects rather than superordinates.)

The attributes listed by the two subjects were tallied in the same manner as has been described for the previous data. Reliability between the two subjects was high; exactly the same attributes were and were not listed six or more times by both subjects in all but one instance.

Results of these tallies were clear-cut. Attributes listed six or more times by the previous 20 subjects responding to one object name and attributes listed by two subjects six or more times to 20 instances of the object were in virtually perfect agreement. For all of the nine categories, every attribute listed in the judge-amended tallies was also listed by both subjects describing concrete objects. Furthermore, few (an average of only one per item) additional attributes were listed. (Added attributes are itemized in Rosch et al., Note 1.)

In summary: The hypothesis that there is a basic level of abstraction in taxonomies of common objects which is the most inclusive level at which the objects of a category possess numbers of attributes in common was supported for attribute listings obtained by three different methods: free listing of attributes for object names, judge-amended tallies of attributes for object names, and free listing of attributes for visually present objects. The one unexpected finding was that, for biological taxonomies, the basic level appeared to be the next higher level in the taxonomy than had been initially proposed by anthropological and linguistic–taxonomic evidence.

An important issue is the extent to which these findings represent descriptions of the correlational structure of attributes which are located in the real world versus in the knowledge and viewpoint of the subjects. That listing of attributes for visually present objects replicates the findings from attributes listed from memory argues that the findings are not an artifact of the way in which object names are stored in memory. However, the degree of expertise of subjects did not vary systematically (see Rosch et al., Note 1), and it is not known to what extent that may have affected location of the basic level, particularly for the biological taxonomies. Would, for example, an ichthiologist, whether presented with an actual example of a category or with a fish name, have been able to list sufficient attributes specific to *trout*, *bass*, and *salmon* that the basic level for fish would have been placed at that level of abstraction? The issue of differential knowledge of correlational structures and the issue of the placement of basic level objects in biological taxonomies will be discussed further after findings of the other experiments have been described.

## Experiment 2: Motor Movements

The major hypothesis of this study was that basic level objects are the most inclusive categories for which highly similar sequences of motor movements are made to objects of the class. Testing the hypothesis required: first, obtaining a corpus of subjects' descriptions of the body and muscle movements which they made in interaction with objects (the level of abstraction of the object names being varied systematically as in Experiment 1); second, the development of a reliable coding system for those sets of descriptions of muscle movements; and, third, a tally of the numbers of motor movements in common for the category terms at the various levels of abstraction.

The major data derive from protocols produced by subjects asked to describe their body and muscle movements when interacting with specified objects. As a check on the validity of the descriptive protocols, naïve models performed the main general activity which had been elicited by the object name with a sample of actual objects (e.g., a model sat down in a chair), and subjects described the actual body and muscle movements which they observed.

## Methods

### Descriptions of Imagined Movements to Object Names

#### SUBJECTS

Subjects were volunteers from psychology classes who received course credit for participation. Protocols were not used if the subject was not a native English speaker, did not complete the test, or clearly and obviously failed to follow instructions for all nine of the items. Two hundred protocols were obtained which met our criteria.

#### STIMULI

Stimuli were the same nine taxonomies used in Experiment 1 (Table 29.1), again divided into 10 sets of nine words. Twenty subjects received each set.

#### PROCEDURES

As in Experiment 1, subjects were tested in groups. The instructions were preceded by a pantomime demonstration by the experimenter of bicycle riding, and by practice in naming movements. The experimenter solicited movement names for the different parts of the body from the subjects, getting every subject to utter at least one answer to a motor movement of a body part. The instructions asked the subjects to "write down the muscle movements that you make when you use or interact with that object, in as much detail as you can." (The text of the instructions is available in Rosch et al., Note 1.)

The name of each item was printed at the top of a blank page. At the end of 3 min, subjects were

asked to stop, turn the page, and proceed with the next item. With the exception of some of the first subjects tested, each subject who received the same set of nine items received them in a different random order.

### Descriptions of Actual Movements of Naïve Models

Subjects were a class of 28 students. Four of the students were chosen at random to be the models. They were asked to wait outside the room while instructions were given to the remainder of the class; thus, they did not know the purpose of the experiment at the time that they performed their actions.

The class was told that previous subjects had been asked to describe the body and muscle movements which they imagined themselves making to objects, but that they would be asked to describe the *actual* body and muscle movements which the models would make when they interacted with actual objects. In order to give this group the same explanation of what was meant by specific body and muscle movements as had been given the previous subjects, the identical instructions were read to them, including their participation in the pantomimed bicycle riding. In addition, the subjects were told to watch the model carefully and to write down the body and muscle movements he or she had made in interacting with the object in as much detail as possible.

The models were called in, one at a time, and each performed with one object. The four activities were: sitting down on a chair, eating a small bunch of grapes, putting on a sock, and hammering a nail. The class was given 3 min following the completion of each modeled action to write down the sequence of movements.

Of the 24 protocols collected, two were eliminated because the subjects were not native English speakers, and two were eliminated at random for computational purposes.

## Results

### Coding of Responses

Considerable effort was required to develop a coding system for reducing the data which was both reliable and yielded similarity scores for units of movement which offered a face valid embodiment of the meaning of our hypothesis concerning similarity of movements.

The steps for coding the protocols were as follows: Each subject's protocol was first divided into the major activities for which that subject described an interaction with that object. For example, while the activity described for chairs was usually the process of sitting down on one, some subjects also described a muscle movement sequence for picking one up and carrying it, and other idiosyncratic responses. A finer coding was then applied separately to each major activity described by each subject. At each point in the description, the activity was segmented into the body part involved (head, eyes, neck, torso, arms, legs, knees, feet, hands, fingers, wrist, etc.). Under the body part, each activity (such as bending, rotating, turning, extending, etc.) described was listed. If the same body part was mentioned again later in the description with the same or a different movement, it was coded again with its new movement. (That movement sequences were not simply analytic descriptions of the meaning of the name of the major activity was demonstrated by the fact that similarly named activities, such as *sitting* or *looking*, received quite different movement lists when applied to different objects—e.g., sitting on a chair versus sitting as part of entering a car; looking at a bird versus looking at a tree.) Reliabilities (percentage of rater agreement) for the coding of nine randomly chosen protocols, each for a different object, three at each of the three levels of abstraction, were all 88% or higher for three independent coders.

The result of primary interest was the degree of similarity between movements made to objects at the three different levels of abstraction. The same movement was considered to have been included in the protocols of two different subjects only if, for the same basic activity in relation to an object, the same movement of the same body part occurred in the same place in the same sequence of movements. For example, if two different subjects mentioned bending their knees as part of the sitting process and that mention occurred between the actions of approaching and/or turning their back to the chair and the actions of touching their buttocks to and/or releasing their weight onto the chair, the bending of the knees was tallied as two occurrences of the same movement. However, if one subject mentioned bending his knees as part of raising his feet to rest them on a desk after hav-

ing already put his weight onto the chair, it was coded as a different movement and not tallied with the other two bendings of knees. For motion sequences which, in fact, occur simultaneously (e.g., steering and food pedal manipulation while driving), sequence requirements for coding movements the same were adjusted to fit that fact. The criterion for counting a common movement was set at four or more responses.

The second count of body part movements was based on a far simpler measure. This tally was obtained to measure the degree of specificity of the descriptions at each level of abstraction regardless of the overlap in descriptions. To obtain this measure, the raters simply counted each specific movement rated, regardless of body part, place in the sequence, place in the major activity, or repetition of mention of the same movement by other subjects. This count was designed to examine the question of the specificity of the movements described for the class of objects named independently from the question of the similarity of movements made to objects of that class.

## Substantive Results

Table 29.3 shows tallies of movements in common for the descriptions of imagined movements for the three levels of abstraction. Examples of some of the movements, listed under their appropriate major activity and in their appropriate sequence are shown in Appendix 2. (A complete listing of all movements for all items is available in Rosch et al., Note 1.) The proportion increase in number of attributes between the hypothesized superordinate and basic level categories differed significantly for the nonbiological and the biological categories: $t(7) = 4.59$, $p < .01$. For the nonbiological taxonomies, significantly more motor movements were given in common for the basic level than for the superordinate, $t(5) = 14.19$, $p < .001$. (As in Experiment 1, this effect could not be tested for the biological taxonomies alone.) The number of motor movements given in common for the subordinate level did not differ significantly from the basic level: nonbiological taxonomies, $t(5) = .92$, ns.; biological taxonomies, $t(2) = 1.83$, ns.

Because each of the motor movements tallied was an individual item in its unique place in a

**TABLE 29.3. Number of Motor Movements in Common at Each Level of Abstraction**

| Category | Number of Motor Movements in Common | | | | |
|---|---|---|---|---|---|
| | Super-ordinate | Basic Level | Subordinate Mean | Subordinate Number Added | Subordinate Number Subtracted |
| | Nonbiological taxonomies | | | | |
| Musical instrument | 0 | 16.7 | 16.2 | 2.2 | 2.6 |
| Fruit | 4 | 21.3 | 20.5 | 2.5 | 3.3 |
| Tool | 2 | 19.2 | 18.0 | 1.2 | 2.7 |
| Clothing | 2 | 19.0 | 19.2 | 1.5 | 1.5 |
| Furniture | 1 | 11.7 | 12.3 | 1.3 | .7 |
| Vehicle | 1 | 18.0 | 18.2 | 2.8 | 2.5 |
| | Biological taxonomies | | | | |
| Tree | 8 | 6.0 | 6.8 | .7 | .8 |
| Fish | 17 | 14.0 | 17.0 | 1.2 | 1.7 |
| Bird | 7 | 7.3 | 7.2 | .3 | .5 |

motor sequence, a tally of the movements to subordinate level objects which averaged movements added to and those omitted from the movement sequences tallied for the basic level object did not seem a totally sufficient test of the possible differences between movements described for basic level and for subordinate level objects. The two right-hand columns of Table 29.3, thus, show, respectively, the mean number of added and the mean number of omitted movements for subordinates in each taxonomy. The significance of the difference between the basic level and the subordinates was tested separately for the case in which only additions to the basic level tallies were counted for the subordinate and for the condition in which only omissions from the basic level tally were counted for the subordinate. None of those $t$-tests reached significance. Thus, even when additions and omissions are analyzed separately, there is no significant difference between the number of movements described in common for basic level and subordinate level categories of objects. The face validity of these results is apparent from the actual movement lists (Rosch et al., Note 1); the movements shown added to or excluded from the

tallies of subordinate over basic level objects, in general, appear to be random fluctuations in the few movements which did or did not reach the criterion tally rather than movements specific to the subordinate object named.

The second measure of motor movements was a specificity count which included all movements listed regardless of whether or not they were listed in common. Table 29.4 shows the means for this tally. As in the count of movements in common, the proportion of increase in number of movements between the hypothesized superordinate and basic level categories differed significantly for the nonbiological and the biological taxonomies: $t(7) = 5.18$, $p < .01$. For the nonbiological taxonomies, the specificity count was significantly greater for the basic level than for superordinate objects: $t(5) = 11.93$, $p < .001$. Far from being more specific than the basic level, the actual means for subordinate level objects for both the nonbiological and biological taxonomies were lower, on the general specificity count, than the means for the basic level objects, a difference which, however, did not reach significance: nonbiological taxonomies, $t(5) = 2.41$, ns.; biological taxonomies, $t(2) = 3.42$, ns.

**TABLE 29.4. Specificity Count at Each Level of Abstraction**

| Category Type | Mean Number of Movements | | |
|---|---|---|---|
| | Superordinate | Basic Level | Subordinate |
| Nonbiological | 18.2 | 49.0 | 45.3 |
| Biological | 28.3 | 25.7 | 22.0 |

These data on motor movements were obtained from subjects' descriptions of imagined movements with object names as stimuli; in the second part of the experiment, the same type of protocols were obtained by asking subjects to observe actual movements with real objects. As in the case of attribute listing, these descriptions varied remarkably little from the imagined descriptions. For three of the four actions performed, all of the movements obtained in the analysis of imagined action were also obtained from protocols based on observed actions. In each case, a small number of additional movements also achieved a frequency of four or greater for the observed actions—an average of 2.7 attributes added to an average of 19 original ones. All additions are listed in Rosch et al., Note 1. Additions were all finer differentiations or extensions of actions already specified in the original sequence. Thus, there is evidence that the protocols on which the conclusions are based, though obtained for imagined actions, would not have been substantially different were they all to have been obtained for observed actions.

In summary: The basic hypothesis of the study was supported both for number of common movements and total number of movements; superordinate categories have few, if any, motor movements that can be made to the category as a whole and few movements in common. Basic level categories receive descriptions of many specific movements made to all members of the category and many of these movements are described by a sufficient number of different subjects to form a picture of movement sequences made in common to all members of the basic level class of objects. Objects subordinate to the basic level did not differ significantly from the basic level either in the specificity of the descriptions or in the number of common movements made to the object. As in Experiment 1, the hypothesized superordinate level for the three biological categories showed all the characteristics of the basic level, and the hypothesized basic level for the biological taxonomies showed the characteristics of subordinates.

## Experiments 3 and 4: Shapes of Objects

To minimize the dependency on linguistic coding (a possible problem in the first two experiments), it is necessary to find a method for analyzing simi-larity in visual aspects of objects which is not dependent upon subjects' descriptions, which is free from effects of using object names, and which goes beyond similarity of the analyzable, listable attributes which have already been explored in Experiment 1.

The basic hypothesis of Experiments 3 and 4 is that shapes of objects show the same correlational structure as do attributes and motor movements. Experiment 3 tests whether the same basic objects identified in Experiments 1 and 2 would prove to be the most inclusive categories in which the shapes of objects would show a gain in objective similarity over the next higher level of abstraction. Experiment 4 tests whether these same basic level objects would be the most inclusive categories in which shapes are sufficiently similar to render the shape of an average of more than one member of the category identifiable as a category member. Before performing these experiments, we demonstrated that shape was a reasonable aspect of an object to use. Several pilot studies were performed (described in Rosch et al., Note 1) that demonstrated that objects were readily identified (at a rate greater than 90%) from the two-dimensional outlines used in the experiments.

### Choice of Stimuli

Choice of the pictures of objects to be used in these experiments was an issue of particular importance. It is clear that the hypotheses of both experiments could easily be confirmed or disconfirmed by a biased choice of the pictures of objects representing each category. Thus, it was necessary to have an essentially random sample of pictures of objects for any category used: however, some of the nine taxonomies used in Experiments 1 and 2 did not lend themselves to such a choice procedure. On the basis of the availability of large numbers of pictures of members of the category, four hypothesized basic level categories from each of four superordinates (a total of 16 basic level categories) were chosen. These categories are shown in Table 29.5.

For each basic level category shown in Table 29.5, a pool of at least 100 pictures was obtained. More than half of the pictures in each category (and almost all of the animal pictures) were taken from books. The rest were obtained by photographing objects in the environment—vehicles on the

**TABLE 29.5. Classifications of Stimuli Used in Experiments 3 and 4**

| Superordinate | Basic Level |
| --- | --- |
| Clothing | pants, shirt, shoes, socks |
| Vehicle | car, truck, airplane, motorcycle |
| Animals[a] | cat, dog, fish, butterfly |
| Furniture | chair, table, sofa, bed |

[a] For an objective measure of shape, the confusion between, the terms *animal* and *mammal* in English is not relevant.

streets and items of furniture and clothing in homes and in stores.

An additional sampling problem was presented by the orientation of the objects in the pictures. There are an infinite number of possible projections of a three-dimensional object in a two-dimensional representation. Rules were, therefore, required for defining and equating the orientations of objects. Fortunately, there is high agreement among subjects concerning the primary (and in many cases, secondary) canonical orientation in which objects are imagined. To obtain normative data, a class of 61 students was asked to list the orientation in which each of the basic level objects in Table 29.5 were imagined. There was high agreement (over 90% of the students) that all of the articles of furniture and two of the articles of clothing (pants and shirts) were imagined primarily in a front view. The other two types of clothing (shoes and socks) were imagined from side as well as front views; however, all subjects agreed that they found imagining shoes and socks from a front view acceptable. For all of the furniture and clothing, front view pictures were, therefore, used. There was high agreement (90%) that all of the vehicles were imagined in a side view. Side views predominated for animals, with some weight given to front views; besides all subjects whose primary orientation for an animal was front agreed that imagining the animals from the side was acceptable. Thus, side view pictures were used for the vehicles and animals. Since none of the hypotheses required comparing items between different superordinates, the difference in the side- and front-oriented categories did not present a problem. (The high agreement on canonical orientation is itself of interest; one may speculate that the canonical imagined orientation represents the most informative perspective in which to view the object by the same definitions of informativeness

used in characterizing basic level objects in the present study.)

From the pool of 100 or more potential pictures, the four pictures to be used for each category were selected in two stages: In the first (non-random) stage, pictures were discarded on the basis of factors which would make them unusable in the study—for example, an object photographed in other than its canonical orientation or the picture of an object interrupted by another object in the foreground. No picture was discarded because of the shape of the object. In the second stage, the four pictures to be used were selected randomly from the remaining pool.

This use of random choice of objects at the basic level had an effect on the availability of subordinate classes; pictures chosen were not always classifiable as a member of any particular subordinate class. To obtain subordinate classifications, four judges gave subordinate names for each of the 64 pictures. Six of the 16 basic level categories used proved divisable into two objects rated as members of one subordinate class with the other two pictures rated as members of a different subordinate class. These six basic level classes were: cars (sports car, sedan car); tables (kitchen table, dining room table); chairs (kitchen chair, living room chair), pants (dress pants, levis); shoes (women's shoes, tennis shoes); and socks (athletic socks, dress socks). Although these were only six out of 16 possible subordinate divisions, these appeared to be naturally occurring subordinates which had come out of a random choice of pictures of basic level objects and, as such, appeared to be of greater validity for testing the hypothesis than nonrandomly chosen subordinates for each basic level classification would have been.

Once the pictures were selected, it was necessary to normalize size and, when needed, to adjust orientation within the picture plane. This normalization took place in two stages. In the first stage, orientation was adjusted and size was approximately normalized photographically. That is, the objects in the photographs were enlarged, reduced and/or rotated to an approximately standard size and orientation by photographic means. At this stage, size was equated only in the sense that the pictures were reduced to the same order of magnitude; all now occupied a 8.89 × 12.70 cm framed space. The outlines of the 64 normalized pictured objects were then traced. These outline shapes were

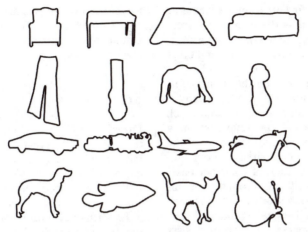

**FIGURE 29.1** ■ Examples of traced outlines of pictures used in Experiment 3. One example of each basic level object from each superordinate category is shown.

the raw material for the stimuli in the pilot studies and in Experiments 3 and 4. Examples of these outlines are shown in Figure 29.1 in which one of the four objects in each basic level category is reproduced. In Figure 29.1 the size of the outlines is reduced to approximately one-eighth of the original size. (To compute the ratio of overlapped areas in Experiment 3, the areas of the shapes were equated more precisely by computer.)

## Experiment 3

### Methods

#### Stimuli and Procedures

The categories used are shown in Table 29.5.

To compute the ratios of overlaps of the normalized shapes, tracings of the shapes were projected by an overhead projector onto a display oscilliscope. Tracings of the two pictures to be compared were overlapped, orientation remaining constant.

Computation of the overlap may be thought of in Venn Diagram terminology. Two juxtaposed shapes, A and B, have an area in common, AB, and areas not in common, A minus AB and B minus AB. For present purposes, it was necessary to compute the ratio of AB to [(A minus AB) plus (B minus AB)]. To do this, the area covered by each shape was first traced with a light pen onto the projections on the display scope. A program com-

puted the ratio of the second shape to the first and adjusted the area of the second by the factor necessary to equalize it to the area of the first. Following this normalization of area, the areas covered by either shape (the union) and by both shapes (the intersection) were traced. The program then computed the ratio of overlap.

Because it was not practical to compute ratios for all possible combinations of the 64 pictures taken four at a time, one of the four basic level object pictures chosen at random from each of the 16 groups of basic level object pictures was compared with each of the other three basic level object pictures in its group. This procedure produced a total of three comparisons within each basic level group of pictures. The mean of these three ratios was taken as a measure of the average overlap within that basic level category.

The same randomly chosen picture that had been compared with the other three pictures within a basic level group was also compared with one randomly chosen member of each of the other three basic level groups within the superordinate (see Table 29.5). The mean of these three comparisons was considered a measure of the ratio of overlap for that basic level group with other members of the superordinate category. For example, if shirt 2 were chosen to represent shirts, it was compared with shirts 1, 3, and 4, and was then compared with one randomly chosen member of each of the other basic level items of clothing—i.e., with one randomly chosen shoe, one sock, and one pair of pants. The means of the first three and second three comparisons were taken as the data points from which to compare the ratio of overlap among shirts with the ratio of overlap between shirts and other clothing.

For comparison of the within subordinate overlap ratios with the within basic level overlap ratios a very similar procedure was followed. Each of the four items in a basic level group containing two subordinates was compared with each of the others, and each item was compared with one randomly chosen item from each of the other basic groups within its superordinate. From these comparisons, 27 mean overlap scores, three for each of the subordinate item pairs, were obtained. The three scores to be compared for each of the six items were: (a) the mean ratio of overlap between the two pairs of subordinate item, (b) the mean ratio of overlap between each of those same items with the other two items, not of the same subordinate, within the same basic level group, and (c) the mean overlap of those same two items with each of the items in the same superordinate class.

## Results

Of the 16 pairs of comparisons between the mean overlap ratios of items within the same basic level category with items within the same superordinate category, 15 were in the direction within-basic-level ratios greater than within-superordinate-level ratios. The one reversal in sign was the smallest difference of the 16. Such results are highly significant by the Wilcoxon Matched-Pairs Signed-Ranks test, $p < .001$. Of the six comparisons of subordinate with basic level overlaps, five showed greater overlap within subordinate categories than within basic level (a difference which reached significance by the $t$ test: $t(5) = 2.91, p < .05$); however, in all six cases, the difference between increase in overlap which was gained by comparing subordinates with each other over comparing basic level objects with each other was far less than the increase in overlap gained by comparing members of the same superordinate with each other: Wilcoxon, $p < .05$; $t(5) = 7.31, p < .001$.

In summary, the basic hypothesis is supported. A large and consistent increase in similarity of the overall look of objects (as measured by increase in the ratio of area of overlap to nonoverlap of normalized shapes of the objects) was obtained

for basic level over superordinate categories. A significant but significantly smaller increase in similarity was obtained for subordinate over basic level categories.

## Experiment 4

Experiment 4 explores one of the possible cognitive effects of the greater similarity in shape within basic level objects shown in Experiment 3. The hypothesis of Experiment 4 is that the basic level is the most general level at which an averaged shape of an object is identifiable as that object.

Experimental confirmation of the hypothesis requires two results. It is necessary to show that averages of different basic level objects which belong to the same superordinate category are not identifiable as members of the superordinate category—that is, that there is not a shape of an average furniture which can be identified as such. In addition, an average based upon the same sort of basic level object must be readily identifiable as such; that is, the average of shapes of two items from the same basic level category should be identifiable as to basic level or superordinate category membership.

## Methods

### Subjects

Subjects were 40 students in undergraduate psychology courses who volunteered to participate in the study for course credit.

### Stimuli

To construct the averages, the two outlines to be averaged were overlapped in the standard orientation as described in Experiment 3. For all points in which the lines of the two outlines did not coincide, the point central between the two lines was taken and the points connected into continuous line segments.

These average drawings were constructed out of the same pictures paired, according to the same rules, as were used for computing the ratios of overlap in Experiment 3. One picture from each basic level category was randomly eliminated. This yielded 32 average drawings consisting of averages of objects within the same basic level category and 32 average drawings consisting of averages of two objects from different basic level but the same superordinate categories. Within the set of within-basic-level averages, six items were averages of objects within the same subordinate category and six were averages of one of those subordinates combined with the other object from the other subordinate class within the basic level category. Tracings of the averaged shapes were copied and given individually to the subjects.

## Procedures

Twenty subjects received the 32 averages of the superordinate categories and 20 different subjects the 32 averages of the basic level (which included the subordinate) categories each in a different random order. Instructions for the basic level set were to "circle the category to which you think the object belongs" and to "write in your best guess about what the object is after the name of the category which you have circled." (The text of the instructions is available in Rosch et al., Note 1.) The four possible categories plus four others to which no objects belonged were listed on each page under the drawing. For superordinates, these were: animal, building(s), clothing, furniture, part of a human body, plant, tool, and vehicle.

Instructions for the superordinate set were the same, with the exception that subjects were told that the pictures consisted of averages of two different objects and that after they had circled the category to which they believed the object belonged, they were to write in guessed names of the two objects of which the outline they were seeing might have been constructed.

## Results and Discussion

The mean number of correct identifications of superordinate categories per subject was 11, i.e., approximately one-third. Since only one-eighth would have been expected by chance, subjects could clearly identify the category from superordinate averages better than chance. However, our pictures consisted of averages of only two outlines, and some of the individual objects remained identifiable at the basic level even when combined with objects of a different basic level category. If superordinate categories are to be

shown identifiable as such, identification should be superior to chance even in those cases when neither of the basic level objects which composed the average was identifiable from the average drawing. To test this, each subject's actual number of correct superordinate category choices made when a basic level object was not named correctly was compared with the number of choices he could have made correctly by chance (one-eighth of the number of items for which that subject did not correctly name a basic level object). A Wilcoxon Matched-Pairs Signed-Ranks test of the difference between these two figures for the 20 subjects was not significant. Thus, it can be concluded that subjects' identifications of the superordinate category membership of averaged shapes was not superior to chance when the shapes composing the average were of different basic level objects and when neither basic level object was itself identifiable. From this experiment there is no evidence for visual features which make superordinate categories identifiable as such.

The mean number identifications correct for the basic level averages was 27 for superordinate category identification (chance would be 4) and 25 for basic level name (78%). For all 32 stimuli, for both superordinate categories correct and basic level name correct, every basic level average shape was guessed correctly more times than its matched superordinate average shape, a result highly significant by any means of analysis.

The same subjects made both basic level and subordinate classifications. The mean correct items per subject were: for superordinate category identification—within subordinate 5.1, across subordinate 5.2; for basic level name identification—within subordinate 5.1, across subordinate 4.9. For neither type of identification was the Wilcoxon Matched-Pairs Signed-Ranks test significant. Thus, although in Experiment 3, within subordinate shapes obtained greater ratios of overlap than cross-sub-ordinates shapes, subjects gave no evidence that they could identify subordinate level averaged shapes better than basic level averaged shapes.

In summary, averages of superordinate objects could not be identified as such better than chance; basic level objects were the most inclusive categories at which objects were readily identified. Furthermore, subordinate object averages were no more identifiable than were the basic level averages.

## Conclusions

The four experiments explore the interrelated aspects of the correlational structure of objects: clusters of co-occurring attributes common to the class, sequences of motor movements common to typical use or interaction with the object, physical similarity in the shape of the object, and high identifiability of averages of shapes of objects of the class. These four aspects of basic objects provide converging operational definitions of basic objects. For all of the taxonomies studied, regardless of whether language dependent variables such as attributes or language independent variables such as shape were used, there was a level of abstraction at which all factors co-occurred and below which further sub-divisions added little information.

The focus was, in one sense, ecological. Psychological processes were only of indirect concern in these experiments. Basic objects, however, have a number of direct implications for psychological processes. We return to a discussion of some of the unresolved issues arising from the converging operational definitions of basic objects—questions of the extent to which basic objects mirror real world structure and the extent to which ignorance and expertise can alter what constitutes a basic level category.

## General Discussion

The categorizations that humans make of the concrete world are not arbitrary, but rather are highly determined. They are determined, in the first place, because the perceived world is not an unstructured total set of equiprobable co-occurring attributes. Unlike the artificial stimulus arrays typically used in concept identification research, the material objects of the world possess high correlational structure. Categories are determined, in the second place, because, in so far as categorization occurs to reduce the infinite differences between stimuli to behaviorally and cognitively useful proportions, the basic category cuts in the world should be those which yield the most information for the least cognitive load. Category cuts should provide the most inclusive categories which can follow the correlational structures perceived in the world. Basic objects are the categories at the level

of abstraction for which the cue validity of categories is maximized. Categories at higher levels of abstraction have lower cue validity than the basic because they have fewer attributes in common; categories subordinate to the basic have lower cue validity than the basic because they share most attributes with contrasting subordinate categories.

The four experiments explored some of the interrelated aspects which make up the correlational structure of objects: clusters of co-occurring attributes common to the category, sequences of motor movements common to typical use or interaction with the object, objective similarity in the shape of the object, and identifiability of an average shape of objects in the class. For all of the taxonomies studied, there was a level of abstraction at which all of these factors co-occurred and below which further subdivisions added little information.[2]

One major issue which these studies raise is the extent to which structure is "given" by the world versus created by the perceiving organism. Such questions can be discussed on a number of levels. In the first place, the present research is empirical and not intended to be related to any of the classical issues of philosophy. Our claim that there is structure "out there" in the world is not a metaphysical claim about the existence of a world without a knower, but an empirical claim which includes the knower. Given a knower who can perceive the complex attributes of feathers, fur, and wings, it is an empirical fact "out there" that wings co-occur with feathers more than with fur. What kinds of attributes can be perceived is, of course, species specific. A dog's sense of smell is more highly differentiated than a human's and the structure of the world for a dog must surely include attributes of smell which, as a species, we are incapable of perceiving. Furthermore, since a dog's body is constructed differently from a human's, his motor interactions with objects are necessarily differently structured. The "out there" of a bat, a frog, or a bee is undoubtedly more different still than that of a human.

On the empirical level, given that a human is capable of perceiving some set of attributes, and that those attributes possess a correlational structure in the world, the state of knowledge of the person may differ from the potential provided by the world in that: (a) The person may be ignorant of (or indifferent or inattentive to) the attributes, or he may know of the attributes but be ignorant of their correlational structure, and (b) He may know of the attributes and their correlational structure but exaggerate that structure, turning partial into complete correlations (as when attributes true only of many members of a category are thought of as true of all members). Basic objects for an individual, subculture, or culture must result from an *interaction* between the potential structure provided by the world and the particular emphases and state of knowlege of the people who are categorizing. However, the environment places constraints on categorizations. Human knowledge cannot provide correlational structure where there is none. Humans can only ignore or exaggerate correlational structures.

## Ignorance and Knowledge of Existing Structure

Different amounts of knowledge about objects can change the classification scheme. Thus, experts in some domain of knowledge make use of attributes that are ignored by the average person. The case of *airplanes* offers a good example. *Airplane* appeared to be the basic level for most of the students participating in our experiments. One subject, however, was a former airplane mechanic. His taxonomy was interesting. The lists of attributes common to airplanes produced by most subjects were paltry compared to the lengthy lists of additional attributes which he could produce. Furthermore, his motor programs as a mechanic were quite distinct for the attributes of the engines of different types of planes. Finally, his visual view of airplanes was not the canonical top and side images of the public; his canonical view was of the undersides and engines.

We used this subject as an informant (in the anthropological sense). His differentiation of airplanes was not infinite; he considered a single and twin engine Cessna to be quite similar, and he thought that they would probably constitute subordinate categories. Furthermore, he considered airplanes as a whole more similar to each other than different vehicles are to each other. He could take the role of the average person and list attributes common to all airplanes, and could imagine an average airplane shape from the outside.

Thus, categories such as airplanes can have differing sets of correlational structures, depending

upon the degree of knowledge of the perceiver. A hypothetical taxonomy of this type and of a potential one-level type are graphed in Figure 29.2. In this figure, basic level objects are depicted as elbows in graphs of common attributes, motor movements, and shapes.

We can now discuss the possible reasons for the disparity between our findings with biological taxonomies and those from anthropological and linguistic data (Berlin, 1972). On the one hand, biological taxonomies might actually be of the type in which only one basic level grouping is possible regardless of degree of knowledge, so that the earlier anthropological findings were in error. In support of such a contention is the fact that when one examines the full range of any genus (for example, *oak*, *maple*, and *birch* in *The Trees of North America*, 1968), one finds that at the genus level, biological classes are not discrete bundles of correlated attributes, but, rather contain many subtypes within the genus whose characteristics merge with those of other genuses. For example, attributes of oaks which one might think would differentiate that genus distinctively from maples—such as tree shape, leaf shape, and seed type—in fact, overlap maples in all of those characteristics when all varieties of the two genuses are considered.

Berlin (Note 2) has countered this argument with the observation that folk biological taxonomies are, by definition, created by the inhabitants of a single

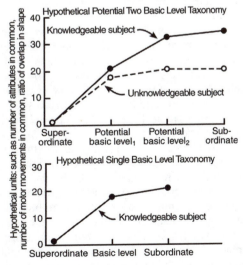

**FIGURE 29.2** ■ Hypothetical one- and two-level taxonomies.

ecological zone who come into contact with only a few of the varieties of each genus. Thus, in folk taxonomies, the genus should be a level of abstraction at which potential correlations of attributes exist. That English speakers once made basic level distinctions at the level of the genus is suggested by the number of monolexemic terms for biological genuses available in English (see the *bird*, *fish*, and *tree* names in Battig & Montague, 1969). Such lists of terms are not similarly available for subordinates of *chair*, *shirt*, *hammer*, or for any of the other nonbiological basic level terms in our taxonomies.

Thus, biological taxonomies are probably of the type in which two basic level groupings are possible, but our city dwelling subjects appeared to be ignorant of the attributes characteristic of the generic level biological categories in their environment.

The effects of expertise on classification requires systematic study. We believe that for all taxonomies there is a level below which further differentiations cannot form basic level categories because, no matter how great the frequency of use of the objects or degree of expertise, there simply is not a sufficient number of attributes to differentiate objects below that level. Thus, for any taxonomy, there should be a level at which the attributes common to objects which are added by further distinctions will be outweighed by the attributes which the newly distinguished classes share with each other. When a further distinction reduces rather than increases the cue validity of categories at the new level of classification, that distinction results in subordinate categories rather than new basic level categories. The only way in which distinctions which are basic level classes can be added indefinitely is to redefine the total set whose structure is at issue to include only the narrowest class under consideration. Thus, *Phillips-screwdrivers-1-in.-long* and *Phillips-screw-drivers-½-in.-long* can be basic level classes if the total set (the universe of discourse) is defined to include only very short Phillips screwdrivers. While this may be a way to characterize the classification system of a specialized machine, it does not seem to be a reasonable way to characterize the cognitive reorganization which takes place in a human mind with increases in expertise. Both theoretical formulation of the change in knowledge structures resulting from a gain in expert knowledge and empiri-

cal studies of the knowledge structures of experts are needed before this question can be discussed intelligently.

One evident aspect of expertise is that the expert's knowledge is probably often confined to specific parts of a taxonomy, thereby, creating unevenness in the expert's categorization of that taxonomy. One can easily imagine a poultry farmer for whom chickens and turkeys (and/or subordinates of these birds) are basic level objects but for whom the rest of the bird class remains undifferentiated. One can imagine an antique furniture dealer for whom Chippendale and Hepplewait chairs are basic level objects, but for whom kitchen and living room chairs, in the average house, are as undifferentiated as for our subjects. Indeed, differentiation of mammals (but not birds, fish, and other major divisions of animals) into basic level objects can be observed in our own culture which is more knowledgeable about mammals than other animal classes. This may be why *mammal* is infrequently used by English speakers; mammals are thought of as members of their basic level classes and are called by their basic names. The names of mammals are one level in the taxonomy lower than are the basic level classes and names for other major animal classifications.

## Exaggeration of Structure: Prototypes

Any person or culture may exaggerate existing structure so that attributes, motor movements, and shapes characteristic of only some members of a category may be thought of as though they were characteristic of all. By such a mechanism, the basic category cuts in the world are made to appear even simpler and more structured than they are in reality. Such simplification may occur through the coding of categories in cognition in terms of prototypes of the most characteristic members of the category. Thus, even when correlational structure in the world is only partial, or when attributes are continuous, categories can be maintained as discrete by their mode of cognitive coding.

At this point, we can comment on the relationship between the present research on the taxonomic structure of categories and earlier research on the internal structure of categories and coding in terms of prototypes. There is considerable evidence that some natural categories are continuous rather than definitively bounded entities (see Lakoff, 1972; Rosch, 1973; Zadeh, 1965). Some natural, continuous categories seem to be structured cognitively into items which differ in their degree of prototypicality—that is, in the degree to which the items match clear classes or good examples of the category (see Rosch, in press, for summary of evidence).

Rosch and Mervis (1975) have shown that the more an item is judged to be prototypical of a category, the more attributes it has in common with other members of the category and the fewer attributes in common with members of contrasting categories. This finding was demonstrated for natural language superordinate categories, for natural language basic level categories, and for artificial categories in which the amount of experience with the items was controlled. Thus, prototypes of categories appear to follow the same principles as basic categories. Prototypes appear to be just those members of a category which most reflect the redundancy structure of the category as a whole. Categories form to maximize the information-rich clusters of attributes in the environment and, thus, the cue validity of the attributes of categories. Prototypes of categories appear to form in such a manner as to maximize the clusters and cue validity within categories.

Given these assumptions, we can now interpret some apparently anomolous data. In Experiment 1, the attributes listed by subjects and verified as true of the category as a whole by the judges, were not true for every example conceivable of the category. A reasonable explanation for this finding is that subjects and judges were thinking of prototypical category members when making the judgments: Attributes that apply to prototypical members need not be true of all items classifiable as members of the category. The experiments of Rosch and Mervis (1975) support this view. They asked subjects to list attributes for 20 members of varying prototypicality from each of six superordinate categories. There were virtually no attributes common to all members of these superordinate categories. However, the five items rated most prototypical within each category tended to have many attributes in common with each other.

The exaggeration of category structure contained in the prototype makes prototypes potentially useful in cognitive processes. Matching to a prototype in categorization would allow humans to make use of their knowledge of the contingency structure of the environment without the laborious process of computing and summing the validities of individual cues (Rosch & Mervis, 1975). The imageability of prototypes of basic level categories may provide additional advantages (Paivio, 1971).

Just as selective ignorance and expertise about categories create unevenness in the categorizations within a taxonomy, variation in basic level classes and coding in terms of prototypes undoubtedly creates unevenness in classifications within basic level categories. Objects nominally within a basic level class may be sufficiently divergent from typical members of the class that they may constitute a separate potential or actual basic level category. For example, consider the objects called *bean bag chairs* in English. These may have attributes, motor movements, and shapes in common with each other and sufficiently different from those of typical chairs that bean bag chairs are thought of as a basic level category separate from and on the same level of abstraction as *chair*. The same is very probably the case for atypical members of biological categories. Although *bird*, *fish*, and *tree* were basic level classes for our subjects, members of these classes such as *penguin*, *lobster*, and *palm tree*, undoubtedly constitute classes differentiated from the basic level categories as a whole. Thus, while a typical looking chair or bird may be perceived and recognized first as a member of the basic level class *chair* or *bird*, a sufficiently deviant member is probably perceived first as a member of its individual class (e.g., *bean bag chair*, *flamingo*). One obvious implication of this is that deviant items should be verified faster for their "subordinate" name than for the name of the basic level category to which they are allied.

## Universality of the Principles of Categorization

From the beginning of the present paper, it has been implied that this is a study of universal principles of categorization. But what aspects of the theory are intended to be universals? The content of categories should not be. It has been argued that categories reflect both real world correlational structure and the state of knowledge of that structure of the people doing the categorizing. Since the structure of the environment differs greatly in different parts of the world, one expects the categories of different cultures to differ. In addition, interest in and knowledge of attributes and their correlation for specific domains differ among cultures, subcultures, and individuals.

It is the principle of category formation that is claimed to be universal. On the most general level, categories form so as to be maximally differentiable from each other. This is accomplished by categories which have maximum cue validity—i.e., categories that have the most attributes common to members of the category and the least attributes shared with members of other categories. While specific principles such as common motor movements and shapes apply only to concrete objects, this most general principle may be applicable to other domains as well. For example, the principle is similar to a recent account of how visual figures are segmented into parts (Palmer, 1975), and it may provide insights into how the stream of experience becomes segmented into events.

In summary: The correlational structure of the environment, modified by selective ignorance and exaggeration of the attributes and structure of that environment, are mirrored in categorization systems. Segmentation of experience occurs to form basic levels which maximize the differentiability of categories. For categories of *concrete* objects, basic objects are the most general classes at which attributes are predictable, objects of the class are used in the same way, objects can be readily identified by shape, and at which classes can be imaged. Basic objects should generally be the most useful level of classification. Universally, basic object categories should be the basic classifications made during perception, the first learned and first named by children, and the most codable, most coded, and most necessary in the language of any people.

## Appendix I

### Examples of Judge-Amended Attribute Lists

Note: Lower levels are assumed to include all attributes listed at higher levels; only attributes new to a lower level are listed.

| Tool | Clothing | Furniture | Bird |
|---|---|---|---|
| make things | you wear it | no attributes | feathers |
| fix things | keeps you warm | *Chair* | wings |
| metal | *Pants* | legs | beak |
| *Saw* | legs | seat | legs |
| handle | buttons | back | feet |
| teeth | belt loops | arms | eyes |
| blade | pockets | comfortable | tail |
| sharp | cloth | four legs | head |
| cuts | two legs | wood | claws |
| edge | *Levis* | holds people—you sit on it | lays eggs |
| wooden handle | blue | | nests |
| *Cross-cutting* | *Double knit* | *Kitchen chair* | flies |
| hand saw | pants | no additional | chirps |
| used in | comfortable | *Living room chair* | eats worms and flies |
| construction | stretchy | large | *Sparrow* |
| *Hack hand saw* | | soft | small |
| no additional | | cushion | brown |
| | | | *Song sparrow* |
| | | | no additional |
| | | | *Field sparrow* |
| | | | no additional |

# Appendix II

### Examples of Motor Movement Sequences

Note: Movements tallied for subordinate classes are the same ones listed in this appendix for the basic level unless otherwise indicated.

"+" indicates a movement which was tallied for the subordinate class that had not been listed for the basic level of that class.

"–" indicates a movement which failed to be tallied for the subordinate class which had been listed for the basic level of that class.

| Tool | | Clothing | | Furniture | | Bird (look at) | |
|---|---|---|---|---|---|---|---|
| Hand: | grasp | Eyes: | scan | Eyes: | scan | Eyes: | scan |
| Fingers: | grasp | Hand: | grasp | *Chair* (sit on) | | | pursue |
| *Hammer* | | *Pants* (put on) | | Head: | turn | | look up |
| Arm: | extend | Hands: | grasp | Body: | turn | | squint |
| Hand: | big grasp | Arms: | extend | | move | | blink |
| | position | Back: | bend | | back | Head: | turn |
| Fingers: | | Feet: | position | | position | | pursue |
| | position | Knee: | bend | Knees: | bend | Neck: | tip back |
| Other hand: | | Leg: | raise | Arm: | extend- | | |
| | position | | extend | | touch | *Sparrow* | |
| Body: | bend | Foot: | raise | Waist: | bend | Eyes: | scan |
| Neck: | bend | | extend | Butt: | touch | | pursue |
| Eyes: | focus | Hand: | raise | Waist: | bend | | pursue |
| | scan | | extend | Body-legs: | | | look up |
| Arm: | raise | Knee: | bend | | release weight | | look down |
| Shoulder: | twist | Leg: | raise | Back-torso: | | Head: | pursue |
| Elbow: | bend | | extend | | straighten | | turn |
| Arm: | lower | Hand: | extend | | lean back | | tilt back |
| Hand: | lower | | raise | *REAL-LIFE* | | *Song sparrow* | |
| Wrist: | tense | Fingers: | grasp | *MODEL* | | +eyes: | focus |
| Arm: | up & down | Elbows: | bend | –head turn | | *Field sparrow* | |
| Hand: | up & down | Arms: | pull up | +feet turn | | –eyes: | look up |
| Elbow: | keep | Fingers: | grasp | +legs touch | | –head: | tilt back |
| | bending | | pull up | body: | squirm | | |
| Shoulder: | keep | | twist | *Kitchen chair* | | | |
| | turning | *Levis* | | –head: | turn | | |
| Wrist: | keep | +toes: | extend | *Living room chair* | | | |
| | flexing | +butt: | rotate | +body: | sink | | |
| *REAL-LIFE* | | *Double knit* | | | | | |
| *MODEL* | | *pants* | | | | | |
| +fingers: manipulate | | –fingers: pull up | | | | | |
| +other | | | | | | | |
| hand: manipulate | | | | | | | |
| +muscles: tense | | | | | | | |
| *Ball-peen hammer* | | | | | | | |
| +fingers: big grasp | | | | | | | |
| *Claw hammer* | | | | | | | |
| –wrist: keep flexing | | | | | | | |

## NOTES

1. Were category cue validity a true probability, the most inclusive category would always have the highest validity. This follows from the fact that if category A includes category B, the probability that object *x* belongs to category A always exceeds the probability at *x* belongs to category B. Category cue validity refers to a psychological factor—the extent to which cues to category membership are available at all (attributes common to the category) and the extent to which those cues are not misleading (attributes which do not belong to other categories). This measure disregards the base rate probabilities of membership in categories—as do most people (Kahneman & Tversky, 1973; Tversky & Kahneman, 1973).

2. It should be emphasized that these claims are made with regard to concrete not abstract objects. To the extent to which categories are not concrete, the overall look of an object and the motor programs for using it may not be necessary concomitants of the attributes and functions of the object. This is true of concrete objects used abstractly as well as of abstract categories as such. The motor movements of sitting on a chair comprise the function of the chair; however, the hand motions made with respect to a rectangle of paper are not the functions of a negotiable check. The separation of shape and motor movements from the attributes of the object are even more obvious for abstract categories such as *causality* or *democracy*. Even for clearly concrete objects, there may be boundary conditions beyond which the present formulation may not be expected to apply. For example, very small objects which have attributes in common and can be used by means of the same motor programs might not necessarily have the similarities in shape which one would expect of larger objects with common attributes and motor programs.

# REFERENCES

Anglin, J. The child's first terms of reference. In S. Ehrlich et E. Tulving (Eds.) *La Memoire Semantique*. Paris: Bulletin de Psychologie, 1976.

Annett, M. The classification of instances of four common class concepts by children and adults. *British Journal of Educational Psychology*, 1959, *29*, 223–236.

Attneave, F. & Arnoult, M. D. The quantitative study of shape and pattern perception. *Psychological Bulletin* 1956, *53*, 452–471.

Battig, W. F., & Montague, W. E. Category norms for verbal items in 56 categories: A replication and extension of the Connecticut category norms. *Journal of Experimental Psychology*, 1969, *80* (Monograph Supplement 3, Part 2).

Beach, L. R. Cue probabilism and inference behavior. *Psychological Monographs*, 1964, *78*, Whole No. 582. (a)

Beach, L. R. Recognition, assimilation, and identification of objects. *Psychological Monographs*, 1964, *78*, Whole No. 583. (b)

Beller, H. K. Priming: Effects of advance information on matching. *Journal of Experimental Psychology* 1971, *87*, 176–182.

Berlin, B. Speculations on the growth of ethnobotanical nomenclature. *Language in Society* 1972, *1*, 51–86.

Berlin, B., Breedlove, D. E., & Raven, P. H. Folk taxonomies and biological classification. *Science* 1966, *154*, 273–275.

Berlin, B., Breedlove, D. E., & Raven, P. H. General principles of classification and nomenclature in folk biology. *American Anthropologist*, 1973, *75*, 214–242.

*Birds of North America: A Guide to Field Identification*. New York: Golden Press, 1966.

Brown, R. *A First Language*. Cambridge, MA: Harvard University Press, 1974.

Bruner, J. S., Olver, R. R., & Greenfield, P. M. *Studies in Cognitive Growth*. New York: Wiley, 1966.

Brunswik, E. *Perception and the Representative Design of Experiments*. Berkeley: University of California Press, 1956.

Bulmer, R. Why is the cassowary not a bird? A problem of zoological taxonomy among the Karam of the New Guinea Highlands. *Man: The Journal of the Royal Anthropological Institute*, 1967, *2*, 5–25.

Bulmer, R. & Tyler, M. J. Karam classification of frogs. *The Journal of the Polynesian Society*, 1968, *77*, 333–385.

Clark, H. H. The language-as-fixed-effect fallacy: A critique of language statistics in psychological research. *Journal of Verbal Learning and Verbal Behavior*, 1973, *12*, 335–359.

*Color Treasury of Acquarium Fish*. New York: Crescent Books, 1972.

Denney, N. W. Evidence for developmental changes in categorization criteria for children and adults. *Human Development*, 1974, *17*, 41–53.

Frake, C. O. The ethnographic study of cognitive systems. In S. A. Tyler (Ed.), *Cognitive Anthropology*. New York: Holt, Rinehart & Winston, 1969.

Garner, W. R. *The Processing of Information and Structure*. New York: Wiley, 1974.

Garrettson, J. Cognitive style and classification. *Journal of Genetic Psychology*, 1971, *119*, 79–87.

Gelman, R. The nature and development of early number concepts. In H. Reese (Ed.), *Advances in Child Development and Behavior*. New York: Academic Press, 1972, Vol. 7.

Goldberg, S., Perlmutter, M., & Myers, W. Recall of related and unrelated lists by 2-year-olds. *Journal of Experimental Child Psychology*, 1974, *18*, 1–8.

*The Golden Book of Bird Stamps*. New York: Golden Press, 1966.

Goldman, A. E. & Levine, M. A developmental study of object-sorting. *Child Development*, 1963, *34*, 649–666.

Kahneman, D. & Tversky, A. On the psychology of prediction. *Psychological Review*, 1973, *80*, 237–251.

Kay, P. Taxonomy and semantic contrast. *Language*, 1971, *47*, 866–887.

Klima, E. S. & Bellugi, U. Perception and production in a visually based language. In D. Aaronson & R. W. Rieber (Eds.) *Developmental Psycholinguistics and Communication Disorders*. New York: New York Academy of Sciences, 1975.

Kucera, H. & Francis, W. N. *Computational Analysis of Present-Day American English*. Providence: Brown University Press, 1967.

Lakoff, G. Hedges: A study in meaning criteria and the logic of fuzzy concepts. *Papers from the Eighth Regional Meeting, Chicago Linguistics Society*, Chicago: University of Chicago Linguistics Department, 1972.

Leach, E. Anthropological aspects of language: Animal categories and verbal abuse. In E. H. Lenneberg (Ed.), *New Directions in the Study of Language*. Cambridge, MA: MIT Press, 1964.

Paivio, A. *Imagery and Verbal Processes*. New York: Holt, Rinehart & Winston, 1971.

Palmer, S. E. Visual perception and world knowledge. In D. A. Norman, D. E. Rumelhart, & the LNR Research Group. *Explorations in Cognition*. San Francisco: W. H. Freeman, 1975.

Peterson, M. J. & Graham, S. E. Visual detection and visual imagery. *Journal of Experimental Psychology*, 1974, *103*, 509–514.

Piaget, J. *The Origins of Intelligence in Children*. New York: International Universities Press, 1952.

Reed, S. K. Pattern recognition and categorization. *Cognitive Psychology*, 1972, *3*, 382–407.

Rosaldo, M. Z. Metaphors and folk classification. *Southwestern Journal of Anthropology*, 1972, *28*, 83–99.

Rosch, E. On the internal structure of perceptual and semantic categories. In T. E. Moore (Ed.), *Cognitive Development and the Acquisition of Language*. New York: Academic Press, 1973.

Rosch, E. Cognitive representations of semantic categories. *Journal of Experimental Psychology: General*, 1975, *104*, 192–233. (a)

Rosch, E. The nature of mental codes for color categories. *Journal of Experimental Psychology: Human Perception and Performance*, 1975, *1*, 303–322. (b)

Rosch, E. Human categorization. In N. Warren (Ed.), *Advances in Cross-Cultural Psychology*. (Vol. 1). London: Academic Press, in press.

Rosch, E. & Mervis, C. B. Family resemblances: Studies in the internal structure of categories. *Cognitive Psychology*, 1975, *7*, 573–605.

Segal, S. J. Processing of the stimulus in imagery and perception. In S. J. Segal (Ed.), *Imagery*. New York: Academic Press, 1971.

Segal, S. J. & Fusella, V. Influence of imaged pictures and sounds on detection of auditory and visual signals. *Journal of Experimental Psychology*, 1970, *83*, 458–464.

Thompson, J. The ability of children of different grade levels to generalize on sorting tests. *Journal of Psychology*, 1941, *11*, 119–126.

*The Trees of North America: A Guide to Field Identification*. New York: The Golden Press, 1968.

Tversky, A. & Kahneman, D. Availability: A heuristic for judging frequency and probability. *Cognitive Psychology*, 1973, *5*, 207–232.

Vygotsky, L. S. *Thought and Language*. New York: Wiley, 1962.

Zadeh, L. A. Fuzzy sets. *Information and Control*, 1965, *8*, 338–353.

## REFERENCE NOTES

1. Rosch, E., Mervis, C. B., Gray, W., Johnson, D., & Boyes-Braem, P. *Basic Objects in Natural Categories*. Working Paper No. 43. The Language Behavior Research Laboratory, University of California, Berkeley, California 94720.
2. Nash, S. C. *The Use of Free Recall to Infer Cognitive Organization in Three, Four, and Five Year Olds*. Unpublished MA thesis, University of Pennsylvania, 1973.
3. Carey, S., DeVilliers, J., & DeVilliers, P. *A New Method for Analyzing Children's Concepts. Cases 1 and 2: The Child's Concept of Life and the Child's Concept of Animal*. Final report for NIMH Grant No. MH24922, 1975.
4. Berlin, B. Personal communication, March 1974.

This research was supported by grants to the first author (under her former name Eleanor Rosch Heider) by the National Science Foundation GB-38245X, by The Grant Foundation, and by the National Institutes of Mental Health 1 R01 MH24316-01. Portions of these data were presented in papers delivered at the meeting of the Psychonomic Society, Boston, November 1974 and at the meeting of the Society for Research in Child Development, Denver, April, 1975. We thank R. Scott Miller, Joseph Romeo, Ross Midgley Clodio Norega, Meriska Huynen, James McLaughlin, Steven Mervis, John Schutz, Buzz Rigsby, Eugene Sanders, Steve Frank, and Denis Fridkis for help in performing the experiments. Our thanks to Oscar Anderson for contributions to the idea of using shape overlap as a measure of similarity and to Carol Simpson for programming the overlap measure. We are grateful to the students and staff of the University of California nursery school and the Pacific Grove public schools for their kindly cooperation in the developmental studies. We are very grateful to Donald Norman for editorial comments.

Carolyn Mervis is now at the University of Illinois. She was a National Science Foundation predoctoral fellow during performance of the research.

Requests for reprints should be sent to Eleanor Rosch, Department of Psychology, University of California at Berkeley, Berkeley, CA 94720.

# On the Genesis of Abstract Ideas[1]

Michael I. Posner and Steven W. Keele • University of Oregon

Previous work has shown that *S*s can learn to classify sets of patterns which are distortions of a prototype, even when they have not seen the prototype. In this paper it is shown that after learning a set of patterns, the prototype (schema) of that set is more easily classified than control patterns which are also within the learned category. As the variability among the memorized patterns increases, so does the ability of *S*s to classify highly distorted new instances. These findings argue that information about the schema is abstracted from the stored instances with very high efficiency. It is unclear whether the abstraction of information involved in classifying the schema occurs while learning the original patterns or whether the abstraction process takes place at the time of the first presentation of the schema.

**W**hen a man correctly recognizes an animal he has never seen before as a dog, he has manifested an ability to generalize from previous experience. What has he learned that allows him to make the classification successfully? This question has been discussed in various forms since Aristotle. Some philosophers suggest a process of abstraction in which *S* builds up a representation of a figure (e.g., triangle) which is different from the instances he has seen. Others have denied the reality of such composite representations or abstractions. For example, Bishop Berkeley pointed out that he could search his imagination in vain for the abstraction of a triangle which was neither equilateral nor scalene but which represented both of these and all other triangles at once. The philosophical idea of abstract representations entered modern psychology from clinical neurology through the work of Barlett (1932) on schema formation (see also Oldfield & Zangwill, 1942).

In the areas of perception and pattern recognition, psychologists have studied questions related to schema formation. Attneave (1957) demonstrated that pretraining on the schema (prototype) of a set of patterns could facilitate later paired-associate learning. Subsequently Hinsey (1963) showed that pretraining on the prototype pattern is superior to pretraining on a peripheral pattern. However, these studies suggest only that knowing the schema can aid later learning and do not reflect on whether *S* in fact abstracts information concerning the schema in the course of learning.

Attneave's (1957) study, like most of the subsequent experiments, used stochastic distortion rules to obtain patterns which varied around a prototype. For rules of this type the prototype represents a kind of average or central tendency of the distortions. Following this same line, Posner, Goldsmith, and Welton (1967) showed that the rate at which *S*s learned to classify a list of patterns was a function of the amount of distortion of the instances from their respective prototypes. As the amount of distortion increased, so did the variability among instances within a category. This increase in variability served to reduce the rate at which the category was learned. Evans and Edmonds (1966) have developed much the same theme. They also showed that Ss could learn a discrimination between patterns generated from different prototypes without having seen the prototypes. This discrimination could be obtained with or without knowledge of results. These studies indicate very little, if anything, about the use of a schema. That Ss can learn to discriminate patterns without seeing a prototype does not indicate that abstraction is involved or that the schema is itself being learned or used.

The philosophical notion of abstract ideas is vague but it does suggest that information which is common to the individual instances is abstracted and stored in some form. In its strongest sense, this might be translated operationally into the hypothesis that the commonalities among a set of patterns are abstracted during learning and that they alone are stored. In the case of patterns obtained by statistical distortion rules, this suggests that S abstracts the prototype. A less extreme hypothesis suggests that S stores the abstracted schema in addition to the individual instances. A still weaker interpretation is that Ss will recognize the schema better than patterns which are similar to the memorized instances but which are not their prototype. This last hypothesis would not necessarily require the abstracting process to take place during learning.

The studies reported in this paper examine various transfer tasks in an effort to understand what S stores during the process of learning to classify distorted patterns. The stimuli are meaningful or nonsense dot patterns which can be distorted by statistical rules. In Exp. I and II, different groups of Ss learned to classify high and low variability distortions of the same prototype. They were then transferred to learning or recognition tasks which involved new distortions not previously seen. In Exp. III all Ss learned to classify distortions of high variability. They were then transferred to the following patterns: old distortions just memorized, the schema of the memorized instances, and control patterns at varying distances from the memorized patterns. Performance in these transfer tasks

was used to infer the role of abstraction and of pattern variability in recognition.

## Experiment I

The original learning in this experiment involved instances of four different prototypes. One group had small distortions of the prototypes, while for the other group the distortions were large. After reaching critieron on the original learning task, both groups were transferred to a list of patterns which were more highly distorted than those in either of the two original lists. Previous work (Posner et al., 1967) demonstrated that the transfer list patterns were equal both in physical and perceived distance from the patterns in the two original lists. Since these new patterns are equally similar to the two original lists, any differences between the groups in transfer must be due either to the distance of the memorized patterns from their prototypes or to their distance from each other (variability). If a clearly defined schema was of primary importance in transfer, the small distortion group should show better transfer. If variability is more important, the larger distortion group should show better transfer. A control group with no original learning was used to assess the direction of the transfer effects.

### Method

#### SUBJECTS

The Ss were 36 introductory psychology students at the University of Wisconsin who received course points for participating in the experiment.

#### MATERIALS

The prototype patterns consisted of a triangle, letters M and F, and a random pattern, all made from nine dots within a 30 × 30 matrix. Pictures of prototypes and some of the distortions were previously published (Posner, Goldsmith, & Welton, 1967). From each of the four originals, six distortions were constructed at each of three different levels (1, 5, and 7.7 bits/dot). The detailed statistical rules and distance data have also been published (Posner et al., 1967). The six distortions were arbitrarily divided into two lists of three distortions each. Each list, therefore, consisted of 12 patterns in total, divided into three distortions of each of the four different prototypes (triangle, M, F, and random). Patterns were placed on 2 × 2 slides and each was duplicated three times, thus providing three independent orders for each list.

### PROCEDURE

The 36 Ss were randomly assigned to one of three conditions and to one of the two lists within the condition. All lists consisted of 12 patterns of one particular level of distortion. The conditions were: learning of Level 1 patterns, learning of Level 5 patterns, and no original learning (control). The exact procedure was reported previously (Posner et al., 1967). Briefly, a slide was presented and remained on until S pressed one of four buttons which represented his choice. Then a feedback light indicating the correct button for that slide came on and remained on during the 8-sec. interstimulus interval. The S continued through trials until he correctly classified two complete lists in a row.

After completing the original learning, the two experimental groups were transferred to a list of 7.7-bit distortions. The control group began its session with the 7.7-bit list. The transfer list was learned by all groups in the same way as the original list except that the learning was terminated at the end of six trials.

## Results

Table 30.1 shows the basic results of the experiment. The two subgroups within each condition were combined since the sublists were arbitrary samplings of the statistical rule which governed the distortions. As expected, the group at Level 5 made more errors in original learning than did the group at Level 1. This replicated findings reported previously (Posner et al., 1967).

During the transfer task Group 1 made more errors on each of the first six trials than did Group 5. The control group showed more errors on each trial than either of the two experimental groups. Analyses of variance of both the first trial and of all six trials were run. For the first trial the overall effects of groups was significant, $F (2, 33) = 10.6$, $p < .01$. Subsequent $t$ tests showed that on the first trial Group 1 was significantly worse than Group 5 but did not differ from the control group. The analysis of all six trials also showed a significant effect of groups, $F (2, 33) = 32$, $p < .01$. Subsequent $t$ tests showed that Group 1 was significantly worse than Group 5 and significantly better than the control.

## Conclusions

The results of this study indicate that transfer from the broader (Level 5) concept was better. This occurs despite the fact that the average distance between corresponding dots and the perceived similarity of the patterns at Levels 1 and 5 to those at Level 7.7 are the same (Posner et al., 1967). Moreover, the minimum distance from Level 5 patterns to any of the new distortions is at least as great, on the average, as the minimum distance of the Level 1 patterns from the new distortions. Thus the superior performance of the groups at Level 5 cannot be due to perceived similarities or actual physical distance between the learned patterns and the new instances. In addition, Ss at Level 1 uniformly reported the correct names of the meaningful patterns, whereas Ss at Level 5 rarely did. Thus having the verbal label does not appear to help as much

**TABLE 30.1. Mean Errors to Criterion for Original Learning and Transfer Tasks, Exp. I**

| Original Learning | Transfer | | | | | | |
|---|---|---|---|---|---|---|---|
| | Trial (Mean Errors) | | | | | | |
| Errors to Criterion | 1 | 2 | 3 | 4 | 5 | 6 | X̄ |
| Group 1 | | | | | | | |
| 4.8 | 8.1 | 6.2 | 5.3 | 5.6 | 4.4 | 3.7 | 5.6 |
| Group 5 | | | | | | | |
| 12.3 | 6.0 | 5.5 | 4.5 | 3.7 | 3.2 | 3.0 | 4.3 |
| Group 7 | | | | | | | |
| — | 8.3 | 7.8 | 7.6 | 6.0 | 5.5 | 5.8 | 6.8 |

as practice in classifying patterns which had considerable noise or variability.

The performance of the control group may have been suppressed somewhat due to lack of warm-up prior to the Level 7 list. However, it seems likely that both Level 1 and 5 are showing positive transfer due to their specific learning experience as well as generalized learning-to-learn. The unpaced nature of the learning situation would probably reduce learning-to-learn effects found in the usual anticipation methods. There are two serious objections which could be raised to the differences between groups at Levels 1 and 5. First, is the initial surprise which Ss at Level 1 had when confronted with highly distorted patterns. This is suggested by the finding that Level 1 is not superior to the control group on the first trial. Even though Level 1 remains below Level 5 on each trial, it might be argued that a learning procedure confounds initial recognition with later performance. Second, is that Level 5 Ss took more trials to learn and it might be argued, therefore, that they have learned methods of how to deal with the storage of information from distorted patterns. Their superior performance would then be due to the appropriateness of the strategies they had previously learned to the new material. Experiment II was designed to eliminate some of these problems.

# Experiment II

In Exp. II the transfer task was pattern recognition rather than learning. It was not necessary for S to memorize the new material and thus storage strategies attained in original learning were not appropriate. Since 24 different patterns were shown, performance on each slide was less dependent upon recognition of previous slides than it is in a learning situation. In order to assess the rela-

tive influence of new learning during the transfer tasks, groups were run with and without feedback.

## Method

### SUBJECTS

The Ss were 32 students in introductory psychology at the University of Oregon who received course points for their participation.

### MATERIAL

The original learning lists were identical to those used in Exp. I. The transfer material consisted of a list of 24 different slides. The 24 slides were six random samples of the 7.7-bit distortion rule for each of the four original patterns.

### PROCEDURE

The learning procedure was the same as in Exp. I. The Ss were divided into two groups. Sixteen Ss learned a list at Level 1 and 16 Ss learned a list at Level 5. Learning was continued until two successful repetitions of the list were completed. The Ss were then given pattern recognition instructions. These instructions indicated that Ss should classify each successive slide as rapidly as possible into one of the four categories that they had learned during the original learning task. For half the Ss in each condition feedback was given after each classification. The other half received no feedback. The Ss were shown the transfer list twice in different random orders. The interslide interval was 9 sec.

## Results

Table 30.2 shows the mean errors to criterion in original learning and the average error in the pattern

TABLE 30.2. Mean Errors in Original Learning and Pattern Recognition, Exp. II

| Condition | Original Learning | Block of Four Trials | | | | | | | | | | | | |
|---|---|---|---|---|---|---|---|---|---|---|---|---|---|---|
| | | 1 | 2 | 3 | 4 | 5 | 6 | 7 | 8 | 9 | 10 | 11 | 12 | X̄ |
| Group 1 | | | | | | | | | | | | | | |
| Feedback | 3.4 | 22 | 16 | 17 | 15 | 13 | 16 | 13 | 12 | 11 | 11 | 11 | 15 | 10.8 |
| No Feedback | 4.1 | 16 | 19 | 15 | 14 | 17 | 21 | 17 | 16 | 11 | 10 | 19 | 13 | 11.9 |
| Group 5 | | | | | | | | | | | | | | |
| Feedback | 16.8 | 15 | 12 | 17 | 10 | 14 | 9 | 8 | 15 | 16 | 12 | 9 | 9 | 9.1 |
| No Feedback | 11.9 | 16 | 11 | 13 | 13 | 17 | 15 | 14 | 17 | 15 | 9 | 14 | 11 | 10.4 |

recognition tasks for all conditions for each block of four trials. As before, Ss in Level 5 took longer in original learning than those in Level 1. There was no significant difference in speed of learning between feedback conditions. Analysis of variance of errors in the pattern recognition task showed that the effect of level was significant. $F(1, 28) = 9$, $p < .01$, and the effect of feedback conditions was also significant, $F(1, 28) = 4.8$, $p < .05$. There were no significant interactions between level and feedback or between either of the two main variables with successive blocks of 24 slides. Table 30.2 also shows the mean errors for successive blocks of four trials in the pattern recognition task. There is a nonsignificant trend for the differences between Levels 1 and 5 to be reduced with practice particularly when feedback is present.

A correlation coefficient was computed between groups at Levels 1 and 5 over the particular slides to which errors were made during pattern recognition. This correlation was .83 indicating that both groups tended to miss the same patterns. A rank order correlation of .97 between distance from the prototype and errors indicated that patterns most distant from the prototype were more difficult to recognize.

## Conclusions

The results of this study confirmed those obtained in Exp. 1. Once again, Ss who had been trained with the high variability patterns did better on transfer than those trained with the low variability patterns. Moreover, they maintained the advantage over the first 24 slides, even though each slide was different. Therefore, it is difficult to argue that the deficiency in transfer for Level 1 Ss was due to an initial startle at seeing patterns which were more distorted than those used in original learning. Moreover the transfer task reduced or eliminated the advantage of general learning strategies attained in the original task (learning-to-learn).

However, it could still be argued that the advantage of Level 5 is primarily in the kinds of criterion which Ss set for admission of a particular pattern into one of the meaningful categories. The use of three highly familiar categories and one nonsense pattern within the same list may have contributed to this. There is a strong tendency for Ss at Level 1 to classify patterns about which they were unsure into the random category. The per-

centage of random responses made during the 48 trials of pattern recognition were 25.5, 37.5, 33.5, and 42.9 for conditions: 5 feedback, 5 nonfeedback, 1 feedback, and 1 nonfeedback, respectively.

Table 30.3 shows a breakdown of the proportion of correct and false alarm responses during pattern recognition for each of the prototypes. The false alarm rate is obtained by dividing the errors in a category by the number of possible errors. In the case of the three meaningful patterns, Level 5 Ss show a higher proportion of correct responses and about equal false alarms. For these distortions, therefore, it is clear that Level 5 Ss are showing better discrimination than those trained on Level 1. For the random patterns, Level 1 Ss have both more correct responses and more false alarms. When these two measures are combined using a graphical method (Norman, 1964) the Level 5 Ss are slightly superior in overall performance. Thus even though Level 1 Ss have a higher proportion of correct responses with the random pattern, when false alarms are taken into consideration, they do not show better discriminability.

The strong tendency of Ss in Level 1 to use the random category suggests that they were somewhat reluctant to classify distorted instances into one of the meaningful categories. While in this study the main differences between groups seem to be in the ability to discriminate the categories, it would seem reasonable to explore changes in criterion particularly in studies where a forced choice between categories is not required.

## Experiment III

The previous two experiments have indicated that Ss do learn something about the variability of in-

**TABLE 30.3. Proportion of Correct and False Alarm Responses for Each Category**

|  | Category | | | | |
|---|---|---|---|---|---|
|  | Triangle | M | F | Random | $\bar{X}$ |
| Cond. 1 |  |  |  |  |  |
|   Correct | .59 | .49 | .50 | .53 | .53 |
|   False Alarm | .10 | .13 | .06 | .33 | .16 |
| Cond. 5 |  |  |  |  |  |
|   Correct | .73 | .71 | .60 | .49 | .64 |
|   False Alarm | .11 | .12 | .05 | .26 | .14 |

stances that they have seen. In both of these experiments, Ss in each group had the same prototypes. If Ss had been storing only the schema, then Level 1 Ss should have shown better performance than Level 5 since it is easier to define the prototype based on Level 1 patterns than based on Level 5 patterns. The results are in the opposite direction, indicating that Ss are learning some information about the individual patterns which they use in their later judgment. In this experiment an effort is made to determine directly whether Ss are also learning information about the prototype.

## Method

### SUBJECTS

The Ss were 30 students recruited from the University of Oregon Employment Service and paid $1.50 per hour for their services.

### MATERIAL

There were two lists of original learning materials. Each list contained 12 slides. The 12 slides were four distortions of three different prototypes. A set of distortions of the same prototype is called a "concept." The prototypes were different for the two lists and were constructed by placing dots in nine randomly selected positions in a 30 × 30 matrix. The four distortions of each prototype were constructed using the same four random samples of a 7.7-bit distortion rule. Thus the distances from each of the prototypes to its four distortions were identical.

The transfer material consisted of two lists of 24 slides. Three of the slides were the prototypes of the patterns in the learning lists. These represent the schema of each concept. Six slides, two from each of the concepts, were patterns memorized during the original learning (old distortions). Six slides, two from each of the concepts, were new 7.7-bit distortions of the prototypes which had not been seen during learning. Six slides, two from each of the concepts, were new 5-bit distortions of the prototypes. Finally, three slides were new random patterns unrelated to any of the concepts which S had learned.

In Table 30.4 the distances from the four memorized patterns of each concept to the respective transfer patterns are shown. The individual patterns are identified by a number or letter. In the case of the old distortions the two transfer patterns are identical to two of the stored patterns. These distance relationships hold for all concepts in both lists, although the prototypes differ from one concept to another and between the two lists. The distances represent the sum of the vertical and horizontal distances from each dot in the stored pattern to the corresponding dot in the transfer patterns. The numbers are in units of 1/20 of an inch. Previous results have shown that, for a given grain size, the logarithm of this measure is linearly related to perceived distance (Posner et al., 1967).

### PROCEDURE

The 30 Ss were divided randomly into two equal groups and assigned to the original learning lists. Original learning proceeded as described in the previous experiments until completion of two correct classifications of the lists. After the original learning was complete, Ss were given their respective transfer lists in the pattern recognition procedure described in the last experiment. On the same

**TABLE 30.4. Distances from Stored Exemplar Pattern to Each Transfer Pattern**

| Stored Pattern | Schema | Old Distortion | | New Level 7s | | New Level 5s | | |
|---|---|---|---|---|---|---|---|---|
| | | 2 | 4 | A | B | C[a] | D | E[b] |
| 1 | 36 | 73 | 66 | 87 | 89 | 49 | 48 | 51 |
| 2 | 43 | 0 | 77 | 104 | 98 | 65 | 71 | 59 |
| 3 | 65 | 88 | 65 | 82 | 60 | 54 | 51 | 56 |
| 4 | 65 | 77 | 0 | 83 | 87 | 51 | 62 | 55 |
| X̄ | 52 | 59 | 52 | 89 | 83 | 54 | 58 | 55 |
| % Errors in Transfer | 15 | 11.5 | 14.7 | 42 | 39 | 26 | 28.5 | 19 |

[a] List B only.
[b] List A only.

day as the original learning they went through the transfer patterns twice, for a total of 48 patterns. Twenty-four hours later Ss returned to the laboratory and ran through the pattern recognition tasks four additional times. During the pattern recognition task, no feedback was provided. Both the classification chosen and the speed of classification were recorded. The Ss were instructed to respond accurately, but to try to respond as rapidly as they could when each new pattern was presented. Concepts were randomly assigned to switches for each S.

## Results

Original learning required an average of 41 and 34 errors to criterion, for List A and List B, respectively. This difference was not significant. The error and speed data for the pattern recognition task are shown in Table 30.5. Since the lists are replications of each other except for the use of different randomly selected original patterns and the results are similar for the two groups, all 30 Ss were combined in subsequent analyses.

The analyses were performed by sign tests because of the high correlation between successive experiences with the same pattern. Separate analyses were run for Day 1 and Day 2. The results of the sign tests are shown in Table 30.6.

On Day 1, it is clear that Ss show no significant differences in proportion of errors between the patterns which they had just finished learning and the prototypes which they had never seen. It is also clear that both the old distortion and the schema have a significantly lower error rate than any of the new distortions seen by S. The Level 5 distortions showed significantly better recognition than the Level 7. No error data can be given for the

new random patterns since there is not any correct classification for these patterns. On Day 2, there is a slightly lower mean error for the old distortions than for the schemas. However, when the data are analysed by individual Ss, 16 show a higher proportion of error on the old distortions and only 11 have a higher proportion on the schema. This difference does not reach significance by a sign test. On Day 2, the new distortions all show significantly more error than either the old distortions or schema patterns. Overall, it is clear that the schema patterns show no greater error than the patterns which S had actually seen and memorized.

On Day 1 the old distortions show faster classification times than the schema patterns. This approaches but does not reach significance by a sign test. In every other respect the Day 1 speeds give the same picture as the error data. On Day 2 there is no significant difference between the old distortion and the schema patterns in speed. The other differences on Day 2 are identical to those discussed previously for errors.

A trial by trial analysis of errors and speeds was performed for the schema vs. old distortions. On the very first trial, 21 Ss have longer RTs to the schema while 8 Ss have longer RTs to the old distortions. This is significant ($p < .01$) by sign test. By the second trial the distribution is 14 RTs longer with the old distortion and 16 with the schema, and on no subsequent trial do more Ss show longer times to the schema. The error data are similar. On the first trial, 13 have a higher proportion of errors on the schema and 7 on the old distortion. This is not significant by sign test; however, this tendency disappears after the first trial.

The transfer lists contain five general types of patterns. These are the old distortions, schema

**TABLE 30.5.** Percentage of Errors and Speeds (in Sec) for Classifying Transfer Patterns for Day 1 and Day 2

| | Day 1 | | | | | Day 2 | | | | |
|---|---|---|---|---|---|---|---|---|---|---|
| | Old | Schema | 5 | 7 | New | Old | Schema | 5 | 7 | New |
| List A | | | | | | | | | | |
| % Error | 10 | 13.3 | 23.3 | 35 | — | 9.7 | 14.4 | 24.1 | 36 | — |
| RT | 2.04 | 2.19 | 2.36 | 2.52 | 2.88 | 1.86 | 1.88 | 2.03 | 2.18 | 2.51 |
| List B | | | | | | | | | | |
| % Error | 16.1 | 16.6 | 30.5 | 41.7 | — | 15.8 | 16.1 | 25.3 | 46.9 | — |
| RT | 1.97 | 2.37 | 2.71 | 3.22 | 2.95 | 1.88 | 2.06 | 2.12 | 2.33 | 2.35 |
| Average % Error | 13.0 | 14.9 | 26.9 | 38.3 | — | 12.8 | 15.3 | 24.5 | 41.9 | — |
| RT | 2.01 | 2.28 | 2.53 | 2.87 | 2.91 | 1.87 | 1.97 | 2.07 | 2.25 | 2.43 |

**TABLE 30.6. Number of Ss with Higher Average Errors or Longer Average Times In Specified Conditions of Transfer**

| Error | | | | | | | | | |
|---|---|---|---|---|---|---|---|---|---|
| Day 1 | | | Sign Test[a] | Day 2 | | | Sign Test | | |
| Old Distort. 9 | Schema 9 | Tie 12 | ns | Old Distort. 16 | Schema 11 | Tie 3 | ns | | |
| Level 5 23 | Schema 5 | Tie 2 | .01 | Level 5 24 | Schema 4 | Tie 2 | .01 | | |
| Level 7 19 | Level 5 6 | Tie 5 | .05 | Level 7 24 | Level 5 5 | Tie 1 | .01 | | |
| Reaction Time | | | | | | | | | |
| Old Distort. 11 | Schema 19 | Tie 0 | ns | Old Distort. 14 | Schema 16 | Tie 0 | ns | | |
| Level 5 22 | Schema 8 | Tie 0 | .05 | Level 5 23 | Schema 7 | Tie 0 | .01 | | |
| Level 7 21 | Level 5 8 | Tie 1 | .05 | Level 7 22 | Level 5 8 | Tie 0 | .05 | | |
| New Randoms 17 | Level 7 13 | Tie 0 | ns | New Randoms 18 | Level 7 12 | Tie 0 | ns | | |

[a] All sign test were two-tailed.

patterns, the new distortions at Level 7, the new distortions at Level 5, and new random patterns. As described earlier, Table 30.4 shows a breakdown of the various patterns used in the transfer list and their distances from each of the patterns shown in the original list. The schema pattern and the 5-bit distortions have roughly the same mean distance from the four stored patterns. Nonetheless, the schema pattern always shows better performance in terms of mean errors than the 5-bit distortions. The distances from the stored patterns also differed among the three 5-bit distortion patterns used in the transfer lists. The performance on those distortions did not seem to be closely related to their mean distance from the stored patterns. Therefore, mean distance does not prove to be a particularly good predictor in the range of distances which include the schema and Level 5 patterns. However, a comparison of Level 5 patterns with the new Level 7.7 patterns shows that the patterns which have the larger mean distance are recognized more poorly. In summary, the old distortions, schema, and new Level 5 patterns have nearly identical mean distances from the memorized patterns, but the old distortions and schema are better recognized than the Level 5s and are not different from each other.

## General Conclusions

### ABSTRACTION

In the introduction some operational statements of the old notion of abstract ideas were suggested.

The data of the present experiments confirm that some form of this proposition is correct. The weakest operational form of this proposition which is consistent with the present authors' findings is that the prototype (schema) of the stored patterns has a higher probability of recognition than other new patterns contained within the concept. This is confirmed both by the finding that the schema is better recognized than transfer patterns with similar distance relationships (Level 5) and by the finding that, after its first presentation, the schema is as well recognized as the patterns which have actually been memorized by Ss. This form of the proposition is consistent with but more explicit than the idea of stimulus generalization. It singles out the prototype of the patterns as unique. In other words, it shows that the maximal generalization for multidimensional patterns of this sort occurs at the prototype even though other patterns are nearly the same average distance from the stored exemplars. Although other patterns may have nearly the same average distance from the distortions, the prototype must share the most common properties with the set of patterns generated from it. This proposition is stronger than a generalization notion because the schema pattern is, on the whole, as well recognized as the exemplars from which it is abstracted.

The first and second experiments allow the authors to reject the idea that only the abstracted prototype is stored. Clearly the information about the individual patterns must also be present in order for a loose concept (high variability) to give better transfer than a tight concept (low variability). Moreover, the variability is of sufficient importance to overcome whatever advantage the tight concept has from a more clearly defined central tendency. The beneficial effect of variability confirms results in other areas of problem solving (Morrisett & Hovland, 1959) and pattern recognition (Dukes & Bevan, 1967) which argue for the importance of variability during training. It is also consistent with Attneave's (1957) suggestion that part of the process of learning to recognize patterns involves acquaintance with the limits of variability.

## TIME OF ABSTRACTION

It is possible to ask when the information is abstracted which allows the efficient recognition of the central tendency. One possibility is that the abstraction of this information takes place during the learning task. This is undoubtedly the notion which philosophers have implied in discussing the genesis of abstract ideas. The present authors cannot either confirm or deny this form of the proposition from the present data. It could be that information concerning the central tendency is stored during learning, but it also could be that the abstraction takes place when the schema pattern is first shown to S. That is, S may not recognize the schema on its first presentation in the direct way in which he identifies the old distortions. Rather he may respond correctly on the basis of a calculation from stored information concerning the exemplars. The finding that RT to the schema is longer than to the old distortions on the first presentation of the transfer list may indicate that S is calculating on the basis of his stored information. However, it could also mean that he has stored abstracted information but that it is not as clearly or completely defined as information concerning the individual exemplars. In either case, once he has seen the schema he recognizes it with the same efficiency as the memorized patterns. If the schema information is not abstracted during learning, then upon its first presentation S must store it as a particularly good example of its concept and treat it on subsequent trials as equivalent to a memorized instance. One way to demonstrate that abstraction occurs during learning would be to find a situation in which the schema, when first introduced, is recognized as well as or better than the patterns memorized during the original learning.

## WHAT IS ABSTRACTED

In the present study the authors have used the word idea in a neutral sense. It is not at all clear what Ss abstract in learning to recognize the transfer patterns. To say Ss learn the central tendency and the variability of the patterns does not tell in what type of a coding system such information is stored. For example, Ss might have an image or mental picture of the individual instances or of the abstracted central tendency. Or perhaps the material is in the form of verbal description, such as has been suggested by various theories of short-term memory (Glanzer & Clark, 1963; Sperling, 1963).

The data obtained here give only a very incomplete answer to these questions. Introspective reports were taken from 15 Ss run in a pilot study with materials identical to one list of Exp. III. These reports suggested that some Ss used verbal rules which related to the patterns. The rules tended to emphasize position of dots, center of gravity, overall orientation of figure, familiar subgroups, and association to familiar objects. The rules were highly idiosyncratic and some Ss verbalized no rules at all. These verbal reports suggest that some of the storage, at least, is by way of rules which are related to the common features of the patterns within a concept. Whether these verbal codes represent all of the information storage or are used in conjunction with other storage codes cannot be determined from the present data.

## NOTE

1. This research was supported in part by National Science Foundation Grant GB 3939 to the University of Oregon. A preliminary version of Exp. I was included in a report presented at the XVIIIth International Congress of Psychology, August 1966. The authors wish to thank Barbara Kerr, William Eichelman, and Stanley Sue for their help in conducting this research.

## REFERENCES

Attneave, F. Transfer of experience with a class-schema to identification-learning of patterns and shapes. *Journal of Experimental Psychology*, 1957, *54*, 81–88.

Bartlett, F. C. *Remembering, a Study in Experimental and Social Psychology*. Cambridge: Cambridge University Press, 1932.

Dukes, W. F. & Bevan, W. Stimulus variation and repetition in the acquisition of naming responses. *Journal of Experimental Psychology*, 1967, *74*, 178–181.

Evans, S. H. & Edmonds, E. M. Schema discrimination as a function of training. *Psychonomic Science*, 1966, *5*, 303–304.

Glanzer, M. & Clark, W. H. Accuracy of perceptual recall: An analysis of organization. *Journal of Verbal Learning and Verbal Behavior*, 1963, *1*, 289–299.

Hinsey, W. C. Identification-learning after pretraining on central and noncentral standards. Unpublished masters thesis, University of Oregon, 1963.

Morrisett, L., Jr. & Hovland, C. I. A comparison of three varieties of training in human problem solving. *Journal of Experimental Psychology*, 1959, *58*, 52–55.

Norman, D. A. A comparison of data with different false alarm rates. *Psychological Review*, 1964, *71*, 243–246.

Oldfield, R. C. & Zangwill, O. L. Head's concept of the schema and its application in contemporary British psychology. *British Journal of Psychology*, 1942, *32*, 267–286.

Posner, M. I., Goldsmith, R., & Welton, K. E., Jr. Perceived distance and the classification of distorted patterns. *Journal of Experimental Psychology*, 1967, *73*, 28–38.

Sperling, G. A model for visual memory tasks. *Human Factors*, 1963, *5*, 19–31.

READING 31

# Concepts and Conceptual Structure

Douglas L. Medin • University of Illinois at Urbana

Research and theory on categorization and conceptual structure have recently undergone two major shifts. The first shift is from the assumption that concepts have defining properties (the classical view) to the idea that concept representations may be based on properties that are only characteristic or typical of category examples (the probabilistic view). Both the probabilistic view and the classical view assume that categorization is driven by similarity relations. A major problem with describing category structure in terms of similarity is that the notion of similarity is too unconstrained to give an account of conceptual coherence. The second major shift is from the idea that concepts are organized by similarity to the idea that concepts are organized around theories. In this article, the evidence and rationale associated with these shifts are described, and one means of integrating similarity-based and theory-driven categorization is outlined.

What good are categories? Categorization involves treating two or more distinct entities as in some way equivalent in the service of accessing knowledge and making predictions. Take psychodiagnostic categories as an example. The need to access relevant knowledge explains why clinical psychologists do not (or could not) treat each individual as unique. Although one would expect treatment plans to be tailored to the needs of individuals, absolute uniqueness imposes the prohibitive cost of ignorance. Clinicians need some way to bring their knowledge and experience to bear on the problem under consideration, and that requires the appreciation of some similarity or relationship between the current situation and what has gone before. Although clinical psychologists may or may not use a specific categorization system, they must find points of contact between previous situations and the current context; that is, they must categorize. Diagnostic categories allow clinicians to predict the efficacy of alternative treat-

ments and to share their experiences with other therapists. Yet another reason to categorize is to learn about etiology. People who show a common manifestation of some problem may share common precipitating conditions or causes. Ironically, the only case in which categorization would not be useful is where all individuals are treated alike; thus, categorization allows diversity.

More generally speaking, concepts and categories serve as building blocks for human thought and behavior. Roughly, a *concept* is an idea that includes all that is characteristically associated with it. A *category* is a partitioning or class to which some assertion or set of assertions might apply. It is tempting to think of categories as existing in the world and of concepts as corresponding to mental representations of them, but this analysis is misleading. It is misleading because concepts need not have real-world counterparts (e.g., unicorns) and because people may impose rather than discover structure in the world. I believe that questions about the nature of categories may be psychological questions as much as metaphysical questions. Indeed, for at least the last decade my colleagues and I have been trying to address the question of why we have the categories we have and not others. The world could be partitioned in a limitless variety of ways, yet people find only a miniscule subset of possible classifications to be meaningful. Part of the answer to the categorization question likely does depend on the nature of the world, but part also surely depends on the nature of the organism and its goals. Dolphins have no use for psychodiagnostic categories.

Given the fundamental character of concepts and categories, one might think that people who study concepts would have converged on a stable consensus with respect to conceptual structure. After all, Plato and Aristotle had quite a bit to say about concepts, medieval philosophers were obsessed with questions about universals and the essence of concepts, and concept representation remains as a cornerstone issue in all aspects of cognitive science. However, we have neither consensus nor stability. The relatively recent past has experienced at least one and probably two major shifts in thought about conceptual structure, and stability is the least salient attribute of the current situation. In the remainder of this article, I will briefly describe these shifts and then outline some ways of integrating the strong points of the various views.

## The First Shift: Classical versus Probabilistic Views

It is difficult to discuss concepts without bringing in the notion of similarity at some point. For example, a common idea is that our classification system tends to maximize within-category similarity relative to between-category similarity. That is, we group things into categories because they are similar. It will be suggested that alternative views of conceptual structure are associated with distinct (though sometimes implicit) theories of the nature of similarity.

### The Classical View

The idea that all instances or examples of a category have some fundamental characteristics in common that determine their membership is very compelling. The classical view of concepts is organized around this notion. The classical view assumes that mental representations of categories consist of summary lists of features or properties that individually are necessary for category membership and collectively are sufficient to determine category membership. The category *triangle* meets these criteria. All triangles are closed geometric forms with three sides and interior angles that sum to 180 degrees. To see if something is a triangle one has only to check for these three properties, and if any one is missing one does not have a triangle.

What about other concepts? The classical view suggests that all categories have defining features. A particular person may not know what these defining features are but an expert certainly should. In our 1981 book, *Categories and Concepts*, Ed Smith and I reviewed the status of the classical view as a theory of conceptual structure. We concluded that the classical view was in grave trouble for a variety of reasons. Many of the arguments and counterarguments are quite detailed, but the most serious problems can be easily summarized:

### 1. FAILURE TO SPECIFY DEFINING FEATURES

One glaring problem is that even experts cannot come up with defining features for most lexical concepts (i.e., those reflected in our language). People may believe that concepts have necessary or sufficient features (McNamara & Sternberg, 1983), but the features given as candidates do not hold up to closer scrutiny. For example, a person may list "made of wood" as a necessary property for violins, but not all violins are made of wood. Linguists, philosophers, biologists, and clinical psychologists alike have been unable to supply a core set of features that all examples of a concept (in their area of expertise) necessarily must share.

### 2. GOODNESS OF EXAMPLE EFFECTS

According to the classical view, all examples of a concept are equally good because they all possess the requisite defining features. Experience and (by now) a considerable body of research undermines this claim. For example, people judge a robin to be a better example of bird than an ostrich is and can answer category membership questions more quickly for good examples than for poor examples (Smith, Shoben, & Rips, 1974). Typicality effects are nearly ubiquitous (for reviews, see Medin & Smith, 1984; Mervis & Rosch, 1981; Oden, 1987); they hold for the artistic style (Hartley & Homa, 1981), chess (Goldin, 1978), emotion terms (Fehr, 1988; Fehr & Russell, 1984), medical diagnosis (Arkes & Harkness, 1980), and person perception (e.g., Cantor & Mischel, 1977).

Typicality effects are not, in principle, fatal for the classical view. One might imagine that some signs or features help to determine the presence of other (defining) features. Some examples may have more signs or clearer signs pointing the way to the defining properties, and this might account for the difference in goodness of example judgments or response times. This distinction between identification procedures (how one identifies an instance of a concept) and a conceptual core (how the concept relates to other concepts) may prove useful if it can be shown that the core is used in some other aspect of thinking. It seems, however, that this distinction serves more to insulate the classical view from empirical findings, and Smith, Rips, and Medin (1984) argued that there are no sharp boundaries between core properties and those used for purposes of identification.

### 3. UNCLEAR CASES

The classical view implies a procedure for unambiguously determining category membership; that is, check for defining features. Yet there are numerous cases in which it is not clear whether an example belongs to a category. Should a rug be considered furniture? What about a clock or radio? People not only disagree with each other concerning category membership but also contradict themselves when asked about membership on separate occasions (Barsalou, 1989; Bellezza, 1984; McCloskey & Glucksberg, 1978).

These and other problems have led to disenchantment with the classical view of concepts. The scholarly consensus has shifted its allegiance to an alternative, the probabilistic view.

## The Probabilistic View

The rejection of the classical view of categories has been associated with the ascendance of the probabilistic view of category structure (Wittgenstein, 1953). This view holds that categories are "fuzzy" or ill-defined and that categories are organized around a set of properties or clusters of correlated attributes (Rosch, 1975) that are only characteristic or typical of category membership. Thus, the probabilistic view rejects the notion of defining features.

The most recent edition of the *Diagnostic and Statistical Manual of Mental Disorders* (*DSM-IIIR*, American Psychiatric Association, 1987) uses criteria based on lists of characteristic symptoms or features to describe diagnostic categories and thereby endorses the probabilistic view. For example, a diagnosis of depression can be made if a dysphoric mood and any five of a set of nine symptoms are present nearly every day for a period of at least two weeks. Thus, two people may both be categorized as depressed and share only a single one of the nine characteristic symptoms!

The probabilistic view is perfectly at home with the typicality effects that were so awkward for the classical view. Membership in probabilistic categories is naturally graded, rather than all or none, and the better or more typical members have more characteristic properties than the poorer ones. It is also easy to see that the probabilistic view may lead to unclear cases. Any one example may have several typical properties of a category but not so many that it clearly qualifies for category membership.

In some pioneering work aimed at clarifying the structural basis of fuzzy categories, Rosch and Mervis (1975) had subjects list properties of exemplars for a variety of concepts such as *bird*, *fruit*, and *tool*. They found that the listed properties for some exemplars occurred frequently in other category members, whereas others had properties that occurred less frequently. Most important, the more frequently an exemplar's properties appeared within a category, the higher was its rated typicality for that category. The correlation between number of characteristic properties possessed and typicality rating was very high and positive. For example, robins have characteristic bird properties of flying, singing, eating worms, and building nests in trees, and they are rated to be very typical birds. Penguins have none of these properties, and they are rated as very atypical birds. In short, the Rosch and Mervis work relating typicality to number of characteristic properties possessed put the probabilistic view on fairly firm footing.

## 1. MENTAL REPRESENTATIONS OF PROBABILISTIC VIEW CATEGORIES

If categories are not represented in terms of definitions, what form do our mental representations take? The term, *probabilistic view,* seems to imply that people organize categories via statistical reasoning. Actually, however, there is a more natural interpretation of fuzzy categories. Intuitively, probabilistic view categories are organized according to a *family resemblance* principle. A simple form of summary representation would be an example or ideal that possessed all of the characteristic features of a category. This summary representation is referred to as the *prototype*, and the prototype can be used to decide category membership. If some candidate example is similar enough to the prototype for a category, then it will be classified as a member of that category. The general notion is that, based on experience with examples of a category, people abstract out the central tendency or prototype that becomes the summary mental representation for the category.

A more radical principle of mental representation, which is also consistent with fuzzy categories, is the exemplar view (Smith & Medin, 1981). The exemplar view denies that there is a single summary representation and instead claims that categories are represented by means of examples. In this view, clients may be diagnosed as suicidal, not because they are similar to some prototype of a suicidal person, but because they remind the clinician of a previous client who was suicidal.

A considerable amount of research effort has been aimed at contrasting exemplar and prototype representations (see Allen, Brooks, Norman, & Rosenthal, 1988; Estes, 1986a, 1986b; Medin, 1986; Medin & Smith, 1984; Nosofsky, 1987, 1988a; and Oden, 1987). Genero and Cantor (1987) suggested that prototypes serve untrained diagnosticians well but that trained diagnosticians may find exemplars to be more helpful. For my present purposes, however, I will blur over this distinction to note that both prototype and exemplar theories rely on roughly the same similarity principle. That is, category membership is determined by whether some candidate is sufficiently similar either to the prototype or to a set of encoded examples, where similarity is based on matches and mismatches of independent, equally abstract, features.

## 2. PROBABILISTIC VIEW AND SIMILARITY

To give meaning to the claim that categorization is based on similarity, it is important to be specific about what one means by similarity. Although the consensus is not uniform, I believe that the modal model of similarity with respect to conceptual structure can be summarized in terms of the four assumptions as follows: (a) Similarity between two things increases as a function of the number of features or properties they share and decreases as a function of mismatching or distinctive features. (b) These features can be treated as independent and additive. (c) The features determining similarity are all roughly the same level of abstractness (as a special case they may be irreducible primitives). (d) These similarity principles are sufficient to describe conceptual structure, and therefore, a concept is more or less equivalent to a list of its features. This theory of similarity is very compatible with the notion that categories are organized around prototypes. Nonetheless, I will later argue that each of these assumptions is wrong or misleading and that to understand conceptual structure theories of similarity are needed that reject each of these assumptions. Before outlining an alternative set of similarity assumptions, however, I will first describe a set of observations that motivate the second, still more recent, shift in thinking concerning conceptual structure.

## Problems for Probabilistic View Theories

### Problems for Prototypes

Although the general idea that concepts are organized around prototypes remains popular, at a more specific, empirical level, prototype theories have not fared very well. First of all, prototype theories treat concepts as context-independent. Roth and Shoben (1983), however, have shown that typicality judgments vary as a function of particular contexts. For example, tea is judged to be a more typical beverage than milk in the context of secretaries taking a break, but this ordering reverses for the context of truck drivers taking a break. Similarly, Shoben and I (Medin & Shoben, 1988) noted that the typicality of combined concepts cannot be predicted from the typicality of the constituents. As an illustrative example, consider the concept of *spoon*. People rate small spoons as more typical spoons than large spoons, and metal spoons as more typical spoons than wooden spoons. If the concept *spoon* is represented by a prototypic spoon, then a small metal spoon should be the most typical spoon, followed by small wooden and large metal spoons, and large wooden spoons should be the least typical. Instead, people find large wooden spoons to be more typical spoons than either small wooden spoons or large metal spoons (see also Malt & Smith, 1983). The only way for a prototype model to handle these results is to posit multiple prototypes. But this strategy creates new problems. Obviously one cannot have a separate prototype for every adjective noun combination because there are simply too many possible combinations. One might suggest that there are distinct subtypes for concepts like *spoon*, but one would need a theory describing how and when subtypes are created. Current prototype models do not provide such a theory. A third problem for prototype theories grows out of Barsalou's work (1985, 1987) on goal-derived categories such as "things to take on a camping trip" and "foods to eat while on a diet." Barsalou has found that goal-derived categories show the same typicality effects as other categories. The basis for these effects, however, is not similarity to an average or prototype but rather similarity to an ideal. For example, for the category of things to eat while on a diet, typicality ratings are determined by how closely an example conforms to the ideal of zero calories.

Laboratory studies of categorization using artificially constructed categories also raise problems for prototypes. Normally many variables relevant to human classification are correlated and therefore confounded with one another. The general rationale for laboratory studies with artificially created categories is that one can isolate some variable or set of variables of interest and unconfound some natural correlations. Salient phenomena associated with fuzzy categories are observed with artificially constructed categories, and several of these are consistent with prototype theories. For example, one observes typicality effects in learning and on transfer tests using both correctness and reaction time as the dependent variable (e.g., Rosch & Mervis, 1975). A striking phenomenon, readily obtained, is that the prototype for a category may be classified more accurately during transfer tests than are the previously seen examples that were used during original category learning (e.g., Homa & Vosburgh, 1976; Medin & Schaffer, 1978; Peterson, Meagher, Chait, & Gillie, 1973).

Typicality effects and excellent classification of prototypes are consistent with the idea that people are learning these ill-defined categories by forming prototypes. More detailed analyses, however, are more problematic. Prototype theory implies that the only information abstracted from categories is the central tendency. A prototype representation discards information concerning category size, the variability of the examples, and information concerning correlations of attributes. The evidence suggests that people are sensitive to all three of these types of information (Estes, 1986b; Flannagan, Fried, & Holyoak, 1986; Fried & Holyoak, 1984; Medin, Altom, Edelson, & Freko, 1982; Medin & Schaffer, 1978). An example involving correlated attributes pinpoints part of the problem. Most people have the intuition that small birds are much more likely to sing than large birds. This intuition cannot be obtained from a single summary prototype for birds. The fact that one can generate large numbers of such correlations is a problem for the idea that people reason using prototypes. More generally, prototype representations seem to discard too much information that can be shown to be relevant to human categorizations.

Yet another problem for prototypes is that they make the wrong predictions about which category structures should be easy or difficult to learn. One way to conceptualize the process of classifying examples on the basis of similarity to prototypes is that it involves a summing of evidence against a criterion. For example, if an instance shows a criterial sum of features (appropriately weighted), then it will be classified as a bird, and the more typical a member is of the category, the more quickly the criterion will be exceeded. The key aspect of this prediction is that there must exist some additive combination of properties and their weights that can be used to correctly assign instances as members or nonmembers. The technical term for this constraint is that categories must be linearly separable (Sebestyn, 1962). For a prototype process to work in the sense of accepting all members and rejecting all nonmembers, the categories must be linearly separable.

If linear separability acts as a constraint on human categorization, then with other factors equal, people should find it easier to learn categories that are linearly separable than categories that are not linearly separable. To make a long story short, however, studies employing a variety of stimulus materials, category sizes, subject populations, and instructions have failed to find any evidence that linear separability acts as a constraint on human classification learning (Kemler-Nelson, 1984; Medin & Schwanenflugel, 1981; see also Sheppard, Hovland, & Jenkins, 1961).

The cumulative effect of these various chunks of evidence has been to raise serious questions concerning the viability of prototype theories. Prototype theories imply constraints that are not observed in human categorization, predict insensitivity to information that people readily use, and fail to reflect the context sensitivity that is evident in human categorization. Rather than getting at the character of human conceptual representation, prototypes appear to be more of a caricature of it. Exemplar models handle some of these phenomena, but they fail to address some of the most fundamental questions concerning conceptual structure.

## Exemplar-Based Theories

The problems just described hold not only for prototype theories in particular but also for any similarity-based categorization model that assumes that the constituent features are independent and additive. To give but one example, one could have an exemplar model of categorization that assumes that, during learning, people store examples but that new examples are classified by "computing" prototypes and determining the similarity of the novel example to the newly constructed prototypes. In short, the central tendency would be abstracted (and other information discarded) at the time of retrieval rather than at the time of storage or initial encoding. Such a model would inherit all the shortcomings of standard prototype theories.

Some exemplar storage theories do not endorse the notion of feature independence (Hintzman, 1986; Medin & Schaffer, 1978), or they assume that classification is based on retrieving only a subset of the stored examples (presumably the most similar ones or, as a special case, the most similar one). The idea that retrieval is limited, similarity-based, and context-sensitive is in accord with much of the memory literature (e.g., Tulving, 1983). In

addition, these exemplar models predict sensitivity to category size, instance variability, context, and correlated attributes. It is my impression that in head-to-head competition, exemplar models have been substantially more successful than prototype models (Barsalou & Medin, 1986; Estes, 1986b; Medin & Ross, 1989; Nosofsky, 1988a, 1988b; but see Homa, 1984, for a different opinion).

Why should exemplar models fare better than prototype models? One of the main functions of classification is that it allows one to make inferences and predictions on the basis of partial information (see Anderson, 1988). Here I am using classification loosely to refer to any means by which prior (relevant) knowledge is brought to bear, ranging from a formal classification scheme to an idiosyncratic reminding of a previous case (which, of course, is in the spirit of exemplar models; see also Kolodner, 1984). In psychotherapy, clinicians are constantly making predictions about the likelihood of future behaviors or the efficacy of a particular treatment based on classification. Relative to prototype models, exemplar models tend to be conservative about discarding information that facilitates predictions. For instance, sensitivity to correlations of properties within a category enables finer predictions: From noting that a bird is large, one can predict that it cannot sing. It may seem that exemplar models do not discard any information at all, but they are incomplete without assumptions concerning retrieval or access. In general, however, the pairs of storage and retrieval assumptions associated with exemplar models preserve much more information than prototype models. In a general review of research on categorization and problem-solving, Brian Ross and I concluded that abstraction is both conservative and tied to the details of specific examples in a manner more in the spirit of exemplar models than prototype models (Medin & Ross, 1989).

Unfortunately, context-sensitive, conservative categorization is not enough. The debate between prototype and exemplar models has taken place on a platform constructed in terms of similarity-based categorization. The second shift is that this platform has started to crumble, and the viability of probabilistic view theories of categorization is being seriously questioned. There are two central problems. One is that probabilistic view theories do not say anything about why we have the categories we have. This problem is most glaringly obvious for exemplar models that appear to allow any set of examples to form a category. The second central problem is with the notion of similarity. Do things belong in the same category because they are similar, or do they seem similar because they are in the same category?

## Does Similarity Explain Categorization?

### 1. FLEXIBILITY

Similarity is a very intuitive notion. Unfortunately, it is even more elusive than it is intuitive. One problem with using similarity to define categories is that similarity is too flexible. Consider, for example, Tversky's (1977) influential contrast model, which defines similarity as a function of common and distinctive features weighted for salience or importance. According to this model, similarity relationships will depend heavily on the particular weights given to individual properties or features. For example, a *zebra* and a *barber pole* would be more similar than a *zebra* and a *horse* if the feature "striped" had sufficient weight. This would not necessarily be a problem if the weights were stable. However, Tversky and others have convincingly shown that the relative weighting of a feature (as well as the relative importance of matching and mismatching features) varies with the stimulus context, experimental task (Gati & Tversky, 1984; Tversky, 1977), and probably even the concept under consideration (Ortony, Vondruska, Foss, & Jones, 1985). For example, common properties shared by a pair of entities may become salient only in the context of some third entity that does not share these properties.

Once one concedes that similarity is dynamic and depends on some (not well-understood) processing principles, earlier work on the structural underpinnings of fuzzy categories can be seen in a somewhat different light. Recall that the Rosch and Mervis (1975) studies asked subjects to list attributes or properties of examples and categories. It would be a mistake to assume that people had the ability to read and report their mental representations of concepts in a veridical manner. Indeed Keil (1979, 1981) pointed out that examples like *robin* and *squirrel* shared many important properties that almost never show up in attribute listings (e.g., has a heart, breathes, sleeps, is an organism, is an object with boundaries, is a physical object, is a thing, can be thought about, and so on). In fact, Keil argued that knowledge about just these sorts of predicates, referred to as ontological knowledge (Sommers, 1971), serves to organize children's conceptual and semantic development. For present purposes, the point is that attribute listings provide a biased sample of people's conceptual knowledge. To take things a step further, one could argue that without constraints on what is to count as a feature, any two things may be arbitrarily similar or dissimilar. Thus, as Murphy and I (Murphy & Medin, 1985) suggested, the number of properties that plums and lawn mowers have in common could be infinite: Both weigh less than 1000 kg, both are found on earth, both are found in our solar system, both cannot hear well, both have an odor, both are not worn by elephants, both are used by people, both can be dropped, and so on (see also Goodman, 1972; Watanabe, 1969). Now consider again the status of attribute listings. They represent a biased subset of stored or readily inferred knowledge. The correlation of attribute listings with typicality judgments is a product of such knowledge and a variety of processes that operate on it. Without a theory of that knowledge and those processes, it simply is not clear what these correlations indicate about mental representations.

The general point is that attempts to describe category structure in terms of similarity will prove useful only to the extent that one specifies which principles determine what is to count as a relevant property and which principles determine the importance of particular properties. It is important to realize that the explanatory work is being done by the principles which specify these constraints rather than the general notion of similarity. In that sense similarity is more like a dependent variable than an independent variable.

### 2. ATTRIBUTE MATCHING AND CATEGORIZATION

The modal model of similarity summarized in Table 31.1 invites one to view categorization as attribute matching. Although that may be part of the story, there are several ways in which the focus on attribute matching may be misleading. First of all, as Armstrong, Gleitman, and Gleitman (1983) emphasized, most concepts are not a simple

TABLE 31.1. Comparison of Two Approaches to Concepts

| Aspect of Conceptual Theory | Similarity-Based Approach | Theory-Based Approach |
|---|---|---|
| Concept representation | Similarity structure, attribute lists, correlated attributes | Correlated attributes plus underlying principles that determine which correlations are noticed |
| Category definition | Various similarity metrics, summation of attributes | An explanatory principle common to category members |
| Units of analysis | Attributes | Attributes plus explicitly represented relations of attributes and concepts |
| Categorization basis | Attribute matching | Matching plus inferential processes supplied by underlying principles |
| Weighting of attributes | Cue validity, salience | Determined in part by importance in the underlying principles |
| Interconceptual structure | Hierarchy based on shared attributes | Network formed by causal and explanatory links, as well as sharing of properties picked out as relevant |
| Conceptual development | Feature accretion | Changing organization and explanations of concepts as a result of world knowledge |

sum of independent features. The features that are characteristically associated with the concept *bird* are just a pile of bird features unless they are held together in a "bird structure." Structure requires both attributes and *relations* binding the attributes together. Typical bird features (laying eggs, flying, having wings and feathers, building nests in trees, and singing) have both an internal structure and an external structure based on interproperty relationships. Building nests is linked to laying eggs, and building nests in trees poses logistical problems whose solution involves other properties such as having wings, flying, and singing. Thus, it makes sense to ask why birds have certain features (e.g., wings and feathers). Although people may not have thought about various interproperty relationships, they can readily reason with them. Thus, one can answer the question of why birds have wings and feathers (i.e., to fly).

In a number of contexts, categorization may be more like problem solving than attribute matching. Inferences and causal attributions may drive the categorization process. Borrowing again from work by Murphy and me (1985), "jumping into a swimming pool with one's clothes on" in all probability is not associated directly with the concept *intoxicated*. However, observing this behavior might lead one to classify the person as drunk. In general, real world knowledge is used to reason about or explain properties, not simply to match them. For example, a teenage boy might show

many of the behaviors associated with an eating disorder, but the further knowledge that the teenager is on the wrestling team and trying to make a lower weight class may undermine any diagnosis of a disorder.

### 3. SUMMARY

It does not appear that similarity, at least in the form it takes in current theories, is going to be at all adequate to explain categorization. Similarity may be a byproduct of conceptual coherence rather than a cause. To use a rough analogy, winning basketball teams have in common scoring more points than their opponents, but one must turn to more basic principles to explain why they score more points. One candidate for a set of deeper principles is the idea that concepts are organized around theories, and theories provide conceptual coherence. In the next section, I will briefly summarize some of the current work on the role of knowledge structures and theories in categorization and then turn to a form of rapprochement between similarity and knowledge-based categorization principle.

## The Second Shift: Concepts as Organized by Theories

### Knowledge-Based Categorization

It is perhaps only a modest exaggeration to say that similarity gets at the shadow rather than the substance of concepts. Something is needed to give concepts life, coherence, and meaning. Although many philosophers of science have argued that observations are necessarily theory-labeled, only recently have researchers begun to stress that the organization of concepts is knowledge-based and driven by theories about the world (e.g., Carey, 1985; S. Gelman, 1988; S. Gelman & Markman, 1986a, 1986b; Keil, 1986, 1987; Keil & Kelly, 1987; Lakoff, 1987; Markman, 1987; Massey & R. Gelman, 1988; Murphy & Medin, 1985; Oden, 1987; Rips, 1989; Schank, Collins, & Hunter, 1986; and others).

The primary differences between the similarity-based and theory-based approaches to categorization are summarized in Table 31.1, taken from Murphy and Medin (1985). Murphy and Medin suggested that the relation between a concept and an example is analogous to the relation between theory and data. That is, classification is not simply based on a direct matching of properties of the concept with those in the example, but rather requires that the example have the right "explanatory relationship" to the theory organizing the concept. In the case of a person diving into a swimming pool with his or her clothes on, one might try to reason back to either causes or predisposing conditions. One might believe that having too much to drink impairs judgment and that going into the pool shows poor judgment. Of course, the presence of other information, such as the fact that another person who cannot swim has fallen into the pool, would radically change the inferences drawn and, as a consequence, the categorization judgment.

One of the more promising aspects of the theory-based approach is that it begins to address the question of why we have the categories we have or why categories are sensible. In fact, coherence may be achieved in the absence of any obvious source of similarity among examples. Consider the category comprised of children, money, photo albums, and pets. Out of context the category seems odd. If one's knowledge base is enriched to include the fact that the category represents "things to take out of one's house in case of a fire," the category becomes sensible (Barsalou, 1983). In addition, one could readily make judgments about whether new examples (e.g., personal papers) belonged to the category, judgments that would not be similarity based.

Similarity effects can be overridden by theory-related strategies even in the judgments of young children. That fact was very nicely demonstrated by Gelman and Markman (1986a) in their studies of induction. Specifically, they pitted category membership against perceptual similarity in an inductive inference task. Young children were taught that different novel properties were true of two examples and then were asked which property was also true of a new example that was similar to one alternative but belonged to a different category, and one that was perceptually different from the other examples but belonged to the same category. For example, children might be taught that a (pictured) flamingo feeds its baby mashed-up food and that a (pictured) bat feeds its baby milk, and then they might be asked how a (pictured) owl feeds its baby. The owl was more perceptually similar to the bat than to the flamingo, but even four-year-olds made inferences on the basis of category membership rather than similarity.

Related work by Susan Carey and Frank Keil shows that children's biological theories guide their conceptual development. For example, Keil has used the ingenious technique of describing transformations or changes such as painting a horse to look like a zebra to examine the extent to which category membership judgments are controlled by superficial perceptual properties. Biological theories determine membership judgments quite early on (Keil, 1987; Keil & Kelly, 1987). Rips (1989) has used the same technique to show that similarity is neither necessary nor sufficient to determine category membership. It even appears to be the case that theories can affect judgments of similarity. For example, Medin and Shoben (1988) found that the terms *white hair* and *grey hair* were judged to be more similar than *grey hair* and *black hair*, but that the terms *white clouds* and *grey clouds* were judged as less similar than *grey clouds* and *black clouds*. Our interpretation is that white and grey hair are linked by a theory (of aging) in a way that white and grey clouds are not.

The above observations are challenging for defenders of the idea that similarity drives conceptual organization. In fact, one might wonder if the notion of similarity is so loose and unconstrained that we might be better off without it. Goodman (1972) epitomized this attitude by calling similarity "a pretender, an imposter, a quack" (p. 437). After reviewing some reasons to continue to take similarity seriously, I outline one possible route for integrating similarity-based and theory-based categorization.

## The Need for Similarity

So far I have suggested that similarity relations do not provide conceptual coherence but that theories do. Because a major problem with similarity is that it is so unconstrained, one might ask what constrains theories. If we cannot identify constraints on theories, that is, say something about why we have the theories we have and not others, then we have not solved the problem of coherence: It simply has been shifted to another level. Although I believe we can specify some general properties of theories and develop a psychology of explanation (e.g., Abelson & Lalljee, 1988; Einhorn & Hogarth, 1986; Hilton & Slugoski, 1986; Leddo, Abelson, & Gross, 1984), I equally believe that a constrained form of similarity will play an important role in our understanding of human concepts. This role is not to provide structure so much as it is to guide learners toward structure.

The impact of more direct perceptual similarity on the development of causal explanations is evident in the structure of people's naive theories. Frazer's (1959) cross-cultural analysis of belief systems pointed to the ubiquity of two principles, homeopathy and contagion. The principle of homeopathy is that causes and effects tend to be similar. One manifestation of this principle is homeopathic medicine, in which the cure (and the cause) are seen to resemble the symptoms. In the Azande culture, for example, the cure for ringworm is to apply fowl's excrement because the excrement looks like the ringworm. Schweder (1977) adduced strong support for the claim that resemblance is a fundamental conceptual tool of everyday thinking in all cultures, not just so-called primitive cultures.

Contagion is the principle that a cause must have some form of contact to transmit its effect. In general, the more contiguous (temporally and spatially similar) events are in time and space, the more likely they are to be perceived as causally related (e.g., Dickinson, Shanks, & Evenden, 1984; Michotte, 1963). People also tend to assume that causes and effects should be of similar magnitude. Einhorn and Hogarth (1986) pointed out that the germ theory of disease initially met with great resistance because people could not imagine how

such tiny organisms could have such devastating effects.

It is important to recognize that homeopathy and contagion often point us in the right direction. Immunization can be seen as a form of homeopathic medicine that has an underlying theoretical principle to support it. My reading of these observations, however, is not that specific theoretical (causal) principles are constraining similarity but rather that similarity (homeopathy and contagion) acts as a constraint on the search for causal explanations. Even in classical conditioning studies, the similarity of the conditioned stimulus and the unconditioned stimulus can have a major influence on the rate of conditioning (Testa, 1974). Of course, similarity must itself be constrained for terms like homeopathy to have a meaning. Shortly, I will suggest some constraints on similarity as part of an effort to define a role for similarity in conceptual development.

Similarity is likely to have a significant effect on explanations in another way. Given the importance of similarity in retrieval, it is likely that explanations that are applied to a novel event are constrained by similar events and their associated explanations. For example, Read (1983) found that people may rely on single, similar instances in making causal attributions about behaviors. Furthermore, Ross (1984) and Gentner and Landers (1985) have found that superficial similarities and not just similarity with respect to deeper principles or relations play a major role in determining the remindings associated with problem solving and the use of analogy.

In brief, it seems that similarity cannot be banished from the world of theories and conceptual structures. But it seems to me that a theory of similarity is needed that is quite different in character from the one summarized in Table 31.1. I will suggest an alternative view of similarity and then attempt to show its value in integrating and explanation with respect to concepts.

## Similarity and Theory in Conceptual Structure

### A Contrasting Similarity Model

The following are key tenets of the type of similarity theory needed to link similarity with knowledge-based categorization: (a) Similarity needs to include attributes, relations, and higher-order relations. (b) Properties in general are not independent but rather are linked by a variety of inter-property relations. (c) Properties exist at multiple levels of abstraction. (d) Concepts are more than lists. Properties and relations create depth or structure. Each of the four main ideas directly conflicts with the corresponding assumption of the theory of similarity outlined earlier. In one way or another all of these assumptions are tied to structure. The general idea I am proposing is far from new. In the psychology of visual perception, the need for structural approaches to similarity has been a continuing, if not major, theme (e.g., Biederman, 1985, 1987; Palmer, 1975, 1978; Pomerantz, Sager, & Stoever, 1977). Oden and Lopes (1982) have argued that this view can inform our understanding of concepts: "Although similarity must function at some level in the induction of concepts, the induced categories are not 'held together' subjectively by the undifferentiated 'force' of similarity, but rather by structural principles" (p. 78). Nonindependence of properties and simple and higher-order relations add a dimension of depth to categorization. Depth has clear implications for many of the observations that seem so problematic for probabilistic view theories. I turn now to the question of how these modified similarity notions may link up with theory-based categorization.

## Psychological Essentialism

Despite the overwhelming evidence against the classical view, there is something about it that is intuitively compelling. Recently I and my colleagues have begun to take this observation seriousl , not for its metaphysical implications but as a piece of psychological data (Medin & Ortony, 1989; Medin & Wattenmaker, 1987; Wattenmaker, Nakamura, & Medin, 1988). One might call this framework "psychological essentialism." The main ideas are as follows: People act as if things (e.g., objects) have essences or underlying natures that make them the thing that they are. Furthermore, the essence constrains or generates properties that may vary in their centrality. One of the things that theories do is to embody or provide causal linkages from deeper properties to more superficial or surface properties. For example, people in our cul-

ture believe that the categories *male* and *female* are genetically determined, but to pick someone out as male or female we rely on characteristics such as hair length, height, facial hair, and clothing that represent a mixture of secondary sexual characteristics and cultural conventions. Although these characteristics are more unreliable than genetic evidence, they are far from arbitrary. Not only do they have some validity in a statistical sense, but also they are tied to our biological and cultural conceptions of *male* and *female*.

It is important to note that psychological essentialism refers not to how the world is but rather to how people approach the world. Wastebaskets probably have no true essence, although we may act as if they do. Both social and psychodiagnostic categories are at least partially culture specific and may have weak if any metaphysical underpinnings (see also Morey & McNamara, 1987).

If psychological essentialism is bad metaphysics, why should people act as if things had essences? The reason is that it may prove to be good epistomology. One could say that people adopt an *essentialist heuristic*, namely, the hypothesis that things that look alike tend to share deeper properties (similarities). Our perceptual and conceptual systems appear to have evolved such that the essentialist heuristic is very often correct (Medin & Wattenmaker, 1987; Shepard, 1984). This is true even for human artifacts such as cars, computers, and camping stoves because structure and function tend to be correlated. Surface characteristics that are perceptually obvious or are readily produced on feature listing tasks may not so much constitute the core of a concept as point toward it. This observation suggests that classifying on the basis of similarity will be relatively effective much of the time, but that similarity will yield to knowledge of deeper principles. Thus, in the work of Gelman and Markman (1986a) discussed earlier, category membership was more important than perceptual similarity in determining inductive inferences.

## Related Evidence

The contrasting similarity principles presented earlier coupled with psychological essentialism provide a framework for integrating knowledge-based and similarity-based categorization. Although it is far short of a formal theory, the framework provides a useful perspective on many of the issues under discussion in this article.

## 1. NONINDEPENDENCE OF FEATURES

Earlier I mentioned that classifying on the basis of similarity to a prototype was functionally equivalent to adding up the evidence favoring a classification and applying some criterion (at least X out of Y features). Recall also that the data ran strongly against this idea. From the perspective currently under consideration, however, there ought to be two ways to produce data consistent with prototype theory. One would be to provide a theory that suggests the prototype as an ideal or that makes summing of evidence more natural. For example, suppose that the characteristic properties for one category were as follows: It is made of metal, has a regular surface, is of medium size, and is easy to grasp. For a contrasting category the characteristic properties were: It is made of rubber, has an irregular surface, is of small size, and is hard to grasp. The categories may not seem sensible or coherent but suppose one adds the information that the objects in one category could serve as substitutes for a hammer. Given this new information, it becomes easy to add up the properties of examples in terms of their utility in supporting hammering. In a series of studies using the above descriptions and related examples, Wattenmaker, Dewey, Murphy, and I (1986) found data consistent with prototype theory when the additional information was supplied, and data inconsistent with prototype theory when only characteristic properties were supplied. Specifically, we found that linearly separable categories were easier to learn than nonlinearly separable categories only when an organizing theme was provided (see also Nakamura, 1985).

One might think that prototypes become important whenever the categories are meaningful. That is not the case. When themes are provided that are not compatible with a summing of evidence, the data are inconsistent with prototype theories. For instance, suppose that the examples consisted of descriptions of animals and that the organizing theme was that one category consisted of prey and the other of predators. It is a good adaptation for prey to be armored and to live in trees, but an animal that is both armored and lives in trees may not be better adapted than an animal with either

characteristic alone. Being armored and living in trees may be somewhat incompatible. Other studies by Wattenmaker et al. using directly analogous materials failed to find any evidence that linear separability (and, presumably, summing of evidence) was important or natural. Only some kinds of interproperty relations are compatible with a summing of evidence, and evidence favoring prototypes may be confined to these cases.

The above studies show that the ease or naturalness of classification tasks cannot be predicted in terms of abstract category structures based on distribution of features, but rather requires an understanding of the knowledge brought to bear on them, for this knowledge determines inter-property relationships. So far only a few types of interproperty relationships have been explored in categorization, and much is to be gained from the careful study of further types of relations (e.g., see Barr & Caplan, 1987; Chaffin & Herrmann, 1987; Rips & Conrad, 1989; Winston, Chaffin, & Herman, 1987).

## 2. LEVELS OF FEATURES

Although experimenters can often contrive to have the features or properties comprising stimulus materials at roughly the same level of abstractness, in more typical circumstances levels may vary substantially. This fact has critical implications for descriptions of category structure (see Barsalou & Billman, 1988). This point may be best represented by an example from some ongoing research I am conducting with Glenn Nakamura and Ed Wisniewski. Our stimulus materials consist of children's drawings of people, a sample of which is shown in Figure 31.1. There are two sets of five drawings, one on the left and one on the right. The task of the participants in this experiment is to come up with a rule that could be used to correctly classify both these drawings and new examples that might be presented later.

One of our primary aims in this study was to examine the effects of different types of knowledge structures on rule induction. Consequently, some participants were told that one set was done by farm children and the other by city children; some were told that one set was done by creative children and the other by noncreative children; and still others were told that one set was done by emotionally disturbed children and the other by

**FIGURE 31.1** ■ Children's drawings of people used in the rule induction studies by Nakamura, Wisniewski, and Medin.

mentally healthy children. The exact assignment of drawings was counterbalanced with respect to the categories such that half the time the drawings on the left of Figure 31.1 were labeled as done by farm children and half the time the drawings on the right were labeled as having been done by farm children.

Although we were obviously expecting differences in the various conditions, in some respects the most striking result is one that held across conditions. Almost without exception the rules that people gave had properties at two or three different levels of abstractness. For example, one person who was told the drawings on the left were done by city children gave the following rule: "The city drawings use more profiles, and are more elaborate. The clothes are more detailed, showing both pockets and buttons, and the hair is drawn in. The drawings put less emphasis on proportion and the legs and torso are off." Another person who was told the same drawings were done by farm children wrote: "The children draw what they see in their normal life. The people have overalls on and some drawings show body muscles as a result of labor. The drawings are also more detailed. One can see more facial details and one drawing has colored the clothes and another one shows the body under the clothes." As one can see, the rules typically consist of a general assertion or assertions coupled with either an operational definition or examples to illustrate and clarify the assertion. In some cases these definitions or examples extend across several levels of abstractness.

One might think that our participants used different levels of description because there was nothing else for them to do. That is, there may have been no low-level perceptual features that would separate the groups. In a followup study we presented examples one at a time and asked people to give their rule after each example. If people are being forced to use multiple levels of description because simple rules will not work, then we should observe a systematic increase in the use of multiple levels across examples. In fact, however, we observed multiple levels of description as the predominant strategy from the first example on. We believe that multiple levels arise when people try to find a link between abstract explanatory principles or ideas (drawings reflect one's experience) and specific details of drawings.

There are several important consequences of multilevel descriptions. First of all, the relation across levels is not necessarily a subset, superset, or a part–whole relation. Most of the time one would say that the lower level property "supports" the higher level property; for example, "jumping into a swimming pool with one's clothes on" supports poor judgment. This underlines the point that categorization often involves more than a simple matching of properties. A related point is that features are ambiguous in the sense that they may support more than one higher level property. When the drawings on the right were associated with the label *mentally healthy*, a common description was "all the faces are smiling." When the label for the same drawing was *noncreative*, a common description was "the faces show little variability in expression." Finally, it should be obvious that whether a category description is disjunctive (e.g., pig's nose or cow's mouth or catlike ears) or conjunctive or defining (e.g., all have animal parts) depends on the level with respect to which the rule is evaluated.

## 3. CENTRALITY

If properties are at different levels of abstraction and linked by a variety of relations, then one might imagine that some properties are more central than others because of the role they play in conceptual structure. An indication that properties differ in their centrality comes from a provocative study by Asch and Zukier (1984). They presented people with trait terms that appeared to be contradictory (e.g., kind and vindictive) and asked participants if these descriptions could be resolved (e.g., how could a person be both kind and vindictive?). Participants had no difficulty integrating the pairs of terms, and Asch and Zukier identified seven major resolution strategies. For present purposes, what is notable is that many of the resolution strategies involve making one trait term more central than the other one. For example, one way of integrating *kind* and *vindictive* was to say that the person was fundamentally evil and was kind only in the service of vindictive ends.

In related work, Shoben and I (Medin & Shoben, 1988) showed that centrality of a property depends on the concept of which it is a part. We asked participants to judge the typicality of adjective noun pairs when the adjective was a property that other participants judged was not true of the noun representing the concept. For example, our participants judged that all bananas and all boomerangs are curved. Based on this observation, other participants were asked to judge the typicality of a straight banana as a banana or a straight boomerang as a boomerang. Other instances of the 20 pairs used include *soft knife* versus *soft diamond* and *polka dot fire hydrant* versus *polka dot yield sign*.

For 19 of the 20 pairs, participants rated one item of a pair as more typical than the other. Straight banana, soft knife, and polka dot fire hydrant were rated as more typical than straight boomerang, soft diamond, and polka dot yield sign. In the case of boomerangs (and probably yield signs), centrality may be driven by structure-function correlations. Soft diamonds are probably rated as very atypical because hardness is linked to many other properties and finding out that diamonds were soft would call a great deal of other knowledge into question.

Most recently, Woo Kyoung Ahn, Joshua Rubenstein, and I have been interviewing clinical psychologists and psychiatrists concerning their understanding of psychodiagnostic categories. Although our project is not far enough along to report any detailed results, it is clear that the *DSM-IIIR* guidebook (American Psychiatric Association, 1987) provides only a skeletal outline that is brought to life by theories and causal scenarios underlying and intertwined with the symptoms that comprise the diagnostic criteria. Symptoms differ in the level of abstractness and the types and number of intersymptom relations in which they participate, and as a consequence, they differ in their centrality.

## CONCLUSIONS

The shift to a focus on knowledge-based categorization does not mean that the notion of similarity must be left behind. But we do need an updated approach to, and interpretation of, similarity. The mounting evidence on the role of theories and explanations in organizing categories is much more compatible with features at varying levels linked by a variety of interproperty relations than it is with independent features at a single level. In addition, similarity may not so much constitute structure as point toward it. There is a dimension of depth to categorization. The conjectures about psychological essentialism may be one way of reconciling classification in terms of perceptual similarity or surface properties with the deeper substance of knowledge-rich, theory-based categorization.

## ACKNOWLEDGMENT

The research described in this article was supported in part by National Science Foundation Grant No. BNS 84–19756 and by National Library of Medicine Grant No. LM 04375. Brian Ross, Edward Shoben, Ellen Markman, Greg Oden, and Dedre Gentner provided helpful comments on an earlier draft of the article.

## REFERENCES

Abelson, R. P., & Lalljee, M. G. (1988). Knowledge-structures and causal explanation. In D. J. Hilton (Ed.), *Contemporary science and natural explanation: Commonsense conceptions of causality* (pp. 175–202). Brighton, England: Harvester Press.

Allen, S. W., Brooks, L. R., Norman, G. R., & Rosenthal, D. (1988, November). *Effect of prior examples on rule-based diagnostic performance.* Paper presented at the meeting of the Psychonomic Society, Chicago.

American Psychiatric Association. (1987). *Diagnostic and statistical manual of mental disorders* (rev. ed.). Washington, DC: Author.

Anderson, J. R. (1988). The place of cognitive architectures in a rational analyses. In *The Tenth Annual Conference of the Cognitive Science Society* (pp. 1–10). Montreal, Canada: University of Montreal.

Arkes, H. R., & Harkness, A. R. (1980). Effect of making a diagnosis on subsequent recognition of symptoms. *Journal of Experimental Psychology: Human Learning and Memory, 6,* 568–575.

Armstrong, S. L., Gleitman, L. R., & Gleitman, H. (1983). What some concepts might not be. *Cognition, 13,* 263–308.

Asch, S. E., & Zukier, H. (1984). Thinking about persons. *Journal of Personality and Social Psychology, 46,* 1230–1240.

Barr, R. A., & Caplan, L. J. (1987). Category representations and their implications for category structure. *Memory and Cognition, 15,* 397–418.

Barsalou, L. W. (1983). Ad hoc categories. *Memory and Cognition, 11,* 211–227.

Barsalou, L. W. (1985). Ideals, central tendency, and frequency of instantiation as determinants of graded structure in categories. *Journal of Experimental Psychology: Learning, Memory and Cognition, 11,* 629–654.

Barsalou, L. W. (1987). The instability of graded structure: Implications for the nature of concepts. In U. Neisser (Ed.), *Concepts and conceptual development: The ecological and intellectual factors in categorization* (pp. 101–140). Cambridge, England: Cambridge University Press.

Barsalou, L. W. (1989). Intra-concept similarity and its implications for inter-concept similarity. In S. Vosniadou & A. Ortony (Eds.), *Similarity and analogical reasoning* (pp. 76–121). Cambridge, England: Cambridge University Press.

Barsalou, L. W., & Billman, D. (1988, April). *Systematicity and semantic ambiguity.* Paper presented at a workshop on semantic ambiguity, Adelphi University.

Barsalou, L. W., & Medin, D. L. (1986). Concepts: Fixed definitions or dynamic context-dependent representations? *Cahiers de Psychologie Cognitive, 6,* 187–202.

Bellezza, F. S. (1984). Reliability of retrieval from semantic memory: Noun meanings. *Bulletin of the Psychonomic Society, 22,* 377–380.

Biederman, I. (1985). Human image understanding: Recent research and a theory. *Computer Vision, Graphics, and Image Processing, 32,* 29–83.

Biederman, I. (1987). Recognition-by-components: A theory of human image understanding. *Psychological Review, 94,* 115–147.

Cantor, N., & Mischel, W. (1977). Traits as prototypes: Effects on recognition memory. *Journal of Personality and Social Psychology, 35,* 38–48.

Carey, S. (1985). *Conceptual change in childhood.* Cambridge, MA: Massachusetts Institute of Technology Press.

Chaffin, R., & Herrmann, D. J. (1987). Relation element theory: A new account of the representation and processing of semantic relations. In D. Gorfein & R. Hoffman (Eds.), *Learning and memory: The Ebbinghaus centennial conference* (pp. 221–245). Hillsdale, NJ: Erlbaum.

Dickinson, A., Shanks, D., & Evenden, J. (1984). Judgment of act-out-comes contingency: The role of selective attribution. *Quarterly Journal of Experimental Psychology, 36A(1),* 29–50.

Einhorn, J. H., & Hogarth, R. M. (1986). Judging probable cause. *Psychological Bulletin, 99,* 3–19.

Estes, W. K. (1986a). Memory storage and retrieval processes in category learning. *Journal of Experimental Psychology: General, 115,* 155–175.

Estes, W. K. (1986b). Array models for category learning. *Cognitive Psychology, 18,* 500–549.

Fehr, B. (1988). Prototype analysis of the concepts of love and commitment. *Journal of Personality and Social Psychology, 55,* 557–579.

Fehr, B., & Russell, J. A. (1984). Concept of emotion viewed from a prototype perspective. *Journal of Experimental Psychology: General, 113,* 464–486.

Flannagan, M. J., Fried, L. S., & Holyoak, K. J. (1986). Distributional expectations and the induction of category structure. *Journal of Experimental Psychology: Learning, Memory and Cognition, 12,* 241–256.

Frazer, J. G. (1959). *The new golden bough.* New York: Criterion Books.

Fried, L. S., & Holyoak, K. J. (1984). Induction of category distribution: A framework for classification learning. *Journal of Experimental Psychology: Learning, Memory and Cognition, 10,* 234–257.

Gati, I., & Tversky, A. (1984). Weighting common and distinctive features in perceptual and conceptual judgments. *Cognitive Psychology, 16,* 341–370.

Gelman, S. A. (1988). The development of induction within natural kind and artifact categories. *Cognitive Psychology, 20,* 65–95.

Gelman, S. A., & Markman, E. M. (1986a). Categories and induction in young children. *Cognition, 23,* 183–209.

Gelman, S. A., & Markman, E. M. (1986b). Young children's inductions from natural kinds: The role of categories and appearances. *Child Development, 58,* 1532–1541.

Genero, N., & Cantor, N. (1987). Exemplar prototypes and clinical diagnosis: Toward a cognitive economy. *Journal of Social and Clinical Psychology, 5,* 59–78.

Gentner, D., & Landers, R. (1985). *Analogical reminding: A good match is hard to find.* Paper presented at the International Conference of Systems, Man and Cybernetics, Tucson, AZ.

Goldin, S. E. (1978). Memory for the ordinary: Typicality effects in chess memory. *Journal of Experimental Psychology: Human Learning and Memory, 4,* 605–616.

Goodman, N. (1972). Seven strictures on similarity. In N. Goodman (Ed.), *Problems and projects.* New York: Bobbs-Merrill.

Hartley, J., & Homa, D. (1981). Abstraction of stylistic concepts. *Journal of Experimental Psychology: Human Learning and Memory, 7,* 33–46.

Hilton, D. J., & Slugoski, B. R. (1986). Knowledge-based causal attribution: The abnormal conditions focus model. *Psychological Review, 93,* 75–88.

Hintzman, D. L. (1986). "Schema abstraction" in a multiple-trace memory model. *Psychological Review, 93,* 411–428.

Homa, D. (1984). On the nature of categories. In G. Bower (Ed.), *The psychology of learning and motivation* (Vol. 18, pp. 49–94). New York: Academic Press.

Homa, D., & Vosburgh, R. (1976). Category breadth and the abstraction of prototypical information. *JEP: Human Learning and Memory, 2,* 322–330.

Keil, F. C. (1979). *Semantic and conceptual development: An ontological perspective.* Cambridge, MA: Harvard University Press.

Keil, F. C. (1981). Constraints on knowledge and cognitive development. *Psychological Review, 88,* 197–227.

Keil, F. C. (1986). The acquisition of natural kind and artifact terms. In W. Demopoulos & A. Marras (Eds.), *Language learning and concept acquisition* (pp. 133–153). Norwood, NJ: Ablex.

Keil, F. C. (1987). Conceptual development and category structure. In U. Neisser (Ed.), *Concepts and conceptual development: Ecological and intellectual factors in categorization* (pp. 175–200). Cambridge, England: Cambridge University Press.

Keil, F. C., & Kelly, M. H. (1987). Developmental changes in category structure. In S. Harnad (Ed.), *Categorical perception: The groundwork of cognition* (pp. 491–510). Cambridge, England: Cambridge University Press.

Kemler-Nelson, D. G. (1984). The effect of intention on what concepts are acquired. *Journal of Verbal Learning and Verbal Behavior, 23,* 734–759.

Kolodner, J. L. (1984). *Retrieval and organizational structures in conceptual memory: A computer model.* Hillsdale, NJ: Erlbaum.

Lakoff, G. (1987). *Women, fire, and dangerous things: What categories tell us about the nature of thought.* Chicago: University of Chicago Press.

Leddo, J., Abelson, R. P., & Gross, P. H. (1984). Conjunctive explanation: When two explanations are better than one. *Journal of Personality and Social Psychology, 47,* 933–943.

Malt, B. C., & Smith, E. E. (1983). Correlated properties in natural categories. *Journal of Verbal Learning and Verbal Behavior, 23,* 250–269.

Markman, E. M. (1987). How children constrain the possible meanings of words. In U. Neisser (Ed.), *Concepts and conceptual development: The ecological and intellectual factors in categorization* (pp. 256–287). Cambridge, England: Cambridge University Press.

Massey, C. M., & Gelman, R. (1988). Preschoolers' ability to decide whether a photographed unfamiliar object can move itself. *Developmental Psychology, 24,* 307–317.

McCloskey, M., & Glucksberg, S. (1978). Natural categories: Well-defined or fuzzy sets? *Memory and Cognition, 6,* 462–472.

McNamara, T. P., & Sternberg, R. J. (1983). Mental models of word meaning. *Journal of Verbal Learning and Verbal Behavior, 22,* 449–474.

Medin, D. L. (1986). Commentary on "Memory storage and retrieval processes in category learning." *Journal of Experimental Psychology: General, 115*(4), 373–381.

Medin, D. L., Altom, M. W., Edelson, S. M., & Freko, D. (1982). Correlated symptoms and simulated medical classification. *Journal of Experimental Psychology: Learning, Memory and Cognition, 8,* 37–50.

Medin, D. L., & Ortony, A. (1989). *Psychological essentialism.* In S. Vosniadou & A. Ortony (Eds.), *Similarity and analogical reasoning* (pp. 179–195). New York: Cambridge University Press.

Medin, D. L., & Ross, B. H. (1989). The specific character of abstract thought: Categorization, problem-solving, and induction. In R. J. Sternberg (Ed.), *Advances in the psychology of human intelligence* (Vol. 5, pp. 189–223). Hillsdale, NJ: Erlbaum.

Medin, D. L., & Schaffer, M. M. (1978). A context theory of classification learning. *Psychological Review, 85,* 207–238.

Medin, D. L., & Schwanenflugel, P. J. (1981). Linear separability in classification learning. *Journal of Experimental Psychology: Human Learning and Memory, 7,* 355–368.

Medin, D. L., & Shoben, E. J. (1988). Context and structure in conceptual combination. *Cognitive Psychology, 20,* 158–190.

Medin, D. L., & Smith, E. E. (1984). Concepts and concept formation. In M. R. Rosenzweig & L. W. Porter (Eds.), *Annual Review of Psychology, 35,* 113–118.

Medin, D. L., & Wattenmaker, W. D. (1987). Category cohesiveness, theories, and cognitive archeology. In U. Neisser (Ed.), *Concepts and conceptual development: The ecological and intellectual factors in categories* (pp. 25–62). Cambridge, England: Cambridge University Press.

Mervis, C. B., & Rosch, E. (1981). Categorization of natural objects. In M. R. Rosenzweig & L. W. Porter (Eds.), *Annual Review of Psychology, 32,* 89–115.

Michotte, A. (1963). *Perception of causality.* London: Methuen.

Morey, L. C., & McNamara, T. P. (1987). On definitions, diagnosis, and DSM-III. *Journal of Abnormal Psychology, 96,* 283–285.

Murphy, G. L., & Medin, D. L. (1985). The role of theories in conceptual coherence. *Psychological Review, 92,* 289–316.

Nakamura, G. V. (1985). Knowledge-based classification of ill-defined categories. *Memory and Cognition, 13,* 377–384.

Nosofsky, R. M. (1987). Attention and learning processes in the identification and categorization of integral stimuli. *Journal of Experimental Psychology: Learning, Memory, and Cognition, 13,* 87–108.

Nosofsky, R. M. (1988a). Exemplar-based accounts of relations between classification, recognition, and typicality. *Journal of Experimental Psychology: Learning, Memory, and Cognition, 14,* 700–708.

Nosofsky, R. M. (1988b). Similarity, frequency, and category representations. *Journal of Experimental Psychology: Learning, Memory, and Cognition, 14,* 54–65.

Oden, G. C. (1987). Concept, knowledge, and thought. In M. R. Rosenzweig & L. W. Porter (Eds.), *Annual Review of Psychology, 38,* 203–227.

Oden, G. C., & Lopes, L. (1982). On the internal structure of fuzzy subjective categories. In R. R. Yager (Ed.), *Recent developments in fuzzy set and possibility theory* (pp. 75–89). Elmsford, NY: Pergamon Press.

Ortony, A., Vondruska, R. J., Foss, M. A., & Jones, L. E. (1985). Salience, similes, and the asymmetry of similarity. *Journal of Memory and Language, 24*, 569–594.

Palmer, S. E. (1975). Visual perception and world knowledge. In D. A. Norman & D. E. Rumelhart (Eds.), *Explorations in cognition* (pp. 279–307). San Francisco: W. H. Freeman.

Palmer, S. E. (1978). Structural aspects of visual similarity. *Memory and Cognition, 6*, 91–97.

Peterson, M. J., Meagher, R. B., Jr., Chait, H., & Gillie, S. (1973). The abstraction and generalization of dot patterns. *Cognitive Psychology, 4*, 378–398.

Pomerantz, J. R., Sager, L. C., & Stoever, R. G. (1977). Perception of wholes and their component parts: Some configural superiority effects. *Journal of Experimental Psychology: Human Perception and Performance, 3*, 422–435.

Read, S. J. (1983). Once is enough: Causal reasoning from a single instance. *Journal of Personality and Social Psychology, 45*, 323–334.

Rips, L. (1989). Similarity, typicality, and categorization. In S. Vosniadou & A. Ortony (Eds.), *Similarity and analogical reasoning* (pp. 21–59). New York: Cambridge University Press.

Rips, L. J., & Conrad, F. G. (1989). The folk psychology of mental activities. *Psychological Review, 96*, 187–207.

Rosch, E. (1975). Cognitive representations of semantic categories. *Journal of Experimental Psychology: General, 104*, 192–233.

Rosch, E., & Mervis, C. B. (1975). Family resemblances: Studies in the internal structure of categories. *Cognitive Psychology, 7*, 573–605.

Ross, B. H. (1984). Remindings and their effects in learning a cognitive skill. *Cognitive Psychology, 16*, 371–416.

Roth, E. M., & Shoben, E. J. (1983). The effect of context on the structure of categories. *Cognitive Psychology, 15*, 346–378.

Schank, R. C., Collins, G. C., & Hunter, L. E. (1986). Transcending induction category formation in learning. *The Behavioral and Brain Sciences, 9*, 639–686.

Schweder, R. A. (1977). Likeness and likelihood in everyday thought: Magical thinking in judgments about personality. *Current Anthropology, 18*, 4.

Sebestyn, G. S. (1962). *Decision-making processes in pattern recognition.* New York: Macmillan.

Shepard, R. H. (1984). Ecological constraints on internal representation: Resonant kinematics of perceiving, imagining, thinking, and dreaming. *Psychological Review, 19*, 417–447.

Shepard, R. N., Hovland, C. I., & Jenkins, H. M. (1961). Learning and memorization of classifications. *Psychological Monographs, 75*, (13, Whole No. 517).

Smith, E. E., & Medin, D. L. (1981). *Categories and concepts.* Cambridge, MA: Harvard University Press.

Smith, E. E., Rips, J. J., & Medin, D. W. (1984). A psychological approach to concepts: Comments on Rey's "Concepts and stereotypes." *Cognition, 17*, 265–274.

Smith, E. E., Shoben, E. J., & Rips, J. J. (1974). Structure and processes in semantic memory: A featural model for semantic decisions. *Psychological Review, 81*, 214–241.

Sommers, F. (1971). Structural ontology. *Philosophia, 1*, 21–42.

Testa, T. J. (1974). Causal relationships and the acquisition of avoidance responses. *Psychological Review, 81*, 491–505.

Tulving, E. (1983). *Elements of episodic memory.* New York: Oxford University Press.

Tversky, A. (1977). Features of similarity. *Psychological Review, 84*, 327–352.

Watanabe, S. (1969). *Knowing and guessing: A formal and quantitative study.* New York: Wiley.

Wattenmaker, W. D., Dewey, G. I., Murphy, T. D., & Medin, D. L. (1986). Linear separability and concept learning: Context, relational properties, and concept naturalness. *Cognitive Psychology, 18*, 158–194.

Wattenmaker, W. D., Nakamura, G. V., & Medin, D. L. (1988). Relationships between similarity-based and explanation-based categorization. In D. Hilton (Ed.), *Contemporary science and natural explanation: Commonsense conceptions of causality* (pp. 205–241). Brighton, England: Harvester Press.

Winston, M. E., Chaffin, R., & Herrmann, D. (1987). A taxonomy of part-whole relations. *Cognitive Science, 11*, 417–444.

Wittgenstein, L. (1953). *Philosophical investigations* (G. E. M. Anscombe, trans.). Oxford, England: Blackwell.

PART VII

# Categorization

## Discussion Questions

1. Describe the difference between what is represented in memory for prototype and exemplar models of categorization. Make an argument for each, drawing upon the ideas of cognitive economy and evolutionary adaptivity.
2. Revisit the pattern recognition chapter, and evaluate the following statement from the classic Neisser (1967) chapter: "I will . . . use 'categorization' as a synonym for 'pattern recognition'" (p. 49).
3. What do you think are the implications for the brain of category-specific deficits (e.g., as described in the methods chapter of this book)? That is, does a lesion for "living things" suggest that there is an area of the brain devoted to that category? Why or why not?
4. Initial theorizing about categories began with natural categories (e.g., birds, trees, insects) and later progressed to include more artificial categories (e.g., both man-made categories like furniture and also goal-derived categories such as "green things"). A good theory of categorization should be able to handle all types of categories. What do you think might be some of the differences between natural and artificial categories? (Hint: here's one difference to start with: people may be less likely to infer that the property of a member of an artificial category characterizes all members of that category.) For each of the theories listed in this chapter, describe any problems they would have with either natural or artificial categories.
5. What are the problems with basing categories on similarity?

## Suggested Readings

F. G. Ashby and E. M. Waldron (2000, The neuropsychological bases of category learning, *Current Directions in Psychological Science, 9,* 10–14) recently wrote a short, easy-to-read summary on the neuropsychology of categorization.

B. C. Malt and E. E. Smith (1984, Correlated properties in natural categories. *Journal of Verbal Learning & Verbal Behavior, 23,* 250–269) showed that people are sensitive to how "typical" or representative an exemplar is of a category. For example, people rate "apple" as a more typical fruit and "raisin" as a less typical fruit.

G. L. Murphy and D. L. Medin (1985, The role of theories in conceptual coherence. *Psychological Review, 92,* 289–316) discuss how people use theories to constrain similarity. As described earlier, similarity is unconstrained. That is, any two objects are always similar on some dimension (e.g., a lawnmower and a swimming pool are both man-made). A theory is needed to determine which features are important for determining similarity.

D. N. Osherson, E. E. Smith, and E. B. Shafir (1986, Some origins of belief. *Cognition, 24,* 197–224) present experiments on category-based reasoning.

L. J. Rips (1989, Similarity, typicality, and categorization. In S. Voisniadou and A. Ortony (Eds.), *Similarity, Analogy, and Thought* [p. 21–29]). New York: Cambridge University Press) provides examples of categorization that do *not* appear to be based on similarity.

A. Tversky provides a model for computing similarity based on sets of common and distinctive features. (1977, Features of similarity. *Psychological Review, 84,* 327–352).

PART VIII

# Language Development

# Introduction to Part VIII: Language Development

Language is arguably the most significant accomplishment of human evolution. In just a few years, a child shifts from being an individual without any language to being a highly competent user of an enormously complex system. Even more remarkable is the manner in which children accomplish this feat, that is, without explicit training. Rather, children appear to naturally extract linguistic principles simply from exposure to language. The crucial issue, as highlighted by the classic debates between B. F. Skinner and Noam Chomsky in the 1950s, concerns the role of environmental influences versus innate structures in language acquisition. That is, can children's acquisition of language be explained by the same kind of principles that govern other types of learning, such that children learn language via environmental exposure and reinforcement? Or, does the difficulty of language acquisition require that we are "pre-wired" or otherwise biologically prepared for the task of language learning? This is, of course, at the very core of the nature/nurture debate central to so many areas of psychology. These basic issues are reflected in the readings in this section.

The work of Lenneberg (1967) spurred interest in biological bases for language. He argued that certain periods of brain development are ideally suited for species-specific learning, and hence this learning is not possible after the end of the critical period. For example, a bird's ability to learn a specific song is tied to a critical period in brain development (e.g., Marler,

1970). If the bird is not exposed to the appropriate song early in life, then it is unlikely that the bird will correctly learn the song. Apparently, the bird can take advantage of the specialized learning device only until the maturation of neural systems specialized for learning birdsong syntax. The notion is that this maturation (and termination of the critical period) is marked by brain lateralization. A similar argument has been made for human learning of language. In particular, Lenneberg argued that the brain is best suited for language acquisition before cerebral dominance is established. After that time, one would not expect normal language acquisition.

By chance, Fromkin, Krashen, Curtiss, Rigler, and Rigler (1974) were afforded a test of Lenneberg's ideas about critical periods. Fromkin et al.'s case study of Genie is important, as it provides a window into what happens if a human is not exposed to language during the presumed critical period (puberty, according to Lenneberg, 1967). Due to a tragic set of circumstances, Genie was exposed to very little (if any) language until after puberty. The important theoretical question is whether Genie could acquire language after this point. If the critical period hypothesis is correct, then one would not expect normal language acquisition. The results were clear: Genie was very good at acquiring a large set of words. However, she had difficulty with syntactic constructions, such as understanding subtle syntactic markers in language. Genie had some difficulty with the difference between active and passive sentences; for example, Genie was confused about the agent in sentences such as "The boy is being pulled by the girl." Also, Genie

had difficulties with production of negative sentences. Genie would be likely to say "No more ear hurt" instead of "My ear doesn't hurt." Unexpectedly, language appeared to be represented in Genie's right hemisphere—even though language in right-handed individuals is normally left-lateralized. Fromkin et al. suggested that Genie's left hemisphere did not develop properly, due to insufficient stimulation during the critical period. Hence, the right hemisphere took over language acquisition, but this prevented Genie from acquiring skilled language use, as the right hemisphere is not specialized for language acquisition.

Genie had problems acquiring grammatical rules; of interest is what healthy children know about grammatical rules in a language. The classic paper by Berko (her dissertation) addresses this issue. Berko's interest was in the rules of morphology. Morphemes are the simplest units of meaning in words. For example, the word *girl* is a single morpheme, but the word *girls* involves two morphemes, the morpheme *girl* and the morpheme /s / for plural. Of interest is how children represent the word *girls*. It could be represented as a whole unit, or a rule could be stored that allows the child to append the pluralization /S/ marker to the end of *girl*. The trick is how to test this empirically, because even adults are relatively poor at describing the rules they use to produce and comprehend language. Berko thought that if children simply memorized different forms of the words, then one might not expect them to do well on a novel nonword form. Thus, Berko created novel situations that used nonwords and asked 4- to 7-year-old children and adults to produce different forms of the stimuli. For example, her classic WUG figure shows a single WUG and the experimenter says *This is a WUG*. Then, the experimenter shows two of the nonsense forms, and says *Now there is another one. There are two of them. There are two _____.* The results were quite clear: young children understood the task and extended their knowledge of morphology to these new stimuli, producing *WUGS*. In addition to pluralization, Berko explored irregular past tense forms. For example, adults and some older children produced the past tense of *gling* as *glang*, but younger children produced *glinged*. The addition of more *ing* words to one's vocabulary (e.g., *ring, sing*) and knowledge of their past tense forms (e.g., *rang, sang*) drives the production of the *glang* response. Although Berko's results suggest a rule system for morphology, this issue is actually quite controversial, as reflected by the debate between Rumelhart and McClelland (1986) and Pinker and Prince (1988).

The notion of a specialized learning device for language is also nicely reflected in two recent papers that appeared in *Science*. Saffran, Aslin, and Newport (1996) examined the ability of infants to segment strings of sounds into words. If the child does not know the words yet, how does the child understand where one word ends and the next word starts? This task is made even more difficult by the lack of consistent breaks between words in fluent speech. Saffran et al. argued that infants are able to segment speech based on the statistical properties of language. In particular, they argued that the transitional probabilities of two sounds are, on average, higher when the sounds occur within a word, as opposed to across words. Saffran et al.

mimicked this regularity with a string of nonsegmented nonsense "words" presented to 8-month-old infants. In the second part of the experiment, of interest was whether the babies would be able to discriminate between the familiar "words" and new nonwords. Of course, one of the tricks to this research is to figure out a way to determine what children know, because you can't simply ask 8-month-olds. So, Saffran et al. took advantage of the fact that babies prefer novel to familiar stimuli. The babies listened longer to the new nonwords than to the familiar "words," suggesting that the babies had segmented the words during the first phase. That is, the infants coded sounds within words (as opposed to across words), making these familiar sound patterns less interesting at test. Amazingly, this learning occurred with only 2 minutes of exposure to the sounds. Thus, it is very clear that young children are equipped with learning systems that pick up the statistical regularities in the language. It is also very important to note that this is precisely the type of statistical learning that simple recurrent connectionist networks (see the Rumelhart & McClelland, 1986, paper, earlier) are ideally suited to capture.

Marcus, Vijayan, Rao, and Vishton (1999) suggest that children may have multiple learning systems. Like Saffran et al., they believe that infants have a system tuned to simple statistical regularities. However, they think infants also have a second learning system, one aimed at solving and applying algebraic-type rules. An algebraic rule describes the relationship between two or more unknowns; use of an algebraic function implies that a child will be able to apply a known rule to novel items. Again, the habituation procedure was employed and infants listened to 2 minutes of nonsense sounds that repeated in a particular pattern (e.g., an ABB pattern: *ga ti ti*). In the test phase, babies were presented with patterns consisting of novel words that followed either the same rule (e.g., a second ABB pattern: *wo fe fe*) or a different rule (e.g., an ABA pattern: *wo fe wo*). Babies looked longer (listened) for the novel pattern, that is, the one that did not follow the grammatical rule. Hence, Marcus et al. concluded that there might be additional learning mechanisms in the repertoire of children that capture rules instead of only statistical regularities.

The results from both the Saffran et al. and the Marcus et al. studies clearly demonstrate that very young children have at their disposal remarkable learning devices. These results fall in the middle of the nature-nuture debate; they can be interpreted as innate mechanisms (nature) that allow the infant to take advantage of environmental exposure (nuture). Both sets of researchers note that it is unclear whether these learning mechanisms are domain-specific, that is, specific to language acquisition. Active debate clearly remains concerning the best way of conceptualizing such learning. It should be clear that the problem of how children represent, acquire, and use language is at the intersection of neuroscience, connectionist modeling, linguistics and cognitive psychology.

## REFERENCES

Berko, J. (1958). The child's learning of English morphology. *Word, 14,* 150–177.

Chomsky, N. (1959). A review of Skinner's "Verbal behavior." *Language, 35,* 26–58.

Fromkin, V., Krashen, S., Curtiss, S., Rigler, D., & Rigler, M. (1974). The development of language in Genie: A case of language acquisition beyond the "critical period." *Brain and Language, 1,* 81–107.

Lenneberg, E. H. (1967). *Biological foundations of Language.* New York: Wiley.

Marcus, G. F., Vijayan, S., Rao, S. B., & Vishton, P. M. (1999). Rule learning by seven-month-old infants. *Science, 283,* 77–80.

Marler, P. (1970). Birdsong and speech development: Could there be parallels? *American Scientist, 58,* 669–673.

Pinker, S., & Prince, A. (1988). On language and connectionism: Analysis of a parallel distributed processing model of language acquisition. *Cognition, 28,* 73–193.

Rumelhart, D. E., & McClelland, J. L., & the PDP Research Group. (1986). *Parallel distributed processing: Explorations in the microstructure of cognition: Vol. 1. Foundations.* Cambridge, MA: MIT Press.

Saffran, J. R., Aslin, R. N., & Newport, E. L. (1996). Statistical learning by 8-month old infants. *Science, 274,* 1926–1928.

Skinner, B. F. (1957). *Verbal behavior.* New York: Appleton-Century Crofts.

# The Development of Language in Genie: A Case of Language Acquisition beyond the "Critical Period"[1,2]

Victoria Fromkin • University of California at Los Angeles
Stephen Krashen • Queens College, C.U.N.Y.
Susan Curtiss • University of California at Los Angeles
David Rigler • Children's Hospital of Los Angeles
Marilyn Rigler • Pacific Oaks College

The present paper reports on a case of a now-16-year-old girl who for most of her life suffered an extreme degree of social isolation and experiential deprivation. It summarizes her language acquisition which is occurring past the hypothesized "critical period" and the implications of this language development as related to hemispheric maturation and the development of lateralization. The results of a series of dichotic listening tests administered to her are included.

When Descartes observed that ". . . there are none so depraved and stupid, without even excepting idiots, that they cannot arrange different words together, forming of them a statement by which they make known their thoughts" he did not consider children who are denied, for a multiplicity of reasons, language input in their formative years. Despite the wide range of views on the subject of language acquisition there is unanimity on one aspect. Neither the empiricist who believes with Locke that we are born with a mental "tabula rasa" with all language the result of "experience," nor the rationalist who supports the Descartian position of a complex, highly specific, innate language mechanism denies that certain environmental conditions are necessary for the acquisition of language. One need not attempt to replicate the apochryphal experiments conducted by Psammeticus or that of the Scottish King John to know that children will not learn any language when deprived of all linguistic input.[3] The cases of children reared in environments of extreme social isolation attest to this.

Ten such children are mentioned by Carl Linneaus in his *System of Nature* published in 1735, and are included by Linnaeus under his subdivision of Homo Sapiens which he called Homo Ferus (Wild Man). One of the defining characteristics of Homo Ferus, according to Linnaeus, was his inability to speak. All the cases of isolated children reported in the literature since his time show this to be a correct observation.

In the 18th century, the interest in such cases was stimulated by the struggle between the "geneticists" and the "environmentalists," and figured sharply in the debate over the theory of innate ideas. The different views continue to be debated today in somewhat different (perhaps more sophisticated) forms. [See, for example, Skinner (1957), Chomsky (1962), Katz and Bever, (1973), Bever (1970), Lenneberg, (1967); see also the *Synthese* Symposium on Innate Ideas, Vol. 17, No. 1, March 1967, pp. 1–28.]

Despite the continuing interest, the study of children reared under conditions of social isolation and sensory deprivation represents a relatively inaccessible area of scientific research. Such children include those who are reported to have undergone a significant period of their development alone in the wilderness or to have been reared with wild animals (Itard, 1962; Singh and Zingg, 1966). The most celebrated of such cases is that of Victor, the "Wild Boy of Aveyron" (Itard, 1962). In addition, there have been studies of children reared within the confines of institutional life (e.g., Spitz, 1949; Dennis and Najarian, 1957; Clarke and Clarke, 1960), and of children whose isolation has been associated with congenital or acquired sensory loss (e.g., Howe and Hall, 1903; Dahl, 1965; Fraiberg and Freedman, 1964). Yet another category is that of children whose isolation resulted from deliberate effort to keep them from normal social intercourse (von Feuerbach, 1833; Mason, 1942; Davis, 1940, 1947; Freedman and Brown, 1968; Koluchova, 1972).

The case discussed in this paper is that of a child who falls into the last category. Genie, the subject of this study, is an adolescent girl who for most of her life underwent a degree of social isolation and experiential deprivation not previously reported in contemporary scientific history. It is a unique case because the other children reported on in contemporary literature were isolated for much shorter periods and emerged from their isolation at much younger ages than did Genie. The only studies of children isolated for periods of time somewhat comparable to that of this case are those of Victor (Itard, 1962) and Kaspar Hauser (Singh and Zingg, 1966).

All cases of such children reveal that experiential deprivation results in a retarded state of development. An important question for scientists of many disciplines is whether a child so deprived

can "catch up" wholly or in part. The answer to this question depends on many factors including the developmental state achieved prior to deprivation, the duration, quality, and intensity of the deprivation, and the early biological adequacy of the isolated child. In addition, the ability of such "recuperation" is closely tied to whether there is a "critical period" beyond which learning cannot take place. The concept of a "critical period" during which certain innately determined faculties can develop derived from experimental embryology. It is hypothesized that should the necessary internal or external conditions be absent during this period, certain developmental abilities will be impossible.

Lenneberg (1967) presents the most specific statement about critical periods in man as it concerns the acquisition of language. He starts with the assumption that language is innately determined, that its acquisition is dependent upon both necessary neurological events and some unspecified minimal exposure to language. He suggests that this critical period lasts from about age two to puberty: language acquisition is impossible before two due to maturational factors, and after puberty because of the loss of "cerebral plasticity" caused by the completion of the development of cerebral dominance, or lateralized specialization of the language function.

The case of Genie is directly related to this question, since Genie was already pubescent at the time of her discovery, and it is to this question that the discussion is primarily directed. The case also has relevance for other linguistic questions such as those concerning distinctions between the comprehension and production of language, between linguistic competence and performance, and between cognition and language.

There are many questions for which we still have no answers. Some we may never have. Others must await the future developments of this remarkable child. The case history as presented is therefore an interim report.

## Case History

Genie was first encountered when she was 13 years, 9 months. At the time of her discovery and hospitalization she was an unsocialized, primitive human being, emotionally disturbed, unlearned, and without language. She had been taken into protective custody by the police and, on November 4, 1970, was admitted into the Children's Hospital of Los Angeles for evaluation with a tentative diagnosis of severe malnutrition. She remained in the Rehabilitation Center of the hospital until August 13, 1971. At that time she entered a foster home where she has been living ever since as a member of the family.

When admitted to the hospital, Genie was a painfully thin child with a distended abdomen who appeared to be six or seven years younger than her age. She was 54.5 inches tall and weighed 62.25 pounds. She was unable to stand erect, could not chew solid or even semi-solid foods, had great difficulty in swallowing, was incontinent of feces and urine, and was mute.

The tragic and bizarre story which was uncovered revealed that for most of her life Genie suffered physical and social restriction, nutritional neglect, and extreme experiential deprivation. There is evidence that from about the age of 20 months until shortly before admission to the hospital Genie had been isolated in a small closed room, tied into a potty chair where she remained most or all hours of the day, sometimes overnight. A cloth harness, constructed to keep her from handling her feces was her only apparel of wear. When not strapped into the chair she was kept in a covered infant crib, also confined from the waist down. The door to the room was kept closed, and the windows were curtained. She was hurriedly fed (only cereal and baby food) and minimally cared for by her mother, who was almost blind during most of the years of Genie's isolation. There was no radio or TV in the house and the father's intolerance of noise of any kind kept any acoustic stimuli which she received behind the closed door to a minimum. (The first child born to this family died from pneumonia when three months old after being put in the garage because of noisy crying.) Genie was physically punished by the father if she made any sounds. According to the mother, the father and older brother never spoke to Genie although they barked at her like dogs. The mother was forbidden to spend more than a few minutes with Genie during feeding.

It is not the purpose of this paper to attempt to explain the psychotic behavior of the parents which created this tragic life for Genie, nor to relate the circumstances which led to the discovery [See Hansen (1972): D. Rigler (1972)]. It is reported that Genie's father regarded her as a hopelessly retarded child who was destined to die at a young age and convinced the mother of this. His prediction was based at least in part on Genie's failure to walk at a normal age. Genie was born with a congenital dislocation of the hips which was treated in the first year by the application of a Frejka pillow splint to hold both legs in abduction, and the father placed the blame for her "retardation" on this device.

On the basis of what is known about the early history, and what has been observed so far, it appears that Genie was normal at the time of birth and that the retardation observed at the time of discovery was due principally to the extreme isolation to which she was subjected, with its accompanying social, perceptual, and sensory deprivation. Very little evidence exists to support a diagnosis of early brain damage, primary mental deficiency, or infantile autism. On the other hand, there is abundant evidence of gross environmental impoverishment and of psychopathological behavior on the part of the parents. This is revealed to some extent in Genie's history and equally by the dramatic changes that have occurred since her emergence. [See D. Rigler (1972); M. Rigler (1972).]

Genie's birth was relatively normal. She was born in April, 1957, delivered by Caesarian section. Her birth problems included an Rh negative incompatibility for which she was exchange transfused (no sequelae were noted), and the hip dislocation spoken of above. Genie's development was otherwise initially normal. At birth she weighed 7 pounds, 7.5 ounces. By three months she had gained 4.5 pounds. According to the pediatrician's report, at 6 months she was doing well and taking food well. At 11 months she was still within normal limits. At 14 months Genie developed an acute illness and was seen by another pediatrician. The only other medical visit occurred when Genie was just over 3.5 years of age.

From the meager medical records at our disposal, then, there is no indication of early retardation. After admission to the hospital, Genie underwent a number of medical diagnostic tests. Radiology reported a "moderate coxa valga deformity of both hips and a narrow rib cage" but no abnormality of the skull. The bone age was reported as approximately 11 years. Simple metabolic disorders were ruled out. The neurologist found no evidence of neurological disease. The electroencephalographic records reported a "normal waking record." A chromosomal analysis was summarized as being "apparently normal."

During the first few months of her hospitalization additional consultations were undertaken. The conclusion from among all of these evaluative efforts may be summarized briefly. Functionally Genie was an extremely retarded child, but her behavior was unlike that of other mentally defective children. Neither, apparently, was she autistic. Although emotionally disturbed behavior was evident there was no discernible evidence of physical or mental disease that would otherwise account for her retarded behavior. It therefore seems plausible to explain her retardation as due to the intensity and duration of her psycho-social and physical deprivation.

The dramatic changes that have occurred since Genie's emergence reinforce this conclusion. Approximately four weeks after her admission to the hospital a consultant described a contrast between her admission status and what he later observed [Shurley (personal communication)]. He wrote that on admission Genie

was pale, thin, ghost-like, apathetic, mute and socially unresponsive. But now she had become alert, bright-eyed, engaged readily in simple social play with balloons, flash-light, and toys, with familiar and unfamiliar adults. . . . She exhibits a lively curiosity, good eye-hand coordination, adequate hearing and vision, and emotional responsivity. . . . She reveals much stimulus hunger. . . . Despite her muteness . . . Genie does not otherwise use autistic defenses, but has ample latent affect and responses. There is no obvious evidence of cerebral damage or intellectual stenosis—only severe (extreme) and prolonged experiential, social and sensory isolation and deprivation during her infancy and childhood. . . . Genie may be regarded as one of the most extreme and prolonged cases of such deprivation to come to light in this century, and as such she is an "experiment in nature."

## Genie's Linguistic Development

Important elements in Genie's history are still unknown and may never be known. We have no reliable information about early linguistic devel-

opments or even the extent of language input. One version has it that Genie began to speak words prior to her isolation and then ceased. Another is that she simply never acquired language at all beyond the level observed on hospital entry. One thing is definite; when Genie was discovered she did not speak. On the day after admission to the hospital she was seen by Dr. James Kent who reports (Kent, 1972):

> Throughout this period she retained saliva and frequently spit it out into a paper towel or into her pajama top. *She made no other sounds except for a kind of throaty whimper.* . . . (Later in the session) . . . she imitated "back" several times, as well as "fall" when I said "The puppet will fall." . . . She could communicate (her) needs nonverbally, at least to a limited extent. . . . Apart from a peculiar laugh, frustration was the only other clear affective behavior we could discern. . . . When very angry she would scratch at her own face, blow her nose violently into her clothes and often void urine. During these tantrums *there was no vocalization.* . . . We felt that the eerie silence that accompanied these reactions was probably due to the fact that she had been whipped by her father when she made noise.

At the outset of our linguistic observations, it was not clear whether Genie's inability to talk was the result solely of physiological and/or emotional factors. We were unable to determine the extent of her language comprehension during the early periods. Within a few days she began to respond to the speech of others and also to imitate single words. Her responses did not however reveal how heavily she was dependent on nonverbal, extra-linguistic cues such as "tone of voice, gestures, hints, guidance, facial and bodily expressions" (Bellugi and Klima, 1971). To determine the extent of her language comprehension it was necessary to devise tests in which all extra-linguistic cues were eliminated.[4] If the comprehension tests administered showed that Genie did comprehend what was said to her, using linguistic information alone, we could assume that she had some knowledge of English, or had acquired some linguistic "competence." In that case, the task facing Genie would not be one of language learning but of learning how to use that knowledge—adding a performance modality—to produce speech. If the tests, on the other hand, in addition to her inability to speak, showed that she had little ability to understand what was said to her when all extra-linguistic cues were eliminated, she would be faced with true first-language acquisition.

## Linguistic Comprehension

The administration of the comprehension tests which we constructed had to wait until Genie was willing and able to cooperate. It was necessary to develop tests which would not require verbal responses since it was her comprehension not her active production of speech to be tested at this stage. The first controlled test was administered in September, 1971, almost 11 months after Genie's emergence. Prior to these tests Genie revealed a growing ability to understand and produce individual words and names. This ability was a necessary precursor to an investigation of her comprehension of grammatical structure, but did not in itself reveal how much language she knew since the ability to relate the sounds and meanings of individual lexical items, while necessary, is not a sufficient criterion for language competence.

It was quite evident that at the beginning of the testing period Genie could understand individual words which she did not utter herself, but, except for such words, she had little if any comprehension of grammatical structures. Genie was thus faced with the complex task of primary language acquisition with a post-pubescent brain. There was no way that a prediction could be made as to whether she could or would accomplish this task. Furthermore, if she did not learn language it would be impossible to determine the reasons. One cannot draw conclusions about children of this kind who fail to develop. One can, however, draw at least some conclusions from the fact that Genie has been acquiring language at this late age. The evidence for this fact is revealed in the results of the 17 different comprehension tests which have been administered almost weekly over the last two years. A slow but steady development is taking place. We are still, of course, unable to predict how much of the adult grammar she will acquire.

Among the grammatical structures that Genie now comprehends are singular-plural contrasts of nouns, negative-affirmative sentence distinctions, possessive constructions, modifications, a number of prepositions (including *under, next to, beside, over*, and probably *on* and *in*), conjunction with *and*, and the comparative and superlative forms of adjectives. [For further details on the comprehension tests, see Curtiss et al. (1973).]

The comprehension tests which are now regularly administered were designed by Susan Curtiss who has been most directly involved in the research of Genie's linguistic development. (New tests are constantly being added.) The nouns, verbs, and adjectives used in all of the tests are used by Genie in her own utterances (see below for discussion on Genie's spontaneous speech production). The response required was primarily a "pointing" response. Genie was familiar with this gesture prior to the onset of testing. One example can illustrate the kinds of tests and the procedures used.

To test Genie's singular/plural distinction in nouns, pairs of pictures are used—a single object on one picture, three of the identical objects on the other. The test sentences differ only by absence or presence of plural markers on the nouns. Genie is asked to point to the appropriate picture. The words used are; balloon(s), pail(s), turtle(s), nose(s), horse(s), dish(es), pot(s), boat(s). Until July, 1972, the responses were no better than chance. Since July, 1972, Genie gives 100% correct responses. It is important to note that at the time when she was not responding correctly to the linguistically marked distinction, she could appropriately use and understand utterances including numbers ("one," "two," "three," etc.) and "many," "more," and "lots of."

## Speech Production and Phonological Development

Genie's ability to comprehend spoken language is a better indication of her linguistic competence than is her production of speech because of the physical difficulties Genie has in speaking. At the age when normal children are learning the necessary neuro-muscular controls over their vocal organs to enable them to produce the sounds of language, Genie was learning to repress any and all sounds because of the physical punishment which accompanied any sounds produced. This can explain why her earliest imitative and spontaneous utterances were often produced as silent articulations or whispered. Her inability to control the laryngeal mechanisms involved in speech resulted in monotonic speech. Her whole body tensed as she struggled to speak, revealing the difficulties she had in the control of air volume and air flow. The intensity of the acoustic signal produced was very low. The strange voice quality of her vocalized utterances is at least partially explainable in reference to these problems.

Because of her speech difficulties, one cannot assess her language competence by her productive utterances alone. But despite the problems which still remain, there has been dramatic improvement in Genie's speech production. Her supra glottal articulations have been more or less normal, and her phonological development does not deviate sharply from that observed in normal children. In addition, she is beginning, both in imitations and in spontaneous utterances to show some intonation and her speech is now being produced with greater intensity.

Like normal children, Genie's first one word utterances consisted of Consonant–Vowel (CV) monosyllables. These soon expanded into a more complex syllable structure which can be diagrammed as (C) (L/G) V (C), where L stands for liquid, G, glide, and the parenthesized elements optional.

Words of two and three syllables entered into her productive vocabulary and in these words stress was correctly marked by intensity and/or duration of the vowel as well as vowel quality (with the unstressed vowel being ə). To date, all of the consonants of Standard American English are included in her utterances (with the inter-dental fricatives occurring only in imitations, and the affricates occurring inconsistently). She still deletes final consonants more often than not. Their correct sporadic presence, however, shows them to be part of her stored representation of the words in which they occur. Consonant clusters were first simplified by the deletion of the /s/ in initial /sp/ /sk/ /st/ clusters; at the present time, in addition to this method of preserving the CV syllable structure, she sometimes adds an epenthetic schwa between the two consonants.

Other changes in Genie's phonological system continue to be observed. At an earlier stage a regular substitution of /t/ for /k/, /n/, and /s/ occurred in all word positions: this now occurs only word medially. /s/ plus nasal clusters are now being produced.

What is of particular interest is that in imitation Genie can produce any English sound and many sound sequences not found in her spontaneous speech. It has been noted by many researchers on child language that children have greater phonetic abilities than are revealed in their utterances. This is also true of Genie; her output reflects phonological constraints rather than her inability to articulate sounds and sound sequences.

Neither Genie nor a normal child learns the sound system of a language totally independent from the syntactic and semantic systems. In fact, the analysis of the syntactic and semantic development of Genie's spontaneous utterances reveals that her performance on the expressive side is parallelling (although lagging behind) her comprehension.

As stated above, within a few weeks after admission to the hospital Genie began to imitate words used to her, and her comprehension of individual words and names increased dramatically. She began to produce single words spontaneously after about five months.

## Sentence Structure

For normal children perception or comprehension of syntactic structures exceeds production; this is even more true in Genie's case possibly for the reasons given above. But even in production it is clear that Genie is acquiring language. Eight months after her emergence Genie began to produce utterances, two words (or morphemes) in length. The structures of her earliest two-word "sentences" were Modifier + Noun and Noun + Noun genitive constructions. These included sentences like "more soup," "yellow car," "Genie purse" and "Mark mouth." After about two months she began to produce strings with verbs—both Noun (subject) + Verb, and Verb + Noun (object), e.g., "Mark paint" (N + V), "Curtiss cough" (N + V), "want milk" (V + N) and "wash car" (V + N). Sentences with a noun followed by a predicate adjective soon followed, e.g., "Dave sick."

In November, 1971, Genie began to produce three and four word strings, including Subject + Verb + Object strings, like "Tori chew glove," modified noun phrases like "little white clear box," subject-object strings, like "big elephant long trunk," and four word predications like "Marilyn car red car." Some of these longer strings are of interest because the syntactic relations which were only assumed to be present in her two-word utterances were now overtly expressed. For example, many of Genie's two-word strings did not contain any expressed subject, but the three-word sentences included both the subject and object: "Love Marilyn" became "Genie love Marilyn." In addition, Modifier–noun Noun Phrases and possessive phrases which were complete utterances at the two-word sentence stage are now used as constituents of her longer strings, e.g., "more soup" occurred in "want more soup" and "Mark mouth" became a constituent in "Mark mouth hurt."

In February, 1972, Genie began to produce negative sentences. The comprehension test involving negative/affirmative distinctions showed that such a distinction was understood many months earlier. (In the tests she had no difficulty in pointing to the correct picture when asked to "show me 'The girl is wearing shoes' " or "Show me the bunny that has a carrot" vs. "Show me the bunny that does not/doesn't have a carrot.") The first negative morpheme used by Genie was "no more." Later she began to use "no" and "not." To date, Genie continues to negate a sentence by attaching the negative morpheme to the beginning of the string. She has not yet acquired the 'Negative movement transformation' which inserts the Negative morpheme inside the sentence in English.

About the same time that the negative sentences were produced, Genie began to produce strings with locative nouns, such as "Cereal kitchen" and "play gym." In recent months prepositions are occurring in her utterances. In answer to the question "Where is your toy radio?" she answered "On chair." She has also produced sentences such as "Like horse behind fence," "Like good Harry at hospital."

In July, 1972, Verb plus Verb-phrase strings were produced: "Want go shopping," "Like chew meat." Such complex VP's began to emerge in sentences that included both a complex Noun-phrase and a complex Verb-phrase, e.g., "Want buy toy refrigerator" and "Want go walk (to) Ralph." Genie has also begun to add the progressive aspect marker "ing" to verbs, always appropriately to denote ongoing action: "Genie laughing," "Tori eating bone."

Grammatical morphemes that are phonologically marked are now used, e.g., plurals as in "bears," "noses," "swings," and possessives such as "Joel's room," "I like Dave's car."

While no definite-indefinite distinction has appeared, Genie now produces the definite article in imitation, and uses the determiner "another" spontaneously, as in "Another house have dog."

At an earlier stage, possession was marked solely by word order; Genie now also expresses possession by the verb "have," as in "Bears have sharp claw," "bathroom have big mirror."

A most important syntactic development is revealed by Genie's use of compound NP's. Prior to December, 1971, she would only name one thing at a time, and would produce two sentences such as: "Cat hurt" followed by "dog hurt." More recently she produced these two strings, and then said "Cat dog hurt." This use of a "recursive" element is also shown by the sentence "Curtiss, Genie, swimming pool" in describing a snapshot.

Genie's ability to combine a finite set of linguistic elements to form new combinations, and the ability to produce sentences consisting of conjoined sentences shows that she has acquired two essential elements of language that permit the generation of an infinite set of sentences.

This is of course an overly sketchy view of the syntactic development evidenced in Genie's utterances. [For further details see Curtiss et al. (1973).] It is clear even from this summary that Genie is learning language. Her speech is rule-governed— she has fixed word-order of basic sentence elements and constituents, and systematic ways of expressing syntactic and semantic relations.

## Linguistic Development in Relation to Normals

Furthermore it is obvious that her development in many ways parallels that of normal first-language acquisition. There are, however, interesting differences between Genie's emerging language and that of normal children. Her vocabulary is much larger than that of normal children whose language exhibits syntactic complexity parallel to Genie's. She has less difficulty in storing lists than she does learning the rules of the grammar. This illustrates very sharply that language acquisition is not simply the ability to store a large number of items in memory.

Genie's performance on the active/passive comprehension test also appears to deviate from that of normal children. Bever (1970) reports on experiments aimed at testing the capacity in young children "to recognize explicitly the concept of predication as exemplified in the appreciation of the difference between subject-action and action-object relations." The children in these experiments were requested to act out using toys both simple active sentences and reversible passive sentences, such as "The cow kisses the horse" and simple passives such as "The horse is kissed by the cow." He reports that "children from 2.0 to 3.0 act out simple active sentences 95 percent correctly, (and) . . . do far better than 5 percent on simple passives." He concludes that "since they perform almost randomly on passives . . . they can at least distinguish sentences they can understand from sentences they cannot understand. Thus, the basic linguistic capacity evidenced by the two-year-old child includes the notion of reference for objects and actions, the notion of basic functional internal relations, and at least a primitive notion of different sentence structures." Genie was similarly tested but with the "point to" response rather than the "acting out" response. That is she was asked to point to "The boy pulls/is pulling the girl" or "The girl is pulled by the boy." For each such test sentence she was presented with two pictures, one depicting the boy as agent, the other with the girl as agent. Unlike the children tested by Bever, Genie's responses to both active and passive sentences have been random, with no better than a chance level of correct responses for either the active or the passive sentences. This is particularly strange when compared with Genie's own utterances which show a consistent word order to indicate Subject Verb Object relations. While she never produces passive constructions, her active sentences always place the object after the verb and the subject before the verb (when they are expressed).

Another difference between Genie and normal children is in the area of linguistic performance. Genie's linguistic competence (her grammar, if we can speak of a grammar at such an early stage of development) is in many ways on a par with a two or two and a half year old child. Her performance—particularly as related to expressive speech—is much poorer than normal children at this level. Because of her particular difficulties in producing speech, however, a number of relatively successful efforts have been directed to teaching her written language. At this point she recognizes,

names, and can print the letters of the alphabet, can read a large number of printed words, can assemble printed words into grammatically correct sentences, and can understand sentences (and questions) constructed of these printed words. On this level of performance, then, she seems to exceed normal children, at a similar stage of language development.

Genie's progress is much slower than that of normals. Few syntactic markers occur in her utterances; there are no question words, no demonstratives, no particles, no rejoinders. In addition, no movement transformations are revealed. Such rules exist in the adult grammar and in normal children's grammars as early as two years. Transformational rules are those which, for example, would move a negative element from the beginning of the sentence to the position after an auxiliary verb. Such a transformational rule would change *I can go* in its negative form from *Neg + I + can + go* to *I + can + neg* (can't) *+ go*. As stated above, Genie continues to produce negative sentences only by the addition of the negative element to the beginning of the sentence, e.g., *No more ear hurt, No stay hospital, No can go*.

Cognitively, however, she seems to be in advance of what would be expected at this syntactic stage. Her earliest productive vocabulary included words cognitively more sophisticated than one usually finds in the descriptions of first vocabulary words. Color words and numbers, for example, were used which usually enter a child's vocabulary at a much later grammatical stage (Castner, 1940; Denckla, 1972).

At the time that Genie began to produce utterances of two-words (June, 1971) she had an active vocabulary of over 200 words, which far exceeds the size of the normal children's lexicon at this stage (about 50 words). This development seems to parallel that found in aphasic children (Eisenson and Ingram, 1972). She comprehends all the WH questions; normal children ordinarily learn HOW, WHY and WHEN questions later than WHO, WHAT, and WHERE (Brown, 1968), although syntactically such questions are similar. Her comprehension of the comparative and superlative, and the differences between "more" and "less" also indicate cognitive sophistication not revealed by her syntax, suggesting at least a partial independence of cognition and language.

## Cognitive Development

The attempt to assess Genie's cognitive development is extremely difficult. All tests purported to measure cognitive abilities, in fact, measure knowledge that has been acquired through experience. In addition, many tests are substantially dependent on verbal response and comprehension. The distinction between cognition and language development is therefore not always possible. A number of tests have however been utilized.

Genie could not easily be psychologically tested by standard instruments at the time of her admission. It is still difficult to administer many of the standard tests. On the Vineland Social Maturity Scale, however, she averaged about 15 months at the time of admission, and on a Gesell Developmental Evaluation, a month and a half later, scores ranged from about one to about three years of age. There was a very high degree of scatter when compared to normal developmental patterns. Consistently, language-related behavior was observed to occur at the lower end of the range of her performance and was judged (by the psychologists at the hospital) to be at about the 15 months level.

Her cognitive growth however seemed to be quite rapid. In a seven month span her score had increased from 15 to 42 months, and six months after admission, on the Leiter International Performance Scale (which depends relatively little on culturally based, specific knowledge, and requires no speech) she passed all the items at the four year level, two at the five year level, and two out of four at the seven year level. In May 1973 her score on this test was on the 6–8 year level. At the same time, the Stanford Binet Intelligence Scale elicited a mental age of 5–8. In all the tests, the subsets which involved language were considerably lower than those assessing other abilities.

From this brief summary of Genie's linguistic development we can conclude the following: (1) When she first emerged from isolation, Genie, a child of 13 years, 9 months had not acquired language; (2) Since there is no evidence of any biological deficiencies, one may assume this was due to the social and linguistic isolation which occurred during 11 years of her life; (3) Since her emergence she has been acquiring her first language primarily by "exposure" alone. This is revealed both by her own speech and by her comprehension of spoken language. (4) Her cognitive development has exceeded her linguistic development.

## The "Critical Age" Hypothesis and Language Lateralization

As mentioned above, Genie's on-going language acquisition is the most direct test of Lenneberg's critical age hypothesis seen thus far. Lenneberg (1967) has presented the view that the ability to acquire primary language (and the acquisition of second languages "by mere exposure") terminates with the completion of the development of cerebral dominance, or lateralization, an event which he argues occurs at around puberty. As we have demonstrated above, however, while Genie's language acquisition differs to some extent from that of normal children, she is in fact in the process of learning language, as shown by the results of tests and by the observations of her spontaneous and elicited speech. Thus, at least some degree of first language acquisition seems to be possible beyond the critical period.

Genie also affords us the opportunity to study the relationship of the development of lateralization and language acquisition.

Lateralization refers to the fact that each hemisphere appears to be specialized for different cognitive functions; that is, some functions seem to be "localized" primarily on one side of the brain. This assumption is based on operational criteria. The discovery, more than a century ago by Broca (1861, and Bonin 1960) that lesions to the left hemisphere produce language problems whereas lesions to the right do not, and that therefore the left hemisphere is dominant for language has been supported by other aphasia studies (Russell and Espir, 1961), by experiments with split-brains (Gazzaniga and Sperry, 1967) and by a variety of other experimental techniques. For example, temporary aphasia is more often the result of left hemisphere anesthetization (Wada, 1949). It has also been shown that the right visual field excels for verbal stimuli (Bryden, 1965). Evoked potential and EEG techniques have confirmed these findings (Wood, Goff, and Day, 1971; McAdam and Whitaker, 1971; Buchsbaum and Fedio, 1970). In addition, dichotic listening tests have consistently shown a right-ear preference when verbal stimuli are presented, which preference is not shown with non-verbal stimuli (Broadbent, 1954; Kimura, 1961; Curry, 1967; Borkowsky, Spreen and Stutz, 1965; Pettit and Noll, 1972; Studdert-Kennedy and Shankweiler, 1970; Berlin et al., 1972; Kimura and Folb, 1968; Zurif and Sait, 1969; Van Lancker and Fromkin, 1973).

There is ample evidence, in addition, to show that certain other cognitive functions are similarly lateralized. In addition to language, the left hemisphere is specialized for temporal order judgments (Carmon and Nachson, 1971) while the right hemisphere is dominant for spatial relations (Bogen, 1969), part to whole judgments (Nebes, 1971), 'gestalt' perception (Kimura, 1966), the perception of musical chords (Gordon, 1970), and the perception of environmental sounds (Curry, 1967). Finally, for certain stimuli, no hemispheric specialization has been found, and hence it is concluded, no lateralization of function (Schulhoff and Goodglass, 1970; Milner, 1962).

That the two sides of the brain appear to show differential abilities seems clear. It is still a matter of debate as to what, if any, the role of the "minor" hemisphere is in carrying out functions associated with the "major" hemisphere. While Lenneberg has maintained that lateralization is complete by puberty and corresponds to the critical period, Krashen and Harshman (1972; see also Krashen, 1972 and 1973a) have argued that lateralization is complete at about five and that this process is not associated with a critical period limiting language acquisition. Instead, they argue that the lateralization and simultaneous maturation of certain mental abilities (e.g., temporal order judgments) underlying the language faculty must precede or at least be simultaneous with language acquisition (argued in greater detail in Krashen, 1972 and 1973b). Whether lateralization has already taken place in Genie is thus of interest. Was her left hemisphere "prepared" for language or would left hemisphere specialization occur along with language acquisition?

Dichotic listening procedures are simple and easy to administer and for this reason such tests were used in our attempt to investigate lateralization development in Genie. In all these tests, a subject is presented with competing simultaneous stimulus pairs. For example, in the right ear he may hear /da/ or "big" and in the left ear /ga/ or "pig." When the stimuli are verbal, items presented

to the right ear are generally reported more accurately by normal right handed subjects. This is assumed to be due to left hemisphere "dominance" for language. When the stimuli are non-verbal (musical chords, Gordon, 1970; environmental sounds, Curry, 1968) a left ear preference is revealed indicating right hemisphere dominance.

The dichotic listening tests administered to Genie were designed, administered and analyzed by Stephen Krashen. The stimuli were prepared at the UCLA Phonetics laboratory using computer programs developed by Lloyd Rice. Two sets of stimuli were prepared; the "verbal" tape consisted of 15 pairs of "point to" words. Each pair of words was preceded by the binaural instructions "point to the _____." Genie pointed to toys or pictures representing the words. [Knox and Kimura (1970) used a similar procedure and found a right ear advantage.] The words were familiar to Genie: baby, boy, car, picture, table, mirror.

The non-verbal tape, prepared by Sarah Spitz, consisted of pairs of environmental sounds recorded from Genie's actual environment (piano chords, car horn, water running, telephone ringing, squeal of toy chimp). She responded by pointing to snapshots of the sound source.

Genie was first tested monaurally; that is, the stimuli were presented to her one ear at a time. She had no difficulty whatsoever in either ear in responding appropriately. Monaural presentation was used as a "warm up" in subsequent sessions and in every case Genie scored 100%. This finding is consistent with her audiometry results of no obvious unilateral hearing loss.

Tables 32.1 and 32.2 present the results of the dichotic tests using verbal stimuli. The results show an extreme left ear advantage, suggesting right hemisphere dominance for language. This is an unusual finding since it is very rare to find a right handed subject who is right dominant, and Genie is right handed. [EEG data that was obtained dur-

TABLE 32.1. Genie's Dichotic Listening Results—Single Pairs of Words Presented Dichotically

| Date | No. of Pairs | No. Correct Right Ear | No. Correct Left Ear |
|---|---|---|---|
| 3/27/72 | 29 | 6 | 29 |
| 5/10/72 | 15 | 1 | 15 |
| 8/16/72 | 30 | 5 | 30 |
| overall % | | 16% | 100% |

**TABLE 32.2. Genie's Dichotic Listening Results—Two Pairs of Words, Presented Dichotically, Separated by ½ Second**

| Date | No. of Pairs | No. Correct Right Ear | No. Correct Left Ear |
|---|---|---|---|
| 6/3/73 | 28 | .0 | 28 |

Controls (N = 21, right handed adults with normal hearing): (p .025, one tail)

| | | | |
|---|---|---|---|
| | 28 | 23.5 | 21.4 |

**TABLE 32.4. Genie's Dichotic Listening Results—Two Pairs of Environmental Sounds, Presented Dichotically, Separated by ½ Second**

| Date | No. of Pairs | No. Correct Rght Ear | No. Correct Left Ear |
|---|---|---|---|
| 6/3/73 | 28 | 15 | 27 |

ing studies of Genie's sleep is described as "typical of a left hemispheric dominance." (Shurley and Natani, 1972)]. Approximately ⅓ of left handers are also right dominant for language. It is clear that the hypothesis that lateralization had not yet been complete because of the language acquisition taking place is not supported by these results.

The degree as well as the direction of lateralization is also unusual. Dichotic listening in normals nearly always produces a slight, but statistically significant, right ear advantage for verbal stimuli. Genie's left ear was perfect while her right ear performed at a chance level.

The results of the tests using dichotically presented environmental sounds, given in Tables 32.3 and 32.4 show that Genie is not simply one of the rare but attested individuals with reversed dominance, with language on the right and certain nonverbal faculties on the left. These show a moderate left ear advantage with her overall accuracy only slightly lower than that of the controls run thus far. This indicates right hemisphere processing of environmental sounds and is a normal finding for right handed subjects (Curry, 1968). It appears that Genie's right hemisphere is doing all the work.

A comparison with other subjects who show similar extreme ear differences, namely split-brain and (right) hemispherectomized patients, may pro-

vide some insight into these unusual results. This is presented in Table 32.5.

A brief examination of the mechanisms thought to underlie dichotic listening may be helpful in attempting to understand the parallel between Genie's verbal results and those of the split-brain and hemispherectomized subjects.

Figure 32.1 is a model of dichotic listening for normal subjects.[5] It has been suggested (Kimura, 1961) that when stimuli are presented dichotically, the contralateral, or crossed auditory pathways suppress the ipsilateral pathways. Thus, in dichotic listening, the uncrossed pathways can be regarded as relatively non-functional. The left primary auditory receiving area then receives only stimuli presented to the right ear while the right primary auditory receiving area receives stimuli presented to the left ear. Since the left primary auditory receiving area is "closer" to the language areas in the left hemisphere, stimuli presented to the right ear have a perceptual advantage. In other words, left ear stimuli must first be routed to the right hemisphere and this gives them a slight disadvantage in competition with the right ear stimuli in the language processing area. In both split-brain and (right) hemispherectomy, as shown in Figure 32.2 there is no input to the language areas from the right hemisphere; thus, any contribution from the left ear is due to the weak (suppressed) ipsilateral pathway.

**TABLE 32.3. Genie's Dichotic Listening Results—Single Pairs of Environmental Sounds Presented Dichotically**

| Date | No. of Pairs | No. Correct Right Ear | No. Correct Left Ear |
|---|---|---|---|
| 8/2/72 | 20 | 12 | 18 |
| 8/16/72 | 20 | 14 | 19 |
| 6/3/73 | 20 | 14 | 20 |
| | | 67% | 95% |

**TABLE 32.5. Comparison of Genie's Verbal Dichotic Listening Results with Normal, Split-Brain, and Hemispherectomized Subjects**

| | % Correct Better Ear | % Correct Weaker Ear |
|---|---|---|
| Normal subjects | 60.3 | 51.9 (Curry, 1968) |
| Genie | 100 | 16 |
| Right hemi- spherectomized | 99 | 24.3 (Berlin et al., 1972) |
| Split-brain | 90.7 | 22.2 (Milner et al., 1968) |

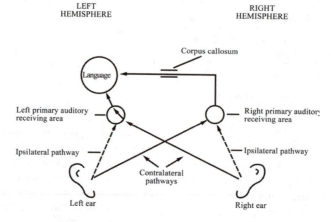

FIGURE 32.1 ■ A model of auditory processing in "normal" dichotic listening. [Taken from Krashen (1972) and Krashen et al. (1972a, b).]

In monotic listening, both split brains and hemispherectomies perform quite well, at or near 100%. For dichotic listening suppression occurs and the ipsilateral pathway is occluded; because of suppression, the right ear does about four times as well as the left ear. The typical scores presented in Table 32.5 have been replicated in other studies (Sparks and Geschwind, 1968; Curry, 1968).

Genie similarly scores 100% in each ear when stimuli are presented monaurally; dichotically she shows the extreme ear difference only paralleled by split brains and hemispherectomies. In a recent study, however, Netley (1972) found that extreme ear differences were found only in hemispherectomized subjects who incurred lesions late (around 17 months), as opposed to those who were injured at birth. It is interesting to note that Genie's case history corresponds more closely to the late lesioned group both with respect to ear difference and onset of lesion.

Genie's results indicate that she in utilizing only her contralateral left ear and ipsilateral right ear pathways in language processing. This does not seem to be true for her non-verbal auditory perception.

In trying to assess this unusual situation it is important to note that Genie seems very proficient in what are considered right hemisphere functions. It was pointed out above that in psychological tests her development can be comprehended more meaningfully when performance on two kinds of test tasks are distinguished: those that require analytic or sequential use of symbols, such as language and number; and those that involve perception of spatial configurations or Gestalts. On the first group of tasks Genie's performance is consistently in the low range, presently approximating an age of two and a half to three years, approximately the age level of her linguistic performance using comparative linguistic criteria. On configurational tests, however, her performance ranges upwards, lying somewhere between eight years and the adult level, depending on the test (see above for Leiter results). The rate of growth on these tests has been very rapid. One year after admission to the hospital, and about two and a half months after she entered the foster home Genie made mental age scores on the French Pictorial Test of intelligence that spanned the range from 4.5 to 9 years. About 3 months later, her performance on the Raven Matrices could not be scored

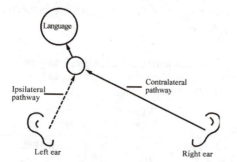

FIGURE 32.2 ■ Dichotic listening for the split-brain and (right) hemispherectomized subject—supression only. [Taken from Krashen (1972) and Krashen et al. (1972a, b).]

in the usual manner but corresponded to the 50th percentile of children aged 8.5 to 9 years. Her performance on the Street Gestalt Test, administered by Dr. Joseph Bogen, also attests to the fact that her right hemisphere is mature. This test is known to be dependent on the ability to make part to whole judgments; patients with right hemisphere lesions perform worse on this test than other brain damaged or normal subjects (De Renzi and Spinnler, 1966). Genie scored 7 and 9 out of 12 on two occasions, an unusual performance in view of the fact that the mean for adults is about 7 and the test is somewhat culture-bound. (For example, one of the items to be recognized on the test is a pot-bellied stove, an object never seen by Genie.) In addition, Genie is quite proficient at finding her way around, a skill that is impaired in cases of right lesion.

It would appear then that Genie is lateralized to the right for both language and non-language functions. This assumes that these nonlinguistic abilities, which have been shown to be right-hemisphere lateralized, are indeed functions of Genie's right hemisphere. We are now in the process of designing tests involving other modalities which will hopefully provide more conclusive evidence on this question.

If this proves to be the case, one tentative hypothesis to explain how this developed is as follows: At the time of her isolation, Genie was a 'normal' right handed child with potential left hemisphere dominance. The inadequate language stimulation during her early life inhibited or interfered with language aspects of left hemisphere development. This would be tantamount to a kind of functional atrophy of the usual language centers, brought about by disuse or suppression. Apparently, what meager stimulation she did receive was sufficient for normal right hemisphere development. (One can imagine her sitting, day after day, week after week, year after year, absorbing every visual stimulus, every crack in the paint, every nuance of color and form.) This is consistent with the suggestion (Carmon et al., 1972) that the right hemisphere is the first to develop since it is more involved with the perception of the environment. Genie's current achievements in language acquisition, according to this reasoning, is occurring in that hemisphere which somehow did mature more normally.

The hypothesis that Genie is using a developed right hemisphere for language also predicts the dichotic listening results. The undeveloped language areas in the left hemisphere prevent the flow of (just language) impulses from the left primary auditory receiving areas to the right hemisphere. This explains why Genie's scores are so similar to split-brain and hemispherectomized subjects: the only auditory pathways that are functional for *verbal* stimuli are the right ipsilateral and left contralateral. The low right score is due to the suppression that occurs under the dichotic condition. Her perfect monotic scores are predicted, since suppression only takes place dichotically.

If this hypothesis is true it modifies the theory of the critical period: while the normal development of lateralization may not play a role in the critical period, lateralization may be involved in a different way; the left hemisphere must perhaps be linguistically stimulated during a specific period of time for it to participate in normal language acquisition. If such stimulation does not take place during this time, normal language acquisition must depend on other cortical areas and will proceed less efficiently due to the previous specialization of these areas for other functions.

A comparison of Genie's case with other instances of right (minor) hemisphere speech in adults implies that Genie's capacity for language acquisition is limited and will cease at some time in the near future. Such cases are rare and not well described from a linguistic point of view. A. Smith's (1966) description of a left hemispherectomized man is the best of these. This man could not speak at all after his left hemisphere was removed but did begin to communicate in 'propositional language' ten weeks later. The patient continued to make linguistic progress but remained severely aphasic 8 months after surgery (see also Bogen, 1969). Similarly, Hillier (1954) reported a left hemispherectomy performed on a 14 year old boy for a tumor whose onset was one year previous to surgery. Again, there was early progress in language learning but after 19 months progress ceased and the deficit became stable.

It is unfortunate that there is no information concerning cerebral dominance for other cases of isolated children—those that acquired language as well as those that didn't. Itard suggests that Victor was about 12 years of age when he was found in the woods of Aveyron, and that "It is . . . almost proved that he had been abandoned at the age of four or five years" (Itard, 1962). If, in those first years he was not genetically deficient, lateralization should have been complete and language should have been acquired. Itard states further that "if, at this time, he already owed some ideas and some words to the beginning of an education, this would all have been effaced from his memory in consequence of his isolation." How, why, and if such "memory effacement" occurs, are questions open to speculation. Despite this "effacement," Victor "did acquire a very considerable reading vocabulary, learning, by means of printed phrases to execute such simple commands as to pick up a key." (Itard, 1962, p. xii) but he never learned to speak. The scar "which (was) visible on his throat" may have damaged his larynx. It is impossible to tell from Itard's reports the exact extent of Victor's comprehension of spoken language.

Another case, similar to some extent to that of Genie, is that of a child who was not exposed to language until she was six and a half years old because of her imprisonment with a mute and totally uneducated aphasic mother (Mason, 1942). Within twenty-two months, she progressed from her first spoken words ("ball," "car," "bye," "baby") to asking such questions as "Why does the paste come out if one upsets the jar?" The rapidity with which she acquired the complex grammar of English provides some support for the hypothesis that the language learning mechanism is more specific than general.

This case is also consistent with a two-to-puberty critical period theory. The language learning capacity of the right hemisphere, then, may be limited either in time or amount of learning. Because we have no grammatical descriptions of right hemisphere speech, we cannot predict how far Genie will progress from comparisons with such cases. On the other hand, Genie's progress in language acquisition impressionistically seems to have far exceeded that of the other reported cases. We intend to continue administering dichotic listening tests to see if the left hemisphere begins to show increasing language function. If this occurs, one plausible conclusion would be that language acquisition and use is a precondition for such lateralization to occur. We note, of course, that this would be contrary to the Krashen and Harshman position that lateralization *precedes* language acquisition. There is also some evidence of lateral-

ity differences in neonates (Wada, quoted in Geschwind, 1970; Molfese, 1972).

It is clear from this report that we have more questions than answers. We are hopeful that Genie's development will provide some of these answers.

As humanists we are hopeful that our tentative prognosis of a slowing down of language and permanent dysphasia will prove to be wrong. For despite the predictions of our hypothesis, Genie continues to make modest but steady progress in language acquisition and is providing us with data in an unexplored area, first language acquisition beyond the "critical period." After all, a discarded hypothesis is a small price to pay for confirmation of the astonishing capabilities and adaptability of the human mind.

## NOTES

1. The research reported on in this paper was supported in part by a grant from the National Institutes of Mental Health, U.S. Department of Health, Education and Welfare, No. MH-21 191-03.
2. This is a combined and expanded version of a number of papers presented before the American Psychological Association, the Linguistic Society of America, the Acoustical Society of America, and the American Speech and Hearing Association, including S. Curtiss (1972); Curtiss et al. (1972, 1973); Krashen et al. (1972a, 1972b); Fromkin (1972); D. Rigler (1972).
3. In the 5th century B.C. the Greek historian Herodotus reported that the Egyptian Pharaoh Psammetichus (664–610 B.C.) sought to determine the most primitive "natural" language by placing two infants in an isolated mountain hut to be cared for by a servant who was cautioned not to speak in their presence on pain of death. According to the story, the first word uttered was "bekos" the Phrygian word for "bread" convincing the Pharaoh that this was the original language. James IV (1473–1513) of Scotland is reported to have attempted the same "experiment." The Scottish children however were said by John to "spak very guid Ebrew." Two hundred years before James, the Holy Roman Emperor Frederick 11 of Hohenstaufen was said to have carried out a similar test but the children died before they spoke at all.
4. The tests were designed, administered, and analyzed by S. Curtiss.

## REFERENCES

Bellugi, U., and Klima, E. 1971. Consultation Report. March.
Berlin, C. I., Lowe-Bell, S. S., Cullen, J. K., and Thompson, C. L. 1972. Dichotic speech perception: An interpretation of right ear advantage and temporal offset effects. *Journal of the Acoustical Society of America* (in press).

Bever, T. G. 1970. The cognitive basis for linguistic structures. In J. R. Hayes (Ed.) *Cognition and the Development of Language*. New York: John Wiley. Pp. 279–362.

Bogen, J. E. 1969. The other side of the brain 1: Dysgraphia and dyscopia following cerebral commissurotomy. *Bulletin of the Los Angeles Neurological Societies*, 34, July, 73–105.

Bonin, G. von 1960. *Some Papers on the Cerebral Cortex*. Springfield, Illinois: C. C. Thomas.

Borkowski, J., Spreen, O., and Stuiz, J. 1965. Ear preference and abstractness in dichotic listening. *Psychonomic Science 3*, 547–548.

Broadbent, D. E. 1954. The role of auditory localization in attention and memory span. *Journal of Experimental Psychology 47*, 191–196.

Broca, P. 1861. Remarques sur le siege de la faculte du language articule, suivies d'une observation d'aphemie. *Bulletin de la Societe d'anatomie 5*. 330–357.

Brown, R. 1968. The development of WH questions in child speech. *Journal of Verbal Learning and Verbal Behavior 7*, 279–290.

Bryden, M. 1963. Far preference in auditory perception. *Journal of Experimental Psychology 65*, 103–105.

Buchsuaum, M. and Fedio, P. 1970. Hemispheric differences in evoked potentials to verbal and nonverbal stimuli in the left and right visual fields. *Physiology and Behavior 5*, 207–210.

Carmon, A., Harishanu, Y., Lowinger, R., and Levy, S. 1972. Assymmetries in hemispheric blood volune and cerebral dominance. *Behavioral Biology* (in press).

Carmon, A. and Nachson, I. 1971. The effect of unilateral brain damage on perception of temporal order. *Cortex 7*, 410–418.

Castner, B. M. 1940. Language development in the first five years of life. Ed. A. Gesell, N. Y.: Harper & Row.

Chomsky, N. 1962. Explanatory models in linguistics. In E. Nagel, P. Suppes, and A. Taiski, (Eds.) *Logic, Methodology, and the Philosophy of Science*. Stanford University Press.

Clarke, A. D. B. and Clarke, A. M. 1960. Some recent advances in the study of early deprivation. *Child Psychology and Psychiatry, 1*.

Curry, F. 1967. A comparison of left-handed and right-handed subjects on verbal and non-verbal dichotic listening tasks. *Cortex 3*, 343–352.

Curry, F. 1968. A comparison of the performance of a right hemispherectomized subject and twenty-five normals on four dichotic listening tasks. *Cortex 4*, 144–153.

Curtiss, S. 1972. The development of language in Genie. Paper presented to the 1972 Annual Convention of the American Speech and Hearing Association, San Francisco, Calif. Nov. 18–20.

Curtiss, S., Fromkin, V., and Krashen, S. 1972. The syntactic development of Genie. Paper presented to the Dec., 1972 Annual meeting of the Linguistic Society of America, Atlanta, Georgia.

Davis, K. 1940. Extreme social isolation of a child. *American Journal of Sociology, 45*, 554–565.

Davis, K. 1947. Final note on a case of extreme isolation. *American Journal of Sociology, 52*, 432–437.

Denckla, M. B. 1972. Performance on color tasks in kindergarten children. *Cortex 8*, 177–190.

Dennis, W. and Najarian, P. 1957. Infant development under developmental handicap. *Psychological Monographs 71*, No. 7.

De Renzi, E., Scotti, G., and Spinnler, H. 1969. Perceptual and associative disorders of visual recognition. *Neurology, 19*.

Eisenson, J. and Ingram, D. 1972. Childhood aphasia—an updated concept based on recent research. *Papers and Reports on Child Language Development*. Standford University, 103–120.

Fraiberg, S. and Freedman, D. A. 1964. Studies in the ego development of the congenitally blind child. *The Psychoanalytic Study of the Child, 19*, 113–169.

Freedman, D. A. and Brown, S. L. 1968. On the role of coenesthetic stimulation in the development of psychic structure.

Fromkin, V. 1972. The development of language in Genie. Paper presented at the 80th Annual Convention of the American Psychological Association. Hunolulu. Hawaii, Sept. 1–8.

Gazzaniga, M. S. and Sperry, R. 1967. Language after section of the cerebral commissures. *Brain, 90*, 131–148.

Geschwind, N. 1970. The organization of language and the brain. *Science 170*, 940–944.

Gordon, H. W. 1970. Hemispheric asymmetries in the perception of musical cords. *Cortex, 6*, 387–398.

Haggard, M. and Parkinson, A. 1971. Stimulus and task factors as determinants of ear advantage. *Quarterly Journal of Experimental Psychology, 23*, 168–177.

Hansen, H. 1972. The first experiences and the emergence of "Genie." Paper presented at the 80th Annual Convention of the American Psychological Association. Honolulu. Hawaii, Sept. 1–8.

Hillier, F. 1954. Total left hemispherectomy for malignant glaucoma. *Neurology, 4*, 718–721.

Howe, M. and Hall, F. G. 1903. *Laura Bridgeman*. Little, Brown and Co.

Itard, J. 1962. *The Wild Boy of Aveyron*. New York: Appleton-Century-Crofts.

Katz, J. J. and Bever, T. G. 1973. The fall and rise of empiricism, or the truth about general semantics. (Forthcoming).

Kent, J. 1972. Eight months in the hospital. Paper presented at the 80th Annual Convention of the American Psychological Association, Honolulu. Hawaii, Sept. 1–8.

Kimura, D. 1961. Cerebral dominance and the perception of verbal stimuli. *Canadian Journal of Psychology, 15*, 166–171.

Kimura, D. 1966. Dual functional asymmetry of the brain in visual perception. *Neuro-psychologia 4*, 275–285.

Kimura, D. and Folb, S. 1968. Neural processing of backwards speech sounds. *Science, 161*, 395–396.

Knox, C. and Kimura, D. 1970. Cerebral processing of nonverbal sounds in boys and girls. *Neuropsychologia, 8*, 227–237.

Koluchova, J. 1972. Severe deprivation in twins. *Child Psychology and Psychiatry, 13*.

Krashen, S. 1972. Language and the left hemisphere. *Working Papers in Phonetics, 24*, UCLA.

Krashen, S. 1973a. Lateralization, language learning, and the critical period: some new evidence. *Language Learning 23*, 63–74.

Krashen, S. 1973b. Mental abilities underlying linguistic and non-linguistic functions. *Linguistics* (in press).

Krashen, S., Fromkin, V., Curtiss, S., Rigler, D., and Spitz, S. (1972a) Language lateralization in a case of extreme psychological deprivation. Paper presented to the 84th meeting of the Acoustical Society of America.

Krashen, S., Fromkin, V., and Curtiss, S. 1972b. A neurolinguistic investigation of language acquisition in the case of an isolated child. Paper presented to the Linguistic Society of America, Winter meeting, Atlanta, Georgia, Dec. 27–29.

Krashen, S. and Harshman, R. 1972. Lateralization and the critical period. *Working Papers in Phonetics 23*, 13–21. UCLA (Abstract in *Journal of the Acoustical Society of America, 52*, 174.)

Lunneberg, E. H. 1967. *Biological Foundations of Language*. New York: Wiley.

McAdam, D. and Whitaker, H. 1971. Language production: Electroencephalographic localization in the normal human brain. *Science, 172*, 499–502.

Mason, M. K. 1942. Learning to speak after six and one-half years. *Journal of Speech Disorders, 7*, 295–304.

Milner, B. 1962. Laterality effects in audition. In V. B. Mountcastle (Ed.) *Interhemispheric Relations and Cerebral Dominance*. Baltimore: Johns Hopkins Press.

Milner, B., Taylor, L., and Sperry. R. 1968. Lateralized suppression of dichotically presented digits after commissural section in man. *Science, 161*, 184–186.

Molfese, D. L. 1972. Cerebral asymmetry in infants, children and adults: auditory evoked responses to speech and musical stimuli. *Journal of the Acoustical Society of America 53*, 363 (A).

Nebes, R. 1971. Superiority of the minor hemisphere in commissurotomized man for the perception of part-whole relations. *Cortex, 7*, 333–349.

Netley, C. 1972. Dichotic listening performance of hemispherectomized patients. *Neuropsychologia, 10*, 233–240.

Petti, J. M. and Noll, J. D. 1972. Cerebral dominance and the process of language recovery in aphasia. Paper presented to the 1972 Annual Convention of the American Speech and Hearing Association, San Francisco, Calif. Nov. 18–20.

Rigler, D. 1972. The Case of Genie. Paper presented to the 1972 Annual Convention of the American Speech and Hearing Association. San Francisco, Calif. Nov. 18–20.

Rigler, M. 1972. Adventure: At home with Genie. Paper presented at the 80th Annual Convention of the American Psychological Association, Honolulu. Hawaii, Sept. 1–8.

Russell, R. and Espir, M. 1961. *Traumatic Aphasia*. Oxford: Oxford University Press.

Schulhoff, C. and Goodglass. H. 1969. Dichotic listening, side of brain injury and cerebral dominance. *Neuropsychologia, 7*, 149–160.

Shurley, J. T. and Natani, K. 1972. Sleep EEG patterns in a fourteen-year old girl with severe developmental retardation. Paper presented at the 80th Annual Convention of the American Psychological Association, Honolulu, Hawaii, Sept. 1–8.

Singh, J. A. L. and Zingg, R. M. 1966. *Wolf-Children and Feral Man*. Archon Books.

Skinner, B. F. 1957. *Verbal Behavior*. New York: Appleton-Century-Crofts.

Smith, A. 1966. Speech and other functions after left (dominant) hemispherectomy. *Journal of Neurology Neurosurgery and Psychiatry, 29*, 467–471.

Sparks, R. and Geschwind, N. 1968. Dichotic listening in man after section of neocortical commissures. *Cortex, 4*, 3–16.

Spitz, R. A. 1949. The role of ecological factors in emotional development. *Child Development, 20*, 145–155.

Studdert-Kennedy, M. and Shankweiler, D. 1970. Hemispheric specialization for speech perception. *Journal of the Acoustical Society of America, 48*, 579–594.

Van Lancker, D. and Fromkin, B. 1973. Hemispheric specialization for pitch and "tone": Evidence from Thai. *Journal of Phonetics, 1*, 101–109.

von Feuerbach, A. 1833. *Casper Hauser*. (Translated from the German) London: Simpkin and Marshall.

Wada, J. 1949. A new method for the determination of the side of cerebral speech dominance: a preliminary report on the intracartoid injection of sodium amytal in man. *Medical Biology, 14*, 221–222.

Wood, C., Goff, W., and Day, R. 1971. Auditory evoked potentials during speech production. *Science, 173*, 1248–1251.

Zurif, E. B. and Mendelsohn, M. 1972. Hemispheric specialization for the perception of speech sounds: the influences of intonation and structure. *Perception and Psychophysics, 11*, 329–332.

Zurif, E. B. and Sait, P. E. 1970. The role of syntax in dichotic listening. *Neuropsychologia, 8*, 239–244.

# The Child's Learning of English Morphology

Jean Berko • Massachusetts Institute of Technology

In this study[1] we set out to discover what is learned by children exposed to English morphology. To test for knowledge of morphological rules, we use nonsense materials. We know that if the subject can supply the correct plural ending, for instance, to a noun we have made up, he has internalized a working system of the plural allomorphs in English, and is able to generalize to new cases and select the right form. If a child knows that the plural of *witch* is *witches*, he may simply have memorized the plural form. If, however, he tells us that the plural of *\*gutch* is *\*gutches*, we have evidence that he actually knows, albeit unconsciously, one of those rules which the descriptive linguist, too, would set forth in his grammar. And if children do have knowledge of morphological rules, how does this knowledge evolve? Is there a progression from simple, regular rules to the more irregular and qualified rules that are adequate fully to describe English? In very general terms, we undertake to discover the psychological status of a certain kind of linguistic description. It is evident that the acquisition of language is more than the storing up of rehearsed utterances, since we are all able to say what we have not practiced and what we have never before heard. In bringing descriptive linguistics to the study of language acquisition, we hope to gain knowledge of the systems and patterns used by the speaker.

In order to test for children's knowledge of this sort, it was necessary to begin with an examination of their actual vocabulary. Accordingly, the 1000 most frequent words in the first-grader's vocabulary were selected from Rinsland's listing.[2] This listing contains the most common words in the elementary school child's vocabulary, as taken from actual conversations, compositions, letters, and similar documents. This list was then examined to see what features of English morphology seem to be most commonly represented in the vocabulary of the first-grade child. From this we could decide what kind of extensions we might expect the child to be able to make. All of the English inflexional morphemes were present.

The areas that seemed to be most promising from this examination were the plural and the two possessives of the noun, the third person singular of the verb, the progressive and the past tense, and the comparative and superlative of the adjective. The pronouns were avoided both because of the difficulty involved in making up a nonsense pronoun, and because the pronouns are so few in number and so irregular that we would hardly expect even adults to have any generalized rules for the handling of new pronouns. Moreover, we do not encounter new pronouns, whereas new verbs, adjectives, and nouns constantly appear in our vocabularies, so that the essential problem is not the same. The past participle of regular or weak verbs in English is identical with the past tense, and since the regular forms were our primary interest, no attempt was made to test for the past participle. A number of forms that might suggest irregular plurals and past tenses were included among the nouns and verbs.

The productive allomorphs of the plural, the

possessive, and the third person singular of the verb are phonologically conditioned and identical with one another. These forms are /-s ~ -z ~-əz/, with the following distribution:

/-əz/ after stems that end in /s z š ž č ǰ/, e.g., *glasses, watches;*

/-s/ after stems that end in /p t k f θ/, e.g., *hops, hits*;

/-z/ after all other stems, viz. those ending in /b d g v ð m ŋ h r l/, vowels, and semivowels, e.g., *bids, goes.*

The productive allomorphs of the past are /-t ~ –d ~ -əd/, and they are also phonologically conditioned, with the following distribution:

/-əd/ after stems that end in /t d/, e.g., *melted*;

/-t/ after stems that end in /p k č f θ š/, e.g., *stopped*;

/-d/ after stems ending in voiced sounds except /-d/, e.g., *climbed, played.*

The progressive *-ing* and the adjective *-er* and *-est* do not have variants. It might also be noted that the possessive has an additional allomorph /-ø/; this occurs after an inflexional /-s/ or /-z/, so that if the form *boy* is made plural, *boys*, the possessive of that plural form is made by adding nothing, and indicated in writing only by the addition of an apostrophe: *boys'.*

The children's vocabulary at the first-grade level also contains a number of words that are made of a free morpheme and a derivational suffix, e.g., *teacher*, or of two free morphemes, e.g., *birthday*. The difficulties encountered in this area are many. First, it might be noted that there are not many contrasts, i.e., not many cases of the same derivational suffix being added to different bases to produce forms of like function. Although *beautiful* and *thankful* both appear on the list, it does not seem that these examples are numerous enough for us to expect a young child to be able to append *-ful* to a new noun in order to produce an adjective. Word derivation and compounding are furthermore often accompanied by changes in stress and pronunciation, so that the picture is additionally complicated. There seemed to be enough examples of the stress pattern ´ `, as in *bláckboàrd* as against *blâck boárd*, and of the diminutive-affectionate *-y*, the adjectival *-y*, and the agentive *-er* to warrant testing for these forms.

So far as the general picture is concerned, all speakers of the language are constrained to use the inflexional endings and apply them appropriately to new forms when they are encountered. We are not so often called upon to derive or compound new words, although by the time we are adults we can all to some extent do this. From the children's actual vocabulary we were able to make an estimate of the kind of morphological rules they might be expected to possess, and from these items a test could be constructed. It was noted, moreover, that in the child's vocabulary there are a number of compound words, like *blackboard* and *birthday*. It is entirely possible to use a compound word correctly and never notice that it is made of two separate and meaningful elements. It is also possible to use it correctly and at the same time have a completely private meaning for one or both of its constituent elements. In order to see what kind of ideas children have about the compound words in their vocabularies, it was decided to ask them directly about a selected number of these words.

Within the framework of the child's vocabulary, a test was devised to explore the child's ability to apply morphological rules to new words. He was called upon to inflect, to derive, to compound, and, lastly, to analyse compound words.

## Materials and Procedures

In order to test for the child's use of morphological rules of different types and under varying phonological conditions, a number of nonsense words were made up, following the rules for possible sound combinations in English. Pictures to represent the nonsense words were then drawn on cards. There were 27 picture cards, and the pictures, which were brightly colored, depicted objects, cartoon-like animals, and men performing various actions. For reasons that will be discussed later, several actual words were also included. A text, omitting the desired form, was typed on each card. An example of the card to test for the regular plural allomorph in /-z/ can be seen in Figure 33.1.

The subjects included 12 adults (seven women and five men), all of whom were college graduates. Many of these adults had also had some graduate training. All were native speakers of English.

The child subjects were obtained at the Harvard Preschool in Cambridge and the Michael Driscoll

1

THIS IS A WUG.

NOW THERE IS ANOTHER ONE.

THERE ARE TWO OF THEM.

THERE ARE TWO _____.

**FIGURE 33.1** ■ The plural allomorph in /-z/.

School, in Brookline, Massachusetts. At the Preschool, each child was brought to the experimenter, introduced, and told that now he was going to look at some pictures. The experimenter would point to the picture and read the text. The child would supply the missing word, and the item he employed was noted phonemically. After all of the pictures had been shown, the child was asked why he thought the things denoted by the compound words were so named. The general form of these questions was "Why do you think a blackboard is called a blackboard?" If the child responded with "Because it's a blackboard", he was asked, "But why do you think it's called that?" The children at the preschool ranged between four and five years in age. Twelve girls and seven boys were asked all items of the completed test, and two groups, one of three boys and three girls and one of five boys and three girls, were each asked half of the inflexional items in preliminary testing.

At the Driscoll School, the experimenter was introduced to the class and it was explained that each child was going to have a turn at looking at some pictures. The procedure from this point, on was the same as for the Preschool. All children in the first grade were interviewed. There were 26 boys and 35 girls in this group. Ages ranged from five and one half to seven years.

The following is the order in which the cards were presented. Included is a statement of what was being tested, a description of the card, and the text that was read. Pronunciation is indicated by regular English orthography; a phonemic transcription is included for first occurrences of nonsense words.

1. Plural. One bird-like animal, then two. "This is a wug /wʌg/. Now there is another one. There are two of them. There are two _____."
2. Plural. One bird, then two. "This is a gulch /gʌè/. Now there is another one. There are two of them. There are two _____."
3. Past tense. Man with a steaming pitcher on his head. "This is a man who knows how to spow /spow/. He is spowing. He did the same thing yesterday. What did he do yesterday? Yesterday he _____."
4. Plural. One animal, then two. "This is a kazh /kæž/. Now there is another one. There are two of them. There are two _____."
5. Past tense. Man swinging an object. "This is a man who knows how to rick /rik/. He is ricking. He did the same thing yesterday. What did he do yesterday? Yesterday he _____."
6. Diminutive and compounded or derived word. One animal, then a miniscule animal. "This is a wug. This is a very tiny wug. What would you call a very tiny wug? This wug lives in a house. What would you call a house that a wug lives in?"
7. Plural. One animal, then two. "This is a tor /tɔr/. Now there is another one. There are two of them. There are two _____."
8. Derived adjective. Dog covered with irregular green spots. "This is a dog with quirks /kwərks/ on him. He is all covered with quirks. What kind of dog is he? He is a _____ dog."
9. Plural. One flower, then two. "This is a lun /lʌn/. Now there is another one. There are two of them. There are two _____."

10. Plural. One animal, then two. "This is a niz /niz/. Now there is another one. There are two of them. There are two _____."
11. Past tense. Man doing calisthenics. "This is a man who knows how to mot /mat/. He is motting. He did the same thing yesterday. What did he do yesterday? Yesterday he _____."
12. Plural. One bird, then two. "This is a cra /kra/. Now there is another one. There are two of them. There are two _____."
13. Plural. One animal, then two. "This is a tass /tæs/. Now there is another one. There are two of them. There are two _____."
14. Past tense. Man dangling an object on a string. "This is a man who knows how to bod /bad/. He is bodding. He did the same thing yesterday. What did he do yesterday? Yesterday he _____."
15. Third person singular. Man shaking an object. "This is a man who knows how to naz /næz/. He is nazzing. He does it every day. Every day he _____."
16. Plural. One insect, then two. "This is a heaf /hiyf/. Now there is another one. There are two of them. There are two _____."
17. Plural. One glass, then two. "This is a glass. Now there is another one. There are two of them. There are two _____."
18. Past tense. Man exercising. "This is a man who knows how to gling /gliŋ/. He is glinging. He did the same thing yesterday. What did he do yesterday? Yesterday he _____."
19. Third person singular. Man holding an object. "This is a man who knows how to loodge /luwdž/. He is loodging. He does it every day. Every day he _____."
20. Past tense. Man standing on the ceiling. "This is a man who knows how to bing /biŋ/. He is binging. He did the same thing yesterday. What did he do yesterday? Yesterday he _____."
21. Singular and plural possessive. One animal wearing a hat, then two wearing hats. "This is a niz who owns a hat. Whose hat is it? It is the _____ hat. Now there are two nizzes. They both own hats. Whose hats are they? They are the _____ hats."
22. Past tense. A bell. "This is a bell that can ring. It is ringing. It did the same thing yesterday. What did it do yesterday? Yesterday it _____."

23. Singular and plural possessive. One animal wearing a hat, then two. "This is a wug who owns a hat. Whose hat is it? It is the _____ hat. Now there are two wugs. They both own hats. Whose hats are they? They are the _____ hats."

24. Comparative and superlative of the adjective. A dog with a few spots, one with several, and one with a great number. "This dog has quirks on him. This dog has more quirks on him. And this dog has even more quirks on him. This dog is quirky. This dog is _____. And this dog is the _____."

25. Progressive and derived agentive or compound. Man balancing a ball on his nose. "This is a man who knows how to zib /zib/. What is he doing? He is _____. What would you call a man whose job is to zib?"

26. Past tense. An ice cube, then a puddle of water. "This is an ice cube. Ice melts. It is melting. Now it is all gone. What happened to it? It _____."

27. Singular and plural possessive. One animal wearing a hat, then two. "This is a bik /bik/ who owns a hat. Whose hat is it? It is the _____ hat. Now there are two biks. They both own hats. Whose hats are they? They are the _____ hats."

28. Compound words. The child was asked why he thought the following were so named. (No pictures were used for these items.)

| | |
|---|---|
| a. afternoon | h. handkerchief |
| b. airplane | i. holiday |
| c. birthday | j. merry-go-round |
| d. breakfast | k. newspaper |
| e. blackboard | l. sunshine |
| f. fireplace | m. Thanksgiving |
| g. football | n. Friday |

It took between ten and fifteen minutes to ask a child all of these questions. Even the youngest children have had experience with picture books, if not actual training in naming things through pictures, and no child failed to understand the nature of the task before him. It was, moreover, evident that a great number of these children thought they were being taught new English words. It was not uncommon for a child to repeat the nonsense word immediately upon hearing it and before being asked any questions. Often, for example, when the experimenter said "This is a *gutch*", the child repeated, "*Gutch*". Answers were willingly, and often insistently, given. These responses will be discussed in the following section.

## Results

Adult answers to the inflexional items were considered correct answers, and it was therefore possible to rate the children's answers. In general, adult opinion was unanimous—everyone said the plural of *wug was *wugs, the plural of *gutch was *gutches; where the adults differed among themselves, except in the possessives, it was along the line of a common but irregular formation, e.g., *heaf became *heaves in the plural for many speakers, and in these cases both responses were considered correct. If a child said that the plural of *heaf was *heafs or *heaves /-vz/, he was considered correct. If he said *heaf (no ending), or *heafes /-fəz/, he was considered incorrect, and a record was kept of each type of response.

## Sex Differences

The first question to be answered was whether there is a sex difference in the ability to handle English morphology at this age level. Since it seemed entirely possible that boys entering the first grade might be on the whole somewhat older than girls entering the first grade, it was necessary to equate the two groups for age.

The children were divided into seven age groups. Since at each of these levels there were more girls than boys, a random selection of the girls was made so that they would match the boys in number. The distribution of these ages and the number in each group can be seen in Table 33.1. This distribution was utilized only in comparing the performance of the boys with that of the girls; in all other instances, the responses of the entire sample were considered.

The groups of 28 boys and 28 girls thus selected were compared with one another on all inflexional items. The chi square criterion with Yates' correction for small frequencies was applied to each item, and on none was there a significant difference between the boys' and girls' performance; boys did as well as girls, or somewhat better, on over half

Table 33.1. Distribution of Children at Each Age Level for Comparison of the Sexes

| Age | Boys | Girls | Total |
|---|---|---|---|
| 4 | 2 | 2 | 4 |
| 4:6 | 1 | 1 | 2 |
| 5 | 2 | 2 | 4 |
| 5:6 | 2 | 2 | 4 |
| 6 | 10 | 10 | 20 |
| 6:6 | 6 | 6 | 12 |
| 7 | 5 | 5 | 10 |
| Total: | 28 | 28 | 56 |

the items, so that there was no evidence of the usual superiority of girls in language matters. From this it would appear that boys and girls in this age range are equal in their ability to handle the English morphology represented by these items.

## Age Differences

Having ascertained that there was no difference between boys' and girls' answers, we combined the sexes and went on to compare the younger with the older children. The oldest children at the Preschool were five years old, and the youngest at the Driscoll School were five and one half years, so that the dividing line was made between the schools. Chi square corrected for small frequencies was again applied to all inflexional items. First graders did significantly better than preschoolers on slightly less than half of these. The differences can be seen in Table 33.2

TABLE 33.2. Age Differences on Inflexional Items

| Item | Percentage of Correct Preschool Answers | Percentage of Correct First-Grade Answers | Significance Level of Difference |
|---|---|---|---|
| *Plural* | | | |
| glasses | 75 | 99 | .01 |
| wugs | 76 | 97 | .02 |
| luns | 68 | 92 | .05 |
| tors | 73 | 90 | — |
| heafs | 79 | 80 | — |
| cras | 58 | 86 | .05 |
| tasses | 28 | 39 | — |
| gutches | 28 | 38 | — |
| kazhes | 25 | 36 | — |
| nizzes | 14 | 33 | — |
| *Progressive* | | | |
| zibbing | 72 | 97 | .01 |
| *Past Tense* | | | |
| binged | 60 | 85 | .05 |
| glinged | 63 | 80 | — |
| ricked | 73 | 73 | — |
| melted | 72 | 74 | — |
| spowed | 36 | 59 | — |
| motted | 32 | 33 | — |
| bodded | 14 | 31 | .05 |
| rang | 0 | 25 | .01 |
| *Third Singular* | | | |
| loodges | 57 | 56 | — |
| nazzes | 47 | 49 | — |
| *Possessive* | | | |
| wug's | 68 | 81 | — |
| bik's | 68 | 95 | .02 |
| niz's | 58 | 46 | — |
| wugs' | 74 | 97 | .02 |
| biks' | 74 | 99 | .01 |
| nizzes' | 53 | 82 | .05 |

## Formation of the Plural

The nature of the children's answers can best be seen through a separate examination of the noun plurals, the verbs, and the possessives. The percentage of all children supplying correct plural endings can be seen in Table 33.3. The general picture indicates that children at this age have in their vocabularies words containing the three plural allomorphs /-s ~ -z ~ -əz/, and can use these words. The real form *glasses* was included here because we knew from a pretest that children at this age generally did not make correct application of /-əz/ to new forms, and we wanted to know if they used this form with a common English word. Evidently they have at least one actual English model for this contingent plural. In uncomplicated cases children at this age can also extend the use of these forms to new words requiring /-s/ or /-z/, as indicated by the high percentage of right answers for *wug and *bik, a form used in the pretest and answered correctly by a correspondingly high number of children. For the items *wugs and *glasses* there is, moreover, a significant difference between the younger and older groups. For *glasses* they progress from 75% right to 99% right in the older group, a change that is significant at the 1% level. The few wrong answers in these cases were either a complete failure to respond, or a repetition of the word in its singular form.

From this it is evident that however poorly children may do on extensions of the rule for forming the plural of *glass*, they do have this item in their vocabulary and can produce it appropriately. During the period from preschool to the first grade, those who do not have this item acquire it. They can also extend the rule for the addition of the /-s/ or /-z/ allomorph where the more general rules of English phonology dictate which of these forms must be used. During this period they perfect this knowledge.

The ability to add /-z/ to *wug and /-s/ to *bik does not alone prove that the child possesses the rule that tells which allomorph of the plural must be used: English phonology decrees that there cannot be a consonant cluster */-kz/ or */-gs/. The final consonant determines whether the sibilant must be voiced or unvoiced. The instances in English where there is a choice are after /l/ /n/ and /r/, and after a vowel or semivowel. Thus we have minimal pairs like: *ells: else; purrs: purse; hens: hence; pews: puce.* In forming the plural of *wug or *bik, the child has only to know that a dental sibilant must be added; which one it is is determined by the invariant rules of combination that govern English consonant clusters. If, however, he is faced with a new word ending in a vowel, semivowel, /-l/, /-n/, or /-r/, he himself must make the choice, because so far as English phonology is concerned he could add either a /-z/ or an /-s/ and still have a possible English word. We would expect him, therefore, to have more difficulty forming the plural of a new word ending in these sounds than in cases where phonology determines the form of the sibilant. These problems are represented by the forms *cra, *tor, and *lun. As Table 33.3 indicates, the percentages correct on these items were respectively 79, 85, and 86. The difference between performance on *wug and *cra is significant at the 5% level.

During the period from preschool to the first grade, they improved markedly in their handling of *cra and *lun. The differences between the younger and older groups were significant at the 5% level. The case of adding /-s/ to these forms did not, however, arise. The child here, as in so many other stages of language learning, answered complexity with silence: the wrong answers were invariably the unaltered form of the singular.

The only other case to be answered correctly by the majority of the children was *heaf. Since adults responded with both *heafs and *heaves /-vz/, both of these answers were considered correct. It must be noted that although 42% of the adults gave *heaves as the plural of this item, employing what would amount to a morphophonemic change along the lines of: *knife: knives: hoof: hooves,* only three children out of a total of 89

**TABLE 33.3. Percentages of Children Supplying Correct Plural Forms**

| Item | Allomorph | Per Cent Correct |
|---|---|---|
| glasses | /-əz/ | 91 |
| wugs | /-z/ | 91 |
| luns | /-z/ | 86 |
| tors | /-z/ | 85 |
| heafs, -ves | /-s/ /-z/ | 82 |
| cras | /-z/ | 79 |
| tasses | /-əz/ | 36 |
| gutches | /-əz/ | 36 |
| kazhes | /-əz/ | 31 |
| nizzes | /-əz/ | 28 |

answering this item said *heaves; 9, or 10% added nothing, and an additional four formed the plural with the wrong allomorph, i.e., they said /hiyfəz/, treating the /-f/ as if it belonged to the sibilant-affricate series. /f/ is, of course, phonetically very similar to /s/, and one of the questions suggested by this problem was whether children would generalize in the direction of phonetic similarity across functional boundaries—/f/ is distinguished phonetically from -/s only in that it is grave and /s/ is acute. It is, so to speak, no more different from /s/ than /z/ is, and it is as similar to /s/ as /ž/ is to /z/. It does not, however, so far as English phonology is concerned, function like /s š z ž č ǰ/, none of which can be immediately followed by another sibilant within the same consonant cluster. The high percentage of correct items indicates that /f/ had already been categorized as belonging to the consonant class that can be followed by /-s/, and the phonetic similarity between /f/ and the sibilants did not lead the children to generalize the rule for the addition of the /-əz/ allomorph in that direction. Nor could any irregular formation be said to be productive for children in this case, although for adults it apparently is.

The proportion of children's right answers suddenly drops when we come to the form *tass. As Table 33.3 shows, 91% of these children when given the form glass could produce the form glasses. When given the form *tass, a new word patterned after glass, only 36% could supply the form *tasses. The picture becomes progressively worse with the other words ending in sibilants or affricates, and by the time we reach the form *niz, only 28% answered correctly. *Niz of these four, is the only one that ends in a sound that is also the commonest plural allomorph, /-z/, and the children did the worst on this item. What is of additional interest, is that on these four items there was no significant improvement from the preschool to the first grade. The difference between performance on *cra, the worst of the other items, and *tass, the best of these, was significant at the .1% level. Again, the wrong answers consisted in doing nothing to the word as given. It must be noted, however, that in these items, the children delivered the wrong form with a great deal of conviction: 62% of them said "one *tass, two *tass" as if there were no question that the plural of *tass should and must be *tass. From this it is evident

that the morphological rules these children have for the plural are not the same as those possessed by adults: the children can add /-s/ or /-z/ to new words with a great deal of success. They do not as yet have the ability to extend the /-əz/ allomorph to new words, even though it has been demonstrated that they have words of this type in their vocabulary.

The form "kazh" /kæž/ was added here once again to see in what direction the children would generalize. /ž/, although it is in the sibilant-affricate group, is very rare as a final consonant in English: it occurs only in some speakers' pronunciation of garage, barrage, and a few other words. As Table 33.3 indicates, the children treated this word like the others of this group. It might also be noted here that for the forms *gutch and *kazh, some few children formed the plural in /-s/, i.e., /gʌčs/ and /kæžs/. 10% did this for *gutch, and 5% for *kazh, errors that indicate that the phonological rules may not yet be perfectly learned. What is clearest from these answers dealing with the plural is that children can and do extend the /-s/ and /-z/ forms to new words, and that they cannot apply the more complicated /-əz/ allomorph of the plural to new words.

## Verb Inflexions

The children's performance on the verb forms can be seen in Table 33.4. It will be observed that the best performance on these items was on the progressive, where they were shown a picture of a man who knew how to *zib and were required to say that he was *zibbing. The difference between *zibbing and the best of the past tense items, *binged, was significant at the 5% level. The improvement from the younger to the older group was significant at the 1% level; fully 97% of the first graders answered this question correctly. Here, there was no question of choice, there is only one allomorph of the progressive morpheme, and the child either knows this -ing form or does not. These results suggest that he does.

The results with the past tense forms indicate that these children can handle the /-t/ and /-d/ allomorphs of the past. On *binged and *glinged the percentages answering correctly were 78 and 77, and the older group did significantly better than the younger group on *binged.

**TABLE 33.4. Percentages of Children Supplying Correct Verb Forms**

| Item | Allomorph | Percentage Correct |
|---|---|---|
| *Progressive* | | |
| zibbing | /-iŋ/ | 90 |
| *Past Tense* | | |
| binged, bang | /-d ~ æ ← (i)/ | 78 |
| glinged, glang | /-d ~ æ ← (i)/ | 77 |
| ricked | /-t/ | 73 |
| melted | /-əd/ | 73 |
| spowed | /-d/ | 52 |
| motted | /-əd/ | 33 |
| bodded | /-əd/ | 31 |
| rang | /æ← (i)/ | 17 |
| *Third Singular* | | |
| loodges | /-əz/ | 56 |
| nazzes | /-əz/ | 48 |

Actually, the forms *gling and *bing were included to test for possible irregular formations. A check of English verbs revealed that virtually all in *-ing* form their past tense irregularly: *sing: sang; ring: rang; cling: clung*, and many others. The only *-ing* verbs that form a past tense in *-ed* are a few poetic forms like *enringed, unkinged*, and *winged*, and onomotopoeias like *pinged* and *zinged*. Adults clearly felt the pull of the irregular pattern, and 50% of them said *bang or *bung for the past tense of *bing, while 75% made *gling into *glang or *glung in the past. Only one child of the 86 interviewed on these items said *bang. One also said *glang, and two said *glanged—changing the vowel and also adding the regular /-d/ for the past.

The great majority on these forms, as well as on *ricked which requires /-t/, formed the past tense regularly. There was a certain amount of room for variation with the past tense, since there is more than one way of expressing what happened in the past. A number of children, for example said "Yesterday he was *ricking". If on these occasions the experimenter tried to force the issue by saying "He only did it once yesterday, so yesterday once he___?" The child usually responded with "once he was *ricking". Taking into account this possible variation, the percentages right on *rick, *gling and *bing represent a substantial grasp of the problem of adding a phonologically determined /-t/ or /-d/.

With *spow the child had to choose one or the other of the allomorphs, and the drop to 52% correct represents this additional complexity. Several children here retained the inflexional /-z/ and said /spowzd/, others repeated the progressive or refused to answer. No child supplied a /-t/.

On *motted, the percentage correct drops to 33, although the subjects were 73% right on the real word *melted*, which is a similar form. On *bodded they were 31% right, and on *rang only 17% right. The older group was significantly better than the younger on *rang and *bodded. What this means is that the younger group could not do them at all—not one preschool child knew *rang—and the older group could barely do them. What emerges here is that children at this age level are not able to extend the rule for forming the past tense of *melted to new forms. They can handle the regular /-d/ and /-t/ allomorphs of the past in new instances, but not /-əd/. Nor do they have control of the irregular past form *rang, and consequently do not form new pasts according to this pattern, although adults do. They have the /-əd/ form in actual words like *melted*, but do not generalize from it. With *ring*, they do not have the actual past *rang*, and, therefore no model for generalization. In the children's responses, the difference between *spowd, the worst of the items requiring /-t/ or /-d/, and *motted, the best requiring /-əd/ is significant at the 2% level. For *mot and *bod, the wrong answers, which were in the majority, were overwhelmingly a repetition of the present stem: "Today he *bods; yesterday he *bod." To the forms ending in /-t/ or /-d/ the children added nothing to form the past.

The third person singular forms require the same allomorphs as the noun plurals. /-s ~ -z ~ -əz/, and only two examples were included in the experiment. These were *loodge and *naz, and required the /-əz/ ending. 56% of the children supplied the correct form *loodges, and 48% supplied *nazzes. The wrong answers were again a failure to add anything to the stem, and there was no improvement whatsoever from the younger to the older group on these two items.

## Formation of the Possessive

The only other inflexional items statistically treated were the regular forms of the possessive. The percentages of children supplying right answers can be seen in Table 33.5. In the singular,

**TABLE 33.5 Percentages of Children Supplying Correct Possessive Forms**

|  | Allomorph | Percentage Correct |
|---|---|---|
| *Singular* | | |
| wug's | /-z/ | 84 |
| bik's | /-s/ | 87 |
| niz's | /-əz/ | 49 |
| *Plural* | | |
| wugs' | /-ø/ | 88 |
| biks' | /-ø/ | 93 |
| nizzes' | /-ø/ | 76 |

the problem was the same as for the noun plurals, and the children's difficulty with the /-əz/ form of the allomorph is mirrored in the low percentage who were able to supply *niz's* /-əz/ when told "This is a *niz* who owns a hat. Whose hat is it? It is the _____?" For *bik's* there was a significant improvement at the 2% level between the younger and older groups. For *niz's* the younger group did no worse than the older group.

In the plural possessives the problem is somewhat different: since these words are already regularly inflected, the possessive is formed by adding a morphological zero. The children did not add an additional /-əz/ to these forms, and in the case of *nizzes'*, they erred on the side of removing the plural *-es*, e.g., for the plural possessive they said simply *niz* in those cases where they gave the wrong answers.

It was the adults who had difficulty with the plural possessives: 33% of them said *wugses* /-zez/ and *bikses* /-sez/, although none said *nizeses* /-əzəz/. This is undoubtedly by analogy with proper nouns in the adults' vocabulary, i.e., no adult would say that if two dogs own hats. They are the *dogses* /-zəz/ hats. However an adult may know a family named *Lyons*, and also a family named *Lyon*. In the first instance, the family are the *Lyonses* /-zəz/ and if they own a house, it is the *Lyonses'* /-zəz/ house; in the second instance, the family are the *Lyons* and their house is the *Lyons'* /-nz/. The confusion resulting from competing forms like these is such that some speakers do not make this distinction, and simply add nothing to a proper noun ending in /-s/ or /-z/ in order to form the possessive—they say "it is Charles' /-lz/ hat". Some speakers seem also to have been taught in school that they must use this latter form. It seems likely that the children interviewed had not enough

grasp of the /-əz/ form for these niceties to affect them.

## Adjectival Inflexion

The last of the inflexional items involved attempting to elicit comparative and superlative endings for the adjective *quirky*. The child was shown dogs that were increasingly *quirky* and expected to say that the second was *quirkier* than the first, and that the third was the *quirkiest*. No statistical count was necessary here since of the 80 children shown this picture, only one answered with these forms. Adults were unanimous in their answers. Children either said they did not know, or they repeated the experimenter's word, and said "*quirky*, too". If the child failed to answer, the experimenter supplied the form *quirkier*, and said "This dog is *quirky*. This dog is *quirkier*. And this dog is the _____?" Under these conditions 35% of the children could supply the *-est* form.

## Derivation and Compounding

The children were also asked several questions that called for compounding or deriving new words. They were asked what they would call a man who *zibbed* for a living, what they would call a very tiny *wug*, what they would call a house a *wug* lives in. and what kind of dog a dog covered with *quirks* is.

Adults unanimously said that a man who *zibs* is a *zibber*. using the common agentive pattern *-er*. Only 11% of the children said *zibber*. 35% gave no answer. 11% said *zíbbingmàn* and 5% said *zíbmàn*, compounds that adults did not utilize. The rest of the children's answers were real words like *clown* or *acrobat*.

For the diminutive of *wug*, 50% of the adults said *wuglet*. Others offered *little *wùg*, *wuggie*, *wugette*, and *wugling*. No child used a diminutive suffix. 52% of the children formed compounds like *báby *wùg*, *teény *wùg*, and *little *wùg*. Two children, moreover, said a little *wug* is a *wig*, employing sound symbolism—a narrower vowel to stand for a smaller animal. For the house a *wug* lives in, 58% of the adults formed the asyntactic compound *wúghoùse*. Others said *wuggery*, *wúgshoùse*, and *wúghùt*. Again, no child used a suffix. The younger children did not understand this question, and where the older children did, they formed compounds. 18% of the first graders said *wughoùse. Others suggested birdcage and similar forms. What emerges from this picture is the fact that whereas adults may derive new words, children at this stage use almost exclusively a compounding pattern, and have the stress pattern ´` at their disposal: the adults unanimously said that a dog covered with *quirks is a *quirky dog. 64% of the children formed the compound *quírk dòg for this item, and again, no child used a derivational suffix.

## Analysis of Compound Words

After the child had been asked all of these questions calling for the manipulation of new forms, he was asked about some of the compound words in his own vocabulary; the object of this questioning was to see if children at this age are aware of the separate morphemes in compound words. The children's explanations fall roughly into four categories. The first is identity: "a blackboard is called a blackboard because it is a blackboard." The second is a statement of the object's salient function or feature: "a blackboard is called a blackboard because you write on it." In the third type of explanation, the salient feature happens to coincide with part of the name: "a blackboard is called a blackboard because it is black;" "a merry-go-round is called a merry-go-round because it goes round and round". Finally, there is the etymological explanation given by adults—it takes into account both parts of the word, and is not necessarily connected with some salient or functional feature: "Thanksgiving is called Thanksgiving because the pilgrims gave thanks."

Of the children's answers, only 13% could be considered etymological. Most of their answers fell into the salient-feature category, while the number of identity responses dropped from the younger to the older group. Many younger children offered no answers at all; of the answers given, 23% were identity. Of the older children, only 9% gave identity answers, a difference that was significant at the 1% level.

As we might expect, the greatest number of etymological responses—23%—was given for Thanksgiving, which is an item that children are explicitly taught. It must be noted, however, that

despite this teaching, for 67% of the children answering this item, Thanksgiving is called Thanksgiving because you eat lots of turkey.

The salient feature answers at first seem to have the nature of an etymological explanation, in those instances where the feature coincides with part of the name—72% of the answers, for instance, said that a fireplace is called a fireplace because you put fire in it. When the salient feature does not coincide with part of the name, however, the etymological aspects also drop out. For birthday, where to the child neither the fact that it is a day nor that it is tied to one's birth is important, the number of functional answers rises: it is called birthday because you get presents or eat cake. Only 2% said anything about its being a day.

The child approaches the etymological view of compound word through those words where the most important thing about the word so far as the child is concerned coincides with part of the name. The outstanding feature of a merry-go-round is that it does, indeed, go round and round, and it is the eminent appropriateness of such names that leads to the expectation of meaningfulness in other compound words.

Although the number of etymological explanations offered by the children was not great, it was clear that many children have what amounts to private meanings for many compound words. These meanings may be unrelated to the word's history, and unshared by other speakers. Examples of this can be seen in the following.

"An airplane is called an airplane because it is a plain thing that goes in the air."
"Breakfast is called breakfast because you have to eat it fast when you rush to school."
"Thanksgiving is called that because people give things to one another." (Thingsgiving?)
"Friday is a day when you have fried fish."
"A handkerchief is a thing you hold in your hand, and you go 'kerchoo'."

These examples suffice to give the general nature of the private meanings children may have about the words in their vocabulary. What is of additional interest, is that the last explanation about the handkerchief was also offered by one of the college-graduate adult subjects.

We must all learn to handle English inflexion and some of the patterns for derivation and compounding. So long as we use a compound word correctly, we can assign any meaning we like to its constituent elements.

## Conclusion

In this experiment, preschool and first grade children, ranging from four to seven years in age, were presented with a number of nonsense words and asked to supply English plurals, verb tenses, possessives, derivations and compounds of those words. Our first and most general question had been: do children possess morphological rules? A previous study of the actual vocabulary of first graders showed that they know real items representing basic English morphological processes. Asking questions about real words, however, might be tapping a process no more abstract than rote memory. We could be sure that our nonsense words were new words to the child, and that if he supplied the right morphological item he knew something more than the individual words in his vocabulary: he had rules of extension that enabled him to deal with new words. Every child interviewed understood what was being asked of him. If knowledge of English consisted of no more than the storing up of many memorized words, the child might be expected to refuse to answer our questions on the grounds that he had never before heard of a *wug, for instance, and could not possibly give us the plural form since no one had ever told him what it was. This was decidedly not the case. The children answered the questions: in some instances they pronounced the inflexional endings they had added with exaggerated care, so that it was obvious that they understood the problem and wanted no mistake made about their solution. Sometimes, they said "That's a hard one," and pondered a while before answering, or answered with one form and then corrected themselves. The answers were not always right so far as English is concerned; but they were consistent and orderly answers, and they demonstrated that there can be no doubt that children in this age range operate with clearly delimited morphological rules.

Our second finding was that boys and girls did equally well on these items. Sometimes the girls had a higher percentage of right answers on an item, and more often the boys did somewhat better, but no pattern of differences could be distinguished and the differences were never statistically significant. These findings are at variance with the results of most other language tests. Usually, girls have been shown to have a slight advantage over boys. In our experiment, girls were no more advanced than boys in their acquisition of English morphology. Since other language tests have not investigated morphology *per se*, it is easy enough to say that this is simply one area in which there are no sex differences. A reason for this lack of difference does, however, suggest itself: and that is the very basic nature of morphology. Throughout childhood, girls are perhaps from a maturational point of view slightly ahead of the boys who are their chronological age mates. But the language differences that have been observed may be culturally induced, and they may be fairly superficial. Some social factor may lead girls to be more facile with words, to use longer sentences, and to talk more. This can be misleading. A girl in an intellectual adult environment may, for instance, acquire a rather sophisticated vocabulary at an early age. This should not be taken to mean that she will learn the minor rules for the formation of the plural before she learns the major ones, or that she will necessarily be precocious in her acquisition of those rules. What is suggested here is that every child is in contact with a sufficiently varied sample of spoken English in order for him to be exposed at an early age to the basic morphological processes. These processes occur in simple sentences as well as in complex ones. Practice with a limited vocabulary may be as effective as practice with an extensive vocabulary, and the factors that influence other aspects of language development may have no effect on morphological acquisition. Since, moreover, this type of inner patterning is clearly a cognitive process, we might expect it to be related to intelligence more than to any other feature. Unfortunately, there were no IQs available for the subjects, so that a comparison could not be made, and this last must remain a speculation.

Our next observation was that there were some differences between the preschoolers and the first graders. These were predominantly on the items that the group as a whole did best and worst on: since no child in the preschool could supply the irregular past *rang*, and a few in the first grade could, this difference was significant. Otherwise, the improvement was in the direction of perfecting knowledge they already had—the simple plurals and possessives, and the progressive tense. The answers of the two groups were not qualitatively different: they both employed the same simplified morphological rules. Since this was true, the answers of both groups were combined for the purpose of further analysis.

Children were able to form the plurals requiring /-s/ or /-z/, and they did best on the items where general English phonology determined which of these allomorphs is required. Although they have in their vocabularies real words that form their plural in /-əz/, in the age range that was interviewed they did not generalize to form new words in /-əz/. Their rule seems to be to add /-s/ or /-z/, unless the word ends in /s z š ž č ǰ/. To words ending in these sounds they add nothing to make the plural—and when asked to form a plural, repeat the stem as if it were already in the plural. This simplification eliminates the least common of the productive allomorphs. We may now ask about the relative status of the remaining allomorphs /-s/ and /-z/. For the items like *lun or *cra, where both of these sounds could produce a phonologically possible English word, but not a plural, no child employed the voiceless alternant /-s/. This is the second least common of the three allomorphs. The only places where this variant occurred were where the speaker of English could not say otherwise. So far as general English phonology is concerned a /-z/ cannot in the same cluster follow a /-k-/ or other voiceless sound. Once the /-k-/ has been said, even if the speaker intended to say /-z/, it would automatically devoice to /-s/. The only morphological rule the child is left with, is the addition of the /-z/ allomorph, which is the most extensive: the /-əz/ form for him is not yet productive, and the /-s/ form can be subsumed under a more general phonological rule.

What we are saying here is that the child's rule for the formation of the plural seems to be: "a final sibilant makes a word plural". The question that arises is, should we not rather say that the child's rule is: "a voiceless sibilant after a voiceless consonant and a voiced sibilant after all other sounds makes a word plural." This latter describes what the child actually does. However, our rule will cover the facts if it is coupled with a prior phonological rule about possible final sound sequences. The choice of the voiceless or voiced variant can generally be subsumed under phonological rules about final sound sequences; the

exceptions are after vowels, semivowels, and /l-n-r-/. In these places where phonology leaves a choice, /-z/ is used, and so the child's conscious rule might be to add /-z/. It would be interesting to find out what the child thinks he is saying—if we could in some way ask him the general question, "how do you make the plural?"

Another point of phonology was illustrated by the children's treatment of the forms *heaf and *kazh. It was demonstrated here that the children have phonological rules, and the direction of their generalizations was dictated by English phonology, and not simple phonetic similarity. /-ž/ is a comparatively rare phoneme, and yet they apparently recognized it as belonging to the sibilant series in English, and they rarely attempted to follow it with another sibilant. The similarity between /f/ and the sibilants, did not, on the contrary cause them to treat it as a member of this class. The final thing to be noted about *heaf is that several children and many adults said the plural was *heaves. This may be by analogy with leaf: leaves. If our speculation that the /-z/ form is the real morphological plural is right, there may be cases where instead of becoming devoiced itself, it causes regressive assimilation of the final voiceless consonant.

The allomorphs of the third person singular of the verb and the possessives of the noun are the same as for the noun plural, except that the plural possessives have an additional zero allomorph. These forms were treated in the same way by the children, with one notable exception: they were more successful in adding the /-əz/ to form possessives and verbs than they were in forming noun plurals. They were asked to produce three nearly identical forms: a man who *nazzes; two *nizzes; and a *niz's hat. On the verb they were 48% right; on the possessive they were 49% right, and on the noun plural they were only 28% right. The difference between their performance on the noun plural and on the other two items was significant at the 1% level. And yet the phonological problem presented by these three forms was the same. For some reason the contingent rule for the formation of the third person singular of the verb and for the possessive is better learned or earlier learned than the same rule for the formation of noun plurals. The morphological rule implies meaning, and forms that are phonologically identical may be learned at different times if they serve different, functions. These forms are not simply the same phonological rule, since their different functions change the percentage of right answers. Perhaps the child does better because he knows more verbs than nouns ending in /s z š ž č ǰ/, and it is possible that he has heard more possessives than noun plurals. It is also possible that for English the noun plural is the least important or most redundant of these inflexions. This is a somewhat surprising conclusion, since nouns must always appear in a singular or plural form and there are ways of avoiding the possessive inflexion: it is generally possible to use an *of* construction in place of a possessive—we can say *the leg of the chair* or *the chair's leg*, or *the chair leg* although in cases involving actual ownership we do not say *of*. A sentence referring to *the hat of John* sounds like an awkward translation from the French. And no child said it was *the hat of the *niz*. The children's facility with these forms seems to indicate that the possessive inflexion is by no means dying out in English.

Of the verb forms, the best performance was with the present progressive: 90% of all the children said that a man who knew how to *zib* was *zibbing*. Undoubtedly, children's speech is mostly in the present tense, and this is a very commonly-heard form. Explanations of what is happening in the present all take this form. "The man is *running*"—or *walking* or *eating* or *doing* something. The additional point is that the *-ing* forms are not only very important; this inflexion has only one allomorph. The rules for its application are completely regular, and it is the most general and regular rules that children prefer.

The children's handling of the past tense parallels their treatment of the plurals, except that they did better on the whole with the plurals. Again, they could not extend the contingent rule. Although they have forms like *melted* in their vocabulary, they were unable to extend the /-əd/ form to new verbs ending in /t d/. They treated these forms as if they were already in the past. They applied the allomorphs /-d/ and /-t/ appropriately where they were phonologically conditioned, and only /-d/ to a form like *spow*, where either was possible. This suggests that their real morphological rule for the formation of the past is to add /-d/, and under certain conditions it will automatically become /-t/. Many adult speakers feel that they are adding a /-d/ in a word like *stopped*; this may be because

of the orthography, and it may be because they are adding a psychological /-d/ that devoices without their noticing it.

Whereas the children all used regular patterns in forming the past tense, we found that for adults strong pasts of the form *rang* and *clung* are productive. Since virtually all English verbs that are in the present of an *-ing* form make their pasts irregularly, this seemed a likely supposition. Adults made *gling* and *bing* into *glang* and *bang* in the past. New words of this general shape may therefore be expected to have a very good chance of being treated according to this pattern—real words like the verb *to string* for instance, have been known the vacillate between the common productive past and this strong subgroup and finally come to be treated according to the less common pattern. The children, however, could not be expected to use this pattern since we could not demonstrate that they had the real form *rang* in their repertory. They said *ringed*. At one point, the experimenter misread the card and told the child that the bell *rang*. When the child was asked what the bell did, he said, "It *ringed*." The experimenter then corrected him and said, "You mean it *rang*." The child said that was what he had said, and when asked again what that was, he repeated, "It *ringed*," as if he had not even heard the difference between these two allomorphs. Perhaps he did not.

The adults did not form irregular pasts with any other pattern, although a form was included that could have been treated according to a less common model. This was the verb *mot, which was of the pattern *cut* or *bet*. There are some 19 verbs in English that form their past with a zero morpheme, but this group does not seem to be productive.

The cases of *gling, which became *glang* in the past and *mot, which became *motted* suggest some correlates of linguistic productivity. About nineteen verbs in English form their past tense with a zero allomorph. About 14 verbs form their past like *cling*, and seven follow the pattern of *ring*. Within these last two groups there are words like *win*, which becomes *won* and *swim*, which becomes *swam*. We can also find words similar to *win* and *swim* that are quite regular in the past: *pin* and *trim*. But virtually all of the verbs that end in *-ing* form their past in *-ang* or *-ung*. There are approximately 10 of these *-ing* verbs.

The productivity of the *-ang* and *-ung* forms proves that new forms are not necessarily assimilated to the largest productive class. Where a small group of common words exist as a category by virtue of their great phonetic similarity and their morphological consistency, a new word having the same degree of phonetic similarity may be treated according to this special rule. *Ox: oxen* is not similarly productive, but probably would be if there were just one other form like *box*: *boxen*, and the competing *fox* : *foxes* did not exist. With *\*mot*, the zero allomorph is not productive because although it applies to more cases than are covered by the *-ing* verbs, it is not so good a rule in the sense that it is not so consistent. The final /-t/, which is the only common phonetic element, does not invariably lead to a zero allomorph, as witness *pit* : *pitted*, *pat* : *patted*, and many others.

Although the adults were uniform in their application of *-er* and *-est* to form the comparative and superlative of the adjective, children did not seem to have these patterns under control unless they were given both the adjective and the comparative form. With this information, some of them could supply the superlative.

Derivation is likewise a process little used by children at this period when the derivational endings would compete with the inflexional suffixes they are in the process of acquiring. Instead, they compound words, using the primary and tertiary accent pattern commonly found in words like *bláckboàrd*.

The last part of the experiment was designed to see if the children were aware of the separate elements in the compound words in their vocabulary. Most of these children were at the stage where they explained an object's name by stating its major function or salient feature: a blackboard is called a *blackboard* because you write on it. In the older group, a few children had noticed the separate parts of the compound words and assigned to them meanings that were not necessarily connected with the word's etymology or with the meaning the morphemes may have in later life. Not many adults feel that Friday is the day for frying things, yet a number admit to having thought so as children.

These last considerations were, however, tangential to the main problem of investigating the child's grasp of English morphological rules and describing the evolution of those rules. The picture that emerged was one of consistency, regularity, and simplicity. The children did not treat new words according to idiosyncratic pattern. They did not model new words on patterns that appear infrequently. Where they provided inflexional endings, their best performance was with those forms that are the most regular and have the fewest variants. With the morphemes that have several allomorphs, they could handle forms calling for the most common of those allomorphs long before they could deal with allomorphs that appear in a limited distribution range.

## NOTES

1. This investigation was supported in part by a fellowship from the Social Science Research Council. During the academic year 1957–58 the writer completed the research while holding an AAUW National Fellowship. A dissertation on this subject was presented by the writer to Radcliffe College in April, 1958. I am indebted to Professor Roger W. Brown for his inspiration and his help in the conduct of this study.
2. H. D. Rinsland, *A Basic Vocabulary of Elementary School Children,* New York, MacMillan, 1945.

# Statistical Learning by 8-Month-Old Infants

Jenny R. Saffran, Richard N. Aslin, and Elissa L. Newport

Learners rely on a combination of experience-independent and experience-dependent mechanisms to extract information from the environment. Language acquisition involves both types of mechanisms, but most theorists emphasize the relative importance of experience-independent mechanisms. The present study shows that a fundamental task of language acquisition, segmentation of words from fluent speech, can be accomplished by 8-month-old infants based solely on the statistical relationships between neighboring speech sounds. Moreover, this word segmentation was based on statistical learning from only 2 minutes of exposure, suggesting that infants have access to a powerful mechanism for the computation of statistical properties of the language input.

During early development, the speed and accuracy with which an organism extracts environmental information can be extremely important for its survival. Some species have evolved highly constrained neural mechanisms to ensure that environmental information is properly interpreted, even in the absence of experience with the environment (1). Other species are dependent on a period of interaction with the environment that clarifies the information to which attention should be directed and the consequences of behaviors guided by that information (2). Depending on the developmental status and the task facing a particular organism, both experience-independent and experience-dependent mechanisms may be involved in the extraction of information and the control of behavior.

In the domain of language acquisition, two facts have supported the interpretation that experience-independent mechanisms are both necessary and dominant. First, highly complex forms of language production develop extremely rapidly (3). Second, the language input available to the young child is both incomplete and sparsely represented compared to the child's eventual linguistic abilities (4). Thus, most theories of language acquisition have emphasized the critical role played by experience-independent internal structures over the role of experience-dependent factors (5).

It is undeniable that experience-dependent mechanisms are also required for the acquisition of language. Many aspects of a particular natural language must be acquired from listening experience. For example, acquiring the specific words and phonological structure of a language requires exposure to a significant corpus of language input. Moreover, long before infants begin to produce their native language, they acquire information about its sound properties (6). Nevertheless, given the daunting task of acquiring linguistic information from listening experience during early development, few theorists have entertained the hypothesis that learning plays a primary role in the acquisition of more complicated aspects of language, favoring instead experience-independent mechanisms (7). Young humans are generally viewed as poor learners, suggesting that innate factors are primarily responsible for the acquisition of language.

Here we investigate the nature of the experience-dependent factors involved in language acquisition. In particular, we ask whether infants are in fact better learners than has previously been assumed, thus potentially reducing the extent to which experience-independent structures must be posited. The results demonstrate that infants possess powerful mechanisms suited to learning the types of structures exemplified in linguistic systems. Experience may therefore play a more important role in the acquisition of language than existing theories suggest.

One task faced by all language learners is the segmentation of fluent speech into words. This process is particularly difficult because word boundaries in fluent speech are marked inconsistently by discrete acoustic events such as pauses (8). Although it has recently been demonstrated that 8-month-old infants can segment words from fluent speech and subsequently recognize them when presented in isolation (9), it is not clear what information is used by infants to discover word boundaries. This problem is complicated by the variable acoustic structure of speech across different languages, suggesting that infants must discover which, if any, acoustic cues correlated with word boundaries are relevant to their native language (10); there is no invariant acoustic cue to word boundaries present in all languages.

One important source of information that can, in principle, define word boundaries in any natural language is the statistical information contained in sequences of sounds. Over a corpus of speech there are measurable statistical regularities that distinguish recurring sound sequences that comprise words from the more accidental sound sequences that occur across word boundaries (11). Within a language, the transitional probability from one sound to the next will generally be highest when the two sounds follow one another within a word, whereas transitional probabilities spanning a word boundary will be relatively low (12). For example, given the sound sequence pretty#baby, the transi-

tional probability from pre to ty is greater than the transitional probability from ty to ba. Previously, we showed that adults and children can use information about transitional probabilities to discover word boundaries in an artificial language corpus of nonsense words presented as continuous speech, with no acoustic cues to word boundaries (13).

We asked whether 8-month-old infants can extract information about word boundaries solely on the basis of the sequential statistics of concatenated speech. We used the familiarization-preference procedure developed by Jusczyk and Aslin (9). In this procedure, infants are exposed to auditory material that serves as a potential learning experience. They are subsequently presented with two types of test stimuli: (i) items that were contained within the familiarization material and (ii) items that are highly similar but (by some critical criterion) were not contained within the familiarization material. During a series of test trials that immediately follows familiarization, infants control the duration of each test trial by their sustained visual fixation on a blinking light (14). If infants have extracted the crucial information about the familiarization items, they may show differential durations of fixation (listening) during the two types of test trials (15). We used this procedure to determine whether infants can acquire the statistical properties of sound sequences from brief exposures.

In our first experiment, 24 8-month-old infants from an American-English language environment were familiarized with 2 min of a continuous speech stream consisting of four three-syllable nonsense words (hereafter, "words") repeated in random order (16). The speech stream was generated by a speech synthesizer in a monotone female voice at a rate of 270 syllables per minute, (180 words in total). The synthesizer provided no acoustic information about word boundaries, resulting in a continuous stream of coarticulated consonant-vowel syllables, with no pauses, stress differences, or any other acoustic or prosodic cues to word boundaries. A sample of the speech stream is the orthographic string *bidakupadotigolabubidaku....* The only cues to word boundaries were the transitional probabilities between syllable pairs, which were higher within words (1.0 in all cases, for example, *bida*) than between words (0.33 in all cases, for example, *kupa*).

To assess learning, each infant was presented with repetitions of one of four three-syllable strings on each test trial. Two of these three-syllable strings were "words" from the artificial language presented during familiarization, and two were three-syllable "nonwords" that contained the same syllables heard during familiarization but not in the order in which they appeared as words (17).

The infants showed a significant test-trial discrimination between word and non-word stimuli (18), with longer listening times for nonwords (Table 34.1). This novelty preference, or dishabituation effect, indicates that 8-month-olds recognized the difference between the novel and the familiar orderings of the three-syllable strings. Thus, 8-month-old infants are capable of extracting serial-order information after only 2 min of listening experience.

Of course, simple serial-order information is an insufficient cue to word boundaries. The learner must also be able to extract the relative frequencies of co-occurrence of sound pairs, where relatively low transitional probabilities signal word boundaries. Our next experiment examined whether 8-month-olds could perform the more difficult statistical computations required to distinguish words (that is, recurrent syllable sequences) from syllable strings spanning word boundaries (that is, syllable sequences occurring more rarely). To take an English example, *pretty#baby*, we wanted to see if infants can distinguish a word-internal syllable pair like *pretty* from a word-external syllable pair like *ty#ba*.

Another 24 8-month-old infants from an American-English language environment were familiarized with 2 min of a continuous speech stream consisting of three-syllable nonsense words similar in structure to the artificial language used in our first experiment (19). This time, however, the test items for each infant consisted of two words and two "part-words." The part-words were created by joining the final syllable of a word to the first two syllables of another word. Thus, the part-words contained three-syllable sequences that the infant had heard during familiarization but statistically, over the corpus, did not correspond to words (20). These part-words could only be judged as novel if the infants had learned the words with sufficient specificity and completeness that sequences crossing a word boundary were relatively unfamiliar.

Despite the difficulty of this word versus part-word discrimination, infants showed a significant test-trial discrimination between the word and part-word stimuli (21), with longer listening times for part-words (Table 34.1). Thus, 2 min of exposure to concatenated speech organized into "words" was sufficient for 8-month-old infants to extract information about the sequential statistics of syllables. Moreover, this novelty preference cannot be attributed to a total lack of experience with the three-syllable sequences forming part-words, as was the case with the nonwords in the first experiment. Rather, infants succeeded in learning and remembering particular groupings of three-syllable strings—those strings containing higher transitional probabilities surrounded by lower transitional probabilities.

The infants' performance in these studies is particularly impressive given the impoverished nature of the familiarization speech stream, which contained no pauses, intonational patterns, or any other cues that, in normal speech, probabilistically supplement the sequential statistics inherent in the structure of words. Equally impressive is the fact that 8-month-old infants in both experiments were able to extract information about sequential statistics from only 2 min of listening experience. Although experience with speech in the real world is unlikely to be as concentrated as it was in these studies, infants in more natural settings presumably benefit from other types of cues correlated with statistical information.

Our results raise the intriguing possibility that

**TABLE 34.1. Mean Time Spent Listening to the Familiar and Novel Stimuli for Experiment 1 (Words versus Nonwords) and Experiment 2 (Words versus Part-Words) and Significance Tests Comparing the Listening Times**

| Experiment | Mean Listening Times (s) | | Matched-Pairs *t* Test |
| --- | --- | --- | --- |
| | Familiar Items | Novel Items | |
| 1 | 7.97 (SE = 0.41) | 8.85 (SE = 0.45) | *t*(23) = 2.3, *P* < 0.04 |
| 2 | 6.77 (SE = 0.44) | 7.60 (SE = 0.42) | *t*(23) = 2.4, *P* < 0.03 |

infants possess experience-dependent mechanisms that may be powerful enough to support not only word segmentation but also the acquisition of other aspects of language. It remains unclear whether the statistical learning we observed is indicative of a mechanism specific to language acquisition or of a general learning mechanism applicable to a broad range of distributional analyses of environmental input (22). Regardless, the existence of computational abilities that extract structure so rapidly suggests that it is premature to assert a priori how much of the striking knowledge base of human infants is primarily a result of experience-independent mechanisms. In particular, some aspects of early development may turn out to be best characterized as resulting from innately biased statistical learning mechanisms rather than innate knowledge. If this is the case, then the massive amount of experience gathered by infants during the first postnatal year may play a far greater role in development than has previously been recognized.

## REFERENCES AND NOTES

1. Certain species-specific skills develop without any experiential input, including bat echolocation [E. Gould, *Dev. Psychobiol.* 8, 33 (1975)] and cricket song [R. Hoy, *Am. Zool.* 14, 1067 (1974)].

2. Examples of behaviors mediated by early experience are imprinting [E. Hess, *Imprinting* (Van Nostrand, New York, 1973); M. Leon, *Physiol. Behav.* 14, 311 (1975)] and suckling responses in newborn rats [M. H. Teicher and E. M. Blass, *Science* 198, 635 (1977)].

3. These milestones have been well-documented both in English [for example, R. Brown, *A First Language* (Harvard Univ. Press, Cambridge, MA, 1973)] and cross-linguistically [for example, E. Lenneberg, *Biological Foundations of Language* (Wiley, New York, 1967); D. Slobin, Ed., vols. 1 to 3 of *The Crosslinguistic Study of Language Acquisition* (Eribaum, Hillsdale, NJ, 1985, 1987, 1992)].

4. This "argument from the poverty of the stimulus" remains widely accepted [for example, N. Chomsky, *Aspects of the Theory of Syntax* (MIT Press, Cambridge, MA, 1965); S. Crain, *Behav. Brain Sci. 14*, 597 (1991)].

5. D. Bickerton, *Behav. Brain Sci.* 7, 173 (1984); N. Chomsky, *Rules and Representations* (Columbia Univ. Press, New York, 1981); J. Fodor, *Modularity of Mind* (MIT Press, Cambridge, MA, 1983); L. Gleitman and E. Newport, in *Language: An Invitation to Cognitive Science*, L. Gleitman and M. Liberman, Eds. (MIT Press, Cambridge, MA, 1995), pp. 1-24.

6. Examples include vowel structure [P. K. Kuhl, K. A. Williams, F. Lacerda, K. N. Stevens, and B. Lindblom, *Science* 255, 606 (1992)], phonotactics [P. Jusczyk, A. Friederici, J. Wessels, V. Svenkerud, and A. Jusczyk, *J.*

*Mem. Lang. 32,* 401 (1993)], and prosodic structure [P. Jusczyk, A. Cutler, and N. Redanz, *Child Dev. 64,* 675 (1993)].

7. Exceptions include research on prenatal exposure to maternal speech [A. DeCasper, J.-P. Lecanuet, M.-C. Busnel, C. Granier-Deferre, and R. Maugeais, *Infant Behav. Dev.* 17, 159 (1994)] and early postnatal preferences [J. Mehler et al., *Cognition 29,* 149 (1988)].

8. R. Cole and J. Jakimik, in *Perception and Production of Fluent Speech*, R. Cole, Ed. (Erlbaum, Hillsdale, NJ, 1980), pp. 133-163.

9. P. Jusczyk and R. Aslin, *Cognitive Psychol. 29,* 1 (1995).

10. A. Christophe, E. Dupoux, J. Bertoncini, and J. Mehler, *J. Acoust. Soc. Am. 95,* 1570 (1994); A. Cutler and D. Carter, *Comput. Speech Lang. 2,* 133 (1987).

11. Z. Harris, *Language 31,* 190 (1955); J. Hayes and H. Clark, in *Cognition and the Development of Language,* J. Hayes, Ed. (Wiley, New York, 1970). See M. Brent and T. Cartwright [*Cognition 61,* 93 (1996)] for a discussion of related statistical cues to word boundaries.

12. The transitional probability of

$$Y \mid X = \frac{\text{frequency of XY}}{\text{frequency of X}}$$

13. J. Saffran, E. Newport, and R. Aslin, *J. Mem. Lang. 35,* 606 (1996); _____, R. Tunick, and S. Barrueco, *Psychol. Sci.*, in press.

14. Each infant was tested individually while seated on the parent's lap in a sound-attenuated booth. Synthetic speech was generated off-line by the Macin-Talk system and stored on disk at a sampling rate of 22 kHz for on-line playback through an Audio-media board in an Apple Quadra 650 computer. An observer outside the testing booth monitored the infant's looking behavior with the use of a color video system, using a buttonbox connected to the computer to initiate trials and score head-turn responses. Both the parent and the observer listened to masking music over headphones to eliminate bias. During the 2-min familiarization phase, the infant's gaze was first directed to a blinking light located on the front wall of the testing booth, and then the sound sequence was presented from two loudspeakers located on the side walls. The infant's gaze was directed to one of two blinking lights on these side walls during familiarization, but there was no relation between lights and sound. Immediately after familiarization, 12 test trials were presented (six words and six nonwords). Each test trial began with the central blinking light. When the observer signaled with a button press that the infant had fixated on the central light, one of the two side blinking lights was turned on and the center light was extinguished. When the infant faced the side light (a head turn of at least 30° in the direction of the light), the three-syllable test string was played and repeated until the infant looked away from the light for 2 s or until 15 s of looking had occurred. The observer simply recorded the direction of the infant's head turn, and the computer measured looking times, determined when the 2-s lookaway criterion had been met, and controlled the randomization and presentation of stimuli. Cumulative looking time across each of the two types of test trials provided the measure of preference.

15. The direction of the fixation preference depends on the degree of familiarity with the stimuli. If the infants have

become highly familiar with the stimuli, they show dishabituation behavior, preferring the novel stimuli.

16. Two counterbalanced stimulus conditions were generated. For each condition, 45 tokens of each of four trisyliabic nonsense words (condition A: *tupiro, golabu, bidaku,* and *padoti*; condition B: *dapiku, tilado, burobi,* and *pagotu*) were spoken in random order to create a 2-min speech stream, with the stipulation that the same word never occurred twice in a row.

17. Test stimuli: *tuplro, golabu, dapiku,* and *tilado*. In condition A, the first two strings were words and the last two strings were nonwords (the transitional probabilities between the syllables in the nonwords were all zero relative to the exposure corpus, as these syllable pairs had never occurred during familiarization). In condition B, the first two strings were nonwords and the last two strings were words. This between-subjects counterbalanced design ensured that any observed preferences for words or nonwords across both conditions would not be artifacts of any general preferences for certain syllable strings. Each of the four test strings were presented (repeated with a 500-ms interval between test strings) on three different trials, resulting in a total of 12 test trials per infant.

18. There were no significant differences between the infants in condition A and condition B: $t(22) = 0.31$. The data from the two groups were thus combined for the other analyses.

19. Condition A words: *pabiku, tibudo, golatu,* and *daropi*; condition B words: *tudaro, pigola, bikuti,* and *budopa*.

20. Test stimuli: *pabiku, tibudo, tudaro,* and *pigola*. In condition A, the first two strings were words and the second two strings were part-words. For example, the part-word *pigola* spanned the word boundary between *daropi#golatu* and thus was heard during exposure. In condition B, the first two strings were part-words and the second two strings were words. The part-words were thus three-syllable sequences that the infants had heard during the course of the exposure period. The difficulty of this test discrimination can be seen by comparing the transitional probabilities between the syllables in the words (1.0 between syllables 1 and 2 and between syllables 2 and 3) to the transitional probabilities between the syllables in the part-words (0.33 between syllables 1 and 2 and 1.0 between syllables 2 and 3).

21. There were no significant differences between the infants in condition A and condition B: $t(22) = 0.49$. The data from the two groups were thus combined for the other analyses.

22. For example, this same general mechanism could be used to find an object, such as a human face, in the environment.

23. We thank J. Gallipeau, J. Hooker, P. Jusczyk, A. Jusczyk, T. Mintz, K. Ruppert, and J. Sawusch for their help with various aspects of this research, and P. Jusczyk, S. Pollak, M. Spivey-Knowlton, and M. Tanenhaus for their helpful comments on a previous draft. Supported by an NSF predoctoral fellowship (J.R.S.), NSF grant SBR9421064 (R.N.A.), and NIH grant DC00167 (E.L.N.). The parents of all participants gave informed consent.

# Rule Learning by 7-Month-Old Infants

Gary F. Marcus, S. Vijayan, S. Bandi Rao, and Peter M. Vishton

A fundamental task of language acquisition is to extract abstract algebraic rules. Three experiments show that 7-month-old infants attend longer to sentences with unfamiliar structures than to sentences with familiar structures. The design of the artificial language task used in these experiments ensured that this discrimination could not be performed by counting, by a system that is sensitive only to transitional probabilities, or by a popular class of simple neural network models. Instead, these results suggest that infants can represent, extract, and generalize abstract algebraic rules.

What learning mechanisms are available to infants on the cusp of language learning? One learning mechanism that young infants can exploit is statistical in nature. For example, Saffran et al. (1) found that the looking behaviors of 8-month-old infants indicated a sensitivity to statistical information inherent in sequences of speech sounds produced in an artificial language—for example, transitional probabilities, which are estimates of how likely one item is to follow another. In the corpus of sentences "The boy loves apples. The boy loves oranges." the transitional probability between the words "the" and "boy" is 1.0 but the transitional probability between the words "loves" and "apples" is ½ = 0.5.

It has been suggested that mechanisms that track statistical information, or connectionist models that rely on similar sorts of information [for example, the simple recurrent network (SRN) (2)], may suffice for language learning (3). The alternative possibility considered here is that children might possess at least two learning mechanisms, one for learning statistical information and another for learn-ing "algebraic" rules (4)—open-ended abstract relationships for which we can substitute arbitrary items. For instance, we can substitute any value of $x$ into the equation $y = x + 2$. Similarly, if we know that in English a sentence can be formed by concatenating any plural noun phrase with any verb phrase with plural agreement, then as soon as we discover that "the three blickets" is a well-formed plural noun phrase and that "reminded Sam of Tibetan art" is a well-formed verb phrase with plural agreement, we can infer that "The three blickets reminded Sam of Tibetan art." is a well-formed sentence.

To date, however, there has been no direct empirical test for determining whether young infants can actually learn simplified versions of such algebraic rules. A number of previous experiments drawn from the literature of speech perception (not aimed at the question of rule learning) are consistent with the possibility that infants might learn algebraic rules, but each of these prior experiments could be accounted for by a system that extracted only statistical tendencies. For example, infants

543

who are habituated to a series of two-syllable words attend longer when confronted with a three-syllable word (5). An infant who attended longer to a three-syllable word might have noticed a violation of a rule (for example, "all the words here are two syllables"), but an infant could also have succeeded with a statistical device that noted that the three-syllable word had more syllables than the average number of syllables in the preceding utterance. Similarly, Gomez and Gerken (6) found that infants who were habituated to a set of sentences constructed from an artificial grammar (VOT-PEL-JIC; PEL-TAM-PEL-JIC) could distinguish between new sentences that were consistent with this grammar. (VOT-PEL-TAM-PEL-JIC) from new sentences that were not consistent (VOT-TAM-PEL-RUD-JIC). Such learning might reflect the acquisition of rules, but because all the test sentences were constructed with the same words as in the habituation sentences (albeit rearranged), in these test sentences it was possible to distinguish the test sentence on the basis of statistical information such as transitional probabilities (for example, in the training corpus, VOT was never followed by TAM)—without recourse to a rule.

We tested infants in three experiments in which simple statistical or counting mechanisms would not suffice to learn the rule that was generating the sequences of words. In each experiment, infants were habituated to three-word sentences constructed from an artificial language (7) and then tested on three-word sentences composed entirely of artificial words that did not appear in the habituation. The test sentences varied as to whether they were consistent or inconsistent with the grammar of the habituation sentences. Because none of the test words appeared in the habituation phase, infants could not distinguish the test sentences based on transitional probabilities, and because the test sentences were the same length and were generated by a computer, the infant could not distinguish them based on statistical properties such as number of syllables or prosody.

We tested infants with the familiarization preference procedure as adapted by Saffran et al. (1, 8, 9); if infants can abstract the underlying structure and generalize it to novel words, they should attend longer during presentation of the inconsistent items than during presentation of consistent items.

Subjects were 7-month-old infants, who were younger than those studied by Saffran et al. but still old enough to be able to distinguish words in a fluent stream of speech (8). In the first experiment, 16 infants were randomly assigned to either an "ABA" condition or an "ABB" condition. In the ABA condition, infants were familiarized with a 2-min speech sample (10) containing three repetitions of each of 16 three-word sentences that followed an ABA grammar, such as "ga ti ga" and "li na li." In condition ABB, infants were familiarized with a comparable speech sample in which all training sentences followed an ABB grammar, such as "ga ti ti" and "Ii na na" (11).

In the test phase, we presented infants with 12 sentences that consisted entirely of new words, such as "wo fe wo" or "wo fe fe" (12). Half the test trials were "consistent sentences," constructed from the same grammar as the one with which the infant was familiarized (an ABA test sentence for infants trained in the ABA condition and an ABB sentence for infants trained in the ABB condition), and half the test trials were "inconsistent sentences" that were constructed from the grammar on which the infant was not trained (13).

We found that 15 of 16 infants showed a preference for the inconsistent sentences (14), which was indicated by their looking longer at the flashing side light during presentations of those sentences (15) (Table 35.1).

Although each of the test words in experiment 1 was new, the sequence of phonetic features in the test overlapped to some extent with the sequence of phonetic features in the habituation items. For example, in the ABA condition three habituation sentences contained a word starting with a voiced consonant followed by a word starting with an unvoiced consonant. Each of these three sequences ended with a word that contained a voiced consonant. An infant who was thus expecting the sequence voiced-unvoiced-voiced would be surprised by the inconsistent tests items (each of which was voiced-unvoiced-unvoiced) but not by the consistent items (each of which was voiced-unvoiced-voiced). To rule out the possibility that infants might rely on learning sequences of particular phonetic features rather than deriving a more abstract rule, we conducted a second experiment with the same grammars as in the first experiment but with a more carefully constructed set

TABLE 35.1. Mean time spent looking in the direction of the consistent and inconsistent stimuli in each condition for experiments 1, 2, and 3, and significance tests comparing the listening times. Mean ages of the infants tested were 6 months 27 days (median, 6 months 24 days) in experiment 1, 7 months 1 day (median, 7 months) in experiment 2, and 7 months (median, 7 months 2 days) in experiment 3.

| | Mean Listening Time (s) (SE) | | Repeated Measures Analysis of Variance |
|---|---|---|---|
| Exp. | Consistent Sentences | Inconsistent Sentences | |
| 1 | 6.3 (0.65) | 9.0 (0.54) | $F(14) = 25.7$, $p < 0.001$ |
| 2 | 5.6 (0.47) | 7.35 (0.68) | $F(14) = 25.6$, $p < 0.005$ |
| 3 | 6.4 (0.38) | 8.5 (0.5) | $F(14) = 40.3$, $p < 0.001$ |

of words. In experiment 2, then, the set of phonetic features that distinguished the test words from each other did not distinguish the words that appeared in the habituation sentences (*16*). For example, the test words varied in the feature of voicing (for example, if the "A" word was +voiced, the "B" word was –voiced), whereas the habituation words did not vary on the feature of voicing (they were all +voiced). Thus, the habituation items provided no direct information about the relationship between voiced and unvoiced consonants; the same holds for each of the phonetic features that varied in the test items. As in experiment 1, 15 of 16 infants looked longer during the presentation of the inconsistent items than during the presentation of the consistent items (*17*) (Table 35.1).

Rather than encoding the entire ABA or ABB rule, the infants could have habituated to a single property that distinguishes these grammars. Strings from the ABB grammar contain immediately reduplicated elements (for example, "ti ti"), whereas strings from the ABA grammar do not. In a third experiment, we compared sentences constructed from the ABB grammar with sentences constructed from an AAB grammar (*18, 19*); because reduplication was contained in both grammars, the infants could not distinguish these grammars solely on the basis of information about reduplication (*20*). As in the first two experiments, infants (this time, 16 of 16) looked longer during presentation of the inconsistent items than during presentation of the consistent items (*21*) (Table 35.1).

Our results do not call into question the existence of statistical learning mechanisms but show that such mechanisms do not exhaust the child's repertoire of learning mechanisms. A system that was sensitive only to transitional probabilities be-

tween words could not account for any of these results, because all the words in the test sentences are novel and, hence, their transitional probabilities (with respect to the familiarization corpus) are all zero. Similarly, a system that noted discrepancies with stored sequences of words could not account for the results in any of the three experiments, because both the consistent items and the inconsistent items differ from any stored sequences of words. A system that noted discrepancies with stored sequences of phonetic features could account for the results in experiment 1 but not those in experiments 2 and 3. A system that could count the number of reduplicated elements and notice sentences that differ in the number of reduplicated elements could account for the results in experiments 1 and 2, but it could not account for infants' performance in experiment 3.

Likewise, we found in a series of simulations that the SRN is unable to distinguish the inconsistent and consistent sentences, because the network, which represents knowledge in terms of a set of connection weights, learns by altering network connection weights for each word independently (*22*). As a result, there is no generalization to novel words. Such networks can simulate knowledge of grammatical rules only by being trained on all items to which they apply; consequently, such mechanisms cannot account for how humans generalize rules to new items that do not overlap with the items that appeared in training (*23, 24*).

We propose that a system that could account for our results is one in which infants extract abstract algebra-like rules that represent relationships between placeholders (variables), such as "the first item X is the same as the third item Y," or more generally, that "item I is the same as item J." In addition to having the capacity to represent such rules, our results appear to show that infants have the ability to extract those rules rapidly from small amounts of input and to generalize those rules to novel instances. If our position is correct, then infants possess at least two distinct tools for learning about the world and attacking the problem of learning language: one device that tracks statistical relationships such as transitional probabilities and another that manipulates variables, allowing children to learn rules. Even taken together, these tools are unlikely to be sufficient for learning language, but both may be necessary prerequisites.

## REFERENCES AND NOTES

1. J. Saffran and R. Aslin, E. Newport, *Science 274,* 1926 (1996).
2. J. L. Elman, *Cogn. Sci. 14,* 179 (1990).
3. E. Bates and J. Elman, *Science 274,* 1849 (1996); M. S. Seidenberg, *ibid. 275,* 1599 (1997).
4. N. A. Chomsky, *Rules and Representations* (Columbia Univ. Press, New York, 1980); S. Pinker and A. Prince, *Cognition 28,* 73 (1988); S. Pinker, *Science 253,* 530 (1991); G. F. Marcus, U. Brinkmann, H. Clahsen, R. Wiese, and S. Pinker, *Cogn. Psychol. 29,* 186 (1995). G. F. Marcus, *The Algebraic Mind* (MIT Press, Cambridge, MA, 1999), in press.
5. R. Bijeljac-Babic, J. Bertoncini, and J. Mehler, *Dev. Psychol. 29,* 711 (1993).
6. R. L. Gomez and L.-A. Gerken, in *Boston University Conference on Language Development 21,* E. Hughes, M. Hughes, and A. Greenhill, Eds. (Cascadilla Press, Somerville, MA, 1997), p. 194.
7. We leave open the question of whether infants interpreted our materials as genuinely linguistic and thus also leave open the question of whether the mechanisms that acquire abstract rules are specific to language learning or are more generally used in many domains.
8. P. Jusczyk and R. N. Aslin, *Cogn. Psychol. 29,* 1 (1995).
9. Infants sat in a three-sided booth on the laps of their parents (parents wore headphones playing classical music so that they could not hear the stimulus materials) and listened to sounds generated off-line by a speech synthesizer. The booth had a yellow bulb on the center panel; each side panel had a red bulb. A speaker was behind each of the red bulbs. The speakers were connected to a G3 Power Macintosh computer that presented the stimuli and controlled the lights. During the familiarization phase, the yellow light flashed to draw the infant's attention to the center panel of the testing booth while the familiarization speech segment played from both speakers. After the familiarization ended, the infant was presented with test trials. At the beginning of each test trial, the central light was flashed. Once an observer (who also wore headphones playing music to mask the stimuli) indicated that the infant had fixated on the flashing light, the central light was turned off and one of the two side lights began flashing. When the observer indicated that the infant had turned toward the side light, the computer played a three-word test sentence from the speaker that was hidden behind the light, which repeated the test sentence over and over (with a 1.2- to 1.5-s pause between presentations of the test sentence) until either the infant had turned away for two continuous seconds or until 15 s had elapsed. The dependent measure was the total time that the Infant spent looking at the light associated with the speaker. Infants who became fussy prior to completion of at least four test trials were not included in the statistical analyses.
10. The first six subjects (three in each condition) were familiarized with 3-min speech samples.
11. The 16 sentences that followed an ABA pattern were "ga ti ga," "ga na ga," "ga gi ga," "ga la ga," "li na li," "li ti li," "li gi li," "li la li," "ni gi ni," "ni ti ni," "ni na ni," "ni la ni," "ta la ta," "ta ti ta," "ta na ta," and "ta gi ta." The 16 sentences that followed the pattern ABB were "ga ti ti," "ga na na," "ga gi gi," "ga la la," "li na na," "li ti ti," "li gi gi," "li la la," "ni gi gi," "ni ti ti," "ni na na," "ni la la," "ta la la," "ta ti ti," "ta na na," and "ta gi gi". Vocalizations of the words used in the above sentences were created with a speech synthesizer, which is available at www.bell-labs.com/ project/tts/voices-java.html. The vocalizations were then combined to form the sentences listed above by using a sound editor. A 250-ms pause was placed between consecutive words in each sentence. The sentences were presented in random order and separated by pauses of 1 s.
12. The 12 test trials, which were randomly ordered, included three repetitions of each of four test sentences, two following the ABB pattern ("wo fe fe" and "de ko ko") and two following the ABA pattern ("wo fe wo" and "de ko de").
13. Similar stimuli were used in a study of children's memory and attention [J. V. Goodsitt, P. A. Morse, and J. N. Ver Hoeve, *Child Dev. 55,* 903 (1984)]. That study does not, however, answer our question about rules, because it tested only how well an infant could remember target B in the context of sequences ABA versus AAB versus ABC and not whether infants familiarized with one of those sequences could distinguish it from another.
14. Results for the ABA and ABB conditions were combined, because there was no significant interaction between them; $F(1,14) = 0.15$.
15. Similar results involving transfer from one finite state grammar to another with the same structure but different words have been reported for adult subjects [A. Reber, *J. Exp. Psychol. 81,* 115 (1969)] and for 11-month-old infants (R. L. Gomez and L-A. Gerken, paper presented at the Annual Meeting of the Psychonomics Society, Philadelphia, PA, November 1997). These researchers, whose focus was not on rule learning, did not include the phonetic control we introduce in experiments 2 and 3.
16. The 16 habituation sentences that followed the ABA pattern were "le di le," "le je le," "le li le," "le we le," "wi di wi," "wi je wi," "wi li wi," "wi we wi," "ji di ji," "ji je ji," "ji li ji," "ji we ji," "de di de," "de je de," "de li de," "de we de"; ABB items were constructed with the same vocabulary. The test trials were "ba po ba," "ko ga ko" (consistent with ABA), "ba po po," and "ko ga ga" (consistent with ABB).

17. Results for the ABA and ABB conditions were combined, because there was no significant interaction between them, $F(1,14) = 1.95$.

18. In principle, an infant who paid attention only to the final two syllables of each sentence could distinguish the AAB grammar from the ABB grammar purely on the basis of reduplication, but they could not have succeeded in the experiment of Saffran et al. (1).

19. We thank an anonymous reviewer for suggesting this comparison. The vocabulary used to construct the test and familiarization items was the same as in experiment 2; hence, as in experiment 2, the phonetic features that distinguished the test words from each other did not vary in the habituation items.

20. The ability to extend reduplication to novel words appears to depend on an algebraic rule. To recognize that an item is reduplicated, a system must have the ability to store the first element and compare the second element to the first; the storage, retrieval, and inferential mechanisms that are involved may appear simple but are outside the scope of most neural network models of language and cognition. Conversely, adults are strongly sensitive to the presence of reduplication and its location in phonological constituents [I. Berent and J. Shimron, *Cognition 64*, 39 (1997)]. For further discussion, see references cited in (22).

21. Results for the AAB and ABB conditions were combined, because there was no significant interaction between them, $F(1,14) = 0.002$.

22. The sort of generalizations that such models can draw are dictated by the choice of input representations. If input nodes correspond to words, the model cannot generalize the abstract pattern to new words; if the input nodes correspond to phonetic features, the model cannot generalize to words containing new phonetic features [G. F. Marcus, *Cognition 66*, 153 (1998); *Cogn. Psychol.*, in press]. An appropriately configured SRN that represented each word by a set of nodes for phonetic features, if it were trained that a voiced consonant followed by an unvoiced consonant was always followed by a voiced consonant, could use memorized sequences of features as a basis to distinguish the test items in experiment 1. However, such a model could not account for the results of experiments 2 and 3, because in those experiments the feature sequences that the network learned about in the familiarization phase would not distinguish the test items.

23. An enhanced version of the SRN [Z. Dienes, G. T. M. Altmann, and S. J. Gao, in *Neural Computation and Psychology*, L. S. Smith and P. J. B. Hancock, Eds. (Springer-Verlag, New York, 1995)] aims to model how speakers who are trained on one artificial language are able to learn a second artificial language that has the same structure more rapidly than a second artificial language that has a different structure. This model would not be able to account for our data, however, because the model relies on being supplied with attested examples of sentences that are acceptable in the second artificial language, whereas our infants succeeded in the absence of such information.

24. The problem is not with neural networks per se but with the kinds of network architectures that are currently popular. These networks eschew explicit representations of variables and relationships between variables; in contrast, some less widely discussed neural networks with a very different architecture do incorporate such machinery and thus might form the basis for learning mechanisms that could account for our data [J. E. Hummel and K. J. Holyoak, *Psychol. Rev. 104*, 427 (1997)]. Our goal is not to deny the importance of neural networks but rather to try to characterize what properties the right sort of neural network architecture must have.

25. Supported in part by an Amherst College Faculty Research Grant to P.M.V. We thank L. Bonatti, M. Brent, S. Carey, J. Dalalakis, P. Gordon, B. Partee, V. Valian, and Z. Zvolenszky for helpful discussion, and P. Marcus and F. Scherer for their assistance in construction of the test apparatus. We also thank Bell Labs for making available to the public the speech synthesizer that we used to create our stimuli. Some subjects in experiment 1 were tested at Amherst College; all other subjects were tested at New York University. The parents of all participants gave informed consent.

PART VIII

# Language Development

## Discussion Questions

1. Berko's results suggest that there are morphological rules that are applied to root forms of words. Her arguments are based on the application of these rules to novel nonword forms. Is it possible that children could use analogies to generate different forms of words? Why would this be a particularly important finding for the "language is special" argument?
2. Genie did acquire some aspects of language just fine but failed to acquire some grammatical rules. What is so special about this aspect of the linguistic system? Given the complexity that we discussed in simple pattern recognition section, why might this system be intact in Genie?
3. Critically evaluate the debate between Saffran et al. and Marcus et al. What are advantages and disadvantages of both perspectives? Take a position and defend it in light of the arguments and data presented in the paper. What precisely is special about the type of learning that 8-month-old children produce?
4. Consider the possibility that there is an innate system that is especially suited for using grammatical rules in infants. Such a system needs to ultimately be implemented in a brain that consists of highly interconnected sets of neurons. How might one envisage such a network that might capture such "rules"?

## Suggested Readings

Bates and Goodman (1997, On the inseparability of grammar and the lexicon: Evidence from acquisition, aphasia and real-time processing, *Language and Cognitive Processes, 12*, 507–584) provide a remarkably comprehensive review of the relations between grammar, the lexicon, acquisition, and specific types of aphasia.

Berko-Gleason (1985, *The Development of Language.* Columbus, OH: Merrill) and MacWhinney (1987, *Mechanisms of Language Acquisition.* Hillsdale, NJ: Erlbaum) have compiled excellent edited volumes that provide overviews of different perspectives on language acquisition.

Kuhl et al. (1992, Kuhl, P. K, Williams, K. A., Lacerda, F., Stevens, K. N., & Lindblom, B. Linguistic experience alters phonetic perception in infants by 6 months of age. *Science, 255*, 606–608) provide a very interesting study of how early experience influences phonetic boundaries across different languages.

P. Marler provides a very thought-provoking piece on the relation between birdsong acquisition and human language acquisition (1970, Birdsong and speech development: Could there be parallels? *American Scientist, 58*, 669–673).

Schlaggar et al. (2002, B. L. Schlaggar, T. T. Brown, H. L. Lugar, K. M. Visscher, F. M. Miezin, & S. E. Petersen, Functional neuroanatomical differences between adults and school-age children in the processing of single words. *Science*, 296, 1476–1479) present a very intriguing neuroimaging study investigating the development of word processing in children learning to read and adults.

Pinker provides a remarkably comprehensive and interesting overview of language processing in *The Language Instinct*. (New York: HarperCollins,1994).

Skinner (1957, *Verbal Behavior*. New York: Appleton-Century Crofts) and Chomsky's (1959, A review of Skinner's Verbal Behavior. *Language, 35*, 26–58) review are exceptional reads and are excellent in specifying many of the current fundamental issues in language acquisition.

PART IX

# Language

# Introduction to Part IX:
# Language

The study of Language has profoundly influenced many of the developments in Cognitive Psychology. For example, as one can see from the readings in each of the sections in this book, linguistic stimuli have been used across virtually all domains of study. Similarly, when pinpointing the primary events of the cognitive science revolution, one of the top candidates is Skinner and Chomsky's historic debate about the nature of language (in the late 1950s). In this light, it is not surprising that it has been difficult to identify a single set of "classic" papers for this section. Thus, instead of identifying "the" critical set of papers, we decided to highlight important papers that take different approaches to developing an understanding of human language.

Although virtually all humans are expert users of language, it has been surprisingly difficult to develop paradigms that explore natural language use. This probably has been most problematic in the area of speech production. How can one manipulate what one produces in speech without making the response so artificial that it limits any extension to natural speech production? Because of this limitation, Fromkin and others have taken the approach of studying natural language production and analyzing naturally-occurring errors for insights into the system. Of course, if the errors were random events, one would not expect much progress in this area. However, it is clear that the errors are not random, and hence the types of errors produced have provided rich insights into the language production system. For example, consider the error of an individual producing *reek long race* instead of *weeklong race*. This relatively common error is called an anticipatory error; the beginning of an upcoming word replaces the beginning of an earlier word as if it were anticipated. What can one learn from such an error? First, such errors suggest that word production is not based on a unitary program for each word. Rather, there are bundles of representations or programs corresponding to the phonetic segments involved in producing a word. If words were not composed of phonetic segments, then how could one anticipate the /r/ in *race* to replace the /w/ in *week*? Of course, this finding also converges with the importance of phonetic segments that were hypothesized in speech perception and described in the earlier section on pattern recognition (see Eimas & Corbit, 1973). This simple error also suggests that the phonetic segments must be held in a buffer and simultaneously activated. If the speaker activated the phonetic segments for only one word at a time, then how could one explain the finding that such errors occur across words? These segments also appear to be tagged by position, that is, the first phoneme is likely to be anticipated by the first phoneme in another word, as opposed to a second or third phoneme.

Fromkin reports many interesting inferences drawn from the regularities of speech error data. For example, one finds that errors in speech production typically keep the original stress pattern, thereby indicating that stress appears to be laid down relatively early in production. Another interesting observation is that speakers often adjust indefinite articles relatively late in the speech production process. For example, one speaker produced *A kice cream cone* instead of *An ice cream cone*, suggesting that the indefinite article (a) was adjusted because of the upcoming /k/ sound, which in fact is an error. Fromkin's paper demonstrates how naturalistic methods can yield considerable insight into the levels of analysis in speech production, and the real time constraints on how these different levels must be implemented. There has been considerable progress made in how humans produce speech, and much of this work has been driven by the databases and sophisticated analyses provided by Fromkin and others.

Let us now consider another problem for the language user, how to determine the meaning of a (produced) word. The classic paper by Swinney (1979) is an example of an experimental approach to answering one question about language comprehension. Of interest is how the language user handles the frequent presence of ambiguous structures in the language. Although ambiguity occurs at many levels in language processing, Swinney focused primarily on the lexical level, for example, the word *bug* can refer to an insect or a type of listening device. When listeners encounter an ambiguous utterance such as *bug,* do they compute all meanings automatically (as in the Posner & Snyder, 1975, manner) or is only one interpretation selected based on the available context? If we attempted to answer this question using naturalistic observation, we might be tempted to conclude that the language user never computes the alternative interpretations. However, a different conclusion was reached using Swinney's experimental approach. In the critical conditions, subjects heard sentences that contained an ambiguous word (e.g., *bug*), which was disambiguated prior to its presentation. Immediately after hearing the ambiguous word, subjects made visual word/nonword decisions about different types of words: contextually related (e.g., *ant*), contextually inappropriate (e.g., *spy*), or unrelated (e.g., *sew*). Compared to the unrelated words, subjects made faster word/nonword decisions about both the contextually related and the contextually inappropriate words. That is, immediately after presentation of the ambiguous word, both of its meanings were equally activated, even when the sentence had biased the subject toward just one of the two interpretations.

The Swinney finding was particularly important because it suggested that some aspects of the language processing system, and the general cognitive system, may be modularized (see Fodor, 1983). That is, systems may be dedicated to a specific type of processing, and this processing can occur independent of processing in other systems. Thus, all interpretations of ambiguous words are accessed automatically, and it is not until later that context serves to select the most appropriate interpretation. Interestingly, the failure of people to notice most of the ambiguity in language suggests that this selection process occurs at a non-conscious (automatic) level of analysis. Although this paper clearly had a large influence on the field, it is also the case that there appear to be strong constraints on this finding (see Tabossi & Sbisa, 2001, for a recent review).

Geschwind also considers the idea of separate language modules or subsystems. In her paper, she develops a neural model of language processing that specifies the relations between various modules. The primary databases in the Geschwind paper are the distinct types of aphasias that have been identified in the literature. She begins with a review of the classic studies by Broca and Wernicke, who over a century ago described individuals with unique patterns of language loss. Individuals with Broca's aphasia produce halting speech but have relatively good comprehension, whereas individuals with Wernicke's aphasia have relatively fluent speech but with limited content and rather severe comprehension deficits. Broca and Wernicke's insight was that these two types of behavior, upon autopsy, appeared to reflect disruptions in distinct brain areas. Based on observations such as these, Geschwind follows Wernicke's lead and develops a framework in which auditorily presented words are first processed in the primary auditory cortex and then transmitted to Wernicke's area. This information is then carried along nerve fibers, called the arcuate fasciculus, to Broca's area, where the articulatory programs are presumably held for speech production. These signals are then sent to the motor areas for speech production.

Such a framework not only allows interpretation of language function, it also makes some interesting predictions. For example, if the lesion is to the tract of fibers connecting Wernicke's area and Broca's area, then the individual should produce relatively fluent speech and also intact comprehension. However, if the individual is asked to repeat auditorily presented words, which would involve the connection between the two areas, performance should be severely impaired—which is precisely what happens in a syndrome called conduction aphasia. The beauty of Geschwind's model is that it makes clear predictions about the behavioral consequences of specific brain lesions. Geschwind even extends this work to understanding distinct types of aphasias in languages that have unique writing systems, such as the Japanese Kanji and Kana system. Although far from a complete understanding of the neural substrates of language processing, the Geschwind paper provides consid-erable historical impetus to better understanding the brain/behavior relations in higher-level pro-cesses such as language.

We conclude with the Robertson et al. paper for two reasons. First, the paper uses functional magnetic resonance imaging (fMRI) techniques; this allows the extension of Geschwind's goal of developing a model of how the brain processes language from studies of aphasics to studies of healthy individuals. Second, the researchers were studying the difficult topic of how language users build a coherent mental representation that interrelates ideas across sentences.

Of course, language users do much more than produce and comprehend single words. Rather, they keep track of and relate ideas across sen-tences. *Discourse mapping* is the term for mentally interrelating ideas that repeat across sentences (Gernsbacher, 1990). In part, the construction of a single mental representation depends upon linguistic cues such as definite articles. For example, the definite article *the* signals that there is

repeated reference to the same object in the discourse (see Robertson et al.'s Table 1 for a nice example). Robertson et al. compared the neural activity underlying comprehension of strings of sentences that were identical except for the very first word of each sentence. In one set, each sentence began with the definite article *the*, whereas sentences in the second set began with the indefinite articles *a* and *an*. One might not expect such a simple manipulation to have much of an effect. However, the psycholinguistic literature indicates that the definite article *the* is important in the mapping processes, which in turn influence comprehension and reading performance. The intriguing new result in the Robertson et al. paper is that there was also a corresponding change in neural activity due to this simple manipulation. Specifically, there was more right frontal activation for the sentences beginning with the word *the,* compared to those sentences beginning with the indefinite articles *a* or *an*. Given the emphasis on the left hemisphere for language dominance, this might be viewed as a bit surprising. However, Robertson et al. suggest that right-frontal activation is consistent with argu-ments that this area is important for episodic retrieval operations and in the internal direction of attention. Both of these processes may be critical for the mapping process in comprehension. Although it is clear that the insights from neuroimaging techniques regarding language processing are still in their infancy, these results are intriguing with respect to potentially helping us understand the nature of the processes involved in comprehension.

The papers in this section introduce you to four methods for studying language: naturalistic observation, behavioral experiments, patient case studies, and neuroimaging experiments. Across the papers, you will also sample a number of different problems facing the language user: speech production, language comprehension, and integration of these into a working language system. However, given the rich literature in this area and the many facets to language, the reader must keep in mind that these papers barely scratch the surface of this fascinating topic.

## REFERENCES

Chomsky, N. (1959). A review of Skinner's "Verbal behavior." *Language, 35,* 26–58.

Eimas, P. D., & Corbit, J. (1973). Selective adaptation of linguistic feature detectors. *Cognitive Psychology, 4,* 99–109.

Fodor, J. A. (1983). *The modularity of mind: An essay on faculty psychology.* Cambridge, MA: MIT Press.

Gernsbacher, M. A. (1990). *Language comprehension as structure building.* Hillsdale, NJ: Erlbaum.

Geschwind, N. (1972). Language and brain. *Scientific American, 226,* 76–83.

Fromkin, V. A. (1971). The non-anomalous nature of anomalous utterances. *Language, 47,* 27–52.

Posner, M. I., & Snyder, C. R. R. (1975). Attention and cognitive control. In R. L. Solso (Ed.), *Information processing and cognition: The Loyola Symposium* (pp. 55–85), Hillsdale, NJ: Erlbaum.

Robertson, D. A., Gernsbacher, M. A., Guidotti, S. J., Robertson, R. R. W., Irwin, W., Mock, B. J., & Campan, M. E. (2000). Functional neuroanatomy of the cognitive process of mapping during discourse comprehension. *Psychological Science, 11,* 255–260.

Skinner, B. F. (1957). *Verbal behavior.* New York: Appleton-Century Crofts.

Swinney, D. A. (1979). Lexical access during sentence comprehension: (Re)consideration of some context effects. *Journal of Verbal Learning and Verbal Behavior, 18,* 645–659.

Tabossi, P., & Sbisa, S. (2001). Methodological issues in the study of lexical ambiguity resolution. In D. Gorfein (Ed.), *On the consequences of meaning selection* (pp. 11–26). Washington, DC: American Psychological Association Press.

# The Non-Anomalous Nature of Anomalous Utterances

Victoria A. Fromkin • University of California, Los Angeles

An analysis of speech errors provides evidence for the psychological reality of theoretical linguistic concepts such as distinctive features, morpheme structure constraints, abstract underlying forms, phonological rules, and syntactic and semantic features. Furthermore, such errors reveal that linguistic performance is highly rule-governed, and that in many cases it is grammatical rules which constrain or monitor actual speech production. While a model of linguistic competence is independent of temporal constraints, a model of linguistic performance must provide information as to the sequencing of events in real time. To explain the occurrence of particular kinds of errors, a specific ordering of rules is posited, which ordering may or may not coincide with the organization of a grammar.

**1.** In current linguistic and psychological literature a sizable number of articles have appeared dealing with 'slips of the tongue' and errors in speech (see References). This interest is not, however, of recent origin. Historically, speech errors have been a source of humor as well as of serious study. In the sixteenth century, Rabelais utilized such errors to display his pungent wit; and in the *Compleat Gentleman* (1622), Henry Peacham refers to a 'melancholy Gentleman' who says 'Sir, I must goe dye a beggar' instead of the intended 'I must goe buy a dagger'.[1] 'Spoonerisms' were uttered before and after the long happy life of the Reverend William A. Spooner, who is credited as the originator of a particular kind of 'lapse'. In fact, if one assumes that the origin of man and the origin of language and speech were simultaneous, then a further assumption follows-that 'spoonerisms' began with Adam.

Speech-error data have been studied as a source of historical linguistic change (Sturtevant, 1917, 1947; Jesperson, 1922; MacKay, 1970d); as a means for understanding the actual mechanisms of the speech production process (Lashley, 1951; Boomer & Laver, 1968; MacKay, 1969, 1970a; Hockett, 1967; Fromkin, 1968; Nooteboom, 1969); and to gain insight into psychological repressions (Freud, 1924). Speech errors have also been investigated in attempts to show the 'reality' of phonological units and rules, and the relationship between linguistic 'competence' and 'performance' (Fromkin, 1968; Green, 1969). Freud, in his *Psychopathology of Everyday Life*, questioned 'whether the mechanisms of this (speech) disturbance cannot also suggest the probable laws of the formation of speech' ([1924] 1938: 71). It is to that general question that this paper is directed.

# Data

**2.** Every book and article which refers to speech errors is replete with examples. The most extensive collection, an estimated 8,800 errors, appears in Meringer & Mayer, 1895 and in Meringer, 1908. A rigorous statistical analysis of these errors is contained in a number of articles by MacKay (1969, 1970a, b, d). This corpus of German errors is augmented by errors in spoken Dutch noted by Cohen (1966), by more than a hundred errors in English tape-recorded by Boomer & Laver, and by other errors cited in various articles listed in the References.

In this paper, while taking into consideration the extensive published data, I will primarily make use of a collection of speech errors collected by myself over the past three years. More than six hundred errors were collected by myself, or by colleagues and friends who reported in detail errors which they either made or heard others produce.[2] For each error which I myself noted, I recorded the name of the speaker and the date, and where possible (particularly in the case of blends) the speaker was questioned as to what he had been thinking of saying. This is scanty information indeed when compared with the data recorded by Meringer for each error in speech which he heard. In true Teutonic style, he also included the birthdate of the speaker, the educational background, the time of day, the state of health and tiredness, the rate of speech etc. Sturtevant reports that Meringer thus became the most unpopular man at the University of Vienna; and since 'no correlations between any of the above factors and the nature of the error were found' (MacKay, 1970d), my own data-collecting omitted such information, in order to protect my personal reputation while maintaining the scientific accuracy of the data. It is important to note, however, that my method of data-collecting has a built-in fault, since many errors occur when it is just not feasible to note them, and unquestionably many errors made are not 'heard' at all. The data-collection method used by Boomer & Laver, in which they analysed tapes of conference discussions, psychiatric interviews etc. for the errors which they contained, is free of this fault. Fortunately, however, there were no sharp discrepancies between the kinds of errors recorded by them and by myself. There are certain kinds of errors included in my corpus which did not seem to occur among the hundred or so errors recorded by them; but I only included such errors when heard and attested by other listeners, or when the speaker himself caught the error and corrected it. I felt this precaution necessary to mitigate my own 'desire' to hear certain kinds of errors.

The aim of this paper, then, is not to treat the errors in the corpus as a random sample of all errors made, but to attempt an explanation for the errors which were recorded.

# Discreteness of Performance Units

**3.** Sturtevant defines a 'lapse' or a 'speech error' as 'an unintentional linguistic innovation' (1947:38). Boomer & Laver's definition echoes Sturtevant's: 'A slip of the tongue . . . is an involuntary deviation in performance from the speaker's current phonological, grammatical or lexical intention' (4). Because such 'unintentional' or 'involuntary' errors may result in utterances which provoke laughter, speakers and writers have also used them intentionally. Such conscious 'creations' will not be considered here, although one finds that these 'intentional errors' usually follow the same 'rules' as do non-intentional errors.[3]

Meringer was mainly interested in classifying the kinds of errors which occurred in spontaneous speech; and since his time, one finds in the literature different classification schemes and varying terminology. In Boomer & Laver's classification scheme, speech errors show a 'MISORDERING of units in the string, OMISSION of a unit, or REPLACEMENT of a unit' (5). According to them, the units so misordered, omitted, or replaced may be segments, morphemes, or words. Nooteboom (1969) classifies segmental errors as 'phonemic speech errors' and 'non-phonemic errors', including in the latter classification 'meaningless combination of phonemes', morphemes (including affixes and root morphemes), and whole words. Nooteboom dismisses the possibility that 'distinctive features' behave 'more or less (like) independent elements just as phonemes do', but Hockett implies the independence of such features (915).

Further classification is not the concern of this paper. The interest is rather in how particular errors shed light on the underlying units of linguistic performance, and on the production of speech. What is apparent, in the analyses and conclusions of all linguists and psychologists dealing with errors in speech, is that, despite the semi-continuous nature of the speech signal, there are discrete units at some level of PERFORMANCE which can be substituted, omitted, transposed, or added. It should be stated here that, were we to find no evidence in actual speech production or perception for such discrete units, this would be insufficient cause to eliminate discrete units in phonology or syntax. The fact that it is impossible to describe the grammars of languages without such units is itself grounds for postulating them in a theory of grammar. But when one finds it similarly impossible to explain speech production (which must include errors made) without discrete performance units, this is further substantiation of the psychological reality of such discrete units. In other words, behavioral data of the kind described here may not be necessary to validate hypotheses about linguistic competence, but they certainly are sufficient for such verification.

**3.1.** THE REALITY OF THE SEGMENT OR PHONE. By far the largest percentage of speech errors of all kinds show substitution, transposition (metathesis), omission, or addition of segments of the size of a phone. These occur both within words and across word boundaries, the latter case being most frequent in our corpus. Most of these segmental errors are errors of anticipation, which is in keeping with the conclusions reached in the literature. Simple anticipations result in a substitution of one sound in anticipation of a sound which occurs later in the utterance, with no other substitutions occurring. The following examples illustrate such errors:

(1) a. John dropped his cup of coffee → ... cuff ... coffee
   b. also share → alsho share [ɔlšo šer]
   c. such observation → sub — such ...
   d. delayed auditory feedback → ... audif — auditory ...
   e. week long race → reek long race
   f. M-U values [ɛm juw væljuwz] → [ɛm vjuw] values
   g. the third and surviving brother → the sird and — the bird — the third ...

Examples 1a–e illustrate the substitution of one segment for another. In 1f, however, anticipating the [v], a segment is added where there is no seg-

ment in the intended word. And in 1g the error is compounded: first the s is anticipated, and then, in an attempt to correct the error, a later b is anticipated.

Perseverance errors are also not uncommon, as exemplified in the following:

(2) a. I'm not allowing any proliferation of nodes → ... proliperation
   b. John gave the boy → ... gave the goy
   c. Spanish speaking people → ... speaping people
   d. irreplaceable → irrepraceable
   e. Chomsky and Halle → Chomsky and Challe

It should be noted that one cannot unambiguously classify the error in 2c, since it could be considered an error of either perseverance or anticipation. As shown by MacKay (1970d), the probability that errors occur when there are repeated phonemes is much greater than chance, and in this case the alliterative structure of the utterance seems to add to the substitution which occurs. As will be seen, this is true of many of the errors to be discussed.

Classic Spoonerisms reveal a more complex error, in that there is a transposition or metathesis of two segments. One possible interpretation is that such errors involve an anticipation plus a perseverance, but it seems more likely that what occurs is a simple (or not so simple) switch in the linear ordering of the sound intended. Such errors, attributed to Spooner, made him famous, as in his purported admonition to an undergraduate student: 'You have hissed all my mystery lectures. I saw you fight a liar in the back quad; in fact, you have tasted a whole worm' (Robbins).

Whether or not the notorious Reverend or his students sat up nights inventing such errors, attested errors reveal the same kind of metathesis, as is shown in these examples:

(3) a. keep a tape → teep a cape
   b. the zipper is narrow → the nipper is zarrow
   c. should serve → [sʊd šərv]
   d. for far more → for mar fore
   e. with this ring I do wed → ... wing ... red
   f. I'm going to die young but I'll die less young → ... yes lung
   g. in the past few weeks → ... fast pew [pjuw] weeks.

In a number of cases, where the speaker catches his error, we cannot be sure whether a mere anticipation and substitution is involved, or whether a transposition is caught before completed, as in the following examples:

(4) a. Kathy can type → tathy — Kathy can type
  b. correct class of → collect — correct . . .
  c. shown in the present slide → shown in the pleasant — I mean present slide
  d. greater pressure → [greyšr̩] — greater pressure
  e. delayed auditory feedback → delayed audif — auditory feedback

All the above examples reflect errors involving consonants. Vowels are also anticipated, metathesized, etc., as shown below:

(5) a. ad hoc [æd hak] → odd hack [ad hæk]
  b. Wang's bibliography → Wing's babliography
  c. turn the corner → torn the kerner [tɔrn] . . . [kərnr̩]
  d. feet moving → [fuwt mijving]
  e. fish and tackle → fash and tickle [fæš] . . . [tɪkl̩]
  f. the new Sony → the no suny [now suwnij]
  g. place the stress → [plɛs] the [strejs]
  h. dissertation topic [dɪsr̩tejšn̩ tapɪk] → [dɪsr̩tašn̩ tejpɪk]
  i. available for exploitation → avoilable for . . .
  j. prevailing temperature → [prejvijlɪŋ] . . .
  k. the waterfall [wɔtr̩fɔl] isn't working → . . . isn't [wɔkɪŋ]

**3.2.** CLUSTERS AS SEQUENCES OF DISCRETE PHONES OR SEGMENTS. The above examples show errors of transposition, substitution, omission, and deletion of individual segments, which may be either vowels or consonants. The error may be either of anticipation (i.e., the interfering segment follows the error), of perseveration (i.e., the interfering segment precedes the error), or of transposition (i.e., the order of sound segments is changed). Further justification for assuming that individual segments are units in speech performance is suggested by the fact that, in many errors where the intended utterance included consonant clusters, only one segment of the cluster is involved:

(6) a. fish grotto → frish gotto
  b. fresh clear water → flesh queer water
  c. split pea soup → plit spea soup
  d. brake fluid → blake fruid
  e. no strings attached → no strings attrached
  f. at the Broadway stores the prices are → . . . spores the prices are
  g. in a split second → . . . slit second
  h. that's a sticky point → . . . spicky point
  i. a car with a stick shift → . . . [štɪk sɪft][4]

As seen in 6a, the intended *fish grotto* has been pronounced *frish gotto* [friš gaDo] (the [D] represents a voiced flap), the addition of an [r] in the first word producing an initial cluster instead of the intended single segment. The substitution of the single [g] for the intended cluster [gr] may be explained by postulating that the cluster [gr] can be 'broken down' into individual segments, [g] followed by [r]. This being so, the individual segments can themselves be transposed. Similarly the error cited in 6b can be explained as an anticipation of the [1] in *clear*, causing the replacement of the intended [fr] in *fresh* by [fl]. The substitution of [kw] in [kwir], for the intended [klir], may again be explained by an anticipation of the [w] in *water*. It is of course true that 6b may be simply an error in word substitution, since *flesh* is a word, as is *queer*. Such an explanation will not, however, explain a number of the other examples given; i.e., [friš] is not a word, nor is [gaDo], [plɪt], [spij], [blejk], [fruwɪd], [ətrætšt], [spɪkij] etc. If we are seeking an explanation for such errors, it seems highly likely that we have here again single segmental errors, the difference being that the segments involved occur in consonant clusters.

The omission of elements or segments in clusters also justifies the conclusion that clusters are not unitary units of performance, as in these examples:

(7) a. two hundred drugs → two hundred [dʌgz]
  b. property that excludes [ɛkskluwdz] → property that [ekskudz]

Errors involving final clusters show that they are also sequences of individual segments, as in the following examples:

(8) a. tab stops → tap [stabz]
  b. weeks and months → [wɪŋks] and . . .

c. great risk → great rist [rɪst]
d. french fried potatoes → frend fried potatoes
e. there's a pest in every class → . . . pet . . .
f. art of the fugue → arg of the [fjuwt]

That some errors reveal the transposition of whole clusters is NOT evidence for the fact that such clusters are indissoluble units. Such errors do, of course, occur very often, as in these examples:

(9) a. at the bottom of the pay scale → at the bottom of the [skej peyl]
b. little island in Brittany → brittle island in litany
c. sweater drying → dreater swying [drɛDr̩ swajɪŋ]
d. throat cutting → coat thrutting

Such movement of whole clusters is but further evidence that the 'syllable' is not a single indissoluble unit in speech production, but is itself composed of a sequence of segments. This is attested by the fact that a CV or a VC sequence which is part of a syllable can be involved in speech errors:

(10) a. pussy cat → cassy put
b. foolish argument → farlish . . .
c. a heap of junk → a hunk of jeep
d. stress and pitch → piss and stretch
e. lost and found → [fawst] and [lɔnd]

Example 10a shows the monosyllable [kæt] as a sequence of three segments [k+æ+t], with the first two segments transposed with the first two segments of [p+ʊ+s+ɪj]. In 10d, the transposition which occurs can easily be explained as

[s t r ɛ s . . p ɪ t š ]

Another explanation is that the word *piss* is substituted for *stress* (the reasons for such a substitution I leave to Freud), and *stretch* for *pitch*; or instead, that the speaker started to say *pitch and stress* and the error is one of final consonant substitutions. There are, however, numerous examples which show errors involving CV or VC sequences which cannot be so explained.

**3.3.** AFFRICATES. The assumption that clusters on a performance level should be interpreted as se-

quences of consonants raises the question of affricates. It is interesting to note that while [str], [pl], [kr], [bl], [fr] etc., as well as final clusters, reveal the splitting of clusters into segments, not a single example in my own data, or the English examples cited by others, shows a splitting of [tš] or [dž] into sequences of stop plus fricative:

(11) a. pinch hit → pinch hitch, but not *[pint hiš]
b. pretty chilly → chitty pilly [tšɪtij pɪlij]
c. entire chapter → enchire [ɛntšajr] . . .
d. further surgery → furger [fərdžr̩] surgery
e. Ray Jackendoff → Jay Rackendoff
f. last cigarette Tim had in June → . . . Jim had in tune
g. in St. Louis John said → in St. Jouis John said

We do not find cases like 'St. [duəs]', or 'St. [žuis]'. One may assume that the old phonemic controversy, as to whether such affricates should be considered one segment or two, is solved for linguistic performance, and that affricates should be considered single segments in the production of speech, for speakers of English.

**3.4.** COMPLEX VOWELS. One finds a similar situation with diphthongs. If [ey] or [uw] or [æw] are interpreted as a succession of V + y, or V + w, one could expect the non-glide section of the diphthong to be subject to substitution without a change of the particular glide. In other words, one would anticipate that *feet moving* might be articulated as [fʊyt mɪwving]. The examples in 12 show that where vowel + glide or [r] is involved, the error always includes the entire diphthong, or the vowel with its 'r-quality':

(12) a. first and goal to go → first and girl to go
b. took part in the first → took pirt [pərt] in the farst
c. dissertation topic → [dɪsr̩tašn̩ tejpɪk]
d. we're going to have to fight very hard → we're going to have to fart very [fayd]
e. feet moving → [fuwt mijving]
f. available for exploitation → avoilable for . . .
g. soup is served → serp is [suwvd]

These examples are, of course, taken only from English, and the conclusions regarding affricates and complex vowel nuclei have meaning only for English.

It is a fact that one never finds an error which results in a 'non-permissible' sequence of, for example, front vowel plus back glide (e.g., [ɪw], [ɛw]), or of back vowel plus front glide (e.g., [ʊj]); but this may have an alternative explanation, which is discussed below. One example above, (5i) 'available [əvejləbl̩] → avoilable [əvɔjləbl̩]', could be interpreted as a switch only in the non-glide portion of the vowel nucleus, as could all examples of errors which involve only tense front vowels or tense back vowels. The errors involving both front and back diphthongs, along with those involving a vowel followed by r, cannot be explained in this way, and seem to suggest that the complex vowels are single units, or that errors which 'violate' phonological constraints are 'corrected' after the substitution occurs. (See below for discussion on this point.)

**3.5.** THE STATUS OF [ŋ] IN ENGLISH. Sapir (1925) and Chomsky & Halle (1968) present arguments for deriving [ŋ] from an underlying sequence of /ng/. Their phonological analysis is justified in itself. It is of interest, however, that behavioral data, found in speech errors, indicate that, at one level of performance, [ŋ] may derive from the sequence of [n + g]—or, because of the constraints which change [n] to [ŋ] before a velar, the sequence of [ŋ + g]:

(13) a. sing for the man [sɪŋ . . . mæn] → [sɪg . . . mæŋ]
b. Chuck Young [tšʌk jʌŋ] → [tšʌŋk jʌg]
c. shilling [šɪlɪŋ] → shingle [šɪŋgl̩]
d. cut the string → [kʌnt] the [strɪg]

A possible explanation for the [g]'s in the actual utterances is to postulate that, prior to the execution of the articulatory commands, the following transposition of segments has occurred:

a. [sɪŋg . . . mæn] → [sɪØg . . . mæŋ]
b. [tšʌk jʌŋg] → [tšʌŋk jʌØg]
c. [šɪlɪŋg] → [šɪŋgəl]
d. [kʌt] . . . [strɪŋg] → [kʌnt] . . . [strɪØg]

If this highly speculative hypothesis can be demonstrated by other experimental data, the postulated phonological rule for English, g → Ø / n__#, may be validated, in that when the nasal is deleted, the [g] emerges.

The data can, however, be given an alternative explanation. Example 13a may show persistence of the velar articulation from [sɪŋ], producing [mæŋ], and a simple loss of the nasality of the final velar in sing. In 13b, since in English a vowel is nasalized preceding a nasal consonant, we may have an example of a transposition of oral vowel with nasal vowel, and a concomitant non-nasalization of the final nasal:

$$[\text{tšʌk jʌ̃ŋ}] \rightarrow [\text{tšʌ̃k jʌg}]$$

Example 13c may be similarly disposed of, but 13d cannot be so easily explained. The only explanation, other than that which postulates an underlying abstract /strɪng/, is to suggest that only the nasality of the vowel is anticipated—which, as we shall see below, is certainly possible. The examples are given, however, since they permit speculation as to the reality of the g in utterances containing [ŋ].

**3.6.** THE REALITY OF PHONETIC FEATURES. Research on the perception of speech has shown that units smaller than the segment, i.e., properties or features of speech sounds, are 'perceived' and confused (Miller & Nicely, 1955; Wickelgren, 1965a,b, 1966). Thirty-two cases in the present corpus can be explained by postulating that certain properties or features also constitute independent elements in the production of speech. The fact that one finds no errors in which consonants and vowels are involved (i.e., vowels do not switch with consonants, etc.) may be explained by suggesting that true vowels ([+vocalic, −consonantal]) constitute one class of segments in a performance model, as opposed to another class composed of true consonants, glides, and liquids ([+consonantal] or [−vocalic]), but that the segments which are members of these two non-intersecting sets cannot be further analysed into independent features.

As we shall see below, there are other explanations for why consonants and vowels do not 'interfere' with each other (e.g., are not transposed, anticipated, etc.). The data, however, suggest that while a HIERARCHY probably exists, other features are independently involved in speech errors:

(14) a. spell mother → smell [bʌðr]
b. pity the new teacher → mity the due teacher—I mean—nity the poor teacher—no—pity the new teacher

c. bang the nail → mang the mail
d. Did you hear what Malcolm said → did
   you hear what balcolm — Malcolm said?
e. Cedars of Lebanon → Cedars of
   Lemadon

These examples show a change in the value of the feature [nasality], acting in many cases independent of other features. In 14a-b, the [–nasal] of [p] becomes [+nasal] (i.e., [p] → [m]). If the [m] of *mother* remained [+nasal], this example could be dismissed as merely an anticipation of the segment [m]. However, since [m] → [b], or since the value of the nasality feature in the [m] of *mother* switches from [+nasal] to [–nasal], all other features remaining the same, a better explanation for the error is that what occurred was a single feature switch. Otherwise, no explanation is provided for the [m] → [b] substitution.

Example 14b illustrates the same phenomenon. [p], which is [–nasal], becomes [m], which is [+nasal], other features remaining intact; and [n] is changed from [+nasal] to [d], which is [–nasal].

Example 14c shows a switch of two features. [b], which is [–nasal, +anterior, –coronal], switches to [+nasal]; and [n] switches from [+coronal] to [–coronal]. Even if one wished to explain the [m] of *mail* as a perseveration of the [m] which has occurred in [mæŋ], the substitution [b] → [m] would be left unexplained. The anticipation of the lowered velum which accompanies the following [n] is a possible explanation.

Example 14d represents a simple substitution, in the first segment of *Malcolm*, from [+nasal] to [–nasal].

The following examples represent a change of value for the feature [voiced]:

(15) a. What does the course consist of → what
       does the gorse consist of
   b. referendum → reverendum
   c. clear blue sky → glear plue sky
   d. reveal → refeel
   e. define → devine
   f. big and fat → pig and vat

In these examples, only the value of the feature [voice] is changed, all other features remaining intact.

Other errors which appear to involve properties or features of whole sounds, rather than whole segments, are as follows:

(16) a. pedestrian → tebestrian ([p] → [t] and
       [d] → [b])
   b. scatterbrain    [skæDr̩brejn]    →
      [spæDr̩grejn]
   c. spaghetti → skabetti
   d. Death Valley [dɛθ vælij] → [fɛθ ðælij]

In 16a, only the value of the feature [coronal]— i.e., only the PLACE of articulation—is changed. It is of course possible to argue that this is rather to be interpreted as segmental transposition, with [p] →[t] in anticipation of the subsequent [t]. But what of [d] → [b]? If we explain [p] → [t] as a switch of labial ([–coronal]) to alveolar ([+coronal]), then [d] → [b] is seen as the result of a change from alveolar ([+coronal]) to labial ([–coronal]).

Similar cases are seen in 16b–c. Again, one can suggest a segment transposition, particularly since the voicing feature of the [g] is neutralized after an [s]. But then how does one explain the [g] → [b] switch? If a mere segment transposition was involved, we would expect [sgəpɛtij] in 16c.

A more complex error is seen in 16d: the switch from [d] → [f] seems to be an anticipation of the subsequent [v]. The coronality of the [d] seems to influence the switch from [v] to [d], with the [+voice] and [+continuant] features remaining.

It is certainly true that errors which involve a substitution of features are rare, compared to errors involving larger units. They nevertheless require some explanation, and one can only conclude that some features appear to be independently extractable as performance units. Many segmental errors may also be examples of such feature errors; but since they can also be accounted for as errors of larger units, we are unable to conclude that individual features are independently involved in all cases. However, the following examples show that feature errors may be obscured in this way:

(17) a. extracted → extrapted ([k] → [p], or
       [+back, –ant] → [–back, +ant])
   b. goofing off → gooping off ([f] → [p], or
      [+cont] → [–cont])
   c. call the girl → gall the curl ([k] → [g], or
      [–voice] → [+voice])
   d. documentation → documendation ([t] →
      [d], or [–voice] → [+voice])

In fact, most of the segmental errors can be so interpreted. In the transposition of *brake fluid* to *brake fruid*, one might suggest that what is involved is a transposition of the feature [lateral] or [anterior] rather than transposition of the two segments. If segmental errors are analysed as feature errors, we will find that many distinctive features other than those cited above do indeed represent a reality, in speech performance.

This suggestion is supported by the findings of Nooteboom: 'In significantly more cases than is to be expected in a random distribution the two elements involved in a substitution error are phonetically similar to one another' (1969: 121). MacKay found that 'most pairs of reversed consonants differed in only one distinctive feature (56 percent) and very few (2 percent) differed in all four distinctive features' (1969).[5] This is in contradiction to the conclusion of Boomer & Laver 'that articulatory similarity is not an important determinant' in speech errors, although they do note two exceptions: 'sequences of voiceless fricatives seemed to encourage mistakes of place of articulation, and (b) alveolar consonants showed a slight tendency to interact' (p. 8, and fn.) But they were examining errors to see if any particular features were involved more often than any others. Their data were not analysed for the degree of similarity of the segments involved. It is interesting to note that an analysis of jargon aphasia errors also shows that most errors involve no more than a confusion of one distinctive feature (Green). Whether or not further analysis of substitution errors confirms or contradicts the MacKay-Nooteboom conclusions regarding the 'similarity' of substituted segments, the only conclusion one can draw from the examples of feature switching given above is that at least some of the proposed distinctive features are independent behavioral units.

But an examination of the errors, whether analysed as errors of whole segments or of independent features, definitely shows a hierarchy and interdependence of certain features. Thus, while there are errors showing just addition or subtraction of nasality, one does not find a 'nasality' switch which results in a voiceless nasal. At least for English, nasality and voicing seem to be interdependent features. This again prevents the occurrence of an 'inadmissible' sound in English.

The claim that certain features are independent units, which must be postulated as such in a model of performance, seems to contradict the earlier hypothesis that segments (or feature complexes) are 'real' performance units. Actually, there is no contradiction. Features cannot exist except as properties of larger segments (just as segments, as we shall see, exist as parts of larger units). In other words, in the generation of speech, there is a hierarchy of different-sized units. A linear ordering of the segments (discussed below) occurs, and this linear ordering may be disrupted. Since the discrete segments are specified by actual physiological properties (or neural commands), some of these properties or features may also get disordered, i.e., 'attached' to other segments. But the claim that all distinctive features (as proposed by Chomsky & Halle) are identical with phonetic properties that can in principle be independently controlled in speech is not borne out by the data of speech errors. Unless 'controllable in speech' is defined in some new strange and abstract way, it would appear that whatever the needs for certain separate phonological features may be, in actual speech performance only certain of these phonological features have their counterpart as phonetic features.[6] Thus, while the two features [consonantal] and [vocalic] very nicely divide segments into four separate classes, needed for phonology, the idea that such features have any independent phonetic reality seems highly improbable. To suggest that a substitution of a [p] for a [k] involves the PHONETIC substitution of [–anterior] for [+anterior], [–high] for [+high], [–back] for [+back], etc., is saying no more, on an articulatory level, than stating that there is a change from a velar articulation to a bilabial articulation. The motor commands to the muscles, specifying a bilabial or velar articulation, specify the part of the tongue to be raised, where it is to be raised, etc. In other words, on a phonetic level a complex of the features [–anterior, +high, +back] is indissolubly a velar place of articulation, and one does not expect to find (and indeed, one doesn't find) a simple switch of the feature [+coronal], for example, without other phonetic effects. In the example 'pedestrian → tebestrian', the error can be specified as a switch in the feature of coronality, but it is obvious that this feature is not 'independently controlled'. What I am suggesting is that segments as feature complexes do exist; that some of these features or properties can be independently controlled, such as nasality, voicing, place of articulation (if considered as a single multi-valued feature) etc.; but that some properties are highly dependent on the existence of other properties of the segment. It is thus that [delayed release] does not seem to be independent of affricates, and one can only suppose that, on the neuro-physiological level, there is some command for a stop closure combined with delayed release, which command cannot be split into two segments. That is, the command for the initial and final consonants of *church* at one level of the generation of speech is a command for just such an affricate. On the other hand, when one says *did you* as [dɪdžuw], in rapid speech the affrication occurs by a different process, i.e., by automatic and mechanical movements of the vocal organs. However, the results at the level of muscle movements are identical.

**3.7.** The reality of the syllabic unit. While it seems plausible to assume, as was done above, that units smaller than syllables (segments and features) have independent status as behavioral units, this does not negate the possibility that syllable-size units are also units of speech performance. In fact, all the evidence from tongue slips supports such a view. Nooteboom (1969:119) suggests that since 'the distance between origin and target (or the substituted segments) does not generally exceed seven syllables, (and) since we know that the short memory span of man may contain about seven units . . . we might interpret our findings as an argument for the syllable to be a unit in the phonemic programming system'. Nooteboom (1969), MacKay (1969, 1970a), and Fromkin (1968) all support the statement that 'segmental slips obey a structural law with regard to syllable-place; that is, initial segments in the origin syllable replace initial segments in the target syllable, nuclear replace nuclear, and final replace final' (Boomer & Laver, 7). Furthermore, Nooteboom points out that 'when the second consonantal element of a CVC form is immediately followed by an initial vowel of the next word . . . final consonantal elements do not tend to become prevocalic' (1969). In other words, in a string CVC#VC . . . CV#CVC, one never finds in errors a substitution of the final consonant of the first word for the initial consonant of the final word. My own English data support the analysis of Nooteboom's Dutch data, and seem to contradict the position taken by Kozhevnikov & Chistovich (1965), where the suggestion is made that in the production of Russian utterances a CVC#VC sequence is reorganized into articulatory programs for each CV sequence. This does not seem to be the case in English or Dutch. The evidence for the syllable suggested by Nooteboom

can, of course, also be used as evidence for the reality of the unit 'word', which will be discussed below.

MacKay (1969) found that the 'syllabic position of reversed consonants was almost invariably identical'. The only examples in my data which do not support this finding are two examples of metathesis occurring within words of two sequential segments:

(18) a. whisper → whipser
     b. ask → aks

It has been suggested (Peter Ladefoged, personal communication) that we should note the rarity of such examples, and the fact that all such errors seem to involve the sibilant *s*. In a number of perception tests, the hiss (such as occurs with [s]) is often 'misplaced'; i.e., it is difficult for subjects to judge where the noise occurs in an utterance. This perceptual difficulty seems to be reflected in production errors of the above kind.

All other examples of errors occurring within the same word show sequential ordering of segments within syllables, as in these examples (a hyphen represents a syllable division):

(19) a. harp-si-chord → carp-si-hord
     b. ma-ga-zine → ma-za-gine
     c. phi-lo-so-phy → phi-so-lo-phy
     d. e-le-phant → e-phe-lant
     e. a-ni-mal → a-mi-nal
     f. spe-ci-fy → spe-fi-cy
     g. Ra-be-lais → Ra-le-bais
     h. pan-cakes → can-pakes
     i. neural mo-de-ling → neural mo-le-ding

Because of the co-articulation effects of segments within a syllable, it is impossible to omit the syllable as a unit of articulation, even if one were to ignore the evidence of the fixed order in the reversal, anticipation, or perseveration of segments (Fromkin, 1968).

There are of course many errors which involve the substitution, omission, replacement, addition etc. of one or more whole syllables, which further substantiates the claim that syllabic units are real performance units:

(20) a. Morton and Broadbent point → Morton and Broadpoint

b. revealed the generalization → reeled the generalization
c. tremendously → tremenly
d. which I analyse as the following → which I analyse as the follow
e. butterfly and caterpillar → butterpillar and catterfly
f. opacity and specificity → opacity and specifity
g. we want to reveal all the facts → we want to feel all . . .

In many of the above, several factors are at work. Some of these examples are what are commonly called 'blends', as are the following:

(21) a. Did you bring your clarinola (a blend of clarinet plus viola)
b. switch and changed → swinged [swindžd]
c. importance of [ədžɔjsn̩t] rules (a blend of 'adjacent' plus 'adjoining')
d. my data consists [monlij] — [mejstlij] (a blend of 'mainly' plus 'mostly')

## The Reality of Phonological and Morphophonemic Constraints

**4.** The speech of jargon aphasics, as well as errors made by non-pathological speakers, reveal that 'normal' slips of the tongue and aphasic jargon utterances are constrained by the linguistic system. One does not find 'phonemes' (or more correctly, 'phones') which are not found in regular utterances. For example, an English speaker does not substitute a rounded front vowel in anticipation of a rounded back vowel, nor a lateral click for a lateral liquid. Furthermore, only permitted segmental sequences occur. Wells (1951) stated this as his 'First law' of tongue slips: 'A slip of the tongue is practically always a phonetically possible noise.' It is obvious that Wells meant a 'phonetically possible noise' in a particular language. As I have stated in an earlier article (Fromkin, 1968): 'The segments constituting each syllable must have sequential ordering, so that only initial consonants, vowels, and final consonants may interchange, IF AND ONLY IF THE TRANSPOSITIONS ARE IN KEEPING WITH THE PHONOLOGICAL RULES OF THE LANGUAGE' (64). This 'First Rule' appears to explain a 'Spoonerism' attributed to Spooner:

sphinx in moonlight → minx in spoonlight.

What is of interest here is the transformation of the [sf] in *sphinx* to [sp] when the cluster is transposed with the [m]. While [sf] does occur in words like *sphincter*, *sphere*, and *sphinx*, such words (and the dozen or other 'technical' words listed in Webster's Third) are 'exceptions' to the regular morpheme-structure rule in English which permits only voiceless stop obstruents after an initial *s*. [sfuwn-light] would thus not be a permitted sequence, and consequently [f] → [p].

All the examples already cited include only permitted English sequences. Further examples will support the 'reality' of such constraints:

(22) a. play the victor → flay the pictor
b. tab stops → tap [stabz]
c. plant the seeds [sijdz] → plan the seats [sijts]
d. bloody students [blʌdij stuwdənts] → [blʌdənt stuwdijz]

There are two ways of interpreting the error shown in 22a. One might suggest that it is simply the manner of articulation (stop vs. fricative) which is switched. If such an interpretation is given, one must also add that, when the [v] is changed to a stop, the place of articulation changes from labiodental to bilabial. Another possible explanation is that the two segments switch (p ↔ v), and that since [vl] is not a permitted sequence in English, the [v] is devoiced. This suggests that these phonological constraints, when learned, become behavioral constraints which occur AFTER the segmental transpositions occur.

A similar example is shown by 22b, in which the final consonant (or just the voicing feature) of the first word is transposed with the penultimate consonant of the second word (or the final stem consonant, prior to the plural morpheme addition). Again, the intended [ps] is changed not to [bs] but to [bz], in keeping with the phonological (and morphological) constraints of English.

Examples 22b–d represent another phenomenon. In these errors, the original syntactic structure of the phrases remains intact, in that the intended plural nouns occurring as the last words of the phrases remain as words with plural endings, despite the errors which occur; but the phonetic realization of the plural morpheme changes, as well as the preceding segments. Thus [stabz] and [sijts] can be explained simply as due to phonological or phonetic constraints, since [bs] and [tz] never occur as final clusters; but the error in 22d is more complex. [js] can occur in English as in *Reese* [rijs], *mice* [majs], *feast* [fijst], *face* [fejs] etc. But [ij + s] cannot occur when the final sibilant represents the plural morpheme. One can then suggest that the phonetic representation of the plural morpheme is specified prior to the automatic phonetic specifications which serve as the units for articulatory commands. If this were not the case, one could not understand the change of the [s] to [z] in [stuwdijz].

Further examples of the reality of morphophonemic rules are evidenced in errors which include the alternation of the non-specific determiner *a/an*:

(23) a. a current argument [ə kʌrn̩t argjumənt] → an arrent curgument [ən arn̩t kʌrgjumənt]
b. an eating marathon → a meeting arathon
c. a history of an ideology → an istory of a hideology
d. an ice cream cone → a kice ream cone

The changes *a* → *an* and *an* → *a* indicate that, in the generation of speech, the segmental errors or transpositions must take place PRIOR to the actual neural muscular commands, since there are possible sound sequences of [ə] plus vowel, as in *America is* [ətz].

Such errors show the separation of morphophonemic rules and phonological rules. In other words, it is not a phonological rule which changes the *a* to *an*, since there is no general restriction on vowel sequences like those of *America is, Rosa and I*. Thus the ordering of events must be as follows: (1) segmental errors, (2) morphophonemic adjustments, (3) P-rules.

The reality of the P-rules is attested by many of the errors cited above, e.g., (8a) [tæb staps] → [tæp stabz]. The transposition of the /b/ and /p/ must have occurred prior to the rule which constrains final clusters to be voiced or voiceless. In 8b, [wijks ən mʌnθs] → [wɪŋks . . . ] can only be explained by the following sequence: /wīks/ → /wīnks/ → [wɪŋks]. The tense /ī/ is not diphthongized because it occurs before a nasal, and the /n/ is made homorganic with the following velar stop by a general rule.

## Stress

5. MacKay, Boomer & Laver, and Nooteboom (1969) all investigate the influence of stress on errors in speech. Boomer & Laver conclude that 'The origin syllable and the target syllable of a slip are metrically similar, in that both are salient (stressed) or both are weak (unstressed), with salient-salient pairings predominating' (7). Nooteboom agrees with this conclusion, stating that 'In significantly more cases than is to be expected in a random distribution the elements involved in a speech error belong to stressed syllables' (1969). He disagrees, however, with Boomer & Laver's finding that 'Slips involve the tonic (primary stressed) word, either as origin or as target, with tonic origins predominating.' But from Nooteboom's own data, the disagreement seems to be the result of a misinterpretation of the difference between primary stress (tonic word) and salient stress. Differences between English and Dutch may also be relevant. MacKay finds that transpositions occurring within words appear in syllables with different stress, while in between-word reversals his findings corroborate those of Boomer & Laver.

What seems to be of greater interest is that, when vowels or syllables or parts of syllables or whole words are substituted or transposed, there is no change in the stress pattern or contour of the sentence. Boomer & Laver cite an example in which a speaker, instead of saying 'how bád things were', said 'how thíngs bad were'. It is evident that there was no transposition of the stress, despite the transposition of the words. The following examples show the same phenomenon (an acute accent [´] represents primary stress, as does '1' above the vowel; a grave accent [`] represents non-primary stress—secondary or tertiary; a '2' above the vowel represents secondary stress, and a '3' tertiary stress).

(24) a. $\overset{3}{\text{hammer}}$ and $\overset{1}{\text{sickle}}$ → $\overset{3}{\text{sickle}}$ and $\overset{1}{\text{hammer}}$
b. $\overset{3}{\text{peoples}}$ $\overset{1}{\text{park}}$ → [$\overset{3}{\text{park}}$l̩z $\overset{1}{\text{pijp}}$]
c. $\overset{2}{\text{verge}}$ of a $\overset{3}{\text{nervous}}$ $\overset{1}{\text{breakdown}}$ → $\overset{2}{\text{nerve}}$ of a $\overset{3}{\text{vergeous}}$ $\overset{1}{\text{breakdown}}$
d. he's been $\overset{2}{\text{around}}$ a $\overset{3}{\text{long}}$ $\overset{1}{\text{time}}$ → he's been $\overset{2}{\text{long}}$ $\overset{3}{\text{around}}$ $\overset{1}{\text{time}}$
e. a $\overset{2}{\text{computer}}$ in our $\overset{3}{\text{own}}$ $\overset{1}{\text{laboratory}}$ → a $\overset{2}{\text{laboratory}}$ in our $\overset{3}{\text{own}}$ $\overset{1}{\text{computer}}$

f. exámine the eýes of the hórse → exámine the hórse of the eýes

g. bróke the crýstal on my wátch → bróke the whistle on my crótch

h. in the theóry of phonólogy → in the phonólogy of theóry

Examples 24e and 24h show that, while the word position of primary stress in the phrase is not transposed, the stressed syllable of the word in isolation is the syllable which receives the sentence stress. That is, if the primary stress is to be placed on 'laboratory', it is placed on the first syllable; and if it is to be placed on 'computer', it is placed on the second syllable.

Thus it seems that two aspects of stress must be accounted for: first, the word stress moves with the word itself (i.e., the syllable of the word which receives main stress in isolation also receives the primary stress when the word is moved); second, the stress contour of the phrase is fixed by the syntactic structure of the phrase itself, and must be generated independently of the word order in the utterance.

One may then suggest that the word stress is stored as part of the articulatory specifications of the stored unit 'word', but that the sentence or phrase stress and over-all intonation contour is generated separately, as part of what Boomer & Laver call the 'tone-group'. I would therefore agree with them that 'The pivotal role of the tonic word in slips suggests that its phonological, syntactic and semantic prominence is matched by an analogous neuro-physiological prominence, coded in the brain as a part of the articulatory programme' (8), and further that 'the tone group is handled in the central nervous system as a unitary behavioral act, and the neural correlates of the separate elements are assembled and partially activated, or 'primed' before the performance of the utterance begins' (9). However, in the construction of a model of linguistic performance, it is necessary to specify the nature, i.e., the syntactic structure, of this tone group, for the 'priming' of the 'tonic' syllable depends on the syntactic structure of the utterance.

The suggestion that the stress placement on words is fixed in the lexicon does not mean that one cannot, or should not, attempt to generalize stress assignment rules in the phonology of English. In fact there may be some evidence from speech errors that not only in a grammar of competence, but also in the actual stored lexicon, words (or perhaps formatives) are stored in a more abstract form than by their actual articulatory specifications. There are speech errors which display a movement of stress, and in certain cases a change in the vowel qualities depending on where the stress is placed:

(25) a. This can viewed altérnately—altérnatively—no—álternately

b. símilarly → [similǽrəlij]

c. homogéneous → [homàdžəníjəs]

d. in favor of [həmádžə - homodžíjniəs]

e. syllabíf—syllábification [sɪləbíf—sɪlǽbəfəkejšn]

f. opácity and specifícity → opácity and spécifity

One may speculate (perhaps wildly) that in the generation of speech a word is selected, stress is assigned, and then the articulatory program is assembled to produce the sounds, reducing unstressed vowels etc. By this hypothesis, the changes [ər] → [ǽr] in 25b, [o] → [a] and [ij] → [ə] in 25c, are 'explained' by the suggestion that the words are stored as stems plus endings, and with their unreduced vowel qualities. While such a suggestion cannot be entirely ruled out, alternative explanations can be provided for all the examples in 25 above, which, from the performance viewpoint, seem more intuitively satisfying. In 25b, for example, the speaker might have begun to say 'similarity', or in Carroll's terms have had 'similarly' and 'similarity' in mind at the same time, just as he clearly had both 'alternately' and 'alternatively' in mind in 25a. It should be clear, without laboring the point, that all the above examples of errors involving stress can be similarly explained. Before one can seriously put forth the hypothesis that the stress of words is generated by phonological rules, and not stored as part of the specification of the word (in one's performance lexicon), a crucial experiment must be found.

## The Reality of Syntactic Word Classes and Syntactic Phrases

**6.** Nooteboom (1969:130) found that 'a mistakenly selected word always or nearly always belongs to the same word class as the intended word [indicating] that the grammatical structure of the phrase under construction imposes imperative restrictions on the selection of words.' In my own corpus of errors, a similar conclusion can be drawn. When words are switched, nouns transpose with nouns, verbs with verbs, etc.:

(26) a. a computer in our own laboratory → a laboratory in our own computer
   b. that no English manufacturer could name these projects — products
   c. naturalness of rules → nationalness of rules
   d. bottom of page five → bottle of page five
   e. I have some additional proposals to hand out → hang out
   f. book of sixes → book of twos
   g. chamber music → chamber maid
   h. a speaker doesn't go through all the worlds — rules he has in his head
   i. while the present — pressure indicates
   j. How come if you're a Scorpio you don't read — wear oriental spice?

The fact that in many cases the substituted word has some phonetic (or phonological) similarity to the target word was also noted by Nooteboom. This suggests that our stored lexicon is ordered in some dictionary-like fashion, and any crossword puzzle addict can confirm this fact. But there must be a complicated addressing system in the computer-like brain mechanism, since each listing must be specified under semantic features, phonological features, number of syllable syntactic features etc. Thus, in 26h, the phonetic similarity of [wərldz] and [rules] is based on two identical segments—which, however, do not have the same sequenced ordering in the words. Of course, this may be a chance error.

The reality of the word as a unit is evidenced by the above. Furthermore, speech errors show that derivationally complex items may be stored as combinations of separate formatives, i.e., stems and affixes. Example 26c, above, *natural +ness* → *national +ness*, attests this, as do the following examples:

(27) a. infinitive clauses → infinity clauses
   b. grouping → groupment
   c. intervening node → intervenient — intervening node

d. and so in conclusion → and so in concludement

Example 27d suggests again that *conclusion* may be stored as *conclude+ion* with rules for *d* → [ž]. It is, however, possible and highly probable that we have here a blend of *concluding* and *conclusion*.

Hockett's analysis would relegate such affix substitutions to what he calls 'analogy'. Unfortunately, this label does not explain how the process takes place. One possible explanation is there are rules of word formation, plus a vocabulary of stems and a vocabulary of affixes which, as the above examples show, can be manipulated to create neologisms which do not occur in the language, such as *groupment*. MacKay's finding (unpublished) that affixes are involved with a probability greater than chance, among syllable errors, would support the hypothesis that affixes do form a separate sub-set of the lexicon.

The constancy of the syntactic structure, and the reality of performance units larger than words, morphemes, stems, etc., is seen in the following:

(28) a. I wouldn't buy macadamia nuts for the kids → I wouldn't buy kids for the macadamia nuts
   b. A fall in pitch occurs at the end of the sentence → an end of the sentence occurs at the fall in pitch
   c. He's a far better man than anyone here → he's a farther man than anyone better here

The displacement of *better* in 28c also results in an adjectival ending added to the adverb *far*, maintaining a correct and intended syntactic structure.

In structures such as $_{NP}[ _{ADJ}[macadamia] _{N}[nuts] ]$ (or, this may be a compound noun), $_{N}[ _{N}[fall] _{PP}[in pitch] ]$, and $_{N}[ _{N}[end] _{PP}[ _{PREP}[of] _{NP}[ _{DET}[the] _{N}[sentence] ] ]$, syntactic phrases can interchange as entire units; similar word classes can also interchange. Furthermore, when (as in 28c) an intended adverb + adjective + noun is involved in an error, a shift of the adjective to another place in the sentence seems simultaneously to change the remaining adverb *far* to an adjective, thus maintaining the over-all structure. Such facts seem to point to the reality of syntactic phrases and of syntactic features of words.

## Semantic Features

**7.** Blends occur in which non-existent words are produced as the result of composites of two words with similar semantic features. These are indeed common errors, not only invented by Lewis Carroll, but occurring naturally. In the examples given in 29 the speaker was questioned as to what he had in mind, or as to what he thought the reason for the blend was. The subject's answers are given in parentheses:

(29) a. My data consists [mownlij]—[mejstlij] . . . (mainly/mostly)
   b. I swindged [swɪndžd] . . . (switch/changed)
   c. It's a lot of [ba]—[brʌðl̩] (bother/trouble)
   d. She's a real [swɪp] chick (swinging/hip)
   e. it's a [spajrətɪv] (spirant/fricative)
   f. a tennis [æθlər] (player/athlete)

Such errors seem to support Carroll's assumptions. A speaker has in mind some meaning which he wishes to convey. In selecting words, it appears that he is matching semantic features. Where there are a number of alternative possibilities, rather than making an immediate selection, he brings them both into a buffer storage compartment, with their phonological specifications. Either a selection occurs at this point, or the words are blended, resulting in the above kind of errors.

The literature and my own data attest the fact that, besides the phonological similarity in substituted words, errors often involve semantic features in common, or substitution of antonyms, i.e., words having the same features with opposite values:

(30) a. I really like to — hate to get up in the morning
   b. It's at the bottom — I mean — top of the stack of books
   c. This room is too damn hot — cold
   d. the oral — written part of the exam

Nooteboom presents a number of examples which seem 'to involve a semantic switch from the space to the time dimension' (1967:14) as in the following:

(31) a. the two contemporary, er — sorry, adjacent buildings

   b. during the apparatus, er — behind the apparatus
   c. the singular, sorry, the present time

Evidence from aphasia studies also show that substituted words often fall into the same semantic class, as in cases where patients will read *tree* for *flower*, *night* for *dark*, *spoon* for *fork*, *liberty* for *democracy* etc. (Marshall & Newcombe, 1966; Luria & Vinogradova, 1959; Jakobson, 1966). Such errors provide important evidence as to the storage of vocabulary and the generation of speech.

## Implications of Speech Errors for a Model of Linguistic Performance

**8.1.** THE LEXICON. When one learns a language, he learns among other things a vocabulary. Judging both from errors of speech and from speakers' ability to form new words by adding derivational affixes to stems (e.g., 'He's a real computerish type') and by inflecting newly coined words in keeping with the rules of the language (e.g., 22d, [stuwdijz]), it seems plausible to assume that the stored lexicon consists of stems and affixes, as well as idioms, compounds, whole words etc. Given the higher than chance probability that prefixes and suffixes are involved in syllable errors (McKay, unpublished), one can further assume that, even if words are stored with their affixes, the stem and affix have a separate status. Thus it is not unlikely that *grouping* is stored as *group + ing*, which permits a substitution of *ment* for the affix *ing*. The fact that one does not find stems substituting for or transposing with affixes further justifies their separate status.

Since phonological or phonetic specifications, semantic features, and syntactic word-class features all play a role in the speech errors that occur, it is obvious that vocabulary items must be stored with such features indicated. But we cannot simply assume that there is one dictionary-like storage starting with all words beginning with A and ending with all words beginning with Z, with other features given. Semantic errors show that words are selected to convey certain meanings as specified by their semantic features. And for literate speakers the listing must also specify the orthography, to account for the ability of people to play 'geography', a game in which one must name a country, river, city etc. beginning with the same LETTER with which the previous word ended: thus, *Passaic* ends with the letter *c*, pronounced [k], and the next player can offer *Charleston*, which begins with *c*, pronounced [tš]. The relationship between orthography and sound must be accounted for. Crossword puzzles, double-crostics, and the 'tip of the tongue' phenomenon (Brown & McNeil, 1966) also attest this fact. For example, it is often the case that in trying to remember someone's name, forgotten at the moment, a speaker will say, 'I know it begins with a C.' The name may be *Cohen*, which begins with a C pronounced [k]. And of course a game like 'geography' is further evidence for the storage of words in semantic classes.

One may then suggest that the vocabulary is stored in a thesaurus-like lattice structure. It is possible to conceive of this network as a listing of all the stems and affixes in some fixed phonological order, each one with all of its feature specifications, and each one with a particular address. The separate semantic section of this lexicon may then be divided into semantic classes, with semantic features under which are listed, not the particular vocabulary item, but the addresses of those items which satisfy the features indicated. One might suggest also that the listings under the semantic headings are grouped under syntactic headings such as [+noun], [+verb] etc., to account for the proper grammatical selection in the generation of utterances.

Since the 'tip of the tongue' phenomenon suggests that speakers recall the number of syllables—the metrical beat of the word—a further division under the full phonological listing is suggested. In other words, it is not impossible to assume that all monosyllables beginning with the same phonological segment constitute one block, followed by disyllables, etc.

The error cited in 30a might then occur in the following way: the speaker wishes to say (at least on a conscious level—we leave the unconscious motivations to be explained by others) *I really hate to get up in the morning*. At the point in the generation of the utterance prior to the selection of the words, in the 'slot' representing *hate*, the features [+verb, –desire . . . ] occur, and an address for a word is sought from the semantic class which includes [±desire]. But either because of unconscious wishes or due to a random error, the ad-

dress for a verb with the feature [+desire] rather than one specified as [–desire] is selected, and the item at that address called forth with its accompanying phonological features turns out as [lajk] rather than [hejt].

The complexity of the stored lexicon is enormous, and it is obvious that there are too many lacunae in our knowledge to suggest anything more than the kinds of sub-parts or components it must contain. I have suggested an 'indirect-addressing' system above with nothing to justify this except a vague appeal to storage simplicity. It seems plausible to assume, however, that any model of a lexicon must include the following sub-parts:

(a) A complete list of formatives with all features specified, i.e., phonological, orthographic, syntactic, and semantic.
(b) A subdivision of the phonological listings according to number of syllables. This is necessitated by the fact that speakers can remember the number of syllables of a word without remembering the phonological shape of the syllables. It is also suggested by the fact that one can get a subject to produce a list of one-, two-, or three-syllable words.
(c) A reverse dictionary sub-component, to account for the ability of speakers to produce a list of words all ending in a particular sound or letter.
(d) A sub-component of phonologically grouped final syllables, to account for the ability of speakers to form rhymes.
(e) Formatives grouped according to syntactic categories, to account for the errors noted above, and the ability of speakers to list nouns, or verbs, or adverbs on command, as well as the more important ability to form grammatical sentences.
(f) Formatives grouped according to hierarchical sets of semantic classes.
(g) Words listed alphabetically by orthographic spelling.

Furthermore, it seems plausible to assume that all these components must be intricately linked in a complicated network.

This highly speculative, oversimplified model of the lexicon is suggested as a first approximation to what must be a most complicated storage mechanism. What seems certain, however, is that any model of the lexicon must account for the observed types of errors, which require the specification of various kinds of properties which we have called phonological, syntactic, and semantic features; no lexicon consisting of a single listing of items can explain what occurs.

**8.2.** THE GENERATION OF UTTERANCES. It seems quite evident from all the examples of speech errors cited above that, in the production of speech, it is not true that 'anything goes,' or that speech performance obeys no rules, or that the errors are totally random and unexplainable (see discussion of this in Fromkin, 1968). While we may not be able to explain as yet the exact mechanisms involved in speech errors, the errors made are not only highly constrained, but provide information about speech performance which non-deviant speech obscures. In other words, if we had no record of errors in which consonant clusters are split into segments, we would not be able to justify the assumption that clusters in performance are strings of individual discrete segments.

Any model of speech performance must therefore account for the kinds of errors which do occur. Such a model must account for the following:

(a) that features, segments, syllables constitute units in the production of a speech utterance;

(b) that segments are ordered within a syllable, and that only segments similarly ordered are involved in the same error;

(c) that 'root morphemes may be interchanged but root morphemes and an affix cannot take each other's places' (Nooteboom, 1967:16), or that words of the same syntactic or morphological class usually interchange with each other;

(d) that intonation contours (including the placement of primary stress) remain fixed, and are generated separately from the individual word stresses;

(e) that morphological constraints and phonetic or phonological constraints must occur at different times in the production of an utterance;

(f) that non-permissible phones or phonetic sequences do not occur;

(g) that errors may be semantic in nature, as in the case of blends or word-substitutions involving similar semantic features; and

(h) that the similarity of the phonological form of words appears to play a role in word substitutions.

To account for such phenomena we may suggest the following (over-simplified) order in the actual generation of an utterance:

STAGE 1. A 'meaning' to be conveyed is generated.

STAGE 2. The 'idea' or 'meaning' is structured syntactically, with semantic features associated with parts of the syntactic structure. For example, if a speaker wishes to convey the fact that 'a ball' rather than 'a bat' was thrown by a boy, the utterance *A ball was thrown* or alternately *He threw a báll* is structured at this stage. If he uses the second structure, part of the features specified for the final nouns must include [+emphasis] together with the features selected for 'ball,' i.e., [–animate, –human, +count, +round, +used in games etc.] This suggests that the STRUCTURE itself is put into buffer storage prior to actual articulation of the utterance; this would account for the switching of noun for noun, verb for verb etc., when such transpositions occur.

STAGE 3. The output of Stage 2 is thus a syntactic structure with semantic and syntactic features specified for the word slots. In order to explain the fact that 'the tone group is handled in the central nervous system as a unitary behavioural act' (Boomer & Laver, 9), one can suggest that the intonation contour, with the placement of primary stress, occurs at this stage. Since a transposition of words in the utterance will cause a transfer of primary stress to the main stressed syllable of the word in a given position, one can posit that only the position of the primary stress is indicated at this stage, and not the particular syllable. That is, the generation of the sentence intonation contour must occur prior to the selection of the words themselves.

STAGE 4. We now have in the buffer a syntactic phrase with semantic features indicated, and with sentence stress assigned. A lexicon look-up now occurs; the semantic class sub-section of the lexicon is first consulted, with features being matched, and the direction is obtained to go to a certain address in the over-all vocabulary. The item in the specified address is then selected, this word being specified as to its phonological segments, which are identified and ordered into syllabic units. At this stage in the process, errors resulting in a choice of a 'wrong' word may occur. Such errors may involve the matching of values of semantic

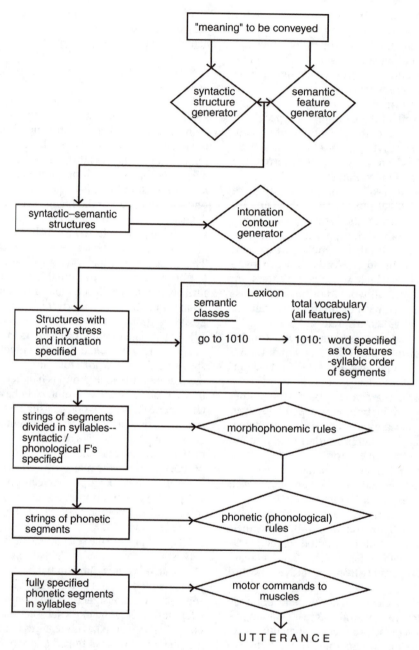

**FIGURE 36.1** ■ Utterance generator.

features, resulting in a wrong address being specified. Or the correct address may be specified, but a different address substituted which is 'in the vicinity' of the intended address. Thus, if the intended word is *like* and the produced word is *hate*, the error occurs in the selection of the wrong address in the semantic component of the lexicon. But if the intended word is *pressure* and the produced word is *present*, the correct address is obtained, but the wrong address selected, given that *pressure* and *present* have addresses in the same section of the vocabulary. This would be due to the phonological similarity of their first three segments. This process thus results in a string of phonological segments, each segment specified by certain features or properties and also specified as to syllabic order, with the syntactic bracketing remaining intact. But it is at this stage, when the string of phonological segments is put into the buffer, that a mis-ordering of segments may occur. In other words, as the segments are 'sent' into the short-term memory buffer, segment 1 of syllable 1 may be substituted for segment 1 of syllable 4. I am not concerned at this stage with an explanation of why and how this occurs, but with the fact that it can occur at this stage without disturbing the syllabic ordering. It is also here that whole syllables or parts of syllables may get transposed or misplaced. These errors must occur before Stage 5, which is where the morphophonemic rules or constraints take over.

STAGE 5. The morphophonemic constraints of the language at this stage change, if necessary, or perhaps 'spell out', the phonological shapes of morphemes. The segmental errors must occur before this stage to account for the alternations of *a*/*an* and *s*/*z* of the plural.

We have now reached the stage where automatic phonetic and phonological rules take over, converting the sequences of segments into actual neuro-motor commands to the muscles in the articulation of the utterance.

The above stages may be diagrammed as shown in Figure 36.1. It must be emphasized that the various 'black-boxes' are highly schematic, and what actually occurs in them is outside the concern of this paper. Rather, the attempt is to show a possible ordering of events in the production of an utterance which can account for non-deviant utterances, as well as for utterances containing errors in speech.[7]

## NOTES

1. Robbins (1966) suggests that the earliest literary example is found in Rabelais, in the following: 'Il n'y a point d'enchantement. Chascun de vous l'a veu. Je y suis *maistre passé*. A brum, a brum, je suis *prestre Macé*.' The contrived error of transposing the *m* and *p* in *maistre passé* (past master) creates *prestre Macé* (priest Macé), 'a monk whose name was synonymous with simple or foolish'. In the same article, Robbins (457-8) cites a 'near-spoonerism' found in the *Lives* of celebrities by John Aubrey (1626-1697), who, discussing a flirtation between Sir Walter Raleigh and a young girl, has the wench's protest 'Sweet Sir Walter' changed into 'swisser Swatter'.

2. Most of the examples cited in the text will be from my own data. In the citation of examples, the arrow is to be interpreted as 'spoken as'. The pronunciation of the utterance will be given in phonetic symbols, within square brackets, only when the orthography may create an ambiguous interpretation or obscure the actual speech errors. A dash represents a pause by the speaker; a series of dots (. . .) indicates that no errors occurred in the intended words.

3. Lewis Carroll, in his preface to *The Hunting of the Snark* (1876), discusses his 'portmanteau' words: '. . . let me take this opportunity of answering a question that has often been asked me, how to pronounce "slithy toves". The "i" in "slithy" is long, as in "writhe"; and "toves" is pronounced so as to rhyme with "groves". Again, the first "o" in "borogoves" is pronounced like the "o" in "borrow". I have heard people try to give it the sound of the "o" in "worry". Such is Human Perversity . . . Humpty-Dumpty's theory, of two meanings packed into one word like a portmanteau, seems to me the right explanation for all. For instance, take the two words "fuming" and "furious". Make up your mind that you will say both words but leave it unsettled which you will say first. Now open your mouth and speak. If your thoughts incline ever so little towards "fuming" you will say "fuming-furious"; if they turn, by even a hair's breadth, towards "furious", you will say "furious-fuming"; but if you have that rarest of gifts, a perfectly balanced mind, you will say "frumious".'

   I have quoted extensively from Lewis Carroll, not only because it is always a delight to read or reread any of his comments, but because in this passage he states that his 'portmanteaus' or 'blends' are possible in natural speech and proposes a hypothesis as to how they occur. As we shall see below, however, these 'complete' blends are seldom found in just this way in 'normal' speech. That is, a blend of [fjurijəs] and [fjumɪŋ] is more apt to occur as [fjumijəs] or [fjurɪŋ], particularly because the first syllables are identical.

4. For the speaker who made this error, [š] followed by a consonant is not an unusual sequence. In fact, this might represent a word substitution, since [štɪk] as a word exists in his dialect as well as *shmuck* [šmʌk], *shtunk* [štʊŋk], *shmo* [šmow] etc.

5. Wickelgren's features were used by MacKay.

6. Chomsky & Halle are of course concerned with the grammatically determined aspects of the signal. The occurrence or lack of occurrence of speech errors involving phonetic features are being discussed in this article as they relate to a model of linguistic performance rather than competence. However, when Chomsky & Halle talk about 'the set of phonetic properties that can in principle be controlled in speech' (295), it is difficult to find the clear separation between competence and performance.

7. This research was supported in part by United States Public Health Services (NIH) grant NB-04595, and in part by Office of Naval Research contract NR-049-226.

# REFERENCES

Applegate, R. B. 1968. Segmental analysis of articulatory errors under delayed auditory feedback. (POLA reports, 8.) Berkeley: University of California.

Bowden, H. H. 1899. A study of lapses. *Psychological Review,* Monograph Supplement 3, no. 4.

Boomer, D. S. and J. D. M. Laver. 1968. Slips of the tongue. *British Journal of Disorders of Communication* 3.1–12.

Broadbent, D. E. 1966. The well ordered mind. *American Educational Research Journal* 3.281-95.

Brown, R. and D. McNeil. 1966. The tip of the tongue phenomenon. *Journal of Verbal Learning and Verbal Behavior* 5.325–37.

Carroll, Lewis. 1876. *The Hunting of the Snark.* London: Macmillan.

Chomsky, N. and M. Halle. 1968. *The Sound Pattern of English.* New York: Harper & Row.

Cohen, A. 1966. Errors of speech and their implication for understanding the strategy of language users. (Instituut voor Perceptie Onderzoek, Annual progress report, 1.) Eindhoven. (To appear in Models of speech, Proceedings of the International Congress of Psychologists, Moscow.)

Freud, Sigmund. 1924. *Zur Psychopathologie des Alltaglebens.* 10th ed. Leipzig: Internationaler Psychoanalytischer Verlag. (English version in Basic writings of Sigmund Freud, ed. by A. A. Brill. New York: Modern Library, 1938.)

Fromkin, V. A. 1968. Speculations on performance models. *Journ. of Ling.* 4.47–68.

Green, E. 1969. Phonological and grammatical aspects of jargon in an aphasic patient: a case study. *Lang. and Speech* 12.80–103.

Hockett, C. F. 1967. Where the tongue slips, there slip I. To honour Roman Jakobson, 2.910–36. (Janua linguarum, series major, 32.) The Hague: Mouton.

Jakobson, R. 1964. Towards a linguistic typology of aphasic impairments. *Disorders of Language,* CIBA Foundation Symposium, 21–46. London.

——. 1966. Linguistic types of aphasia. *Brain Function,* ed. by E. C. Carterette, 67–91. Berkeley & Los Angeles: University of California Press.

Jespersen, O. 1922. *Language: Its Nature, Development, and Origin.* London: Allen and Unwin.

Kozhevnikov, V. A. and L. A. Chistovich. 1965. Speech: articulation and perception (revised). (Joint Publications Research Service, 30,543.) Washington: U.S. Department of Commerce.

Lashley, K. S. 1951. The problem of serial order in behavior. *Cerebral Mechanisms in Behavior,* ed. by L. A. Jeffress, 112–36. New York: Wiley.

Laver, J. 1969. The detection and correction of slips of the tongue. Work in progress no. 3, Dept. of Phonetics and Linguistics, Edinburgh University, 1–13.

Luria, A. R. and O. S. Vinogradova. 1959. An objective investigation of the dynamic of semantic systems. *Brit. Journ. of Psych.* 50.89–105.

MacKay, D. G. 1969. Forward and backward masking in motor systems. *Kybernetik* 6.57–64.

——. 1970a. Spoonerisms: the anatomy of errors in the serial order of speech. To appear in *Neuropsychologia.*

——. 1970b. Context dependent stuttering. To appear in *Kybernetik.*

——. 1970c. Spoonerisms of children. To appear in *Neuropsychologia.*

——. 1970d. Sound change and errors in speech. Unpublished.

Marshall, J. C. and F. Newcombe. 1966. Syntactic and semantic errors in paralexia. *Neuropsychologia* 4.169–76.

Meringer, R. 1908. Aus dem Leben der Sprache. Berlin.

—— and K. Mayer. 1895. Versprechen und Verlesen, eine psychologisch linguistische Studie. Vienna.

Miller, G. A. 1962. Decision units in the perception of speech. *IRE Transactions on Information Theory,* IT-8, 81–3.

—— and P. E. Nicely. 1955. An analysis of perceptual confusions among some English consonants. *Journal of the Acoustical Society of America* 27.338–52.

Nooteboom, S. G. 1967. Some regularities in phonemic speech errors. (Instituut voor Perceptie Onderzoek, Annual progress report, 2.) Eindhoven.

——. 1969. The tongue slips into patterns. *Nomen: Leyden Studies in Linguistics and Phonetics,* ed. by A. G. Sciarone et al., 114–32. The Hague: Mouton.

Robbins, Rossell Hope. 1966. The warden's wordplay: toward a redefinition of the spoonerism. *Dalhousie Review* 46.457–65.

Sapir, Edward. 1925. Sound patterns in language. Lg. 1.37–51.

Sturtevant, E. H. 1917 *Linguistic Change.* Chicago: University of Chicago Press.

——. 1947. An introduction to linguistic science. New Haven: Yale University Press.

Wells, R. 1951. Predicting slips of the tongue. *Yale Scientific Magazine,* December, pp. 9–12.

Wickelgren, W. A. 1965a. Acoustic similarity and intrusion errors in short-term memory *Journal of Experimental Pscyhology* 70.102–8.

——. 1965b. Distinctive features and errors in short-term memory for English vowels. *Journal of the Acoustical Society of America* 38.583–8.

——. 1966. Distinctive features and errors in short-term memory for English consonants. *Journal of the Acoustical Society of America* 39.388–98.

# Lexical Access during Sentence Comphrehension: (Re)Consideration of Context Effects

David A. Swinney • Tufts University

The effects of prior semantic context upon lexical access during sentence comprehension were examined in two experiments. In both studies, subjects comprehended auditorily presented sentences containing lexical ambiguities and simultaneously performed a lexical decision task upon visually presented letter strings. Lexical decisions for visual words related to each of the meanings of the ambiguity were facilitated when these words were presented simultaneous with the end of the ambiguity (Experiment 1). This effect held even when a strong biasing context was present. When presented four syllables following the ambiguity, only lexical decisions for visual words related to the contextually appropriate meaning of the ambiguity were facilitated (Experiment 2). Arguments are made for autonomy of the lexical access process of a model of semantic context effects is offered.

Sentence comprehension requires the integration of information derived from a number of ongoing cognitive processes. It is clear, for example, that semantic and syntactic contexts interact with moment-to-moment comprehension processes to affect our interpretation of individual words and sentences; observations that contexts act to determine sentential interpretations abound in the literature. However, while this effect is well documented, the process by which it occurs is not. Until the manner in which contexts exert their effects (i.e., the nature of information interaction) can be detailed, claims relying on the concept of "contextual determination" are empty and merely beg the question. Certainly, any attempt at a performative description of sentence comprehen-

sion must incorporate the details of this process. One of the important debates arising from concern over how (and when) contexts have their effects involves the question of whether comprehension processes are, in general, of a highly interactive, directable, nature (so that any stage of a process can come under the direction of some other, contextual, process; e.g., Marslen-Wilson, 1975; Marslen-Wilson & Welsh, 1978; Swinney & Hakes, 1976; Jenkins, Note 1) or whether these processes are basically isolable and autonomous (so that context effects exert themselves only on the output of these processes; see, e.g., Forster, 1976; Garrett, 1978).

One domain in which some effort has been made to examine this question is that of lexical access.

The studies of interest have typically examined the processing of lexical ambiguities during sentence comprehension. Experiments involving a number of different tasks have shown that the occurrence of an ambiguous word, in comparison with that of an unambiguous control word, increases the processing complexity of an unbiased sentence (e.g., Foss, 1970; Foss & Jenkins, 1973; Holmes, Arwas, & Garrett, 1977; Chodorow, Note 2). Such an increase presumably reflects comprehension processes which, at least momentarily, are involved in the retrieval and consideration of the several meanings of an ambiguous word. This effect occurs even though most people eventually become aware of only a single meaning for ambiguities in these conditions. The question of interest, then, is one of exactly how and when a biasing context aids in the final selection of a single relevant reading for an ambiguous word. It is particularly important to examine the nature of these effects for the most critical of contextual conditions for the issues raised here, that in which the biasing context occurs prior to the ambiguity.

Two general classes of hypotheses have been offered in explanation of such effects. The first of these, which have variously been termed "prior decision" (Foss & Jenkins, 1973) or "unitary perception" hypotheses are all versions of the highly interactive sentence processing view (see also Hogaboam & Perfetti, 1975; MacKay, 1970; Schvaneveldt, Meyer, & Becker, 1976). These hold that prior contextual information can act to direct lexical access so that only a single, relevant reading is ever accessed for an ambiguity. It is important to note that the nature of the claim made by such hypotheses is not limited to ambiguity alone; rather, it is a claim that lexical access, in general, is a contextually restricted, nonindependent process. The alternative class of hypotheses—postdecision or multiple-meaning hypotheses—holds that prior context has its effect only after all information is accessed for an ambiguity. Under these hypotheses, lexical access is viewed as an independent and relatively autonomous process in which context has its effects only following complete access of all the information about a word.

Data exist which appear to support both classes of hypotheses. Several studies (e.g., Conrad, 1974; Foss & Jenkins, 1973; Holmes et al., 1977; Lackner & Garrett, 1972; Cutler & Foss, Note 3) have reported support for the Postdecision Hypothesis.

However, a number of these utilized tasks which appear likely to have led subjects to employ some very specialized processing strategies (see Swinney & Hakes, 1976, for further discussion). Further, even the most compelling of the remainder have supported the Postdecision Hypothesis largely by virtue of failing to find support for the Prior Decision Hypothesis; they have not actually demonstrated the access of more than a single meaning for an ambiguity in the presence of a prior, biasing context.[1] Studies by Foss & Jenkins (1973) and Cutler & Foss (Note 3) provide good examples of this point. Both papers reported that phoneme monitoring latencies increased in the presence of an ambiguity (in comparison with an unambiguous control word) in an unbiased sentential context. Further, both studies failed to find any decrement in the ambiguity effect when a biasing context was introduced. Because such a decrement was expected if the Prior Decision Hypothesis was true, they interpreted this failure as support for the Postdecision Hypothesis. Unfortunately, support by default can often prove, for a number of reasons, to be a treacherous position to take. The work of Swinney & Hakes (1976), in fact, demonstrated that the ambiguity effect does decrease significantly in the presence of a *strongly* biased context, a result which forced reinterpretation of these previous results. The Swinney & Hakes (1976) result thus appeared to provide strong evidence that context can, at least under some conditions, direct the lexical access process; context would appear to be capable of interaction with lexical information during the access phase.

In spite of the intuitive appeal of this result, and its accordance with the highly interactive view of sentence perception, two problems deserve some consideration. First, it is obvious that the tasks used to study any process, and particularly those used to obtain on-line measures of comprehension (i.e., tasks examining the process during its operation, in contrast to examinations made after it is finished), must be appropriately applied in order to detect that process. This fact would appear to hold particular importance for examinations of ambiguity processing which use the phoneme monitoring task. The phoneme target in such monitoring studies, of necessity, occurs "downstream" from the ambiguity which is being examined (it usually begins the word following the ambiguity). The temporal gap between occurrence of the ambiguity and detection of the phoneme target in a following word is, thus, fairly extensive relative to the magnitude of the effects reported with this task. It is hoped that the problem here is self-evident: Claims related to lexical access which rely on monitoring data all contain the key assumption that the task actually measures lexical *access* and not some process that occurs *following* access. However, it is at least possible that the phoneme monitoring task actually reflects some type of postaccess decision process. If so, in situations where a prior biasing context is not very strong (as was the case in the Foss & Jenkins (1973) study) this postaccess decision process might take a relatively long time to complete, long enough so that the phoneme monitor decision for the following word is engaged while this process is still at work. Such a situation would thus produce the typical ambiguity effect. However, in the presence of a very strong biasing context (the Swinney & Hakes (1976) study) this postaccess decision process could occur sufficiently quickly so as to reduce the processing load caused by the ambiguity prior to the time when the phoneme monitor task comes into play. In short, it may be that the phoneme monitoring task does not actually reflect the access of information for ambiguous (or other) words preceding the phoneme target but, rather, that it reflects postaccess processing (see Cairns & Hsu (1979) and Swinney (Note 4) for related arguments). If true, the task is not appropriate for examination of the hypotheses under question.

The second of the problems surrounding some of the previous work has arisen from recent examinations of the phoneme monitoring task (which has provided the bulk of the on-line evidence in this field). Both Mehler, Segui, & Carey (1978) and Newman & Dell (1978) have convincingly demonstrated that the ambiguity effects reported by Foss (1970), Foss & Jenkins (1973), and Cairns & Kamerman (1975) are all confounded with length and phonological properties of the initial phoneme of the ambiguity, its control, and the word preceding the ambiguity. When these factors were carefully examined it appeared as though the ambiguity processing effects could be accounted for largely on the basis of these confounding variables. While the existence of some effect of ambiguity upon sentential processing has not been disproved, the role of the phoneme monitoring task in reflecting such an effect is certainly open to question. (It should be noted that the claims of confounding asserted for the above-mentioned studies do not apply as strongly to the Swinney & Hakes (1976) results.)[2]

The key to examining the experimental hypotheses in question, and to resolving the problems raised above, lies in increasing the sensitivity of the experimental task. In order to be able to provide positive evidence for the Postdecision Hypothesis, the experimental task should be capable of reflecting access of each of the several meanings of an ambiguous word. In addition, the task must be flexible enough to minimize the temporal gap between occurrence of the ambiguous word and the measure of access. Finally, the task must be applicable during sentence comprehension, and not just after the sentence has already been processed. To these ends, a task was devised which coupled the auditory presentation of an ambiguous sentence with a visual, lexical decision task. Recent work with cross-modality semantic priming has demonstrated that visual lexical decisions are facilitated following auditory processing of a related word (Swinney, Onifer, Prather, & Hirshkowitz, 1979). This finding fits well with the visual mode priming effect reported by Meyer and his associates (e.g., Meyer, Schvaneveldt, & Ruddy, 1975, Note 5) and others (Fishler, 1977; Tweedy, Lapinski, & Schvaneveldt, 1977). In fact, the data suggest that cross-modal facilitation effects are at least as robust as those found solely within the visual modality. Several characteristics of the cross-modal priming task are worthy of note. One is that semantic priming holds when the primed (facilitated) word is presented visually during auditory sentence comprehension. The second is that subjects in this task are typically not aware of any particular relationship between the visually presented material and the auditory sentential material. (See Results and Discussion sections for further explanation.) The semantic priming effect to be used here, much like that demonstrated in other studies, can thus occur as an automatic process, one not under control of conscious direction (see, e.g., Fishler, 1977; Neely, 1977). In short, the task reflects the access of auditory (priming) words through the relative facilitation of lexical decisions made to visual words, without drawing particular attention to the relationships involved.

The major advantages of this task are, first, that

the visual word can be presented simultaneously with the offset of the ambiguous word in the sentence (thus overcoming distance problems faced by the phoneme monitoring task), second, that it can be used during (rather than after) comprehension, and third, that it minimizes the possibility of attention being drawn to the experimental variables, a situation that has often compromised the results of previous experiments. Finally, this task can be used to measure activation of *each* of the meanings of an auditorily presented ambiguity. If a strong sentential context causes only a single reading to ever be accessed for an ambiguity in a sentence then only lexical decisions for visually presented words related to *that* reading of the ambiguity will be facilitated. On the other hand, if both (or several) readings of an ambiguity are accessed, even in the presence of a strong biasing context, then visual words related to each reading will display some facilitation in the concurrent lexical decision task.

In order to give the hypotheses under investigation a strong test, materials used in this first experiment were taken from the Swinney & Hakes (1976) study which had produced results supporting the Prior Effect Hypothesis.

## Experiment 1

### Method

#### DESIGN AND MATERIALS

Sentential materials for this study were taken, with a few changes and additions, from those used in the Swinney & Hakes (1976) study. These consisted of 36 sets of sentence pairs (two sentences presented sequentially) each set having four variations. The four variations derive from a factorial combination of two variables: Ambiguity and Context.

The Ambiguity variable was comprised of two conditions: inclusion of either an ambiguous word or an unambiguous control word which was roughly synonymous with one reading of the ambiguity. These words were all nouns and all appeared in the predicate of the second sentence of each sentence pair. Ambiguous and control words were matched for frequency, using the Kučera and Francis (1967) norms, and for length in syllables. All ambiguous words were approximately

equibiased, as determined by a pretest in which 44 subjects recorded their first interpretation of auditorily presented experimental sentences from the "no context" condition (see below). The maximum proportion attained for any single reading of any of the ambiguities ranged between .50 and .70.

The context variable comprised two conditions: either no disambiguating context, or a prior, strongly predictive, disambiguating context. The latter was determined using a criterion (discussed at length in Swinney & Hakes, 1976) in which the context was not only more related to one meaning of the ambiguity than the others, but, as judged by two judges, was strongly predictive of one meaning of the ambiguity by virtue of being highly associated with that meaning and being incompatible with other possible meanings.

For each sentence pair, a set of three words (to be presented visually) was prepared. One of these words was related to the contextually biased reading of the ambiguity in the sentence, one was related to the "other," contextually inappropriate reading of the ambiguity, and the third was not related to any meaning of the ambiguity. The specific degree of relatedness of each visual word to its paired reading of the ambiguity was not specifically controlled. (All such materials, however, appeared to hold a moderate degree of relatedness.) The three words of each set were yoked for length and frequency. (Only moderate-frequency words were utilized.) All words used in these conditions were then compared in an independent, isolated lexical decision task. The experimental words, along with 36 other words and 44 nonword letter strings, were presented visually in random order to 24 subjects. Reaction times to make a word/nonword (lexical) decision were compared for words comprising the three conditions of experimental words. The mean times for these conditions were 0.661, 0.664, and 0.657 second, respectively. Both multiple $t$ test comparisons and analysis of variance, $F(2, 46) = 0.918$, revealed no significant differences between reaction times to words in these three conditions.

The four sentence variations and the set of three words paired with them are presented schematically in Table 37.1. "Δ" represents the point at which one of the three words would be presented visually during the auditory comprehension of the sentence.

Four tape recordings were made from the

**TABLE 37.1. Schematized Sample of Experimental Materials**

| Context Condition | Ambiguity Condition | |
|---|---|---|
| | Ambiguous | Unambiguous |
| No context | Rumor had it that, for years, the government building had been plagued with problems. The man was not surprised when he found several bugs$_\Delta$ in the corner of his room. | Rumor had it that, for years, the government building had been plagued with problems. The man was not surprised when he found several insects$_\Delta$ in the corner of his room. |
| Biasing context | Rumor had it that, for years, the government building had been plagued with problems. The man was not surprised when he found several spiders, roaches, and other bugs$_\Delta$ in the corner of his room. | Rumor had it that, for years, the government building had been plagued with problems. The man was not surprised when he found several spiders, roaches, and other insects$_\Delta$ in the corner of his room. |
| | Visual words* ANT | (contextually related) |
| | Displayed at "$\Delta$" SPY | (contextually inappropriate) |
| | SEW | (unrelated) |

sentential materials. Each tape contained one variation of each of the 36 sentence pairs chosen so that the four types of variation were equally represented on each tape. All tapes also included 46 filler sentence pairs, randomly interspersed among the test sentence pairs. Filler sentence pairs were identical for each tape.

For presentation purposes three separate lists were created from the words and nonwords which were to be presented visually. Each list contained only one of the three visual words which were created in conjunction with each sentence pair. The three visual word conditions were equally represented on each list. Half of the materials on each list were words (36 experimental materials, and 2 words which were paired with filler sentences) and the other half (32) were nonwords (paired with filler sentences). For six of the filler sentences, no visual word appeared on the screen.

Thus, there were 12 presentation conditions: each of 3 lists paired with each of the 4 tape conditions. A 1000-Hz signal was placed on a separate channel of the tape exactly coincident with the *offset* of each ambiguous or control word in the experimental sentential materials, and with the offset of a pseudorandomly chosen word in the filler sentences. These signals, inaudible to the subjects, signaled a PDP8/e computer to present the appropriate visual word and to start the timing mechanism which measured the latencies for the subject's lexical decisions. (See Onifer, Hirshkowitz, & Swinney (1978) for discussion of hardware and software involved in this procedure.)

## SUBJECTS

Eighty-four undergraduates from Tufts University participated in partial fulfillment of a course requirement. Seven subjects were randomly assigned to each of the 12 experimental conditions. Data for six additional subjects were omitted from analysis for failure to achieve a score of at least 85% correct on the comprehension test.

## PROCEDURE

The subjects were seated in front of a CRT screen and listened through headphones to the 82 binaurally presented sentence pairs. Subjects were tested in groups of up to 3 at a time: each subject was in a booth isolating him/her from other subjects in a group. Subjects were instructed to listen carefully to each sentence and to understand it. They were told that they would be tested on their comprehension during the experiment, and that the result of this test was crucial to their successful participation in this experiment.

In addition, subjects were told that they had a second task. It was explained that a string of letters would appear on the screen during some of the sentences they listened to, and that they were to decide as quickly as possible whether each letter string formed a word or not. No hint was given that words and sentences might be related and, in the five practice trials, no such relationship existed.

At both the midpoint and the end of the experimental session, subjects were given a sheet of paper containing 21 sentence pairs. They were required to decide whether each of these was either identical or similar to sentences they had heard, or whether the sentence had not occurred at all in the experiment. These materials were scored on a percentage correct basis. At the end of the experimental session, subjects were questioned about whether they had noticed ambiguities in the sentence material and about whether they thought the words on the screen related in any specific fashion to the sentences they had heard.

## Results

The mean reaction times for the 12 experimental conditions, calculated across all materials and subjects, are presented in Table 37.2. It is apparent that lexical decisions for words related to *both* readings of the ambiguity are facilitated (relative to decisions for an unrelated control word) in conditions containing a lexical ambiguity and no biasing context. Similarly, and of greatest interest, this same effect holds for the condition in which there is a strongly biasing semantic context present; lexical decisions for words related to both the contextually relevant and the contextually inappropriate meanings of the ambiguity appear to be facilitated compared to decisions for unrelated control words. The effects for both of the unambiguous conditions also appear quite straightforward: Lexical decisions for the "related" word appear to be facilitated, but those for the other two words are not. Thus, by inspection, the results appear to support the Postdecision Hypothesis; even a very strong semantic context apparently does not direct lexical access. Statistical analysis supports this contention.

An analysis of variance revealed that main effects for Context, Ambiguity, and Visual Word Type were each significant for analyses employing both subjects and materials as random factors,

min $F'(1, 79) = 7.01$, $p < .01$; Min $F'(1, 86) = 6.32$, $p < .025$; Min $F'(2, 188) = 52.6$, $p < .001$, respectively. Both the Context × Visual Word Type and the Context × Ambiguity interactions failed to reach significance, Min $F'(1, 119) = 0.42$; Min $F'(1, 74) = 0.1$, respectively. Most revealing for the present purposes, however, was the fact that Ambiguity interacted significantly with Visual Word Type, Min $F'(2, 157) = 4.71$, $p < .01$, but that the Context × Ambiguity × Visual Word Type interaction was not significant, Min $F(2, 161) = 0.04$.

In order to examine the predicted effects, planned multiple comparisons were made on the relevant Visual Word Type categories for each of the Ambiguity × Context conditions. For the condition containing a biasing context and an ambiguity, reaction times to visual words in both the contextually related and contextually inappropriate categories were significantly faster than latencies for unrelated words, $t(83) = -6.1$, $p < .0009$; $t(83) = -5.04$, $p < .0009$, respectively. The contextually related and contextually inappropriate categories, however, did not differ from each other in this condition, $t(83) = -1.05$. This same overall configuration of results held for the no context condition containing an ambiguity, $t(83) = -5.2$, $p < .0009$; $t(83) = -4.94$, $p < .0009$, $t(83) = -0.98$, respectively. In the unambiguous conditions, reaction times to the contextually related words were significantly faster than those for the unrelated words in both the biasing context, $t(83) = -7.4$, $p < .0009$, and no context, $t(83) = -5.16$, $p < .0009$, conditions. However, reaction times to contextually related words differed significantly from contextually inappropriate words in each context condition, $t(83) = -7.2$, $p < .0009$; $t(83) = -5.2$, $p < .0009$, respectively. In neither case did reaction times to the contextually inappropriate words differ from those to the unrelated words, $t(83) = -0.55$; $t(83) = -0.6$, respectively.[3,4]

**TABLE 37.2. Mean Reaction Times, in Milliseconds, for Conditions of the Ambiguity × Context × Visual Word Interaction: Experiment 1**

| Ambiguity Condition | Context Condition | Visually Presented Words | | |
| --- | --- | --- | --- | --- |
| | | Contextually Related | Contextually Inappropriate | Unrelated |
| Ambiguous | Biasing context | 890 | 910 | 960 |
| | No context | 916 | 925 | 974 |
| Unambiguous | Biasing context | 887 | 958 | 963 |
| | No context | 914 | 967 | 972 |

The post-test questionnaires were evaluated in order to determine whether subjects noticed any specific relationship between words in the sentence and the visually presented words. Of the 84 subjects, only 11 thought they noticed any time-locked relationship between materials in the sentence and the visual words. However, the relationships these subjects reported were almost entirely unrelated to the experimental manipulations; it appears that perceptual displacement typically occurs in this task, and that subjects report seeing the visual words one to two syllables downstream from where they actually occur. Thus, reported relationships are most typically unrelated to the experimental manipulations. (Because the ratio of related materials to unrelated materials is kept low, a strategy of attempting to relate visual words to immediately preceding auditory material would actually be detrimental rather than facilatory to task performance.) Because these 11 "aware" subjects came from eight different materials conditions, analysis of their data could only be made by comparison with data obtained from the same subject-group conditions. In these comparisons there was only a single case in which the basic direction of effects for Ambiguity, Context, and Visual Word Type did not hold. However, it is notable that the facilitation for the contextually inappropriate visual word condition did not appear to be nearly so robust for "aware" subjects as it was for the "unaware" subjects, although these differences were not statistically significant.

Similarly, only 3 of the 84 subjects reported that they had noticed ambiguities in the materials during the experiment; due to the small number of cases no further analysis of this factor was undertaken.

## Discussion

The results of Experiment 1 provide fairly strong support for a model of sentential processing in which lexical *access* is an autonomous process; because semantic facilitation was observed for lexical decisions to words related to both the contextually relevant and the contextually inappropriate meaning of the ambiguity, even in the presence of the very strong prior semantic contexts, it appears reasonable to conclude that semantic context does not *direct* lexical access. Rather, immediately following occurrence of an ambiguous

word all meanings for that word seem to be momentarily accessed during sentence comprehension. Thus, the results which were previously obtained with the phoneme monitoring task would appear to be the consequence of some process which occurred following lexical access rather than a reflection of the access process itself (see also Cairns & Hsu (1979) for arguments supporting this position). It seems likely that semantic context has its effects upon a postaccess decision process, one which eventuates in the choosing of a single reading for an ambiguity. Certainly, a number of intriguing questions now present themselves. Foremost among these is one concerning the nature of the information interaction which occurs during this posited postaccess decision process.

In order to further investigate this, a second experiment was performed which focused on the time course of this process. The experiment also had the goal of providing further information concerning the cross-modal priming task. Cairns & Kamerman (1976) reported that the increased sentential processing complexity caused by an ambiguity disappears approximately two syllables following the ambiguity, when measured by the phoneme monitoring task. If these results are valid (again, see Newman & Dell, 1978) then any lexical ambiguity is apparently resolved by that time, even when no overtly biasing context is present. Even if these phoneme monitoring data are questionable, it is clear that lexical ambiguity must be resolved relatively quickly, certainly by the end of the clause containing that ambiguity (see, e.g., Foss, Bever, & Silver, 1968; Bever, Garrett, & Hurtig, 1973). It is thus important to determine the rate and manner in which the nonrelevant reading(s) of an ambiguity is discarded during this postaccess decision process. Available data do not permit us to even determine whether contextually irrelevant readings remain available at some level for processing or whether they are irretrievably lost to the comprehension device. Experiment 2 examines these questions utilizing the same basic experimental design as was used in Experiment 1. In this experiment, however, the visual (primed) materials appear three syllables following occurrence of the ambiguous word in the sentence as well as immediately following it. If the contextually inappropriate meanings of an ambiguous word are immediately discarded or suppressed, then we should find that only the contextually relevant visual materials will be facilitated in this experiment. On the other hand, if all meanings of the ambiguous word remain under consideration until the end of the clause containing the ambiguity, then words related to both the contextually appropriate and the contextually inappropriate meanings of the ambiguous word should be facilitated.

## Experiment 2

### Method

#### DESIGN AND MATERIALS

This experiment was designed in two parts: a replication of Experiment 1 and an extension of that experiment. The replication was quite straightforward involving only minor changes in materials used in Experiment 1. The extension duplicated this replication experiment with the single change being that the visual (lexical decision) materials appeared three syllables following the ambiguous (or control) word during the course of the sentence. Because the design of each of these studies is nearly identical to that for Experiment 1, only the important changes will be noted. Thirty-six sets of experimental sentences (not sentence pairs as were presented in Experiment 1) were used in each study. Each set contained four variations derived, controlled, and counter-balanced for presentation as in Experiment 1. In addition, half of the biasing semantic contexts were chosen to be in accord with the a priori more likely meaning of the ambiguity (as determined in pretests of materials for Experiment 1), and half were in accord with one of the less likely meanings of the ambiguous word. All lexical ambiguities were, however, chosen for their approximate equibias as measured in the pretest described in Experiment 1. There were 44 filler sentences interspersed among the experimental materials. For 8 of these, visual words were displayed during their presentation; during the other 36 filler sentences visual nonwords were displayed.

Visual words and tape recordings were constructed as in Experiment 1, and the three types of visual words (contextually related, contextually inappropriate, and unrelated) were again compared on an isolated lexical decision pretest using 33 subjects. The mean reaction times to each of these conditions (647, 641, and 650 milliseconds, re-

spectively) did not differ significantly. Planned $t$ test comparisons of the contextually related and contextually inappropriate, $t(32) = 0.68$, and of the contextually related and unrelated, $t(32) = -0.38$, as well as the contextually inappropriate and unrelated categories, $t(32) = -0.79$, all revealed no significant differences.

#### SUBJECTS

One hundred and forty-four subjects participated in this experiment, half of these in the replication and half in the extension portion of the study. Six subjects were randomly assigned to each of the 12 experimental conditions in each half of the study.

#### PROCEDURE

The procedure was identical to that for Experiment 1, except that no formal post-test for awareness of ambiguity was given.

### Results

The mean reaction times for the critical conditions of the replication portion of the experiment, calculated across subject groups and materials conditions, are given in Table 37.3. Inspection of these data suggests that the results reported in Experiment 1 did, indeed, replicate in this second study. Analysis of individual subjects' data for this portion of the study substantiated this observation. An analysis of variance revealed that, overall, all main effects and interactions were nonsignificant except for a significant main effect for Visual Word. Type (which was significant for an analysis utilizing both subject and material as random factors), Min $F'(2, 164) = 4.83$, $p < .01$, and for the Ambiguity × Visual Word Type interaction, Min $F(2, 141) = 3.09$, $p < .05$. Planned comparisons of relevant cells in this interaction revealed the following effects in this design: Lexical decisions made to words in the contextually related and contextually inappropriate categories were each significantly faster than those of unrelated visual materials in the sentential conditions containing an ambiguous word and a biasing context, $t(71) = 2.676$, $p < .01$; $t(71) = 2.131$, $p < .04$, respectively. Reaction times to contextually related and contextually inappropriate conditions did not differ significantly, however, $t(71) = 1.60$. These same

**TABLE 37.3. Mean Reaction Times, in Milliseconds, for Conditions of the Ambiguity × Context × Visual Word Interaction: Experiment 2 (Replication)**

| Ambiguity Condition | Context Condition | Visually Presented Word | | |
| --- | --- | --- | --- | --- |
| | | Contextually Related | Contextually Inappropriate | Unrelated |
| Ambiguous | Biasing context | 708 | 715 | 746 |
| | No context | 703 | 708 | 743 |
| Unambiguous | Biasing context | 710 | 747 | 744 |
| | No context | 702 | 732 | 742 |

relationships held for the sentential materials containing an ambiguity and no biasing context, $t(71) = 2.57, p < .015; t(71) = 2.56, p < .015; t(71) = 0.469$, respectively. In the sentential conditions containing unambiguous control words, lexical decisions were significantly faster for the contextually related category words than for the unrelated words in both the biasing context, $t(71) = 2.43, p < .015$, and no context $t(71) = 2.61, p < .01$, conditions. Similarly, reaction times to contextually related words were significantly faster than to contextually inappropriate words in both the biasing context and no context conditions, $t(71) = 2.35, p < .02; t(71) = 2.07, p < .05$, respectively. Reaction times to the contextually inappropriate words did not differ significantly from the unrelated words in either of these conditions, $t(71) = 0.05; t(71) = 0.075$, respectively.[5]

The results of the extension portion of this study differ markedly from those of the replication portion. Table 37.4 presents mean reaction times for the 12 major experimental conditions, calculated across materials and subjects' conditions, for the extension study. It can be seen that facilitation of lexical decisions appears to occur only for the contextually related word category; this effect, however, occurs for each of the relevant experimental conditions. This observation is confirmed by the results of planned $t$ tests and an analysis of variance. The analysis of variance performed on these data (again, with both subjects and materials as random factors) revealed significant main effects for Visual Word Type, Min $F'(2, 172) = 19.87$, $p < .001$, but no significant main effects for Ambiguity, Min $F'(1, 80) = 0.46$, or Context, Min $F'(1, 53) = 0.008$, and no significant interaction of Visual Word Type with Ambiguity and Context, Min $F'(2, 161) = 0.06$. Planned comparisons for the three Visual Word Type categories in sentential conditions containing an ambiguous word and a biasing context revealed that lexical decisions for contextually related words are significantly faster than those both for contextually inappropriate words, $t(71) = -4.76, p < .001$, and for unrelated words, $t(71) = -4.389, p < .001$. Additionally, reaction times for words in the contextually inappropriate and unrelated categories do not differ, $t(71) = 0.08$. The same set of effects holds for each of the other three Context × Ambiguity conditions. That is, when the sentence contained an ambiguous word and no biasing context, lexical decisions to contextually related words were significantly faster than those for both contextually inappropriate words, $t(71) = -4.24, p < .001$, and unrelated words, $t(71) = -2.42, p < .02$, but words in the latter two categories did not differ, $t(71) = 0.79$. When the sentential materials contained an unambiguous control word and a biasing context, lexical decisions to words in the contextually related condition were faster than for those in the contextually inappropriate, $t(71) = -3.10, p < .003$, or unrelated, $t(71) = -3.30, p < .002$, conditions, but the latter

**TABLE 37.4. Mean Reaction Times, in Milliseconds, for Conditions of the Ambiguity × Context × Visual Word Interaction: Experiment 2 (Extension)**

| Ambiguity Condition | Context Condition | Visual Word Condition | | |
| --- | --- | --- | --- | --- |
| | | Contextually Related | Contextually Inappropriate | Unrelated |
| Ambiguous | Biasing context | 795 | 849 | 848 |
| | No context | 800 | 846 | 845 |
| Unambiguous | Biasing context | 808 | 843 | 849 |
| | No context | 811 | 847 | 846 |

two categories did not differ significantly, $t(71) = -0.6$. Finally, in the sentential conditions containing an unambiguous control word and no biasing context, lexical decisions to words in the contextually related condition were responded to faster than those in the contextually inappropriate, $t(71) = -3.4$, $p < .001$, and unrelated, $t(71) = -3.2$, $p < .002$, conditions, but, again, the latter two categories did not differ significantly, $t(71) = 0.02$.[6]

## Discussion

The results of the second experiment replicate those of the first, demonstrating that lexical decisions for words related to both the relevant and the contextually inappropriate meanings of an ambiguous word are facilitated, even in the presence of a strong, prior, biasing context, when these decisions are made immediately following occurrence of the ambiguity in a sentence. In addition, the experiment shows that when this test is applied three syllables following occurrence of the ambiguous word, only lexical decisions for words related to the contextually relevant meaning of the ambiguity are facilitated; at this point lexical decisions for words related to contextually inappropriate meanings of an ambiguity no longer show facilitation.

It might be noted that in the extension portion of Experiment 2 (where the test point was three syllables following the ambiguity) only the "relevant" meanings of the ambiguities were found to be facilitated in the materials containing no biasing context. Because half of the materials had originally been chosen to have a priori biases toward the interpretation picked as the "related" meaning, and the other half chosen to have a priori biases toward the other (inappropriate) meaning, one might have expected that each of these interpretations would have shown some facilitation in the unbiased context condition. However, although all ambiguities were originally chosen to be approximately equibiased, with a balanced representation of whatever a priori biases they contained, interpretations of words change over time. The bias ratings used in Experiment 2 were based on those used for Experiment 1. Thus, at least 2 years separated the gathering of bias ratings and performance on those materials in Experiment 2. In order to discover whether changes in these biases had taken place over this period of time, a post-test was performed (for the unbiased context sentences) using 35 Tufts University undergraduates. It was found that, of the 36 experimental ambiguities, 29 actually had biases favoring the reading which had been chosen as the "related" meaning in the experiment (although some of these were very small). Adding this information to the fact that all biases, whatever their direction, were relatively small, leads to the conclusion that the "related" meanings of the ambiguity were still facilitated at a point three syllables following the ambiguity, but the "inappropriate" meanings were not, even when no biasing context was present, because (overall) the a priori preferred interpretation for the ambiguities at the time of test tended to be those designated as "related" in this study. This fact, however, does not change the conclusions that have been drawn based on these results. In fact, the evidence suggests that not only are both (all) meanings for an ambiguity momentarily accessed, even in the presence of a strong biasing context, when the ambiguities are approximately balanced for most likely a priori interpretation (Experiment 1), but that all meanings are also immediately and momentarily accessed even when materials have a priori biases largely toward just one of the "senses" of the word tested. The fact that two meanings are available upon immediate access but that only one meaning is available three syllables later suggests that a very rapid postaccess decision process is at work. (In addition, it suggests that the task used in this experiment is sensitive to the "active" meanings of a word throughout their time course.)

An additional note should be made of the "drift" which we found for our bias ratings. The degree of drift which occurred over a 2-year period suggests that far more than sampling error is at work here. The favored interpretations of ambiguities do not remain fixed, at least for the words examined in this study. This recalls the old (and apparently true) theme in language research that, due to the rapidity of change in the language, reliance of preestablished norms must be done with care, and avoided where possible.

## General Discussion

In all, the results from both of these experiments provide strong support for the conclusion that the *access* process for lexical items is isolable and autonomous at least with respect to effects of semantic context. That is, semantic contexts do not appear to direct lexical access, as was predicted by the Prior Decision Hypothesis. Thus, the access operation appears to be a stimulus (form)-driven process for which the entire inventory of information stored for a lexical form is made available to the sentence comprehension device. The results also support the existence of a postaccess decision process which acts to select a single meaning from those originally and momentarily accessed for involvement in further processing. This decision process apparently is completed at least by the time that three syllables of additional information have been processed (approximately 750–1000 milliseconds), even when no biasing context is present.

A few general comments concerning the posited postaccess decision process are in order. First, the normal time course of access, activation, and deactivation (for inappropriate meanings) in this process is clearly underestimated in this study. It is likely to be far less than the approximately 750–1000 milliseconds found in Experiment 2. Further as this decision process takes place within a 1000-millisecond period even for conditions containing no biasing context, one would expect it to be far faster in normal situations, where a context is typically present. Second, the nature of the decision process which chooses the relevant meaning of the ambiguity deserves some consideration. It may be that the process acts to suppress the level of activation of unchosen meanings. On the other hand, it may be that the single meaning which is chosen for an ambiguity is somehow made available to further (higher order) sentential processes in a manner which simply ignores the unchosen meanings. (For example, it could be that both meanings of the ambiguity are still somewhat activated following access, but that the relevant meaning is shifted to what might be considered the "current" level of processing; presumably, it would be just this "current" level which can provide automatic semantic priming.) At present, there are no data which will allow us to directly choose between these quite different alternatives, and it is clear that further work on the nature of this decision process is in order.

Finally, because most words can, in fact, have different meanings (be these merely the different senses of a word or the totally different meanings comprising an unsystematic lexical ambiguity), it seems reasonable to suggest that the postaccess decision process posited here may be a general process. For any word, some subset of all the information which is originally accessed for that word may be selected for further processing and integration into ongoing sentential analysis. If so, only a single meaning for an ambiguous word, and only a single "sense" of an unambiguous word, would thus come to conscious awareness following this postaccess decision process. Semantic contexts apparently aid this selection process; the more the context restricts or determines the relevant sense of a word, the quicker the decision process will presumably take place. This model would fit with approaches taken by a number of authors (e.g., Collins & Loftus, 1975; Morton, 1969) on the access of semantic memory. It should be noted that while semantic contexts apparently do not affect access, there may be other types of information that will act upon the access phase of word recognition. Syntactic information, for example, may well serve to direct access in a way that semantic context cannot (see, e.g., Garrett, 1978; Fay, Note 6; Prather & Swinney, Note 7; Ryder, Note 8).

The model just sketched is, admittedly, underdetermined by the data. The nature of the claim being made is that sentence comprehension is not a totally interactive process; that is, that all kinds of information do not interact at all levels of processing. Certainly, it suggests that lexical access is basically a "bottom-up" or stimulus-driven process. This, however, is not at all to claim that this accessed information does not interact with other information. In fact, the data presented here could fit well with certain types of interactive models, such as that presented by Marslen-Wilson and his associates (e.g., Marslen-Wilson, 1975; Marslen-Wilson & Welsh, 1978), provided that certain constraints are placed on the interactions occurring around the access phase. In sum, however, these data appear to provide some evidence for autonomy of the lexical access process during sentence comprehension.

## NOTES

This research was supported in part by Grant 1-ROH MH29885–01 from NIMH to the author. The author expresses his appreciation to Max Hirshkowitz and Bill Onifer for their valuable assistance in developing the technology for the experiments, and to Marie Banich, Janet Dorfzahn, Sara Robinowitz, and Susan Sklover for their assistance in data collection. In addition, the critical discussions and valuable advice given by Donald Foss, David Hakes; and Penny Prather on earlier drafts of this paper are appreciated and gratefully acknowledged. Requests for reprints should be sent to David A. Swinney, Psychology Department, Paige Hall, Tufts University, Medford, Mass. 02155.

1. The experiment by Lackner and Garrett (1972) may be an exception to the particular problems stated here. However, their data do not actually allow a decision concerning whether context acted in a prior access or post access fashion (see comments in Holmes, Arwas, & Garrett (1977) and Lackner & Garrett (1972)).

2. Newman and Dell (1978) point to the apparent direct relationship between the magnitude of the obtained ambiguity effect and the magnitude of the difference in the number of phonological features shared between the target phoneme and the initial phoneme of the ambiguous and unambiguous control words. A similar direct relationship was shown to hold between the magnitude of the obtained ambiguity effect and the amount by which the length of the unambiguous control word exceeded that of the ambiguous word. The Swinney and Hakes (1976) materials have smaller differences between ambiguous and nonambiguous control words (on both the phonological and the length criteria) than any of the studies examined by Newman and Dell, and yet their data show the *largest* ambiguity effect of any of these studies. Further, and perhaps most importantly, the Swinney and Hakes (1976) results showed a decrement in this ambiguity effect in the face of a strong biasing context. Note that this change in the ambiguity effect occurs over sets of materials in which the critical phonemic and length features are identical. If the phoneme monitoring data is not reflecting an ambiguity processing effect, it is difficult to see what the basis for the observed decrement could be. Newman and Dell suggest that the semantic contexts may be attenuating a phonological search effect associated with the phoneme monitoring task rather than an ambiguity processing effect. However, that claim appears rather unlikely, particularly given that the decrement in processing latency occurs in the presence of semantic contexts which are in sentences which precede those containing the ambiguity and target phoneme. It would appear that a more parsimonious account of the results is that while length and phonological properties of the word preceding the target phoneme undoubtedly effect the phoneme monitoring task, the task also, given appropriate circumstances, reflects lexical processing complexity.

3. It should be noted that the only appropriate comparisons to make for these data are those given. Because the level of associativity of the contextually related and contextually inappropriate words to each of the meanings of the ambiguity are not equated (a nearly impossible task given the other, more critical, constraints required in matching these words; see Design and Materials section), the appropriate comparisons are just those which examine for evidence of facilitation/priming between each of these visual words and its control. Levels of such facilitation cannot be meaningfully examined by direct comparison of reaction times to the "related" and "inappropriate" words or by comparison of the relative degree of facilitation for each of these words compared to its control (although these have been given in a few cases above, just for general interest purposes). This is, again, because the absolute degree of associativity of each visual word to its related sense of the ambiguity differ by an unknown amount. In addition, although the reaction times for the contextually related words are beguilingly similar for the ambiguous and nonambiguous conditions, no interpretable comparisons between these conditions are possible; the facilitation of the "contextually related" words occurs in response to different auditory contexts in the ambiguous and unambiguous conditions (e.g., to the word "bug" in the one and "insect" in the other, in the materials sample in Table 37.1). It is interesting to note that reaction times to the control words, which are legitimate sources for comparison, are remarkably similar for the ambiguous and unambiguous conditions. However, overall, the only relevant and interpretable comparisons are those involving the search for presence or absence of significant facilitation/priming for the "related" and "inappropriate" visual words in each of the individual experimental conditions; such evidence is sufficient and appropriate for examining the issues addressed in this paper.

4. Although all paired comparisons made by multiple $t$ tests were both planned and necessary in order to examine the hypotheses under question, a more conservative test, the Bonferroni $t$ (Kirk, 1968), was also applied to the data. For this test, the critical value of $d$ for $\alpha = .05$, was 46.1. As can be seen by inspection, all comparisons which were significant under the standard $t$ tests were also significant under the Bonferroni $t$ analysis.

5. All comparisons found to be significant under standard $t$ were also significant under the Bonferroni correction ($d = 36.2$, $\alpha = .05$) with two exceptions. Comparisons in the unambiguous condition involving contrasts of the contextually related words to the unrelated words when no context was present, and the contrast of contextually related words to inappropriate words when a biasing context was present, both just failed to reach significance at $\alpha = .05$. Both are significant at $\alpha = .07$.

6. Under Bonferroni $t$ analysis (for $\alpha = .05$, $d = 28.4$), all significant effects reported for the multiple $t$ tests are also significant under the more conservative Bonferroni $t$ analysis.

## REFERENCES

Bever, T. G., Garrett, M. F., & Hurtig, R. The interaction of perceptual processes and ambiguous sentences. *Memory and Cognition*, 1973, *1*, 227–286.

Cairns, H. S. & Hsu, J. R. Effects of prior context upon lexical access during sentence comprehension: A replication and reinterpretation. *Journal of Psycholinguistic Research*, 1979, in press.

Cairns, H. S. & Kamerman, J. Lexical information processing during sentence comprehension. *Journal of Verbal Learning and Verbal Behavior*, 1975, *14*, 170–179.

Collins, A. M. & Loftus, E. F. A spreading activation theory of semantic processing. *Psychological Review*, 1975, *82*, 407–428.

Conrad, C. Context effects in sentence comprehension: A study of the subjective lexicon. *Memory and Cognition*, 1974, *2*, No. 1A, 130–138.

Fishler, I. Semantic facilitation without association in a lexical decision task. *Memory and Cognition*, 1977, *5*, 333–339.

Forster, K. I. Accessing the mental lexicon. In R. J. Wales & E. Walker (Eds.), *New Approaches to Language Mechanisms*. Amsterdam: North–Holland, 1976.

Foss, D. J. Some effects of ambiguity upon sentence comprehension. *Journal of Verbal Learning and Verbal Behavior*, 1970, *9*, 699–706.

Foss, D. J., Bever, T. G., & Silver, M. The comprehension and verification of ambiguous sentences. *Perception and Psychophysics*, 1968, *4*, 304–306.

Foss, D. J. & Jenkins, C. Some effects of context on the comprehension of ambiguous sentences. *Journal of Verbal Learning and Verbal Behavior*, 1973, *12*, 577–589.

Foss, D. J. & Swinney, D. On the psychological reality of the phoneme: Perception, identification and consciousness. *Journal of Verbal Learning and Verbal Behavior*, 1973, *12*, 246–257.

Garrett, M. F. Word and sentence perception. In R. Held, H. W. Liebowitz, & H. L. Teuber (Eds.), *Handbook of Sensory Physiology*, Vol. VIII: *Perception*. Berlin: Springer-Verlag, 1978.

Hogaboam, T. & Perfetti, C. Lexical ambiguity and sentence comprehension. *Journal of Verbal Learning and Verbal Behavior*, 1975, *14*, 265–274.

Holmes, V. M., Arwas, R., & Garrett, M. F. Prior context and the perception of lexically ambiguous sentences. *Memory and Cognition*, 1977, *5*, 103–110.

Kirk, R. *Experimental Design: Procedures for the Behavioral Sciences*. Belmont, Calif.: Brooks/Cole, 1968.

Kučera, H. & Francis, W. *Computational Analysis of Present-day American English*. Providence, R.I.: Brown Univ. Press, 1967.

Lackner, J. R. & Garrett, M. F. Resolving ambiguity: Effects of biasing context in the unattended ear. *Cognition*, 1972, *1*, 359–372.

MacKay, D. G. Mental diplopia: Towards a model of speech perception at the semantic level. In G. B. Flores d'Arcais & W. J. Levelt (Eds.), *Advances in Psycholinguistics*. Amsterdam: North–Holland, 1970.

Marslen-Wilson, W. D. Sentence perception as an interactive parallel process. *Science*, 1975, *189*, 226–228.

Marslen-Wilson, W. D. & Welsh, A. Processing interactions and lexical access during word recognition in continuous speech. *Cognitive Psychology*, 1978, *10*.

Mehler, J., Segui, J., & Carey, P. Tails of words: Monitoring ambiguity. *Journal of Verbal Learning and Verbal Behavior*, 1978, *17*, 29–35.

Meyer, D. E., Schvaneveldt, R. W., & Ruddy, M. G. Loci of contextual effects on visual word recognition. In P. M. A. Rabbit & S. Dornic (Eds.), *Attention and Performance V*. London/New York: Academic Press, 1975.

Morton, J. The interaction of information in word recognition. *Psychological Review*, 1969, *60*, 329–346.

Neely, J. Semantic priming and retrieval from lexical memory: Roles of inhibitionless spreading activation and limited capacity attention. *Journal of Experimental Psychology: General*, 1977, *106*, 226–254.

Newman, J. E. & Dell, G. S. The phonological nature of phoneme monitoring: A critique of some ambiguity studies. *Journal of Verbal Learning and Verbal Behavior*, 1978, *17*, 359–374.

Onifer, W., Hirshkowitz, M., & Swinney, D. A mini-processor PDP8/e-based system for investigations of on-line language processing: Automated program for psycholinguistic experiments (APPLE). *Behavior Research Methods and Instrumentation*, 1978, *10*(2), 307–308.

Schvaneveldt, R., Meyer, D., & Becker, C. Lexical ambiguity, semantic context, and visual word recognition. *Journal of Experimental Psychology: Human Perception and Performance*, 1976, *2*, 243–256.

Swinney, D. & Hakes, D. Effects of prior context upon lexical access during sentence comprehension. *Journal of Verbal Learning and Verbal Behavior*, 1976, *15*, 681–689.

Swinney, D., Onifer, W., Prather, P., & Hirshkowitz, M. Semantic facilitation across sensory modalities in the processing of individual words and sentences. *Memory and Cognition*, 1979, *7*(3), 159–165.

Tweedy, L., Lapinski, R., & Schvaneveldt, R. Semantic context effects upon word recognition. *Memory and Cognition*, 1977, *5*, 84–89.

## REFERENCE NOTES

1. Jenkins, J. *Context Conditions Meaning*. Invited address delivered at Midwestern Psychological Association, Chicago, Ill., May 1977.

2. Chodorow, M. *Using Time-Compressed Speech to Measure the Effects of Ambiguity*. Quarterly Progress Report No. 116, Massachusetts Institute of Technology, 1973, Pp. 235–240.

3. Cutler, A. & Foss, D. J. *Comprehension of Ambiguous Sentences. The Locus of Context Effects*. Paper presented at the Midwestern Psychological Association, Chicago, Ill., May 1974.

4. Swinney, D. *Does Context Direct Lexical Access?* Paper presented at Midwestern Psychological Association, Chicago, Ill., May 1976.

5. Meyer, D., Schvaneveldt, R., & Ruddy, M. *Activation of Lexical Memory*. Paper presented at the Meeting of the Psychonomic Society, St. Louis, Mo., 1972.

6. Fay, D. *The Role of Grammatical Category in the Mental Lexicon*. Paper presented at the Midwestern Psychological Association, Chicago, Ill., May 1976.

7. Prather, P. & Swinney, D. *Some Effects of Syntactic Context upon Lexical Access*. Paper presented at the American Psychological Association, San Francisco, August 1977.

8. Ryder, J. The effects of semantic and syntactic ambiguity on lexical processing. Unpublished paper, Psychology Department, Brandeis University, 1978.

# Language and the Brain

Norman Geschwind

Aphasias are speech disorders caused by brain damage. The relations between these disorders and specific kinds of brain damage suggest a model of how the language areas of the human brain are organized.

Virtually everything we know of how the functions of language are organized in the human brain has been learned from abnormal conditions or under abnormal circumstances: brain damage, brain surgery, electrical stimulation of brains exposed during surgery and the effects of drugs on the brain. Of these the most fruitful has been the study of language disorders, followed by postmortem analysis of the brain, in patients who have suffered brain damage. From these studies has emerged a model of how the language areas of the brain are interconnected and what each area does.

A disturbance of language resulting from damage to the brain is called aphasia. Such disorders are not rare. Aphasia is a common aftereffect of the obstruction or rupture of blood vessels in the brain, which is the third leading cause of death in the U.S. Although loss of speech from damage to the brain had been described occasionally before the 19th century, the medical study of such cases was begun by a remarkable Frenchman, Paul Broca, who in 1861 published the first of a series of papers on language and the brain. Broca was the first to point out that damage to a specific portion of the brain results in disturbance of language output. The portion he identified, lying in the third frontal gyrus of the cerebral cortex, is now called Broca's area [Figure 38.2].

Broca's area lies immediately in front of the portion of the motor cortex that controls the muscles of the face, the jaw, the tongue, the palate and the larynx, in other words, the muscles involved in speech production. The region is often called the "motor face area." It might therefore seem that loss of speech from damage to Broca's area is the result of paralysis of these muscles. This explanation, however, is not the correct one. Direct damage to the area that controls these muscles often produces only mild weakness of the lower facial muscles on the side opposite the damage and no permanent weakness of the jaw, the tongue, the palate or the vocal cords. The reason is that most

FIGURE 38.1 ■ Location of some lesions in the brain can be determined by injecting into the bloodstream a radioactive isotope of mercury, which is taken up by damaged brain tissue. The damaged region is identified by scanning the head for areas of high radioactivity. The top scan on the opposite page was made from the back of the head; the white area on the left shows that the damage is in the left hemisphere. The bottom scan is of the left side of the head and shows that the uptake of mercury was predominantly in the first temporal gyrus, indicating damage to Wernicke's speech area by occlusion of blood vessels. David Patten and Martin Albert of the Boston Veterans Administration Hospital supplied the scans.

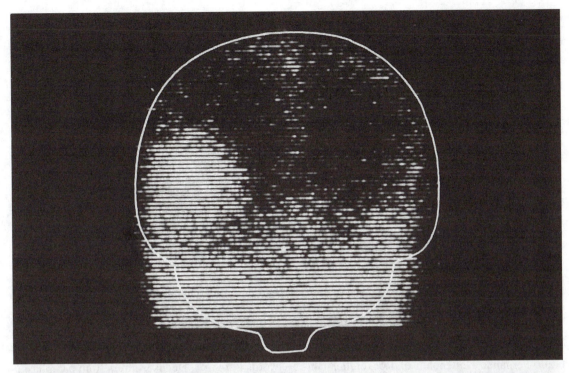

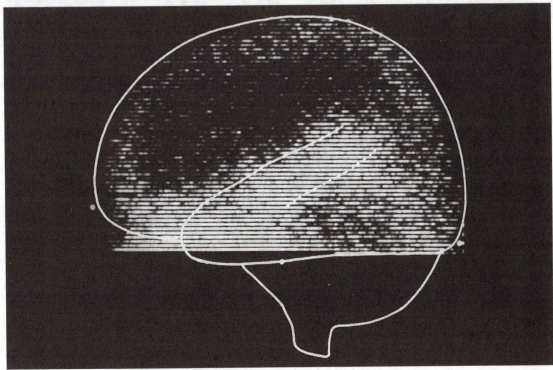

of these muscles can be controlled by either side of the brain. Damage to the motor face area on one side of the brain can be compensated by the control center on the opposite side. Broca named the lesion-produced language disorder "aphemia," but this term was soon replaced by "aphasia," which was suggested by Armand Trousseau.

In 1865 Broca made a second major contribution to the study of language and the brain. He reported that damage to specific areas of the left half of the brain led to disorder of spoken language but that destruction of corresponding areas in the right side of the brain left language abilities intact. Broca based his conclusion on eight consecutive cases of aphasia, and in the century since his report his observation has been amply confirmed. Only rarely does damage to the right hemisphere of the brain lead to language disorder; out of 100 people with permanent language disorder caused by brain lesions approximately 97 will have damage on the left side. This unilateral control of certain functions is called cerebral dominance. As far as we know man is the only mammal in which learned behavior is controlled by one half of the brain. Fernando Nottebohm of Rockefeller University has found unilateral neural control of birdsong. It is an interesting fact that a person with aphasia of the Broca type who can utter at most only one or two slurred words may be able to sing a melody rapidly, correctly and even with elegance. This is another proof that aphasia is not the result of muscle paralysis.

In the decade following Broca's first report on brain lesions and language there was a profusion of papers on aphasias of the Broca type. In fact, there was a tendency to believe all aphasias were the result of damage to Broca's area. At this point another great pioneer of the brain appeared on the scene. Unlike Broca, who already had a reputation at the time of his first paper on aphasia, Carl Wernicke was an unknown with no previous publications; he was only 26 years old and a junior assistant in the neurological service in Breslau. In spite of his youth and obscurity his paper on aphasia, published in 1874, gained immediate attention. Wernicke described damage at a site in the left hemisphere outside Broca's area that results in a language disorder differing from Broca's aphasia.

In Broca's aphasia speech is slow and labored. Articulation is crude. Characteristically, small grammatical words and the endings of nouns and verbs are omitted, so that the speech has a telegraphic style. Asked to describe a trip he has taken, the patient may say "New York." When urged to produce a sentence, he may do no better than "Go . . . New York." This difficulty is not simply a desire to economize effort, as some have suggested. Even when the patient does his best to cooperate in repeating words, he has difficulty with certain grammatical words and phrases. "If he were here, I would go" is more difficult than "The general commands the army." The hardest phrase for such patients to repeat is "No ifs, ands or buts."

The aphasia described by Wernicke is quite different. The patient may speak very rapidly, preserving rhythm, grammar and articulation. The speech, if not listened to closely, may almost sound normal. For example, the patient may say: "Before I was in the one here, I was over in the other one. My sister had the department in the other one." It is abnormal in that it is remarkably devoid of content. The patient fails to use the correct word and substitutes for it by circumlocutory phrases ("what you use to cut with" for "knife") and empty words ("thing"). He also suffers from paraphasia, which is of two kinds. Verbal paraphasia is the substitution of one word or phrase for another, sometimes related in meaning ("knife" for "fork") and sometimes unrelated ("hammer" for "paper"). Literal or phonemic paraphasia is the substitution of incorrect sounds in otherwise correct words ("kench" for "wrench"). If there are several incorrect sounds in a word, it becomes a neologism, for example "pluver" or "flieber."

Wernicke also noted another difference between these aphasic patients and those with Broca's aphasia. A person with Broca's aphasia may have an essentially normal comprehension of language. Indeed, Broca had argued that no single lesion in the brain could cause a loss of comprehension. He was wrong. A lesion in Wernicke's area can produce a severe loss of understanding, even though hearing of nonverbal sounds and music may be fully normal.

Perhaps the most important contribution made by Wernicke was his model of how the language areas in the brain are connected. Wernicke modestly stated that his ideas were based on the teachings of Meynert, a Viennese Theodor neuroanatomist who had attempted to correlate the nervous system's structure with its function. Since Broca's area was adjacent to the cortical region of the brain that controlled the muscles of speech, it was reasonable to assume, Wernicke argued, that Broca's area incorporated the programs for complex coordination of these muscles. In addition Wernicke's area lay adjacent to the cortical region that received auditory stimuli [Figure 38.2]. Wernicke made the natural assumption that Broca's area and Wernicke's area must be connected. We now know that the two areas are indeed connected, by a bundle of nerve fibers known as the arcuate fasciculus. One can hypothesize that in the repetition

of a heard word the auditory patterns are relayed from Wernicke's area to Broca's area.

Comprehension of written language would require connections from the visual regions to the speech regions. This function is served by the angular gyrus, a cortical region just behind Wernicke's area. It acts in some way to convert a visual stimulus into the appropriate auditory form.

We can now deduce from the model what happens in the brain during the production of language. When a word is heard, the output from the primary auditory area of the cortex is received by

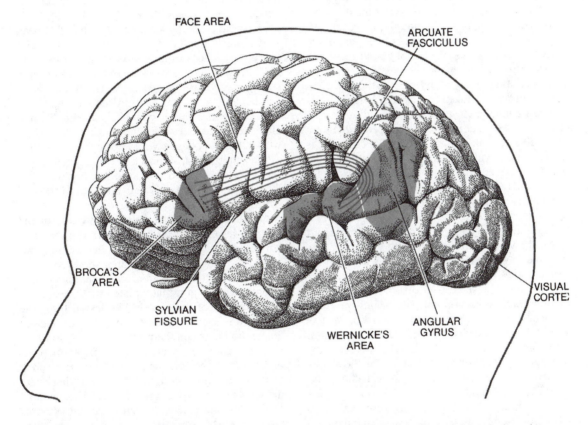

**FIGURE 38.2** ■ Primary language areas of the human brain are thought to be located in the left hemisphere, because only rarely does damage to the right hemisphere cause language disorders. Broca's area, which is adjacent to the region of the motor cortex that controls the movement of the muscles of the lips, the jaw, the tongue, the soft palate and the vocal cords, apparently incorporates programs for the coordination of these muscles in speech. Damage to Broca's area results in slow and labored speech, but comprehension of language remains intact. Wernicke's area lies between Heschl's gyrus, which is the primary receiver of auditory stimuli, and the angular gyrus, which acts as a way station between the auditory and the visual regions. When Wernicke's area is damaged, speech is fluent but has little content and comprehension is usually lost. Wernicke and Broca areas are joined by a nerve bundle called the arcuate fasciculus. When it is damaged, speech is fluent but abnormal, and patient can comprehend words but cannot repeat them.

Wernicke's area. If the word is to be spoken, the pattern is transmitted from Wernicke's area to Broca's area, where the articulatory form is aroused and passed on to the motor area that controls the movement of the muscles of speech. If the spoken word is to be spelled, the auditory pattern is passed to the angular gyrus, where it elicits the visual pattern. When a word is read, the output from the primary visual areas passes to the angular gyrus, which in turn arouses the corresponding auditory form of the word in Wernicke's area. It should be noted that in most people comprehension of a written word involves arousal of the auditory form in Wernicke's area. Wernicke argued that this was the result of the way most people learn written language. He thought, however, that in people who were born deaf, but had learned to read, Wernicke's area would not be in the circuit.

According to this model, if Wernicke's area is damaged, the person would have difficulty comprehending both spoken and written language. He should be unable to speak, repeat and write correctly. The fact that in such cases speech is fluent and well articulated suggests that Broca's area is intact but receiving inadequate information. If the damage were in Broca's area, the effect of the lesion would be to disrupt articulation. Speech would be slow and labored but comprehension should remain intact.

This model may appear to be rather simple, but it has shown itself to be remarkably fruitful. It is possible to use it to predict the sites of brain lesions on the basis of the type of language disorder. Moreover, it gave rise to some definite predictions that lesions in certain sites should produce types of aphasia not previously described. For example, if a lesion disconnected Wernicke's area from Broca's area while leaving the two areas intact, a special type of aphasia should be the result. Since Broca's area is preserved, speech should be fluent but abnormal. On the other hand, comprehension should be intact because Wernicke's area is still functioning. Repetition of spoken language, however, should be grossly impaired. This syndrome has in fact been found. It is termed conduction aphasia.

The basic pattern of speech localization in the brain has been supported by the work of many investigators. A. R. Luria of the U.S.S.R. studied a large number of patients who suffered brain wounds during World War II [see "The Functional Organization of the Brain," by A. R. Luria; *Scientific American*, March, 1970]. When the wound site lay over Wernicke's or Broca's area, Luria found that the result was almost always severe and permanent aphasia. When the wounds were in other areas, aphasia was less frequent and less severe.

A remarkable case of aphasia has provided striking confirmation of Wernicke's model. The case, described by Fred Quadfasel, Jose Segarra and myself, involved a woman who had suffered from accidental carbon monoxide poisoning. During the nine years we studied her she was totally helpless and required complete nursing care. She never uttered speech spontaneously and showed no evidence of comprehending words. She could, however, repeat perfectly sentences that had just been said to her. In addition she would complete certain phrases. For example, if she heard "Roses are red," she would say "Roses are red, violets are blue, sugar is sweet and so are you." Even more surprising was her ability to learn songs. A song that had been written after her illness would be played to her and after a few repetitions she would begin to sing along with it. Eventually she would begin to sing as soon as the song started. If the song was stopped after a few bars, she would continue singing the song through to the end, making no errors in either words or melody.

On the basis of Wernicke's model we predicted that the lesions caused by the carbon monoxide poisoning lay outside the speech and auditory regions, and that both Broca's area and Wernicke's area were intact. Postmortem examination revealed a remarkable lesion that isolated the speech area from the rest of the cortex. The lesion fitted the prediction. Broca's area, Wernicke's area and the connection between them were intact. Also intact were the auditory pathways and the motor pathways to the speech organs. Around the speech area, however, either the cortex or the underlying white matter was destroyed [Figure 38.4]. The woman could not comprehend speech because the words did not arouse associations in other portions of the cortex. She could repeat speech correctly because the internal connections of the speech region were intact. Presumably well-learned word sequences stored in Broca's area could be triggered by the beginning phrases. This syndrome is called isolation of the speech area.

Two important extensions of the Wernicke model were advanced by a French neurologist,

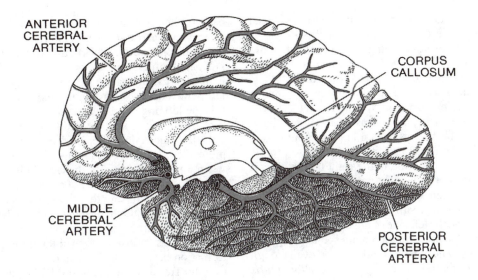

ANTERIOR
CEREBRAL
ARTERY

CORPUS
CALLOSUM

MIDDLE
CEREBRAL
ARTERY

POSTERIOR
CEREBRAL
ARTERY

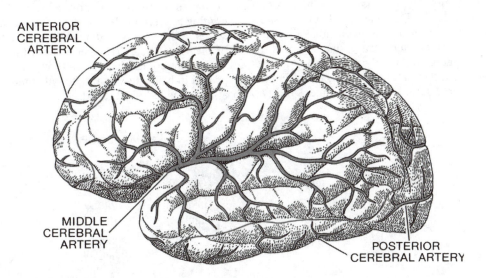

ANTERIOR
CEREBRAL
ARTERY

MIDDLE
CEREBRAL
ARTERY

POSTERIOR
CEREBRAL ARTERY

**FIGURE 38.3** ■ Cerebral areas are nourished by several arteries, each supplying blood to a specific region. The speech and auditory region is nourished by the middle cerebral artery. The visual areas at the rear are supplied by the posterior cerebral artery. In patients who suffer from inadequate oxygen supply to the brain the damage is often not within the area of a single blood vessel but rather in the "border zones" (*colored lines*). These are the regions between the areas served by the major arteries where the blood supply is marginal.

Joseph Jules Dejerine. In 1891 he described a disorder called alexia with agraphia: the loss of the ability to read and write. The patient could, however, speak and understand spoken language. Postmortem examination showed that there was a lesion in the angular gyrus of the left hemisphere, the area of the brain that acts as a way station between the visual and the auditory region. A lesion here would separate the visual and auditory language areas. Although words and letters would be seen correctly, they would be meaningless visual patterns, since the visual pattern must first be converted to the auditory form before the word can be comprehended. Conversely, the auditory pattern for a word must be transformed into the visual pattern before the word can be spelled. Patients suffering from alexia with agraphia cannot recognize words spelled aloud to them nor can they themselves spell aloud a spoken word.

Dejerine's second contribution was showing the importance of information transfer between the hemispheres. His patient was an intelligent businessman who had awakened one morning to discover that he could no longer read. It was found that the man was blind in the right half of the visual field. Since the right half of the field is projected to the left cerebral hemisphere, it was obvious that the man suffered damage to the visual pathways on the left side of the brain [Figure 38.5]. He could speak and comprehend spoken language and could write, but he could not read even though he had normal visual acuity. In fact, although he could not comprehend written words, he could copy them correctly. Postmortem examination of the man's brain by Dejerine revealed two lesions that were the result of the occlusion of the left posterior cerebral artery. The visual cortex of the left hemisphere was totally destroyed. Also destroyed was a portion of the corpus callosum: the mass of nerve fibers that interconnect the two cerebral hemispheres. That portion was the splenium, which carries the visual information between the hemispheres. The destruction of the splenium prevented stimuli from the visual cortex of the right hemisphere from reaching the angular gyrus of the left hemisphere. According to Wernicke's model, it is the left angular gyrus that converts the visual pattern of a word into the auditory pattern; without such conversion a seen word cannot be comprehended. Other workers have since shown that when a person is blind in the right half of the visual field but is still capable of reading, the portion of the corpus callosum that transfers visual information between the hemispheres is not damaged.

In 1937 the first case in which surgical section of the corpus callosum stopped the transfer of information between the hemispheres was reported by John Trescher and Frank Ford. The patient had the rear portion of his corpus callosum severed during an operation to remove a brain tumor. According to Wernicke's model, this should have resulted in the loss of reading ability in the left half of the visual field. Trescher and Ford found that the patient could read normally when words appeared in his right visual field but could not read at all in his left visual field.

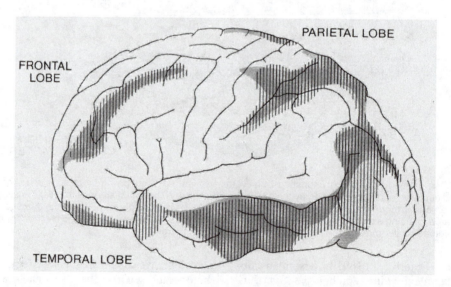

**FIGURE 38.4** ■ Isolation of speech area by a large *C*-shaped lesion produced a remarkable syndrome in a woman who suffered from severe carbon monoxide poisoning. She could repeat words and learn new songs but could not comprehend the meaning of words. Postmortem examination of her brain revealed that in the regions surrounding the speech areas of the left hemisphere, either the cortex (*colored areas*) or the underlying white matter (*hatched areas*) was destroyed but that the cortical structures related to the production of language (Broca's area and Wernicke's area) and the connections between them were left intact.

**FIGURE 38.5** ■ Classic case of a man who lost the ability to read even though he had normal visual acuity and could copy written words was described in 1892 by Joseph Jules Dejerine. Postmortem analysis of the man's brain showed that the left visual cortex and the splenium (*dark colored areas*) were destroyed as a result of an occlusion of the left posterior cerebral artery. The splenium is the section of the corpus callosum that transfers visual information between the two hemispheres. The man's left visual cortex was inoperative, making him blind in his right visual field. Words in his left visual field were properly received by the right visual cortex, but could not cross over to the language areas in the left hemisphere because of the damaged splenium. Thus words seen by the man remained as meaningless patterns.

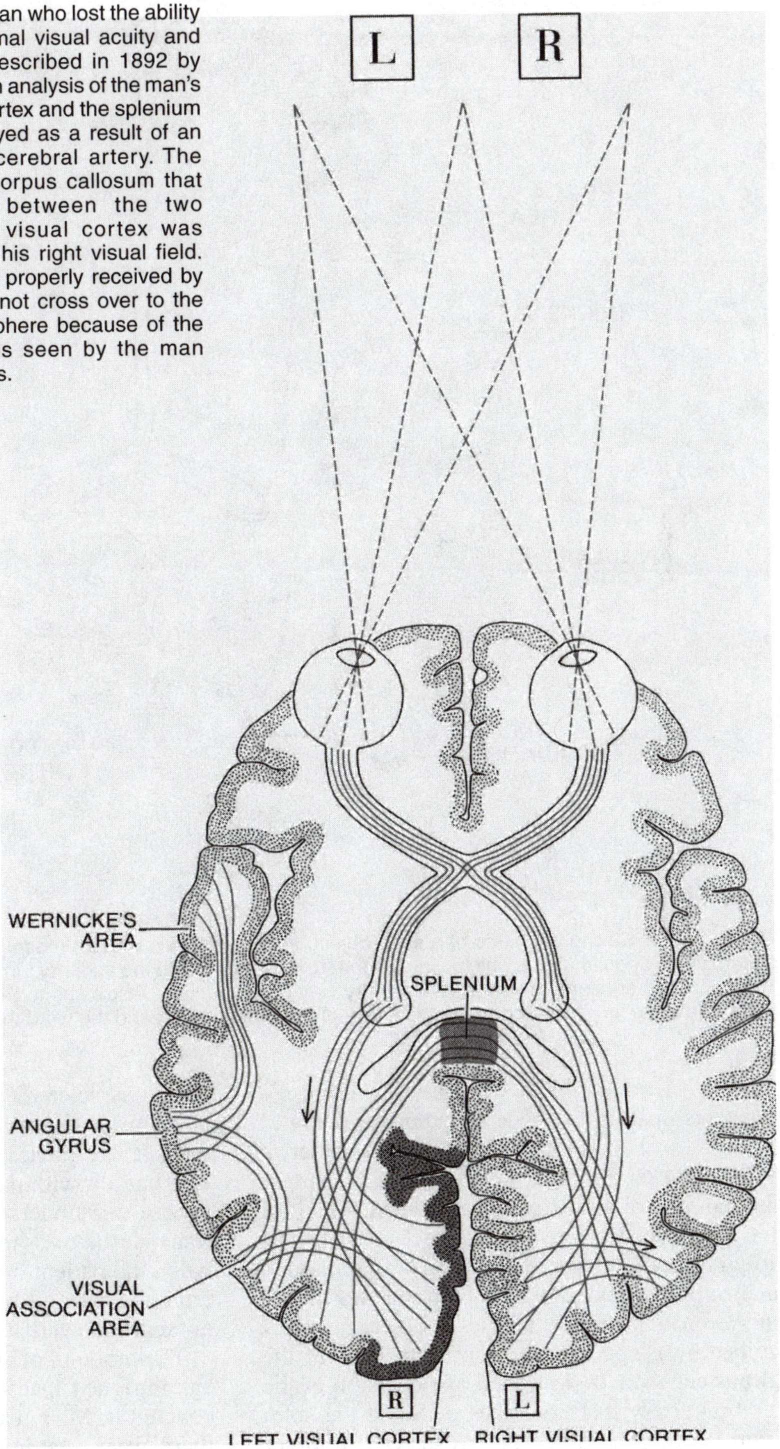

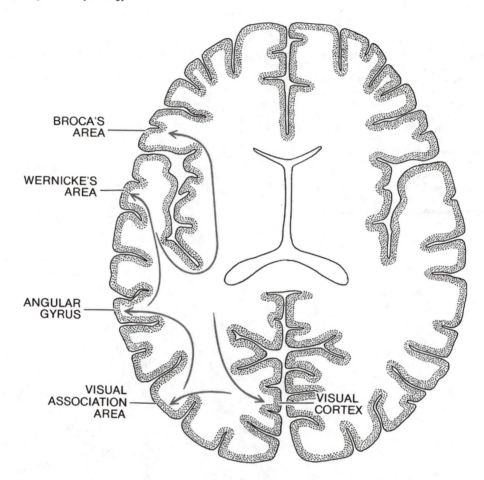

BROCA'S
AREA

WERNICKE'S
AREA

ANGULAR
GYRUS

VISUAL
ASSOCIATION
AREA

VISUAL
CORTEX

**FIGURE 38.6** ■ Saying the name of a seen object, according to Wernicke's model, involves the transfer of the visual pattern to the angular gyrus, which contains the "rules" for arousing the auditory form of the pattern in Wernicke's area. From here the auditory form is transmitted by way of the accuate fasciculus to Broca's area. There the articulatory form is aroused, is passed on to the face area of the motor cortex and the word then is spoken.

Hugo Liepmann, who was one of Wernicke's assistants in Breslau, made an extensive study of syndromes of the corpus callosum, and descriptions of these disorders were a standard part of German neurology before World War I. Much of this work was neglected, and only recently has its full importance been appreciated. Liepmann's analysis of corpus callosum syndromes was based on Wernicke's model. In cases such as those described by Liepmann the front four-fifths of the corpus callosum is destroyed by occlusion of the cerebral artery that nourishes it. Since the splenium is preserved the patient can read in either visual field. Such a lesion, however, gives rise to

three characteristic disorders. The patient writes correctly with his right hand but incorrectly with the left. He carries out commands with his right arm but not with the left; although the left hemisphere can understand the command, it cannot transmit the message to the right hemisphere. Finally, the patient cannot name objects held in his left hand because the somesthetic sensations cannot reach the verbal centers in the left hemisphere.

The problem of cerebral dominance in humans has intrigued investigators since Broca first discovered it. Many early neurologists claimed that there were anatomical differences between the hemispheres, but in the past few decades there has

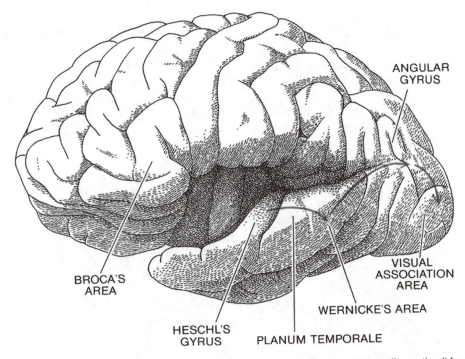

ANGULAR
GYRUS

VISUAL
ASSOCIATION
AREA

WERNICKE'S AREA

BROCA'S
AREA

HESCHL'S
GYRUS

PLANUM TEMPORALE

**FIGURE 38.7** ■ Understanding the spoken name of an object involves the transfer of the auditory stimuli from Heschl's gyrus (the primary auditory cortex) to Wernicke's area and then to the angular gyrus, which arouses the comparable visual pattern in the visual association cortex. Here the Sylvian fissure has been spread apart to show the pathway more clearly.

been a tendency to assume that the left and right hemispheres are symmetrical. It has been thought that cerebral dominance is based on undetected subtle physiological differences not reflected in gross structure. Walter Levitsky and I decided to look again into the possibility that the human brain is anatomically asymmetrical. We studied 100 normal human brains, and we were surprised to find that striking asymmetries were readily visible. The area we studied was the upper surface of the temporal lobe, which is not seen in the intact brain because it lies within the depths of the Sylvian fissure. The asymmetrical area we found and measured was the planum temporale, an extension of Wernicke's area [Figure 38.8]. This region was larger on the left side of the brain in 65 percent of the cases, equal in 24 percent and larger on the right side in 11 percent. In absolute terms the left planum was nine millimeters longer on the average than the right planum. In relative terms the left planum was one-third longer than the right.

Statistically all the differences were highly significant. Juhn A. Wada of the University of British Columbia subsequently reported a study that confirmed our results. In addition Wada studied a series of brains from infants who had died soon after birth and found that the planum asymmetry was present. It seems likely that the asymmetries of the brain are genetically determined.

It is sometimes asserted that the anatomical approach neglects the plasticity of the nervous system and makes the likelihood of therapy for language disorders rather hopeless. This is not the case. Even the earliest investigators of aphasia were aware that some patients developed symptoms that were much milder than expected. Other patients recovered completely from a lesion that normally would have produced permanent aphasia. There is recovery or partial recovery of language functions in some cases, as Luria's large-scale study of the war wounded has shown. Of all the patients with wounds in the primary speech area of the left

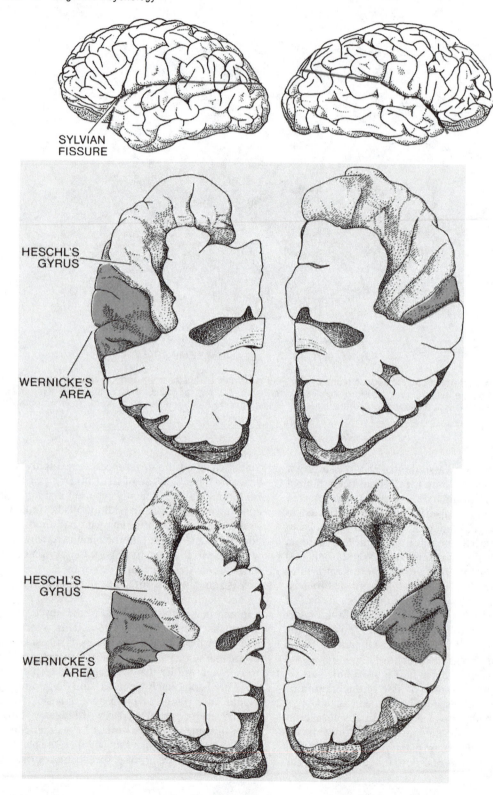

SYLVIAN
FISSURE

HESCHL'S
GYRUS

WERNICKE'S
AREA

HESCHL'S
GYRUS

WERNICKE'S
AREA

**FIGURE 38.8** ■ Anatomical differences between the two hemispheres of the human brain are found on the upper surface of the temporal lobe, which cannot be seen in an intact brain because it lies within the Sylvian fissure. Typically the Sylvian fissure in the left hemisphere appears to be pushed down compared with the Sylvian fissure on the right side *(top illustration)*. In order to expose the surface of the temporal lobe a knife is moved along the fissure *(broken line)* and then through the brain, cutting away the top portion *(solid line)*. The region studied was the planum temporale *(colored areas)*, an extension of Wernicke's area. The middle illustration shows a brain with a larger left planum; the bottom illustration shows left and right planums of about the same size. In a study of 100 normal human brains planum temporale was larger on the left side in 65 percent of the cases, equal on both sides in 24 percent of the cases and larger on the right side in 11 percent.

hemisphere, 97.2 percent were aphasic when Luria first examined them. A follow-up examination found that 93.3 percent were still aphasic, although in most cases they were aphasic to a lesser degree.

How does one account for the apparent recovery of language function in some cases? Some partial answers are available. Children have been known to make a much better recovery than adults with the same type of lesion. This suggests that at least in childhood the right hemisphere has some capacity to take over speech functions. Some cases of adult recovery are patients who had suffered brain damage in childhood. A number of patients who have undergone surgical removal of portions of the speech area for the control of epileptic seizures often show milder language disorders than had been expected. This probably is owing to the fact that the patients had suffered from left temporal epilepsy involving the left side of the brain from childhood and had been using the right hemisphere for language functions to a considerable degree.

Left-handed people also show on the average milder disorders than expected when the speech regions are damaged, even though for most left-handers the left hemisphere is dominant for speech just as it is for right-handers. It is an interesting fact that right-handers with a strong family history of left-handedness show better speech recovery than people without left-handed inheritance.

Effective and safe methods for studying cerebral dominance and localization of language function in the intact, normal human brain have begun to appear. Doreen Kimura of the University of West-

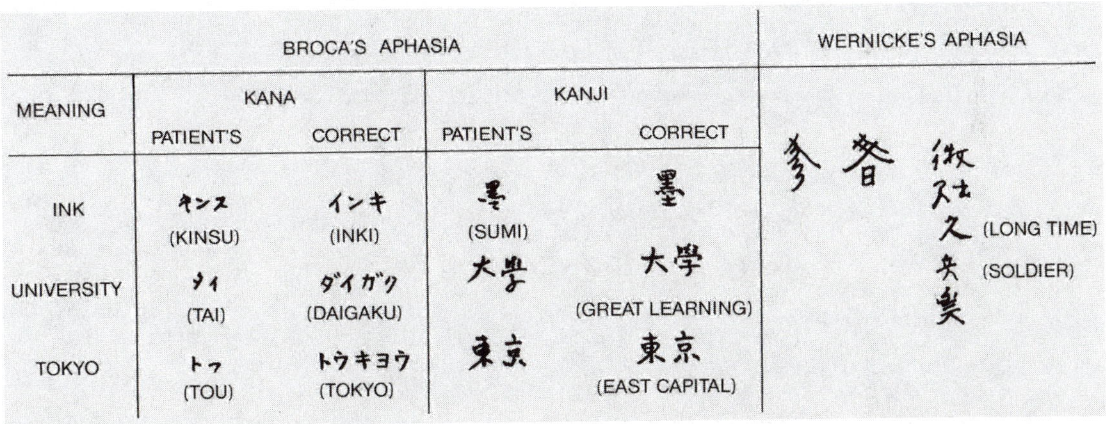

| | BROCA'S APHASIA | | | | WERNICKE'S APHASIA | |
|---|---|---|---|---|---|---|
| MEANING | KANA | | KANJI | | | |
| | PATIENT'S | CORRECT | PATIENT'S | CORRECT | | |
| INK | キンス (KINSU) | インキ (INKI) | 墨 (SUMI) | 墨 | 参 答 | 微社 久 矢莫 (LONG TIME) (SOLDIER) |
| UNIVERSITY | タイ (TAI) | ダイガク (DAIGAKU) | 大學 | 大学 (GREAT LEARNING) | | |
| TOKYO | トウ (TOU) | トウキヨウ (TOKYO) | 東京 | 東京 (EAST CAPITAL) | | |

**FIGURE 38.9** ■ Japanese aphasics display some characteristics rarely found in Western patients because of the unique writing system used in Japan. There are two separate forms of such writing. One is Kana, which is syllabic. The other is Kanji, which is ideographic. Kana words are articulated syllable by syllable and are not easily identified at a glance, whereas each Kanji character simultaneously represents both a sound and a meaning. A patient with Broca's aphasia, studied by Tsuneo Imura and his colleagues at the Nihon University College of Medicine, was able to write a dictated word correctly in Kanji but not in Kana *(top left)*. When the patient was asked to write the word "ink," even though there is no Kanji character for the word, his first effort was the Kanji character "sumi," which means india ink. When required to write in Kana, the symbols he produced were correct but the word was wrong. Another patient who had Wernicke's aphasia wrote Kanji quickly and without hesitation. He was completely unaware that he was producing meaningless ideograms, as are patients who exhibit paraphasias in speech. Only two of characters had meaning *(top right)*.

ern Ontario has adapted the technique of dichotic listening to investigate the auditory asymmetries of the brain. More recently several investigators have found increased electrical activity over the speech areas of the left hemisphere during the production or perception of speech. Refinement of these techniques could lead to a better understanding of how the normal human brain is organized for language. A deeper understanding of the neural mechanisms of speech should lead in turn to more precise methods of dealing with disorders of man's most characteristic attribute, language.

READING 39

# Functional Neuroanatomy of the Cognitive Process of Mapping during Discourse Comprehension

David A. Robertson, Morton Ann Gernsbacher, Seline J. Guidotti,
Rachel R. W. Robertson, William Irwin,
• University of Wisconsin-Madison
Bryan J. Mock • GE Medical Systems
Mary E. Campana • University of Wisconsin-Madison

We used functional magnetic resonance imaging (fMRI) to identify brain regions involved in the process of mapping coherent discourse onto a developing mental representation. We manipulated discourse coherence by presenting sentences with definite articles (which lead to more coherent discourse) or indefinite articles (which lead to less coherent discourse). Comprehending connected discourse, compared with reading unrelated sentences, produced more neural activity in the right than left hemisphere of the frontal lobe. Thus, the right hemisphere of the frontal lobe is involved in some of the processes underlying mapping. In contrast, left-hemisphere structures were associated with lower-level processes in reading (such as word recognition and syntactic processing). Our results demonstrate the utility of using fMRI to investigate the neural substrates of higher-level cognitive processes such as discourse comprehension.

A hallmark of coherent discourse is the recurrence and interrelations of key concepts. To build a similarly coherent mental representation, readers and listeners must identify those recurring concepts and have a means for mentally interrelating them; we call this cognitive process *mapping* (Gernsbacher, 1990). In the experiment reported here, we used functional magnetic resonance imaging (fMRI) to identify brain regions

underlying this putative cognitive process of mapping.

We isolated the cognitive process of mapping during discourse comprehension from lower-level sentence-comprehension processes (e.g., letter recognition, word identification, syntactic parsing) by manipulating a subtle marker of discourse coherence: the definite article *the*. In languages that employ an article system, the definite article signals

**TABLE 39.1. Example Sentence Sets Containing Indefinite and Definite Articles**

| Sentences Containing Indefinite Articles | Sentences Containing the Definite Article |
|---|---|
| A grandmother sat at a table. | The grandmother sat at the table. |
| A child played in a backyard. | The child played in the backyard. |
| A mother talked on a telephone. | The mother talked on the telephone. |
| A husband drove a tractor. | The husband drove the tractor. |
| A grandchild walked up to a door. | The grandchild walked up to the door. |
| A little boy pouted and acted bored. | The little boy pouted and acted bored. |
| A grandmother promised to bake cookies. | The grandmother promised to bake cookies. |
| A wife looked out at a field. | The wife looked out at the field. |
| Some dark clouds were rapidly accumulating. | The dark clouds were rapidly accumulating. |
| A mother worried about a harvest. | The mother worried about the harvest. |
| A grandfather opened a door. | The grandfather opened the door. |
| Some rain began to pour down. | The rain began to pour down. |
| A day's work ended early. | The day's work ended early. |
| A grandmother tried to lighten a mood. | The grandmother tried to lighten the mood. |
| An elderly woman led some others outside. | The elderly woman led the others outside. |
| A family ran through a wet field. | The family ran through the wet field. |

repeated reference. Consider the two series of sentences in Table 39.1. The series on the left contains only indefinite articles (*a, an,* and *some*), whereas the series on the right contains only the definite article, *the*. The sentences on the left seem less related to one another, more independent; the sentences on the right seem more coherent and interrelated.

Behavioral data confirm these intuitions. The same sentences are read more rapidly (Haviland & Clark, 1974), recalled in a more integrative fashion (Gernsbacher & Robertson, 2002), and rated as more coherent (de Villiers, 1974) when their articles are definite rather than indefinite. Moreover, sentences with definite articles produce a priming-in-item-recognition phenomenon. After several series of sentences with definite articles have been read, recognition memory for a sentence is facilitated if it is preceded by another sentence from the same series. This priming, which is not evident if the sentences contain only indefinite articles, suggests that a more interrelated and coherent mental representation is fostered by the definite article (Gernsbacher & Robertson, 2002). We have suggested that the definite article *the* is a cue to discourse coherence, which serves as the basis for the cognitive process of mapping (Gernsbacher, 1997; Gernsbacher & Robertson, 2002). When readers encounter the definite article, it cues them to map a representation of the current information onto a representation of previous information.

The general cognitive process of mapping most likely comprises several discourse-level structure-building operations (e.g., co-reference, alignment, integration), and discourse coherence can certainly be cued by devices other than the article system. We chose to manipulate the article system to assay a general cognitive process of mapping because the manipulation involves altering only one word.

Participants read series of sentences in which all the articles were definite (*the*), thus signaling the recurrence and interrelation of concepts (i.e., connected discourse) and enabling the cognitive process of mapping, or all the articles were indefinite (*a, an, some*). The participants also alternated between reading series of sentences and viewing series of nonletter character strings (e.g., @#$)\&@/$%% @ = = }\~ =/'$/). We used fMRI to identify regions of neural activity associated with comprehending connected discourse (sentences containing the definite article) versus comprehending unconnected discourse (sentences containing only indefinite articles). During periods of increased neural activity in the brain, the local ratio of oxygenated to deoxygenated hemoglobin increases (Malonek et al., 1997), resulting in an increase in the MR signal (Ogawa et al., 1992).

Regions of increased neural activity are determined by statistical analysis.

## Method

### Participants

Eight neurologically normal participants (4 female) participated in exchange for payment. All participants answered "right-hand" to every question on the Chapman and Chapman (1987) handedness questionnaire. Two participants contributed data to only the first two blocks.

### Stimuli and Design

We constructed numerous sets of sentence, based on the one set presented by de Villiers (1974) and the sets presented in our earlier work (Gernsbacher & Robertson, 2002). (Two example sets are shown in Table 39.1, and all the stimuli can be seen on the World Wide Web at http://psych.wisc. edu/lang/material.html.) Each set comprised 16 sentences and totaled 140 (±2) syllables. The experiment presented three blocks; during each block, the participant viewed 11 sets of sentences and nonletter character strings. During the first block, sets of sentences containing only indefinite articles were alternated with sets of nonletter strings. During the second block, sets of sentences containing only the definite article were alternated with sets of sentences containing only indefinite articles; during the third block, sets of sentences containing only the definite article were alternated with sets of nonletter strings. The nonletter strings were derived from the sentences by replacing all letters with nonletter characters, retaining interword spacing, and equating for length. For the block that alternated reading sets of sentences with indefinite versus definite articles, two versions of each set of sentences were constructed—one version with only the definite article and one with indefinite articles: each participant was presented with only one version of each set, and the versions were counterbalanced across participants. Block order was held constant for all participants to minimize possible carryover effects (e.g., interpreting sentences that contained indefinite articles as more "storylike" after experiencing sets of the storylike sentences containing the definite article).

### Procedure

Prior to scanning, participants were acclimated to the environment and procedures in a mock MR scanner. Stimuli were displayed with fiber-optic goggles (Avotec. Inc., Jensen Beach, Florida). Sentences were displayed one whole sentence at a time. Display time per syllable was equalized. Each set lasted for 48 s (i.e., an average rate of 0.34 s/ syllable). Head movements were restricted by use of a padded head coil and a dental impression bitebar. Estimated head movements were less than 1 mm within a block and less than 2 mm over the whole scan session. Participants were instructed to read the sentences: no mention was made of the sentences potentially composing narratives. For the nonletter character strings, participants were instructed to visually scan the lines. After each block, participants performed a recognition test, judging whether test sentences were "old" or "new"; no image data were collected during the recognition tests.[1]

### Scanning Protocol

Functional images were collected in the coronal plane using a gradient-echo, echo-planar imaging sequence sufficient to cover the whole brain (echo time/repetition time = 50/3,000 ms, $64 \times 64$ matrix, field of view = 240 mm, slice/gap = 7/1 mm, flip angle = 90°, 23 interleaved slices). A total of 191 images was collected for each slice in each block. The first 5 non-steady-state images were excluded from analysis to allow for signal stabilization. Additional high-resolution. T1-weighted spin-echo images in the coronal plane, directly corresponding to the functional images, and a three-dimensional image volume ($256 \times 256 \times 124$, Spoiled Gradient Recalled) were collected prior to the functional scans.

### Data Processing

The data were analyzed with Statistical Parametric Mapping (SPM96) software (Wellcome Department of Cognitive Neurology, London. United Kingdom) implemented in Matlab (Mathworks, Inc., Sherborn, Massachusetts). SPM96 combines the general linear model (to create the statistical map, or SPM) and the theory of Gaussian fields to make statistical inferences about regional effects while controlling for multiple comparisons

(Friston, Worsley, Frackowiak, Mazziotta, & Evans, 1994; Friston et al., 1995; Worsley, Evans, Marrett, & Neelin, 1992). Data were realigned using the first scan of the experiment as a reference, spatially normalized to a standard stereotactic space approximating the Talairach and Tournoux (1988) atlas, and smoothed (spatially using an isotropic Gaussian kernel, 5-mm full width at half maximum [FWHM], and temporally using a 2.8-s FWHM kernel). Analyses were conducted using a 6-s delayed boxcar corresponding to the task paradigm, using proportional global scaling, treating subjects as fixed effects.

To test the hemispheric asymmetry of neural activity for the block comparing sentences containing the definite article with sentences containing indefinite articles, we calculated activation maps using a three-parameter least squares fitting procedure (cf. Sorenson & Wang, 1996). Anatomical regions of interest were selected using T1-weighted high-resolution images as an underlay to the activation maps, and were defined for the frontal lobe as the seven most anterior coronal slices. To avoid regions of the temporal lobe that showed signal loss due to susceptibility artifact, we considered only the first three slices of the temporal lobe. No statistically reliable hemispheric differences were detected in the temporal regions.

We computed an activation index by counting the number of voxels with signal change exceeding a threshold ($t \geq 2$, $p < .05$, uncorrected), excluding the two columns of voxels adjacent to the longitudinal and Sylvian fissures, and deriving the mean $r$-statistic value of these voxels. This value was then divided by the total number of voxels in the volume. Activation indices were statistically compared using region, hemisphere, and sex as predictors (for similar approaches, see Bavelier et al., 1997; Pugh et al., 1996). We did not detect any effect of or interactions with sex.

## Results

### Functional Neuroanatomy of Sentence Reading

Analyses of the two blocks that alternated reading sentences with viewing nonletter strings allowed us to identify neural regions involved in reading sentences, while equating approximately for vi-

sual stimulation. As shown in Figure 39.1 and Table 39.2, these comparisons produced robust regions of activation in the left hemisphere, extending from the angular gyrus rostrally to the left anterior temporal pole along the middle temporal gyrus. A smaller region of activation was also observed in the right hemisphere. These results corroborate other brain-imaging studies of sentence reading (Bavelier et al., 1997; Helenius, Salmelin, Service, & Connolly, 1998; Just, Carpenter, Keller, Eddy, & Thulborn, 1996), and are suggestive of a language-processing circuit primarily localized to the left hemisphere.

### Functional Neuroanatomy of the Cognitive Process of Mapping

Analyses of the block that alternated reading sentences containing the definite article with reading sentences containing indefinite articles allowed us to identify neural regions involved in comprehending connected discourse. This manipulation isolated the cognitive process of mapping from basic sentence-reading processes. Indeed, the comparison of reading sentences with definite articles versus indefinite articles revealed virtually no differences in activation in the left-hemisphere regions that are typically thought to underlie sentence processing and that we identified in the comparisons of sentence versus nonletter-string blocks. Instead, differential activation was observed in frontal regions, particularly in the right superior and medial frontal gyri. Table 39.3 shows that the two most prominent clusters of activation for sentences with definite articles were in the right hemisphere of the frontal lobe, whereas the two most prominent clusters of activation for sentences with indefinite articles were in the left hemisphere.

To statistically assess the hemispheric asymmetry, we computed an activation index for each hemisphere in seven homotopic regions of the frontal lobe based on activation maps calculated for each participant while reading sentences with definite articles and while reading sentences with indefinite articles. These regional activation-index values were analyzed in a hemisphere-by-region repeated measures analysis of variance, which revealed greater activation in the right than the left frontal lobe during the reading of sentences containing the definite article,[2] as indicated in Figure 39.2. Note that whereas there was marginally

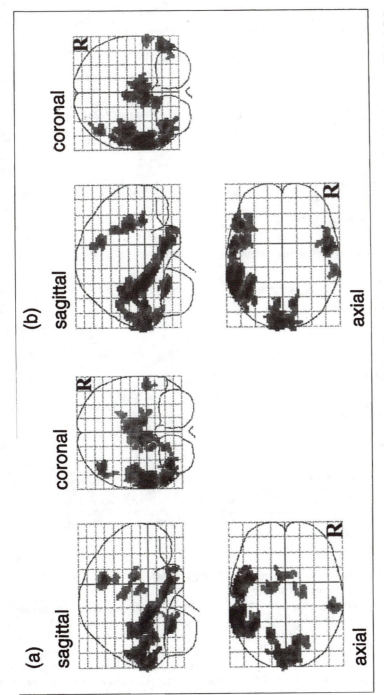

**FIGURE 39.1** ■ Glass brain projections of the statistical parametric maps (SPMs) showing regions of activation for (a) sentences with indefinite articles versus nonletter character strings and (b) sentences with the definite article versus nonletter character strings. Each SPM is displayed in a standard format as a maximum-intensity projection viewed from the back, the right-hand side, and the top of the brain. The SPM has been extent-thresholded at $p < .05$, corrected for multiple comparisons.

**TABLE 39.2. Table of Regional Differences for the Blocks That Alternated Sentences with Nonletter Strings**

| Location | Hemisphere | Volume (cm³) | Intensity (Z) | Coordinates (mm) x | y | z |
|---|---|---|---|---|---|---|
| *Sentences with indefinite articles versus nonletter character strings* | | | | | | |
| *Positive activations* | | | | | | |
| Middle temporal gyrus, BA 21 | Left | 15.50 | 8.44 | −66 | −38 | 0 |
| Cerebellum | Left | 2.51 | 7.50 | −40 | −52 | −26 |
| Lingual gyrus, BA 19 | | 12.08 | 6.94 | 12 | −72 | 4 |
| Middle frontal gyrus, BA 6, 8 | Left | 2.25 | 6.83 | −40 | 6 | 52 |
| Inferior frontal gyrus, BA 45 | Left | 0.52 | 6.48 | −56 | 26 | 0 |
| Middle temporal gyrus, BA 21 | Right | 1.54 | 5.83 | 54 | −28 | 0 |
| Parahippocampal gyrus | Left | 0.62 | 5.64 | −20 | −2 | −20 |
| Anterior cingulate, BA 24 | | 1.24 | 5.35 | −6 | 6 | 16 |
| *Negative activations* | | | | | | |
| Superior parietal lobule, BA 7, 19 | Right | 4.70 | −7.85 | 22 | −74 | 52 |
| Cerebellum/fusiform gyrus | Right | 5.76 | −7.29 | 30 | −52 | −16 |
| Precuneus, BA 7 | | 6.68 | −7.11 | −6 | −74 | 56 |
| Lateral and superior occipital gyrus, BA 18 | Right | 2.58 | −7.09 | 34 | −88 | 12 |
| Cerebellum/fusiform gyrus | Left | 0.96 | −6.76 | −26 | −50 | −20 |
| *Sentences with definite article versus nonletter character strings* | | | | | | |
| *Positive activations* | | | | | | |
| Middle temporal gyrus, BA 22 | Left | 18.99 | 8.02 | −62 | −42 | 4 |
| Cerebellum | Left | 2.47 | 7.59 | −40 | −54 | −24 |
| Middle temporal gyrus, BA 21 | Right | 3.07 | 7.36 | 54 | −8 | −20 |
| Inferior/mid frontal gyrus, BA 8, 9, 10 | Left | 7.38 | 7.02 | −48 | 22 | 20 |
| Lingual gyrus, BA 17, 18 | | 12.38 | 6.92 | −4 | −92 | −4 |
| Cerebellum/fusiform gyrus | Right | 0.47 | 6.06 | 38 | −46 | −26 |
| Superior temporal gyrus, BA 22 | Right | 0.26 | 5.85 | 52 | −44 | 14 |
| Superior frontal gyrus, BA 6 | Left | 0.34 | 5.81 | −36 | 12 | 60 |
| *Negative activations* | | | | | | |
| Superior parietal lobule, BA 7, 19 | Right | 4.03 | −7.10 | 16 | −76 | 54 |
| Superior parietal lobule, BA 7, 40 | Left | 1.17 | −6.07 | −38 | −48 | 48 |
| Medial frontal gyrus, BA 9 | Left | 0.64 | −6.04 | −34 | 38 | 40 |
| Supramarginal gyrus, BA 7, 40 | Right | 1.21 | −5.70 | 46 | −38 | 60 |
| Anterior cingulate gyrus, BA 32 | | 0.70 | −5.46 | −2 | 36 | 22 |

*Note.* Coordinates are estimated locations of the primary maxima in stereotactic space. All regions are statistically reliable based on peak height of 3.09 ($p < .001$, uncorrected) and spatial extent ($p < .05$, corrected). The eight clusters with the greatest primary maxima for positive activations and the five greatest deactivations are reported for both blocks. For the comparison of sentences with indefinite articles versus nonletter character strings. $N = 8$, $df = 612$, smoothness full width at half maximum = 6.3, 8.8, 6.4 mm. For the comparison of sentences with the definite article versus nonletter character strings. $N = 6$, $df = 459$, smoothness full width at half maximum = 7.2, 9.5, 7.2 mm. BA = Brodmann's Area.

greater right-hemisphere activation for sentences with the definite article at all locations, the laterality difference was statistically reliable only in the more caudal portions of the frontal lobe: $F(1, 7) = 1.76$, $p = .19$; $F(1, 7) = 2.53$, $p = .13$; $F(1, 7) = 9.72$, $p < .02$; $F(1, 7) = 6.63$, $p < .04$; $F(1, 7) = 10.62$, $p < .01$; $F(1, 7) = 5.30$, $p < .05$; and $F(1, 7) = 21.73$, $p < .01$, for each region, listed anterior to posterior.

# Discussion

We observed that the cognitive process of mapping during discourse comprehension was accompanied by more neural activity in the right than the left hemisphere. This observation challenges conventional beliefs about language lateralization. All early theories of brain organization emphasized left-hemisphere dominance for language, most

**TABLE 39.3 Two Most Prominent Activations and Deactivations from the Block That Alternated Sentences That Contained the Definite Article with Sentences That Contained Only Indefinite Articles**

| Location | Volume (mm³) | Intensity (Z) | Coordinates (mm) | | |
|---|---|---|---|---|---|
| | | | x | y | z |
| *Positive activations* | | | | | |
| Right inferior frontal sulcus | 232 | 4.70 | 38 | 14 | 16 |
| Right inferior frontal gyrus | 192 | 4.30 | 46 | 12 | 4 |
| *Negative activations* | | | | | |
| Left inferior frontal gyrus | 120 | −3.98 | −34 | 22 | 0 |
| Left anterior cingulate gyrus | 144 | −3.61 | −10 | 20 | 36 |

*Note.* The table presents the results of an analysis using SPM96, using a minimum peak threshold of $p < .001$, uncorrected for spatial extent. $N = 8$; $df = 611$: smoothness = 6.3, 8.6, 6.2 mm.

likely because most aphasias are associated with left-hemisphere lesions. Recent neuroimaging studies have buttressed the long-held belief about left-hemisphere dominance for language by reporting greater left-hemisphere activation during language tasks (Bavelier et al., 1997; Helenius et al., 1998; Just et al., 1996; Price, 1997; Pugh et al., 1996).

However, people with right-hemisphere lesions experience difficulty processing more complex language, particularly the pragmatic (intentional), prosodic (intonational), figurative, and idiomatic aspects of discourse (Brownell, Carroll, Rehak, & Wingfield, 1992; van Lancker & Kempler, 1987; Winner & Gardner, 1977; Zaidel, Zaidel. Oxbury,

& Oxbury, 1995). Further, increased right-hemisphere activity has been reported during discourse tasks such as judging the aptness of metaphors (Bottini et al., 1994) or evaluating each sentence's fit in an ongoing narrative (Robertson, Gernsbacher, & Guidotti, 1999), compared with tasks requiring only simple sentence judgments.

Based on the neuropsychological and psycholinguistic literatures, we did not expect to identify a single brain location per se underlying the cognitive process of mapping during discourse comprehension.[3] We did expect to find frontal lobe involvement because frontal lobe damage is often associated with a reduced ability to generate mental

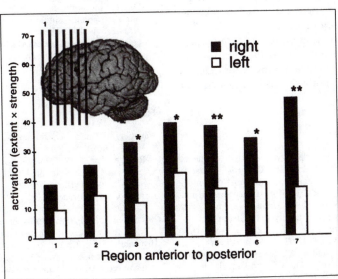

**FIGURE 39.2 ■** Activation for sentences with the definite article compared with sentences with indefinite articles. Activations are shown for seven regions in the left and right hemispheres separately. The lines on the inlay are approximate centers of the regions analyzed. Units are the mean proportion of voxels in each hemisphere that were activated. multiplied by the mean *t*-statistic value. *$p < .05$, **$p < .01$.(using Greenhouse-Geisser adjustment).

representations of situations, and the right frontal lobe is hypothesized to be dominant for allocating internal attention (Knight & Grabowecky, 1995). Allocating internal attention must be an important subcomponent of the process of mapping (e.g., interpreting the definite article as a discourse cue to direct attention to previous information). Thus, our finding of right-frontal dominance for the cognitive process of mapping is consistent with the literature, despite its apparent contradiction of traditional accounts of left-hemisphere dominance for language processing.

Although many psychologists are skeptical that knowing the answer to "where?" will illuminate the answer to "how?" we feel optimistic that studying functional neuroanatomy will help us investigate cognitive processes. For example, our finding of right-hemisphere frontal dominance for our putative process of mapping suggests that mapping definite reference is more related to episodic memory retrieval than episodic encoding or semantic retrieval, according to neuroimaging studies (Gabrieli et al., 1996; Nyberg, Cabeza, & Tulving, 1996; Tulving, Kapur, Craik, Moscovitch, & Houle, 1994). Such speculations, of course, await further behavioral and neuroanatomical investigations.

Our results demonstrate that altering a single word in the language input can result in qualitatively different activity in the brain, provided that single word carries an important cue for comprehension processes. Thus, our results demonstrate the efficacy of using neuroimaging techniques to test psychological hypotheses about higher-order cognition.

## ACKNOWLEDGMENTS

We thank Mark Beeman and Alex Shackman for comments on the manuscript; Michael Anderle, Richard Davidson. Diermar Cordes, Melissa Rosenkranz, and James Sorenson for assistance in the design and execution of the research; and two anonymous reviewers for helpful comments on the manuscript. This research was supported by grants from the National Institutes of Health (RO1 NS 29926) and the Army Research Institute (DASW0194-K-004, DASW0196-K-0013, and DAAG55-97-1-0224), and by a University of Wisconsin Faculty Development Award to Morton Ann Gernsbacher, a National Institute of Mental Health (T32-MH18931) predoctoral traineeship to David Robertson, and a National Science Foundation graduate research fellowship to William Irwin.

## NOTES

1. Average correct response was 83%, with no statistically reliable differences. We did not predict a difference on this gross measure of recognition memory because in another study (Gernsbacher & Robertson, in press) we found no differences in the quantity of sentences recalled by participants who read them with definite versus indefinite articles: we found striking differences in the forms of the sentences recalled (reading sentences with definite articles led participants to recall more integrative sentences, more synonym substitutions, and more insertions of pronominal anaphora, all of which are discourse markers of greater coherence).

2. We interpreted increases in MR signal during the reading of sentences with definite articles compared with the reading of sentences with indefinite articles as reflecting increased right-frontal neural activity reflecting the mapping process. However, according to the strict statistical threshold presented in Table 39.3, no significant right-frontal activity was observed in the blocks that alternated between sentences and nonletter strings, so it could be that reading sentences with definite articles does not result in increased activity relative to a low-level baseline. In another neuroimaging study, we observed increased activity in this region for reading sentences that promote mapping relative to a low-level baseline task (Robertson. Gernsbacher, & Guidotti, 1999). The data from this study are equivocal in that respect: as with any observed difference between two experimental treatments (either physiological or behavioral mesurements), one cannot tell if the difference is an increase for one treatment or a decrease for the other. The interaction between article and hemisphere, rather than main effect, is of primary concern for this report.

3. One region implicated in the mapping process for most of our participants' single-subject analyses is Brodmann's Area 8, which has been reported as activated during the comprehension of stories (Mazoyer et al., 1993), tasks that require judgments about characters' mental states (Fletcher et al., 1995), and narrative comprehension (Robertson et al., 1999).

## REFERENCES

Bavelier, D., Corina, D., Jezzard, P., Padmanabhan, S., Clark, V. P., Karni, A., Prinster, A., Braun, A., Lalwani, A., Rauscheeker, J. P., Turner, R., & Neville, H. (1997). Sentence reading: A functional MRI study at 4 Tesla. *Journal of Cognitive Neuroscience, 9,* 664–686.

Bottini, G., Corcoran, R., Sterzi, R., Paulesu, E., Schenone, P., Scarpa, P., Frackowiak, R. S. J., & Frith, C. D. (1994). The role of the right hemisphere in the interpretation of figurative aspects of language. *Brain, 117,* 1241–1253.

Brownell, H. H., Carroll, J. J., Rehak, A., & Wingfield, A. (1992). The use of pronoun anaphora and speaker mood in the interpretation of conversational utterances by right hemisphere brain-damaged patients. *Brain & Language, 43,* 121–147.

Chapman, L. J., & Chapman, J. P. (1987). The measurement of handedness. *Brain & Cognition, 6,* 175–183.

de Villiers, P. A. (1974). Imagery and theme in recall of connected discourse. *Journal of Experimental Psychology, 103,* 263–268.

Fletcher, P. C., Happe, F., Frith, U., Buker, S. C., Dolun, R. J., Frackowiak, R. S. J., & Frith, C. D. (1995). Other minds in the brain: A functional imaging study of "theory of mind" in story comprehension. *Cognition, 57,* 109–128.

Friston, K. J., Holmes, A. P., Worsley, K. J., Pollne, J. B., Frith, C. D., & Frackowiak, R. S. J. (1995). Statistical parametric maps in functional imaging: A general approach. *Human Brain Mapping, 2,* 189–210.

Friston, K. J., Worsley, K. J., Frackowiak, R. S. J., Mazziotta, J. C., & Evans, A. C. (1994). Assessing the significance of focal activations using their spatial extent. *Human Brain Mapping, 1,* 214–220.

Gubrieli, J. D. E., Desmond, J. E., Demb, J. B., Wagner, A. D., Stone, M. V., Vaidya, C. J., & Glover, G. H. (1996). Functional magnetic resonance imaging of semantic memory processes in the frontal lobes. *Psychological Science, 7,* 278–283.

Gernsbacher, M. A. (1990). *Language comprehension as structure building,* Hillsdale, NJ: Erlbaum.

Gernsbacher, M. A. (1997). Two decades of structure building. *Discourse Processes, 23,* 265–304.

Gernsbacher, M. A., & Robertson, R. R. W. (2002). The definite article *the* as a cue to map thematic information. In W. van Peer & M. M. Louwerse (Eds.), *Thematics: Interdisciplinary studies.* Philadelphia: John Benjamins.

Haviland, S. E., & Clark, H. H. (1974). What's new? Acquiring new information as a process in comprehension. *Journal of Verbal Learning and Verbal Behavior, 13,* 512–521.

Helenius, P., Sulmelin, R., Service, E., & Connolly, J. F. (1998). Distinct time courses of word and context comprehension in the left temporal cortex. *Brain, 121,* 1133–1142.

Just, M. A., Carpenter, P. A., Keller, T. A., Eddy, W. F., & Thulborn, K. R. (1996). Brain activation modulated by sentence comprehension. *Science, 274,* 114–116.

Knight, R. T., & Grabowecky, M. (1995). Escape from linear time: Prefrontal cortex and conscious experience. In M. S. Gazzuniga (Ed.), *The cognitive neurosciences* (pp. 1357–1371). Cambridge, MA: MIT Press.

Malonek, D., Dirnagl, U., Lindauer, U., Yamada, K., Kanno, I., & Grinvald, A. (1997). Vascular imprints of neuronal activity: Relationships between the dynamics of cortical blood flow, oxygenation, and volume changes following sensory stimulation. *Proceedings of the National Academy of Sciences, USA, 94,* 14826–14831.

Mazoyer, B. M., Tzourio, N., Frak, V., Syrota, A., Murayama, N., Levrier, O., Salamon, G., Dehuence, S., Cohen, L., &

Mehler, J. (1993). The cortical representation of speech. *Journal of Cognitive Neuroscience, 5,* 467–479.

Nyberg, L., Cabeza, R. & Tulving, E. (1996). PET studies of encoding and retrieval: The HERA model. *Psychonomic Bulletin & Review, 3,* 135–148.

Ogawa, S., Menon, R. S., Tank, D. W., Kim, S. G., Merkle, H., Ellermann, J. M., & Ugurbil, K. (1992). Intrinsic signal changes accompanying sensory stimulation: Functional brain mapping with magnetic resonance imaging. *Proceedings of the National Academy of Sciences, USA, 89,* 5951–5955.

Price, C. J. (1997). Functional anatomy of reading. In R. S. J. Frackowiak, K. J. Friston, R. J. Dolan, & J. C. Mazziotm (Eds.), *Human brain function* (pp. 301–328). San Diego: Academic Press.

Pugh, K. R., Shaywitz, B. A., Shaywitz, S. E., Constable, R. T., Skudlarski, P., Fulbright, R. K., Bronen, R. A., Shunkweiler, D. P., Katz, L., Fletcher, J. M., & Gore, J. C. (1996), Cerebral organization of component processes in reading. *Brain, 119,* 1221–1238.

Robertson, D. A., Gernsbacher, M. A., & Guidotti, S. J. (1999, April). *FMRI Investigation of the comprehension of written versus picture narratives.* Paper presented at the annual meeting of the Cognitive Neuroscience Society, Washington, DC.

Sorenson, J. A., & Wang, X. (1996). ROC methods for evaluation of FMRI techniques. *Magnetic Resonance in Medicine, 36,* 737–744.

Talairach, J., & Tournoux, P. (1988). *Coplanar stereotaxic atlas of the human brain.* New York: Thieme.

Tulving, E., Kapur, S., Craik, F. J. M., Moseovitch, M., & Houle, S. (1994), Hemispheric encoding/retrieval asymmetry in episodic memory: Positron emission tomography findings. *Proceedings of the National Academy of Sciences, USA, 91,* 2016–2020.

van Lancker, D. R., & Kempler, D. (1987). Comprehension of familiar phrases by left- but not by right-hemisphere damaged patients. *Brain & Language, 32,* 265–277.

Winner, E., & Gardner, H. (1977). The comprehension of metaphor in brain-damaged patients. *Brain, 100,* 717–729.

Worsley, K. J., Evans, A. C., Marrell, S., & Neelin, P. (1992). A three-dimensional statistical analysis for rCBF activation studies in the human brain. *Journal of Cerebral Blood Flow Metabolism, 12,* 900–918.

Zaidel, D. W., Zaidel, E., Oxbury, S. M., & Oxbury, J. M. (1995). The interpretation of sentence ambiguity in patients with unilateral focal brain surgery. *Brain & Language, 51,* 458–468.

# Language

## Discussion Questions

1. Describe the steps in speech production uncovered by Fromkin. Be sure to indicate the evidence from speech error data regarding each of the steps. How can one make such forceful arguments from error-prone behavior? What are the limitations of relying on naturally occurring speech errors?

2. The work by Swinney could easily be related to the two-process perspective of attentional control described by Posner and Snyder in the "Attention" readings. Delineate the relation between Swinney's results and the Posner and Snyder theoretical distinction between automatic and attentional processes (in particular, the speed with which the operations are engaged and the influence of conscious expectancies). Do the Swinney results provide more information about language per se or simply attentional control?

3. A number of distinct types of aphasias are described by Geschwind. Describe five different sets of aphasias and the underlying neurological substrates of each. Would this relation fulfill Marr's three levels of analysis, and if not, where are the major limitations?

4. Consider the processes involved in comprehension that were addressed in the Robertson et al. paper. What specifically have we learned about the bridging operation necessary for comprehension from knowing the pattern of underlying neural activation?

5. Each of the papers in the present section has employed a distinct approach to better understanding language. However, in order to build confidence in theory, one needs to have converging operations. Consider some component of language processing, and discuss how the results from at least two of the different approaches provide constraints on the understanding of that component.

## Suggested Readings

G. S. Dell (1986, A spreading activation theory of sentence production, *Psychological Review, 93,* 283–321) provides an integration of the speech error data within an interactive activation model of speech production. He nicely specifies how linguistic frames can be related to spreading activation mechanisms.

H. H. Clark and E. V. Clark's book (1977, *Psychology and Language*. New York: Harcourt Brace Jovanovich) is still an excellent overview of linguistic principles, written in a very engaging style. Chapter 1 is still a classic.

F. Dick, E. Bates, B. Wulfeck, J. A. Utman, N. Dronkers, and M. A. Gernsbacher (2001, Language deficits, localization, and grammar: Evidence for a distributive model of language breakdown in aphasic patients and neurologically intact individuals, *Psychological Review, 108,* 759–788) provide a recent theoretical discussion of the interpretation of localization of lesion and the type of language deficit that one observes. This work shows that there are multiple ways in which a lesion can express itself and also that an apparent lesion-produced deficit can be produced.

D. Gorfein's (2001, Edited volume entitled *On the Consequences of Meaning Selection: Perspectives on Resolving Lexical Ambiguity*. Washington, DC: American Psychological Association Press) recent book on ambiguity resolution provides more recent overviews of the work on ambiguity resolution, which involves methodological issues, behavioral studies, neuropsychological studies, and computational perspectives.

L. R. Gleitman and M. Liberman (Eds., 1995: *An Invitation to Cognitive Science. Volume 1: Language*. Cambridge, MA: MIT Press) provide an excellent and relatively recent compilation of interesting papers dealing with central issues in language processing.

M. Kutas, K. D. Federmeier, S. Coulson, J. W. King, and T. F. Munte (2000, Language. In J. T. Cacioppo, L. G. Tassinary, & G. G. Berntson [Eds.], *Handbook of Psychophysiology*, 2nd ed., pp. 576–601, Cambridge University Press) provide an important recent review of the electrophysiological work on language processing.

W. J. M. Levelt's book (1989, *Speaking: From Intention to Articulation*. Cambridge, MA: MIT Press) is simply the most comprehensive treatment of the processes involved in speech production.

S. Pinker (1994, *The Language Instinct*. New York: HarperCollins) provides a remarkably comprehensive and interesting overview of language processing.

K. Rayner and A. Pollatsek (1989, *The Psychology of Reading*. Englewood Cliffs, NJ: Prentice Hall) provide a detailed review of the many aspects of linguistic processing that are involved in reading. They give overviews of basic work related to perception all the way up to higher order aspects of syntax and comprehension.

M. K. Tanenhaus, M. J. Spivey-Knowlton, K. M. Eberhard, and J. C. Sedivy (1995, Integration of visual and linguistic information in spoken language comprehension, *Science, 268,* 1632–1634) and Z. M. Griffin and K. Bock (2000, What the eyes say about speaking, *Psychological Science, 11,* 274–279) provide excellent examples of a new approach to tracking comprehension and speech production, respectively, by measuring where and when the eyes are looking at particular referents in a relatively naturally occurring scene.

# Judgment and Decision Making

# Introduction to Part X:
# Judgment and Decision Making

We make countless decisions and judgments every day, some seemingly without much thought. When passing the ball during a pick-up basketball game, you are unlikely to have time to deliberately consider the alternatives. But you might deliberately weigh the pluses and minuses in other situations, such as when deciding which of two sound systems is a better bargain or which of two companies is more likely to turn a profit next year. In other situations, more visceral and affective components are likely to play a role, such as when you assess the likelihood of a plane crash before getting on an airplane. As these examples illustrate, different types of processes appear to be engaged in different types of decision-making situations.

One idea about how people make decisions is that they choose the option that has the higher expected value (Expected Utility Theory). That is, if Option A involves an 80% chance to win $100 and Option B involves a 70% chance to win $200, Option B has the higher expected value ($140) and hence should be chosen. Thus, one way to make a decision is to compute the expected value of each of the options (by multiplying the outcome by its probability), and then select the highest. According to this model, the decision maker should not be affected by the order of the options or the way in which the two options are presented (von Neumann & Morgenstern, 1947).

Much research has shown that people do not always behave according to Expected Utility Theory. For example, the classic paper by Tversky and Kahneman (1981) describes several examples of how people are affected by the framing or the wording of choices. In one study, subjects evaluated two alternative responses to a disease expected to kill 600 people. In Option A, 200 people would be saved. In Option B, there would be a 33% chance of saving all 600 people and a 67% chance of saving no one. Overwhelmingly, subjects preferred Option A, in which 200 people would be saved for sure. However, people's preferences switched when the options were framed as deaths rather than as saved lives. When asked to choose between 400 deaths for sure (the complement of Option A) and a 33% chance of no deaths combined with a 67% chance of 600 deaths (the complement of Option B), people chose the second option. The framing of responses as deaths versus saved lives reversed people's preferences; this is not the hallmark of a rational decision maker.

Instead, it appears that people rely on a number of shortcuts, or heuristics, when making decisions. The use of such heuristics has advantages; it is cognitively efficient and often leads people to the same answer as would be obtained via Expected Utility Theory. However, sometimes heuristics lead to different answers than would be expected from a strictly rational decision maker. The classic paper by Tversky and Kahneman (1974) describes several famous examples of reliance on heuristics. One heuristic is availability, that is, basing one's judgment on how easy it is to think of instances of the to-be-judged event. For example, in one experiment, subjects were asked which are more frequent in the English language: words beginning with the letter r or words with the letter r in the 3rd position. Subjects named the first option as more frequent, presumably because it was easier for them to generate words beginning with r. In fact, words with r in the 3rd position are more frequent, albeit less retrievable to subjects (Tversky & Kahneman, 1973).

Some researchers have suggested that people simply do not have enough knowledge about probability, statistics, and chance to follow a normative model of decision making. For example, a clever demonstration of people's misconceptions of chance is provided in Tversky and Gilovich (1989). The paper evaluates the alleged "hot hand" in basketball; this refers to the belief that basketball players are more likely to make a shot after having just made one. The shooting records of the 1980–1981 Philadelphia 76ers were examined. Several different statistics were computed in the search for the hot hand; none supported its existence. For example, players were actually slightly more likely to make a shot after a miss than after scoring. Similar findings were obtained in a controlled experiment in which varsity basketball players predicted the likelihood of making each of 100 free throws: the players (and observers) predicted greater success following a basket, but, again, players were no more likely to score following a hit than a miss. Be it fans or players, people misinterpret runs of successful shots as a "hot hand," rather than what they really are, the natural sequences that occur due to chance.

Tversky and Kahneman (1981) developed

Prospect Theory as an alternative to Expected Utility Theory; Prospect Theory follows from the results on heuristics and framing effects. In 2002, Kahneman won a Nobel Prize in Economics in part for his work on Prospect Theory. Of interest is the relationship between outcome (which ranges from loss to gain) and value (which ranges from negative to positive). This is graphically portrayed in the Tverksy and Kahneman (1981) paper. The key points are summarized here. As expected, gains lead to increases in value, whereas losses lead to decreases in value. The function is *s*-shaped; the relationship between outcome and value, is asymptotic. At first, changes in outcome lead to large changes in value, but, eventually, changes in outcome do not affect value as much. There is a large difference in value between $5 and $10 but not between $105 and $110; people appear to take into consideration the relative change in value. Finally, the function is much steeper for losses than for gains; people are risk-averse. Thus, different behaviors emerge when choices are framed as gains versus losses.

There has clearly been a considerable amount of work addressing how individuals make decisions, with an emphasis on situations in which the use of heuristics would yield different outputs than would be predicted by Expected Utility Theory.

We do not, however, wish to leave the reader with the idea that people are irrational decision makers. Although heuristics may sometimes mislead, they often represent a faster and more cognitively efficient route to the same decision as would a more explicit computation. In fact, Gigerenzer and colleagues (1999) have argued for the existence of "simple heuristics that make us smart," that lead to equal or even more adaptive conclusions.

In closing, it is useful to note a few applications and extensions of basic decision-making research. For example, there has been much work on how clinicians diagnose mental illnesses (e.g., Dawes, Faust, & Meehl, 1989) and more generally how people reach diagnostic decisions (e.g., Swets, Dawes, & Monahan, 2000). There has been research within the medical field regarding how patients make judgments of pain (e.g., Kahneman, Fredrickson, Schreiber, & Redelmeier, 1993). Work on decision making has been extended to different populations, such as older adults (e.g., Mather & Johnson, 2000), and to look at different types of decisions, such as more emotional ones (e.g., Mellers, 2000; Mellers, Schwartz, & Ritov, 1999). These extensions of decision-making research clearly will nurture this burgeoning and important field.

## REFERENCES

Dawes, R. M., Faust, D., & Meehl, P. E. (1989). Clinical versus actuarial judgment. *Science, 243,* 1668–1674.

Gigerenzer, G. & Todd, P. (1999). *Simple heuristics that make us smart.* New York: Oxford University Press.

Kahneman, D., Fredrickson, B. L., Schreiber, C. A., & Redelmeier, D. A. (1993). When more pain is preferred to less: Adding a better end. *Psychological Science, 4,* 401–405.

Mather, M., & Johnson, M. K. (2000). Choice-supportive source monitoring: Do our decisions seem better to us as we age? *Psychological & Aging, 15,* 596–606.

Mellers, B. A. (2000). Choice and the relative pleasure of consequences. *Psychological Bulletin, 126,* 910–924.

Mellers, B. A., Schwartz, A., & Ritov, I. (1999). Emotion-based choice. *Journal of Experimental Psychology: General, 128,* 332–345.

Swets, J. A., Dawes, R. M., & Monahan, J. (2000). Psychological science can improve diagnostic decisions. *Psychological Science in the Public Interest, 1,* 1–26.

Tversky, A., & Gilovitch, T. (1989). The cold facts about the "hot hand" in basketball. *Chance: New directions for statistics and computing, 2,* 16–21.

Tversky, A., & Kahneman, D. (1973). Availability: A heuristic for judging frequency and probability. *Cognitive Psychology, 5,* 207–232.

Tversky, A. & Kahneman, D. (1974). Judgment under uncertainty: Heuristics and biases. *Science, 185,* 1124–1131.

Tversky, A. & Kahneman, D. (1981). The framing of decisions and the psychology of choice. *Science, 211,* 453–458.

von Neumann, J., & Morgenstern, O. (1947). *Theory of games and economic behavior.* Princeton, NJ: Princeton University Press.

# The Framing of Decisions and the Psychology of Choice

Amos Tversky and Daniel Kahneman

*Summary.* The psychological principles that govern the perception of decision problems and the evaluation of probabilities and outcomes produce predictable shifts of preference when the same problem is framed in different ways. Reversals of preference are demonstrated in choices regarding monetary outcomes, both hypothetical and real, and in questions pertaining to the loss of human lives. The effects of frames on preferences are compared to the effects of perspectives on perceptual appearance. The dependence of preferences on the formulation of decision problems is a significant concern for the theory of rational choice.

Explanations and predictions of people's choices, in everyday life as well as in the social sciences, are often founded on the assumption of human rationality. The definition of rationality has been much debated, but there is general agreement that rational choices should satisfy some elementary requirements of consistency and coherence. In this article we describe decision problems in which people systematically violate the requirements of consistency and coherence, and we trace these violations to the psychological principles that govern the perception of decision problems and the evaluation of options.

A decision problem is defined by the acts or options among which one must choose, the possible outcomes or consequences of these acts, and the contingencies or conditional probabilities that relate outcomes to acts. We use the term "decision frame" to refer to the decision-maker's conception of the acts, outcomes, and contingencies associated with a particular choice. The frame that a decision-maker adopts is controlled partly by the formulation of the problem and partly by the norms, habits, and personal characteristics of the decision-maker.

It is often possible to frame a given decision problem in more than one way. Alternative frames for a decision problem may be compared to alternative perspectives on a visual scene. Veridical perception requires that the perceived relative height of two neighboring mountains, say, should not reverse with changes of vantage point. Similarly, rational choice requires that the preference between options should not reverse with changes of frame. Because of imperfections of human perception and decision, however, changes of perspective often reverse the relative apparent size of objects and the relative desirability of options.

We have obtained systematic reversals of preference by variations in the framing of acts, contingencies, or outcomes. These effects have been observed in a variety of problems and in the choices of different groups of respondents. Here we present selected illustrations of preference reversals, with data obtained from students at Stanford University and at the University of British Columbia who answered brief questionnaires in a classroom setting. The total number of respondents for each problem is denoted by $N$, and the percentage who chose each option is indicated in brackets.

The effect of variations in framing is illustrated in problems 1 and 2.

Problem 1 [$N = 152$]: Imagine that the U.S. is preparing for the outbreak of an unusual Asian disease, which is expected to kill 600 people. Two alternative programs to combat the disease have been proposed. Assume that the exact scientific estimate of the consequences of the programs are as follows:

> If Program A is adopted, 200 people will be saved. [72 percent]
> If Program B is adopted, there is $1/3$ probability that 600 people will be saved, and $2/3$ probability that no people will be saved. [28 percent]
> Which of the two programs would you favor?

The majority choice in this problem risk averse: the prospect of certainly saving 200 lives is more attractive than a risky prospect of equal expected value that is a one-in-three chance of saving 600 lives.

A second group of respondents was given the cover story of problem 1 with a different formulation of the alternative programs, as follows:

> Problem 2 [$N = 155$]:
> If Program C is adopted 400 people will die, [22 percent]
> If Program D is adopted there is $1/3$ probability that nobody will die, and $2/3$ probability that 600 people will die. [78 percent]
> Which of the two programs would you favor?

The majority choice in problem 2 is risk taking: the certain death of 400 people is less acceptable than the two-in-three chance that 600 will die. The preferences in problems 1 and 2 illustrate a common pattern: choices involving gains are often risk averse and choices involving losses are often risk taking. However, it is easy to see that the two problems are effectively identical. The only difference between them is that the outcomes are described in problem 1 by the number of lives saved and in problem 2 by the number of lives lost. The change is accompanied by a pronounced shift from risk aversion to risk taking. We have observed this reversal in several groups of respondents, including university faculty and physicians. Inconsistent responses to problems 1 and 2 arise from the conjunction of a framing effect with contradictory attitudes toward risks involving gains and losses. We turn now to an analysis of these attitudes.

## The Evaluation of Prospects

The major theory of decision-making under risk is the expected utility model. This model is based on a set of axioms, for example, transitivity of preferences, which provide criteria for the rationality of choices. The choices of an individual who conforms to the axioms can be described in terms of the utilities of various outcomes for that individual. The utility of a risky prospect is equal to the expected utility of its outcomes, obtained by weighting the utility of each possible outcome by its probability. When faced with a choice, a rational decision-maker will prefer the prospect that offers the highest expected utility (1, 2).

As will be illustrated below, people exhibit patterns of preference which appear incompatible with expected utility theory. We have presented elsewhere (3) a descriptive model, called prospect theory, which modifies expected utility theory so as to accommodate these observations. We distinguish two phases in the choice process: an initial phase in which acts, outcomes, and contingencies are framed, and a subsequent phase of evaluation (4). For simplicity, we restrict the formal treatment of the theory to choices involving stated numerical probabilities and quantitative outcomes, such as money, time, or number of lives.

Consider a prospect that yields outcome $x$ with probability $p$, outcome $y$ with probability $q$, and the status quo with probability $1 - p - q$. According to prospect theory, there are values $v(.)$ associated with outcomes, and decision weights $\pi(.)$ associated with probabilities, such that the overall value of the prospect equals $\pi(p) v(x) + \pi(q) v(y)$. A slightly different equation should be applied if all outcomes of a prospect are on the same side of the zero point (5).

In prospect theory, outcomes are expressed as positive or negative deviations (gains or losses)

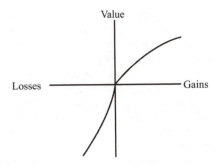

Value

Losses ——————————————— Gains

**FIGURE 40.1** ■ A hypothetical value function.

from a neutral reference outcome, which is as-signed a value of zero. Although subjective val-ues differ among individuals and attributes, we propose that the value function is commonly S-shaped, concave above the reference point and convex below it, as illustrated in Figure 40.1. For example, the difference in subjective value be-tween gains of $10 and $20 is greater than the subjective difference between gains of $110 and $120. The same relation between value differences holds for the corresponding losses. Another prop-erty of the value function is that the response to losses is more extreme than the response to gains. The displeasure associated with losing a sum of money is generally greater than the pleasure asso-ciated with winning the same amount, as is re-flected in people's reluctance to accept fair bets on a toss of a coin. Several studies of decision *(3, 6)* and judgment *(7)* have confirmed these proper-ties of the value function *(8)*.

The second major departure of prospect theory from the expected utility model involves the treat-ment of probabilities. In expected utility theory the utility of an uncertain outcome is weighted by its probability; in prospect theory the value of an uncertain outcome is multiplied by a decision weight $\pi(p)$, which is a monotonic function of $p$ but is not a probability. The weighting function $\pi$ has the following properties. First, impossible events are discarded, that is, $\pi(0) = 0$, and the scale is normalized so that $\pi(1) = 1$, but the function is not well behaved near the endpoints. Second, for low probabilities $\pi(p) > p$, but $\pi(p) + \pi(1-p) \leq 1$. Thus low probabilities are overweighted, moder-ate and high probabilities are underweighted, and the latter effect is more pronounced than the former. Third, $\pi(pq)/\pi(p) < \pi(pqr)/\pi(pr)$ for all $0 < p, q, r \leq 1$. That is, for any fixed probability

ratio $q$, the ratio of decision weights is closer to unity when the probabilities are low than when they are high, for example, $\pi(.1)/\pi(.2) > \pi(.4)/\pi(.8)$. A hypothetical weighting function which satisfies these properties is shown in Figure 40.2. The major qualitative properties of decision weights can be extended to cases in which the prob-abilities of outcomes are subjectively assessed rather than explicitly given. In these situations, however, decision weights may also be affected by other characteristics of an event, such as ambi-guity or vagueness *(9)*.

Prospect theory, and the scales illustrated in Figures 40.1 and 40.2, should be viewed as an approximate, incomplete, and simplified descrip-tion of the evaluation of risky prospects. Although the properties of v and $\pi$ summarize a common pattern of choice, they are not universal: the pref-erences of some individuals are not well described by an S-shaped value function and a consistent set of decision weights. The simultaneous measure-ment of values and decision weights involves se-rious experimental and statistical difficulties *(10)*.

If $\pi$ and v were linear throughout, the prefer-ence order between options would be independent of the framing of acts, outcomes, or contingencies. Because of the characteristic nonlinearities of $\pi$ and v, however, different frames can lead to differ-ent choices. The following three sections describe reversals of preference caused by variations in the framing of acts, contingencies, and outcomes.

## The Framing of Acts

Problem 3 [$N = 150$]: Imagine that you face the following pair of concurrent decisions. First

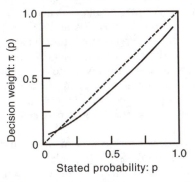

**FIGURE 40.2** ■ A hypothetical weighting function.

examine both decisions, then indicate the options you prefer.

Decision (i). Choose between:

A. a sure gain of $240 [84 percent]
B. 25% chance to gain $1000, and 75% chance to gain nothing [16 percent]

Decision (ii). Choose between:

C. a sure loss of $750 [13 percent]
D. 75% chance to lose $1000, and 25% chance to lose nothing [87 percent]

The majority choice in decision (i) is risk averse: a riskless prospect is preferred to a risky prospect of equal or greater expected value. In contrast, the majority choice in decision (ii) is risk taking: a risky prospect is preferred to a riskless prospect of equal expected value. This pattern of risk aversion in choices involving gains and risk seeking in choices involving losses is attributable to the properties of $v$ and $\pi$. Because the value function is S-shaped, the value associated with a gain of $240 is greater than 24 percent of the value associated with a gain of $1000, and the (negative) value associated with a loss of $750 is smaller than 75 percent of the value associated with a loss of $1000. Thus the shape of the value function contributes to risk aversion in decision (i) and to risk seeking in decision (ii). Moreover, the underweighting of moderate and high probabilities contributes to the relative attractiveness of the sure gain in (i) and to the relative aversiveness of the sure loss in (ii). The same analysis applies to problems 1 and 2.

Because (i) and (ii) were presented together, the respondents had in effect to choose one prospect from the set: A and C, B and C, A and D, B and D. The most common pattern (A and D) was chosen by 73 percent of respondents, while the least popular pattern (B and C) was chosen by only 3 percent of respondents. However, the combination of B and C is definitely superior to the combination A and D, as is readily seen in problem 4.

Problem 4 [$N$ = 86]. Choose between:

A & D. 25% chance to win $240, and 75% chance to lose $760. [0 percent]
B & C. 25% chance to win $250, and 75% chance to lose $750. [100 percent]

When the prospects were combined and the dominance of the second option became obvious, all respondents chose the superior option. The popularity of the inferior option in problem 3 implies that this problem was framed as a pair of separate choices. The respondents apparently failed to entertain the possibility that the conjunction of two seemingly reasonable choices could lead to an untenable result.

The violations of dominance observed in problem 3 do not disappear in the presence of monetary incentives. A different group of respondents who answered a modified version of problem 3, with real payoffs, produced a similar pattern of choices (11). Other authors have also reported that violations of the rules of rational choice, originally observed in hypothetical questions, were not eliminated by payoffs (12).

We suspect that many concurrent decisions in the real world are framed independently, and that the preference order would often be reversed if the decisions were combined. The respondents in problem 3 failed to combine options, although the integration was relatively simple and was encouraged by instructions (13). The complexity of practical problems of concurrent decisions, such as portfolio selection, would prevent people from integrating options without computational aids, even if they were inclined to do so.

## The Framing of Contingencies

The following triple of problems illustrates the framing of contingencies. Each problem was presented to a different group of respondents. Each group was told that one participant in ten, preselected at random, would actually be playing for money. Chance events were realized, in the respondents' presence, by drawing a single ball from a bag containing a known proportion of balls of the winning color, and the winners were paid immediately.

Problem 5 [$N$ = 77]: Which of the following options do you prefer?

A. a sure win of $30 [78 percent]
B. 80% chance to win $45 [22 percent]

Problem 6 [$N$ = 85]: Consider the following two-stage game. In the first stage, there is a 75% chance to end the game without winning anything, and a 25% chance to move into the second stage. If you reach the second stage you have a choice between:

C. a sure win of $30 [74 percent]
D. 80% chance to win $45 [26 percent]

Your choice must be made before the game starts, i.e., before the outcome of the first stage is known. Please indicate the option you prefer.

Problem 7 [$N = 81$]: Which of the following options do you prefer?

E. 25% chance to win $30 [42 percent]
F. 20% chance to win $45 [58 percent]

Let us examine the structure of these problems. First, note that problems 6 and 7 are identical in terms of probabilities and outcomes, because prospect C offers a .25 chance to win $30 and prospect D offers a probability of .25 × .80 = .20 to win $45. Consistency therefore requires that the same choice be made in problems 6 and 7. Second, note that problem 6 differs from problem 5 only by the introduction of a preliminary stage. If the second stage of the game is reached, then problem 6 reduces to problem 5; if the game ends at the first stage, the decision does not affect the outcome. Hence there seems to be no reason to make a different choice in problems 5 and 6. By this logical analysis, problem 6 is equivalent to problem 7 on the one hand and problem 5 on the other. The participants, however, responded similarly to problems 5 and 6 but differently to problem 7. This pattern of responses exhibits two phenomena of choice: the certainty effect and the pseudocertainty effect.

The contrast between problems 5 and 7 illustrates a phenomenon discovered by Allais (14), which we have labeled the certainty effect: a reduction of the probability of an outcome by a constant factor has more impact when the outcome was initially certain than when it was merely probable. Prospect theory attributes this effect to the properties of π. It is easy to verify, by applying the equation of prospect theory to problems 5 and 7, that people for whom the value ratio $v(30)/v(45)$ lies between the weight ratios $\pi(.20)/\pi(.25)$ and $\pi(.80)/\pi(1.0)$ will prefer A to B and F to E, contrary to expected utility theory. Prospect theory does not predict a reversal of preference for every

individual in problems 5 and 7. It only requires that an individual who has no preference between A and B prefer F to E. For group data, the theory predicts the observed directional shift of preference between the two problems.

The first stage of problem 6 yields the same outcome (no gain) for both acts. Consequently, we propose, people evaluate the options conditionally, as if the second stage had been reached. In this framing, of course, problem 6 reduces to problem 5. More generally, we suggest that a decision problem is evaluated conditionally when (i) there is a state in which all acts yield the same outcome, such as failing to reach the second stage of the game in problem 6, and (ii) the stated probabilities of other outcomes are conditional on the nonoccurrence of this state.

The striking discrepancy between the responses to problems 6 and 7, which are identical in outcomes and probabilities, could be described as a pseudocertainty effect. The prospect yielding $30 is relatively more attractive in problem 6 than in problem 7, as if it had the advantage of certainty. The sense of certainty associated with option C is illusory, however, since the gain is in fact contingent on reaching the second stage of the game (15).

We have observed the certainty effect in several sets of problems, with outcomes ranging from vacation trips to the loss of human lives. In the negative domain, certainty exaggerates the aversiveness of losses that are certain relative to losses that are merely probable. In a question dealing with the response to an epidemic, for example, most respondents found "a sure loss of 75 lives" more aversive than "80% chance to lose 100 lives" but preferred "10% chance to lose 75 lives" over "8% chance to lose 100 lives," contrary to expected utility theory.

We also obtained the pseudocertainty effect in several studies where the description of the decision problems favored conditional evaluation. Pseudocertainty can be induced either by a sequential formulation, as in problem 6, or by the introduction of causal contingencies. In another version of the epidemic problem, for instance, respondents were told that risk to life existed only in the event (probability .10) that the disease was carried by a particular virus. Two alternative programs were said to yield "a sure loss of 75 lives" or "80% chance to lose 100 lives" if the critical virus was involved, and no loss of life in the event (probability .90) that the disease was carried by another virus. In effect, the respondents were asked to choose between 10 percent chance of losing 75 lives and 8 percent chance of losing 100 lives, but their preferences were the same as when the choice was between a sure loss of 75 lives and 80 percent chance of losing 100 lives. A conditional framing was evidently adopted in which the contingency of the noncritical virus was eliminated, giving rise to a pseudocertainty effect. The certainty effect reveals attitudes toward risk that are inconsistent with the axioms of rational choice, whereas the pseudocertainty effect violates the more fundamental requirement that preferences should be independent of problem description.

Many significant decisions concern actions that reduce or eliminate the probability of a hazard, at some cost. The shape of $\pi$ in the range of low probabilities suggests that a protective action which reduces the probability of a harm from 1 percent to zero, say, will be valued more highly than an action that reduces the probability of the same harm from 2 percent to 1 percent. Indeed, probabilistic insurance, which reduces the probability of loss by half, is judged to be worth less than half the price of regular insurance that eliminates the risk altogether (3).

It is often possible to frame protective action in either conditional or unconditional form. For example, an insurance policy that covers fire but not flood could be evaluated either as full protection against the specific risk of fire or as a reduction in the overall probability of property loss. The preceding analysis suggests that insurance should appear more attractive when it is presented as the elimination of risk than when it is described as a reduction of risk. P. Slovic, B. Fischhoff, and S. Lichtenstein, in an unpublished study, found that a hypothetical vaccine which reduces the probability of contracting a disease from .20 to .10 is less attractive if it is described as effective in half the cases than if it is presented as fully effective against one of two (exclusive and equiprobable) virus strains that produce identical symptoms. In accord with the present analysis of pseudocertainty, the respondents valued full protection against an identified virus more than probabilistic protection against the disease.

The preceding discussion highlights the sharp contrast between lay responses to the reduction and the elimination of risk. Because no form of protective action can cover all risks to human welfare, all insurance is essentially probabilistic: it reduces but does not eliminate risk. The probabilistic nature of insurance is commonly masked by formulations that emphasize the completeness of protection against identified harms, but the sense of security that such formulations provide is an illusion of conditional framing. It appears that insurance is bought as protection against worry, not only against risk, and that worry can be manipulated by the labelling of outcomes and by the framing of contingencies. It is not easy to determine whether people value the elimination of risk too much or the reduction of risk too little. The contrasting attitudes to the two forms of protective action, however, are difficult to justify on normative grounds (16).

## The Framing of Outcomes

Outcomes are commonly perceived as positive or negative in relation to a reference outcome that is judged neutral. Variations of the reference point can therefore determine whether a given outcome is evaluated as a gain or as a loss. Because the value function is generally concave for gains, convex for losses, and steeper for losses than for gains, shifts of reference can change the value difference between outcomes and thereby reverse the preference order between options (6). Problems 1 and 2 illustrated a preference reversal induced by a shift of reference that transformed gains into losses.

For another example, consider a person who has spent an afternoon at the race track, has already lost $140, and is considering a $10 bet on a 15:1 long shot in the last race. This decision can be framed in two ways, which correspond to two natural reference points. If the status quo is the reference point, the outcomes of the bet are framed as a gain of $140 and a loss of $10. On the other hand, it may be more natural to view the present state as a loss of $140, for the betting day, and accordingly frame the last bet as a chance to return to the reference point or to increase the loss to $150. Prospect theory implies that the latter frame will produce more risk seeking than the former. Hence, people who do not adjust their reference point as they lose are expected to take bets that they would normally find unacceptable. This analysis is supported by the observation that bets on long shots are most popular on the last race of the day (17).

Because the value function is steeper for losses than for gains, a difference between options will loom larger when it is framed as a disadvantage of one option rather than as an advantage of the other option. An interesting example of such an effect in a riskless context has been noted by Thaler (18). In a debate on a proposal to pass to the consumer some of the costs associated with the processing of credit-card purchases, representatives of the credit-card industry requested that the price difference be labeled a cash discount rather than a credit-card surcharge. The two labels induce different reference points by implicitly designating as normal reference the higher or the lower of the two prices. Because losses loom larger than gains, consumers are less willing to accept a surcharge than to forego a discount. A similar effect has been observed in experimental studies of insurance: the proportion of respondents who preferred a sure loss to a larger probable loss was significantly greater when the former was called an insurance premium (19, 20).

These observations highlight the lability of reference outcomes, as well as their role in decision-making. In the examples discussed so far, the neutral reference point was identified by the labeling of outcomes. A diversity of factors determine the reference outcome in everyday life. The reference outcome is usually a state to which one has adapted; it is sometimes set by social norms and expectations; it sometimes corresponds to a level of aspiration, which may or may not be realistic.

We have dealt so far with elementary outcomes, such as gains or losses in a single attribute. In many situations, however, an action gives rise to a compound outcome, which joins a series of changes in a single attribute, such as a sequence of monetary gains and losses, or a set of concurrent changes in several attributes. To describe the framing and evaluation of compound outcomes, we use the notion of a psychological account, defined as an outcome frame which specifies (i) the set of elementary outcomes that are evaluated jointly and the manner in which they are combined and (ii) a reference outcome that is considered neutral or normal. In the account that is set up for the purchase of a car, for example, the cost of the purchase is not treated as a loss nor is the car viewed as a gift. Rather, the transaction as a whole is evaluated as positive, negative, or neutral, depending on such factors as the performance of the car and the price of similar cars in the market. A closely related treatment has been offered by Thaler (18).

We propose that people generally evaluate acts in terms of a minimal account, which includes only the direct consequences of the act. The minimal account associated with the decision to accept a gamble, for example, includes the money won or lost in that gamble and excludes other assets or the outcome of previous gambles. People commonly adopt minimal accounts because this mode of framing (i) simplifies evaluation and reduces cognitive strain, (ii) reflects the intuition that consequences should be causally linked to acts, and (iii) matches the properties of hedonic experience, which is more sensitive to desirable and undesirable changes than to steady states.

There are situations, however, in which the outcomes of an act affect the balance in an account that was previously set up by a related act. In these cases, the decision at hand may be evaluated in terms of a more inclusive account, as in the case of the bettor who views the last race in the context of earlier losses. More generally, a sunk-cost effect arises when a decision is referred to an existing account in which the current balance is negative. Because of the nonlinearities of the evaluation process, the minimal account and a more inclusive one often lead to different choices.

Problems 8 and 9 illustrate another class of situations in which an existing account affects a decision:

Problem 8 [$N = 183$]: Imagine that you have decided to see a play where admission is $10 per ticket. As you enter the theater you discover that you have lost a $10 bill.

Would you still pay $10 for a ticket for the play?
Yes [88 percent]                    No [12 percent]

Problem 9 [$N = 200$]: Imagine that you have decided to see a play and paid the admission price of $10 per ticket. As you enter the theater you discover that you have lost the ticket. The seat was not marked and the ticket cannot be recovered.

Would you pay $10 for another ticket?
Yes [46 percent]                    No [54 percent]

The marked difference between the responses to problems 8 and 9 is an effect of psychological accounting. We propose that the purchase of a new ticket in problem 9 is entered in the account that was set up by the purchase of the original ticket. In terms of this account, the expense required to see the show is $20, a cost which many of our respondents apparently found excessive. In problem 8, on the other hand, the loss of $10 is not linked specifically to the ticket purchase and its effect on the decision is accordingly slight.

The following problem, based on examples by Savage (2, p. 103) and Thaler (18), further illustrates the effect of embedding an option in different accounts. Two versions of this problem were presented to different groups of subjects. One group (N = 93) was given the values that appear in parentheses, and the other group (N = 88) the values shown in brackets.

Problem 10: Imagine that you are about to purchase a jacket for ($125) [$15], and a calculator for ($15) [$125]. The calculator salesman informs you that the calculator you wish to buy is on sale for ($10) [$120] at the other branch of the store, located 20 minutes drive away. Would you make the trip to the other store?

The response to the two versions of problem 10 were markedly different: 68 percent of the respondents were willing to make an extra trip to save $5 on a $15 calculator; only 29 percent were willing to exert the same effort when the price of the calculator was $125. Evidently the respondents do not frame problem 10 in the minimal account, which involves only a benefit of $5 and a cost of some inconvenience. Instead, they evaluate the potential saving in a more inclusive account, which includes the purchase of the calculator but not of the jacket. By the curvature of v, a discount of $5 has a greater impact when the price of the calculator is low than when it is high.

A closely related observation has been reported by Pratt, Wise, and Zeckhauser (21), who found that the variability of the prices at which a given product is sold by different stores is roughly proportional to the mean price of that product. The same pattern was observed for both frequently and infrequently purchased items. Overall, a ratio of 2:1 in the mean price of two products is associated with a ratio of 1.86:1 in the standard deviation of the respective quoted prices. If the effort that consumers exert to save each dollar on a purchase, for instance by a phone call, were independent of price, the dispersion of quoted prices should be about the same for all products. In contrast, the data of Pratt et al. (21) are consistent with the hypothesis that consumers hardly exert more effort to save $15 on a $150 purchase than to save $5 on a $50 purchase (18). Many readers will recognize the temporary devaluation of money which facilitates extra spending and reduces the significance of small discounts in the context of a large expenditure, such as buying a house or a car. This paradoxical variation in the value of money is incompatible with the standard analysis of consumer behavior.

## Discussion

In this reading we have presented a series of demonstrations in which seemingly inconsequential changes in the formulation of choice problems caused significant shifts of preference. The inconsistencies were traced to the interaction of two sets of factors: variations in the framing of acts, contingencies, and outcomes, and the characteristic non-linearities of values and decision weights. The demonstrated effects are large and systematic, although by no means universal. They occur when the outcomes concern the loss of human lives as well as in choices about money; they are not restricted to hypothetical questions and are not eliminated by monetary incentives.

Earlier we compared the dependence of preferences on frames to the dependence of perceptual appearance on perspective. If while traveling in a mountain range you notice that the apparent relative height of mountain peaks varies with your vantage point, you will conclude that some impressions of relative height must be erroneous, even when you have no access to the correct answer. Similarly, one may discover that the relative attractiveness of options varies when the same decision problem is framed in different ways. Such a discovery will normally lead the decision-maker to reconsider the original preferences, even when there is no simple way to resolve the inconsistency. The susceptibility to perspective effects is of special concern in the domain of decision-making because of the absence of objective standards such as the true height of mountains.

The metaphor of changing perspective can be applied to other phenomena of choice, in addition to the framing effects with which we have been concerned here (19). The problem of self-control is naturally construed in these terms. The story of

Ulysses' request to be bound to the mast of the ship in anticipation of the irresistible temptation of the Sirens' call is often used as a paradigm case *(22)*. In this example of precommitment, an action taken in the present renders inoperative an anticipated future preference. An unusual feature of the problem of intertemporal conflict is that the agent who views a problem from a particular temporal perspective is also aware of the conflicting views that future perspectives will offer. In most other situations, decision-makers are not normally aware of the potential effects of different decision frames on their preferences.

The perspective metaphor highlights the following aspects of the psychology of choice. Individuals who face a decision problem and have a definite preference (i) might have a different preference in a different framing of the same problem, (ii) are normally unaware of alternative frames and of their potential effects on the relative attractiveness of options, (iii) would wish their preferences to be independent of frame, but (iv) are often uncertain how to resolve detected inconsistencies *(23)*. In some cases (such as problems 3 and 4 and perhaps problems 8 and 9) the advantage of one frame becomes evident once the competing frames are compared, but in other cases (problems 1 and 2 and problems 6 and 7) it is not obvious which preferences should be abandoned.

These observations do not imply that preference reversals, or other errors of choice or judgment *(24)*, are necessarily irrational. Like other intellectual limitations, discussed by Simon *(25)* under the heading of "bounded rationality," the practice of acting on the most readily available frame can sometimes be justified by reference to the mental effort required to explore alternative frames and avoid potential inconsistencies. However, we propose that the details of the phenomena described in this article are better explained by prospect theory and by an analysis of framing than by ad hoc appeals to the notion of cost of thinking.

The present work has been concerned primarily with the descriptive question of how decisions are made, but the psychology of choice is also relevant to the normative question of how decisions ought to be made. In order to avoid the difficult problem of justifying values, the modern theory of rational choice has adopted the coherence of specific preferences as the sole criterion of rationality. This approach enjoins the decision-maker to resolve inconsistencies but offers no guidance on how to do so. It implicitly assumes that the decision-maker who carefully answers the question "What do I really want?" will eventually achieve coherent preferences. However, the susceptibility of preferences to variations of framing raises doubt about the feasibility and adequacy of the coherence criterion.

Consistency is only one aspect of the lay notion of rational behavior. As noted by March *(26)*, the common conception of rationality also requires that preferences or utilities for particular outcomes should be predictive of the experiences of satisfaction or displeasure associated with their occurrence. Thus, a man could be judged irrational either because his preferences are contradictory or because his desires and aversions do not reflect his pleasures and pains. The predictive criterion of rationality can be applied to resolve inconsistent preferences and to improve the quality of decisions. A predictive orientation encourages the decision-maker to focus on future experience and to ask "What will I feel then?" rather than "What do I want now?" The former question, when answered with care, can be the more useful guide in difficult decisions. In particular, predictive considerations may be applied to select the decision frame that best represents the hedonic experience of outcomes.

Further complexities arise in the normative analysis because the framing of an action sometimes affects the actual experience of its outcomes. For example, framing outcomes in terms of overall wealth or welfare rather than in terms of specific gains and losses may attenuate one's emotional response to an occasional loss. Similarly, the experience of a change for the worse may vary if the change is framed as an uncompensated loss or as a cost incurred to achieve some benefit. The framing of acts and outcomes can also reflect the acceptance or rejection of responsibility for particular consequences, and the deliberate manipulation of framing is commonly used as an instrument of self-control *(22)*, When framing influences the experience of consequences, the adoption of a decision frame is an ethically significant act.

## REFERENCES AND NOTES

1. J. Von Neumann and O. Morgenstern, *Theory of Games and Economic Behavior* (Princeton Univ. Press, Princeton, N.J., 1947); H. Raiffa, *Decision Analysis: Lectures on Choices Under Uncertainty* (Addison-Wesley, Reading, Mass., 1968); P. Fishburn, *Utility Theory for Decision Making* (Wiley, New York, 1970).

2. L. J. Savage, *The Foundations of Statistics* (Wiley, New York, 1954).

3. D. Kahneman and A. Tversky, *Econometrica* 47, 263 (1979).

4. The framing phase includes various editing operations that are applied to simplify prospects, for example by combining events or outcomes or by discarding negligible components (3).

5. If $p + q = $ [and either $x > y > 0$ or $x < y < 0$, the equation in the text is replaced by $v(y) + \pi(p) [v(x) - v(y)]$, so that decision weights are not applied to sure outcomes.

6. P. Fishburn and G. Kochenberger, *Decision Sci.* 10, 503 (1979); D. J. Laughhunn, J. W. Payne, R. Crum, *Manage. Sci.*, in press; J. W. Payne, D. J. Laughhunn, R. Crum, ibid., in press; S. A. Eraker and H. C. Sox, *Med. Decision Making*, in press. In the last study several hundred clinic patients made hypothetical choices between drug therapies for severe headaches, hypertension, and chest pain. Most patients were risk averse when the outcomes were described as positive (for example, reduced pain or increased life expectancy) and risk taking when the outcomes were described as negative (increased pain or reduced life expectancy). No significant differences were found between patients who actually suffered from the ailments described and patients who did not.

7. E. Galanter and P. Pliner, in *Sensation and Measurement*, H. R. Moskowitz et al., Eds. (Reidel, Dordrecht, 1974), pp. 65–76.

8. The extension of the proposed value function to multiattribute options, with or without risk, deserves careful analysis. In particular, indifference curves between dimensions of loss may be concave upward, even when the value functions for the separate losses are both convex, because of marked subadditivity between dimensions.

9. D. Ellsberg, *Q. J. Econ.* 75, 643 (1961); W. Fellner, *Probability and Profit—A Study of Economic Behavior Along Bayesian Lines* (Irwia, Homewood, Ill., 1965).

10. The scaling of v and π by pair comparisons requires a large number of observations. The procedure of pricing gambles is more convenient for scaling purposes, but it is subject to a severe anchoring bias: the ordering of gambles by their cash equivalents diverges systematically from the preference order observed in direct comparisons [S. Lichtenstein and P. Slovic, *J. Exp. Psychol.* 89, 46 (1971)].

11. A new group of respondents ($N = 126$) was presented with a modified version of problem 3, in which the outcomes were reduced by a factor of 50. The participants were informed that the gambles would actually be played by tossing a pair of fair coins, that one participant in ten would be selected at random to play the gambles of his or her choice. To ensure a positive return for the entire set, a third decision, yielding only positive outcomes, was added. These payoff conditions did not alter the pattern of preferences observed in the hypothetical problem: 67 percent of respondents chose prospect A and 86 percent chose prospect D. The dominated combination of A and D was chosen by 60 percent of respondents, and only 6 percent favored the dominant combination of B and C.

12. S. Lichtenstein and P. Slovic, *J. Exp. Psychol.* 101, 16 (1973); D. M. Grether and C. R. Plott, *Am. Econ. Rev.* 69, 623 (1979); I. Lieblich and A. Lieblich, *Percept. Mot. Skills* 29, 467 (1969); D. M. Grether, *Social Science Working Paper No. 245* (California Institute of Technology, Pasadena, 1979).

13. Other demonstrations of a reluctance to integrate concurrent options have been reported: P. Slovic and S. Lichtenstein, *J. Exp. Psychol.* 78, 646 (1968); J. W. Payne and M. L. Braunstein, *Ibid.* 87, 13 (1971).

14. M. Allais, *Econometrica* 21, 503 (1953); K. McCrimmon and S. Larsson, In *Expected Utility Hypotheses and the Allais Paradox*, M. Allais and O. Hagan, Eds. (Reidel, Dordrecht, 1979).

15. Another group of respondents ($N = 205$) was presented with all three problems, in different orders, without monetary payoffs. The joint frequency distribution of choices in problems 5, 6, and 7 was as follows: ACE, 22; ACF, 65; ADE, 4; ADF, 20; BCE, 7; BCF, 18; BDE, 17; BDF, 52. These data confirm in a within-subject design the analysis of conditional evaluation proposed in the text. More than 75 percent of respondents made compatible choices (AC or BD) in problems 5 and 6, and less than half made compatible choices in problems 6 and 7 (CE or DF) or 5 and 7 (AE or BF). The elimination of payoffs in these questions reduced risk aversion but did not substantially alter the effects of certainty and pseudocertainty.

16. For further discussion of rationality in protective action see H. Kunreuther, *Disaster Insurance Protection: Public Policy Lessons* (Wiley, New York, 1978).

17. W. H. McGlothlin, *Am. J. Psychol.* 69, 604 (1956).

18. R. Thaler, *J. Econ. Behav. Organ.* 1, 39 (1980).

19. B. Fischhoff, P. Slovic, S. Lichtenstein, in *Cognitive Processes in Choice and Decision Behavior*, T. Wallsten, Ed. (Erlbaum, Hillsdale, N. J., 1980).

20. J. C. Hershey and P. J. H. Schoemaker, *J. Risk Insur.*, in press.

21. J. Pratt, A. Wise, R. Zeckhauser, *Q. J. Econ.* 93, 189 (1979).

22. R. H. Strotz, *Rev. Econ. Stud.* 23, 165 (1955); G. Ainslie. *Psychol. Bull.* 82, 463 (1975); J. Elster, *Ulysses and the Sirens: Studies in Rationality and Irrationality* (Cambridge Univ. Press, London, 1979); R: Thaler and H. M. Shifrin, *J. Polit. Econ.*, in press.

23. P. Slovic and A. Tversky, *Behav. Sci.* 19, 368 (1974).

24. A. Tversky and D. Kahneman, *Science* 185, 1124 (1974); P. Slovic, B. Fischhoff, S. Lichtenstein, *Annu. Rev. Psychol.* 28, 1 (1977); R. Nisbett and L. Ross, *Human Inference: Strategies and Shortcomings of Social Judgment* (Prentice-Hall, Englewood Cliffs, N. J., 1980); H. Einhorn and R. Hogarth, *Annu. Rev. Psychol.* 32, 53 (1981).

25. H. A. Simon, *Q. J. Econ.* 69, 99 (1955); *Psychol. Rev.* 63, 129 (1956).

26. J. March, *Bell J. Econ.* 9, 587 (1978).

27. This work was supported by the Office of Naval Research under contract N00014–79–C–0077 to Stanford University.

Dr. Tversky is a professor of psychology at Stanford University, Stanford, California 94305, and Dr. Kahneman is a professor of psychology at the University of British Columbia, Vancouver, Canada V6T 1W5.

# Judgment under Uncertainty: Heuristics and Biases
## Biases in Judgments Reveal Some Heuristics of Thinking under Uncertainity

Amos Tversky and Daniel Kahneman

Many decisions are based on beliefs concerning the likelihood of uncertain events such as the outcome of an election, the guilt of a defendant, or the future value of the dollar. These beliefs are usually expressed in statements such as, "I think that . . . ," "chances are . . . ," "it is unlikely that . . . ," and so forth. Occasionally, beliefs concerning uncertain events are expressed in numerical form as odds or subjective probabilities. What determines such beliefs? How do people assess the probability of an uncertain event or the value of an uncertain quantity? This article shows that people rely on a limited number of heuristic principles which reduce the complex tasks of assessing probabilities and predicting values to simpler judgmental operations. In general, these heuristics are quite useful, but sometimes they lead to severe and systematic errors.

The subjective assessment of probability resembles the subjective assessment of physical quantities such as distance or size. These judgments are all based on data of limited validity, which are processed according to heuristic rules. For example, the apparent distance of an object is determined in part by its clarity. The more sharply the object is seen, the closer it appears to be. This rule has some validity, because in any given scene the more distant objects are seen less sharply than nearer objects. However, the reliance on this rule leads to systematic errors in the estimation of distance. Specifically, distances are often overestimated when visibility is poor because the contours of objects are blurred. On the other hand, distances are often underestimated when visibility is good because the objects are seen sharply. Thus, the reliance on clarity as an indication of distance leads to common biases. Such biases are also found in the intuitive judgment of probability. This article describes three heuristics that are employed to assess probabilities and to predict values. Biases to which these heuristics load are enumerated, and the applied and theoretical implications of these observations are discussed.

## Representativeness

Many of the probabilistic questions with which people are concerned belong to one of the following types: What is the probability that object A belongs to class B? What is the probability that event A originates from process B? What is the probability that process B will generate event A?

In answering such questions, people typically rely on the representativeness heuristic, in which probabilities are evaluated by the degree to which A is representative of B, that is by the degree to which A resembles B. For example when A is highly representative of B, the probability that A originates from B is judged to be high. On the other hand, if A is not similar to B, the probability that A originates from B is judged to be low.

For an illustration of judgment by representativeness, consider an individual who has been described by a former neighbor as follows: "Steve is very shy and withdrawn, invariably helpful, but with little interest in people or in the world of reality. A meek and tidy soul, he has a need for order and structure, and a passion for detail." How do people assess the probability that Steve is engaged in a particular occupation from a list of possibilities (for example, farmer, salesman, airline pilot, librarian, or physician)? How do people order these occupations from most to least likely? In the representativeness heuristic, the probability that Steve is a librarian, for example, is assessed by the degree to which he is representative of, or similar to, the stereotype of a librarian. Indeed, research with problems of this type has shown that people order the occupations by probability and by similarity in exactly the same way (1). This approach to the judgment of probability leads to serious errors, because similarity, or representativeness, is not influenced by several factors that should affect judgments of probability.

### INSENSITIVITY TO PRIOR PROBABILITY OF OUTCOMES

One of the factors that have no effect, on representativeness but should have a major effect on probability is the prior probability, or base-rate frequency, of the outcomes. In the case of Steve, for example, the fact that there are many more farmers than librarians in the population should enter into any reasonable estimate of the probability that Steve is a librarian rather than a farmer. Considerations of base rate frequency, however, do not affect the similarity of Steve to the stereotypes of librarians and farmers. If people evaluate probability by representativeness, therefore, prior probabilities will be neglected. This hypothesis was tested in an experiment where prior probabilities were manipulated (1). Subjects were shown brief personality descriptions of several individuals, allegedly sampled at random from a group of 100 professionals—engineers and lawyers. The subjects were asked to assess for each description, the probability that it belonged to an engineer rather than to a lawyer. In one experimental condition, subjects were told that the group from which the descriptions had been drawn consisted of 70 engineers and 30 lawyers. In another condition, subjects were told that the group consisted of 30 engineers and 70 lawyers. The odds that any particular description belongs to an engineer rather than to a lawyer should be higher in the first condition, where there is a majority of engineers, than in the second condition, where there is a majority of lawyers. Specifically, it can be shown by applying Bayes' rule that the ratio of these odds should be $(.7/.3)^2$, or 5.44, for each description. In a sharp violation of Bayes' rule, the subjects in the two conditions produced essentially the same probability judgments. Apparently, subjects evaluated the likelihood that a particular description belonged to an engineer rather than to a lawyer by the degree to which this description was representative of the two stereotypes, with little or no regard for the prior probabilities of the categories.

The subjects used prior probabilities correctly when they had no other information. In the absence of a personality sketch, they judged the probability that an unknown individual is an engineer to be .7 and .3, respectively, in the two base-rate conditions. However, prior probabilities were effectively ignored when a description was introduced, even when this description was totally uninformative. The responses to the following description illustrate this phenomenon:

> Dick is a 30 year old man. He is married with no children. A man of high ability and high motivation, he promises to be quite successful in his field. He is well liked by his colleagues.

This description was intended to convey no information relevant to the question of whether Dick is an engineer or a lawyer. Consequently, the probability that Dick is an engineer should equal the proportion of engineers in the group, as if no description had been given. The subjects, however, judged the probability of Dick being an engineer to be .5 regardless of whether the stated proportion of engineers in the group was .7 or .3. Evidently, people respond differently when given no evidence and when given worthless evidence. When no specific evidence is given, prior probabilities are properly utilized; when worthless evidence is given, prior probabilities are ignored (*1*).

## INSENSITIVITY TO SAMPLE SIZE

To evaluate the probability of obtaining a particular result in a sample drawn from a specified population, people typically apply the representativeness heuristic. That is, they assess the likelihood of a sample result, for example, that the average height in a random sample of ten men will be 6 feet (180 centimeters), by the similarity of this result to the corresponding parameter (that is, to the average height in the population of men). The similarity of a sample statistic to a population parameter does not depend on the size of the sample. Consequently, if probabilities are assessed by representativeness, then the judged probability of a sample statistic will be essentially independent of sample size. Indeed, when subjects assessed the distributions of average height for samples of various sizes, they produced identical distributions. For example, the probability of obtaining an average height greater than 6 feet was assigned the same value for samples of 1000, 100, and 10 men (*2*). Moreover, subjects failed to appreciate the role of sample size even when it was emphasized in the formulation of the problem. Consider the following question:

A certain town is served by two hospitals. In the larger hospital about 45 babies are born each day, and in the smaller hospital about 15 babies are born each day. As you know, about 50 percent of all babies are boys. However, the exact percentage varies from day to day. Sometimes it may be higher than 50 percent, sometimes lower.

For a period of 1 year, each hospital recorded the days on which more than 60 percent of the babies born were boys. Which hospital do you think recorded more such days?

- The larger hospital (21)
- The smaller hospital (21)
- About the same (that is, within 5 percent of each other) (53)

The values in parentheses are the number of undergraduate students who chose each answer.

Most subjects judged the probability of obtaining more than 60 percent boys to be the same in the small and in the large hospital presumably because these events are described by the same statistic and are therefore equally representative of the general population. In contrast, sampling theory entails that the expected number of days on which more than 60 percent of the babies are boys is much greater in the small hospital than in the large one, because a large sample is less likely to stray from 50 percent. This fundamental notion of statistics is evidently not part of people's repertoire of intuitions.

A similar insensitivity to sample size has been reported in judgments of posterior probability, that is, of the probability that a sample has been drawn from one population rather than from another. Consider the following example.

Imagine an urn filled with balls, of which $2/3$ are of one color and $1/3$ of another. One individual has drawn 5 balls from the urn, and found that 4 were red and 1 was white. Another individual has drawn 20 balls and found that 12 were red and 8 were white. Which of the two individuals should feel more confident that the urn contains $2/3$ red balls and $1/3$ white balls, rather than the opposite? What odds should each individual give?

In this problem, the correct posterior odds are 8 to 1 for the 4 : 1 sample and 16 to 1 for the 12 : 8 sample, assuming equal prior probabilities. However, most people feel that the first sample provides much stronger evidence for the hypothesis that the urn is predominantly red, because the proportion of red balls is larger in the first than in the second sample. Here again, intuitive judgments are dominated by the sample proportion and are essentially unaffected by the size of the sample, which plays a crucial role in the determination of the actual posterior odds (*2*). In addition, intuitive estimates of posterior odds are far less extreme than the correct values. The underestimation of the impact of evidence has been observed repeatedly in problems of this type (*3, 4*). It has been labeled "conservatism."

## MISCONCEPTIONS OF CHANCE

People expect that a sequence of events generated by a random process will represent the essential characteristics of that process even when the sequence is short. In considering tosses of a coin for heads or tails, for example, people regard the sequence H-T-H-T-T-H to be more likely than the sequence H-H-H-T-T-T, which does not appear random, and also more likely than the sequence H-H-H-H-T-H, which does not represent the fairness of the coin (2). Thus, people expect that the essential characteristics of the process will be represented, not only globally in the entire sequence, but also locally in each of its parts. A locally representative sequence, however, deviates systematically from chance expectation: it contains too many alternations and too few runs. Another consequence of the belief in local representativeness is the well-known gambler's fallacy. After observing a long run of red on the roulette wheel, for example, most people erroneously believe that black is now due, presumably because the occurrence of black will result in a more representative sequence than the occurrence of an additional red. Chance is commonly viewed as a self-correcting process in which a deviation in one direction induces a deviation in the opposite direction to restore the equilibrium. In fact, deviations are not "corrected" as a chance process unfolds, they are merely diluted.

Misconceptions of chance are not limited to naive subjects. A study of the statistical intuitions of experienced research psychologists (5) revealed a lingering belief in what may be called the "law of small numbers," according to which even small samples are highly representative of the populations from which they are drawn. The responses of these investigators reflected the expectation that a valid hypothesis about a population will be represented by a statistically significant result in a sample—with little regard for its size. As a consequence, the researchers put too much faith in the results of small samples and grossly overestimated the replicability of such results. In the actual conduct of research, this bias leads to the selection of samples of inadequate size and to overinterpretation of findings.

## INSENSITIVITY TO PREDICTABILITY

People are sometimes called upon to make such numerical predictions as the future value of a stock, the demand for a commodity, or the outcome of a football game. Such predictions are often made by representativeness. For example, suppose one is given a description of a company and is asked to predict its future profit. If the description of the company is very favorable, a very high profit will appear most representative of that description; if the description is mediocre, a mediocre performance will appear most representative. The degree to which the description is favorable is unaffected by the reliability of that description or by the degree to which it permits accurate prediction. Hence, if people predict solely in terms of the favorableness of the description, their predictions will be insensitive to the reliability of the evidence and to the expected accuracy of the prediction.

This mode of judgment violates the normative statistical theory in which the extremeness and the range of predictions are controlled by considerations of predictability. When predictability is nil, the same prediction should be made in all cases. For example, if the descriptions of companies provide no information relevant to profit, then the same value (such as average profit) should be predicted for all companies. If predictability is perfect, of course, the values predicted will match the actual values and the range of predictions will equal the range of outcomes. In general, the higher the predictability, the wider the range of predicted values.

Several studies of numerical prediction have demonstrated, that intuitive predictions violate this rule, and that subjects show little or no regard for considerations of predictability (1). In one of these studies, subjects were presented with several paragraphs, each describing the performance of a student teacher during a particular practice lesson. Some subjects were asked to *evaluate* the quality of the lesson described in the paragraph in percentile scores, relative to a specified population. Other subjects were asked to *predict*, also in percentile scores, the standing of each student teacher 5 years after the practice lesson. The judgments made under the two conditions were identical. That is, the prediction of a remote criterion (success of a teacher after 5 years) was identical to the evaluation of the information on which the prediction was based (the quality of the practice lesson). The students who made these predictions were undoubtedly aware of the limited predictability of teaching competence on the basis of a single trial lesson 5 years earlier; nevertheless, their predictions were as extreme as their evaluations.

## THE ILLUSION OF VALIDITY

As we have seen, people often predict by selecting the outcome (for example, an occupation) that is most representative of the input (for example, the description of a person). The confidence they have in their prediction depends primarily on the degree of representativeness (that is, on the quality of the match between the selected outcome and the input) with little or no regard for the factors that limit predictive accuracy. Thus, people express great confidence in the prediction that a person is a librarian when given a description of his personality which matches the stereotype of librarians, even if the description is scanty, unreliable, or outdated. The unwarranted confidence which is produced by a good fit between the predicted outcome and the input information may be called the illusion of validity. This illusion persists even when the judge is aware of the factors that limit the accuracy of his predictions. It is a common observation that psychologists who conduct selection interviews often experience considerable confidence in their predictions, even when they know of the vast literature that shows selection interviews to be highly fallible. The continued reliance on the clinical interview for selection, despite repeated demonstrations of its inadequacy, amply attests to the strength of this effect.

The internal consistency of a pattern of inputs is a major determinant of one's confidence in predictions based on these inputs. For example, people express more confidence in predicting the final grade point average of a student whose first-year record consists entirely of Bs than in predicting the grade-point average of a student whose first-year record includes many As and Cs. Highly consistent patterns are most often observed when the input variables are highly redundant or correlated. Hence, people tend to have great confidence in predictions based on redundant input variables. However, an elementary result in the statistics of correlation asserts that, given input variables of stated validity, a prediction based on several such inputs can achieve higher accuracy when they are independent of each other than when they are redundant or correlated. Thus, redundancy among inputs decreases accuracy even as it increases confidence, and people are often confident in predictions that are quite likely to be off the mark (1).

## MISCONCEPTIONS OF REGRESSION

Suppose a large group of children has been examined on two equivalent versions of an aptitude test. If one selects ten children from among those who did best on one of the two versions, he will usually find their performance on the second version to be somewhat disappointing. Conversely, if one selects ten children from among those who did worst on one version, they will be found, on the average, to do somewhat better on the other version. More generally, consider two variables $X$ and $Y$ which have the same distribution. If one selects individuals whose average $X$ score deviates from the mean of $X$ by $k$ units, then the average of their $Y$ scores will usually deviate from the mean of $Y$ by less than $k$ units. These observations illustrate a general phenomenon known as regression toward the mean, which was first documented by Galton more than 100 years ago.

In the normal course of life, one encounters many instances of regression toward the mean, in the comparison of the height of fathers and sons, of the intelligence of husbands and wives, or of the performance of individuals on consecutive examinations. Nevertheless, people do not develop correct intuitions about this phenomenon. First, they do not expect regression in many contexts where it is bound to occur. Second, when they recognize the occurrence of regression, they often invent spurious causal explanations for it (1). We suggest that the phenomenon of regression remains elusive because it is incompatible with the belief that the predicted outcome should be maximally representative of the input, and, hence, that the value of the outcome variable should be as extreme as the value of the input variable.

The failure to recognize the import of regression can have pernicious consequences, as illustrated by the following observation (1). In a discussion of flight training, experienced instructors noted that praise for an exceptionally smooth landing is typically followed by a poorer landing on the next try, while harsh criticism after a rough landing is usually followed by an improvement on the next try. The instructors concluded that verbal rewards are detrimental to learning, while verbal punishments are beneficial, contrary to accepted psychological doctrine. This conclusion is unwarranted because of the presence of regression toward the mean. As in other cases of repeated examination, an improvement will usually follow a poor performance and a deterioration will usually follow an outstanding performance, even if the instructor does not respond to the trainee's achievement on the first attempt. Because the instructors had praised their trainees after good landings and admonished them after poor ones they reached the erroneous and potentially harmful conclusion that punishment is more effective than reward.

Thus, the failure to understand the effect of regression leads one to overestimate the effectiveness of punishment and to underestimate the effectiveness of reward. In social interaction, as well as in training, rewards are typically administered when performance is good, and punishments are typically administered when performance is poor. By regression alone, therefore, behavior is most likely to improve after punishment and most likely to deteriorate after reward. Consequently, the human condition is such that, by chance alone, one is most often rewarded for punishing others and most often punished for rewarding them. People are generally not aware of this contingency. In fact, the elusive role of regression in determining the apparent consequences of reward and punishment seems to have escaped the notice of students of this area.

## Availability

There are situations in which people assess the frequency of a class or the probability of an event by the ease with which instances or occurrences can be brought to mind. For example, one may assess the risk of heart attack among middle-aged people by recalling such occurrences among one's acquaintances. Similarly, one may evaluate the probability that a given business venture will fail by imagining various difficulties it could encounter. This judgmental heuristic is called availability. Availability is a useful clue for assessing frequency or probability, because instances of large classes are usually recalled better and faster than instances of less frequent classes. However, availability is affected by factors other than frequency and probability. Consequently, the reliance on availability leads to predictable biases, some of which are illustrated below.

## BIASES DUE TO THE RETRIEVABILITY OF INSTANCES

When the size of a class is judged by the availability of its instances, a class whose instances are easily retrieved will appear more numerous than a class of equal frequency whose instances are less retrievable. In an elementary demonstration of this effect, subjects heard a list of well-known personalities of both sexes and were subsequently asked to judge whether the list contained more names of men than of women. Different lists were presented to different groups of subjects. In some of the lists the men were relatively more famous than the women and in others the women were relatively more famous than the men. In each of the lists, the subjects erroneously judged that the class (sex) that had the more famous personalities was the more numerous (6).

In addition to familiarity, there are other factors, such as salience, which affect the retrievability of instances. For example, the impact of seeing a house burning on the subjective probability of such accidents is probably greater than the impact of reading about a fire in the local paper. Furthermore, recent occurrences are likely to be relatively more available than earlier occurrences. It is a common experience that the subjective probability of traffic accidents rises temporarily when one sees a car overturned by the side of the road.

## BIASES DUE TO THE EFFECTIVENESS OF A SEARCH SET

Suppose one samples a word (of three letters or more) at random from an English text. Is it more likely that the word starts with r or that r is the third letter? People approach this problem by recalling words that begin with r (road) and words that have r in the third position (car) and assess the relative frequency by the ease with which words of the two types come to mind. Because it is much easier to search for words by their first letter than by their third letter, most people judge words that begin with a given consonant to be more numerous than words in which the same consonant appears in the third position. They do so even for consonants, such as r or k, that are more frequent in the third position than in the first (6).

Different tasks elicit different search sets. For example, suppose you are asked to rate the frequency with which abstract words (thought, love) and concrete words (door, water) appear in written English. A natural way to answer this question is to search for contexts in which the word could appear. It seems easier to think of contexts in which an abstract concept is mentioned (love in love stories) than to think of contexts in which a concrete word (such as door) is mentioned. If the frequency of words is judged by the availability of the contexts in which they appear, abstract words will be judged as relatively more numerous than concrete words. This bias has been observed in a recent study (7) which showed that the judged frequency of occurrence of abstract words was much higher than that of concrete words, equated in objective frequency. Abstract words were also judged to appear in a much greater variety of contexts than concrete words.

## BIASES OF IMAGINABILITY

Sometimes one has to assess the frequency of a class whose instances are not stored in memory but can be generated according to a given rule. In such situations, one typically generates several instances and evaluates frequency or probability by the ease with which the relevant instances can be constructed. However, the ease of constructing instances does not always reflect their actual frequency, and this mode of evaluation is prone to biases. To illustrate, consider a group of 10 people who form committees of $k$ members: $2 \leq k \leq 8$. How many different committees of $k$ members can be formed? The correct answer to this problem is given by the binomial coefficient $(10_k)$ which reaches a maximum of 252 for $k = 5$. Clearly, the number of committees of $k$ members equals the number of committees of $(10 - k)$ members, because any committee of $k$ members defines a unique group of $(10 - k)$ nonmembers.

One way to answer this question without computation is to mentally construct committees of $k$ members and to evaluate their number by the ease with which they come to mind. Committees of few members, say 2, are more available than committees of many members, say 8. The simplest scheme for the construction of committees is a partition of the group into disjoint sets. One readily sees that it is easy to construct five disjoint committees of 2 members, while it is impossible to generate even two disjoint committees of 8 members. Consequently, if frequency is assessed by imaginability, or by availability for construction, the small committees will appear more numerous than larger committees, in contrast to the correct bell-shaped function. Indeed, when naive subjects were asked to estimate the number of distinct committees of various sizes, their estimates were a decreasing monotonic function of committee size (6). For example, the median estimate of the number of committees of 2 members was 70, while the estimate for committees of 8 members was 20 (the correct answer is 45 in both cases).

Imaginability plays an important role in the evaluation of probabilities in real-life situations. The risk involved in an adventurous expedition, for example, is evaluated by imagining contingencies with which the expedition is not equipped to cope. If many such difficulties are vividly portrayed, the expedition can be made to appear exceedingly dangerous, although the ease with which disasters are imagined need not reflect their actual likelihood. Conversely, the risk involved in an undertaking may be grossly underestimated if some possible dangers are either difficult to conceive of, or simply do not come to mind.

## ILLUSORY CORRELATION

Chapman and Chapman (8) have described an interesting bias in the judgment of the frequency with which two events co-occur. They presented naive judges with information concerning several hypothetical mental patients. The data for each patient consisted of a clinical diagnosis and a drawing of a person made by the patient. Later the judges estimated the frequency with which each diagnosis (such as paranoia or suspiciousness) had been accompanied by various features of the drawing (such as peculiar eyes). The subjects markedly overestimated the frequency of co-occurrence of natural associates, such as suspiciousness and peculiar eyes. This effect was labeled illusory correlation. In their erroneous judgments of the data to which they had been exposed, naive subjects "rediscovered" much of the common, but unfounded, clinical lore concerning the interpretation of the draw-a-person test. The illusory correlation effect was extremely resistant to contradictory data. It persisted even when the correlation between symptom and diagnosis was actually negative, and it prevented the judges from detecting relationships that were in fact present.

Availability provides a natural account for the illusory-correlation effect. The judgment of how frequently two events co-occur could be based on the strength of the associative bond between them. When the association is strong, one is likely to conclude that the events have been frequently paired. Consequently, strong associates will be judged to have occurred together frequently. According to this view, the illusory correlation between suspiciousness and peculiar drawing of the eyes, for example, is due to the fact that suspiciousness is more readily associated with the eyes than with any other part of the body.

Lifelong experience has taught us that, in general, instances of large classes are recalled better and faster than instances of less frequent classes; that likely occurrences are easier to imagine than unlikely ones; and that the associative connections between events are strengthened when the events frequently co-occur. As a result, man has at his disposal a procedure (the availability heuristic) for estimating the numerosity of a class, the likelihood of an event, or the frequency of co-occurrences, by the ease with which the relevant mental operations of retrieval construction, or association can be performed. However, as the preceding examples have demonstrated, this valuable estimation procedure results in systematic errors.

## Adjustment and Anchoring

In many situations, people make estimates by starting from an initial value that is adjusted to yield the final answer. The initial value, or starting point, may be suggested by the formulation of the problem, or it may be the result of a partial computation. In either case, adjustments are typically insufficient (4). That is, different starting points yield different estimates, which are biased toward the initial values. We call this phenomenon anchoring.

### INSUFFICIENT ADJUSTMENT

In a demonstration of the anchoring effect, subjects were asked to estimate various quantities, stated in percentages (for example, the percentage of African countries in the United Nations). For each quantity, a number between 0 and 100

was determined by spinning a wheel of fortune in the subjects' presence. The subjects were instructed to indicate first whether that number was higher or lower than the value of the quantity, and then to estimate the value of the quantity by moving upward or downward from the given number. Different groups were given different numbers for each quantity, and these arbitrary numbers had a marked effect on estimates. For example, the median estimates of the percentage of African countries in the United Nations were 25 and 45 for groups that received 10 and 65, respectively, as starting points. Payoffs for accuracy did not reduce the anchoring effect.

Anchoring occurs not only when the starting point is given to the subject but also when the subject based his estimate on the result of some incomplete computation. A study of intuitive numerical estimation illustrates this effect. Two groups of high school students estimated, within 5 seconds, a numerical expression that was written on the blackboard. One group estimated the product.

$$8 \times 7 \times 6 \times 5 \times 4 \times 3 \times 2 \times 1$$

while another group estimated the product

$$1 \times 2 \times 3 \times 4 \times 5 \times 6 \times 7 \times 8$$

To rapidly answer such questions, people may perform a few steps of computation and estimate the product by extrapolation or adjustment. Because adjustments are typically insufficient, this procedure should lead to underestimation. Furthermore, because the result of the first few steps of multiplication (performed from left to right) is higher in the descending sequence than in the ascending sequence, the former expression should be judged larger than the latter. Both predictions were confirmed. The median estimate for the ascending sequence was 512, while the median estimate for the descending sequence was 2,250. The correct answer is 40,320.

### BIASES IN THE EVALUATION OF CONJUNCTIVE AND DISJUNCTIVE EVENTS

In a recent study by Bar-Hillel (9) subjects were given the opportunity to bet on one of two events. Three types of events were used: (i) simple events, such as drawing a red marble from a bag containing 50 percent red marbles and 50 percent white marbles; (ii) conjunctive events, such as drawing a red marble seven times in succession, with replacement, from a bag containing 90 percent red marbles and 10 percent white marbles; and (iii) disjunctive events, such as drawing a red marble at least once in seven successive tries, with replacement, from a bag containing 10 percent red marbles and 90 percent white marbles. In this problem, a significant majority of subjects preferred to bet on the conjunctive event (the probability of which is .48) rather than on the simple event (the probability of which is .50). Subjects also preferred to bet on the simple event rather than on the disjunctive event, which has a probability of .52. Thus, most subjects bet on the less likely event in both comparisons. This pattern of choices illustrates a general finding. Studies of choice among gambles and of judgments of probability indicate that people tend to overestimate the probability of conjunctive events (10) and to underestimate the probability of disjunctive events. These biases are readily explained as effects of anchoring. The stated probability of the elementary event (success at any one stage) provides a natural starting point for the estimation of the probabilities of both conjunctive and disjunctive events. Since adjustment from the starting point is typically insufficient, the final estimates remain too close to the probabilities of the elementary events in both cases. Note that the overall probabilities of a conjunctive event is lower than the probability of each elementary event, whereas the overall probability of a disjunctive event is higher than the probability of each elementary event. As a consequence of anchoring, the overall probability will be overestimated in conjunctive problems and underestimated in disjunctive problems.

Biases in the evaluation of compound events are particularly significant in the context of planning. The successful completion of an undertaking, such as the development of a new product, typically has a conjunctive character: for the undertaking to succeed, each of a series of events must occur. Even when each of these events is very likely, the overall probability of success can be quite low if the number of events is large. The general tendency to overestimate the probability of conjunctive events leads to unwarranted optimism in the evaluation of the likelihood that a plan will succeed or that a project will be completed on time. Conversely, disjunctive structures are typically encountered in the evaluation of risks. A complex system, such as a nuclear reactor or a human body, will malfunction if any of its essential components fails. Even when the likelihood of failure in each component is slight, the probability of an overall failure can be high if many components are involved. Because of anchoring, people will tend to underestimate the probabilities of failure in complex systems. Thus, the direction of the anchoring bias can sometimes be inferred from the structure of the event. The chain-like structure of conjunctions leads to overestimation, the funnel-like structure of disjunctions leads to underestimation.

## ANCHORING IN THE ASSESSMENT OF SUBJECTIVE PROBABILITY DISTRIBUTIONS

In decision analysis, experts are often required to express their beliefs about a quantity, such as the value of the Dow-Jones average on a particular day, in the form of a probability distribution. Such a distribution is usually constructed by asking the person to select values of the quantity that correspond to specified percentiles of his subjective probability distribution. For example, the judge may be asked to select a number, $X_{90}$, such that his subjective probability that this number will be higher than the value of the Dow-Jones average is .90. That is, he should select the value $X_{90}$ so that he is just willing to accept 9 to 1 odds that the Dow-Jones average will not exceed it. A subjective probability distribution for the value of the Dow-Jones average can be constructed from several such judgments corresponding to different percentiles.

By collecting subjective probability distributions for many different quantities, it is possible to test the judge for proper calibration. A judge is properly (or externally) calibrated in a set of problems if exactly $n$ percent of the true values of the assessed quantities falls below his stated values of $X_n$. For example, the true values should fall below $X_{01}$ for 1 percent of the quantities and above $X_{00}$ for 1 percent of the quantities. Thus, the true values should fall in the confidence interval between $X_{01}$ and $X_{00}$ on 98 percent of the problems.

Several investigators (11) have obtained probability distributions for many quantities from a large number of judges. These distributions indicated large and systematic departures from proper calibration. In most studies, the actual values of the assessed quantities are either smaller than $X_{01}$ or greater than $X_{00}$ for about 30 percent of the problems. That is, the subjects state overly narrow confidence intervals which reflect more certainty than is justified by their knowledge about the assessed quantities. This bias is common to naive and to sophisticated subjects, and it is not eliminated by introducing proper scoring rules, which provide incentives for external calibration. This effect is attributable, in part at least, to anchoring.

To select $X_{90}$ for the value of the Dow-Jones average, for example, it is natural to begin by thinking about one's best estimate of the Dow-Jones and to adjust this value upward. If this adjustment—like most others—is insufficient, then $X_{90}$ will not be sufficiently extreme. A similar anchoring effect will occur in the selection of $X_{10}$, which is presumably obtained by adjusting one's best estimate downward. Consequently the confidence interval between $X_{10}$ and $X_{90}$ will be too narrow, and the assessed probability distribution will be too tight. In support of this interpretation it can be shown that subjective probabilities are systematically altered by a procedure in which one's best estimate does not serve as an anchor.

Subjective probability distributions for a given quantity (the Dow-Jones average) can be obtained in two different ways: (i) by asking the subject to select values of the Dow-Jones that correspond to specified percentiles of his probability distribution and (ii) by asking the subject to assess the probabilities that the true value of the Dow-Jones will exceed some specified values. The two procedures are formally equivalent and should yield identical distributions. However, they suggest different modes of adjustment from different anchors. In procedure (i), the natural starting point is one's best estimate of the quantity. In procedure (ii), on the other hand, the subject may be anchored on the value stated in the question. Alternatively, he may be anchored on even odds, or 50–50 chances, which is a natural starting point in the estimation of likelihood. In either case, procedure (ii) should yield less extreme odds than procedure (i).

To contrast the two procedures, a set of 24 quantities (such as the air distance from New Delhi to Peking) was presented to a group of subjects who assessed either $X_{10}$ or $X_{90}$ for each problem. Another group of subjects received the median judgment of the first group for each of the 24 quanti-

ties. They were asked to assess the odds that each of the given values exceeded the true value of the relevant quantity. In the absence of any bias, the second group should retrieve the odds specified to the first group, that is, 9:1. However, if even odds or the stated value serve as anchors, the odds of the second group should be less extreme, that is, closer to 1:1. Indeed, the median odds stated by this group, across all problems, were 3:1. When the judgments of the two groups were tested for external calibration, it was found that subjects in the first group were too extreme, in accord with earlier studies. The events that they defined as having a probability of 10 actually obtained in 24 percent of the cases. In contrast, subjects in the second group were too conservative. Events to which they assigned an average probability of .34 actually obtained in 26 percent of the cases. These results illustrate the manner in which the degree of calibration depends on the procedure of elicitation.

## Discussion

This article has been concerned with cognitive biases that stem from the reliance on judgmental heuristics. These biases are not attributable to motivational effects such as wishful thinking or the distortion of judgments by payoffs and penalties. Indeed, several of the severe errors of judgment reported earlier occurred despite the fact that subjects were encouraged to be accurate and were rewarded for the correct answers (2, 6).

The reliance on heuristics and the prevalence of biases are not restricted to laymen. Experienced researchers are also prone to the same biases—when they think intuitively. For example, the tendency to predict the outcome that best represents the data, with insufficient regard for prior probability, has been observed in the intuitive judgments of individuals who have had extensive training in statistics (1, 5). Although the statistically sophisticated avoid elementary errors, such as the gambler's fallacy, their intuitive judgments are liable to similar fallacies in more intricate and less transparent problems.

It is not surprising that useful heuristics such as representativeness and availability are retained, even though they occasionally lead to errors in prediction or estimation. What is perhaps surprising is the failure of people to infer from lifelong experience such fundamental statistical rules as regression toward the mean, or the effect of sample size on sampling variability. Although everyone is exposed, in the normal course of life, to numerous examples from which these rules could have been induced, very few people discover the principles of sampling and regression on their own. Statistical principles are not learned from everyday experience because the relevant instances are not coded appropriately. For example, people do not discover that successive lines in a text differ more in average word length than do successive pages, because they simply do not attend to the average word length of individual lines or pages. Thus, people do not learn the relation between sample size and sampling variability, although the data for such learning are abundant.

The lack of an appropriate code also explains why people usually do not detect the biases in their judgments of probability. A person could conceivably learn whether his judgments are externally calibrated by keeping a tally of the proportion of events that actually occur among those to which he assigns the same probability. However, it is not natural to group events by their judged probability. In the absence of such grouping it is impossible for an individual to discover, for example, that only 50 percent of the predictions to which he has assigned a probability of 9 or higher actually came true.

The empirical analysis of cognitive biases has implications for the theoretical and applied role of judged probabilities. Modern decision theory (12, 13) regards subjective probability as the quantified opinion of an idealized person. Specifically, the subjective probability of a given event is defined by the set of bets about this event that such a person is willing to accept. An internally consistent, or coherent, subjective probability measure can be derived for an individual if his choices among bets satisfy certain principles, that is, the axioms of the theory. The derived probability is subjective in the sense that different individuals are allowed to have different probabilities for the same event. The major contribution of this approach is that it provides a rigorous subjective interpretation of probability that is applicable to unique events and is embedded in a general theory of rational decision.

It should perhaps be noted that, while subjective probabilities can sometimes be inferred from preferences among bets, they are normally not formed in this fashion. A person bets on team A rather than on team B because he believes that team A is more likely to win; he does not infer this belief from his betting preferences. Thus, in reality, subjective probabilities determine preferences among bets and are not derived from them, as in the axiomatic theory of rational decision (12).

The inherently subjective nature of probability has led many students to the belief that coherence, or internal consistency, is the only valid criterion by which judged probabilities should be evaluated. From the standpoint of the formal theory of subjective probability, any set of internally consistent probability judgments is as good as any other. This criterion is not entirely satisfactory, because an internally consistent set of subjective probabilities can be incompatible with other beliefs held by the individual. Consider a person whose subjective probabilities for all possible outcomes of a coin-tossing game reflect the gambler's fallacy. That is, his estimate of the probability of tails on a particular toss increases with the number of consecutive heads that preceded that toss. The judgments of such a person could be internally consistent and therefore acceptable as adequate subjective probabilities according to the criterion of the formal theory. These probabilities, however, are incompatible with the generally held belief that a coin has no memory and is therefore incapable of generating sequential dependencies. For judged probabilities to be considered adequate, or rational, internal consistency is not enough. The judgments must be compatible with the entire web of beliefs held by the individual. Unfortunately, there can be no simple formal procedure for assessing the compatibility of a set of probability judgments with the judge's total system of beliefs. The rational judge will nevertheless strive for compatibility, even though internal consistency is more easily achieved and assessed. In particular, he will attempt to make his probability judgments compatible with his knowledge about the subject matter, the laws of probability, and his own judgmental heuristics and biases.

## Summary

This article described three heuristics that are employed in making judgments under uncertainty: (i) representativeness, which is usually employed when people are asked to judge the probability that an object or event A belongs to class or process B; (ii) availability of instances or scenarios, which is often employed when people are asked to assess the frequency of a class or the plausibility of a particular development; and (iii) adjustment from an anchor, which is usually employed in numerical prediction when a relevant value is available. These heuristics are highly economical and usually effective, but they lead to systematic and predictable errors. A better understanding of these heuristics and of the biases to which they lead could improve judgments and decisions in situations of uncertainty.

## REFERENCES AND NOTES

1 D. Kahneman and A. Tversky, *Psychol. Rev. 80,* 237 (1973).

2 ——, *Cognitive Psychol. 3,* 430 (1972).

3 W. Edwards, in *Formal Representation of Human Judgment,* H. Kleinmuntz, Ed. (Wiley, New York, 1968), pp. 17–52.

P. Slovic and S. Lichtenstein, *Organ. Behav. Hum. Performance 6,* 649 (1971).

5 A. Tversky and D. Kahneman, *Psychol. Bull. 76,* 105 (1971).

6 ——, *Cognitive Psychol. 5,* 207 (1973).

7 R. C. Galbraith and B. J. Underwood, *Mein. Cognition 1,* 56 (1973).

8 L. J. Chapman and J. P. Chapman, *J. Abnorm. Psychol. 73,* 193 (1967); *ibid.,* 74, 271 (1969).

9 M. Bar-Hillel, *Organ. Behav. Hum. Performance 9,* 396 (1973).

10 J. Cohen, E. I. Chesnick, and D. Haran, *Br. J. Psychol. 63,* 41 (1972).

11 M. Alpert and H. Raiffa, unpublished manuscript; C. A. S. von Holstein, *Acta Psychol. 35,* 478 (1971): R. L. Winkler, *J. Am. Stat. Assoc. 62,* 776 (1967).

12 L. J. Savage, *The Foundation of Statistics* (Wiley, New York, 1954).

13 B. De Finetti, in *International Encyclopedia of the Social Sciences,* D. E. Sills, Ed. (Macmillan, New York, 1968), vol. 12, pp. 496–504.

14 This research was supported by the Advanced Research Projects Agency of the Department of Defense and was monitored by the Office of Naval Research under contract N00014-73-C-0438 to the Oregon Research Institute, Eugene. Additional support for this research was provided by the Research and Development Authority of the Hebrew University, Jerusalem, Israel.

The authors are members of the department of psychology at the Hebrew University, Jerusalem, Israel.

# The Cold Facts about the "Hot Hand" in Basketball

## Do basketball players tend to shoot in streaks? Contrary to the belief of fans and commentators, analysis shows that the chances of hitting a shot are as good after a miss as after a hit.

Amos Tversky and Thomas Gilovich

You're in a world all your own. It's hard to describe. But the basket seems to be so wide. No matter what you do, you know the ball is going to go in.

—Purvis Short, of the NBA's
Golden State Warriors

This statement describes a phenomenon known to everyone who plays or watches the game of basketball, a phenomenon known as the "hot hand." The term refers to the putative tendency for success (and failure) in basketball to be self-promoting or self-sustaining. After making a couple of shots, players are thought to become relaxed, to feel confident, and to "get in a groove" such that subsequent success becomes more likely. The belief in the hot hand, then, is really one version of a wider conviction that "success breeds success" and "failure breeds failure" in many walks of life. In certain domains it surely does—particularly those in which a person's reputation can play

a decisive role. However, there are other areas, such as most gambling games, in which the belief can be just as strongly held, but where the phenomenon clearly does not exist.

What about the game of basketball? Does success in this sport tend to be self-promoting? Do players occasionally get a "hot hand"?

## Misconceptions of Chance Processes

One reason for questioning the widespread belief in the hot hand comes from research indicating that people's intuitive conceptions of randomness do not conform to the laws of chance. People commonly believe that the essential characteristics of a chance process are represented not only globally in a large sample, but also locally in each of its parts. For example, people expect even short sequences of heads and tails to reflect the fairness of a coin and to contain roughly 50% heads and 50% tails. Such a locally representative sequence,

643

however, contains too many alternations and not enough long runs.

This misconception produces two systematic errors. First, it leads many people to believe that the probability of heads is greater after a long sequence of tails than after a long sequence of heads; this is the notorious gamblers' fallacy. Second, it leads people to question the randomness of sequences that contain the expected number of runs because even the occurrence of, say, four heads in a row—which is quite likely in even relatively small samples—makes the sequence appear nonrepresentative. Random sequences just do not look random.

Perhaps, then, the belief in the hot hand is merely one manifestation of this fundamental misconception of the laws of chance. Maybe the streaks of consecutive hits that lead players and fans to believe in the hot hand do not exceed, in length or frequency, those expected in any random sequence.

To examine this possibility, we first asked a group of 100 knowledgeable basketball fans to classify sequences of 21-hits and misses (supposedly taken from a basketball player's performance record) as *streak shooting, chance shooting,* or *alternating shooting.* Chance shooting was defined as runs of hits and misses that are just like those generated by coin tossing. Streak shooting and alternating shooting were defined as runs of hits and misses that are longer or shorter, respectively, than those observed in coin tossing. All sequences contained 11 hits and 10 misses, but differed in the probability of alternation, $p(a)$, or the probability that the outcome of a given shot would be different from the outcome of the previous shot. In a random (i.e., independent) sequence, $p(a) = .5$; streak shooting and alternating shooting arise when $p(a)$ is less than or greater than .5, respectively. Each respondent evaluated six sequences, with $p(a)$ ranging from .4 to .9. Two (mirror image) sequences were used for each level of $p(a)$ and presented to different respondents.

The percentage of respondents who classified each sequence as "streak shooting" or "chance shooting" is presented in Figure 42.1 as a function of $p(a)$. (The percentage of "alternating shooting" is the complement of these values.) As expected, people perceive streak shooting where it does not exist. The sequence of $p(a) = .5$, representing a perfectly random sequence, was classified as streak shooting by 65% of the respondents. Moreover, the perception of chance shooting was strongly biased against long runs: The sequences selected as the best examples of chance shooting were those with probabilities of alternation of .7 and .8 instead of .5.

It is clear, then, that a common misconception about the laws of chance can distort people's ob-

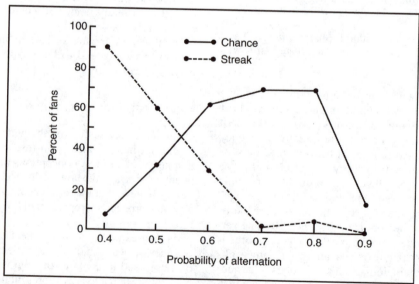

**FIGURE 42.1** ■ Percentage of basketball fans classifying sequences of hits and misses as examples of streak shooting or chance shooting, as a function of the probability of alternation within the sequences.

servations of the game of basketball: Basketball fans "detect" evidence of the hot hand in perfectly random sequences. But is this the main determinant of the widespread conviction that basketball players shoot in streaks? The answer to this question requires an analysis of shooting statistics in real basketball games.

## Cold Facts from the NBA

Although the precise meaning of terms like "the hot hand" and "streak shooting" is unclear, their common use implies a shooting record that departs from coin tossing in two essential respects (see accompanying box). First, the frequency of streaks (i.e., moderate or long runs of successive hits) must exceed what is expected by a chance process with a constant hit rate. Second, the probability of a hit should be greater following a hit than following a miss, yielding a positive serial correlation between the outcomes of successive shots.

To examine whether these patterns accurately describe the performance of players in the nba, the field-goal records of individual players were obtained for 48 home games of the Philadelphia 76ers during the 1980–81 season. Table 42.1 presents, for the nine major players of the 76ers, the probability of a hit conditioned on 1, 2, and 3 hits and misses. The overall hit rate for each player, and the number of shots he took, are presented in column 5. A comparison of columns 4 and 6 indicates that for eight of the nine players the prob-

ability of a hit is actually higher following a miss (mean = .54) than following a hit (mean = .51), contrary to the stated beliefs of both players and fans. Column 9 presents the (serial) correlations between the outcomes of successive shots. These correlations are not significantly different than zero except for one player (Dawkins) whose correlation is negative. Comparisons of the other matching columns (7 vs. 3, and 8 vs. 2) provide further evidence against streak shooting. Additional analyses show that the probability of a hit (mean = .57) following a "cold" period (0 or 1 hits in the last 4 shots) is higher than the probability of a hit (mean = .50) following a "hot" period (3 or 4 hits in the last 4 shots). Finally, a series of Wald-Wolfowitz runs tests revealed that the observed number of runs in the players' shooting records does not depart from chance expectation except for one player (Dawkins) whose data, again, run counter to the streak-shooting hypothesis. Parallel analyses of data from two other teams, the New Jersey Nets and the New York Knicks, yielded similar results.

Although streak shooting entails a positive dependence between the outcomes of successive shots, it could be argued that both the runs test and the test for a positive correlation are not sufficiently powerful to detect occasional "hot" stretches embedded in longer stretches of normal performance. To obtain a more sensitive test of stationarity (suggested by David Freedman) we partitioned the entire record of each player into non-overlapping series of four consecutive shots. We then counted the number of series in which the player's performance was high (3 or 4 hits),

**TABLE 42.1. Probability of Making a Shot Conditioned on the Outcome of Previous Shots for Nine Members of the Philadelphia 76ers; Hits Are Denoted H, Misses Are M.**

| Player | P(H/3M) | P(H/2M) | P(H/1M) | P(H) | P(H/1H) | P(H/2H) | P(H/3H) | Serial Correlation r |
|---|---|---|---|---|---|---|---|---|
| Clint Richardson | .50 | .47 | .58 | .50 (248) | .49 | .50 | .48 | −.020 |
| Julius Erving | .52 | .51 | .51 | .52 (384) | .53 | .52 | .48 | .016 |
| Lionel Hollins | .50 | .49 | .46 | .48 (419) | .46 | .46 | .32 | −.004 |
| Maurice Cheeks | .77 | .60 | .80 | .56 (339) | .55 | .64 | .69 | −.038 |
| Caldwell Jones | .50 | .48 | .47 | .47 (272) | .45 | .48 | .27 | −.016 |
| Andrew Toney | .52 | .58 | .51 | .46 (451) | .43 | .40 | .34 | −.083 |
| Bobby Jones | .81 | .58 | .58 | .64 (433) | .53 | .47 | .53 | −.049 |
| Steve Mix | .70 | .58 | .52 | .52 (351) | .51 | .48 | .36 | −.015 |
| Darryl Dawkins | .88 | .78 | .71 | .62 (403) | .57 | .58 | .51 | −.142* |
| Weighted Mean | .56 | .53 | .54 | .52 | .51 | .50 | .46 | −.039 |

Note: The number of shots taken by each player is given in parentheses in Column 5.
* p < .01.

moderate (2 hits) or low (0 or 1 hits). If a player is occasionally "hot," his record must include more high-performance series than expected by chance. The numbers of high, moderate, and low series for each of the nine Philadelphia 76ers were compared to the expected values, assuming independent shots with a constant hit rate (taken from column 5 of Table 42.1). For example, the expected percentages of high-, moderate-, and low-performance series for a player with a hit rate of .50 are 31.25%, 37.5%, and 31.25%, respectively. The results provided no evidence for non-stationarity or streak shooting as none of the nine chisquares approached statistical significance. The analysis was repeated four times (starting the partition into quadruples at the first, second, third, and fourth shot of each player), but the results were the same. Combining the four analyses, the overall observed percentages of high, medium, and low series are 33.5%, 39.4%, and 27.1%, respectively, whereas the expected percentages are 34.4%, 36.8%, and

28.8%. The aggregate data yield slightly fewer high and low series than expected by independence, which is the exact opposite of the pattern implied by the presence of hot and cold streaks.

At this point, the lack of evidence for streak shooting could be attributed to the contaminating effects of shot selection and defensive strategy. Streak shooting may exist, the argument goes, but it may be masked by a hot player's tendency to take more difficult shots and to receive more attention from the defensive team. Indeed, the best shooters on the team (e.g., Andrew Toney) do not have the highest hit rate, presumably because they take more difficult shots. This argument however, does not explain why players and fans erroneously believe that the probability of a hit is greater following a hit than following a miss, nor can it account for the tendency of knowledgeable observers to classify random sequences as instances of streak shooting. Nevertheless, it is instructive to examine the performance of players when the diffi-

---

## What People Mean by the "Hot Hand" and "Streak Shooting"

Although all that people mean by streak shooting and the hot hand can be rather complex, there is a strong consensus among those close to the game about the core features of non-stationarity and serial dependence. To document this consensus, we interviewed a sample of 100 avid basketball fans from Cornell and Stanford. A summary of their responses are given below. We asked similar questions of the players whose data we analyzed—members of the Philadelphia 76ers—and their responses matched those we report here.

Does a player have a better chance of making a shot after having just made his last two or three shots than he does after having just missed his last two or three shots?

Yes 91%
No 9%

When shooting free throws, does a player have a better chance of making his second shot after making his first shot than after missing his first shot?

Yes 68%
No 32%

Is it important to pass the ball to someone who has just made several (2, 3, or 4) shots in a row?

Yes 84%
No 16%

Consider a hypothetical player who shoots 50% from the field.

What is your estimate of his field goal percentage for those shots that he takes after having just made a shot?

Mean = 61%

What is your estimate of his field goal percentage for those shots that he takes after having just missed a shot?

Mean = 42%

culty of the shot and the defensive pressure are held constant. Free-throw records provide such data. Free throws are shot, usually in pairs, from the same location and without defensive pressure. If players shoot in streaks, their shooting percentage on the second free throws should be higher after having made their first shot than after having missed their first shot, Table 42.2 presents the probability of hitting the second free throw conditioned on the outcome of the first free throw for nine Boston Celtics players during the 1980–81 and the 1981–82 seasons.

These data provide no evidence that the outcome of the second shot depends on the outcome of the first. The correlation is negative for five players and positive for the remaining four, and in no case does it approach statistical significance.

## The Cold Facts from Controlled Experiments

To test the hot hand hypothesis, under controlled conditions, we recruited 14 members of the men's varsity team and 12 members of the women's varsity team at Cornell University to participate in a shooting experiment. For each player, we determined a distance from which his or her shooting percentage was roughly 50%, and we drew two 15-foot arcs at this distance from which the player took 100 shots, 50 from each arc. When shooting baskets, the players were required to move along the arc so that consecutive shots were never taken from exactly the same spot.

The analysis of the Cornell data parallels that of the 76ers. The overall probability of a hit following a hit was .47, and the probability of a hit following a miss was .48. The serial correlation was positive for 12 players and negative for 14 (mean $r = .02$). With the exception of one player ($r = .37$) who produced a significant positive correlation (and we might expect one significant result out of 26 just by chance), both the serial correlations and the distribution of runs indicated that the outcomes of successive shots are statistically independent.

We also asked the Cornell players to predict their hits and misses by betting on the outcome of each upcoming shot. Before every shot, each player chose whether to bet high, in which case he or she would win 5 cents for a hit and lose 4 cents for a

**TABLE 42.2. Probability of Hitting a Second Free Throw ($H_2$) Conditioned on the Outcome of the First Free Throw ($H_1$ or $M_1$) for Nine Members of the Boston Celtics.**

| Player | $P(H_2/M_1)$ | $P(H_2/H_1)$ | Serial Correlation $r$ |
|---|---|---|---|
| Larry Bird | .91 (53) | .88 (285) | −.032 |
| Cedric Maxwell | .76 (128) | .81 (302) | .061 |
| Robert Parish | .72 (105) | .77 (213) | .056 |
| Nate Archibald | .82 (76) | .83 (245) | .014 |
| Chris Ford | .77 (22) | .71 (51) | −.069 |
| Kevin McHale | .59 (49) | .73 (128) | .130 |
| M. L. Carr | .81 (26) | .68 (57) | −.128 |
| Rick Robey | .61 (80) | .59 (91) | −.019 |
| Gerald Henderson | .78 (37) | .76 (101) | −.022 |

Note: The number of shots on which each probability is based is given in parentheses.

miss, or to bet low, in which case he or she would win 2 cents for a hit and lose 1 cent for a miss. The players were advised to bet high when they felt confident in their shooting ability and to bet low when they did not. We also obtained betting data from another player who observed the shooter and decided, independently, whether to bet high or low on each trial. The players' payoffs included the amount of money won or lost on the bets made as shooters and as observers.

The players were generally unsuccessful in predicting their performance. The average correlation between the shooters' bets and their performance was .02, and the highest positive correlation was .22. The observers were also unsuccessful in predicting the shooter's performance (mean $r = .04$). However, the bets made by both shooters and observers were correlated with the outcome of the shooters' previous shot (mean $r = .40$ for the shooters and .42 for the observers). Evidently, both shooters and observers relied on the outcome of the previous shot in making their predictions, in accord with the hot-hand hypothesis. Because the correlation between successive shots was negligible (again, mean $r = .02$), this betting strategy was not superior to chance, although it did produce moderate agreement between the bets of the shooters and the observers (mean $r = .22$).

## The Hot Hand as Cognitive Illusion

To summarize what we have found, we think it may be helpful to clarify what we have not found.

Most importantly, our research does not indicate that basketball shooting is a purely chance process, like coin tossing. Obviously, it requires a great deal of talent and skill. What we have found is that, contrary to common belief, a player's chances of hitting are largely independent of the outcome of his or her previous shots. Naturally, every now and then, a player may make, say, nine of ten shots, and one may wish to claim—after the fact—that he was hot. Such use, however, is misleading if the length and frequency of such streaks do not exceed chance expectation.

Our research likewise does not imply that the number of points that a player scores in different games or in different periods within a game is roughly the same. The data merely indicate that the probability of making a given shot (i.e., a player's shooting percentage) is unaffected by the player's prior performance. However, players' willingness to shoot may well be affected by the outcomes of previous shots. As a result, a player may score more points in one period than in another not because he shoots better, but simply because he shoots more often. The absence of streak shooting does not rule out the possibility that other aspects of a player's performance, such as defense, rebounding, shots attempted, or points scored, could be subject to hot and cold periods. Furthermore, the present analysis of basketball data does not say whether baseball or tennis players, for example, go through hot and cold periods. Our research does not tell us anything general about sports, but it does suggest a generalization about people, namely that they tend to "detect" patterns even where none exist, and to overestimate the degree of clustering in sports events, as in other sequential data. We attribute the discrepancy between the observed basketball statistics and the intuitions of highly interested and informed observers to a general misconception of the laws of chance that induces the expectation that random sequences will be far more balanced than they generally are, and creates the illusion that there are patterns or streaks in independent sequences.

This account explains both the formation and maintenance of the belief in the hot hand. If independent sequences are perceived as streak shooting, no amount of exposure to such sequences will convince the player, the coach, or the fan that the sequences are actually independent. In fact, the more basketball one watches, the more one encounters what appears to be streak shooting. This misconception of chance has direct consequences for the conduct of the game. Passing the ball to the hot player, who is guarded closely by the opposing team, may be a non-optimal strategy if other players who do not appear hot have a better chance of scoring. Like other cognitive illusions, the belief in the hot hand could be costly.

## ADDITIONAL READING

Gilovich, T., Vallone, R., and Tversky, A. (1985). "The hot hand in basketball: On the misperception of random sequences." *Cognitive Psychology, 17,* 295–314.

Kahneman, D., Slovic, P., and Tversky, A. (1982). "Judgment under uncertainty: Heuristics and biases." New York: Cambridge University Press.

Tversky, A. and Kahneman, D. (1971). "Belief in the law of small numbers." *Psychological Bulletin, 76,* 105–110.

Tversky, A. and Kahneman, D. (1974). "Judgment under uncertainty: Heuristics and biases." *Science, 185,* 1124–1131.

Wagenaar, W. A. (1972). "Generation of random sequences by human subjects: A critical survey of literature." *Psychological Bulletin, 77,* 65–72.

PART X

# Judgment and Decision Making

## Discussion Questions

1. What are the pros and cons of heuristics? That is, lay out how simple heuristics can make us smart (also see Gigerenzer's book of a similar title) and contrast that to the kinds of errors observed by Tversky and Kahneman. How adaptive are heuristics?
2. Do you think any of the decision-making results described in this chapter would change if the situation were a more emotional one? That is, do you think there is anything different about emotional decisions?
3. Does the person have to behave according to the "rational" model (that is, Expected Utility Theory) to be rational?
4. What are the implications of Framing Effects for polling (e.g., political questionnaires)?
5. Do you see any relationship between the heuristics discussed in the decision-making chapter and the schemas discussed in other chapters (e.g., the type of knowledge structure utilized in the Bransford and Johnson reading)?

## Suggested Readings

L. R. Brooks, V. R. LeBlanc, and R. Geoffrey (2000, On the difficulty of noticing obvious features in patient appearance. *Psychological Science, 11,* 112–117) write on the difficult decisions faced by medical doctors. When reading this, think about how making such a decision draws upon many different cognitive processes, including pattern recognition and categorization.

L. Chapman and J. Chapman (1967, Genesis of popular but erroneous psychodiagnostic observations. *Journal of Abnormal Psychology, 72,* 193–204) show experimentally that people see the symptoms that they expect even if not present.

B. Fischhoff (1975, Hindsight is not equal to foresight: The effect of outcome knowledge on judgment under uncertainty. *Journal of Experimental Psychology: Human Perception & Performance, 1,* 288–299) studies another bias, the hindsight bias. When judging what they would have known in the past, people are biased by what they currently know.

G. Gigerenzer and P. Todd's (1999, *Simple Heuristics That Make Us Smart.* New York: Oxford University Press) book argues for the importance of heuristics in the real world.

S. Plous's 1993 book (*The Psychology of Judgment and Decision Making*. New York: McGraw-Hill) is a wonderful short introduction to the field of decision making. Plous does a nice job of tying the issues discussed in this chapter to other topics, such as memory and social psychology.

D. A. Schkade and D. Kahneman (1998, Does living in California make people happy? A focusing illusion in judgments of life satisfaction. *Psychological Science, 9,* 340–346) provide a fun example of how people are biased when judging the preferences of others. That is, we focus on different factors than the target people would. Schkade and Kahneman study how California's warm climate biased Midwesterners' judgments of Californians' happiness.

H. Simon (1955, A behavioral model of rational choice. *Quarterly Journal of Economics, 69,* 99–118) describes a model of decision making, promoting selection of the highest expected value. It is noteworthy that Simon is a Nobel Laureate.

P. Slovic (1995, The construction of preference. *American Psychologist, 50,* 364–371) discusses how people come to hold preferences, noting that these are not hard-and-fast rules (e.g., question framing affects people's choice).

PART XI

# Reasoning and Problem Solving

# Introduction to Part XI:
# Reasoning and Problem Solving

Researchers of reasoning and problem solving work with many seemingly disparate paradigms. Of interest are such diverse problems as how a chess master remembers a briefly flashed chess board; how a physicist solves a complicated equation; how a bartender verifies that everyone drinking beer is 21 or older; and how students solve brainteasers. What commonalities underlie all these situations? Across paradigms, researchers study how subjects approach and represent problems, draw on prior experience, and the route by which they finally reach (or fail to reach) a solution. Some problems are naturally more amenable to answering certain questions; for example, people vary in chess and physics ability and thus these problems are good ones for studying expertise. Some problems are interesting ones due to educational applications; for example, analogical reasoning is of interest to educators who want students to transfer knowledge across domains. Some problems are easy to manipulate in the lab (e.g., expertise in digit learning) whereas others depend on pre-existing differences in skill (e.g., physics expertise). Thus, different problems might be appropriate for study depending on the researcher's goal. Many problems have been studied extensively, and we sample only a few of them in this section.

We begin with the classic series of studies by Gick and Holyoak (1980, 1983), who examined subjects' ability to apply a solution from one problem to a second, thematically unrelated problem. For example, subjects read a description of a military attack that suggested a solution to a medical problem; both solutions involved attacking an enemy (a fortress or a tumor) from multiple directions. If subjects were given an explicit hint to use the military story, they could apply that story's solution to the medical problem. In everyday life, however, situations are often not explicitly related. Rather, one needs to notice the similarity between two experiences to take advantage of prior experience. Without a hint about the connection between problems, subjects failed to take advantage of the solution in the military story under numerous conditions. Only when subjects read multiple stories with corresponding solutions did they solve the medical problem at rates comparable to subjects who had received a hint.

Gick and Holyoak's subjects benefited from multiple experiences with the problem. More generally, we can consider how familiarity with the topic (or problem) affects problem solving. Among other paradigms, such issues have been explored using the Wason (1966) card selection task. In this task, subjects see one side of each of 4 double-sided cards; each card has a letter on one side and a number on the other. The 4 visible sides show the letter A, the letter D, the number 4, and the number 7. The subject's task is to identify which cards need to be turned over to determine the validity of the statement "*If a card has an A on one side, it must have a 4 on the other side.*" The most common answers are either "A and 4" or "A only." The correct answer is "A and 7." There is no need to turn over the 4 card—if it doesn't have an A on the other side, it does not violate the rule. However, if the 7 card has an A on the other side, then the rule is violated. Students have a hard time with this task. However, consider the following equivalent task: envision 4 double-sided cards, each with an age on one side and a drink on the other side. The 4 visible sides show BEER, COKE, 25, and 16. Now the task is to verify which cards need to be turned over to determine the validity of the statement "*If a person is drinking beer, he or she must be 21 or older.*" Now, subjects can correctly select the BEER and 16 cards. They realized it was not necessary to check the drink of the 25-year-old, even though this is functionally equivalent to checking the 4 card in the previous task (Cox & Griggs, 1982). It can be easier to reason in a familiar context than in an unfamiliar abstract context.

The previous results from the Wason card selection task suggest it is easier to reason in a familiar context, but it is not clear that students will apply their knowledge of familiar problems to later similar abstract problems. Remember that in the Gick and Holyoak (1983) experiments, people often failed to spontaneously apply a prior problem's solution to a new problem. The Kaiser et al. (1986) experiments bridge these two problems. Of interest was transfer from a familiar physics situation (in which better performance was expected) to an analogous abstract physics problem. For example, in the first experiment, subjects were queried about the future pathway of a ball rolled out of an elevated curving tube (see their Figure 44.1). Subjects often erred and reported that the ball's exit from the tube would continue to follow the tube's circular path. However, when the problem was presented as water's movement through a hose (a more familiar situation), there was an increase in ability to describe its exit from the tube (a straight path).

Of interest was whether subjects would be better at solving the ball problem if it was preceded by the water problem. That is, would subjects recognize the similarity between the two problem and correctly apply the solution of water's straight movement to the ball problem? Kaiser et al. did not find significant levels of improvement—subjects failed to notice similarities between the two problems and thus did not transfer knowledge from the familiar situation.

The Kaiser et al. (1986) subjects were undergraduates with limited physics knowledge. They were misled by irrelevant differences between the ball and water situations. Similar results have been found in studies of students' approach to physics word problems. When sorting problems into groups, they focus on surface features rather than underlying principles (Chi, Feltovich, & Glaser, 1981). When attempting to solve problems, they work backward from the goal (i.e., I want velocity, what formula do I know that will let me figure that out? e.g., Larkin, McDermott, Simon, & Simon, 1980). Of interest is how such novices differ from experts. Physics experts spend more time analyzing the deep structure of the problem; group physics problems based on principles, rather than on surface similarities; and work forward toward the desired answer. Some of the differences between physics novices and experts are described in the Ericsson and Charness (1994) reading in this book.

We had several reasons for placing the paper on expertise by Ericsson and Charness (1994) in the reasoning and problem-solving chapter of this book. Oftentimes, an expert does reason differently (and more appropriately) than a novice—consider how experts versus novices approach physics problems. But we should be clear that expertise in a domain does not involve only reasoning and problem-solving skills. In addition to differences in reasoning processes, expertise in a domain may involve faster or even qualitatively different processing in attention, memory, and other domains. The chess master, for example, is estimated to have memorized thousands of chess patterns (Simon & Gilmartin, 1973); when these board positions occur during a chess match, the chess master is able to respond from memory, rather than reasoning out the next best move. Expertise involves many different cognitive processes, and as such belongs at the end of a book such as this one.

Note that we wrote "expertise in a domain." As argued by Ericsson and Charness, expertise is very specific and the result of much training and experience in a domain. The chess master's advantage at remembering and reconstructing briefly presented chess boards disappears when the to-be-remembered patterns are random (DeGroot, 1965). Similar results are obtained when expertise is cultivated in the lab. For example, with considerable practice, subjects can be trained to do such tasks as remembering extremely long series of digits—but this does not transfer to remembering long series of letters (Ericsson, Chase, & Faloon, 1980).

We end this introduction by reiterating a theme that should sound familiar by now: Good performance in one domain or on one problem does not ensure success in another domain or on a different problem. Expertise is domain-specific and does not easily transfer to other nonpracticed domains. This is similar to the subjects' difficulty in transferring problem solutions across stories and the physics novices' difficulty in using solutions from familiar problems in novel situations.

## REFERENCES

Chi, M. T. H., Feltovich, P. J., & Glaser, R. (1981). Categorization and representation of physics problems by experts and novices. *Cognitive Science, 5,* 121–152.

Cox, J. R., & Griggs, R. A. (1982). The effects of experience on performance in Wason's selection task. *Memory & Cognition, 10,* 496–502.

DeGroot, A. D. (1965). *Thought and choice in chess.* The Hague: Mouton.

Ericsson, K. A., & Charness, N. (1994). Expert performance: Its structure and acquisition. *American Psychologist, 49,* 725–747.

Ericsson, K. A., Chase, W. G., & Faloon, S. (1980). Acquistion of a memory skill. *Science, 208,* 1181–1182.

Gick, M. L., & Holyoak, K. J. (1980). Analogical problem solving. *Cognitive Psychology, 12,* 306–355.

Gick, M. L., & Holyoak, K. J. (1983). Schema induction and analogical transfer. *Cognitive Psychology, 15,* 1–38.

Kaiser, M. K., Jonides, J., & Alexander, J. (1986). Intuitive reasoning about abstract and familiar physics problems. *Memory & Cognition, 14,* 308–312.

Larkin, J., McDermott, J., Simon, D. P., & Simon, H. A. (1980). Expert and novice performance in solving physics problems. *Science, 208,* 1335–1342.

Simon, H. A., & Gilmartin, K. (1973). A simulation of memory for chess patterns. *Cognitive Psychology, 5,* 29–46.

Wason, P. C. (1966). Reasoning. In B. M. Foss (Ed.), *New horizons in psychology.* Harmondsworth: Penguin.

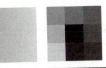

# Schema Induction and Analogical Transfer

Mary L. Gick and Keith J. Holyoak • University of Michigan

An analysis of the process of analogical thinking predicts that analogies will be noticed on the basis of semantic retrieval cues and that the induction of a general schema from concrete analogs will facilitate analogical transfer. These predictions were tested in experiments in which subjects first read one or more stories illustrating problems and their solutions and then attempted to solve a disparate but analogous transfer problem. The studies in Part I attempted to foster the abstraction of a problem schema from a single story analog by means of summarization instructions, a verbal statement of the underlying principle, or a diagrammatic representation of it. None of these devices achieved a notable degree of success. In contrast, the experiments in Part II demonstrated that if two prior analogs were given, subjects often derived a problem schema as an incidental product of describing the similarities of the analogs. The quality of the induced schema was highly predictive of subsequent transfer performance. Furthermore, the verbal statements and diagrams that had failed to facilitate transfer from one analog proved highly beneficial when paired with two. The function of examples in learning was discussed in light of the present study.

Analogy pervades thought. When a John Donne proposes that "no man is an island," we feel an intuitive grasp of the interconnectedness of human relations. When a William Harvey compares a biological organ to a water pump, a productive scientific model of blood circulation is created; in addition, the meaning of "pump" may take on a new, more abstract form. When a student is told that the atom resembles a miniature solar system, a complex new concept may take root in the learner's mind. To make the novel seem familiar by relating it to prior knowledge, to make the familiar seem strange by viewing it from a new perspective—these are fundamental aspects of human intelligence that depend on the ability to reason by analogy. This ability is used to construct new

scientific models, to design experiments, to solve new problems in terms of old ones, to make predictions, to construct arguments, and to interpret literary metaphors. (See Miller, 1979, for a recent defense of the classical view that metaphor should be analyzed in terms of analogy.)

The essence of analogical thinking is the transfer of knowledge from one situation to another by a process of *mapping*—finding a set of one-to-one correspondences (often incomplete) between aspects of one body of information and aspects of another. A central psychological issue concerns the mechanisms underlying analogical transfer. Reasoning by analogy typically implies a comparison of two concepts ("analogs") at the same (usually quite concrete) level of abstraction (e.g., the heart

657

and a water pump). However, a similar mapping process may be required to compare a specific concept to a more general schema (e.g., the heart and the abstract concept of "pump"). Furthermore, mapping may also be involved in the induction of schemas from examples (e.g., learning the abstract sense of "pump" by comparing hearts and water pumps). Such a close relationship between the processing of concrete analogs and general schemas is supported both by experimental evidence (Schustack & Anderson, 1979) and computational analysis (Winston, 1980).[1]

The present study was designed to investigate the mechanisms that govern analogical transfer between semantically disparate problems. The central empirical questions concern how analogies are noticed and then applied to generate solutions to novel problems. In addressing these questions the experiments explore the induction of a problem schema from concrete analogs and the role of the schema in fostering subsequent transfer. To provide a context for the empirical work, we will first briefly review our previous research on analogical problem solving and then provide a theoretical analysis of the nature of analogy and its relationship to schema induction. In addition to generating predictions regarding the determinants of analogical transfer, this analysis may serve to clarify the concept of "schema," which has been widely applied in cognitive models, but also widely criticized for its vagueness.

## Background Research

Most psychological research on analogical reasoning has used four-term "proportions" as stimuli (i.e., A:B::C:?; for a review see Sternberg, 1977). The adequacy of the proportion framework as a model of analogical thinking has been questioned by Hesse (1966) and Weitzenfeld and Klein (Note 2). A major limitation is that such stimuli obviate any need for the subject to spontaneously notice the analogy, which is often a prerequisite for successful transfer in realistic problem situations. A few studies have investigated the use of analogies to solve problems. For example, Gentner and Gentner (in press) have demonstrated that alternative analogies, known by subjects prior to the experiment, produce systematically varying patterns of difficulty among types of electricity prob-

lems. Other studies have indicated that potential analogies presented in the experimental context are often not used (Reed, Ernst, & Banerji, 1974) or even noticed, especially when the problem analogs are from different semantic domains (Duncker, 1926; Gick & Holyoak, 1980). We will discuss the Gick and Holyoak study in more detail, since it led directly to the present investigation. We had subjects attempt to solve Duncker's (1945) "radiation problem," which was the primary problem used in the present study.

Suppose you are a doctor faced with a patient who has a malignant tumor in his stomach. It is impossible to operate on the patient, but unless the tumor is destroyed the patient will die. There is a kind of ray that can be used to destroy the tumor. If the rays reach the tumor all at once at a sufficiently high intensity, the tumor will be destroyed. Unfortunately, at this intensity the healthy tissue that the rays pass through on the way to the tumor will also be destroyed. At lower intensities the rays are harmless to healthy tissue, but they will not affect the tumor either. What type of procedure might be used to destroy the tumor with the rays, and at the same time avoid destroying the healthy tissue?

Prior to their attempt to solve the radiation problem, our subjects often read a story about an analogous military problem and its solution (see "The General" in Appendix II). In this story a general wishes to capture a fortress located in the center of a country. There are many roads radiating outward from the fortress. All have been mined so that while small groups of men can pass over the roads safely, any large force will detonate the mines. A full-scale direct attack is therefore impossible. The general's solution is to divide his army into small groups, send each group to the head of a different road, and have the groups converge simultaneously on the fortress. As you may have already noticed, there is an analogous "convergence" solution to the radiation problem. The doctor could direct multiple low-intensity rays toward the tumor simultaneously from different directions, so that the healthy tissue will be left unharmed, but the effects of the low-intensity rays will summate and destroy the tumor.[2]

A paradigm for investigating analogical problem solving must satisfy two basic requirements. First, a relevant known analog must be available to the subject. Provision of a story analog prior to the radiation problem fulfilled this prerequisite. Second, the target problem must be sufficiently novel and challenging that an analogy could potentially be useful. Subjects are unlikely to bother to apply an analogy if a solution to the target problem is already known or can be easily achieved by means–ends analysis. The radiation problem, due to its ill-defined nature, meets the second requirement. The problem admits of a variety of potential solution plans, and we were able to exploit this feature to demonstrate the influence of an analogy. By varying the solution provided in the military story, we were able to selectively facilitate the discovery of various alternative potential solutions to the radiation problem. The influence of the analogy was very pronounced. For example, about 75% of those subjects who received the appropriate military analog produced the convergence solution to the radiation problem, as compared to less than 10% of control subjects who did not receive the analogy.

The above results were obtained when subjects were given an explicit hint to use the prior story to help solve the radiation problem. The hint was quite nonspecific, as subjects were told nothing about *how* the story might help; however, it obviated any need for subjects to spontaneously notice the potential analogy. In further experiments we attempted to assess subjects' ability to *notice* the analogy separately from their ability to subsequently *apply* it to generate an analogous solution to the target problem. The study of noticing raises some tricky methodological issues. Ideally, one would like to provide an ecologically natural context for the prior analog; however, the range of such contexts is not readily delimited. Subjects must be led to process the analog in such a way that the information will be potentially retrievable when they later encounter the target problem. Task demands should neither make it obvious to subjects that they should use the analogy, nor preclude the possibility of their noticing its relevance.

To approximate the above requirements we had subjects first memorize the military story analog in the guise of a study of story recall and then immediately go on to work on the radiation problem, without any hint to use the prior story. Under these conditions only about 30% of our subjects produced the convergence solution, as opposed to about 75% who produced it when a hint was given. Assuming that about 10% of subjects would pro-

duce the solution in the absence of any analogy (a figure based on several replications), these results indicate that only a third or less of the subjects who could potentially apply the analogy spontaneously noticed it. We found this striking gap between noticing and application quite surprising, although, as noted above, comparable outcomes have been obtained in other transfer paradigms (Kohler, 1940; Reed et al., 1974). Our procedure did not involve any deception; subjects were told at the outset that the experiment would have two parts, story recall and then problem solving. The delay between the two tasks was minimal. One might well have supposed that the demand characteristics of being in a psychology experiment would have led virtually all subjects to consider how the first part might be related to the second. Indeed, a participant in one of our earlier experiments had complained to us that giving a hint to use the story was an insult to our subjects' intelligence!

It is thus no easy matter to spontaneously notice an analogy between two superficially dissimilar situations, even in our highly simplified experimental paradigm. The present study investigates factors that influence the likelihood that subjects will notice and apply analogies. To derive specific predictions we first need to analyze the structure of analogy and the relationship between specific analogs and more abstract schemas.

## Analogical Thinking and Schemas

### Structure of Analogy

It is important to recognize that the structure of analogy is dictated by its function. In analogical problem solving, one problem and its solution are already known. The analogist notes correspondences between the known problem and a new unsolved one, and on that basis derives an analogous potential solution. More generally, the function of an analogy is to derive a new solution, hypothesis, or prediction; this is done by finding an *initial partial mapping* between the two analogs and then *extending* the mapping by retrieving or creating additional knowledge about, the analog that was initially less well understood.

Each analog is thus conceptually divided into two parts: that which provides the initial basis for mapping, and that which constitutes the "conclusion." As Hesse (1966) has argued, analogy involves two distinct types of relationships: the "horizontal" mapping relationship between aspects of the two analogs, and the "vertical" relationship between the two parts of a single analog. At the most general level, the latter relationship is between relevant antecedent conditions and their correlated consequences.[3] In many cases, including analogies between problems, the vertical relationships will correspond to causal relations within the person's mental model of each situation (Winston, 1980). For example, certain aspects of an initial problem situation will be viewed as sufficient conditions for the attainment of a particular solution. The vertical and horizontal relationships in an analogy are inextricably linked. For while it is not essential to map *all* aspects of the two analogs (indeed, this will seldom be possible), those aspects which constitute the causal antecedents of the known outcome obtained in the referent analog must be mappable. If these causal elements cannot be mapped, the putative analogy can be rejected as misleading.

## Analogical Mapping and Schema Induction

To understand the process of reasoning by analogy and the relationship between an analog and a schema, it is necessary to examine the concept of "mapping" in some detail. While many important questions about the mapping process must remain unanswered, several general points deserve emphasis. First, mappings may involve aspects of the analogs that have never been explicitly presented to the analogist. Consequently, the various inference processes required for everyday understanding will often play important roles in analogical thinking. Second, the mapping process will often involve a search for "alternative views" of one of the analogs (Moore & Newell, 1973; Schon, 1979). For example, in order to use the military story to help solve the radiation problem, subjects must presumably view the story as a problem and its solution, rather than as, say, an anecdote about a populist hero. In addition, mappings can be defined at multiple levels of abstraction, which may correspond to "macrostructures" in the sense of Kintsch and van Dijk (1978) and van Dijk (1980). The optimal level of representation will be that

which maximizes the degree of correspondence between causally relevant features of the analogs. Finally, since mapped elements (relations and properties and their arguments) are typically similar but not identical, they must be decomposable into *identities* and *differences* (Hesse, 1966; Tversky, 1977).

To make our discussion more concrete, we present in Table 43.1 an informal description of the mapping relations between the military story and the radiation problem. The correspondences are stated at a fairly abstract level of macrostructure (for a description at a more concrete level, see Gick & Holyoak, 1980). We assume that each of the two analogs is an instance of a very general "problem schema," which is organized hierarchically into an initial state (goals, available resources, and constraints), a solution plan, and an actual or anticipated outcome of realizing the plan. The problem schema reflects the vertical organization of the analogs, as we discussed earlier; the initial state includes relevant antecedent conditions, of which the solution plan and outcome are consequences. These problem components thus have a natural procedural interpretation as "situation–action" rules (Winston, 1980). The task of the analogist is to construct a partial mapping between the two initial states, which can be used to construct the analogous solution plan and expected outcome for the radiation problem.

At the level of macrostructure assumed in Table 43.1 the two problems can be *completely* mapped, i.e., a one-to-one correspondence can be found between their components. For example, the goal of using the army to capture the fortress maps onto the goal of using the rays to destroy the tumor. The basis of such a mapping relation is an abstract "core idea" that both mapped propositions instantiate, which we will term a "mapped identity." (See Holyoak, in press, for a more detailed taxonomy of mapping relations.) In each problem the goal, for example, is to use a force to overcome a central target. At the bottom of Table 43.1 these mapped identities are abstracted and stated as a "convergence schema"; i.e., a representation of the *type* of problem for which convergence solutions are feasible. Such a schema can be abstracted from the two analogs by "eliminative induction" (Mackie, 1974; see Winston, 1980, for a computational implementation). In essence, the process of schema induction involves deleting the differ-

**TABLE 43.1. Correspondences among Two Convergence Problems and Their Schema**

Military problem
    Initial state
        Goal: Use army to capture forces.
        Resources: Sufficiently large army.
        Constraint: Unable to send entire army along one road.
    Solution plan: Send small groups along multiple roads simultaneously.
    Outcome: Fortress captured by army.
Radiation problem
    Initial state
        Goal: Use rays to destroy tumor.
        Resources: Sufficiently powerful rays.
        Constraint: Unable to administer high-intensity rays from one direction.
    Solution plan: Administer low-intensity rays from multiple directions simultaneously.
    Outcome: Tumor destroyed by rays.
Convergence schema
    Initial state
        Goal: Use force to overcome a central target.
        Resources: Sufficiently great force.
        Constraint: Unable to apply full force along one path.
    Solution plan: Apply weak forces along multiple paths simultaneously.
    Outcome: Central target overcome by force.

ences between the analogs while preserving their commonalities.[4]

The schema can be viewed as an abstract category that the individual analogs instantiate in different ways. For example, the goal of "overcoming a target" is instantiated as "capturing a fortress" in the military story, and as "destroying a tumor" in the radiation problem. Such domain-specific instantiations of the schema can be termed "structure-preserving differences" between the two analogs (Holyoak, in press). In our example, the military analog can be viewed as a transformation of the convergence schema into concepts appropriate to a military domain, and the medical analog can be viewed as a transformation of the same schema into concepts appropriate to a medical domain. Since the schema is implicitly embedded in each analog, and assuming the mapped identities are causally sufficient to yield the outcome associated with the schema, it follows that structure-preserving differences do not alter the causal relations in the schema. Such differences make the problems analogous rather than identical.

The distinction between mapped identities and structure-preserving differences helps to elucidate the intuitive notion that analogs differ in their similarity to one another. The similarity of any pair of mapped concepts will increase with the extent of the meaning captured by a mapped identity (Tversky, 1977). In general, if the mapped concepts are either identical or instances of a close superordinate concept, the analogs will be very similar (yielding, one might say, a "literal" rather than a "metaphorical" analogy). Thus, a story about a doctor treating a brain tumor with multiple lasers would obviously be more similar to the radiation problem than is our military problem. A "deep" analogy, the sort that captures our admiration, is an analogy between disparate situations in which the essential causal relations are maintained.

Differences between analogs are not always structure preserving. A "structure-violating" difference is one that does not conform to the general transformation relating the schema to its analog (Holyoak, in press). Such differences make the analogy incomplete. While our convergence analogy is complete at the level of macrostructure represented in Table 43.1, it is incomplete at more specific levels (see Gick & Holyoak, 1980). For example, the role of the *army* in the military story usually corresponds to the role of the *rays* in the medical problem. But whereas a direct attack on the fortress would endanger the army, direct treatment of the tumor would *not* endanger the rays. (Rather, it would harm healthy tissue.) This violation of role parallelism constitutes a structure-violating difference between the two analogs. Normatively, a structure-violating difference should lead to rejection of the analogy as inappropriate *if* such a difference alters an element causally necessary for the solution to the known problem (which is not the case for the above example).

In general, increasing the level of representational abstraction will increase the completeness of an analogy, by deleting mismatching details (both structure-preserving and structure-violating differences). Note, however, that greater completeness need not be entirely a virtue. For example, one might claim that any two problems are completely analogous at the level of the abstract problem schema corresponding to the headings used in Table 43.1. But such abstract analogies will seldom trigger development of a realizable solution procedure. In general, increasing the level of abstraction will at some point delete corresponding identities as well as mismatches, and consequently diminish the similarity of the analogy. A tendency to maximize the completeness of an analogy by moving to a more abstract level of macrostructure may therefore often compete with a tendency to maximize the extensiveness of the mapping between causal relations by moving to a more detailed representational level. As a result, the "optimal" level of representation for successful analogical thinking may typically lie at an intermediate level of abstraction, and it may yield an analogy that is less than complete.

## Schemas as Mediators of Analogical Transfer

The above analysis suggests how analogical transfer may take place. The schema (mapped identities) affords the basis for analogical transfer. However, we can distinguish two conceptually distinct ways in which the schema could be used in solving a problem with reference to information obtained from prior analogs. First, the new problem may be mapped directly with a prior analog to generate the analogous solution. While the mapped identities will mediate the transfer process, the schema need not exist as a separate concept independent of the two analogs (although an independent schema may be incidentally induced in the course of the mapping process). We will refer to this case as "reasoning from an analog." Second, an independent schema may already have been

induced from one or more prior analogs and stored in memory. The person can therefore map the new analog directly with the schema in order to construct a solution. This case will be termed "reasoning from a schema."

There are several reasons why our analysis predicts a processing advantage for reasoning for a schema rather than an analog. Consider first how an analogy might be initially noticed. It is well established that human memory search is guided by semantic retrieval cues. We might suppose, then, that any semantic aspect of the novel problem could potentially provide a link to a relevant analog. There will be many potential cues to retrieve a very similar problem from the same semantic domain; for example, the radiation problem is likely to call to mind prior knowledge about related medical procedures. But by its very nature, an analog from a disparate domain will lack such transparent resemblances. Consequently, the potential semantic links between two dissimilar analogs will simply correspond to the basis of the analogy: the identities that comprise the implicit schema embedded within each analog.

It follows that if an appropriate schema has not been at least partially abstracted, it will be relatively difficult to retrieve a prior analog when given the target problem, because it is the schema that affords potential retrieval cues. Tversky's (1977) analysis of similarity implies that an analog will be more similar to its schema than to another analog, because the schema contains all the aspects common to the two analogs (mapped identities) and none of the differences between them. An independent schema will therefore facilitate the retrieval and noticing of an analogy.

In addition, it should be easier to apply a schema than an analog. An explicit problem schema will make salient those causal aspects of a situation that should trigger a particular plan of action. When two analogs are drawn from disparate domains, the inference processes underlying the mapping process will be difficult to execute; if the optimal mapping is therefore not found, the analogist may fail to generate the corresponding solution to the target problem. In general, mapping an analog to a schema will be simpler than mapping one analog with another, because in the former case it will only be necessary to map identities, rather than both identities and differences. We therefore predict that factors favoring schema induction will facilitate generation of the intended solution even if a "teacher" is available to call the person's attention to the relevant analogy.

## Overview of Experiments

### Methodological Issues

The basic procedure used to separate spontaneous noticing of an analogy from its application after a hint was adapted from Gick and Holyoak (1980) and was used in all of the present experiments. This procedure has three steps: (1) subjects process a story analog in the guise of a task such as story comprehension; (2) they then attempt to solve the radiation problem without any explicit hint to use the prior story; and (3) they are explicitly asked to propose a solution suggested by the story. The percentage of subjects producing the analogous solution to the target problem on their first pass provides a measure of spontaneous noticing and application; the total percentage of subjects producing the solution on either pass provides a measure of potential application given that the analogy has been noticed. The difference between these two percentages is a measure of the importance of having a "teacher" to point out the relevance of the prior analog.

This procedure is particularly sensitive to the effect of a hint, because each subject attempts to solve the problem both before and after receiving the hint. However, it also has limitations. The total percentage of subjects producing the analogous solution is not as pure a measure of potential application as would be provided by a separate group of subjects who were given a hint on their first encounter with the radiation problem. Subjects who do not immediately notice the relevance of the prior analog may tend to forget it during their initial attempts to solve the target problem. In addition, their initial attempts may produce a "set" effect that interferes with later application of the analogy. Our within-subject procedure may thus make it difficult for a condition that produces a relatively low rate of initial noticing to later "catch-up" and achieve an equal rate of total application. We should note, however, that Gick and Holyoak (1980) used both between-subject and within-subject procedures in different experiments and obtained essentially the same estimates of the percentage of subjects who could apply the analogy

(compare their Experiments II and V). There is therefore reason to think the potential bias associated with a within-subject procedure is not a serious one, at least for the radiation problem; nevertheless, it necessitates a degree of caution in interpreting certain of our results.

We should also note that the present study does not include any control groups that attempted to solve the radiation problem without receiving a story analog. Gick and Holyoak (1980) tested a variety of such control groups, which received either an irrelevant story that was not analogous to the radiation problem or no story at all; no more than 10% of such subjects ever produced the convergence solution. Because the present experiments used subjects drawn from essentially the same subject population, we assumed a base rate of 10% for producing the critical solution without an analogy.

The experimental manipulations used in the present study involve variations in the processing of the prior analog, rather than of the target problem. The target problem is explicitly presented as a "problem"; the subject can try out alternative representations of it in the course of the solution attempt. The analogous story, however, has been encoded in memory prior to presentation of the target problem. It is presented as a "story" rather than as a "problem"; subjects are never given any impetus to search for alternative representations of it, nor are they led to expect the story to later serve as the basis for a potential analogy. More generally, the analogist is free to mentally transform the representation of a situation currently being considered; but the memory representations of potential analogs will presumably have been "fixed" at the times of their original encodings and cannot be processed further until they have been retrieved and their pertinence noticed. The later accessibility of an analog should therefore be especially dependent on the nature of its initial encoding. Accordingly, all of the present experiments involve manipulations of the encodings of story analogs that are presented prior to the target problem.

### Manipulations of Schema Induction

All of the present experiments investigated the effects of manipulations that might influence the induction of a problem schema. One major manipulation, which serves to organize the experiments, follows directly from our theoretical analysis. This basic variation is extremely simple—we presented subjects with either one prior story analog or else two. Our earlier analysis of schema induction suggests that this distinction is potentially crucial. A schema can be formed by abstracting the mapped identities common to two analogs. Such a mechanism clearly hinges on the provision of *two* prior analogs, which can be mapped together to induce the schema. Indeed, the schema is defined by the correspondences between two analogs. Accordingly, provision of two analogs should foster induction of an independent schema, and hence facilitate subsequent transfer.

Nevertheless, the schema will be implicit within the representation of an individual analog. It is therefore conceivable that a schema *could* be abstracted in whole or in part from a single example. What would be required is some mechanism, other than mapping with a further example, which could make the schema explicit. Part I of the empirical section below includes three experiments that explored encoding manipulations that might promote schema induction from a single analog. The manipulations used were summarization of the prior analog (as opposed to rote recall), provision of a verbal statement of the implicit schema as part of the story, and provision of a diagrammatic representation of the schema. Part II includes three further experiments in which two prior analogs were presented. Two of the latter experiments also investigated the effects of provision of a verbal or diagrammatic representation of the schema.

## Part I: Reasoning from a Single Analog

### Experiment 1

As noted above, Gick and Holyoak (1980) presented an initial story analogy to subjects in the guise of a recall experiment. It could be argued that the type of encoding encouraged by recall instructions may be particularly ill-suited for producing subsequent transfer to an analogous problem. Because the instructions emphasized verbatim recall, subjects may have refrained from doing any kind of abstraction that might have highlighted the convergence schema implicit in the story. Perhaps subjects would be more likely to abstract the un-

derlying solution principle if they were required to summarize the story, rather than to recall it. The notion that summarization might foster schema abstraction acquires a degree of plausibility from evidence that summaries, as compared with recall protocols, typically include a proportionately greater number of propositions drawn from higher levels of a representational hierarchy (Thorndyke, 1977; Kintsch & van Dijk, 1978).

Gick (Note 1) compared transfer from a story to the radiation problem when the story was presented in the context of either a recall or summarization task. She found no firm evidence that summarization instructions facilitated either abstraction of a convergence schema or subsequent transfer. Experiment 1 investigated this same issue using a different transfer problem (since the exclusive use of the radiation problem is an obvious limitation of our previous research).

#### METHOD

In choosing a new target problem we followed a conservative tack, selecting a problem that shared many of the major properties of the radiation problem. In particular, the new problem was also spatial in its nature, did not tax working memory, and allowed a variety of potential solution plans. Our choice was Maier's (1930, 1931) "cord problem":

Suppose you are in a room, where two cords are hung from the ceiling. The two cords are of such a length that when you hold one cord in either hand, you cannot reach the other. Your task is to tie the ends of these cords together. To help you in this task, you may use any of the objects listed below, which are also in this room: poles, clamps, pliers, extension cords, tables, chairs.

Maier distinguished among several types of solutions to this problem, of which he was mainly interested in the "pendulum" solution. This is to tie a weight to one cord and swing it so it becomes a pendulum. The other cord can then be brought toward the center, the swinging cord can be caught as it approaches the midpoint, and then the two cords can be tied together. Maier found that 39% of his subjects produced the pendulum solution without any hints from the experimenter. This suggests that in the absence of an analogy, the pendulum solution to the cord problem is easier to discover than is the convergence solution to the radiation problem.

To provide a potential analogy, we wrote a story called "The Birthday Party" (see Appendix I), in which two ribbons are tied together after a pair of scissors is used to turn one of them into a pendulum. The story was embellished with various details more or less irrelevant to its problem-solving component. If summarization instructions lend subjects to focus on the problem-solving aspects of the story, the presence of extra details should make it more likely that summarization instructions will improve transfer performance relative to recall instructions.

The experiment was administered in booklet form to high school classes (grades 10 to 12) in Bloomfield, Michigan. Subjects were divided into three conditions: analog recall, analog summary, and control summary. The analog conditions either recalled or summarized the story analog prior to attempting the cord problem. The control-summary condition served to establish the base rate for production of the pendulum solution in the absence of an analogy. Subjects in the latter condition received a story that was not analogous to the cord problem ("The Wine Merchants"; see Appendix IV in Gick & Holyoak, 1980); in other respects they received the same treatment as did those in the analog-summary condition.

Subjects were told they were participating in a two-part experiment, involving story comprehension and problem solving. Before distribution of the stories, subjects were told either that they would have to summarize or else recall the story later, so they should pay attention to the major points of the story (summary conditions), or else learn it in as much detail as possible (analog-recall condition). Following the 3-min period during which they studied the story, they were given detailed instructions about how to either summarize or recall it. After the protocols were written, the cord problem was distributed and subjects were required to produce as many solutions as possible.

A questionnaire that queried subjects about their noticing of the story's relevance, the solution that was suggested by the story, and their prior familiarity with this solution was then distributed. Sixty-nine subjects served in the experiment: 25 in the analog-recall condition, 24 in the analog-summary condition, and 20 in the control-summary condition.

## RESULTS AND DISCUSSION

Table 43.2 presents the percentage of subjects in each condition who produced the pendulum solution to the cord problem before the hint, after the hint, and in total. Maximum likelihood chi squares ($G^2$) were calculated for the frequency data (Bishop, Fienberg, & Holland, 1975; Hays, 1973, p. 737, Eq. 17.8.2). The facilitative effect of a prior story analog was at least as striking as it had been in our earlier studies using the radiation problem. Combining the two analog conditions, subjects who received the analogous story produced more pendulum solutions prior to the hint than did those who received the control story (71 vs. 20%), $G^2(1) = 15.8, p < .001$. The advantage of the analog conditions was maintained in a comparison of total solution frequencies (98 vs. 30%), $G^2(1) = 30.1, p < .001$. However, the two analog conditions, recall and summary, did not differ significantly either in solutions prior to the hint (68 vs. 75%), $G^2(1) < 1$, or in total solution frequencies (96 vs. 100%).

The results of Experiment 1 thus yielded no evidence that summarization of the analog facilitates either noticing or applying an analogy more than does recall. While the lack of a difference in total solution frequencies could obviously be attributable to a ceiling effect, the absence of a reliable summarization advantage in initial noticing cannot. As in the comparable experiment using the radiation problem (Gick, Note 1), scrutiny of the story protocols revealed few differences between

**TABLE 43.2. Percentage of Subjects Producing Pendulum Solution to Cord Problem (Experiment 1)**

|  | Before Hint | After Hint | Total | N |
|---|---|---|---|---|
| Analog recall | 68 (17) | 29 (7) | 96 (24) | 25 |
| Analog summary | 25 (18) | 25 (6) | 100 (24) | 24 |
| Control summary | 20 (4) | 10 (2) | 30 (6) | 20 |

Note. Frequencies are given in parentheses.

summaries and recall protocols, except that the summaries were shorter. Neither experiment yielded any clear indication that instructions to summarize are more likely to foster either abstraction of an explicit problem schema or subsequent analogical transfer. Encoding for recall may often involve a degree of abstraction similar to that associated with encoding for summarization, particularly when study time is limited, as in the present experiment. For example, the Kintsch and van Dijk (1978) model suggests that multiple levels of macrostructure are derived in either case; summaries may be briefer than recall protocols due to differences in output processes, rather than to differences in the internal representations of the story.

The "gap" between initial noticing and eventual application of the analogy was much smaller in the present experiment with the cord problem than in prior experiments with the radiation problem. Because the experimental situations differed in many ways (e.g., the cord problem is somewhat easier to solve in the absence of an analogy), strong conclusions are unwarranted. But while we do not have a formal metric of analogical similarity with which to compare such diverse analogies as the military and radiation problems versus the ribbon and cord problems, it is intuitively compelling that the analog is semantically closer to the target problem in the latter case. For example, ribbons and cords are much more similar than are armies and rays; both pendulum solutions accomplish a goal of "tying," while the analogous convergence solutions serve either to "capture" or to "destroy." In terms of our earlier theoretical analysis, the former mapping seems to be characterized by a greater degree of identity relative to difference. The present results are thus consistent with our prediction that more similar analogs will have a greater number of potential retrieval cues to link them, so that the prior analog will more often be noticed without an explicit hint.

## Experiment 2

The failure of summarization instructions to foster abstraction of a problem schema from a story analog is not surprising, given the nondirective nature of the manipulation. Experiment 2 introduced what would seem to be a more direct approach: the story analog was augmented by an explicit verbal statement of the principle underlying the implicit problem schema. Kohler (1940) found that explaining the abstract principle upon which the solution to an algebra problem depended sometimes facilitated analogical transfer more than did provision of the initial example alone. There was therefore some reason to expect the addition of a verbal principle to be of benefit in our paradigm.

### METHOD

The basic story analog used in Experiment 2 was "The General" (see Appendix II), with the radiation problem as the transfer task. Subjects served in one of three conditions, which differed only in the material initially studied. Those in the analog-only condition read "The General"; those in the analog-plus-principle condition read the same story, except that the following sentence was added as a final paragraph: "The general attributed his success to an important principle: If you need a large force to accomplish some purpose, but are prevented from applying such a force directly, many smaller forces applied simultaneously from different directions may work just as well." This verbal principle was meant to be an explicit statement of the essential aspects of the schema for convergence problems. Finally, subjects in the principle-alone condition did not receive the story, but only the bare statement of the principle ("If you need . . ."). If the verbal statement can effectively convey the convergence schema to subjects, even without an accompanying specific example, then subjects in the latter condition should produce the convergence solution to the radiation problem more frequently than the base rate.

Subjects were tested in small groups. Those in the analog-only and analog-plus-principle conditions were told they were first to learn a story; they then were allowed 3 min to read the story, after which they were asked to recall it. Subjects in the principle-only condition were given a slightly different task. They were told the first part of the experiment involved "selecting statements to use in a study of comprehension" and that they were to first read a statement and prepare to paraphrase it. After studying the statement for 3 min, they were asked to paraphrase it and to rate its plausibility and comprehensibility. After their initial task was completed, subjects in all conditions attempted to solve the radiation problem in the usual two-pass manner: first without a hint to use the prior story or statement, and then with such a hint.

Eighty-eight subjects participated in the experiment, distributed approximately equally across the three conditions.

## RESULTS AND DISCUSSION

Table 43.3 presents the percentage of subjects in each of the three conditions who produced the convergence solution before the hint, after it, and in total. The results were straightforward: solution frequencies did not differ significantly among the conditions, either before the hint, $G^2(2) < 1$, or in total, $G^2(2) = 2.05$, $p = .36$. In particular, the performance of subjects in the analog-plus-principle condition was virtually identical to that of those in the analog-only condition: about 30% produced the convergence solution without a hint, and about 80% produced it in total. These figures are comparable to those obtained in previous experiments that used the military story and radiation problem. Experiment 2 thus yielded no support for the hypothesis that augmenting the story analog with a verbal principle would increase analogical transfer.

This does not mean, however, that the verbal principle was totally ineffective, because a substantial proportion of subjects in the principle-only condition also produced the convergence solution. In all three conditions (considered separately) the 95% confidence limits for the percentage of such successful subjects excluded the base rate of 10%, even prior to the hint. It is therefore clear that the information in the verbal statement was often sufficient to allow generation of the convergence solution to the transfer problem; however, once the subject received a specific story analog, addition of the abstract principle conveyed no further benefit.

It therefore seems that the verbal principle did not foster abstraction of the convergence schema from the analog. One possibility is that subjects who received the story simply ignored the concluding statement. However, inspection of the recall protocols for the analog-plus-principle subjects suggested otherwise. All but three of the 31 subjects included at least one aspect of the abstract statement of the convergence principle in their recall of the story. It is possible, however, that subjects did not attend carefully to the relationship between the final statement and the concrete instantiation of a convergence solution embedded in the story. That is, they may not have mapped the story and the statement to abstract the convergence schema implicit in the story itself. This seems particularly plausible given that they were simply asked to learn the story and did not expect to have to apply the information in a subsequent problem-solving task. The present findings therefore should not be taken as evidence that a verbal principle can never aid in clarifying an example. Augmenting an example with a principle may be beneficial when the information is presented in an explicit problem-solving context (Kohler, 1940), rather than in an incidental task. However, our results indicate that simply adding a principle to a specific analog by no means guarantees that an abstract schema will be abstracted.

## Experiment 3

Although the problems used in our experiments have always been stated verbally, they are fundamentally spatial in nature. Perhaps an abstract principle would better serve to highlight the convergence schema implicit in a single analog if the principle were presented in a spatial rather than a verbal mode. To test this possibility, Experiment 3 used a design analogous to that of Experiment 2, but with visual diagrams instead of a verbal statement of the principle.

**TABLE 43.3. Percentage of Subjects Producing Convergence Solution (Experiment 2)**

|  | Before Hint | After Hint | Total | N |
|---|---|---|---|---|
| Analog plus principle | 32 (10) | 48 (15) | 80 (25) | 31 |
| Analog only | 29 (8) | 50 (14) | 79 (22) | 28 |
| Principle only | 28 (8) | 38 (11) | 66 (19) | 29 |

*Note.* Frequencies are given in parentheses.

METHOD

Subjects again served in one of three conditions. Those in the analog-only condition read the same military story as had been used in the comparable condition of Experiment 2. Subjects in the analog-plus-diagrams condition also read the same story, but modified slightly to refer to a pair of accompanying diagrams, depicted in Figure 43.1. Diagram A, a single large arrow, represents the desirable but blocked plan of sending a large force from a single direction. The story referred to this diagram as an illustration of the general's initial plan "to launch a full-scale direct attack." Diagram B, several smaller converging arrows, represents the alternative, successful plan of sending small forces from multiple directions. The story referred to the latter diagram as an illustration of the general's solution in a sentence inserted immediately before the last sentence of the story (see Appendix II). These simple arrow diagrams were intended to represent the convergence principle at an abstract level, not necessarily tied to the story's specific military context.

Subjects in both of the above conditions were told to pay attention to the major points of the story during their 3-min study period and that they would later have to summarize it. Those in the analog-plus-diagrams condition were told in addition to pay attention to the diagrams and to incorporate them into their summaries. After the study period subjects in both analog conditions were asked to write a summary and to rate the story's plausibility and comprehensibility. Subjects in a third condition, diagrams only, received the diagrams without any accompanying story. They were told that the first part of the experiment involved pattern recognition; they were to study the diagrams for 3 min so that they could later reproduce them. These subjects then drew the diagrams from memory and rated their perceptual complexity and the difficulty of reproducing them.

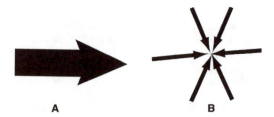

**FIGURE 43.1** ■ The two diagrams used in Experiments 3 and 6 to illustrate the principle underlying the convergence solution.

After completing their initial task, all subjects received the radiation problem and final questionnaire in the usual two-pass manner. The final questionnaire for the diagrams-only condition asked subjects to give a solution suggested by the prior diagrams. Sixty-six subjects served in the experiment: 26 in the analog-plus diagrams condition, 25 in the analog-only condition, and 15 in the diagrams-only condition.

RESULTS AND DISCUSSION

Table 43.4 presents the percentage of subjects in each condition who produced the convergence solution to the radiation problem. There was no indication that spatial diagrams, any more than the verbal statement used in Experiment 2, constituted an effective addition to the basic story analog. The percentage of subjects producing the convergence solution prior to the hint was actually lower in the analog-plus-diagrams condition than in the analog-only condition, although not significantly so, $G^2(1) = 1.71$, $p = .19$. The total solution frequencies in both conditions were very similar (approximately 80%), $G^2(1) < 1$.

Although both analog conditions yielded results much like those in previous comparable experiments, the diagrams-only condition provided an interesting contrast. Combining the two analog

**TABLE 43.4. Percentage of Subjects Producing Convergence Solution (Experiment 3)**

|  | Before Hint | After Hint | Total | N |
|---|---|---|---|---|
| Analog plus diagrams | 23 (6) | 58 (15) | 81 (21) | 26 |
| Analog only | 40 (10) | 36 (9) | 76 (19) | 25 |
| Diagrams only | 7 (1) | 60 (9) | 67 (10) | 15 |

Note. Frequencies are given in parentheses.

conditions, 31% of their subjects produced the convergence solution without the hint, as compared to only one of the 15 diagrams-only subjects (7%). The latter subject reported solving the radiation problem without thinking of the diagrams. However, nine additional diagrams-only subjects generated the target solution once the hint was given; the total for that condition, 67%, was not significantly less than the figure of 78% obtained for the analog conditions, $G^2(1) < 1$. The diagrams-only condition thus yielded the most striking discrepancy between initial noticing and eventual application we have yet observed: information in memory, sufficient to trigger the convergence solution for most subjects, was literally never spontaneously noticed.

This result in fact supports our semantic retrieval-cue analysis of noticing analogies. When the diagrams were presented alone in the context of a "pattern recognition" task, it is unlikely that subjects assigned any semantic interpretation to them, and surely none even approximating the convergence schema. As a result, no semantic retrieval cues were subsequently available to link the radiation problem with the diagrams. But once subjects had been explicitly told to consider the prior diagrams, they were able to interpret them by means of a mapping process. For example, they may have noticed the abstract similarity of the large unidirectional arrow to the desirable but blocked possibility of directing high-intensity rays at the tumor. Once the initial arrow had been interpreted as a representation of the intensity and direction of rays, the relationship between the two diagrams could be construed as a transformation of one large unidirectional ray into several small converging ones, thus illustrating the convergence solution. Such a chain of reasoning might be termed "analogical bootstrapping." The antecedent conditions given in the statement of the transfer problem are first used to interpret the "antecedent" diagram; once the components of the first diagram have been interpreted by constructing an initial mapping, the "consequence" represented by the second diagram can be decoded.

But if the diagrams can indeed be interpreted as an abstract analog to the radiation problem, why did they not facilitate analogical transfer when presented in the context of the military story? They certainly were not ignored; every subject reproduced them accurately after the study period. One might have expected the diagrams to highlight the abstract convergence schema implicit in the story. But as was the case with the verbal statement used in Experiment 2, scrutiny of subjects' story protocols indicated that nothing of the sort actually occurred. Except for references to the diagrams, there were no obvious differences between the summaries written by subjects in the analog-plus-diagrams conditions and those written by subjects in the analog-only condition. In neither case was there anything in the protocols to suggest a more abstract interpretation of the general's solution strategy, which might apply to disparate problems. In fact, there were signs that rather than the diagrams providing a more abstract interpretation of the story, the story provided a more specific interpretation of the diagrams. Two subjects stated that the general divided his men into six groups, which were dispatched to six roads, "as illustrated in the diagram." The story does not say how many roads were used, but the second diagram indeed shows six arrows. It seems that in the story context the diagrams were simply taken to represent roads, rather than abstract directions of force. Given that the diagrams did not encourage abstraction of the convergence schema from the story analogy, their failure to increase analogical transfer is entirely in accord with our earlier analysis.

## Part II: Formation and Use of Schemas

We have examined three manipulations—summarization instructions, addition of a verbal statement of the underlying principle, and addition of a diagrammatic representation of it—that were designed to promote spontaneous transfer by making the schema latent in the story analog more explicit. These all failed to facilitate transfer from a single analog. Furthermore, none of these manipulations appeared to foster abstraction of a general problem schema from one example, even though the verbal statement amounted to an explicit statement of such a schema, and both the verbal statement and the diagram produced transfer when presented alone (although in the latter case only with a hint). A common limitation of all these procedures is that they do not allow induction of a schema by mapping, since only one example was provided. The experiments in Part II investigated the induction of a problem schema from multiple analogs.

## Experiment 4

Experiment 4 explicitly compared the effectiveness of two vs. one prior analogs in producing analogical transfer. In addition, the experimental procedure gave subjects an opportunity to write down a description that could approximate the convergence schema. The quality of their schema descriptions could then be related to their subsequent performance in solving the transfer problem.

As well as simply providing a second analog, we varied whether the two story analogs were drawn from similar or dissimilar domains (where the analog domains were always dissimilar to the medical domain of the radiation problem). There is reason to expect the effect of analog similarity to be complex. Studies of perceptual category learning have often found that training with relatively diverse examples leads to superior transfer performance (Posner & Keele, 1968; Fried & Holyoak, Note 3); comparable effects have been demonstrated with artificial semantic concepts (Nitsch, Note 4). On the other hand, perceptual categories are learned more slowly when the training exemplars are highly variable (Fried & Holyoak, Note 3); and when the number of initial exemplars is very small, high variability can actually impair transfer performance (Peterson, Meagher, Chait, & Gillie, 1973; Homa & Vosburgh, 1976).

The general picture appears to be that dissimilar training examples make it more difficult to learn a concept, but allow it to be used more flexibly once acquired. A comparable pattern might be expected in the present paradigm. In terms of our earlier analysis, the optimal schema for a set of analogs will be a representation that captures the essential relations relevant to the solution, while excluding irrelevant domain-specific details. The schema that can be abstracted from two analogs will depend on the set of mapped identities they share. Because the optimal convergence schema is quite abstract, it would seem that the mapped identities linking two relatively dissimilar analogs would more likely correspond to an optimal schema (because they are similar only at an abstract level). A schema induced from two similar examples would often include information too specific to apply to a disparate transfer problem. However, the mapping process may be substantially more difficult to accomplish if the analogs

are dissimilar, because the differences will be many and the identities few and abstract. In contrast, it will be relatively easy to map two similar analogs, which will afford salient and specific points of correspondence. Thus, while a mapping between dissimilar analogs may potentially yield relatively optimal schemas, the actual schema that results may fall short of that which emerges from a mapping between two similar analogs.

### METHOD

Four story analogs to the radiation problem were used (see Appendix II). One was "The General" (by now a veteran of many campaigns in our previous experiments); the other three were written for this experiment. "The Commander," a story involving an attack on an island using multiple bridges, provided a second military analog. The other pair of stories shared a fire-fighting theme. "Red Adair" had the resourceful hero extinguish an oil-well fire by using multiple hoses; "The Fire Chief" accomplished a similar feat with the aid of a bucket brigade.

All subjects initially read two stories. Subjects were divided into three basic groups, each of which received a different type of story pair. Those in the two-similar-analogs condition received either the two military stories or the two fire-fighting stories, while those in the two-dissimilar-analogs condition received one of each. Subjects in the analog-plus-control condition received just one story analog, plus a disanalogous control story ("The Identical Twins") that had proved useless as a prompt for the convergence solution in earlier experiments (Gick & Holyoak, 1980). Across different subjects, all four story analogs were used about equally often within each of these three conditions, and the order of the stories was counterbalanced.

Subjects were told that the first part of the experiment involved screening some stories for use in a study of story comprehension. They were asked to read each story in the given order and to write brief summaries of each, with the stories still available for reference. Subjects were allowed to keep the stories while answering questions about them in order to facilitate comparison of one to the other. The subjects also rated the comprehensibility of each story. Then, in what may be the most critical aspect of the procedure, subjects were asked to describe in writing, as clearly as possible, ways in which the stories were similar. This task was intended to elicit a mapping between one story and the other, and hence to potentially lead to abstraction of a convergence schema. Furthermore, the written descriptions could later be scored for presence and quality of the schema. Finally, subjects were asked to rate the similarity of the two stories on a 7-point scale. The radiation problem was then presented in the usual two-pass manner, except that the final questionnaire asked subjects to write down a solution suggested by either one or both of the prior stories.

A total of 98 subjects were tested: 28 in the two-similar-analogs condition, 23 in the two-dissimilar-analogs condition, and 47 in the analog-plus-control condition. Subjects in the latter condition were divided into four approximately equal subgroups, each of which read a different story analog, plus the irrelevant story.

## RESULTS AND DISCUSSION

Table 43.5 presents the percentage of subjects in each condition who produced the convergence solution prior to the hint, after it, and in total. While there was a small trend toward a greater frequency of unprompted solutions when the two prior analogs were dissimilar rather than similar (52 vs. 39%), this difference did not approach significance, $G^2(1) < 1$. Because these two conditions that received two analogs also did not differ in total solution frequencies, they were combined in order to make a comparison with the one-analog-plus-control condition. This comparison yielded clear differences. Forty-five percent of subjects in the two-analog conditions generated the convergence solution prior to the hint, as opposed to only 21% of subjects in the one-analog condition, $G^2(1) = 6.35$, $p < .01$. A comparable advantage for the two-analog conditions was obtained when total solution frequencies were compared (80 vs. 53%),

$G^2(1) = 8.36$, $p < .003$. It was clearly the case that two analogs were better than one.

We next sought to assess the relationship between quality of the schemas induced by subjects, as evidenced by their descriptions of the similarities between the two stories, and analogical transfer. This analysis was performed only for the two-analog conditions. The descriptions were categorized into three levels of schema quality. In order for a description to qualify as a "good" schema, the basic idea of having forces converge from different directions had to be present either explicitly or as an inference. (The idea of using different directions was inferred if the subject mentioned the simultaneous use of multiple forces.) In addition, at least one other major aspect of the analogy had to be expressed: either the use of multiple small forces or the parallels in the initial problem situations (e.g., centrally located targets). An example of a good schema is: "Both stories used the same concept to solve a problem, which was to use many small forces applied together to add up to one large force necessary to destroy the object." An "intermediate" schema contained only one of these major features; e.g., "In both cases many small forces were used." "Poor" schemas contained none of the basic aspects of the convergence principle. They usually either alluded to a similarity between the solutions that was abstract to the point of vacuity (e.g., "In both stories a problem was solved using logical means.") or did not focus on the problem-solving aspects of the stories at all (e.g., "In both stories a hero was rewarded for his efforts."). The descriptions were evaluated by two independent judges, and disagreements, which were infrequent, were resolved by discussion.

The schema analysis revealed no significant differences as a function of similarity of the two analogs; nor did the relationship between schema quality and transfer performance vary reliably across the two conditions (although the cell frequencies

**TABLE 43.5. Percentage of Subjects Producing Convergence Solution (Experiment 4)**

|  | Before Hint | After Hint | Total | N |
|---|---|---|---|---|
| Two similar analogs | 39 (11) | 39 (11) | 79 (22) | 28 |
| Two dissimilar analogs | 52 (12) | 31 (7) | 83 (19) | 23 |
| One analog plus control | 21 (10) | 32 (15) | 53 (25) | 47 |

*Note.* Frequencies are given in parentheses.

were too low for the latter null result to be taken at all seriously). Combining both conditions, 21% of subjects produced good schemas, 20% produced intermediate schemas, and the majority, 59%, produced poor schemas. The question of central interest is whether schema quality was at all predictive of success in generating the convergence solution to the radiation problem. As the data in Table 43.6 indicate, such a relationship is strikingly evident. The cell frequencies presented in Table 43.6 differ reliably, $G^2(4) = 15.8$, $p < .005$, and the pattern of difference is quite simple: the better the schema, the more successful was transfer performance. Thus, fully 91% of subjects scored as having good schemas generated the convergence solution *without a hint*; none failed to produce it eventually. Forty percent of subjects with intermediate schemas produced the target solution without a hint, and 90% produced it in total. The comparable figures for those with poor schemas were 30% unprompted and 70% in total. To state the results in different terms, 90% of the subjects who failed to ever produce the convergence solution were scored as having poor schemas.

One must be cautious in suggesting a causal basis for this strong relationship between schema quality and transfer performance; it may be that people who are skillful problem solvers write good schemas and also apply analogies well. However, our subsequent experiments will lend a degree of support for a causal interpretation. The observed pattern is certainly consistent with the view that the task of evaluating story similarities invokes a mapping process which may lead to the incidental abstraction of a problem schema; the more closely the induced schema approximates the optimal convergence schema, the more likely the person is to notice its relevance to the subsequent transfer problem and to be able to derive the appropriate solution.

The schema analysis also suggests explanations of what would otherwise seem to be puzzling aspects of the performance levels observed in the present transfer task. First, the two-analog conditions yielded solution frequencies of 45% without a hint and 80% in total. At least the latter figure is not remarkably different from figures obtained in previous experiments with a single prior analog, which might seem to contradict our prediction that reasoning from a schema will be more effective than reasoning from an analog. However, the schema analysis revealed that virtually 60% of the subjects in the two-analog conditions produced poor schemas, which is to say no part at all of the convergence schema. Those subjects who wrote intermediate or good schemas indeed outperformed any of our previous one-analog conditions.

A second and related puzzle is why the present one-analog condition did so poorly: 21% solutions without a hint, 53% in total, as opposed to the usual figures of roughly 30 and 75%. Although three of the four story analogies had not been used in previous experiments, the new stories were no less effective than the old one. However, note that the present one-analog-plus-control condition actually involved two stories, only one of which was an analogy to the radiation problem; furthermore, subjects in this condition also described the similarities between the two stories, just as did those in the two-analog conditions. The procedure thus encouraged analog-plus-control subjects to also abstract some sort of schema linking their two stories. But because the two stories were totally disanalogous, except that both described problem situations, the resulting schemas were invariably poor—indeed, very poor—approximations to the convergence schema. For these subjects, the induced schema may have actually interfered with their ability to later retrieve and apply the actual analog during the transfer task.

**TABLE 43.6. Percentage of Subjects Producing Convergence Solution at Each Stage as a Function of Schema Quality (Experiment 4)**

| Schema Quality | Timing of Convergence Solution | | | |
| --- | --- | --- | --- | --- |
| | Before Hint | After Hint | Not Produced | N |
| Good | 91 (10) | 9 (1) | 0 (0) | 11 |
| Intermediate | 40 (4) | 50 (5) | 10 (1) | 10 |
| Poor | 30 (9) | 40 (12) | 30 (9) | 30 |

*Note.* Frequencies are given in parentheses.

# Experiment 5

Experiment 4 yielded clear evidence that a problem schema can be induced by mapping two analogs and that the quality of that schema predicts subsequent transfer performance. However, only about 40% of the subjects described the similarities between the two analogs in terms that approximated the convergence schema. Our analysis predicts that any manipulation that can facilitate schema formation will boost analogical transfer. Once the subject has been given two analogs, the mapping process should be aided by any device that calls attention to the critical correspondences. We have already introduced two such devices in earlier experiments: a verbal statement of the convergence principle and a diagrammatic representation of it. Neither manipulation facilitated schema abstraction from a single analog. However, these negative results may simply reflect the fact that a mapping process requires two analogs in order to operate at all. Once this prerequisite is met, highlighting devices should have a positive effect. Experiment 5 therefore examined the effect of adding the verbal statement, used previously in Experiment 2, to two prior analogs.

## METHOD

To simplify the experimental design only one pair of dissimilar story analogs were used: "The General" and "The Fire Chief." Subjects served in one of two conditions. Those in the without-principle condition read the two stories just as they appear in Appendix II. Those in the with-principle condition read the identical stories, except that the verbal statement of the convergence principle, previously used in Experiment 2, was appended as the final paragraph of each. The statement was worded exactly as it had been in the earlier experiment (except, of course, that the corresponding sentence for "The Fire Chief" began, "The fire chief attributed his success . . ."). The statement was thus designed to focus the subjects' attention on the critical aspects of the schema implicit in each of the two analogs.

The two-analog procedure of Experiment 4 was modified slightly so as to be more comparable with that of Experiment 2. Subjects were first told to study the two stories carefully for 5 min in preparation for answering questions about them. The stories were then collected, and the remainder of the initial story task was done from memory. Subjects were asked to briefly summarize each story, rate the comprehensibility of each, describe as clearly as possible the ways in which the situations in the two stories seemed similar, and rate their overall similarity. After this initial task was completed, the radiation problem was administered in the usual two-pass manner.

Subjects were tested in several different classrooms. A total of 143 subjects were divided about evenly between the two conditions.

## RESULTS AND DISCUSSION

In sharp contrast to the comparable one-analog study (Experiment 2), addition of the verbal statement had a clear positive effect on transfer from a pair of analogs. As is shown in Table 43.7A, 62% of the subjects in the with-principle condition produced the convergence solution without a hint, as compared to only 40% of those in the without-principle condition, $G^2(1) = 6.75$, $p < .01$. The

**TABLE 43.7. A. Percentage of Subjects Producing Convergence Solution (Experiment 5)**

|  | Before Hint | After Hint | Total | N |
|---|---|---|---|---|
| With principle | 62 (45) | 20 (15) | 82 (60) | 73 |
| Without principle | 40 (28) | 27 (19) | 67 (47) | 70 |

**B. Percentage of Subjects at Each Level of Schema Quality**

|  | Schema Quality | | | |
|---|---|---|---|---|
|  | Good | Intermediate | Poor | N |
| With principle | 44 (32) | 33 (24) | 23 (17) | 73 |
| Without principle | 10 (7) | 30 (21) | 60 (42) | 70 |

*Note.* Frequencies are given in parentheses.

frequency of noticing in the former condition is in fact higher than that obtained in any of our previous experiments with the radiation problem. The with-principle condition maintained a slightly smaller advantage in total solution frequency (82 vs. 67%), $G^2(1) = 4.34$, $p < .05$.

Subjects' similarity descriptions were scored for schema quality in essentially the same manner as in Experiment 4. A few subjects in the with-principle condition simply said that the two stories illustrated the same principle; such descriptions were counted as good schemas only if the principle was clearly stated in their summary of each story. As the data in Table 43.7B indicate, addition of the principle had a strong influence on schema quality, $G^2(2) = 28.4$, $p < .001$. Sixty percent of subjects in the without-principle condition wrote poor schemas, just as in the comparable condition of Experiment 4; only 10% gave good schemas. In contrast, only 23% of those in the with-principle condition produced poor schemas, whereas 44% produced schemas scored as good.

Table 43.8 presents data regarding the relationship between schema quality and transfer performance. Data for the two experimental conditions were tabulated and analyzed separately. For the with-principle condition, schema quality had a strong influence on generation of the convergence solution, $G^2(4) = 13.0$, $p < .02$. For example, fully 94% of the subjects who wrote good schemas eventually produced the solution, as opposed to only 53% of those who wrote poor schemas. The overall relationship between schema quality and solution generation was less robust for the without-principle condition, $G^2(4) = 7.00$, $p = .14$, due to the lack of clear differences between subjects who

gave good versus intermediate schemas. However, little weight can be attached to this null finding, because only seven subjects in this condition wrote good schemas. When subjects with good and intermediate schemas were combined, schema quality had a significant positive effect for the without-principle condition as well, $G^2(2) = 6.89$, $p < .05$. Eighty-six percent of the subjects who gave descriptions relevant to the convergence principle eventually produced the target solution, as opposed to only 57% of those who gave poor schemas.

## Experiment 6

The results of Experiment 5 again provided clear evidence of the formation and use of schemas in analogical problem solving; furthermore, they demonstrated that a verbal statement of the solution principle can aid in the induction of a schema from two analogs and substantially improve both noticing and application of the information in a subsequent transfer task. Experiment 6 was designed to seek comparable effects of a visual representation of the principle. The diagrams previously used in Experiment 3, where they failed to facilitate abstraction of a schema from one analog, were now presented along with two analogs. In addition, Experiment 6 obtained further evidence regarding the influence of similarity between the two prior analogs, which had yielded no clear effects in Experiment 4.

As we argued in connection with Experiment 4, there are reasons to expect variations in similarity of the analogs to have complex and sometimes offsetting effects. We would expect provision

**TABLE 43.8. Percentage of Subjects Producing Convergence Solution at Each Stage as a Function of Schema Quality (Experiment 5)**

| Schema Quality | Timing of Convergence Solution | | | |
|---|---|---|---|---|
| | Before Hint | After Hint | Not Produced | N |
| With principle | | | | |
| Good | 75 (24) | 19 (6) | 6 (2) | 32 |
| Intermediate | 58 (14) | 29 (7) | 13 (3) | 24 |
| Poor | 41 (7) | 12 (2) | 47 (8) | 17 |
| Without principle | | | | |
| Good | 57 (4) | 29 (2) | 14 (1) | 7 |
| Intermediate | 57 (12) | 24 (5) | 19 (4) | 21 |
| Poor | 29 (12) | 29 (12) | 43 (18) | 42 |

*Note.* Frequencies are given in parentheses.

of diagrams or other devices that highlight the problem schema implicit in each analog to foster induction of the schema from either similar or dissimilar analogs, but for somewhat different reasons. The danger with similar analogs is that the mapping process will yield a set of mapped identities that includes domain-specific details irrelevant to the more general schema. The diagrams in Figure 43.1 should reduce this problem, by focusing the subject's attention on those central correspondences causally related to the analogous solution plans. The difficulty raised by a pair of dissimilar analogs is essentially the converse: the analogical correspondences will be few and relatively abstract, so that the mapping process may simply fail to find them. In this case the diagrams should also prove helpful, because they will serve to isolate the essential correspondences which they abstractly represent.

## METHOD

Subjects served in one of four basic conditions, all of which received two story analogies. The four stories used in Experiment 4 were again used in Experiment 6. Subjects read either two similar analogs (both from either the military or the firefighting domain) or else two dissimilar analogs (one from each domain). The assignment of stories to conditions, and the order of the two stories in a pair, were fully counterbalanced, so that across subjects each story was used about equally often in similar and dissimilar pairs. Subjects in the without-diagrams conditions read the stories as they are presented in Appendix II. Those in the with-diagrams conditions received a separate sheet of paper with the two arrow diagrams illustrated in Figure 43.1. The stories in these conditions were each modified slightly to refer to the diagrams appropriately, just as in Experiment 3.

The procedure of Experiment 6 was essentially the same as that of Experiment 5. Subjects first studied the stories for 5 min and then summarized them and described their similarities from memory. Subjects in the with-diagrams conditions were also asked to draw the diagrams. Following the story task the radiation problem was administered as usual. The subjects, 189 in all, were run in small groups; approximately equal numbers of subjects served in each of the four conditions.

## RESULTS AND DISCUSSION

Table 43.9A presents the percentage of subjects in each condition who produced the convergence solution before the hint, after it, and in total. Provision of a diagram resulted in a higher frequency of initial solutions (57 vs. 37%), $G^2(1) = 7.55$, $p < .01$, as well as of total solutions (92 vs. 79%), $G^2(1) = 6.66$, $p < .01$. This total solution frequency obtained when subjects received two analogs plus the diagrams, 92%, is higher than that observed in any previous experiment with the radiation problem: nine times higher than the base rate for generation of the solution without any analog, it is clearly close to the maximum any manipulation could achieve.[5] The facilitating effects of the diagrams were essentially the same for similar and

**TABLE 43.9.  A. Percentage of Subjects Producing Convergence Solution (Experiment 6)**

|  | Before Hint | After Hint | Total | *N* |
|---|---|---|---|---|
| Similar analogs with diagrams | 61 (29) | 33 (16) | 94 (45) | 48 |
| Dissimilar analogs with diagrams | 53 (27) | 37 (19) | 90 (46) | 51 |
| Similar analogs without diagrams | 40 (17) | 40 (17) | 79 (34) | 43 |
| Dissimilar analogs without diagrams | 34 (16) | 45 (21) | 79 (37) | 47 |

**B. Percentage of Subjects at Each Level of Schema Quality**

|  | Schema Quality | | | |
|---|---|---|---|---|
|  | Good | Intermediate | Poor | *N* |
| Similar analogs with diagrams | 44 (21) | 29 (14) | 27 (13) | 48 |
| Dissimilar analogs with diagrams | 65 (33) | 18 (9) | 18 (9) | 51 |
| Similar analogs without diagrams | 26 (11) | 30 (13) | 44 (19) | 43 |
| Dissimilar analogs without diagrams | 30 (14) | 36 (17) | 34 (16) | 47 |

*Note.* Frequencies given in parentheses.

dissimilar analogs; analog similarity had no significant influence on solution frequencies.

Subjects' descriptions of the similarities between the two stories were again scored for schema quality. A few subjects in the with-diagrams conditions explicitly referred to the diagrams as representing the similar aspects of the two situations. We made the assumption that such subjects understood the underlying principle, and scored them as having good schemas. (If this assumption were unduly generous, it should reduce the relationship between schema quality and transfer performance for the with-diagrams conditions.) Table 43.9B presents the percentages of subjects at the three levels of schema quality, for each of the four conditions. Provision of the diagrams improved the quality of the schemas derived from both similar and dissimilar analogs, $G^2(2) = 14.4, p < .001$. Of subjects who received diagrams, 55% wrote good schemas and only 22% wrote poor ones; of those who did not receive diagrams, only 28% gave good schemas while 39% gave poor ones. Thus, once again, as in Experiment 5, a manipulation that facilitated schema induction also increased the degree of analogical transfer.

When no diagrams were given, analog similarity did not influence schema quality, $G^2(2) < 1$. However, when the diagrams were presented, there was a tendency for dissimilar analogs to yield a higher frequency of good schemas than was the case for similar analogs (65 vs. 44%). This trend was in fact significant, $G^2(1) = 4.41, p < .05$; it provides a hint that a mapping between relatively disparate analogs, when guided by a device that highlights the underlying solution principle, may be more likely to generate the optimal schema.

However, as noted above, this increase in the proportion of good schemas did not translate into superior transfer performance for subjects given dissimilar analogs. The data reported below will shed light on this apparent discrepancy.

The data in Table 43.10 convey the relationship between schema quality and success in generating the analogous solution to the transfer problem. Because this pattern did not differ significantly as a function of whether diagrams were provided, the data have been collapsed across that variable. When the prior analogs were dissimilar to each other, the usual positive relationship was found: the better the schema, the more likely the convergence solution was to be produced, especially prior to the hint, $G^2(4) = 21.5, p < .001$. But somewhat surprisingly, the relationship was far less strong when the prior analogs were similar, $G^2(4) = 5.16, p = .27$. Some degree of positive relationship was still apparent, which was significant when the most extreme cells were compared (the frequencies with which solutions were produced before the hint vs. not at all, for subjects with good vs. poor schemas), $G^2(1) = 3.98, p < .05$.

In fact, the only substantial difference in Table 43.10 between the patterns obtained for similar vs. dissimilar analogs involved the relative frequencies with which subjects who wrote poor schemas produced the solution without a hint (44% for similar analogs vs. 12% for dissimilar analogs). There is a sense in which our measure of schema quality establishes only a lower bound on what subjects have learned from the prior analogs; they may write down less than they know. Those who receive similar analogs may sometimes write down only similarities irrelevant to the convergence principle, and

**TABLE 43.10.** Percentage of Subjects Producing Convergence Solutions at Each Stage as a Function of Schema Quality and Similarity of the Prior Analogs (Experiment 6)

| Schema Quality | Timing of Convergence Solution | | | |
|---|---|---|---|---|
| | Before Hint | After Hint | Not Produced | N |
| Similar analogs | | | | |
| Good | 63 (20) | 31 (10) | 6 (2) | 32 |
| Intermediate | 44 (12) | 45 (12) | 11 (3) | 27 |
| Poor | 44 (14) | 34 (11) | 22 (7) | 32 |
| Dissimilar analogs | | | | |
| Good | 64 (30) | 28 (13) | 8 (4) | 47 |
| Intermediate | 39 (10) | 50 (13) | 11 (3) | 26 |
| Poor | 12 (3) | 56 (14) | 32 (8) | 25 |

*Note.* Frequencies given in parentheses.

hence be scored as having poor schemas; nevertheless, they may have actually abstracted the critical correspondences to some degree. This is less likely in the case of subjects who receive dissimilar analogs; because there are few superficial resemblances to describe, those who write poor schemas have probably really missed the basic analogy. Thus, while dissimilar stories, when accompanied by the diagrams, yielded a higher frequency of good schemas, those subjects who wrote poor schemas on the basis of dissimilar analogs were less successful at transfer than were their counterparts who wrote poor schemas on the basis of similar analogs. This pattern is in accord with our hypothesis regarding analog similarity: while dissimilar analogs have greater potential to yield optimal schemas, they are also more likely to fail to produce any useful schema. At a descriptive level, this tradeoff accounts for the absence of differences in overall transfer performance as a function of similarity of the prior analogs.

## General Discussion

### Summary and Implications

The experiments in Part I attempted to foster the abstraction of a problem schema from a single story analog by means of summarization instructions, or else either verbal or visual statements of the underlying principle. We found no evidence that any of these devices yielded more abstract representations of the story, nor did any consistently facilitate analogical transfer. In contrast, the results obtained in Part II were dramatically more positive. Once two prior analogs were given, subjects often derived an approximation to the convergence schema as the incidental product of describing the similarities of the analogs; furthermore, the quality of the induced schema was highly predictive of subsequent transfer performance. In addition, the same verbal statements and diagrams that had failed to influence transfer from a single analog proved highly beneficial when paired with two.

These central results, as well as other more detailed findings (e.g., the extreme separation of noticing from application in the case of a diagrammatic analogy presented alone) support our analyses of analogical mapping, schema formation, and

semantically driven retrieval. A mapping process cannot operate on only a single prior analog to derive a schema; consequently, the most direct mechanism for schema induction is inapplicable. Two analogs, on the other hand, can be mapped together to derive a more general schema; furthermore, any device that highlights the causally relevant correspondences will facilitate abstraction of a more optimal schema. To the extent that the schema implicit in the prior analogs has been made explicit, analysis of a disparate transfer problem may yield semantic retrieval cues that prompt recall of the prior information. Schema induction will thus increase the probability that an analogy will subsequently be noticed; in addition, a problem schema will simplify the process of mapping the prior information with the new problem in order to generate an analogous solution.

It should be noted that in all of our experiments the critical prior analogs were presented in a context in which their problem-oriented character was incidental. Subjects were never explicitly encouraged to use the stories to learn about a novel kind of problem. In many situations, such as an instructional context, more directive guidance in the application of an analogy is often given. It is quite likely that more intentional learning procedures could improve transfer performance in our paradigm. In particular, explicit guidance might facilitate transfer from a single analog. In the absence of such guidance, failure to derive a general schema from a single instance may only reflect appropriate conservatism; without either further examples or direct instruction, the person may have no principled way to isolate the essential causal aspects of the situation.

Given the difficulty of schema abstraction from a single analog (at least without the guidance of a teacher), one might ask how anyone could spontaneously notice an analogy between one initial analog and a semantically remote transfer problem. After all, we obtained consistent estimates that about 20% of our subjects solved the radiation problem by using the military story without receiving an explicit suggestion to do so. In part, this minority may simply consist of subjects sensitive to demand characteristics that suggest the two parts of the experiment might be related. However, there are more basic reasons why at least a few people may spontaneously represent the initial story in a way that would enable subsequent transfer. Our subjects may have often brought relevant prior knowledge to the experiment. One subject in an earlier experiment (Gick & Holyoak, 1980) immediately mapped the story analog with another, previously known convergence problem (in which multiple weak lasers were used to fuse the filament of a lightbulb without breaking the surrounding glass). While few subjects are likely to be reminded of such a complete analogy to the story, many may bring some type of prior knowledge to bear on it. For example, college students are likely to already know the abstract concept of "force," and a few may spontaneously encode a military attack as an instance of the application of force. If such subjects later see the radiation problem as one involving a search for a method of applying force, this shared semantic component may trigger recall of the prior story and initiation of a mapping process. More generally, if a current situation can be related to prior knowledge, so that its causally relevant aspects are encoded at an abstract level, then the situation has the potential to be subsequently related to a new analog from a remote domain. Because experts tend to encode problems at a relatively abstract level (Chi, Feltovich, & Glaser, 1981), it follows that expert knowledge of one domain should tend to enable analogical transfer to another. (See Holyoak, in press, for discussion of the relationship between analogical thinking and problem-solving expertise.)

Given our emphasis on schema induction as a basis for analogical transfer, it is worth considering what, if anything, specific analogs can *add* to a general schema. It might seem that if a schema could be somehow directly taught, examples would not be of any use at all. However, the present study provides evidence against this hypothesis. The provision of a verbal statement of the convergence principle without any accompanying story (Experiment 2) could be viewed as an attempt to teach the schema directly. The total percentage of subjects producing the target solution in this condition was not exceptionally high (66%), at least when compared to the levels of transfer obtained in the later experiments with multiple analogs. This might seem to contradict our prediction that reasoning from a schema will be more effective than reasoning from an analog. However, the discrepancy is only apparent. Our prediction refers to the benefit provided by a schema abstracted from specific analogs; there is no reason to assume that the ver-

bal statement used in Experiment 2 conveys the same information as could be induced from the story analogs. Indeed, the verbal principle does not in fact allow as complete a mapping with the radiation problem as do the stories. For example, the principle refers to "accomplishing some purpose," whereas the corresponding core idea in the stories is the more specific relation of "overcoming." In addition, the stories may allow a more detailed mapping that generates information about how the abstract convergence solution could be realized in a medical situation. For instance, the use of multiple hoses in "Red Adair" could suggest the idea of introducing multiple ray-emitting machines.

More generally, the more detailed information implicit in the representation of a specific analog may in part account for the intuitive view that examples are often critical for learning; for a teacher to simply "explain the principle" is not enough. To be put to use, a general schema must always be instantiated as a set of specific concepts appropriate to a particular domain; an example, even from a different domain, may suggest how the process of instantiation could proceed. Furthermore, in complex domains much of the detailed knowledge shared by experts, particularly procedural knowledge, is likely to be implicit and not easily verbalized. A teacher may therefore have difficulty explicitly teaching such knowledge. However, by presenting the student with selected examples, the knowledge may be conveyed implicitly.

## Toward a Computational Model

A great deal remains to be learned before it will be possible to formulate a computationally adequate model of analogical thinking. Without such a model, it is difficult to know how to optimize people's use of analogies. For example, Polya (1957) suggests searching for similar examples as a problem-solving heuristic; a worthy goal without doubt, but how to find the relevant examples and apply them? Perhaps analogical thinking can be developed by appropriate training; however, this educational goal is handicapped by our lack of knowledge regarding the essential processes underlying the skill. The mapping process presents particularly formidable problems that must be solved in order to construct a process model of analogical thinking, and computational implementations have tended to invoke algorithms that would unduly strain the capacity limits of human working memory. For example, Evan's (1968) program to solve proportional analogies between geometrical figures finds the optimal level of abstraction for representing the figures by computing all possible levels.

A related mapping problem arises from the fact that the number of potential pairings between two sets of concepts quickly becomes very large as the number of concepts in each set grows. Winston's (1980) program to compare story scenarios must either test all possible matches, or else prune away all except those between concepts that share some arbitrary feature (e.g., characters of the same gender). As Winston notes, this algorithm will never discover a male Cinderella. Psychological process models must strive to capture the remarkable flexibility that people exhibit in their use of analogy. The curtains have scarcely parted on this particular window to the mind.

## Appendix I

## Analog to the Cord Problem (Experiment 1)

### The Birthday Party

It was Jane's sixth birthday and her mother wanted to make it a very special day for her. So she organized a big surprise party and invited the neighborhood children without Jane knowing about it. The plan was that the mother who usually picked up Jane after school would be late in order to allow the children time to arrive before Jane. The big day finally arrived. Everything was just about ready, and it was fifteen minutes before the children were supposed to come. Jane's mother was putting the final touches on the decorations for the party room. She was covering the walls and ceiling with balloons and party streamers made of crepe paper and ribbons. Jane's mother was finishing up a decoration pattern. Two final pieces were left that were dangling from the wood paneling above. She had originally planned to knot these two pieces of ribbon together in order to attach balloons to them. However, whenever she grabbed the end of one ribbon, colored blue, she was not able to grasp the other ribbon, colored pink, at the

same time. The ribbons simply were not long enough to be knotted together in this way. It seemed that she would have to abandon her final bit of decoration.

Jane's mother was just about to give up when she had an idea. She took the pair of scissors that she had been using to cut the various ribbons and crepe paper, and attached the scissors to the end of the ribbon. Next, she took hold of the scissors, and pointing them in the direction of the pink ribbon, swung them vigorously so that this blue ribbon now swayed alternately between the pink ribbon and a nearby wall. She then ran quickly and took the end of the dangling pink ribbon and walked as close to the swinging blue ribbon as possible without letting go of the pink ribbon. She then waited until the swinging blue ribbon came her way and caught it on the upswing. While still holding the pink ribbon, she then removed the scissors from the other blue ribbon and knotted the two ribbons together. Jane's mother just managed to attach all her balloons on these ribbons, completing her decorations, before the children started pouring in. Soon Jane arrived and was genuinely surprised. The party was a great success, and all the mothers complimented Jane's mother on the decorations.

## Appendix II

## Four Analogs to the Radiation Problem

### The General

A small country was ruled from a strong fortress by a dictator. The fortress was situated in the middle of the country, surrounded by farms and villages. Many roads led to the fortress through the countryside. A rebel general vowed to capture the fortress. The general knew that an attack by his entire army would capture the fortress. He gathered his army at the head of one of the roads, ready to launch a full-scale direct attack. However, the general then learned that the dictator had planted mines on each of the roads. The mines were set so that small bodies of men could pass over them safely, since the dictator needed to move his troops and workers to and from the fortress. However, any large force would detonate the mines. Not only would this blow up the road, but it would also destroy many neighboring villages. It therefore seemed impossible to capture the fortress.

However, the general devised a simple plan. He divided his army into small groups and dispatched each group to the head of a different road. When all was ready he gave the signal and each group marched down a different road. Each group continued down its road to the fortress so that the entire army arrived together at the fortress at the same time. In this way, the general captured the fortress and overthrew the dictator.

## The Commander

A military government was established after the elected government was toppled in a coup. The military imposed martial law and abolished all civil liberties. A tank corp commander and his forces remained loyal to the overthrown civilian government. They hid in a forest waiting for a chance to launch a counterattack. The commander felt he could succeed if only the military headquarters could be captured. The headquarters was located on a heavily guarded island situated in the center of a lake. The only way to reach the island was by way of several pontoon bridges that connected it to the surrounding area. However, each bridge was so narrow and unstable that only a few tanks could cross at once. Such a small force would easily be repulsed by the defending troops. The headquarters therefore appeared invincible.

However, the tank commander tried an unexpected tactic. He secretly sent a number of tanks to locations near each bridge leading to the island. Then under cover of darkness the attack was launched simultaneously across each bridge. All of the groups of tanks arrived on the island together and immediately converged on the military headquarters. They managed to capture the headquarters and eventually restore the civilian government.

## Red Adair

An oil well in Saudi Arabia exploded and caught fire. The result was a blazing inferno that consumed an enormous quantity of oil each day. After initial efforts to extinguish it failed, famed firefighter Red Adair was called in. Red knew that the fire could be put out if a huge amount of fire retardant foam could be dumped on the base of the well. There was enough foam available at the site to do the job. However, there was no hose large enough to put all the foam on the fire fast enough. The small hoses that were available could not shoot the foam quickly enough to do any good. It looked like there would have to be a costly delay before a serious attempt could be made.

However, Red Adair knew just what to do. He stationed men in a circle all around the fire, with all of the available small hoses. When everyone was ready all of the hoses were opened up and foam was directed at the fire from all directions. In this way a huge amount of foam quickly struck the source of the fire. The blaze was extinguished, and the Saudis were satisfied that Red had earned his three million dollar fee.

## The Fire Chief

One night a fire broke out in a wood shed full of timber on Mr. Johnson's place. As soon as he saw flames he sounded the alarm, and within minutes dozens of neighbors were on the scene armed with buckets. The shed was already burning fiercely, and everyone was afraid that if it wasn't controlled quickly the house would go up next. Fortunately, the shed was right beside a lake, so there was plenty of water available. If a large volume of water could hit the fire at the same time, it would be extinguished. But with only small buckets to work with, it was hard to make any headway. The fire seemed to evaporate each bucket of water before it hit the wood. It looked like the house was doomed.

Just then the fire chief arrived. He immediately took charge and organized everyone. He had everyone fill their bucket and then wait in a circle surrounding the burning shed. As soon as the last man was prepared, the chief gave a shout and everone threw their bucket of water at the fire. The force of all the water together dampened the fire right down, and it was quickly brought under control. Mr. Johnson was relieved that his house was saved, and the village council voted the fire chief a raise in pay.

## NOTES

1. The present distinction between a general schema and a specific analog is close to that between the first and second senses of the term "model" as it is used by Hesse (1966).
2. In our earlier paper (Gick and Holyoak, 1980) we referred

to this as the "dispersion" solution, emphasizing the initial division of the single large force into several small ones and their dispersal to multiple locations. However, in some forms of the problem a single large force may not initially exist (see "Red Adair" in Appendix II), making our original name for the solution quite misleading. Calling it the convergence solution emphasizes its central property, the convergence of multiple forces on the target.

3. Metaphors typically produce an initial partial mapping that creates an expectation that additional correspondences can be found, involving correlated aspects of the referent. For example, suppose we assert that "Analogy is a window on the mind." The most salient attribute of a window is probably that it is something one sees through; accordingly, in appropriate context (such as a psychological report) we might interpret the remark to mean that studying analogy is a way to gain understanding of ("see") the mind. The initial maping then constitutes an "invitation" to pursue the metaphor further. Thus, one might note that a window is typically a relatively small opening in an opaque wall, suggesting that the mind is generally difficult to study. Furthermore, a small window often allows only partial view of what lies beyond, intimating that analogy may provide limited and selective insights, and so on. The interpretation of metaphor thus seems to begin with detection of salient initial correspondences, followed by the construction of others (Jaynes, 1976, Chap. 2).

4. In the case of metaphor, the formation of a schema from mapped identities, so that the subject and referent can be viewed as instances of a more general concept, may provide a basis for the "interaction view" of metaphorical interpretation (Black, 1962).

5. In an earlier experiment using one pair of dissimilar analogs (Gick, Note 1), the addition of the diagrams yielded solution frequencies of 68% without a hint and 95% in total ($N = 37$). The results of this study were replicated in all comparable respects by those of Experiment 6.

# REFERENCES

Bishop, Y. M. M., Fienberg, S. E., & Holland, P. W. *Discrete Multivariate Analysis: Theory and Practice.* Cambridge, MA: MIT Press, 1975.

Black, M. Metaphor. In M. Black, *Models and Metaphors.* Ithaca, NY: Cornell Univ. Press, 1962.

Chi, M. T. H., Feltovich, P. J., & Glaser, R. Categorization and representation of physics problems by experts and novices. *Cognitive Science*, 1981, *5*, 121–152.

Duncker, K. A qualitative (experimental and theoretical) study of productive thinking (solving of comprehensible problems). *Journal of Genetic Psychology, 33*, 1926, 642–708.

Duncker, K. On problem solving. *Psychological Monographs*, 1945, *58* (Whole No. 270).

Evans, T. G. A. A program for the solution of geometric-analogy intelligence test questions. In M. Minsky (Ed.), *Semantic Information Processing.* Cambridge, MA: MIT Press, 1968.

Gentner, D. & Gentner, D. R. Flowing waters or teeming crowds: Mental models of electricity. In D. Gentner & A. Stevens (Eds.), *Mental Models.* Hillsdale, NJ: Erlbaum, in press.

Gick, M. L. & Holyoak, K. J. Analogical problem solving. *Cognitive Psychology*, 1980, *12*, 306–355.

Hays, W. L. *Statistics for the Social Sciences* New York: Holt, Rinehart & Winston, 1973. 2nd ed.

Hesse, M. B. *Models and Analogies in Science.* Notre Dame, IN: Univ. of Notre Dame Press, 1966.

Holyoak, K. J. Analogical thinking and human intelligence. In R. J. Sternberg (Ed.), *Advances in the Psychology of Human Intelligence.* Hillsdale, NJ: Erlbaum, in press. Vol. 2.

Homa, D. & Vosburgh, R. Category breadth and the abstraction of prototypical information. *Journal of Experimental Psychology: Human Learning and Memory*, 1976, *2*, 322–330.

Jaynes, J. *The Origin of Consciousness in the Breakdown of the Bicameral Mind.* Boston: Houghton Mifflin, 1976.

Kintsch, W. & van Dijk, T. A. Toward a model of text comprehension and production. *Psychological Review*, 1978, *85*, 363–394.

Kohler, W. *Dynamics in Psychology.* New York: Liveright, 1940.

Mackie, J. L. *The Cement of the Universe.* London/New York: Oxford Univ. Press, 1974.

Maier, N. Reasoning in humans. I. On direction. *Journal of Comparative Psychology*, 1930, *10*, 15–43.

Maier, N. Reasoning in humans. II. The solution of a problem and its appearance in consciousness. *Journal of Comparative Psychology*, 1931, *12*, 181–194.

Miller, G. A. Images and models, similes and metaphors. In A. Ortony (Ed.), *Metaphor and Thought.* London/New York: Cambridge Univ. Press, 1979.

Moore, J. & Newell, A. How can MERLIN understand? In L. W. Gregg (Ed.), *Knowledge and Cognition.* Hillsdale, NJ: Erlbaum, 1973.

Peterson, M. J., Meagher, R. B., Chait, H., & Gillie, S. The abstraction and generalization of dot patterns. *Cognitive Psychology*, 1973, *4*, 378–398.

Polya, G. *How to Solve It.* Princeton, NJ: Princeton Univ. Press, 1957.

Posner, M. I. & Keele, S. W. On the genesis of abstract ideas. *Journal of Experimental Psychology*, 1968, *77*, 353–363.

Reed, S. K., Ernst, G. W., & Banerji, R. The role of analogy in transfer between similar problem states. *Cognitive Psychology*, 1974, *6*, 436–450.

Schon, D. A. Generative metaphor: A perspective on problem-setting in social policy. In A. Ortony (Ed.), *Metaphor and Thought.* London/New York: Cambridge Univ. Press 1979.

Shustack, M. & Anderson, J. R. Effects of analogy to prior knowledge on memory for new information. *Journal of Verbal Learning and Verbal Behavior*, 1979, *18*, 565–583.

Sternberg, R. J. *Intelligence, Information Processing, and Analogical Reasoning: The Componential Analysis of Human Abilities.* Hillsdale, NJ: Erlbaum, 1977.

Thorndyke, P. W. Cognitive structures in comprehension and memory of narrative discourse. *Cognitive Psychology*, 1977, *9*, 77–110.

Tversky, A. Features of similarity. *Psychological Review*, 1977, *84*, 327–352.

van Dijk, T. A. *Macrostructures.* Hillsdale, NJ: Erlbaum, 1980.

Winston, P. H. Learning and reasoning by analogy. *Communications of the ACM*, 1980, *23*, 689–703.

## REFERENCE NOTES

1. Gick, M. L. *Analogical Reasoning and Schema Formation.* PhD dissertation, University of Michigan, 1981.
2. Weitzenfeld, J. & Klein, G. A. *Analogical Reasoning as a Discovery Logic.* Technical Report TR-SCR-79-5, Klein Associates, Yellow Springs, OH, 1979.
3. Fried, L. S. & Holyoak, K. J. *Induction of Category Distributions: A Framework for Classification Learning.* Michigan/Chicago Cognitive Science Technical Report 38, 1982.
4. Nitsch, K. E. *Structuring Decontextualized Forms of Knowledge.* PhD dissertation, Vanderbilt University, 1977.

This paper is largely based on a PhD dissertation completed by Gick (Note 1) under the direction of Holyoak, together with additional collaborative experiments and analyses. The work benefitted from the guidance of the members of the dissertation committee: John Jonides, Manfred Kochen, David Krantz, and substitute member John Holland. Patricia Cheng provided incisive criticisms of an early draft; a subsequent draft benefitted from the reviews of Dedre Gentner, Earl Hunt, and an anonymous referee. Terra Albert, Holly Brewer, Tim Carroll, Teresa Frankovich, and Michael Smith ably assisted in testing subjects. Susan Petersen and Jean Schtokal assisted with both subject testing and scoring of data. Experiment 4 was reported at the 20th meeting of the Psychonomic Society, Phoenix, November 1979. This research was supported by a University of Michigan Rackham Dissertation Grant to Gick, and by National Institute for Mental Health Grant 5-R01-MH332878-03 and National Institute for Mental Health Research Scientist Development Award 1-K02-MH00342-02, both to Holyoak. Reprint requests may be sent to K. Holyoak, University of Michigan, Human Performance Center, 330 Packard Road, Ann Arbor, MI 48104.

# Intuitive Reasoning about Abstract and Familiar Physics Problems

Mary Kister Kaiser • NASA Ames Research Center
John Jonides and Joanne Alexander
• University of Michigan, Ann Arbor

Previous research has demonstrated that many people have misconceptions about basic properties of motion. In two experiments, we examined whether people are more likely to produce dynamically correct predictions about basic motion problems involving situations with which they are familiar, and whether solving such problems enhances performance on a subsequent abstract problem. In Experiment 1, college students were asked to predict the trajectories of objects exiting a curved tube. Subjects were more accurate on the familiar version of the problem, and there was no evidence of transfer to the abstract problem. In Experiment 2, two familiar problems were provided in an attempt to enhance subjects' tendency to extract the general structure of the problems. Once again, they gave more correct responses to the familiar problems but failed to generalize to the abstract problem. Formal physics training was associated with correct predictions for the abstract problem but was unrelated to performance on the familiar problems.

Recent studies have demonstrated that many adults hold erroneous beliefs concerning fundamental laws of motion (McCloskey, 1983; McCloskey, Caramazza, & Green, 1980). For example, when asked to predict the trajectory of a ball exiting a curved tube, many college students respond that the ball will continue to curve, at least for some period of time. McCloskey and his colleagues explain such erroneous predictions as evidence that, when people are asked to reason abstractly about motion, their intuitive models frequently resemble a medieval impetus theory rather than a Newtonian model. The Newtonian model holds that, in the absence of external force, objects maintain a linear path. Alternatively, the impetus theory holds that setting an object in motion imparts to the object an internal energy, or impetus, that maintains the object's motion along its initial trajectory, be it linear or curvilinear.

Suppose people were asked to reason about problems that evoked actual motion events with which they are familiar. Would they make the same impetus-like error? Research in other cognitive domains raises the possibility that they would not: whereas many adults make errors in reasoning about abstract logic problems, performance is much better on problems that are logically equivalent to the abstract problems but that make reference to familiar situations. For example, in Wason's (1966) selection task, subjects were presented with cards showing a letter on one side and a number on the other. They were required to choose which cards needed to be examined to determine the validity of the statement: "If a card has an A on one side, then it has a 4 on the other." When presented four cards showing an "A," a "B," a "4," and a "7," many subjects responded that the "A" and "4" cards must be examined (instead of the logically correct "A" and "7"), an error termed "affirming the consequent." Other logical errors, such as insisting that all cards must be examined, were also observed. This would suggest that adults make systematic errors in logical reasoning, much as McCloskey's work suggests that adults make systematic errors in mechanical reasoning.

However, research has shown that subjects can solve problems that are formally identical to the selection task if they are presented in realistic, thematic contexts (see Evans, 1982). Drawing on the now-defunct British postal rule requiring more postage for sealed than unsealed envelopes, Johnson-Laird, P. Legrenzi, and M. S. Legrenzi (1972) asked subjects to examine letters for violations of the rule, "If a letter is sealed, then it has a 5d stamp on it." This problem is formally identical to Wason's (1966) selection task. Older subjects, familiar with the postal system, performed far better on the envelope task than on Wason's task. Younger subjects who had no previous experience with the postal rule performed no better on the envelope task.

Our Experiment 1 is concerned with the possibility that familiarity may breed success: We examined whether or not people would give more accurate trajectory predictions on a somewhat familiar motion problem than on a more abstract version of the problem. In addition to examining performance on the two problems, we were interested in whether or not subjects would recognize the similarity between the problems and perform better on the abstract problem if it was presented after the familiar one.

## Experiment 1

### Method

#### SUBJECTS

Eighty college students (40 males and 40 females) were recruited in the hallway of a classroom build-

ing at the University of Michigan. Half of the students (20 males and 20 females) had taken physics courses in either high school or college.

### MATERIALS AND PROCEDURES

A clear plastic spiral tube was mounted on a 60 × 80 cm plywood board that lay flat on a level table. The tube was 2.2 cm in diameter and formed a spiral of 540° rotation with an interior diameter of 25 cm (see Figure 44.1a). One end of the tube was elevated such that it appeared that a ball or liquid inserted in the elevated end would travel through the tube at a moderate speed. Half of the subjects were given the following instructions: "Suppose I take this ball bearing and place it in this (the elevated) end of the tube. It would roll around the tube and come out here (indicate mouth of tube). I'd like you to draw the path that the ball would take when it exited the tube." Once the subject had produced a response, a second problem was presented: "Okay, now imagine that we connect a hose to the elevated end of the tube and send water through it. The water would flow through the tube and come out here (at the mouth of the tube). Could you draw the path that the main part of the stream

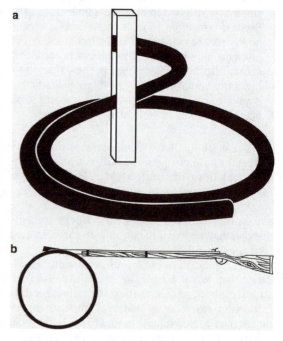

**FIGURE 44.1** ■ Schematics of apparatus employed in Experiment 1 (a) and Experiment 2 (a and b).

of water would take when it came out of the tube?" The other half of the subjects were administered the problems in the opposite order.

The ball problem has been used by a number of researchers to investigate people's understanding of curvilinear motion (e.g., McCloskey et al., 1980). Typically, a sizable proportion of subjects' answers include references to nonexistent forces and influences (e.g., curvilinear momentum). The water problem was chosen since water shooting from a curved garden hose is a closely related event that is familiar to most people. Since most subjects have seen that the curvature of the hose does not affect the water's path, we hoped that people would draw upon this experience in solving the problem.

Subjects made their predictions by drawing a path on a 28 × 55 cm piece of paper placed on the board at the mouth of the tube. Subjects were asked to describe verbally the path they drew to clarify any ambiguity. The experimenter recorded the subject's gender, and inquired about his or her coursework in physics. Subjects were thanked and paid for their participation.

## Results

A response was coded as correct if the path arced no more than 10° throughout its length and was tangent to the point of exit. Examples of correct and incorrect responses are illustrated in Figure 44.2. Subjects produced far more correct predictions for the water problem than for the ball problem. Fifty-three people (31 men and 22 women) drew linear paths for the water problem, compared with 31 subjects (22 men and 9 women) for the ball problem. This effect was highly significant ($\chi^2(1) = 12.13, p < .005$). Log-linear analyses demonstrated a strong gender effect for the ball problem [$\chi^2(1) = 9.45, p < .005$] and a lesser gender effect for the water problem [$\chi^2(1) = 4.59, p < .05$]. Physics training had a marginal effect on performance on the ball problem [$\chi^2(1) = 2.93, p < .10$] but no significant effect on performance on the water problem [$\chi^2(1) = 1.21$].

To examine whether or not subjects transferred their correct solutions on the water problem to the more abstract ball problem, we tested for a problem-order effect among those subjects who answered the water problem correctly. Were subjects who demonstrated a correct understanding of the

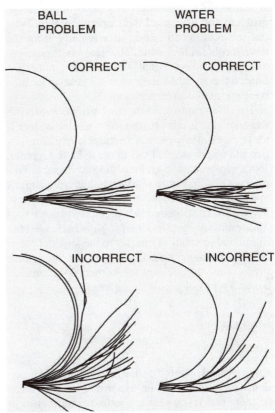

BALL PROBLEM      WATER PROBLEM

CORRECT      CORRECT

INCORRECT      INCORRECT

**FIGURE 44.2** ■ Examples of correct and incorrect responses on the Water and Ball problems in Experiment 1.

water problem more likely to answer the ball problem correctly if it was administered second? Of the 53 subjects who gave a correct response to the water problem, 27 were administered the ball problem first. Ten of these subjects (37%) were correct on the ball problem. The other 26 subjects answered the ball problem after correctly answering the water problem. Fifteen of them (58%) were correct on the ball problem. This difference is not significant ($\chi^2 = 2.26, p > .10$). Thus, correctly solving a familiar problem on curvilinear motion immediately prior to attempting an abstract curvilinear problem did not significantly enhance performance on the latter.

## Experiment 2

The lack of transfer in Experiment 1 is quite striking, especially since the abstract problem was administered immediately after the common-sense problem and even used the same apparatus. Why did subjects fail to reason analogically from the water problem to the ball problem? Is it possible to improve subjects' transfer by offering more than one common-sense exemplar? These questions were addressed in Experiment 2.

The literature on analogical problem solving suggests that a critical obstacle to solution transfer is the failure to recognize the relevant similarities among problems (D. Gentner & D. R. Gentner, 1983; Holyoak, 1984). Providing multiple exemplars of a solution type often enhances people's ability to recognize abstract similarities (Holyoak, 1984). We investigated whether providing a second common-sense motion problem increased the likelihood of solution transfer to the abstract problem. Furthermore, we asked subjects to justify their predictions, particularly when their solutions for the two types of problems differed.

## Method

### SUBJECTS

Eighty-one University of Michigan female students participated in the experiment. Forty-three of them had taken physics courses in either high school or college. Subjects were recruited from a subject pool at the university and were paid for their participation.

### MATERIALS AND PROCEDURE

Subjects were administered one abstract and two familiar curvilinear motion problems. The ball problem from Experiment 1 was the abstract problem. One of the familiar problems was the water problem of Experiment 1. The other problem required subjects to predict the path of a bullet when

fired from a rifle with a curved barrel. The rifle was oriented such that the curved barrel lay flat on a horizontal surface, similar to the curved-tube apparatus. A pilot study indicated that, although people had never used such a weapon, many insisted that they had seen them used (in cartoons and movies) and professed an intuitive understanding that bullets would have to travel straight regardless of the shape of the barrel. The experimental apparatus is schematized in Figures 44.1a and 44.1b.

Subjects were instructed to draw the path of the ball, the water, or the bullet upon exiting the curved tube or barrel. Forty of the subjects were given the two familiar problems (water and rifle) first, followed by the abstract (ball) problem. The other subjects were administered the abstract problem first. The order of presentation for the two familiar problems was counterbalanced across subjects. After they had made all three predictions, 41 of the subjects (every other subject) were asked to explain their predictions and to justify any discrepancies in the paths.

## Results

Subjects' responses were coded as in Experiment 1. The patterns of subjects' predictions are shown in Table 44.1. It should be noted that a fairly conservative classification scheme was used for the familiar problems: Subjects had to produce correct predictions for both familiar problems to be classified as accurate on that problem type. Very few subjects (12) gave incorrect predictions for both familiar problems.

Even with such a classification scheme, subjects were found to give more accurate predictions for the familiar problems than for the abstract problem [$\chi^2(1) = 4.24$, $p < .05$]. As in Experiment 1, there was no evidence of transfer of correct solu-

**TABLE 44.1.** Patterns of Subjects' Responses for Abstract and Common-Sense Curvilinear Motion Problems (Experiment 2)

| Pattern of Responses | Number of Subjects | | |
|---|---|---|---|
| | Common-Sense Problems First | Abstract Problem First | Total |
| Accurate Predictions for all Problems | 11 (6) | 17 (14) | 28 (20) |
| More Accurate Predictions for Common-Sense Problems | 10 (7) | 13 (5) | 23 (12) |
| More Accurate Prediction for Abstract Problem | 8 (2) | 3 (2) | 11 (4) |
| Inaccurate Predictions for Common-Sense and Abstract Problems | 13 (3) | 6 (4) | 19 (7) |

Note—Numbers in parentheses indicate number of subjects with formal physics training.

tions from the familiar to the abstract problems [$\chi^2(1) = 1.29$]. Having correctly solved two familiar curvilinear problems did not enhance subjects' performance on the abstract problem.

How did subjects who gave correct responses for the familiar problems justify their erroneous responses to the ball problem? Examination of these subjects' protocols indicated three basic justifications: First, in the case of the rifle, subjects noted that the barrel had less curvature (360°) than did the ball apparatus (540°). Second, in the case of the water, subjects contended that liquids and solids had different motion properties; water would not acquire curvilinear "momentum" the way a ball would. Finally, subjects cited several irrelevant dynamic properties, notably speed, pressure, and weight. Speed was most often seen as a determining factor. Subjects reported that since the bullet (and sometimes the water) would travel faster than the ball, there would be less tendency for the bullet (and water) to "pick up" curvature from the tube. Two examples of subjects' protocols are given in the Appendix. Both of these subjects gave correct responses to the two common-sense problems but curvilinear responses to the abstract problem.

Most subjects who gave correct responses to all three problems noted the underlying similarity. Newton's first law of motion (or some more vernacular version) was often cited, as was the tendency of objects to move in a "natural" path (i.e., a straight line). The remainder of these subjects either were unable to justify their correct responses or acknowledged that they were just guessing.

Experience-based explanations were given for all problems, although more were given for the familiar problems than for the ball problem. Interestingly, incorrect responses were sometimes justified with inappropriate experiences, such as citing whirlpools as a basis for a curvilinear path for water.

## General Discussion

The data from both experiments indicate that people give more accurate predictions to some curvilinear motion problems than to others. Furthermore, a correct solution on one type of problem is not generalized to another, usually because irrelevant differences are noted in the problems.

One model that is generally consistent with the data holds that subjects apply formal physical principles to both kinds of problems, but that their principles are inaccurate and include such irrelevant factors as the object's velocity and the amount of tube curvature. Certainly, protocols indicate that subjects employ a number of inappropriate physical properties in their justifications. Subjects' allusions to specific experiences may merely reflect an attempt to provide concrete examples of their basic, abstract beliefs. However, if such a model is correct, it is not clear why these misconceptions should impact on subjects' ball predictions more often than on their water or rifle predictions. It would be rather serendipitous that the familiar problems we selected tapped more accurate formal physical principles than did the abstract problem we chose.

An alternative interpretation of the data is that people are able to reason more appropriately about motion problems when they are related to specific, concrete, familiar experiences. The facilitation of reasoning that results from placing an abstract problem in a familiar context has been examined in other cognitive domains, notably in the area of deductive reasoning. Context effects, or "facilitation by realism," have been found to affect performance on syllogistic reasoning (Wilkins, 1928) as well as on a number of variations of the Wason selection task (see Evans, 1982, for a summary). As in our motion problems, however, the facilitation did not generalize to subsequent abstract problems.

Evans (1982) has discussed context effects and the lack of solution transfer from the familiar to the abstract deductive reasoning problem. He argues that the studies that demonstrate the greatest context effects (e.g., Johnson-Laird et al., 1972) may present problems that are too realistic. That is, they do not require subjects to reason at all, but rather allow for a solution based on specific experiences. Such a model would certainly explain the lack of transfer: the relevant similarity in the problems is not recognized since the familiar problem is never processed in formal terms.

We propose a similar model for our subjects' performance. Subjects draw on specific experiences to solve the common-sense problems, and need not employ formal reasoning. The abstract problem, evoking no specific memory, requires subjects to draw upon their formal understanding of physics (which is often erroneous). Thus, we suggest that subjects apply a two-stage approach to solving these problems. First, they search for a specific solution based on relevant experiences. If this search fails, they default to a reasoning process employing formal understanding of mechanics. Such default reasoning models have been proposed in many areas of cognitive psychology (e.g., Siegler, 1981) and artificial intelligence (e.g., Reiter, 1980).

The striking lack of transfer can also be accounted for by such a model. Reasoning by analogy is dependent upon recognizing the relevant similarities of the base problem and the target problem (D. Gentner, 1982). Since the relevant similarities of the common-sense and abstract problems exist only at the level of formal analysis, it is necessary that the common-sense problems be viewed in formal terms for transfer to occur. However, subjects' protocols suggest that most people are able to map the common-sense problem to experience-based solutions on a very concrete level. Since the common-sense problems are only considered on a concrete level, similarity recognition is not possible. The use of two common-sense problems in our Experiment 2 did not improve subjects' solution transfer, although other researchers have found the provision of multiple exemplars to enhance subjects' awareness of formal similarities among problems (Holyoak, 1984).

Finally, our model explains why people demonstrate inconsistency in their reasoning concerning motion problems. Many people who give impetus-type responses to one problem will provide a correct prediction on the next. We suggest that this is because people do not always draw upon their formal representation of physics, but only do so when they are unable to find an acceptable solution based on specific experiences in their memories. The problem of deciding what is or is not a relevant experience is still an issue, but our main point is that people draw on their formal models only after such a solution-by-analogy method fails. In the problems we employed, subjects usually failed to find a relevant experience for the abstract problem and dismissed the common-sense problems as irrelevant based on extraneous factors (e.g., velocity, substance). What we propose, therefore,

is that reasoning by analogy is the default strategy most people apply to motion problems (particularly if they lack formal physics training). Only when people are unable to map the target problem to an appropriate base do they draw upon formal representations. It is then that errors reflecting an impetus model of physics emerge from many individuals.

## ACKNOWLEDGMENTS

This research was supported in part by NIMH Training Grant T32-MH16892 to the first author and in part by a grant from AFOSR to the second author. Portions of this paper were presented at the Annual Meeting of the Midwestern Psychological Association, Chicago, May, 1985.

We would like to thank Michelene Chi, Alice Healy, and Michael McCloskey for their helpful comments. Requests for reprints should be sent to Mary Kaiser, NASA Ames Research Center, Mail Stop 239–3, Moffett Field, CA 94035.

## REFERENCES

Evans, J. St. B. T. (1982). *The psychology of deductive reasoning*. London: Routledge & Kegan Paul.

Gentner, D. (1982). Are scientific analogies metaphors? In D. S. Miall (Ed.), *Metaphor: Problems and perspectives* (pp. 106–132). Brighton, Sussex, England: Harvester Press.

Gentner, D., & Gentner, D. R. (1983). Flowing waters or teeming crowds: Mental models of electricity. In D. Gentner & A. Steven (Eds.), *Mental models* (pp. 99–130). Hillsdale, NJ: Erlbaum.

Holyoak, K. J. (1984). Analogical thinking and human intelligence. In R. J. Sternberg (Ed.), *Advances in the psychology of human intelligence* (Vol. 2, pp. 199–230). Hillsdale, NJ: Erlbaum.

Johnson-Laird, P. N., Legrenzi, P., & Legrenzi, M. S. (1972). Reasoning and a sense of reality. *British Journal of Psychology, 63,* 395–400.

McCloskey, M. (1983). Intuitive physics. *Scientific American*, 248(4), 122–130.

McCloskey, M., Caramazza, A., & Green, B. (1980). Curvilinear motion in the absence of external forces: Naive beliefs about the motion of objects. *Science, 210,* 1139–1141.

Reiter, R. (1980). A logic for default reasoning. *Artificial Intelligence,* **13**, 81–132.

Siegler, R. (1981). Developmental sequences within and between concepts. *Monographs of the Society for Research in Child Development, 46*(2).

Wason, P. C. (1966). Reasoning. In B. M. Foss (Ed.), *New horizons in psychology I* (pp. 135–151). Harmondsworth, England: Penguin.

Wilkins, M. C. (1928). The effect of changed material on the ability to do formal syllogistic reasoning. *Archives of Psychology* (New York) No. 102.

# Appendix

## Sample Subject Protocols from Experiment 2

### Subject 20

Q: Could you explain for each of the situations why you thought the objects took the paths you drew?

A: I guess when I think in terms of bullets, bullets always go straight; when it came out of the gun, I figure it would go straight. And the water, water also seems to go straight out, no matter how much like a garden hose is twisted around, so I imagine the water coming out straight. The ball, I imagine, staying next to the tube, like just following around the tube.

Q: Could you tell me how the speed of the object affects the path it takes?

A: If it were going really fast, it would go straighter than if it were going slow.

Q: Why is that?

A: When you roll a ball very slowly, it tends to go off to the side, where if you throw it faster, it takes a straighter path. I guess maybe it's the gravity behind it . . . well, it's not even gravity, I guess; it's more like inertia, or the energy it has.

Q: Could you tell me your background in physics?

A: Two years in high school. I got As.

### Subject 21

Q: Could you explain why you thought the objects took the paths you drew?

A: I'm going to assume that the ball's going to come out slower here, and because it's been going around and not going real fast, it's going to take the path it had, and curve around. With the gun, the curve was less on the tube, and there's more force, so it's going to be going more straight forward. I don't known the physics behind it, but since it hadn't been going real slow, it's going to take the most direct path, which will be straight. With the water, it's the same reasoning as with the shotgun, it's coming out faster, so it's going to take the direct path, and that's more out straight.

Q: How does the speed of the object affect the path it takes?

A: The faster the object goes, the straighter or more direct path it will take.

Q: Why is that? What about its going faster makes it take a straighter path?

A: Gravity's going to want to hold it in more to the circular path, but when it's going faster, then you get away from the effects of gravity.

Q: What's your physics background?

A: Very limited. Just reading on my own, and what they threw in chemistry. . . . I got an A in chemistry.

# Expert Performance:
# Its Structure and Acquisition

K. Anders Ericsson and Neil Charness

Counter to the common belief that expert performance reflects innate abilities and capacities, recent research in different domains of expertise has shown that expert performance is predominantly mediated by acquired complex skills and physiological adaptations. For elite performers, supervised practice starts at very young ages and is maintained at high daily levels for more than a decade. The effects of extended deliberate practice are more far-reaching than is commonly believed. Performers can acquire skills that circumvent basic limits on working memory capacity and sequential processing. Deliberate practice can also lead to anatomical changes resulting from adaptations to intense physical activity. The study of expert performance has important implications for our understanding of the structure and limits of human adaptation and optimal learning.

In nearly every field of human endeavor, the performance of the best practitioners is so outstanding, so superior even to the performance of other highly experienced individuals in the field, that most people believe a unique, qualitative attribute, commonly called innate talent, must be invoked to account for this highest level of performance. Although these differences in performance are by far the largest psychologists have been able to reliably measure among healthy adults, exceptional performance has not, until recently, been extensively studied by scientists.

In the last decade, interest in outstanding and exceptional achievements and performance has increased dramatically. Many books have been recently published on the topic of genius (for example, Gardner, 1993a; Murray, 1989a; Simonton, 1984, 1988b; Weisberg, 1986, 1993), exception-

ally creative individuals (D. B. Wallace & Gruber, 1989), prodigies (Feldman, 1986; A. Wallace, 1986), and exceptional performance and performers (Howe, 1990; Radford, 1990; Smith, 1983). Of particular interest to the general public has been the remarkable ability of idiot savants or savants, who in spite of a very low general intellectual functioning display superior performance in specific tasks and domains, such as mental multiplication and recall of music (Howe, 1990; Treffert, 1989). The pioneering research comparing the performance of experts and beginners (novices) by de Groot (1946/1978) and Chase and Simon (1973) has generated a great deal of research (Chi, Glaser, & Farr, 1988; Ericsson & Smith, 1991b). A parallel development in computer science has sought to extract the knowledge of experts by interviews (Hoffman, 1992) to build expert systems, which are computer models that are designed to duplicate the performance of these experts and make their expertise generally available. These efforts at artificial intelligence have been most successful in domains that have established symbolic representations, such as mathematical calculation, chess, and music (Barr & Feigenbaum, 1981–1982: Cohen & Feigenbaum, 1982), which incidentally are the main domains in which prodigies and savants have been able to display clearly superior performance (Feldman, 1980, 1986).[1]

The recent advances in our understanding of exceptional performance have had little impact on general theories in psychology. The new knowledge has not fulfilled the humanistic goals of gaining insights from the lives of outstanding people about how people might improve their lives. Maslow (1971) long ago eloquently expressed these goals:

> If we want to know how fast a human being can run, then it is no use to average out the speed of a "good sample" of the population; it is far better to collect Olympic gold medal winners and see how well they can do. If we want to know the possibilities for spiritual growth, value growth, or moral development in human beings, then I maintain that we can learn most by studying our moral, ethical, or saintly people. . . . Even when "good specimens," the saints and sages and great leaders of history, have been available for study, the temptation too often has been to consider them not human but supernaturally endowed. (p. 7)

The reasons for the lack of impact become clear when we consider the two most dominant approaches and their respective goals. The human information-processing approach, or the skills approach, has attempted to explain exceptional performance in terms of knowledge and skills acquired through experience. This approach, originally developed by Newell and Simon (1972), has tried to show that the basic information-processing system with its elementary information processes and basic capacities remains intact during skill acquisition and that outstanding performance results from incremental increases in knowledge and skill due to the extended effects of experience. By constraining the changes to acquired knowledge and skill, this approach has been able to account for exceptional performance within existing general theories of human cognition. According to this approach the mechanisms identified in laboratory studies of learning can be extrapolated to account for expertise and expert performance by an incremental accumulation of knowledge and skill over a decade of intense experience in the domain. The long duration of the necessary period of experience and the presumed vast complexity of the accumulated knowledge has discouraged investigators from empirically studying the acquisition of expert performance. Similarly, individual differences in expert performance, when the amount of experience is controlled, have not been of major interest and have been typically assumed to reflect differences in the original structure of basic processes, capacities, and abilities.

The other major approach focuses on the individual differences of exceptional performers that would allow them to succeed in a specific domain. One of the most influential representatives of this approach is Howard Gardner, who in 1983 presented his theory of multiple intelligence in his book *Frames of Mind: The Theory of Multiple Intelligences* (hereinafter referred to as *Frames of Mind*). Gardner (1983, 1993a, 1993b) drew on the recent advances in biology and brain physiology about neural mechanisms and localization of brain activity to propose an account of the achievements of savants; prodigies, and geniuses in specific domains. He argued that exceptional performance results from a close match between the individual's intelligence profile and the demands of the particular domain. A major concern in this approach is the early identification and nurturing of children with high levels of the required intelligence for a specific domain. Findings within this approach have limited implications for the lives of the vast majority of children and adults of average abilities and talents.

In this article we propose a different approach to the study of exceptional performance and achievement, which we refer to as the study of expert performance. Drawing on our earlier published research, we focus on reproducible, empirical phenomena of superior performance. We will thus not seriously consider anecdotes or unique events, including major artistic and scientific innovations, because they cannot be repeatedly reproduced on demand and hence fall outside the class of phenomena that can be studied by experimental methods. Our approach involves the identification of reproducible superior performance in the everyday life of exceptional performers and the capture of this performance under laboratory conditions. Later we show that the analysis of captured superior performance reveals that extended training alters the cognitive and physiological processes of experts to a greater degree than is commonly believed possible. In the final section of the article we review results from studying the lives of expert performers and identify the central role of large amounts of focused training (deliberate practice), which we distinguish from other forms of experience in a domain. The recent evidence for far-reaching effects of training leads us to start by reexamining the available evidence for innate talent and specific gifts as necessary conditions for attaining the highest levels of performance in a domain.

## Traditional View of the Role of Talent in Exceptional Performance

Since the emergence of civilization, philosophers have speculated about the origin of highly desirable individual attributes, such as poetic ability, physical beauty, strength, wisdom, and skill in handiwork (Murray, 1989b). It was generally believed that these attributes were gifts from the gods, and it was commonly recognized that "On the whole the gods do not bestow more than one gift on a person" (Murray, 1989b, p. 11). This view persisted in early Greek thought, although direct divine intervention was replaced by natural causes. Ever since, there has been a bias toward attributing high abilities to gifts rather than experience, as expressed by John Stuart Mill, there is "a common tendency among mankind to consider all power which is not visibly the effect of practice, all skill which is not capable of being reduced to mechanical rules, as the result of a particular gift" (quoted in Murray, 1989b, p. 12).

One important reason for this bias in attribution, we believe, is linked to immediate legitimatization of various activities associated with the gifts. If the gods have bestowed a child with a special gift in a given art form, who would dare to oppose its development, and who would not facilitate its expression so everyone could enjoy its wonderful creations? This argument may appear strange today, but before the French Revolution the privileged status of kings and nobility and the birthright of their children were primarily based on such claims.

The first systematic development of this argument for gaining social recognition to artists can be found in classic work on *The Lives of the Artist* by Vasari (Bull, 1987), originally published in 1568. This book provided the first major biography of artists and is generally recognized as a major indirect influence on the layman's conceptions of artists even today (Barolsky, 1991). Although Vasari's expressed goal was simply to provide a factual history of art, modern scholars argue that "the *Lives* were partly designed to propagate ideas of the artist as someone providentially born with a vocation from heaven, entitled to high recognition, remuneration and respect" (Bull, 1987, Vol. 2, p. xxvi). To support his claim, Vasari tried to identify early signs of talent and ability in the lives of the artists he described. When facts were missing, he is now known to have added or distorted material (Barolsky, 1991). For example, Vasari dated his own first public demonstration of high ability to the age of 9, although historians now know that he was 13 years old at that event (Boase, 1979). His evaluations of specific pieces of art expressed his beliefs in divine gifts. Michelangelo's famous painting in the Sistine Chapel, the *Final Judgment*, was described by Vasari as "the great example sent by God to men so that they can perceive what can be done when intellects of the highest grade descend upon the earth" (quoted in Boase, 1979, pp. 251–252). Vasari also tried to establish a link between the noble families and the families of outstanding artists by tracing the heritage and family trees of the artists of his time to the great families of antiquity and to earlier great artists. However, much of the reported evidence is now considered to have been invented by Vasari (Barolsky, 1992). In the centuries following Vasari, our civilization underwent major social changes leading to a greater social mobility through the development of a skilled middle class and major progress in the accumulation of scientific knowledge. It became increasingly clear that individuals could dramatically increase their performance through education and training, if they had the necessary drive and motivation. Speculation on the nature of talent started to distinguish achievements due to innate gifts from other achievements resulting from learning and training. In 1759 Edward Young published a famous book on the origin of creative products, in which he argued that "An *Original* may be said to be of *vegetable* nature: it rises spontaneously from the vital root of Genius; it *grows*, it is not *made*" (quoted with original italics in Murray, 1989b, p. 28). Hence, an important characteristic of genius and talent was the apparent absence of learning and training, and thus talent and acquired skill became opposites (Bate, 1989). A century later Galton (1869/1979) presented a comprehensive scientific theory integrating talent and training that has continued to influence the conception of exceptional performance among the general population.

Sir Francis Galton was the first scientist to investigate empirically the possibility that excellence in diverse fields and domains has a common set of causes. On the basis of an analysis of eminent men in a wide range of domains and of their relatives, Galton (1869/1979) argued that three factors had to be present: innate ability, eagerness to work, and "an adequate power of doing a great deal of very laborious work" (p. 37). Because the importance of the last two factors—motivation and effort—had already been recognized (Ericsson, Krampe, & Heizmann, 1993), later investigators concentrated primarily on showing that innate abilities and capacities are necessary to attain the highest levels of performance.

Galton (1869/1979) acknowledged a necessary but not sufficient role for instruction and practice in achieving exceptional performance. According to this view, performance increases monotonically as a function of practice toward an asymptote representing a fixed upper bound on performance. Like Galton, contemporary researchers generally assume that training can affect some of the components mediating performance but cannot affect others. If performance achieved after extensive training is limited by components that cannot be modified, it is reasonable to assert that stable, genetically determined factors determine the ultimate level of performance. If all possible changes in performance related to training are attained after a fairly limited period of practice, this argument logically implies that individual differences in final performance must reflect innate talents and natural abilities.

The view that talent or giftedness for a given activity is necessary to attain the highest levels of performance in that activity is widely held among people in general. This view is particularly dominant in such domains of expertise as chess, sports, music, and visual arts, where millions of individuals are active but only a very small number reach the highest levels of performance.

One of the most prominent and influential scientists who draw on evidence from exceptional performance of artists, scientists, and athletes for a biological theory of talent is Howard Gardner. In *Frames of Mind*, Gardner (1983) proposed seven intelligences: linguistic, musical, spatial, logical-mathematical, bodily kinesthetic, and interpersonal and intrapersonal intelligence—each an independent system with its own biological bases (p. 68). This theory is a refinement and development of ideas expressed in an earlier book (Gardner, 1973), in which the talent position was more explicitly articulated, especially in the case of music. Gardner (1973) wrote,

> Further evidence of the strong hereditary basis of musical talent comes from a number of sources. Most outstanding musicians are discovered at an early age, usually before 6 and often as early as 2 or 3, even in households where relatively little music is heard. Individual differences are tremendous among children, and training seems to have comparatively little effect in reducing these differences. (p. 188)

He discussed possible mechanisms for talent in the context of music savants, who in spite of low intellectual functioning display impressive music ability as children: "it seems possible that the children are reflecting a rhythmic and melodic capacity that is primarily hereditary, and which needs as little external stimulation as does walking and talking in the normal child" (Gardner, 1973, p. 189). Although Gardner (1983) did not explicitly discuss his earlier positions, the evidence from prodigies and savants remains central. *Frames of Mind* contains a careful review of the then available research on the dramatic effects of training on performance. In particular, he reviewed the exceptional music performance of young children trained with the Suzuki method and noted that many of these children who began training without previous signs of musical talent attained levels comparable to music prodigies of earlier times and gained access to the best music teachers in the world. The salient aspect of talent, according to Gardner (1983), is no longer the innate structure (gift) but rather the potential for achievement and the capacity to rapidly learn material relevant to one of the intelligences. Gardner's (1983) view is consistent with Suzuki's rejection of inborn talent in music and Suzuki's (1963/1981) early belief in individual differences in innate general ability to learn, although Suzuki's innate abilities were not specific to a particular domain, such as music. However, in his later writings, Suzuki (1980/1981) argued that "every child can be highly educated if he is given the proper training" (p. 233), and he blamed earlier training failures on incorrect training methods and their inability to induce enthusiasm and motivation in the children. The clearest explication of Gardner's (1983) view is found when he discussed his proposal for empirical assessments of individuals' profiles in terms of the seven intelligences. He proposed a test in which "individuals were given the opportunity to learn to recognize certain patterns [relevant to the particular domain] and were tested on their capacities to remember these from one day to the next" (p. 385). On the basis of tests for each of the intelligences, "intellectual profiles could be drawn up in the first year or two of life" (p. 386), although reliable assessments may have to wait until the preschool years because of "early neural and functional plasticity" (p. 386). Gardner's own hunch about strong intellectual abilities was that "an individual so blessed does not merely have an easy time learning new patterns; he learns them so readily that *it is virtually impossible for him to forget them*" (pp. 385–386).

Our reading of Gardner's (1993a, 1993b)[2] most recent books leads us to conclude that his ideas on talent have not fundamentally changed. According to Gardner's (1983) influential view, the evidence for the talent view is based on two major sources of data on performance: the performance of prodigies and savants and the ability to predict future success of individuals on the basis of early test results. Given that our knowledge about the exceptional performance of savants and prodigies and the predictive validity of tests of basic abilities and talents have increased considerably in the past decade, we briefly review the evidence or rather the lack of evidence for innate abilities and talent.

## Performance of Prodigies and Savants

When the large collection of reports of amazing and inexplicable performance is surveyed, one finds that most of them cannot even be firmly substantiated and can only rarely be replicated under controlled laboratory conditions. Probably the best established phenomenon linked to talent in music is perfect pitch, or more accurately absolute pitch (AP). Only approximately 0.01% of the general population have AP and are able to correctly name each of the 64 different tones, whereas average musicians without AP can distinguish only approximately five or six categories of pitches when the pitches are presented in isolation (Takeuchi & Hulse, 1993). Many outstanding musicians display AP, and they first reveal their ability in early childhood. With a few exceptions, adults appear to be unable to attain AP in spite of extended efforts. Hence the characteristics of absolute pitch would seem to meet all of the criteria of innate talent, although there is some controversy about how useful this ability is to the expert musicians. In a recent review of AP, Takeuchi and Hulse (1993) concluded that the best account of the extensive and varied evidence points toward a theory that "states AP can be *acquired by anyone* [italics added], but only during a limited period of development" (p. 355). They found that all individuals with AP had started with music instruction early—nearly always before age five or six—and that several studies had been successful in teaching AP to three- to six-year-old children. At older ages children perceive relations between pitches, which leads to accurate relative pitch, something all skilled musicians have. "Young children *prefer* to process absolute rather than the relative pitches of musical stimuli" (p. 356). Similar developmental trends from individual features to relational attributes are found in other forms of perception during the same age period (Takeuchi & Hulse, 1993). Rather than being a sign of innate talent, AP appears to be a natural consequence of appropriate instruction and of ample opportunities to interact with a musical instrument, such as a piano, at very young ages.

Other proposed evidence for innate talent comes from studies of prodigies in music and chess who are able to attain high levels of performance even as young children. In two influential books, Feldman (1980, 1986) showed that acquisition of skills in prodigies follows the same sequence of stages as in other individuals in the same domain. The primary difference is that prodigies attain higher levels faster and at younger ages. For example, an analysis of Picasso's early drawings as a child shows that he encountered and mastered problems in drawing in ways similar to less gifted individuals (Pariser, 1987). Feldman (1986) also refuted the myth that prodigies acquire their skills irrespective of the environment. In fact, he found evidence for the exact opposite, namely that "the more powerful and specific the gift, the more need for active, sustained and specialized intervention" (p. 123) from skilled teachers and parents. He described the classic view of gifts, in which parents are compelled to support their development, when he wrote, "When extreme talent shows itself it demands nothing less than the willingness of one or both of the parents to give up almost everything else to make sure that the talent is developed" (p. 122). A nice case in point is the child art prodigy Yani (Ho, 1989), whose father gave up his own painting career so as not to interfere with the novel style that his daughter was developing. Feldman (1980, 1986) argued that prodigious performance is rare because extreme talent for a specific activity in a particular child and the necessary environmental support and instruction rarely coincide.

Contrary to common belief, most child prodigies never attain exceptional levels of performance as adults (Barlow, 1952; Feldman, 1986). When Scheinfeld (1939) examined the reported basis of the initial talent assessment by parents of famous musicians, he found signs of interest in music rather than objective evidence of unusual capacity. For example, Fritz Kreisler was "playing violin" (p. 239) with two sticks at age four, and Yehudi Menuhin had a "response to violins at concerts" (p. 239) at the age of one and a half years. Very early start of music instruction would then lead to the acquisition of absolute pitch. Furthermore, the vast majority of exceptional adult performers were never child prodigies, but instead they started instruction early and increased their performance due to a sustained high level of training (Bloom, 1985). The role of early instruction and maximal parental support appears to be much more important than innate talent, and there are many examples of parents of exceptional performers who successfully designed optimal environments for their children

without any concern about innate talent (see Ericsson, Krampe, & Tesch-Römer, 1993, and Howe, 1990). For example, as part of an educational experiment, Laslo and Klara Polgar (Forbes, 1992) raised one of their daughters to become the youngest international chess grand master ever— she was even younger than Bobby Fischer, who was the youngest male achieving that exceptional level of chess-playing skill. In 1992 the three Polgar daughters were ranked first, second, and sixth in the world among women chess players, respectively.

Although scientists and the popular press have been interested in the performance of prodigies, they have been especially intrigued by so-called savants. Savants are individuals with a low level of general intellectual functioning who are able to perform at high levels in some special tasks. In a few cases the parents have reported that these abilities made their appearances suddenly, and they cited them as gifts from God (Ericsson & Faivre, 1988; Feldman, 1986). More careful study of the emergence of these and other cases shows that their detection may in some cases have been sudden, but the opportunities, support, and encouragement for learning had preceded the original performance by years or even decades (Ericsson & Faivre, 1988; Howe, 1990; Treffert, 1989). Subsequent laboratory studies of the performance of savants have shown them to reflect acquired skills. For example, savants who can name the day of the week of an arbitrary date (e.g., November 5, 1923) generate their answers using instructable methods that allow their performance to be reproduced by a college student after a month of training (for a review see Ericsson & Faivre, 1988). The only ability that cannot be reproduced after brief training concerns some savants' reputed ability to play a piece of music after a single hearing.

However, in a carefully controlled study of a music savant (J.L.), Charness, Clifton, and MacDonald (1988) showed that reproduction of short (2- to 12-note) tonal sequences and recall of from two to four chords (4 notes each) depended on whether the sequences or chords followed Western scale structure. Unfamiliar sequences that violated musical conventions were poorly recalled past 6 notes. Short, familiar sequences of notes and chords were accurately recalled, although recall dropped with length of sequence so that only

3 (of 24) 12-note familiar sequences were completely correct. Attempts to train J.L. to learn temporally static 16-note melodies were unsuccessful. Even in the case of the musical savant studied by Sloboda, Hermelin, and O'Connor (1985), who was able to memorize a new piece of music, there was a marked difference in success with a conventional versus a tonally unconventional piece. Thus, music savants, like their normally intelligent expert counterparts, need access to stored patterns and retrieval structures to enable them to retain long, unfamiliar musical patterns. Given that savants cannot read music—most of them are blind—they have to acquire new music by listening, which would provide motivation and opportunities for the development of domain-specific memory skills.

In summary, the evidence from systematic laboratory research on prodigies and savants provides no evidence for giftedness or innate talent but shows that exceptional abilities are acquired often under optimal environmental conditions.

## Prediction of Future Success Based on Innate Abilities and Talent

The importance of basic processes and capacities is central to many theorists in the human information-processing tradition. In conceptual analogies with computers, investigators often distinguish between hardware (the physical components of the computer) and software (computer programs and stored data). In models of human performance, "software" corresponds to knowledge and strategies that can be readily changed as a function of training and learning, and "hardware" refers to the basic elements that cannot be changed through training. Even theorists such as Chase and Simon (1973), who acknowledge that "practice is the major independent variable in the acquisition of skill" (p. 279), argue in favor of individual differences in talent that predispose people to be successful in different domains: "Although there clearly must be a set of specific aptitudes (e.g., aptitudes for handling spatial relations) that together comprise a talent for chess, individual differences in such aptitudes are largely overshadowed by immense differences in chess experience" (p. 297). Bloom (1985) went through many different domains to point out some necessary qualities that are likely to be mostly inborn, such as

"*motor coordination*, *speed of reflexes* and *hand-eye coordination*" (p. 546). These views were consistent with the available information at the time, such as high heritabilities for many of these characteristics. In their review of sport psychology, Browne and Mahoney (1984) argued for the importance of fixed physiological traits for elite performance of athletes and wrote that "there is good evidence that the limits of physiological capacity to become more efficient with training is determined by genetics" (p. 609). They cited research reporting that percentage of muscle fibers and aerobic capacity "are more than 90% determined by heredity for both male and female" (p. 609). However, more recent reviews have shown that heritabilities in random samples of twins are much lower and range between zero and 40% (Malina & Bouchard, 1991).

It is curious how little empirical evidence supports the talent view of expert and exceptional performance. Ever since Galton, investigators have tried to measure individual differences in unmodifiable abilities and basic cognitive and perceptual capacities. To minimize any influence from prior experience, they typically base their tests on simple tasks. They measure simple reaction time and detection of sensory stimuli and present meaningless materials, such as nonsense syllables and lists of digits, in tests of memory capacity. A recent review (Ericsson, Krampe, & Tesch-Römer, 1993) showed that efforts to measure talent with objective tests for basic cognitive and perceptual motor abilities have been remarkably unsuccessful in predicting final performance in specific domains. For example, elite athletes are able to react much faster and make better perceptual discriminations to representative situations in their respective domains, but their simple reaction times and perceptual acuity to simple stimuli during laboratory tests do not differ systematically from those of other athletes or control subjects (for reviews see Regnier, Salmela, & Russell, 1993, and Starkes & Deakin, 1985). Chess players' and other experts' superior memory for brief presentation of representative stimuli from their domains compared with that of novices is eliminated when the elements of the same stimuli are presented in a randomly arranged format (Chase & Simon, 1973; see Ericsson & Smith, 1991a, for a review). The performance of elite chess players on standard tests of spatial ability is not reliably different from control subjects (Doll & Mayr, 1987). The domain specificity of superior performance is striking and is observed in many different domains of expertise (Ericsson, Krampe, & Tesch-Römer, 1993).

This conclusion can be generalized with some qualifications to current tests of such general abilities as verbal and quantitative intelligence. These tests typically measure acquired knowledge of mathematics, vocabulary, and grammar by successful performance on items testing problem solving and comprehension. Performance during and immediately after training is correlated with IQ, but the correlations between this type of ability test and performance in the domain many months and years later is reduced (even after corrections for restriction of range) to such low values that Hulin, Henry, and Noon (1990) questioned their usefulness and predictive validity. At the same time, the average IQ of expert performers, especially in domains of expertise requiring thinking, such as chess, has been found to be higher than the average of the normal population and corresponds roughly to that of college students. However, IQ does not reliably discriminate the best adult performers from less accomplished adult performers in the same domain.

Even physiological and anatomical attributes can change dramatically in response to physical training. Almost everyone recognizes that regular endurance and strength training uniformly improves aerobic endurance and strength, respectively. As the amount and intensity or physical training is increased and maintained for long periods, far-reaching adaptations of the body result (see Ericsson, Krampe, & Tesch-Römer, 1993, for a review). For example, the sizes of hearts and lungs, the flexibility of joints, and the strength of bones increase as the result of training, and the nature and extent of these changes appear to be magnified when training overlaps with physical development during childhood and adolescence. Furthermore, the number of capillaries supplying blood to trained muscles increases, and muscle fibers can change their metabolic properties from fast twitch to slow twitch. With the clear exception of height, a surprisingly large number of anatomical characteristics show specific changes and adaptations to the specific nature of extended intense training, which we describe in more detail later in this article.

If one accepts the necessity of extended intense training for attaining expert performance—a claim that is empirically supported later in this article—then it follows that currently available estimates of heritability of human characteristics do not generalize to expert performance. An estimate of heritability is valid only for the range of environmental effects for which the studied subjects have been exposed. With a few exceptions, studies of heritabilities have looked only at random samples of subjects in the general population and have not restricted their analyses to individuals exposed to extended training in a domain. The remaining data on exceptional and expert performers have not been able to demonstrate systematic genetic influences. Explanations based on selective access to instruction and early training in a domain provide as good or in some cases better accounts of familial relations of expert performers, such as the lineage of musicians in the Bach family (see Ericsson, Krampe, & Tesch-Römer, 1993, for a review).

In summary, we argue that the traditional assumptions of basic abilities and capacities (talent) that may remain stable in studies of limited and short-term practice do not generalize to superior performance acquired over years and decades in a specific domain. In addition, we will later review evidence showing that acquired skill can allow experts to circumvent basic capacity limits of short-term memory and of the speed of basic reactions, making potential basic limits irrelevant. Once the potential for change through practice is recognized, we believe that a search for individual differences that might be predictive of exceptional and expert performance should refocus on the factors advocated by Charles Darwin (quoted in Galton, 1908) in a letter to Galton after reading the first part of Galton's (1869/1979) book: "You have made a convert of an opponent in one sense, for I have always maintained that excepting fools, men did not differ much in intellect, only in zeal and hard work; I still think this is an *eminently* important difference" (p. 290). In commenting on Darwin's remark, Galton (1908) agreed but argued that "character, including the aptitude for work, is heritable" (p. 291). On the basis of their review, Ericsson, Krampe, and Tesch-Römer (1993) found that motivational factors are more likely to be the locus of heritable influences than is innate talent. We explicate the connection between these "motivational" factors and the rate of improving performance in a specific domain in the last section of this article.

There are two parts to the remaining portion of this article. First, we show that it is possible to study and analyze the mechanisms that mediate expert performance. We also show that the critical mechanisms reflect complex, domain-specific cognitive structures and skills that performers have acquired over extended periods of time. Hence, individuals do not achieve expert performance by gradually refining and extrapolating the performance they exhibited before starting to practice but instead by restructuring the performance and acquiring new methods and skills. In the final section, we show that individuals improve their performance and attain an expert level, not as an automatic consequence of more experience with an activity but rather through structured learning and effortful adaptation.

## The Study of Expert Performance

The conceptions of expert performance as primarily an acquired skill versus a reflection of innate talents influence how expert performance and expert performers are studied. When the goal is to identify critical talents and capacities, investigators have located experts and then compared measurements of their abilities with those of control subjects on standard laboratory tests. Tests involve simple stimuli and tasks in order to minimize any effects of previously acquired knowledge and skill. Given the lack of success of this line of research, we advocate a different approach that identifies the crucial aspects of experts' performance that these experts exhibit regularly at a superior level in their domain. If experts have acquired their superior performance by extended adaptation to the specific constraints in their domains, we need to identify representative tasks that incorporate these constraints to be able to reproduce the natural performance of experts under controlled conditions in the laboratory. We illustrate this method of designing representative test situations with several examples later in this section. Once the superior performance of experts can be reliably reproduced in a test situation, this performance can then be analyzed to assess its mediating acquired mechanisms. Following Ericsson and Smith (1991a), we define expert performance as consistently superior performance on a specified set of representative tasks for the domain that can be administered to any subject. The virtue of defining expert performance in this restricted sense is that the definition both meets all the criteria of laboratory studies of performance and comes close to meeting those for evaluating performance in many domains of expertise.

## Perceived Experts versus Consistent Expert Performance

In many domains, rules have evolved and standardized conditions, and fair methods have been designed for measuring performance. The conditions of testing in many sports and other activities, such as typing competitions, are the same for all participating individuals. In other domains, the criteria for expert performance cannot be easily translated into a set of standardized tasks that captures and measures that performance. In some domains, expert performance is determined by judges or by the results of competitive tournaments. Psychometric methods based on tournament results, most notably in chess (Elo, 1986), have successfully derived latent measures of performance on an interval scale. In the arts and sciences, selected individuals are awarded prizes and honors by their peers, typically on the basis of significant achievements such as published books and research articles and specific artistic performances.

Some type of metric is of course required to identify *superior performance*. The statistical term *outlier* may be a useful heuristic for judging superior performance. Usually, if someone is performing at least two standard deviations above the mean level in the population, that individual can be said to be performing at an expert level. In the domain of chess (Elo, 1986), the term *expert* is defined as a range of chess ratings (2000–2199) approximately two to three standard deviations (200 rating points) above the mean (1600 rating points) and five to six standard deviations above the mean of chess players starting to play in chess tournaments.

In most domains it is easier to identify individuals who are socially recognized as experts than it is to specify observable performance at which these individuals excel. The distinction between the perception of expertise and actual expert performance becomes increasingly important as research has shown that the performance of some individuals who are nominated as experts is not measurably superior. For example, studies have found that financial experts' stock investments yield returns that are not consistently better than the average of the stock market, that is, financial experts' performance does not differ from the result of essentially random selection of stocks. When successful investors are identified and their subsequent investments are tracked, there is no evidence for sustained superiority. A large body of evidence has been accumulated showing that experts frequently do not outperform other people in many relevant tasks in their domains of expertise (Camerer & Johnson, 1991). Experts may have much more knowledge and experience than others, yet their performance on critical tasks may not be reliably better than that of nonexperts. In summary, researchers cannot seek out experts and simply assume that their performance on relevant tasks is superior; they must instead demonstrate this superior performance.

## Identifying and Capturing Expert Performance

For most domains of expertise, people have at least an intuitive conception of the kind of activities at which an expert should excel. In everyday life, however, these activities rarely have clearly defined starting and end points, nor do the exact external conditions of a specific activity reoccur. The main challenge is thus to identify particular well-defined tasks that frequently occur and that capture the essence of expert performance in a specific domain. It is then possible to determine the contexts in which each task naturally occurs and to present these tasks in a controlled context to a larger group of other experts.

De Groot's (1946/1978) research on expertise in chess is generally considered the pioneering effort to capture expert performance. Ability in chess playing is determined by the outcomes of chess games between opponents competing in tournaments. Each game is different and is rarely repeated exactly except for the case of moves in the opening phase of the game. De Groot, who was himself a chess master, determined that the ability to play chess is best captured in the task of selecting the next move for a given chess position taken from the middle of the game between two chess

masters. Consistently superior performance on this task for arbitrary chess positions logically implies a very high level of skill. Researchers can therefore elicit experts' superiority in performing a critical task by presenting the same unfamiliar chess position to any number of chess players and asking them to find the best next move. De Groot demonstrated that performance on this task discriminates well between chess players at different levels of skill and thus captures the essential phenomenon of ability to play this game.

In numerous subsequent studies, researchers have used a similar approach to study the highest levels of thinking in accepted experts in various domains of expertise (Chi et al., 1988; Ericsson & Smith, 1991b). If expert performance reflects extended adaptation to the demands of naturally occurring situations, it is important that researchers capture the structure of these situations in order to elicit maximal performance from the experts. Furthermore, if the tasks designed for research are sufficiently similar to normal situations, experts can rely on their existing skills, and no experiment-specific changes are necessary. How similar these situations have to be to real-life situations is an empirical question. In general, researchers should strive to define the simplest situation in which experts' superior performance can still be reliably reproduced.

## Description and Analysis of Expert Performance

The mere fact that it is possible to identify a set of representative tasks that can elicit superior performance from experts under standardized conditions is important. It dramatically reduces the number of contextual factors that can logically be essential for reproducing that superior performance. More important, it allows researchers to reproduce the phenomenon of expert performance under controlled conditions and in a reliable fashion. Researchers can thus precisely describe the tasks and stimuli and can theoretically determine which mechanisms are capable of reliably producing accurate performance across the set of tasks. Part of the standard methodology in cognitive psychology is to analyze the possible methods subjects could use to generate the correct response to a specific task, given their knowledge about procedures and facts in the domain. The same methodology

can be applied to tasks that capture expert performance. Because, however, the knowledge experts
may apply to a specific task is quite extensive and
complex, it is virtually impossible for nonexperts
to understand an analysis of such a task. Instead
of describing such a case, we illustrate the methodology and related issues with a relatively simple
skill, mental multiplication.

## Mental Multiplication: An Illustration of Text Analysis

In a study of mental multiplication, the experimenter typically reads a problem to a subject: What
is the result of multiplying 24 by 36? The subject
then reports the correct answer—864. It may be
possible that highly experienced subjects recognize that particular problem and retrieve the answer immediately from memory. That possibility
is remote for normal subjects, and one can surmise that they must calculate the answer by relying on their knowledge of the multiplication table
and familiar methods for complex multiplication.
The most likely method is the paper-and-pencil
method taught in the schools, where $24 \times 36$ is
broken down into $24 \times 6$ and $24 \times 30$ and the products are added together (illustrated as Case B in
Table 45.1). Often students are told to put the highest number first. By this rule, the first step in solving $24 \times 36$ is to rearrange it as $36 \times 24$ and then
to break it down as $36 \times 4$ and $36 \times 20$ (Case A).
More sophisticated subjects may recognize that 24
$\times 36$ is equivalent to $(30 - 6) \times (30 + 6)$ and use
the formula $(a - b) \times (a + b) = a^2 - b^2$, thus calculating $24 \times 36$ as $30^2 - 6^2 = 900 - 36 = 864$ (Case
C). Other subjects may recognize other shortcuts,
such as $24 \times 36 = (2 \times 12) \times (3 \times 12) = 6 \times 12^2 = 6$
$\times 144$ (Case D). Skilled mental calculators often
prefer to calculate the answer in the reverse order,
as is illustrated in Case E. Especially for more complex problems this procedure allows them to report the first digit of the final result long before
they have completed the calculation of the remaining digits. Because most people expect that the
entire answer has to be available before the first
digit can be announced, the last method gives the
appearance of faster calculation speeds.

An investigator cannot determine on which of
the methods in Table 45.1 a subject relied. However, if the subject was instructed to think aloud
(see Ericsson & Simon, 1993, for the detailed pro-

**TABLE 45.1. Five Possible Methods of Mentally Multiplying 24 by 36 and a Think-Aloud Protocol from a Subject Generating the Correct Answer**

| Mental Multiplication | Think-Aloud Protocol |
|---|---|
| Method A | 36 times 24 |
| 24 | 4 |
| × 36 | carry the—no wait |
| 144 | 4 |
| 72 | carry the 2 |
| 864 | 14 |
|  | 144 |
|  | 0 |
|  | 36 times 2 is |
| Method B | 12 |
| 36 | 6 |
| × 24 | 72 |
| 144 | 720 plus 144 |
| 72 | 4 |
| 864 | uh, uh |
|  | 6 |
|  | 8 |
| Method C | uh, 864 |
| $24 \times 36 =$ | |
| $= (30 - 6) \times (30 + 6) =$ | |
| $= 30^2 - 6^2 =$ | |
| $= 900 - 36 = 864$ | |
| Method D | |
| $24 \times 36 = 2 \times 12 \times 3 \times 12 =$ | |
| $= 6 \times 12^2 = 6 \times 144 = 864$ | |
| Method E | |
| AB            24 | |
| × CD         × 36 | |
| $100 \times A \times C$     600 | |
| $10 \times A \times D$      120 | |
| $10 \times C \times B$      120 | |
| $B \times D$           24 | |
| 864 | |

cedure) while completing the mental multiplication, the investigator could record in detail the
mediating sequences of the subject's thoughts, as
is illustrated in the right panel of Table 45.1. Although methodologically rigorous methods for
encoding and evaluating think-aloud protocols are
available (Ericsson & Simon, 1993), the visual
match between Case B and the protocol in Table
45.1 is sufficiently clear for the purposes of our
illustration. Even with a less detailed record of the
verbalized intermediate products in the calculation,
it is possible to reject most of the alternative methods as being inconsistent with a recorded protocol.

## Think-Aloud Protocols and Task Analysis in Research on Expert Performance

Since the demise of introspective analysis of consciousness around the turn of the century, investigators have been reluctant to consider any type of verbal report as valid data on subjects' cognitive processes. More recently investigators have been particularly concerned that having subjects generate verbal reports changes the underlying processes. In a recent review of more than 40 experimental studies comparing performance with and without verbalization, Ericsson and Simon (1993) showed that the structure of cognitive processes can change if subjects are required to explain their cognitive processes. In contrast, if subjects were asked simply to verbalize the thoughts that come to their attention (think aloud), Ericsson and Simon found no reliable evidence that structural changes to cognitive processing occurred. Thinking aloud appears only to require additional time for subjects to complete verbalization and therefore leads to somewhat longer solution times in some cases.

A critical concern in applying this methodology to expert performance is how much information the think-aloud protocols of experts contain about the mediating cognitive processes. Obviously many forms of skilled perceptual-motor performance are so rapid that concurrent verbalization of thought would seem impossible. We later consider alternative methodologies for such cases; but for a wide range of expert performance, think-aloud protocols have provided a rich source of information on expert performance. In his work on chess masters, de Groot (1946/1978) instructed his subjects to think aloud as they identified the best move for chess positions. From an analysis of the verbal reports, de Groot was able to describe how his subjects selected their moves. First they familiarized themselves with the position and extracted the strengths and weaknesses of its structure. Then they systematically explored the consequences of promising moves and the opponent's likely countermoves by planning several moves ahead. From subjects' verbalizations, de Groot and subsequent investigators (Charness, 1981a) have been able to represent the sequences of moves subjects explored as search trees and to measure the amount and depth of planning for chess players at different

levels of expertise (see Figure 45.1). The results of these analyses show that the amount and depth of search increase as a function of chess expertise to a given point (the level of chess experts); thereafter, no further systematic differences were found (Charness, 1989). That the very best chess players still differ in their ability to find and selectively explore the most promising moves suggests that the structure of their internal representation of chess positions differs.

The central importance of experts' representation of solutions is revealed by verbal reports in other domains such as physics and medical diagnosis. When novices in physics solve a problem, they typically start with the question that asks for, say, a velocity; then they try to recall formulas for calculating velocities and then construct step by step a sequence of formulas by reasoning backward from the goal to the information given in the problem. In contrast, more experienced subjects proceed by forward reasoning. As they read the description of the problem situation, an integrated representation is generated and updated, so when they finally encounter the question in the problem text, they simply retrieve a solution plan from memory (Larkin, McDermott, Simon, & Simon, 1980). This finding suggests that experts form an immediate representation of the problem that systematically cues their knowledge, whereas novices do not have this kind of orderly and efficient access to their knowledge. Similarly, medical experts comprehend and integrate the information they receive about patients to find the correct diagnosis by reasoning forward, whereas less accomplished practitioners tend to generate plausible diagnoses that aid their search for confirming and disconfirming evidence (Patel & Groen, 1991).

Experts' internal representation of the relevant information about the situation is critical to their ability to reason, to plan out, and to evaluate consequences of possible actions. Approximately 100 years ago Binet was intrigued by some chess players' claims that they could visualize chess positions clearly when they played chess games without a visible chessboard (blindfold chess). Binet (1894) and subsequently Luria (1968) studied individuals with exceptional memory abilities, who claimed to visualize as a mental image the information presented to them. These claims, if substantiated, would imply that some individuals have a sensory-based memory akin to a photographic

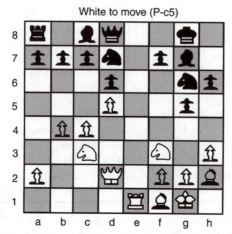

White to move (P-c5)

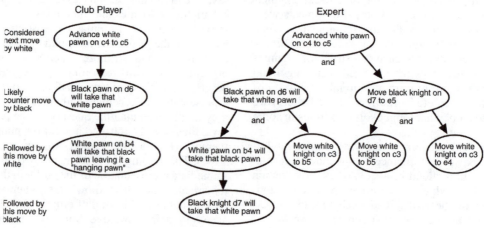

**FIGURE 45.1** ■ Chess Position Presented to Players with Instruction to Select Best Next Move by White (Top Panel). *Note.* Think-aloud protocols of a good club player (chess rating = 1657) and a chess expert (chess rating = 2004) collected by Charness (1981a) are shown in bottom panel to illustrate differences in evaluation and planning for one specific move, P-c5 (white pawn from c4 to c5), the best move for this position. Reported considerations for other potential moves have been omitted. The chess expert considers more alternative move sequences, some of them to a greater depth than the club player does. (From "Search in Chess: Age and Skill Differences" by N. Charness, 1981, *Journal of Experimental Psychology: Human Perception and Performance, 7*, p. 469. Copyright 1981 by American Psychological Association.)

memory, making them qualitatively different from the vast majority of human adults. To gain understanding of these processes and capacities, investigators have turned to tests of perception and memory.

## Immediate Memory of Perceived Situations

To study subjects' immediate perception of chess positions, de Groot (1946/1978) restricted the pre-sentation to 2–15 seconds and then removed the chess position from view. Even after such a brief exposure, the best chess players were able to describe the structure of the chess position and could reproduce the locations of all the chess pieces almost perfectly. Weaker chess players' memory was much worse, and generally the amount of information chess players could recall was found to be a function of skill. In a classic study Chase and Simon (1973) studied subjects' memory for briefly presented chess positions and replicated de Groot's findings under controlled conditions. To the same subjects Chase and Simon also presented chess positions with randomly rearranged chess pieces. Memory for these scrambled positions was uniformly poor and did not differ as a function of skill. This finding has been frequently replicated and shows that the superior memory for briefly presented chess positions in not due to any general memory ability, such as photographic memory, but depends critically on subjects' ability to perceive meaningful patterns and relations between chess pieces. Originally Chase and Simon proposed that experts' superior short-term memory for chess positions was due to their ability to recognize configurations of chess pieces on the basis of their knowledge of vast numbers of specific patterns of pieces. With greater knowledge of more complex and larger configurations of chess pieces (chunks), an expert could recall more individual chess pieces with the same number of chunks. Hence Chase and Simon could account for very large individual differences in memory for chess positions within the limits of the capacity of normal short-term memory (STM), which is approximately seven chunks (Miller, 1956).

The Chase-Simon theory has been very influential. It gives an elegant account of experts' superior memory only for representative stimuli from their domain, and not even for randomly rearranged versions of the same stimuli (see Ericsson & J. Smith, 1991a, for a summary of the various domains of expertise in which this finding has been demonstrated). At that time Chase and Simon (1973) believed that storage of new information in long-term memory (LTM) was quite time consuming and that memory for briefly presented information could be maintained only in STM for experts and nonexperts alike. However, subsequent research by Chase and Ericsson (1982) on the effects of practice on a specific task measuring the capacity of STM has shown that through extended practice (more than 200 hours), it is possible for subjects to improve performance by more than 1,000%. These improvements are not mediated by increasingly larger chunks in STM but reflect the acquisition of memory skills that enable subjects to store information in LTM and thereby circumvent the capacity constraint of STM. Hence with extensive practice it is possible to attain skills that lead to qualitative, not simply quantitative, differences in memory performance for a specific type of presented information.

From experimental analyses of their trained subjects and from a review of data on other individuals with exceptional memory, Chase and Ericsson (1982; Ericsson, 1985) extracted several general findings of skilled memory that apply to all subjects. Exceptional memory is nearly always restricted to one type of material, frequently random sequences of digits. The convergence of acquired memory skills and alleged exceptional memory was demonstrated when the trained subjects performed tasks given previously to "exceptional" subjects. Figure 45.2 (middle panel) shows a matrix that Binet presented visually to his subjects. Below the matrix are several orders in which the same subjects were asked to recall the numbers from the matrix that they memorized. Ericsson and Chase (1982) found that their subjects matched or surpassed the exceptional subjects both in the speed of initial memorization and in the speed of subsequent recall. A detailed analysis contrasting the speed for different orders of recall showed the same pattern in trained and exceptional subjects, both of whom recalled by rows faster than by columns. Consistent with their acquired memory skill, the trained subjects encoded each row of the matrix as a group by relying on their extensive knowledge of facts relevant to numbers. They then associated a cue corresponding to the spatial location of each row with a retrieval structure illustrated in the top panel of Figure 45.1. To recall numbers in flexible order, subjects retrieved the relevant row using the corresponding retrieval cue and then extracted the desired next digit or digits. The high correlation between the recall times predicted from this method and the recall times observed for both exceptional and trained subjects imply that these groups have a similar memory representation. When the biographical background of individuals exhibiting exceptional memory performance was examined, Ericsson (1985, 1988) found evidence for extended experience and practice with related memory tasks. Hence, these exceptional individuals and the trained college students should be viewed as expert performers on these laboratory tasks, where the same type of memory skills has been acquired during extended prior experience.

Acquired memory skill (skilled memory theory, Ericsson & Staszewski, 1989; and long-term

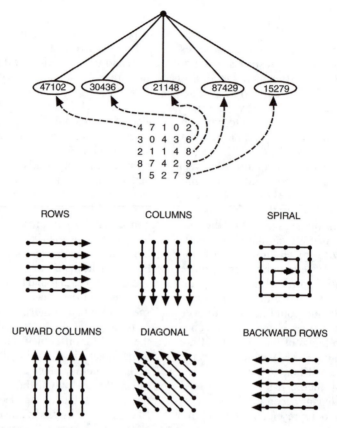

**FIGURE 45.2** ■ 25-Digit Matrix Used by Binet to Test Memory Experts.
*Note.* Binet asked subjects to repeat entire matrix in various orders shown at bottom or to repeat individual rows as five-digit numbers. Top shows trained subjects' representation of matrix as a sequence of rows, with all digits in a row stored together in an integrated memory encoding.

working memory, Ericsson & Kintsch, 1994) accounts well even for the superior memory of experts. In many types of expert performance, research has shown that working memory is essentially unaffected by interruptions, during which the experts are forced to engage in an unrelated activity designed to eliminate any continued storage of information in STM. After the interruption and after a brief delay involving recall and reactivation of relevant information stored in LTM, experts can resume activity without decrements in performance. Storage in LTM is further evidenced by experts' ability to recall relevant information about the task even when they are unexpectedly asked for recall after the task has been completed. The amount recalled is found to in-

crease as a function of the level of expert performance in chess (Charness, 1991).

The critical aspect of experts' working memory is not the amount of information stored per se but rather how the information is stored and indexed in LTM. In support of this claim, several cases have been reported in which nonexperts have been able to match the amount of domain-specific information recalled by experts, but without attaining the expert's sophisticated representation of the information. After 50 hours of training on memory for presented chess positions, a college student with minimal knowledge of chess was able to match the performance of chess masters (Ericsson & Harris, 1990). However, an analysis of how the chess position was encoded revealed that the trained subject focused on perceptually salient patterns in the periphery of the chessboard, whereas the chess master attended to the central aspects critical to the selection of the next moves (Ericsson & Harris, 1990). When told explicitly to memorize presented medical information, medical students match or even surpass medical experts (Patel & Groen, 1991; Schmidt & Boshuizen, 1993). However, the medical experts are more able than medical students to identify and recall the important pieces of presented information. Medical experts also encode more general clinical findings, which are sufficient for reasoning about the case but not specific enough to recall or reconstruct the detailed facts presented about the medical patient (Boshuizen & Schmidt, 1992; Groen & Patel, 1988).

Experts acquire skill in memory to meet specific demands of encoding and accessibility in specific activities in a given domain. For this reason their skill does not transfer from one domain to another. The demands for storage of intermediate products in mental calculation differ from the demands of blindfold chess, wherein the chess master must be able not simply to access the current position but also to plan and accurately select the best chess moves. The acquisition of memory skill in a domain is integrated with the acquisition of skill in organizing acquired knowledge and refining of procedures and strategies, and it allows experts to circumvent limits on working memory imposed by the limited capacity of STM.

## Perceptual–Motor Skill in Expert Performance

In many domains it is critical that experts respond not just accurately but also rapidly in dynamically changing situations. A skilled performer needs to be able to perceive and encode the current situation as well as to select and execute an action or a series of actions rapidly. In laboratory studies of skill acquisition, investigators have been able to demonstrate an increase in the speed of perceptual–motor reactions as a direct function of practice. With extensive amounts of practice, subjects are able to evoke automatically the correct reaction to familiar stimulus situations. This analysis of perceived situations and automatically evoked responses is central to our understanding of skilled performance, yet it seems to be insufficient to account for the speeds observed in many types of expert performance. The time it takes to respond to a stimulus even after extensive training is often between 0.5 and 1.0 seconds, which is too slow to account for a return of a hard tennis serve, a goalie's catching a hockey puck, and fluent motor activities in typing and music.

The standard paradigm in laboratory psychology relies on independent trials in which the occurrence of the presented stimulus, which the subject does not control, defines the beginning of a trial. In contrast, in the perceptual environment in everyday life, expert performance is continuous and changing, and experts must be able to recognize if and when a particular action is required. Most important, it is possible for the expert to analyze the current situation and thereby anticipate future events. Research on the return of a tennis serve shows that experts do not wait until they can see the ball approaching them. Instead they carefully study the action of the server's racquet and are able to predict approximately where in the service area the tennis ball will land even before the server has hit the ball. Abernethy (1991) has recently reviewed the critical role of anticipation in expert performance in many racquet sports. Similarly, expert typists are looking well ahead at the text they are typing in any particular instant. The difference between the text visually fixated and the letters typed in a given instant (eye-hand span) increases with the typists' typing speed. High-speed filming of the movements of expert typists' fingers shows that their fingers are simultaneously moved toward the relevant keys well ahead of when they are actually struck. The largest differences in speed between expert and novice typists are found for successive keystrokes made with fingers of different hands because the corresponding movements can overlap completely after extended typing practice. When the typing situation is artificially changed to eliminate looking ahead at the text to be typed, the speed advantage of expert typists is virtually eliminated (Salthouse, 1991a). Similar findings relating the amount of looking ahead and speed of performance apply to reading aloud (Levin & Addis, 1979) and sight-reading in music (Sloboda, 1985).

In summary, by successfully anticipating future events and skillfully coordinating overlapping movements, the expert performer is able to circumvent potential limits on basic elements of serial reactions.

## General Comments on the Structure of Expert Performance

Recent studies of expert performance have questioned the talent-based view that expert performance becomes increasingly dependent on unmodifiable innate components. Although these studies have revealed how beginners acquire complex cognitive structures and skills that circumvent the basic limits confronting them, researchers have not uncovered some simple strategies that would allow nonexperts to rapidly acquire expert performance, except in a few isolated case, such as the sexing of chickens (Biederman & Shiffrar, 1987). Analyses of exceptional performance, such as exceptional memory and absolute pitch, have shown how it differs from the performance of beginners and how beginners can acquire skill through instruction in the correct general strategy and corresponding training procedures (Howe, 1990). However, to attain exceptional levels of performance, subjects must in addition undergo a very long period of active learning, during which they refine and improve their skill, ideally under the supervision of a teacher or coach. In the following section we describe the particular activities (deliberate practice) that appear to be necessary to attain these improvements (Ericsson, Krampe, & Tesch-Römer, 1993).

By acquiring new methods and skills, expert performers are able to circumvent basic, most likely physiological, limits imposed on serial reactions and working memory. The traditional distinction between physiological (unmodifiable physical) and cognitive (modifiable mental) factors that influence performance does not seem valid in studies of expert performance. For the purposes of the typical one-hour experiment in psychology, changes in physiological factors might be negligible; but once we consider extended activities, physiological adaptations and changes are not just likely but virtually inevitable. Hence we also consider the possibility that most of the physiological attributes that distinguish experts are not innately determined characteristics but rather the results of extended, intense practice.

## Acquisition of Expert Performance

A relatively uncontroversial assertion is that attaining an expert level of performance in a domain requires mastery of all of the relevant knowledge and prerequisite skills. Our analysis has shown that the central mechanisms mediating the superior performance of experts are acquired; therefore acquisition of relevant knowledge and skills may be the major limiting factor in attaining expert performance. Some of the strongest evidence for this claim comes from a historical description of how domains of expertise evolved with increased specialization within each domain. To measure the duration of the acquisition process, we analyze the length of time it takes for the best individuals to attain the highest levels of performance within a domain. Finally we specify the type of practice that seems to be necessary to acquire expert performance in a domain.

## Evolution of Domains of Expertise and the Emergence of Specialization

Most domains of expertise today have a fairly long history of continued development. The knowledge in natural science and calculus that represented the cutting edge of mathematics a few centuries ago and that only the experts of that time were able to master is today taught in high school and college (Feldman, 1980). Many experts today are struggling to master the developments in a small subarea of one of the many natural sciences. Before the 20th century it was common for musicians to compose and play their own music; since then, distinct career patterns have emerged for composers, solo performers, accompanists, teachers, and conductors. When Tchaikovsky asked two of the greatest violinists of his day to play his violin concerto, they refused, deeming the score unplayable (Platt, 1966). Today, elite violinists consider the concerto part of their standard repertory. The improvement in music training has been so considerable that according to Roth (1982), the virtuoso Paganini "would indeed cut a sorry figure if placed upon the modern concert stage" (p. 23). Paganini's techniques and Tchaikovsky's concerto were deemed impossible until other musicians figured out how to master and describe them so that students could learn them as well. Almost 100 years ago the first Olympic Games were held, and results on standardized events were recorded. Since then records for events have been continuously broken and improved. For example, the winning time for the first Olympic Marathon is comparable to the current qualifying time for the Boston Marathon, attained by many thousands of amateur runners every year. Today amateur athletes cannot successfully compete with individuals training full time, and training methods for specific events are continuously refined by professional coaches and trainers.

In all major domains there has been a steady accumulation of knowledge about the domain and about the skills and techniques that mediate superior performance. This accumulated experience is documented and regularly updated in books, encyclopedias, and instructional material written by masters and professional teachers in the domain. During the last centuries the levels of performance have increased, in some domains dramatically so. To attain the highest level of performance possible in this decade, it is necessary both to specialize and to engage in the activity full time.

## Minimum Period of Attainment of Expert Performance

Another measure of the complexity of a domain is the length of time it takes an individual to master it and attain a very high level of performance or make outstanding achievements. Of particular interest is how fast the most "talented" or best performers can attain an international level of performance. In their classic study on chess, Simon and Chase (1973) argued that a 10-year period of intense preparation is necessary to reach the level of an international chess master and suggested similar requirements in other domains. In a review of subsequent research, Ericsson, Krampe, and Tesch-Römer (1993) showed that the 10-year rule is remarkably accurate, although there are at least some exceptions. However, even those exceptions, such as Bobby Fischer, who started playing chess very early and attained an international level at age 15, are only about a year shy of the 10-year requirement. Winning international competitions in sports, arts, and science appears to require at least 10 years of preparation and typically substantially longer. In the sciences and some of the arts, such

as literature, the necessary preparation overlaps so much with regular education that it is often difficult to determine a precise starting point. However, when the time interval between scientists' and authors' first accepted publication and their most valued publication is measured, it averages more than 10 years and implies an even longer preparation period (Raskin, 1936). Even for the most successful ("talented") individuals, the major domains of expertise are sufficiently complex that mastery of them requires approximately 10 years of essentially full-time preparation, which corresponds to several thousands of hours of practice.

## Practice Activities to Attain Expert Performance

In almost every domain, methods for instruction and efficient training have developed in parallel with the accumulation of relevant knowledge and techniques. For many sports and performance arts in particular, professional teachers and coaches monitor training programs tailored to the needs of individuals ranging from beginners to experts. The training activities are designed to improve specific aspects of performance through repetition and successive refinement. To receive maximal benefit from feedback, individuals have to monitor their training with full concentration, which is effortful and limits the duration of daily training. Ericsson, Krampe, and Tesch-Römer (1993) referred to individualized training on tasks selected by a qualified teacher as deliberate practice. They argued that the amount of this type of practice should be closely related to the level of acquired performance.

From surveys of the kinds of activities individuals engage in for the popular domains, such as tennis and golf, it is clear that the vast majority of active individuals spends very little if any time on deliberate practice. Once amateurs have attained an acceptable level of performance, their primary goal becomes inherent enjoyment of the activity, and most of their time is spent on playful interaction. The most enjoyable states of play are characterized as flow (Csikszentmihalyi, 1990), when the individual is absorbed in effortless engagement in a continuously changing situation. During play even individuals who desire to improve their performance do not encounter the same or similar situations on a frequent and predictable basis. For example, a tennis player wanting to improve a weakness, such as a backhand volley, might encounter a relevant situation only once per game. In contrast, a tennis coach would give that individual many hundreds of opportunities to improve and refine that type of shot during a training session.

Work, another type of activity, refers to public performances, competitions, and other performances motivated by external social and monetary rewards. Although work activities offer some opportunities for learning, they are far from optimal. In work activities, the goal is to generate a quality product reliably. In several domains, such as performance arts and sports, there is a clear distinction between training before a performance and the performance itself. During the performance itself, opportunities for learning and improvements are minimal, although the problems encountered can be addressed during training following the performance. Most occupations and professional domains pay individuals to generate efficiently services and products of consistently high quality. To give their best performance in work activities, individuals rely on previously well-entrenched methods rather than exploring new methods with unknown reliability. In summary, deliberate practice is an effortful activity motivated by the goal of improving performance. Unlike play, deliberate practice is not inherently motivating; and unlike work, it does not lead to immediate social and monetary rewards (Ericsson, Krampe, & Tesch-Römer, 1993).

Individualized training of students, who begin as very young children under the supervision of professional teachers and coaches, is a relatively recent trend in most major domains. It was only in 1756, for example, that Wolfgang Amadeus Mozart's father published the first book in German on teaching students to play the violin. Before organized education became the norm, people acquired skill through apprenticeship, working as adolescents with a skilled performer, frequently one of their parents. Recently there has been a lot of interest in this type of learning environment within the framework of situated cognition (Lave, 1988; Lave & Wenger, 1991). A significant element of apprenticeship is the imitation of skilled performers and careful study and copying of their work. In the arts the study and imitation of mas-

terpieces has a long history. For example, Benjamin Franklin (1788/1986) described in his autobiography how he tried to learn to write in a clear and logical fashion. He would read through a passage in a good book to understand it rather than memorize it and then try to reproduce its structure and content. Then he would compare his reproduction with the original to identify differences. By repeated application of this cycle of study, reproduction, and comparison with a well-structured original, Franklin argued that he acquired his skill in organizing thoughts for speaking and writing.

With the advent of audio and video recording, which have opened new possibilities for repeated study of master artists' performance, reproduction and comparison have been extended to allow individualized study and improvement of performance. This general method is central to achieving expert performance in chess. Advanced chess players spend as many as four hours a day studying published games between international chess masters (Forbes, 1992). The effective component of this type of study is predicting the chess master's next move without looking ahead. If the prediction is wrong, the advanced player examines the chess position more deeply to identify the reasons for the chess master's move. The activity of planning and extended evaluation of chess games is likely to improve a player's ability to internally represent chess positions, a memory skill that we discussed earlier in this article. This form of self-directed study has most of the characteristics of deliberate practice, but it is probably not as effective as individualized study guided by a skilled teacher. It is interesting to note that most of the recent world champions in chess were at one time tutored by chess masters (Ericsson, Krampe, & Tesch-Römer, 1993).

Deliberate practice differs from other domain-related activities because it provides optimal opportunities for learning and skill acquisition. If the regular activities in a domain did not offer accurate and preferably immediate feedback or opportunities for corrected repetitions, improvements in performance with further experience would not be expected from learning theory. Most amateurs and employees spend a very small amount of time on deliberate efforts to improve their performance, once it has reached an acceptable level. Under these conditions only weak relations between amount of experience and performance would be predicted, which is consistent with the empirical data. Recent research has explored the question whether deliberate practice can account for the attainment of elite performance levels and for individual differences among expert-level performers. According to the framework proposed by Ericsson, Krampe, and Tesch-Römer (1993), the primary mechanism creating expert-level performance in a domain is deliberate practice.

## Acquiring Elite Performance

Why do individuals even begin to engage in deliberate practice, when this activity is not inherently enjoyable? From many interviews, Bloom (1985) found that international-level performers in several domains start out as children by engaging in playful activities in the domain (see Phase 1 in Figure 45.3). After a period of playful and enjoyable experience they reveal "talent" or promise. At this point parents typically suggest that their children take lessons from a teacher and engage in limited amounts of deliberate practice. The parents help their children acquire regular habits of practice and teach them that this activity has instrumental value by noticing improvements in performance. The next phase (Bloom, 1985) is an extended period of preparation and ends with the individual's commitment to pursue activities in the domain on a full-time basis. During this period

the daily amounts of deliberate practice are increased, and more advanced teachers and training facilities are sought out. Occasionally parents even move to a different region of the country to provide their children with the best training environment. In the next phase, the individual makes a full-time commitment to improving performance. This phase ends when the individual either can make a living as a professional performer in the domain or terminates full-time engagement in the activity. Bloom (1985) found that during this phase nearly all of the individuals who ultimately reach an international level performance work with master teachers who either themselves had reached that level or had previously trained other individuals to that level. All through their development, international-level performers are provided with the best teachers for their current level of performance and engage in a great amount of deliberate practice.

The dilemma in most domains of expertise is that millions of young individuals enter these domains with aspirations to reach the highest levels of performance, but by definition only a very small number can succeed. Given the low probability of ultimate success, parents and coaches have been very much interested in identifying these select individuals as early as possible and giving them encouragement, support, and the best learning opportunities. The consistent failures to identify

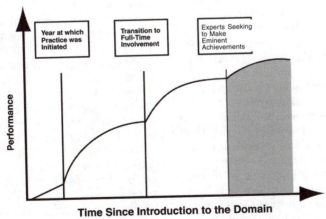

**FIGURE 45.3** ■ Three Phases of Development of Expert Performance Followed by a Qualitatively Different Phase of Efforts to Attain Eminent Achievements.
*Note.* From "Can We Create Gifted People?" by K. A. Ericsson, R. Th. Krompe, and S. Heizmann in *The Origins and Development of High Ability* (pp. 222–249), 1993, Chichester, England: Wiley. Copyright 1993 by Ciba Foundation. Adapted by permission.

specific "talents" in children is not surprising when one considers the qualitative changes occurring during the long period of development. In many domains international performers start practice at age 4 to 6, when it is unclear what kind of objective evidence of talent and promise they could possibly display. Available descriptions suggest that children this young display interest and motivation to practice rather than exceptional performance. Once deliberate practice has begun, the primary measure of acquired skill and talent is the current level of performance compared with that of other children of comparable ages in the neighborhood. Only later at age 10 to 12 do the children typically start participating in competitions, where their performance is compared with that of other successful children from a larger geographical area. As performance level and age increase, the criteria for evaluating performance also change. In the arts and sciences, technical proficiency is no longer enough, and adult criteria of abstract understanding and artistic expression are applied.

During the first three phases of development, individuals master the knowledge and skills that master teachers and coaches know how to convey. To achieve the highest level (eminent performance), individuals must enter a fourth phase, going beyond the available knowledge in the domain to produce a unique contribution to the domain. Eminent scientists make major discoveries and propose new theories that permanently change the concepts and knowledge in the domain. Similarly eminent artists generate new techniques and interpretations that extend the boundaries for future art. The process of generating innovations differs from the acquisition of expertise and mastery. Major innovations by definition go beyond anything even the master teachers know and could possibly teach. Furthermore, innovations are rare, and it is unusual that eminent individuals make more than a single major innovation during their entire lives. Unlike consistently superior expert performance, innovation occurs so infrequently and unpredictably that the likelihood of its ever being captured in the laboratory is small. However, it is still possible through retrospective analysis of concurrent records, such as notebooks and diaries (Gruber, 1981; D. B. Wallace & Gruber, 1989), to reconstruct the processes leading up to major discoveries. Once the context of a particular discovery has been identified, it is possible to

reconstruct the situation and study how other naive subjects with the necessary knowledge can uncover the original discovery (Qin & Simon, 1990). Let us now turn back to expert performance, which we consider both reproducible and instructable.

## Individual Differences in Expert Performance

Biographies of international-level performers indicate that a long period of intense, supervised practice preceded their achievements. The simple assumption that these levels of deliberate practice are necessary accounts for the fact that the vast majority of active individuals who prematurely stop practicing never reach the highest levels of performance. However, in most major domains a relatively large number of individuals continue deliberate practice and thus meet the criterion of necessity. Within this group striking individual differences in adult performance nonetheless remain.

Ericsson, Krampe, and Tesch-Römer (1993) hypothesized that differences in the amount of deliberate practice could account for even the individual differences among the select group of people who continue a regimen of deliberate practice. The main assumption, which they called the *monotonic benefits assumption*, is that individuals' performances are a monotonic function of the amount of deliberate practice accumulated since these individuals began deliberate practice in a domain. The accumulated amount of deliberate practice and the level of performance an individual achieves at a given age is thus a function of the starting age for practice and the weekly amount of practice during the intervening years. This function is illustrated in Figure 45.4. The second curve has been simply moved horizontally to reflect a later starting age, and the third curve reflects in addition a lower weekly rate of practice.

To evaluate these predictions empirically, it is necessary to measure the amount of time individuals spend on various activities, in particular deliberate practice. One way of doing so, which is to have them keep detailed diaries, has a fairly long tradition in studies of time budgeting in sociology (Juster & Stafford, 1985). In most domains with teachers and coaches, deliberate practice is regularly scheduled on a daily basis, and advanced performers can accurately estimate their current and

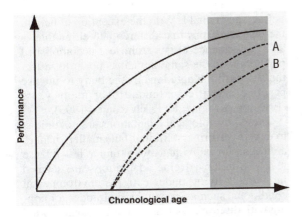

**FIGURE 45.4** ■ Relations between Age and Performance. *Note.* Late period involving selection to the best music academies has been shaded. Solid line: performance associated with early starting age and high level of practice. Dashed line A: performance for equally high level of practice but later starting age. Dashed line B: performance associated with the same late starting age but lower level of practice. The slope of the dashed line appears steeper than that of the solid line. However, the horizontal distance between these two curves is constant. From "Can We Create Gifted People?" by K. A. Ericsson, R. Th. Krampe, and S. Heizmann in *The Origins and Development of High Ability* (pp. 222–249), 1993, Chichester, England: Wiley. Copyright 1993 by Ciba Foundation. Adapted by permission.

past amounts of practice as well as their starting ages and other characteristics of their practice history.

In a comprehensive review of studies comparing starting ages and amount of weekly practice for international, national, and regional-level performers in many different domains, Ericsson, Krampe, and Tesch-Römer (1993) found that performers who reached higher levels tended to start practicing as many as from two to five years earlier than did less accomplished performers. Individuals who attained higher levels of performance often spent more time on deliberate practice than did less accomplished individuals, even when there was no difference in the total time both groups spent on domain-related activities. Differences in the amount of deliberate practice accumulated during their development differentiated groups of expert performers at various current levels of performance. The three graphs in Figure 45.4 illustrate how simple differences in starting ages and weekly amounts of practice can yield very stable differences in amounts of training and performance levels.

Everyone recognizes that maturational factors affect performance. For this reason competitions are nearly always structured by groups of contestants with the same ages. By the time individuals approach their middle to late teens (the shaded area in Figure 45.4) and are applying for scholarships and admission to the studios of master teachers and the best training environments, large differences in past practice and acquired skill are already present. Ericsson, Krampe, and Tesch-Römer (1993) found that by age 20, the top-level violinists in their study had practiced an average of more than 10,000 hours, approximately 2,500 hours more than the next most accomplished group of expert violinists and 5,000 hours more than the group who performed at the lowest expert level.

In summary, evidence from a wide range of domains shows that the top-level experts have spent a very large amount of time improving their performance and that the total amount accumulated during development is several years of additional full-time practice more than that of other less accomplished performers. This difference is roughly equivalent to the difference between freshmen and seniors in a highly competitive college. In these environments, where the best opportunities for further development are offered only to the individuals with the best current performance, it may be difficult for individuals with less prior practice and lower levels of performance even to secure situations in which they can practice full time. It is virtually impossible for them to catch up with the best performers because those performers maintain their lead through continuous practice at optimal levels.

## Structure of Practice in the Daily Lives of Elite Performers

From analyses of diaries and other sources of biographical material, Ericsson, Krampe, and Tesch-Römer (1993) concluded that expert performers design their lives to optimize their engagement in deliberate practice. Expert musicians in their study spent approximately four hours a day—every day including weekends—on deliberate practice. Practice sessions were approximately one hour long, followed by a period of rest. Performers practiced most frequently during the morning, when independent research indicates that individuals have the highest capacity for complex, demanding activity during the day (Folkard & Monk, 1985). All the expert musicians reported on the importance of sleep and rest in maintaining their high levels of daily practice. The expert musicians in the two best groups, who practiced longer each day, slept more than those in the least accomplished group and also slept more than other reference groups of subjects of comparable age. The additional sleep was primarily from an afternoon nap. Expert subjects maximize the amount of time they can spend on deliberate practice when they can fully focus on their training goals without fatigue. Many master teachers and coaches consider practice while fatigued and unfocused not only wasteful but even harmful to sustained improvements.

Focused, effortful practice of limited duration has been found to be important in a wide range of domains of expertise. Interestingly the estimated amount of deliberate practice that individuals can sustain for extended periods of time does not seem to vary across domains and is close to four hours a day (Ericsson, Krampe, & Tesch-Römer, 1993).

The effort and intensity of deliberate practice is most readily observable for perceptual-motor behavior in sports and performance arts. One goal of most of the practice activities is to push the limits of performance to higher levels by, for example, stretching in ballet, or repeated maximal efforts until exhaustion during interval training in running and weight lifting. It is well-known that intense exercise increases endurance and the size of muscles. However, recent research in sports physiology has shown that anatomical changes in response to extended intense exercise are more far-reaching than commonly believed. Within a few weeks of vigorous training, the number of capillaries supplying blood to the trained muscles increases. Longitudinal studies show that after years of "elite-level" endurance training, the heart adapts and increases in size to values outside the normal range for healthy adults. The metabolism and general characteristics of muscle fibers also change— from slow-twitch to fast-twitch or vice versa. Most interestingly these changes are limited only to those muscles that are trained and critical to the particular sports event for which the athlete is preparing. Many of these changes appear to increase when practice overlaps with the body's development during childhood and adolescence. For example the flexibility required for elite performance in ballet requires that dancers begin practicing

before age 10 or 11. With the exception of height, the characteristics that differentiate elite athletes and performance artists from less accomplished performers in the same domains appear to reflect the successful adaptations of the body to intense practice activities extended over many years (Ericsson, Krampe, & Tesch-Römer, 1993).

These physiological adaptations are not unique to expert performers. Similar but smaller changes are found for individuals who train at less intense levels. Similar extreme adaptations are seen in individuals living under extreme environmental conditions, such as at very high altitudes, or coping with diseases, such as partial blockages of the blood supply to the heart. Many occupation-specific problems that expert performers experience in middle age also seem to result from related types of (mal)adaptive processes.

It is becoming increasingly clear that maximizing the intensity and duration of training is not necessarily good. Expert performers have a constant problem with avoiding strains and injuries and allowing the body enough time to adapt and recuperate. Even in the absence of physical injuries, an increasing number of athletes and musicians overtrain and do not allow themselves enough rest to maintain a stable equilibrium from day to day. Sustained overtraining leads to burnout, for which the only known remedy is to terminate practice completely for long periods. It appears that top-level adult experts practice at the highest possible level that can be sustained for extended periods without burnout or injury. Hence, it may be extremely difficult to consistently practice harder and improve faster than these individuals already do.

## Expert Performance from a Life Span Perspective

Elite performers in most domains are engaged essentially full time from childhood and adolescence to late adulthood. The study of expert performers therefore offers a unique perspective on life span development and especially on the effects of aging. Many studies have examined the performance of experts as a function of age or of the ages when experts attained their best performance or their highest achievement. It is extremely rare for performers to attain their best performance before reaching adulthood, but it is not necessarily the case that performance continues to improve in those who keep exercising their skills across the life span. Rather, a peak age for performance seems to fall in the 20s, 30s, and 40s, as Lehman (1953) first noted. The age distributions for peak performance in vigorous sports are remarkably narrow and centered in the 20s with systematic differences between different types of sports (Schulz & Curnow, 1988). In vigorous sports it is rare for elite athletes above age 30 to reach their personal best or even in many cases remain competitive with younger colleagues. Although less pronounced, similar age distributions centered somewhere in the 30s are found for fine motor skills and even predominantly cognitive activities, such as chess, science, and the arts. Simonton (1988a) has argued that the relative decline with age may be slight and may be attributable to the fact that total creative output for artists and scientists declines, al-

though the probability of achieving an outstanding performance remains constant. Thus the frequency of producing an outstanding work declines with age. Perhaps the best evidence for decline with age is Elo's (1965) analysis of the careers of grand master chess players. As seen in Figure 45.5 (from Charness & Bosman, 1990), there is a peak for chess players in their 30s, although performance at 63 years of age is no worse than that at 21 years. The peak age for creative achievement differs considerably between domains. In pure mathematics, theoretical physics, and lyric poetry, the peak ages for contributions occur in the late 20s and early 30s. In novel writing, history, and philosophy, the peaks are less pronounced and occur in the 40s and early 50s (Simonton, 1988a). Even within domains the peak age for performance seems to vary systematically with the types of demands placed on the performer. In international-

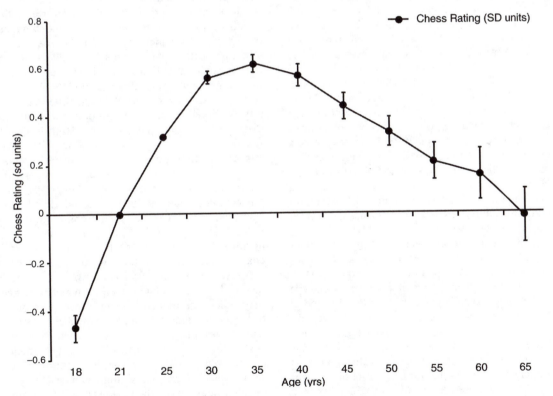

**FIGURE 45.5** ■ Grand Master Performance by Age.
*Note.* Chess ratings scaled in standard deviation units, with performance at age 21 for each individual set to zero (data from Elo, 1965). Averaged scores across grand masters shown with standard error bars. From "Expertise and Aging: Life in the Lab" (p. 358) by N. Charness and E. A. Bosman in *Aging and Cognition: Knowledge Organization and Utilization*, T. H. Hess (Ed.), 1990, Amsterdam. Elsevier. Copyright 1990 by Elsevier. Adapted by permission.

level tournament chess, individuals typically play chess games for four to five hours daily for more than a week. Furthermore, tournament chess makes strong demands on working memory and, to some extent, on speed of processing, when players attempt to choose the best move by searching through the problem space of possible moves. On average, a tournament chess player has approximately three minutes to consider each move (when normal time controls are used). In "postal chess," players have several days to make a move. Because deliberation times are longer and the players can use external memory to maintain the results of analysis, ascension to the world postal chess championship occurs much later, near 46 years of age as compared with 30 years of age for tournament chess (Charness & Bosman, 1990).

To researchers on aging, the decline in expert performance in old age, which in many domains is often relatively slight, is less interesting than expert performers' ability to maintain a very high level of performance during ages when beginners and less accomplished performers display clear effects of aging. A common hypothesis related to the notion of innate talent is that experts generally age more slowly than other performers, and thus no observable impairments would be expected. However, this hypothesis is not consistent with recent research on expert performance in chess (Charness, 1981b), typing (Bosman, 1993; Salthouse, 1984), and music (Krampe, 1994). The superior performance of older experts is found to be restricted to relevant tasks in their domains of expertise. For unrelated psychometric tasks and some tasks related to occupational activities, normal age-related decline is observed (Salthouse, 1991b).

The mediating mechanisms in younger and older experts' performance have been examined in laboratory studies developed under the expert performance approach. in typing, older experts who type at the same speed as younger experts are found to have larger eye-hand spans that permit older experts to compensate through advance preparation (Bosman, 1993; Salthouse, 1984). Older chess experts' ability to select the best chess move is associated with less planning than that of younger experts at an equivalent skill level. This suggests that older chess experts compensate through more extensive knowledge of chess (Charness, 1981a). Comparisons of older and younger expert pianists' ability to perform simple and complex sequences of key strokes requiring bimanual coordination reveal no or small differences, whereas the same comparisons between older and younger amateur pianists reveal clear decrements with age that increase with the complexity of the tasks (Krampe, 1994). Such age effects require greater diversity in the models proposed to explain expertise. It is now evident that at least in typing and chess, two individuals at the same level of skill can achieve their performance through mechanisms with different structure. Although it is convenient to collapse a measure of expertise onto a unidimensional scale (such as chess rating or net words per minute for typing), this is an oversimplification that may obscure individual differences in the underlying processes that mediate same level-performance.

## The Role of Deliberate Practice

In the previous sections we described the evidence for the necessity of deliberate practice for initially acquiring expert performance. The maintenance of expert performance could be due to the unique structure of the mechanisms acquired in expert performance or to a level of deliberate practice maintained during adulthood or both.

The most marked age-related decline is generally observed in perceptual-motor performance displayed in many types of sports. High levels of practice are necessary to attain the physiological adaptations that are found in expert performers, and the effects of practice appear to be particularly large when intense practice overlaps with physical development during childhood and adolescence. Most of these adaptations require that practice is maintained; if not, the changes revert to normal values, although for some anatomical changes many years of no practice appear necessary before the reversion is completed. Hence, much of the age-related decline in performance may reflect the reduction or termination of practice. Studies of master athletes show that older athletes do not practice at the same intensity as the best young athletes. When older master athletes are compared with young athletes training at a similar level, many physiological measurements do not differ between them. However, at least some physiological functions, such as maximal heart rate, show an age-related decline independent of past or current practice. In summary, the ability to retain superior performance in sports appears to depend critically on maintaining practice during adulthood (Ericsson, 1990).

Evidence on the role of early and maintained practice in retaining cognitive aspects of expertise is much less extensive. Takeuchi and Hulse's (1993) recent review of absolute (perfect) pitch shows that children can easily acquire this ability at around the ages of three to five. Acquisition of the same ability during adulthood is very difficult and time consuming. Some other abilities, such as the acquisition of second languages (especially accents and pronunciation), appear easier to acquire at young rather than adult ages. Whether early acquisition of abilities, per se, translates into better retention into old age is currently not known.

Virtually by definition expert performers remain highly active in their domains of expertise. With increasing age, they typically reduce their intensive work schedules, a change in life style that is consistent with the decrease observed in their productivity (Simonton, 1988a). Roe (1953) found that eminent scientists reduce their level of work during evenings and weekends. Information about the distribution of time among different types of activities and especially the amount of time spent on maintaining and improving performance is essentially lacking. However, Krampe (1994) collected both diaries and retrospective estimates of past practice for older expert pianists. Consistent with the lack of performance differences between younger and older pianists in tasks relevant to piano playing, Krampe found that the older experts still practiced approximately 10 hours a week and spent more than 40 additional hours a week on other music-related activities. In addition he found that individual differences in performance among older pianists could be predicted well by the amount of practice during the past 10 years. Whether a reduction in practice by older chess players and typists accounts for the differences between younger and older experts in these fields cannot currently be answered, given the lack of longitudinal data on performance and practice.

The study of expert performance over the life span of the performers is needed. This perspective is quite likely to provide new insights into the plasticity of the structure of human performance as a function of different developmental phases. Through investigation of focused sustained practice, it may be possible to determine which aspects can and, at least with the current training methods, cannot be modified to enhance current and future performance. Of particular practical and theoretical interest are those factors that enable experts to retain and maintain superior performance into old age.

## Summary and Conclusion

The differences in performance between experts and beginners are the largest that have been reliably reproduced with healthy, normal adults under controlled test conditions. From the life-long efforts of expert performers who continuously strive to improve and reach their best performance, one can infer that expert performance represents the highest performance possible, given current knowledge and training methods in the domain. Individuals' acquisition of expert performance is thus a naturally occurring experiment for identifying the limits of human performance. It is hard to imagine better empirical evidence on maximal performance except for one critical flaw. As children, future international-level performers are not randomly assigned to their training condition. Hence one cannot rule out the possibility that there is something different about those individuals who ultimately reach expert-level performance.

Nevertheless the traditional view of talent, which concludes that successful individuals have special innate abilities and basic capacities, is not consistent with the reviewed evidence. Efforts to specify and measure characteristics of talent that allow early identification and successful prediction of adult performance have failed. Differences between expert and less accomplished performers reflect acquired knowledge and skills or physiological adaptations effected by training, with the only confirmed exception being height.

More plausible loci of individual differences are factors that predispose individuals toward engaging in deliberate practice and enable them to sustain high levels of practice for many years. Differences in these factors clearly have, in part, an environmental origin and can be modified as the level of practice is slowly increased with further experience. However, some of these factors, such as preferred activity level and temperament, may have a large genetic component. Furthermore, there may need to be a good fit between such predisposing factors and the task environment (along the lines of Thomas & Chess's, 1984, temperament-environment fit model) for expert-level performance to develop.

For a long time the study of exceptional and expert performance has been considered outside the scope of general psychology because such performance has been attributed to innate characteristics possessed by outstanding individuals. A better explanation is that expert performance reflects extreme adaptations, accomplished through life-long effort, to demands in restricted, well-defined domains. By capturing and examining the performance of experts in a given domain, researchers have identified adaptive changes with physiological components as well as the acquisition of domain-specific skills that circumvent basic limits on speed and memory. Experts with different teachers and training histories attain their superior performance after many years of continued effort by acquiring skills and making adaptations with the same general structure. These findings imply that in each domain, there is only a limited number of ways in which individuals can make large improvements in performance. When mediating mechanisms of the same type are found in experts in very different domains that have evolved independently from each other, an account of this structure based on shared training methods is highly unlikely.

There is no reason to believe that changes in the structure of human performance and skill are restricted to the traditional domains of expertise. Similar changes should be expected in many everyday activities, such as thinking, comprehension, and problem solving, studied in general psychology. However, people acquire everyday skills under less structured conditions that lack strict and generalizable criteria for evaluation. These conditions also vary among individuals because of their specific living situations. In contrast, stable expert performance is typically restricted to standardized situations in a domain. Hence, the criteria for expert performance offer a shared goal for individuals in a domain that directs and constrains their life-long efforts to attain their maximal performance. Even when scientific investigators' ultimate goal is to describe and understand everyday skills, they are more likely to succeed by studying expert performance than by examining everyday skills because the former is acquired under much more controlled and better understood conditions

and achieved at higher levels of proficiency in a specific domain.

We believe that studies of the acquisition and structure of expert performance offer unique evidence on many general theoretical and applied issues in psychology. Extended deliberate practice gives near maximal values on the possible effects of environmental variables (in interaction with developmental variables) relevant to theoretical claims for invariant cognitive capacities and general laws of performance. We will significantly advance our knowledge of the interaction between environment and development by observing the effects of training during the early development of expert performers and the effects of maintaining training for older experts in late adulthood. The study of expert performance complements cross-cultural studies of environmental influences on thinking and cognition. The relation between language and thinking, traditionally restricted to comparisons between different languages (Hunt & Agnoli, 1991), should be particularly suitable for study in the context of expertise, where domain-specific names, concepts, and knowledge are explicated in training manuals and books and subjects with differing levels of mastery of the vocabulary and where "language" of the domain can be easily found.

For applied psychologists the study of expert performers and their master teachers and coaches offers a nearly untapped reservoir of knowledge about optimal training and specific training methods that has been accumulated in many domains for a long time. Across very different domains of expert performance, Ericsson, Krampe, and Tesch-Römer (1993) uncovered evidence for intriguing invariances in the duration and daily scheduling of practice activities. Further efforts to investigate training and development of training methods and to derive principles that generalize across domains should be particularly fruitful. Most important, a better understanding of social and other factors that motivate and sustain future expert performers at an optimal level of deliberate practice should have direct relevance to motivational problems in education, especially in our school system.

In conclusion, an analysis of the acquired characteristics and skills of expert performers as well as their developmental history and training methods will provide us with general insights into the structure and limits of human adaptations.

## ACKNOWLEDGMENTS

Lyle E. Bourne served as action editor for this article.

K. Anders Ericsson, Department of Psychology, Florida State University; Neil Charness, Department of Psychology, University of Waterloo, Waterloo, Ontario, Canada (now at Department of Psychology, Florida State University).

We wish to thank Janet Grassia, Andreas Lehmann, William Oliver, and Michael Rashotte for their valuable comments on drafts of this article.

## NOTES

1. The field of visual art may offer at least one recent exception (Feldman, 1986). The Chinese girl Yani produced some acclaimed paintings between the ages of three and six (Ho, 1989), but matters are complicated by the fact that these paintings were selected by her father (a professional painter) from more than 4,000 paintings completed by Yani during this three-year period (Feng, 1984).

2. In his recent book *Creating Minds*, Gardner (1993a) examined the lives of seven great innovators, such as Einstein, Picasso, Stravinsky, and Gandhi. Each was selected to exemplify outstanding achievements in one of seven different intelligences. Gardner's careful analysis reveals that the achievements of each individual required a long period of intense preparation and required the coincidence of many environmental factors. Striking evidence for traditional talent, such as prodigious achievements as a child, is notably absent, with the exception of Picasso. The best evidence for talent, according to Gardner, is their rapid progress once they made a commitment to a particular domain of expertise. These findings are not inconsistent with Gardner's views on talent because innovation and creation of new ideas are fundamentally different from high achievements in a domain due to talent. Gardner wrote, "in the case of a universally acclaimed prodigy, the prodigy's talents mesh perfectly with current structure of the domain and the current tastes of the field. Creativity, however, does not result from such perfect meshes" (pp. 40–41).

## REFERENCES

Abernethy, B. (1991). Visual search strategies and decision-making in sport. *International Journal of Sport Psychology*, 22, 189–210.

Barlow, F. (1952). *Mental prodigies*. New York: Greenwood Press.

Barolsky, P. (1991). *Why Mona Lisa smiles and other tales by Vasari*. University Park: Pennsylvania State University Press.

Barolsky, P. (1992). *Giotto's father and the family of Vasari's Lives*. University Park: Pennsylvania State University Press.

Barr, A., & Feigenbaum, E. A. (Eds.). (1981–1982). *The handbook of artificial intelligence* (Vols. 1–2). Stanford, CA: HeurisTech Press.

Bate, J. (1989). Shakespeare and original genius. In P. Murray (Ed.), *Genius: The history of an idea* (pp. 76–97). Oxford, England: Basil Blackwell.

Biederman, I., & Shiffrar, M. M. (1987). Sexing day-old chicks: A case study and expert systems analysis of a difficult perceptual-learning task. *Journal of Experimental Psychology: Learning, Memory, and Cognition*, 13, 640–645.

Binet, A. (1894). *Psychologie des grands calculateurs et joueurs d'echecs* [Psychology of great mental calculators and chess players]. Paris: Libraire Hachette.

Bloom, B. S. (1985). Generalizations about talent development. In B. S. Bloom (Ed.), *Developing talent in young people* (pp. 507–549). New York: Ballantine Books.

Boase, T. S. R. (1979). *Giorgio Vasari: The man and the book*. Princeton, NJ: Princeton University Press.

Boshuizen, H. P. A., & Schmidt, H. G. (1992). On the role of biomedical knowledge in clinical reasoning by experts, intermediates and novices. *Cognitive Science*, 16, 153–184.

Bosman, E. A. (1993). Age-related differences in motoric aspects of transcription typing skill. *Psychology and Aging*, 8, 87–102.

Browne, M. A., & Mahoney, M. J. (1984). Sport psychology. *Annual Review of Psychology*, 35, 605–625.

Bull, G. (1987). *A translation of Giorgio Vasari's lives of the artists* (2 vols.). New York: Viking Penguin.

Camerer, C. F., & Johnson, E. J. (1991). The process-performance paradox in expert judgment: How can the experts know so much and predict so badly? In K. A. Ericsson & J. Smith (Eds.), *Toward a general theory of expertise: Prospects and limits* (pp. 195–217). Cambridge, England: Cambridge University Press.

Charness, N. (1981a). Search in chess: Age and skill differences. *Journal of Experimental Psychology: Human Perception and Performance*, 7, 467–476.

Charness, N. (1981b). Visual short-term memory and aging in chess players. *Journal of Gerontology*, 36, 615–619.

Charness, N. (1989). Expertise in chess and bridge. In D. Klahr & K. Kotovsky (Eds.), *Complex information processing: The impact of Herbert A. Simon* (pp. 183–208). Hillsdale, NJ: Erlbaum.

Charness, N. (1991). Expertise in chess: The balance between knowledge and search. In K. A. Ericsson & J. Smith (Eds.), *Toward a general theory of expertise: Prospects and limits* (pp. 39–63). Cambridge, England: Cambridge University Press.

Charness, N., & Bosman, E. A. (1990). Expertise and aging: Life in the lab. In T. H. Hess (Ed.), *Aging and cognition: Knowledge organization and utilization* (pp. 343–385). Amsterdam: Elsevier.

Charness, N., Clifton, J., & MacDonald, L. (1988). Case study of a musical mono-savant. In L. K. Obler & D. A. Fein (Eds.), *The exceptional brain: Neuropsychology of talent and special abilities* (pp. 277–293). New York: Guilford Press.

Chase, W. G., & Ericsson, K. A. (1982). Skill and working memory. In G. H. Bower (Ed.), *The psychology of learning and motivation* (Vol. 16, pp. 1–58). New York: Academic Press.

Chase, W. G., & Simon, H. A. (1973). The mind's eye in chess. In W. G. Chase (Ed.), *Visual information processing* (pp. 215–281). New York: Academic Press.

Chi, M. T. H., Glaser, R., & Farr, M. J. (Eds.). (1988). *The nature of expertise*. Hillsdale, NJ: Erlbaum.

Cohen, P. R., & Feigenbaum, E. A. (Eds.). (1982). *The handbook of artificial intelligence* (Vol. 3). Stanford, CA: HeurisTech Press.

Csikszentmihalyi, M. (1990). *Flow: The psychology of optimal experience*. New York: Harper & Row.

de Groot, A. (1978). *Thought and choice and chess*. The Hague, The Netherlands: Mouton. (Original work published 1946.)

Doll, J., & Mayr, U. (1987). Intelligenz und Schachleistung— Eine Untersuchung an Schachexperten [Intelligence and achievement in chess: A study of chess masters]. *Psychologische Beiträge, 29*, 270–289.

Elo, A. E. (1965). Age changes in master chess performances. *Journal of Gerontology, 20*, 289–299.

Elo, A. E. (1986). *The rating of chessplayers, past and present* (2nd ed.). New York: Arco.

Ericsson, K. A. (1985). Memory skill. *Canadian Journal of Psychology, 39*(2), 188–231.

Ericsson, K. A. (1988). Analysis of memory performance in terms of memory skill. In R. J. Sternberg (Ed.), *Advances in the psychology of human intelligence* (Vol. 4, pp. 137–179). Hillsdale, NJ: Erlbaum.

Ericsson, K. A. (1990). Peak performance and age: An examination of peak performance in sports. P. B. Baltes & M. M. Baltes (Eds.), *Successful aging: Perspectives from the behavioral sciences* (pp. 164–195). New York: Cambridge University Press.

Ericsson, K. A., & Chase, W. G. (1982). Exceptional memory. *American Scientist, 70*, 607–615.

Ericsson, K. A., & Faivre, I. A. (1988). What's exceptional about exceptional abilities? In I. K. Obler & D. Fein (Eds.), *The exceptional brain: Neuropsychology of talent and special abilities* (pp. 436–473). New York: Guilford Press.

Ericsson, K. A., & Harris, M. S. (1990, November). *Expert chess memory without chess knowledge: A training study.* Poster presented at the 31st Annual Meeting of the Psychonomic Society, New Orleans, LA.

Ericsson, K. A., & Kintsch, W. (1994). *Long-term working memory* (ICS Tech. Report No. 94–01). Boulder: University of Colorado, Institute of Cognitive Science.

Ericsson, K. A., Krampe, R. Th., & Heizmann, S. (1993). Can we create gifted people? In CIBA Foundation Symposium 178, *The origins and development of high ability* (pp. 222–249). Chichester, England: Wiley.

Ericsson, K. A., Krampe, R. Th., & Tesch-Römer, C. (1993). The role of deliberate practice in the acquisition of expert performance. *Psychological Review, 100*, 363–406.

Ericsson, K. A., & Simon, H. A. (1993). *Protocol analysis: Verbal reports as data* (rev. ed.). Cambridge, MA: MIT Press.

Ericsson, K. A., & Smith, J. (1991a). Prospects and limits of the empirical study of expertise: An introduction. In K. A. Ericsson & J. Smith (Eds.), *Toward a general theory of expertise: Prospects and limits* (pp. 1–39). Cambridge, England: Cambridge University Press.

Ericsson, K. A., & Smith, J. (Eds.). (1991b). *Toward a general theory of expertise: Prospects and limits*. Cambridge, England: Cambridge University Press.

Ericsson, K. A., & Staszewski, J. (1989). Skilled memory and expertise: Mechanisms of exceptional performance. In D. Klahr & K. Kotovsky (Eds.), *Complex information processing: The impact of Herbert A. Simon* (pp. 235–267). Hillsdale, NJ: Erlbaum.

Feldman, D. H. (1980). *Beyond universals in cognitive development*. Norwood, NJ: Ablex.

Feldman, D. H. (1986). *Nature's gambit: Child prodigies and the development of human potential*. New York: Basic Books.

Feng, J. (1984). Foreword. In L. Shufen & J. Cheng'an (Eds.), *Yani's monkeys* (pp. 1–2). Beijing, China: Foreign Languages Press.

Folkard, S., & Monk, T. H. (1985). Circadian performance rhythms. In S. Folkard & T. H. Monk (Eds.), *Hours of work* (pp. 37–52). Chichester, England: Wiley.

Forbes, C. (1992). *The Polgar sisters: Training or genius?* New York: Henry Holt.

Franklin, B. (1986). *The autobiography and other writings*. New York: Penguin Books. (Autobiography originally published 1788)

Galton, F. (1979). *Hereditary genius: An inquiry into its laws and consequences*. London: Julian Friedman. (Original work published 1869.)

Galton, F. (1908). *Memories of my life*. London: Methuen.

Gardner, H. (1973). *The arts and human development*. New York: Wiley.

Gardner, H. (1983). *Frames of mind: The theory of multiple intelligences*. New York: Basic Books.

Gardner, H. (1993a). *Creating minds*. New York: Basic Books.

Gardner, H. (1993b). *Multiple intelligences: The theory in practice*. New York: Basic Books.

Groen, G. J., & Patel, V. L. (1988). The relationship between comprehension and reasoning in medical expertise. In M. T. H. Chi, R. Glaser, & M. J. Farr (Eds.), *The nature of expertise* (pp. 287–310). Hillsdale, NJ: Erlbaum.

Gruber, H. E. (1981). *Darwin on man: A psychological study of scientific creativity* (2nd ed.). Chicago: University of Chicago Press.

Ho, W.-C. (Ed.). (1989). *Yani: The brush of innocence*. New York: Hudson Hills.

Hoffman, R. R. (Ed.). (1992). *The psychology of expertise: Cognitive research and empirical AI*. New York: Springer-Verlag.

Howe, M. J. A. (1990). *The origins of exceptional abilities*. Oxford, England: Basil Blackwell.

Hulin, C. L., Henry, R. A., & Noon, S. L. (1990). Adding a dimension: Time as a factor in the generalizability of predictive relationships. *Psychological Bulletin, 107*, 328–340.

Hunt, E., & Agnoli, F. (1991). The Whorfian hypothesis: A cognitive psychology perspective. *Psychological Review, 98*, 377–389.

Juster, F. T., & Stafford, F. P. (Eds.). (1985). *Time, goods and well-being*. Ann Arbor: University of Michigan, Institute for Social Research.

Krampe, R. Th. (1994). *Maintaining excellence: Cognitive-motor performance in pianists differing in age and skill level*. Berlin, Germany: Edition Sigma.

Larkin, J. H., McDermott, J., Simon, D. P., & Simon, H. A. (1980). Models of competence in solving physics problems. *Cognitive Science, 4*, 317–345.

Lave, J. (1988). *Cognition in practice*. Cambridge, England: Cambridge University Press.

Lave, J., & Wenger, E. (1991). *Situated learning: Legitimate peripheral participation*. Cambridge, England: Cambridge University Press.

Lehman, H. C. (1953). *Age and achievement*. Princeton, NJ: Princeton University Press.

Levin, H., & Addis, A. B. (1979). *The eye-voice span*. Cambridge, MA: MIT Press.

Luria, A. R. (1968). *The mind of a mnemonist*. New York: Avon.

Malina, R. M., & Bouchard, C. (1991). *Growth, maturity, and physical activity*. Champaign, IL: Human Kinetics.

Maslow, A. H. (1971). *The farther reaches of human nature*. New York: Viking.

Miller, G. A. (1956). The magical number seven, plus or minus two: Some limits on our capacity for processing information. *Psychological Review, 63*, 81–97.

Murray, P. (Ed.). (1989a). *Genius: The history of an idea*. Oxford, England: Basil Blackwell.

Murray, P. (1989b). Poetic genius and its classic origins. In P. Murray (Ed.), *Genius: The history of an idea* (pp. 9–31). Oxford, England: Basil Blackwell.

Newell, A., & Simon, H. A. (1972). *Human problem solving*. Englewood Cliffs, NJ: Prentice-Hall.

Pariser, D. (1987). The juvenile drawings of Klee, Toulouse-Lautrec and Picasso. *Visual Arts Research, 13*, 53–67.

Patel, V. L., & Groen, G. J. (1991). The general and specific nature of medical expertise: A critical look. In K. A. Ericsson & J. Smith (Eds.), *Toward a general theory of expertise* (pp. 93–125). Cambridge, England: Cambridge University Press.

Platt, R. (1966). General introduction. In J. E. Meade & A. S. Parkes (Eds.), *Genetic and environmental factors in human ability* (pp. ix–xi). Edinburgh, Scotland: Oliver & Boyd.

Qin, Y., & Simon, H. A. (1990). Laboratory replication of scientific discovery processes. *Cognitive Science, 14*, 281–312.

Radford, J. (1990). *Child prodigies and exceptional early achievers*. New York: Free Press.

Raskin, E. (1936). Comparison of scientific and literary ability: A biographical study of eminent scientists and letters of the nineteenth century. *Journal of Abnormal and Social Psychology, 31*, 20–35.

Regnier, G., Salmela, J., & Russell, S. J. (1993). Talent detection and development in sport. In R. N. Singer, M. Murphy, & L. K. Tennant (Eds.), *Handbook of research in sport psychology* (pp. 290–313). New York: Macmillan.

Roe, A. (1953). A psychological study of eminent psychologists and anthropologists, and a comparison with biological and physical scientists. *Psychological Monographs: General and Applied, 67* (Whole No. 352), 1–55.

Roth, H. (1982). *Master violinists in performance*. Neptune City, NJ: Paganinia.

Salthouse, T. A. (1984). Effects of age and skill in typing. *Journal of Experimental Psychology: General, 13*, 345–371.

Salthouse, T. A. (1991a). Expertise as the circumvention of human processing limitations. In K. A. Ericsson & J. Smith (Eds.), *Toward a general theory of expertise: Prospects and limits* (pp. 286–300). Cambridge, England: Cambridge University Press.

Salthouse, T. A. (1991b). *Theoretical perspectives on cognitive aging*. Hillsdale, NJ: Erlbaum.

Scheinfeld, A. (1939). *You and heredity*. New York: Frederick A. Stokes.

Schmidt, H. G., & Boshuizen, H. P. A. (1993). On the origin of intermediate effects in clinical case recall. *Memory & Cognition, 21*, 338–351.

Schulz, R., & Curnow, C. (1988). Peak performance and age among superathletes: Track and field, swimming, baseball, tennis, and golf. *Journal of Gerontology: Psychological Sciences, 43*, 113–120.

Simon, H. A., & Chase, W. G. (1973). Skill in chess. *American Scientist, 61*, 394–403.

Simonton, D. K. (1984). *Genius, creativity, and leadership: Historiometric inquiries*. Cambridge, MA: Harvard University Press

Simonton, D. K. (1988a). Age and outstanding achievement: What do we know after a century of research? *Psychological Bulletin, 104*, 251–267.

Simonton, D. K. (1988b). *Scientific genius: A psychology of science*. Cambridge, England: Cambridge University Press.

Sloboda, J. A. (1985). *The musical mind: The cognitive psychology of music*. Oxford, England: Oxford University Press.

Sloboda, J. A., Hermelin, B., & O'Connor, N. (1985). An exceptional musical memory. *Music Perception, 3*, 155–170.

Smith, S. B. (1983). *The great mental calculators*. New York: Columbia University Press.

Starkes, J. L., & Deakin, J. M. (1985). Perception in sport: A cognitive approach to skilled performance, in W. F. Straub & J. M. Williams (Eds.), *Cognitive sport psychology* (pp. 115–128). Lansing, NY: Sports Science Associates.

Suzuki, S. (1981). Every child can become rich in musical sense. In E. Hermann (Ed.), *Shinichi Suzuki: The man and his philosophy* (pp. 136–141). Athens, OH; Ability Development Associates. (Originally presented in 1963.)

Suzuki, S. (1981). Discovery of the law of ability and the principle of ability development: Proof that talent is not inborn. In E. Hermann (Ed.), *Shinichi Suzuki: The man and his philosophy* (pp. 233–246). Athens, OH; Ability Development Associates. (Originally presented in 1980.)

Takeuchi, A. H., & Hulse, S. H. (1993). Absolute pitch. *Psychological Bulletin, 113*, 345–361.

Thomas, A., & Chess, S. (1984). Genesis and evolution of behavioral disorders: From infancy to early adult life. *American Journal of Psychiatry, 141*, 1–9.

Treffert, D. A. (1989). *Extraordinary people: Understanding "Idiot savants."* New York: Harper & Row.

Wallace, A. (1986). *The prodigy*. New York: Dutton.

Wallace, D. B., & Gruber, H. E. (Eds.). (1989). *Creative people at work*. New York: Oxford University Press.

Weisberg, R. W. (1986). *Creativity: Genius and other myths*. New York: Freeman.

Weisberg, R. W. (1993). *Creativity: Beyond the myth of genius*. New York: Freeman.

# PART XI

# Reasoning and Problem Solving

## Discussion Questions

1. How general is problem-solving? That is, can we come up with global rules of problem-solving that apply to such diverse domains as physics, driving behavior, chess, and bingo? What are some distinctions between problems that you think might influence the type of cognitive processes involved? We'll start you with an example: Some researchers distinguish between technical knowledge domains like physics and everyday knowledge domains.

2. Evaluate the role of background knowledge in reasoning and expertise. By background knowledge, we mean previously known information that one brings into a given situation (e.g., the chess master comes to the match prepared with thousands of memorized patterns).

3. After reading the papers included in this chapter, what advice would you give to a high school science teacher?

4. In contrast to this book, some textbooks place decision making and problem solving in the same chapter. In what ways do you think these two fields of research are related?

## Suggested Readings

L. Boroditsky and M. Ramscar (2002, The roles of body and mind in abstract thought, *Psychological Science, 13,* 185–189) provide a series of clever demonstrations of how people's knowledge of a familiar domain (physical space) affects how they think about a more abstract domain (time). Read this paper to see how people's physical position in a lunch line influenced how they answered an ambiguous question about time!

D. Gentner (1983, Structure-mapping: A theoretical framework on analogy, *Cognitive Science, 7,* 155–170) wrote this classic on analogy. This paper describes how subjects connect knowledge from one domain (e.g., the solar system) to a second domain (e.g., the atom).

P. A. Kolers and H. L. Roediger (1984, Procedures of mind, *Journal of Verbal Learning & Verbal Behavior, 23,* 425–449) provide an account of expertise in memory as involving the acquisition of procedures. When reading this paper, think generally about the role of practice in expertise, and how expertise may involve the acquisition of specific procedural skills.

J. Metcalfe and D. Wiebe (1987, Intuition in insight and noninsight problem solving, *Memory & Cognition, 15,* 238–246) compare problems that tend to be solved with a sudden feeling of insight (aha! experiences) versus problems that tend to be solved after a more standard application of steps (e.g., algebra problems).

M. Scheerer's (1963, Problem-solving, *Scientific American, 208,* 118–128) paper contains the famous 9-dot problem; in this problem, you are given 9 dots arranged in a 3 × 3 matrix, and the task is to draw 4 continuous straight lines to connect all 9 dots, without lifting your pencil from the paper. Try it, and then see Scheerer for the solution and a discussion of how people often fail to solve problems that require "thinking outside of the box."

B. Tversky (1981, Distortion in memory for maps, *Cognitive Psychology, 13,* 407–433) provides examples of shortcuts people use when solving spatial problems. In some cases, people's background knowledge can lead to errors in reasoning.

# Appendix: How to Read a Journal Article in Cognitive Psychology

Henry L. Roediger and David A. Gallo

Research in cognitive psychology and cognitive neuroscience is aimed at understanding the workings of the mind/brain. Cognitive processes are those involved in knowing the world, and cognitive scientists are interested in all facets—from sensing and perceiving, to attending and remembering, and on to thinking, reasoning, and solving problems. Language processes are often a central part of the study of cognition, as language is regarded as "the light of the mind." Therefore, processes involved in listening to speech and in reading are frequently studied.

The study of cognition can proceed through use of purely behavioral methods or by methods from cognitive neuroscience. In the first approach, researchers control and manipulate stimulation to the senses and measure behavioral responses, often focusing on the speed of responses or the patterns of errors generated on a task. From these data, they make inferences about the mental processes involved in a task. The cognitive neuroscience approach involves the study of cognitive processes through use of neuroimaging techniques or from studying patients who have suffered various types of brain damage. The patients and people whose brains are scanned are usually given tests much like those in purely behavioral experiments, but interest centers on specifying neural correlates of performance.

As in all sciences, the journal article is the dominant form of communication among researchers in cognitive psychology. Many journals exist to report findings in the fields of cognitive psychology and cognitive neuroscience, and most subscribe to a similar format. The form of scientific journal articles is unlike that of forms of literature you have already experienced as students; journal articles are not like magazine articles, expository essays, short stories, or novels. The one feature in common is that the journal article, like these other forms, is intended to communicate information and tell a story about the research that was conducted.

The purpose of this appendix is to give you advice on how to approach the journal article. We assume that most readers will have had little more than a first course in psychology. Entering the world of scientific literature is, in our experience, rather like embarking on a journey in a foreign country where the language and customs are strange. To be sure, the words in these journal articles may be English, but often the terms (even ones that seem familiar, like *perceiving* or *paying attention*) are used in ways that take on technical meanings. Scientists, like members of all subcultures, have their own private languages to discuss the phenomena of their fields. You must learn their language for them to communicate with you, or vice versa. The jargon and format of the writing can be daunting.

Journal articles serve many functions and come in many forms. Some journals specialize in papers that review the literature or present theories. Other journals present findings in brief form and are intended for a wider audience than specialists. However, the standard article in most journals is written for specialists. This means that the authors assume quite a bit of knowledge and they will not bother to explain some terms that "everybody" in the field is supposed to know (e.g., between-subjects design, analysis of variance, or double-blind experiment). If some of the articles you read seem hard to follow or assume too much knowledge, it is probably because they were written for another specialist and not for a novice to the field. Most of the articles in the book you are holding were carefully selected by the editors to be appropriate for undergraduate students without much background in the topic. Nonetheless, some terms will be unfamiliar. If the article you are reading has terms that you do not understand, our advice is to look them up or to ask your professor or a graduate student in the field. However, as noted below, you will not necessarily be able to understand every aspect of each paper perfectly if you are just starting out in the field. Concentrate on the main points.

Scientific articles in psychology come in distinct parts, which usually appear in a systematic order. The main purpose of this chapter is to acquaint you with these sections and to let you know what to expect. These parts include the title and authors, the abstract, the introduction, the method, the results, the discussion, and the references. We cover these in the order they appear in a paper, but as you gain experience in the field, you may elect to read the parts of articles in a different order from their arrangement in the paper. For example, if you just want to know the main conclusions, you can usually get these by reading the discussion.

If you are unfamiliar with journal articles, it is important to avoid getting bogged down by details that are difficult for you to understand. Often you do not need to know these details (e.g., the details of some complicated statistical test) in order to understand the main points of the article. Concentrating on the complex details may only interfere with your grasp of the main points in the article (and you probably won't remember the details, anyway). So, keep your eyes on the forest (what are the important points to be gleaned from this article?) and do not let some scraggly trees (what is multiple regression, anyway?) interfere with your overall comprehension of the main thrust of the article.

## Title and Authors

A good title should give you an accurate idea as to an article's content. The author who made the most significant contribution (i.e., to the research and writing) is typically listed first, and in a footnote, you can find out where the research was performed.

## Abstract

The abstract represents a brief summary of the article. It usually tells what the research was about, what methods were used to study the issue under investigation, and what results were obtained. Finally, the abstract provides a brief assessment of either the practical value or theoretical importance of the findings. If properly written, the abstract entices you into the paper and gives you a framework for understanding it.

## Introduction

The introduction specifies the problem to be studied and tells why it is important. A good introduction will have you involved in a fascinating scientific journey, so that by the end you will know the theory guiding the research and the hypotheses that were tested. In addition, the author also reviews the relevant research literature on the topic in the introduction. In citing relevant literature, psychologists put the name of the prior author doing the work right in the text (e.g., Jacoby, 1991), rather than in a footnote.[1] (The reference can be found at the end of the paper.) Depending on how much prior work has been done (and how extensively the authors report it), the introduction may vary in length. By the end of a good introduction, you should be ready (even eager) to learn about the methods, results and conclusions that will be delivered in the remaining sections.

## Method

The *method* section describes exactly how the experimenter conducted the study, and it should contain enough information so that another researcher could replicate the work. Although it is sometimes printed in smaller type to conserve space, it is still a critical part of the article, because it tells how the researchers approached the problem and what they did. Knowing the method is essential if you want to completely understand results of an experiment and form your own interpretation of them.

The method section is usually divided into subsections that cover the participants (or subjects), the design of the experiment, the apparatus or materials, and the procedure that the participants experienced. The *participant* or *subject* section tells how many people (or animals) were studied, how they were selected and assigned to conditions (at random or by specified criteria), and who they were (college undergraduates taking introductory psychology, paid volunteers obtained by a newspaper ad, patients undergoing a certain medical procedure, etc.). Depending on the nature of the study, more or less detail may be provided. For example, in studies of aging it is typical to give quite a bit of detail about ages, education, and other characteristics of the group of people being tested.

The *design* section provides a crisp description of the conditions that will be involved. For example, in an experiment on remembering, it might be that old, middle-aged, and young subjects were asked to study pictures, words (i.e., the names of the pictures), or both types of material simultaneously. Thus, the design would be described as a 3 (age: young, middle, or old) × 3 (materials: pictures, words, or pictures + words) design. The dependent variable would be the number of items recalled on the memory test. The idea for the design section is to present the logic of the experiment concisely. The design just described has two independent variables or "factors" (age and type of material) with three levels of each factor. Recall that independent variables in experiments are those that the experimenters manipulate and dependent variables are the measures of behavior that are taken. The design section typically specifies the independent and dependent variables used.

The *apparatus* subsection of the method section describes any equipment used to test the subjects. This section might include such details as the model number of a computer or the resolution of a viewing apparatus. This section is referred to as the *materials* section when questionnaires, written or videotaped sketches, and similar means are used to test subjects. If they are long, lists of special materials may be placed in an appendix section,

---

[1] Footnotes are used for asides, like this one, or to qualify the point under discussion with new information. However, in psychology (unlike some fields) they are not used for primary references. Footnotes are generally discouraged, but some authors cannot live without them.

usually set in smaller type, or placed on the Internet with an address provided. (The difficulty with this last practice is that the website may become unavailable as technologies change.)

The *procedure* section explains what happened to subjects in relatively great detail, so that the experimental techniques could be replicated. Therefore, the critical features must be clearly enumerated. Many "failures to replicate" past work often hinge on factors that were not well specified in the original procedure but that are discovered, after much later work, to have been critical. The procedure section should include instructions subjects received, the timing of events, the responses participants were required to make, the number of trials or events experienced, and so on. When you read the procedure, it is often helpful to imagine being a subject in the experiment to form an intuitive understanding of the task and the demands that were placed upon the participant.

## Results

The results section tells the outcome obtained in the research. It is unusual to find raw data or individual subjects' scores reported in a journal article; instead, descriptive statistics are presented that summarize the data. Typical descriptive statistics are the mean of a distribution of scores, reflecting a central tendency or "average" score, and some measure of variance (the standard deviation or standard error of the mean) about the mean value. Inferential statistics provide the probability that the observed differences between the various experimental conditions could have been produced by random, or chance, factors. Statistically significant results are those that are judged unlikely to have occurred by chance; they are said to be reliable, which means that they can probably be replicated. This information helps both the researcher and the reader determine how confident to be that the independent variable(s) produced a change in the dependant variable. Both kinds of statistics are important to help psychologists understand the outcome of an experiment.

Either *tables* or *graphs* may be used to describe and summarize data. In the typical *table*, such as Table A.1, data appear under various headings. The experiment required students to answer one of three types of questions about words they saw one at a time. Questions given before each word directed attention to simple perceptual features (Is the word in uppercase letters?), to what it sounded like (Does the word rhyme with *chair*?), or to its meaning (Does the word refer to a type of animal?). If the word to be judged were BEAR, then the answer to any of the questions would have been *yes*. In actuality, half the time the presented word required a *yes* response and half the time it required a *no* response. After subjects had answered a question for each of the words, they were given a recognition memory test.

Before you look at the data, you should first read the title of the table. The title should be explicit enough to tell you what type of data appears in the table. The title of Table A.1 tells you that it contains information about recognition of the words as a function of the ques-

**TABLE A.1. Mean Proportion of Words Recognized, as a Function of Question Type at Study (Case, Rhyme, or Semantic) and Response Type ("Yes" or "No").**

| Response Type | Question Type | | |
| --- | --- | --- | --- |
| | Case | Rhyme | Category |
| Yes | .42 | .65 | .90 |
| No | .37 | .50 | .65 |

*Note.* Adapted from Craik and Tulving (1975, Experiment 9).

tions that people were asked about the words. Sometimes you will also find a note at the bottom of the table, which is used to give more specific information about the data than is provided in the title. Next, you should examine the headings and subheadings carefully. These will tell you about the conditions or variables that are relevant to the data in the table. Across the top of Table A.1 is the Question Type, with three subheadings and columns representing the three types (Case, Rhyme, and Category). On the side are the responses people made to each question (*Yes* or *No*).

The data in the table show that the type of question asked had a powerful effect on probability of recognition, with category questions leading to better retention of words than the rhyme questions, which in turn produced better recognition than the case questions. This main effect is a replication of a result that has been well documented in the memory literature: items encoded with respect to meaning were better remembered than those encoded with respect to their surface features (the levels of processing effect; Craik & Tulving, 1975). Further, although the effect of type of question occurred with both responses, this effect was larger when the answer was *yes* than when it was *no*. This pattern represents an interaction between the two variables. That is, the effect of one independent variable (question type) on the dependent variable (recognition performance) depended on the other independent variable (response type). In these data, the levels of processing effect was greater for *yes* than for *no* responses.

Tables are useful to present numerous data points from various conditions. *Graphs* or *figures* are very effective ways of highlighting important aspects of the data and of showing trends. In Figure A.1, we have graphed the data from Table A.1 that we just discussed. The mean proportion of recognized items is represented on the vertical axis, or *ordinate*. On the horizontal axis, also called the *x-axis* or the *abscissa*, are the six question/answer conditions (that is, three questions to which there could be two answers). On the vertical axis (the *y-axis* or the ordinate), the proportion of items recognized is represented. Nearly all figures from any type of psychological research have a scale of the dependent variable (what is measured) on the ordinate. In figures from experiments, the independent variable (what is manipulated) is on the abscissa. In correlational research, where an independent variable is not manipulated, there is a dependent variable on both the ordinate and the abscissa. (If you have trouble remembering which axis is the ordinate and which is the abscissa, a good mnemonic or memory aid is that your mouth moves in the appropriate direction when you say the words: it widens side to side when you say *abscissa* and lengthens up and down when you say *ordinate*.)

Be sure to examine the labels on the ordinate and the abscissa so you know what data are plotted in the figure. In Figure A.1, the heights of the bars tell you the proportion of items recognized in each condition. The main effect of question type is represented by the fact that the bars increase from left to right, as the question was varied. Also, there is an effect of response type, so that words that required a *yes* response are generally better recognized than are those that required a *no* response. The interaction between these two independent variables can be seen by the fact that the difference between the *yes* and *no* bars varies from one question type to the next.

Figure A.1 is a bar graph, and the data from an experiment are plotted as bars when the levels of the independent variable are not given in a measurable dimension. That is, the conditions here are qualitatively different and have different names, but they cannot be ordered on a quantitative dimension. A different way to plot data is shown in Figure A.2. The data appear as points (triangles) connected by lines. A function like this is drawn when the independent variable is on a measurable dimension, so that an ordering of the measures is possible. In Figure A.2, the graph represents the effect of study time (shown on the abscissa) on correct recall of words from a list (measured on the ordinate). Greater time to study each item (i.e., slower presentation rates) results in greater recall.

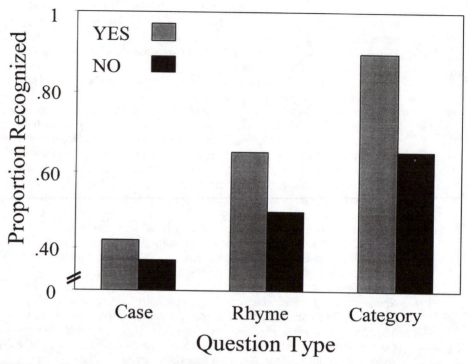

**FIGURE A.1** ■ Mean proportion of items recognized for each of the three question types in Craik and Tulving (1975, Experiment 9). The dependent variable (mean proportion of recognized items) is on the ordinate, or vertical axis, and one independent variable (question type) is on the abscissa, or horizontal axis. The other independent variable (response type) is represented by the different colored bars, as specified in the upper-left hand key. Note how the main effect of each independent variable, and their interaction, can be seen from the figure.

When you are trying to understand the data in a figure, be sure that you pay close attention to the scale of the dependant variable on the ordinate. Sometimes the scale can be misleading: An exaggerated scale with widely spaced numbers will tend to make differences appear more impressive, and a scale with numbers jammed close together will tend to make differences appear smaller. To see how this works, look back to Figure A.2. Here we put breaks along the ordinate so that the scale could be widely spaced from .60 to .80, thereby exaggerating the differences in the data to highlight the effect of study time on recall. However, if we had simply allowed the scale to range from 0 to 1, as in Figure A.3, one gets a much different impression from the data. Here the differences among the conditions are not emphasized as much, and a casual glance might lead to the conclusion that the manipulation was not nearly as effective as it appeared in Figure A.2. However, exactly the same data are accurately plotted in both figures.

Both of these graphing techniques are common, and you should always look carefully to see what the scale is in a graph. But which way of graphing the results is right? In a sense, both are, because both can be argued to portray matters accurately. However, if statistical tests have shown a difference to exist between the three conditions, then Figure A.2 would more accurately capture the relation between measures and show up the differences obtained. With experimental data, it is more important to determine whether a difference is statistically reliable than to determine whether the difference appears large when graphed,

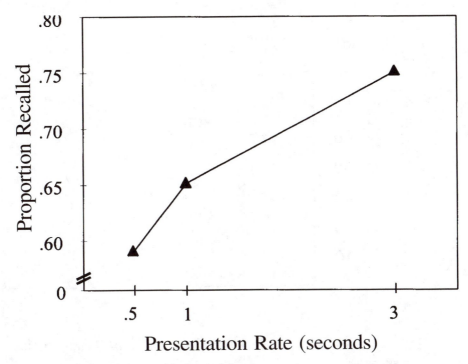

**FIGURE A.2** ■ Mean proportion of items recalled at each of the three presentation rates in Gallo and Roediger (2000, Experiment 2). Slowing presentation rate appears to result in a dramatic increase in recall.

because whether a result appears large or small depends on the scale of the dependent variable on the ordinate.

Inferential statistics permit the assessment of whether differences that appear between conditions are the result of the experimental manipulations as opposed to unknown or chance factors. Inferential statistics about the data appear in such statements as "$F_{(4, 60)} = 2.03$, $MSe = 3.40$, $p < .05$." This means that the odds for obtaining by chance an $F$-statistic at least as large as 2.03 would be less than 5% if the experiments were repeated (that's the $p < .05$ part of the reporting of the statistical test). That is, if the experiment were conducted 100 times, the direction of difference in the results should be the same in at least 95 out of the 100 repetitions. You do not necessarily need to know a lot about the statistical tests to survive as a consumer of the research being reported. By convention, results that meet the .05 level of confidence are deemed statistically significant; if you see $p < .05$ that means there is less than a 1 in 20 probability that these results occurred by chance, a good indicator that they are reliable.

## Discussion

The discussion section is often the most creative part of an article. At the beginning of the section, the author will typically provide a concise statement of the outcome of the experiment, summarizing the results. Then the author will go on to draw theoretical or practical implications from the results and to relate them to the rest of the literature on this topic. How do these results change what we know about the topic at hand? How do these results fit in with past results? Besides answering these sorts of questions, the author may go on to

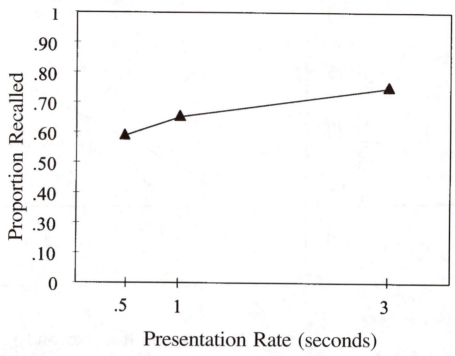

**FIGURE A.3** ■ Data from Figure A.2 that have been plotted using the full range (from 0 to 1) of the dependent variable. Note that although the data are the same as in Figure A.2, the effects of presentation rate on recall do not appear to be as "dramatic" in this figure, due to the change of scale.

describe future research that might be useful in answering questions that are left unresolved by the current research.

## References

References are found at the end of the article, and include only those articles that are cited in the text. This is different from a bibliography, which includes as many relevant citations as feasible. In contrast to journals in other disciplines, psychology journals list full titles of referenced articles. This practice helps to tell the reader what the article is about, making this section a valuable guide for related information. Furthermore, the references in an article can also be used as a good starting place to find out more about the topic. The cited articles usually refer to the most recently published works in the area before the current one you are reading, as well as including the most important previous publications.

## Checklist for the Critical Reader

In this section, we offer some hints that have helped us to become better consumers of the information presented in psychological journals. Keep this checklist handy as you read through the journal articles included in this book. Although many of the points should seem redundant to you by now, going through them will help you identify which sections you may not be reading as effectively as possible, and will sharpen your skills at extracting the critical pieces of information from these sections.

## Introduction

1. *What is the author's goal?* The introduction explains the reasons behind the research and reviews the earlier literature on the phenomena of interest. If one or more theories are related to the research, the introduction gives the predictions the theories make. As with scientists in other areas, psychologists do not necessarily agree as to the underlying mechanisms and theoretical interpretations of behavior. The author may present a particular theory that he or she thinks provides a useful explanation of behavior. Although the author may present more than one theory in the introduction, he or she will proceed later on to demonstrate that they do not all help equally to predict and explain the obtained results. Try to figure out which of the several theories the author believes and which are slated for subsequent rejection.
2. *What hypothesis will be tested in the experiment?* The answer to this should be obvious and stated directly within the introduction section.
3. *If I had to design an experiment to test this hypothesis, what would I do?* This is the key question for the introduction. You must try to answer this *before* continuing on the method section of the article. Many experiments are done within the context of a systematic investigation of behavior to test and support a particular theoretical framework developed by the author. If the author has any skill as a wordsmith, once you have finished the method section, you are likely to agree with the method that the author has advocated in the article. A clever author will plant the seeds to this answer in the introduction itself; this practice makes it harder for you to state a method independently. Write down your ideas for testing the hypothesis.

## Method

Compare your answer to question 3 with the method used by the author. They probably will differ, if you have not peeked. Now answer questions 4a-c.

4a. *Is my proposed method better than the author's?* Regardless of who has the better method, you or the author, this forced comparison will make you think about the method section critically, instead of passively accepting it.
4b. *Does the author's method actually test the hypothesis?* The hypothesis is sometimes an early casualty, disappearing between the introduction and the methods sections. Always check that the method used is adequate and relevant to the hypothesis at hand.
4c. *What are the independent, dependent, and control variables?* This is an obvious question and can be answered quickly. Listing the variables helps you avoid passive reading of the methods section. After you have resolved differences between your proposed method and the author's, answer the next question.
5. *Using the participants, apparatus, materials, and procedures described by the author, what results would I predict for this experiment?* You must answer this on your own before reading the results section. Think about the procedure of the experiment, and how the different processes involved in the task would have influenced your performance had you been a participant. State your prediction in terms of the hypothesis and the independent and dependent variables. You may find it impossible to predict a single outcome. This is not really a problem, because the author probably also had more than one prediction originally. He or she may have done some preliminary investigations to narrow down possible outcomes; alternatively, he or she may have been surprised by the results and had to rethink the introduction

**TABLE A.2. Questions for Critical Readers**

*Introduction*
1.  What is the author's goal?
2.  What hypothesis will be tested in the experiment?
3.  If I had to design an experiment to test this hypothesis, what would I do?

*Method*
4a.  Is my proposed method better than the author's?
4b.  Does the author's method actually test the hypothesis?
4c.  What are the independent, dependent, and control variables?
5.  Using the participants, apparatus, materials, and procedures described by the author, what results would I predict for this experiment?

*Results*
6.  How did the author analyze the data?
7.  Did I expect the obtained results?
8a.  How would I interpret these results?
8b.  What applications and implications would I draw from my interpretation of the results?

*Discussion*
9a.  Does my interpretation, or the author's, best represent the data?
9b.  Do I or does the author offer the most cogent discussion of the applications and implications of the results?
10.  Am I being too critical?

once the results were in. Draw a rough sketch illustrating the most likely outcomes you have predicted.

## Results

6.  *How did the author analyze the data?* Although you may not be totally comfortable with statistics yet, a good exercise is to note how the author presented and analyzed the data. Note *which* conditions are being compared and *why*. Data from experiments never come out exactly as anticipated, and authors will often focus on presenting data that they feel are important to convey their main point, while downplaying other data. Do try to understand the author's point of view, but also try to form your own impression about the data as a whole. Are there some unexplained puzzles in the results that the author overlooks?

7.  *Did I expect the obtained results?* If not, then you will reach one of two conclusions: either your prediction was wrong, or the results are hard to believe. Perhaps the method the author selected was inappropriate and did not adequately test the stated hypotheses or introduced sources of uncontrolled variance. Or perhaps these results would not be obtained again if the experiment were repeated. Still, even if you did not expect the results, the author obtained them and clearly believes them. Also, if the editors selected the paper for this book of readings, the results are probably considered important to the field.

8a.  *How would I interpret these results?*

8b.  *What applications and implications would I draw from my interpretation of the results?* Try to answer these questions on your own, before reading the discussion.

## Discussion

The discussion section includes the author's interpretation of the data in the form of conclusions. A good discussion section brings the reader full circle in that it provides a narrative response to the questions posed in the introduction. In addition, the author expands on his or her conclusions by offering insight regarding the applications and implications of the experimental results.

As a critical reader, you have constructed your own interpretation of the results. Compare the merits of your interpretation with the merits of the author's. Which one do you prefer? Answer questions 9a and 9b to help you critically assess yours and the author's interpretation of the results.

9a. *Does my interpretation or the author's best represent the data?* Because authors are allowed more latitude in the discussion section than in other sections, it is conceivable that an author has drawn conclusions that may not be warranted by the data. In other cases, authors draw conclusions that are largely appropriate but may proceed to extend these conclusions beyond what the data can support. The latter situation typically occurs when a researcher fails to recognize the limitations of the dependent variable. Still, the author has doubtless thought longer and harder than you have about the problem. Think critically about issues, but don't become nihilistic and believe nothing from what you read.

9b. *Do I or does the author offer the most cogent discussion of the applications and implications of the results?* This question is secondary to the question posed in 9a. Nonetheless, a researcher's responsibilities extend beyond that of conducting a tightly controlled experiment. He or she must also consider the rationale and theory that underlie the research. The extent to which an author identifies applications and implications of the results contributes to the overall integrity of the research process.

10. *Am I being too critical?* Although critical evaluation of a particular set of findings is an important element of science, it is equally important to be willing to accept new ideas and discoveries. Keep in mind that, with practice, anyone should be able to find problems or limitations of a particular piece of research. Only the best scientists are capable of acknowledging these limitations while, at the same time, recognizing the novel contributions an article may offer. The research glass may be mostly full, so you shouldn't necessarily see it as partly empty.

## Authors' Note

Portions of this chapter have been adapted from D. G. Elmes, B. H. Kantowitz, and H. L. Roediger, *Research Methods in Psychology*, 6e. Belmont, CA: Wadsworth. We thank the authors and Wadsworth Publishing Co. for permission to adapt pages 159–171 of the text.

## REFERENCES

Craik, F. I. M., & Tulving, E. (1975). Depth of processing and the recognition of words in episodic memory. *Journal of Experimental Psychology: General, 104,* 268–294.

Gallo, D. A., & Roediger, H. L., III. (2000). *Variability among word lists in eliciting false memories: The roles of associative activation and decision processes.* Manuscript in preparation.

Jacoby, L. L. (1991). A process dissociation framework: Separating automatic from intentional uses of memory. *Journal of Memory & Language, 30,* 513–541.

# Author Index

# Subject Index

stage theory in, 58–59
subtraction method in, 48–50
Reaction times, 24
additivity of effects on, 56
for ambiguity conditions, 582, 585
in image scanning experiments, 241–242
and knowledge retrieval, 396–397, 399
in knowledge retrieval experiments, 399
in mental rotation, 254, 257
with negative priming, 225
Reading, interactive model of, 98–99
Reading color names test, effects of practice on, 201
Reasoning, *see also* Problem solving
by analogy, 657, 658–659
intuitive, 683
research in, 653
and working memory, 357
Recall, *see also* Tip of tongue phenomenon
comprehension and, 434
false, 338, 343
in false memories experiments, 341–342, 346, 349
generic, 425, 428–430
in LOP experiments, 303
in memory process, 5–6
and recognition, 369–370
search process in, 71
*vs.* recognition, 68–70
Recognition, *see also* Pattern recognition; Word recognition
in category-specific deficit, 103
false, 338
in false memories experiments, 342–343, 346–348, 349
and fragment completion, 371
impaired, 105
in memory process, 5–6
and naming procedures, 101
persistence of, 130
and recall, 369–370
search process in, 71
of speech, 122–123, 186–192
visual, 106
*vs.* recall, 68–70
Recognition experiments
anagram solutions in, 372
shadow face identification in, 372–373
stochastic independence in, 370–373
Recognition memory, and fragment completion, 368, 370
Recognition performance, in LOP experiments, 300–301, 302
Recognition tasks, and visible surfaces, 45
Recognition test procedure, 310
Recollection
conscious, 323, 334–336
effect of divided attention on, 324
"spontaneous," 335
Recollective memory, and childhood amnesia, 379
Regression, misconceptions of, 635–636
Rehearsal process
involving covert spech, 71
in memory, 54
Remembering
false, 351
processes involved in, 296
Representation, 35
abstract, 472
and abstract expectations, 165

active, 91
for analogical thinking, 662
in analysis of process, 37
and change blindness, 159–160
in computational theory, 38–39
connectionist *vs.* symbolic, 15–16
formed via imagery, 237
image as, 41–42
in information-processing problems, 35
knowledge, 391, 392
local *vs.* distributed, 92–93
and mental imagery, 235, 258
organization of internal, 106
in PDP models, 91–97
psychophysics, 38–39
of shape from images, 45
transformation of, 311 (*see also* Witnessing experiments)
usefulness of, 42
Representativeness, 641–642
heuristic for, 631–632, 640
and illusion of validity, 635
and insensitivity to predictability, 634
and insensitivity to sample size, 633
and misconceptions of chance, 633–634
and misconceptions of regression, 635
Response, in subtraction method, 49
Response bias, in signal detection theory, 4
Response latencies, *see also* Reaction-time experiments
insight into, 24
in LOP experiments, 303, 307
Retention
in learning experiments, 297
in memory process, 5
Retention interval, in witnessing experiments, 314
Retention/storage, in memory research, 291
Retinal neurons, selectivity of, 30
Retrieval, 5
and analogical thinking, 657
and automatic activation processes, 222
default assignment in, 91
graceful degradation in, 90–91
from inactive *vs.* active memory, 61–63
independent from active memory, 66–68
interference with, 292
in memory research, 291
of nonsymbolic *vs.* symbolic information, 60–61
PDP models for, 88–91
semantically, 677
spontaneous generalization in, 91
spreading activation, 403
and stage theory, 49
Risk, in decision-making experiments, 626
Robots, programming, 83
Rotation, in pattern recognition, 130–133, *see also* Mental rotation
Rule induction
effects of knowledge on, 493–494
studies, 493–494

**S**
Savants, 690
music, 693, 695–696
performance of, 694
Savings-in-learning technique, 5